Karen Kearns

SUPPORTING EDUCATION

4TH EDITION

Karen Kearns

SUPPORTING EDUCATION

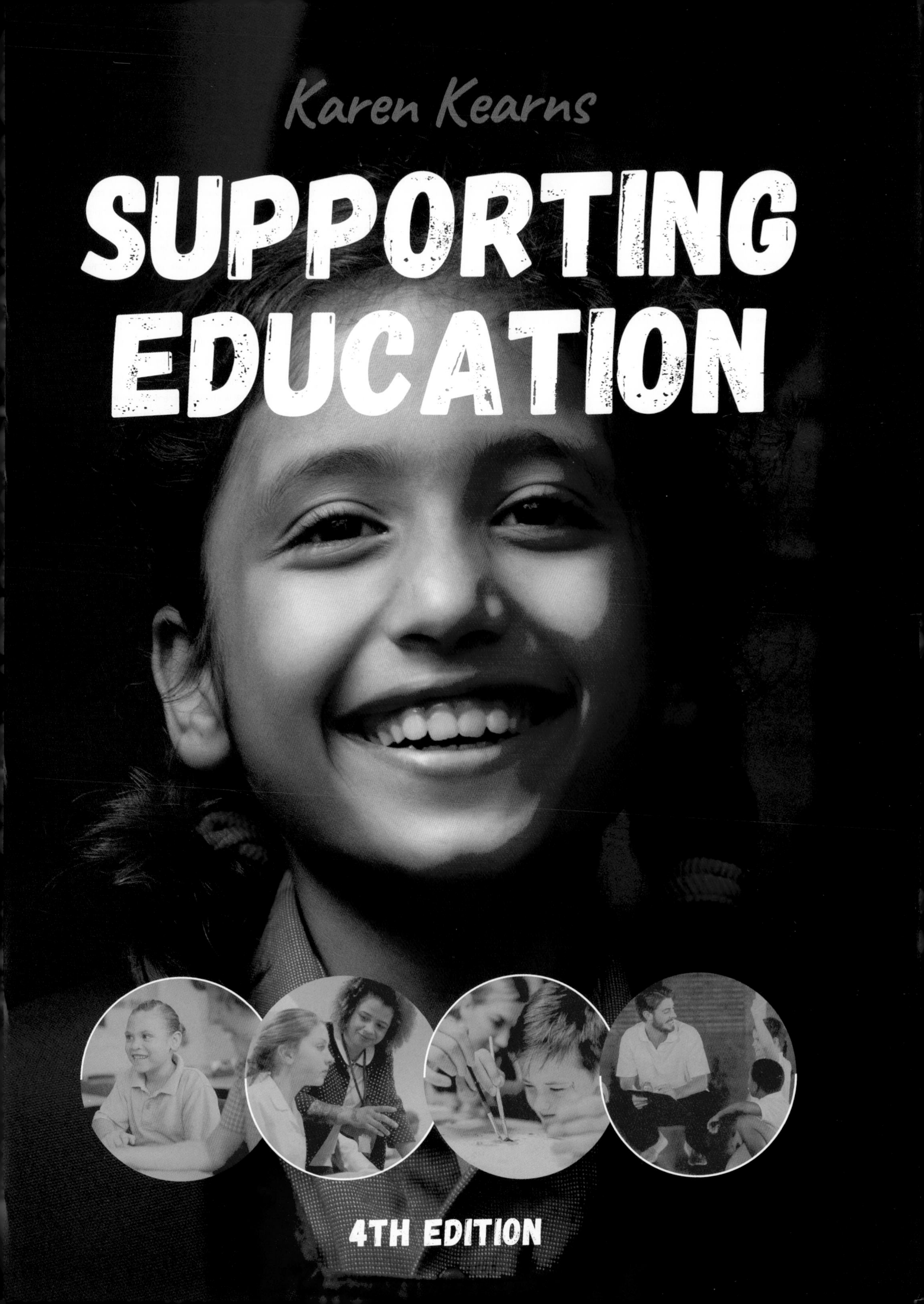

4TH EDITION

CENGAGE

Supporting Education
4th Edition
Karen Kearns

Portfolio manager: Sophie Kaliniecki
Senior content developer: Kylie Scott
Senior project editor: Nathan Katz
Text designer: Jenna Lee Fai (Jenki)
Cover designer: Linda Davidson
Permissions/Photo researcher: Liz McShane
Editor: Anne Mulvaney
Proofreader: James Anderson
Indexer: KnowledgeWorks Global Ltd.
Art direction: Nikita Bansal
Cover: Courtesy Adobe Stock/Claire Bonnor/Austockphoto; Alamy Stock Photo/EyeEm; stock.adobe.com/dglimages; stock.adobe.com/Iryna; stock.adobe.com/WavebreakMediaMicro.
Typeset by KnowledgeWorks Global Ltd.

This fourth edition published in 2024

For product information and technology assistance,
in Australia call **1300 790 853**;
in New Zealand call **0800 449 725**

For permission to use material from this text or product, please email
aust.permissions@cengage.com

National Library of Australia Cataloguing-in-Publication Data
ISBN: 9780170458658
A catalogue record for this book is available from the National Library of Australia.

Cengage Learning Australia
Level 5, 80 Dorcas Street
Southbank VIC 3006 Australia

For learning solutions, visit **cengage.com.au**

Printed in China by 1010 Printing International Limited.
1 2 3 4 5 6 7 27 26 25 24 23

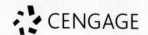

BRIEF CONTENTS

CONTENTS

PART C LITERACY AND NUMERACY

PART D SUPPORTING STUDENTS WITH ADDITIONAL NEEDS

Guide to the text

As you read this text you will find a number of features in every chapter to enhance your study of education support and help you understand how the theory is applied in the real world.

CHAPTER-OPENING FEATURES

Identify the key concepts that the chapter will cover with the **Learning objectives** at the start of each chapter.

PART A

WORKING IN A SCHOOL ENVIRONMENT

Chapter 1

THE ROLE OF THE EDUCATION SUPPORT WORKER

LEARNING OBJECTIVES

When you have completed this chapter, you should be able to demonstrate that, in relation to working in a school environment, you can:

1.1 identify the role and responsibilities of an education support worker (ESW) and specific understanding of own work role and responsibilities

1.2 describe the skills and knowledge need by an ESW, including teamwork, collaboration, flexibility, empathy and initiative

1.3 work in an ethical and professional manner, meet obligations for privacy and confidentiality, and identify and manage conflicts of interest.

GO FURTHER

Go Further icons link to extra content for this chapter. Ask your instructor for the **Go Further** resource and deepen your understanding of the topic.

Online resources icons refer to useful weblinks. Ask your instructor for these **Online Resources.**

FEATURES WITHIN CHAPTERS

Gain insight into real-world experiences using the **Scenario** boxes. Challenge the theory you have learned by considering the discussion questions and 'What does this tell us?' prompts.

SCENARIO

WHS TRAINING WORKSHOP

As part of their annual training obligations, ESWs **Michael** and **Zahra** have recently attended a one-day workshop conducted by the state WHS authority. The aim of the workshop was to provide employees with up-to-date information on their WHS obligations and responsibilities. Michael and Zahra have come away with a greater understanding of their legal obligations, and the importance of knowing and understanding the range of WHS policies and procedures in place at the school.

▶ DISCUSSION

How does regular WHS training support workplace safety?

FEATURES WITHIN CHAPTERS

Consider this boxes provide key facts, tips and research. Pause for self-reflection about the different issues you might encounter in your role using the discussion questions.

CONSIDER THIS

CULTURAL RESPONSIVITY

Cultural responsivity refers to 'the ability to learn from and relate respectfully to people from your own and other cultures'. It includes modifying your approach to people based on your knowledge of other cultures. It also includes demonstrating and accepting an open attitude towards other points of view. To be culturally responsive, you must demonstrate that you:

- have become culturally self-aware
- value a range of diverse views
- do not impose your own values on others
- avoid stereotyping
- examine your beliefs for bias
- learn what you can from others by attending their celebrations, reading information about other cultures and talking with members of a culture
- accept that learning about and understanding other cultures is a lifelong journey (Zion, Kozleski & Fulton, 2005, pp. 15, 16–17).

▶ DISCUSSION

Are you culturally responsive? What do you do that demonstrates this?

Analyse in-depth **Case studies** that build upon concepts as you progress through the chapter.

CASE STUDY | Lavindra

Part 2

The classroom teacher, specialist EAL/D teacher and ESW have identified a range of teaching strategies that can be used with **Lavindra**.

Teaching strategies for Lavindra

- Role-playing part of a story using repetitious dialogue from the text – for example, a picture book.
- Naming and displaying real objects and asking Lavindra to choose a similar thing from a set of picture cards: *'This is a plate. Show me another plate.'*
- Using a repetitive chorus with visual cues or prompts to model target language: *'My name is Miss Jenkins, hello, hello, hello. My name is Lavindra, hello, hello, hello.'*
- Naming colour cards and matching objects to colour cards – crayons, counters, teddies.
- Sitting opposite Lavindra and using the whole hand to point to your own eyes, nose, mouth, etc. Indicate that Lavindra should mirror and say words.
- Using common objects for 'feely box' activities. Lavindra pulls an object from the box, the ESW labels the object, then Lavindra repeats, *'This is a dog.' 'This is a spoon.' 'This is a pen.'*

Gain insight into real working practices and documents using **example templates** and **checklists**.

ASSESSING WRITING SKILLS

Student name:	Class:
Date:	

Planning skills (pre-writing)	
▪ Able to articulate the purpose/reason for the written task	☐
▪ Able to identify the most appropriate genre	☐
▪ Able to plan a beginning, middle and end	☐
▪ Able to identify key words, phrases or concepts	☐
Written task	
▪ Writing reflects the purpose/reason for the written task	☐
▪ Writing shows an awareness of the audience	☐
▪ Writing reflects pre-planning	☐

Examples of children's work demonstrate how chapter concepts can be applied to real examples from the classroom.

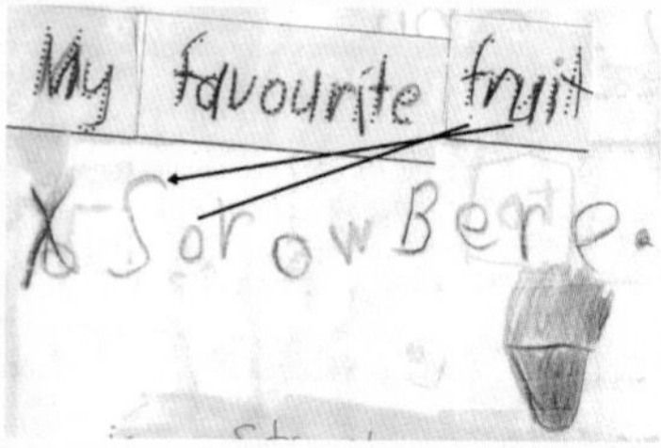

FEATURES WITHIN CHAPTERS

Aboriginal and Torres Strait Islander icons indicate where content is related to the Aboriginal and Torres Strait Islander context.

Aboriginal and Torres Strait Islander

Australian Curriculum icons refer directly to Australian Curriculum content.

AC

NEW

NEW Online resources icons direct you to curated lists of online resources to further your understanding of particular topics. Ask your instructor for these online resources.

Go further icons link to additional learning content. Ask your instructor for the Go Further resource to deepen your understanding of the topic.

GO FURTHER

END-OF-CHAPTER FEATURES

At the end of each chapter you will find several tools to help you to review, practise and extend your knowledge of the key learning objectives.

Review your understanding of the key chapter topics with the **Summary**.

Summary

This chapter provided an overview of the key legislative frameworks within which schools operate. Legislation both dictates and guides policies and procedures designed to ensure schools deliver programs that meet the diverse needs of learners in a fair and ethical manner while at the same time ensuring the safety and wellbeing of students, teachers and support staff. ESWs must ensure they comply with the school's policies and procedures at all times.

Test your knowledge and consolidate your learning through the **self-check questions, discussion questions** and **activities.**

Self-check questions

1 In what ways do the Disability Standards for Education 2005 assist students?
2 What is the definition of duty of care when working with children as an ESW?
3 Who is responsible in schools for ensuring compliance with WHS legislation? List two responsibilities of this individual.
4 What is the *Privacy Act 1988*? List five key components in the Act.
5 As an ESW, what is your responsibility in relation to sharing of information?
6 How do workplace policies guide employees?
7 What are the responsibilities of employees regarding workplace policies and procedures?

Discussion questions

1 For this task, refer to the 'Ella Jones' Scenario earlier in this chapter.
You are Ella's ESW for orientation day, a day where all children who are coming to primary school next year attend. You have been given the information in the scenario about Ella and know that they will be completing a sport session in the gym after lunch.
a What could you do to prepare yourself, knowing Ella's medical needs, so she can get the best out of the session?

where Samuel is only to be collected from the school by his father and paternal grandparents.
a Who do you advise Marcus to speak with at the school so that Marcus and Samuel are supported in this process?
3 Your role as an ESW outreach worker requires you to be accessible at all times via mobile phone. Your workplace has supplied you with a work phone. While you are driving to visit a student, your personal phone rings.

Activities

1 Investigate at your school how the following records and information are maintained:
a Student records
b Accidents and injuries
c Assets/inventory register
2 In times gone by, all paper records were destroyed after a certain number of years had passed. Investigate what length of time records are now kept for, where and how they are kept.
3 Discover what policy documents you are introduced to during an induction day at your local school.

Guide to the online resources

FOR THE INSTRUCTOR

Cengage is pleased to provide you with a selection of resources that will help you to prepare your lectures and assessments when you choose this textbook for your course. Contact your Cengage learning consultant for more information.

GO FURTHER

Provide your students with the **Go further** resource to help deepen their understanding of the topic. It contains further readings to support the text.

ONLINE RESOURCES

Provide your students with the curated **Online resources** lists for each chapter to help deepen their understanding of the topic.

SOLUTIONS MANUAL

The **Solutions manual** provides detailed solutions to every question in the text.

MAPPING GRID

The **Mapping grid** is a simple grid that shows how the content of this book relates to the units of competency needed to complete the Certificate III in School-based Education Support (CHC30221) and the units of competency in the Certificate IV in Education Support (CHC40221).

INSTRUCTOR RESOURCES PACK

Premium resources that provide additional instructor support are available for this text, including:

- Cognero® Testbank
- PowerPoint presentations
- Instructor's handbook (including interactive diagrams, case studies and competency-based activity sheets)
- Artwork from the text.

These resources save you time and are a convenient way to add more depth to your classes, covering additional content and with an exclusive selection of engaging features aligned with the text. The Instructor Resource Pack is included for institutional adoptions of this text when certain conditions are met.

The pack is available to purchase for course-level adoptions of the text or as a standalone resource.

Contact your Cengage learning consultant for more information.

PREFACE

The 4th Edition of this text focuses on key knowledge required by students undertaking CHC30221 – Certificate III in School Based Education Support. It also addresses some core knowledge required for students undertaking CHC40221 – Certificate IV in School Based Education Support.

This new edition incorporates references and online links to V9 of the Australian Curriculum. An exciting addition is the inclusion of an extensive list of online resources curated to extend learner knowledge and create opportunities for learners to build their own resource bank.

Teaching Assistants (TAs) play a vital role in supporting foundation to Year 12 students to participate and engage in learning in the classroom. TAs are employed across public and private education settings and undertake a wide variety of roles.

The experience of the pandemic has had a lasting impact on students, teachers and families. The ongoing shortage of teachers, along with increased workloads has seen a rise in stress and mental health issues in the teaching profession. There has also been a reported increase in students presenting with anxiety and other mental health issues. Now more than ever, TAs perform a critical role in the classroom supporting not only learning but student wellbeing.

I trust that this new edition will support TAs to continue to make a significant contribution to student learning and wellbeing.

Karen Kearns

ABOUT THE AUTHOR

Karen Kearns M.Ed. (EC), B Ed. (EC) Grad. Dip. Ed (Spec. Ed.) Dip. Teach.

Karen is CEO of International Child Care College, based in Newcastle, NSW. Karen has been a passionate educator for over forty years, working in early childhood education, primary school, university and vocational education. Karen also has extensive experience at state government level implementing early childhood education policy.

Karen believes that the learning journey of each student is unique and as educators we must strive to make the learning experience of every student positive and productive. As an educator Karen believes that one of the greatest challenges is supporting learners to make the vital connection between theory and practice. Karen has always believed that the key to supporting students in the classroom is for educators to know, understand and apply our knowledge of child – adolescent development and learning. Karen is also an advocate of emotional intelligence as a foundation skill for all educators.

ACKNOWLEDGEMENTS

Cengage Learning and the author would like to thank the following reviewers for their incisive and helpful feedback.

- Gabby Johnstone, CRTAFE, Kalgoorlie
- Franki Ford, TAFE Digital
- Renee McCormack, TAFE Digital
- Sarah Berwick, TasTAFE
- Adrienne Champness, Private RTO and a Learn Local
- Leanne Hillman, Bolster Education
- Alexandra Jennes, Charles Darwin University.

Writing any textbook is always a collaborative affair. I would like to thank the following people for getting this new edition across the line.

My Cengage Learning support team: Kylie Scott, Senior Content Developer; Nathan Katz, Senior Project Editor; and Anne Mulvaney, copyeditor.

With very special thanks to Sophie Kaliniecki, Portfolio Lead – Vocational, Cengage Learning. Sophie had been my long-time project manager, mentor, supporter and sharer of my angst! Thank you, Sophie, for always being in my corner.

I would also like to thank two people who made a significant contribution to this textbook:

- Letitia Okely, Education Support Worker. Tish has shared her wealth of knowledge, experience and practical expertise with me, which has helped me to gain a deeper understanding of the role and the challenges of TAs. Tish provided many of the new photographs for the book, which I know was not an easy task! A big thank you Tish.
- Azadeh Motevali Zadeh Ardakani (Azi) Educator, PHD student. Azi has been my research assistant and has helped me to navigate current research in education. Azi also took on the task of updating the end of chapter questions. Thank you Azi, it's been a pleasure working with you.

I would like to say a big thank you to my team at International Child Care College (ICCC) who have accommodated my continual absences from the College and have lent me their moral support, acting as a sounding board and cheering me on when needed. Thanks guys.

Thank you, my wonderful family, for always supporting me. Love you.

PART A WORKING IN A SCHOOL ENVIRONMENT

Chapter 1

THE ROLE OF THE EDUCATION SUPPORT WORKER

LEARNING OBJECTIVES

When you have completed this chapter, you should be able to demonstrate that, in relation to working in a school environment, you can:

1.1 identify the role and responsibilities of an education support worker (ESW) and specific understanding of own work role and responsibilities

1.2 describe the skills and knowledge need by an ESW, including teamwork, collaboration, flexibility, empathy and initiative

1.3 work in an ethical and professional manner, meet obligations for privacy and confidentiality, and identify and manage conflicts of interest.

GO FURTHER

Go Further icons link to extra content for this chapter. Ask your instructor for the **Go Further** resource and deepen your understanding of the topic.

Online resources icons refer to useful weblinks. Ask your instructor for these **Online Resources.**

Introduction

Throughout this text the term education support worker (ESW) will be used to cover the many titles given to this job role throughout Australia, as shown in **Figure 1.1**.

This chapter explores the role and responsibilities of the ESW in working with teachers, students and colleagues. Every ESW will bring their individual values and beliefs to the job, and these will shape how they undertake their duties and the relationships they develop with other people in the workplace.

Figure 1.1 Examples of titles given to education support workers

School learning and support officer	Integration aide
Student support officer	Multicultural aide
Ethnic assistant	School services officer
Education assistant/aide (e.g. special needs, Braille, behaviour, orthopaedic, hearing)	EAL (English as additional language) student support officer
Education assistant/aide (mainstream)	Teacher aide: generic; identified; educational interpreter – Auslan; language model – Auslan
Aboriginal and Torres Strait Islander education officer	Learning support assistant
Aboriginal community education officer	Teaching assistant
Community liaison officer	School assistant (mainstream, autism spectrum disorder, vision, communication, bilingual)

Job roles and titles

ESWs must be well organised, able to work with minimum supervision and demonstrate the ability to be flexible, adaptable and use their initiative. They must also take responsibility for managing their own time to ensure work is carried out efficiently and to the standard required by the employer.

Effective communication is an essential workplace skill for ESWs. This includes written information, speaking, active listening and paying attention to body language.

ESWs are expected to conduct themselves in a professional and ethical manner, particularly when working with students and families. The ESW's role is to provide care and support to students with diverse abilities and behaviours, and the skills and knowledge required to do this well are quite broad and diverse.

1.1 The role of the ESW

ESWs are an integral part of the school community, in both public and independent education systems. The role of the ESW can be quite diverse and may, for example, include administration, in-class support in a regular classroom, working in a special unit and supporting students with English as a second language or dialect.

ESWs who work in the classroom are employed to assist the teacher to support the learning, wellbeing and care of students. This may include working with students who have been identified with specific learning/behaviour/language needs and/or students with physical disabilities. It may also include working alongside the classroom teacher in a more generalist role of supporting classroom learning activities. In classroom settings, the ESW plays an important role supporting students to participate as active, independent learners (see **Figure 1.2**). Supporting students to become active learners also builds **self-esteem**, **self-confidence** and **resilience**, and facilitates **social interactions**.

In the Scenario 'My role', ESWs describe their diverse roles.

Figure 1.2 An ESW supporting a student with an activity

Source: Media Bakery/John Lund/Marc Romanelli

SCENARIO

MY ROLE

Freddy: *'I work with my mob at a school in Arnhem Land. It's called a Community Education Centre, but we just call it school. We got kids from little ones to high school. Most kids speak Ndjebbana or Burarra. English is a second language around here. We do lots of things outside. The kids don't like the classroom so we gotta think of ways to get them interested in comin' to school. I get the kids to read to me outside – they like that better.'*

Casey: *'I work in a mainstream public school with two students with additional needs. Kirra is eight years old. She has spina bifida and is confined to a wheelchair. I mainly help her with personal care. We have a purpose-built toilet that has wheelchair access, which is great as we are encouraging Kirra to be more independent. Kirra is very bright and is doing well academically. She does, however, struggle with her social skills and finds it difficult to make friends. Kirra says that the other kids don't like her because she is in a wheelchair but I don't agree. Kirra tends to be quite loud and bossy. She needs to learn how to be a friend. I also work with Brock, who is 11 and has Down syndrome. I usually help him with his work in the classroom. He has been given a special program and is going really well, but he needs my help to stay on track and finish his work. Brock is a delightful student. He is well liked by his peers because he is friendly, kind and considerate.'*

Adam: *'I work in a special school for older students with severe physical disabilities. Part of my role is to work one-on-one with students to support their literacy skills. I enjoy working with teenagers and most of the kids have a great sense of humour, which is handy when they are struggling with basic physical tasks – it makes the day less stressful. We've got quite a bit of special equipment at the school that helps the students with their mobility. My days are full on, and by the end of each day I am exhausted!'*

Eshe: *'I work at a high school in the city. We have around 70 different nationalities at the school. It's like a mini United Nations! For most of the students, English is their second language. I speak Farsi as well as English. Mostly things are harmonious, but we do have to work hard on anti-bias, inclusion and acceptance of differences. My role is to work with small groups to help the students learn conversational English. It's such a rewarding job. The girls like to learn about movie stars, singers and fashion while the boys are focused on sports, cars, Aussie slang and swear words!'*

WHAT DOES THIS TELL US?

The role of an ESW will vary from one school to another, and the range of skills and knowledge needed to work successfully with students can be quite complex and demanding.

▶ DISCUSSION

Discuss what each of these settings may be like. What might be the rewards and challenges? What specific skills/qualities would you need to work successfully in each setting?

The role of the ESW will be unique to each school setting. For example, an ESW employed in a rural community would likely have a role and relationships that are very different from those experienced by an ESW in a large regional or city school. ESWs employed in high schools will also have different experiences and challenges from those working in primary schools or in special education environments. ESWs working in remote areas are likely to have multiple responsibilities in both student support and administration.

GO FURTHER

Examples of ESW duty statements can be found in your **Go Further** resource, available through your instructor.

SCENARIO

WHAT ESWs SHOULD NOT DO!

At a recent ESW professional development workshop, ESWs shared their various roles and responsibilities. ESW **Katrina** was amazed to hear that some ESWs were expected to assist in marking assessment tasks, taking over the whole class for extended periods of time while the teacher attended to administrative tasks, take primary responsibility for student **Individual Educational Plans (IEPs)** and attend IEP meetings in place of the teacher.

Katrina feels relieved that she has never been asked to do any of these things. She wonders how such situations have been allowed to come about.

WHAT DOES THIS TELL US?

There may be occasions when ESWs are asked to perform tasks outside their scope of duties and responsibilities. Where this happens, it is important to clarify your role and make it known that you are not comfortable with taking on such tasks.

► DISCUSSION

If you were asked to perform any of the above duties, how would you respond? Can you think of a circumstance where a teacher might ask you to perform tasks that are clearly outside your role?

Working collaboratively

Videos: Job roles

Working collaboratively with the teacher will help to ensure the best possible outcomes for the teacher, the ESW and the student/s. **Figure 1.3** identifies how the roles and responsibilities of the teacher and the ESW typically are allocated.

Figure 1.3 Areas of responsibilities of teachers and ESWs

	Teacher	ESW
Teaching and learning philosophy	Establishes teaching and learning philosophy, such as collaborative learning, problem solving, respectful relationships, positive reinforcement and confidentiality.	Discusses the teaching and learning philosophy with the teacher and applies this in the classroom.
Student support	Develops IEPs, **Learning Support Plans (LSPs)** and/or **Individual Behaviour Management Plans (IBMPs)** for students as required. Shares information about the IEP/IBMP with the ESW: background information, diagnosis, identified strengths and weaknesses, agencies and personnel involved with the student/family, long-term and short-term goals, home–school liaison strategies, classroom strategies and major teaching strategies.	Assists in the delivery, monitoring and assessment of the IEP as directed by the teacher. Provides feedback to the teacher on student performance, management and care issues. Attends planning and review meetings as requested by the teacher. Liaises with agency personnel as required and/or directed by the teacher.
Lesson planning	Lesson planning based on curriculum and learning outcomes or Key Learning Areas (KLAs). Includes teaching strategies, instructional design, daily goals and objectives. Identifies language/terminology to be used to support learning.	Works with individuals and small groups as directed by the teacher, using content and teaching/instructional design strategies and language/terminology provided by the teacher. For example, listens to students read aloud.
Learning materials and resources	Identifies learning materials and resources to be used to support student learning. These may include special equipment/aids and adaptive technology. Reviews learning materials and resources. Provides information on safety procedures.	Prepares, accesses, sets up and uses learning materials and resources as directed by the teacher. Provides feedback to teacher in relation to students' use of learning materials and resources. Uses special equipment/aids and adaptive technology.
Classroom rules and behaviour management	Establishes classroom rules and behaviour-management strategies.	Reinforces classroom rules and uses behaviour-management strategies as directed by the teacher. Provides feedback on student behaviour and identifies any behaviour issues or concerns.
Assessment	Determines assessment requirements, including reporting and documentation requirements. Identifies assessment tools and strategies.	Undertakes student assessment, such as observations, under the direction of the teacher.

	Teacher	ESW
Relationships with families	Establishes positive and respectful relationships with families. Provides written and verbal feedback to parents. Works with family when developing goals for the student.	Establishes positive and respectful relationships with families. Only provides feedback to families under the direction of the teacher.
Reviewing the educational program	Undertakes regular reviews of all aspects of the educational programs.	Assists as directed in regular reviews of the educational programs.
Professional development	Provides professional supervision and support to the ESW. Shares professional learning resources, knowledge and skills with the ESW. Supports the ESW to undertake ongoing professional development.	Asks questions and accesses professional learning resources to improve skills and knowledge. Engages in ongoing professional learning opportunities.
WHS	Ensures due diligence in relation to work health and safety (WHS). Actively conveys the need to comply with all policies and procedures.	Ensures due diligence in relation to WHS. Actively complies with all policies and procedures.

To work effectively as an ESW, there must be clearly defined roles, responsibilities and expectations in relation to work standards. Your job description will typically be broad and generic and won't include all of the tasks you'll be expected to perform. It may not include the level of autonomy you have in decision-making and is unlikely to include how to address challenges you may face when performing your duties.

The classroom teacher is responsible for managing the work of the ESW, providing direct instruction as well as guidance and supervision (**Figure 1.4**). The teacher will identify how the ESW will be used in the classroom – for example, working one-to-one with students with special needs; working alongside a student who has difficulty staying on task; working with a small group of students to support a teacher-planned lesson; working with a few students to revise and consolidate skills and knowledge; assisting the teacher to undertake assessment tasks with students; observing and documenting student learning and/or behaviour; preparing teaching materials; setting up classroom resources and/or learning centres; adapting or preparing resources to meet specific learner needs; supporting a student's personal care; and providing behaviour and/or social support.

Figure 1.4 An ESW working collaboratively with a teacher in the classroom

Source: Photo by Tish Okely © Cengage

Before commencing work in a classroom, make time to meet with the teacher to discuss your role. You may like to do this in your own time prior to your first day in the workplace. The classroom teacher is typically responsible for assigning the duties of the ESW in the classroom. The teacher will usually determine how these duties are to be carried out, when they are to be performed and how the ESW will work with the students in the classroom. The best way to understand these expectations is to meet with the teacher, discuss your job role and ask questions to clarify what the teacher is expecting, including boundaries and limits – for example:

- the task/s to be undertaken (what)
- the timeframe (when and how long)
- with whom (an individual student, a small group of students)
- the goals and outcomes (why the task is being done)

- the learning strategies to be used (how to do the task)
- the materials/resource to be used
- the documentation required
- how, and how often, information is to be communicated/exchanged with the teacher (e.g. morning briefing for allocation of tasks, and/or a weekly meeting to review student progress and plans for the following week, sharing an electronic calendar).

Meeting with the teacher provides you with the opportunity to gather information about the students (their needs, strengths, likes, communication style and behaviour-specific learning goals or IEPs), share information about behaviour-management strategies and become familiar with the daily timetable as well as your daily schedule and the resources available.

To maximise the ESW's time and effectiveness in the classroom, teachers will incorporate the ESW's schedule into the daily timetable. The weekly timetable in **Figure 1.5** shows that the teacher is planning for the ESW to work with both individual students (1:1) as well as small groups.

Figure 1.5 ESW weekly timetable

	Monday	Tuesday	Wednesday	Thursday	Friday
9.00	Singing	Spelling	Spelling	Spelling	Spelling
9.30	Spelling Writing/Grammar **ESW: 1:1**	Literacy **ESW: 1:1**	Numeracy Computer Lab **ESW: Group**	Literacy Vocabulary, oral language **ESW: 1:1**	Music
10.00					STEM Projects **ESW: Group**
10.30				Silent Reading	
11.00			**RECESS**		
11.30	Mental Maths Numeracy **ESW: 1:1**	Science **ESW: Group**	Literacy **ESW: 1:1**	Maths numeracy **ESW: Group**	Grammar Writing **ESW: 1:1**
			LUNCH		
2.00 3.00	HSIE	Numeracy Games	Creative Arts	Literacy games	PDHPE

Effective collaboration

Effective collaboration requires clear, unambiguous communication, including active listening. While it is the responsibility of the teacher to provide specific directions and clear instructions related to daily tasks, the ESW must also take responsibility for clarifying the teacher's expectations. **Figure 1.6** provides examples of how this can be achieved.

Effective collaboration also requires a positive mindset by maintaining a 'can do' attitude and staying motivated. For example, 'I do find myself challenged by Izzy but I'm also finding the little gains she is making every day very rewarding', 'Are there areas of my work that I can improve on?' and 'Are there any other tasks you would like me to perform each day as part of the daily routine?'

Acknowledging and validating feedback and support is also an important tool when collaborating with others. For example, 'Thanks for sharing the learning goals with me. It gives me a better understanding of my role.' It's also important to be open to feedback and see it as an

Figure 1.6 Working collaboratively and clarifying expectations

Ask questions	'If the students finish early, what options can I give them?'
Clarify instructions	'Do you want him to attempt the whole text or just one page?'
Address potential problems	'What would you like me to do if Izzy starts to disrupt other students like she did yesterday?'
Clarify goals	'The goal for Izzy is to stay on task'
Clarify support strategies	'Do you want me to prompt Zane as he's reading?'

opportunity to learn and develop. Where feedback implies criticism, it can be difficult not to become defensive or look for excuses to justify poor performance. **Figure 1.7** provides some ideas for responding to feedback, even when it seems negative.

Figure 1.7 Responding to feedback

Ask questions	Shed light on what specifically you can do to fix the issue or improve your performance.
Be aware that negative feedback isn't a personal attack	Good negative feedback is about your actions or your behaviour, not about who you are as a person.
Don't always wait for feedback	Be proactive and seek feedback as needed, and in time this will support the development of a positive and professional working relationship.
Try not to react with strong emotions	Give yourself time to process the feedback by reflecting on it and how the information might be used to improve your practices. Eurich (2018) states that processing and acting on negative feedback is not always easy. It can **make us** defensive, angry and self-conscious, which subsequently **impairs** our effectiveness.
Consider the feedback from the speaker's perspective	This can help you to understand why the feedback was given.
Put feedback into perspective	You are not your job and you have many skills.
Use self-talk to help you process the feedback	For example, 'Wow, I feel like the teacher really appreciates the challenges I face', 'Wow! I wasn't expecting such harsh criticism. I feel so deflated!'
Feedback is simply that	You can act on it or you can reject it. Constructive (even where the feedback is negative) feedback typically leads to positive change and/or opportunity for growth. Destructive feedback or criticism can lower your self-confidence and leave you questioning your own worth. Such feedback is unhelpful and while difficult to do, it should be discarded. Perhaps consider that the speaker is having a bad day and try not to allow the person's words to upset you.

Source: Adapted from: How to handle negative feedback: 6 ways to accept criticism. https://www.masterclass.com/articles/how-to-handle-negative-feedback#why-is-it-important-to-accept-negative-feedback; Eurich, T. (2018). The right way to respond to negative feedback. *Harvard Business Review*. https://hbr.org/2018/05/the-right-way-to-respond-to-negative-feedback

To ensure the best possible outcomes for students, ESWs and teachers must work as a team. There must be a relationship of mutual trust and respect as well as clearly defined roles and boundaries. Working collaboratively requires the ESW and the teacher to work towards a common set of goals, share and exchange information, clarify expectations and set clear roles boundaries. Effective collaboration builds trust, respect and rapport, which are necessary for establishing sound professional relationships.

Videos: Active listening and feedback

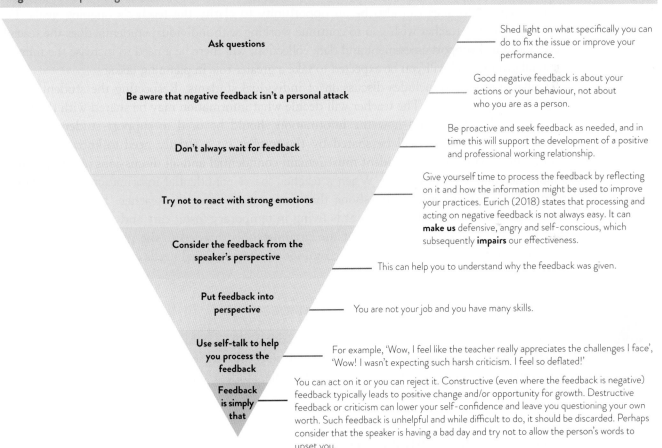

Collaboration also requires a willingness to engage in problem-solving. ESWs will quickly discover that even the most well-thought-out lesson can go wrong. For example, students can be uncooperative, upset, tired, bored or anxious; the resources or learning materials may not meet the needs of the students; there may be an unexpected disruption to the daily schedule; or you may be presented with an issue or problem that you are unsure how to resolve. When problems arise, it's important to respond in ways that minimise disruption to student learning and/or ensure their safety and wellbeing. Having a backup strategy or contingency plan is helpful. For example, introduce a language or memory game, a brain teaser, or engage the students in a conversation.

Collaborating with the teacher also means that plans are in place to meet daily, weekly and monthly/bimonthly. A daily meeting may only take five minutes to clarify the day's work and address any changes or modifications that need to be made to the planned schedule. Weekly meetings of 10 to 15 minutes can be used to review the week, exchange information and identify any tasks for follow-up. Monthly/bimonthly meetings might include meeting over the lunch break to review and seek feedback on your performance, identify areas for improvement and celebrate achievements. Meetings can also be an opportunity to clarify the teacher's ongoing goals. For example, does the teacher wish you to continue working with individual students; does the teacher need additional support assessment and data collection; will there be a need to increase the number of small groups; and will you be expected to take a greater role in planning tasks?

Collaboration also includes discussion of individual students. Respecting the student's right to privacy is paramount. The teacher will decide what information may be shared with the ESW, how it will be shared and how the information should be used to support student learning. Remember, information will be shared by the teacher on a strictly need-to-know basis. Any information shared about a student must remain confidential and all discussions about a student should be conducted in private. When a teacher shares confidential information, ESWs should refrain from asking probing questions that may compromise the teacher. For example, if a teacher shares with you that a student is living in temporary foster care and as a result is 'acting out', it's not appropriate to ask about the circumstances that led to the placement. Rather, it's important to focus on how you might accommodate the emotional needs of the student.

Other roles and responsibilities

Other roles in schools

An ESW may have a number of roles and responsibilities, which will vary according to their specific employment contract. Some ESWs will be employed solely to work with students while others may perform a variety of roles – for example, student support, resource support and non-teaching/administrative roles.

ESW student health care role

- Assisting students with special needs; in certain circumstances, this may extend to supporting mobility, such as assisting with positioning, toileting and dressing of students unable to care for themselves.
- Assisting with feeding via a gastronomy or nasogastric tube; shallow suctioning of secretions from the mouth, nose or tracheostomy tube; administering a student's healthcare plan; implementing procedures to minimise infection; catheterisation; nappy change; washing, bathing, changing clothes.
- Preparing drinks, meals and snacks for students.

- Daily cleaning of materials used for art and craft, wiping tables and chairs, mopping toilets and wet areas.
- Supporting students to use a range of assistive technology, mobility aids and adaptive equipment to support daily living skills development, and supporting the use of augmentative or alternative communication aids and equipment.
- Administering medications, administering first aid (if qualified), providing temporary care for children who are unwell.
- Assisting students to and from motor vehicles at arrival and departure times.
- Working with the teacher to undertake a risk management plan for students with additional needs.

ESW resource-support role

- Preparing learning materials.
- Assisting students who communicate using sign language, audio-visual aids and augmentative and alternative communication.
- Working as an aide to visiting therapists.
- Assisting with recording audio-visual learning tools.
- Transcribing print to Braille or large print.

ESW non-teaching role

- Assisting teachers and students with sporting activities and school excursions.
- Compiling and supervising class rolls.
- Assisting teaching staff with playground and bus supervision.
- Collecting money from students for school activities as required.
- Contributing to the welfare, health and safety of students, including the delivery of first aid.
- Laundering linens.
- Caring of equipment.
- Assisting with organising off-site activities, such as excursions and performances.

ESW administrative role

- Performing a range of general clerical duties at a basic level – for example, filing, handling mail, maintaining records and data entry.
- Operating routine office equipment, such as computers, photocopiers, scanners, facsimile machines, binding machines, guillotines, franking machines, calculators.
- Performing a reception function, including providing information and making referrals in accordance with school procedures.
- Carrying out minor cash transactions, including receipting, balancing and banking.
- Monitoring and maintaining stock levels of stationery/materials within established parameters, including reordering.
- Initiating and handling correspondence, which may include confidential correspondence.

Source: Fair Work Ombudsman. Australian Government https://www.fairwork.gov.au/employee-entitlements/national-employment-standards. Accessed April 2018.

You should also clarify your specific role and responsibilities in key policies such as confidentiality, child protection, discipline and behaviour management.

Employment awards

Employment awards

In Australia employment options may include: full-time; part-time; casual; fixed term; shift workers; daily hire and weekly hire; probation and outworkers (© Fair Work Ombudsman. www.fairwork.gov.au). ESWs may be employed on a fixed-term, full-time or part-time basis.

At the time of writing, the national award for ESWs in Australia was the Educational Services (Schools) General Staff Award 2020. Each state and territory also has its own award, which can be found by searching online. Exploring awards is a good place to start when considering a career as an ESW.

Understanding the award conditions and the terms and conditions set out in an **employment contract** will ensure the employee is aware of their entitlements and the obligations of both the employee and employer. It should be noted that the Educational Services (Schools) General Staff Award 2020 does not cover employees who are covered by a modern enterprise award or an enterprise instrument – for example, state public sector modern awards.

In Australia, all employees are protected by the National Employment Standards (NES) set up as part of the *Fair Work Act 2009*. The NES are designed to provide a safety net in relation to a minimum of 10 workplace entitlements. These are:

1. maximum weekly hours
2. requests for flexible working arrangements
3. parental leave and related entitlements
4. annual leave
5. personal carer's leave and compassionate leave
6. community service leave
7. long service leave
8. public holidays
9. notice of termination and redundancy pay
10. Fair Work Information Statement.

GO FURTHER

Learn more about employment awards and find links to access award information in your **Go Further** resource, available through your instructor.

SCENARIO

EMPLOYMENT CONTRACT

Lucy, the assistant principal, greets **Max** as he walks into the foyer. This is the first day for Max as a part-time ESW and he is rather nervous. Fortunately, Lucy makes him feel welcome and relaxed.

Lucy: *'Hello Max, I'm Lucy James, assistant principal. It's my job to supervise all our ESWs. Welcome aboard! I hope you'll enjoy working with us – it's a great school. Now first things first, Kate, our Admin Officer, will show you where to sign in and out and give a rundown of housekeeping matters. I'll leave you in her capable hands and see you in around 15 minutes in my office.'*

When Max rejoins Lucy, she begins his orientation process.

Lucy: *'We'll go through your employment contract, Max, just to make sure you fully understand the conditions of your employment, such as work hours, start and finish times, sick leave, etc. We will also talk about your specific duties and responsibilities, and later I'll introduce you to the teachers you'll be most closely working with – Tom and Jesse.'*

When concluding the interview, Lucy states: *'I've put together a folder of key policies and procedures for you, Max. You'll see I've included Child Protection, Confidentiality, Professional Conduct, WHS, School Discipline and Communication with Families. I'll highlight the key information for you now, but I don't expect you'll remember everything and I'm sure you'll have some questions for me. This is your folder to keep, so you can read it at your leisure. It's very important that you familiarise yourself with school policies and procedures. They are there to guide you and ensure that everyone acts in the best interests of the school.'*

By the time Lucy has finished talking to Max, it is 10.30 a.m. and Max is more than ready for a coffee. He is pleased that Lucy has explained his contract, roles and responsibilities. He now feels much more confident about being an ESW.

WHAT DOES THIS TELL US?

The assistant principal has clearly explained both the conditions of employment and the specific requirements of the job role. When entering into any new employment arrangement, it is essential to have the job role, expectations and conditions of employment in writing.

1.2 Skills and knowledge

ESWs are often required to work with students who have a range of special needs that influence their ability to learn, behave in an appropriate manner, communicate effectively, relate to others in a socially acceptable and age-appropriate manner, use learning resources, access physical facilities and manage their own personal care.

Increasingly, students with additional needs are supported within the regular classroom or in an additional classroom or program within a mainstream school. ESWs will typically work under the direction and supervision of a classroom teacher. ESWs will work in the classroom alongside the teacher by withdrawing students for one-to-one support, or work with students in small groups (see **Figure 1.8**).

Figure 1.8 ESWs may be required to work with students in small groups

Important attributes for an ESW include effective communication and interpersonal skills, patience, a sense of humour, self-motivation, good organisational and time-management skills, a willingness to be flexible and work effectively as part of a team, an ability to accept direction and supervision, and a willingness to engage in ongoing education and professional learning. Above all, ESWs need to enjoy working with children and young people. They also need to be resilient and willing to persist in supporting students whose progress may be marginal or who may act out and resist support. Importantly, ESWs must also be aware of the critical importance of maintaining privacy and confidentiality, and respecting the student and their family at all times.

SCENARIO

PERSONAL COMPETENCE

Arna: *'I work four days per week at a local high school, primarily with young people who are struggling readers. My biggest challenge is communication. I work really hard to keep my students motivated. It's not an easy task to work with teenagers who have low self-esteem!'*

Jude: *'The high school where I work is in a socially disadvantaged area. The kids have to be resilient to survive. I find that I spend much of my time trying to manage behaviour issues. I need to be patient, respectful and understanding.'*

Megan: *'I work at two schools – a high school and a primary school. I have to plan ahead and be really well organised. I use a daily diary and 'Things to Do Today' list. I write everything down that I need to do so that I don't forget anything. My own children laugh at me and say, 'Mum, why don't you use your phone or your iPad for your notes?' I tell them I like pen and paper. It may be old-fashioned, but it works for me!'*

Saafie: *'I find that being courteous and respectful even to the most challenging students is a good strategy. I remind myself that these kids are doing it tough and many of them don't have a very happy home life. When a student gets angry or frustrated and takes it out on me, I do my best to stay calm and positive. Getting angry back doesn't help – it's my job to model coping strategies.'*

Dion: *'If you want to be an ESW, you need to be able to cope with change. Some days nothing goes to plan, and you just have to go with the flow. You can't get stressed because you planned to have an hour with students and end up being allocated 30 minutes because of a special assembly, for example. Sometimes the students won't cooperate and so you end up wasting valuable time just getting them settled. Sometimes I just scrap what I've planned and do something completely different, depending on the mood of the students. It's the sort of job where you have to think on your feet. You can't get caught up in sticking to your plans. That's never going to work!'*

WHAT DOES THIS TELL US?

ESWs need to plan ahead, but also should be flexible and willing to adapt, adjust or even abandon planned activities in response to changing situations.

▶ DISCUSSION

Which of these situations would you find most challenging? What resources could you access to support you when working in challenging situations?

GO FURTHER

Learn more about employability skills in your **Go Further** resource, available through your instructor.

Employability skills

Employability skills is the term used to describe a set of generic or interpersonal skills identified as essential for all employees if they are to be effective and productive in the workplace. These employability skills, also known as 'soft skills', are often referred to as Skills for the 21st Century.

Organising your work

A key skill for ESWs is the ability to be organised. Being well organised may vary from person to person and school to school. Being organised comes naturally to some people, but for others it requires careful thought and planning. Organised people tend not to procrastinate and can usually achieve more in a limited time by having a range of 'mini-routines' or systems that they stick to each day. Schools, large or small, are always busy places. Being organised does not make them less busy, but it certainly makes the work more manageable. Being organised means:

- having a thorough knowledge of your job description – understand your responsibilities, roles and associated tasks and be clear about your supervising teacher's expectations
- being aware of the roles and duties of others within the organisation
- being aware of timetables and school schedules
- being aware of the equipment and resources available, where they are stored, how they can be accessed and whether they must be returned to storage at the end of each day or can be left in the classroom (see **Figure 1.9**)
- prioritising – knowing what is important, and not wasting time on trivial tasks
- using a diary or organiser to forward-plan known commitments
- having a 'to do' list to ensure extra tasks are carried out as required – this takes the pressure off remembering everything and clears your mind for the day ahead
- arriving at work on time by making sure that you are up early enough to prepare yourself for the day

Figure 1.9 Find out where equipment is stored before you need to use it

Source: Photo by Tish Okely © Cengage

- asking for direction and support when needed
- knowing when you are becoming 'snowed under' – learn to say 'no' when you need to, and do not take on the work of others when your own jobs are incomplete
- pacing yourself and keeping an eye on the time throughout the day without becoming a 'clock watcher'.

Being organised and well prepared leads to greater productivity, which in turn leads to improved workplace performance and a greater sense of achievement and wellbeing. Being organised reduces workplace stress that, if allowed to accumulate, can lead to serious health issues. See the following Scenario for an example.

SCENARIO

BE PREPARED!

Vicki has been an ESW for seven years. Today she is a guest speaker at an orientation/training course for new ESWs. Vicki's topic is 'Be Prepared!' Vicki shares her experiences with the group and outlines some interesting scenarios to highlight the importance of being organised and expecting the unexpected. Vicki has brought along her basket, which she has with her every day and refers to as her 'tools of trade'. She unpacks the basket and, one by one, discusses the contents with the group. Vicki explains that the items in her basket are essential work tools for an ESW – her motto is 'Never leave home without it'. Her basket contains the following items:

- diary, including a 'to do list', school timetable and class timetables and class list – Vicki tells the group this is a must-have item
- pens, pencils, pencil sharpener, eraser, paperclips, notebook, hole punch, stapler, sticky tape, masking tape, glue, scissors, ruler, sticky notes pad, felt pens, whiteboard marker and eraser, spare manila folders, spare paper, felt pens, stickers for rewards, reward charts – Vicki explains that these items make her self-reliant. She doesn't have to go hunting for things, which saves her precious classroom time
- use-and-wipe game books, football cards, fun work sheets for different age groups, egg timer, games such as a set of magnets, dominoes, collection of plastic figures, babushka dolls, handheld electronic games, magic marker boards – Vicki shares with the group that these items are her 'sanity savers'. She uses them to calm students, as rewards for staying on task, as brain breaks and as time fillers if needed
- hand wipes, a box of tissues, hat and sunscreen – Vicki emphasises the need to look after yourself and take basic healthcare measures.

Vicki tells the group that they must be self-reliant and well prepared, and that having a well-stocked toolbox is a good starting point.

WHAT DOES THIS TELL US?

Vicki has emphasised the need to think about the job role and to be as self-sufficient as possible to save time and enable her to get on with the job.

Managing your time

Time is a limited resource. Juggling competing priorities and demands for their time has become an ongoing challenge for many people. Being able to set priorities and manage time are essential skills for an ESW, as evidenced by the timetable in **Figure 1.10**.

There are many things that can impact on our ability to get the job done in a timely and efficient manner. Common 'time stealers', which can interfere with the 'best-laid plans' at home and at work, include unforeseen interruptions, procrastination and indecision, acting with incomplete information, poor communication, unclear goals and priorities, poor planning, taking on too many tasks (the inability to say 'no') and poor organisational skills.

Videos: Time management

Figure 1.10 Example of a weekly plan

WEEK 8						
Week beginning: 21-3-20XX						
Activity	Monday	Tuesday	Wednesday	Thursday	Friday	Weekend
Personal	3–4 School football practice	4.30 Cardio Netball practice	4.15 Dentist Netball practice	4.30 Cardio Netball practice	3–4 Football prac	Netball Family break
Reading 9–10.30 a.m.	Jack/Lylla */ch/sound *Read 'Choo choo train'	Harry *CVC initial chart *Term assessment	Harry * Set goals *Identify goal strategies *Draft deskmat	Robots *Read 'Insects' *Discuss new terminology	Robots 'Insects' comprehension tasks 1–7	
Reporting 11–12 p.m.	Class week's preparation	Finalising CVC data to MS Mae	Email specialists with student goals	~~Finalise term report~~ Stand in for Nick's group	Class prep Sport Grade 4	
Maths 2–3 p.m.	General assistance in 8F INTEGERS	Jack/Lillya *Catch up on Surds	Jack/Lillya *Surds activities × 8 qtns	Penguins *Adding fractions	Sloths *Fraction pie puzzles	
Follow-up 3–3.30 p.m.	Write up observations	Write up observations	Write up observations	Write up observations	Write up observations	

TO DO	NOTES
☐ ______	______
☐ ______	______
☐ ______	______
☐ ______	______
☐ ______	______
☐ ______	______
☐ ______	______

This is a summative document that provides visual notes for a quick reference. More detailed notes would be located in a planner or diary.

GO FURTHER

Learn more about maintaining a work–life balance in your **Go Further** resource, available through your instructor.

Of the time stealers listed above, one of the most common is procrastination. Everyone will procrastinate over a task or decision at some time. Many people use procrastination as a strategy to allow time for further thought and consideration. However, when procrastination occurs regularly in relation to daily tasks, it can become a real problem. Putting off 'must do' small tasks can quickly lead to an overwhelming 'mountain' of tasks.

If you are a procrastinator, you need to make a list of all the tasks that you need to do, set a timeframe and identify a realistic amount of time each day to tackle one task. To manage your time effectively, you can try creating a daily/weekly 'to do' list, be realistic about what you can achieve each day, delegate tasks where possible and learn to be assertive – it's okay to say 'no'!

Keeping a work diary

A diary is a simple and effective way to document and maintain a record of day-to-day activities in the workplace. You may choose to use a paper-based diary or an electronic diary/planner for an iPhone or iPad that can be shared with others. **Figure 1.11** shows some of the uses of a work diary.

Figure 1.11 Uses of a work diary

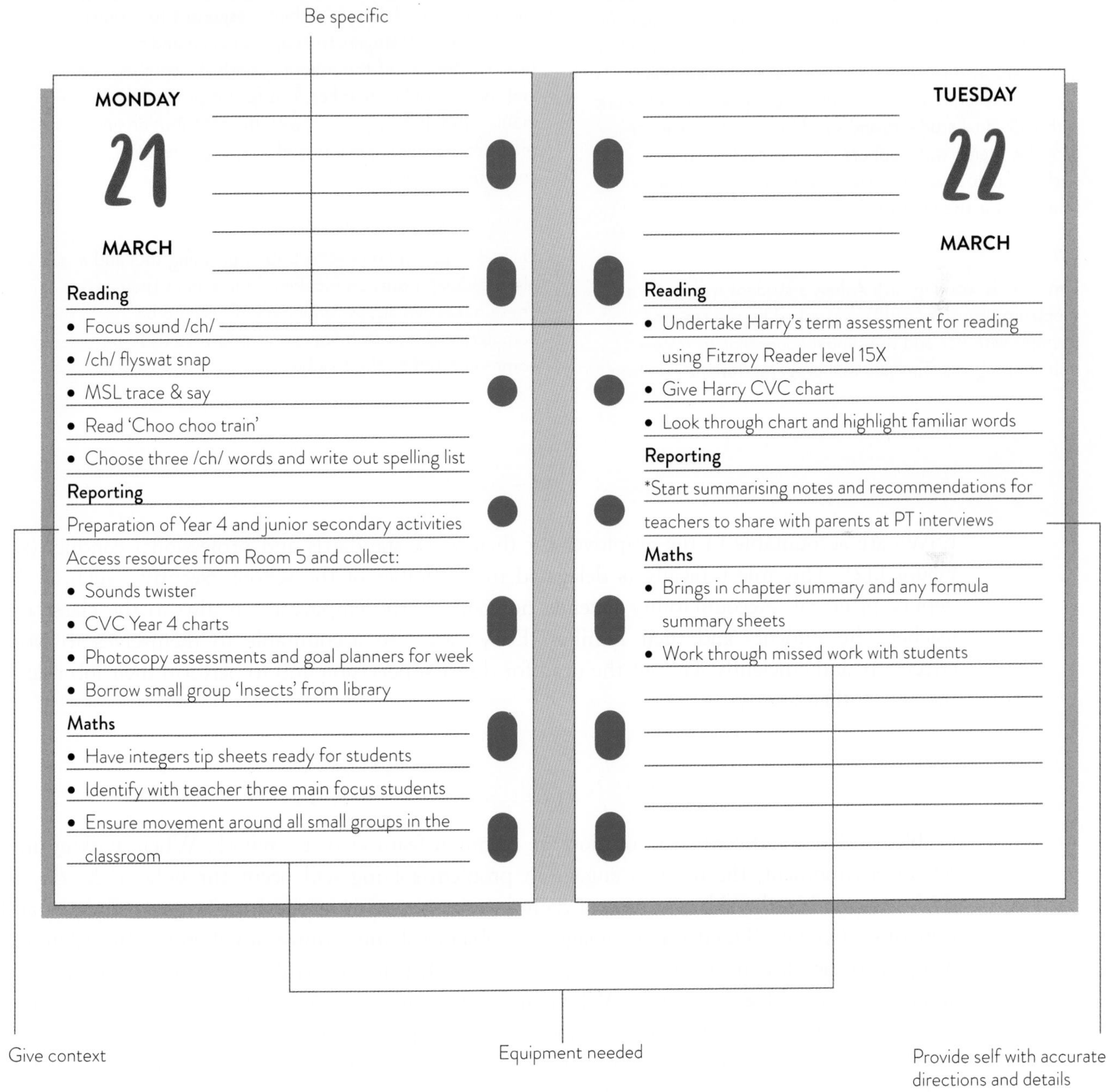

Be specific
MONDAY
21
MARCH
Reading
• Focus sound /ch/
• /ch/ flyswat snap
• MSL trace & say
• Read 'Choo choo train'
• Choose three /ch/ words and write out spelling list
Reporting
Preparation of Year 4 and junior secondary activities
Access resources from Room 5 and collect:
• Sounds twister
• CVC Year 4 charts
• Photocopy assessments and goal planners for week
• Borrow small group 'Insects' from library
Maths
• Have integers tip sheets ready for students
• Identify with teacher three main focus students
• Ensure movement around all small groups in the classroom
TUESDAY
22
MARCH
Reading
• Undertake Harry's term assessment for reading using Fitzroy Reader level 15X
• Give Harry CVC chart
• Look through chart and highlight familiar words
Reporting
*Start summarising notes and recommendations for teachers to share with parents at PT interviews
Maths
• Brings in chapter summary and any formula summary sheets
• Work through missed work with students
Give context
Equipment needed
Provide self with accurate directions and details

Accurate detail here also enables you to revisit what was completed and use this to document in any reporting that your school uses.

Accurate details in your diary can also enable you to revisit what was completed and use this document in any reporting that your school uses. Your diary is confidential and should not be left lying around for students to read.

SCENARIO

DAILY DIARY

HELEN

Each morning ESW **Helen** spends 10 minutes reviewing her schedule of tasks with the teacher. At these meetings, Helen can ask questions to clarify her role and/or specific tasks that are to be performed. Helen makes notes in her daily diary as they talk. At the end of the week, Helen gives the teacher a written and verbal update on her work with individual students and small groups. The teacher provides Helen with support and feedback on her performance. This information is used to plan Helen's schedule for the next week.

TIM

Tim, who is working with **Asher**, a student with autism spectrum disorder (ASD), was asked by the teacher to meet with her and the school counsellor to review Asher's progress. Tim was well prepared for the meeting because he had his daily planning and evaluation sheets as well as notes he had made in his diary. Tim was able to make a significant contribution to the meeting, particularly in relation to Asher's responses to various management strategies to keep him calm and on task. At the end of the meeting, both the teacher and the counsellor thanked Tim for his professional input. Tim felt very pleased with his contribution and reflected on the importance of keeping objective and timely records.

WHAT DOES THIS TELL US?

Daily diaries can be used as both a planning tool and a place to keep notes on incidental matters as they arise. These notes can act as reminders of tasks to be completed, things to follow up or information to be communicated to the teacher.

Accountability

ESWs are accountable to the employer for their work standards and professional conduct (see **Figure 1.12**). This role typically is delegated to a member of the school executive, such as the deputy principal. Accountability extends not only to the employer but also to the classroom teacher, the students and their families. ESWs are also accountable to themselves to work effectively and efficiently without the need for direct supervision and to perform their job role to the best of their ability.

Problem-solving, collaboration and conflict resolution

Problem-solving and conflict resolution are common features of teamwork. When working in a school environment, the need to engage in problem-solving will occur throughout the day as ESWs respond to the ebb and flow of daily interactions with teachers, colleagues, students and sometimes families. To effectivly engage in problem-solving requires a willingness to listen and be open to the ideas of others; there will be times when team members have differing opinions about how to resolve a problem. When this occurs, it is important to be prepared to listen, explore and discuss the problems from varying perspectives to reach a satisfactory solution. Problem-solving is also an opportunity to learn from others as they share different ways of thinking and different solutions. The goal when problem-solving is to reach a consensus. This does not mean that everyone must agree with the solution; rather, it means that everyone agrees to accept and implement the solution. **Figure 1.13** shows the key steps in problem-solving.

Figure 1.12 ESW key areas of accountability

Accountability to students

- Support learning and inclusion
- Support safety, health and self-care

Accountability to teachers

- Build professional relationships
- Follow directions
- Share information
- Support learning goals

Accountability to families

- Communicate with families following school protocols
- Treat all families with dignity and respect

Accountability to employer

- Comply with all policies and procedures
- Act in an ethical manner
- Work collaboratively with all staff

Accountability to self

- Understand own role/responsibilities
- Act in a professional manner
- Communicate effectively
- Engage in ongoing learning

Figure 1.13 Steps in problem-solving

Step 1 Identify or clarify the problem or issue. Be specific – identify the cause of the problem, why it's a problem and for whom it is a problem? When/how often is it a problem?

Step 2 Identify and understand the outcomes that must be achieved

Step 3 Analyse the problem – gather all relevant information and facts

Step 4 Generate and evaluate ideas/solutions – discuss pros and cons. Will this solution work? Will it achieve the desired outcome? How can the solution be implemented?

Step 5 Select one solution and develop an implementation plan – how, when, who

Step 6 Implement the plan and monitor it – did the solution work?

The following Scenario demonstrates how helpful these steps can be and how important it is to work as a team to problem-solve.

SCENARIO

PROBLEM-SOLVING COMMUNICATION

Each day ESW **Harry** writes an evaluation of his support sessions with **Selina** (14 years) who struggles with literacy. Harry records how Selina responded, what worked well and how Selina is progressing. At the end of the week Harry meets with teacher **Anna** to discuss Selina's work.

Harry's evaluations are written in a notebook, where he also records his work with other students, reminders of things he needs to do and resources he has accessed.

At the end-of-week meeting, Harry refers to his notes when discussing Selina's progress with Anna.

At today's meeting, Anna asks if Harry could photocopy his notes and give them to her for her records. Harry feels a little uncomfortable about this as his notes include his reflections on his own performance and goals for self-improvement. Moving forward, Anna suggests they develop a template which Harry can use to transcribe his notes and for ongoing evaluations. Together Harry and Anna work on a template that meets both their needs.

WHAT DOES THIS TELL US?

By collaborating, Harry and Anna were able develop a solution that met both their needs.

Conflict resolution

Conflict can occur in any workplace. Often it stems from poor communication, lack of respect, differences in values and beliefs, resistance to change, inability to be flexible or differences in motivation.

Videos: Resolving conflict

The Conflict Resolution Network has identified 12 skills necessary for effective conflict resolution, which are shown in **Figure 1.14**.

The goal when engaging in conflict resolution is to create a win–win situation where all parties feel they have been listened to and able to contribute towards a satisfactory resolution. A win–win approach focuses on resolving the problem. In the workplace, the goal of conflict resolution should not be about power (being right, having a better idea, exerting seniority); rather, it should be about finding a solution that best fits the needs of the organisation. It requires participants to actively listen to others and try to consider the perspectives of others. It requires all participants to be objective, keep their emotions in check and avoid attacking others on a personal level (see **Figure 1.14**). It also requires an open mind – conflict resolution can be an opportunity for learning and innovation.

Figure 1.14 Twelve steps to conflict resolution

1. Win–win approach: how can we solve this as partners rather than opponents?
2. Creative response: transform problems into creative opportunities
3. Empathy: develop communication tools to build rapport. Use listening to clarify understanding
4. Appropriate assertiveness: apply strategies to attack the problem not the person
5. Cooperative power: eliminate 'power over' to build 'power with' others
6. Managing emotions: express fear, anger, hurt and frustration wisely to effect change
7. Willingness to resolve: name personal issues that cloud the picture

8 Mapping the conflict: define the issues needed to chart common needs and concerns

9 Development of options: design creative solutions together

10 Introduction to negotiation: plan and apply effective strategies to reach agreement

11 Introduction to mediation: help conflicting parties to move towards solutions

12 Broadening perspectives: try to see the problem from a range of viewing points, other points of view and wider perspectives. Respect and value differences. Consider the wider context, the longer term, and reflect on what you can and cannot change

Source: Conflict Resolution Network (n.d.). Conflict resolution skills: 12 skill summary. https://www.crnhq.org/12-skill-summary

SCENARIO

CONFLICT RESOLUTION

Narnia and **Josie** are experienced ESWs but have very different personalities. Narnia is best described as a quiet achiever. She goes about her duties calmly and efficiently. She is quietly spoken, friendly and helpful. Josie, on the other hand, is quite dominant, loud and inflexible. With Josie it's a case of 'my way or the highway!'

Narnia and Josie are currently assigned to work with students in three kindergarten classes. While they work with different children, they are required to work collaboratively and share ideas and plan the use of various resources. Josie tends to dominate any planning discussions. She tells Narnia what resources she has planned to use for the week and expects Narnia to adapt her own plans to fit in with Narnia.

Narnia: *'Josie, we are supposed to be working together on the use of resources. I find it difficult when you expect me to plan my week around your needs. I would like to work more collaboratively so that the resources can be shared fairly.'*

Josie: *'That's exactly what I'm doing. I've told you when I need the resources so that you know when they're not available.'*

Narnia: *'Josie, that's not working collaboratively, that's you ensuring your needs are met without any consideration of my needs.'*

Josie: *'That's rubbish! One of us has to have first choice otherwise we'll be here all day. It's always worked well in the past, I don't know what you're complaining about. Let's just get on with it!'*

Since this exchange, Josie speaks to Narnia only when necessary. Narnia is feeling rather defeated. She had hoped Josie would see that she was being selfish and unfair.

▶ DISCUSSION

Discuss the conflict from the perspective of both Narnia and Josie. What outcome are both Narnia and Josie wanting to achieve? Suggest why it would be important to resolve this conflict as quickly as possible.

It is essential to have in place well-defined strategies to resolve conflicts or problems. Equally important are a positive attitude and a willingness by all team members to work collaboratively towards a win–win outcome.

1.3 Professional conduct

Schools are busy workplaces. ESWs work as part of a diverse team of teaching and non-teaching staff. Each member of the team will have a specific role and responsibilities that contribute to the overall operation of the school. To be effective and efficient, and to deliver quality educational experiences, all members of the team must work collaboratively, follow policies and procedures, and respect all other members of the school community.

Accountability can be demonstrated as part of a performance review process that allows ESWs to review their skills, practices and knowledge, critically reflect on performance and set goals for future development. Performance reviews allow both the employee and the supervisor to reflect on individual achievements and identify areas where additional support, information, resources, guidance or training may be required. It is also an opportunity to identify longer-term career goals and how these might be achieved.

CAREER PLANNING

SCENARIO

David has been working as an ESW at an independent boys' school for almost 10 years. His primary role has been IT support. Over the last three years, David has gained a Diploma in Education Support. He now wants to enrol part-time at university to complete a teaching degree. David is a very independent person and has not shared this information with his supervisor.

At his performance review, David is asked by his supervisor, **John**, if he has any long-term career goals and is surprised when David tells him of his achievements and aspirations.

John responds: *'Wow David, that's fantastic. You'll make a great teacher! How about we schedule some regular classroom experiences so you can work on practical teaching skills?'*

David is delighted and surprised by John's enthusiastic response. He wishes he had asked John for support when he was doing his Diploma course.

WHAT DOES THIS TELL US?

Professional development is best achieved when the employee and the employer/supervisor work collaboratively to set goals and devise learning strategies.

Professional knowledge

Working with students can be both rewarding and challenging, particularly when students have additional needs. Each student will be unique in terms of their personality, strengths, areas of need and preferred learning style. Being well informed about each student's particular strengths and needs is essential to ensure optimal support. It is also important to understand how children and young people learn, and how learning can be supported in a formal school setting.

Professional knowledge is a term used to describe specialised knowledge and its application to practice. In the case of ESWs, professional knowledge is required to ensure high standards and quality outcomes when supporting teachers, students, parents and the broader school community. Working with children and young people requires the highest possible standards of professional conduct. The 'Consider this' box provides you with the opportunity to reflect on the range of professional knowledge you may need when working in school settings.

PROFESSIONAL KNOWLEDGE

CONSIDER THIS

What skills and knowledge might you require in each of the following situations? Where could you go to access resources and support?

- Observe and document the social skills of a student.
- Guide and support a student with behaviour issues.
- Work with a small group of students to support numeracy skills.
- Assist a student to complete a program of exercises that has been developed by a physiotherapist.
- Support high school students with daily living skills to promote independence in areas such as dressing, toileting, handwashing and meals.
- Work one-on-one with a student who is visually impaired.
- Support students who have limited mobility to navigate the classroom, outdoors, toilet, bus stop and so on.
- Assist a student to use augmentative communication.
- Assist a student to use mobility aids.
- Plan a small group reading activity for a group of Year 7 students.

Professional knowledge usually is acquired through formal training, self-directed reading, working alongside an experienced colleague, engaging in a mentoring program and undertaking formal professional development activities. Professional knowledge assists in understanding:

- how students develop and learn – for example, understanding literacy or numeracy development
- brain development – for example, understanding how adolescent brain development can provide insight into adolescent behaviour
- children's and young people's behaviour and the effective application of behaviour management strategies – for example, understanding adolescent social development
- the principles of supervision and how these can be applied both inside and outside the classroom – for example, understanding that supervision includes looking, listening, anticipating and setting clear behaviour limits
- how to use effective communication with adults and students – for example, adapting your communication style so that it reflects the developmental level of a kindergarten or a high school student
- legal and ethical obligations, school policies and procedures – for example, understanding child protection legislation, policies and procedures to provide you with instructions on what to do if you suspect a child or young person is at risk
- how learning materials can be used to enhance and support classroom learning – for example, creating a bank of age-appropriate resource materials for young people with reading problems
- the Australian Curriculum and the seven general capabilities – this knowledge is essential when working with the classroom teacher to deliver supported learning programs for students
- how to observe, document, record and interpret students' behaviour – for example, the strategies a 14-year-old struggling reader uses when confronted with challenging text
- how to develop technical expertise to support the use of supplementary aids to assist students with disabilities, such as adaptive equipment, structural aids and adaptive technology.

GO FURTHER

Learn more about communication skills in your **Go Further** resource, available through your instructor.

SCENARIO

PROFESSIONAL KNOWLEDGE AND SKILLS

Astarlin (14 years) has limited mobility and poor muscle control. To support her head and neck, she wears a foam wrap-around collar. She also wears a lightweight helmet to protect her skull. Astarlin can use her hands to operate her electric wheelchair but needs assistance at mealtimes and when toileting. Astarlin uses assistive technology as her main form of communication.

WHAT DOES THIS TELL US?

To work effectively with Astarlin, ESW **Zenni** must have the following skills and knowledge:

- personal care skills – assisting with toileting, handwashing and meals
- correct fitting of aids – for example, neck collar and helmet
- knowledge about use of personal protective equipment (PPE) and back-care strategies
- correct lifting techniques
- physical care – managing and monitoring mobility needs
- operation of an electric wheelchair
- use of assistive technology
- ethical conduct.

Professional knowledge informs best practice – that is, it equips you with the underpinning knowledge upon which you can build your skills as an ESW. It is important to be aware that no two classrooms will be the same and no two students – even those with similar abilities and/or disabilities – will be the same. The key to being an effective ESW is to continually build your knowledge and skills.

Acting ethically

All employees working with students must conduct themselves in an ethical manner, respecting the rights of students and their families. Ethics are shaped by morals, principles, values and beliefs about 'the right thing to do' that guide our decision-making. Ethical decision-making involves:

- creating the greatest balance between good and harm – that is, using moral reasoning to ensure the greatest benefits for all those involved. For example, even though one student did not complete all tasks as agreed, ESW Jenna decides to allow all of the students in her group to play a fun game. Excluding the student would have made everyone feel uncomfortable
- acknowledging and respecting the individual's right to make choices. For example, ESW Maggie accepts that her co-worker, Zoya, chooses not to participate in the end of year Christmas celebrations because it is not part of her religious tradition
- consideration of the common good according to expected standards of behaviour – for example, mandatory vaccination as a condition of employment
- courage, honesty, integrity, compassion, dignity and social justice – for example, compassion for students whose home life is violent or chaotic.

The Markkula Center for Applied Ethics states:

> Ethics is based on well-founded standards of right and wrong that prescribe what humans ought to do, usually in terms of rights, obligations, benefits to society, fairness, or specific virtues.

Source: Markkula Center for Applied Ethics (2010). What is ethics? https://www.scu.edu/ethics/ethics-resources/ethical-decision-making/what-is-ethics/ (accessed November 2021).

Various professional bodies have developed codes of ethics that guide ethical decision-making. According to the Australian Human Rights Commission, a code of ethics is a set of core ethical principles that informs and guides ethical practice within a profession. It defines the values and responsibilities that are fundamental to a particular profession (AHRC, 2016).

Having a code of ethics in place can:

- assist in making clear what is important among conflicting workplace demands
- specify core values, beliefs and practices that are fundamental to the wellbeing and education of children and young people
- assist to ensure quality education and wellbeing practices by identifying what cannot be compromised
- educate the community about standards of good practice
- demonstrate the complexity of the school's role in supporting the wellbeing of children and young people
- promote appreciation of **diversity**.

Typically, a code of ethics includes a statement of underpinning values, such as integrity, respect, justice, empathy and dignity. In contrast, a code of conduct will describe a range of professional behaviours and competence expected of a teacher. A code of conduct may include directives such as managing **conflicts of interest**, protecting confidential information, duty of care, use of drugs, alcohol and tobacco, professional relationships between employees and students, dress code and statement of ethics.

Videos: Ethics in the workplace

At the time of writing, Australian Teacher Aide was developing the Australian Standards for Paraprofessional Educators in Schools. These seven professional standards will guide professional practice, support reflection and skills development. They are:

Professional Knowledge Standard 1: Know students and how they learn
Professional Knowledge Standard 2: Know how to support teaching and learning
Professional Practice Standard 3: Collaborate with teachers to implement effective teaching and learning
Professional Practice Standard 4: Contribute to, and maintain supportive and safe learning environments
Professional Practice Standard 5: Contribute to assessment and provide feedback on student learning
Professional Engagement Standard 6: Engage in professional learning
Professional Engagement Standard 7: Engage and communicate professionally with colleagues and the school community

Source: Australian Teacher Aide (2023). Australian Standards for Paraprofessional Educators in Schools. https://www.australianteacheraide.com.au/

Ethical dilemmas

Inevitably, ethical issues in relation to students, families and colleagues will arise in the workplace. These can lead to ethical dilemmas. **Ethical dilemmas** present conflicting perspectives related to personal values and beliefs, professional and legal obligations, fairness, privacy and social justice. As you read the following examples of ethical dilemmas, think about how you might respond:

- A student who is known to be at risk of harm by her mother's abusive partner asks for your mobile number.
- A student makes a friend request on your Facebook page.
- The parent of a student who is a casual acquaintance and who lives around the corner from you asks if you can give her son a lift to and from school so that he doesn't have to catch two buses each way.
- You attend a compulsory professional day for ESWs with a colleague. Your colleague doesn't return after lunch. You know she has taken the afternoon off to go shopping. You are asked by the trainer if you know why your colleague is not present.
- You and your partner go for a late dinner to a local restaurant where you see six-year-old Lim sitting at a table folding napkins. You leave at 10 p.m. and notice that Lim is still working on the napkins. You know that Lim's teacher is concerned that he doesn't pay attention in class and tends to daydream. Should you tell Lim's teacher what you have witnessed?

When faced with ethical dilemmas, there are no firm rules about how to respond. However, ESWs have a moral and legal obligation to comply with their employer's code of conduct and act in the best interests of children and young people. Useful strategies to work through an ethical dilemma might include:

- exploring the issue from each party's perspective – what are the needs, rights and beliefs of each party?
- considering your moral and legal obligations to each party, including yourself as an employee, your duty of care to the students and the family's right to privacy
- seeking guidance and support from a mentor, supervisor or trusted colleague.

The following Scenario highlights the challenges of addressing an ethical dilemma.

EDEN AND MANDY

SCENARIO

Eden, an ESW, is concerned that her colleague **Mandy** is consuming alcohol while working at the school. On several occasions, Eden has been able to smell alcohol on Mandy's breath. Eden suspects that Mandy puts alcohol in her water bottle, which she carries with her at all times. Mandy is a single parent with three teenage children. She gets little financial support from her ex-husband and often tells Eden how lucky she is to have such a wonderful job.

Eden knows that if she reports Mandy and it is found that she is drinking on the job, Mandy will be dismissed immediately and is unlikely to be employed by any other school in the area.

Eden grapples with her conscience – on the one hand, she knows she has a duty of care to students and a responsibility to act in accordance with the school's code of conduct. On the other hand, she knows that if Mandy is dismissed she will probably spiral into binge drinking, putting herself and her children at risk.

WHAT DOES THIS TELL US?

Acting ethically is not always easy to do. In this situation, Eden is torn between her responsibility to her employer (and students) and the wellbeing of her colleague and her family.

▶ DISCUSSION

If you were in Eden's shoes, what would you do? Why? Would you base your decision on consideration of the common good according to expected standards of behaviour? Would you show compassion for Mandy and ask her to seek help to address her alcohol addiction?

The interrelationship between legal and ethical issues

Ethics are sets of principles that guide decision-making. They set out what is considered to be best practice in relation to morals, values and beliefs. Ethical behaviours are often argued in the context of the 'right thing to do' rather than simply complying with a set of laws or rules.

Laws and regulations are the enforceable rules or standards of behaviour of a society. Failure to comply may result in penalties and sanctions. For example, employees and employers are bound by employment, WHS and anti-discrimination legislation.

Ethics and laws clash when rules and laws are thought to be unethical by the society in which those laws and rules are imposed. Consider, for example, the decriminalisation of homosexuality in many Western societies, the dismantling of segregation and apartheid laws, the decriminalisation of abortion, the rights of women to vote or the repatriation of land to its Indigenous custodians. All of these changes came about in part because the intent of the existing laws was considered to be unethical, unjust, unfair and discriminatory.

While ethics and laws are separate and distinct, there is also a relationship between the two. This relationship exists because laws are often formulated as a result of ethics (the right thing to do). For example, the legislation that exists to ensure every child has access to a public education (Disability Standards for Education 2005; DET, 2005) reflects the ethical belief that every child, regardless of their financial circumstances and abilities, is entitled to an education on the same basis as other students; employment laws related to unfair dismissal exist because governments are ethically bound to protect vulnerable workers.

While laws can be challenged, they are widely accepted as the rules by which society operates and is governed. When these laws or rules are broken, penalties, which are also embodied in law, are imposed by the courts. In contrast, where there are deemed to be breaches in ethical conduct, sanctions may be imposed by professional bodies, the employer and, in some instances, by the courts (where the breach is also deemed to be unlawful). For example, an ESW who 'friends' a young high school student for the purposes of conducting a close personal relationship is breaching ethical standards of professional conduct and also breaking the law. An ESW who swears at a student is breaching ethical standards but is not breaking the law. However, in both cases, it is likely that the ESW would be deemed unfit to continue their employment.

In the Scenario 'Eden and Mandy', it could be argued that consuming alcohol while working with students means Mandy is breaking the law by breaching her employment contract.

As previously stated, ethical standards for a particular profession are typically embodied in a code of ethics. However, not every professional may hold the same set of values and beliefs, and therefore may not always agree with or comply with the standards set by a code of ethics. Consider the following Scenario.

SCENARIO

ETHICS VS THE LAW

Aidan lives close to the local high school where he is employed as an ESW. He walks to and from work and often calls in at the local shopping centre to pick up groceries on his way home. Today he witnesses two students steal a loaf of bread from a rack at the front of a hot bread shop. The boys are brothers aged 13 and 15. Aidan knows the family struggle to make ends meet. The boys' father is unemployed and known to be violent, and their mother has chronic health issues. Aidan is aware that the boys regularly come to school without having had breakfast and often are without lunch. Later that evening Aidan recounts the incident to his partner. Should he speak to the boys? Should he report the incident to the principal? Should the boys' parents be informed? Whose rights should be addressed – the shop owner who is simply trying to make a living and must bear the cost of shoplifters or the boys who often go hungry?

WHAT DOES THIS TELL US?

In this scenario, Aidan has witnessed the boys stealing, which is clearly against the law. Is Aidan acting ethically if he reports the incident? Is Aidan acting ethically if he doesn't report the incident? Is this an example where compassion and 'doing the right thing' means ignoring evidence of a crime?

Privacy and confidentiality

The *Privacy Act 1988* (Privacy Act) was introduced to promote and protect the privacy of individuals and to regulate Australian Government agencies and organisations with an annual turnover of more than $3 million, and some other organisations, in relation to the collection, storage, access to, use and disclosure of personal information.

The Privacy Act includes the Australian Privacy Principles, which govern standards, rights and obligations regarding:

- the collection, use and disclosure of personal information
- an organisation or agency's governance and accountability
- integrity and correction of personal information
- the rights of individuals to access their personal information

Source: Office of the Australian Information Commissioner (n.d.). Australian Privacy Principles. https://www.oaic.gov.au/privacy/australian-privacy-principles (accessed November 2021).

Privacy and policy guidelines

ESWs are required to act in a legal and ethical manner to ensure privacy and confidentiality in relation to all aspects of the work role. This extends to all employees, students, parents/carers and visitors to the school. Examples of confidential information relating to students and their families include student behaviour, academic results, formal and informal assessment outcomes and family circumstances. Examples of confidential information relating to employees include telephone numbers and addresses, family details and workplace performance.

The role of an ESW is a position of trust. ESWs must never provide information about a student or their family to other agencies/services – this is the role of the teacher, who will follow the school's privacy/confidentiality policy when sharing information. Typically, the school will be required to have written permission from the parent or guardian to share information about a student with relevant agencies and support services.

Any in-school discussion about students and their families with colleagues should be on a need-to-know basis. The ESW should avoid commenting on students and/or their families in informal settings such as the staffroom, as this can sometimes lead to gossiping, which is extremely unethical. When talking about your work role with family and friends, you should avoid using teachers' or students' names, and also avoid sharing information of a specific nature.

Confidentiality and privacy should also be maintained in relation to written documentation. Documents of a confidential nature that are in your possession should never be left lying around in the classroom or staffroom. Best practice is to store these documents in a lockable filing cabinet. If this is not possible, you should seek direction from the classroom teacher about safe storage options.

Student records are typically accessible only by teachers who may choose to share information with the ESW as relevant to their work role – for example, goals for the student or assessment outcomes relevant to planning/IEPs.

Schools are dynamic environments. This means that while most often the school day runs smoothly and without incident, there will be occasions when this is not the case. For example, a student may act aggressively or have a serious meltdown, a student or colleague may accidentally be injured, a parent may become angry or upset, or conflict may occur between staff members. Where you witness or are exposed to such situations, you should avoid becoming involved unless directed to do so by the teacher and/or where the student is in danger and no teachers are available to assist. Details of any such situations should remain confidential and should only be discussed if you are directed to do so by a teacher or school executive.

Conflict of interest

Video: Australian Privacy law

The principle of a conflict of interest in the workplace is a simple one. When you're making an important decision at work that impacts on others, you should only be influenced in that decision by factors that are genuinely relevant to it. You shouldn't be influenced by the impact that it might have on you, members of your family or your friends. Your only motivation must be the best interests of the workplace. When your private interests affect the decisions you make as an employee or you consider any benefits to others, then you have a conflict of interest (**Figure 1.15**).

Figure 1.15 Conflict of interest

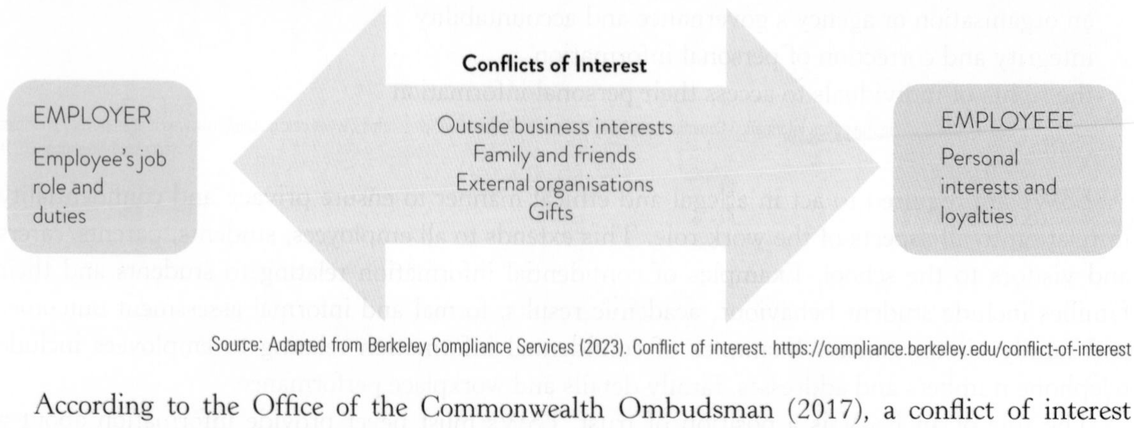

Source: Adapted from Berkeley Compliance Services (2023). Conflict of interest. https://compliance.berkeley.edu/conflict-of-interest

According to the Office of the Commonwealth Ombudsman (2017), a conflict of interest exists when it appears likely that an employee could be influenced, or where it could be perceived that they are influenced, by a personal interest in carrying out their duty.

Conflicts of interest may be real, apparent or potential:

- Real – where a direct conflict exists between current official duties and existing private interests.
- Apparent – where it appears or could be perceived that private interests are improperly influencing the performance of official duties whether or not that is actually the case.
- Potential – where private interests are not but could come into direct conflict with official duties.

Source: Office of the Commonwealth Ombudsman. (September 2017). Conflict of Interest Guideline. https://www.ombudsman.gov.au/__data/assets/pdf_file/0030/29919/Conflict-of-Interest-Guidelines-September-2017.pdf, p. 3.

A conflict of interest that involves actual or perceived financial benefits or loss is referred to as a pecuniary interest. Money does not need to change hands for an interest to be pecuniary. For example, you would have a pecuniary interest if you (or your relative or close associate) owned property, held shares, had a position in a company bidding for work, or received benefits such as concessions, discounts, gifts or hospitality from a particular source (Victoria State Government Education and Training, 2017, p. 10).

How do you identify a conflict of interest?

Even when you are absolutely sure that your decisions and motives are beyond reproach, if a reasonable bystander may think your private interests affect the decisions you make, then you have a perceived conflict of interest. A perceived conflict of interest can be just as damaging as an actual conflict of interest. Examples of a conflict of interest are:

- a member of an interview panel is a close, personal friend of one of the applicants and does not disclose this at the time of the interviews
- the senior teacher responsible for allocating the workloads to ESWs is in a relationship with one of the ESWs
- you are asked to source some equipment and you recommend your brother-in-law's company without disclosing your relationship
- your partner has a tutoring franchise and gives you cards to hand to parents whose children would benefit from after-school tutoring
- you are involved in the purchase of resources for students with additional needs, and order from the sales representative who always gives you small gifts
- you are required to regularly purchase supplies at a local supermarket, and the person at the checkout suggests you use your own card to collect points
- you are required to seek quotes for a venue for the end-of-year school awards. Your neighbour is chairperson of the local hall and tells you he will undercut any quotes you may receive. The quotes are confidential.

Responding to conflicts of interest

If you are aware that there is a conflict of interest or there may be a perceived conflict of interest, it must be declared to your employer. Government and non-government schools will typically have policies and procedures to manage conflicts of interest. Declaring a conflict of interest may or may not result in having to withdraw from the task. How a conflict of interest is managed will depend on the nature of the conflict. Conflicts of interest are usually assessed using a risk management approach, which may include:

- registering the conflict of interest
- appointing a third party to oversee the task to ensure fairness
- directing the person to step down and have no further involvement in the task.

Where you are unsure if a conflict of interest exists, always err on the side of honesty and discuss the matter with your employer.

Summary

This chapter has provided an overview of the diverse roles and responsibilities of an ESW. The role of the ESW was explored in the context of the importance of professional and ethical behaviour, acting within the law and identifying conflicts of interest. While each workplace will impose different accountability requirements, it's important to be aware that documenting your work provides evidence of how, and under what conditions, your work was carried out. This is particularly important where ESWs are working with minimal supervision. Communication is a critical aspect of the job role. This chapter explored the importance of non-verbal communication, active listening and the range of factors that impact on effective communication.

Self-check questions

1. Describe your understanding of what the ESW's role may be in a classroom.
2. You have just started working with a new teacher at your school. What can you do to ensure that you and the teacher work together as effectively as possible?
3. ESWs are required to work under the direction and supervision of a classroom teacher. What are other skills and important attributes for an ESW?
4. Why is personal time management important in your classroom?
5. List five things you would include in your daily work diary/planner.
6. What is effective communication? List some of its outcomes for school setting.
7. Explain how you would respond as an ESW when faced with an ethical dilemma. Provide two useful strategies for dealing with ethical dilemmas.

Discussion questions

1. Your Year 10 student, Annabel, has a busy schedule outside of school, which includes participating in a theatre company with you three nights a week and alternate weekend practices. Annabel has not submitted any work in the past two weeks and her teachers have raised concerns.
   a. How do you support Annabel in completing her tasks, knowing that she has strict deadlines to adhere to?
2. You have arrived later than usual to work and find out that Mr. Higgenbottom is replacing your regular teacher. You are aware that change for 3 of your students is difficult and can lead to a more difficult day.
   a. In relation to being organised, what could you have done do to ensure that your lateness and a change of teacher creates less impact on the students and yourself for the day?
3. As a trained Multi-Sensory Language (MSL) specialist, the majority of your work is in a withdrawal program that provides more intensive work with students. You collect each student from the classroom and move to your office to work through the phonic session. At the completion, you walk the student back to class and signal to the teacher that the student has returned.
   a. What effective communication strategies could you implement to ensure that you and the teacher are sharing progress and notes on the students you work with?

Activities

1. Look up your state's employment award and identify 5 workplace entitlements that are listed within it.
2. Look through the employability skills and identify two that you feel you need to work on. Chat with a partner about your response and seek their feedback.
3. Investigate within your school how ESWs and other staff effectively communicate about students.

Chapter 2

WORKING IN A LEGISLATIVE ENVIRONMENT

LEARNING OBJECTIVES

When you have completed this chapter, you should be able to demonstrate that, in relation to working in a school environment, you can:

2.1 identify and comply with legislative and policy requirements relating to the school workplace environment

2.2 understand the duty-of-care responsibilities and obligations of both the educational support worker (ESW) and the school in maintaining student safety

2.3 identify and comply with organisational policies and procedures as they apply to record-keeping, privacy and information systems

2.4 comply with organisational policies and procedures as they relate to student health and wellbeing.

GO FURTHER

Go Further icons link to extra content for this chapter. Ask your instructor for the **Go Further** resource and deepen your understanding of the topic.

Online resources icons refer to useful weblinks. Ask your instructor for these **Online Resources.**

Introduction

As an employee in a public or independent school, you are required to be aware of and comply with a range of legislative requirements, policies and procedures. You are required to conduct yourself in a professional manner and reflect the core values of the school. You also have a legal and ethical obligation to act in the best interests of children and young people.

2.1 Legislation

Schools operate within a legislative framework. All schools must comply with state/territory and Commonwealth legislation to ensure accountability, ethical conduct and to safeguard and protect the rights of all stakeholders. Schools – both public and independent – are funded under the provision of Commonwealth legislation, which includes:

- the ***Australian Education Act 2013*** – the principal legislation for the provision of Australian Government funding to government and non-government schools. The Act also sets out broad expectations for compliance to ensure funding accountability to the Commonwealth and to school communities. Under the Act, the Schooling Resource Standard (SRS) provides a base amount per student and additional funding for disadvantage. The Act was last amended on 23 June 2017 to give effect to the Quality Schools package, a needs-based funding model to expand successful programs such as specialist teacher or targeted intervention for children falling behind (Australian Government Department of Education, 2022)
- the **Australian Education Regulation 2013**, which outlines the financial accountability and other conditions that are required by approved authorities in order to receive funding under the *Australian Education Act 2013* (© The Department of Education and Training. CC-BY-4.0 licence).

Approved authorities include government schools (administered by relevant state or territory governments) and non-government schools (administered by a body corporate approved by the minister).

Legislative compliance in the education environment is the responsibility of the employer, the principal and all employees.

Human rights, anti-discrimination and equal opportunity legislation

The Australian Human Rights Commission (AHRC) is responsible for the implementation of federal human rights and anti-discrimination law in Australia. The key role of the AHRC is to assist in the resolution of complaints about **discrimination** and other breaches of human rights. The priorities of the Commission (AHRC, 2012, p. 8) are 'building understanding and respect for rights in our community' and 'tackling violence, harassment and bullying'.

Figure 2.1 describes Commonwealth legislation that addresses discrimination.

Figure 2.1 Legislation and grounds for discrimination

Legislation	Summary	Areas covered
Australian Human Rights Commission Act 1986	Discrimination based on race, colour, sex, religion, political opinion, national extraction, social origin, age, medical record, criminal record, marital or relationship status, impairment, mental, intellectual or psychiatric disability, physical disability, nationality, sexual orientation, and trade union activity. Also covers discrimination based on the imputation of one of the above grounds.	Discrimination in employment or occupation.

Legislation	Summary	Areas covered
Age Discrimination Act 2004	Discrimination based on age – protects both younger and older Australians. Also includes discrimination based on age-specific characteristics or characteristics that are generally imputed to a person of a particular age.	Discrimination in employment, education, access to premises, provision of goods, services and facilities, accommodation, disposal of land, administration of Commonwealth laws and programs, and requests for information.
Disability Discrimination Act 1992	Discrimination based on physical, intellectual, psychiatric, sensory, neurological or learning disability, physical disfigurement, disorder, illness or disease that affects thought processes, perception of reality, emotions or judgement, or results in disturbed behaviour, and presence in body of organisms causing or capable of causing disease or illness (e.g. HIV virus). Also covers discrimination involving harassment in employment, education or the provision of goods and services.	Discrimination in employment, education, access to premises, provision of goods, services and facilities, accommodation, disposal of land, activities of clubs, sport, and administration of Commonwealth laws and programs.
Racial Discrimination Act 1975	Discrimination based on race, colour, descent or national or ethnic origin, and in some circumstances immigrant status. Racial hatred, defined as a public act or acts likely to offend, insult, humiliate or intimidate based on race, is also prohibited under this Act unless an exemption applies.	Discrimination in all areas of public life including employment, provision of goods and services, right to join trade unions, access to places and facilities, land, housing and other accommodation, and advertisements.
Sex Discrimination Act 1984	Discrimination based on sex, marital or relationship status, pregnancy or potential pregnancy, breastfeeding, family responsibilities, sexual orientation, gender identity and intersex status. Sexual harassment is also prohibited under this Act.	Discrimination in employment.
Fair Work Act 2009	Discrimination based on race, colour, sex, sexual orientation, age, physical or mental disability, marital status, family or carer responsibilities, pregnancy, religion, political opinion, national extraction, and social origin.	Discrimination, via adverse action, in employment.

Source: © Australian Human Rights Commission 2019. licensed under the Creative Commons Attribution 4.0 International Licence, https://creativecommons.org/licenses/by/4.0/legalcode

Schools must also comply with state or territory anti-discrimination legislation shown in **Figure 2.2**.

Figure 2.2 State/territory equal employment opportunity and anti-discrimination legislation

Region	Equal opportunity legislation
Australian Capital Territory	*Discrimination Act 1991* ACT Human Rights Commission: **http://hrc.act.gov.au**
New South Wales	*Anti-Discrimination Act 1977* Anti-Discrimination Board of NSW: **http://www.antidiscrimination.justice.nsw.gov.au**
Northern Territory	*Anti-Discrimination Act 1996* Northern Territory Anti-Discrimination Commission: **http://www.adc.nt.gov.au**

Region	Equal opportunity legislation
Queensland	*Anti-Discrimination Act 1991* Anti-Discrimination Commission Queensland: **http://www.adcq.qld.gov.au**
South Australia	*Equal Opportunity Act 1984* Equal Opportunity Commission of South Australia: **http://www.eoc.sa.gov.au**
Tasmania	*Anti-Discrimination Act 1998* Office of the Anti-Discrimination Commissioner: **http://equalopportunity.tas.gov.au/home**
Victoria	*Equal Opportunity Act 2010* Equal Opportunity and Human Rights Commission: **http://www.humanrightscommission.vic.gov.au**
Western Australia	*Equal Opportunity Act 1984* Equal Opportunity Commission: **http://www.eoc.wa.gov.au**

Children's rights

Currently, there is no single national law in relation to the care and protection of children. However, each state and territory has legislation that seeks to protect the special interests and vulnerability of children and young people under the age of 18 years. Each state and territory has also a Children's Commissioner and/or a Children's Guardian to promote the safety, welfare and wellbeing of all children and young people in that state or territory.

In 2013, a National Children's Commissioner was appointed. The role of the Commissioner is to promote public discussion and awareness of issues affecting children, conduct research and education programs, and consult directly with children and representative organisations. The Commissioner also examines relevant existing and proposed Commonwealth legislation to determine if it recognises and protects children's human rights in Australia (Department of Families, Housing, Community Services and Indigenous Affairs, 2013. © Commonwealth of Australia. Released under CC BY 3.0 AU, link to licence: https://creativecommons.org/licenses/by/3.0/au).

The Children's Commissioner also focuses on vulnerable and at-risk groups of children, such as children with disability, Aboriginal and Torres Strait Islander children, homeless children and those who experience violence.

United Nations Convention on the Rights of the Child (1991)

United Nations Convention on the Rights of the Child

The AHRC is responsible for monitoring Australia's commitments under the United Nations Convention on the Rights of the Child, which was ratified by Australia in 1990. The Convention includes 54 Articles (statements) that set out the rights of children to education, health care and economic opportunity, as well as protection from abuse, neglect, and sexual and economic exploitation.

Article 23 states that children with a disability have the right to special education and care; Article 28 states that children have the right to a good-quality education; and Article 29 states that education should support every child to reach their full potential, learn to live peacefully, protect the environment and respect other people.

Disability, inclusion and education legislation

The Disability Standards for Education 2005 (Department of Education and Training [DET], 2005) were developed to clarify the obligations and responsibilities of educational institutions under the *Disability Discrimination Act 1992* and are designed to ensure that students with a disability can access and participate in education on the same basis as other students.

> The Standards apply to preschools and kindergartens, public and independent schools, public and independent education and training places and tertiary institutions including TAFEs and universities. (p. 1)

Source: © The Department of Education and Training. CC-BY-4.0 licence.

The Standards seek to ensure that students are not discriminated against in relation to enrolment, access to services and facilities and participation in learning programs (see **Figure 2.3**).

> The Standards cover enrolment, participation, curriculum development, accreditation and delivery, student support services and elimination of harassment and victimisation. (p. 1)

Source: © The Department of Education and Training. CC-BY-4.0 licence.

Figure 2.3 Facilities available at school for students with disability

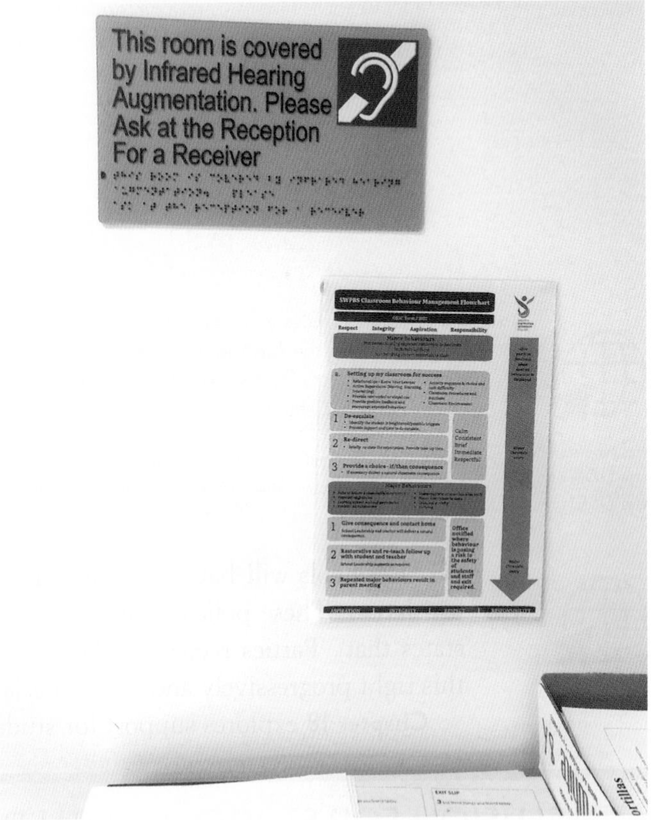

Source: Photo by Tish Okely © Cengage

The Standards support the concept of **inclusion** by promoting participation and accessibility for students with disabilities, advocating for facilities and resources that allow for universal access and promoting practices to eliminate discrimination, harassment and victimisation.

Figure 2.4 describes the key elements of the *Disability Discrimination Act 1992* (DDA) and the Disability Standards for Education 2005 (DSE).

Figure 2.4 Key elements of the DDA and DSE

Disability Discrimination Act 1992 (DDA)	Disability Standards for Education 2005 (DSE)
The DDA makes it against the law to treat people unfairly because of a disability.	The Standards seek to ensure that students with disability can access and participate in education on the same basis as other students.
Defines the meaning of disability for the purposes of the DDA	The Standards clarify the obligations of education and training providers, and the rights of people with disability, under the DDA.

Disability Discrimination Act 1992 (DDA)	Disability Standards for Education 2005 (DSE)
The DDA implements Australia's international human rights obligations under the Convention on the Rights of Persons with Disabilities	A primary objective of the Standards is to make rights and responsibilities in education and training easier to understand. The Standards cover: > enrolment > participation > curriculum development > accreditation and delivery > student support services > elimination of harassment and victimisation.
The DDA provides a mechanism for individuals to make complaints to the Australian Human Rights Commission and seek redress for disability discrimination in certain areas of public life, including education.	The Standards reflect the DDA – i.e., the right of children with disability to have the same educational opportunities as other children.

Factsheets about the DDA and the DSE

Source: Fact Sheet 2: Disability Standards for Education 2005 © Commonwealth of Australia. Licensed under Creative Commons Attribution 4.0 International Licence, https://creativecommons.org/licenses/by/4.0/; Fact Sheet 1: Disability Discrimination Act 1992 © Commonwealth of Australia. Licensed under Creative Commons Attribution 4.0 International Licence, https://creativecommons.org/licenses/by/4.0/

Examples of inclusion policies

All schools will have an inclusion policy that reflects both the DSE and anti-discrimination legislation. These policies will also reflect Article 28 of the UN Convention. In part, Article 28 states that, 'Parties recognize the right of the child to education, and with a view to achieving this right progressively and on the basis of equal opportunity'.

Chapter 18 explores support for students with disability in greater detail.

INCLUSION FOR STUDENTS WITH DISABILITIES

SCENARIO

ELLA JONES

Ella (5 years, 10 months) has Down syndrome and has been attending her local preschool for three years. The preschool director has provided a comprehensive report to the family on Ella's developmental progress. Ella is a happy and confident child with a mild intellectual disability. She has well-developed expressive and receptive language skills and manages her own personal hygiene needs. At times she can be quite impulsive and overexcited. She has a congenital heart condition that causes her to become breathless and fatigued if she overexerts herself.

Mr and Mrs Jones want Ella to attend the local school with her older siblings. They know that, over time, Ella will gradually fall behind her peers academically; however, they believe this will be outweighed by the benefits of inclusion in her local school community. Today, Ella and her parents are attending a pre-enrolment interview at the school. The school is located in a growing suburb and this year there will be three Kindergarten classes. The junior school principal is concerned that Ella may not cope with the size of the school campus. He is also concerned that funding for ESWs is scarce and is worried about how the teacher will cope with the demands of a student with additional needs.

The interview goes well. Ella is very excited and insists on wearing one of her sister's old uniforms. The principal later reflects that he had perhaps unfairly prejudged Ella. He reminds himself that every child with a disability also has many abilities and strengths.

WHAT DOES THIS TELL US?

The benefits of inclusion for students with disabilities go well beyond the individual's right to quality education. The social and emotional wellbeing of the child and family should be a primary consideration.

▶ DISCUSSION

What first comes to mind when thinking about a student with a disability? Do you immediately begin to think about the *dis*abilities the child may have? If your answer is yes, you are not alone, as we tend to be conditioned to think of the negatives rather than potential of those with disabilities.

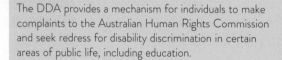

Child protection legislation

Each state and territory has child protection legislation governing key areas such as mandatory reporting requirements, investigation, registration, legal proceedings, protection orders, ongoing intervention, supervision and the collection of statistical data. Occupations where mandatory reporting is required vary across jurisdictions, but typically include medical professionals, police, teachers, disability workers and Family Court officers. Western Australia requires mandatory reporting only for suspected child sexual abuse.

All schools will have policies and procedures for reporting students who are suspected of being at serious risk of harm. Typically, any employees – including ESWs – who suspect a student is at risk of harm would report those concerns in line with the school's child protection policy and procedures.

Mandatory pre-employment screening

Pre-employment screening, such as the Working with Children Check, is designed to identify and prevent unsuitable individuals from working in occupations where they come into direct and regular contact with children and young people. Currently, there is no single national strategy in place setting out the requirements for pre-employment screening for adults working with children. However, all employees and volunteers employed in schools in every state and territory are usually screened as part of the recruitment process.

Chapter 6 explores child protection in greater detail, including your obligations in relation to legislation and policy.

2.2 Duty of care

Duty of care

All teachers have a **duty of care** and must take reasonable measures to protect students from **risk** of harm. Duty of care requires adults working with students to assess potential risks in a range of situations. The Department of Education WA (2018, p. 3) states: 'The duty owed to students is not a duty to ensure that no harm will ever occur, but rather a duty to take *reasonable care* to avoid harm being suffered.' (© Department of Education, Western Australia. CC-BY-4.0 licence.)

Duty of care extends to ESWs where this responsibility is included in the duty statement or job description. However, regardless of this legal position, all adults working with children and young people should take reasonable care to reduce the risk of harm. Reasonable care is difficult to define, and will often depend on particular circumstances. The Department of Education and Children's Services SA (2007) states:

> Generally speaking a teacher owes a student a duty to take reasonable care to protect him or her from foreseeable risk of injury. This duty may be manifested in many ways including:
> - the duty to supervise the students so that they comply with rules and practices designed for their own safety and that of other students;
> - the duty to design and implement appropriate programmes and procedures to ensure the safety of students;
> - the duty to ensure that school buildings, equipment and facilities are safe;
> - the duty to warn students about dangerous situations or practices.

A **risk assessment** can be undertaken to determine reasonable care. Factors that must be taken into account include the nature of the experience, the physical setting, the abilities of the students, the typical behaviour of students and the equipment being used. Any risk assessment must also take into account the roles and other duties of any adults caring for or supervising the students. A risk assessment will include identifying any hazards, assessing the risks, controlling, managing or eliminating the risks, and monitoring and evaluating the outcomes.

> To determine a breach of duty of care, it must be established that, on the balance of probabilities:
> - a duty of care was owed to them at the time of the injury, and
> - the risk of injury was reasonably foreseeable, and
> - the likelihood of the injury occurring was more than insignificant, and
> - there was a breach of the duty of care or a failure to observe a reasonable standard of care; and
> - this breach or failure caused or contributed to the injury, loss or damage suffered.
>
> Source: © State of Victoria (Department of Education and Training). CC-BY-4.0 licence.

SCENARIO

REASONABLE CARE

ESW **Matt** notices a group of Year 10 boys climbing on and jumping from the roof of the sports shed. As well as putting themselves in danger, Matt knows that this area is off limits to the students. Matt tells the students to get down and go back to the main playground. One of the boys laughs at Matt. *'You're not a teacher. You can't tell us what to do!'* Rather than arguing with the boys, Matt goes in search of the teacher on outdoor lunch duty.

WHAT DOES THIS TELL US?

Matt has conducted himself in the expected manner. He took immediate action to eliminate the risk. When his directions were ignored, he immediately notified the supervising teacher. Matt demonstrated that he was aware of the duty of care owed to students by school employees.

Family law

Examples of duty of care policies

Decision making responsibilities for students

All schools have a duty of care to their students. Where there are court orders, parenting orders (i.e. Family Law Act orders), family violence intervention orders, protection orders or parenting plans related to a child enrolled in a school, parents have an obligation (but are not required by law) to notify the school. Sharing this information ensures that the school is aware of:

- who has legal responsibility for the child – for example, signing permission forms, payment of any school fees, who to notify in case of sickness or injury
- who may pick up the child at the end of the school day
- any restrictions in relation to access/restraining orders – for example, attendance at school events, collecting a child early from school
- who should receive official information such as the child's assessment reports.

Most schools will have policy guidelines to manage orders made by the Family Court where it directly impacts on the school's duty-of-care obligations.

Work health and safety legislation

Every person conducting a business or undertaking has a duty to ensure, as far as is reasonably practicable, the health, safety and welfare of all employees and others who come into the workplace. In Australia, legislation in relation to work health and safety (WHS) includes:

- the *Model Work Health and Safety (WHS) Act 2011* (Model WHS Act)
- the Model Work Health and Safety (WHS) Regulations 2011 (Model WHS Regulations).

Incorporated under this legislation are Model Codes of Practice and a National Compliance and Enforcement Policy.

In schools, the principal is responsible for ensuring, as far as is reasonably practicable, that all legal requirements relating to WHS are met. These responsibilities include:

- acquiring and disseminating up-to-date knowledge of WHS best practice
- identifying risks and hazards in the workplace
- taking action to eliminate or minimise risks to health and safety for employees, visitors, and students
- ensuring adequate supply of and training in the use of personal protective equipment (PPE)
- consulting with employees to plan and implement WHS policies and procedures
- following legislative requirements in relation to notification of WHS incidents and workplace injuries
- providing access to WHS training for all employees.

Example of an EPR template for schools

Emergency procedures

All schools will have an emergency response plan (EPR) designed to prepare for and respond to a disaster or emergency situations, such as severe weather events, and geological, biological or human events that pose risks to life, property or the environment (see **Figure 2.5**).

EPRs will include plans for:

- evacuation
- lockdown
- temporary closure
- pre-emptive actions where a major emergency is forecast such as flooding or a bushfire.

The EPR reflects the employer obligation of Regulation 43 of the Model WHS Regulations which requires every workplace to have emergency procedures in place. This obligation extends to testing the emergency procedures, including how often they should be tested, as well as information, training and instruction to relevant workers in relation to implementing the emergency procedures. WHS and emergency procedures are examined in detail in **Chapter 4**.

Figure 2.5 An example of an emergency plan at school

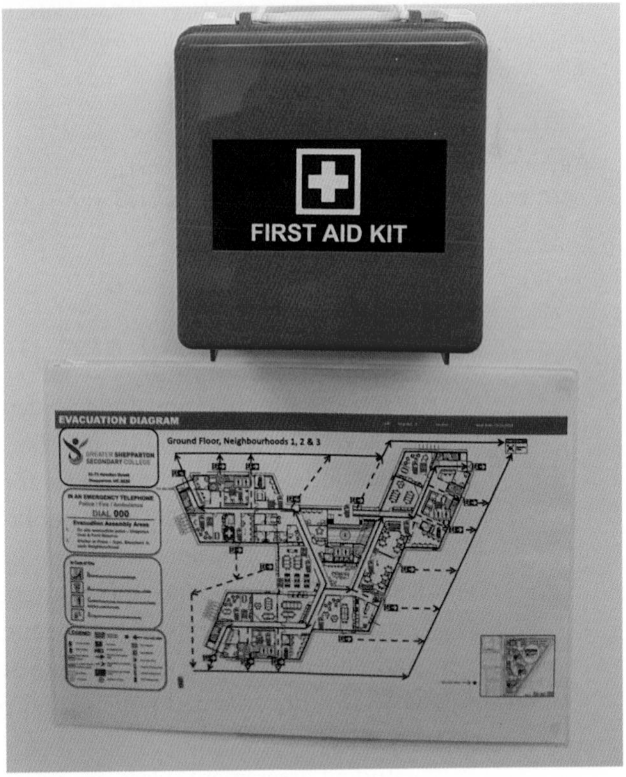

Source: Photo by Tish Okely © Cengage

2.3 Privacy legislation

Within Australia, the *Privacy Act 1988* relates to the protection of personal information and applies to all states and territories. The Privacy Act regulates how personal information is handled, covering:

- how personal information is collected
- how it is used and disclosed
- its accuracy
- how securely it is kept
- the individual's general right to access their personal information.

There is no legislation that specifically identifies a child's right to privacy. However, Article 16 of the UN Convention on the Rights of the Child, to which Australia is a signatory, states that children have the right to privacy. All adults working in the school environment have a responsibility to treat every student and family with dignity and respect and ensure that all private information relating to the student and family remains confidential. The Privacy Act is administered by the Office of the Australian Information Commissioner: http://www.oaic.gov.au.

SCENARIO

PRIVACY AND PERSONAL INFORMATION

Connie is an ESW at the local high school and works with a student whose family was involved in a drug raid that was reported in the local news. While out shopping, Connie runs into a friend who has a child at Connie's school. Over coffee, the friend asks Connie what she knows about the family: *'You work with the son of that family involved in the drug bust, don't you? I've heard they are a violent family. How did the boy react?'*
Connie: *'I'm sorry, I'm not allowed to discuss the students and their families. Can we talk about something else? How's Ellie going with her soccer?'*

DID CONNIE DO THE RIGHT THING?

Yes: information about the students and families must be treated as confidential and only shared with relevant people (e.g. a school counsellor) on a need-to-know basis. Even though Connie was not at work, she still observed the school's confidentiality and privacy policy.

WHAT DOES THIS TELL US?

As an employee, you are required to be familiar with and comply with school policies related to student privacy, welfare and safety. This extends to your responsibilities both within and outside the school. In this scenario, Connie also demonstrated that she was able to act in an ethical manner to protect the privacy of the student.

Record-keeping and privacy

All schools – public and independent – operate within a regulatory framework that requires a high level of accountability for the education and welfare of students and the expenditure of public funds. While requirements for record-keeping may vary between each state and territory, and between independent and public schools, most schools will maintain the following types of records and information:

- student records – enrolment, attendance, immunisation status, specialist assessment reports, student progress reports (academic and welfare), records of attendance, records relating to the administration of medications to students
- WHS – documented policies and procedures related to all operational aspects of school services
- student assessment, class programs
- personnel records – details of staff qualifications, including compliance with child protection legislation, employment records, sick leave
- accidents and injuries to students, serious incidents
- financial records (income and expenditure) – petty cash, monies collected from parents for various school functions or student resources/equipment
- assets/inventory register (important for taxation and depreciation purposes and provides a dollar value for the purposes of insurance), with details such as:
  - name, brand, serial number and description of item
  - date and place of purchase – name, address and telephone number (and name of contact person if applicable)
  - cost (including GST)
  - details of guarantee, return options and after-sales service.

The content of records kept will be prescribed in related school policy and procedure documents – for example, a Records Management Policy, an Attendance Policy, Data Protocols: Student Information, a Performance and Development Policy, a Risk Management Policy, an ICT Policy. The school principal will usually delegate record-keeping responsibilities to staff as appropriate. Privacy and confidentiality policies and procedures will apply to most records kept by the school.

SCENARIO

ACCIDENTS

As part of the annual risk management review of student safety, the **principal** and **senior executives** reviewed the accidents and injury-to-students reports for the previous 12 months. They found that most accidents had occurred during the lunch break or as students were moving from one classroom to another. Boys in the 13–15 years age bracket had the highest number of accidental injuries. This led to new supervision procedures being put in place during the high-risk periods.

WHAT DOES THIS TELL US IN RELATION TO RECORD-KEEPING?

By documenting and reviewing accidental injury records, the principal can gain an accurate picture of when most accidents occur and, in this case, the gender and age group for which most accidents occur. This information can be used to make changes to supervision practices and target those students at high risk of accidental injury.

Managing information and privacy

Technology allows for the storage of large amounts of data and makes inputting, processing and accessing information quick and easy. Storing information electronically also leaves it vulnerable to unauthorised access. To address this risk, most schools will have an information and communications technology (ICT) policy (or similar). This policy typically provides clear guidelines on the use of technology such as security, privacy, confidentiality and authorised access; records management, retrieval and archiving; email protocols; social media; and copyright infringement. The Department of Education and Early Childhood Development Victoria's ICT Policy (2011, p. 3) states that its purpose is

> to ensure that all use of Department of Education and Early Childhood Development (DEECD) Information, Communications and Technology (ICT) resources is legal, ethical and consistent with the aims, values and objectives of DEECD and its responsibilities to the students in its care. DEECD is an institution charged with the safety and education of children …

DEECD ICT resources must be used properly and efficiently. They are not to be used for inappropriate activities – for example, pornography, fraud, defamation, breach of copyright, unlawful discrimination or vilification, harassment (including sexual harassment), stalking, privacy violations and illegal activity, including illegal peer-to-peer file sharing. Non-compliance with the policy is regarded as a serious matter and may result in dismissal or criminal charges.

Administrative staff will be required to prepare and disseminate a wide range of information to members of the school community and the public. The distribution or dissemination of information should be in accordance with the school's policies and procedures. For example, information of a general nature, such as enrolment procedures, behaviour management policy or procedures for giving medication to a student, is usually provided in the form of a written policy or procedure that is available in print or freely accessible via the school's website.

Each teacher and senior administrator will have a school email account where information can be directed or disseminated as required. Many schools also have an intranet where internal documents and resources are stored and can only be accessed by designated staff. Many schools now have a website that is used to disseminate information to parents, students and the public. Management of the website is typically allocated to one individual, who is responsible for keeping the website updated. There will be strict protocols in place around the type of information that can be posted on the website.

It is essential that ESWs become familiar with school policies and procedures regarding the sharing of information. Even information of a general nature should be authorised by the relevant staff member prior to dissemination.

An extract from an information security policy is shown in **Figure 2.6**.

Figure 2.6 Information security policy extract

For the employee	An employee is defined as:
Employees will manage and maintain the security of the information in their care by understanding their obligations under relevant departmental policies, legislation and guidelines including the Code of Conduct for the Queensland public service and departmental procedures, and by undertaking annual training.	Any permanent, temporary, seconded or contracted staff member, contractors and consultants, volunteers or other person who provides services on a paid or voluntary basis to the department that are required to comply with the department's policies and procedures. Within schools this includes Principals, Deputy Principals, heads of departments, head of curriculums, guidance officers, teachers and other school staff who manage information.

Source: Information security policy. Version number 1.1; Version effective 12 May 2022; © The State of Queensland (Department of Education) 2023; Licensed under Creative Commons 4.0, https://creativecommons.org/licenses/by/4.0/

To ensure security of information, most schools will have two access points – one that is publicly accessible, such as a website, and one that is accessible only via an intranet. Intranet access requires authentication (identifying the users) and authorisation (granting authenticated users access via a password, pin code or security number).

Intranets are used to share information such as policies, templates and forms, internal emails, information dissemination such as memos or newsletters, wikis, conferencing and webinars. To protect information, there will be firewalls (hardware and software) in place, which Williams and McWilliams (2014, p. 291) explain 'sit between the computers in an internal organisational network and outside network, such as the internet [and] filter and check incoming and outgoing data'.

Information that is stored manually should be easy to access and retrieve. All confidential information will be stored in a manner that ensures security and confidentiality. For example, confidential e-records should be password protected and backed up on a regular scheduled basis. Hard copies of confidential information should be stored in lockable filing cabinets.

Once collected, information will need to be stored on a short-, medium- or long-term basis. Some information will be of short-term value and may only need to be stored for the life of the task and then destroyed – for example, names of families planning to attend a family disco evening. Some information may need to be stored for many years. Requirements for each state and territory will usually stipulate the length of time for which records are required to be stored.

Archiving and disposal of information

Information that is no longer required or out of date should be archived or destroyed. All schools have a legal requirement to retain and archive some records for specific periods of time – for example, student accidents or staff accidents/workplace injuries. The length of time for which records need to be retained will depend on the specific legislation. Records that are not required to be maintained by law, and which are out of date, should be destroyed.

When destroying records, care should be taken to make certain that the information contained in the records cannot be retrieved. For example, students' confidential records should be shredded rather than simply placed in the recycling bin. This will ensure that the information contained in the documents cannot be accessed, either accidentally or deliberately.

GO FURTHER

Learn more about privacy and correspondence in your **Go Further** resource, available through your instructor.

SCENARIO

MANAGING ELECTRONIC COMMUNICATIONS – UNAUTHORISED USE

Recently, **Kate** was approached by a parent, **Mrs Hughes**, requesting that an electronic brochure be sent as a bulk email to all parents. Mrs Hughes had set up an authorised before- and after-school program and wanted Kate to notify all parents via email. Kate explained that the email policy did not allow her to disseminate any information to parents on behalf of other organisations. Mrs Hughes began to argue with Kate, stating that the service was for the benefit of students and families from the school community. Kate resolved the matter by offering to include information about the after-school program in the next school newsletter.

WHAT DOES THIS TELL US?

Even though the information about the after-school program was obviously relevant to the school community, Kate acted in accordance with the school's policy in refusing Mrs Hughes' request. Kate was, however, able to offer an acceptable alternative.

▶ DISCUSSION

Social media is now an accepted form of communication and is used widely for both personal and business purposes. Does Facebook, for example, have a legitimate role to play in sharing information about the school community with families? What might be the benefits and risks?

2.4 Health and wellbeing

All schools have a responsibility to ensure, as far as practicable, the health and wellbeing of students and employees. Each state and territory has legislation relating to the collection of the immunisation status of students, the requirement to notify the public health department if a student has a vaccine preventable disease; how to manage the outbreak of infectious diseases in schools.

Schools must also follow the state/territory requirements related to the exclusion of students (and staff) who have contracted a vaccine-preventable disease or a contagious disease such as conjunctivitis, gastroenteritis, hand, foot and mouth disease, hepatitis A or impetigo.

Schools will also have wellbeing programs to support the mental health and wellbeing of students, such as the Australian Student Wellbeing Framework. Student health and wellbeing are explored in **Chapter 5** of this text.

Workplace policies

Workplace policies and procedures are designed to direct and/or guide day-to-day decision-making and practices. In school-based settings, they direct, inform and guide employers, employees, students and families. They are designed to:

- provide unambiguous information that ensures consistency of education, student care and wellbeing
- ensure consistency in relation to information provided to employees, students and families

- ensure consistency in decision-making with employees, students and families
- provide evidence of legislative compliance with state, territory and Commonwealth laws
- reflect knowledge and evidence of best practice
- support ethical and consistent decisions and allow the organisation to operate in a manner that is open, transparent, equitable and free of bias
- ensure effective risk management.

In many cases, policies and procedures will reflect the legislative requirements of the organisation. For example, a child protection policy will reflect the requirements of state/territory child protection legislation, including mandatory pre-employment screening; a manual handling policy or procedures for use of PPE will directly reflect the requirements of WHS and DSE legislation.

Employers have an obligation to ensure all employees are aware of, understand and implement all relevant policies related to their employment. Employers are also responsible for:

- ensuring that school policies and procedures are easily accessible and written in plain English
- training employees to understand and translate policies and procedures into workplace practices
- updating policies and procedures to reflect current legislation and best practice.

The employer is also required to provide initial and ongoing training to ensure employees are able to comply with all policies. This will include a wide range of targeted training, such as in the use of specialist equipment, machinery and tools; IT equipment and devices; medical equipment and aids used to support the health and wellbeing of students with physical disabilities; safe use and storage of chemicals; personal protective behaviours; communication protocols; recognition of signs a student may be at risk of harm or self-harm; and ethical and professional conduct.

For employees, policies and procedures set out and clarify expected standards of behaviour, protect the employees' rights, health and welfare, guide day-to-day decision-making, and define the standards and values under which the organisation operates to ensure consistency and fairness for all stakeholders.

Employees have a legal obligation to make themselves aware of and comply with all lawful directions given by the employer. Employees are responsible for:

- knowing, understanding and complying with school policies and procedures
- undertaking training as directed
- where possible, engaging in consultation where policies and procedures are updated or newly introduced
- becoming familiar with employee legal obligations in relation to policy compliance – for example, WHS policies and procedures
- alerting the employer where a policy or procedure is not working as intended.

Examples of policies and procedures relevant to the role of an ESW may include:

- grievance policy and procedures
- information privacy and rights
- information security
- manual handling
- managing unsatisfactory performance
- occupational violence prevention
- social media use
- preventing workplace bullying, sexual harassment and unlawful discrimination
- managing students' health support needs at school
- manual tasks – for example, assisting students how have physical impairments.

An ESW is expected to be familiar with school policies such as these, and to comply with the policies as they apply to their work with teachers and specialist staff, students and families. Most schools will make their policies available on the school website and/or intranet.

Translating policies and procedures into workplace practices

ESWs will implement and use policies and procedures on a daily basis as they work with teachers, other colleagues, students and families. **Figure 2.7** provides some examples of policies and procedures and how they relate to work practices.

Figure 2.7 Examples of school policies, procedures and work practices

Policies and procedures	Examples of work practices
WHS	Setting up the classroom, accessing and moving equipment and resources, or providing physical assistance to students
Assisting students with learning difficulties	Ensuring that the specific learning needs of students experiencing difficulties in learning are met
DDA and DSE	
Child protection	Reporting any concerns of possible risk of harm to the teacher
Digital devices and online services – staff use safety, security and privacy	Accessing and using online tools to prepare learning resources and/or support student learning
Environmental sustainability	Where possible recycle, reuse or repurpose materials to minimise waste
Information security	Ensuring any documents relating to individual students are stored securely to protect privacy and confidentiality
Professional development	Participating in mandatory professional development training
Student welfare	Reporting concerns in relation to student wellbeing
Student behaviour	Applying behaviour management strategies when working with students
Complaints/grievance resolution	Following the processes in place to address and resolve a workplace conflict or grievance
Staff induction	Completing a mandatory induction program before commencing employment

Policies are typically developed, disseminated, monitored and evaluated at the government or organisation level. For example, in public schools, policies are developed by state and territory education departments. In non-government schools, policies may be developed by, for example, the Catholic Education Commission, which oversees the Catholic education system, or the Anglican Schools Corporation.

In some instances, legislation requires that employees be consulted in relation to policies and procedures. For example, WHS legislation requires employers to consult with employees where there are changes in workplace practices that directly impact on workers. Including employees in monitoring and evaluating policies can ensure that related procedures address the workplace performance.

You can access policy information for public schools in all states and territories through the relevant education department websites.

GO FURTHER

View an example school social media policy in your **Go Further** resource, available through your instructor.

Public school policy information

Summary

This chapter provided an overview of the key legislative frameworks within which schools operate. Legislation both dictates and guides policies and procedures designed to ensure schools deliver programs that meet the diverse needs of learners in a fair and ethical manner while at the same time ensuring the safety and wellbeing of students, teachers and support staff. ESWs must ensure they comply with the school's policies and procedures at all times.

Self-check questions

1. In what ways do the Disability Standards for Education 2005 assist students?
2. What is the definition of duty of care when working with children as an ESW?
3. Who is responsible in schools for ensuring compliance with WHS legislation? List two responsibilities of this individual.
4. What is the *Privacy Act 1988*? List five key components in the Act.
5. As an ESW, what is your responsibility in relation to sharing of information?
6. How do workplace policies guide employees?
7. What are the responsibilities of employees regarding workplace policies and procedures?

Discussion questions

1. For this task, refer to the 'Ella Jones' Scenario earlier in this chapter.

   You are Ella's ESW for orientation day, a day where all children who are coming to primary school next year attend. You have been given the information in the scenario about Ella and know that they will be completing a sport session in the gym after lunch.

   a. What could you do to prepare yourself, knowing Ella's medical needs, so she can get the best out of the session?
2. Samuel's dad, Marcus, has just informed you that both he and Samuel's mum have separated. This has not been an amicable situation and restraining orders are in place where Samuel is only to be collected from the school by his father and paternal grandparents.

   a. Who do you advise Marcus to speak with at the school so that Marcus and Samuel are supported in this process?
3. Your role as an ESW outreach worker requires you to be accessible at all times via mobile phone. Your workplace has supplied you with a work phone. While you are driving to visit a student, your personal phone rings.

   a. To which policy would you refer for detailed information about use of your personal mobile phone during work hours?

Activities

1. Investigate at your school how the following records and information are maintained:

   a. Student records

   b. Accidents and injuries

   c. Assets/inventory register

   d. Personal records
2. In times gone by, all paper records were destroyed after a certain number of years had passed. Investigate what length of time records are now kept for, where and how they are kept.
3. Discover what policy documents you are introduced to during an induction day at your local school.

Chapter 3

WORKING WITH DIVERSE PEOPLE

LEARNING OBJECTIVES

When you have completed this chapter, you should be able to demonstrate that, in relation to working in a school environment, you can:

3.1 describe the concepts of diversity and inclusion as they apply to the workplace

3.2 identify cultural diversity and develop cultural competence, and understand the concepts of cultural identity and cultural safety, as well as strategies for effective cross-cultural communication

3.3 reflect on your own cultural identity and biases, and how they may affect your interactions with others

3.4 understand the depth of cultural diversity in the community and work in an inclusive and culturally safe manner

3.5 reflect on the complex histories and cultures of Aboriginal and Torres Strait Islander peoples, and understand the importance of working in inclusive and culturally safe ways.

Online resources icons refer to useful weblinks. Ask your instructor for these **Online Resources.**

Introduction

This chapter explores the importance of diversity and inclusion in the workplace and the school community. Workplace and school diversity extends to many elements, such as ethnicity, gender, religious beliefs, language, sexuality, lifestyle, health, abilities, disposition and education.

Inclusion in the workplace 'occurs when a diversity of people (e.g. of different ages, cultural backgrounds, genders) feel valued and respected, have access to opportunities and resources, and can contribute their perspectives and talents to improve their organisation' (Diversity Council of Australia, 2023).

3.1 Diversity

Diversity goes far beyond differences of race, ethnicity or country of origin. Understanding diversity means understanding that every individual is unique and different. Samson, Donnet and Daft (2018, p. 204) describe diversity in terms of two key dimensions. *Primary dimensions* include inborn differences, or differences that have an impact throughout one's life – for example, sexual orientation, gender, ethnicity or race. *Secondary dimensions* are those that can be acquired or changed throughout one's life – for example, socioeconomic status, marital status or religious beliefs.

The Universal Declaration of Human Rights

Australia is a signatory to the United Nations (UN) Universal Declaration of Human Rights (UDHR). The UDHR describes the basic rights and fundamental freedoms to which all human beings are entitled, including civil and political rights, among them the right to life, liberty, free speech, legal protection and privacy. It also includes economic, social and cultural rights, including the right to social security, health and education, and the right to be free from discrimination.

Article 2 of the UDHR states:

> Everyone is entitled to all the rights and freedoms set forth in this Declaration, without distinction of any kind, such as race, colour, sex, language, religion, political or other opinion, national or social origin, property, birth or other status.

Universal Declaration of Human Rights

The UDHR is not legally binding; rather, it sets out the values shared by UN members in recognition of the minimum components that must be in place to ensure the essential human dignity of all people.

The relationship between human needs and human rights

In 1943, Abraham Maslow developed a 'hierarchy of needs', which included five levels or hierarchies, as shown in **Figure 3.1**.

Figure 3.1 Maslow's hierarchy of needs

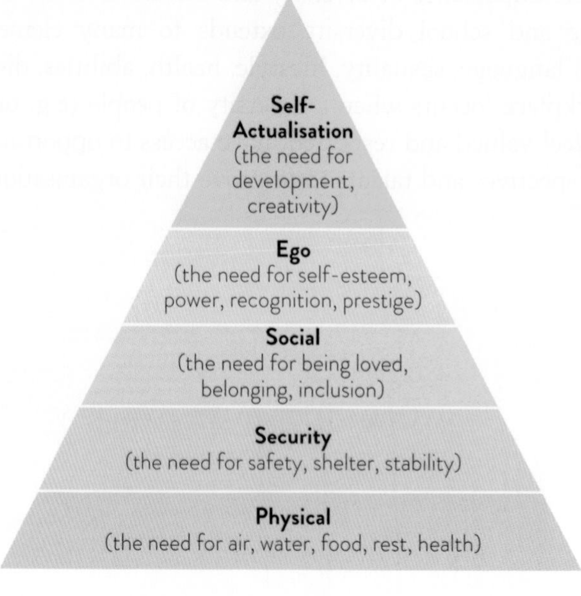

Maslow argued that higher-order needs can only be addressed if basic human needs such as food, shelter, rest, health and security are met. At the apex of this hierarchy is self-actualisation, which Maslow described as the opportunity for the individual to reach their maximum potential. Maslow's theory is still relevant today, although additional higher-order needs have been suggested, such as knowledge, meaning, self-awareness, beauty, inner balance and helping others.

In comparison, human rights go beyond needs to include human aspirations and desires. Human rights focus on entitlement with dignity, worth, justice and freedoms. Human rights are regarded as a collective responsibility of communities, governments and countries. They are something to be fought for and protected. Violations of human rights often lead to protest, prosecution and direct action. In comparison, the absence of the provision of basic human needs tends to be addressed through government welfare and charities.

Australia has a range of legislation to protect human rights in the workplace. These rights are embodied in anti-discrimination and workplace legislation. According to the Fair Work Ombudsman (2016), discrimination in the workplace is defined as any occasion when an employer takes adverse action against an employee or prospective employee because of a protected attribute. Protected attributes include:

- race, colour, national extraction
- sex and sexual orientation
- age
- physical or mental disability
- marital status, family or carer's responsibilities
- pregnancy
- religion, political opinion
- social origin.

Adverse action is defined as doing, threatening or organising any of the following:

- firing an employee
- injuring the employee in their employment – for example, not giving an employee legal entitlements such as pay or leave
- changing an employee's job to their disadvantage
- treating an employee differently from others
- not hiring someone
- offering a potential employee different and unfair terms and conditions for the job compared with other employees.

Discrimination can happen to:

- someone applying for a job
- a new employee who has not started work
- an employee at any time during employment.

Areas in which anti-discrimination legislation makes it illegal to discriminate are shown in **Figure 3.2**. In November 2021, the population of Australia was approximately 25.7 million people; **Figure 3.3** shows a snapshot of the diversity within that population.

Figure 3.2 Anti-discrimination and workplace law

Figure 3.3 A snapshot of the Australian population

Cultural diversity	For the year ended 30 June 2020: > 7.6 million migrants living in Australia > 29.8% of Australia's population was born overseas. As at 30 June 2016, Aboriginal and Torres Strait Islander people make up 3.3% of the total population.

Disability	In 2018 there were 4.4 million Australians with disability – 17.7% of the population. Almost one-quarter (23.2%) of all people with disability reported a mental or behavioural disorder as their main condition. 7.7% of children under 15 were reported as having disability; of these children, 4.5% had profound or severe disability and 1.6% had moderate or mild disability. Boys were more likely than girls to have disability (9.6% compared with 5.7% girls). In 2018, among school aged children (5 to 14 years) with disability, almost all (95.8%) attended school. Of these, nearly one-third attended special classes or special schools.
Age	In 2018, 1 in every 6 Australians (15.9%) was aged 65 years and over.

Sources: Based on Australian Bureau of Statistics data: Australian Bureau of Statistics (2022). Statistics. https://www.abs.gov.au/statistics/people/population; Australian Bureau of Statistics (2018). Estimates of Aboriginal and Torres Strait Islander Australians. https://www.abs.gov.au/statistics/people/aboriginal-and-torres-strait-islander-peoples/estimates-aboriginal-and-torres-strait-islander-australians/jun-2016; Australian Bureau of Statistics (2019). Disability, Ageing and Carers, Australia: Summary of Findings. https://www.abs.gov.au/statistics/health/disability/disability-ageing-and-carers-australia-summary-findings/latest-release.

3.2 Cultural diversity

The Australian Human Rights Commission (AHRC, 2016) refers to **culture** as 'a common set of norms and values shared by a group' and **cultural diversity** as 'the variation between people in terms of ancestry, ethnicity, ethno-religiosity, language, national origin, race and/or religion'. Cultural diversity also includes a diverse range of beliefs and practices, ways of communicating, style of dress, gender roles and parenting/child-rearing practices (see **Figure 3.4**).

Figure 3.5 highlights the key differences between culture, race and ethnicity.

Figure 3.4 The school environment celebrates cultural diversity

Source: Photo by Tish Okely © Cengage

Cultural competence

Cultural competence is the ability to understand, communicate and interact with people across cultures. It is a complex skill that can only be acquired over time, and includes:

- developing a knowledge of diverse cultures
- understanding the challenges faced by members of non-dominant cultures (particularly where there are significant differences in beliefs and practices)
- developing a set of values that focus on the positive nature of cultural diversity.

Figure 3.6 shows the steps involved in acquiring cultural competence.

Being culturally competent requires *cultural proficiency*, which can be described as the ability to 'identify and challenge one's own cultural assumptions, values and beliefs and to make a commitment to communicating at the cultural interface' (SNAICC, 2012, p. 1).

Videos: Cultural competence

An individual who can demonstrate cultural competence and cultural proficiency will be aware of their own cultural practices and values, and be able to reflect on these. For example,

Figure 3.5 Culture, race and ethnicity

Culture

Culture is not about superficial group differences or just a way to label a group of people.
It is an abstract concept.
It is diverse, dynamic and ever-changing.
It is the shared system of learned and shared values, beliefs and rules of conduct that make people behave in a certain way.
It is the standard for perceiving, believing, evaluating and acting.
Not everyone knows everything about their own culture.

Race

The term 'race' is not appropriate when applied to national, religious, geographic, linguistic or ethnic groups.
Race does not relate to mental characteristics such as intelligence, personality or character.
Race is a term applied to people purely because of the way they look.
It is considered by many to be predominantly a social construct.
It is difficult to say a person belongs to a specific race because there are so many variations such as skin colour.
All human groups belong to the same species (*Homo sapiens*).

Ethnicity

Ethnicity is a sense of peoplehood, when people feel close because of sharing a similarity.
It is when people share the same things, for example:
- physical characteristics such as skin colour or bloodline, linguistic characteristics such as language or dialect, behavioural or cultural characteristics such as religion or customs or environmental characteristics such as living in the same area or sharing the same place of origin.

Source: Department of Home Affairs (n.d.). Lesson plan – culture, race & ethnicity. Australian Government Harmony Week: https://www.harmony.gov.au/get-involved/schools/lesson-plans/lesson-plan-culture-race-ethnicity. Licensed under a Creative Commons Attribution 3.0 Australia licence, https://creativecommons.org/licenses/by/3.0/au/deed.en.
Image sources: Shutterstock.com/Brown Camel Studios; Shutterstock.com/Lightspring; Shutterstock.com/Lightspring.

Figure 3.6 Steps to acquiring cultural competence

Step 1: Self-awareness

- Strive to understand how your background has shaped beliefs, values and attitudes.
- Challenge some of your own assumptions.
- Realise that everyone has biases.
- Consider how your fear of doing or saying the wrong thing can inhibit interactions with others and therefore decrease your cultural competence over time.

Step 2: Seeking to understand

- Learn more about others' cultural and sociocultural perspectives.
- Recognise that cultures differ.
- Learn about cultural values, beliefs and behaviours.

Step 3: Putting what was learned into practice

- Honour other cultures in your daily practice.
- Cast yourself in the role of the learner.
- Realise that curriculum is not neutral.

Source: Adapted from Jalongo & Isenberg (2012), p. 77.

how does your culture view gender roles and sexual orientation? How are issues of ethnicity and race dealt with? What about social class and socioeconomic status? Your culture will have a series of 'norms', or accepted beliefs, about all these aspects and others, including geography (where you live), age, abilities and disabilities, religion, educational beliefs and language (Cooper, He & Levin, 2011).

Cultural competence self-assessment

CONSIDER THIS

CULTURAL RESPONSIVITY

Cultural responsivity refers to 'the ability to learn from and relate respectfully to people from your own and other cultures'. It includes modifying your approach to people based on your knowledge of other cultures. It also includes demonstrating an accepting and open attitude towards other points of view. To be culturally responsive, you must demonstrate that you:

- have become culturally self-aware
- value a range of diverse views
- do not impose your own values on others
- avoid stereotyping
- examine your beliefs for bias
- learn what you can from others by attending their celebrations, reading information about other cultures and talking with members of a culture
- accept that learning about and understanding other cultures is a lifelong journey (Zion, Kozleski & Fulton, 2005, pp. 15, 16–17).

▶ DISCUSSION

Are you culturally responsive? What do you do that demonstrates this?

Cultural identity

While Australia is regarded as a multicultural society, the dominant culture traditionally has been Anglo-Australian, and Anglo-Australian laws continue to shape Australian society. Australia remains a member of the British Commonwealth. The process of colonisation assumed superiority over Aboriginal and Torres Strait Islander peoples, and the consequences are still being felt today.

Aboriginal and Torres Strait Islander

Anglo-Australian cultural heritage includes national values such as a sense of justice, fairness, honesty, integrity, optimism and humour. Yet, each member of Australian society has an individual story about their own cultural heritage. Some of these stories are very recent, while others go back several generations. Aboriginal and Torres Strait Islander peoples, in contrast, have stories about their cultural heritage that go back through thousands of years of habitation in Australia.

Video: Cultural identity

Typically, people will look first to their immediate family when reflecting on their cultural heritage. For example, what do we value as a family? What traditions are practised in our family? What do we know about our family's story? This connection to family is extremely important. When family connection is lost – as evidenced by stories of individuals who have experienced adoption, displacement or, in the case of Aboriginal and Torres Strait Islander peoples, forced removal – the consequences can be significant.

The richness, diversity and complexity of our cultural identity shape the ways in which each of us views the world and influence how we engage and interact with others.

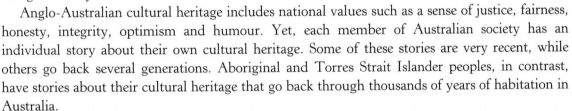

CULTURAL IDENTITY

CONSIDER THIS

Zion, Kozleski and Fulton (2005, pp. 5–9) list a range of factors that influence each individual's cultural identity:

- *language* – not only spoken and written words, but also non-verbal communication forms such as the use of eyes, hands, and body
- *attitudes towards time* – being early, on time or late; some cultures stress the importance of being on time, while for others it is not important
- *space/proximity* – accepted distances between individuals within the culture; appropriateness of physical contact
- *gender roles* – the way a person views, understands and relates to members of the opposite sex; what behaviours are deemed appropriate
- *familial roles* – beliefs about providing for oneself, the young, the old; who protects whom
- *taboos* – attitudes and beliefs about doing things against culturally accepted patterns
- *family ties* – how people see themselves in the context of family; who is considered part of the family; roles within the family; responsibility towards family members
- *grooming and presence* – cultural differences in personal behaviour and appearance, such as laughter, smile, voice quality, gait, poise and style of dress, hair or cosmetics
- *autonomy* – beliefs about the priority given to individual needs in relation to group needs
- *status of age* – accepted manners and attitudes toward older persons, peers, younger persons
- *education* – purpose of education, kinds of learning that are favoured, methods of learning used in home and community.

▶ DISCUSSION

What factors make up your cultural identity?

Culturally safe workplaces

Cultural safety

The Secretariat of National Aboriginal and Islander Child Care (SNAICC, 2012) defines **cultural safety** as 'an environment that is safe for people: where there is no assault, challenge or denial of their identity, of who they are and what they need. It is about shared respect, shared meaning, shared knowledge and experience, of learning, living and working together with dignity and truly listening'.

Martin (1999) uses the term 'cultural safety' to describe the level of acceptance, understanding and respect that families who are not from the dominant culture must feel before they will access a children's service. Martin believes that cultural safety must also include a non-judgemental acceptance of family values and child-rearing practices, and argues that non-Aboriginal people, for example, may not understand that Aboriginal children, by and large, are afforded the status of young adults, are expected to behave as such and are treated accordingly. They are expected to be independent, self-regulating and respectful from an early age.

This lack of understanding of cultural beliefs and practices can lead to culturally biased value judgements.

Ball (2015) believes that 'cultural safety' is characterised by respectful relationships; equitable partnerships in which 'all parties have the right to influence the terms of engagement' and quality interactions that 'contribute to positive outcomes'. Ball suggests that there are five key principles related to cultural safety, which include protocols, process, personal knowledge, positive purpose and partnerships, as described in **Figure 3.7**.

Figure 3.7 Five principles of cultural safety

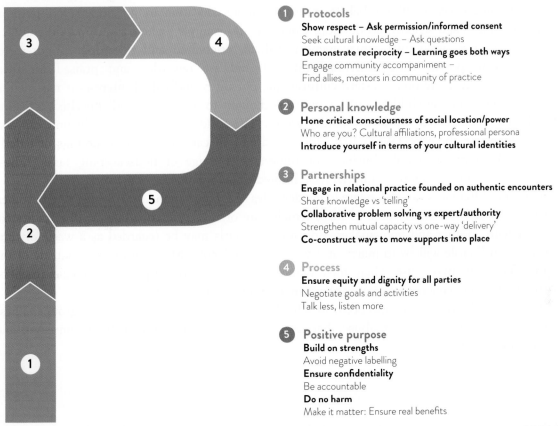

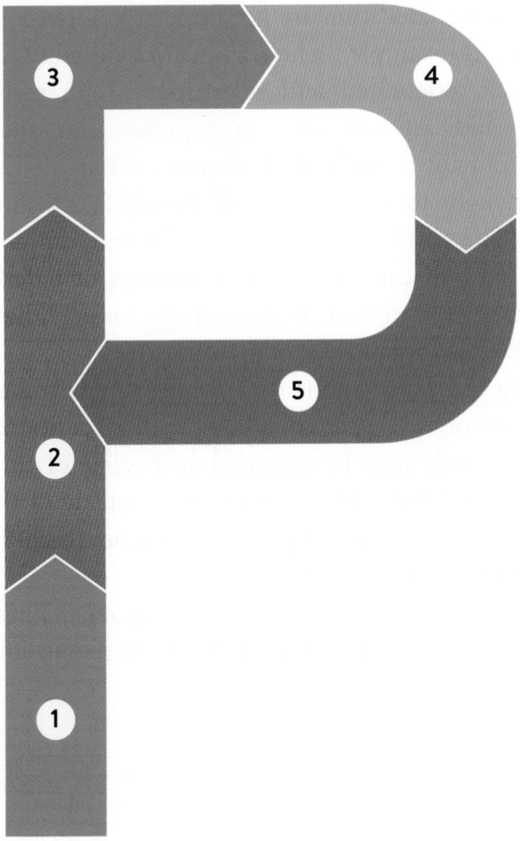

1 Protocols
Show respect – Ask permission/informed consent
Seek cultural knowledge – Ask questions
Demonstrate reciprocity – Learning goes both ways
Engage community accompaniment –
Find allies, mentors in community of practice

2 Personal knowledge
Hone critical consciousness of social location/power
Who are you? Cultural affiliations, professional persona
Introduce yourself in terms of your cultural identities

3 Partnerships
Engage in relational practice founded on authentic encounters
Share knowledge vs 'telling'
Collaborative problem solving vs expert/authority
Strengthen mutual capacity vs one-way 'delivery'
Co-construct ways to move supports into place

4 Process
Ensure equity and dignity for all parties
Negotiate goals and activities
Talk less, listen more

5 Positive purpose
Build on strengths
Avoid negative labelling
Ensure confidentiality
Be accountable
Do no harm
Make it matter: Ensure real benefits

Source: Ball (2015).

CONSIDER THIS

CULTURAL SAFETY

It is the right of our families to be able to express and be proud of their culture. We, as Kooris, acknowledge that western culture is no more or less important than our own culture. We do not force or inflict our views on others and we ask that our families be afforded the same courtesy – without the expectation that they conform to non-Aboriginal ways.

Source: Koori Human Services Unit (2008).

WHAT DOES THIS TELL US?

This statement tells us that cultural safety is a right enjoyed by all members of society. It is the responsibility of members of the dominant culture to acknowledge and respect the rights of minority cultures to their customs, values, beliefs and practices.

Cultural tensions and education

The aspirations that families have for their children will influence their educational expectations both of the child and educators. In some cultures, academic achievement is valued from a very young age, which may result in unrealistic parental expectations and pressure on the child.

Aboriginal and Torres Strait Islander cultural safety framework

Cultural differences also exist in relation to beliefs about how children learn. In some cultures, children are expected to learn by observing and copying adults, or may be children given detailed verbal instructions; in other cultures, including many Western cultures, children are expected to learn by engaging in investigation, experimentation, problem-solving, exploration and direct instruction. In contrast, in many Eastern cultures, such as in China and Vietnam, students are expected to sit quietly and receive instruction without interrupting the teacher with questions.

Where differences in cultural beliefs and values about education are not understood, tensions between families and schools can develop. Consider, for example, beliefs about individuality. In Western cultures, individual achievement is valued, celebrated and rewarded. Children are encouraged to pursue their individual interests and are rewarded and praised for their achievements. In many non-Western cultures, the pursuit of individual interests is regarded as inappropriate. Singling children out for praise is thought to make the child conceited, affecting the child's relationships within the family group. The child's role in the family unit can also vary. There may be expectations that older children will care for younger siblings or elderly relatives, help in the family business or undertake a range of housekeeping tasks. These responsibilities may mean that children have limited time for study or homework.

Cultural differences can also relate to gender roles and expectations. In cultures where women are not afforded the same status as men, females are often expected to take on the traditional roles of wife, mother and homemaker. Education for girls may be regarded as a waste of time because a girl's role will be to marry at a young age and not participate in work outside of the home. Tensions may arise when men demonstrate a lack of respect for female teachers, particularly where concerns are raised about male children's behaviour.

Intercultural tensions can also occur in schools where there is a mix of cultural groups. These tensions may result in racist abuse, harassment and discrimination at both conscious and unconscious levels.

Cross-cultural communication

Videos: Cultural discrimination and racism

All communication is culturally bound. It draws on the ways in which we have learned to speak and give non-verbal messages. LeBaron (2003, p. 7) suggests 'the challenge is that even with all the good will in the world, miscommunication is likely to happen, especially when there are significant cultural differences between communicators. Miscommunication may lead to conflict, or aggravate conflict that already exists'. Every culture has variations in the ways in which both verbal and **non-verbal communication** are used. LeBaron (2003) suggests that differences in how people within a culture communicate can be grouped into key areas, as outlined below.

It should be remembered that while one culture may have tendencies to display a certain style of communication, there will always be differences among people and not all individuals from a particular culture will conform to these generalisations – they should be used as a guide only.

Direct vs indirect context

High context and low context are used to describe differences in styles of communication practised by various cultures. Cultures that use a high-context style of communication, such as Aboriginal and Torres Strait Islander, Asian and African cultures, tend to use an indirect style of communication. Information is indirect, and meaning is often conveyed through subtle non-verbal communication. In contrast, Western cultures, such as in the United States, United Kingdom and Australia, tend to use low-context communication, which is more direct and explicit. Conflict can arise in the workplace when employees have different styles of communication.

Time

Variations in time relate to the timing of communication and the way information is communicated. In many Western cultures, time is of the essence, and the goal is to say what needs to be said quickly and succinctly. In contrast, in cultures where time is viewed in a much more relaxed manner (or as having little or no importance), the approach to conversation, negotiations and sharing information tends to be slow-paced and relaxed.

Personal space

The concept of personal space also varies between cultures. In many Western cultures, standing too close to others when engaged in conversation is regarded as impolite and tends to make individuals feel uncomfortable. This is commonly referred to as invading someone's personal space. In other cultures, being close to the speaker is regarded as polite and necessary to ensure that the conversation is interpreted correctly.

Fate and personal responsibility

This refers to the things we feel we have control over (personal responsibility) and those things we feel we have no control over in our life (fate). For example, many children from a white, Anglo-Saxon background in Australia are raised to dream big, have goals and believe in free will. If they encounter failure when trying to achieve their goals, they are encouraged to keep trying until they are successful. Children raised in some other countries – in Mexico, as just one example – may have a more fatalistic view of the world: if they encounter failure or accidents, they accept them as unavoidable or inevitable. In the workplace, two individuals with these differing beliefs may come into conflict if they are faced with a problem to solve.

Face and face-saving

The concepts of *face* and *face-saving* relate to issues of respect, power and status. In some cultures, saving face and enabling others to save face (i.e. not be embarrassed) are extremely important cultural practices. In many Western societies, individuals are generally less concerned with saving face – individuals say what they mean and are not afraid of conflict. In China, Japan and Iran, for example, group harmony is often the main goal, so individuals will avoid saying what they mean if it is likely to cause conflict.

Non-verbal communication

Non-verbal communication can be even more powerful than verbal communication, and can easily be misinterpreted by colleagues of culturally diverse backgrounds. Non-verbal communication includes body language, facial expressions and gestures. There are also variations in cultural rules in the use of gestures or touching the other person while talking. **Figure 3.8** sets out some examples of non-verbal communication, and how different meanings can be conveyed depending on the cultural background of the participants.

Figure 3.8 Examples of non-verbal communication and meanings

	Different meanings	Potential misunderstanding
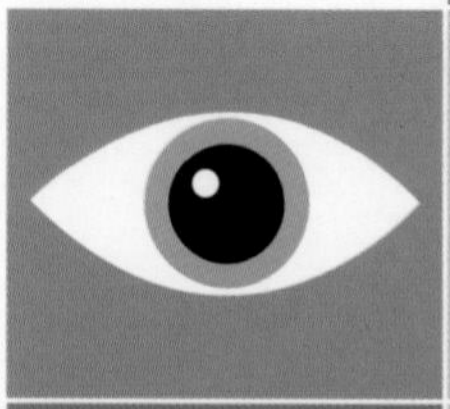	In Western cultures, speakers tend to look into each other's eyes. If someone avoids eye contact, this can be interpreted as uninterest or deception. In many Asian and Australian Aboriginal cultures, however, avoiding eye contact is a sign of respect and humility.	If a person from a Western culture is speaking with a colleague from an Asian or Aboriginal culture, they may believe that the listener is not interested in what they are saying.
	Some gestures that are commonly used in Western cultures can be offensive in others. For example, pointing with one finger is considered rude in some Asian cultures. In some Latin cultures, hand gestures can be exaggerated compared with those used by other cultures.	It might be incorrectly assumed that a colleague from a Latin background is angry or over-excited if they wave their hands around a lot during a conversation.
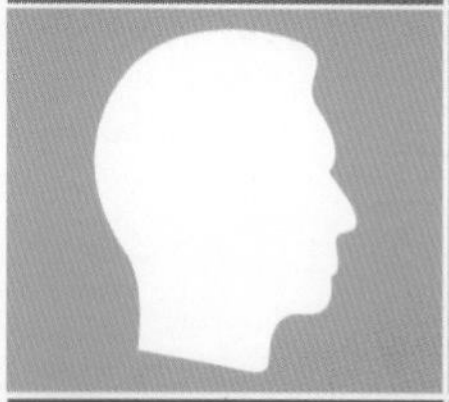	In some cultures, a listener who nods their head is conveying the message that they are listening to what you are saying – it does not necessarily mean they agree with you.	A worker might fail to seek verbal agreement from their colleague and simply assume they agree because they have nodded their head.
	For some cultures, if a listener remains silent, the speaker assumes that the other person does not understand. In other cultures, such as Aboriginal cultures, listeners often prefer to remain silent and delay their response until they have had time to think or listen to others' opinions first.	A worker might incorrectly assume that their colleague doesn't understand what they are saying, or will rush to fill the other person's silence and not give them a chance to contribute.

Communication strategies

Any strategies that may be put in place to communicate with people from diverse language backgrounds should be based on mutual respect and acceptance of differences. Being polite, patient and respectful should be a general rule of thumb when communicating with others in the workplace.

Strategies that may be used include:

- talking slowly so that the listener has time to hear and interpret what is being said
- when explaining a task, breaking it down into smaller steps
- keeping the message simple and to the point – avoid 'information overload'
- avoiding jargon, slang, swearing and jokes – these can be confusing or even offensive to others
- maintaining a respectful distance – avoid invading the personal space of others
- not touching the other person when speaking
- remaining aware of non-verbal communication
- understanding that gestures can be useful if not overdone – don't wave your hands around when speaking
- checking for understanding – ask questions to clarify understanding, or ask person to demonstrate the task.

Language barriers

Australia's population is very linguistically diverse. If you are from an English-speaking background, it is important to be aware of misunderstandings that might arise when communicating with colleagues for whom English is a second language. Workers from non-English-speaking backgrounds (NESB) may have difficulty understanding others or making themselves understood. Idioms, slang and jargon can be a source of misunderstanding for NESB workers. Consider the following Australian idioms (adapted from Australian Catholic University, 2015):

Video: Studying intercultural communication

- 'I'm feeling under the weather' – meaning you are feeling sick.
- 'It was a piece of cake' – meaning something was easy.
- 'That's the last straw' – meaning you've had enough of something.
- 'Please bring a plate' – meaning please bring some food to share.

Australian slang can also present challenges – for example, 'g'day' (hello), 'hooroo' (goodbye), 'sunnies' (sunglasses) and 'chook' (a chicken). *Australianisms* or slang can make it extremely challenging for individuals learning to speak English, but also quite challenging in terms of embracing the Australian culture.

Dealing with language barriers

There are strategies you can implement to help overcome language barriers:

- Ask families to teach you key words in their first language and make a note of how to pronounce these words and phrases.
- Ask whether the child's name is a family name. Ensure that all names are pronounced correctly.
- Download a translator app on your phone or tablet.
- Use visual methods, such as photos or demonstration, to share key information.
- If you are working with a person from a NESB, you could also take the time to learn a few words in their language – for example, the words for hello and thank you.

Translator and interpreter services

Where there are significant language barriers, the school may need to access a translator and/or interpreter services. Translators can convert written materials from one language to another. This is particularly helpful in assisting the family to understand the enrolment process and sharing information about the child, such as immunisation status. It can also be helpful for translating information about the family's right to privacy and confidentiality.

Interpreters orally restate in one language what has been said in another language. The Department of Social Services provides free interpreter services for Australian citizens and permanent residents to assist with communication between eligible organisations and individuals. These services can be used to share and exchange general information relating to enrolment, school attendance and how parents can engage with the school. Interpreters can also assist when teachers need to share information about a child or young person's learning, identified needs or behaviour issues.

When determining whether to use a professional interpreting service or a non-professional interpreter, such as another parent or family friend, it is important to consider:

- whether or not the information or discussion is of a personal or confidential nature
- the degree of impartiality of the non-professional interpreter
- the English language skills of the non-professional interpreter.

ACCESSING TRANSLATION AND INTERPRETER SERVICES

CONSIDER THIS

The Translating and Interpreting Service (TIS National) is for people who do not speak English and for agencies and businesses that need to communicate with their non-English-speaking clients. The service is available 24 hours a day, seven days a week (fees apply, although some people may be eligible for free interpreting services – see the website for more information): https://www.tisnational.gov.au.

3.3 A personal perspective: values and beliefs

Each of us is a product of our own culture and experiences. Our culture guides our thinking, our behaviour and our values. It influences what and how we eat, what customs are celebrated and how they are celebrated, our concept of family and family values, and our attitudes towards work and education.

Your own values, attitudes and beliefs will significantly influence and shape your role as an ESW. Consider your beliefs about children and young people – for example, what are your expectations in relation to behaviour in public places, dress, manners, access to money, taking on responsibilities around the home, teenagers going to parties or teenage drinking? Your beliefs will be shaped by your own life experiences, upbringing and culture.

When working with children and young people, your values and beliefs can be challenged when you are confronted by situations and behaviours that you consider to be unacceptable, provocative, sad or shocking. Being able to manage these challenges, so that you respond in a positive and professional manner, can be quite testing.

Attitudes

Attitudes are learned predispositions of thinking or reacting towards a situation, group or concept. Attitudes are difficult to change, and have a strong influence on our behaviour. For example, some people have a positive attitude towards adversity – they believe things will get better (the glass half-full); while others have a negative attitude towards adversity – they believe that bad things always happen to them (the glass half-empty).

Having a positive attitude is critical when working with children and young people, particularly where students are faced with adversity or learning challenges. Promoting an 'I can do this' attitude will assist children and young people to persist at tasks and contribute to building resilience and essential long-term success.

Beliefs

Beliefs are things that we accept as true. Beliefs can be positive or negative and often have no factual basis, yet they can be quite powerful and may need to be challenged or examined carefully.

Our beliefs may determine our response to major issues, such as whether young unemployed people should work for unemployment benefits, what responsibility our local council should take for household recycling or whether mothers should stay at home to look after their children rather than using child care. Our beliefs are also reflected in many of the day-to-day tasks that we carry out at work and at home – for example, is the television left on or turned off during dinner? What time should a 16-year-old be home from a party?

Beliefs can shape how we perceive ourselves and how we view the actions of others. Children and young people who are challenged by the school environment will often develop self-defeating beliefs about themselves: 'I can't read. I'm stupid. Everyone is better than me.' Challenging these beliefs can assist children and young people to recognise their own strengths and develop a more balanced view of themselves – for example, 'There are some words that you can't read yet but there are lots of words that you can read' or 'You're not stupid. You find some things hard to do but you are good at lots of other things.'

Values

Ashman and Elkins (2012, p. 9) define **values** as 'the principles or standards of behaviour that reflect judgements about what is held to be important in life. These standards of behaviour are affected by cultural influences and personal preferences and beliefs'. Examples of personal values include honesty, a belief in always doing your very best, spirituality, the importance of family and friendships, kindness, freedom and democracy, integrity, respect, fairness and equality. Personal values impact all aspects of life.

In school settings, our values have a powerful influence on children and young people. For example, if fairness is valued, all students will be treated with respect. If respect for differences is valued, we will strive to ensure that students do not engage in bullying or racial taunts. When working with children and young people, it is important to reflect on your personal values and consider how they impact your daily practices. See the following Scenario box.

SCENARIO

VALUES, ATTITUDES AND BELIEFS

John, an ESW, is working with a group of Year 6 students. The students are working on a project about river systems. John notices that **Liam** and **Dillan** are teasing **Armin** because of his accent.

Liam: *'Hey listen to Armin – he says riber. A riber sis-tom!'*

Liam and Dillan laugh.

Dillan: *'Yeah, he can no speak English.'*

Armin walks back to his desk and sits down.

John takes Liam and Dillan aside. *'Why are you making fun of Armin?'*

Liam: *'It's just a joke.'*

Dillan: *'Yeah, he knows we're only joking.'*

John: *'Take a look at Armin. It looks to me like he's pretty upset.'*

The boys look at Armin and then look to the floor.

John: *'It's not okay to make fun of the way other people speak. What can you do to fix this situation?'*

Liam: *'I'll go and say sorry.'*

Dillan: *'Me too.'*

John watches as the boys talk to Armin and reflects what it must be like to be 12 years old and made to feel different. John makes a mental note to report the incident to the classroom teacher.

WHAT DOES THIS TELL US?

Students act in ways that are hurtful to others. What Liam and Dillan considered to be a harmless joke is in fact a demonstration of racial bias. John acted quickly and appropriately to address this behaviour. By reporting the incident, John is demonstrating to the teacher that he understands the importance of addressing bias.

Exploring your own cultural identity

The way individuals perceive their own culture is shaped first by their family. Family values, beliefs, traditions and home language play a critical role in shaping one's cultural identity. How are relationships maintained in our family? What roles are assigned to family members? What do we know about our family's story? The transmission of cultural values and norms begins at birth and remains a powerful influence on cultural identity throughout life.

Many Australians would also acknowledge that Australian culture is shaped by national values such as mateship, social justice, fairness, optimism and a sense of humour. You can explore your own cultural identity by asking yourself the series of questions in the Consider this box.

CONSIDER THIS

EXPLORING MY CULTURAL IDENTITY

- What is my nationality?
- With which race/s do I identify/feel I belong?
- Do I consider myself to belong to a specific ethnic group?
- What role does religion/spirituality play in my cultural identity?

The following questions explore how your family has shaped your cultural identity.

- Who is included in my family (this may include relatives and non-relatives)?
- What roles are assigned to family members?
- How do we communicate? What language do we speak at home? What role does non-verbal communication play in our family?
- What behaviour standards are expected in our family – manners, behaviour in public, etc.?
- What are our family beliefs about community, religion/spirituality, education, work, law, mental health?
- What traditions are celebrated in our family?

▶ DISCUSSION

The factors that contribute to one's sense of cultural identity will vary between cultures and between families. Use the above questions to explore your cultural identity. What factors do you consider to be most important in shaping your cultural identity?

Diversity and bias

Everyone will have some degree of personal **bias** based on their own unique belief system, values, attitudes and traditions, which have been shaped over time by family, cultural and social influences.

Personal bias extends to **stereotypes** – one way in which individuals assign certain traits to groups of people or cultures. Stereotyping reflects our personal beliefs in relation to race, religion, disability, gender or ethnic background. Some examples of stereotyping include:

- 'All women are maternal.'
- 'All Indians love cricket.'
- 'People with a mental illness are unstable and can't be trusted in the workplace.'
- 'People with a learning disability have low intelligence.'

These stereotypes often remained fixed until they are challenged. Addressing our own bias can be quite confronting: often, we may not be consciously aware of our bias until challenged by others. Some ways to address personal bias are engaging in critical self-reflection and discussion with family and trusted colleagues.

Figure 3.9 provides examples of questions that can be used to reflect on our own beliefs and bias.

Bias and racism in Australia

Racism can take many forms, such as jokes or comments that cause offence or hurt, sometimes unintentionally; name-calling or verbal abuse; harassment or intimidation, or commentary in the media or online that inflames hostility towards certain groups (Understanding Racism, 2023). Racism can be overt – a conscious and intentional act aiming to harm someone based on their race – or covert. An example of overt racism is an employer refusing to hire someone because of their race or linguistic background. Covert racism is a subtle and sometimes unconscious act, and is not always intended – for example, laughing at a joke that enforces racist stereotypes. The effects of racism,

Figure 3.9 Self-reflective questions

Question	Points to reflect on
What personal values and beliefs do I hold?	Consider how you would respond to questions such as: > Should all first tertiary qualifications be paid for by the government? > How do you feel about same-sex marriage? > Is religion an important part of my belief system?
How do I feel and react when I am confronted with an unfamiliar experience?	Think about a time when you found yourself in an unfamiliar situation. For example, have you ever attended a wedding of a friend who had different religious beliefs to yours, or found yourself in a foreign country where no one spoke your language?
What stereotypes do I uphold?	We consciously or unconsciously uphold many positive and negative stereotypes. You could begin by reading the following stereotypes and examining your own beliefs about them: > Asian people are smart. > People with tattoos are not professional. > Older people are not good with technology. > Men are better at sport than women.

whether overt or covert, include increased stress; feelings of resentment, shame, fear and insecurity; harm to physical and mental health; and undermined confidence (Victorian Equal Opportunity and Human Rights Commission [VEOHRC], 2013).

Unfortunately, cultural bias and racism are still prevalent in Australian society. A report by the AHRC (2014) found the following:

- People born in countries where English is not the main spoken language are three times as likely to experience discrimination in the workplace.
- Around 20 per cent of Australians have experienced race-hate talk.
- Some 19 per cent of Australians have reported discrimination because of their skin colour, ethnic origin or religion.
- One in 10 Australians (1.5 million of the nation's adult population) believes that some races are inferior or superior to others.

According to VEOHRC (2013), most people do not report the racism they witness or experience themselves because they feel that nothing will be done to fix it anyway or they are afraid of retribution. However, if racism or discrimination in your workplace is not reported, it is effectively being accepted. If you witness acts of discrimination or racism in the workplace, it is important not to ignore it. You should discuss the incident with your supervisor and follow the school's anti-discrimination policy.

CONSIDER THIS

EXPERIENCING RACISM

The AHRC suggests that there are a number of ways you might respond to racism or discrimination:

- React calmly and try not to follow your initial emotional response. You may feel hurt and angry, but in this situation it is best to remain calm. If you feel up to it, you should let the person know that what they have said or done has upset you and/or is offensive.
- Alternatively, don't react at all. Racist comments are usually designed to gain attention. By ignoring the person, you are not giving them what they want.

If you do not want to deal with the situation yourself, you should report the incident to your supervisor or school executive. If you are not satisfied with the result, you can make a complaint to the AHRC or seek legal advice.

Source: Racism. It stops with me. https://itstopswithme.humanrights.gov.au

3.4 Working with diverse people

The school community will include students and their families, teachers and ESWs, administrative staff, support staff and sometimes volunteers and tertiary students. ESWs may also be required to liaise with visiting specialist professionals, such as educational psychologists, itinerant teachers for students with vision and hearing impairment, physiotherapists, social workers, welfare officers and specialist officers from police units.

In medium to large schools, the school community may also include several sub-teams: for example, the school executive, administration team, and teaching teams based on subjects, grades or specialist areas, such as literacy, sports and music. In large schools, there may be a team of ESWs. Depending on their job roles, ESWs will typically be part of the administration team or the teaching team.

Within these various school communities, there will be a great deal of diversity – social, cultural, religious, language, sexual identity, level of education and expertise, age and gender. With this diversity will come differences in values, beliefs and attitudes. Working effectively within such a diverse community requires teamwork, mutual trust and acceptance, and respect for differences. This is demonstrated when all members of the school community:

- have a clear understanding and commitment to the educational and social goals of the school
- are familiar with and comply with all policies and procedures necessary for the safe and effective operation of the school
- are willing to be flexible, adaptable and open to change
- are cooperative and willing to share information and address issues as they arise in a spirit of collaboration
- use effective communication, including active listening, with adults and children
- comply with all lawful directions to ensure the safety and wellbeing of members of the school community
- are willing to use their initiative to address or prevent issues as they arise
- are able to acknowledge and appreciate that each individual has the right to respectfully express their own point of view.

The effectiveness of the school team will depend largely on the leadership skills of the executive team and a willingness by all team members to work towards a set of common goals.

Working with culturally diverse colleagues

An **inclusive workplace** provides opportunities to experience and benefit from a wide range of skills, abilities, cultures, life experiences, knowledge and expertise. Where there is a collective willingness to embrace diversity, and to explore and respect differences, bringing people from diverse backgrounds together can enrich any workplace. Everyone in the workplace, regardless of their role/status, deserves to be treated with dignity and respect. Every individual can make a positive contribution to the workplace if they are supported and encouraged to do so.

It is highly likely that, at some point in your career, you will work with colleagues whose cultural background is different from your own. For most people, cultural differences present very few problems in the workplace. Wentling and Palma-Rivas (1998), however, identify a number of relevant factors, such as negative attitudes and discomfort towards people who are different; discrimination and prejudice; stereotyping; racism; and personal bias as cultural barriers in the workplace. Where such barriers exist, specific interventions – such as workplace training – are often needed to overcome these barriers and ensure the workplace is culturally safe.

Cultural safety in the workplace

Cultural safety in the workplace is a process that, according to Eckermann, Dowd and Jeffs (2009), includes two elements:

Cultural awareness + Cultural sensitivity = Cultural safety.

Cultural awareness involves recognising and acknowledging that cultural differences exist. **Cultural sensitivity** is awareness of the sensitivities around cultural differences; it requires critical self-reflection on one's own cultural values, attitudes and beliefs, as well as the beliefs and biases of other cultures.

Achieving cultural safety in the workplace can be a challenging task, and may never be fully achieved simply because the dominant culture will always be entrenched in every aspect of the workplace. Williams (1998, p. 4) suggests that organisations should begin the process of evaluating cultural safety by first examining preconceived ideas and stereotypes held by members of the organisation. Williams (1998, p. 6) describes the 'nuts and bolts' of cultural safety for organisations working with or employing Aboriginal and Torres Strait Islander Australians as involving the following principles:

- respecting the individual's culture, knowledge, experience and cultural obligations
- treating cultural differences with dignity and ensuring culturally appropriate programs and environments
- recognition that there is more than one way of doing things
- debunking of the myth that all Aboriginal and Torres Strait Islander peoples are the same.

Cultural safety issues in the workplace

All employees should have the opportunity to participate fully in the workplace and be treated with dignity and respect. According to the Equal Opportunity Commission of South Australia (2011), diversity in the workplace may include:

- dress – for example, some cultures have specific clothing such as head scarves or turbans that are worn at all times
- religious practices – some religions require time during work each day for prayer or time off for special religious days
- customs – some cultures restrict the foods that may be consumed, including the way foods are prepared
- intergenerational protocols – in some cultures older people must be addressed by their title, such as Mrs/Mr, or be referred to as Sir/Madam, while in other cultures there may be a more relaxed approach such as using the person's first name or the term aunty/uncle
- social values – differences will exist in relation to what is considered appropriate social and sexual behaviour and work ethics
- family obligations – in some cultures family commitments take priority over work commitments
- taboos in relation to non-verbal communication, such as eye contact, facial expressions and hand gestures.

PROTOCOLS

SCENARIO

ESW **Trinh** is in her mid-forties and has worked at the school on and off for around five years. The school recently employed a new ESW, **Susan Pearce**, who is in her mid-twenties. When introduced to Trinh, Susan smiled and said, *'Nice to meet you, Trinh.'*

Later in the day Trinh approached the teacher: *'Mr Brown, may I speak with you about Miss Pearce? I am not comfortable being called by my first name. As a young person, she must show respect. I would prefer that she call me Miss Phan. I think also that she should not call you by your first name. It is disrespectful to your position as teacher.'*

WHAT DOES THIS TELL US?

Being aware of and respecting differences in social protocols is important in the workplace. In this situation, Susan has inadvertently offended Miss Phan.

Working with people with disability

The right of people with disability to work on an equal basis with others is protected by Article 27 of the UN Convention on the Rights of Persons with Disabilities. The *Disability Discrimination Act 1992* (Cth) makes it illegal to discriminate against someone based on their disability. Discrimination includes direct and indirect discrimination. Direct discrimination involves treating a person with disability less favourably than a person without disability in the same or similar circumstances. Indirect discrimination occurs when there is a rule or policy that is the same for everyone but has an unfair effect on people with disability.

DISABILITY DISCRIMINATION ACT 1992 (CTH) EXEMPTIONS

CONSIDER THIS

Under the *Disability Discrimination Act 1992* (AHRC, 2016, pp. 9–10), it is not unlawful to refuse to employ or promote a person based on their disability if they are unable to carry out the essential or 'inherent' requirements of the job, even with reasonable adjustments. It is also not unlawful for an employer to terminate a person's employment if they are unable to carry out the inherent requirements of the job because of disability.

Employment barriers for people with disability

The National Inquiry into Employment Discrimination Against Older Australians and Australians with Disability (AHRC, 2016, pp. 12–13) found that some possible barriers to gaining and keeping employment faced by Australians with disability included:

- discriminatory attitudes and behaviours during recruitment, and in the workplace, from employers and others
- low levels of awareness of rights at work
- a lack of availability of jobs
- a lack of assistance in finding, securing and maintaining employment
- difficulty in accessing skills training and education
- potential reduction or loss of the Disability Support Pension as a result of increased employment
- difficulty experienced in accessing flexible work arrangements
- health issues
- difficulty in negotiating reasonable adjustments/accommodation in the workplace

- a lack of availability of accessible transport and technology in the workplace
- poor workplace design.

Some possible barriers that employers may face in employing people with disability include:

- low levels of awareness of legal obligations in relation to discrimination against people with disability
- difficulties ensuring access and flexibility for workers with disability
- limited resources, particularly for small business
- difficulties in complying with multiple laws and regulations related to anti-discrimination, employment, work, health and safety, workers' compensation and insurance
- difficulties associated with compliance with monitoring and reporting requirements
- a lack of knowledge or confidence regarding what is needed to support workers with disability.

Source: AHRC (2016). Willing to Work. © Australian Human Rights Commission 2016.

Employment of a person with disability

Studies conducted in Australia and overseas have found no differences in performance and productivity of people with disability and people without disability, and found that employees with disability have fewer scheduled absences as well as increased tenure. On average, employing people with disability does not cost any more than employing people without disability (Australian Network on Disability, 2016).

The Australian Government has invested in several support mechanisms to assist people with disability to participate in the workforce. These include:

- *disability employment services* – a network of service providers that support job seekers with disability to find and keep a job, and assist employers to implement practices that support employees with disability
- *Australian disability enterprises* – government-supported commercial enterprises that provide supported employment for people with disability
- *Employment Assistance Fund* – a fund to provide financial assistance for workplace modifications and services
- *JobAccess* – an advisory service that provides information about the employment of people with disability to people with disability, employers, service providers and workplace solutions (AHRC, 2016, p. 11).

Source: AHRC (2016). Willing to Work. © Australian Human Rights Commission 2016.

Mental health

Mental health is an issue that can significantly affect how a person feels, thinks, behaves and interacts with other people. Mental health issues include:

- mood disorders (such as depression)
- anxiety and stress
- psychotic disorders (such as schizophrenia and some forms of bipolar disorder) (AHRC, 2010, p. 7).

According to Safe Work Australia (2018, p. 4), the most common workplace-related mental health disorders are linked to workplace stress.

MENTAL ILLNESS

CONSIDER THIS

- One in five Australians aged 16–85 years experiences a mental health issue in any one year.
- One in seven Australians will experience depression in their lifetime.
- One in six Australian workers will experience a mental health issue.
- Depression and anxiety are now the leading causes of long-term sickness absence in the developed world.
- The most common mental health issues are depression, anxiety and substance use disorder. These three types of mental illnesses often occur in combination.
- Of the 20 per cent of Australians with a mental health issue in any one year, 11.5 per cent have one disorder and 8.5 per cent have two or more disorders.
- Almost half (45 per cent) of Australians will experience a mental health issue in their lifetime.
- Around 54 per cent of people with a mental health issue do not access any treatment.

The Black Dog Institute (2020) states that jobs characterised by high emotional and/or cognitive demands have a higher rate of sickness absence due to mental health issues. Typical examples of these workforces include teachers, nurses, lawyers and industrial workers.

WHAT DOES THIS TELL US?

We know that working in a support role in a school setting can be physically and emotionally demanding. These figures tell us that there are likely to be teachers and ESWs currently working in schools who have a mental health issue.

Individuals with anxiety may experience the symptoms shown in **Figure 3.10**.

Figure 3.10 Symptoms of anxiety

Psychological symptoms	Physical symptoms
Frequent or excessive worry Poor concentration Specific fears or phobias (e.g. fear of dying or fear of losing control)	Fatigue Irritability Sleeping difficulties General restlessness Muscle tension Upset stomach Sweating and difficulty breathing Behavioural changes – including procrastination, avoidance, difficulty making decisions and social withdrawal

Source: Black Dog Institute (2019).

As an employee and workplace colleague you can reduce the stigma of mental health issues by talking about the importance of mental health and wellbeing and taking a zero-tolerance approach to stigmatisation.

Gender diversity

The acronym LGBTIQ+ refers to people who identify as lesbian, gay, bisexual, transgender, intersex, queer, asexual and questioning. The Department of Education, Queensland (2018, p. 7) states that, nationally, research highlights the following in relationship to LGBTIQ+ experiences in education environments:

- One third of people who worked in Australian schools felt they were unable to name their partner on forms or use their preferred gender.

- Some 56 per cent indicated that they were not supported to 'be out'.
- Around 79 per cent of LGBTIQ+ staff in Australian schools indicated that their sexual orientation or gender identity made them feel uncomfortable at work and they harboured fears of discrimination and job loss.

In school settings, LGBTIQ+ people also face potential discrimination from parents and families. According to Pride in Diversity (2013), discrimination may be a result of deeply held religious convictions, cultural norms, conservative mindsets or a lack of understanding of inclusion and diversity.

Discrimination based on gender and sexuality

LGBTIQ+ people represent part of the rich diversity that exists within the Australian community. Yet, despite widespread support for same-sex marriage in Australia, the AHRC (2015) states that LGBTIQ+ people in Australia still experience discrimination, harassment and hostility in many parts of everyday life: in public, at work and study, in accessing health and other services, and in securing proper recognition of their sex in official documents. Pride in Diversity (2013, pp. 10, 18) reports that:

- 53 per cent of gay and lesbian people experience workplace harassment and discrimination
- 50 per cent experience homophobic remarks/jokes in the workplace
- 28 per cent experience aggressive or unwelcome questions about their status and 22 per cent report having been 'outed' in the workplace against their wishes
- 17 per cent report having a restricted career due to their sexual orientation.

LGBTIQ+ stereotyping and experiences

CONSIDER THIS

SEXUAL DISCRIMINATION

DIRECT DISCRIMINATION

In terms of sexual discrimination, direct discrimination is treating another person less favourably, based on their sexual orientation, gender identity or intersex status, than someone without that attribute would be treated in the same or similar circumstances.

INDIRECT DISCRIMINATION

Indirect discrimination is imposing, or proposing to impose, a requirement, condition or practice that has, or is likely to have, disadvantaged people based on sexual orientation or gender identity or intersex status, and which is not reasonable in the circumstances.

VILIFICATION

Vilification includes where an individual publicly incites hatred towards, contempt for, or ridicule of, staff members because of their sexuality; and/or threatens physical harm to property or persons.

SCENARIO

HOMOPHOBIA

ESW **Cahya**, originally from Indonesia, is quiet and polite. He has been assigned to work with a new ESW, **Ethan**, to support a group of students for whom English is a second language. Ethan is pleased that he will be working with a more experienced ESW, as his experience with English language learners is limited.

Ethan is gay and does not hide his sexual identity. Cahya believes that homosexuality is a sin and he is shocked to learn that the school has employed Ethan, knowing that he is gay. Cahya complains to his supervisor that he should not be expected to work with Ethan, who he describes as an abomination.

His supervisor tells Cahya that such comments are discriminatory and have no place in the school. She tells Cahya that he has no choice and must work respectfully with Ethan. Cahya is not happy but can't afford not to work.

Over the next several weeks, the tension between Cahya and Ethan grows. Finally, Ethan goes to his supervisor, telling her that Cahya is difficult to work with and extremely unfriendly. He suspects Cahya is homophobic but has no direct evidence to back his suspicions.

WHAT DOES THIS TELL US?

In this scenario, discrimination against Ethan has been indirect. Cahya has been unfriendly and difficult to work with, but he has not engaged in any direct acts of discrimination.

▶ DISCUSSION

If you were the supervisor, how would you respond to Ethan's complaints about Cahya's behaviour? How would you resolve the situation?

Religious and spiritual diversity

According to the AHRC (n.d.), discrimination in employment on the basis of religion occurs when someone does not experience equality of opportunity in employment because of their religion. This may include being refused a job, being dismissed from employment, being denied training opportunities or being harassed at work. Discrimination on the basis of religion alone is not unlawful under federal anti-discrimination law, although it may be unlawful under some state/territory legislation.

RELIGION AND SPIRITUALITY

CONSIDER THIS

Religion is a set of organized beliefs, practices, and systems that most often relate to the belief and worship of a controlling force, such as a personal god or another supernatural being. Religion often involves cultural beliefs, worldviews, texts, prophecies, revelations, and morals that have spiritual meaning to members of the particular faith, and it can encompass a range of practices, including sermons, rituals, prayer, meditation, holy places, symbols, trances, and feasts.

Source: Stibich, M. (2022). What is Religion? The Psychology of Why People Believe. https://www.verywellmind.com/religion-improves-health-2224007

Spirituality is the broad concept of a belief in something beyond the self . . . It may involve religious traditions centering on the belief in a higher. It can also involve a holistic belief in an individual connection to others and to the world as a whole.

Source: Scott, E. (2022). What is spirituality? The Very Well Mind. https://www.verywellmind.com/how-spirituality-can-benefit-mental-and-physical-health-3144807

Religion and human rights

Employers can accommodate religious rights by providing a quiet room or space for employees to observe prayer or for private reflection in employees' break times. Employers can also allow employees to use holiday entitlements to engage in religious and cultural celebrations. Schools can acknowledge and celebrate various religious and cultural days as a part of their whole school diversity strategy.

3.5 Australia's First Nations people

Aboriginal and Torres Strait Islander

Aboriginal and Torres Strait Islander peoples are 'persons of Aboriginal and/or Torres Strait Islander descent, who identify as Aboriginal and/or Torres Strait Islander and are accepted as such by the community in which they live' (National Mental Health Consumer & Carer Forum, 2018, p. 1).

The impact of colonisation

Aboriginal and Torres Strait Islander people have a cultural history dating back 50 000 to 65 000 years, making theirs the oldest known civilisations in the world. As the first inhabitants, Aboriginal and Torres Strait Islander people are the traditional owners of the land. However, Aboriginal and Torres Strait Islander people did not have the same perspective on land ownership as the white settlers. Aboriginal and Torres Strait Islander people believed themselves to be part of the land – not 'owners' in the colonialist sense, but rather caretakers of the land. This belief allowed Aboriginal and Torres Strait Islander communities to successfully live in harmony with the environment for thousands of years.

White settlement systematically stripped Aboriginal and Torres Strait Islander people of their traditional land rights, and they have suffered abuse, massacres, racism and the forced removal of children from the family unit. Aboriginal and Torres Strait Islander people were forced off their traditional lands, away from their active hunter-gatherer lifestyle. Those who resisted faced violence. Furthermore:

- A treaty has never been negotiated as part of the colonisation process.
- Many Aboriginal and Torres Strait Islander people died from infectious diseases brought into the country by Europeans.
- Many Aboriginal and Torres Strait Islander people were moved to missions or reserves, where they were forbidden to speak their own language or maintain their cultural practices.
- Laws were enacted, limiting the rights of Aboriginal and Torres Strait Islander people, segregating them from other Australians and giving them little or no self-determination.
- Aboriginal and Torres Strait Islander children were removed forcibly from their families and communities, to be raised in institutions or by foster families of European background; they were also forced to give up their Aboriginal or Torres Strait Islander identity.
- Aboriginal and Torres Strait Islander people suffered physical or sexual abuse in institutions or lived in servitude or poverty as labourers and domestic workers.
- Many people lost their language and cultural identity, as they were expected to adopt European dress, language, religion, lifestyle and cultural values.
- Many were prevented from having any contact with their Aboriginal and Torres Strait Islander family, even by letter.

Aboriginal and Torres Strait Islander people have been denied basic human rights and continue to be disadvantaged in all aspects of life. The need to address and acknowledge the treatment of Aboriginal and Torres Strait Islander people led to the appointment of the Aboriginal and Torres Strait Islander Social Justice Commissioner. The role of the Commissioner is to advocate for the recognition of the rights of Aboriginal and Torres Strait Islander Australians and to promote respect and understanding of these rights among the broader Australian community. A life of opportunity and dignity, free from discrimination and disadvantage, should not be an ideal. It is a basic human right – one that we all share. **Social justice** (AHRC, 2003) also means recognising the distinctive rights that Aboriginal and Torres Strait Islander Australians hold as the original peoples of this land, including:

- the right to a distinct status and culture, which helps maintain and strengthen the identity and spiritual and cultural practices of Indigenous communities
- the right to self-determination, which is a process whereby Indigenous communities take control of their future and decide how they will address the issues facing them
- the right to land, which provides the spiritual and cultural basis of Indigenous communities.

Social justice for Aboriginal and Torres Strait Islander people has focused on both fundamental human rights such as education, health and housing as well as land rights. For example, the 1992

High Court's Mabo decision recognised the common law right of Aboriginal and Torres Strait Islander peoples to land, based on their continuing use and connection to land. The 1997 *Bringing Them Home* report (AHRC, 2010) revealed the extent of government policy and laws that resulted in the systematic removal of Aboriginal and Torres Strait Islander children from their families between 1910 and 1970. Mick Dodson, an Aboriginal rights activist, reminds us that we still have a long way to go to make right our treatment of Aboriginal and Torres Strait Islander people:

> Social justice is what faces you in the morning. It is awakening in a house with adequate water supply, cooking facilities and sanitation. It is the ability to nourish your children and send them to school where their education not only equips them for employment but reinforces their knowledge and understanding of their cultural inheritance. It is the prospect of genuine employment and good health: a life of choices and opportunity, free from discrimination.

Source: Dodson, M. (1993), Australian Human Rights Commission 2015, licensed under Creative Commons Attribution 4.0 International (CC BY 4.0).

CONSIDER THIS

Successive governments have failed to address the inequities between Aboriginal and Torres Strait Islander people and other Australians. Why has this occurred?

Social justice

The statement by the then Social Justice Commissioner, Mick Dodson, brings into focus the glaring gap between the human rights of Aboriginal and Torres Strait Islander people and other Australians. Australia is a wealthy country with a high standard of living. Most Australians would regard food, shelter, education and cultural respect as part of their birthright. Yet many Aboriginal and Torres Strait Islander people are living in developing world conditions, which contribute to poor physical and mental health, poor education and a lack of job opportunities.

Policy of assimilation

In the late nineteenth and early twentieth century, the government adopted a policy of **assimilation** based on the false belief that Aboriginal people were a doomed race that would eventually die out through interracial marriage. The aim of assimilation was to make the so-called 'Aboriginal problem' gradually disappear so that Aboriginal people would lose their identity in the wider community.

The government of the day changed the definition of 'Aboriginality' to identify differences between 'full-bloods' and 'half-castes', allowing the separation of different groups. Those defined as having a certain amount of European blood were prevented from living on the reserves and forced either to live in camps or in areas not designated as being for Aboriginal and Torres Strait Islander people. By the turn of the twentieth century, it was decided to merge the mixed-descent population into non-Aboriginal society. So-called 'half-caste' Aboriginal and Torres Strait Islander children were also sent to missions, special schools and training institutions, where Aboriginal and Torres Strait Islander languages and cultural practices were usually forbidden and the discipline was severe.

Children who 'looked white' were put up for adoption with white families without the consent of their families. Referred to as members of the Stolen Generations, as adults these children have reported that they:

- were forbidden to speak in their own languages
- were told their parents did not want them
- experienced neglect, as well as physical, emotional and sexual abuse

- received little or no education
- were refused contact with their families (Australian Human Rights Commission, 2019. Released under CC BY 4.0 International, link to licence: https://creativecommons.org/licenses/by/4.0/legalcode).

Chief Protectors were appointed and given wide powers to control the lives of Aboriginal and Torres Strait Islander people. These powers included:

- managing and controlling the reserves
- the power to remove people from the reserves
- the power to decide who could (or could not) marry (Australian Human Rights Commission, 2019. Released under CC BY 4.0 International, link to licence: https://creativecommons.org/licenses/by/4.0/legalcode).

Children of the Stolen Generations were forcibly removed from their families and placed in group homes to be trained in domestic service or placed with white families and forced to work. As the AHRC has described, these policies had a devastating effect on the children who were forcibly taken away and on their families.

Changing perspectives

During the 1990s, a number of decisions and reforms took place that helped to change the way Aboriginal and Torres Strait Islander people were viewed by other Australians. These were:

- the establishment of the Council for Aboriginal Reconciliation by law of the federal Parliament
- the findings of the 1991Royal Commission into Aboriginal Deaths in Custody
- the decision of the High Court in *Mabo v Queensland*
- the *Native Title Act*, passed by the federal Parliament in 1993
- the establishment of the National Inquiry into the Separation of Aboriginal and Torres Strait Islander Children from Their Families and the Human Rights and Equal Opportunity Commission's *Bringing Them Home* report
- the High Court's Wik decision
- the introduction of the *Native Title Amendment Act 1998* (Cth)
- the People's Walk for Reconciliation in 2000.

While these reforms have attempted to address historical injustices, Australia still has a long way to go in the process of justice and reconciliation. as evidenced by the Black Lives Matter (BLM) movement in Australia. The BLM movement was created in 2013 by activists Alicia Garza, Patrisse Cullors and Opal Tometi following the murder of Trayvon Martin by George Zimmerman in the United States. In 2020, the death of George Floyd at the hands of Minneapolis police sparked worldwide condemnation and ignited the BLM movement into a global issue.

The BLM movement in Australia is focused on providing evidence to expose and address racism in the criminal justice system and police misconduct and prejudice. The movement has also highlighted the lack of progress in relation to the findings and recommendations of the Royal Commission into Aboriginal Deaths in Custody in 1991. 'Since the Royal Commission into Aboriginal Deaths in Custody in 1991, more than 470 people have died in police custody without a single conviction recorded and Indigenous people remain grossly over-represented in Australia's prison system' (Roth & McCracken Jarrar, 2021).

Aboriginal and Torres Strait Islander social justice issues

The BLM movement has also highlighted what many in the movement regard as 'The Great Australian Silence' in relation to Aboriginal deaths in custody. Darumbal and South Sea Islander journalist Amy McQuire stated: 'When Aboriginal people die in custody there is a national silence' (*The Conversation*, 2021).

Working with Aboriginal and Torres Strait Islander people

Aboriginal and Torres Strait Islander peoples are not a single homogeneous group. They speak different languages, identify with different tribal groups and experience a deep connection to different parts of Australia and the Torres Strait Islands. Like all Australians, individuals have different skin tones and facial features. Sharron 'Mirii' Lindh, proud Gamilaroi Wiradjuri woman, states:

> Most people have the perception that all Aboriginal people are dark skinned, but we come in all beautiful colours, shapes and sizes, just as non-Aboriginal people do. Black is my culture, not my colour. It is not the colour of my skin that matters but what comes from within.

Source: Lindh (2012), p. 6.

Use of the term 'Aboriginal and Torres Strait Islander'

The terms 'Aboriginal', 'Indigenous' and 'Torres Strait Islander' are a legacy of colonisation. 'Aboriginal' refers to Australia's First Nations people (including Darug, Gandangarra, Tharawal, Eora, Kamilaroi, Wiradjuri). 'Torres Strait Islander' refers to the traditional people of these islands. The term 'Indigenous' is commonly used to refer to both Australia's First Nations people and Torres Strait Islander people.

Aboriginal people typically refer to each other by their boundary, and to their mob by their nation name, as shown in **Figure 3.11** (note that not all nations are listed).

Figure 3.11 Some Aboriginal nation names

State	Name
New South Wales	Koori/Goorie/Koorie/Coorie/Murri
Victoria	Koorie
South Australia	Nunga/Nyungar/Nyoongah
Western Australia	Nyungar/Nyoongar
Northern Territory	Yolngu (top end), Anangu (central)
Queensland	Murri
Tasmania	Palawa/Koori

Nation Name	Areas
Bundjalung	Grafton, Yamba, Gold Coast
Dunghutti/Thungutti	Kempsey
Eora	Sydney, La Perouse
Kamilaroi/Gamilaraay/Gomeroi	Goondiwindi, Lighting Ridge, Tamworth
Tharawal/Dharawal	Wollongong, Kiama
Wiradjuri	Gilgandra, Dubbo, Wagga Wagga, Bathurst

When referring to Aboriginal and Torres Strait Islander people in your own community, it is important to clarify the preferred name of that community and of individuals. This not only demonstrates respect, but also helps you to better understand the importance of these titles to the people concerned.

Understanding kinship

Understanding the nature and role that kinship plays in Aboriginal and Torres Strait Islander communities is essential in reaching a deeper understanding of these cultures. Relationships among Aboriginal and Torres Strait Islander people are not only defined by family, but also by kinship – their birthplace or place of origin, which is referred to as their mob (see **Figure 3.12**).

Figure 3.12 Kinship

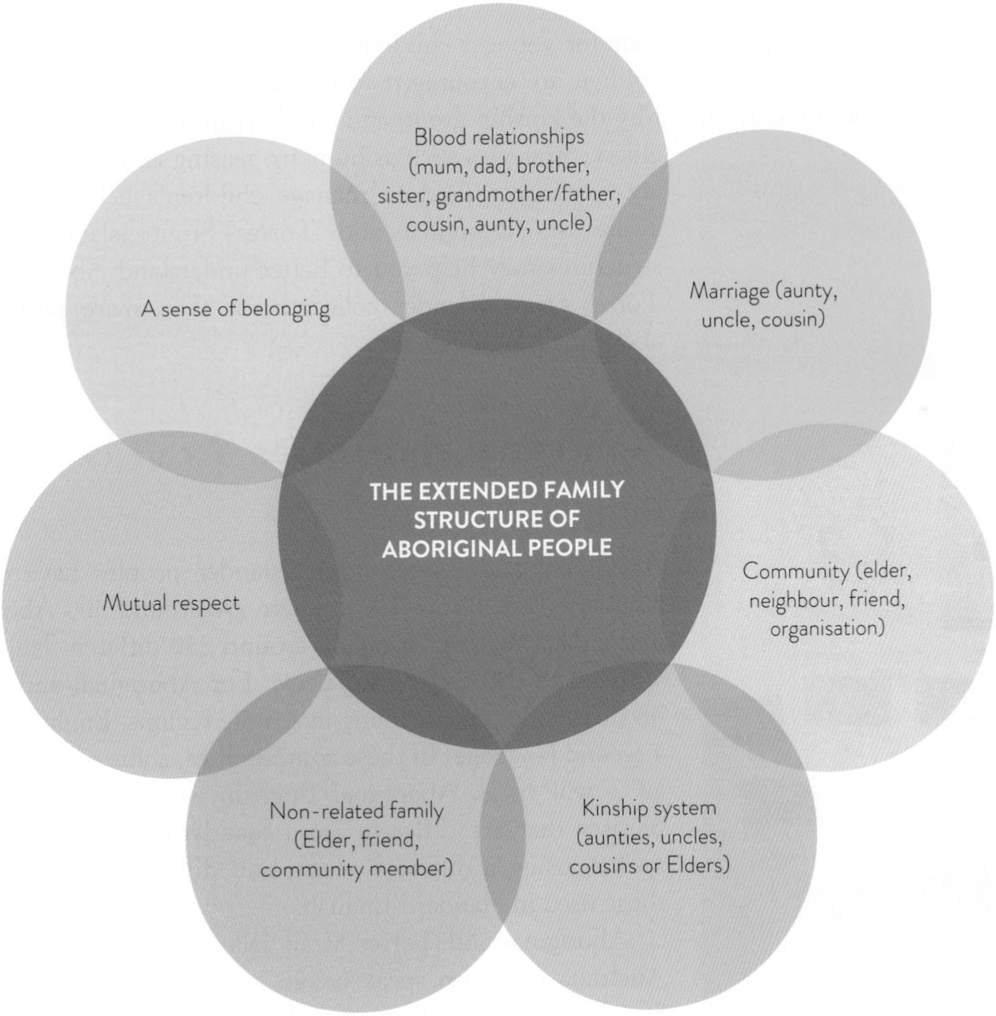

Many Aboriginal people identify as belonging to several nations and kinship groups as a result of parents'/grandparents' place of birth, marriage and identity with locations where these individuals have lived. These kinship groups play an important role in raising children and teaching cultural beliefs and practices. Kinship groups also provide both moral and financial support. The responsibility of caring for and raising children is shared by the extended family and community, who play an important role in the transmission of cultural traditions and values. Many Aboriginal and Torres Strait Islander children live in households that not only include immediate relatives such as parents and siblings, but can extend to aunties, uncles, cousins, grandparents and family established by kinship systems and other members of the community (Australian Institute of Health and Welfare [AIHW], 2012).

In recognition of this extended family network, children may refer to more than one person as 'mother', and will use the terms 'auntie', 'uncle' and 'sis'(ter) to refer to members of the extended kinship group. As part of the kinship group, children are included in most family events and discussions – there may not be the same distinction between adults' and children's 'business' that is typically seen in Anglo-Australian society. Aboriginal and Torres Strait Islander children traditionally engage in a wide range of social activities and spend much of their time in groups. The members of the kinship group share in celebrations, and also share in honouring the deceased. Funerals are often a large kinship affair, and the inclusion of children is seen as natural.

Older children are expected to care for younger children, and younger children are expected to learn from their older peers. Children are encouraged to be independent and to learn from their mistakes. Discipline is shared by the kinship group and children are taught to respect their elders. Strategies such as humour, teasing and acting surprised are commonly used to manage children's behaviour. Being aware of Aboriginal and Torres Strait Islander kinship structures may help you to better understand Aboriginal and Torres Strait Islander colleagues if they share information about their family.

Figure 3.13 An example of an Aboriginal language signs display at a school

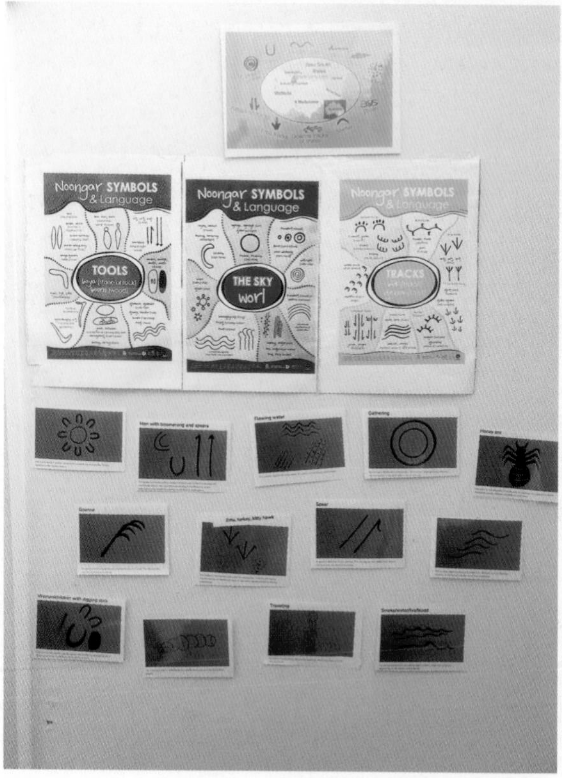

Source: Photo by Tish Okely © Cengage

Aboriginal and Torres Strait Islander languages

Aboriginal and Torres Strait Islander peoples have diverse languages (see **Figure 3.13**). There are around 300 Aboriginal nations in Australia speaking around 250 different languages, with up to 600 different dialects. For Aboriginal and Torres Strait Islander people living in remote regions, English is often a second language. In these communities, some – although not all – will speak Aboriginal English, which uses words and phrases that are different from Standard English. It is also spoken using a different accent and different grammar from those used in Standard English.

Aboriginal and Torres Strait Islander people in Northern Australia may also speak creole – a language that combines Standard English with a native language. The vowel sound for 'h' is usually dropped so that 'house' becomes 'ouse', 'heavy' becomes 'eavy' and so on. This is thought to be because traditional Aboriginal languages do not contain an 'h' sound. It is also common for Aboriginal English questions to end with a question tag, such as 'eh', 'inna' or 'unna' – for example, 'You goin' to the dance, eh?'

Gaining a better understanding of Aboriginal and Torres Strait Islander culture and history, and being aware of the differences in cultures, is a first step towards improving intercultural working relationships. As with any culturally diverse workforce, it is important to be aware of barriers to effective communication that may cause misunderstandings or conflict. For example, for some Indigenous people, looking someone directly in the eye is a sign of disrespect. While many Westerners are uncomfortable with silences during conversations, an Aboriginal or Torres Strait Islander person might leave more time to think or consider someone else's opinion before responding. Their silence is not a sign that they do not understand what is being said.

When meeting with Aboriginal and Torres Strait Islander people, it is considered polite to build a relationship before talking business. For example, ask about family, where the person is from and who their mob is, and share information about yourself.

As in all cultures, Aboriginal and Torres Strait Islander people have developed words and phrases that have a particular meaning within the cultural group, examples of which are shown in **Figure 3.14**.

Figure 3.14 Examples of Aboriginal English

Aboriginal English	Standard Australian English
country	land, home
mob	family, kin, group of people
lingo	Aboriginal language
Sorry Business	ceremony and rituals associated with death
grow [a child] up	raise [a child]
growl	scold, chastise
gammon	pretending, kidding, joking
cheeky	mischievous, aggressive, dangerous
deadly	fantastic, great, awesome
shame	embarrass, humiliate
tidda girl	female friend, best friend, peer
sista/sister girl	female friend, cousin, peer
brotha/brother boy	male friend, cousin, peer
gunja, yaandii	marijuana
dubbay, dub	girlfriend, female partner
gubba	non-Aboriginal person
duri (doori)	sex
charge-up, charge	drink alcohol
goomi	alcoholic
goom	alcohol
gungi, gungy	police
jillawah, jillabah	toilet
durri (durry)	cigarette, smoke

Source: Working With Aboriginal People and Communities: A Practice Resource, © State of New South Wales through Department of Family and Community Services. Licensed under Creative Commons Attribution 4.0 License, https://www.dcj.nsw.gov.au/statements/copyright-and-disclaimer.html

ABORIGINAL AND TORRES STRAIT ISLANDER TERMINOLOGY

CONSIDER THIS

- Traditionally, an Aboriginal Elder is someone who has gained recognition within their community as a custodian of knowledge and lore, and who has permission to disclose cultural knowledge and beliefs.
- 'Our mob' is a term identifying a group of Aboriginal people associated with a particular place or country – it is used to identify who they are and where they are from.
- A traditional owner is an Aboriginal person (or group of Aboriginal people) directly descended from the original Aboriginal inhabitants of a culturally defined area of land or country, who has a cultural association with this country that derives from the traditions, observances, customs, beliefs or history of the original Aboriginal inhabitants of the area.
- The following terms are considered offensive to Aboriginal and Torres Strait Islander people: native, mixed blood, half-caste, quarter-caste, full-blood, part-Aboriginal, 25 per cent, 50 per cent Aboriginal, them, them people, those people, those folk, you people.
- Aboriginal and Torres Strait Islander people may refer to themselves as blackfellas, but it is not appropriate for other people to use this term.

Source: NSW Health (2004), pp. 1–2. Reproduced by permission, NSW Ministry of Health © 2016.

Understanding Aboriginal and Torres Strait Islander protocols

A primary barrier when working with Aboriginal and Torres Strait Islander people is a lack of understanding of Aboriginal and Torres Strait Islander **cultural protocols**. These are ethical principles that guide behaviour in a particular situation. These protocols are designed to protect Aboriginal and Torres Strait Islander cultural and intellectual property rights. Cultural protocols assist in understanding and respecting Aboriginal and Torres Strait Islander culture (see **Figure 3.15**).

Figure 3.15 Displaying images of flags is an effective way of acknowledging cultures

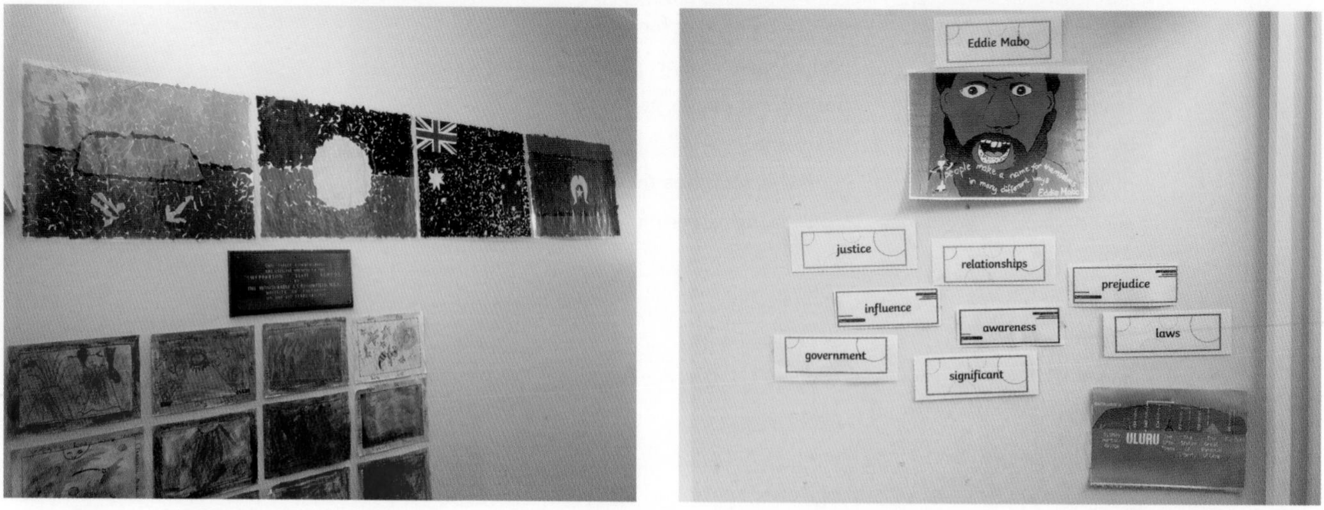

Source: Photos by Tish Okely © Cengage

In a review of nine Aboriginal and Torres Strait Islander and non-Aboriginal and Torres Strait Islander-controlled early childhood services (SNAICC, 2012), all services reported concerns relating to not knowing protocols, being afraid of doing the wrong thing and causing offence when interacting with Aboriginal and Torres Strait Islander families and the Aboriginal and Torres Strait Islander community.

Oxfam Australia (2015) describes a number of key values and principles that should be observed in relation to Aboriginal and Torres Strait Islander cultural protocols. These are outlined in **Figure 3.16**.

Figure 3.16 Aboriginal and Torres Strait Islander cultural protocols

Respect	The rights of Aboriginal and Torres Strait Islander people to own and control their cultural heritage, and their rights and interests in how they are portrayed (in images, text or the like) must at all times be respected and protected.
Aboriginal and Torres Strait Islander control	Aboriginal and Torres Strait Islander people should be consulted and involved in all decisions affecting their cultural heritage, and in particular on the ways in which their history, community, stories and interviews, lives, families and cultural and intellectual property are represented and used.
Interpretation and integrity	Aboriginal and Torres Strait Islander people should be recognised as the primary guardians and interpreters of their cultures. Representation of Aboriginal and Torres Strait Islander cultures should reflect their cultural values and respect their customary laws.
Secrecy and confidentiality	Indigenous people have the right to keep secret their sacred and ritual knowledge in accordance with their customary laws.
Attribution	Aboriginal and Torres Strait Islander people should be given proper credit or appropriate acknowledgement for their achievements, contributions and roles in the development of media stories and/or use of cultural material.
Sharing of benefits	Aboriginal and Torres Strait Islander people have the right to share in the benefits from use of their culture, especially where it is being commercially applied.
Legal recognition and protection	Australian laws and policies should be in place that respect and protect Indigenous rights to cultural and intellectual property.

Source: Oxfam Australia (2015), pp. 3–6.

The following are examples of the protocols:

- As a sign of respect, capital letters should always be used when writing Aboriginal, Torres Strait Islander and Indigenous.
- Welcome to Country – performed by an Elder or designated member of the Aboriginal and Torres Strait Islander community – may include speeches of welcome, traditional dance and smoking ceremonies.
- Traditional custodians of the land should be acknowledged – for example, 'I would like to acknowledge the … people who are the traditional custodians of this land we meet on today. I would also like to pay my respects to all Elders, past and present.'
- Honour the importance of Elders – recognised Elders are highly respected people within Aboriginal and Torres Strait Islander communities. Elders are usually referred to by Aboriginal and Torres Strait Islander people as 'Aunty' and 'Uncle'. Other people should always seek permission before using these terms.
- Aboriginal and Torres Strait Islander people avoid speaking the name of a person who has recently died and showing images of those who have died.
- It is considered disrespectful to make eye contact during conversations with others.
- Verbal communication may include periods of silence, which should not be misinterpreted as a lack of understanding.
- Women's business and men's business relate to gender-specific knowledge and practices (specifically health, wellbeing and religious matters) that cannot be known or observed by the opposite sex. It is a mark of cultural respect not to discuss traditionally female issues (women's business) in the presence of men and vice versa.

Sorry Business is a term used by Indigenous Australians to refer to the death of a family or community member and the mourning process. Sorry Business includes attending funerals and taking part in mourning activities with community. This can take an extended period of time, such as a week or more, and may also involve travelling long distances. It is extremely important in Indigenous cultures that people participate in Sorry Business.

Shame refers to feeling ashamed or embarrassed. Indigenous Australians can often be shy and feel 'shame' if singled out or laughed at. Even when the singling out is for positive reasons it may still leave them feeling shamed because they do not want to appear better than others, particularly other Indigenous persons (Charles Sturt University, n.d., p. 4).

Be aware that community members may prefer to deal with people of their own gender. As a mark of respect, your initial approach should be to a person of the same gender. While Aboriginal and Torres Strait Islander people refer to each other by their boundary, this right may not automatically be extended to non-Aboriginal and Torres Strait Islander people, and permission should be sought to use boundary names when referring to the local Aboriginal or Torres Strait Islander community.

Each year, Aboriginal and Torres Strait Islander people participate in special days/events for celebration or remembrance. Children's education and care services can participate in these events by attending activities, by inviting local Aboriginal and Torres Strait Islander people to share their stories and by helping the children to celebrate events as a service.

CELEBRATIONS AND OBSERVANCES

CONSIDER THIS

- Why an Acknowledgement of Country is important (and advice on how to give one): https://www.abc.net.au/everyday/why-acknowledgement-of-country-is-important-and-how-to-give-one/11881902

Source: Reproduced with permission from NAIDOC

- NAIDOC Week (National Aborigines and Islanders Day Observance Committee) celebrates the history, culture and achievements of Aboriginal and Torres Strait Islander peoples. Research it online at: https://www.naidoc.org.au
- National Aboriginal and Torres Strait Islander Children's Day is held on 4 August each year. It celebrates the strengths and culture of Aboriginal and Torres Strait Islander children. Children's Day is coordinated by the Secretariat of National Aboriginal and Islander Child Care (SNAICC). Research it online at: http://aboriginalchildrensday.com.au
- National Reconciliation Week focuses on promoting respectful relationships between the wider Australian community and Aboriginal and Torres Strait Islander peoples: https://www.reconciliation.org.au/national-reconciliation-week

Summary

Consideration of workplace diversity extends to a wide variety of elements, such as ethnicity, gender, religious beliefs, language, sexuality, lifestyle, health, abilities, disposition and education. An inclusive workplace embraces and respects diversity and accommodates, as far as possible, the diverse needs of employees.

Every person in the workplace deserves to be treated with empathy, dignity and respect regardless of their status in the organisation. In this regard, schools are no different to any other workplace – employees will have different cultural and social values and beliefs; they will have differing skills areas such as communication, teamwork and problem-solving. Employees will have differences in opinions, ideas and ways of working.

- treating each person with politeness, kindness and courtesy
- being fair and reasonable when negotiating with others
- being open to the ideas of others by listening without interruption before commenting
- not engaging in gossip, or bullying, patronising or criticising others
- communicating openly and being aware of your own body language
- meeting your work commitments on a daily basis
- including co-workers in discussion and decision-making where this impacts on their work role
- giving positive feedback when appropriate without being patronising
- being willing to share information about your culture to promote greater understanding of similarities and differences.

Respecting and getting along with other employees means:

ESWs will encounter diversity among colleagues, students and their families. You may find this exciting, challenging or even confronting. Your role as an ESW is to work in ways that demonstrate respect for diversity and a willingness to accommodate individual differences.

Self-check questions

1 What is included in the Universal Declaration of Human Rights?

2 How does the Australian Human Rights Commission define cultural diversity?

3 Connect each term to its correct definition.

Culture	It is not appropriate when applied to national, religious, geographic, linguistic or ethnic groups.
Race	A sense of peoplehood, when people feel close because of sharing a similarity.
Ethnicity	The ability to understand, communicate and interact with people across cultures.
Cultural responsivity	The shared system of learned and shared values, beliefs and rules of conduct that make people behave in a certain way.
Cultural competence	The ability to learn from and relate respectfully to people from your own and other cultures.

4 List two strategies an ESW could use to overcome language barriers when working with families from diverse backgrounds.

5 Define cultural safety in the workplace and its elements.

6 What are Aboriginal and Torres Strait Islander cultural protocols? List two examples.

7 How can schools participate in Aboriginal and Torres Strait Islander peoples' celebrations? List two events or days.

Discussion questions

1 You notice that Ismael has attended school the last three days with the same torn pants and T-shirt in winter and there is a distinct odour coming from his clothes as he passes you. During fruit break, you notice that he does not go to get his lunchbox, and at lunch you see his lunchbox contains a mouldy sandwich.

   a Where would Ismael fall within Maslow's hierarchy of needs? What action could you take to ensure his immediate needs are met and what follow-up might you take?

2 There is a buzz in the classroom today as Mohammad's father is coming to share his profession with the children. Akeel arrives and you greet him at the door by extending your hand for him to shake. Instead, he places his hands in prayer position and bows. You sheepishly withdraw your hand as you feel embarrassed to have not prepared yourself for the appropriate cultural greeting.

   a What could you do next time to better prepare yourself for greeting another person from a culturally diverse background?

3 The school that you are working at values respect and, as such, students call the staff by their first name. In Chinese culture, a person's name is written as [surname] [first name]. When asking for Tang Deyu, you would use the full name. It would be up to the individual if they were okay that you called them only by their first name.

   a How would you explain such differences to students in your classroom in a respectful manner?

Activities

1 For this activity, refer to **Figure 3.1** on page 46 and identify where you sit within the pyramid of Maslow's hierarchy of needs. What do you need to do to move up to the next level?

2 In relation to the principles of cultural safety in **Figure 3.7**, partnerships is the third listed. What partnerships does your school have with culturally diverse communities in your locality?

3 For this activity, refer to the values, attitudes and beliefs scenario on page 64. Identify a cultural bias that you have. Note down how this may impact on a relationship with another person. Identify two ways you can work at neutralising that bias.

Chapter 4

WORKPLACE HEALTH AND SAFETY

LEARNING OBJECTIVES

When you have completed this chapter, you should be able to demonstrate that, in relation to working in a school environment, you can:

4.1 understand and apply state/territory WHS legislation and how it impacts on workplace regulations, codes of practice and industry standards

4.2 understand and apply workplace policies and procedures for WHS

4.3 understand hazard identification, risk management and safety signs and their meanings

4.4 identify and manage infection and disease risks to yourself, other staff and students in the school

4.5 contribute to safe work practices in the workplace through correct office ergonomics, manual handling procedures, equipment use and operation of electrical devices

4.6 understand and apply workplace emergency procedures

4.7 identify and respond appropriately to sources of stress, bullying, violence or abuse in the workplace.

GO FURTHER

Go Further icons link to extra content for this chapter. Ask your instructor for the **Go Further** resource and deepen your understanding of the topic.

Online resources icons refer to useful weblinks. Ask your instructor for these **Online Resources.**

Introduction

This chapter provides an overview of **work health and safety (WHS) legislation** and identifies the roles and responsibilities of employers and employees in relation to their health, safety and wellbeing. The chapter also explores the roles and responsibilities of all employees working in a school in relation to the health, safety and wellbeing of students.

Health and safety in a school environment must address the health, safety and wellbeing of students, employees and visitors to the school. Working with children and young people can be physically and emotionally demanding. The physical demands of the ESW's role can be quite diverse – for example, lifting and carrying equipment, cleaning spilled body fluids, working with chemicals, using photocopiers, working at tables that are not at adult height, assisting with the personal care of students with severe disabilities and working with students with behaviour issues. All of these tasks require compliance with WHS policies and procedures.

WHS in schools also has a flow-on effect in relation to the health and safety of students. While student health and safety is addressed in Chapter 5, the two areas are interdependent – that is, when employees engage in safe work practices it creates a safe environment for both themselves and students.

4.1 WHS legislation

Work health and safety is everyone's responsibility. The primary aim of WHS is to ensure that risks are minimised so that everyone who enters the workplace is safe. In a school setting, this includes students, employees, parents and visitors. The goal of every workplace is to minimise workplace injuries by complying with WHS legislation. **Figure 4.1** describes what you are required to know as an employee about WHS.

Figure 4.1 Understanding WHS

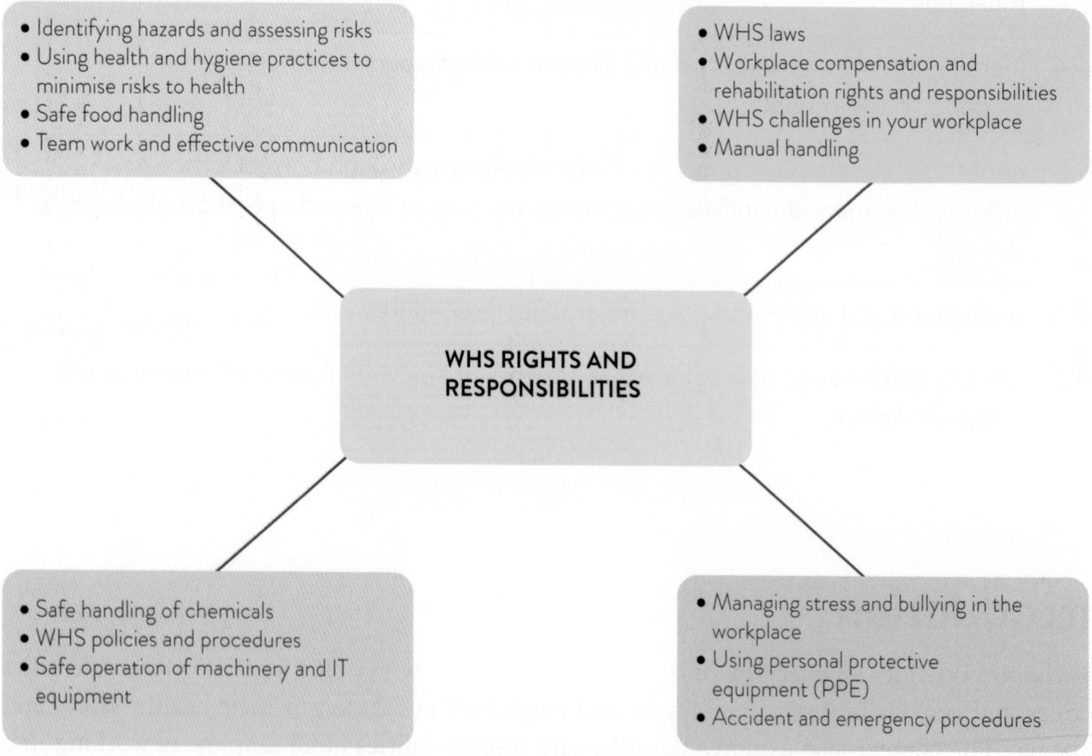

With the support of the states and territories, the Australian Government has established the federal statutory agency Safe Work Australia. The primary purposes of Safe Work Australia are to harmonise WHS laws throughout Australia; develop national work health, safety and workers' compensation policy; and promote awareness of WHS issues. As a result, it has developed:

- the *Model Work Health and Safety (WHS) Act 2011* (Model WHS Act)
- the Model Work Health and Safety (WHS) Regulations 2019 (Model WHS Regulations)
- Model Codes of Practice
- a National Compliance and Enforcement Policy.

At the time of writing, all states and territories except for Victoria and Western Australia had adopted the legislation (as shown in **Figure 4.2**).

Figure 4.2 Principal WHS legislation for Commonwealth and states and territories

Jurisdiction	Principal legislation	WHS regulatory authority
Commonwealth	*Work Health and Safety (WHS) Act 2011* Work Health and Safety (WHS) Regulations 2019 Model Codes of Practice National Compliance and Enforcement Policy	Safe Work Australia: **http://www.safeworkaustralia.gov.au**
Australian Capital Territory	*Work Health and Safety Act 2011* Work Health and Safety Regulation 2011	WorkSafe ACT: **http://www.worksafe.act.gov.au**
New South Wales	*Work Health and Safety Act 2011* Work Health and Safety Regulation 2019	SafeWork NSW: **https://www.safework.nsw.gov.au**
Queensland	*Work Health and Safety (National Uniform Legislation) Act 2011* Work Health and Safety (National Uniform Legislation) Regulations	Workplace Health and Safety Queensland: **http://www.deir.qld.gov.au/workplace**
Northern Territory	*Work Health and Safety Act 2011* Work Health and Safety Regulation 2011	NT WorkSafe: **http://www.worksafe.nt.gov.au**
South Australia	*Work Health and Safety Act 2012* Work Health and Safety Regulations 2012	SafeWork SA: **http://www.safework.sa.gov.au**
Tasmania	*Work Health and Safety Act 2012* Work Health and Safety Regulations 2012	WorkSafe Tasmania: **https://www.worksafe.tas.gov.au**
Victoria	Currently has not adopted Commonwealth legislation *Occupational Health and Safety Act 2004* Occupational Health and Safety Regulations 2007	WorkSafe Victoria: **http://www.worksafe.vic.gov.au**
Western Australia	Currently has not adopted Commonwealth legislation *Occupational Safety and Health Act 1984* Occupational Safety and Health Regulations 1996	WorkSafe WA: **http://www.commerce.wa.gov.au/WorkSafe**

Model Work Health and Safety Act and Regulations

The aims of the Model WHS Act are to:

- protect the health and safety of workers and other people by eliminating or minimising risks arising from work or workplaces
- ensure fair and effective representation, consultation and cooperation to address and resolve health and safety issues in the workplace
- encourage unions and employer organisations to take a constructive role in improving WHS practices
- assist businesses and workers to achieve a healthier and safer working environment
- promote information, education and training on WHS
- provide effective compliance and enforcement measures
- deliver continuous improvement and progressively higher standards of WHS (Safe Work Australia, 2019, © Commonwealth of Australia 2018 CC-BY-3.0 licence).

The Model WHS Regulations provide a 'how to' for the implementation of the Act, and provide specific details of responsibilities and requirements to ensure compliance with the Act.

A key principle of the Model WHS Act is that all people are given the highest level of health and safety protection from hazards arising from work, so far as is *reasonably practicable*.

WHAT DOES REASONABLY PRACTICABLE MEAN?

CONSIDER THIS

To determine what is reasonably practicable, it is necessary to take into account:

- the probability that a person will be exposed to harm as a result of a workplace hazard or risk
- the potential for serious injury or harm
- how much knowledge the person has about the hazard, the risk or strategies, which they could use to remove/ minimise that risk
- the ways available to remove or minimise the hazard/risk
- how much it would cost to remove or minimise the hazard/risk.

Source: Safe Work Australia (2019),

Safe Work Australia

Approved Safe Work Australia Model Codes of Practice that may be applied in school settings include:

- Work health and safety consultation cooperation and coordination
- Managing the risk of falls at workplaces
- Managing the work environment and facilities
- First aid in the workplace
- Labelling of workplace hazardous chemicals
- Preparation of safety data sheets for hazardous chemicals
- Managing risks of hazardous chemicals in the workplace
- How to manage work health and safety risks.

State and territory WHS legislation

While most states and territories have adopted the Commonwealth legislation described above, it is the states and territories that are responsible for administering and enforcing WHS legislation, regulating WHS practices, and administering the systems of workers' compensation and rehabilitation. They also develop resources and provide training to assist anyone conducting a business and their employees to manage WHS.

THE FUNCTIONS OF WHS REGULATORY AUTHORITIES

CONSIDER THIS

- Monitoring and enforcing compliance with the Model WHS Act and Model WHS Regulations
- Providing advice and information on WHS to duty holders and the community
- Fostering a cooperative, consultative relationship between duty holders and the people to whom they owe WHS duties, and their representatives
- Promoting and supporting education and training on matters relating to WHS
- Engaging in, promoting and coordinating the sharing of information to achieve the object of the Model WHS Act, including the sharing of information with other WHS regulators
- Conducting and defending legal proceedings under the Model WHS Act
- Collecting, analysing and publishing statistics relating to WHS
- Promoting public awareness and discussion of WHS matters in the community

Source: Safe Work Australia (2019),

If the regulatory authority believes there has been a contravention of the Model WHS Act in a workplace, it has the power to investigate that workplace and obtain written evidence. Regulatory authorities also have the power to monitor a workplace to ensure WHS compliance.

WHS responsibilities of the employer

WHS legislation is designed to reduce the incidence of workplace injuries and disease by prescribing the general requirements for workplace safety that must be met to manage risks in the workplace. WHS legislation also defines the legal responsibilities of all persons conducting a business – workers, the self-employed, manufacturers and suppliers – and people in control of workplaces used by non-employees.

Every **person conducting a business or undertaking (PCBU)** has a duty to ensure – as far as is reasonably practicable – the health, safety and welfare of all employees and others who come into the workplace. The employer must ensure that all 'reasonably practicable' measures and actions have been taken to control risks against possible injuries in the workplace, and to avoid anyone causing harm to themselves or to others in the workplace.

The PCBU (employer), or a delegated employee, has a duty to ensure:

- the provision and maintenance of a working environment that is safe and without risks to health, including safe access to and exit from the workplace
- the provision and maintenance of plant, structure and systems of work that are safe and do not pose health risks
- the safe use, handling, storage and transport of plant, structure and substances
- the provision of adequate facilities for the welfare of workers at work
- the provision of information, instruction, training or supervision to workers needed for them to work without risks to their health and safety and that of others around them
- the monitoring of the health of workers and the conditions of the workplace to prevent injury or illness arising out of the conduct of the business or undertaking
- the maintenance of any accommodation owned or under their management and control to ensure the health and safety of workers occupying the premises (Safe Work Australia (2019), © Commonwealth of Australia. 2018 CC-BY-3.0 licence.).

Employers are also required to provide adequate first aid equipment and facilities, and to ensure that an adequate number of workers have a current senior first aid certificate issued by an approved registered training organisation (see **Figure 4.3**).

Figure 4.3 The school has a designated area for first aid equipment

Source: Photo by Tish Okely © Cengage

Employers must ensure consultation with all workers who are directly affected by health and safety in the workplace. Consultation must also take place when:

- employers are changing systems of work that may impact on WHS, such as rosters or work practices
- employers are considering changes, additions or modifications to employee facilities
- employers are introducing new equipment or chemicals into a workplace
- decisions about health and safety issues are being made, including changes to WHS policies and procedures

- strategies are being developed to eliminate or modify risks when hazards in workplace are identified
- any health and safety issues that have arisen in the workplace are being addressed
- the WHS training needs of workers are being reassessed
- new strategies to monitor employee health and safety are being implemented.

Due diligence

The employer must exercise **due diligence** by taking reasonable steps to ensure that the workplace supervisor (school principal) is able to:

- acquire and update their knowledge of WHS issues so their knowledge stays current
- identify the hazards and risks associated with the school, including bullying or harassment in the workplace.

DUE DILIGENCE

SCENARIO

DUE DILIGENCE 1

Erin and **Tom** (WHS representatives [WHSRs]) are attending a one-day workshop conducted by their state WHS authority. The aim of the workshop is to provide WHSRs with up-to-date information on their WHS obligations and responsibilities. Driving home that evening, Erin and Tom review the day. Even though the school has in place quite comprehensive WHS policies and procedures, they both agree that the workshop was extremely worthwhile and have both come away with a greater understanding of their legal obligations and maintaining rigorous WHS procedures.

DUE DILIGENCE 2

As a follow-up to the workshop, Erin and Tom are required to provide feedback at the staff meeting. They decide to put together a short PowerPoint presentation of the key points. To make it more interesting and relevant, they have included some WHS scenarios that require staff to work together in small groups to problem-solve solutions. Through open discussion, it is revealed that many of the staff pay little or no attention to WHS and are not aware of their basic responsibilities. The workshop demonstrates that regular training in WHS is essential for all employees.

WHAT DOES THIS TELL US?

Providing access to training contributes to meeting due diligence requirements. While all employees have a legal obligation to be aware of their WHS responsibilities, it can never be assumed that all employees comply.

WHS training

The employer is responsible for providing information about WHS policies and practices at the time of employee induction. This information should include the WHS obligations and responsibilities of both the employer and the worker. It may include a wide range of WHS information related to the particular school and the person's work role, such as procedures for reporting hazards, identification of first aid officers, correct use of personal protective equipment (PPE), a copy of all WHS policies and procedures, and information on handwashing and manual handling. It may also include information about emergency evacuation procedures, emergency exits, the location of fire extinguishers, fire blankets, first aid kits and disposable gloves, the use and storage of hazardous chemicals, and security.

Ongoing WHS training may include access to WHS email alerts from the state/territory regulatory authority, and to specific in-house training on key areas such as emergency evacuation, use of fire extinguishers, correct hand-washing procedures, use and storage of chemicals, and responding to student violence.

Employees may also attend training on a broad range of skills related to WHS, such as bullying and harassment in the workplace, manual handling, first aid or responding to intruders.

> **SCENARIO**
>
> ### WHS TRAINING WORKSHOP
>
> As part of their annual training obligations, ESWs **Michael** and **Zahra** have recently attended a one-day workshop conducted by the state WHS authority. The aim of the workshop was to provide employees with up-to-date information on their WHS obligations and responsibilities. Michael and Zahra have come away with a greater understanding of their legal obligations, and the importance of knowing and understanding the range of WHS policies and procedures in place at the school.
>
> ▶ DISCUSSION
>
> How does regular WHS training support workplace safety?

WHS responsibilities of the worker

All workers must take reasonable care to ensure their own health and safety, and the health and safety of others in the workplace. Workers are obligated to:

- cooperate with their employer's attempts to meet their WHS responsibilities
- comply with all lawful instructions in relation to WHS
- follow all WHS policies and procedures
- report all workplace hazards to the nominated supervisor
- undertake WHS training as directed.

Safe work procedures are defined by WorkSafe ACT (2010, p. 1) as directions on how work is to be carried out safely. They identify hazards and clarify what must be done to eliminate or minimise risks – for example, correct lifting procedures to minimise the risk of back, neck and leg injury.

WorkSafe ACT (2023) suggests that the process for developing a written safe work procedure for a hazardous task may include the following steps:

1. Determine the overall task that requires a safe work procedure.
2. Break down the task into its basic steps.
3. Identify the hazards associated with each step, and ways to eliminate or minimise the risks to workers from these hazards.
4. Write the safe work procedure – the list of actions that workers must do when performing the task.

Examples in a school environment where safe work procedures are documented may include:

- hazardous tasks, such as exposure and cleaning up of body fluids, chemicals or broken glass
- tasks that must be carried out following a specific sequence, such as setting up and packing away science experiments, assisting a student with toileting or meals, decanting bulk chemicals into smaller containers for daily use
- tasks that are performed on a daily basis, such as setting up a classroom for specific learning activities
- management of classroom pets and cleaning their enclosures of faecal matter.

WHS notifiable incidents

Regardless of how well WHS policies and procedures are implemented, there is a potential for accidents or near-misses to occur in any workplace.

The Model WHS Act defines a **notifiable incident** – that is, something that must be reported to the relevant state/territory regulatory authority – as an incident involving the death of a person, the 'serious injury or illness' of a person or a 'dangerous incident' (or near miss) (as defined in Part 3 of the Act).

A serious injury or illness under the Act (section 36) includes an injury that requires any immediate treatment in a hospital, or immediate treatment for:

- amputation of any part of the body
- a serious head, spinal or eye injury
- a serious burn
- an injury in which skin is separated from underlying tissue
- the loss of a bodily function
- serious lacerations
- exposure to a dangerous substance (within 48 hours of exposure)
- any infection to which the carrying out of work is a 'significant contributing factor', which in children's education and care services may include infections arising from contact with micro-organisms, providing treatment or care to a person or contact with human blood or body substances.

A **dangerous incident** (or **'near-miss'**) is defined under the Model WHS Act (section 37) as any incident in relation to a workplace that exposes a worker or any other person to a serious risk to health or safety (either immediately or soon after), such as exposure to asbestos or chemicals, the collapse of a structure, an electric shock, an explosion or a fire.

A record of the notification and details of the incident must be kept by the employer for at least five years. The report should include the following information:

- a detailed description of what happened and when, how and where (date, time and place)
- the injured person's name, address, contact number, age, gender, occupation and relationship to the organisation
- a description of the injury sustained, the immediate treatment given and where the injured person was taken for treatment
- contact details of the person conducting the business and the person notifying the state/territory authority.

The Work Safe authority for each state and territory has definitions of notifiable incidents and the requirements for reporting the workplace details on action taken to ensure prevention of a recurrence. All schools also will have policies and procedures for reporting and documenting incidents, accidents and near-misses. **Figure 4.4** provides an example of the details that may be recorded in relation to an incident/accident or near-miss in the workplace.

NOTIFIABLE INCIDENT

SCENARIO

Dali and **Adrian**, both ESWs, have acted as school first aid officers for the last three years. To date they have only had to deal with minor injuries; however, today they were faced with a major incident when four students and two teachers were injured when a 5-metre-high platform on which they were standing collapsed. Injuries included fractures, broken bones, a punctured lung and suspected head injuries. While waiting for ambulances to arrive, Dali and Adrian took responsibility for applying first aid and directing other staff to assist.

WHAT DOES THIS TELL US?

A serious incident may occur at any time, requiring a prompt and calm response from staff. In a situation where there are multiple casualties, it is important to delegate control to trained first aid staff.

Figure 4.4 Incident report form template

Hazard/incident report form

Use this form in your workplace to report health and safety hazards and incidents. To notify SafeWork NSW of an incident, call 13 10 50.

Hazard/Incident

Brief description of hazard/incident: (Describe the task, equipment, tools and people involved. Use sketches, if necessary. Include any action taken to ensure the safety of those who may be affected.)

____

____

____

Where is the hazard located in the workplace?

____

____

When was the hazard identified? Date: ___/___/___ Time: ___am/pm

Recommended action to fix hazard/incident: (List any suggestions you may have for reducing or eliminating the problem – for example re-design mechanical devices, update procedures, improve training, maintenance work)

____

____

____

____

____

Date submitted to manager: Date: ___/___/___ Time: ___ am/pm

Action taken

Has the hazard/incident been acknowledged by management? Yes/ No
Describe what has been done to resolve the hazard/incident:

____

____

____

Do you consider the hazard/incident fixed? Yes/ No

Name: ______________ Position: ______________

Signature: ______________

Date: ___/___/___

Source: © State of New South Wales (SafeWork NSW). For current information go to safework.nsw.gov.au. Licensed under the Creative Commons Attribution 4.0 licence, https://creativecommons.org/licenses/by/4.0/

Workers' compensation and rehabilitation

Workers' compensation laws are designed to assist in managing workplace injuries. The legislation covers reporting of injuries, appropriate ways to manage the injuries, income support for injured workers and planning workers' return to work. While Safe Work Australia is working towards national harmonisation of workers' compensation laws, currently the Commonwealth Government, as well as each state and territory, has its own workers' compensation legislation. Workers' compensation is administered by each state and territory's WHS authority.

Workers' compensation typically covers work-related injuries and diseases that occur:

- while undertaking duties as directed in the workplace
- as a result of an incident arising from employment
- on a journey to or from work.

Employers are required to take out workers' compensation insurance with an approved insurer. The WHS authority for each state and territory provides an easily accessible website where employees and employers can access detailed information relating to workers' compensation, reporting requirements, managing injured workers and standardised report forms.

4.2 WHS systems, policies and procedures

The primary goal of WHS policies in the workplace is to minimise risks to health and safety as far as is reasonably practicable. WHS policies will typically be accompanied by written procedures with clear, step-by-step instructions for WHS-related tasks.

Every workplace should have systems in place to manage and monitor the health, safety and welfare of workers. Individual workplaces will have specific WHS factors that reflect the physical environment, the nature of the work being carried out, and the skills and experience of those conducting the work or engaging in services provided by workers. The primary goal of WHS systems in workplaces is to minimise the risks to health and safety as far as is reasonably practicable. WHS systems should reflect the requirements of WHS legislation and codes of practice. They may also take into account Australian Standards or published safety guidelines.

WHS workplace systems will vary from one workplace to another, but may include:

- recruitment and selection procedures that ensure all new employees have the knowledge and skills to undertake the job role
- a WHS induction program to ensure that all workers are properly oriented to the workplace
- job descriptions that provide workers with a clear allocation of roles and responsibilities
- ongoing training to maintain up-to-date workplace knowledge and competencies
- clearly defined lines of authority, supervision and support to ensure workers are adequately supervised, have their workplace skills monitored and are provided with clear instructions
- management of physical facilities and equipment to ensure they are maintained in a safe manner and provide workers with the resources, meal breaks and rest periods needed for them to do the job in a safe manner
- provision of first aid kits that reflect the needs of the workplace and the task being undertaken, as well as access to qualified first aid officers

- an emergency evacuation plan, with exits and assembly points clearly indicated, and regular scheduled emergency evacuation practice conducted for all workers
- a security system, where necessary, to protect workers and visitors from intruders
- clear procedures to identify hazards and assess risks
- clear procedures to manage and use chemicals in the workplace
- clear procedures for lifting and manual handling
- provision of PPE – this must also include instruction and/or training on use.

A WHS workplace system ensures that WHS is managed methodically so all members of the workplace understand how to identify and manage hazards in the workplace. It also makes sure that everyone in a workplace understands how they can contribute to making that workplace safe and healthy. A properly managed WHS workplace system can also be used by the employer to demonstrate workplace compliance with WHS legislation.

Accurate WHS records must be maintained at all times and should include:

- copies of all WHS policies and procedures
- an incident, illness and near-miss register (containing records of incidents, near-misses and workplace-related illnesses)
- maintenance records, such as checking and tagging, fire extinguisher maintenance and replenishment of first-aid supplies
- details of training and employee resources to support WHS posters that may be displayed and written procedures and instructions given to employees in relation to WHS procedures and directions
- records of workers' compensation and any rehabilitation programs
- copies of current workers' compensation premiums
- a record of employee immunisations (if required as part of conditions of employment)
- evidence of WHS consultation with workers
- evidence of WHS continuous improvement actions
- safety audit checklists and inspections carried out internally or by external sources
- processes in relation to hazard identification, risk assessment, controlling risks and reviewing controls.

The intent of WHS policies is to identify workplace practices where there are potential hazards and to provide clear directions or procedures to minimise risks. Written WHS procedures aim to ensure consistency in workplace practices. The purpose of each WHS policy can be incorporated into a rationale and/or goals – for example, using a team lift when moving heavy or bulky equipment minimises the risk of back and neck injury.

Written policies and procedures protect both workers and employers. Workers are protected because clearly written policies and procedures direct work practices and take away any element of uncertainty or guesswork when performing a potentially hazardous task. Employers are protected because they can demonstrate due diligence by taking reasonable steps to provide workers with lawful directions in relation to WHS procedures.

To be effective, WHS policies and procedures are dependent on compliance by all workers, and for this reason employers must also ensure adequate training and supervision of workers as they carry out WHS tasks. In schools, the number and range of WHS policies and procedures will vary depending on the type of school, the nature of the tasks being undertaken and the physical environment. For example, staff working with physically disabled students in a special

GO FURTHER

Learn more about WHS policies from the NSW Department of Education in your Go Further resource, available through your instructor.

school would need to be trained in the use of mechanical aids, correct lifting techniques and PPE, while staff working in a science lab or with woodwork or metalwork would need to be trained in the use of machinery operation and PPE.

While WHS policies are specifically written to ensure the health, safety and wellbeing of workers in schools, many WHS policies also serve to protect the health and safety of students. However, it is important to distinguish between policies aimed primarily at WHS and those aimed at ensuring the health and safety of students. In some instances, one policy may cover both WHS and students' health and safety. For example, emergency evacuation and lockdown, first aid, sun protection and code of conduct for staff members. **Figure 4.5** lists WHS policies and student health and welfare policies that are commonly found in most schools.

Figure 4.5 WHS policies

WHS policies	Student health and welfare policies
> Anti-bullying, anti-racism, anti-discrimination	> Administration of prescribed medication, catheters and injections to students
> Child protection	> Anaphylaxis
> Code of conduct	> Asthma-management plan
> Complaints handling	> Behaviour policy
> Conduct and performance	> Child protection
> Critical/non-critical incident management and reporting	> Drugs in schools
> First aid	> Excursions
> Homophobia in schools	> Family law
> Sexual harassment	> Head lice
> Social inclusion	> Healthy school canteen
> Sun safety	> Home–school liaison support
> Use of alcohol, tobacco and other drugs on school premises	> Homophobia in schools
> WHS	> Hydrotherapy pools – school use
> Workforce diversity	> Management of eating and drinking support (for students with disability)
> Working with Children Check	> Nutrition in schools
> Workplace accidents, injuries and illness	> Playground supervision
	> School accidents, injuries and illness
	> Social inclusion
	> Sports and physical activity safety
	> Student discipline and welfare
	> Student grievance procedures
	> Student immunisation record keeping
	> Student suspension and expulsion
	> Students with disability
	> Sun safety
	> Swimming pool and water park based aquatic activities
	> Violent behaviour
	> Welfare policy

4.3 Identifying hazards and managing risks

A key strategy in the management of WHS is the identification, assessment and management of hazards and associated risks. According to Safe Work Australia's Code of Practice, 'a **hazard** is a situation or thing that has the potential to harm a person' while 'a **risk** is the possibility that harm (death, injury or illness) might occur when exposed to a hazard' (Safe Work Australia, 2011a, p. 4; © Commonwealth of Australia 2018 CC-BY-4.0 licence).

Hazards can be found in any workplace. Their nature will depend largely on the type of work being conducted, the facilities, the processes used to carry out the work and the equipment used as part of that process. Some common hazards that can be encountered in school settings are:

- *biological* – exposure to infectious diseases; exposure to fungus from damp or poorly ventilated areas
- *chemical* – fumes from photocopiers; skin, eye, throat irritation from contact with chemicals or chemical fumes, such as bleach, cleaning products, chemicals used in science labs
- *ergonomic* – manual handling; lifting heavy or bulky items; poorly designed workstations that result in muscle strain; repetitive movements; bending, lifting, sitting on small chairs resulting in back/neck strain
- *physical* – noise pollution where schools are located on busy roads; temperature extremes of heat/cold (not all schools are adequately ventilated or have air-conditioning installed); inadequately maintained electrical equipment; poor light in classrooms, storage areas, stairwells and walkways; lack of trolleys to move heavy equipment, and a lack of training in manual handling, use of special education aids and mechanical lifts; lack of availability of sufficient PPE
- *psychosocial* – bullying, racism, sexual harassment; student violence.

Principles of risk management

The Model Work Health and Safety Regulations set out the requirements for the management of WHS risk in the workplace. Risk management includes four key steps that can be applied to any workplace situation (see **Figure 4.6**).

Figure 4.6 The four steps of risk management

Step	Requirement
1 Identify all hazards in the workplace	Identify all hazards related to the work that is done and the environment in which it is conducted. In schools this also includes potential hazards and risks to students
2 Assess the risk of each hazard	Decide how likely it is to happen (its probability) and how great (the severity) the resulting injuries or ill health are likely to be
3 Control, manage or eliminate the risk	Do something about the hazards – reduce the severity of the hazards and the probability of injury to health
4 Monitor and evaluate	Ensure all hazards, accidents and near misses are recorded as part of a continuous improvement process

Figure 4.7 The risk-management process

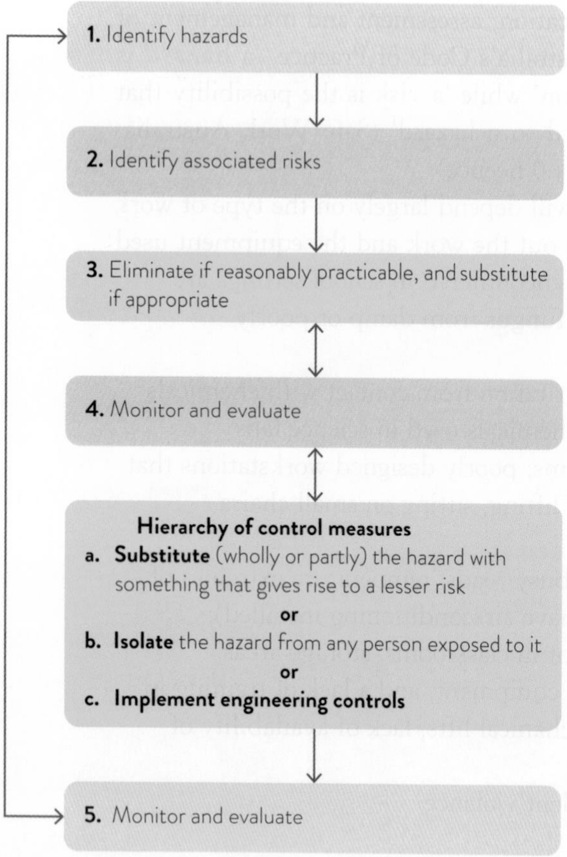
1. Identify hazards
2. Identify associated risks
3. Eliminate if reasonably practicable, and substitute if appropriate
4. Monitor and evaluate
Hierarchy of control measures
a. Substitute (wholly or partly) the hazard with something that gives rise to a lesser risk
or
b. Isolate the hazard from any person exposed to it
or
c. Implement engineering controls
5. Monitor and evaluate

Figure 4.8 The SAFE risk-management guide

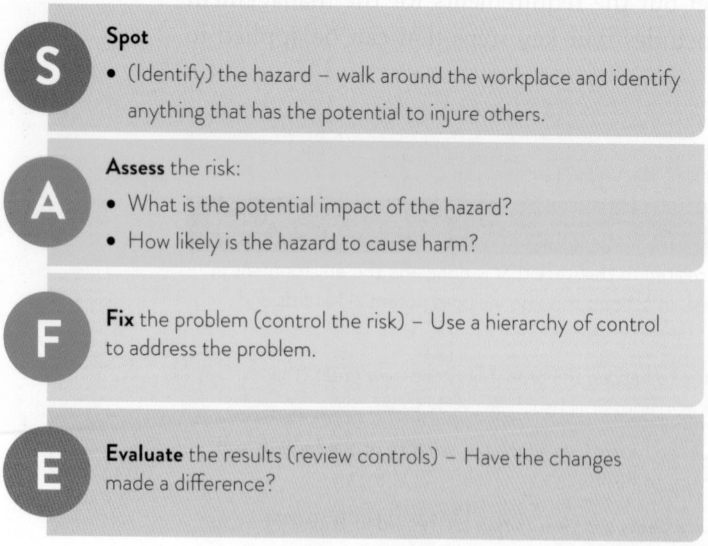
S
Spot
• (Identify) the hazard – walk around the workplace and identify anything that has the potential to injure others.
A
Assess the risk:
• What is the potential impact of the hazard?
• How likely is the hazard to cause harm?
F
Fix the problem (control the risk) – Use a hierarchy of control to address the problem.
E
Evaluate the results (review controls) – Have the changes made a difference?

Source: Adapted from WorkSafe ACT (2012).

Figure 4.7 shows risk management as a continuous cycle. Hazards should be prioritised according to the level of risk they involve, and those with the highest degree of risk should be addressed first.

WorkSafe ACT suggests a very simple and effective strategy to manage hazards and associated risks in the workplace by using the SAFE Risk-Management Model. This method, shown in **Figure 4.8**, is easy to remember and easy to implement.

Identify hazards and risks

Some hazards, such as a cracked and uneven footpath or a frayed electrical cord, are easy to spot. Others require much closer examination of:

- the processes being used to undertake the task
- the skills and knowledge required to undertake the task
- the equipment/resources/tools being used to perform a task
- the physical environment in which the task is being performed.

Using a risk-assessment matrix allows workers to systematically identify hazards, assess risks and work towards a solution. Each part of the process can then be documented and retained as evidence of compliance with WHS legislation. **Figure 4.9** is an example of a risk-assessment matrix.

There are two key considerations when assessing risks, as presented in **Figure 4.10**.

Control or manage the risk

The primary goal in any workplace is to identify and eliminate as many hazards as possible; however, this is not always practicable. Where hazards can't be eliminated, they must be minimised or controlled. Risk control can be achieved by using a technique known as the hierarchy of control. This approach assigns a

Figure 4.9 Risk-rating matrix

Likelihood of harm	Insignificant	Minor	Moderate	Major	Catastrophic
	Consequences				
Almost Certain	Moderate	High	High	Catastrophic	Catastrophic
Likely	Moderate	Moderate	High	Catastrophic	Catastrophic
Possible	Low	Moderate	Moderate	High	High
Unlikely	Low	Moderate	Moderate	Moderate	High
Rare	Low	Low	Low	Moderate	Moderate

Figure 4.10 Key considerations when assessing risks

What is the consequence of the risk?

- *Insignificant*. There are no injuries.
- *Minor*. The worker may require first aid.
- *Moderate*. The worker may require medical attention and several days off work.
- *Major*. The worker may suffer long-term illness, serious injury, permanent disability or ill-health.
- *Catastrophic*. The risk can cause death.

What is the likelihood of harm?

- *Almost certain*. Harm is expected to occur in most circumstances.
- *Likely*. Could easily happen.
- *Possible*. Harm might occur occasionally.
- *Unlikely*. Harm could happen at some time.
- *Rare*. Harm may happen only in exceptional circumstances.

ranking to the ways of controlling a risk, from the most effective and reliable measures down to the least effective and reliable, as shown in **Figures 4.11** and **4.12**.

Control measures must be practicable and cost-effective. They must also be easy to implement, otherwise they are unlikely to be used by workers. For example, two simple control measures in schools that can be used to minimise infection being passed from students to ESWs are using disposable gloves and washing hands frequently. For this to be practicable, ESWs must have easy access to disposable gloves, both indoors and outdoors.

The final stage in the management process is to evaluate and monitor WHS improvements. This allows the organisation to measure the effectiveness of WHS policies and procedures, and identify any areas where better risk management is needed. For example, review all accidental injuries and near-misses in the workplace for the previous year by considering the following:

- Has the number of accidents/near misses decreased or increased?
- What was the nature of the accidents/near-misses?
- What preventative measures have been put in place?
- Is there evidence of patterns of behaviour that contributed to accidents/near-misses?
- Where have the accidents/near-misses occurred? Who was involved?
- What WHS training has been undertaken by employees?
- Have any WHS policies/procedures been reviewed/updated?

Figure 4.11 The hierarchy of control

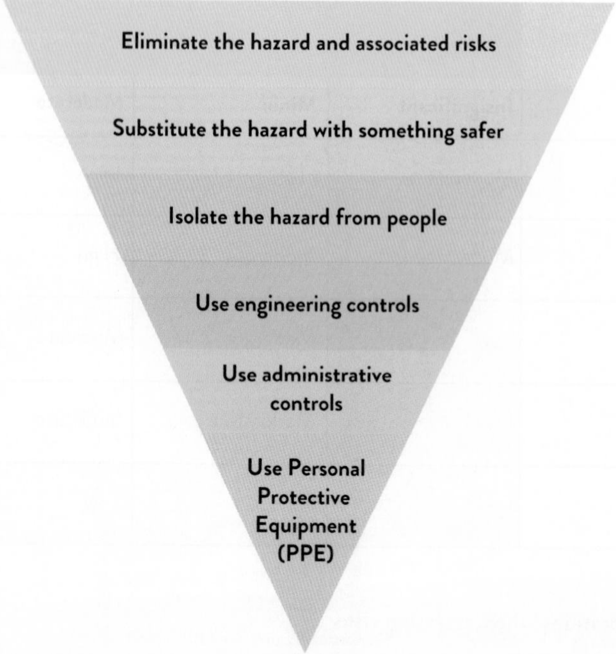
Eliminate the hazard and associated risks
Substitute the hazard with something safer
Isolate the hazard from people
Use engineering controls
Use administrative controls
Use Personal Protective Equipment (PPE)

Figure 4.12 Examples of hierarchy of control

Hierarchy	Hazard	Control measures
Eliminate the hazard associated with the risk	The rug in the staffroom is beginning to curl up and is a trip hazard	Level 1 control: Eliminate by removing the rug
Substitute the hazard with something safer	The Zip hot water tank in the staffroom is constantly dripping creating a risk of splash burns	Level 2 control: Replace with an electric kettle until the system is repaired or replaced
Isolate the hazard from people	The path at the side of the administration building is cracked and uneven	Level 3 control: Place a barrier around the path with a 'danger' trip hazard sign
Use engineering controls	Power boards in the office are overloaded and do not have individual on/off switches	Level 4 control: Replace with power boards with individual switches and install additional power points
Use administrative controls	Administrative controls don't control the hazard at the source. They rely on human behaviour and tend to be least effective in minimising risks Example: Address risk of back injury from daily bending and lifting	Level 4 control: Train all workers in correct manual handling techniques
Use PPE	Address risk of blood contamination when applying first aid to student who has fallen and has a bloody knee	Train all first aid officers to wear PPE such as disposable gloves

Reviewing and monitoring WHS may also include observation of employees as they undertake WHS tasks to ensure procedures are being followed correctly and to identify any gaps in employees' skills and knowledge.

Safety signs

Safety signs are an effective control measure and are used to warn of hazards, identify desired behaviour and provide emergency information. Australian Standards set out the requirements for the design and use of safety signs in the workplace. These signs may include a combination of pictures, symbols and text to communicate:

- information on hazards
- the need to use PPE (where other control strategies are inadequate or impractical)
- the location of safety equipment/emergency facilities (such as a first aid kit, fire blanket, fire extinguisher)
- guidance and instruction in an emergency.

Figure 4.13 Safety sign commonly found in schools

Source: Shutterstock.com/Andrey_Popov

Safety signs draw attention to hazards or potential hazards in the environment, and are also used to indicate the location of safety equipment. In Australia, all safety signs are colour-coded and divided into categories, as the sample shows in **Figure 4.13**.

Key safety information for education and training providers.

Personal protective equipment

Personal protective equipment (PPE) is an important control measure that minimises the risk of injury or infection to workers, and should be used as directed according to WHS policies and procedures in the workplace. Commonly used PPE includes disposable gloves, closed-in shoes, face masks, face shields, eye protection goggles, disposable aprons, wide-brimmed hats, sun screen, noise protection such as ear plugs or earmuffs, hard hats and high-vis vests.

PPE is only effective if it is used consistently, correctly and under the appropriate conditions. WHS policies and procedures will identify when PPE must be used. It's not possible to know the current infection status of all students and adults in a setting. For this reason, ESWs should always apply universal precautions when dealing with body fluids, including faeces, urine, saliva, vomit or blood. The best form of protection from body fluids is disposable gloves, eye protection and handwashing.

To minimise the risk of infection, ESWs should also:

- cover all open wounds
- immediately wash any part of the body that comes into contact with blood or body fluids; if necessary, flush eyes and mouth with clean water
- clean body fluid spills on any surfaces with disinfectant or bleach solution
- treat all contaminated linen or clothing as infectious.

The following Scenario addresses the importance of wearing appropriate clothing in the workplace as a form of PPE.

SCENARIO

WEARING APPROPRIATE CLOTHING

Elana is undertaking work placement at a school for students with cognitive and physical disabilities as part of her Certificate 3 in Education Support studies. It's a hot day and Elana arrives at the centre wearing a T-shirt, an above-the-knee skirt and sandals. She is also wearing large hoop earrings. Her supervising teacher asks her to go home and change into joggers, trousers or long shorts and studs instead of hoop earrings. She was also asked to apply sunscreen and bring a wide-brimmed hat to wear in the playground.

▶ DISCUSSION

Why did the supervising teacher make this request?

Figure 4.14 An example of an organised, clean and tidy classroom

Source: Photo by Tish Okely © Cengage

Housekeeping

A school is typically a shared workspace, where a team of staff work together to provide an education for students. WHS practices therefore protect not only workers but also the health and safety of students and visitors to the school. Keeping the workplace clean and tidy is essential (see **Figure 4.14**). Good housekeeping includes:

- returning equipment and resources to the correct storage location after use
- storing equipment and resources safely (and neatly), ready for use
- ensuring that lids on containers are secure before they are returned to storage
- refilling expendable items such as toilet rolls, paper towels or liquid soap as they run low (or alerting the person responsible for this task)
- wiping spills on floor or tables as and when they occur
- emptying rubbish bins as they become full
- ensuring that doorways and emergency exits are kept clear at all times
- removing equipment that may become hazardous from wear and tear
- returning cleaning materials and equipment to the correct storage area so that they don't become a trip hazard.

Hazardous chemicals

The use, handling, storage and labelling of hazardous chemicals are subject to strict legislative requirements. A range of chemicals may be used in schools, such as detergent, washing powder or liquid, abrasive cream cleaning products, bleach disinfectants and gardening products. Some chemicals will be classified as dangerous goods and/or hazardous substances (DGHS), and may cause serious harm to human health through ingestion, inhalation or absorption through the skin or eyes. Examples of such chemicals include solvents and thinners, herbicides and pesticides, gas storage tanks, acids and other caustic substances. These chemicals may also pose a threat to the immediate environment. Using them will require PPE, such as protective clothing (e.g. gloves) and footwear, dust masks, and respirators or breathing apparatus.

Chemicals may be used in science labs, art rooms and dark rooms, technology/engineering classrooms and outdoors. They may be stored in classrooms, labs, cleaners' rooms and gardeners' sheds.

Whenever a hazardous chemical is used in the workplace, a **Safety Data Sheet (SDS)** must be provided, free of charge, by the supplier or manufacturer of a hazardous chemical on first supply to the workplace or when asked to do so.

A Safety Data Sheet (Safe Work Australia, 2012, p. 1) is a document that provides detailed information about a hazardous chemical, including:

- the identity of the chemical product and its ingredients
- the hazards related to the chemical, including health hazards, physical hazards and environmental hazards
- physical properties of the chemical, like boiling point, flash point and incompatibilities with other chemicals
- workplace exposure standards for airborne contaminants
- safe handling and storage procedures for the chemical
- what to do in the event of an emergency or spill
- first aid information
- transport information.

Product Safety Australia (2015) suggests that if used inappropriately, products containing toxic chemicals can cause:

- serious illness if swallowed
- severe irritation on contact with the eyes or skin
- respiratory and other illnesses if inhaled
- allergic reactions in consumers with high sensitivity to small amounts of certain chemicals.

For people who may have a high degree of sensitivity or allergy to chemicals, the effects can include mild skin irritation, dermatitis and/or life-threatening anaphylaxis.

A number of strategies can be used to reduce the risk of injury or illness when handling hazardous chemicals. ESWs, teachers and students who use chemicals must be trained in their correct handling, use and storage. Training should also include how to access, read and interpret labels and SDS. All chemicals should be used in accordance with written directions and warnings. This includes the use of recommended PPE.

It is also essential that workers are familiar with the signs and symptoms of poisoning or adverse reactions to chemicals and the administration of emergency first aid.

GO FURTHER

Learn more about WHS in a school science lab in your **Go Further** resource, available through your instructor.

Electrical hazards

Operating machinery and IT equipment in the workplace can be hazardous if the correct safety instructions are not followed or if the equipment is faulty or stored incorrectly. Equipment and machinery that may be used by ESWs in schools includes computers, printers, scanners, projectors and electronic whiteboards.

Hazards associated with this machinery and equipment include electrocution, laser printer particle emissions, poor ventilation and noise. Key strategies to minimise risks associated with the operation of machinery include training, demonstration and clearly written, step-by-step instructions.

When operating equipment, it is important to:

- read the manufacturer's instructions, warnings and suggested maintenance schedule
- identify hazards, potential risks and risk control measures
- identify PPE that may be required
- follow safe start-up and shutdown procedures
- learn specific skills recommended by the manufacturer to safely operate the equipment
- assess ergonomic hazards.

Electrocution is a possibility in any workplace. Safe Work Australia (2012, p. 7) defines the risk as 'risks of death, electric shock or other injury caused directly or indirectly by electricity'. The most common electrical risks and causes of injury are:

- electric shock causing injury or death
- arcing, explosion or fire, causing burns
- electric shock from 'step-and-touch potentials' (step potential is the risk of injury during an electrical fault simply by standing near the grounding point; touch potential is the voltage between the energised object and the feet of a person in contact with the object)
- toxic gases causing illness or death
- fire resulting from an electrical fault.

All equipment where electricity is supplied through an electrical socket should be inspected regularly for damage such as frayed or bent cords, discoloration that may indicate burning or broken switches. Safe Work Australia (2012, p. 17) states that testing and tagging by a licensed electrician or electrical inspector is only required where such plug-in electrical equipment is 'used in an environment in which its normal use exposes the equipment to operating conditions that are likely to result in damage to the equipment or a reduction in its expected life span. This includes conditions that involve exposing the electrical equipment to moisture, heat, vibration, mechanical damage, corrosive chemicals or dust'.

Residual current devices (RCDs) or safety switches such as circuit breakers reduce the risk of electrical shock because they are designed to immediately switch off the supply of electricity when electricity 'leaking' to earth is detected at harmful levels. WHS Regulation 164 requires RCDs to be used in workplaces where electrical equipment is portable (that is, it can be used in different parts of the workplace) or handheld, or moved from one location to another.

Electrical hazards in schools may include any plug-in device, particularly where equipment is used frequently and moved – for example, vacuum cleaners, shared CD players or laptops. A risk assessment should be carried out on electrical devices, which should be based around the potential likelihood of a risk occurring and the potential severity of that risk.

Control measures may include providing in-house training for workers and students, providing written step-by-step safety instructions and close supervision, restricting the use of the equipment, restricting the unnecessary movement of equipment around the school, regular visual safety inspections, testing and tagging of equipment by a licensed electrician or electrical inspector, not using extension cords, only using power boards with a built-in RCD, using a cord organiser to keep cords off the floor, and ensuring that electrical cords are not placed across a room or walkway.

RCD

SCENARIO

The cord on one of the electric mixers used by food technology students has begun to fray. The ESW makes a mental note to arrange for it to be repaired. Two weeks later, the cord has still not been replaced. It is a busy morning and Year 7 students are making desserts. **Eddie**, a student, turns on the mixer. The circuit breaker immediately cuts the power to the power point. The ESW is quietly thankful for the RCD and decides to immediately remove the mixer until it is repaired.

WHAT DOES THIS TELL US?

Any equipment that is damaged should be immediately removed from use until it can be repaired or replaced.

▶ DISCUSSION

Had Eddie been electrocuted, who would have been responsible for this accident?

4.4 Identify and manage infection and disease

Working in schools exposes staff to the risk of infection and disease. ESWs working with students with disability who require a high level of personal care are at higher risk of contracting infections and contagious diseases.

Infection can be spread in a variety of ways:

- *Airborne droplets:* some infections occur by transfer of bacteria or viruses via mucus or saliva, through the air by coughing or sneezing or nose-blowing. Droplets are then spread to hands, furniture, equipment and books. ESWs who do not wash their hands after wiping a student's nose may also spread airborne droplets. Examples of infections spread by airborne droplets include the influenza virus and meningococcus.
- *Airborne transmission:* germs are spread by breathing contaminated air. Small particles can be spread on air currents, and through ventilation systems and air-conditioning systems. Examples of infections spread by airborne transmission include the measles virus and the *varicella* (chickenpox) virus.
- *Direct contact:* organisms can be transferred from one person to another when the secretions (urine, blood, saliva, tears, vaginal secretions and semen) of an infected person come into direct contact with the broken, cut or scratched skin of another person.
- *Organisms spread by faeces:* these include bacteria, viruses and parasites. Surfaces most commonly contaminated with faeces include the hands, floors, tap handles, toilet flush areas, hand towels, equipment and table tops. Examples of infections spread by faeces include viral gastroenteritis, giardia (diarrhoea) and hepatitis A.
- *Organisms transferred via contaminated surfaces:* surfaces are easily contaminated by an infected person through coughing, sneezing or touching. Infection occurs when others touch the contaminated surface and then touch their mouth, eyes or nose. Examples of infections spread by direct contact include head lice (head-to-head contact), scabies and fungal infections of the skin (skin-to-skin contact).
- *Animals:* infections from animal faeces spread into the environment and may then be passed on to humans through direct contact – such as with a dog, a hand or face – or indirectly – such as with contaminated sand or soil. Infection can also be spread by flies and vermin.
- *Food:* germs can spread when people eat food that has not been heated or chilled properly, and where good hygiene such as hand washing or sneezing etiquette is not practised.

Source: National Health and Medical Research Council (2012), CC-BY-3.0 licence.

COVID-19

The COVID-19 pandemic has highlighted the need for clear guidelines to manage the spread of infection in school communities. The directions around COVID management have changed over time as more people become immunised and scientists gain a deeper understanding of the virus.

Keeping up-to-date with guidelines can be challenging. The Australian Government has a 'Coronavirus (COVID-19) information for schools and students' website (**https://www.dese.gov.au/covid-19/schools**), which includes a range of information for the school community, including:

- National Framework for Managing COVID-19 in Schools and Early Childhood Education and Care
- National Code for Boarding School Students

- 2021 Statement of Intent for Australian Schools
- Emerging Priorities Program
- reducing potential risk of COVID-19 transmission in schools
- resources for teachers and school leaders
- new research
- National Principles for School Education
- support for students with disability
- COVID-19 support available to non-government schools
- senior secondary arrangements and university admissions
- information about NAPLAN
- international students.

Due to the behaviour and mutation of the SARS-CoV-2 virus (which causes COVID-19), information needs to be regularly updated. The website is a useful first stop for information about the latest advice. Many states and territory health departments also publish continually updated advice for school communities.

Remember, it is impossible to know the current infection status of every student and adult in a school environment. For this reason, ESWs should always apply universal precautions when dealing with body fluids such as blood, vomit, saliva and nose secretions. The best form of protection from body fluids is disposable gloves and handwashing. Disposable gloves must be worn when dealing with any body fluids (including body fluids on clothing, carpets, hard surfaces, equipment and sand). To minimise the risk of infection, educators should also:

- cover all open wounds
- wash any part of the body that comes in contact with blood or body fluids immediately; if necessary, flush eyes and mouth with clean water
- clean body fluid spills on any surfaces with disinfectants or bleach solution
- treat all contaminated linen or clothing as infectious.

Infectious diseases and exclusion periods

All schools will have a range of procedures to minimise the spread of infection. Examples of these procedures include hand hygiene, PPE, disposal of used or discarded needles and syringes, food hygiene, management of blood and body fluids, cough etiquette, cleaning surfaces and equipment. Beginning ESWs should familiarise themselves with their school's policies and procedures.

Handwashing

Handwashing is an extremely effective first-line defence strategy to minimise the spread of infectious disease. To be effective, handwashing throughout the day should be a regular part of the daily routine for ESWs.

Follow these steps for effective handwashing procedure:

1. Use liquid soap to minimise the risk of transferring germs on bars of soap.
2. Place hands under running water. Thoroughly wash the palms, backs of the hand down past the wrists, between the fingers, around the thumbs and under the nails for at least 15 seconds (sing a song while doing this to ensure you wash your hands for an extended amount of time).
3. Rinse hands with water.
4. Minimise contact with the tap handle by using a paper towel as a barrier when turning the tap off.
5. Pat hands thoroughly dry with disposable paper towel.

Figure 4.15 shows correct handwashing procedure.

Figure 4.15 Correct handwashing technique

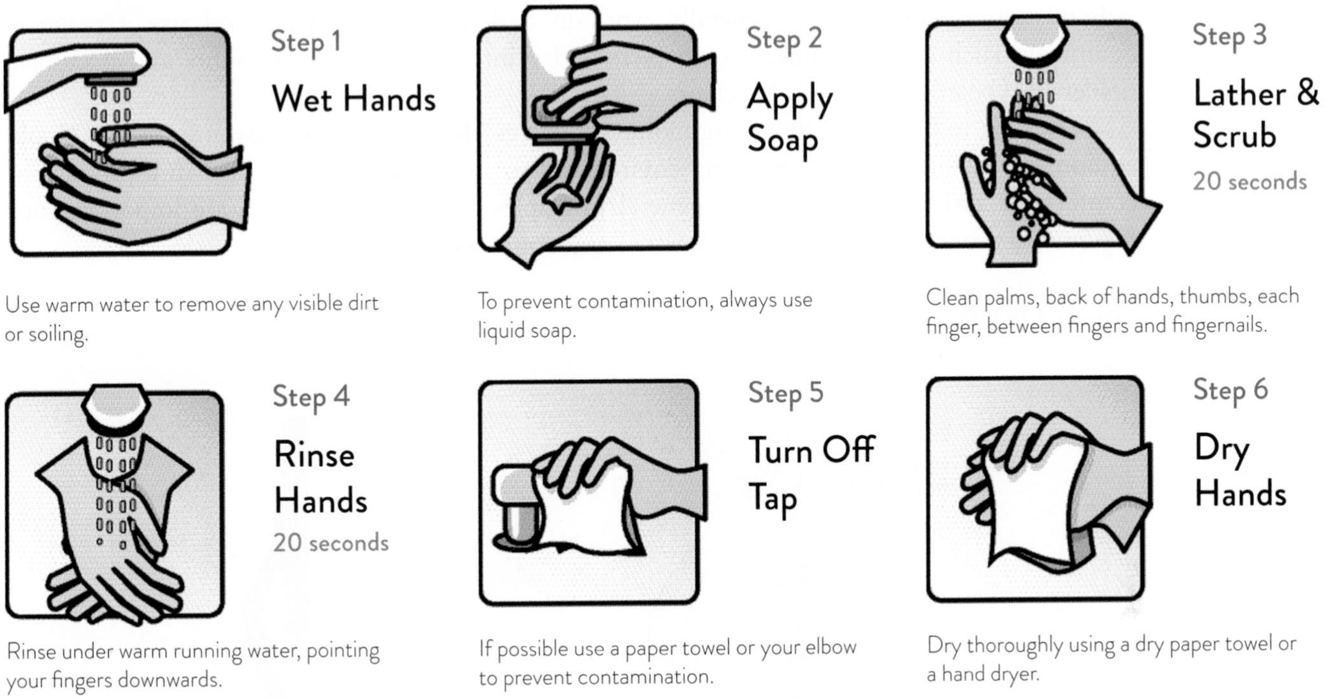

Step 1
Wet Hands
Use warm water to remove any visible dirt or soiling.
Step 2
Apply Soap
To prevent contamination, always use liquid soap.
Step 3
Lather & Scrub
20 seconds
Clean palms, back of hands, thumbs, each finger, between fingers and fingernails.
Step 4
Rinse Hands
20 seconds
Rinse under warm running water, pointing your fingers downwards.
Step 5
Turn Off Tap
If possible use a paper towel or your elbow to prevent contamination.
Step 6
Dry Hands
Dry thoroughly using a dry paper towel or a hand dryer.

Source: https://www.foodsafety.com.au/resources/posters/a-guide-to-washing-your-hands

Worker immunisation

Immunisation can protect ESWs from a range of communicable diseases. The National Health and Medical Research Council (NHMRC, 2012) recommends that adults working with children be vaccinated against:

- pertussis (whooping cough)
- measles–mumps–rubella
- varicella (herpes virus that causes chickenpox)
- hepatitis A
- coronavirus (COVID-19).

The NHMRC also recommends a yearly influenza vaccination, and that additional precautions should be taken for pregnant people working with children.

Exposure to ultraviolet (UV) radiation

Schools will have policies and safe practices to limit the risk of exposure to the harmful effects of the sun. Cancer Council Australia warns that ultraviolet radiation is the major cause of sunburn and increased skin cancer risk, and also contributes to ageing of the skin.

ESWs can protect themselves from sunburn by applying a broad-spectrum sunscreen to all exposed skin 20 minutes before going outdoors, and wearing a broad-brimmed hat and clothing that covers the neck and shoulders. The PCBU is responsible for ensuring that there is adequate shading in the outdoor area for workers (and students).

4.5 Office ergonomics

Administrative support staff generally work in a defined office space and use a range of equipment such as telephones, photocopiers and printers, computers, monitors and document holders, keyboards and adjustable chairs.

According to Comcare (2008), ergonomics involves 'designing tasks, jobs, information, tools, equipment, facilities and the working environment so work can be performed in a productive, comfortable and safe manner'. The general principles of office ergonomics are important, and **Figure 4.16** provides a detailed breakdown of ergonomic assessment.

Figure 4.16 Office ergonomics

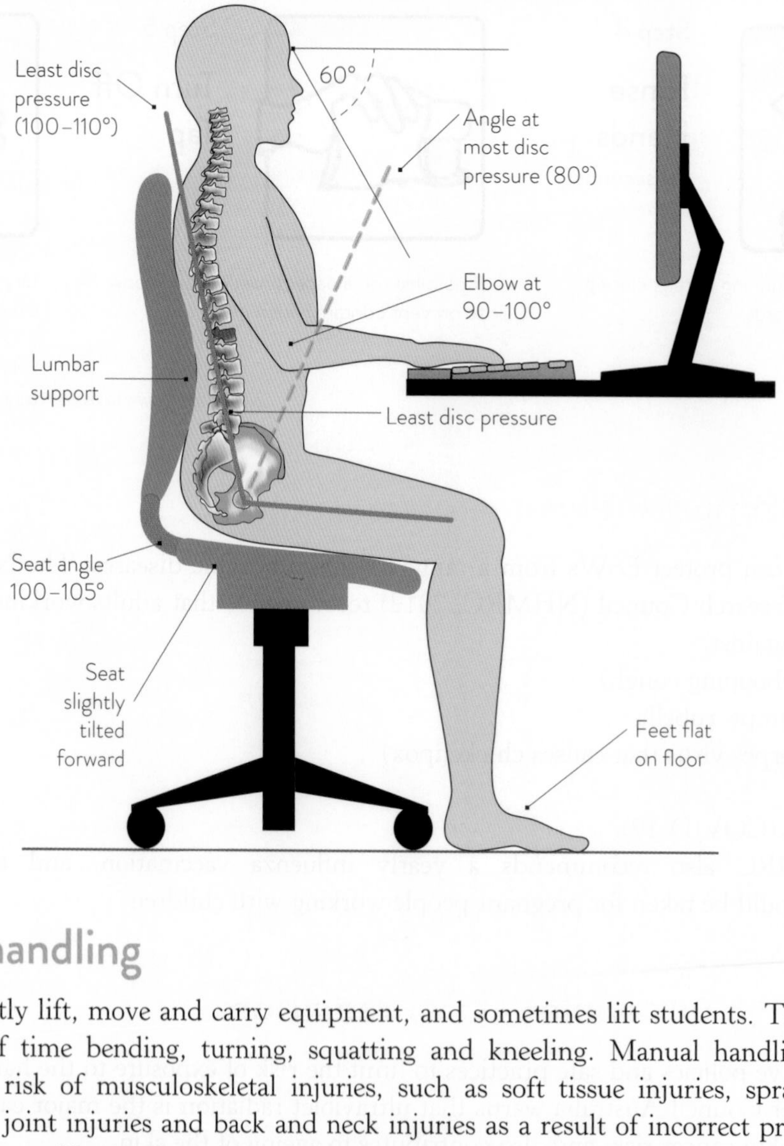

Manual handling

ESWs frequently lift, move and carry equipment, and sometimes lift students. They also spend a great deal of time bending, turning, squatting and kneeling. Manual handling and lifting present a real risk of musculoskeletal injuries, such as soft tissue injuries, sprains, repetitive strain injuries, joint injuries and back and neck injuries as a result of incorrect procedures when lifting, carrying, pulling and pushing. Injuries may occur immediately or as the result of wear and tear over a period of time.

The strategies to identify hazardous manual tasks are the same as those used to identify any workplace hazard: consult with workers, closely examine workplace tasks and break down each task into steps. Workers can also identify tasks that are physically challenging or tiring, or that require awkward or unnatural movements that cause discomfort or pain. An important strategy in identifying hazardous manual tasks is to observe how such tasks typically are performed in the workplace. **Figure 4.17** lists the questions recommended by Safe Work Australia's 'Model code of practice: Hazardous manual tasks' to assist in determining whether a task poses a risk of a musculoskeletal injury.

Figure 4.17 Does this task pose a risk of musculoskeletal injury?

1. Does the task involve any of the following?
   - repetitive movement
   - sustained or awkward postures
   - repetitive or sustained forces
2. Does the task involve long duration?
   - The duration of the task is how long it takes to carry out the task over a whole shift or continually at any time during a shift. Tasks that continue over a long period (30 or more minutes), or are repeated over the work day (two or more hours), increase the risk of injury.
3. Does the task involve high or sudden force? The risk in tasks involving high force is related to:
   - the intensity of the force needed
   - the speed involved
   - whether the force is jerky or sudden
4. Does the task involve vibration?
5. Is there a risk [of musculoskeletal disorder]?

Source: Adapted from 'Hazardous Model Code of Practice: Manual Tasks', October 2018 © Commonwealth of Australia 2018, Released under CC BY 4.0, link to licence: https://creativecommons.org/licenses/by/4.0/

Consideration should also be given to the physical environment, the tools, machinery or equipment being used, and the strategies or practices being utilised to perform a task.

It is possible to reduce the risk of injury when undertaking hazardous manual tasks in the school workplace:

- Use mechanical devices such as mobile storage crates, trolleys, porter's trolleys, large plastic garden trolleys that can be easily moved, and shelving with wheels (it will be necessary to use devices to immobilise this type of storage while it is being used by the students).
- Use chairs and workbenches that can be height adjusted.
- Use mechanical lifting devices for students with a physical disability.
- Ensure that storage facilities are designed to minimise the need to bend, twist or reach above shoulder height.
- Plan daily routines to minimise the number of times equipment is moved.
- Regularly stretch and flex throughout the day with gentle movements such as turning the head from side to side and stretching arms towards the ceiling.
- Always use a buddy system when moving heavy or bulky objects.
- Where possible, encourage students to help pack away equipment and keep the room tidy.

Training in the management of and procedures for hazardous manual tasks – for example, correct lifting techniques (**Figure 4.18**), team lifts and using alternative manual strategies such as

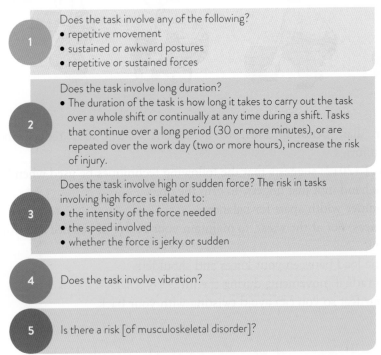

Figure 4.18 Correct lifting procedures

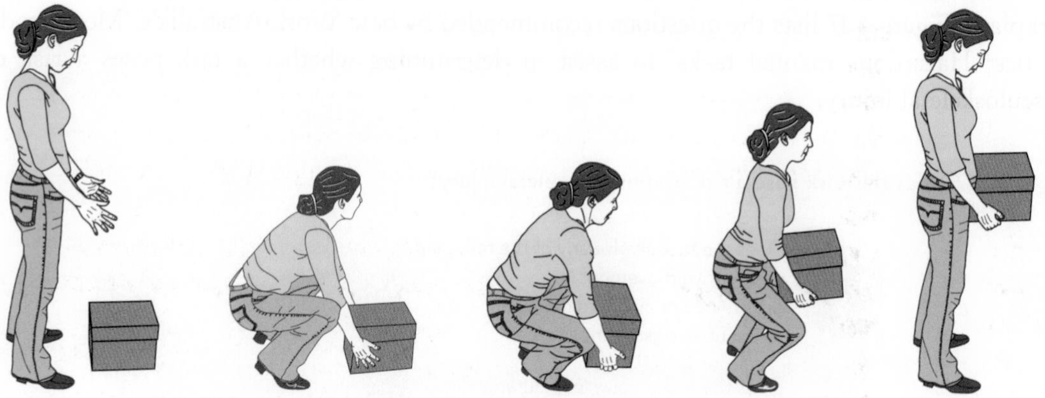

Source: Workfast (2017).

squatting rather than bending down to a student – will also reduce the likelihood of musculoskeletal injuries.

WorkSafe ACT (2012) suggests that the following techniques be used when lifting:

- Use the whole hand, not just fingers, to grip the object.
- Place feet shoulder-width apart for balance.
- Bend at the knees, not at the waist, to maintain your centre of balance and utilise leg muscles to do the lifting.
- Try to keep the load between your knees and shoulders.
- Use smooth, gradual movements during the lift.
- Pivot with your feet so you can avoid twisting with your back.

Manual handling and students with disability

ESWs involved in the physical and personal care of students with disability are required to undertake a range of tasks that may pose a risk of neck, back or other musculoskeletal injuries. Manual handling of students may include lifting the student from a chair, undressing/dressing, assisting with toileting or nappy change, helping to transfer a student to or from a car or bus, moving a student in a wheelchair, or physically supporting a student who may be engaged in physical therapy or using climbing equipment. These tasks may require a range of movements such as bending, squatting, twisting, reaching, gripping, lifting or forceful exertion.

Factors that may contribute to the risk of injury to the ESW when assisting a student include the degree of mobility, flexibility and head control of the student, the degree of involuntary movement, the student's weight, size and degree of alertness, the ability or willingness of the student to cooperate with the ESW, and the student's level of communication skills (expressive and receptive). Students with chronic health conditions that require regular medication – for example, epilepsy, cystic fibrosis or diabetes – may display symptoms such as fatigue, sluggish mobility and a lack of concentration.

Some students with physical impairments must be moved with the assistance of a hoist and sling. These mechanical devices reduce the risk of injury to ESWs and the student. Safe Work

Australia (2011a, p. 28) suggests a number of controls that can be used to reduce the risk of injury. These controls include:

Safe manual handling

- undertaking a mobility risk assessment to identify the most appropriate mechanical or assistive device
- moving the person to a place that does not constrain the movement of the worker
- performing the task – for example, when toileting a student ensure that the toilet area is large enough so that the door can be closed to respect the dignity and privacy of the student without restricting the movement of the ESW
- where handling is required, assessing the needs of the task including the specific type of mechanical aids and personnel needed, and planning it in a manner that avoids the hazardous manual task
- where the use of a hoist requires two or more people, providing adequate supervision and resources to eliminate the risk of workers being under time pressure and attempting the task on their own
- planning how to handle a person attached to medical or other equipment
- ensuring the location and storage of mechanical aids and assistive devices enables easy access
- providing training in the safe use of mechanical aids and assistive devices (see **Figure 4.19**).

Sometimes lifts and larger bed-style chairs need to be moved while the student is not in them. It is important for the ESW to give careful thought to their own safety in this situation.

Figure 4.19 A device used to enhance mobility

Source: Shutterstock.com/Goldsithney

Developing a care plan

Students who require physical and personal care should have a care plan in place. The care plan should outline the degree of support the student will need from the ESW to help them move, the equipment the ESW will need to use in assisting the student (e.g. a hoist) and the equipment the student will need (such as a wheelchair or walking frame), as well as personal care requirements. The plan may also include the assistance required by the student when lifting and positioning their body for toileting or moving from a mobility device to a chair or onto the floor.

ESWs who are responsible for lifting and positioning should be provided with formal training by the employer in manual handling of people to ensure best practice in transferring and positioning students and the safe use of mechanical lifts and assistive devices. Formal training will also minimise the risk of injury to both the ESW and the student.

SCENARIO

ASSISTIVE DEVICES

WHEELCHAIRS

'Until I went to the training day I didn't really think there was much to know about pushing a student round in a wheelchair. We learnt how to maintain a wheelchair, the best way to move a wheelchair over uneven surfaces, on grass and on thick pile carpet. We practised things like moving wheelchairs up and down ramps, over curbs, manoeuvring in tight spaces, accessing toilets, and transferring people to and from

chairs, folding chairs and putting them into a boot and getting them out again. I was amazed how much there was to learn!'

MOBILITY DEVICES

'This week I have been working with the physiotherapist so that I can learn about how to support students who use walking frames, chest harnesses and head supports, splints and braces, standing frames and crutches. I've also learnt how to use slings and hoists. It's been great – I feel confident that I know what to do to make it easier for the students and also to make sure I keep myself safe. The physio showed me how to move and brace myself so that I don't end up with an injury.

'The physio said I'd also need these skills when assisting students with mobility challenges for school-based activities such as swimming and excursions, as well as daily tasks like getting out of and into buses or cars.'

WHAT DOES THIS TELL US?

When working with students with limited mobility, it is essential that ESWs are competent in and confident about the use of mobility devices.

▶ DISCUSSION

What should you do and be aware of in order to protect your back in the workplace?

Figure 4.20 Emergency evacuation plans must be clearly displayed

Source: Photo by Tish Okely © Cengage

4.6 Workplace emergency procedures

By their nature, emergencies can occur with little or no warning. It is essential to have a well-planned and well-rehearsed emergency plan. All schools are required by law to have set procedures that can immediately be activated in an emergency (see **Figure 4.20**).

Emergencies that may impact on schools include:

- natural disasters such as flood, bushfire, earthquake, severe electrical or dust storms
- power failures, gas leaks, loss of water supply
- spills of hazardous or toxic materials on the roadside or the release of toxic chemicals into the atmosphere
- a medical emergency involving serious sudden illness or injury to a staff member or student
- a parent, guardian, intruder or student who presents as threatening, angry, abusive or under the influence of drugs or alcohol.

A PCBU must ensure that an emergency plan is prepared for the workplace that provides for emergencies, drills and training.

The 'Managing the work environment and facilities code of practice' (Safe Work Australia, 2011b, p. 28) recommends that emergency procedures be written clearly and that they be easy to understand. Where relevant, the emergency procedures should address evacuation procedures and appropriate staff training, assembly locations and protocols for an emergency, and lockdown procedures. There are many other considerations that are important to understand – the full code of practice can be found for perusal at: https://www.safeworkaustralia.gov.au.

GO FURTHER

Learn more about emergency procedures in your **Go Further** resource, available through your instructor.

CONSIDER THIS

EMERGENCY EVACUATION OR LOCKDOWN

Procedures in relation to emergency evacuation and lockdown will usually include (see **Figure 4.21**):

- responsibilities of individual staff members to ensure all students are safely evacuated or contained (in the case of a lockdown)
- clearly designated assembly point/s and evacuation routes – these should be familiar to all staff and students with signs posted at strategic points around the school facilities
- a system for identifying all students in attendance (class rolls)
- a designated signal for evacuation or lockdown
- clearly stated procedures to follow such as closing doors (if there is a fire) or leaving doors open if there's a bomb threat

Figure 4.21 An emergency evacuation poster

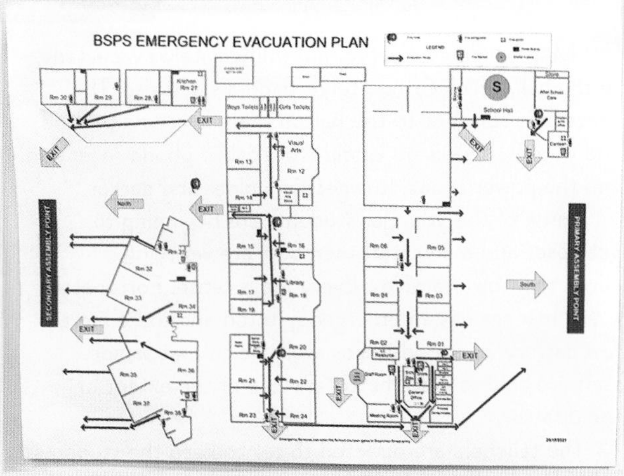

Source: Photo by Tish Okely © Cengage

- identification of who will check areas such as toilets, canteen, meeting rooms and the sick bay; who will be responsible for visitors, parents who may be on the premises and volunteers or students; who will contact emergency services; who will collect the first aid kit and mobile phone; who will contact head office
- procedures for checking on 'missing' students or staff
- procedures for assisting students with disability, particularly where mobility is an issue or students are not able to understand the evacuation procedures. This may include an individual evacuation plan for each student with a disability, which takes into account the specific mobility, health and medical needs of each student. Generally, the evacuation route would need to be wheelchair-friendly and also take into account students who are sight or hearing impaired. Where students must be evacuated via a staircase, it would be necessary for the school to have a wheelchair especially designed for use on stairs. Evacuation procedures for students with a disability may need to be practised more frequently than for students in the general population
- procedures for ensuring that students with disability are familiar with the evacuation procedure from all areas of the school premises accessed by students
- procedures for ensuring staff have access to keyed locks on doors and fences (particularly in specialised settings where absconding is prevalent).

WHAT DOES THIS TELL US?

A wide range of factors need to be taken into account and carefully planned in the event of an emergency evacuation or lockdown. Preparation and regular practice are an essential part of the planning process.

Selecting assembly areas

Establishing a safe assembly area for a whole school can be a challenge, particularly where there are large numbers of students of different ages and abilities. In the event of a widespread emergency where whole streets must be evacuated, such as a flood or bushfire, it is likely that the assembly point will be nominated by emergency personnel.

Evacuation

When evacuating, all staff must remain calm and in control. Forward planning will assist staff to act promptly and efficiently and may include doing the following:

- Plan ahead by selecting and clearly marking exits from the building. Ensure that exits are always kept clear. If some gates are kept locked, ensure keys are readily available.

- Choose a route to the assembly location. Ideally, the assembly place will be within easy walking distance.
- Decide what signals will be used to alert staff (and students) to the need to evacuate or commence lockdown procedures.
- Have specific procedures in place where there are younger students or students with disability. This will assist the orderly progress to the assembly place or complying with lockdown procedures. It is important to be aware that in the event of a real emergency, younger students or those with a disability may become distressed or even hysterical.
- Ensure procedures account for all people, including students, staff and visitors who may be there at the time of the emergency. A visitor sign-in/sign-out book will help with this task.
- Ensure all staff know and understand their specific role as part of the preparation for emergencies – for example, a person nominated to take charge of overall evacuation, a person nominated to take charge of evacuation of designated areas, a person nominated to search and check the building to ensure no one is left behind, persons nominated as first aid officers.
- All staff must be trained adequately in emergency procedures, including the location and use of fire extinguishers and fire blankets.

SCENARIO

EMERGENCY PROCEDURES

LOCKDOWN

It is just after 9 a.m. and classes have commenced for the day. ESW **Liz** is walking along the verandah, accompanying four students to the special reading unit room, when she notices two men in the playground; one appears to be carrying a crossbow and the other is carrying what looks like a machete. Liz quickly diverts the students into the closest classroom and quietly says 'lockdown' to the teacher. The teacher uses her mobile phone to alert the office to the situation. The signal for lockdown is issued and the police are called.

DISASTER!

It is 2.40 p.m. and the sky is an eerie greenish-black colour. Large hailstones begin to fall, followed by heavy rain and lashing winds. The storm is still raging at 3 p.m. and it is evident that this is no ordinary storm. News has come through that a cargo ship has run aground on the beach, stormwater drains all over the city and surrounding suburbs have overflowed, roads are blocked, cars have been swept into drains and houses and businesses have been inundated.

Parents are not able to get to the school and many of the cars in the staff car park are now under water. It is clear that students and staff will have to remain at the school. Water is starting to creep into several of the low-lying buildings. Everyone is immediately evacuated to the hall, which fortunately sits on a slight rise. The canteen is adjacent to the hall so there is access to food and water. There is no landline or mobile phone reception and the power is out. It is getting colder and darker.

Some of the younger students are beginning to get upset and many staff members are worrying about their own families. Everyone is tense. Fortunately, every teacher has an emergency torch and there are a few battery-operated radios available so that senior staff are able to get a better picture of the extent of the disaster.

The teachers are directed to try to keep the students calm. Some classes decide to sing songs or tell stories, but the fading light makes this difficult. Several teachers are gathering snacks from the canteen to distribute to the students before the light is completely gone. It is going to be a very long night!

WHAT DOES THIS TELL US?

Staying calm and following procedure is the key to managing emergency situations. Students will look to the adults for reassurance and direction. The adults remaining calm will help students to remain calm also and listen to and follow instructions.

It is impossible to be totally prepared for all emergencies. The very nature of an 'emergency' makes it unpredictable and often brings with it unforeseen circumstances that cannot be anticipated. However, schools can ensure that all staff are trained in emergency procedures.

4.7 Stress, bullying and workplace violence

Work-related stress has been identified as the most common health issue for staff in school settings. Working in a school setting can also present a risk to mental health. Reducing stress should be part of the school's **WHS management system**.

According to Comcare (2008, p. 12), there are six primary causes of workplace stress:

- *demands* – includes workload, work patterns and the work environment
- *control* – how much say the person has in the way they do their work
- *support* – includes the encouragement, sponsorship and resources provided by the organisation, line management and colleagues
- *relationships* – includes promoting positive working to avoid conflict and dealing with unacceptable behaviour
- *role* – whether people understand their role within the organisation and whether the organisation ensures that they do not have conflicting roles
- *change* – how organisational change (large or small) is managed and communicated in the organisation.

Psychosocial hazards

Working with children and young people is very demanding and requires all staff to be healthy, alert and energetic. There will be times when individuals experience personal stress in addition to the everyday pressures of work. Each individual's physical and emotional wellbeing, and the level of support available both outside and in the workplace, will have an impact on how well they cope with and manage stress.

Workers who are stressed present a risk to themselves and others in the workplace. Employers have an obligation to reduce stress by identifying possible sources of stress and, where practicable, developing procedures and strategies to eliminate or reduce the causes of stress.

When people are stressed, they respond in different ways. Physical, mental or emotional symptoms of stress are identified in the Consider this box.

CONSIDER THIS

STRESS

SYMPTOMS OF STRESS

- *Physical symptoms of stress* – common symptoms include fatigue, back pain, a rise in blood pressure and/or heart rate, insomnia, stomach ulcers, digestive disorders, headaches, sweating and dry mouth.
- *Mental symptoms of stress* – common symptoms include racing thoughts, anxiety, irritability, poor memory and concentration, and an inability to make decisions.
- *Emotional symptoms of stress* – common symptoms include irrational fear and/or anger, panic and depression.

HOW TO IMPROVE PERSONAL HEALTH AND WELLBEING

According to the Black Dog Institute (2014, p. 4), strategies to improve personal health and wellbeing include:

- meditation, listening to music and other techniques to calm the mind
- getting involved in a hobby/interest
- sleeping and eating well
- using exercise as a stress release
- doing things in moderation – avoid the use of alcohol to 'wind down'
- recognising the importance of work–life balance.

Source: Adapted from Black Dog Institute (2014).

▶ DISCUSSION

1 Can you list the symptoms you experience when you become stressed?
2 Does everyone experience the same symptoms?
3 What can you do to minimise stress in your life?

Figure 4.22 An example of warning sign about bullying at school

Source: Reproduced with permission of Kids Helpline, kidshelpline.com.au

Harassment and bullying in the workplace

Like workplace stress, workplace bullying and harassment can result in physical, emotional and mental illness, and can also result in serious injury. Symptoms will vary but may include a sense of helplessness, a decrease in self-confidence, feelings of isolation, anxiety and depression, insomnia and a decrease in work performance (see **Figure 4.22**).

Workplace bullying is defined by Safe Work Australia (2016, p. 2) as 'unreasonable behaviour directed towards a worker or a group of workers that creates a risk to health and safety'. It includes repeated and unreasonable behaviour:

> Repeated behaviour refers to the persistent nature of the behaviour and can involve a range of behaviours over time. Unreasonable behaviour means behaviour that a reasonable person, having considered the circumstances, would see as unreasonable including behaviour that is victimising, humiliating, intimidating or threatening.

Bullying in the workplace can take on many forms. It can be overt or covert, subtle or openly aggressive. Whatever form it takes, workplace bullying – previously referred to as workplace harassment – will have an adverse impact on the workplace and those in it. Bullying may include behaviours such as verbal abuse – swearing, yelling at a person, ridicule, constant criticism, sarcasm, threats of violence, negative body language, dismissal, harm, sabotaging the person's work, spreading gossip, name calling, laughing at a person, excluding the person from the team by ignoring, not communicating information or messages, sending threatening texts or emails.

Safe Work Australia states that the responsibility to prevent workplace bullying, harassment and discrimination is covered in the *Work Health and Safety Act 2011* by the duty of the organisation to provide a healthy and safe working environment and safe systems of work. As Safe Work Australia (2016, p. 6) states 'a single incident of unreasonable behaviour is not considered to be workplace bullying, however it may have the potential to escalate and should not be ignored'.

Sexual harassment

According to ComCare, sexual harassment is a known workplace hazard that can cause psychological and physical harm. It can include unwelcome hugging, kissing or other types of inappropriate physical contact, staring or leering, intrusive questions about a person's private life or physical appearance, repeated unwanted invitations to go out on dates, requests for sex, or explicit emails, calls, text messages or online interactions (Comcare, 2021).

Discrimination and sexual harassment in employment are unlawful under anti-discrimination, equal employment opportunity, workplace relations and human rights laws (Safe Work Australia, 2016, p. 25).

SCENARIO

SEXUAL HARASSMENT

Catherine is a newly appointed ESW at a local high school. She is young, single and attractive. Catherine has been receiving unwanted attention from a male teacher, who comments on Catherine's physical appearance and tells jokes of a sexual nature.

Catherine's response A: Catherine makes it clear to the teacher that she is not comfortable with his behaviour towards her and asks him to stop. However, when the behaviour continues Catherine keeps a record of incidents and reports the teacher's behaviour to the principal, who instigates action in accordance with the school's Sexual Harassment Policy.

Catherine's response B: at first, Catherine tries to ignore the teacher's behaviour. As the behaviour continues, she tells him it makes her feel uncomfortable and asks him to stop. She then tries to avoid being alone with the teacher. Catherine wants to make a complaint, but fears she will not be believed and that she will ultimately lose her job.

WHAT DOES THIS TELL US?

Harassment is unacceptable in any workplace. Every school will have policies and procedures to address bullying and harassment.

SCENARIO

EXAMPLES OF HARASSMENT

QUASAM

Quasam is originally from India and wears the traditional Sikh turban as a symbol of his religious values. Quasam has recently started work as an ESW in a high school. One of his colleagues teases him about his turban: *'What have you got hidden under that turban, Quasam?'*

JUDITH

ESW **Judith** rings her husband every day at morning tea and lunch. Judith's husband is retired due to a heart condition. Her work colleagues have started to make sarcastic comments that are loud enough for Judith to hear. *'There she goes again, calling Bill. I don't know why she doesn't just stay home with him!'*

AMY

ESW **Amy** is recently divorced. Although Amy has made it clear that she is not interested in dating, one of her work colleagues constantly asks her out: *'Hey sexy, want to come to the pub with me tonight for dinner?'*

TRISH

Trish, aged 54 years, is a quietly spoken ESW and goes about her work diligently and efficiently. She has been at the school for students with disability for five years and is well respected by the teaching staff and parents. This year, **Mark** has joined the ESW team. Mark is very outspoken and continually talks about the way things were done at his last school. Mark often puts Trish down, saying she needs to 'get with the program' and update her skills and knowledge or consider retirement.

WHAT DOES THIS TELL US?

Harassment can take many forms – it can be overt or covert. Often those engaged in harassment are surprised when the recipient makes a complaint.

▶ DISCUSSION

Each of the above examples of harassment demonstrates a lack of respect for the victim. Discuss why each situation is unacceptable. Suggest what could be said to the perpetrators to make them aware that their behaviour is inappropriate and unacceptable.

In the first instance, formal complaints about bullying or harassment must be raised with the employer. If the situation is not addressed satisfactorily and the bullying either continues or results in further harassment, workers can seek help from Fair Work Australia. The Fair Work Ombudsman can address harassment or bullying where it relates to unlawful discrimination in the workplace. The Ombudsman's scope includes resolving collective and individual workplace disputes through conciliation, mediation and, in some cases, arbitration.

Workplace bullying and sexual harrassment

Addressing workplace bullying and harassment can be difficult because of fear of how the perpetrator/s might react. The worker who is being bullied or harassed may have concerns that they won't be believed or will be regarded as a 'whinger'. The worker may be concerned about putting into place a chain of events that are outside the worker's control. There may also be concerns about how they will be perceived by workplace colleagues, or whether a complaint will result in job loss or being overlooked for promotion.

Workplace violence

WorkSafe Victoria (2014, p. 3) defines workplace violence as:

> Work-related violence involves incidents in which a person is abused, threatened or assaulted in circumstances relating to their work. This definition covers a broad range of actions and behaviours that can create a risk to the health and safety of employees. It includes behaviour often described as acting out, challenging behaviour and behaviours of concern.
>
> Examples of work-related violence include biting, spitting, scratching, hitting, kicking, pushing, shoving, tripping, grabbing, throwing objects, verbal threats, threatening someone with a weapon, armed robbery and sexual assault. It may also include harassing telephone calls, sending of threatening emails, website postings and SMS texting using mobile phones, and stalking.

Responding to threatening behaviour by co-workers or parents

All employees have a right to be and feel safe in the workplace. Unfortunately, there may be occasions when staff are threatened by colleagues or a parent. Any threats of violence should be taken seriously, documented and reported immediately to your supervisor, or if this is not an option, to an executive member of the school. PCBUs have a duty of care to investigate any reported threats and act in accordance with the school's policy and procedures.

Violence and agression against teachers

If faced with an imminent threat, it is important to take action to ensure your own safety and that of students or other adults who may be nearby. Retreat is often the best and safest course of action. If retreat is not an option, call or send for help. Arguing or engaging in a confrontation may only escalate the threat or result in the threat being acted upon. Where threats are made by a parent, it is often best to seek the help of a senior teacher or member of the school executive as they will have greater expertise in responding to, managing and following up as needed.

SCENARIO

VIOLENCE

Mrs James, **Carl**'s mother is angry – very angry! She approaches **Toni**, an ESW in the Special Behaviour Unit, who is busily preparing for tomorrow's lessons. Toni is alone in the classroom.

Mrs James: *'I see Carl has yet more misdemeanour points again today, Toni. What's going on? You teachers are supposed to be the great behaviour experts and all you're doing is putting him down. I have to say I'm getting sick of it. I'm so angry I could really hurt you!'*

Toni: *'I'm sorry you're upset, Mrs James. We do try to do our best with Carl. He has been struggling with his aggression today and unfortunately he has hit several students.'*

Mrs James: *'Well they must have done something to provoke him. Did they get misdemeanour points too?'*

Mrs James advances towards Toni: *'That's right, just brush me off, you smug bitch!'*

Toni: *'Mrs James, I'll go and get the teacher to come and talk to you.'*

Toni quickly ducks past Mrs James and goes outside to get the teacher.

After the students have left for the day Toni and the teacher discuss the incident.

Toni: *'I was really scared of Mrs James, especially when she stepped towards me. She was so angry I thought she was going to hit me.'*

Teacher: *'It must have been very frightening. Mrs James can be quite intimidating when she's angry. You did the right thing coming to get me. I'm pleased to see you have documented what happened. Hopefully she will apologise to you tomorrow. She told me she just wants to see some improvement in Carl's behaviour. I reminded her that the misdemeanour points were there as a visual aid to help Carl understand when his behaviour is unacceptable. I pointed out to her that he also has quite a few positive behaviour stickers.'*

WHAT DOES THIS TELL US?

When threatened by others, it is important to try to remain calm, remove yourself from the situation, and document and report the incident as soon as possible.

▶ DISCUSSION

What strategies could you use if confronted with a threat of verbal or physical violence in the workplace?

Student violence

The Standing Council on School Education and Early Childhood's (SCSEEC) National Safe Schools Framework (SCSEEC, 2013, p. 3) has as its vision 'All Australian schools are safe, supportive and respectful teaching and learning communities that promote student wellbeing'. The guiding principles of the Framework emphasise the importance of student safety and wellbeing as a prerequisite for effective learning in all school settings. Australian schools:

- affirm the rights of all members of the school community to feel safe and be safe at school
- acknowledge that being safe and supported at school is essential for student wellbeing and effective learning
- accept responsibility for developing and sustaining safe and supportive learning and teaching communities that also fulfil the school's child protection responsibilities
- encourage the active participation of all school community members in developing and maintaining a safe school community where diversity is valued
- actively support young people to develop understanding and skills to keep themselves and others safe
- commit to developing a safe school community through a whole-school and evidence-based approach.

Student wellbeing hub

Source: SCSEEC (2013), p. 3, © 2010 Education Services Australia as the legal entity for the Standing Council on School Education and Early Childhood (SCSEEC) http://www.safeschoolshub.edu.au/documents/nationalsafeschoolsframework.pdf CC-BY-4.0 licence.

Responding to violence or threats of violence by students

Schools will have policies and procedures to respond to violence or threats of violence by students. This will typically include actions to ensure the immediate safety of staff, other students and the student of concern. The management of violence or threats of violence is usually undertaken as a collaborative process with teachers, senior executive staff, parents, a school counsellor and other professionals as relevant. It may also include police.

A risk assessment should identify strategies to eliminate or control the risks. It will take into account the student's age, gender, abilities, family, and social and cultural context. It will also include the student's behavioural history, the context of the violent behaviours and the triggers that led to the behaviour, and will take into account the nature of the violent behaviour, the degree of harm caused (or threatened), patterns of behaviour, others involved (or targeted), the physical and social environment of the school, and any underlying conditions or significant circumstance that may contribute to the student's behaviour, such as disability, medical condition, drugs, living with domestic violence or the subject of abuse or bullying. For more information, see NSW Department of Education and Training (2018).

At worst, students who engage in violence or serious threats of violence may be subject to suspension, expulsion and criminal charges. At best, they will require intensive behavioural support in order to continue their education and may also require a range of interventions from other agencies, such as family intervention.

When responding to a physical attack by a student, using physical force to restrain the student should be avoided and used only as an absolute last resort. The NSW Department of Education and Communities (2012, p. 2) states that:

> If staff determine that physical intervention is an appropriate response to a particular situation, then any force used in that intervention must be reasonable having regard to the circumstances and any force used must be proportional to the nature of the threat. Reasonable force in dealing with a young infant or primary school student will be significantly different from that in dealing with a senior secondary school student. Staff who use physical intervention to diffuse dangerous situations are occasionally subject to complaint. It is also possible that staff who use physical intervention may be subject to criminal assault proceedings by the police or by private prosecution.

Being confronted by a violent or out-of-control student can be frightening. You must act to protect yourself, other students and, if possible, the aggressor. The best strategy is to leave the area, taking other students with you, and seek immediate help by asking a student (if possible) to run to the nearest classroom and alert a teacher to get help.

When confronted with student violence, Guetzloe (2006) suggests adults use the following strategies:

- Play the role of 'calm, cool and composed'. Acting in this manner actually helps a person to remain calm.
- Be assertive and directive but not aggressive. Do not threaten the student, either verbally or physically.
- Be as non-intrusive and non-invasive as possible. Do not move towards the student or invade their space.
- Communicate expectations verbally and non-verbally. Always tell the student to stop (with an accompanying hand signal) and give a directive statement, as explained below. For example, 'Sit down now', 'Step back', 'Stand still'.
- Send for help and get rid of the audience (the rest of the students).
- Wait for help (if possible).
- Do not argue and do not respond to verbal abuse.
- Use physical intervention only as a last resort, and then only if policies permit and you are well trained in its use.

Where violence occurs between students, such as a physical fight, it is often better to wait for assistance rather than attempt to intervene. Many schools offer training, such as non-violent crisis intervention, to assist adults working with students to implement strategies to de-escalate challenging situations.

SCENARIO

CRISIS INTERVENTION

JB

JB (14 years), who we met in the Scenario 'Crisis intervention', is learning skills to manage his anger. When JB arrived at school this morning, it was clear that he was in a bad mood. He threw his bag on the floor, kicked his chair back with his foot and then began to pace around. He angrily yelled at another student who happened to glance at him, *'What are you looking at, moron?'* The ESW, **Peter**, suggested to JB that he might like to spend some time alone and practise some relaxation techniques. JB responded by deliberately bumping his shoulder into Peter as he walked away. Peter ignored this provocation as he knew that if he confronted JB in his present mood things could get out of hand.

Richard, a colleague who witnessed this display from JB commented: *'Are you just going to let him get away with treating you like that? He deliberately bumped into you and that's assault. You should follow school policy on student violence and report him.'*

Peter responded: *'Yes, it probably does fit the legal definition of assault. I'd like the chance to talk to JB before I take any action. I'm not condoning his behaviour but reporting him and having him suspended or expelled isn't going to help him. I will talk to Kate (school counsellor) about it and see what she thinks we should do.'*

▶ DISCUSSION

Discuss Peter's decision not to immediately respond to JB's shoulder-bumping provocation. Was it a wise decision? Why or why not?

ALICIA

Alicia (9 years) is prone to violent outbursts. She will throw things, push and hit others, and scream abuse. Other students know to steer clear of Alicia when she is in a bad mood.

Today, while working in a small group with ESW, **Rachel** and three other students, Alicia became enraged because the program on her iPad would not load. She slammed it onto the desk and began to abuse Rachel.

Alicia: *'You idiot, you've given me a broken iPad. I'm not doing this stupid game!'*

Rachel: *'Alicia, please sit down and take some deep breaths. When you have calmed down, I'll see what I can do to help you.'*

Alicia: *'No, I don't want your help!'* Alicia throws her pencil case at Rachel, which hits her in the chest. Rachel calmly tells the other students to move to the library area.

The teacher is alert to the situation and is ready to intervene. All the students in the class are now looking at Alicia. Rachel then tells Alicia that she needs to stop, sit down and rest her head on the table. This is a strategy that has worked in the past with Alicia.

WHAT DOES THIS TELL US?

Responding with anger when a student is out of control or very angry does not help to de-escalate the situation. Often students who are out of control are frightened by their own anger and need an adult to respond calmly. This can help the student to regain control and feel safe.

▶ DISCUSSION

Should the teacher have intervened immediately?
Why might the teacher have chosen not to intervene?

Summary

Key to WHS is the consistent application of WHS policies and practices in the workplace. This application is the responsibility of everyone – workers and employers alike. It is essential beginning ESWs take the time to become familiar with the potential hazards in the workplace and the associated risks and apply appropriate strategies to eliminate or minimise these hazards. This includes risks from infection, disease, physical activity and the physical work environment, as well as recognising and responding appropriately to harassment, bullying and stress.

▶

This chapter has explored WHS and student health and safety, both of which require a safe physical environment and safe work practices. WHS is the responsibility of adults – policymakers, school executive, teachers, ESWs and other school staff. Responsibility for student health and safety also includes parents and carers as well as the students themselves (where appropriate).

All members of the school community, including visitors, have the right to be in a safe environment. Documented health and safety policies and procedures provide a framework for keeping staff and students safe. However, to be effective, all employers must be familiar with and comply with these policies and procedures.

Self-check questions

1 What is the primary purpose of Safe Work Australia?
2 What is a key principle of the Model WHS Act?
3 Why must the employer exercise due diligence?
4 All workers must take reasonable care to ensure their own health and safety. List three responsibilities of the employee.
5 Define WHS notifiable incidents.
6 Determine whether each of the following statements is true or false.
   a WHS workplace systems may vary from one workplace to another.
   b Risk is a situation or thing that has the potential to harm a person.
   c Bullying, racism, sexual harassment and student violence are psychological hazards in school settings.
   d Personal protective equipment (PPE) is an important control measure that minimises the risk of injury or infection to workers and is always effective.
7 What are four key steps of risk management?
8 How are dangerous chemicals regulated in the workplace?
9 What does 'care plan' refer to in terms of students with disability?
10 As an ESW, how should you respond to a physical attack at school?

Discussion questions

1 You are in the classroom and there are several posters displayed higher than you can reach. You locate a ladder and position it carefully under the posters. As you take the poster off the wall, the swing of the poster puts you off balance and you topple off the ladder. Luckily, nothing is broken – you just have dented pride and a broken chair.
   a Who is responsible for the care, health and safety of you, the ESW, in this case?
2 On your way into the office this morning, you noticed that the stormwater grate was elevated in one corner, creating a hazard. With your hands full you were not able to tend to it on the way in.
   a Now that you have reached your classroom, what action should you take to make the storm water drain safe?
3 Gastro is going around the school. One of your students comes to class after morning break and explains she has a pain in the stomach. You make the decision to take her to sick bay where the nurse will provide supportive care. Unfortunately, on the way over, Melissa vomits in the hallway. Not only is she now embarrassed in front of the class of students, but you need to clean the area. Before moving on, you segregate the area with chairs and inform the nearest teacher to keep an eye out for passing students.
   a What PPE will you need to take back to the hallway with you to clean up the vomit?

Activities

1 At your school, what is the procedure for reporting a notifiable incident, such as an accident or a near miss?

2 Looking around at your classroom or workspace, identify hazards that may fall into the following categories:

- a Chemical
- b Biological
- c Physical
- d Ergonomic
- e Psychological

3 Take the time to look over **Figure 4.16** Office ergonomics. Using it as a prompt, arrange your workstation according to the principles of office ergonomics as listed in the image.

4 Participate in an emergency procedure with your classmates or at your school. This may be a lockdown or emergency evacuation. Take note of the role an ESW has.

5 What process does your school have in place for when you need to respond to violence or threats by students?

Chapter 5

STUDENT HEALTH, SAFETY AND WELLBEING

LEARNING OBJECTIVES

When you have completed this chapter, you should be able to demonstrate that, in relation to working in a school environment, you can:

5.1 provide guidance and support and take appropriate steps to maintain a safe environment

5.2 provide assistance with the general care and wellbeing of students, attend to students with minor illnesses and identify health issues according to organisational policies and procedures

5.3 maintain the classroom in a clean and tidy condition and respond appropriately to students who require assistance with personal care or hygiene

5.4 identify physical, psychological and logistical risks that may impede the active supervision of students

5.5 supervise students outside the classroom according to teacher direction and school policy and procedures

5.6 use verbal and non-verbal techniques that acknowledge and influence student behaviour

5.7 establish expectations for student behaviour according to student wellbeing models.

Online resources icons refer to useful weblinks. Ask your instructor for these **Online Resources.**

Introduction

This chapter explores the role of the ESW in supporting the health, safety and wellbeing of children and young people. The health and wellbeing of the student population will vary significantly and is influenced by a range of factors, such as:

- ability/disability
- medical conditions
- socioeconomic status – which impact on income, housing, geographic location, nutrition, access to health and social services, opportunities for entertainment and sports, and for teenagers in particular, access to technology

- family life and life experiences – including supportive and nurturing adults, stability, exposure to drugs/alcohol and domestic violence, child abuse, caring for disabled parent, parental attitudes to education
- personality and temperament
- sexual orientation.

Each student will have unique strengths and needs. All students benefit from the care and support of positive, nurturing adults who have the child's or young person's best interests as central to their thinking and actions.

Schools can be a safe haven for many students, offering a degree of respite from family stress and challenging life situations. ESWs are in the unique position of being able to provide support and act as a positive role model as they work with students. Supporting all children and young people to build their self-esteem, confidence and resilience should underpin all interactions.

Before exploring the health, safety and wellbeing of children and young people, it is important to take a moment to reflect on what is known about Australia's children and young people. As you read the snapshots in **Figure 5.1**, think about how this knowledge will assist you when working with students in your care.

Figure 5.1 A snapshot of children and young people in Australia

English as a second language

Approximately **9%** of children born overseas

Personal injury

Leading cause of death and a major cause of disability among adolescents

22% of 16–17-year-olds missed multiple days of school or work due to an injury in the previous two years

Alcohol consumption

Around **28%** of teens aged 16–17 allowed to drink alcohol at home

Approximately **18%** permitted to take alcohol to parties or social events

Discrimination

Many teenagers experience discrimination on multiple grounds (e.g. race and sex)

Body discrimination (due to body size, shape or physical appearance) the most widespread type of discrimination among teens overall

Mental health

Most young people are happy, feel positive about the future and are satisfied with their lives overall

Almost 1 in 7 4–17-year-olds assessed as having mental health disorders (2013–14)

4 in 10 15–19-year-olds identified mental health as a top issue (2018)

Sources: Based on Australian Bureau of Statistics data: Australian Bureau of Statistics (2022). ABS 2071.0 – Census of Population and Housing: Reflecting Australia – Stories from the Census, 2016 (June 2017); Australian Institute of Family Studies, Growing Up in Australia: The Longitudinal Study of Australian: Children Annual Statistical Report 2017 (2018); Australian Human Rights Commission. *Children's Rights Report 2019.* In Their Own Right: Children's Rights in Australia. https://www.humanrights.gov.au/our-work/childrens-rights/publications, pp. 28–30.

CONSIDER THIS

Reflect on the information provided in the snapshot about children and young people in **Figure 5.1**. What situations would you find most challenging?

5.1 Maintaining a safe environment

There are many policies, procedures and laws to help ESWs maintain a safe environment for children and young people.

School policies

All schools will have a range of policies and procedures related to the health, safety and wellbeing of students. According to the Association of Independent Schools South Australia (2016), the aim of these policies is to:

- develop a shared understanding across the whole school community of the importance of student health, safety and wellbeing
- provide clear advice on the roles and responsibilities of students, parents, caregivers and teachers in relation to student health, safety and wellbeing
- identify specific responses to and management strategies relating to certain student health, safety and wellbeing issues
- include strategies for developing and implementing whole school health, safety and wellbeing programs
- develop a communications plan to promote the policy and ensure the whole school is aware of and understands the content of the policy.

Health, safety and welfare policies are typically underpinned by a philosophy of care and support, for example:

- to reinforce that the emotional and physical wellbeing of students is pivotal to their success at school, as children and adolescents, and in their future lives
- to promote the provision of a safe, healthy and secure learning environment for all
- to ensure awareness of relevant health, safety and wellbeing strategies and practices implemented by the school
- to ensure that all reported incidents relating to student health, safety and wellbeing are dealt with in an appropriate manner
- to identify how a school will develop environments that are engaging, supportive and conducive to learning
- to identify links to other relevant policies within the school, i.e. anti-bullying and harassment, and encourage students to take active steps in tackling bullying, prejudice and other behaviours that have a negative impact on wellbeing.

Source: Association of Independent Schools South Australia (2016). Student Health, *Safety & Wellbeing: Policy Guidelines*. https://www.ais.sa.edu.au/wp-content/uploads/Pages/Policy_Resources/Student-Health-Safety-Wellbeing-Policy-Guidelines.pdf, pp. 5–6.

Figure 5.2 lists examples of school policies related to student health, safety and wellbeing. Links to policy information can be found on your state/territory public schools website.

Respect, privacy and confidentiality

All students and families have a right to be treated with dignity and respect. Student and family information that is personal, sensitive or relates to health needs (including mental health) should only be shared on a need-to-know basis and, if possible, with the consent of the student and/or parent/guardian.

Figure 5.2 Student health, safety and wellbeing policies

Health	Duty of care (see also Chapter 2)	Student support services
> Administration of medications > Anaphylaxis management > Asthma management > First aid > Head lice screening > Immunisation status > Management of prescribed contagious conditions > Management of students with specialised health needs > Road safety > Sun safety and managing excessive heat in schools	> Child protection > Emergency evacuation/lockdown > Excursions > Photographing, filming or recording students > Privacy and confidentiality > Safe food handling > Safe use of equipment and machinery > Undertaking sports such as bushwalking, surfing, swimming, horse riding, paddling, etc. > Use of social media	> Anti-discrimination/racism > Bullying > Child and family violence > Child-safe organisations > Cyber safety > Drug education and intervention > Supporting students' mental health and wellbeing

All parents are required to disclose specific information about their child and the family at the time of enrolment. Examples of information that must be provided include the immunisation status of the child, any medical conditions the child may have and details of court orders, parenting orders or parenting plans.

The primary purpose of collecting information about students and families is to meet legal obligations and make informed decisions/reasonable adjustment in relation to student education, health and wellbeing needs in consultation with families and students.

Legal information that must be supplied at the time of enrolment includes:

- child's birth certificate or identity documents
- proof of address, such as current council rates notice, residential lease, electricity bill
- immunisation history statement from the Australian Immunisation Register
- any family law or other relevant court orders, if applicable
- copies of medical/healthcare or emergency action plan and evidence of any disability and learning and support plans (NSW Government, 2020).

Examples of information of a personal nature that a parent or guardian may share at the time of enrolment (or when the need arises) include challenging behaviours, personality/temperament issues, anxieties, phobias, family circumstances that have impacted on the child or young person's wellbeing, traumatic life experiences such as loss of home due to bushfire, floods or financial insecurity, and issues around sexual identity.

Sharing information of a sensitive nature can be quite difficult for parents, especially when such information is emotionally distressing. Consider, for example, how a parent may feel about confiding information about family breakdown, domestic violence, custody orders, financial hardship or health issues such as parental mental illness or addiction. Of course, not all families and/or students wish to share sensitive information and this should be respected.

Privacy legislation

While there is no legislation that specifically identifies a child's right to privacy, Article 16 of the UN Convention on the Rights of the Child states that children have the right to privacy.

In Australia, the *Privacy Act 1988* provides for the protection of personal information and applies to all states and territories. The Privacy Act regulates how personal information is managed, including:

- how personal information is collected
- how it is used and disclosed
- its accuracy
- how securely it is kept
- the individual's general right to access their personal information.

Examples of school privacy/ confidentiality policies and guidelines

Alongside the Privacy Act, all states and territories have legislation related to privacy and personal information protection (and complaints related to breach of privacy), as well as the privacy and confidentiality of health records. Schools may also have a records management policy and an internal policy for the handling and storage of sensitive information which also aims to protect the student and family's right to privacy. School privacy and confidentiality policies must comply with this legislation.

NEED TO KNOW

SCENARIO

During an executive meeting, the **Deputy Principal** advised team members that **Evan** (6 years) Brown's father can now only see his son on supervised access visits. His father is not allowed to collect Evan from school or attend any school events. Any telephone calls from **Mr Brown** must be directed to the Deputy Principal. The school was also advised by the police that Mr Brown can be extremely aggressive and had threatened to *'take Evan from school and disappear'*. The police advised that if Mr Brown goes to the school or is seen waiting outside the school the police should be contacted immediately.

The Deputy Principal stated he would inform Evan's teacher and Evan's ESW and stress that the information was strictly confidential and not to be shared with other staff. The Deputy Principal also stated that Evan had witnessed several episodes of domestic violence and it was important that his behaviour and emotional wellbeing be closely monitored.

WHAT DOES THIS TELL US?

There will be occasions when confidential information about a child and family must be shared with members of staff. Often this information is of a highly sensitive and personal nature and should always be regarded as confidential. Information typically is shared on a need-to-know basis. In this scenario, information is shared to ensure that Evan is protected from exposure to further trauma and violence. The information will also alert the teacher and ESW that any changes in behaviour or Evan's emotional state should be closely monitored and support provided as needed.

When sensitive information about a student/family is shared with an ESW, it should always be treated as confidential. Necessary professional discussions about the student should only take place in private, where it can be assured that such discussion will not be overheard by students, other teachers, administrators, parents or visitors to the school.

Immunisation

Schools are required to maintain records of each child's immunisation status and to notify health authorities should there be an outbreak of immunisation-preventable disease. Parents are required by law to provide evidence of the immunisation status of their children prior to enrolment.

At the time of enrolment (or transfer), parents must provide an approved immunisation certificate that shows their child's immunisation status, including that the child:

- is fully immunised for their age, or
- is not fully immunised for their age, or

- has a medical reason not to be vaccinated, or
- is on a recognised catch-up schedule if the child has fallen behind with their immunisations.

Schools are required to:

- record each child's immunisation status in a register and retain copies of approved immunisation certificates for a period of three years after the child has ceased to attend the school
- provide a copy of a child's immunisation certificate to another school that the child has transferred to (upon request)
- notify the public health unit if an enrolled child has a vaccine-preventable disease, or if they reasonably believe that an unimmunised enrolled child has come into contact with someone who has a vaccine-preventable disease
- exclude unimmunised children at risk of contracting a disease from attending school on the direction of a public health officer.

Figure 5.3 provides a list of vaccine-preventable diseases that must be notified by the school to the public health authority.

Figure 5.3 Notification of vaccine-preventable disease

Disease	Description
Diphtheria	Bacterial disease spread by respiratory droplets – causes severe throat and breathing difficulties, nerve paralysis and heart failure
Tetanus	Caused by toxin of bacteria in soil – causes painful muscle spasms, convulsions and lockjaw
Pertussis (whooping cough)	Bacterial disease spread by respiratory droplets – causes 'whooping cough' with prolonged cough lasting up to three months
Haemophilus influenzae type b (Hib)	Bacterial disease spread by respiratory droplets – causes meningitis (infection of tissues around brain), epiglottitis (blockage of airway), septicaemia (blood infection) and septic arthritis (joint infection)
Polio	Virus spread in faeces and saliva – causes fever, headache and vomiting and may progress to paralysis
Measles	Highly infectious virus spread by respiratory droplets – causes fever, cough and rash
Mumps	Virus spread by saliva – causes swollen neck and salivary glands and fever
Rubella	Virus spread by respiratory droplets and causes fever, rash and swollen glands but can cause severe birth defects in babies of infected pregnant women
Meningococcal C	Bacteria spread by respiratory droplets – causes septicaemia (blood infection) and meningitis (infection of tissues around brain)

Source: NSW Ministry of Health (2018). Immunisation Enrolment Toolkit. For Primary and Secondary Schools from 1 April 2018. https://www.health.nsw.gov.au/immunisation/Pages/school-immunisation-enrolment-toolkit.aspx

School vaccination programs currently include:

- *12–13 years:* human papillomavirus (HPV); diphtheria, tetanus, pertussis (whooping cough)
- *14–16 years:* meningococcal ACWY.

The National Health and Medical Research Council (NHMRC) recommends that teachers and others working in schools be protected against vaccine-preventable diseases including: measles; mumps; rubella; pertussis (whooping cough); varicella (chickenpox); and influenza (NSW Ministry of Health, 2018, p. 13).

Immunisation programs and requirements

Food safety standards and school canteens

School canteens that are privately operated may, in some states and territories, be considered a retail food business and must therefore comply with food safety legislation. Food safety is particularly important in the prevention of food-borne diseases.

Food poisoning can be caused by eating food contaminated with bacteria, viruses, chemicals or poisonous metals such as lead or cadmium. Food can become contaminated when:

- a person preparing or serving food does not wash their hands properly, or has poor hygiene
- food is touched by someone who is ill with gastroenteritis
- food comes into contact with animals, flies or other pests
- ready-to-eat foods come into contact with raw meat – called 'cross-contamination'
- food is cooked or stored at the incorrect temperature (Department of Health (WA), 2013).

Most food poisoning is caused by one of four bacteria:

- *Staphylococcus*: these bacteria are found on the skin, in sores, in infected eyes and in the nose, throat, saliva and bowel of humans.
- *Salmonella*: there are hundreds of different types of salmonella bacteria, but not all are harmful to humans. They are found mainly in the intestines, bowels and faeces of humans and other animals. It is the salmonella bacteria themselves that can cause salmonella food poisoning.
- *Clostridium*: these bacteria are found in soil and in the intestines of animals, including cattle, poultry, fish and humans.
- *Campylobacter*: these bacteria are found in many animals, including dogs, cats, cattle and poultry.

Key practices to minimise the risk of food contamination include:

- personal hygiene practices such as handwashing
- cleaning and sanitising
- storing food at the correct temperature
- cooking and reheating food correctly
- correct procedures for taking delivery of and storing foods delivered.

For children and young people with food allergies, it's also important to ensure the staff and volunteers working in the canteen are aware of what can cause allergies.

Figure 5.4 Emergency first aid kits are placed in strategic locations around the school

Source: Photo by Tish Okely © Cengage

5.2 Supporting student health and wellbeing

First aid

Often ESWs take on the role of first aid officer in schools. Responsibilities for this role may typically include providing first aid for minor injuries to students and adults, assessing students for signs of minor illnesses, administering prescribed medications, supervising younger children who require asthma prevention or are having an asthma episode, administering adrenaline auto-injectors in the event of an anaphylaxis emergency, and checking and maintaining first aid supplies (see **Figure 5.4**).

Minor illness and health screening

A quick scan of a student who presents as unwell can be a valuable tool for preventing the spread of infectious disease. **Figure 5.5** shows what signs to look for in students when scanning for illness.

Figure 5.5 Signs and symptoms of illness

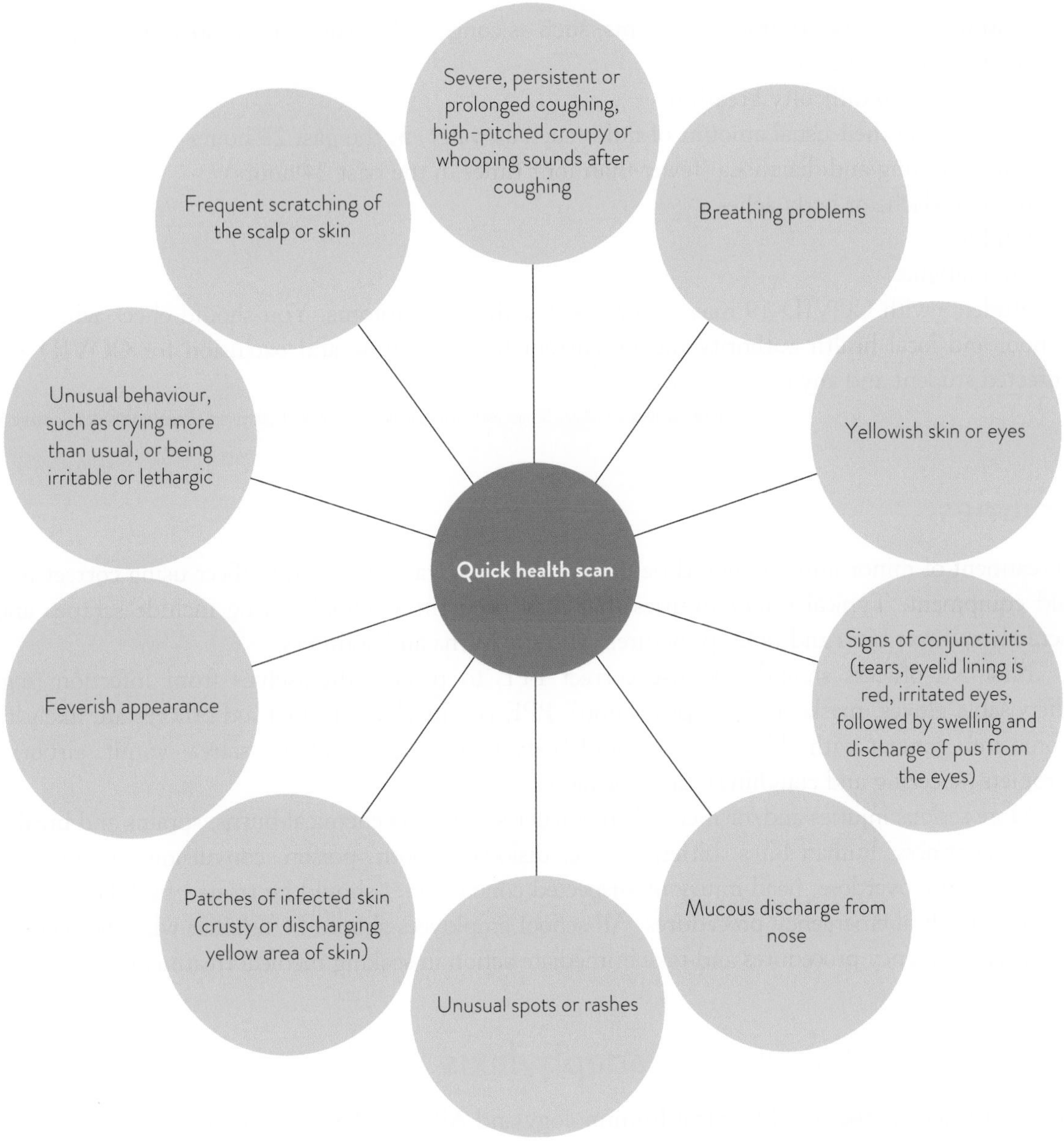

Source: Robertson (1998), p. 65

Minor illnesses in school settings may include:

- slight fever – temperature (over 38°C)
- slight cold and cough, sore throat
- tooth or earache
- sore eyes – may be conjunctivitis (redness, sore and watery eyes, with pus swelling)
- 'non severe' stomach ache, headache
- rash

- scabies – an infestation of mites (tiny insects) that burrow under the skin causing intense itching and sometimes a rash
- hand, foot and mouth disease – symptoms include fever and tiny blisters on the cheeks and gums, inside the mouth and on the hands and feet
- head lice (while not a disease is easily and quickly spread).

COVID-19 symptoms range in severity. The following are considered mild symptoms in children:

- mild upper respiratory tract symptoms, such as congested or runny nose, sneezing, or a scratchy or sore throat
- cough with no difficulty breathing
- not drinking their usual amount of fluid (such as water) in the past 24 hours
- mild vomiting and diarrhoea (fewer than four times in the past 24 hours)
- mild headache or body aches
- mild fever
- mild fatigue.

Students with COVID-19 may also present with no symptoms. You should check with your school and local health authority on the current testing regime and exclusion for COVID-19-infected student and any close contacts.

Source: healthdirect (2022). School exclusion periods. https://www.healthdirect.gov.au/school-exclusion-periods

Injuries

Treatment of minor injuries should be undertaken by a trained first aid officer using correct first aid equipment. Typical minor injuries that may occur in a school setting include scrapes and scratches, insect bites and ticks, punctures, blisters, burns and splinters.

First aid officers should also use correct PPE to protect themselves from infection (e.g. disposable gloves, masks and eye protection). PPE is critical where first aid officers are likely to come into contact with skin infections and body fluids such as blood, saliva, vomit, airborne droplets (sneezing and coughing), urine or faeces.

Calling an ambulance

More serious injuries and/or medical emergencies – such as chemical burns, sprains and breaks, unconsciousness, human bites, bitten tongue, dislodged tooth, poison, convulsion, eye injuries, choking, drug overdose, head injury or suspected concussion – should be treated by following the school's medical emergency procedures. All school employees should be familiar with the school's medical emergency procedures and take immediate action in seeking medical treatment.

Managing allergies and anaphylaxis

The Australasian Society of Clinical Immunology and Allergy (ASCIA) states:

> An allergy is when the immune system reacts to a substance (allergen) in the environment which is usually harmless (e.g. a food, pollen, animal, dust mites), or to an insect bite or sting, or to a medication. The most common causes of allergic reactions in Australia are to foods (most commonly, peanut, egg, milk, tree nuts, soy, wheat, fish, shellfish and sesame), insect stings or bites (e.g. bee, wasp, jack jumper ant) and medications (e.g. painkillers and antibiotics).

Source: Australasian Society of Clinical Immunology and Allergy Ltd (ASCIA). https://www.allergy.org.au

Severe allergies can be life-threatening, as reactions can be sudden and violent. In serious cases, reactions can occur as a result of ingestion or absorption through the skin. Where children and young people are known to have serious allergies or intolerances to food, it is essential that employees working with the student are aware of the foods or products that may cause a severe allergic reaction.

Anaphylaxis is the most severe form of allergic reaction, and it often involves more than one body system (e.g. skin, respiratory, gastrointestinal, cardiovascular). It usually occurs within 20 minutes to two hours of exposure to the trigger and can rapidly become life-threatening, so it must be treated immediately. The most common causes of anaphylaxis are allergies to some foods, such as eggs, cow's milk, soy, peanuts, sesame, shellfish, food additives and preservatives. In extreme cases, anaphylaxis can occur from skin contact or even the smell of certain foods.

The signs and symptoms of anaphylaxis (see **Figure 5.6**) may occur almost immediately after exposure or within the first 20 minutes after exposure. Information on the symptoms and treatment of allergies and anaphylaxis is updated regularly. Refer to the ASCIA website (**https://www.allergy.org.au**) for current information and advice.

Figure 5.6 Common symptoms of anaphylaxis

Mild to moderate allergic reaction	Watch for any one of the following signs of anaphylaxis
• Swelling of lips, face, eyes • Hives or welts • Tingling mouth • Abdominal pain, vomiting (These are signs of a severe allergic reaction to insects.) Mild to moderate allergic reactions may or may not precede anaphylaxis.	• Difficult/noisy breathing • Swelling of tongue • Swelling/tightness in throat • Difficulty talking and/or hoarse voice • Wheeze or persistent cough • Persistent dizziness or collapse • Pale and floppy (young children).

Where a student is known to have a severe allergy, a written Anaphylaxis Action Plan must be put in place, in consultation with the student's parents and doctor. The plan will usually include:

ASCIA action plans for anaphylaxis

- a photo of the student
- parent/guardian contact details
- details of the medical practitioner completing the Action Plan
- a list of confirmed allergens
- the required the first aid response
- the prescribed medication
- instructions on AAI (adrenaline [epinephrine] autoinjectors) administration (if prescribed).

ASCIA's guidelines for prevention of anaphylaxis recommend the following steps:

1. Obtain up-to-date medical information and develop a health-care plan.
2. Staff training in recognition and management of acute allergic reactions.
3. Awareness that unexpected allergic reactions might occur for the first time outside of home in those not previously identified as being at high risk.
4. Age-appropriate education of children and young people with severe allergies and their peers.
5. Implementation of practical strategies to reduce the risk of accidental exposure to known allergic triggers.
6. Consideration of institutional provision of AAIs for general use.

An emergency kit with an AAI (e.g. Epi-pen), containing a single, fixed dose of adrenaline, will typically be kept at the school. There should be at least one person on duty at all times who is trained to administer the device. ASCIA also provides a form that can be used to record an allergic event.

Reducing allergens in schools

By school age, most children who are known to have a severe allergy have been taught to eat only food given to them by the parent. However, for children and young people with additional needs, their ability to know which foods are a danger will be limited.

Asthma management

Asthma information for schools

Asthma is a reversible narrowing of the airways in the lungs where the lining of the airways swells and produces sticky mucus. Asthma attacks may be triggered by a range of things, including dust mites, pollen, animal hair/skin, mould, cigarette smoke, viral infections (colds, flu, etc.), weather conditions (such as cold air, changes in temperature, thunderstorms), some medicines, stress/crying, wood dust, chemicals, metals and salts (National Asthma Council Australia, 2013a).

Asthma symptoms include wheezing, coughing (particularly at night), chest tightness, difficulty breathing and shortness of breath. The National Asthma Council Australia (2013b) also advises that younger children with asthma may present with other symptoms, such as not eating or drinking as much as usual, crying, stomach ache and vomiting, tiring quickly and getting more puffed out than usual when running and playing.

Children and young people who are known to suffer from asthma should have an Asthma Action Plan that has been prepared by their doctor. It will include the following information:

- a list of the child's usual asthma preventer and other medicines, including doses
- instructions for what to do when asthma is getting worse (including when to take extra doses or extra medicines, and when to contact a doctor or go to the emergency department)
- what to do in an asthma emergency
- name and contact details of the child's or young person's doctor
- emergency contact details
- date of the plan.

Schools should have a person on duty at all times who has completed approved emergency asthma management training and anaphylaxis management training. In the case of asthma management training, this includes the use of relievers, such as puffer and spacer devices.

Managing medications

According to the Australian Institute of Health and Welfare (AIHW), chronic conditions, also known as long-term conditions or non-communicable diseases, refer to a wide range of conditions, illnesses and diseases that tend to be long lasting with persistent effects. The AIHW (2022) reports that:

- for 2017–18, asthma, hay fever and allergic rhinitis, anxiety-related problems and psychological development problems were the four leading chronic conditions for children aged 0–14, based on self-reported proxy data from the ABS National Health Survey
- among all children aged 5–14, asthma was the leading cause of disease burden followed by mental health disorders
- the fifth most commonly reported chronic condition was food allergies.

Source: Australian Institute of Health and Welfare (2022). Chronic conditions and burden of disease. Australia's children. 25 February. https://www.aihw.gov.au/reports/children-youth/australias-children/contents/health/chronic-conditions-and-burden-of-disease

To manage both chronic and short-term disease, schools must have a range of policies and procedures, such as:

- authorisation forms for prescribed and non-prescribed medications (see **Figure 5.7**)
- administration of medications and medications records (see **Figure 5.8**)

Chronic conditions and burden of disease

Figure 5.7 Authorisation for administration of medication prescribed and non-prescribed

ASPIRATION GROWTH COURAGE RESPECT

DEPARTMENT OF EDUCATION learners first

AUTHORISATION FOR ADMINISTRATION OF STUDENT MEDICATION

FORM A: Non-prescription medication – to be completed by Parent/Carer

Student name: ______________________ Date of birth: ______________________

School: ______________________ Year level: ______________________

NON-PRESCRIBED medication to be given to student during school hours:

Name of medication	Expiry date	Dose	Route (mouth, nasal spray etc.)	Frequency or Time	Relation to meals or N/A	In original container?*	Student permitted to self-administer?
						Yes / No	Yes / No
						Yes / No	Yes / No
						Yes / No	Yes / No
						Yes / No	Yes / No
						Yes / No	Yes / No
						Yes / No	Yes / No
						Yes / No	Yes / No

I understand that this form provides authorisation for administration, or self-administration (if indicated) of non-prescribed medication to the student named. I understand that I should notify the school IMMEDIATELY if this information changes. *I understand that all medication MUST be supplied in the original container or Webster-pak, and that the school cannot administer medication if it is not supplied in the original container or Webster-pak.

Parent/Carer Name: ______________________ Relationship to student: ______________________

Address: ______________________ Phone number: ______________________

Signature: ______________________ Date: ______________________

Personal information collected on this form is used to provide support services for your child. This will only be used for the primary purpose for which it is gathered, except where authorised or mandated by legislative requirements (e.g. Mandatory Reporting). For further information, contact Learning Services.

Tasmanian Government

ASPIRATION GROWTH COURAGE RESPECT

DEPARTMENT OF EDUCATION learners first

AUTHORISATION FOR ADMINISTRATION OF STUDENT MEDICATION

FORM B: Prescription medication – to be completed by Doctor/Pharmacist/Practise Nurse

Student name: ______________________ Date of birth: ______________________

School: ______________________ Year level: ______________________

PRESCRIBED medication to be given to student during school hours:

Name of medication	Expiry date	Type of medication (e.g. S8, S4d)	Dose and route	Frequency or Time	Relation to meals or N/A	Side effects, if any	In original container with instructions?*	Student permitted to self-administer?
							Yes / No	Yes / No
							Yes / No	Yes / No
							Yes / No	Yes / No
							Yes / No	Yes / No
							Yes / No	Yes / No
							Yes / No	Yes / No

I understand that this form provides authorisation for administration, or self -administration (if indicated) of prescribed medication to the student named. I understand that I should notify the school IMMEDIATELY if this information changes. *I understand that all medication MUST be supplied in the original container or Webster-pak, and that the school cannot administer medication if it is not supplied in the original container or Webster -pak.

Name: ______________________ Profession (circle): Doctor / Pharmacist / Practise Nurse

Address: ______________________ Phone number: ______________________

Signature: ______________________ Date: ______________________

Parent/Guardian Signature: ______________________ Date: ______________________

Personal information collected on this form is used to provide support services for your child. This will only be used for the primary purpose for which it is gathered, except where authorised or mandated by legislative requirements (e.g. Mandatory Reporting). For further information, contact Learning Services.

Tasmanian Government

Source: © Government of Tasmania, Department for Education, Children and Young People. Licensed under a Creative Commons Attribution 4.0 International (CC BY 4.0) licence, https://creativecommons.org/licenses/by/4.0/

Figure 5.8 Medications record form

Record of medication administration (routine medication)

<Insert/attach student photo if required for identification purposes>

Student name		Date of birth		Class		Dosage time/s	
Medication						Route	

On receipt of the medication:

1. *Check that the medication is in the original container and is intact (e.g. tablets in blister packs are sealed)*
2. *Check for medical authorisation e.g. pharmacy label, other written authorisation*
3. *Advise the parent/carer that they will need to collect any unused medication when it is no longer required to be administered at school*
4. *Attach the completed* ***Consent to administer medication*** *form*
5. *Attach Individual Health Plan if one is required*
6. *Refer to all information when administering medication.*

Initial the appropriate box below to confirm when the medication was administered, or enter the appropriate code from the key below.

KEY: A – Student absent; **S** – Student self-administration; **P** – Parent/carer administered medication; **X** – School closed; **O** – Student off campus; **N/S** – No supply of medication→contact parent/carer; **R** – Student refused medication→contact parent/carer; **V** – Student vomited following medication→contact parent/carer

Note: The table allows for the recording of up to two doses of the medication per day. Amend the document electronically to add additional lines if more than two doses per day are required.

If a student requires multiple doses of the same medication at differing strengths, use one form per dose strength e.g. one form for Lamotrigine 25 mg and one form for Lamotrigine 50 mg.

MTH	DOSAGE TIME/S	DATE																														
		1	2	3	4	5	6	7	8	9	10	11	12	13	14	15	16	17	18	19	20	21	22	23	24	25	26	27	28	29	30	31
Jan																																
Feb																																
Mar																																

Student name		Date of birth		Class		Dosage time/s	
Medication						Route	

Uncontrolled copy. Refer to the Department of Education Policy and Procedure Register at https://ppr.qed.qld.gov.au/pp/administration-of-medications-in-schools-procedure to ensure you have the most current version of this document.

- storage of medications
- self-medication (e.g. ventolin, insulin)
- emergency medications (e.g. AAIs).

Medication should only be given with the written consent of the parent/guardian by completing the school's medication form. Management of medications must include correct and secure storage. This means:

- medications must be stored according to the product's written storage directions (in the case of medicines that must be refrigerated, these should be stored in a lock container)
- medications should be stored in a secure location that is accessible only to teachers, ESWs and/or first aid officers
- medications should not be stored in a first aid kit.

The Guidelines for the Administration of Medications in Schools state that some students require medication to be kept with them (or close by) to manage their individual health needs (Department of Education Queensland, n.d., p. 23). For this to occur the principal and parent/s must sign a written agreement. For example, 'The school has agreed to (student's name) carrying this medication to and at school. I have outlined below how this arrangement will occur at school (insert agreed details of how and where the student will carry their medication)' (Education NSW, 2020).

Regardless of storage requirements, educators must be aware of, and monitor the safe storage and use of these medications.

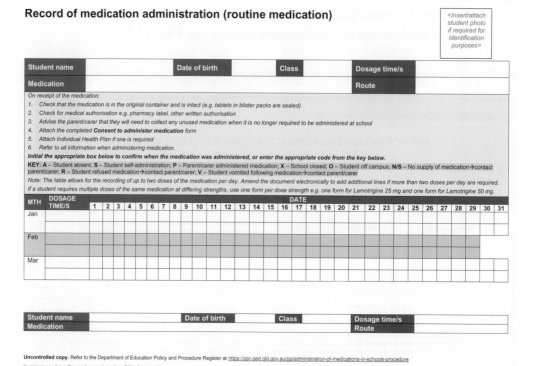

Administering medications

Before administering a medication, the person responsible should check the following:

- ☑ medication is in the original container
- ☑ the name on the medication matches the names of the student
- ☑ the expiry date – medication that has expired should not be administered
- ☑ the dosage instruction – amount, when and under what circumstance (e.g. with food)
- ☑ the route – how the medication should be administered.

The 'five rights' for administering medication is an effective safety guide that can be used by schools (see **Figure 5.9**).

Figure 5.9 The 'five rights' of medication administration

1 Right person	Check the identity of the student – i.e. use of a photograph, ask student their full name and/or their date of birth
2 Right drug	Drugs have both a trade and generic name, which can cause confusion. Refer to the medication container for the 'generic' name, to match the medication identified on authorisation form Check it is the right drug when the drug is taken from the secure location – check the name printed on the medication and the expiry date
3 Right dose	Medications are designed to be given with specific intervals between doses to ensure consistent therapeutic blood levels. If given at times different to those ordered, the drug may be less effective or may cause side effects
4 Right time	The label may say, for example, 'three times daily' – check the authorisation form to see when the medication was last administered. It may say 'with food' or 'before food'
5 Right route	Medications have specific 'routes of administration'. Common routes of administration include: topical (apply to skin); oral (by mouth) – ensure medication has been swallowed; injection (subcutaneous injection – i.e. insulin injection under the skin); sublingual (under the tongue); gastric feeding tube; nasal (through the nose); inhalation – i.e. asthma medication (puffer or spacer).

Source: Adapted from Diocese of Broken Bay (2016). Administration of medication in schools procedures. https://www.skmvdbb.catholic.edu.au/wp-content/uploads/2017/12/Medication-Procedures-2016.pdf, pp. 6–7.

Non-compliance

Non-compliance may occur for several reasons – for example, acting-out behaviour, cognitive disability, the student feeling unwell or fear of side effects. Where a student refuses the administration of medication, the incident should be documented and reported to the student's teacher, who in turn will notify the parent/guardian. Where non-compliance is an ongoing issue, it will be necessary to collaborate with the parent/guardian, treating doctor and, if possible, the student to resolve the issue.

Non-prescribed medications

Families may use non-prescribed medications, such as over-the-counter cough and cold medication or herbal/naturopathic medications, to treat children's minor illnesses. Each school will have a policy in place in relation to non-prescribed medications. It is common for schools to prohibit the administration of non-prescribed medications, as part of their duty of care obligation, due to risks such as overmedicating, poisoning, allergic reaction and lack of knowledge about ingredients (especially in relation to herbal/naturopathic medications).

Self-medication

There will be circumstances where the child or young person is able to self-administer their own medication. In these situations, written consent must be given by the parent/guardian and supported with a letter from the student's treating doctor. According to Education NSW (2020), the principal's decision to allow self-medication must be based on the following considerations:

- the ability and maturity level of the student
- relevant parental and medical advice
- the complexity of the administration of the prescribed medication procedure
- the willingness of the student to self administer
- the level of support required in an emergency.

An example of a self-medication assessment checklist is shown in **Figure 5.10**.

Medication management and specific health issues

Where a student is approved to self-medicate, the medication is usually stored following the same procedures used to store prescribed medications. An exception to this may be asthma reliever medications used by young people. Education NSW (n.d.) states: 'For some medications and some students it can be appropriate for them to carry their own medication to school and at school, for example, EpiPen® or Anapen® for anaphylaxis and asthma reliever medication for asthma.' Students may carry this medication on their person, in a medical pouch or bum bag.

It should be remembered that schools have a duty of care to ensure the safety and wellbeing of students. Where a student is approved to self-medicate, the school should arrange for the student to be supervised and monitored.

5.3 Meeting personal care and hygiene needs

Under the *Disability Discrimination Act 1992* (Cth) and the *Disability Standards for Education 2005*, education providers have three main types of obligations. They must consult, make reasonable adjustments and eliminate harassment and victimisation.

'Reasonable adjustments' for students with disability requires schools to put in place strategies to allow students with disability to participate in education *on the same basis* as students without disability.

'Consultation' could include:

- talking with the student and their family members or carers, to get ideas about the type of assistance that is needed
- discussing ways to overcome the barriers and the adjustments that could be made by the education provider, and whether these adjustments are reasonable
- providing any relevant medical and therapist reports that help to explain the disability (Department of Education and Training, 2014).

Figure 5.10 Self-medication assessment checklist

FACTORS FOR CONSIDERATION	Yes/No
The student can:	
• follow a timetable for administering medication (where it is required routinely at set times)	
• recognise signs and symptoms that indicate they need to administer their medication (when it is required 'as-needed')	
• confidently, competently and safely administer their own medication following all instructions (e.g. on pharmacy label, in health plans)	
• follow infection control guidelines	
• demonstrate safe storage of medication as medication may be potentially harmful to other students	
• demonstrate appropriate storage of medication e.g. when medication is required to be kept at a certain temperature	
• safely dispose of sharps, equipment or other medication consumables (where relevant)	
• ensure their medication is in-date.	
Other students who are in the proximity of a student self-administering can behave appropriately to maintain a safe and respectful environment for the student self-administering medication.	

Source: Adapted from 'Guidelines for the administration of medications in schools', https://ppr.qed.qld.gov.au/pp/administration-of-medications-in-schools-procedure. Licensed under the Creative Commons Attribution 4.0 International licence (CC BY 4.0), https://creativecommons.org/licenses/by/4.0/deed.en

According to the Department of Education and Training (n.d.), effective consultation is based on the following principles:

- *student focused* – the needs and wishes of the student are central to the consultation process
- *mutual respect* – there is respect for all stakeholders (student, family, school, other professionals)
- *accessibility and transparency* – information and information sources are shared
- *balancing power* – the role of the student, the family and the school are respected
- *fairness* – there is a commitment to fairness, equity and reaching a mutually agreed consensus
- *accountability* – consultations and decisions are documented and there is a process for ongoing review.

Schools will also have personal hygiene learning plans for students in need of hygiene and personal care. These plans detail how the school will support the student – for example, blowing and wiping nose, washing hands, washing face after eating, dressing/undressing and toileting care (including menstrual health management). Plans are developed in collaboration with a parent/guardian, the student (where possible) and any health professionals involved with the student. The plan identifies the student's hygiene and personal care needs and the strategies that will be used by the ESW in carrying out the care. The plan may also indicate what the student can do for themselves and/or how the student can assist in the care routines.

Supporting student health and personal hygiene

It is also important that the plan identifies how the dignity and rights of the student will be protected – for example, providing a private area where care routines can be completed, talking quietly and respectfully to the student and showing patience and empathy for the student.

A student who soils or wets themselves should be cleaned and changed in a private space with access to a toilet, washing facilities, a sink for handwashing and sealable plastic bags for soiled clothing. There should also be accessible PPE for ESWs, such as disposable gloves and apron, mask and eye protection.

Procedures for hygiene and personal care needs should also include adequate supervision that ensures students are not subjected to any form of verbal or physical abuse. It is also important that ESWs are aware of the importance of acting in a professional and ethical manner at all times.

Infection control

Schools are ideal environments for the spread of infection. Students are indoors for extended periods of time, many classrooms lack handwashing facilities, and students may fail to follow basic hygiene practices when sneezing, coughing, blowing their nose, and handwashing before eating and after toileting.

In the school setting, infection risk management can include:

- daily cleaning of facilities and hard surfaces
- regular handwashing
- health screening and exclusion of students and adults who are unwell
- monitoring of students' immunisation status
- implementation of health and hygiene programs
- compliance with WHS policies and procedures.

Infection can be spread in a variety of ways:

- *Airborne droplets.* Some infections occur by transfer of bacteria or viruses via mucus or saliva, through the air, or via coughing, sneezing or nose blowing. Droplets are then spread to hands, furniture, equipment, books and food. ESWs who do not wash their hands after wiping a child's nose may also spread airborne droplets. Examples of infections spread by airborne droplets include the influenza (flu) virus and the meningococcal virus.
- *Airborne transmission.* Germs are spread by breathing contaminated air. Small particles can be spread on air currents, and through ventilation and air-conditioning systems. Examples of infections spread by airborne transmission include the measles virus and the varicella (chickenpox) virus.
- *Direct contact.* Organisms can be transferred from one person to another when the secretions (urine, blood, saliva, tears, vaginal secretions and semen) of an infected person come into direct contact with the broken, cut or scratched skin of another person. Surfaces can be contaminated through coughing, sneezing or touching; if a person touches the surface then touches their eyes, mouth or nose, infection can be transferred. Organisms spread by faeces include bacteria, viruses and parasites. Surfaces most commonly contaminated with faeces in a school setting may include the hands, doors, tap handles, toilet-flush areas and tabletops. Examples of infections spread by faeces include viral gastroenteritis, giardia (diarrhoea) and hepatitis A. Infections spread by other direct contact include head lice, scabies and fungal skin infections.
- *Animals.* Infections from animal faeces spread into the environment and may then be passed on to humans through direct contact via a hand or face, or indirectly, such as by contact with contaminated sand or soil. Infection can also be spread by flies and vermin.
- *Food.* Germs can spread when people eat food that has not been heated or chilled properly, and where good hygiene, such as handwashing or sneezing etiquette, is not practised.

The NHMRC (2013, p. 10) refers to the way in which germs are spread as the chain of infection (see also **Figure 5.11**):

1 The germ has a source.
2 The germ spreads from the source.
3 The germ infects another person.

The chain of infection can be broken at any stage by the implementation of three key strategies:

1 effective handwashing
2 excluding students and staff who are ill
3 ensuring students and adults are up-to-date with their immunisations.

Additional strategies include the appropriate use of disposable gloves, appropriate cough/sneezing etiquette and effective cleaning (NHMRC, 2013).

Figure 5.11 The chain of infection

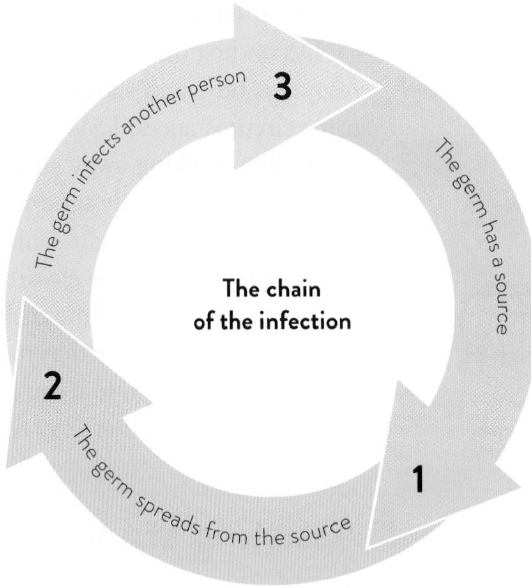

Source: NHMRC (2013). Licensed under a Creative Commons (CC) BY Attribution 3.4 international licence, http://creativecommons.org/licenses/by/4.0/.

Handwashing

Washing hands with soap and water at key times is the most effective way to prevent the spread of gastrointestinal and respiratory infections in community settings. According to Hand Hygiene Australia, hand hygiene includes:

> – applying an alcohol-based handrub to the surface of hands (including liquids, gels and foams) OR
> – washing hands with the use of a water and soap or a soap solution, either non-antimicrobial or antimicrobial.
>
> Source: Hand Hygiene Australia (n.d.). What is hand hygiene? https://www.hha.org.au/hand-hygiene/what-is-hand-hygiene

Hand hygiene posters

Cleaning

All public schools are required to engage professional cleaning services to clean (and disinfect some surfaces) on a daily basis. Cleaning using detergent and warm water removes germs, dirt, grime and impurities from surfaces using a detergent. Chemical disinfectants kill germs on hard surfaces. It is best to disinfect after cleaning (Australian Government, 2022).

A clean and tidy classroom minimises the spread of infection, reduces accidental injury caused by trips and builds a sense of community and responsibility among students (see **Figure 5.12**). Everyone – students, teachers and ESWs – is responsible for a tidy classroom. Developing positive habits, such as putting equipment into its designated container and

Figure 5.12 A clean and tidy classroom minimises the spread of infection

Source: Photo by Tish Okely © Cengage

returning it to the correct storage space, helps to keep busy classrooms tidy and reduces time wasted searching for equipment when it is needed. Students can also be taught to alert the teacher if equipment/resources are broken, missing or require replenishment.

Video: Classroom organisation

Depending on the setting, ESWs may be required to assist in keeping the room and equipment/resources tidy, and should role-model and encourage students to tidy the room or activity areas. In some circumstances, ESWs may be required to undertake cleaning duties, such as:

- tidying/packing away equipment, such as instruments, paper, scissors, glue
- cleaning frequently used high-touch surfaces, such as tabletops, computer keyboards, door handles, fan and light switches
- cleaning areas of the classroom, such as sinks and wet areas, wiping bag lockers, cleaning paint pots and washing dishes
- cleaning equipment that may be frequently mouthed by children and young people
- assisting children to clean school bags where food has spilled or spoiled
- cleaning an outdoor play space, such as hosing tables after use for chalk drawing or painting.

Cleanliness in the classroom

Assisting students with physical impairments and/or medical disabilities

ESWs may be required to undertake a range of care duties – for example, assisting a student to move to or from a wheelchair or walker, assisting with dressing/undressing, assisting with nappy change or toileting, assisting to transfer a student to or from a bus or motor vehicle, physically supporting a student with limited mobility, and supporting a student to use equipment. These actions involve bending, squatting, twisting, reaching, gripping and lifting, and pose a risk of muscle strain or skeletal injuries. When caring for a student, ESWs must assess factors such as the student's degree of mobility, flexibility and head control; the degree of involuntary movement; the student's weight, size and degree of alertness; the ability or willingness of the student to cooperate; and the student's communication skills (receptive and expressive).

Manual tasks - assisting people

Some students with physical impairments may be moved with the assistance of mechanical devices (e.g. a hoist and sling), which reduce the risk of accidental injury to both the student and the ESW.

Individual health care plans

All schools will have policies and procedures for the development of health care plans for students with complex medical needs, including, for example:

- oncology care plan
- intravenous care instructions
- continence care plan
- ileostomy, colostomy, urostomy care and learning plan
- intermittent catheterisation care and learning plan
- toileting care and learning plan
- menstruation management care and learning plan
- cystic fibrosis care plan
- twice daily injections school action and management plan
- multiple daily injections school action and management plan
- insulin pump school action and management plan
- oral eating and drinking care plan

- osteogenesis imperfecta care plan
- seizures management plan
- spina bifida care plan
- hydrocephalus and shunt care plan (Department of Education SA, 2022).

Typically, an individual health care plan will include:

- an emergency care/response plan
- a statement of the responsibilities of those involved in the student's support
- a schedule for the administration of prescribed medication as provided by the treating medical practitioner
- a schedule for the administration of health care procedures as provided by the treating medical practitioner
- an authorisation to contact the medical practitioner
- other relevant documents.

Individual health care plans

SCENARIO

TRAINING TO ASSIST STUDENTS' MOVEMENT

WHEELCHAIRS

'Until I went to the training day I didn't really think there was much to know about pushing a student around in a wheelchair. We learnt how to maintain a wheelchair, the best way to move a wheelchair over uneven surfaces, on grass and on thick pile carpet. We practised things like moving wheelchairs up and down ramps, over curbs, manoeuvring in tight spaces, accessing toilets and transferring people to and from chairs; folding chairs and putting them into a boot and getting them out again. I was amazed there was so much to learn!'

MOBILITY DEVICES

'This week I have been working with the physiotherapists so that I can learn about how to support students who use walking frames, chest harnesses and head supports, splints and braces, standing frames and crutches. I've also learnt how to use slings and hoists. It's been great – I feel confident that I know what to do to make it easier for students and to make sure I keep myself safe. The physio showed me how to move and brace myself so that I don't get injured.'

▶ DISCUSSION

Think about the wide range of physical impairments that students may present. Why is it important to ensure that ESWs receive the correct training needed to ensure the safety of the student and the worker?

Sun safety

Australia has one of the highest rates of skin cancer in the world. Damage to the skin from the sun's ultraviolet (UV) radiation during childhood increases the later risk of skin cancer. UV radiation cannot be seen or felt, and levels can be high enough to damage skin on cool as well as warm days. Schools have a duty of care to protect students from the effects of UV radiation and should have a sun-protection policy to provide adequate shade in outdoor areas and for younger students to wear a hat when outside. Cancer Council Australia has developed a national SunSmart Membership Program for schools, which promotes using a combination of sun protection measures from 'September to the end of April' or 'whenever UV levels reach three or higher'.

The Cancer Council Victoria's SunSmart (2014, pp. 1–2) membership program for primary schools recommends that:

- all students and staff wear hats that protect their face, neck and ears – legionnaire, broad brimmed or bucket hats – whenever they are outside
- students who do not have appropriate hats or outdoor clothing are asked to play in the shade or a suitable area protected from the sun

Sample sun protection policy

- school uniforms provide sun protection – for example, collared shirts with elbow-length sleeves and longer-style dresses
- the outdoor play space should include a sufficient number of shelters and trees providing shade in the school grounds, particularly where students congregate
- students should provide their own SPF 30 or higher broad-spectrum, water-resistant sunscreen (applied 20 minutes before going outdoors and reapplied every two hours)
- students should be encouraged to wear close-fitting, wrap-around sunglasses that meet Australian Standards
- SunSmart education should be provided to students and parents.

5.4 Students and risk management

The role of the ESW as it relates to managing the risks to student health and safety may vary from school to school; however, the role may typically include:

- supporting students with additional needs in a range of tasks – for example, eating, toileting, handwashing
- providing first aid (including emergency care)
- providing temporary care when students become unwell at school
- administering medications and health care procedures by following individual health care plans – this may include students diagnosed with severe asthma, type 1 diabetes, epilepsy or anaphylaxis
- monitoring students who are able to self-medicate to ensure correct procedures are followed
- supporting students to develop the knowledge, skills and understandings relevant to managing their own health care needs
- liaising with families, medical practitioners, health services, other relevant agencies and local community resources to support the health of students
- ensuring every student is treated with dignity and respect.

There are a wide range of potential hazards in any school environment. These may include: uneven or rough paths or play spaces; hazardous chemicals or substances; electrical equipment; dust; noise; classroom equipment and machinery; using materials such as wood, metal and plastics; risks associated with excursions and incursions; special events such as fairs, discos, family BBQs; use of vehicles; natural disasters and emergencies; manual handling and physical activities such as sport; the spread of infection, disease and illness; and the application of first aid.

Minimising the risk of accidental injury to students is a whole-of-school responsibility and must include the cooperation of teachers, ESWs and other support staff, students, administration, families and visitors.

Assessing risks to students

As part of their risk management framework, schools are required to undertake risk assessments to ensure the safe delivery of curriculum activities. According to Queensland's Curriculum Activity Risks Assessment (CARA) guidelines, those responsible for any school curriculum activities have legal obligations and a common law duty of care to ensure the safety of all those involved in the activity through curriculum activity risk management. **Figure 5.13** shows the risk assessment process for curriculum activities.

Figure 5.13 Curriculum Activity Risks Assessment

Step	Process
Identify hazards	> Consider the physical environment, any equipment used, the activity itself and its design, prior knowledge and skills of participants, and the management of the activity.
Assess the level of risk for each hazard in context	> Use the CARA risk matrix to identify the risk level of each foreseeable risk and hazard of the activity by considering the 'likelihood' of an incident occurring in conjunction with the 'consequence' (e.g. injury) if the incident did occur. > Consider the students involved in the activity, the location of the activity, which students will be participating, and which adult supervisors will be required.
Determine the inherent risk level for the activity	> Document the inherent risk level of the activity. This is the same level of risk as the hazard with the highest level of risk in the activity.
Decide on control measures	> Identify the control measures that will be put in place: – eliminate – substitute – isolate – engineering control – administrative control – PPE.
Document the risk assessment	> All activities must be documented, typically in unit planning as part of the three levels of planning. > Further documentation may be required, depending upon the risk level of the activity. > Consult the CARA flowchart for further information.

Source: Adapted from Department of Education, Qld (2022). Curriculum Activity Risk Assessment (CARA) process. CARA Planner. © State of Queensland, (Department of Education). Licensed under the Creative Commons Attribution 4.0 International licence (CC BY 4.0), https://creativecommons.org/licenses/by/4.0/deed.en

Risk assessment of student activities will include consideration of:

- Which students will be involved? (e.g. the number of participants, size of student groups and students' capabilities, such as age, experience, competence, fitness or maturity; individual supervision requirements
- Where will the students be? (environmental factors)
- What will the students be doing? (the nature and duration of the activity; the need for first aid kits, first aid trained personnel, Ventolin®, Epipen®, and students' personal prescribed medications as required in health plans)
- What will the students be using? (use of equipment)
- Who will be leading the activity? (the expertise or competence of the supervisor) (Department of Education, Qld, 2022).

Where students have a medical condition and/or a disability, the risk assessment must include provision for adequate supervision. The CARA guidelines state:

> During the activity, all adult supervisors:
> – **must** be readily identifiable
> – **must** closely monitor students with health support needs
> – **must** comply with control measures from the CARA record and adapt as hazards arise
> – **must** suspend the activity if the conditions become unfavourable (e.g. poor visibility, extreme temperatures, thunderstorms).

Source: Queensland Government (2021). Managing risks in school curriculum activities procedure. CARA information sheet. https://education.qld.gov.au/curriculum/stages-of-schooling/CARA.

Most schools will also have a risk-management procedure for planning physical activities to ensure the safety of both adults and students. These procedures will typically include: assessing risks by following WHS policy and procedures (ensuring employees are safe); undertaking a risk assessment for student safety that includes consideration of the inherent risks associated with the type of activity; consideration of student risk factors such as age, maturity, special needs and behaviour (in the case of students with a disability, this may include reasonable adjustments and/or an Individual Learning Plan).

An example of a completed curriculum activity risk assessment is shown in **Figure 5.14**. The form shows that the ESW has anticipated and planned for a range of possible risks:

- potential physical risk (location and equipment) – the area is free from hazards; there is sufficient equipment
- logistical risks related to supervision (transitioning to and from classroom; accessing the toilets; accessing support in the event of a medical emergency or behaviour challenge
- impediments to the active supervision – the form shows that there are no impediments to active supervision
- health and medical needs of students has been accommodated
- de-escalating conflict and strategies to calm and refocus students if needed.

Figure 5.14 Sample curriculum activity risk assessment

Curriculum Activity Risk Assessment		
Description of Activity		
Date: 23/05/xx	**Time:** 11.30 a.m.	**Completed by:** James Parry (ESW) Class 6M
Ball games > Throwing ball at target (individual) > Throwing and catching ball (in pairs) > Playing a ball game in a circle (group of 10 students)		
Location and Equipment		
> Lower playground – covered outdoor learning area; asphalt surface; away from roads and carpark; fenced perimeter; access to drinking water and toilets > Equipment – balls of various sizes, 4 large tubs, chalk to draw circle, water bottles; clipboard with list of student names and any medical conditions, whistle > Mobile phone		
Students		
8 students (10–12 years) > mild cognitive disability and some with physical disability > students are typically compliant and well-behaved > students are able to interact socially and engage in group experiences > able to follow directions and understand simple rules > familiar with play area > able to access and use toilets independently > able to communicate verbally > 2 students with medical conditions (asthma and epilepsy)		
Supervision Requirements		
Supervision risk level: Low risk level > An adult supervisor, working under the direct supervision of a registered teacher, with competence (knowledge and skills) in the activity > The play area is easily accessible, provide shelter from the sun; there are no 'blind spots' – the students will be visible at all times > Students are able to independently access the toilet block which is visible from the play area		

Curriculum Activity Risk Assessment	
Hazards and control measures (physical, psychological and logistical risks)	
Considering environmental hazards	**Planned control measures**
Covered area for sun protection	> Students must remain under cover
Asphalt surface – students may graze hands, elbows, knees if they fall	> Students reminded of hard surface and not to hurry/rush > Area checked for any trip hazards – remove/isolate
Considering facilities and equipment hazards	**Planned control measures**
Toilets and drinking water	> Students to ask permission to go to toilet; time student leaves to go to toilet noted on clipboard; students instructed to return promptly > Students will carry their own water bottle
Considering students	**Planned control measures**
Students with medication conditions	> Take asthma reliever and administer if necessary by referring to Asthma Management Plan > Monitor student with epilepsy and implement first aid plan if required
Transitioning to and from classroom	> The equipment will be taken to the play area and set up prior to the activity > Tell the students what we are going to do and where we are going > Remind students of rules – walk to area; ask to go to toilet; ask for help if needed; stop, stand still and look at ESW when she blows the whistle > Students will be taken from the classroom and escorted to the covered outdoor learning area > Students will be reminded to walk
Contingency Planning: Incident and emergency	> Should there be a medical emergency or a behaviour challenge use the mobile phone to call for help (classroom or office) Note: I have advised the admin. staff of my planned experience following the school's risk management policy and procedures > Should there be a conflict between two students, use a firm, calm tone of voice, give clear, short instructions asking each student look at me, move away from each other, close eyes and take 5 deep breaths (a familiar technique used in the classroom); when students are calm, redirect them or join in with them and model appropriate behaviour > Use the school's Incident and Emergency Report Form should this be needed

Curriculum Activity Risk Assessment			
Managing behaviour		Remind students of rules > Actively engage in the ball games with the students and role-model required behaviours > Praise desired behaviours using verbal and non-verbal positive reinforcement > If students become unsettled or disruptive de-escalate by blowing whistle to gain their attention, do some calming down stretches and start over	
Supervising Teacher Approval			
Name: Lin Miller	**Class:** 6M	**Date:** 23/05/xx	**Signature:** L Miller
Evaluation			
Have additional hazards been identified?		☐ yes ☑ no	
Were the control measures effective?		☑ yes ☐ no	
Are further or different actions required?		☐ yes ☑ no	

Source: Adapted from Queensland Government (2021). Managing risks in school curriculum activities procedure. CARA information sheet. https://ppr.qed.qld.gov.au/pp/managing-risks-in-school-curriculum-activities-procedure; https://education.qld.gov.au/curriculum/stages-of-schooling/CARA

Figure 5.15 provides an example of a risk-assessment evaluation.

Figure 5.15 Risk evaluation

Evaluation of risk management strategies and own performance

The risk assessment allowed me to plan ahead and anticipate possible risks and actions I could take to mitigate these risks.

The students followed my directions and complied with the behaviour guidelines.

I used the whistle once when I saw that some of the students were becoming over-excited. I was able to use the planned calming technique and redirect the play.

Having my mobile phone at hand provided reassurance that I could call for help if needed.

I managed the group effectively and was able to achieve the following learning outcomes for the students:

> Positive social interactions, fun, cooperation and collaboration
> Practising coordination and ball handling skills
> Remembering and following simple rules – games/behaviour expectations
> Listening to and following directions

Incidents and emergency reporting

As part of the school's risk management policy, staff would be required to report any incident or emergency (such as a medical emergency) involving students using the procedures in place.

Education Victoria defines an incident as an actual or alleged event or situation that:

- causes harm or creates a risk of causing harm to a student's health, safety or wellbeing either directly or indirectly while under the care or supervision of the school, including international students
- impacts a student and is brought to the attention of the school, regardless of when or where it occurred, provided it is impacting on the student or other students within the school environment
- causes harm or creates a risk of causing harm to an employee's health, safety or wellbeing either directly or indirectly in the work setting
- affects or risks affecting the continuity of school operations, including matters of security (including cyber security), property damage and emergencies
- requires police notification or involves matters of serious conduct
- is a WorkSafe notifiable incident.

Source: Education Victoria (2022). Managing and Reporting School Incidents (including emergencies). 20 June. https://www2.education.vic.gov.au/pal/reporting-and-managing-school-incidents-including-emergencies/policy

To respond to an incident, schools will have a system to report, investigate and make recommendations that may reduce the likelihood of a reoccurrence. Education Victoria uses a mechanism called School Incident Management System (SIMS), which includes six actions/stages:

1 Identifying incident and immediate response
2 Reporting an incident (Report for Support)
3 Ongoing support and recovery
4 Investigation
5 Incident review and closure
6 Analyse and learn (Education Victoria, 2022).

Managing and reporting incidents

ACT Education's policy to respond to student accidents/incidents sets out the occasions when an accident/incident involving a student must be reported by the school principal:

- a student breaks a bone or suffers an injury to the eyes, head, or mouth
- a student is injured at school or in a school organised activity and first aid and/or medical attention is provided or such treatment is reported by the student or a parent at a later date
- a student has to leave school early as a consequence of an accident/incident
- a parent or other emergency contact is advised by the school of an accident/incident
- in other instances when a principal or his/her delegate considers it appropriate to do so.

Source: ACT Government (n.d.). Responding to student accidents/incidents: Support, reporting and insurance arrangements procedure. https://www.education.act.gov.au/__data/assets/pdf_file/0019/810136/RespondingStudentsAccidentsIncidentsProcedure.pdf, p. 2.

An extract of an accident report form is shown in **Figure 5.16**.

Involving students in reducing risks

According to the Department of Employment and Workplace Relations (2006), students can be taught to act in ways that reduce the risk of accidental injury if:

- they are taught to be alert to potential risks and hazards (to others as well as oneself)
- they know what to do in risky and hazardous situations (at an age appropriate/abilities level), and have the self-confidence to do it
- they know how to minimise risks and hazards (p. 8).

Kidsafe Queensland (2016) recommends working with students to teach them how to use playground equipment safely. It also suggests that active zones be created for ball games and quiet zones for no running, and that a process be implemented to check the playground and playing fields regularly for hazards such as broken glass, used syringes, broken or worn equipment and unwelcome visitors such as stinging or biting insects and snakes.

Figure 5.16 Accident report form

ACCIDENT TO SCHOOL STUDENT/VISITOR

Name of school

Region ....

PERSONAL DETAILS OF STUDENT/VISITOR

Full Name: ....

Age: .... Date of Birth: ....

Name(s) of Parent(s)/Carer(s): ....

Address: ....

.... Postcode: ....

Contact telephone number: ....

ACCIDENT DETAILS

Date of injury: .... Day of Week: ....

Time: .... am/pm

Location of accident: ....

Describe the injuries sustained by the student/visitor: ....

....

....

State exactly what happened ....

....

....

Was first aid given by school? Y/N Was further medical attention given Y/N

Name of doctor/hospital: ....

On whose authority teacher's/parent's? ....

Subsequent treatment of student (if known) ....

Name of person completing this report...

Serial number (if appropriate) ....

Privacy Notice The information provided on this form is being obtained for the purpose of ascertaining the details of the accident. It will be used by the Department of Education and Training for the purpose of obtaining legal advice as to any liability it may have arising out of the accident, and for use in the course of any litigation that may eventuate. This information will be stored securely. You may correct any personal information provided at this time by contacting the school.

Source: Reporting School Accidents support document, https://education.nsw.gov.au/policy-library/policies/pd-2002-0064. Licensed under a Creative Commons Attribution 4.0 International (CC BY 4.0) licence © State of New South Wales (Department of Education), 2023

ESWs and personal safety

The role of an ESW can be satisfying and rewarding. It can also be stressful and demanding. Being aware of how to ensure your own safety and wellbeing in the workplace is essential for a long and fulfilling career. An ESW's safety and wellbeing may be threatened by exposure to:

- bacterial and viral infection
- musculoskeletal injury related to manual handling
- student verbal abuse, threats and physical violence
- workplace stress due to competing demands, limited time, limited resources and limited support

- unclear or inappropriate expectations of the work role
- workplace bullying
- risk of injury from the use of hazardous chemicals
- risks of injury associated with the use of electrical equipment and machinery.

Being aware of, and putting in place, strategies to minimise personal risk is an important consideration for ESWs. Maximising personal safety can be supported by:

- understanding and implementing the school's WHS policy and procedures
- wearing clothing that is comfortable and provides ease of movement, including suitable footwear such as joggers; avoiding wearing dangling earrings or necklaces that could be pulled by a student; using PPE as instructed; using universal precautions when handling any body fluids (e.g. disposable gloves, protective goggles)
- understanding and following the school's behaviour management/discipline policy
- being aware of the temperament and behaviour triggers of students with whom you are working
- establishing and maintaining effective communication with classroom teachers to establish clear strategies for responding to challenging and/or aggressive students
- understanding your responsibilities and the limitations of responsibilities
- asking for help, direction and support as needed
- being prepared – have the physical environment setup and all resources/equipment ready to start work with students; be clear about your goals/objectives and the steps you will engage in with the students; tell students what is expected and set boundaries for acceptable behaviour – for example: 'Remain seated', 'Ask for help if needed', 'Share resources/equipment'
- providing students with clear instructions for safe use of equipment – clarify that students understand and can apply the instruction through demonstration, and if working outside with students, take a mobile phone for emergencies; ensure that the classroom teacher knows your location and the time you are expected to return to the classroom.

Being aware of your surroundings, noticing potential hazards and being aware of the likely behaviours of students will help to keep you safe.

5.5 Student supervision

All schools will have a supervision policy that reflects their duty of care obligations. Supervision polices will include:

- expectations and requirements for general supervision of students (indoors/outdoors and while moving around the school; 10–15 minutes before and after school; students accessing buses at home time)
- supervision expectations and requirements for special activities/occasions/visitors to the school
- supervision expectations and requirements for excursions
- supervision expectations and requirements for sports/change rooms
- supervision expectations and requirements for religious instruction
- school grounds and facilities – out of bounds areas.

Supervision and yard duty

Effective supervision is critical for ensuring students' safety. For a supervision strategy to be effective, all supervising adults must be aware of their role, responsibilities and obligations. ESWs must consider a range of factors in relation to the physical setting, and in terms of the abilities and typical behaviours of students. Good supervision involves constant vigilance. Supervision should never be knowingly compromised. For example, engaging in lengthy

Figure 5.17 Fixed equipment presents supervision challenges

Source: Dreamstime.com/KrystynaWojciechowska-Czarnik.

conversations with other adults or undertaking other duties should be avoided when supervising students.

Supervision strategies will vary according to variables such as age, maturity, abilities, temperament and activities being undertaken. Environmental factors should also be considered, such as the weather, the fixed equipment (see **Figure 5.17**), open spaces, enclosed spaces, fencing, proximity to busy roads, and hazards such as on-site grounds or buildings work. In relation to the behaviour of students, factors that contribute to accidents or incidents may include:

- the student's level of mastery, especially in relation to physical skills – for example, the student's ability to remain seated while completing a task
- the mobility of the student – for example, where a student has a disability that limits or restricts mobility, it is important to ensure that the physical space is free of obstacles that may cause the student to fall or trip, or that will make manoeuvring a wheelchair or walker difficult
- the ability of the student to understand cause and effect and anticipate the consequences of their behaviour. Some students may act recklessly or impulsively without any thought of danger to themselves or others
- the student's ability to concentrate and stay on task, or a propensity to be distracted easily. These students may attempt to distract or annoy others, which can lead to retaliation by other students
- the student's temperament – while most students are compliant, there will be students whose temperament causes them to be argumentative or defiant, or to act the 'class clown'. Always take immediate action if students are engaging in risky behaviours that are unsafe – for example, throwing things at others; climbing on gates or fences; using equipment in a dangerous manner
- the student's level of competence – students who struggle academically can easily become frustrated and resist participating – or even refuse to participate – in class activities
- the student's health – awareness of students with medical conditions such as asthma, allergies or epilepsy
- students for whom English is a second language
- students who are new to the school.

The gender factor

Gender plays a role in the likelihood of accidental injury. Generally, the rate of accidental injuries is far higher in males than in females. This may be explained by the type of play in which males and females typically engage – for example, males are likely to be more active and engage in greater risk-taking and showing-off behaviour. Males also tend to engage in greater physical contact, such as pushing, poking and tapping.

Getting to know students allows you to adapt your supervision to accommodate, anticipate or at least be alert to possible challenging behaviours. **Figure 5.18** identifies the key principles of active supervision, which requires focused attention and intentional observation.

Figure 5.18 Key principles of active supervision

Knowing	Be aware of the location of all students being supervised, and of all activities and equipment that may require special supervision. You should know the number of students under your direct supervision so you can do regular head counts as a quick and effective way to ensure all students are present and accounted for – e.g. when students have transitioned from outside to inside.
Positioning	Make sure you position yourself to get the best possible view of the areas being supervised so you can see and hear the students you are supervising.
Scanning	Watch and be aware of all activities occurring in the supervision area. Look around regularly and be aware of all students in the area you are supervising.
Listening	Listen for unusual sounds, raised voices; crying or silence – these are a good indicator that something unusual may be happening.
Anticipating	Be aware of: individual students' risky behaviours; students with medical conditions; risk factors associated with particular equipment, activities, play or recreation spaces.
Engaging and redirecting	Engage and interact with students – this allows you to model and discuss safe play behaviours as needed.
Communicating	Effective supervision requires ESWs to communicate and be aware of the position of other supervising adults.

How the principles of supervision are applied will depend on the age and abilities of the students. For example, scanning is an appropriate strategy if supervising a regular group of high school students, while anticipating, engaging and redirecting would be more appropriate when supervising high school students with sensory or cognitive disabilities.

The impact of group dynamics

The concept of group dynamics, first developed in the 1940s by Kurt Lewin, explores the behaviours and attitudes of people in a group situation. Lewin noticed that people take on different roles and behaviours when working in, or being part of a social group, such as leader or follower, information giver, coordinator, negotiator, doer, time-waster or critic.

In the classroom, good team dynamics rely on effective communication and clearly defined goals. The group must be clear about individual roles as well as the outcome that is expected. It is also important to define the expected standards of behaviour, such as active listening, respecting the ideas and opinions of others, and contributing positively.

While learning occurs best in a social context, working together as a team to achieve a shared outcome is not an easy task for children and young people. When selecting students to work in small groups, it is essential to think about the individuals within the group and how they will influence each other or the group as a whole. For example, allocating two students who are known to be disruptive to the same small group may result in a negative group dynamic, such as conflict, disharmony and frustration. Alternatively, allocating a student who has good leadership skills to a group with students who are less confident can create a positive group dynamic.

Group dynamics can be improved by observing individual behaviours within groups and taking action to build skills by acting as a role model, providing direct instruction or posing questions or problems for discussion. For example, 'I hear that Axle and Anshu don't agree on how to find the information needed. Let's talk over the options'; 'Samir, when Sara is sharing her ideas you need to listen'; 'Ishmal, the job you agreed to do was go to the bookcase and find some books on whales. You need to do that right now.'

In a social context, group dynamics can play a powerful role in student behaviour and attitudes towards others. This is particularly true for teenagers, where group dynamics can lead to bullying behaviours, such as taunting, name-calling, meanness, shaming and threatening behaviours. Conversely, group dynamics can also lead to positive behaviours, such as helping others, displaying empathy and kindness, and positive leadership.

Students will need support and encouragement when working in a group – for example, reinforcing positive behaviours, helping to address differences or conflict or sharing feelings. Being aware of group dynamics when working with students can assist you to anticipate behaviours, avoid student conflict or frustration and support positive opportunities for learning.

Supporting age-appropriate safe behaviours

While it is essential for ESWs to implement safe supervision practices to minimise risks to student safety, it is also important to encourage students to develop age-appropriate practices to keep themselves safe. Younger students or students with limited cognitive skills need reminding and prompting if they are to consistently engage in age-appropriate safe behaviours. This can be achieved when adults tell students *what to do*, rather than what *not to do* – for example, 'Remember to keep your hands by your side when walking into the classroom'; 'Always hold on with at least one hand and look up/down when on climbing equipment'. Students with disabilities that restrict their ability to apply safe behaviours will require close and constant supervision.

Assisting students to develop age-appropriate safe behaviours must take the individual student's stage of development into account. It is also important to remember that children and young people do not think in the same way as adults. Younger children and children with cognitive disabilities or poor impulse control may lack the skills necessary to anticipate danger. These students have not yet developed logical thinking skills and may act impulsively. For example, a six-year-old child may remember not to push others when walking up/downstairs at school but may forget this rule when excitedly rushing into a cinema.

Expectations for age-appropriate safe behaviours when supervising high school students, particularly teenage boys, can be a challenge. Like younger students, teenagers can be impulsive and may engage in risky behaviours, taunting/teasing others and sometimes violence. When supervising teenagers it is important to be seen as fair and consistent but not authoritarian; provide choices; set clear boundaries and behaviour expectations; role-model kindness, patience and problem-solving; be respectful and avoid 'talking down' to students; avoid threats of punishment; follow through on behaviour expectations by talking to students about their behaviour and actively listening to their response; use humour (if appropriate) to defuse tense situations; occasionally turn a blind eye and pick your battles; and, finally, recognise students' strengths and have fun with them.

Figure 5.19 An example of classroom rules for safe behaviour

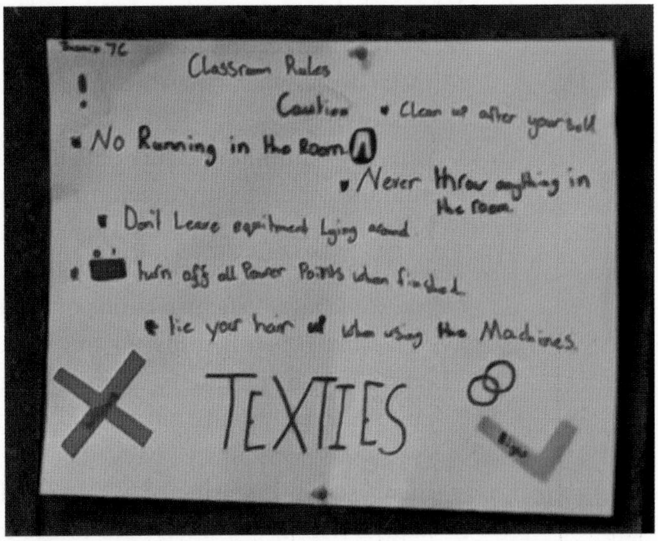

Source: Photo by Tish Okely © Cengage

Establishing rules for safe behaviour

The classroom teacher will have established rules for classroom behaviour. Before ESWs begin working with students, they must be clear about how the teacher manages student behaviour and the rules that have been established to guide behaviour. Where possible, to provide consistency, ESWs should use the same behaviour-management strategies that are used by the teacher (see **Figure 5.19**).

Depending on the age of the students, ESWs should ensure that students understand and follow basic rules for listening and speaking – for example:

- Wait for instructions before beginning work – 'Look at me while I am talking, listen, concentrate and ask if you are unsure about what to do.' Promoting active listening skills is a key strategy for keeping students safe in the classroom.
- Look at, and listen to, the person speaking and allow the person to speak without interruption.
- Use a quiet voice when speaking.
- Be respectful of others – everyone has a right to their own opinion if it is respectful of others. Older students can be encouraged to use 'I' messages when challenging the opinions of others – for example, 'I believe that …'; 'I think that …'

Reinforcing courteous and respectful interactions and active listening contributes to a safe environment.

SCENARIO

RULES

Edward (10 years) has several learning difficulties and easily becomes agitated. Before commencing the small-group activity, the ESW reminds Edward of the class rules and also of the consequences of breaking the rules. Edward and the ESW have worked on some strategies that Edward can use to calm himself down. The ESW and Edward have also worked out some signals that the ESW can use when she thinks Edward's behaviour needs to be modified. This strategy gives Edward a sense of control over his own actions.

WHAT DOES THIS TELL US?

Safe behaviours can be established by working with individual students to assist them to regulate and modify their behaviours as needed. In this Scenario, the ESW supports Edward to take responsibility for his own behaviours.

5.6 Using verbal and non-verbal communication

Non-verbal communication can be a fast and effective way to convey messages to students. Non-verbal communication includes:

- *facial expressions* – there are four universal facial expressions: anger, happiness, fear and sadness
- *gestures* – common gestures include waving, pointing, using fingers to indicate numeric amounts, thumbs up/down, hand up with palm facing out means stop
- *paralinguistics* – such as loudness, tone of voice, inflection and pitch. For example, 'I'm just *fine!* (meaning 'I am not fine at all!')
- *body language* – such as hands on hips, arms folded across chest, pointing, tapping
- *proxemics or personal space* – the amount of distance we need and the amount of space we perceive as belonging to us is influenced by a number of factors, including social norms, cultural expectations, situational factors, personality characteristics and level of familiarity
- *eye gaze* – normal, steady eye contact shows trust; inability to maintain eye contact conveys mistrust; while staring or excessive blinking may be signs of anger or fear
- *haptics (touch)* – women tend to use touch to convey care, concern and nurturance. Men, on the other hand, are more likely to use touch to assert power or control over others
- *appearance* – style and colour of clothing, hairstyles and other factors affecting appearance can convey power, confidence and trust (e.g. uniforms) social status and personality
- *artefacts* – can be used as status symbols (e.g. diamond or gold jewellery) or to convey beliefs, such as religion, political affiliation or social convictions (Cherry, 2022).

When supervising students, gestures can communicate powerful messages. For example, frowning at a student, raising your eyebrows, pursing your mouth, scowling or shaking your head with hands on hips will communicate that you are unhappy with the student's behaviour; smiling and nodding will positively reinforce desired behaviours; a light touch on the shoulder may signal you want the student to settle down or stop interrupting others; standing near a student can help them to settle and stay on task.

Verbal communication using paralinguistics can also be an effective way to modify unacceptable behaviour or encourage positive behaviour. For example, speaking in a clear firm, voice communicates that you want the student to listen and follow your instructions; raising the pitch of your voice can convey concern about a danger, such as shouting 'Stop' in a high-pitched voice. Once you have the attention of the student, using a soft, calm voice or whispering, can help the student to focus and listen. Using a relaxed stance, smiling and being upbeat when verbally communicating conveys to the student that you are non-threatening and genuinely interested (Cherry, 2022).

Health promotion activities

The International Union for Health Promotion and Education states:

> Health promotion in a school setting could be defined as any activity undertaken to improve and/or protect the health of all school users. It is a broader concept than health education and it includes provision and activities relating to: healthy school policies, the school's physical and social environment, the curriculum, community links and health services.

Source: International Union for Health Promotion and Education (n.d.). *Promoting Health in Schools: From Evidence to Action.* https://doh.health.tas.gov.au/__data/assets/pdf_file/0007/117385/PHiSFromEvidenceToAction_WEB1.pdf, p. 2.

The Health Promoting Schools Framework, an initiative of the World Health Organization (WHO), defines a health promoting school as 'one that constantly strengthens its capacity as a healthy setting for living, learning and working' and all members of a school community work together to make the school a healthy place to spend time, learn and work in. According to the WHO, a health-promoting school:

Health promotion programs in schools

- Fosters health and learning with all the measures at its disposal.
- Engages health and education officials, teachers, teachers' unions, students, parents, health providers and community leaders in efforts to make the school a healthy place.
- Strives to provide a healthy environment, school health education, and school health services along with school/community projects and outreach, health promotion programmes for staff, nutrition and food safety programmes, opportunities for physical education and recreation, and programmes for counselling, social support and mental health promotion.
- Implements policies and practices that respect an individual's wellbeing and dignity, provide multiple opportunities for success, and acknowledge good efforts and intentions as well as personal achievements.

Source: Reproduced from World Health Organization (2022). Health promoting schools. https://www.who.int/health-topics/health-promoting-schools#tab=tab_1

All Australian state and territory government schools have adopted the Health Promoting Schools Framework. Examples of health promotion activities in schools are shown in **Figure 5.20**.

Figure 5.20 Examples of health promotion activities

Program	Aims
Live Life Well @ School	To get more students, more active, more often and improve healthy eating habits: **https://www.health.nsw.gov.au/heal/schools/Pages/llw-at-school.aspx**
Deadly Choices	Health, lifestyle and physical activity aimed at Indigenous students and their families: **https://deadlychoices.com.au**
School-Wide Positive Behaviour Support Framework	Brings together school communities to develop positive, safe, supportive learning cultures: **https://www.pbisrewards.com/?utm_source=google&utm_medium=cpc&utm_content=PBIS%2520General%2520-%2520Search_Pbis&utm_campaign=PBISR-K12-CPC-Q1-2023-Google-AUS**
Life Ed. Program (Primary Schools)	**https://lifeed.org.au/teachers-and-schools/the-life-ed-program/primary-program**
Life Ed. Program (Secondary Schools)	Life Ed for secondary students includes: > Reality Now (NSW & SA) – Smoking – Tobacco/Cannabis/Vaping, Alcohol, Illicit drugs, Perception of young people's use of alcohol and other drugs > Talk About It – Building and maintaining healthy relationships (Qld, Vic & SA) – Consent, Managing peer pressure, Protective behaviours and hygiene, Diversity and inclusivity **https://lifeed.org.au/teachers-and-schools/the-life-ed-program/secondary-program**
Be You	Supporting children's and young people's mental health: **https://beyou.edu.au**
Crunch&Sip®	An initiative to encourage students to take a break and eat fruit (or salad and vegetables) and drink water: **https://www.health.nsw.gov.au/heal/schools/Pages/crunch-and-sip.aspx**

Figure 5.21 An example of student wellbeing plans in a school

Source: Photo by Tish Okely © Cengage

Figure 5.22 Australian Student Wellbeing Framework

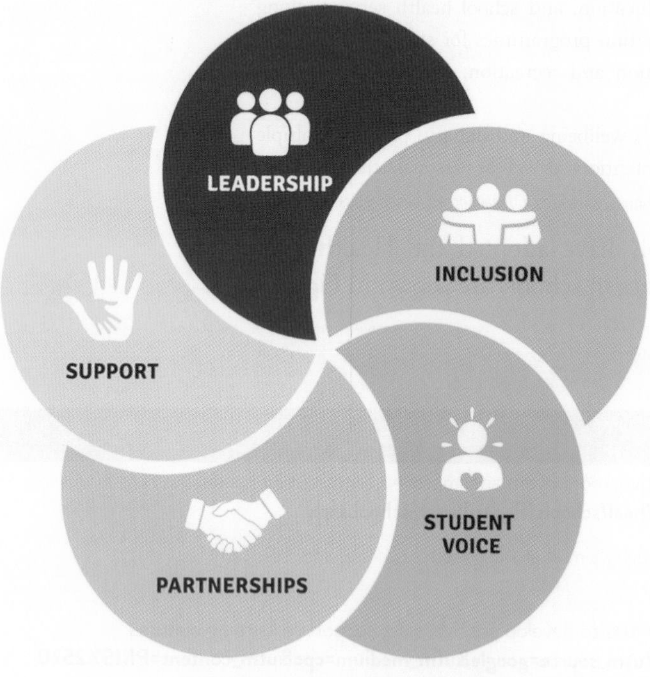

Source: Australian Student Wellbeing Framework. https://studentwellbeinghub.edu.au/educators/framework. Licensed under Creative Commons Attribution 4.0 International (CC BY 4.0) licence, https://creativecommons.org/licenses/by/4.0/

ESWs may be involved in supporting students to participate in a range of health promotion programs. Involvement may include accessing and preparing resources/activities, creating posters and displays and/or participation in instructional programs.

5.7 Student wellbeing frameworks

An essential component of students' health and safety is mental wellbeing. All schools will have strategies to support the mental wellbeing of students (see **Figure 5.21**).

The Australian Student Wellbeing Framework includes five key principles (see also **Figure 5.22**):

- Leadership – Principals and school leaders play an active role in building a positive learning environment where the whole school community feels included, connected, safe and respected.
- Student Voice – Students are active participants in their own learning and wellbeing, feel connected and use their social and emotional skills to be respectful, resilient and safe.
- Support – School staff, students and families share and cultivate an understanding of wellbeing and positive behaviour and how this supports effective teaching and learning.
- Inclusion – All members of the school community are active participants in building a welcoming school culture that values diversity, and fosters positive, respectful relationships.
- Partnerships – Families and communities collaborate as partners with the school to support student learning, safety and wellbeing.

Source: Student Wellbeing Hub (2020). Australian Student Wellbeing Framework. https://studentwellbeinghub.edu.au/educators/framework

The Wellbeing Framework for Schools (NSW Department of Education and Communities, 2020, p. 9) states:

> Students, teachers and staff, and members of the wider school community have a shared understanding of the behaviours, attitudes and expectations that enhance wellbeing and lead to improved student outcomes.

The Framework includes five domains of wellbeing, as shown in **Figure 5.23**. The key principles of the Wellbeing Framework are shown in **Figure 5.24**.

Figure 5.23 Five domains of wellbeing

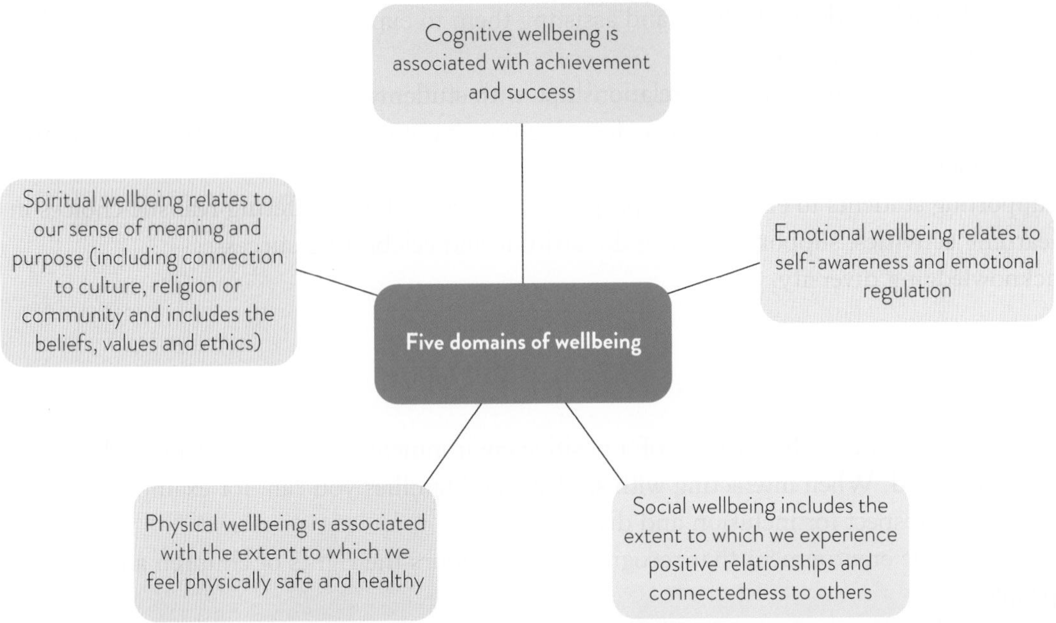

Source: Adapted from NSW Department of Education and Communities (2015). The Wellbeing Framework for Schools. https://education.nsw.gov.au/content/dam/main-education/student-wellbeing/whole-school-approach/Wellbeing_Framework_for_Schools.pdf, p. 5.

Figure 5.24 Key principles of the Wellbeing Framework for Schools

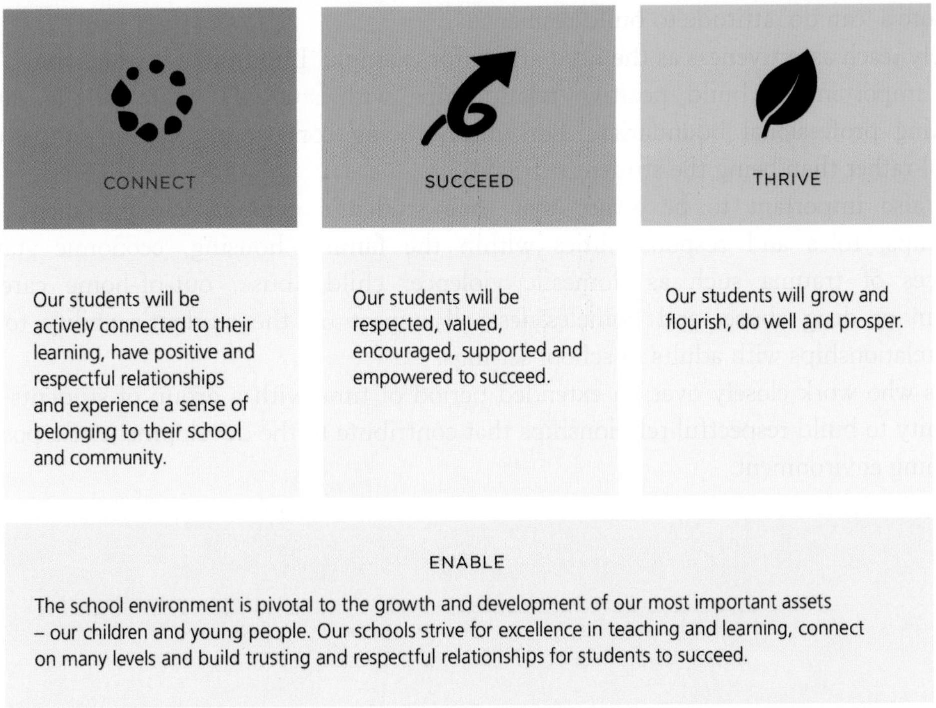

NSW Department of Education and Communities (2015). The Wellbeing Framework for Schools. https://education.nsw.gov.au/content/dam/main-education/student-wellbeing/whole-school-approach/Wellbeing_Framework_for_Schools.pdf, p. 5.

Australian Student Wellbeing Framework videos and information

ESWs can support wellbeing by:

- modelling respect for others
- acknowledging students' feelings and assisting them to express these feelings in a socially and culturally acceptable manner
- building positive and respectful relationships with students
- encouraging student achievement by focusing on what students can do rather than on their limitations
- supporting students to engage in appropriate problem-solving, offering realistic choices in learning activities, supporting a 'can do' attitude and celebrating successes
- acknowledging diversity.

Student wellbeing: the role of ESWs

ESWs can contribute to the creation of a positive environment in which students feel emotionally safe and respected. When interacting with students and families you can, for example:

- role-model respect for inclusion and diversity
- provide a safe environment that recognises and honours the rights of children and young people
- role-model and encourage active listening
- foster positive relationships with peers
- provide students with choices that are realistic and authentic
- engage students in discussion and decision-making
- acknowledge kindness and empathy when displayed by a student
- address bullying and bias when it occurs
- promote a 'can do' attitude to build resilience
- actively teach assertiveness as the need arises, for example 'I don't like it when you…'.

It is important to build positive relationships with students while at the same time maintaining professional boundaries. This means being consistently caring, empathetic and respectful rather than being the student's 'friend'.

It is also important to be aware that each student's personal circumstances – family relationships, roles and responsibilities within the family, housing, economic status, and experiences of trauma such as domestic violence, child abuse, out-of-home care, parent alcoholism or drug abuse, and homelessness all impact on the student's ability to develop trusting relationships with adults in school settings.

ESWs who work closely over an extended period of time with a group of students have the opportunity to build respectful relationships that contribute to the development of a positive and safe learning environment.

Summary

This chapter has explored the factors that contribute to a safe and healthy environment for children and young people in school settings. School policies and procedures guide employees when making decisions that may impact on student health and safety. Duty-of-care obligations also guide decision-making and practices to ensure students are safe within the context of the school environment.

Student wellbeing is also guided by policies and procedures that highlight the critical role of student mental health as a key contributing factor in the creation of a respectful and trusting learning environment.

Self-check questions

1. What are the key practices to minimise the risk of food contamination in schools?
2. What are your responsibilities as an ESW acting as a first aid officer?
3. What is the difference between allergies and anaphylaxis?
4. What responsibilities do schools have towards asthmatic children?
5. What are the five rights of medication administration in the school setting?
6. As an ESW responsible for medication administration, what is your responsibility when a student is non-compliant?
7. What are the most common means of infection transmission?
8. What factors must an ESW assess when caring for students with physical impairments and/or medical disabilities?
9. As part of the overall risk management framework, schools are required to undertake risk assessments to ensure the safe delivery of curriculum activities. What are the five steps of the risk assessment process for curriculum activities?
10. How can you maximise personal safety as an ESW? List two strategies.
11. What are the key principles of active supervision?
12. All schools have strategies to support the mental wellbeing of students. What are the five key principles of the Australian Student Wellbeing Framework?

Discussion questions

1. It is Sean's birthday, and his dad makes the best cupcakes Lisa, the ESW, has tasted. Sean's dad, Bart, forgot to call the school on Friday and let them know he would be bringing in a tray of homemade cupcakes to share among the students. Sean's dad arrives just as morning break is about to happen and walks into the classroom with the cupcakes. The children are abuzz.
   a. Joanne-Louise has anaphylaxis to egg and egg products when ingested. How would you manage this situation?
2. It is early, and everyone is excited as they arrive at their country camp for the week. The camp nurse has asked you to bring over the children and their medications. As you are handing over the collection, you notice that Ali has a small canister of tablets broken in half, unlabelled and not in their original packet. There is also his asthma puffer. Alongside this is the completed and signed form from his parent advising what each of the medications are for and the dosage.
   a. If you applied the 'five rights' safety protocol to this situation, where would the gaps be and what would you need to do about this?
3. The classroom teacher is absent for the day and, being a Friday afternoon, the children are a little noisy and unsettled. You have noted that the relief teacher has been raising her voice all morning and the kids reciprocate by getting louder. In your classroom, you use both verbal and non-verbal cues to direct and obtain the attention of the children.
   a. What three non-verbal strategies might you suggest to your relief teacher to try after morning break?

Activities

1 Investigate your school's policy on sharing food and bringing in catering from parents.

2 Obtain your school's risk assessment documents and complete them for these two hazards:

   a The carpet in your classroom has started to fray and there are several loose strands that are connected at both ends.

   b The newly installed playground has a bolt head that sticks up in the landing platform at the end of the slide.

3 Ask the teachers at your school and students in your classroom about the range of programs used to support wellbeing. Compile this as a reference list to use during your placement and employment.

Chapter 6

CHILD PROTECTION

LEARNING OBJECTIVES

When you have completed this chapter you should be able to demonstrate that, in relation to working in a school environment, you can:

6.1 define child abuse and identify the legislative requirements for child protection in your state/territory

6.2 identify the four interrelated factors that are commonly used to explain why abuse occurs

6.3 describe indicators of the different types and dynamics of abuse as they may apply to age, gender, disability and culture and understand the consequences of child maltreatment

6.4 describe your legal obligations, and notification procedures and protocols within a school-based setting, and identify the ethical issues in relation to child protection.

Online resources icons refer to useful weblinks. Ask your instructor for these **Online Resources.**

Introduction

This chapter explores the sensitive issue of child protection. It examines current child protection legislation and legal responsibilities for reporting suspected risk of harm. It also explores the complex factors that contribute to risk of harm, the possible indicators of risk of harm and the consequences of abuse and neglect for children, young people and families.

Child protection legislation cannot prevent child abuse from occurring, but it can put measures in place to minimise the risk of abuse and neglect, provide appropriate responses to support victims of abuse and impose punitive measures against perpetrators of abuse. Child protection legislation can also raise public awareness of child abuse and neglect, and support training in preventative measures. Protecting children and young people from abuse and neglect requires all members of the community to be vigilant and to act in the best interest of children and young people at all times.

6.1 What is child abuse?

Child maltreatment, which encompasses both abuse and neglect of a child, can be defined as 'any non-accidental behaviour by parents, caregivers, other adults or older adolescents that is outside the norms of conduct and entails a substantial risk of causing physical or emotional harm to a child or young person' (Price-Robertson, 2015). The **maltreatment** may be intentional or unintentional.

Generally, child protection legislation identifies the following types of abuse:

- physical abuse
- emotional abuse
- neglect
- witnessing domestic violence
- sexual abuse.

Child abuse continues to be a growing social and public health issue in Australia. Typically, indicators of abuse and neglect (see **Figure 6.1**) occur in a cluster or pattern, rather than being a single indicator, and will usually manifest over a period of time.

Figure 6.1 Indicators of abuse and neglect

Physical abuse

- Bruising
- Lacerations or welts
- Burns
- Fractures
- Dislocations

Psychological harm and emotional abuse

- Feelings of worthlessness about life or themselves
- Inability to value or trust others
- Lack of interpersonal skills
- Extreme attention-seeking or risk-taking
- Being markedly disruptive or bullying

Neglect

- General appearance of neglect
- Ongoing poor standard of hygiene
- Excessive anxiety about being abandoned
- Unexpected delay in reaching developmental milestones
- Extreme craving for adult attention and affection

Sexual abuse

- Child verbalising the sexual act
- Child describing sexual acts from watching adult videos
- Direct or indirect disclosure
- Bleeding from the vagina, external genitalia or anus

It should be remembered that many of the indicators of abuse may be attributed to other causal factors. For example, young children may display separation anxiety due to their temperament or simply because they are adjusting to a new situation. A young child may display regressive behaviours because there is a new baby in the family or a parent is absent from the home. When considering possible indicators of abuse, it is essential to consider the context in which they occur, the child's temperament, typical behaviours, family situation and any history of abuse. It is important for educators to be alert to persistent atypical behaviours, and suspicious or unexplained physical injuries.

CONSIDER THIS

CHILD PROTECTION

According to Child Protection Australia's 2016–17 annual report:

- During 2019–20, 174 700 (31 per 1000) Australian children received child protection services (investigation, care and protection order and/or were in out-of-home care).
- Around 3 per cent of all children aged 0–17 are assisted by Australia's child protection systems (age 5–9 years: 8.3%; 10–14 years: 8.1%; 15–17 years: 4.8%).
- Children from geographically remote areas were more likely to be the subject of a substantiation or be in out-of-home care than those from major cities.
- Sixty-seven per cent of children who received child protection services were repeat clients.
- A total of 30 600 children had been in out-of-home care for two years or more.
- A higher proportion of girls (13%) were subject to sexual abuse than boys (6%), while boys had slightly higher percentages of substantiations for neglect and physical abuse.
- At 30 June 2020, of the approximately 46 000 children in out-of-home care, 92 per cent were in home-based care.
- The number of children in out-of-home care rose by 7 per cent between 30 June 2017 and 30 June 2020.
- Indigenous children continue to be overrepresented among children receiving child protection services, including for substantiated child abuse and neglect, children on care and protection orders and children in out-of-home care.
- In 2019–20, 55 300 Indigenous children received child protection services, a rate of 166 per 1000 Indigenous children – an increase from 151 per 1000 in 2016–17.
- 1 in 18 Indigenous children (around 18 900) were in out-of-home care at 30 June 2020, almost two-thirds (63%) of whom were living with relatives, kin or other Indigenous caregivers.
- Over 4 in 5 Indigenous children (84%) who exited out-of-home care to a permanency outcome in 2018–19 did not return to care within 12 months.

Aboriginal and Torres Strait Islander

Source: Australian Institute of Health and Welfare (2021a). Child protection Australia 2019–20. Child welfare series no. 74. Cat. no. CWS 78. Canberra: AIHW. Released under CC BY 3.0, link to license: https://creativecommons.org/licenses/by/3.0/au/

WHAT DOES THIS TELL US?

The rate of notifications and substantiations of child abuse and neglect continues to grow. This is likely to be a result of greater community awareness of the importance of notifying concerns about the welfare of children and young people. It is also likely to be a result of increased social isolation of families, financial stress, housing stress, domestic violence and the complexities and challenges of living in a consumer-driven society. It may also reflect the stress faced by families as a result of the COVID-19 pandemic, which resulted in families being forced to spend long periods of time together without any respite.

Figure 6.2 shows the prevalence of abuse by primary substantiated harm types.

Child abuse occurs for many different reasons. Although there are factors that may commonly contribute to abuse, these will vary from one case to another. The triggers for abuse will be unique to each individual and each situation. Perpetrators of abuse do not fit a specific profile – we cannot say that one person will abuse their children and that another person will not. Child abuse occurs across all socioeconomic groups, religions and cultures.

Four interrelated factors are commonly cited to explain why abuse occurs:

1. *Individual characteristics.* Child abuse happens because of 'personality' problems.
2. *An individual's interpersonal relationships.* Abuse happens because of poor relations with family members and social networks.
3. *Individual history.* Abuse happens because of the abuse or neglect of a person as a child.
4. *Sociocultural factors.* Abuse happens because of the beliefs created by society in relation to children's behaviour, families, gender and power.

Abuse may occur for a variety of reasons that, when combined, may cause a parent or carer to use inappropriate force, neglect or physical punishment. These triggers may include vulnerable adults, unclear or unrealistic expectations of children and young people, relationship difficulties, social/cultural issues and issues surrounding the child. Circumstances surrounding a child's

Figure 6.2 Percentage breakdown of primary substantiated harm types in Australia in 2019/20

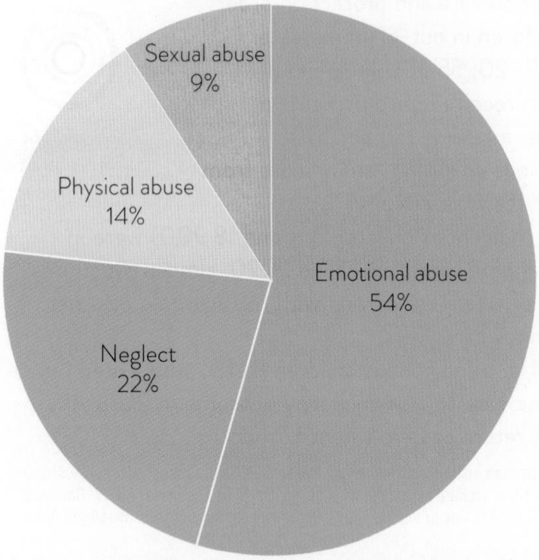

Source: Based on Australian Institute of Health and Welfare (2021b). Child Protection Australia 2019–20 (18 May). https://www.aihw.gov.au/publication-detail/?id=60129558626&tab=3. CC-BY-3.0 licence.

birth, such as prolonged hospitalisation at birth, may result in a disruption to the bonding process and act as triggers for abuse and neglect.

Child abuse and neglect occur across all sectors of the community and are not restricted to a particular socioeconomic group, culture, race, gender or religious group. Perpetrators of abuse can be parents (including step-parents, a partner in a de facto relationship or a casual partner), community leaders, religious figures, teachers, doctors, counsellors, community workers, plumbers, cleaners, shop assistants, or people from any other walk of life. From the evidence available, it is clear that, with the exception of child sexual abuse, children and young people are most likely to be abused or neglected by parents and/or caregivers (Australian Institute of Health and Welfare [AIHW], 2018a).

Most perpetrators of sexual abuse are people known to the child, such as parents, relatives, family friends or other adults who have regular contact with the child (Lamont, 2011). Although perpetrators of abuse are more likely to be male, females also abuse children.

In 2019–20, of children and young people who were the subject of a substantiation, 35 per cent were from the lowest socioeconomic areas (AIHW, 2021a). It is important to be aware that families who live in poverty, are dependent on welfare and use a range of social services are more likely to come to the notice of authorities than families within higher socioeconomic groups. It should be noted that the true incidence of abuse to children and young people in our society is unknown, simply because much of it may go unreported.

United Nations Convention on the Rights of the Child

In February 2013, Australia appointed its first National Children's Commissioner, whose role is to focus on the rights and interests of children and young people, and the laws, policies and programs that impact on them. Australia is also a signatory to the United Nations Convention on the Rights of the Child, which sets out the rights of children to education, health care and economic opportunity; and protection from abuse, neglect, and sexual and economic exploitation. Article 19 of the Convention states:

> Parties shall take all appropriate legislative, administrative, social and educational measures to protect the child from all forms of physical or mental violence, injury or abuse, neglect or negligent treatment, maltreatment or exploitation, including sexual abuse, while in the care of parent(s), legal guardian(s) or any other person who has the care of the child.

Source: United Nations (1990).

Every child has the right to live in a safe, secure environment, free from harm. By maintaining child-focused practices, educators can ensure that the safety and wellbeing of children remains their highest priority.

Child abuse occurs on a global level. It happens at a macro level when governments fail to provide essential health, education and welfare services for families and children, and at a micro level when families fail to act in the best interests of the child or young person.

The National Principles for Child Safe Organisations

The National Principles for Child Safe Organisations were developed to assist organisations engaged with children and young people to build a culture of safety. The 10 principles guide organisations to adopt strategies and take action to promote child wellbeing and prevent harm to children and young people. They are designed to build capacity and deliver child safety and wellbeing, and are shown in **Figure 6.3**.

Figure 6.3 National Principles for Child Safe Organisations

Principle 1	Child safety and wellbeing is embedded in organisational leadership, governance and culture.
Principle 2	Children and young people are informed about their rights, participate in decisions affecting them and are taken seriously.
Principle 3	Families and communities are informed and involved in promoting child safety and wellbeing.
Principle 4	Equity is upheld and diverse needs respected in policy and practice.
Principle 5	People working with children and young people are suitable and supported to reflect child safety and wellbeing values in practice.
Principle 6	Processes to respond to complaints and concerns are child focused.
Principle 7	Staff and volunteers are equipped with the knowledge, skills and awareness to keep children and young people safe through ongoing education and training.
Principle 8	Physical and online environments promote safety and wellbeing while minimising the opportunity for children and young people to be harmed.
Principle 9	Implementation of the national child safe principles is regularly reviewed and improved.
Principle 10	Policies and procedures document how the organisation is safe for children and young people.

Source: National Principles for Child Safe Organisations © Australian Human Rights Commission 2018. Licensed under the Creative Commons Attribution 4.0 International Licence, http://creativecommons.org/licenses/by/4.0/legalcode

All states and territories have signed a commitment to the National Principles for Child Safe Organisations. This involves a commitment to promoting safe, happy and engaged children, as shown in the Wheel of Child Safety (**Figure 6.4**).

Child Safe Standards

Child Safe Standards in schools

The New South Wales Child Safe Standards were developed in response to the Royal Commission into Institutional Responses to Child Sexual Abuse, which identified both historical and current sexual abuse of children within a range of organisations engaged with children and young people, including schools, religious, social, sporting and disability support groups. The Child Safe Standards are designed to be proactive – stopping the harm before it occurs – and are legislated in the *Office of the Children's Guardian Act 2019* for organisations working with children to implement into their practice and designed to:

- help drive cultural change in organisations
- be principle-based and outcome-focused

Figure 6.4 Wheel of Child Safety

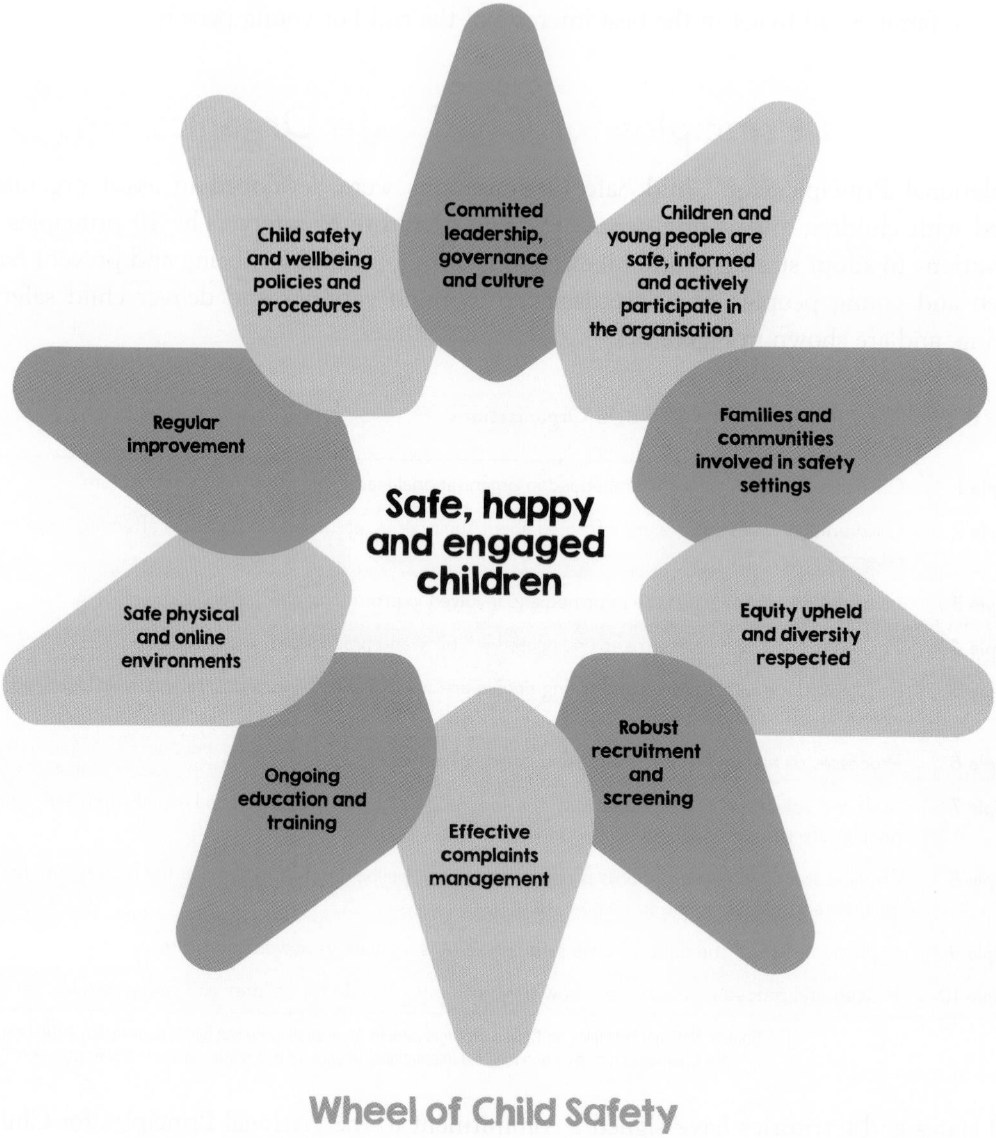

Source: National Principles for Child Safe Organisations © Australian Human Rights Commission 2018. Licensed under the Creative Commons Attribution 4.0 International Licence, http://creativecommons.org/licenses/by/4.0/legalcode

- be flexible enough that they can be adapted by organisations of varying sizes and characteristics
- avoid placing undue burden on organisations
- help organisations address multiple risks
- balance caution and caring
- be a benchmark against which organisations can assess their child-safe capability and set performance targets
- be of equal importance and interrelated.

Source: NSW Government, Office of the Children's Guardian (2020). The Child Safe Standards. https://ocg.nsw.gov.au/sites/default/files/2021-12/g_CSS_GuidetotheStandards.pdf?Embed=Y, p. 4.

Figure 6.5 describes the NSW 10 Child Safe Standards.

Figure 6.5 The NSW Child Safe Standards

STANDARD 1
Child safety is embedded in organisational leadership, governance and culture
STANDARD 2
Children participate in decisions affecting them and are taken seriously
STANDARD 3
Families and communities are informed and involved
STANDARD 4
Equity is upheld and diverse needs are taken into account
STANDARD 5
People working with children are suitable and supported
STANDARD 6
Processes to respond to complaints of child abuse are child focused
STANDARD 7
Staff are equipped with the knowledge, skills and awareness to keep children safe through continual education and training
STANDARD 8
Physical and online environments minimise the opportunity for abuse to occur
STANDARD 9
Implementation of the Child Safe Standards is continuously reviewed and improved
STANDARD 10
Policies and procedures document how the organisation is child safe

Source: NSW Government, Office of the Children's Guardian (2020). A guide to the Child Safe Standards. https://ocg.nsw.gov.au/sites/default/files/2021-12/g_CSS_GuidetotheStandards.pdf?Embed=Y, p. 2.

Terminology

As a specialist area, child protection uses a range of terminology that you are likely to hear or read when developing your knowledge of child protection. **Figure 6.6** describes a number of key terms commonly used in relation to child protection.

Figure 6.6 Child protection: key terms

Term	Definition
Notification	Contacts made to an authorised department by persons or other bodies making allegations of child abuse or neglect, child maltreatment or harm to a child.
Disclosure	Revealing that some form of abuse has occurred. A child may fully disclose – that is, tell someone they have been or are being abused and provide details of the abuse and the perpetrator. Partial disclosure means the child will hint at or allude to being abused, but does not provide specific details.
Allegation	A statement without proof that someone has perpetrated abuse against a child or young person.
Investigation	The process whereby the relevant department obtains more detailed information about a child who is the subject of a notification.
Substantiated	After investigation, it is concluded that there is reasonable cause to believe that the child has been, was being or was likely to be abused, neglected or otherwise harmed.
Not substantiated	A notification received . . . where an investigation concludes that there was no reasonable cause to suspect prior, current or future abuse, neglect or harm to the child.
Perpetrator	A person who has been determined to have caused (intentionally or unintentionally) by acts of omission or knowingly the maltreatment of a child.
Guardianship order	Conveys responsibility for the welfare of the child to the guardian (for example, regarding the child's education, health, religion, accommodation and financial matters). Does not necessarily grant the right to the daily care and control of the child, or the right to make decisions about the daily care and control of the child, which are granted under custody orders.
Custody order	Generally refers to orders that place children and young people in the custody of the state or territory department responsible for child protection, or a non-government agency. These orders usually involve the child protection department being responsible for the daily care and requirements of the child, while the parent retains legal guardianship. Custody alone does not bestow any responsibility regarding the long-term welfare of the child.
Care and protection order	A legal order or arrangement that gives child protection departments some responsibility for a child's welfare.
Finalised guardianship or custody order	Order involving the transfer of legal guardianship to the relevant state or territory department or non-government agency.
Foster care	A form of out-of-home care where the caregiver is authorised and reimbursed (or was offered but declined reimbursement) by the state/territory for the care of the child (excludes relatives/kin who are reimbursed).

Source: AIHW (2014).

Child protection legislation

Each state and territory has child protection legislation governing key areas such as mandatory reporting requirements, investigation, registration, legal proceedings, protection orders, ongoing intervention, supervision and the collection of statistical data (see **Figure 6.7**). In addition,

Australia now has the National Framework for Protecting Australia's Children 2009–2020. This framework aims to develop a long-term approach to ensuring the safety and wellbeing of Australia's children and young people, and to deliver 'a substantial and sustained reduction in levels of child abuse and neglect in Australia' over time (AIHW, 2013, pp. 4–5). The six outcome areas under the framework are:

1. Children live in safe and supportive communities.
2. Children and families access adequate support to promote safety and intervene early.
3. Risk factors for child abuse and neglect are addressed.
4. Children who have been abused or neglected receive the support and care they need for their safety and wellbeing.
5. Indigenous children are supported and safe in their families and communities.
6. Child sexual abuse and exploitation are prevented, and survivors receive adequate support.

Source: National Framework for Protecting Australia's Children 2009–2020, August 2013 © Australian Institute of Health and Welfare 2013. Released under CC BY 3.0 AU, link to license: https://creativecommons.org/licenses/by/3.0/au/

Mandatory reporting requirements

Child protection legislation identifies people who are required by law to report suspected child abuse and neglect. Those nominated as mandatory reporters vary across jurisdictions, but typically include people such as medical professionals, police officers, teachers, disability workers and Family Court officers. Western Australia requires mandatory reporting only for suspected child sexual abuse.

Mandatory reporting is the legal requirement to report abuse and/or neglect where there are reasonable grounds to suspect that a child is at risk (or significant risk) of harm. Those mandated by child protection legislation must report their concerns to the relevant state/territory authority. **Figure 6.7** lists mandatory reporters for each state and territory. As you can see, ESWs are not identified as mandatory reporters. However, if you have any concerns about a student, you should report your concerns to the teacher.

Working with children screening

As **Figure 6.7** also shows, currently there is no single national strategy that sets out the requirements for pre-employment screening for adults working with children. The aim of a Working with Children Check is to assess the level of risk a person poses to children's and young people's safety. In general, these checks consider:

- criminal convictions, including those dating from a person's childhood
- any court orders, such as apprehended violence orders, prohibitions, reporting orders
- criminal charges where a conviction was not recorded or charges were dismissed/withdrawn
- any allegations or police investigations
- relevant employment proceedings and records from professional organisations of any disciplinary actions (Scott, 2012).

Figure 6.7 Principal child protection legislation – Australian states and territories

Australian states and territories	
Australian Capital Territory	**Legislation** *Children and Young People Act 2008* (ACT) **Government agency/department** Office for Children, Youth and Family Support: **https://www.communityservices.act.gov.au/ocyfs** **Mandatory reporters** > A person caring for a child at a child care centre (including paid assistants/aides but not unpaid volunteers); a person coordinating or > monitoring home-based care for a family day care scheme proprietor; teachers at a school (including paid aides/assistants); a person authorised to inspect education programs, materials or other records used for home education of a child or young person under the *Education Act 2004* (ACT) > Doctors, dentists, nurses, enrolled nurses and midwives > Police officers; school counsellors; a public servant who works with children and families or provides services to them; the public advocate; the official visitor; a person who, in the course of the person's employment, has contact with or provides services to children, young people and their families and is prescribed by regulation **Mandatory pre-employment screening** Working with Vulnerable People (Background Checking): **https://www.accesscanberra.act.gov.au/s/article/working-with-vulnerable-people-wwvp-registration-tab-overview**
New South Wales	**Legislation** *Children and Young Persons (Care and Protection) Act 1998* (NSW) **Government agency/department** Department of Communities and Justice: **https://www.dcj.nsw.gov.au** **Mandatory reporters** > Child care educators, family day care educators and home-based carers; teachers > Doctors, nurses, dentists and other health workers; psychologists; social workers and youth workers; refuge workers; community housing providers; police officers **Mandatory pre-employment screening** Working with Children Check: **https://ocg.nsw.gov.au/working-children-check**
Northern Territory	**Legislation** *Care and Protection of Children Act 2007* (NT) **Government agency/department** Office of Children and Families: **https://nt.gov.au/law/crime/report-child-abuse** **Mandatory reporters** > Any person with reasonable grounds; registered health professionals **Mandatory pre-employment screening** Working with Children (Ochre Card) Clearance Screening: **https://nt.gov.au/emergency/community-safety/working-with-children-clearance-before-you-apply**

Australian states and territories	
Queensland	**Legislation** *Child Protection Act 1999* (Qld) **Government agency/department** Department of Children, Youth Justice and Multicultural Affairs **https://www.cyjma.qld.gov.au/protecting-children** **Mandatory reporters** > An authorised officer, employee of the department or a person employed in a departmental care service or licensed care service; staff of the Commission for Children and Young People and Child Guardian (CCYPCG); doctors and registered nurses; Family Court personnel and counsellors; teachers and early childhood education and care professionals **Mandatory pre-employment screening** Blue Card screening system: **https://www.qld.gov.au/law/laws-regulated-industries-andaccountability/queensland-laws-and-regulations/regulatedindustries-and-licensing/blue-card-services**
South Australia	**Legislation** *Children's Protection Act 1993* (SA) **Government agency/department** Department for Child Protection: **https://www.childprotection.sa.gov.au** **Mandatory reporters** > Medical practitioners; pharmacists; registered or enrolled nurses; dentists; psychologists > Police officers; community corrections officers and public service employees whose duties include supervising young or adult offenders in the community; social workers; ministers of religion; employees or volunteers in a religious/spiritual organisation > Teachers in an educational institution (including a kindergarten); approved family day care providers > Any employee or volunteer in an organisation that provides health, welfare, education, sporting, recreational, child care or residential services for children, and who is engaged in delivering services to children or whose duties include direct responsibility for, or direct supervision of, the provision of services to children **Mandatory pre-employment screening** Employers and responsible authorities are required to obtain criminal history checks for those engaging in child-related occupations/volunteering: **https://screening.sa.gov.au**
Tasmania	**Legislation** *Children, Young Persons and their Families Act 1997* (Tas); *Children, Young Persons and Their Families Amendment Act 2009* (Tas) **Government agency/department** Department for Education, Children and Young People: Child Safety Service: **https://www.decyp.tas.gov.au/children/child-safety-service/** **Mandatory reporters** > Child care providers; school principals and teachers > Registered medical practitioners and nurses; psychologists; dentists, dental therapists or dental hygienists > Police officers and probation officers > Department of Health and Human Services employees; volunteers and employees of any organisation that provides health, welfare, education, care or residential services and which receives government funding **Mandatory pre-employment screening** Registration to work with vulnerable people: **https://www.cbos.tas.gov.au/topics/licensing-and-registration/registrations/work-with-vulnerable-people**

Australian states and territories	
Victoria	**Legislation** *Children, Youth and Families Act 2005* (Vic); *Child Wellbeing and Safety Act 2005* (Vic) **Government agency/department** Child Protection Service, Department of Human Services: **https://services.dhhs.vic.gov.au/child-protection** **Mandatory reporters** > *Doctors, nurses, midwives, teachers and principals, police officers* **Mandatory pre-employment screening** Working with Children Check: **http://www.workingwithchildren.vic.gov.au** **Other legislation** *Child Wellbeing and Safety Act 2018* (Vic) Child Safe Standards **Government agency/department** Department of Human Services: **http://providers.dhhs.vic.gov.au/child-safe-standards** Child Safe Standards: **https://www.vrqa.vic.gov.au/childsafe/Pages/Home.aspx**
Western Australia	**Legislation** *Children and Community Services Act 2004* (WA); *Children and Community Services Amendment (Reporting Sexual Abuse of Children) Act 2008* (WA) **Government agency/department** Department for Child Protection and Family Support: **http://www.dcp.wa.gov.au** **Mandatory reporters (child sexual abuse only)** > *Doctors, nurses, midwives, teachers and police officers* **Mandatory pre-employment screening** Working with Children Check: **https://workingwithchildren.wa.gov.au**

Note: Correct at time of printing – always check your state/territory website for any updates or changes.

Ethical considerations

All children, young people and their families should be treated with dignity and respect. Where a child or young person is suspected of being at risk of harm, it is critical that the ESW behaves in a professional and ethical manner. The role of all adults working with children and young people is to act in the best interests of the child or young person – the protection and wellbeing of the child or young person are paramount.

Under normal circumstances, information about children and families should be treated as confidential. However, in the case of suspected risk of harm, child protection authorities will have interagency protocols to allow relevant information to be shared on an as-needs basis without the consent of the individual or family.

Working with other agencies

Child protection requires the close cooperation and goodwill of a range of government and non-government agencies. Each state and territory has well-defined inter-agency guidelines and protocols so that investigating officers work with all relevant agencies to ensure, as far as possible, that processes are put in place to minimise ongoing risks to the child. Confidentiality, high standards of ethical practice and a genuine willingness to act in the best interests of the child and family are necessary to ensure that children and young people are provided with the best possible protection against abuse and neglect.

Legal definitions

Generally, child protection legislation recognises and defines several types of abuse, including:

- physical abuse
- emotional abuse
- neglect
- witnessing domestic violence
- sexual abuse.

Child protection legislation in each state and territory includes a legal definition of child abuse and neglect that is used to determine when and under what circumstances state and territory authorities are mandated to intervene on behalf of a child or young person. **Figure 6.8** provides conceptual definitions of abusive and neglectful behaviours.

Figure 6.8 Definitions of abusive and neglectful behaviours

Term	Definition
Maltreatment	Refers to non-accidental behaviour towards another person that is outside the norms of conduct and entails a substantial risk of causing physical or emotional harm. Behaviours may be intentional or unintentional and include acts of omission and commission. Specifically, abuse refers to acts of commission and neglect to acts of omission.
Physically abusive behaviour	Any non-accidental physically aggressive act towards a child. Physical abuse may be intentional or may be the inadvertent result of physical punishment. Physically abusive behaviours include shoving, hitting, slapping, beating, shaking, throwing, punching, kicking, biting, burning, scalding, strangling, poisoning and suffocating the child (Butchart et al., 2006). The definition of **physically abusive behaviours** extends to and includes the fabrication, exaggeration and inducing of illness symptoms in a child (previously known as Munchausen Syndrome by Proxy – see Lasher and Sheridan, 2009).
Sexually abusive behaviour	Refers to any sexual activity between an adult and a child below the age of consent; non-consensual sexual activity between minors (e.g. a 14-year-old and a 10-year-old); sexual activity between a child under 18 years and a person in a position of power or authority (e.g. parent, teacher); or any sexual activity that a child does not fully comprehend, is unable to give informed consent to or for which the child is not developmentally prepared (Butchart et al., 2006; Higgins, 1998).Sexual activity includes fondling genitals, masturbation, oral sex, vaginal or anal penetration by a penis, finger or any other object, fondling of breasts, voyeurism, exhibitionism and exposing the child to or involving them in pornography (Butchart et al., 2006; Higgins, 1998).

Term	Definition
Neglectful behaviour	Refers to the failure (usually by a parent) to provide for a child's basic needs. Physically **neglectful behaviours** include a failure to provide adequate food, shelter, clothing, supervision, hygiene, medical attention, safe living conditions, education or emotional development (Butchart et al., 2006).
Witnessing family violence	A form of psychologically abusive behaviour; however, there is growing support for the inclusion of family violence as a distinct maltreatment sub-type. With this in mind, **witnessing family violence** refers to 'a child being present (hearing or seeing) while a parent or sibling is subjected to physical abuse, sexual abuse or psychological maltreatment, or is visually exposed to the damage caused to persons or property by a family member's violent behaviour' (Higgins, 1998, p. 104).

Source: AIFS (2014a).

Defining 'risk of harm' or significant risk of harm

The definition of 'risk of harm/significant risk of harm' varies across each jurisdiction. Generally, *reasonable grounds* to suspect that a child or young person is at risk of harm (or significant risk of harm) will include concerns that:

- the basic physical or psychological needs of the child are not being met
- the parent/s is unwilling or unable to arrange necessary medical care
- the child is being physically or sexually abused or neglected
- the child is witnessing domestic violence.

The Consider this box provides a definition of risk of harm as defined in the Queensland *Child Protection Act 1999*.

HARM AND UNACCEPTABLE RISK OF SIGNIFICANT HARM

CONSIDER THIS

Unacceptable risk of significant harm refers to significant harm that has not yet occurred but is likely in the future, given risk factors identified in the present. A child may be assessed as in need of protection if the level of future risk is identified as likely (probable), not just possible (may occur); the probable harm will have a significant detrimental effect on the child if it does occur; and there is not a parent able and willing to protect the child from future significant harm.

Where abuse is an action against a child, **harm** refers to the detrimental effect or impact of that action on the child. Therefore, to assess harm, parental actions, behaviour, motivation or intent are identified to determine the impact on the child, which may be cumulative in nature.

Source: Department of Communities, Child Safety and Disability Services Qld, 2015, pp. 2–3.

6.2 Why abuse occurs

Child abuse occurs for many different reasons. Although there are 'common' factors that may contribute to abuse, these will vary from one situation to another. It is likely that the 'triggers' for abuse will be unique to each individual and each situation.

While any adult faced with a screaming baby, a toddler throwing a tantrum or a sullen teenager has the potential to abuse a child, most adults are able to show appropriate restraint. **Perpetrators** of abuse do not fit a specific profile, and child abuse occurs across all socioeconomic groups, religions and cultures.

SCENARIO

THE NEXT GENERATION

Leylak (16 years) has four younger brothers. The family lives in an inner-city area populated by families who have emigrated from the Middle East. Leylak attends a school for academically gifted students. Although her father doesn't believe that girls need to be well educated, Leylak's mother is determined that her daughter will go to university. Each term, Leylak's school has a supervised school dance but Leylak's father refuses to allow her to attend. Tonight there is a huge argument, which results in Leylak being slapped across the face by her father. Leylak runs to her room screaming that her father lives in the past. She tells him she is Australian and wants to be treated like her friends.

WHAT DOES THIS TELL US?

Leylak has been physically assaulted by her father. The slap constitutes physical abuse. The reason for the slap is complex. Leylak's father is drawing on his traditional cultural values in not allowing her to attend the school dance. Leylak clearly rejects these values and wants her father to embrace 'Australian' values. As Leylak matures into young adulthood, the clash between the two cultures is likely to escalate.

▶ DISCUSSION

If you were aware of this situation, would you make a notification? Why or why not?

Triggers for abuse

Abuse may occur due to a variety of precipitating factors that, when combined, may cause a parent or carer to use inappropriate force, neglect or physical punishment. **Figure 6.9** lists the wide range of factors that may, *given a range of particular circumstances,* trigger abuse and neglect.

SCENARIO

JUST LIKE YOUR FATHER!

Marco (13 years) lives with his mother, **Maria**, and two older sisters. His parents are divorced. Marco spends every second weekend with his father, **Peter**, his new partner, **Nell**, and their three-year-old daughter. Marco loves going to his father's house and wishes he could live with Peter and Nell full-time, but he is afraid to tell his mother. His mother makes it clear that she loathes Peter and endlessly tells her children that Peter and his new wife enjoy 'the good life' while they struggle to make ends meet. Today, when he gets home from visiting his father, Maria is in a bad mood. When Marco takes his weekend washing and tips it into the laundry basket, his mother yells: *'That's right, just come home and dump me with a load of washing. You are so selfish, just like your father! Get out of my sight!'* Marco runs to his room and slams the door, muttering to himself, *'Yeah I know you hate me like you hate Dad!'*

WHAT DOES THIS TELL US?

Maria still harbours resentment towards Peter and seems unable to separate these feelings from her relationship with her son. This type of emotional abuse can have long-term consequences for children.

▶ DISCUSSION

What impact might this situation have on Marco's behaviour at school?

Figure 6.9 Triggers or risk factors for abuse

Vulnerable adults

- Low self-esteem
- A low tolerance or frustration level
- Drug or alcohol abuse
- Chronic physical illness/complex medical needs
- Mental health disorders
- A history of family and/or domestic violence
- Family crisis
- Little or no preparation for parenting
- Poor parenting models as a child
- Poor physical or emotional health
- Involvement in a violent relationship
- Disability/developmental delay
- Personal history of abuse and/or neglect
- Personal history of complex trauma
- An inability to manage stress

Parenting risk factors

- Under 20 years of age at birth of first child
- Little or no knowledge of child development and child behaviour
- Fear that the child will be spoiled or disobedient
- A view of children as inherently bad or naughty
- Unrealistic expectations of the child
- Unwilling and/or unable to put the child's needs before own needs
- Rejection or scapegoating of the child (blaming child for own misfortune/poor health)
- A lack of understanding about and/or ability to supervise the safety of the child
- Inadequate or no antenatal support
- Alcohol/substance abuser

Relationship difficulties

- Domestic violence
- Few or no supportive friends
- Poor relationship with own parent/s
- Single parent and/or multiple partners who are emotionally unsupportive
- Reliance on the child to meet emotional needs
- Social isolation

Social/cultural factors

- Homelessness, poor housing and no safe play areas
- Poverty/unemployment
- A lack of reliable transport
- Life crises, such as the death of a family member or friend, or a recent separation
- Unwanted/unplanned pregnancy
- Constant illness of children
- Social changes, such as breakdown of family support and social isolation
- Belonging to a member of a minority group
- Community attitudes towards violence
- A lack of affordable child care

Characteristics of the child

- Born prematurely
- Has a disability
- Has learning difficulties
- Experiences chronic health issues
- Considered to be the 'wrong' gender
- Resembles a disliked family member
- Has feeding problems
- Is difficult to settle or a poor sleeper

Physical abuse

Physical abuse refers to non-accidental injury of a child by a parent, caregiver or any other person, and includes injuries resulting from excessive discipline, severe beatings or shaking, and attempted suffocation or attempted strangulation. Injuries include bruising, lacerations or welts, burns, fractures and dislocations.

Indicators of physical abuse may vary according to the age of the child or young person and may include:

- facial, head and neck bruising
- lacerations and welts from excessive discipline or physical restraint
- the explanation offered by the child being inconsistent with the injury or the parent's explanation
- other bruising and marks that may show the shape of the object that caused them, such as a hand or belt buckle
- bite marks and scratches where the bruise may show a print of adult teeth
- multiple injuries and bruises of varying colours
- ingestion of poisonous substances, alcohol or other harmful drugs
- ruptured organs without a history of trauma
- dislocations, sprains or twisting
- fractures of bones, especially in children aged under three years
- burns, especially on the back of the legs, lower legs or buttocks, consistent with immersion and scalding
- head injuries where the child may have indicators of drowsiness, vomiting or retinal haemorrhage, suggesting the possibility of the child having been shaken violently.

Psychological harm/emotional abuse

Psychological harm/emotional abuse occurs when a child has been, or is at risk of being, harmed, because of the parent or carer's behaviour or attitude.

Behaviours considered to be psychologically harmful or emotionally abusive include repeated rejection and using threats to frighten the child. This may involve constantly criticising, belittling and teasing, as well as ignoring or withholding praise and affection. It can also include being persistently hostile and verbally abusive, rejecting and blaming the child unnecessarily, making excessive or unreasonable demands and isolating and/or preventing the young child from engaging in normal peer relationships.

Sometimes emotional abuse occurs when the needs of children and young people are overlooked or misunderstood, and parental expectations far exceed the child's ability to achieve. Emotional abuse occurs when parental expectations significantly affect the child's quality of life and the right of the child to be a child. Psychological harm/emotional abuse is also likely to occur where there is domestic violence, untreated mental problems (of the parent/s) and drug and alcohol abuse.

Psychological/emotional abuse can have lifelong consequences. Confidence and self-esteem can be shattered, and social, emotional and behavioural problems can result – for example, difficulty forming relationships, a lack of trust and acting-out behaviours such as physical assault, violence or vandalism. Because it can easily be hidden by perpetrators, psychological/emotional abuse is a particularly difficult issue to address (Family and Community Services (NSW), 2011, p. 5).

Indicators of emotional abuse may include:

- feelings of worthlessness about life and themselves
- inability to value others or show empathy
- inability to trust others
- lack of interpersonal skills necessary for age-appropriate functioning
- extreme attention-seeking behaviour
- extreme risk-taking behaviour
- being markedly disruptive, bullying or aggressive
- teenagers having suicidal thoughts.

SCENARIO

EXPECTATIONS

JACK

Jack (12 years) is the youngest of four children and the only boy. Jack's sisters are all involved in team sports. Jack's father, **Dan**, has always been good at sports, he was captain of his high school football team and was a competitive swimmer. Dan swims each morning and goes for a run each evening. Jack is very shy and quiet. He prefers indoor games and doesn't like sport. Dan is disappointed that Jack isn't more outgoing. He tells Jack that he needs to toughen up and stop being a wimp.

EVA

Eva's mother had a difficult labour. As a result, Eva (now nine) suffered brain damage and has a number of learning difficulties. Eva has two older siblings, both of whom are high achievers. Eva's parents are high achievers with professional careers and have found it difficult to come to terms with Eva's learning difficulties. They describe Eva as their 'mistake'.

▶ DISCUSSION

What might be the emotional consequences for Jack and Eva in relation to their parents' attitude towards them?

Neglect

Neglect occurs when the basic needs of a child or young person – for shelter, food, medical care and education – have not been, or are at risk of not being, met to the point where this may have a significant adverse impact on the safety, welfare or wellbeing of the child or young person. This lack of care could be constituted by a single act or omission or a pattern of acts or omissions. It may also include a lack of adequate supervision and abandonment (Family and Community Services (NSW), 2011, p. 8).

Neglect can occur in a variety of ways and is not restricted to the absence of physical care. According to Dwyer and colleagues (2012, p. 4), neglect may include the following forms:

- *Physical neglect.* This encompasses poor hygiene, inadequate food or clothing and inadequate shelter, which may involve environmental neglect where the standards of living are unsafe or unhygienic.
- *Medical neglect.* This is where the parent or carer fails to ensure basic health care.
- *Supervisory neglect.* This occurs when a responsible adult fails to ensure supervision for a child that is appropriate for their age and development. This might include leaving the child unattended or leaving the child with an inappropriate person.
- *Developmental neglect.* This relates to a number of aspects of care that are required for stimulation, and physical and social development. Neglect in these areas means a child is left without adequate stimulation or educational opportunity.
- *Emotional neglect.* This relates to the nature of the parent or carer's emotional relationship with the child, and a failure to meet the child's emotional needs.

Indicators of neglect may include:

- an ongoing poor standard of hygiene
- scavenging for or hoarding food
- an extreme craving for adult attention and affection
- excessive anxiety about being abandoned
- excessive self-comforting behaviour, such as rocking
- failure to thrive that can't be traced to another source
- an unexplained delay in reaching developmental milestones
- a general appearance of neglect – dirty clothing, unclean appearance, poor skin tone, poor hair condition.

SCENARIO

ABSENCES

ASHER

Asher (10 years) is one of four children living with his mother and her partner. Asher is often left to care for his two younger siblings at night when his mother and her partner go out to clubs and pubs, often coming home drunk. The parents often sleep late, leaving Asher to prepare breakfast and get himself and his sisters to school. Often there is little or no food in the house. Most evenings Asher is sent to the shop to buy hot chips for the children's evening meal. To avoid hearing his parents' drunken behaviour, Asher has begun climbing out of his bedroom window when his parents get home and walking around the streets late at night. He has been picked up by the police and returned home on two occasions.

LUCY AND JASMINE

Lucy and **Jasmine** are six-year-old twins. Their parents run a successful physiotherapy practice, which operates from 7 a.m. until 6 p.m. Monday to Friday and 9 a.m. until noon Saturdays. Saturday afternoon is usually taken up with paperwork while Sunday is spent grocery shopping, washing and cleaning. Because their parents work long hours, the girls are cared for by a nanny. Often the girls are asleep by the time their parents get home. The girls ask their nanny why Mummy and Daddy are never home: *'Don't they like us any more?'*

▶ DISCUSSION

Can it be argued that Asher, his siblings and the twins are equally neglected?

Living with family and domestic violence

Family violence refers to violence between family members, typically where the perpetrator exercises power and control over another person. The most common and pervasive instances occur in intimate (current or former) partner relationships and are usually referred to as domestic violence. Family violence may also include sexual violence, which includes behaviours of a sexual nature carried out against a person's will. It can be perpetrated by a current or former partner, other people known to the victim, or strangers. Family, domestic and sexual violence happens repeatedly – more than half (54%) of the women who had experienced current partner violence, experienced more than one violent incident. Those at greater risk of family, domestic and sexual violence include Aboriginal and Torres Strait Islander women, young women, pregnant women, women separating from their partners, women with disability and women experiencing financial hardship (AIHW, 2018b).

Domestic and family violence can affect children's behaviour, schooling, cognitive development, mental and physical wellbeing, and is the leading cause of homelessness for children (Campo, 2015). Disturbingly, people who as children witnessed partner violence against their parents were two to four times as likely to experience partner violence themselves (as adults) as people who had not (ABS, 2017b, cited in AIHW, 2018b).

SCENARIO

DOMESTIC VIOLENCE

Saari (14 years), **Eddie** (8 years) and **Oscar** (6 years) live with their mother, **Cara** and father, **Dan**. Their father was seriously injured in a workplace accident three years ago and is unable to work. Dan has become increasingly depressed but refuses to seek help. Cara and Dan constantly argue and Dan is becoming increasingly aggressive towards his wife. Saari knows the warning signs and always tries to get Eddie and Oscar into her bedroom or out of the house when the arguments start. Last night, for the first time, Dan pushed Cara, knocking her to the ▶

floor. When Saari heard the noise she rushed to her mother's side, screaming at her father to stop. Eddie and Oscar hid under Saari's bed.

WHAT DOES THIS TELL US?

Children who are caught up in domestic violence are victims of emotional abuse. Older children may feel they need to protect the parent who is subject to the abuse and/or to protect younger siblings. Younger children and their older siblings are placed in a situation where they no longer feel safe and protected.

► DISCUSSION

What would you do if you were made aware of Saari's situation?

Sexual abuse

Sexual abuse is defined by the AIHW (2021a) as 'any act by a person having the care of a child that exposes the child to, or involves the child in, sexual processes beyond his or her understanding, or contrary to accepted community standards' (p. 93).

Sexual abuse may include sexual acts; exposure to sexually explicit material; inducing or coercing the child or young person to engage in, or assist any other person to engage in, sexually explicit conduct for any reason and exposing the child or young person to circumstances where there is risk that they may be sexually abused (Family and Community Services (NSW), 2011, p. 3).

The Australian Institute of Family Studies (AIFS) (2014b) reports that child sexual abuse is the least **substantiated** form of abuse. Of substantiated cases, girls are more likely to be victims of sexual abuse than boys. The AIFS (2014b, n.p.) also reports that 'a far greater number of child sexual abuse offences are perpetrated by adults who are not in a caregiver role but may be known to the child or young person'. Children and young people with a disability are a particularly vulnerable group, especially those in the out-of-home care system (Royal Commission into Institutional Responses to Child Sexual Abuse, 2016).

Sexual abuse is usually premeditated, planned and progressive, often moving from inappropriate touching to sexual penetration. Perpetrators will usually bribe, coerce or physically and/or emotionally threaten the victim into keeping the abuse a secret. Children and young people can be very confused about sexual abuse, especially when the perpetrator is a significant person in the child's life, such as a parent, de facto partner of mother, foster parent, uncle, grandfather, teacher/instructor, coach, family friend or neighbour.

Perpetrators (predominantly male) use deliberate strategies to target children and young people. They may bribe, coerce or physically and/or emotionally threaten the victim into keeping the abuse a secret.

The AIFS (2014b) describes three main types of child sex abuse offenders:

- **Serial perpetrator predators** – high-frequency chronic offenders who choose victims based on situational factors and are likely to actively manipulate environments to create opportunities to abuse. Serial perpetrators usually engage in grooming behaviours by befriending, spending increasing amounts of time with the child or young person to win trust, offering gifts and moving from hugs to inappropriate touching to sexual penetration.
- **Opportunistic occasional predators** – more likely to commit abuse when a lack of appropriate controls, such as a code of conduct or reporting procedures, obscures personal responsibility for the abuse.

- **Situational perpetrators** – commit abuse in reaction to environmental factors and often behave impulsively when overcome by temptation or a temporary failure of self-control.

Indicators of sexual abuse may include:

- the child verbalising the sexual act, such as 'Daddy hurt my wee-wee'
- the child describing sexual acts from watching adult videos
- a young person becoming extremely withdrawn, aggressive, suicidal, absconding from home or care.

Consequences of sexual abuse

Sexual abuse of children and young people is perhaps the ultimate act of betrayal and breach of trust. The secretive nature of child sexual abuse usually leads to children and young people feeling that they are to blame for the abuse. They come to see themselves as bad, useless, hopeless and dirty. Children and young people will often experience guilt that they did not tell anyone about the abuse and feel responsible for the ongoing nature of the abuse.

Many perpetrators tell their victims that they will not be believed if they report the abuse, and that they will be sent away for telling lies. Victims may also be told by the perpetrator that they will cause the family unit to be split up if they tell.

Child sexual abuse has devastating lifelong consequences, the most extreme of which may include self-harm and suicide. Children may display indicators such as extreme acting-out behaviours, regression, phobias, nightmares and sleep disturbances, pseudo-maturity, persistent, inappropriate sexual play and provocative sexual behaviour, an overly sophisticated and detailed understanding of sexual behaviour, depression and anxiety. Young people who are victims of sexual abuse may display indicators such as promiscuity, prostitution, drug and/or alcohol abuse, eating disorders and suicidal or self-mutilating behaviours. Children and young people who have been sexually abused are likely to have difficulty forming satisfying adult relationships and are more likely to choose partners who are violent and abusive.

It must be remembered that while curiosity about genitalia is normal in most young children, it is extremely rare for children to make up stories of sexual abuse. Detailed knowledge of sexual behaviour is normally outside a young child's realm of knowledge. In order for young children to have explicit knowledge of sexual behaviour, they must be exposed to it or experience it.

SCENARIO

SARAH

Sarah (12 years) is being sexually abused by her stepfather, **Paul**. The abuse started when Sarah was eight. Sarah's mother is a nurse, and when she is on night shift, Paul goes into Sarah's room. He tells Sarah that he loves her and that she is his 'special girl'. Paul tells Sarah that what they do is a secret and that she must never tell because everyone will think she is a liar and she will be put into care or sent to a children's home. Sarah knows that her stepfather is not like other fathers. She loves her stepfather, but she wishes he would stop.

Sarah's teacher has expressed concern that Sarah is becoming increasingly withdrawn at school – she sits alone at lunchtime and refuses to join in any activities with her peers. Recently, Sarah told her teacher that she wished she could die. When asked why she felt this way, she said that she 'did bad things', but would make no further comment. Her teacher reported the conversation to the principal and Sarah was referred to the school counsellor for urgent follow-up.

WHAT DOES THIS TELL US?

Victims of child sexual abuse are often told that they are 'special' and they must keep it a secret. They are typically threatened that they will be sent away and/or they will break up the family if they tell. Victims often blame themselves or see themselves as 'bad'.

6.3 Indicators of abuse

Figure 6.10 lists common indicators of abuse and neglect. These indicators should be considered in the context of what is already known about the child and family. Indicators of abuse and neglect typically present in clusters (that is, the child or young person will display a number of indicators).

Figure 6.10 Indicators of abuse

Type of abuse	Possible indicators
Physical	> Facial, head and neck bruising > Lacerations and welts from excessive discipline or physical restraint > An explanation offered by the child or young person that is inconsistent with the injury or the parent's explanation > Other bruising and marks that may show the shape of the object that caused it – e.g. a handprint or belt buckle > Bite marks and scratches where the bruise may show a print of adult teeth > Multiple injuries and bruises of varying colours > Ingestion of poisonous substances, alcohol or other harmful drugs > Ruptured organs without a history of trauma > Dislocations, sprains, twisting > Fractures of bones, especially in children under three years > Burns, especially on the back of the legs, lower legs or buttocks, consistent with immersion and scalding > Head injuries where the child or young person may have indicators of drowsiness, vomiting, fits or retinal haemorrhages, suggesting the possibility of the child having been shaken violently
Sexual	> The young child verbalising the sexual act – for example, 'Daddy hurt my wee-wee' > The young child describing sexual acts from watching adult videos > Direct or indirect disclosure (such as role-playing sexual acts) > Age-inappropriate behaviour and/or persistent sexual behaviour > Regression in developmental skills > Bleeding from the vagina, external genitalia or anus – for example, blood on the underpants or nappy > Trauma to buttocks, lower abdomen or thighs > Regressive behaviour – for example, wetting or soiling
Neglect	> Ongoing poor standard of hygiene > Scavenging for food or hoarding food > Extreme craving for adult attention and affection > Excessive anxiety about being abandoned > Excessive self-comforting behaviour – for example, rocking > Non-organic failure to thrive > Unexplained delay in reaching developmental milestones > General appearance of neglect – dirty clothing, unclean appearance, poor skin tone, poor hair condition

Type of abuse	Possible indicators
Psychological/emotional abuse	> Feelings of worthlessness about life and themselves > Inability to value others or show empathy > Inability to trust others > Lack of interpersonal skills necessary for age-appropriate functioning > Extreme attention-seeking > Taking extreme risks > Being markedly disruptive, bullying or aggressive
Children living with domestic violence	> Atypical aggressive or violent behaviour > Persistent separation anxiety > Frequent absences from service > Regressive behaviour > Reduced social competence skills, including low levels of empathy, anxiety, depression, low self-esteem

Remember that, as discussed earlier in the chapter, many of the possible indicators of abuse listed in **Figure 6.10** may be attributed to a range of non-abusive causal factors. It is important to be alert to persistent atypical behaviours, or suspicious or unexplained physical injuries.

The consequences of child maltreatment

The long-term consequences of abuse and neglect are not the same for every child, and depend on a number of contributing or contextual factors. Although the outcomes for each child may be unique, there is no doubt that child abuse always has extremely damaging consequences for children and young people.

Contextual factors that contribute to the negative consequences of abuse include social isolation of the family, geographical location (such as a high-crime neighbourhood or a remote community), low socioeconomic status, partner/caregiver with alcohol or drug dependence or psychological problems, and children with a disability.

Other factors contributing to the consequences of abuse and neglect are the child's/young person's level of resilience, self-esteem and independence; the severity, frequency, duration and type/s of the abuse; the child/young person's age and developmental stage; the child/young person's own perception of the abuse (e.g. self-blaming); and the relationship/attachment of the child/young person and perpetrator of abuse (AIFS, 2014b, pp. 2, 3). Mitigating factors may include positive relationships with extended family or friends and the support of teachers or other figures of authority.

The consequences of abuse include a range of health and social problems, as shown in **Figure 6.11**.

Figure 6.11 Possible consequences of abuse and neglect for a child or young person

Outcomes	Example
Attachment issues	Babies and children exposed to abuse and neglect are more likely to experience attachment problems, which can negatively impact on lifelong social and emotional development – an inability to trust others and difficulty forming healthy relationships throughout life.

Outcomes	Example
Physical and mental health problems	Severe physical trauma may have long-term consequences. An example is Shaken Baby Syndrome, where the baby is shaken vigorously, causing tiny blood vessels inside the baby's brain to tear and bleed. As a result of such trauma, babies may suffer brain damage, hearing loss, spinal cord injuries, seizures, blindness, speech problems and even death. Exposure to prolonged abuse and/or neglect can have a profound effect on the developing brains of young children, and may result in learning and developmental problems, behavioural problems, depression and anxiety. Children who have been abused are more likely to develop depression and anxiety disorders in their teenage years. During adolescence, children who have been abused are: > twice the risk of youth suicide > more likely to develop eating disorders > more likely to engage in drug and alcohol abuse > more likely to display aggression and violence > more likely to engage in criminal activity > more likely (if sexually abused) to engage in risky sexual activity and have a higher risk of becoming homeless.

Source: Children's Hospital Westmead (2014); CFCA (2014) CC-BY-4.0 licence.

Dolgin (2014, pp. 254–5) states that neglect, or physical, sexual or emotional abuse, during adolescence has serious long-term consequences for young people as they are moving into early adulthood. Adolescents who have been physically abused may display pathological fear, shyness, passive dispositions, deep-seated hostility, sullenness and a cold and indifferent inability to love others. They are more likely to use violence themselves and more likely to develop clinical depression and have suicidal thoughts. Teenage girls who have been physically abused are more likely to choose partners who are physically abusive and so continue to be abused. Adolescents who have been sexually abused (including victims of incest) will manifest similar symptoms but are also more likely to engage in self-harm, substance abuse, truancy, running away, hostility and aggression. They may also turn to prostitution. The most extreme consequence of abuse is death (Lamont, 2010). (See the Scenario box.)

SCENARIO

SEXUAL ABUSE

When **Casey** was 13, she told her mother that **Jayden**, her mother's current partner, was sexually abusing her. Casey's mother accused her of lying and said she was just trying to ruin her mother's life. Casey tried to tell one of her teachers about the abuse but felt too ashamed.

At 15, Casey ran away from home and now lives on the streets. Casey sees herself as worthless and 'unlovable'. She daydreams about having a loving family and living in a nice safe home.

WHAT DOES THIS TELL US?

Children and young people who are abused feel isolated. They often won't seek help outside of the family – especially when those who are meant to safeguard them are the perpetrators. The long-term consequences are often feelings of worthlessness and hopelessness.

The most powerful consequence of abuse is the breach of trust between the child and the trusted adult. The role of adults is to nurture, love and protect children and young people so that they can grow up with a sense of being valued as individuals. Child abuse takes away the joy and innocence of childhood and replaces it with fear and anxiety. Sadly, children who are abused and/or neglected by a parent or parents are at risk of becoming abusers themselves as adults. Victims of child abuse often lack positive parenting role models and may repeat the abusive behaviours to which they were subjected as children.

Video: The science of neglect'

Children and young people with disabilities

Any child or young person may be the subject of abuse or neglect. As we have explored, abuse occurs in all cultural and socioeconomic groups. There are, however, some children and young people who, for a range of reasons, are at greater risk of abuse than others. Miller and Brown (2014, p. 8) report on findings from research undertaken by the National Society for the Prevention of Cruelty to Children (NSPCC), London, that:

> disabled children are three times more likely to be abused than non-disabled children ... are at significantly greater risk of physical, sexual and emotional abuse and neglect than non-disabled children ... Disabled children at greatest risk of abuse are those with behaviour/conduct disorders. Other high-risk groups include children with learning difficulties/disabilities, children with speech and language difficulties, children with health-related conditions and deaf children.

Based on international research, a number of factors contribute to this greater level of risk, including:

- a tendency not to believe children with disabilities when they report abuse
- children with disabilities and their families tending to be more isolated within the community, meaning that abuse may go unreported
- the child's or young person's inability to understand, resist and communicate abuse
- the child's or young person's inability to seek help
- a general assumption that children and young people with disabilities will not be at risk in the care of parents, carers or professionals.

This research also shows that children and young people with disabilities are more likely to be abused by a family member, carer or someone known to the child.

Children and young people with disabilities face multiple barriers in disclosing abuse. They may lack the cognitive skills to understand what is happening to them or to be aware that they have the right to be protected. They may not have the necessary vocabulary or language skills to communicate what is happening and may not have access to a wider network of caring adults to whom they can turn for support. See the following Consider this and Scenario boxes.

ABUSE AND DISABILITY

CONSIDER THIS

- Boys who are disabled are at greater risk of abuse (physical and sexual abuse and neglect) than girls who are disabled.
- Children and young people with disabilities are more likely to be bullied than their non-disabled peers because they are seen as different, an easy target, easily exploited, or easily hurt or upset (Miller & Brown, 2014, p. 24).
- Most common reasons for not reporting given by children and young people with disabilities were fear of violent retribution, embarrassment and not being believed (Miller & Brown, 2014, p. 25).
- Children and young people with disabilities find it difficult to report sexual abuse or sexual misbehaviour perpetrated by their peers.

- Children and young people with disabilities are more likely to experience multiple kinds of abuse and multiple episodes of abuse (Miller & Brown, 2014, p. 22).
- Despite explicit sex education, neither boys nor girls with disabilities readily associated sex with pregnancy or sexually transmitted diseases (Miller & Brown, 2014, p. 27).
- The majority of children and young people with disabilities accepted sexual misbehaviour (among peers) as the norm and did not think it worth reporting (Miller & Brown, 2014, p. 27).

Source: Miller & Brown (2014). Copyright © 2019 NSPCC.

SCENARIO

BARRIERS

JORDAN

Jordan (14 years) has learning and physical disabilities as well as a range of health problems. Jordan's communication is very restricted – he uses a limited number of pictures and symbols to make his needs known. Jordan has a new carer, **Tom**, who takes him to and from hydrotherapy. Tom has begun sexually abusing Jordan when he is changing him after hydrotherapy. Jordan becomes distressed each time Tom comes to collect him for hydrotherapy but his teacher puts this down to Jordan reacting to the presence of a new carer.

MICHAEL

Michael (11 years) has a severe hearing impairment and is academically gifted. He has just started at his local high school but is finding the large number of students challenging. Several Year 8 boys have targeted Michael and taunt him daily by pointing and shaking their fists at him and indicating that they are going to hurt him. Michael tries to ignore the boys but he is becoming worried that they will carry out their threats.

CASSIE

Cassie (16 years) has Down syndrome. She attends a living skills program at a special school. Cassie tells her mother that one of the boys in her class, **Elliot**, who also has Down syndrome, is her boyfriend and they are 'sexing'. When questioned, Cassie tells her mother that they kiss and hold hands but they don't cuddle 'because that's how you get a baby'. Cassie giggles as she says this and her mother realises that Cassie has not understood the many discussions they have had about sex.

WHAT DOES THIS TELL US?

Children and young people with disabilities are at greater risk of abuse by perpetrators who prey on their vulnerabilities.

Child abuse in Aboriginal and Torres Strait Islander communities

Aboriginal and Torres Strait Islander

Violence and the incidence of child abuse in Aboriginal and Torres Strait Islander communities is disproportionately higher than in the general population. The AIHW (2018a) found that Aboriginal and Torres Strait Islander children were seven times more likely to be the subject of substantiated child abuse and neglect than other Australian children. Aboriginal and Torres Strait Islander children living in remote areas were 10 times more likely to be in out-of-home care, while Aboriginal and Torres Strait Islander children living in major cities were 15 times more likely than other Australian children to be in out-of-home care. Neglect is the most common form of substantiated abuse for Aboriginal and Torres Strait Islander children (AIHW, 2018a). At 30 June 2020, 38 per cent (23 300) of children on **care and protection orders** were Indigenous (AIHW, 2021a).

The high rate of substantiated abuse of Aboriginal and Torres Strait Islander children is the result of multiple historical, social, community, family and individual factors (Scott & Nair, 2013). Historical events, including the poor treatment and lack of respect for Aboriginal and Torres Strait Islander communities, the forced removal of Aboriginal and Torres Strait Islander children from their families (the Stolen Generations), forced assimilation, racism and the removal of Aboriginal and Torres Strait Islander communities from their lands, have resulted in Aboriginal and Torres Strait Islander communities feeling disempowered. Ongoing trauma and community problems have resulted in alcohol and drug abuse, domestic violence, sexual abuse, and overcrowded and inadequate housing.

SCENARIO

CORRINE

Corrine (9 years) is being sexually abused by her uncle, who shares the home with Corrine's mother, brothers, younger sister and grandfather. Corrine's remote community is extremely poor, with a high rate of unemployment, low school attendance, alcohol and drug abuse, domestic violence and child abuse among the Aboriginal population. Corrine wishes her uncle would stop. Her uncle tells her that if she tells she will be taken away from her community and placed in a home with white people and she will never see her mother again.

WHAT DOES THIS TELL US?

Aboriginal and Torres Strait Islander families living in remote communities are often disconnected from their culture and face a lifetime of unemployment and welfare dependency. The reasons for this are complex and can be traced back to the breakdown of traditional communities as a consequence of white settlement.

6.4 Protecting children and young people

The challenge in protecting children and young people from abuse, neglect and bullying becomes significantly more complex when children and young people have disabilities that limit their understanding of what is happening to them, have no understanding of their rights and/or cannot communicate with an appropriate adult.

All children and young people have the right to be protected from abuse and neglect. This right is enshrined in the UN Convention on the Rights of the Child. The Consider this box details Articles 19 and 23 of the Convention.

CONSIDER THIS

UN CONVENTION ON THE RIGHTS OF THE CHILD

Article 19: Governments should ensure that children are properly cared for and protect them from violence, abuse and neglect by their parents, or anyone else who looks after them.

Article 23: Children who have any kind of disability should receive special care and support so that they can live a full and independent life.

Source: UNICEF (2018).

The responsibility to protect children and young people with disabilities from abuse rests with the community. In particular, it rests with those adults who have regular, ongoing contact with these children and are in a position to identify possible indicators of abuse and/or neglect.

PANTS: The underwear rule

The report by Miller and Brown (2014, p. 26) found that teaching explicit 'keeping safe' skills (building self-esteem, assertiveness and relationship skills) was effective in assisting children and young people with disabilities to identify and report abuse. An excellent example of a 'keeping safe' strategy is described in **Figure 6.12**. The strategy, developed by the National Society for the Prevention of Cruelty to Children (NSPCC), is called 'The Underwear Rule'. It is designed to assist parents, teachers and carers to teach children and young people with disabilities about how to keep themselves safe.

Figure 6.12 The NSPCC Talk Pants initiative

Source: Reproduced with permission from National Society for the Prevention of Cruelty to Children (NSPCC).

Miller and Brown (2014, p. 27) also report that peer support programs have been found to be successful (or at least to create greater awareness) in reducing bullying of children and young people with disabilities. Anecdotal results of peer support programs in schools showed:

- fewer friendship problems
- a drop in the number of 'petty' incidents reported to staff
- the school feeling safer for pupils
- vulnerable and lonely pupils spotted earlier and supported
- a more pleasant playground
- fewer complaints about pupil behaviour from lunchtime supervisors
- learning time no longer lost in following up lunchtime incidents.

Protecting children and young people with disabilities from harm is the responsibility of the whole community. The ESW's role is to always act in the best interests of the child or young person and always report any concerns or suspicions of potential risk of harm immediately.

If a child or young person discloses abuse

Disclosure of abuse can be an extremely stressful situation for both the adult and the child. Children and young people who are being abused will often be extremely secretive or protective of the perpetrator if that person is a parent or close family member. Many child victims are threatened with dire consequences if they disclose abuse, such as being taken away from the family or causing the perpetrator to be removed from the home. Even very young children may sense that 'telling' is being disloyal (even though they are not able to articulate such thoughts). Children and young people will only disclose to a person they trust, such as a teacher, an ESW or a carer.

Younger children or children with a cognitive disability may not have the language to describe their abuse with any clarity. In relation to sexual abuse, younger children will often lack the vocabulary to describe what is happening to them. It is important to be alert to children's attempts to tell you they are being abused; however, it is equally important not to jump to conclusions. Disclosure for young children may include generalised statements – for example,

'I don't like it when my Daddy hurts me'; 'My Mummy said I'm naughty and I get a smack'; 'My Poppy makes my wee-wee hurt'; 'Mummy pulls my hair'; 'I don't like my Uncle Rob'.

When children make these kinds of statements, it can be helpful to ask for more information, but this must be done in a very careful manner – for example, 'I'm sorry you are feeling upset/unhappy. Can you tell me what Daddy/Mummy/Poppy does?' If the child refuses to say more (as they often do), don't probe. You might simply say, 'Thank you for sharing with me. It's good to talk about feelings.'

If a child or young person makes a disclosure, you must always act in the best interests of the child or young person. You should follow the school's child protection policy and procedures. Remember that your role is to listen to and support the child. You are not required to investigate nor are you required to determine whether or not the information given is accurate. You should also refrain from judging the alleged perpetrator. You must put your own feelings of shock, dismay or anger to one side – the child must be your primary concern at the time of disclosure. **Figure 6.13** shows the steps that may be followed if a child or young person discloses abuse. (You should also refer to your school's child protection policy for the procedures that should be followed.)

Figure 6.13 Steps to take if a child or young person discloses

1. React calmly
2. Listen without judging
3. Don't ask leading questions – e.g. 'Did your mother hit you with a belt?'
4. Reassure the child that they have done the right thing – e.g. 'I'm pleased that you have told me about what's worrying you Sarah'
5. Don't make promises that can't be kept – e.g. the child may ask you not to tell others
6. Provide comfort to the child
7. Don't confront the alleged perpetrator – this is the role of the investigating authorities
8. Don't leave the child alone

9 Report the disclosure to the person nominated in your school's policy and procedures

10 In the case of sexual abuse where the alleged perpetrator is a family member living in the family home, it would be important to ensure immediate action is taken so that the child does not have to return to the family home that evening

11 As soon as possible, make note of what the child said and include a description of any visible injuries

SCENARIO

DISCLOSURE

Zola (13 years) has learning difficulties and attends a special unit at her local high school. ESW **Kelly** has been working with Zola for a number of years in the unit and the two have developed a good relationship. It is the first day back after the summer break and Kelly is chatting to a group of students about their holidays. Kelly notices that Zola is not her usual happy self and doesn't join in the conversation. Later Kelly asks Zola about her holidays.

Kelly: *'What did you do in your holidays, Zola?'*

Zola: *'We went to my uncle's because he lives at the beach.'*

Kelly: *'Wow, that must have been fun.'*

Zola: *'I don't like Uncle Peter. He scares me.'*

Kelly: *'Why does he scare you?'*

Zola: *'He comes into my bedroom at night and wants to get in bed with me but I don't like it and he gets angry.'*

Kelly: *'Have you told your mum or dad about Uncle Peter?'*

Zola: *'No because they like Uncle Peter and Mum gets mad at me when I say I don't like him.'*

WHAT DOES THIS TELL US?

Children and young people are often uncertain or even fearful about disclosure. They worry they may be in trouble or accused of lying. They often sense that telling will create family tensions or family breakdown, for which they will be responsible.

▶ DISCUSSION

What action should Kelly take?

Documenting concerns

Documenting signs of possible risk of harm is an extremely important role for all adults working with children and young people. Such documentation can assist in identifying a pattern of unexplained changes in behaviour and/or unexplained injuries (see **Figure 6.14** for an example of a template). Again, your school's child protection policy should include procedures for documentation.

It is important to always act promptly and in the best interests of the child or young person. Always report any concerns you may have to your supervisor and/or follow your school's child protection reporting policies and procedures.

Suspected abuse of children and young people by school employees/volunteers

Any adult has the potential to abuse a child. Some children and young people can be extremely challenging, and at times it can be difficult to form a positive relationship with a child. All adults working with children and young people need to be aware of their own stress levels and take time

Figure 6.14 Document template

Date: ______________ **Time:** ______________

Description of the visible injury:

> e.g. size (use a comparison, such as the size of a 50-cent coin), shape (round, elongated, hand-shape), colour (this will indicate the age of the bruise: red, purple, brown, yellow)

Location of visible injury/ injuries:

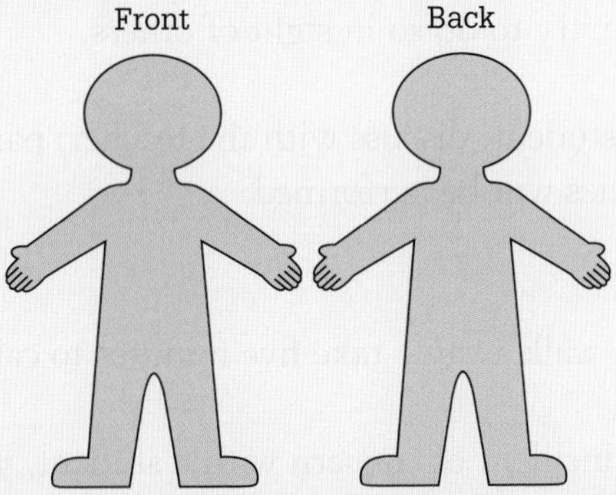

> the easiest way to do this is to draw a simple body outline and mark the position of the injury on the outline

Any explanation of the injury given by the child, young person, carer or parent:

> this can be particularly important if conflicting explanations are given

Observations of the child or young person's behaviour:

Direct or indirect comments made by the child or young person that may indicate abuse has occurred:

Uncharacteristic behaviours of the child or young person:

out if needed. Abuse by an adult entrusted with the care of a child is regarded by the community as an extreme breach of trust. The perpetrator usually suffers the full weight of the law.

Every child and young person has the right to a safe, secure environment free from harm. By maintaining child-focused practices, all adults can ensure that the safety and wellbeing of children and young people remain the highest priority.

Where there is suspected abuse of a student by a teacher, other member of staff or a visitor to the school, it should immediately be reported to the principal. Where this is not possible, it should immediately be reported to the state or territory child protection authorities.

Child protection policies and procedures

Protective behaviours

As an adult working with children and young people, it is important for ESWs to be aware of behaviours that they can adopt to ensure they are not vulnerable to false allegations of incorrect or inappropriate behaviour in relation to students.

The following are some strategies that you can put into place to minimise the likelihood of false allegations:

- Always follow policies and procedures in relation to behaviour-management practices.
- Where possible, minimise physical contact with students.
- If you need to take a student aside to address an issue, try to do so in sight of others.
- Under no circumstances use physical punishment.
- Where you are responsible for the personal care of a student, discuss with the teacher, parents and student (if appropriate) how and where these duties will be performed.
- Always treat each student with dignity and respect.
- Avoid engaging in arguments with students.
- Remember that if you get angry or upset, it is best to walk away – take five minutes to calm down.
- Where you have been involved in a confrontation or incident of concern with a student, you should report the situation as soon as possible and try to accurately record the incident.

The Government of South Australia (2017) has published an excellent resource on protective behaviours: *Protective Practices for Staff in Their Interactions with Children and Young People*.

Summary

Your responsibilities as an ESW include understanding the legislative requirements for child protection in your state or territory. Child abuse is a complex problem that occurs for many different reasons. Although there can be common factors that contribute to abuse, every situation is unique.

It is important that you can recognise the different types and dynamics of abuse as they apply to age, gender, disability and culture, and understand your legal and ethical obligations to report suspected abuse. You should ensure that you are familiar with the notification procedures and protocols within your school.

Child protection is a challenging issue that can generate a range of emotional responses, such as anger, shock, disbelief and sadness. It may also raise personal issues for adults who have themselves been the subject of abuse or neglect. Every adult who works with children and young people has a responsibility to act always in the best interests of the child. Remember, it is the right of every child to feel and be safe.

Self-check questions

1 What does Article 19 of the United Nations Convention on the Rights of the Child state?

2 Identify whether each of the following statements is true or false:

a Aboriginal and Torres Strait Islander children are seven times more likely to be the subject of substantiated child abuse and neglect than other Australian children.

▶

b ESWs are identified as mandatory reporters.

c Psychological harm/emotional abuse occurs when a child has been, or is at risk of being, harmed because of the parent's or carer's behaviour or attitude.

d A far greater number of child sexual abuse offences are perpetrated by adults who are in a caregiver role.

3 What does child protection legislation in each state and territory include?

4 What is the aim of National Framework for Protecting Australia's Children 2009–2020?

5 Who is nominated as a mandatory reporter under the child protection legislation?

6 What states in Australia have exceptions to their child protection legislation?

7 What are reasonable grounds to suspect that a child or young person is at risk of harm? List four concerns.

8 Define neglect and list its different forms.

9 What is the role of a keeping safe strategy with regard to protecting children and young people?

Discussion questions

1 Sian has arrived at school today with her hair in a low ponytail and scruffy hair, looking like she slept in it last night. At morning break you notice that there is only a badly bruised and very smelly banana in her lunch box and nothing else. After speaking with the teacher, your discussion reveals that you have both noticed similar things, including a poor hygiene smell and filthy clothes over the last two weeks.

a You feel this needs to be reported. Who do you report this to and what key points would you raise?

2 While on duty in the playground you notice 15-year-old Seth hit his 12-year old brother Nevil several times. After you and another teacher separate them, you work with Nevil as you have already formed a relationship with him because of the work you do to help him in his classes. As you walk away, you hear Seth say to the teacher, 'Dad says I have to knock sense into his dumbass – or he will never amount to anything.'

a What do you suspect is happening here and what would be your next course of action?

Activities

1 Investigate what the process is for reporting abuse at your school. Who do you need to speak with about the process?

2 What professional development opportunities are there for you to participate in that will assist you in developing skills for identifying and working with children who experience abuse?

3 The indicators of abuse are different for different age groups. Ensure that you are aware of those that are applicable to the students you work with. Visit the Department of Education Victoria's website 'Identify signs of child abuse': **https://www.education.vic.gov.au/childhood/professionals/health/childprotection/Pages/ecidentifying.aspx**

PART B SUPPORTING LEARNING AND DEVELOPMENT

Chapter 7

INTRODUCTION TO CHILD AND ADOLESCENT DEVELOPMENT

LEARNING OBJECTIVES

When you have completed this chapter, you should be able to demonstrate that, in relation to working in a school environment, you can:

7.1 identify the domains and principles of child and adolescent development

7.2 identify the environmental and biological factors that influence development

7.3 identify the interrelationship between the domains of development, the developing brain and the environment.

Online resources icons refer to useful weblinks. Ask your instructor for these **Online Resources.**

Introduction

Chapter 7 provides an introductory overview of child and adolescent development. The study of child development is a large and complex area, and acquiring an in-depth knowledge of child development will require ongoing study and research. This chapter examines the key principles of child development and introduces you to the domains of development. Key theories of development are also presented at an introductory level.

The aim is to assist you to better understand the reciprocal relationship between growth, development and learning. This understanding is essential for you to work with children and young people to support their acquisition of skills and knowledge in a developmentally appropriate manner. Knowledge of child development can contribute to appropriate planning and implementation of learning activities.

7.1 Learning and development

The study of human development is complex and challenging, but at the same time it is quite amazing. Theorists have been studying human development for many years, and there is now a substantial body of foundation knowledge and a set of underlying principles to help us to understand how humans grow, develop and learn.

Learning and development are intricately intertwined – we cannot understand one without understanding the other. While there is no single, universally accepted theory of human development, collectively the various theories can be used to help us to better understand the complex nature of development, which in turn informs and influences educational practices. A theory is a set of general principles or beliefs that can be applied consistently to explain or describe something – in this case, human development. Theorists study these principles by testing, challenging, adding to and modifying them, or offering new theories or explanations about human development. Theories of development and learning influence curriculum design and pedagogical (teaching) practices so that children and young people can be supported to reach their full potential.

It is important to be aware that each child develops at their own unique pace. Ages and stages of development associated with various theories of development and developmental charts should therefore be regarded as approximate. The degree to which varying factors shape and influence development is also unique to each child.

The journey from childhood to adolescence and, finally, adulthood is marked by significant developmental milestones. This period is typically divided into five stages, as shown in **Figure 7.1**. While an age range is assigned to each stage, these should be regarded as a rough guide only, as each child will develop at their own unique developmental pace.

Figure 7.1 Stages of child and adolescent development (approximate ages)

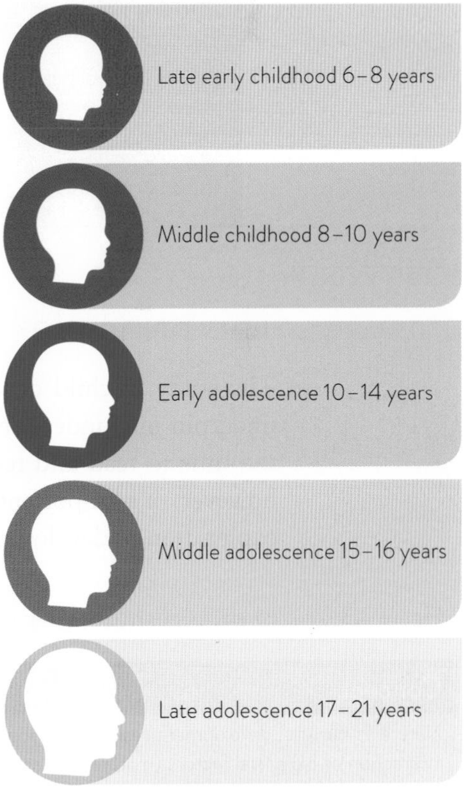

Domains of development

The study of child development typically begins with an understanding of the **domains of development**, typically referred to as physical, social, emotional, cognitive and language development.

As a beginning learner of child development, it is critical that you have a thorough understanding of each domain, the typical sequence of each domain and the interrelationship between domains – that is, how each domain is dependent on and influenced by the others. It is also important to consider the biological, social and cultural context of each child in order to build a realistic understanding of the unique nature of each child's development.

A sound knowledge of developmental domains will help you gain an understanding of how children develop and what typically can be expected during each stage of development as the child matures. The traditional domains of development are outlined in **Figure 7.2**.

Figure 7.2 Traditional domains of development

Domains of development	Details
Physical development	Gross motor development – the large muscles in the body, such as legs, arms and chest Fine motor development – the small muscles such as those in the hands, fingers, lips and tongue. Hand–eye coordination is an example of fine motor development Growth and maturation
Social/emotional development	Self-regulation, self-concept, self-esteem, emotional intelligence, relationships with others
Language development	Speech – production of sounds (articulation) and voice quality Receptive language (understanding or comprehending) and expressive language (verbal and non-verbal communication)
Cognitive (intellectual) development	Information processing (thinking, concentrating, imagining, problem-solving, using logic, organising information and using symbols) memory and recall Language and cognitive development are closely linked

The principles of child development

The study of child development has resulted in the establishment of several core concepts that underpin our understanding of development. These concepts are explained in **Figure 7.3**. Take the time to read and reflect on these concepts. Some of the language may be unfamiliar to you; however, it's important to familiarise yourself with these concepts as a foundation to further exploration of development.

Figure 7.3 Core concepts of child development

Concept	Explanation
Nature vs nurture: development results from the interaction of biological factors (maturation) and environmental factors (learning) – for example, intelligence and temperament are shaped by both nature and nurture.	Nature: the role of genes and biology which predetermine some developmental outcomes from conception, such as hair colour, skin tone, eye colour; they may also determine, for example, whether or not a child is born with a disability. Nurture: refers to the social, emotional and physical environment such as relationships within the family, culture, education, life experiences, etc.
Plasticity	The ability of the brain and nervous system to change their structure, functions and connections in response to both biological and external stimuli.
Continuity vs discontinuity	Continuity: development occurs gradually and continuously. Discontinuity: development occurs in predictable stages. Rapid development occurs as the child transitions to each stage followed by a period of little change until transition to the next stage.

Concept	Explanation
Development builds on development	Earlier development lays the foundation for new development – for example, babbling to talking, or crawling to walking.
Development moves from simple to complex and from general to specific	Children's development becomes more complex in all areas as they develop; the child moves through a developmental sequence for each developmental domain.
One area of development affects and influences another area of development	Physical, cognitive, emotional and social development are integrated and are all equally important.
Development occurs in a predictable sequence	Individuals develop according to a timetable and pace. The timing and length of each stage can vary from one individual to another; however, the sequence for most children remains the same.
There are optimal periods in development; critical and sensitive periods Learning occurs most easily when children are developmentally 'ready'	A critical period is a limited time that begins and ends abruptly during which a specific function develops – for example, the development of language in the first five years of life. A sensitive period is a time when it is easiest for children to acquire certain skills. Critical and sensitive periods are best understood as optimal windows of opportunity and are important for encouraging positive developmental outcomes that are most likely (and possibly can only occur) during certain ages.

Source: Guerra, N.G., Williamson, A.A., Lucas-Molina, B. (2012). Normal development: Infancy, childhood, and adolescence. In Rey, J.M. (ed.), *IACAPAP e-Textbook of Child and Adolescent Mental Health*. Geneva: International Association for Child and Adolescent Psychiatry and Allied Professions (pp. 4 and 5).

The study of child development includes a range of terminology and phrases that you will need to know and understand. **Figure 7.4** describes this terminology.

Figure 7.4 Typical terms and phrases used in the study of child development

Definitions	
Basic human needs	All humans have basic needs that must be met if they are to thrive and develop to their potential. These include: > physical needs: shelter, protection, food, warmth, health care, rest and activity > psychological needs: affection, consistency, security, trust, quality interactions, appropriate expectations, acceptance and positive attitudes towards unique characteristics; for example, cultural, ethnic and developmental differences > opportunities to learn: access to developmentally appropriate play that fosters development in all areas > respect and self-esteem: a respectful and supportive environment, where efforts and accomplishments are appreciated and acknowledged.
Growth and development	
Growth	Physical changes – for example, height, weight. Growth occurs throughout a person's life and the rate of growth varies, with infancy and adolescence identified as rapid growth periods.
Development	The changes that take place as part of growth and development are the result of two processes: maturation and learning. For example, a 12-month-old has developed the fine motor skills to hold a spoon and with this new skill will attempt to feed herself.
Learning	A permanent change in behaviour that occurs as a result of experience. For example, Anshu (7 years) can now tie her shoelaces.
Maturation	Changes that result from a person's individual, biologically determined developmental pathway. It's determined by internal signals and not influenced by the environment. For example, when teeth erupt, an infant is ready to eat solid food.

Changes in development can be measured in two ways:	
Quantitative change	Changes that involve an increase or decrease and can be measured by: > comparing an individual's development at different times in their life – for example, comparing language at two years and language at four years > comparing an individual's development with that of other children of the same age – for example, comparing the reading skill of same age students.
Qualitative change	Changes to the 'quality' of a function or process. For example, the gradual improvement in handwriting.

The pace of development	
Sequence of development	Refers to the predictable series of steps or stages through which most children typically progress as part of the developmental process. For example: sitting to creeping to crawling to walking.
Individual differences	Each child's developmental timetable is unique – while most children will progress through the same sequence of development, the timing of this development is unique to each individual. For example, Teddy began walking at 11 months. His brother Ollie did not walk until 14 months. Both are considered to be within the 'normal range'.
Readiness	Refers to the period when a child has all the prerequisite skills and opportunities to master the next step in the developmental sequence. For example, if a child's motor skills are not sufficiently developed to hold and guide a pen the child would not be considered as 'ready' for learning to write letters. Readiness is linked to maturation. One term you are likely to hear often is 'school readiness', which refers to the emotional and social skills necessary for children to confidently transition to a formal school setting.
Normal or 'typical' growth and development or 'age-appropriate' development	These terms are often used when exploring child development to describe development that falls within what has come to be regarded as typical development for an age range. For example, a two-year old who speaks in three- to four-word sentences and a two-year old who uses single words or two-word phrases would both be considered to be within the normal range of development.
Developmental milestones	This refers to the acquisition of significant skills or events in a child's life. For example, when babies take their first steps, they have reached an important milestone that signals that they are entering the toddler stage.
Developmental profiles	Refers to a group of understandings, skills or behaviours that can normally be expected of children of a particular age or stage.
Stages of development	Each stage of development is related to an approximate age range and a set of behaviours and skills that generally are thought to be 'typical' of an age/stage of development. However, it is important to be aware that a wide range of factors influence each child's developmental pathway and progression. For example, a two-year-old who is striving for independence and expresses her frustration through tantrums is considered to be demonstrating age-stage typical behaviour.
Environment	The physical, cultural, social and emotional influences experienced by the child. It includes the critical role that relationships play in shaping development. For example, the family play a critical role in shaping a child's development.
Context	The circumstances or situation experienced by the child. For example, 'the social context' refers to factors such as relationships within the family, friends, religion, cultural practices, etc.
Culture	The common way in which participants in a community share skills and knowledge. For example, language, beliefs and values, food, etc.

Theories of child and adolescent development

Developmental theories (also referred to as learning theories) are ways of explaining how development occurs, what influences development and how this information can be used to understand how children and young people learn. Developmental theories show that development is a continuous process that moves from the simple to the more complex. Most theorists believe that development occurs in stages. We also know that development can be interrupted by a range of physiological and external factors. Importantly, we know that each individual develops at their own unique rate.

Theories of development and learning typically seek to answer the following questions:

- How does learning occur?
- Which factors influence learning?
- What is the role of memory?
- How does transfer occur?
- What types of learning are best explained by the theory?
- What basic assumptions/principles of this theory are relevant to instructional design?
- How should instruction be structured to facilitate learning? (Ertmer & Newby, 2013).

In this text, we will explore child development from the perspective of a range of theories and theorists, as listed in **Figure 7.5**. These theories will be introduced as you work through Chapters 7 to 10.

Figure 7.5 Theories of child development

Theory	Examples of theorist
Ecological theory	Urie Bronfenbrenner (1917–2005)
Psychosocial theory	Erik Erikson (1902–94)
Social learning theory	Lev Vygotsky (1896–1934) Albert Bandura (1925–2021)
Moral reasoning theory	Lawrence Kohlberg (1927–87) Carol Gilligan (1936–)
Cognitive theory	Jean Piaget (1896–1980) Jerome Bruner (1915–2016) Howard Gardner (1943–) Benjamin Bloom (1913–99)

The concept of the 'whole child'

While the study of child and adolescent development necessitates an examination of growth and development in each domain (see **Figure 7.2**), it is important to keep the concept of the **whole child** in mind – the idea that each domain of development is influenced by and dependent on all other domains of development, and all development is influenced by genetic and environmental factors unique to each child. This concept is particularly important when working with students with disabilities. For example, a student with a language delay or speech impairment may, as a direct influence of that delay/impairment, have poor social skills and find it difficult to form friendships because other students may avoid or exclude a student who is difficult to understand.

Child development and developmental milestones

The concept of the whole child also emphasises a balanced assessment of the student – not simply focusing on the student's disabilities or weakness, but also focusing on the student's strengths and interests. **Figure 7.6** shows the concept of the whole child.

Figure 7.6 The whole child

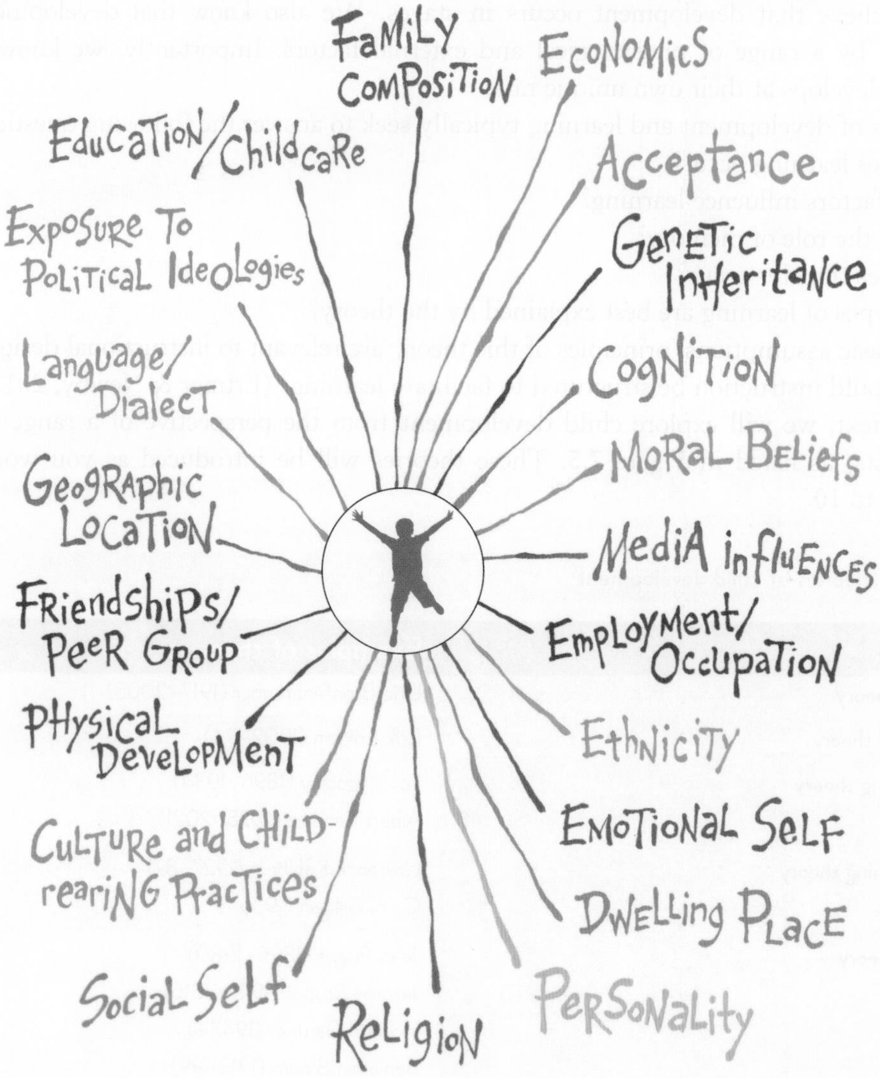

Every child and adolescent will have common developmental characteristics as they grow and develop; however, no two children will be exactly alike and no two children will follow the same developmental pathway. Even children born into the same family, living in the same home with the same parents and experiencing the same upbringing will develop at their own unique pace. This is best understood by studying Uri Bronfenbrenner's (1979) ecological systems theory of development. Bronfenbrenner believed that development was influenced by the child's interaction with the environment, which occurs within the context of the child's culture.

Bronfenbrenner's theory focuses on a sociocultural view of development and suggests that there are five layers or systems of sociocultural influences on the developing child. Each system is further removed from the child and reflects the broader social, political and economic factors that operate within a society. It also argues that the individual's interactions at each level demonstrate that the individual is actively engaged in constructing their own social meaning and not merely a passive agent.

Bronfenbrenner compared his ecological systems theory (**Figure 7.7**) with babushka dolls that nest one inside the other – separate yet connected. Each system is influenced by the other systems and represents a dynamic model of development.

Figure 7.7 Ecological systems theory

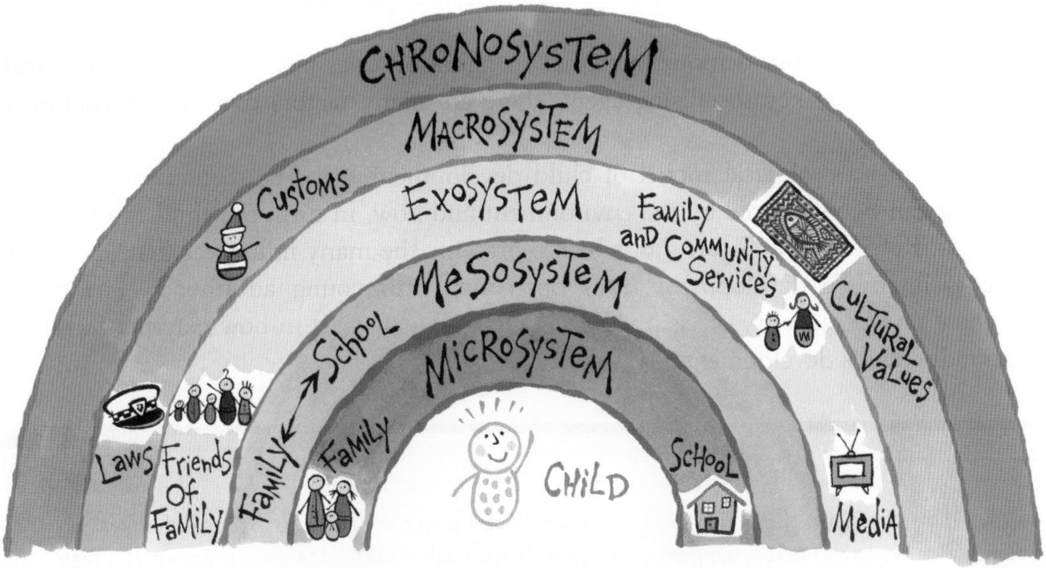

Source: Based on Bronfenbrenner (1979).

At the heart of Bronfenbrenner's ecological systems theory is the child within the family. Bronfenbrenner argues that the family is the primary socialising agent, and even though external factors become increasingly important as the child matures *the family remains the cornerstone for social and emotional development*.

Radiating outwards from the family are the social and cultural systems that influence and shape the child's development. Bronfenbrenner uses the term 'bi-directional influences' to describe the relationships that exist within and between the child and the various **microsystems**. These relationships both influence and are influenced by the child. **Figure 7.8** describes Bronfenbrenner's five ecological systems.

Figure 7.8 Bronfenbrenner's five ecological systems

Ecological system	Description
Microsystem	The first and most critical system, which includes roles and interpersonal relationships, such as family, childcare services, school, the local neighbourhood and memberships of organisations or clubs.
Mesosystem	This system links the microsystems, such as the relationship between home and school, parents and friends.

Ecological system	Description
Exosystem	This is the social system one step removed from the child. The **exosystem** has an indirect impact on the child's development because of the connection with the family unit – for example, a parent's place of employment, and access to family and community services.
Macrosystem	Radiating further from the child and family this system includes the cultural values, laws and customs of the community in which the child and family live.
Chronosystem	The final system reflects the social and historical timeframe in which the child's life is set.

Bronfenbrenner's theory demonstrates that socialisation does not occur in isolation, and that while the family is the key socialising agent, there are many factors that may impact on social development.

Bronfenbrenner's ecological model of child development helps us to understand how child development can be influenced by the environment and how, in turn, the child can influence the environment. Refer back to **Figure 7.6**, which represents the many influences that impact on and influence each child's development from birth well into young adulthood. The individual temperament and personality of each child are significant factors in how external factors might shape an individual's development.

SCENARIO

INFLUENCES ON DEVELOPMENT

Ali (12 years) has resettled in Australia after spending two years in a detention centre with his aunt, uncle, younger brothers and cousins. Four years ago, Ali's parents, grandparents and two older sisters were killed when a bomb landed on their house while they were sleeping. Ali will carry the horror of his experiences with him for the rest of his life. Ali last went to school when he was six years old. He is quiet and withdrawn – he rarely smiles and only contributes to class discussion if the teacher directs a question specifically to him.

Rhett (12 years) lives with his parents and two younger brothers in an affluent inner-city area. Rhett attends a private school and has enjoyed a happy, secure childhood. The family spends weekends going on picnics with the extended family, bike rides and various cultural and sporting events. Rhett is a struggling reader and attends a special reading intervention program at his school. Rhett is becoming increasingly embarrassed and frustrated by his poor reading skills.

Myles (12 years) lives with his mother and two younger stepsisters in a high-rise public housing estate. Myles has never had contact with his father. Myles misses a great deal of school because his mother has a chronic health condition and he stays at home to care for her and his sisters. Myles can barely read or write. He is described by his mother as 'an old head on young shoulders'.

Nasser (12 years) has Down syndrome. He lives at home with his parents and three older siblings. Nasser is a much-loved member of a large extended family. Next year, Nasser will attend a life skills program at a high school a few suburbs away. His family is very positive about Nasser's future.

Evan (12 years) has a chronic health condition that requires frequent bouts of hospital care. Over the years, Evan has missed the equivalent of four years of schooling. His mother has tried home schooling but finds it difficult to manage as she also has two younger children and a husband who is a long-distance truck driver. Because he is often housebound, Evan has very few friends. He presents as shy and lacking in confidence when around other children his own age.

WHAT DOES THIS TELL US?

Each of these 12-year-olds is in the early adolescent stage of development. Each child has a unique set of factors that have influenced and shaped their development. Each child will face unique learning challenges that will need to be considered in the classroom environment.

▶ DISCUSSION

Taking into account the diversity of children and young people's development and life experiences, is the current age/grade system the best option for teachers and students? What might be a better option?

7.2 Child development and culture: environmental and biological factors

When studying child development, it is also important to be aware that development does not occur in isolation but rather in a dynamic social and cultural context that is unique to each individual. Even within a family unit, social and cultural influences may be unique for each child. This is also true in the broader context of the community – that is, each family is unique in terms of its values, beliefs and practices.

Rogoff (2003) defines culture as the common way in which participants in a community share skills and knowledge. She claims that both individual and group functions contribute to the concept of culture, and that culture should be viewed as dynamic rather than static. She believes that the traditional view of culture as a static collection of traditions, values, beliefs and practices is too simplistic, and that culture is better described as a complex and dynamic process of relationships between the individual and their sociocultural context. Culture is thus an interwoven series of interactions between an individual and the community in which they live. Rogoff also believes that biology and culture function together and contribute to both similarities and differences in human behaviour. The process of learning is also viewed as both biological and sociocultural in nature. That is, we learn because of our biological predisposition to learn and through socialisation within our cultural setting.

Cultural identity

The term **sociocultural context** refers to all the external factors that influence a person's development and behaviour. Each of us belongs to a cultural group that is made up of people who share a common language, as well as a common set of values, beliefs and behaviours that have been learned from other people within the cultural group. Other factors often used to identify a cultural group include class, race, nationality, ethnicity, customs and artefacts. A strong cultural identity gives people a sense of belonging and promotes positive self-esteem and self-confidence. People feel most comfortable within their own cultural group. Our culture influences all aspects of our life – for example, the way we think and learn, how we relate to others, our beliefs about the roles of males and females, motherhood and fatherhood, and our beliefs about the role of the family. Importantly, our culture also shapes our sense of self as part of the family and the broader community.

SCENARIO

MY CULTURE

An inner-city high school with a large Aboriginal population has adopted a range of strategies to create a sense of belonging for Aboriginal students. There are images of Aboriginal culture displayed throughout the school, Aboriginal dance groups, an Aboriginal student council supported by community Elders, and several staff, including the school principal, are Aboriginal.

What the students say:

'I like it here because there's lots of my mob here.'

'Mr Kennell, the bossman, is the best! He can play the didg.'

'Yeah, Mr Kennell makes us work hard you know. But that's good because we can grow up to be leaders.'

'The teachers listen to us, you know. We respect them, and they respect us. It's good, man.'

WHAT DOES THIS TELL US?

A sense of belonging is essential if students are to feel connected to their school, want to come to school and want to learn. For Aboriginal and Torres Strait Islander students, this extends to an environment that acknowledges and respects Aboriginal and Torres Strait Islander culture.

Biological factors

As well as social and cultural influences, child development is shaped by biological factors. The significant developmental changes from middle childhood to young adulthood are marked by physical growth, strength and agility, sexual maturity, and the ability to think abstractly, engage in self-reflection and address moral issues, and use language in more complex ways. During adolescence, the brain moves into its final stage of development of the frontal lobe, which controls behaviour, reasoning and rational thinking.

Feinstein (2009, p. 125) reports that 'the volatility of adolescent behaviour is, in part, caused by lack of emotional regulation in the frontal cortex'. The brain continues to refine itself but does not reach full maturity until 23–25 years of age.

Each person is born with an inherited genetic blueprint that will determine many, although not all, developmental outcomes. These biological (or **heredity**) factors are shown in **Figure 7.9**.

Figure 7.9 Biological factors

Sex	Boys traditionally mature later than girls
Physical attributes	Body shape, agility, strength, athleticism
Personality	Children are born with a personality type and, while this can't be changed, it can be modified by relationships with nurturing adults
Intelligence	The brain continues to develop well into young adulthood. Amazingly, brain research has demonstrated that our genetic makeup can be altered by experience. This occurs as a direct result of human interactions and sensory stimulation. It has now been established that while our genes determine when specific brain circuits or wiring occur, it is sensory experience that shapes their formation.

While many of these biological factors – for example, physical characteristics such as eye colour or shape of face – are predetermined and cannot be changed easily, other biological factors can be shaped or modified by the environment. How the child interacts with and experiences the social environment and the physical environment will thus affect the child's development.

Environmental factors that can shape or influence biological factors include:

- the presence of consistent nurturing relationships, first and most importantly within the family unit and later extending to significant others (teachers, peers, coaches). Nurturing relationships are critical to healthy emotional development and have a significant impact on the developing brain
- the way in which the physical environment supports the child's health and wellbeing – for example, adequate nutrition, a physical environment that provides adequate safety and shelter
- trauma – significant or prolonged childhood trauma can directly influence how the brain develops in response to the trauma. Childhood trauma may include child abuse, war, displacement such as becoming a refugee, natural disasters, persistent bullying, exposure to domestic violence, terrorism or medical trauma.

Brain development

Early brain development

Neuroscience has shaped the way we understand human development. It has reinforced the belief that human development is dynamic, interactive and sensitive to environmental factors. To begin your study of brain development, it is important to understand the core principles that provide the foundation of the growing body of knowledge in relation to how the brain develops and in turn shapes development.

The book *From Neurons to Neighborhoods: The Science of Early Childhood Development* (Shonkoff & Phillips, 2000) identified 10 core concepts that are critical to our understanding of brain development. Take your time to read and think about these concepts. You may be unfamiliar with some of the terminology. The scenarios are designed to help you understand these concepts, which are described in **Figure 7.10**.

Figure 7.10 The core concepts of brain development

Human development is shaped by a dynamic and continuous interaction between biology and experience.	In essence, this means child development is influenced by the child's genetic and biological makeup. In addition, how the child reacts to their environment (relationships and experiences) will impact on their development.
Culture influences every aspect of human development.	The values, beliefs and child-rearing practices of the family will have a significant influence on child development.
The growth of self-regulation is a cornerstone of early childhood development.	Self-regulation includes the ability to pay attention, express feelings and control impulses at an age-appropriate level. Self-regulation influences all domains of development.
Children are active participants in their own development.	They learn by observing and imitating others, exploring, practising, investigating and experimenting.
Human relationships have a critical influence on brain development.	Warm, caring and nurturing relationships will have a positive influence on emotional and social development. Conversely, inconsistent, emotionally absent, abusive or neglectful relationships will have a negative impact on social and emotional development.
Each child develops at their own unique pace.	Comparing children's developmental progress at a specific age is not an effective way to identify delays or impairments in development.
Child development occurs along a continuum.	Each child's progress along this continuum is unique, and is characterised by a series of back-and-forth progressions where the child acquires and practises new skills. For example, a child who has just learned to walk will often revert to crawling until they feel confident as a walker.
Child development is shaped by both positive influences and negative influences.	Examples of positive influences are outgoing temperament, a nurturing family environment, a healthy diet. Examples of negative influences are medical condition, poor nutrition, parental mental health issues.
The timing of early experiences can matter.	However, child development can be supported by positive experiences throughout childhood.
The course of development can be altered in early childhood by effective interventions.	Early intervention can have a positive influence on children's development, particularly where children are at risk of abuse or neglect.

Source: Based on Shonkoff & Phillips (2000).

Neuroscience research

Brain development has a significant impact on learning and behaviour, as well as physical and mental health. Brain research is providing new knowledge about how the brain interacts with the external environment to influence human development and learning. Understanding the architecture of the brain, and how human relationships and the environment impact brain development, is critical for all educators.

The brain is the only organ in the body that is unfinished at birth. The primary task of the brain in early childhood is making connections between brain cells. Babies are born with 100 billion nerve cells, called neurons (**Figure 7.11**). Every neuron has an axon that sends information out to other neurons and several dendrites that receive information. As axons 'wire up' to dendrites, trillions of connections called synapses are formed.

Figure 7.11 The neuron

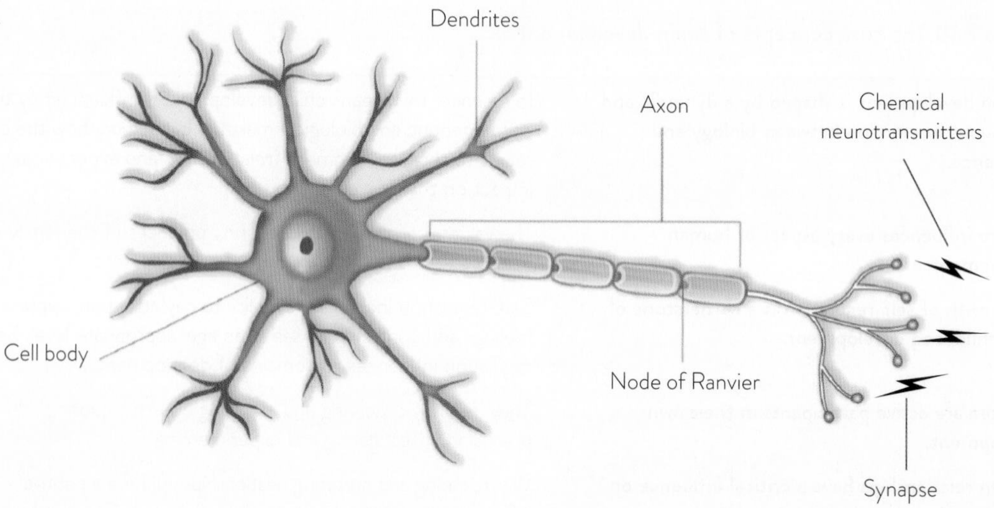

The synapses are activated when stimulation occurs. The first three years of life are the most critical for the development of synapses. Synapses that are used repeatedly become permanent; those that are not used are eliminated. By age 10, the number of synapses decreases to about 500 trillion. The exact number of synapses depends on the degree of stimulation the brain receives in early childhood.

Research (Mustard, 2008; Shonkoff & Phillips, 2000) tells us that during the early years the brain makes more connections than are required for optimal functioning, and these are pruned back over time. The brain will also prune incorrect connections and shape brain circuitry before becoming fully mature. The 'wiring' that takes place in a very young child's brain depends not only upon genetic factors but also on environmental factors, including critical relationships between the child and their parents, and between the child and their teachers.

James Fraser Mustard (2008), a prominent researcher in early brain development, has found that experiences in early childhood have a critical impact on later learning because early experiences:

- affect gene expression, the function of sensing neurons and the development of neural pathways
- shape emotion, and regulate temperament and social development
- shape language and literacy capability
- shape perceptual and cognitive ability
- shape how children cope with their daily experiences
- shape physical and mental health in later life
- shape physical activity and performance.

Research also tells us that the brain develops in an hierarchical manner. Earlier brain development impacts on later brain development.

Mustard (2008, p. 12) states:

> The brain is composed of billions of neurons and trillions of nerve connections (synapses). The neurons in an individual all have the same genetic coding and are shaped for their different functions by sensory experiences. Experience transmitted to the brain in early life by the sensing pathways assists in the later development of the architecture and function of the brain.

Figure 7.12 provides an overview of brain development from around age five to 20 years and beyond.

Figure 7.12 Stages of brain development

EARLY CHILDHOOD: Sensory and motor regions are becoming more efficient and interconnected. These include regions involved in speaking, listening, and understanding language and social communication; feeling and perceiving emotions; manipulating objects to learn simple concepts; and understanding time and sequence.

MIDDLE TO LATE CHILDHOOD: Association brain regions are especially developing–bringing together information from different senses and sources to help build conceptual understanding across social, emotional, and cognitive contexts.

EARLY TO MIDDLE ADOLESCENCE: Regions involved in emotional reward, sensitivity to social reputation, and higher-order thinking are maturing, allowing new capacities for emotional regulation, in-depth interests, identity development, long-term planning, and abstract thinking.

LATE ADOLESCENCE TO EARLY ADULTHOOD: Association areas, and their underlying networks, are continuing to mature, which supports increasingly complex cultural, ethical, and scholarly thinking about how the world works, why, and how it could work differently.

Source: Immordino-Yang, M.H., Darling-Hammond, L. & Krone, C. (2018). *The Brain Basis for Integrated Social, Emotional, and Academic Development: How emotions and social relationships drive learning.* The Aspen Institute National Commission on Social, Emotional, and Academic Development, https://www.aspeninstitute.org/wp-content/uploads/2018/09/Aspen_research_FINAL_web.pdf, p. 5.
Image sources: Shutterstock.com/CroMary; Shutterstock.com/Monkey Business Images; Shutterstock.com/Monkey Business Images; Photo by Jessica Podraza on Unsplash.

After infancy, the most dramatic period of brain development is adolescence. The frontal lobes, involved in planning, decision-making, executive functioning, and higher-order thinking, begin a protracted period of intense development (lasting into the mid-twenties). It is also during this period that puberty-related hormonal changes also make the brain more vulnerable to the effects of stress, social rejection, and sleep deprivation (Immordino-Yang, Darling-Hammond & Krone, 2018, p. 7).

Critical periods, sensitive periods and plasticity

Critical periods and **sensitive periods** in brain development have important implications for educators.

These terms are defined as follows:

> Critical periods represent a narrow window of time during which a specific part of the body is most vulnerable to the absence of stimulation or to environmental influences. Vision is a good example: unless a baby sees light during the first six months, the nerves leading from the eye to the visual cortex of the brain that processes those signals will degenerate and die. Critical periods of brain development occur at the time when the brain is most influenced by sensory information, and are essential for the development of specific neural circuitry.
>
> Sensitive periods are the broad windows of opportunity for certain types of learning. They represent a less precise and often longer period of time when skills, such as acquiring a second language, are influenced. If the opportunity for learning does not arise, however, these potential new skills are not lost forever. Individuals learn new languages at many different times in their lives.
>
> Source: Gable & Hunting (2001).

Sensitive periods of brain development occur at the time when environmental influences have the greatest impact on the development of neural circuitry. Research into brain development has highlighted that the years from birth to age three are a sensitive period for development and learning in all areas. Like other areas of development, the brain moves from simple to complex – lower-order functions lay down the foundation for the development of higher-order functions.

Plasticity is the brain's ability to reorganise and adapt to influences, interactions and challenges in the environment. While the human brain remains plastic throughout life, plasticity is greatest in the first years of life, and decreases with age as the brain becomes more complex.

We now know that the brain development that supports higher-order functions, such as complex behaviour, thinking and problem-solving, depends on the prior development of lower-level neural pathway circuits. These lower-level pathways are formed during the first four years of life, and they lay the foundations for the higher-order brain functions. By the time a child is school-aged, these foundations have lost plasticity and are difficult to change.

Brain development or function at the lower level that directly impacts on later brain development is referred to as the limbic–hypothalamus–pituitary–adrenal (LHPA) pathway. This is often called the stress or behaviour emotional pathway. Mustard (2008, p. 12) states that:

> This pathway (LHPA) works as a stress, emotional and behaviour thermostat. It is vital for everyday existence and we are now learning how the development of this pathway and its function in early life affects cognition, emotions and behaviour and risks for diseases (physical and mental) throughout life.

Amazingly, neuroscience research has demonstrated that our genetic makeup can be altered by experience. This occurs as a direct result of human interactions and sensory stimulation. It has been established that, while our genes determine when specific brain circuits or wiring occur, it is sensory experience that shapes how they are formed. Early sensory experiences involving touch, sound and vision act as stimulants for the brain. Babies respond to this stimulation by staring intently at human faces, using facial gestures such as smiling and responding to the sound of a human voice. The baby's response reinforces this adult stimulation, which helps to build a mutually pleasant and reciprocal relationship between the baby and the adult.

Research on the impact of supportive, nurturing relationships between adults and children undertaken by the National Scientific Council on the Developing Child (NSCDC, 2004, p. 1) highlights the importance of these relationships in children's development:

> relationships are the active ingredients of the environment's influence on healthy human development. They incorporate the qualities that best promote competence and wellbeing – individualised responsiveness, mutual action and interaction, and an emotional connection to another human being … relationships engage children in the human community in ways that help them define who they are, what they can become, and how and why they are important to other people.

Brain architecture

This research concluded that early, secure attachments enhance emotional development and social competence, and support the brain's early foundations for cognitive and language development.

Brain development and the environment

Environmental factors (the child's lived experiences and relationships) play a critical role in brain development. **Figure 7.13** shows both positive and negative environmental factors.

Figure 7.13 Environmental factors that influence brain development

Positive factors that support brain development	Negative factors that disrupt brain development
The consistent presence of significant adults who nurture and support the child Adequate nutrition and health care Safe, stable and predictable living conditions Quality, age-appropriate experiences	Inconsistency in caregiving Lack of consistently nurturing parent/carer Poor nutrition Poor health care Lack of appropriate stimulation Toxic stress – child abuse; exposure to domestic violence; parent/carer engaged in drug/alcohol abuse; parent/carer with a serious mental illness or addiction; war; extreme poverty; loss of home

As brain plasticity differs between lower-order and higher-order functions, different experiences at different ages are necessary for optimal brain development. The complexity of brain development is not easy to grasp, and cannot easily be simplified. It is incorrect to make a simple assumption that 'missing' these sensitive periods means that the 'window of opportunity' is lost forever. It must be remembered that higher-order functions of the brain, such as social, cognitive and emotional functions, continue to develop well into early adulthood. However, the timeframe for optimal brain development in these sensitive periods will vary from one individual to another and will be shaped by experience over a period of time. It is also incorrect to assume that children who have had limited stimulation in early childhood or who have been exposed to toxic stress can simply undergo an intensive enrichment program to help improve brain development.

There is also no scientific evidence to suggest that intensive exposure to particular media, such as music or intensive early learning programs to teach babies to read, have any impact on brain development. As the NSCDC (2004, p. 5) states:

> evidence from decades of scientific investigation of experience-induced changes in brain development makes it highly unlikely that the potential benefits of such media would even come close to matching (much less exceeding) the more important influences of attentive, nurturing, and growing-promoting interactions with invested adults.

Trauma and childhood development

In essence, children's ability to interpret, understand and make sense of their experiences will change over time as the brain develops and matures. This means that parents and educators have an important role to play in providing age-appropriate experiences that help the developing brain to lay down the foundation for higher-level functioning.

Executive functioning

During early adolescence, the brain undergoes its second major phase of increased production of grey matter, which is responsible for executive functioning (thinking and processing information, decision-making, impulse control, focusing, holding and working with information in mind, filtering distractions and switching gears. Executive functions help to make connections between existing knowledge and current actions.

The NSCDC (2011) states that having executive function in the brain is like having an air traffic control system at a busy airport to manage the arrivals and departures of dozens of planes on multiple runways.

Three executive functions are particularly important:

1. **Working memory** – the ability to remember and recall information. It includes:
   - holding and manipulating information in our heads over short periods
   - remembering and connecting information
   - performing tasks/problems that have several steps and keeping track of our steps
   - identifying what comes next
   - remembering and following multi-step directions.
2. **Inhibitory/Impulse control** – the ability to control our own behaviour. It includes:
   - resisting temptations, distractions and habits by taking control of our thoughts
   - controlling our impulses (pause and think before acting)
   - ignoring distractions and focus on the task at hand
   - prioritising our thoughts and subsequent actions.
3. **Flexible thinking** – the ability to think outside of the box, adapt to change or the unexpected. It includes:
   - changing our thinking in response to changing demands, priorities or new perspectives
   - applying different sets of rules to suit different settings
   - identifying our mistakes in thinking, fixing them and revising ways of doing things in light of new information.

Other executive functions include:

- *emotional control* – the ability to manage feelings and keep them under control
- *self-monitoring* – the ability to monitor and evaluate your own performance/behaviour and make changes in the future or avoid repeating errors
- *planning/prioritising* – the ability to identify future needs/actions and set goals to achieve the planned outcomes; it includes being able to analyse the steps involved in the planned actions

- *task initiation* – the ability to independently engage in problem-solving, think of new ideas, recognise when it's time to get started on something and begin without procrastinating
- *time management* – the ability to understand time and how to use it effectively. It includes developing efficient time management skills by understanding how long a task may take and allocating sufficient time for completion, managing and meeting deadlines, developing daily routines or schedules to ensure all tasks are completed in a timely manner
- *organisation* – the ability to create and maintain systems to keep track of information or materials (Understood, 2013, pp. 5–6).

Executive functions provide the foundation skills needed for the process (the how) of learning – focusing, remembering, planning – which enables children to effectively and efficiently, master the content (the what) of learning – reading, writing and computation. Executive functioning skills are boosted when learning occurs in a social context (with others) that provides opportunities for students to draw on existing skills and knowledge to build new skills and knowledge (**scaffolding**).

The development of executive functioning skills occurs over time. It is important to be aware that each child will develop executive functioning skills at their own unique pace and that individual development will depend on a range of factors that are unique to each child.

Development of executive functioning skills

Children and young people who have not yet developed executive functioning skills in one or more areas are likely to experience difficulties both academically and socially. **Figure 7.14** provides examples of what poor executive functioning may look like in children and young people.

Figure 7.14 Examples of poor executive functioning

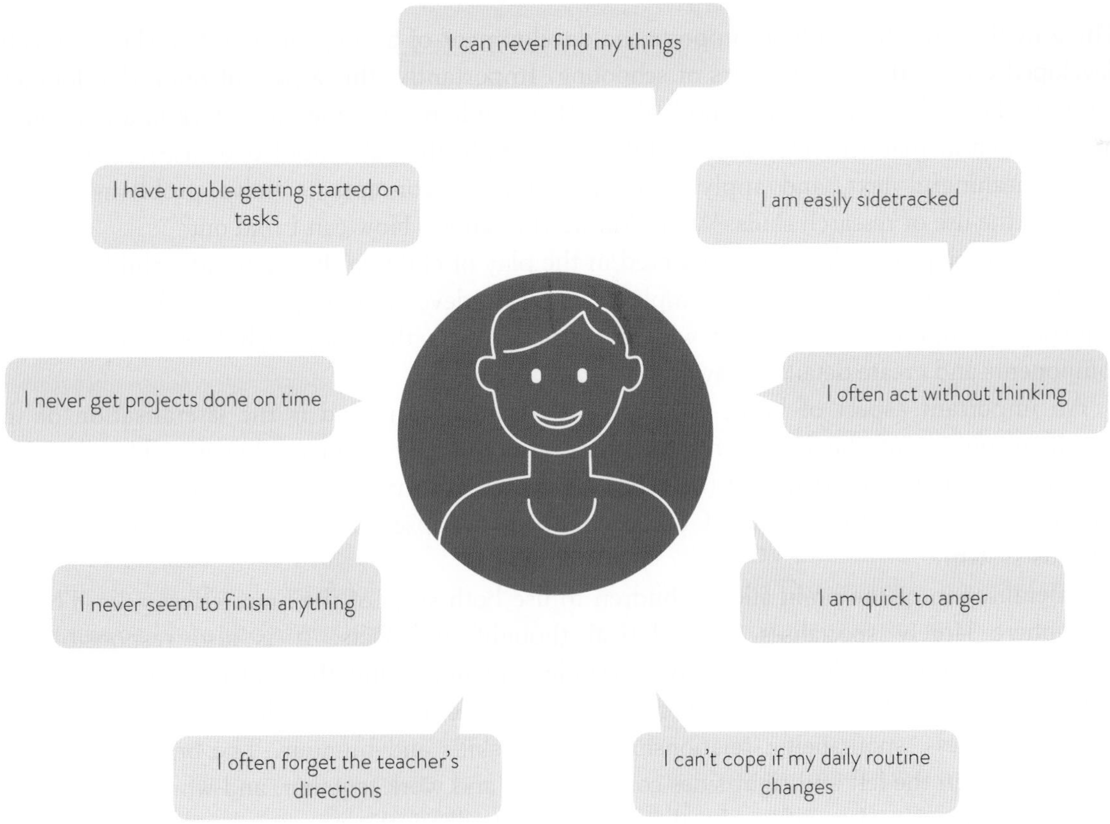

I can never find my things
I have trouble getting started on tasks
I am easily sidetracked
I never get projects done on time
I often act without thinking
I never seem to finish anything
I am quick to anger
I often forget the teacher's directions
I can't cope if my daily routine changes

SCENARIO

EXECUTIVE FUNCTIONING

Edward (11 years) is working his way through a task that each student is required to complete independently. Edward becomes very anxious whenever the class is required to work on independent tasks. He finds it difficult to focus and get himself organised. Edward reads the task to himself and then reads it aloud. He's already forgotten what he's supposed to do, so he reads it again. He decides to make a list of what he needs to do. He writes 'Step 1' and then rereads the task. Still unsure, Edward decides he could get started by getting together the things he needs for the task. He thinks this will be easy as there is already a list called 'What you need to complete this task'. Edward reads the list and goes off to get his materials but returns to his desk empty-handed as he has forgotten the three items on the list. He decides to take the list with him to remind him what he needs. As he moves around the room getting his materials, Edward becomes distracted by what other students are doing. By the time he returns to his desk, the teacher tells the class that the allotted time for the task is nearly up and to finish off what they are doing. Edward slumps down on his chair. He is disappointed with himself and wonders why he can't keep up with the other students.

WHAT DOES THIS TELL US?

Edward has poor executive function skills. He has poor planning/prioritising skills, poor organisational skills and a poor working memory; he is also easily distracted. Without appropriate intervention, Edward will not reach his full potential and will lag behind his classmates. Edward is already comparing himself adversely with his peers. This may lead to feelings of hopelessness and decrease his motivation to learn.

▶ DISCUSSION

As an ESW, what could you do to support Edward to organise his thoughts, recall what he needs to do and complete the task in a timely manner?

The brain from middle childhood to young adulthood

The growth in the frontal lobe supports the development of a range of cognitive skills typically developed during the middle years of schooling. Importantly, this aspect of brain development supports the application of order and logic, so that children can undertake a task in an organised and methodical manner. This allows children to apply the rules needed to learn to read and create meaningful text, and apply basic mathematical concepts to solve problems. It also supports the use of research skills: What do I need to know? How can I find out?

These developing skills can be observed in the play of children during middle childhood. For example, they invent increasingly complex role-plays, develop and apply rules for games, play sequenced computer games, build with construction sets that may include simple electronic components and create detailed drawings.

An important aspect of brain development during this period is the lateralisation of the two hemispheres of the brain and the maturation of the corpus callosum. This involves maturation of both the brain and the synapses, which are the connections between the cells in the nervous system. Over time, if not used, these synapses are gradually pruned from the nervous system.

Lateralisation of the brain allows children to use both sides of the brain effectively. The left hemisphere largely specialises in analytical thought and facts. It is also responsible for mathematical thinking, logic, deductive reasoning, planning and the understanding of spoken and written words. The right hemisphere specialises in feelings and emotions, creativity, rhythm, spatial awareness, spontaneity, relationships, motor skills and humour. The brain works most effectively when the left and right sides communicate and work together, and while the left/right brain are each assigned specific tasks, they are not mutually exclusive.

The brain: five to six years of age

According to Sprenger (2008), the following are the key features of brain development that occur at five to six years:

- development of the frontal lobes, allowing for an increase in short-term memory skills
- acceleration of the language and skills necessary for reading
- improved ability to plan and organise – children are able to set long-term goals
- development of an ability to understand and use strategies for remembering
- improvement in long-term memory
- improvement in reading and the understanding of word meaning.

The brain: seven to eight years of age

Sprenger (2008) suggests that the development of the brain by eight years allows for more sophisticated thinking, including:

- increased impulse control and improved ability to plan, support developing independence and accept responsibility for oneself
- improved ability to understand irony and sarcasm
- significantly improved ability to organise stored memories
- automatic reading and writing, which allows the brain to focus on comprehension and content. By eight years of age, the brain has reached 90 per cent of its adult weight.

The adolescent brain

According to Sprenger (2008), during adolescence the brain undergoes a period of reconstruction, which partly contributes to the impulsive and seemingly reckless behaviour that is typical of adolescent development:

- At around 10 to 12 years of age, the brain has a final growth spurt.
- By the time children reach adolescence, the brain begins the reorganisation of regulatory systems. Unused neurons and connections are pruned.
- It is thought that many of the undesirable attributes of adolescent development, such as recklessness, challenging rules, poor organisational skills and emotional outbursts, are related to the pruning process.
- The adolescent brain is still in the process of developing higher-order thinking skills, which are not fully developed until the prefrontal cortex matures in the mid-twenties.
- The part of the brain that controls emotions tends to dominate the adolescent brain. This can lead to irrational and risky behaviours.

The most significant cognitive advancement in adolescence is the refinement of the executive function of the brain, which allows young people to think logically, engage in abstract thought and use metacognition skills such as planning, monitoring and evaluating their own learning. Increasingly, when guided by adults, young people are able to engage in critical reflection – they begin to question and challenge ethical, moral and social issues. They are able to consider more than just their own perspective and can apply creative ideas to solve problems and learning challenges.

The transition to young adulthood

Great gains in cognitive skills are evident by early adolescence.

Dolgin (2014, p. 155) reports the following improvements in cognition:

- improvement in deductive reasoning – allowing students to find answers more quickly
- improved ability to think hypothetically – allowing students to engage in reflective thinking, predict and consider a range of possibilities and alternatives
- greater use of prepositional logic – using reason based on logical inference, which allows students to engage in more complex problem-solving tasks
- the development of reasoning and probability – used to explore problems and find logical solutions; such skills are necessary for higher-order mathematical thinking
- improved metacognition – the ability to think about one's own thoughts, which allows students to examine their own thinking and consider alternative ways of thinking about a problem
- greater command of language – meaning students are therefore better able to express thoughts, feelings and ideas.

The teenage brain

Brain research and education

Brain research has led to a better understanding of how the brain is built over time, how learning occurs and the factors that influence learning and brain development. Applying what we know about the brain can assist educators to create more effective learning environments and develop better strategies to support learning. **Figure 7.15** summarises a number of key brain facts that can assist educators when working with students (Schiller, 2010).

Figure 7.15 Brain facts and the classroom

Brain development is both genetically predetermined and dependent upon the child's interactions and stimulation within the environment.	Brain development can be influenced positively when educators provide timely and stimulating learning experiences.
Sensory stimulation is food for the rapidly growing brain.	Providing students with 'hands-on' learning experiences is a critical learning strategy.
The quality, quantity and consistency of stimulating experiences influence brain development.	Learning experiences allow time for students to explore and practise concepts on multiple occasions.
Positive interactions affect brain wiring and healthy brain development.	Positive and respectful relationships with students allow for two-way communication to support brain development.

There are critical or sensitive periods in which a greater 'window of opportunity' exists for learning certain skills and knowledge.	Learning opportunities must be sequenced in ways that reflect our knowledge of child development and the developing brain.
A child's brain is two and a half times more active than an adult's brain.	Children and young people are biologically pre-programmed to learn.
Positive early childhood experiences are likely to prevent or reduce the likelihood of later learning, social and emotional problems.	During the early primary school years learning should be social, playful and hands-on.

Source: Adapted from Schiller (2010), pp. 14–18.

Being aware of brain development research also supports our understanding of how to support learning. The research tells us that as the brain matures learning and development gradually progresses along a continuum from simple to complex. That is, the brain is built over time and scaffolds its development by using existing knowledge, understanding and skills to build new knowledge, understanding and skills. **Figure 7.16** demonstrates this concept.

Figure 7.16 Progression of learning

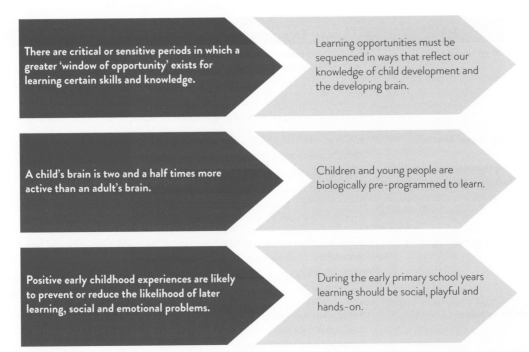

Progression	Teaching concept
Known to unknown	When trying to teach a concept, the teacher connects the concept to something familiar to the child and then builds a bridge from what the child knows to what the child does not know.
Self to others	Children must understand how the concept relates to them before they can generalise their knowledge to understanding others. This is especially relevant in social situations.
Whole to part	Children must understand the big picture before they can understand the small parts that make up the big picture. When teachers understand the whole-to-part needs of children, they provide repetition of activities, time for exploring concepts and ideas, and teach specific pieces rather than general ideas.
Concrete to abstract	For young children, learning stems from concrete experiences in which they can touch, taste, see, smell and hear. Teachers utilise a variety of approaches to teaching a concept that includes both concrete experiences and more abstract teaching strategies, such as bringing real leaves to the classroom before showing pictures of leaves.

Progression	Teaching concept
Enactive to symbolic	Enactive representation occurs when children act out situations in their lives (role play, quacking like a duck after they see a duck). Symbolic representation, on the other hand, refers to using words or symbols (writing) to interpret experiences. Children need time to explore concepts through all modes of representation instead of relying on symbolic representation alone.
Exploratory to goal directed	Children need time to explore materials (spaces, concepts) before they are given specific directions about how to use the material in the appropriate way. Children need time to explore paint before being able to focus on completing the task desired by the teacher that uses the paint. In the same way, children need time to explore the new books about leaves before they are expected to look closely at the books.
Less accurate to more accurate	Children utilise trial and error to learn about the world. Over time and with experience, children learn the accurate information. The role of the teacher is to provide experiences and supports that help children revisit their misconceptions about concepts and build more accurate knowledge.
Simple to complex	Tasks are presented to children in the simplest manner possible. This makes the task easier for children to navigate and helps them understand the task. Tasks are simplified when they are: > closely tied to what children know > more focused on self than others > more focused on the whole than the parts > more concrete than abstract > more enactive than symbolic > more exploratory than goal directed > more tolerant of inaccuracies.

Source: Table I. Examples of each developmental direction from Brain Development and Learning in the Primary Years by Gerdes, J., Durden, T. & Poppe, L. (June 2013). University of Nebraska–Lincoln Extension, Institute of Agriculture and Natural Resources. https://extensionpublications.unl.edu/assets/pdf/g2198.pdf

CONSIDER THIS

THE DEVELOPING BRAIN

We know that emerging readers' brains change in two fundamental ways: circuits that adapted at very early ages to recognise faces and objects reconfigure to recognise thousands of visual words. And circuits for language that developed early to hear and pronounce words adapt to recognise sounds associated with syllables and letters (McCandliss & Toomarian, 2020).

WHAT DOES THIS TELL US?

The brain's ability to engage in increasingly complex tasks relies on the foundations already laid down in earlier development.

Source: McCandliss, B. & Toomarian, E. (April 2020). Putting Neuroscience in the Classroom: How the Brain Changes as We Learn. Pew. https://www.pewtrusts.org/en/trend/archive/spring-2020/putting-neuroscience-in-the-classroom-how-the-brain-changes-as-we-learn

Encouraging a growth mindset

Helping children reach their potential

According to Briceño (2015) a growth mindset is the belief that [personal] qualities [and abilities] can change and that we can develop our intelligence and abilities. The opposite of having a growth mindset is having a fixed mindset, which is the belief that intelligence and abilities cannot be developed. In essence, this means that praising students for the techniques they use as a learner rather than praising overall effort creates a growth mindset. For example, a student who works hard and doesn't progress in her learning but is praised for her effort (e.g. 'I can see you are trying') will develop a fixed mindset (i.e. 'I've worked really hard but I'm just not smart enough'). A student who works hard and is praised for applying a range of learning strategies (e.g. 'It's great that you're not just relying on one source of information to get the answers') creates a growth mindset (i.e. 'I don't know the answer but I can use research to help me.').

Supporting a growth mindset encourages students to persevere and engage in creative thinking and problem-solving when faced with learning challenges. Focusing on developing a range of learning skills that students can apply to learning builds their confidence as learners (see **Figure 7.17**).

Having a growth mindset doesn't mean that every student will be a successful learner. First, as you are now aware, learning does not occur in isolation but in the social context of the classroom and school community, as well as the cultural context of the family, all of which must work together to support a growth mindset. Second, the curriculum and its delivery in the classroom are important factors in determining whether students are supported to develop a growth mindset.

Figure 7.17 Students who can apply a range of learning strategies will be more confident learners

Source: Photo by Tish Okely © Cengage

7.3 Development, learning and the curriculum

A **curriculum** typically describes content and skills – that is, what children should know (knowledge content) and be able to do (skills content). It often describes the type of learning that will take place and the expected outcomes that will be achieved by learners. Curricula are usually written around subject or knowledge areas, such as numeracy or literacy, and typically describe a progression of skills, knowledge and capabilities from beginning or foundation level to the final year of school.

The Australian Curriculum is presented as a developmental sequence of learning from Foundation to Year 10 (AC). It includes three dimensions:

1 learning areas – disciplinary knowledge, skills and understanding
2 general capabilities
3 cross-curriculum priorities.

Figure 7.18 provides an outline of the Australian Curriculum.

In Australia, the learning areas are specific to a year level or a two- or three-year band. Students are typically grouped by age from Foundation (also called Prep or Kindergarten) to Year 10. Curriculum content has been developed along a continuum that allows students to build on their knowledge, understandings and skills as they progress through each year level. The integration of general capabilities and cross-curriculum priorities recognises that to prepare students to be successful members of society, learning must extend beyond subject content. The continuum approach and the integration of dispositions for learning reflect child development knowledge and brain development research. Importantly, they also recognise that learning occurs in a social context and is built on shared understandings.

Australian Curriculum

Figure 7.18 Three dimensions of the Australian Curriculum (V9.0)

Dimension
Eight learning areas > English > Mathematics > Science > Health and Physical Education > Humanities and Social Sciences (HASS) – comprising the subjects of Civics and Citizenship, Economics and Business, Geography and History > The Arts – comprising the subjects of Dance, Drama, Media Arts, Music and Visual Arts > Technologies – comprising the subjects of Design and Technologies, and Digital Technologies > Languages
General capabilities In the Australian Curriculum, general capabilities equip young Australians with the knowledge, skills, behaviours and dispositions to live and work successfully. General capabilities are developed through the content of the learning area. The seven general capabilities in the Australian Curriculum are: > Critical and Creative Thinking > Digital Literacy > Ethical Understanding > Intercultural Understanding > Literacy > Numeracy > Personal and Social capability.
Cross-curriculum priorities The three cross-curriculum priorities in the Australian Curriculum are: > Aboriginal and Torres Strait Islander Histories and Cultures > Asia and Australia's Engagement with Asia > Sustainability.

Source: Eight learning areas: https://v9.australiancurriculum.edu.au/f-10-curriculum/f-10-curriculum-overview/learning-areas; General capabilities: https://v9.australiancurriculum.edu.au/f-10-curriculum/f-10-curriculum-overview/general-capabilities; cross-curriculum priorities: https://v9.australiancurriculum.edu.au/f-10-curriculum/f-10-curriculum-overview/cross-curriculum-priorities. AC

Implications for ESWs

Child development research tells us that learning occurs in a social context and children learn best when they can engage in learning with others – family, peers, teachers and ESWs. Research also tells us that each child develops and learns at their own unique pace and that new knowledge, understanding and skills are built by drawing on existing knowledge, understanding and skill. Just like building a house – beginning with a solid foundation, scaffolding is added to provide a strong framework to support the structure and layers, and details are added so that the house is functional. The process continues – rooms are filled with things both functional and aesthetic, paths are laid and gardens developed. Over time, the house is maintained, renovated and loved.

The analogy of a house is a useful way for thinking about how the brain develops. The brain is built over time, with layer upon layer that are interconnected. It requires ongoing input to be maintained, and each house is similar but also unique, shaped by its occupants and the amount of love and attention they are able to contribute. In a school setting, the role of teachers, ESWs and others is to support the development of the brain by providing learning experiences that allow the brain to continue building itself, keeping in mind the 'whole child' concept and remembering that all domains of development influence and are influenced by all other domains of development. We know that learning is multidimensional and can occur in many different ways. We also know that for children to develop key concepts they must have many opportunities to explore, experiment and practise in ways that are meaningful to the child or young person. Underpinning our knowledge of child development is the critical importance of the warm, trusting and respectful relationships without which children will not reach their full potential.

The Pittsburgh University Child Development Center used child development knowledge as the foundation for a set of guiding principles for teaching that serve as a useful framework for ESWs. These principles are shown in **Figure 7.19**.

Figure 7.19 Guiding principles for teaching

Guiding principles	*What this means in practice*
Social Learning: Social learning is the foundation for growth in all developmental and academic learning.	Learning occurs in a social context – children learn about themselves and the world firstly from their family and later from school, teachers, peers, etc.).
Process: How children learn is as important as what they learn.	Learning involves, knowing (facts, concepts, procedures), understanding (facts, concepts, procedures) and doing (applying facts, concepts, procedures to explore, problem solve, create and discover).
Social Interaction: The greatest cognitive growth occurs through social interaction with peers, teachers and other adults.	Learning is a social skill. Learning happens when students are given the opportunity to work alongside others, ask and pose questions, generate ideas and engage in problem-solving.
Emotional Development: Children engage in daily opportunities to learn about cooperation, responsibility, empathy, self-control and what it means to be an individual and part of a group.	Social interactions allow children and young people to build their skills so that they develop trust, respect, self-confidence and resilience.
Relationships	**What this means in practice**
Teacher-Child Relationships: Teachers' knowledge of the children they teach – individually, culturally, and developmentally, is the basis for curricular development. Teacher-Family Relationships: Teachers and administration partner with parents/guardians to ensure that communication supports the growth and education of children and young people Staff Relationships: A sense of community, support, and modelling is embraced as an approach to staying current and connected with each other.	Human relationships have a critical influence on brain development. Children who experience positive, nurturing and respectful relationships are able to build resilience, and develop a 'can do' attitude which will allow them to strive towards reaching their full potential. Children who experience negative, unpredictable, abusive or violent relationships learn that the world is not a safe place, they tend to have low self-esteem and may grow up feeling angry, sad and mistrustful of the world. These children rarely reach their full potential.

Source: University of Pittsburgh (2022). Curriculum: Guiding Principles. University Child Development Center. http://www.childdevelopment.pitt.edu/node/225

The principles described in **Figure 7.19** are a good reminder that adults who support and guide children and young people's learning must do so in ways that acknowledge the concept of 'the whole child', build positive and respectful relationships and understand the social nature of learning.

The ESW's role is to support students' acquisition and application of, knowledge, understanding and skills. This is best achieved when your practices reflect the needs of the learner and are delivered at a pace that best suits the learner. When ESWs and teachers have a professional working relationship, the needs of the students can be the central focus of discussion and planning.

To understand and support students as learners, ESWs must have a sound knowledge of child development and understand the many factors that influence development. Being aware of the critical role of relationships and social interactions as a cornerstone for successful learning experiences and outcomes is essential.

Developmental red flags

Developmental red flags

Developmental red flags is a term used to describe behaviours of concern in relation to a child's development, particularly developmental milestones. Being familiar with what might typically be expected in each domain of development will assist you to identify 'red flags' – to be alert to signs that indicate a need for further investigation by the teacher and or specialist. For example, a six-year-old who has not established hand dominance and has poor fine motor and hand–eye coordination would present as a red flag.

Developmental delay is a term used to describe children who are slower to reach developmental milestones in one or more domains of development. Where a child or young person has delays in two or more domains, the term 'significant developmental delay' is used.

Being familiar with the concept of 'the whole child', the unique nature of child development and knowing that each domain of development both influences, and is influenced by, all other domains of development is critical when thinking about developmental delays. As you gain experience working with children and young people of different ages, you will build on your knowledge of child development and begin to identify what might typically be expected of students within a particular age range. Building this knowledge will help you to identify developmental red flags.

Signs of developmental delay typically present in early childhood – for example, a baby or young child who lags in developing motor skills such as sitting, crawling or walking; a baby who is always fussy, doesn't like to be cuddled and avoids eye contact; a toddler who doesn't use single words, shows no interest in exploring their surrounding or can't identify common objects (e.g. 'Where's the ball?').

There are a range of known factors that may contribute to developmental delay. Conversely, there may be no known cause for a child's developmental delay. Known factors include: premature birth or complications at birth such as breathing difficulties; brain injury caused by lack of oxygen to the brain; a brain infection or damage caused by toxins; genetic conditions such as Down syndrome or Fragile X syndrome; and the mother's health and nutrition during pregnancy.

Summary

The principles of child development introduced in this chapter may appear quite overwhelming. The language and concepts used to describe development can seem complex; however, as you continue your study of child development, you will become more familiar and comfortable with the terminology. A sound knowledge of child and adolescent development will assist you to better understand what can reasonably be expected as each student progresses along the developmental continuum. Knowledge of child development is a huge area of study. This chapter has provided a brief introduction.

Self-check questions

1 Explain the two types of physical development.
2 What does 'developmental milestones' refer to? Give one example.
3 Define the following key terms/statements:
   a Whole child
   b Sociocultural context
   c Culture influences every aspect of human development
   d Each child develops at their own unique pace
4 List two positive and two negative factors that support brain development.
5 Explain the Australian Curriculum and list its three elements.
6 What is the role of the ESW in supporting the brain development of children in the school setting?
7 There are a range of known factors that may contribute to developmental delay. Give two examples.

Discussion questions

1 Akhmal, who is 17 years old, has experienced both physical and emotional trauma between ages four to 10. He has been with his adoptive family for the past three years, after spending a long time in foster care and homes.
   a Using Bronfenbrenner's ecological systems theory, consider the impacts from the abuse Akhmal has experienced at each of the five levels. This will inform how you can work most effectively with Akhmal during your sessions.
2 Billy has experienced three foster homes in his seven years. Most disturbing was the limited care that he received during his time with his parents, where there was limited food provided and he was left in his cot for hours at a time. It wasn't until he was with his first foster placement that he had the freedom to move and learned to crawl at 15 months.
   a Revisit the section on brain development and consider which of the negative factors that interrupt the developing brain Billy experienced.

Activities

1 Imagine you are working with young teenagers. Knowing what you do about executive functioning, what activities could you use to develop planning and prioritising as well as time management?
2 Classify each of the following statements as true or false:
   a Sensory stimulation deprives the brain of growth.
   b Providing students with 'hands-on' learning experiences is a critical learning strategy.
   c The quality, quantity and consistency of stimulating experiences influence brain development.
   d Positive interactions affect brain wiring and healthy brain development
   e There are critical or sensitive periods in which a greater 'window of opportunity' exists for learning certain skills and knowledge.
   f A child's brain is three and a half times more active than an adult's brain.
   g Every single childhood experience is likely to prevent or reduce the likelihood of later learning, social and emotional problems.

Chapter 8

PHYSICAL GROWTH, DEVELOPMENT AND LEARNING

LEARNING OBJECTIVES

When you have completed this chapter, you should be able to demonstrate that, in relation to working in a school environment, you can:

8.1 identify the stages of physical development

8.2 describe the factors that influence physical development

8.3 identify the relationship between physical development and the current curriculum

8.4 access information on strategies, materials and resources that support physical development.

Online resources icons refer to useful weblinks. Ask your instructor for these **Online Resources.**

Introduction

When beginning the study of child and adolescent development, a good starting point is physical development because it is easily observable. Physical development is most rapid during the first three years of life. During this relatively short period, children move from total dependency on others for all of their physical needs to being able to do many things for themselves. Healthy physical development during this period is dependent not only on good nutrition, adequate health care and opportunities for physical activity, but also on a loving, supportive and nurturing environment.

Remember, development does not occur in isolation. It occurs in a social context (experiences with family, culture, education, etc.). Each domain of development is affected and influenced by all other domains of development.

8.1 The process of physical development

Physical development (also referred to as **motor development**) is a complex process that begins in the womb, involving muscle tissue, tendons, bones, joints and nerves. Brain development influences and is also influenced by motor development.

Physical growth occurs in a predictable pattern – motor skills tend to develop in the same universal sequence across all cultures. Females usually reach physical maturity around 16 years of age while for males it is at around 18 years of age. Mastery of motor skills will vary according to genetic predisposition and environmental factors.

Motor development includes both *quantitative physiological change* (increased strength allows walking to develop) and *qualitative change* (motor skills improve with practice).

Two of the basic principles related to growth are **cephalocaudal development** and **proximodistal development** (see **Figure 8.1**).

Cephalocaudal development refers to the direction of the body's physical growth, reflected in the order in which parts of the body become larger and the functions and structures become more complex. Cephalocaudal development progresses from head to foot. The infant gains control of their head movement, then their neck, shoulders, back, hips, legs and feet (see **Figure 8.2**).

Figure 8.1 Cephalocaudal (A) and proximodistal (B)

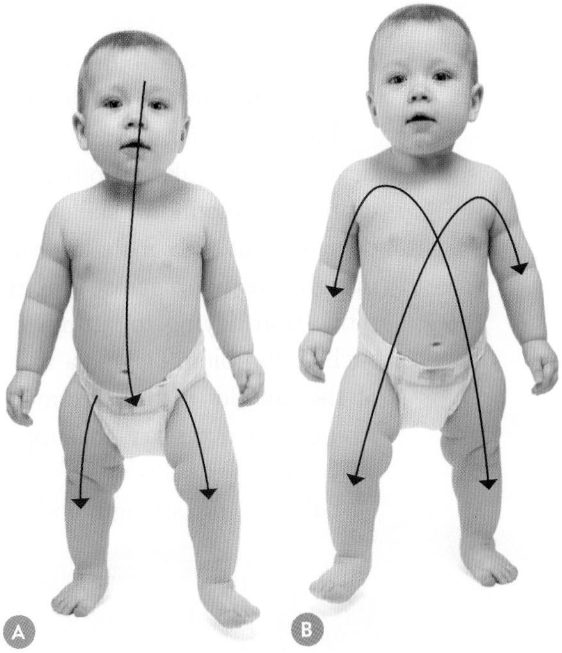

Shutterstock.com/irin-k

Figure 8.2 Cephalocaudal development: changes in body proportions (prenatal to adult)

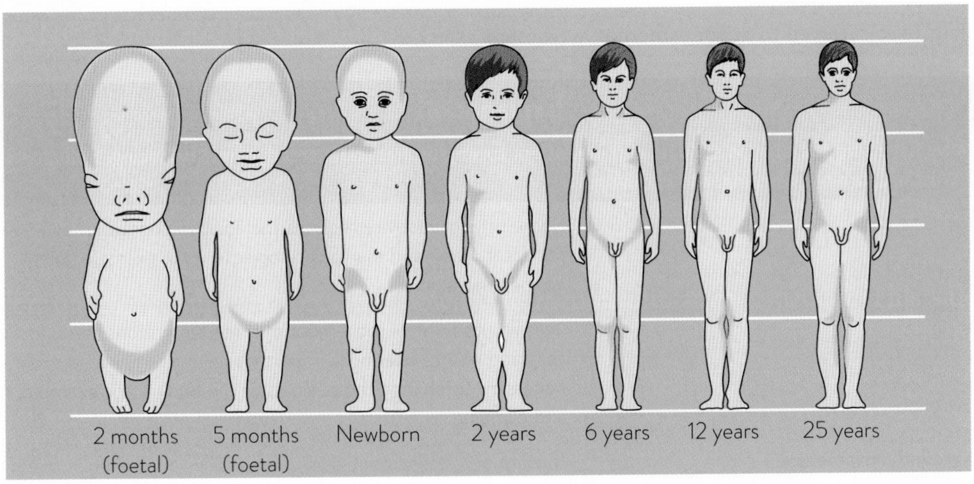

Source: Cengage Learning Inc. Reproduced by permission. www.cengage.com/permissions

Proximodistal development is the progression of physical and motor development from the centre of the body towards the extremities. For example, an infant learns to control the muscles of their chest and shoulders before they can control their arms, hands or fingers.

The study of physical development includes three broad areas:

1. **gross motor development** – the development and coordination of large muscles such as those in the arms, legs, back, chest and abdominals
2. **fine motor development** – the development and coordination of small muscles such as those in fingers, hands, toes, eyes and the face
3. **sensorimotor development** (also referred to as perceptual motor development or motor planning) – the ability to receive, interpret and respond successfully to sensory information. Perceptual motor development is critical to cognitive development.

Each area of motor development influences, and is influenced by, all other areas of motor development. Like all other areas of development, motor skills develop at uneven rates – for example, gross motor skills develop and are refined more quickly than fine motor skills. Physical development also includes balance and core strength. **Balance** is the ability to maintain an upright position against gravity without falling over. Babies gradually develop balance as they move from laying to sitting to standing to walking. Balance is necessary for later motor skills such as climbing, kicking a ball, hopping and jumping. **Core strength** involves the development of the muscles in the abdomen, pelvis, shoulders and back necessary for posture control. Core strength is necessary to support the spine and stabilise the body for fine and gross motor movement.

Balance, core strength and motor planning are essential motor development skills.

Gross motor development

Gross motor development refers to the development of large muscles used for walking, running, climbing, jumping, hopping and so on. Gross motor development precedes fine motor development and includes the skills outlined in **Figure 8.3**.

Figure 8.3 Gross motor skills (also referred to as fundamental movement skills)

Skill	Explanation
'Body-management skills involve balancing the body in stillness and in motion. Examples are: static and dynamic balancing, rolling, stopping, landing, bending, stretching, twisting, turning, swinging, and climbing.'	
Stability and mobility	Some physical activity requires the ability to control movement in a purposeful way and manipulate objects – for example, join connecting blocks.
Weight shift and weight bearing	Learning to control movement in three dimensions through weight shift and weight bearing is important for movements where it is necessary to change the position of the body – for example, running and climbing.
Reduction of unwanted background movement	Moving only those body parts required for purposeful movement – for example, keeping the legs still while sitting at a table completing a writing task.

Skill	Explanation
Balancing muscle length and strength	This skill is necessary for control of the head and trunk and for reaching. It is essential that each muscle group be flexed and stretched to full use. Preschool children who have not refined this skill may, for example, persistently run on their tiptoes.
Proprioceptive development	This is an understanding of where the body is in space – the sense of extremities and how to move the body within a defined space.
'Locomotor skills involve transporting the body in any direction from one point to another. Examples are crawling, walking, running, hopping, leaping, jumping, galloping, skipping, dodging and swimming.'	
Moving one body part independently of another	Children without body control will have difficulty coordinating their movements, such as swinging arms in opposite directions or using alternate feet and hands when climbing.
Strength	This refers to having the power, strength or endurance necessary for movement.
Agility	This is the ability to move quickly and easily.
Flexibility	This refers to having flexible muscles and joints for easy movement.
'Object-control skills require controlling implements (for example, bats, racquets or hoops) or objects (such as balls), either by hand or foot. Examples are throwing, catching, kicking, striking, bouncing, and dribbling.'	
Sequencing and scaling of muscle activity	Learning to sequence and coordinate the movement of muscles so that the correct amount of force is used in a complex task. Children who have not refined this skill can look awkward or clumsy. Children with poor sequencing and scaling of muscle activity may, for example, have a great deal of difficulty applying the correct pressure when writing with a pen.
'Fundamental Movement Skills (FMS) are movement patterns that involve different body parts such as the legs, arms, trunk and head, and include such skills as running, hopping, catching, throwing, striking and balancing.'	

Source: Fundamental Movement Skills: Learning Teaching and Assessment, Preparing Children For An Active And Healthy Lifestyle (2013), Department of Education Western Australia

Fundamental movement skills

Fundamental movement skills provide the foundation for the more complex movements required when playing various sports or when engaged in more complex motor tasks. Fundamental movement skills include those shown in **Figure 8.4**.

Figure 8.4 Fundamental movement skills

Locomotor skills involve moving the body in any direction from one point to another
Crawling, walking, running, marching, galloping, skipping, hopping, leaping, jumping, swimming, dodging – stepping forwards, backwards and sideways

Non-locomotor skills are body-management skills that involve balancing the body in stillness (static) and in motion (dynamic)
Bending, stretching, twisting, balancing, swinging, spinning

Object control involves small muscle skills required for controlling objects such as a ball or bat
Throwing, catching, bouncing, dribbling, kicking

LINK TO THE AUSTRALIAN CURRICULUM

HEALTH AND PHYSICAL EDUCATION CURRICULUM (VERSION 9.0)

Strand: Movement and physical activity

SUB-STRAND: MOVING OUR BODIES

- Foundation: practise fundamental movement skills in minor game and play situations (AC9HPFM01)
- Years 1 and 2: practise fundamental movement skills and apply them in a variety of movement situations (AC9HP2M01)
- Years 3–4: refine and apply fundamental movement skills in new movement situations (AC9HP4M01)
- Years 5–6: adapt and modify movement skills across a variety of situations (AC9HP6M01)
- Years 7–8: analyse, refine and transfer movement skills in a variety of movement situations (AC9HP8M01)
- Years 9–10: analyse, adapt and refine their own and others' movement skills in a range of challenging movement situations to enhance performance (AC9HP10M01)

Source: Australian Curriculum: Health and Physical Education F–10 Version 9.0, Scope and sequence (accessed 2 December 2022); https://v9.australiancurriculum.edu.au/content/dam/en/curriculum/ac-version-9/downloads/health-and-physical-education/health-and-physical-education-scope-and-sequence-f-10-v9.docx

Fundamental movement skills videos and resources

There is no evidence that improvement in movement skills directly improves academic performance. However, increased movement competence can improve self-esteem, self-confidence, self-management and self-control. In turn, this can affect academic performance and willingness to tackle new challenges, provided that the tasks required are meaningful, relevant, purposeful and appropriate for the child (© Northern Territory of Australia (Department of Education) 2017. CC-BY-4.0 licence.).

Fine motor development

Fine motor development involves all functions related to the use of small muscle groups, such as wrist movement or using the palm of the hand and fingers. Mastery of fine motor skills is necessary for children to develop independent self-help skills, such as using utensils for eating, toileting and handwashing, dressing and undressing. Fine motor skills tend to lag behind cognitive development, which can result in frustration. For example, a child may know the letters needed to form their name but lack the fine motor control needed to write it.

During the preschool years, there can be great variation in children's fine motor capabilities. For example, some four-year-olds will be able to cut around shapes while others have difficulty opening and closing scissors. This variation in fine motor skills is evident when children commence school. However, fine motor skills are usually well developed by six to seven years.

The development of fine motor skills is outlined in **Figure 8.5**.

Figure 8.5 Skills needed for fine motor development

Skill	Explanation
Bilateral integration	Using two hands together with one hand leading (e.g. holding a sheet of paper with one hand while holding a pencil and drawing in the other hand).
Crossing the midline	The ability to cross the imaginary line running from a child's nose to pelvis that divides the body into left and right sides.

Skill	Explanation
Hand and finger strength	An ability to exert force against resistance using the hands and fingers that allows the necessary muscle power for controlled movement (e.g. applying force with the fingers to grip and lift an object). Hand and finger strength is essential for precise movement and control when learning to write.
Hand-eye coordination	The ability to process information received from the eyes to control, guide and direct the hands in the performance of a task such as drawing.
Hand dominance	The consistent use of one (usually the same) hand for task performance, which allows refined skills to develop.
Hand division	Using just the thumb, index and middle finger for manipulation, leaving the fourth and little finger tucked into the palm not participating but providing stability for the other three fingers (e.g. holding a pencil when drawing).
Object manipulation	The ability to skilfully manipulate tools (such as the ability to hold and move pencils and scissors with control) and the controlled use of everyday tools such as a toothbrush, hairbrush and cutlery.
Body awareness (proprioception)	Information that the brain receives from our muscles and joints to make us aware of our body position and body movement, so we can accurately control our movements.

Source: 'Fine motor skills' from Kid Sense, https://childdevelopment.com.au/, Kid Sense Child Development Corporation Pty Ltd © 2019.

Healthy physical development is an important school-readiness factor. Children who arrive at school with age-appropriate fine and gross motor skills are better able to engage in a learning environment that requires them to move around the room, sit for extended periods of time, engage in movement games and manipulate materials for literacy and numeracy.

Fine motor activities

Sensorimotor development

Sensorimotor development refers to the brain's use of sensory information including taste, touch, smell, hearing, vision, detection of movement, balance and proprioception (awareness of where your body is as you move around) to produce movement. The use of sensory information by the brain is referred to as **sensory input** and using this information to produce movement is referred to as a **motor response** or **motor output**. For example, a baby may track the movement of their mother with their eyes or bring their hand to their mouth; a toddler will turn their head to the sound of their name being called or look to and locate an object to which an adult is pointing (see **Figure 8.6**).

Sensory information carried by the nervous system allows the brain to coordinate movement so that the body remains upright and balanced during movement. This process occurs at a subconscious level. Types of sensory information are shown in **Figure 8.7**.

Figure 8.6 Sensory input

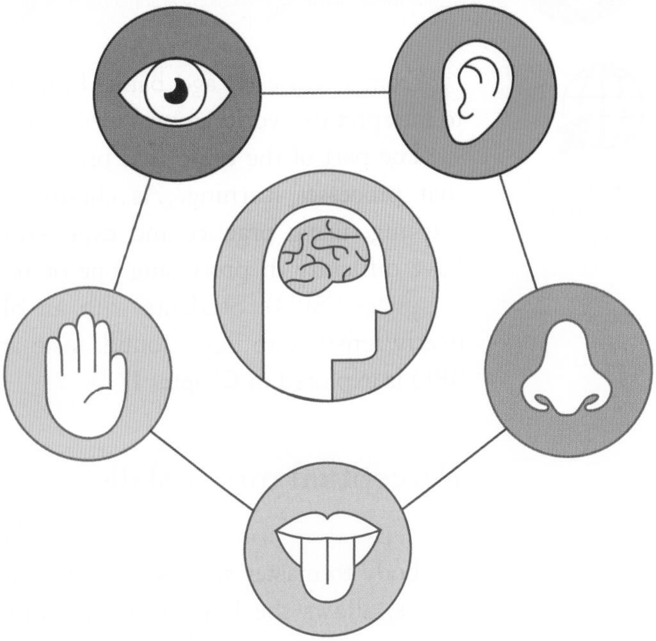

Figure 8.7 Sensory information

Tactile
Used to obtain information about everything that is touched by or touches the body. It tells us when something is rough, smooth, sharp, hard, prickly and so on. Tactile information also alerts us to danger such as the 'flight/fight' process, for example, pulling away from a hot or sharp surface.

Oral
The sense of taste.

Visual
Involves detection of light, colour, depth perception and movement.

Auditory
The detection of sound. Children can develop hypersensitivity to sounds.

Olfactory
Relates to detecting scents/smells.

Proprioceptive
Awareness of the body's position in space. It is essential for coordination of movement such as eye–hand and eye–foot coordination, necessary for running, jumping, climbing, balancing, writing and so on. Children with poor proprioceptivity are often described as clumsy.

Vestibular
Involves the structures in the inner ear that allow for the detection of movement, head position and balance, speed and direction of movement, and eye tracking. Children with a poor vestibular sense may have difficulty with coordinated movement, such as writing, jumping, climbing or walking along a balance beam.

Physical activity and cognitive function

From a very early age, babies begin to store, recall and use information obtained from the senses to interpret the world around them. Sensory stimulation is critical to healthy brain development.

The part of the brain that processes movement, the cerebellum, is the same part of the brain that processes learning. As children develop their motor skills, they also engage in motor learning, using practice and experience to continually refine their motor skills. Children who have difficulty in processing one or more of their senses are said to have **Sensory Processing Disorder** (SPD). Students with an SPD may present as awkward, clumsy, tactile defensive, overly sensitive to light, sound, taste and/or movement, unable to sit still and easily distracted. SPD is explored in **Chapter 17**.

Perceptual motor skills

Perceptual motor development skills involve connecting the brain's sensory functions with the body to master skills such as timing and direction of movement. Perception, using all of the senses, allows the brain to collect information from the environment to plan for and control movement (motor skills). Perceptual motor skills incorporate timing, spatial awareness and direction of movement necessary for complex movement such as hand–eye coordination, static balance, auditory language skills (expressive and receptive language) and visual-auditory skills (recognising written symbols as spoken words). Development of perceptual motor skills lays the foundation for literacy and numeracy learning.

Motor planning is the ability to plan, organise and carry out movements. Motor planning requires the integration of the brain and the senses. It usually occurs at a subconscious level – for example, using a knife and fork to eat, picking up a pencil dropped on the floor or walking up stairs. As we carry out these movements, our brain is busy planning and directing them almost instantaneously. It calculates how to move, how to balance while moving, the sequence of movements, the speed of movements and so on.

Perceptual motor learning involves all senses: seeing, hearing, touching, smelling and moving, or kinaesthetics. Perceptual development begins with *proprioception*. **Proprioception** is an innate sensory motor skill that allows babies to become aware of their body by receiving sensory feedback from involuntary movement of the joints and muscles. At this early stage, the brain is simply processing sensory and vestibular (sense of balance – i.e. which way is up) information. Perceptual motor skills are outlined in **Figure 8.8**.

Perceptual motor difficulties

Figure 8.8 Perceptual motor skills

Skill	Explanation
Hand–eye coordination	Using the eye to assist in accurate movement such as writing, drawing, using scissors, grasping and gripping objects, throwing and catching, and coordinating movements for climbing.
Foot–eye coordination	This refers to a child's ability to use their eyes and feet together to accomplish a task.
Laterality	Internalising the awareness of the difference between right and left and the ability to control the two sides of the body together or separately.
Directionality	An awareness of external space outside the body and knowledge of directions in relation to left and right, in and out, up and down. This is often confused with laterality.
Kinaesthesia	The function of the senses that sends messages from joints, muscles and ligaments to the brain. Kinaesthesia provides information about the position and movement of limbs and bodies without conscious thought.
Static balance	The ability to maintain balance while remaining stationary. This skill requires vestibular development, which is linked to the inner ear, balance and coordination. Balance refers to the ability to assume and maintain any position against the force of gravity. Maintenance of balance results from the interaction of the muscles working to keep the body on its base.
Body image	This refers to an individual's concept of their body and its parts.
Visual motor control	The ability to successfully integrate visual and motor responses into a physical action. It enables an individual to control movement and move easily and smoothly from place to place.
Coordination	The ability of the body to integrate the action of the muscles of the body to accomplish a specific movement or a series of skilled movements in the most efficient manner.
Gross motor coordination	This results from the development of the skeletal or large muscles to produce efficient total body movement.
Fine motor coordination	The coordinated use of small muscles resulting from the development of the muscles to the degree that they can perform specific small movements – for example, cutting, writing and grasping.
Spatial awareness/ orientation	This involves the ability to select a reference point to stabilise functions and organise objects into the correct perspective. It involves knowledge of the body and its position, as well as the positions of other people and objects in relation to your body in space. It is closely associated with body image.

Source: Capon (1984), pp. 6–7.

Figure 8.9 Crossing the midline

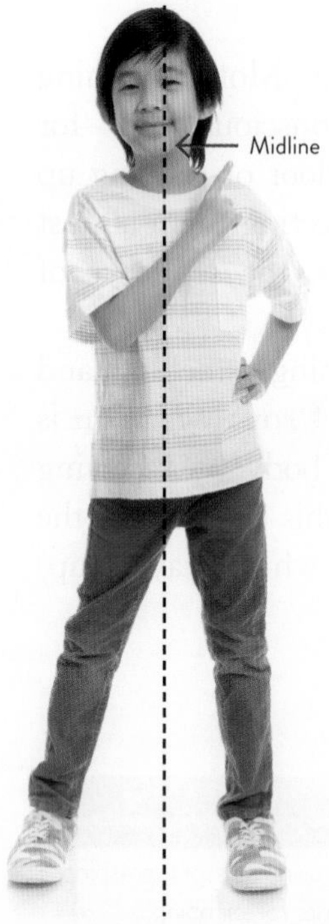

Source: Shutterstock.com/ANURAK PONGPATIMET

CROSSING THE MIDLINE (BILATERAL INTEGRATION)

The midline is an imaginary line down the centre of the body (**Figure 8.9**). Crossing the midline means moving an arm and/or a leg across the body to perform a tasks. It also includes shifting the eye gaze from one side of the body to the other. Examples of crossing the midline include putting on socks and shoes, turning the page of a book and reaching across to pick up cards. Crossing the midline requires both sides of the brain to work together.

When children use their dominant hand or foot to cross the midline, they are strengthening the muscles on their dominant side and also reinforcing a preference for a dominant hand or foot.

Children who use both left/right hand and foot equally are not developing dominance, which can lead to later problems with tasks such as holding a pen and writing tracking from left to right with their eyes when reading. The Consider this box describes behaviours that may indicate a child is having difficulties with crossing the midline.

CROSSING THE MIDLINE

CONSIDER THIS

You can tell there are problems with crossing the body's midline if the child:

- frequently switches hands when writing, drawing, painting and colouring
- uses their left hand for activities on the left side of the body and their right hand for activities on the right-hand side
- rotates their trunk to the opposite side when reaching across the body
- has difficulty tracking an object from one side of the body to the other
- uses different feet to kick a ball
- has difficulty coordinating gross motor patterns (e.g. crawling, skipping, star-jumps).

Poor early literacy and pencil skills can also be an indicator.

Activities for crossing the midline

Activities for visual perception

Visual and auditory perception skills

Visual and auditory perceptual skills are gradually refined as the child matures and the developing brain is able to process or make sense of the information being received. **Visual perception** is the ability to make sense and meaning out of what you see. **Visual discrimination** includes the ability to perceive depth, colour and movement.

Auditory perception is the process of making sense of what we hear. The ability to detect, locate and discriminate sounds begins to develop prenatally, and is essential for speech and language development. It includes listening to speech sounds, looking towards the speaker and beginning to experiment with phonemes (speech sounds). **Figures 8.10** and **8.11** describe the key visual and auditory perception skills.

Figure 8.10 Visual perception skills

Skill	Description
Visual discrimination	The ability to detect small differences between objects and things
Figure ground	The ability to screen out irrelevant visual details and focus selectively on chosen details
Spatial relations	The ability to understand how objects relate spatially to one another
Visual memory	The ability to recall visual images and information
Visual closure	The ability to visualise a whole when only fragments are visible

Figure 8.11 Auditory perception skills

Skill	Description
Auditory awareness	The simple recognition of the presence of sound
Auditory decoding	The ability to understand sounds or spoken words
Auditory discrimination	The ability to distinguish between sounds
Auditory memory	The ability to remember and recall auditory information
Auditory sequencing	The ability to reproduce a sequence of sounds in the correct order

Visual and auditory perception skills have obvious implications for language development, reading, writing and spelling. For example, a child who is not able to decode auditory information will have difficulty with verbal communication. A child who has poor visual discrimination skills will find learning to read and write a challenge.

Auditory memory and auditory processing activities

Having an awareness of physical development will assist the ESW to better understand and support students who have motor skills problems. Being aware that there is an established connection between physical development and cognitive development will also provide you with an understanding of the learning challenges faced by many students with poor physical development.

DOMINANCE AND HANDWRITING

Handwriting activities and resources

Most people have a dominant side. For example, when asked to write their name, kick a ball, use scissors, look through a tube or step onto a platform, people consistently use one side of their body. Some people will always use their right eye, hand, foot and ear while others will always use the left. This preference for one side of the body is referred to as *dominance*. Some people use a mixture of right and left – this is referred to as *mixed dominance*.

Dominance also occurs in the left and right hemispheres of the brain. The right hemisphere focuses on the big picture and breaking down information into smaller details. This side of the brain deals with patterns, shapes and images, estimates, possibilities, colour and the beat and rhythm of music. The right hemisphere helps us to remember faces and voices. It is also the emotional side of the brain, and responds best to events as they are happening. Individuals who are more right-brain thinkers are said to be creative, spontaneous and intuitive, and favour a hands-on approach to learning. The left hemisphere focuses on identifying and processing detail in a logical and sequential manner in order to create the bigger picture. The left hemisphere is the decoding side of our brain. It deals with facts, analysis of numbers, sound, words and complex sentences. The left hemisphere is the centre for reading, spelling and comprehension. Individuals who are more left-brain thinkers are said to be logical and planned in their thinking.

Figure 8.12 The child is confidently using their dominant hand to write

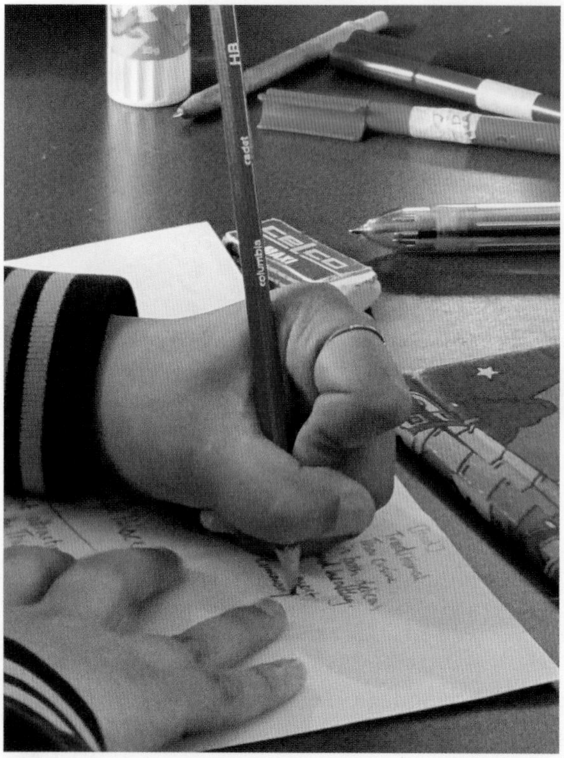

Source: Photo by Tish Okely © Cengage

While most individuals will favour either the left or right hemisphere of the brain, as indicated by eye, hand, foot and ear dominance, there are many different dominance profiles, and dominance of one hemisphere does not occur to the exclusion of the other hemisphere.

Establishing dominance assists children to accomplish many tasks, including writing and reading. By three years of age, most children develop a preference for a particular hand (see **Figure 8.12**) and are able to hold writing tools in a more mature grip. Children who have not developed a hand preference by the time they are three or four years old may have difficulty with tasks that require the coordination of two hands.

During the preschool years, children develop an intense interest in learning to write letters and words. Typically, they begin by learning to write their own names. This is a complex skill and is also an excellent example of the interrelated nature of the domains of development. Handwriting requires children to understand that symbols (letters), when grouped together, form words that represent spoken language. Often this knowledge precedes the refinement of their fine motor skills. Children often understand the concept of print before they are able to reproduce recognisable print.

Figure 8.13 describes the perceptual motor skills that are needed for handwriting.

Figure 8.13 Perceptual motor skills for handwriting

Postural control and shoulder stability

Essential to control arm movements on a table or desktop.

Development of postural control can be supported by experiences such as pulling or pushing heavy objects, crawling and kneading play dough or clay.

Wrist extension

Necessary to guide the direction of the pen.

Can be developed by working on vertical surfaces such as an easel, walls or fences; rolling play dough or clay; or clapping hands with a child standing opposite.

Hand and finger coordination

Necessary to hold and guide a pen.

Can be developed by thumb-finger activities: threading beads, paper tearing, manipulating tweezers and tongs, using eye droppers for painting and finger painting.

Visual motor control

Required for fine motor control and hand–eye coordination. Developed when children copy patterns made from blocks, draw in the sand or finger paint.

Bilateral integration. Using both hands together to hold the paper with one hand and write with the other hand.

Spatial awareness

Able to place letters from left to right with spaces between words.

Kinaesthetic awareness

Sensitivity to the pressure and movement of a pen.

USING SCISSORS

Developing cutting skills

Mastery of scissors is another complex developmental task that will only be accomplished when the child is physically ready. For most children, using scissors with accuracy begins to be refined at around six years of age. The following abilities are necessary to use scissors:

- *Open and close hands.* Children need to have the ability to open and close their hands, and to grasp and release objects.
- *Use a leading and a helping hand.* Children need the ability to use their hands together in a leading and helping way. The leading hand holds the scissors and makes the cutting movement, while the helping hand must hold and manoeuvre the paper.
- *Isolate fingers.* Children need the flexibility to isolate or combine the movements of the thumb, index and middle fingers, and to keep these fingers moving separately from the ring and little fingers.
- *Put movements together.* Children need the ability to coordinate arm, hand and eye movements towards an end goal.
- *Achieve stability.* Children need to be able to keep the joints in their wrist, elbow and shoulder stable, so that the scissors can be well controlled. Joint stability can be related to strength.

Figure 8.14 illustrates the sequence of difficulty of cutting.

Developing the skills necessary to cut with scissors can be supported by providing children with a range of activities that strengthen small muscles and develop specific skills, such as using fingers in isolation, opening and closing the hand, putting movements together and using two hands together.

Figure 8.14 The sequence of difficulty in cutting shapes

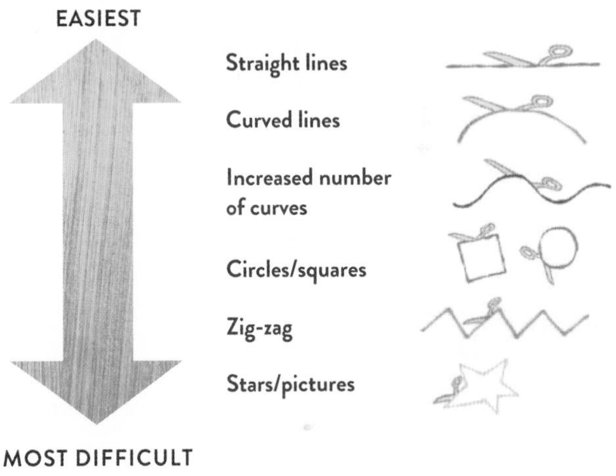

PHYSICAL DEVELOPMENT: KEY FACTS TO REMEMBER

CONSIDER THIS

Physical development occurs in a predictable pattern:

- Head to toe – head, shoulders, trunk and lastly legs.
- Large to small – large muscles (gross motor) are the first to develop; these include muscles in the neck, trunk, arms and legs. Small muscles (fine motor) then develop in the hands, fingers, wrist and eyes.
- Trunk to extremities – babies develop strength and movement of the trunk to roll and sit well before they develop purposeful coordination of arms, hands and legs.
- Differentiation – in order to develop purposeful movement and coordination, babies first need to become aware of their limbs. For example, you may have noticed how babies will gaze at their hands. At this stage, babies are beginning to explore how their body fits together.
- Integration – movement gradually becomes coordinated and purposeful. For example, hand–eye coordination allows a baby to grasp a spoon and bring it to their mouth at around six months.
- General to specific – at first, movement is random and uncoordinated, but with maturity, movement becomes purposeful (e.g. purposefully moving the hand to the mouth).
- Continuity and discontinuity – physical growth is continuous until adulthood, but there are periods when growth slows to allow for refinement of skills.

8.2 Factors that influence physical development

Like all other areas of development, physical development is influenced by biological and environmental factors (see **Figure 8.15**).

Figure 8.15 Factors that influence physical development

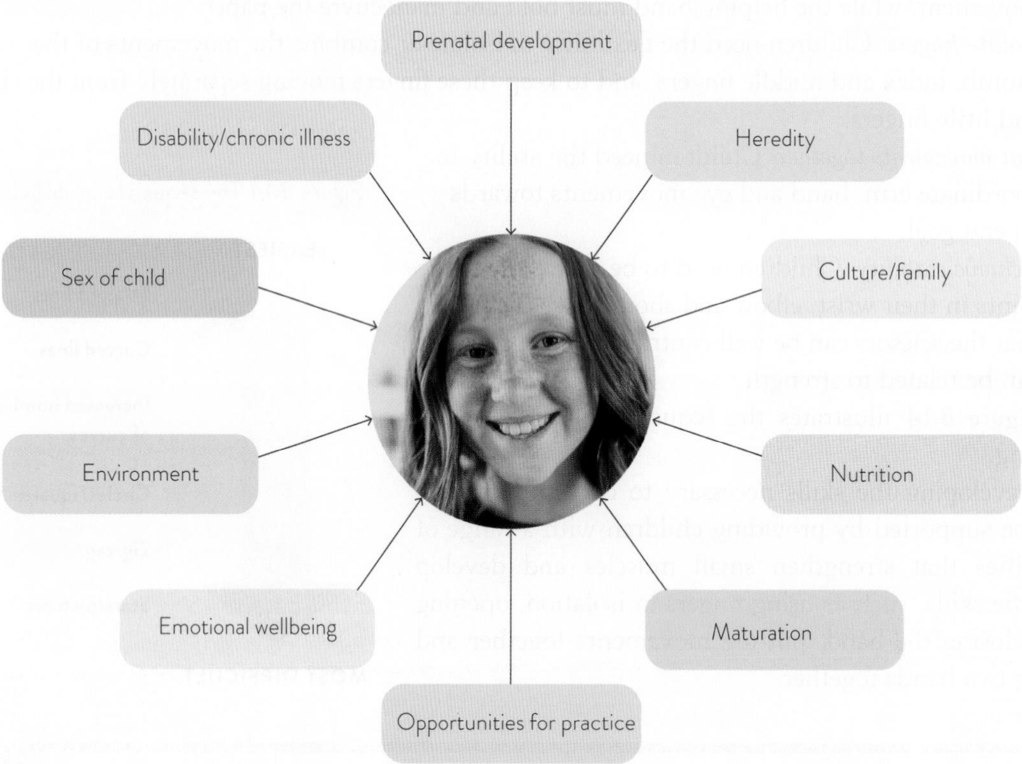

Source: iStock.com/eyecrave productions

The factors influencing physical development shown in **Figure 8.15** include:

- *Prenatal development.* The health and wellbeing of a mother during pregnancy can be linked directly to a child's physical growth. For example, pregnant women who smoke heavily, abuse alcohol, have a poor diet, drink excessive caffeine or are drug abusers are more likely to give birth to an infant with a low birth weight. These children often have poor fine motor and coordination skills compared with their same-age peers.
- *Heredity factors.* These include body shape, size and growth rate. Children will look similar to their parents and experience similar growth rates to their parents. By middle childhood, body image is a significant factor in self-esteem, self-concept and peer relationships. Body image will also influence young people's participation in physical activities. For example, a student who perceives that they are athletic is more likely to attempt ball games with a greater sense of self-confidence than a student whose body image is one of being awkward, clumsy or overweight.

- *Culture/family.* A range of cultural and family factors will influence physical growth and development. Parental attitudes related to gender expectations and physical activity will greatly influence children's and young people's participation in outdoor games and sports. Attitudes towards immunisation may also leave some children more vulnerable to disease and poor health.
- *Nutrition.* Nutrition influences individual growth rates as well as the growth rates of whole populations. For example, children and young people living in extreme poverty are likely to have reduced growth rates due to poor nutrition; children and young people who have poor role models and consume large amounts of processed and fast foods are at risk of obesity and its associated health risks. Poor nutrition can also have a negative influence on the developing brain.
- *Maturation (readiness).* Readiness is an important factor in physical development. For example, if a child has not yet developed the fine motor control and hand–eye coordination necessary to be able to manipulate scissors, no amount of practice will help the child to achieve this skill.
- *Opportunities for practice.* While physical development occurs naturally through maturation, providing opportunities for children to practise their physical skills also contributes to the rate of physical development. For example, an infant who is left in a cot for long periods is likely to reach physical milestones later than an infant who is placed in different positions, and encouraged and stimulated to begin to move about, reach and look around.
- *Emotional wellbeing.* Children who suffer physical, emotional or sexual abuse are likely to have delayed physical development. There is a direct link between a lack of emotional availability and consistency of love and care and conditions such as 'failure to thrive'. Failure-to-thrive children may have experienced an unpredictable and frightening relationship with their primary carer. This condition affects all areas of development, including brain development. For older children and young people, a lack of emotional support and/or abuse have both short-term and long-term negative psychological consequences, which may include behaviours such as extreme acting-out, self-harm and promiscuity, as well as homelessness.
- *Environment.* Socioeconomic status: children of low-income families are unlikely to have the same opportunities to engage in a wide variety of sports as children from more affluent families due to cost, lack of transport, low priority when funds are limited. Children living in rural/remote areas or children living in high-rise apartments are likely to experience differences in access to and participation in a variety of physical activities.
- *Sex of child.* Males and females develop and mature at different rates – males become physically stronger, while females mature at a faster rate.
- *Disability/chronic illness.* Children may be born with physical disability or may acquire a physical disability due to an accident or illness; chronic health issues may also influence physical development.

Healthy growth and development

Middle childhood

Middle childhood is the developmental phase that leads from prepubescence (the period prior to commencement of the physiological processes and changes associated with puberty) to pubescence (the period during which the child begins to experience diverse and gradual physical processes associated with puberty). Children of the same chronological age may vary greatly in stature, weight and sexual development (Charlesworth, Wood & Viggian, 2011, pp. 183, 184).

It is a time of complex physical change and the refinement of existing motor skills. Due to uneven rates of physical development, some children may appear awkward when attempting one skill, while appearing quite accomplished at other skills – for example, they may swim well but have poor ball skills. At this age, children often focus on developing specific physical skills of interest to them – for example, ball-handling skills associated with games such as soccer and football or fine motor skills needed for online gaming or playing a musical instrument.

During middle childhood, growth rate slows and there is steady weight gain. While children at this stage may appear to have endless energy, they can still tire easily, so a balance of rest and activity is still necessary.

During the second half of middle childhood, children may become very interested in organised games and team sports. Some children may have the necessary physical skills but find participation in organised group activities cognitively and socially challenging. Children who are not so good at sport begin to notice that they are physically less competent than their peers. This may lead to feelings of inferiority.

Physical development in middle childhood

The key physical changes that occur during middle childhood are shown in **Figure 8.16**.

Figure 8.16 Physical development in middle childhood

Growth spurts	Coordination and sport skills	Visual and auditory
At around 8 years of age, the head size has reached 90 per cent of its adult size, the stomach flattens and the chest size increases.	Greater strength, agility and balance, which require coordination, speed, reflexes and strength.	Visual skills continue to develop but children will still have difficulty judging distance and speed.
Until nine to 10 years, males tend to be slightly taller and heavier than females.	Refinement of running, climbing, jumping, throwing, hopping, skipping and bicycle riding.	The Eustachian tube in the ear grows, resulting in improved hearing.
At around 10 years, girls begin to grow and develop more rapidly than boys.	Greater strength, speed and control with physical activities.	Refinement of hand–eye coordination allows students to begin to incorporate 3D images into their drawings.
Girls have a growth spurt at around 10–12 years while boys have a growth spurt around 13–14 years of age.	Most children master foot–eye coordination and can kick a ball with a degree of accuracy.	Fluency in handwriting increases; however, some students may show a great deal of irregularity in their handwriting style.

Gender differences

At around nine to 10 years of age, girls begin to grow and develop more rapidly than boys. Secondary sex characteristics begin to appear in females, particularly breasts, pubic hair and/or menstruation. During the later stage of middle childhood, children – particularly girls, but increasingly boys too – begin to become conscious of their body image and take greater responsibility for personal hygiene. Some may become quite self-conscious.

Risk-taking and experimentation

Along with changes in body size and shape, middle childhood is also a time when children will test their mastery of physical skills. Peers become more influential, and there is greater competition among peers. Children are likely to extend themselves to their physical limits or show off to impress their friends and ensure acceptance by their peers.

At around nine to 12 years of age, children increase in strength and refine their coordination. Children are prepared to devote time to practising and testing their skills. Close supervision is still required as greater confidence in their physical abilities, and increased endurance and stamina, are accompanied by greater risk-taking behaviour, especially in boys. Gross motor development still precedes fine motor development, although greater control of small muscles is achieved.

Risk-taking

SCENARIO

AWKWARD!

Frank and **Nic** (both 12 years) are each keen to invite a girl to be their partner at the end-of-year farewell dance for Year 6 students. The problem with which they are struggling is that the girls they like are much taller than the boys. In fact, most of the girls in their class are taller than the boys. Frank and Nic have discussed this issue on a number of occasions and can't quite decide whether being shorter than their partner is something they should worry about. Frank's older brother teases Frank and says he will look like he's dancing with his big sister instead of a girlfriend!

WHAT DOES THIS TELL US?

At around 12 years, girls tend to be taller than their male peers due to a growth spurt between 10 and 12 years of age.

Adolescence

Adolescence is the period of the life span between the time puberty begins and the time adult status is approached, when young people are preparing to take on the roles and responsibilities of adulthood in their culture.

The transition from middle childhood to adolescence is characterised by changes in physical appearance as a result of **maturation**. Adolescents will become more self-conscious – body odour, pimples, acne, body shape, clothing and hairstyle are central concerns. Growth spurts during this period include not only an increase in height and weight, but also the hands, feet, arms, legs, trunk and chest. Often the limbs seem to grow disproportionately in comparison to the trunk, making adolescents appear gangly and awkward. Some males and females will become so anxious about appearance and body shape that they may become bulimic or anorexic. This is a period of a heightened sense of one's own sexuality and sexual experimentation.

Adolescent development

Puberty

Puberty refers to the changes in physiology, anatomy and physical functioning that develop a person into a mature adult biologically and prepare the body for sexual reproduction. Puberty may begin as young as 10 years in females, while boys typically mature 12 to 18 months later than girls. Hormonal changes contribute to mood swings, which lead to emotional outbursts, sullenness, anger and 'attitude' in relation to authority figures such as parents and teachers.

The characteristics of puberty for females include enlargement of breasts, the development of pubic hair, enlargement of the uterus and the commencement of menstruation, as well as an increase in height and weight. For males, puberty includes changes to the testes and scrotum, enlargement of the penis and the growth of pubic hair. It also includes the growth of facial hair, lengthening of the jaw and chin, enlargement of the nose and deepening of the voice. Boys also gain height, increased bone density and increased muscle size (Jensen Arnett & Jensen Arnett, 2019, p. 342).

Body image

According to The Butterfly Foundation (2022), body image is formed by the thoughts, feelings, attitudes and beliefs we have about our bodies and how we look. This includes our shape, size, weight, gender identity and the way our body functions for us.

Body image is a significant issue for most teenagers, who are very aware of their own appearance compared with that of their peers. In relation to body image, Dolgin (2014, p. 118) states that

> physical attractiveness and body image have an important relationship to the adolescent's positive self-evaluation, popularity, and peer acceptance … attractive adolescents appear to have higher self-esteem and healthy personality attributes, are better adjusted socially, and possess a wider variety of interpersonal skills than their less attractive peers.

Beyond Blue (2022) states: 'Australian young people describe body image as one of their top five personal concerns. It's estimated about 28% of males and 35% of females ages 11–24 years are dissatisfied with their appearance'.

Each young person will go through puberty at their own individual rate, which may result in feelings of inadequacy and a lack of self-confidence – particularly when a young person compares their underdeveloped body with the more mature physique of some of their peers or with media images of the 'perfect body'.

EATING DISORDERS AND AGE

CONSIDER THIS

- Eating disorders can affect people of all ages and have been diagnosed in those younger than five years and older than 80 years (NEDC, 2017).
- Research shows that adolescents are at greatest risk, with the average age of onset for an eating disorder between 12 and 25 years (Volpe et al., 2016).
- Seventy-five per cent of people diagnosed with anorexia nervosa and 83 per cent of people diagnosed with bulimia nervosa are between 12 and 25 years (Volpe et al., 2016).
- Fifty-seven per cent of contacts to the Butterfly Foundation National Helpline in 2018–19 were from young people aged up to 25 years (Butterfly Foundation 2020).

Source: Eating Disorders Victoria (2023). Key research and statistics. https://www.eatingdisorders.org.au/eating-disorders-a-z/eating-disorder-statistics-and-key-research/?gclid=EAIaIQobChMIoIWxmrqu9wIVLplmAh3oyQOQEAAYAiAAEgK67_D_BwE

Children and young people's focus on body image is driven by social media – cosmetics, fashion, sports and music tend to portray 'beautiful' people as being slim, tanned, toned and with flawless complexions. These images present both females and males in a way that is unrealistic, unachievable and unhealthy for young people. The focus on body image may result in poor self-esteem and can also lead to obsessive dieting and eating disorders, such as binge eating, bulimia nervosa or anorexia nervosa. These disorders are treated as serious mental health issues that can have long-term negative physical and psychological consequences. For young children, they can lead to stunted growth and negatively impact on normal development.

Binge eating disorder is a mental illness characterised by regular episodes of binge eating. Binge eating involves eating an excessive amount of food, which may take place in a rapid space of time, or may be more of an extended grazing. These episodes can feel chaotic, uncontrollable and highly distressing (Eating Disorders Victoria, 2022b). *Anorexia nervosa* is described by Eating Disorders Victoria (2022a) as a psychological illness that has devastating physical consequences. It is characterised by low body weight and body image distortion with an obsessive fear of gaining weight, which manifests itself through depriving the body of food. It often coincides with increased levels of exercise. *Bulimia nervosa* is also a serious mental health illness. It is characterised by recurrent binge-eating episodes (the consumption of abnormally large amounts of food in a short period of time), immediately followed by self-induced vomiting, fasting, over-exercising and/or the misuse of laxatives, enemas or diuretics (Eating Disorders Victoria, 2022c).

According to Dolgin (2014, p. 443), young people with eating disorders typically 'have a pervasive sense of inadequacy and distorted body images and this often leads to depression'. Discouraging negative self-talk, promoting acceptance of differences and focusing on each students' strengths can assist in building self-esteem.

Positive body image

Childhood obesity

Overweight and obesity (the abnormal or excessive accumulation of fat in the body), increases a child's risk of poor physical health. Health problems and consequences of obesity in children include musculoskeletal problems, cardiovascular disease, some cancers, sleep apnoea, type 2 diabetes and hypertension. Childhood obesity can also lead to poor self-esteem, self-loathing and a higher risk of being a victim of bullying.

CONSIDER THIS

OVERWEIGHT AND OBESITY

- In 2017–18, around 1 in 4 (24%) children aged 5–14 were overweight (17%) or obese (7.7%).
- Children living in a regional and remote area were more likely to be overweight or obese (29%) than children living in major cities (23%).
- The prevalence of overweight and obesity among children aged 5–14 was similar between those living in the lowest socioeconomic areas (27%) and those in the highest areas (22%).
- According to a national snapshot of pre-teen health and disease development, 11–12-year-olds spend an average of 11 hours each day sedentary.

Source: Murdoch Children's Research Institute (2019). Aussie pre-teens spend most of their day sitting still, study shows. https://www.mcri.edu.au/news/aussie-pre-teens-spend-most-their-day-sitting-still-study-shows

Behavioural factors that contribute to childhood obesity include:

- a lack of exercise and a sedentary lifestyle (being driven to school rather than walking or cycling)
- spending long periods of time watching television, videos and playing computer games
- a high intake of energy-dense, low-nutrient foods and sugar-sweetened beverages and highly processed foods, caused by peer group and media pressure to consume fast foods in order to collect various 'toys'; poor food choices by families, family lifestyle
- insufficient sleep.

Obesity in children

Biological, environmental and social factors also influence the likelihood of a child gaining excess weight, including:

- genetic differences in appetite and metabolism
- accessibility of fresh and healthy food
- fewer options for safe outdoor play (AIHW, 2020).

HEALTH RISKS

SCENARIO

Annita (6 years) is obese and is already wearing size 10–12 clothing. Her mother, father and older brother are also obese. The family eats fast foods three to four times per week. Annita does not participate in outdoor games because her breathing becomes laboured. She is often teased about her weight by other students.

Dane (9 years) lives with his mother and two younger siblings. Mum is a shift worker and often leaves money for Dane to buy hot chips for dinner. The children usually buy their lunch from the school canteen. Dane tells his teacher her never eats fruit or vegetables. Dane is thin, pale and very lethargic.

Larnie (12 years) is the tallest student at the school. She inherited her tallness from her father, who was a professional basketball player. Until recently, Larnie was not worried about her height. Now that she is almost a teenager, though, she is beginning to regard her height as a disadvantage. She tells her mother that she just wants to be the same as all the other girls in the class. Larnie is constantly measuring her height and asking her parents how tall they think she might grow.

Eric (14 years) is an academically gifted student. His goal is to become a medical research scientist. Eric is obese. He eats lots of junk foods and does very little in the way of physical activity. He spends most of his free time playing online games. Eric has very few friends at school, but is proud of the fact that he has many online friends who are also 'gamers'.

WHAT DOES THIS TELL US?

The physical and mental wellbeing of children and young people can be affected by a wide range of factors. These factors are very often outside the control of the school, but can play a significant role in the opportunities each child has to reach their full potential.

▶ DISCUSSION

The physical development of Annita, Dane, Larnie and Eric presents unique issues in relation to their physical wellbeing and mental health. Who is responsible for addressing these issues to support each student? Is it the parent/s, a teacher, the school counsellor or a combination of these people?

Sex and gender identity

A person's sex is assigned at birth by physical characteristics – females have a vagina and males have a penis. Gender and sex are different. Gender is an individual's feeling about themselves as either male, female or somewhere in between. Children and young people who identify with a gender not assigned by their sex at birth are referred to as transgender or gender diverse. According to the Royal Children's Hospital Melbourne (2020), about 1.2 per cent of Australian school children (about 45 000 children) are thought to identify as transgender.

Sexual orientation is a major developmental marker of adolescence. Jackson and Goossens (2006, p. 292) state that 'the development and acknowledgement of sexual orientation plays an important role in the formation of adult identity. Sexual fantasies, emotional attraction, sexual behaviour and self-identification are considered to be dimensions of sexual orientation'.

Adolescents who identify as homosexual can experience extreme anxiety and confusion if not supported by the family unit and friends. Homophobia and the uncertainty faced by young people in telling their parents of their sexual orientation can be extremely difficult. Dolgin (2014, p. 361) reports that these adolescents 'fear abandonment or even abuse, especially from their fathers'. Dolgin also reminds us that gay and lesbian students are at greater risk of bullying and victimisation than their heterosexual peers.

Diversity in gender and sexuality

Children and young people who experience distress, confusion and anxiety because their body doesn't match the gender to which they identify are experiencing gender dysphoria.

According to the Queensland Human Rights Commission (2020):

> being supportive and inclusive of trans and gender diverse students should be embedded in the school's culture, and not just 'on show' in the presence of people who belong to the trans and gender diverse community. There may be many students in a school community who have not 'come out', or who have family and friends who are trans and gender diverse. Behaviours, attitudes, and language should always be inclusive in order to avoid hurting or offending others.

Source: Queensland Human Rights Commission (2020). Trans@School. https://www.qhrc.qld.gov.au/__data/assets/pdf_file/0019/24535/QHRC_TransAtSchool_forschools.pdf, p. 8.

8.3 Health and Physical Education curriculum

The Australian Curriculum: Health and Physical Education enables students to develop skills, understanding and willingness to positively influence the health and wellbeing of themselves and their communities (ACARA, 2022b) AC. Integral to Health and Physical Education is the acquisition and application of movement skills, concepts and strategies across a range of physical activity contexts. This enables students to participate confidently and competently when moving (ACARA, 2022b) AC.

The Australian Curriculum: Health and Physical Education aims to enable students to:

- access, evaluate and synthesise information to make informed choices and act to enhance and advocate for their own and others' health, wellbeing, safety and physical activity participation
- develop and use personal, social and cognitive skills and strategies to promote self-identity and wellbeing, and to build and manage respectful relationships
- acquire, apply and evaluate movement skills, concepts and strategies to respond confidently, competently and creatively in various physical activity settings
- engage in and create opportunities for regular physical activity participation as individuals and for the communities to which they belong
- analyse how varied and changing personal and contextual factors shape opportunities for health and physical activity. AC

The curriculum is shaped by five propositions that are informed by a strong and diverse research base for a futures-oriented curriculum, as described in **Figure 8.17**.

Figure 8.17 Health and Physical Education propositions

Proposition	Description
Focus on educative purposes	Health and Physical Education emphasises the importance of learning opportunities that explicitly teach the knowledge, understanding and skills described in the standards and content through authentic and meaningful learning contexts.
Take a strengths-based approach	A strengths-based approach recognises that students have varying levels of access to personal skills, strengths, assets and community resources to maintain and promote their own and others' wellbeing.
Value movement	Valuing movement promotes appreciation of how movement in all its forms is central to daily life.
Develop health literacy	Health literacy is an individual's ability to access, understand, interrogate and use health information and services to promote their own and others' health and wellbeing.
Include a critical inquiry approach	Health and Physical Education promotes a critical inquiry approach to examining information, ideas and views that are commonly expressed in the media and society.

Source: Australian Curriculum, Assessment and Reporting Authority (ACARA) (2022b). Understand this learning area: Health and Physical Education. Key Considerations: Health and Physical Education propositions. AC

Content in Health and Physical Education is organised under two strands as shown in **Figure 8.18**.

Figure 8.18 Australian Curriculum Health and Physical Education content structure

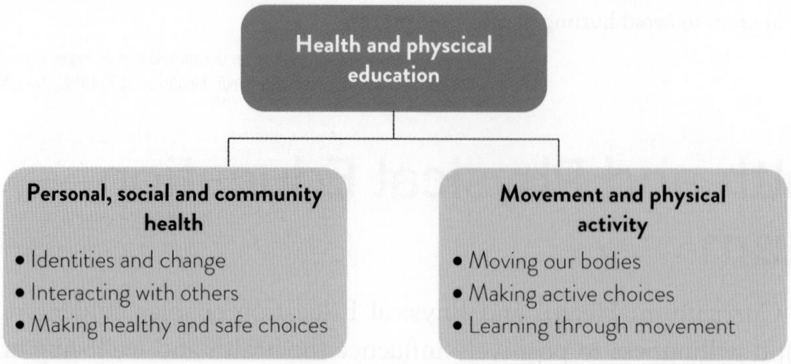

Source: Australian Curriculum, Assessment and Reporting Authority (ACARA) (2022b). Understand this learning area: Health and Physical Education. Key Considerations: Health and Physical Education propositions. AC

The two strands are interrelated and inform and support each other. Both strands must be taught in each year from Foundation to Year 10 (ACARA, 2022b) AC. The content descriptions in Health and Physical Education must be taught through the 12 focus areas shown in **Figure 8.19**.

Figure 8.19 Health and Physical Education focus areas

Source: Australian Curriculum, Assessment and Reporting Authority (ACARA) (2022b). Health and Physical Education (Version 9). 'Understand this learning area: Health and Physical Education', Structure: Focus areas. AC

8.4 Supporting physical development

Physical activity is essential for healthy development. Engaging in a range of physical games, movements and other activities not only helps children and young people to maintain a healthy weight, but also helps to develop strong bones and muscles, fitness, flexibility and posture. It supports brain development and improves a child's balance, movement and coordination skills. ESWs should use strategies, materials and resources that support physical development according to the school's organisational policies and procedures.

When children and young people interact with others during physical games and sports, they build their social skills, confidence and self-esteem, and improve their thinking and concentration skills. Encouraging and supporting participation in physical activity throughout childhood and adolescence reinforces the value of general fitness as an essential life skill.

Supporting physical development

Physical development influences all domains of development, including the brain. Physical development also plays an important role in learning. In fact, the area of the brain (the cerebellum) that contributes most to learning is also responsible for movement (see **Figure 8.20**).

Figure 8.20 Children engaging in physical activity

Source: Alamy Stock Photo/Rob Walls

Jensen (2005, p. 61) reminds us that movement involves mental processes such as predicting, sequencing, ordering, timing, and practising or rehearsing a task before carrying it out. Strong evidence supports the connection between movement and learning and shows that moderate exercise enhances cognitive processing.

Being aware of physical development and how it might influence the student's ability to participate in learning activities is an important skill for ESWs. Strategies that can easily be used in the classroom to support physical development are described in **Figure 8.21**.

Figure 8.21 Supporting physical development in the classroom

Strategy	Examples
Alternative seating positions	Provide therapy balls, large cushions, bean bags. Encourage standing and working at a benchtop.
Writing utensils	Provide a range of pencil grips, weighted pens, jumbo grip pencils.
Adapt the physical environment	Minimise distractions by creating a quiet zone that allows students to face away from others in the classroom. Provide headphones to screen out background noise. Create small work spaces by using shelving and dividers.

Strategy	Examples
Brain breaks	The brain learns best in short bursts because this allows time for information to be processed, so having a five-minute break from learning is good teaching practice. Jog on the spot, push-ups (floor/wall/desk), stretching, sit-ups, star jumps, dance and wiggle, move and freeze, Simon Says, keep a beach ball in the air, give yourself a bear hug, arm squeezes (use right hand to tightly squeeze left arm moving from bottom-to-top-to-bottom then swap arms).
Finger aerobics	Stretch and curl fingers, spider push-ups (fingers of each hand touching at tips pressing and out), finger lifts (press hands flat on desk and raise each finger independently while other fingers remain on desk), fingertip touch (touch each finger to thumb as quickly as possible).
Relaxation	Yoga stretches, meditation, breathing exercises, stillness, listen to calming music with eyes closed.
Movement	Movement increases the heartrate and increases blood circulation and oxygen to the brain. Movement relaxes tense muscles and increases energy and alertness.

Supporting physical development

Including movement and brain breaks as a routine learning strategy acknowledges and supports the powerful role of movement in the learning process. Children and young people are not designed to sit still for long periods – accepting this and incorporating movement into daily learning activities recognises the fundamental role that movement plays in learning.

Red flags in physical development

Red flags in physical development

Keep in mind that red flags in relation to physical development may also indicate issues in other developmental domains (see **Chapter 7**). Concerns about development should be based on observations over a period of time and in different situations that show a persistent pattern of behaviours. It is also essential to take into account other influential factors, such as age, fatigue, illness, family issues and temperament. **Figure 8.22** highlights examples of red flags that may be observed in relation to physical development. As you read these red flags, try to assign an approximate age range for the development of these skills.

Figure 8.22 Examples of red flags for physical development

Skill	Red flag
Movement sequence and pattern	Difficulties combining physical movements into a controlled sequence, learning basic movement patterns and/or remembering the next movement in a sequence
Writing	Difficulties establishing the correct pencil grip and age-appropriate speed of writing
Balance	Poor balance (sometimes even falling over in mid-step)
Spatial awareness	Problems with spatial awareness (e.g. fitting objects into appropriate sized spaces such as puzzles, and knowing left from right)
Handling objects	Trouble picking up and holding onto simple objects due to poor muscle tone

Skill	Red flag
Body awareness	Trouble with body awareness, such as applying more force than intended, determining the distance between themselves and objects and invading other people's personal space without recognising this
Coordination	Uncoordinated physical movements, awkward postures and running styles
Gross motor control	Inadequate whole body (gross motor) control skills (e.g. they may find it difficult to stand on one leg or handle equipment like a bat or racquet)
Mastery of new skills	Requiring more than typical time and effort to master a new physical skill

Source: Kids Sense (2022). Developmental delay. https://childdevelopment.com.au/areas-of-concern/diagnoses/developmental-delay

Identify and always report concerns about a student's physical development to the teacher, according to organisational policies and procedures.

Summary

This chapter provides a broad overview of the significant changes in physical development from middle childhood to 18 years. As with all other domains of development, physical development follows a predictable sequence and includes periods where development slows as well as periods of rapid change. This chapter also highlights the interconnections of the domains of development. For example, alongside physical changes in the body during adolescence, young people become more preoccupied with body image, self-identity and self-confidence, all of which can have a positive or negative influence on their self-esteem. Brain development during this period also impacts on young people's ability to assess risk, and they tend to engage in risk-taking behaviours. It is a time when young people are seeking greater independence, but they still require the presence and protection of nurturing and supportive adults.

This chapter has also provided links to the Health and Physical Education curriculum, which will be further explored in Chapter 9. Links to online resources and activities provide an opportunity for you to begin to build your own resources to support physical development.

Self-check questions

1. Define the following concepts:
   a. Perceptual motor development
   b. Proprioceptive development
   c. Fundamental movement skills
   d. Sensory motor skills
   e. Motor planning
2. What is the difference between visual perception and auditory perception?
3. What factors influence physical development?
4. What are the potential health problems and consequences of childhood obesity?
5. What is the aim of the Australian Curriculum: Health and Physical Education?
6. List two examples of red flags for physical development.
7. What are the benefits of physical development for children?

Discussion questions

1 Merrick has been in and out of foster care homes right through his schooling. He is now in his third year of high school.

a How might this regular transition between foster care homes influence his physical development?

Activities

1 Categorise each of the examples below into one of the three movement skills: locomotor, non-locomotor or object control.

Balancing	Kicking	Stretching
Bending	Leaping	Swimming
Bouncing	Marching	Swinging
Catching	Running	Throwing
Crawling	Skipping	Twisting
Dodging	Spinning	Walking
Hopping	Stepping forwards	
Jumping	Stepping sideways	

2 Match the following terms to their definition.

Term	Possible definitions
Fine motor skills	the brain's use of sensory information
Sensorimotor development	the developing brain is able to process or make sense of the information being received and these are gradually refined as the child matures
Perceptual motor skills	all functions related to the use of small muscle groups
Visual and auditory perception skills	connecting the brain's sensory functions to the body to master skills such as timing and direction of movement

3 Handwriting investigation.

a Look around at your peers and their writing styles:
- How do they hold their pen/pencil?
- Do they write with their left or right hand?
- Is their book square to the table or on an angle?
- Do they need lines to write on or can they write in a straight line without lined paper?

b Investigate the reasons for the responses you found to the questions. Is there a right and wrong way to write on paper? Who decides this?

Chapter 9

SOCIAL AND EMOTIONAL DEVELOPMENT AND LEARNING

LEARNING OBJECTIVES

When you have completed this chapter, you should be able to demonstrate that, in relation to working in a school environment, you can:

9.1 identify the key elements of social and emotional development

9.2 identify the factors that influence social and emotional development

9.3 interpret key theories of social and emotional development as they relate to classroom practice

9.4 identify how to support students' mental health and wellbeing

9.5 identify concerns in relation to social and emotional development

9.6 access aspects of the Australian Curriculum as they relate to social and emotional development.

GO FURTHER

Go Further icons link to extra content for this chapter. Ask your instructor for the **Go Further** resource and deepen your understanding of the topic.

Online resources icons refer to useful weblinks. Ask your instructor for these **Online Resources.**

Introduction

Social development is about children and young people learning the values, knowledge and skills that enable them to relate to others. **Emotional development** is closely related to social development. It involves learning what feelings and emotions are, understanding how and why they occur, recognising your own feelings and those of others, and developing effective ways for managing those feelings. The process of social and emotional development begins at birth and continues throughout the lifespan (Be You, n.d.a, n.d.b).

Children and young people's social and emotional development – how they behave, how they understand the world, how they interact with others, how they determine right from wrong, their ethical and moral behaviours, attitudes and values – is learned within a social-cultural context of relationships, first within the family and later with friends, educators, teachers and significant others in the child's life. Socialisation also occurs in the context of the child's environment and is influenced by family (including child-rearing practices), culture, ethnicity, religious beliefs and practices, language, political beliefs, humanitarian beliefs and geographical location.

The relationships children and young people have with significant others (parents, carers, extended family, teachers) profoundly influence and shape their social and emotional development and wellbeing. Alberg (2018), in **Figure 9.1**, summarises the skills and knowledge required for healthy social and emotional development. These skills begin to develop in the early years; however, the majority of them develop over many years – often well into young adulthood.

Figure 9.1 Skills for social and emotional development (birth to adulthood)

Foundation skills	Interaction skills	Affective skills	Cognitive skills
Maintain eye contact	Resolving conflict	Identifying own feelings	Social perception
Recognise and respect personal space	Taking turns	Recognising the feelings of others	Making choices
Understand gestures and facial expressions	Beginning and ending conversations	Demonstrating empathy	Self-monitoring
	Determining appropriate topics for conversations	Decoding body language and facial expressions	Understanding community norms
	Interacting with authority figures	Determining whether someone is trustworthy	Determining appropriate behaviour for different situations

Source: Alberg (2018, p. 2).

The process of social and emotional development also includes:

- building and sustaining mutually nurturing relationships
- identifying and naming one's own feelings, such as happiness, surprise, anger, sadness, fear, sympathy, empathy, negativity/positivity, frustration, shyness, anxiety, elation, embarrassment, aggression, shame, guilt and pride
- awareness of physical responses to one's emotions, such as increased heart rate, laughter, physical aggression, tears, sweating, outrage, fight or flight response
- awareness of one's own thoughts about feelings
- awareness of how feelings are judged by self and others
- awareness of action signals – for example, a desire to approach, escape or fight
- awareness of how one's expression of emotions impacts self and others
- self-regulation (self-efficacy – managing emotions).

9.1 Social and emotional health and wellbeing

Emotional wellness can be described as:

> the developing capacity of children (birth through age eight) to: experience, regulate, and express emotion; form close, secure, interpersonal relationships; and explore the environment and learn – all in the cultural context of family and community. Emotional wellness might also be called mental health, emotional intelligence, relationships for learning, and social/emotional development.

Source: The Pennsylvania State University (2016). Emotional wellness: Understanding its importance. 2016. http://bkc-od-media.vmhost.psu.edu/documents/tips1303.pdf

Social health reflects a child's developing ability to form close, secure relationships with other familiar people in their lives, such as parents, relatives and other nurturing caregivers. This trusting bond helps children to feel safe in exploring their world. When children's social and emotional health is compromised, it can create significant challenges for children, leading to failure in school, inability to make and sustain friendships, and negative feelings about themselves (Georgetown University Center for Child and Human Development, n.d.).

CONSIDER THIS

THE BRAIN AND SOCIAL AND EMOTIONAL DEVELOPMENT

- Human brain development requires social relationships, emotional experiences and cognitive opportunities – and the quality of these relationships, experiences and opportunities influences how the brain develops, and hence how a person thinks and feels.
- Throughout life, and to an extraordinary degree in young people, the brain develops differently based on opportunities to engage actively and safely with rich and meaningful environments, social relationships and ideas.
- Emotional development is actually built into the architecture of young children's brains in response to their individual personal experiences and the influences of the environments in which they live.
- A growing body of scientific evidence tells us that emotional development begins early in life, that it is a critical aspect of the development of overall brain architecture, and that it has enormous consequences over the course of a lifetime.
- The foundations of social competence that are developed in the first five years are linked to emotional wellbeing and affect a child's later ability to functionally adapt in school and to form successful relationships throughout life.
- Young children who grow up in homes that are troubled by parental mental-health problems, substance abuse, or family violence face significant threats to their own emotional development.

Source: Immordino-Yang, Darling-Hammond & Krone (n.d.); National Scientific Council on the Developing Child (2004).

It is important to be aware that every experience a child or young person has with others contributes to shaping their long-term social and emotional wellbeing. A strong social and emotional foundation also supports children's learning and academic performance.

Brain development and adolescent development

9.2 Factors that influence social and emotional development

Social and emotional development is influenced by a range of factors, identified in **Figure 9.2**. How a child experiences and reacts to these factors will be unique to that child. Many of these factors have lifelong implications for social and emotional wellbeing.

Family and culture

The family is at the heart of the **socialisation** process and provides the child or young person with the emotional support necessary for healthy development. Relationships and **relationship skills** are the key not only to healthy social and emotional development but to all areas of development. Family units may include children and young people living with a single parent (mother or father); blended families (step-parent and step-siblings); adoptive parent/s; same-sex parents; grandparent/s; extended family and friends; foster care or group care.

Figure 9.2 Factors that influence social and emotional development

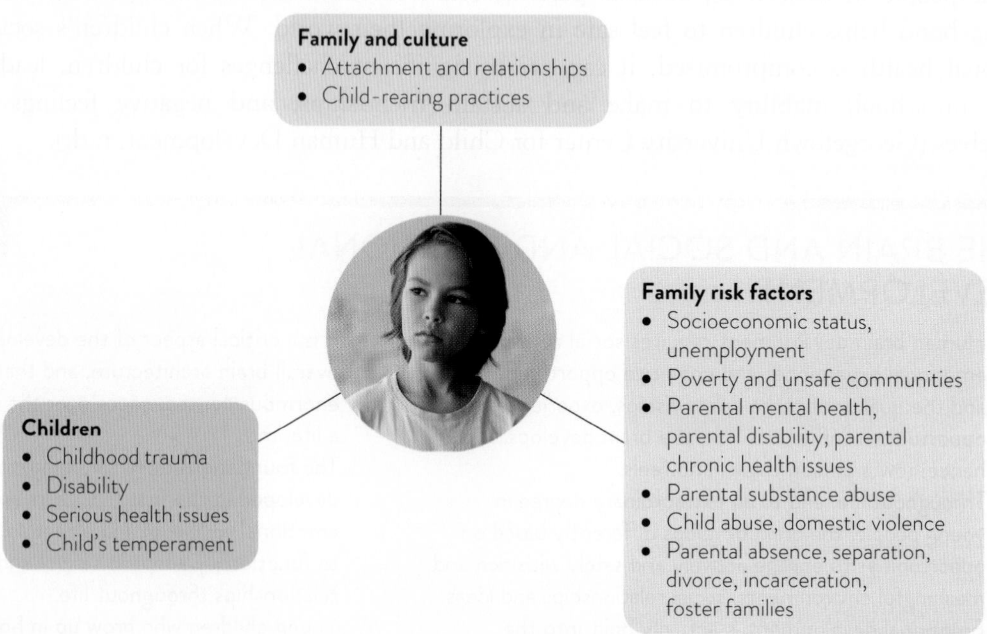

Family and culture
• Attachment and relationships
• Child-rearing practices
Children
• Childhood trauma
• Disability
• Serious health issues
• Child's temperament
Family risk factors
• Socioeconomic status, unemployment
• Poverty and unsafe communities
• Parental mental health, parental disability, parental chronic health issues
• Parental substance abuse
• Child abuse, domestic violence
• Parental absence, separation, divorce, incarceration, foster families

Source: (image) iStock.com/fizkes

FAMILY DIVERSITY

SCENARIO

AJ (13 years) now lives with his mother and two brothers in a caravan park. His parents separated after years of drunken violence and spouse abuse. AJ's mother often gambles her single parent benefit on poker machines, and as a result AJ and his brothers frequently go without meals. AJ tells his best friend that he is going to leave home as soon as he can.

Jalena (13 years) lives with her mother and her mother's partner and her two children. Jalena sees her father regularly. Her parents have a good relationship and Jalena presents as a happy and well-adjusted teenager. Jalena plans to study veterinary nursing when she finishes school.

Saleh (13 years) has three younger siblings and lives with his parents and grandmother in a three-bedroom high-rise apartment. Saleh's mother is chronically ill and his father works two jobs to bring in enough income to support the family. Saleh helps his grandmother to care for his mother and siblings. Saleh dreams of having a bedroom of his own.

Macy (13 years) lives with her brother, sister and parents in a five-bedroom home in a leafy inner-city suburb. Macy and her family enjoy overseas holidays each year. Macy plans to take a gap year when she finishes school before deciding on a career.

WHAT DOES THIS TELL US?

These 13-year-olds come from very different family situations. Their different life experiences will have a unique influence on how they see themselves and their long-term future aspirations.

▶ DISCUSSION

As an ESW, it is unlikely that you will have any background knowledge of the students with whom you are working. What difference would it make to you if you had such information? Would it help you to better understand each student? Would it assist you to build relationships with students?

Attachment

A critical first role in emotional development that occurs within the family unit is attachment. The process of attachment is one of the most important developmental tasks in infancy. The emotional bond that develops between parent (typically mother) and baby and the ongoing quality of the relationship provides a lifelong foundation for healthy (or unhealthy) emotional development. Babies begin the process of attachment from birth – they already know the sound of their mother's voice and will quickly be able to identify their mother by her scent. The development of healthy attachment has four distinct stages (**Figure 9.3**).

Figure 9.3 Overview of types of attachment

Pre-attachment stage: birth to around 3 months	Baby doesn't demonstrate attachment to a specific carer
Indiscriminate attachment: around 6 weeks to 7 months	Baby begins to display attachment to primary carer (usually mother) and secondary carer/s Baby shows preference for primary carer
Discriminate attachment: around 7 to 11 months	Baby shows strong preference for primary carer Baby begins to show separation anxiety if left in the care of others Baby also begins to show stranger anxiety in the presence of unfamiliar adults
Multiple attachments: around 11 months +	Baby begins to form strong emotional bonds with other familiar adults

Secure attachment forms the cornerstone of social and emotional development. Developing a trusting relationship and secure attachments to primary carers is critical for the healthy social and emotional development of children and young people. When children and young people sense they are secure and valued, they feel good about themselves and are more likely to develop positive relationships with other people. A sense of trust develops in infancy when the baby's needs are met by a parent/carer who has a relationship with them that 'guarantees' their needs will be met quickly and consistently in a loving, nurturing way.

Attachment theory

In the 1950s, British psychiatrist John Bowlby (1969) attempted to explain the importance of first relationships to human development. Bowlby's research was not readily accepted at the time, as much of it was based on observation and anecdotal evidence from his experiences working with hospitalised and homeless children after World War II. His experiences highlighted the profound and long-lasting effects of separation and maternal deprivation on young children. He felt that traditional theory did not adequately explain the intensity of a child's attachment relationship to a mother figure or the young child's often dramatic response to separation.

Bowlby suggests that attachment behaviour was originally a 'survival mechanism', which ensured children would stay close to their mothers, thus ensuring their safety. Babies and children use observable behaviours such as rooting, grasping, sucking, smiling, crying, following, approaching and clinging to increase contact with significant adults. These behaviours are usually directed to the person with whom the child has the most interaction. Bowlby points out that separation anxiety is only experienced when attachment behaviour is 'activated' or established. He also suggests that excessive separation anxiety is the result of family experiences such as repeated threats of abandonment, rejection by parents, or sibling/parent illness or death for which the child feels responsible.

Bowlby believed attachment and exploration were linked. When a child is focused on having their need for emotional security met, the 'attachment system' is activated. When the child feels secure, they are able to 'switch off' the attachment system and focus on exploration and play.

Types of attachment

Expanding on Bowlby's work in the 1970s, Mary Ainsworth described three styles of attachment: secure, insecure-avoidant and insecure ambivalent (Mcleod, 2023). A fourth style of attachment, called the disorganised model, was added in the mid 1980s by researchers Main and Solomon (Mcleod, 2023). These styles of attachment are described in **Figure 9.4**.

Figure 9.4 Styles of attachment

Secure attachment

A secure child knows their attachment figure will be available if and when needed. The child will:

- develop a sense of trust
- confidently explore their environment
- develop a sense of independence.

Insecure attachment

Children who are insecurely attached tend to be less able to openly express their attachment needs. They may minimise or exaggerate their emotional expressions, making it difficult for others to meet their needs.

Avoidant-Insecure

- Children tend to either avoid conflict or create conflict but ignore the consequences
- The child appears 'impersonal' in their peer interactions
- Their avoidant strategies may result in them being disliked, rejected or isolated from their peers

Ambivalent-Insecure

- Children may appear as helpless or passive
- Alternatively, they may seek emotional support but then reject it when it is offered

Disorganised Model

- Children seem to be in a 'world of their own' (Harrison, 2003)
- They are unaware of other children's feelings and are emotionally disconnected
- Disorganised children can be challenging and controlling or distant, and have a low threshold for distress

CONSIDER THIS

WHY IS ATTACHMENT THEORY IMPORTANT?

- Research suggests that failure to form secure attachments early in life can have a negative impact on behaviour in later childhood and throughout life.
- Children diagnosed with oppositional defiant disorder (ODD), conduct disorder (CD) or post-traumatic stress disorder (PTSD) frequently display attachment problems, possibly due to early abuse, neglect or trauma.
- Children who have experienced secure attachment are shown to have positive self-esteem and self-confidence which allows them to form friendships, have a positive attitude towards learning and are less likely to suffer from anxiety or depression as they mature.

Source: Cherry, K. (2022). What Is Attachment Theory? The Importance of Early Emotional Bonds. Very Well Minds. https://www.verywellmind.com/what-is-attachment-theory-2795337

Video: Attachment theory

Child-rearing practices

Child-rearing practices typically reflect the values, beliefs and traditions of the family's culture. Expectations in relation to how children should behave within and outside the family unit, the roles of family members, displays of affection and respect and how behaviour is managed will all reflect the cultural values and beliefs of the family.

Child-rearing practices are culturally bound – that is, the family's culture, values and beliefs will significantly influence how children are raised. Cultural factors that influence child-rearing practices may include:

- beliefs related to morality, discipline and manners
- quality of relationships:
  - positive relationships such as communicating and spending quality time together, working together to resolve issues and conflict
  - negative relationships such as physical and verbal violence, ridicule and threats, unrealistic expectations
- the roles assigned to family members – sharing household tasks, caring for others, the expected degree of independence of children at various ages
- gender roles and expectations
- the importance of family status in the community – in some cultures, the status of the family unit is determined by the behaviour of individual family members, which means that a child who acts out or misbehaves in public may be seen as bringing shame/embarrassment on the family.

Parental role modelling has a very powerful influence on the socialisation process. Children whose parent/s act as a positive role model will imitate desired behaviours and begin to understand the 'rules' around social interactions. For example, through role modelling children learn how affection is shown, how adults and children communicate and interact, how emotions are expressed, how disappointment and setbacks are managed or how conflict is resolved.

How children and young people are parented will directly impact on emerging skills such as:

- developing positive relationships – developing friendships and trust in educators and peers; demonstrating care and empathy for others
- learning to get along with others – conflict-resolution skills, learning collaboration, cooperation and compromise; respecting diversity
- managing and expressing feelings in a socially and culturally appropriate manner – emotional self-regulation
- developing the skills necessary for independence and a positive self-esteem
- building confidence – a positive attitude to learning; asking and answering questions; accepting challenges and directing one's own learning
- developing a sense of community – working as a team, accepting shared responsibility to care for the environment.

Each student will arrive at school having experienced a unique set of child-rearing experiences. These will have shaped the child's sense of self and wellbeing. For example, 'I am loved, valued, capable and confident' or, at the other end of the spectrum, 'I am a disappointment, I am incompetent'.

SCENARIO

CULTURAL VALUES

ISHWOR

Ishwor (7 years) is timid and withdrawn. In his family, children must only speak when asked a direct question by an adult. His father is the head of the household and is a strict disciplinarian. Ishwor's mother is forbidden by her husband to work outside of the home. Ishwor's mother always make a point of telling him at drop-off to act responsibly and not do anything to shame the family.

BELLA

Bella (10 years) is impulsive and lives life at full speed. She is easily distracted and rarely completes a task before moving on to something new. Her family delights in her quirky character and encourages her individuality. Bella's parents address behaviour concerns by talking to her about the strategies she can use to behave in a socially acceptable manner.

STEFAN

Stefan (13 years) is very serious, rarely smiles and is easily upset with himself if he can't complete a task. On these occasions he will refer to himself as 'stupid'. Stefan is an only child and his parents have set high standards for his academic achievements. Stefan is enrolled in an after-school tutoring program three days per week. Each evening, as well as his homework, Stefan is expected to spend one hour on his studies, which are supervised by his father.

▶ DISCUSSION

Discuss how each parenting style might influence the child's emotional and/or social development.

Behaviour management and discipline

How children and young people behave, how they relate to others and their view of themselves as worthwhile are shaped by the family. From early childhood, children observe and imitate the behaviour of significant adults. Children who experience age-appropriate rules and limits, positive emotional reinforcement and observe behaviours such as persuasion, discussion and collaboration to resolve problems learn resilience and self-confidence. Children who experience shaming, threatening, verbal and physical punishment/abuse, sarcasm, ridicule and withdrawal of emotional support will develop poor self-esteem, shame and a sense of hopelessness.

These positive or negative influences will profoundly affect the child's view of themselves as socially competent and will shape the way the child responds to social and emotional challenges. **Figure 9.5** shows how diverse child-rearing and discipline techniques might influence and shape behaviour.

Figure 9.5 Contrasting child-rearing practices

Child-rearing based on positive relationships	Child-rearing based on fixed beliefs
Strong moral rules – discipline is based on importance of manners, religious beliefs and/or family code of conduct.	Poor moral rules – little or no consideration, concern or empathy shown for other members of the community.
Loving family relationships – frequent hugs, kisses, encouragement and positive statements.	Poor family relationships – frequent physical and verbal violence, ridicule and threats.
Family imposes clear, consistent rules and limits that reflect the child's age/stage of development.	Family imposes inconsistent and inappropriate rules and limits that do not reflect the child's age/stage of development.
Discipline is based on the child's development – punishment focuses on assisting the child or young person to learn from their behaviour in a positive, non-punitive manner.	Discipline is based on family pride – children are punished if their behaviour is seen to embarrass the family.
The family gradually promotes independence and a sense of responsibility.	Independence is expected at an early age; children are not supported emotionally.

Gender roles

The cultural and social background of families will influence beliefs about how boys and girls are expected to behave. Research has shown that from the age of four, boys are more likely than girls to engage in antisocial behaviour and are overrepresented in relation to aggressive behaviour compared with girls. As children mature, boys are more likely to engage in physical aggression, while girls are more likely to use other forms of aggression (alienating and ostracising others, defaming character, gossip, etc.) (NSW Centre for Parenting and Research, 2004).

While most parents are simply happy to have a child who is healthy, some cultures place great value on the sex of the child. For example, in some cultures male children are more highly valued than female children. Also, in some cultures, very clearly defined roles are assigned to males and females. The Scenario box highlights the link between cultural/**social values** and gender-linked behaviour.

SCENARIO

CHILD-REARING PRACTICES

UMAY

Umay (13 years) has two older brothers and two younger brothers. Her parents emigrated from Turkey as newlyweds and have retained their cultural practices and beliefs in their new country. As the only female child, Umay is expected to help her mother around the house, assist with meal preparation and care for her younger siblings. Her older brothers see their role as protecting Umay and often criticise her friends as unsuitable because they are not Turkish. Umay complains that this is unfair, and this has led to Umay becoming increasingly rebellious. Umay tells her mother that she wants to become a strong, independent woman and will not become a slave to the old ways like her mother.

MY VALUES

Ankica and her two older sisters were raised by their grandmother because her mother and father worked long hours in the family business. Ankica's grandmother was born in Poland. She is devoutly religious and is a strong believer in strictness and respect for elders. Ankica was expected to respect her sisters and do what she was told without question. Grandmother seldom demonstrated any physical affection to the girls but was devoted to ensuring that they were raised to be well mannered and hard working.

Ankica, now a parent of two girls, reflects on what she wants for her own children. She says: *'Obviously, I am influenced by the Australian culture and way of life, which seems to me to be very relaxed and easy-going. Children in Australia seem to have it pretty easy; they get what they want and are allowed to do many things. My childhood was very strict, and we didn't get many hugs or cuddles. However, I can't help thinking that being brought up strictly was a good thing. We learnt to be independent and respectful of our elders, something that is certainly lacking in today's society. I want my girls to be strong and independent but I also want them to know the value of working hard and caring for others.'*

WHAT DOES THIS TELL US?

In the first scenario, Umay, who was born in Australia, rebels against the traditional values of her parents. Umay is fighting against long-held traditions and beliefs, which will continue to put her at odds with her family. In the second scenario, Ankica is able to verbalise how her own upbringing has influenced her parenting style.

Traditional cultural values can significantly influence child-rearing practices. As educators, it is important to be aware that family values and expectations will vary, and that in turn this will impact how children behave and how they are expected to behave.

Family risk factors

The crucial role of the family in children's social and emotional development can be shaped by a range of risk factors (described in **Figure 9.6**), and the circumstances will be unique to each family. How these risk factors impact on children and young people's emotional development will vary and will depend on, for example:

- the love, nurturance and dependability of one parent or significant adult (extended family member or close family friend)
- support from community services organisations and or church/cultural/welfare groups
- the child or young person's temperament
- opportunities for respite where the child or young person can feel safe for a period of time.

Video: The science of neglect

Figure 9.6 Family risk factors

Family risk factor	Influence on social-emotional development
Socioeconomic status (income, education and employment)	Poverty in childhood is associated with a decline in the use of imaginative play, poor attitudes towards school and learning, low self-esteem and a shorter attention span. Low income limits children and young people's: • opportunity to engage in social/community activities • access to common status symbols during adolescence such as brand clothing, footwear, iPhone, etc. • access to nutritious foods and health care Children and young people may feel embarrassed, ashamed or resentful of their family's economic circumstance.
Parental health problems	May include disability; chronic, debilitating health issues; mental health problems, including severe stress and depression; substance abuse. Children and young people living in these circumstances are more likely to experience stress and mental health issues; feel unsafe and insecure; may take on the role of parent carer and/or parenting of younger siblings.
Family violence	May include domestic violence, child abuse and/or neglect. Children and young people living in these circumstances will feel unsafe, frightened, hyper-alert to danger, anger towards abusive parent.
Parental absence	May include separation, divorce, desertion by a parent, incarceration of a parent, parent working away for long periods, parent whose presence is intermittent. Children and young people living in these circumstances may feel abandoned, unsafe, insecure or worried about their future (not all children experience these negative consequences).

Childhood disability/chronic health issues

Anxiety and depression in children and teens with chronic conditions

Children and young people living with disability and/or chronic illness have an increased risk of being developmentally vulnerable. They may face barriers to participation in recreational and sporting activities, have fewer opportunities to develop friendships and engage socially with same-age peers, experience disruption to school participation, and experience social isolation, discrimination and bullying. According to Yeo and Sawyer (2005), visible signs of illness or its treatment mark young people out as different at a time when such differences are important to young people and their peers. Body image issues related to height, weight, pubertal stage and scarring can contribute to reduced self-esteem and negative self-image, problems that may persist into adult life.

Childhood trauma

What is child trauma?

The Center for Child Trauma Assessment Services and Interventions (CCTASI), Chicago, states: '"Child trauma" refers to a scary, dangerous, violent, or life-threatening event that happens to a child (0–18 years of age).' CCTASI point out that each child experiences a traumatic event in their own unique way – the same event may be traumatic for one child while not being traumatic for another child (CCTASI, 2023).

One way of understanding childhood trauma is referred to as 'The three Es of trauma', as shown in **Figure 9.7**.

Traumatic events may include:

- bullying
- community violence

Figure 9.7 The three Es of trauma

EVENT
The actual event or threat that has taken place

→

EXPERIENCE
The emotional response to the event

→

EFFECT
The short- and long-term adverse effects of the traumatic event

- complex trauma
- disasters
- early childhood trauma (children 0–6 years)
- intimate partner violence (e.g. domestic violence)
- medical trauma
- physical abuse
- refugee trauma
- sexual abuse
- sex trafficking
- terrorism and violence
- traumatic grief (National Child Traumatic Stress Network, n.d.).

The range of events that can be regarded as traumatic indicates the broad nature of these events, some of which may be a 'one-off' experience, such as a natural disaster, while others may be a recurring experience, such as child abuse, domestic violence or refugee trauma. Children and young people who develop traumatic stress as a result of a traumatic event do so because their ability is overwhelmed. **Figure 9.8** lists the common signs and symptoms of traumatic stress that may be displayed by children and young people.

Figure 9.8 The common signs and symptoms of traumatic stress

Preschool children

- Feel helpless and uncertain
- Fear of being separated from their parent/caregiver
- Cry and/or scream a lot
- Eat poorly and lose weight
- Return to bedwetting
- Return to using baby talk
- Develop new fears
- Have nightmares
- Recreate the trauma through play
- Are not developing to the next growth stage
- Have changes in behaviour
- Ask questions about death

Primary school children

- Become anxious and fearful
- Worry about their own or others' safety
- Become clingy with a teacher or a parent
- Feel guilt or shame
- Tell others about the traumatic event again and again
- Become upset if they get a small bump or bruise
- Have a hard time concentrating
- Experience numbness
- Have fears that the event will happen again
- Have difficulties sleeping
- Show changes in school performance
- Become easily startled

Middle and high school children

- Feel depressed and alone
- Discuss the traumatic events in detail
- Develop eating disorders and self-harming behaviours such as cutting
- Start using or abusing alcohol or drugs
- Become sexually active
- Feel like they're going crazy
- Feel different from everyone else
- Take too many risks
- Have sleep disturbances
- Don't want to go to places that remind them of the event
- Say they have no feeling about the event
- Show changes in behaviour

Source: Center for Child Trauma Assessment Services and Intervention (2023). What is child trauma? Chicago. https://cctasi.northwestern.edu/child-trauma

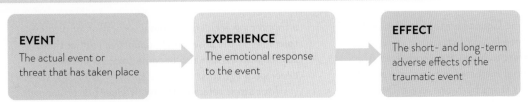

STRESS

CONSIDER THIS

The National Scientific Council on the Developing Child (2005) identifies three levels of stress.

Positive stress refers to moderate, short-lived stress responses, such as brief increases in heart rate or mild changes in the body's stress hormone levels. This kind of stress is a normal part of life and learning to adjust to it is an essential feature of healthy development.

Tolerable stress refers to stress responses that have the potential to negatively affect the architecture of the developing brain, but generally occur over limited time periods that allow the brain to recover and thereby reverse potentially harmful effect.

The presence of supportive adults who create safe environments that help children learn to cope with and recover from major adverse experiences is one of the critical ingredients that make serious stressful events (such as the death or illness of a loved one, a frightening accident, parental separation or divorce) tolerable. In the absence of supportive relationships, tolerable stress can also become toxic to the body's developing systems.

Toxic stress refers to strong, frequent or prolonged activation of the body's stress-management system.

Stressful events that are chronic, uncontrollable and/or experienced without the child having access to support from caring adults tend to provoke these types of toxic stress responses. Studies indicate that toxic stress can have an adverse impact on brain architecture. Stress hormone levels have been shown to be significantly elevated in children who experience economic hardship and insecure, neglectful or abusive relationships in the home.

Source: National Scientific Council on the Developing Child (2005), pp. 1–2. Used by permission of the Center on the Developing Child at Harvard University.

JAKE'S STRESS

SCENARIO

Jake (8 years) often arrives at school in a subdued mood but typically by mid-morning his mood has brightened. Jake finds it difficult to concentrate, is easily distracted and rarely finishes any set tasks. Jake deals with conflict by swearing, name calling or sulking. He will tell his adversaries that he'll tell his father and his father will 'get them'.

Jake and his mother have experienced a long history of domestic violence. Jake has fled the family home with his mother on at least 10 occasions over the past three years. Jake never talks about these events to his teacher or friends. Jake tells his mother that Dad doesn't really mean to hurt her: 'He just gets mad sometimes'.

Even though it's a warm spring day Jake arrives at school in the company of his older cousin, **Sara** (11 years). Jake is wearing a thick, padded jacket. As the morning gets progressively warmer Jake's teacher, **Lara**, suggests he remove his jacket so that he'll be more comfortable. Jake refuses and by lunchtime, he is red in the face and perspiring. Lara takes Jake aside and again suggests he remove his jacket. Jake begins to cry and Lara decides not to pursue the matter. Jake barely participates in the afternoon activities and is quiet and subdued throughout the afternoon.

At home time, Jake's Aunt Beth arrives to collect him, and Lara takes the opportunity to mention to Beth that Jake has been upset and has refused to remove his jacket. Beth tells Lara that Jake's mother had been physically abused by her partner on the weekend, and Jake and his mother had been thrown out onto the street. Jake and his mother are now staying with Beth who explains that Jake was wearing the jacket when she rescued them on the Saturday night. She explained that he has been reluctant to take off the jacket which his father recently had given him as a birthday present. Beth tells Lara that Jake and his mother will be staying with her for the remainder of the week. She then expects Jake's mother will follow her usual pattern of returning to the family home 'to start over'.

Lara had no idea that Jake was being exposed to domestic violence over such a long period of time.

▶ DISCUSSION

1. What signs of stress is Jake displaying?
2. What might have motivated Jake not to remove his jacket?
3. Jake and his mother have fled domestic violence on at least 10 occasions, yet Jake's mother continues to return to the family home to 'start over'. How is this behaviour contributing to Jake's traumatic stress?

Temperament

Temperament is part of personality – it refers to individual differences in the way individuals react to other people, situations and events. Temperament influences the quality of the relationships with others. Our temperament is present at birth. Although the way a child reacts to situations can be modified, the temperament we are born with remains constant throughout life. Temperament is an excellent example of how each individual contributes to and shapes their own development. This is because the way a child reacts to various situations and events in turn influences the way an adult might respond. **Figure 9.9** describes other dimensions of temperament.

Figure 9.9 Dimensions of temperament

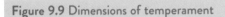

Sensory threshold – Degree of sensitivity to physical stimuli such as clothing, light, temperature, sounds, textures, tastes
Mood – whether positive or negative on a day-to-day basis
Activity – the amount of body movement and activity level on a day-to-day basis
Persistence – the ability to remain focused on an activity or a task
Distractibility – the ease with which a child can be distracted or comforted when necessary
Intensity – of responses to everyday occurrences and experiences, such as crying or protesting very lustily, or responding in a mild way
Reactivity – the readiness with which a child reacts to a particular stimulus or event
Rhythmicity – the regularity and predictability of the child's usual pattern of activities, including eating and sleeping schedules
Sociability – tendency to approach new people and situations versus shyness and withdrawal
Adaptability – ability to adapt over time to new foods, experiences and life challenges

Source: (text) Adapted from Prior et al. (2000), p. 9; (inset): iStock.com/Ridofranz

Researchers from the mid 1960s to 1970s (see Thomas, Chess & Birch, 1970) grouped temperament into three key patterns that are thought to remain constant throughput life. These patterns of temperament are shown in **Figure 9.10**.

Figure 9.10 Temperament patterns

Temperament	Characteristics	Behaviours
Easy	Adaptable, happy, calm, not easily upset; able to persist at tasks; accepts rules and limits; gets along well with others	Easy-going, adapts to change; accepts new challenges; has regular sleep patterns
Difficult	Irritable, shy, uncooperative, easily upset, does not cope with new situations, irritated by noise or other sensory distractions	Tend to be fussy eaters; reacts to situations in extreme/intense ways – highly excitable/easy to anger; high energy levels
Slow to warm up	Cautious, wary; slow to adapt to change	Can be quietly negative and slow to respond; resists new challenges; doesn't cope with change in routines

SCENARIO

INDIVIDUAL TEMPERAMENT

ADAPTABILITY

Richard (8 years) insists on having a cheese sandwich every day for his lunch, while his twin sister Amy is happy to try a variety of foods.

SENSITIVITY

Mia (13 years) is sensitive to sound and is easily upset by a noisy environment. **Daisy** (13 years) thrives in a group setting – the noisier the better!

CONSISTENCY

Owen (9 years) likes to follow a regular daily routine and becomes very upset if these routines are interrupted. Owen does not cope well with change. **Jay** (9 years) comes from a large family where routines are flexible. Jay copes well with change.

ACTIVITY LEVELS

Stuart (11 years) is always on the move – he talks quickly and never seems to sit still. He plays several different sports. **Barney** (11 years) is quiet and a bit of a dreamer. He doesn't like any sports, preferring to be an observer rather than a participant.

INTENSITY

When upset, **Carly** (16 years) will become quiet and withdrawn. When **Zoe** (16 years) is upset, everybody around her knows it! She yells, screams and slams doors.

WHAT DOES THIS TELL US?

A child's or young person's temperament influences the way they behave and the way they relate to others. Knowing a student's temperament can be useful when planning learning activities, and also when responding to inappropriate or challenging behaviours.

Video: Understanding children's behaviour through temperament

Temperament influences *how* children and young people react and behave rather than *what* they do in a situation. For example, it can refer to the way in which children show their likes and dislikes. Vera (11 years) doesn't like the skirt and top her grandmother gives her for her birthday. However, she accepts the gift graciously: 'Thank you Grandma for my present.' Bridy (11 years) doesn't like the skirt and top her grandmother gives her for her birthday: 'Grandma why did you give me these? You know I hate green!'

Temperament can also refer to the child's ability to get along with others (see **Figure 9.11**). Children and young people who have a high level of irritability can be difficult to get along with and difficult to please. They may find it difficult to form friendships, struggle to play/work cooperatively with others and may often be engaged in conflict with others.

SCENARIO

TEMPERAMENT

Samuel (13 years) has a 'difficult' temperament. He doesn't like changes to his daily routine and becomes angry and upset if he can't manage a task in class. He is easily frustrated and in class will quite often put his head in his hands and say, *'It's too hard. I can't do it!'*. To support Samuel, the ESW sits with Samuel and breaks down the task into small manageable steps, allowing Samuel to experience success and control as he progresses through the task.

Maisie (13 years) has an easy temperament. She is friendly, outgoing and copes well with change. She is happy to attempt challenging tasks and ask for help if needed.

WHAT DOES THIS TELL US?

Temperament influences how children and young people respond to daily life challenges and their willingness to attempt and persist at new tasks. Knowing which students can take things in their stride and which students require additional support allows teachers and ESWs to adjust the level of support needed for the student to achieve the desired outcomes.

▶ DISCUSSION

Reflect on your own temperament. What are your temperament traits? How does your temperament influence your life choices – socialising, friendships, coping with new situations, etc.? How might understanding your own temperament help you as an ESW when working with children and young people?

Think about the children or young people you know – you can probably identify those who fit into each of these classifications and many who display a combination of temperament traits. It is important to be aware that not every individual will fit neatly into any one temperament type or pattern.

Prior and colleagues (2000) found that the key characteristics of temperament were persistence, flexibility and reactivity, which they referred to as temperamental 'self-regulation'. This is the ability to control and manage responses and behaviours to various events and situations. Prior and colleagues report that children who have poor temperamental 'self-regulation' are most likely to be at risk of poor behaviour as a reaction to stress or frustration.

Being aware of each student's temperament can assist teachers and ESWs to better understand behaviours and respond to the child's social and emotional needs as a learner in ways that take into account temperament traits. Keogh (2009) explains the relationship between temperament and academic achievement. Consider how a child must adapt to a reading or math assignment, especially if the assignment is long and demanding. The child must 'settle down', focus energy and attention, adapt to new directions, resist distraction and persist, even when the task may be boring or difficult – these skills are part of the process of self-regulation.

Figure 9.11 Temperament can influence how young people react to different situations

Source: Photo by Tish Okely © Cengage

Self-regulation and executive function

The executive function skills of the brain filter distractions, prioritise tasks, set and achieve goals, and control impulses. The Center on the Developing Child, Harvard University (n.d.) likens these skills to the role of an air traffic control system at a busy airport safely managing the arrivals and departures of many aircraft on multiple runways. They include the mental processes that enable us to plan, focus attention, remember instructions, and juggle multiple tasks successfully.

Executive function includes three key mental skills:

1. *Working memory* governs our ability to retain and manipulate distinct pieces of information over short periods of time.
2. *Mental flexibility* helps us to sustain or shift attention in response to different demands or to apply different rules in different settings.
3. *Self-control* enables us to set priorities and resist impulsive actions or responses.

These functions are highly interrelated, and the successful application of executive function skills requires them to operate in coordination with each other. Children and young people who do not have opportunities to use and strengthen these skills have a very hard time managing the routine tasks of daily life, studying, sustaining friendships, holding down a job, or managing a crisis and pose even bigger challenges (Center on the Developing Child, Harvard University (n.d.).

Self-regulation is a component of temperament. It's the ability to pay attention, express feelings and control impulses at an age-appropriate level. It includes a range of pro-social skills such as cooperation, taking turns, sharing, showing kindness and compassion, and accepting responsibility for one's actions. Self-regulation is dependent on the successful development of executive function, both of which are critical skills in relation to social and emotional development. Being able to self-regulate in response to situations, people or events is an essential skill that all children and young people must acquire if they are to function successfully in a classroom environment.

Like all other areas of development, self-regulation occurs in a social context as children and young people build relationships – first with the family and later with significant others such as teachers, peer groups and close friends. Executive function and self-regulation improves as the child matures, but is also dependent on, and influenced by, temperament, gender, cultural factors such as child-rearing practices, life experience, cultural expectations in relation to the expression of emotions, parental expectations and role models.

The process of self-regulation takes time, and for some children the process continues well into adolescence (or even adulthood). The process of self-regulation starts as young children begin to understand that emotions have both a cause and an effect. For example, a seven-year-old might learn that being unkind to a friend is likely to result in that friend not wanting to play. A teenager might learn that bragging to her peers about her good looks does not in fact win friends.

Children and young people who have poor self-regulation will be at risk of social isolation and school failure. In later years, they may be more likely to engage in antisocial behaviours, which in turn may have lifelong consequences.

Based on the work of Goleman (2006) and Gardner (1993), the Collaborative for Academic, Social, and Emotional Learning (CASEL, 2007) has identified five core groups of social and emotional competencies that contribute to the development of self-regulation:

1. self-awareness – recognising and managing our emotions
2. self-management – making responsible decisions

3 social awareness – developing caring and concern for others (empathy)
4 relationship skills – establishing positive relationships
5 responsible decision-making – handling challenging situations constructively and ethically.

These competencies allow children and young people to calm themselves when angry, make friends, resolve conflicts respectfully, and make ethical and safe choices. **Figure 9.12** shows the general progression of these competencies from middle childhood to adolescence.

Figure 9.12 Five core groups of social and emotional competencies

Competency: Self-awareness Accurately assessing one's feelings, interests, values and strengths; maintaining a well-grounded sense of self-confidence	**Examples of development** **Middle childhood (around 6 to 9 years):** recognise and accurately label simple emotions such as sadness, anger and happiness **Pre-pubescence (around 9 to 12 years):** analyse factors that trigger their stress reactions **Adolescence (12 years+):** analyse how various expressions of emotion affect other people
Competency: Self-management Regulating one's emotions to handle stress, control impulses and persevere in overcoming obstacles; setting and monitoring progress towards personal and academic goals; expressing emotions appropriately	**Examples of development** **Middle childhood (around 6 to 9 years):** describe the steps of setting and working towards goals **Adolescence (12 years+):** identify strategies to make use of available school and community resources and overcome obstacles to achieving a long-term goal
Competency: Social awareness Being able to take the perspective of and empathise with others; recognising and appreciating individual and group similarities and differences; recognising and using family, school and community resources	**Examples of development** **Middle childhood (around 6 to 9 years):** identify verbal, physical and situational cues indicating how others feel **Pre-pubescence (around 9 to 12 years):** predict others' feelings and perspectives in various situations **Adolescence (12 years+):** evaluate their ability to empathise with others
Competency: Relationship skills Establishing and maintaining healthy and rewarding relationships based on cooperation; resisting inappropriate social pressure; preventing, managing and resolving interpersonal conflict; seeking help when needed	**Examples of development** **Middle childhood (around 6 to 9 years):** describe approaches to making and keeping friends **Pre-pubescence (around 9 to 12 years):** demonstrate cooperation and teamwork to promote group goals **Adolescence (12 years+):** evaluate uses of communication skills with peers, teachers and family members
Competency: Responsible decision-making Making decisions based on consideration of ethical standards, safety concerns, appropriate social norms, respect for others and likely consequences of various actions; applying decision-making skills to academic and social situations; contributing to the wellbeing of one's school and community	**Examples of development** **Middle childhood (around 6 to 9 years):** identify a range of decisions they make at school **Pre-pubescence (around 9 to 12 years):** evaluate strategies for resisting peer pressure to engage in unsafe or unethical activities **Adolescence (12 years+):** analyse how current decision-making affects their university and career prospects

Source: © CASEL, https://casel.org.

Video: Social and emotional development

9.3 Social emotional learning (SEL)

Social and emotional learning (SEL) is how children and young people learn to understand and manage their emotions, set goals, show empathy for others, establish positive relationships and make responsible decisions. These skills are based on five strategies: **self-awareness**, **self-management**, **social awareness**, **relationship skills** and responsible decision-making. The Collaborative for Academic, Social, and Emotional Learning (CASEL) states that social and emotional learning (SEL) is the process through which all young people and adults acquire and apply the knowledge, skills and attitudes to develop healthy identities, manage emotions and achieve personal and collective goals, feel and show empathy for others, establish and maintain supportive relationships, and make responsible and caring decisions. The SEL competencies are briefly described in **Figure 9.13** (CASEL, 2020).

Figure 9.13 SEL skills

Self-awareness	The ability to understand one's own emotions, thoughts, and values and how they influence behaviour across contexts. For example, being aware of how our own expressions of emotions can impact on others.
Self-management	The ability to manage one's emotions, thoughts and behaviours effectively in different situations and to achieve goals and aspirations. For example, manage disappointment.
Social awareness	The ability to make caring and constructive choices about personal behaviour and social interactions across diverse situations. For example, thinking about the consequences of an action and then modifying behaviour.
Relationship skills	The ability to establish and maintain healthy and supportive relationships and to effectively navigate settings with diverse individuals and groups. For example working collaboratively with other to achieve a common goal.
Responsible decision-making	The ability to understand the perspectives of and empathise with others, including those from diverse backgrounds, cultures, and contexts. For example, avoid making assumptions about others based on cultural stereotypes.

Source: Adapted from: Interactive CASEL Wheel: https://casel.org/fundamentals-of-sel/what-is-the-casel-framework/#self-awareness

Resilience

Video: Executive function and self-regulation

Resilience is also related to self-regulation and executive function and refers to a person's ability to overcome setbacks and persevere in the presence of challenge or hardship. Children and young people who are resilient tend to have an easy temperament, high self-esteem and live in environments where there is a high level of emotional support. A child who is resilient is able to attempt and persist in trying new tasks without the fear or disappointment of failure, and will strive to do their best and work towards success with a 'can do' attitude and a degree of optimism.

Children and young people who lack resilience tend to focus on failure and dwell on what they can't do. They will often avoid tasks for fear of failure or give up easily when faced with a challenge. They are likely to become very disappointed and negative towards their own abilities:

'I can't do it. It's too hard for me.' Sometimes these children will blame others for their limitations: 'The other kids never pass me the ball!'

The skills required to develop resilience include:

- self-control – the ability to manage disappointment without losing control (self-regulation)
- **thinking and problem-solving** – the ability to engage in problem-solving and finding new ways to approach challenges
- self-confidence – believing in self and willingness to persist
- a **positive outlook** – a focus on positives rather than negatives; having a 'can do' attitude
- a **sense of responsibility/participation** – a sense of purpose and self-motivation to attempt challenges.

Figure 9.14 identifies the internal and external factors that can support the development of resilience.

According to Be You (2019a), a national mental health in education initiative led by Beyond Blue, children and young people 'with greater levels of resilience are better able to manage stress'. While resilience is thought to have a genetic component, protective factors such as helping children to manage their emotions, family support, friendships and a sense of belonging to the school community support the development of resilience. Building resilience supports good mental health for children and young people.

Figure 9.14 Internal and external factors that can support the development of resilience

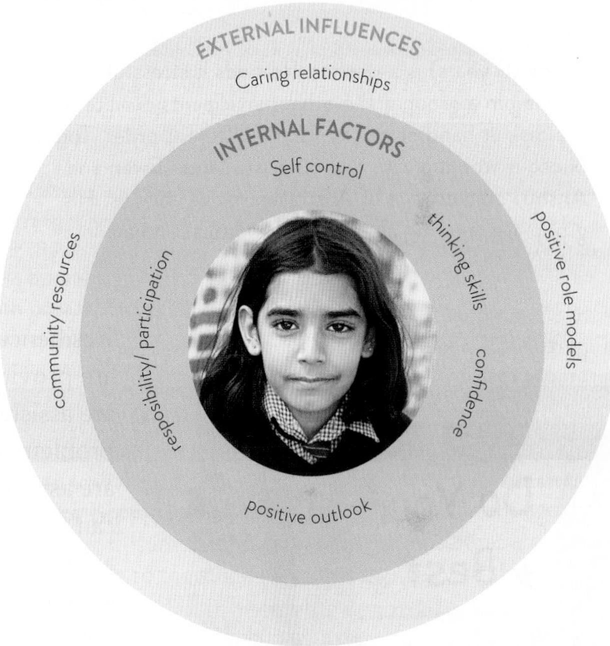

Source: Ontario Maternal, Newborn and Early Child Development Resource Centre (2012). iStock.com/pixelfusion3d.

Supporting resilience

ESWs can promote resilience by actively assisting children and young people to understand that mistakes are opportunities for learning and disappointment is part of life. It can also be helpful to identify what the child or young can do and how these skills can be used to build new skills. It's also helpful to put disappointment or mistakes into perspective: 'Remember last year you weren't even asked to try out for the rep. team, this year you made it through to the final selection round. That is a great achievement.'

Developing strategies to cope with disappointment requires adults to talk about the experience and encourage the child or young person to verbalise how they are feeling. Acknowledging the feelings related to disappointment assists children and young people to build resilience – for example, 'I was upset at the time but now I'm feeling okay.' or 'It's not as bad as I first thought!' As children's resilience matures, they begin to understand that they may not always have what they want when they want it. They are able to defer their need for immediate gratification. They begin to realise that they may have to wait or accept that things may not always turn out as they want. They also begin to realise that they can work towards or contribute to having their needs met by sharing, helping others or developing new skills. Children and young people who are continually sheltered or rescued from disappointment by well-meaning adults may find that as adults they don't have the skills to cope with life's challenges.

SCENARIO

RESILIENCE

KARRIE

Karrie (6 years): *'I can't write all these words. It's too hard for me.'*
ESW: *'How about I help you? We could do it together.'*
Karrie (becoming upset): *'Can you write the words for me?'*
ESW: *'No Karrie, I can help you but you need to keep trying.'*
Karrie (still visibly upset): *'But my hand hurts.'*

NICCO

Nicco (8 years) is a worrier. He finds it stressful when working in a group if the other participants deviate from the task at hand or do things in a different order. Today Nicco is working with two other students (**Ewen** and **Anshu**) on a collage of Australian native animals. His group are creating an echidna, a wombat and a bilby.

Ewen is working on the echidna. *'I'm drawing some ants because echidnas eat ants.'*

Nicco: *'No Ewen. You're not allowed to draw ants. Ants are insects!'*

Anshu: *'Yes he can if he wants to! I'm going to draw a snake going into the wombat's burrow.'*
Nicco: *'No! You're ruining it. I'm telling!'*
Nicco rushes to the teacher, visibly distressed.

WHAT DOES THIS TELL US?

Karrie and Nicco both lack resilience. Karrie is not willing to persist with her writing and wants the ESW to do it for her. Nicco is unable to tolerate the other students deviating from the task. He's unable to compromise and seeks adult support to 'correct' the situation.

Figure 9.15 Encouraging messages can promote resilience

Source: Photo by Tish Okely © Cengage

Resilience is supported when children and young people:

- are provided with frequent and constructive feedback
- are assisted to acquire process skills such as planning, concentration, problem-solving, collaborating with others and self-reflection
- are assisted to identify their strengths rather than focus on what they can't do/control
- are provided with tasks that assist in the development of new skills
- are encouraged to take calculated risks – a 'have a go' attitude
- are assisted to understand that learning is a process of trial and error – mistakes are opportunities for learning
- are given honest feedback and genuine praise (otherwise it becomes meaningless).

Encouragement, as illustrated in **Figure 9.15**, also promotes resilience.

Resilience is related to temperament – some children and young people will struggle to build age-appropriate resilience without support.

Self-concept, self-esteem and self-efficacy

How children and young people see and like themselves and how they feel about their own abilities and potential are critical factors in social and emotional development. Self-esteem, self-efficacy and self-concept contribute to our sense of self (see **Figure 9.16**).

Self-concept is the process of evaluating oneself – 'Who am I, what am I like, what do others think of me, what will I become?' Self-concept is multidimensional – it is a process of thinking critically in order to evaluate oneself in a range of areas. Duchesne and colleagues (2019) discuss four factors relating to the self-concept of school-age children and young people:

- **physical self** – What do I look like compared with others? What physical skills do I have? Am I attractive?
- **psychological/emotional self** – Am I likeable? How do I manage my emotions? How do I deal with disappointment or conflict? Am I happy, kind, friendly, helpful, empathic?
- **social self** – Do I have a range of social networks and friendships? Do I participate in a range of activities and experiences with others? Can I communicate effectively with people of different ages? What are my core values and beliefs?
- **academic self** – How do I perform at school? What subjects do I like. What am I good at? What are my goals for the future? Duchesne et al. (2019, p. 157) report that having a positive academic self has a positive effective on academic achievement.

Figure 9.16 Three critical factors in sense of self

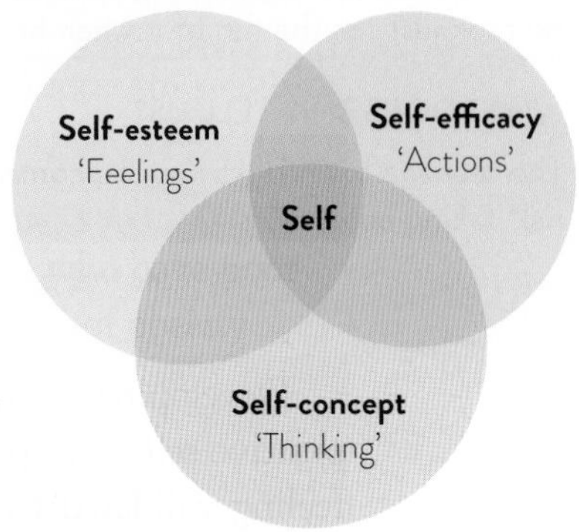

Self-concept, or how young people 'see' themselves, is a primary concern for adolescents. They are preoccupied by how they fit in, which group they belong to at school, their physical appearance, their physical prowess, their reputation among their peers and what they can do well. How adolescents see themselves as competent individuals will to a large extent shape their interactions with family, peers and teachers. Self-image may also impact on participation in sport, social functions or part-time work.

Adolescence is also a time when young people may experiment with drugs, alcohol and sex. They may engage in risk-taking behaviour with little or no thought given to the possible consequences. Adolescents are dealing with surges in hormones and major physical changes, while the frontal lobe – which manages the executive functions of the brain, such as behaviour and impulse control – is not yet fully developed. This combination of an immature frontal lobe, which limits the ability to problem-solve, combined with the surge in hormones, often results in risk-taking behaviour. Jackson and Goossens (2006, p. 286) suggest that much of adolescent behaviour described as 'risky' is in fact characteristically developmental for adolescents and experimental in nature. They state that 'very often risk behaviours arise more because of situations which bring about new and unexpected challenges to an inexperienced youngster, than [due] to characteristics inherent in the individual'.

SCENARIO

RISKY

Asher (15 years) and his mates have two dozen eggs and are out for a good time. It's 9 p.m. and the boys are walking around the neighbourhood throwing eggs at cars, houses and shopfronts. They find this behaviour exhilarating, especially if chased or challenged by someone in the neighbourhood.

When his father hears what Asher has done, he makes him help to wash the dried egg off the damaged property.

Although annoyed, Asher's father is aware that his son's behaviour is typical for his age and recalls the many risks he took just for the fun of it when he was a teenager.

WHAT DOES THIS TELL US?

The teenage brain lacks impulse control, which leads to risk-taking behaviours.

► DISCUSSION

Young people often engage in behaviours that are annoying and borderline unacceptable, but can be explained by the need to show off or conform to the peer group – for example, swearing, risk-taking behaviours, answering back, showing off. Should these behaviours be addressed formally or is it more effective to simply ignore them?

Developing a positive self-concept is an integral part of the socialisation process. To develop a positive self-concept, children and young people need to feel they are competent and to have this feeling validated by significant people in their lives. Feeling good about oneself is essential for establishing successful interactions with other people. The ways in which adults respond to and guide children's and young people's behaviour will significantly affect their self-concept.

Self-esteem

Self-esteem is the measure of how much an individual likes or values the characteristics that make up the image they have of themselves. Self-esteem reflects the judgements children make about themselves when they compare their self-concept with what they believe is their **ideal self**.

From infancy, self-esteem is shaped by the degree of unconditional love and nurturance received from parents or primary attachment figure/s. This attachment is a critical factor and continues to have a strong influence on self-esteem throughout adolescence. As babies begin to interact with their environment, their self-esteem is shaped by adult responses to their attempts to become more independent. It is not until around three years of age that children develop the cognitive skills to understand that other people can have different thoughts and feelings from them.

A child's self-esteem in turn plays a role in how they behave and how successfully they interact with others. Children and young people who do not have their self-esteem validated find the world untrustworthy and unreliable, and often use unacceptable or extreme behaviour to have their emotional needs met. Negative behaviours such as bullying and aggression are often symptoms of poor self-esteem.

Children and young people with poor self-esteem are less likely to be proactive in taking responsibility for their own actions or to respect the rights of others. They may find it difficult to form trusting relationships with adults. Self-esteem is also closely linked to the development of friendships, and children with poor self-esteem are less likely to develop friendships and more likely to be easily led or manipulated by others.

A child's self-esteem develops in response to the experiences they have and the feedback they get from significant people in their lives (family members, friends, teachers, ESWs). The concept of self-esteem as the foundation for emotional health is supported by the work of several theorists. For example, pyscho-social theorist Erikson (1963) believed it was essential that children be given 'the right messages' at each stage of development in order to develop:

- a sense of trust in the world
- a feeling of control over actions and decisions

- a sense of responsibility
- a feeling of competence.

Children and young people behave according to the way they see themselves (see **Figure 9.17**); their belief about what they can and cannot achieve will influence how they approach new situations.

Self-esteem also influences life chances and life choices – what you do and what you can become. If children and young people are given genuine, positive feedback, such as 'You're kind, responsible, creative, helpful, thoughtful', they are more likely to develop positive, healthy attitudes and beliefs about themselves and to have positive self-esteem. It is critical that children and young people hear 'the right messages' so they see themselves as worthwhile and valued: 'I am loveable, I am valued, I am worthwhile, I can handle myself and my environment with confidence. I know I have something to offer to others'.

Figure 9.17 Self-esteem – how children and young people see themselves

Healthy self-esteem	Poor self-esteem
Respected	Anxious
Valued	Unhappy
Happy	Anti-social
Productive	Feeling of hopelessness
Optimistic	Mistrustful
Risk-taker	Focuses on failure
Perseveres	Avoids risks
Cooperative	
Capable	
Resourceful	

The attributes of children and young people with high self-esteem and low self-esteem are shown in **Figures 9.18** and **9.19**, respectively.

Figure 9.18 Signs of high self-esteem

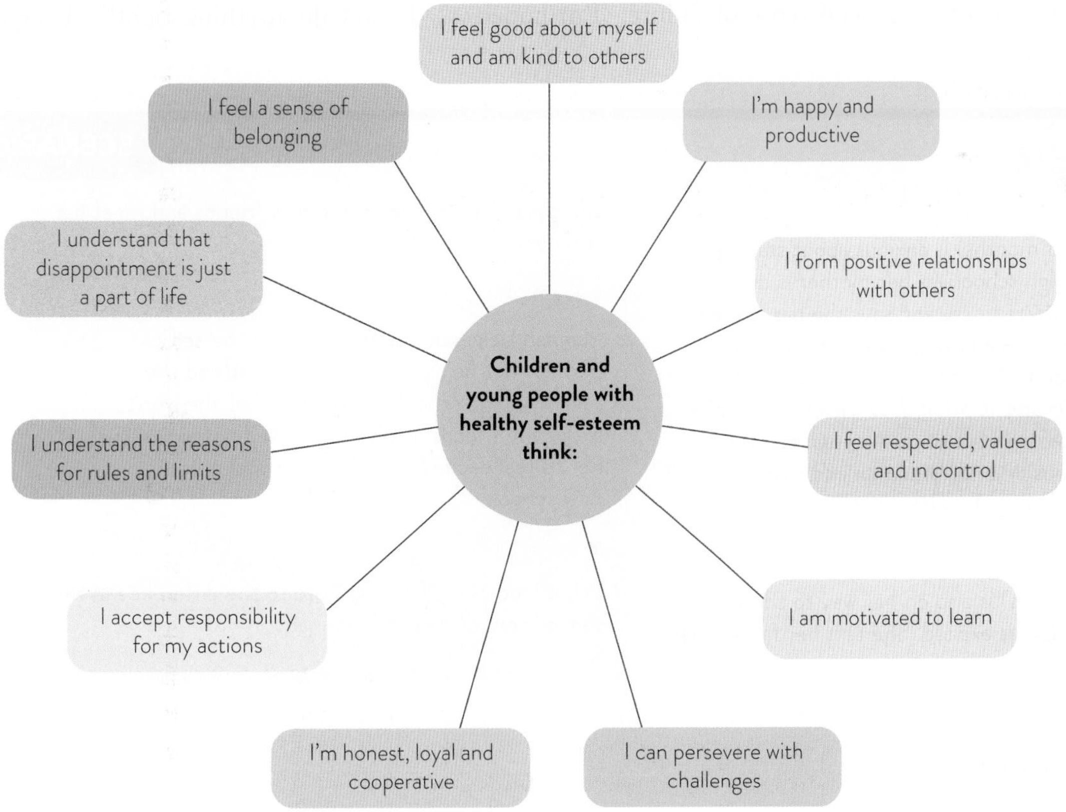
Children and young people with healthy self-esteem think:
I feel good about myself and am kind to others
I'm happy and productive
I form positive relationships with others
I feel respected, valued and in control
I am motivated to learn
I can persevere with challenges
I'm honest, loyal and cooperative
I accept responsibility for my actions
I understand the reasons for rules and limits
I understand that disappointment is just a part of life
I feel a sense of belonging

Figure 9.19 Signs of low self-esteem

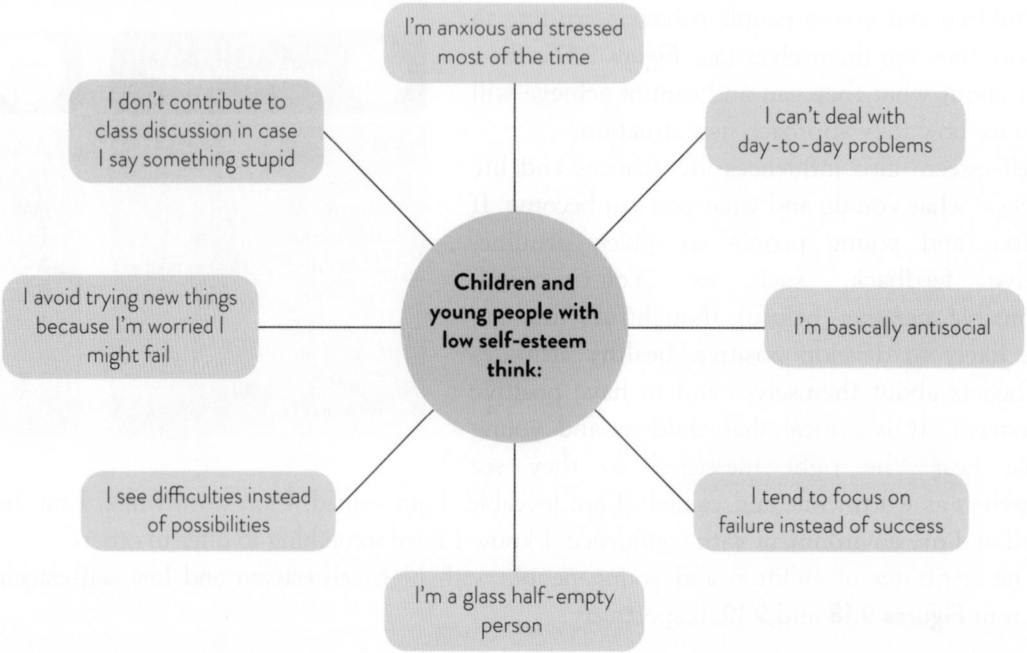

Children and young people with low self-esteem will often generalise difficulties or challenges in one area to a general sense of failure: 'I'm hopeless', 'I can't do anything right!', 'Everyone hates me.'

SELF-ESTEEM

SCENARIO

NERVES

Hannah (11 years, 8 months) is anxious about starting at her new selective high school. As her mother is driving her to school, she starts to cry and says she has made the wrong decision and should have gone to her local high school with her friends: *'I won't be as smart as the other kids. They'll think I'm stupid. What if no one likes me?'* Her mother tries to reassure Hannah, telling her that it is normal to be nervous in a new situation and that there will be other students feeling the same way.

SELF-CONFIDENCE

Eva (11 years, 9 months) is also on her way to the same school as Hannah. Eva is excited. She tells her father that she can't wait to make some new friends and meet her teachers: *'It's going to be so exciting!'*

WHAT DOES THIS TELL US?

Hannah lacks self-esteem. She sees herself as perhaps not being good enough to attend the selective high school and worries that she won't make any friends. Eva's positive self-esteem allows her to feel excited and confident about her new school.

▶ DISCUSSION

What factors might contribute to the difference in the self-esteem of Eva and Hannah?

Self-efficacy

Self-efficacy is an individual's belief in their ability to achieve and to 'have a go' – for example, 'I think I could learn how to do that' versus 'I'll never be able to do that!' Self-efficacy is based on the individual's **sense of agency** (sense of control or self-confidence) – the individual's perception of their ability to influence/control their own fate by making deliberate choices and decisions.

Self-efficacy involves an individual's belief about their own competence and power to be in control and take purposeful action to achieve desired outcomes – for example, 'If I practise every day I might be selected for the first division team'; 'I'm going to study hard so that I get lots of options for my future.'

Low self-efficacy can lead to a sense of powerlessness, helplessness and despair. As described by Bandura (1986), low self-efficacy can create a cycle of continuous low achievement: 'I can't do this so there is no point trying', with resulting failure reinforcing the 'I can't do this' belief. Students caught in this cycle will often avoid new challenges and use a range of avoidance strategies – for example, 'I have a headache; My tummy hurts; I feel sick; My hand is sore.'

Students with low self-efficacy can be supported by the following strategies:

- Break tasks down into small, manageable steps. This helps the student to see that completing a task need not be overwhelming if it is broken down into small chunks.
- Talk about the task with the student and allow them to ask questions. This encourages the student to think through the task and visualise a positive outcome.
- Ask open-ended questions to clarify the student's thinking (think aloud) – for example, 'Tell me what you know about …; What can you do if you don't' know how to spell a word? What can you do if you get stuck?'
- Use specific, positive reinforcement by commenting on what the student does – for example, 'Good, you remembered to start your sentence with a capital letter.'
- Provide a range of resources (depending on age/interests) – for example, coloured paper, special pens, iPad, apps.
- Where possible, offer choices – for example, choose a book for reading; choose a topic for writing; choose where to sit.
- Set short-term goals with the student – for example, 'By next Friday I will write a sentence with at least six words.'
- Offer rewards/motivation for effort – 'When you have written your sentence, you can choose …'
- Start with what the student can do and gradually build on these skills.
- Give the student specific tips, such as a visual reminder of the structure of a sentence, or teach rhymes – for example, when rounding up or down, chant, 'Four or less let it rest, five or more raise the score!'

SCENARIO

'CAN DO!' VERSUS 'NO WAY!'

Mitch (10 years) and his sister **Callie** (8 years) have been enrolled in the local swimming club.

Callie is looking forward to improving her swimming and says she might be able to go to the Olympics one day. Callie always sees the glass as half full. She is an eternal optimist and will have a go at almost anything. As a result, she is a good all-rounder who achieves well, both academically and in sport. She is popular with other students and teachers.

Mitch, on the other hand, is a fatalist – he always thinks about what might go wrong. This attitude has limited Mitch's opportunities to reach his full potential. He lacks self-confidence and complains whenever he is faced with a new challenge. He tells his father he doesn't want to be in the swimming club as he's 'hopeless at swimming' and it will be a waste of time and money.

WHAT DOES THIS TELL US?

Mitch and Callie are siblings but have very different levels of self-belief. Callie's optimism will support her to reach her full potential in life; conversely, Mitch's low self-efficacy will limit his ability to reach his full potential.

▶ DISCUSSION

What could the children's father do to build Mitch's low self-efficacy?

Social competence and the importance of friendships

Social competence is the ability to get along with others, adapt to new situations and engage as a productive member of society. Social competence develops when children and young people have a positive self-esteem, are self-confident and have positive self-efficacy. The ability to form and sustain friendships contributes to the development of social competence.

Friendships developed at school are typically the first relationships formed independently of the family. Friends are often chosen on the basis of similarity – gender, age, sporting skills, common interests, socioeconomic status and ethnicity. Children and young people are acutely aware of how they compare with and are different from their peers. Awareness of these differences will play an increasing role in whether or not children and young people regard themselves as competent and confident individuals.

By middle childhood, children are increasingly becoming focused on body image, and are anxious to 'fit in' and be part of a friendship group. Being 'different' or not being accepted within the peer group can cause great anxiety and undermine confidence at this age. Negative experiences with their peer group can have a significant impact on self-esteem.

Children and young people use various strategies to 'fit in' or be part of a group. They may adopt the same dress, likes or dislikes, behaviour and even speech patterns of more popular children to ensure acceptance. The positive opinion of peers exerts a powerful influence over how children and young people see themselves and how they behave.

By adolescence, friendships can influence the development of values such as trust, empathy, loyalty, problem-solving and conflict resolution. Friendships also support emotional development – to have a friend, you must be a friend. The interdependent and reciprocal nature of friendships provides children and young people with the opportunity to explore and gain valuable experience in building and sustaining mutually beneficial relationships. They learn that friendship can mean compromising or putting the needs of others before one's own needs.

During adolescence, friendships provide an important source of emotional support. There will be occasions during early adolescence when young people may prefer to share their intimate concerns, thoughts and feeling with their friends rather than with a supportive adult. By high school, young people usually have an established group of friends. Membership of these groups is usually achieved by mutual consent and there is usually a natural group leader.

Dolgin (2014) reminds us that a teenager's definition of *popular* is not the same as an adult's definition (kind, generous, thoughtful, outgoing, friendly). Young people who are regarded as popular are typically natural leaders who are perceived as being cool – they usually have their own style of dress and way of talking, and they are usually good-looking, persuasive and charismatic. They can also be manipulative, dismissive and judgemental – for example, controlling others by spreading malicious rumours, making unkind comments or excluding others from the group.

Young people who have not been able to establish special friendships during their primary school years may find it difficult to do so in high school. Children in mainstream education who have a disability that impacts on their ability to form and sustain relationships may also become loners at high school. For example, a young person with mild autism who does not have the **social skills** necessary to effectively interact on an ongoing basis with their peers may find it difficult to establish friendships.

Duchesne and colleagues (2019, p. 195) remind us that 'a history of peer rejection and a lack of supportive friendships is associated with a risk of poor school performance, early school dropout, antisocial behaviour, criminality and poor relationships in adulthood'. These authors also state that friendship, particularly during adolescence, is a source of protection – that is, friends look out for each other, care for each other, help each other out and provide a source of security.

SCENARIO

BFF

Harley and **Adam** (both 17 years) have been best friends since kindergarten. As they get ready to leave school and begin a new phase in their lives, they reflect on their friendship and how it has helped them to navigate their way to adulthood. They know they will remain friends forever, even as they go on their separate journeys – one to university, the other on a 12-month student exchange to Germany.

Lan and **Mei** (both 15 years) are Chinese-Australians. Their parents are close friends and the families socialise on weekends. Lan's parents have very traditional views on gender roles and want Lan to marry well. Mei's parents are more Westernised and tell Mei she is free to choose her own path in life. Lan has a boyfriend at school but keeps it a secret from her parents because she knows they would disapprove as he is not Chinese. Lan and Mei collaborate on stories to tell Lan's mother about where they are going and what they are doing so Lan can spend time with her boyfriend. Lan is so grateful to have Mei as her best friend.

WHAT DOES THIS TELL US?

Forming and sustaining friendships is an important part of the socialisation process, particularly as young people move towards greater independence.

9.4 Theories of social and emotional development

Theories of development help educators to develop pedagogical strategies (teaching practices) that best meet the developmental needs of children and young people. Traditional theories of social development include the work of Bandura, Erikson, Vygotsky and Kohlberg.

It is important to be aware that while theorists are typically assigned to broad principles (e.g. developmental, sociocultural, psychosocial, behaviourist, etc.), all theories of development acknowledge the complex interactions between each domain of development. **Figure 9.20** provides a brief summary of key theories/theorists.

GO FURTHER

Learn more about the theories of Bandura, Erikson, Vygotsky and Kohlberg in your **Go Further** resource, available through your instructor.

Figure 9.20 Key theorists and theories

Theorist	Theory
Albert Bandura (1925–2021)	Social learning theory is based on the belief that learning occurs as a result of observation, imitation and modelling.
Erik Erikson (1902–94)	Erikson's psychosocial theory proposes that development is driven by a combination of an individual's biological makeup and the environment (Bee & Boyd, 2004).
Lev Vygotsky (1896–1934)	Sociocultural theory learning and knowledge acquisition is a collaborative partnership between adults and children, facilitated by adults and/or more knowledgeable learners, such as older siblings.
Lawrence Kohlberg (1927–87)	Kohlberg believed that morality was based on the ability to reflect, debate, question and challenge rules, laws and practices. It requires the ability to be empathic – to understand the feelings of others and consider situations from the perspective of others.

Supporting moral development

Moral development provides the foundation for ethical behaviour. To support moral development and ethical behaviour, schools generally have in place a range of rules, policies and procedures to promote fairness, equity, natural justice, empathy and wellbeing. A key driver is the National Framework for Values Education in Australian Schools, which includes nine core values based on Australia's common democratic way of life – for example, equality, freedom, the rule of law, compassion, integrity, respect, inclusion, environmental sustainability and social justice.

Values education requires a whole-of-school approach, which engages all key stakeholders – students, parents, teachers and support staff, and the governing body. Students learn about the core values when they are modelled and practised by teachers and parents, and, importantly, when they are able to experience these values in their day-to-day life – for example, being treated with dignity and respect, being acknowledged as worthwhile individuals or having opportunities to work towards the common good.

The final report on the National Framework for Values Education in Australian Schools (Values Education Good Practice Schools Project, 2008) highlights the 10 good practices in values education from Stage 2 of the project. One of these practices is explicitly teaching values so students know what the values mean and how the values are lived. This allows the teacher to reinforce the importance of respecting differences in values and beliefs. Strategies such as a 'value of the month', weekly values assemblies, community forums, newsletters, dramatic presentations and lunchtime clubs have been used to focus on values.

Another practice involves teachers implicitly modelling the values that have been explicitly taught. This creates opportunities for teachers to actively reinforce values learning. The report states that such pervasive modelling of values helps to create more positive classrooms and school cultures. Modelling values also reinforces the importance of respectful relationships between teachers and students, students and students, and teachers and teachers.

9.5 Mental health and emotional wellbeing

Videos: Mental health and emotional wellbeing in children

Emotional development, like all other domains of development, occurs in a social context. Children's and young people's emotional wellbeing is shaped by their immediate environment – family, school and the broader community.

The Center on the Developing Child, Harvard University states that a growing body of scientific evidence tells us emotional development begins early in life, that it is a critical aspect of the development of overall brain architecture, and that it has enormous consequences over the course of a lifetime. The core features of emotional development include the ability to:

- identify and understand one's own feelings
- accurately read and comprehend emotional states in others to manage strong emotions and their expression in a constructive manner
- regulate one's own behaviour
- develop empathy for others
- establish and sustain relationships.

Source: National Scientific Council on the Developing Child (2004). Children's emotional development is built into the architecture of their brains: Working paper no. 2 (p. 1). Center on the Developing Child, Harvard University. http://www.developingchild.net

Mental health can be defined as 'a positive capacity relating to the social and emotional wellbeing of individuals and communities' (Hunter Institute of Mental Health, 2010, p. 2). How it is defined depends on cultural understandings, but it generally includes elements such as our enjoyment of life, how we cope with stress, sadness, grief and difficulties, our goals and ambitions, how we go about achieving them and our connections with other people. Mental health encompasses 'our thoughts, our emotions, our social functioning, and the overall coherence or purpose in our lives. Mental health is an integral part of a person's overall health and wellbeing' (Hunter Institute of Mental Health, 2010, p. 2).

According to Health Direct (2021) about one in seven children and adolescents aged four to 17 have recently experienced a mental health disorder in Australia. The most common mental health-related issues experienced by children and adolescents include:

- relationship problems (for example family, peers)
- eating or body-image issues
- bullying (including cyberbullying)
- abuse (physical, emotional or sexual)
- feeling sad or depressed
- worry or anxiety
- self-harm or suicide.

Source: Health Direct (2021). Kids and mental health. https://www.healthdirect.gov.au/kids-mental-health (accessed May 2022).

ONLINE RESOURCES

- Kids Helpline – 1800 55 1800 (telephone and online counselling for ages 5–25): **https://kidshelpline.com.au**
- Parentline – search online for the Parentline phone number in your state or territory for counselling and support for parents and carers
- headspace: phone or online support those aged 12–25: **https://headspace.org.au**
- SANE Australia (people living with a mental illness and their carers) – call 1800 18 7263: **https://www.sane.org**
- ReachOut (youth mental health service) – visit the website for info or use the online forum: **https://au.reachout.com**
- Raising Healthy Minds app – a free app with evidence-based information to help parents or carers with the wellbeing of their child: **https://raisingchildren.net.au/guides/raising-healthy-minds**
- Beyond Blue – 1300 22 4636. Call or chat online with a trained mental health professional: **https://www.beyondblue.org.au**
- Lifeline – 13 11 14: **https://www.lifeline.org.au**

Risk factors

Risk factors associated with young people with a mental health disorder include smoking, excessive alcohol consumption, use of cannabis and other drugs, problem-eating behaviours, risky/promiscuous sexual behaviours, bullying and excessive use of or addiction to internet/electronic games.

The report on the mental health and wellbeing of children indicates that educators need to be aware of the mental health of children and young people. Schools can be a source of support for students with mental health issues. This may include identification, counselling and/or referral to health services. Teachers are often the first people outside the family to identify children and young people with emotional and behavioural problems.

It is important to actively assist students to deal with disappointment or mistakes, and to help them understand that these are a part of life. This support can be achieved by talking to students and helping them to see how they can work towards building their skills or working through their mistakes. It is important not to dismiss students' concerns, but rather to acknowledge them in a respectful manner – for example, 'I know you're disappointed, William. How about we work through it together?'

Students should not always be 'rescued' from disappointment or failure, but should be supported to cope, take responsibility for their own actions and identify and draw on their own strengths. Sometimes students will need to simply accept disappointment or failure: 'You did your very best and I know you are upset. You won't always succeed at what you do but you can always feel good about trying your best. Let's think about the things you can do well.' Help students to put disappointment or mistakes into perspective: 'Remember last year you couldn't write your name and now you can!'

Children and young people who present with mental health issues may present in many different ways. For example, they may exhibit acting-out behaviours such as persistent defiance, physical or verbal aggression, including verbal threats, inability to inhibit or control behaviour impulses or remain on task without constantly being distracted. Alternatively, they may become quiet and withdrawn from the family and from their peers. They may present as anxious, uncertain or unsure of themselves. They may also see the world in very negative ways and present with a sense of hopelessness.

It is important to be aware that determining a child's or young person's mental health status requires specialised expertise. Labelling a student as having mental health issues is not helpful and can be quite damaging for the student and the family. As an ESW, your role is to be aware of the student's needs and support the student in the classroom under the guidance of the teacher and/or other professionals engaged with the student.

Anxiety

All children and young people will experience a degree of **anxiety** from time to time – for example, when starting school, joining a sporting team, completing exams or going to a party. This type of anxiety is normal, healthy and usually overcome by support from the family. Children and young people who suffer from anxiety disorder are constantly anxious. They may feel overwhelmed by the expectations of themselves and others, they may have irrational fears and they generally lack self-confidence. They can be overwhelmed by a task simply because they are not able to break the task into manageable chunks and often are not able to visualise themselves as competent, capable and resourceful. They are unable to relax, and this creates a cycle of worry, stress and anxiety that becomes all-consuming. They lack the resilience needed to attempt tasks or move from their comfort zone because they fear failure, sense danger or simply regard themselves as incapable.

According to Be You (2019b), behaviours that might indicate higher than average levels of anxiety may include separation anxiety and clingy behaviour; frequent, severe tantrums; low interest in social situations; unwillingness to get involved in unfamiliar activities; and significant difficulty with change or transitions. Ultimately, chronic anxiety in children and young people stops them from participating fully in their life and enjoying it. Anxieties that may manifest in childhood include:

- **separation anxiety** – while this is appropriate in younger children, in older children the inability to separate from the family without becoming anxious will reduce the child's opportunities to participate in normal social activities such as sleepovers, attending parties or school camps/excursions

- **phobias** (including social phobia) – a phobia is an intense and irrational fear of an object, thing or event. It becomes debilitating when the child obsesses over the phobia. For example, a social phobia may mean that the child refuses to attend social outings with others
- **generalised anxiety disorder** – the child worries about almost everything. For example, being late, forgetting their homework, what to wear, how many friends they have, etc.
- **post-traumatic stress disorder** (PTSD) – this disorder can develop as a consequence of a traumatic experience or event such as a serious accident, a natural disaster, witnessing extreme violence, being attacked or bullied. PTSD is often accompanied by flashbacks and extreme mood swings
- **obsessive compulsive disorder** (OCD) – this can be an extremely debilitating disorder as the child obsesses over a particular action or ritual such as hand-washing, touching certain objects before leaving the house, checking that certain items are in the backpack and so on. Children with OCD will repeat the same action over and over again, even if this means returning to the house multiple times
- **school refusal** – children who develop school refusal are usually so anxious about going to school that they will develop psychosomatic illnesses such as a headache or upset stomach.

Accommodations

Students who suffer from an anxiety disorder require adults to be supportive and patient. It may take a child several false starts before they are prepared to try to overcome their anxieties. **Accommodations** may include:

- allowing students to talk about their anxieties and helping them to verbalise what makes them feel anxious
- teaching calming techniques, such as self-affirmations, deep breathing or rehearsal
- collaborating with the children rather than taking over or acting on behalf of the child
- facing anxieties with a trusted person to reduce fears
- encouraging a 'can do' attitude. Teach resilience by talking about failure and the importance of having a go, learning from the experience and trying again.

Childhood trauma

As discussed earlier in the chapter, **childhood trauma** refers to 'a scary, dangerous, violent, or life-threatening event that happens to a child' (CCSTASI, 2023). Children who suffer from child traumatic stress are those who have been exposed to one or more traumas over the course of their lives and develop reactions that persist and affect their daily lives after the events have ended. **Figure 9.8** lists common signs and symptoms exhibited by children suffering traumatic stress.

Not all children who experience the same trauma will develop traumatic stress or experience the same level of traumatic stress. This will depend on the nature of the traumatic experience, previous traumatic experiences, the response and support of the family, the child's culture, living conditions, community support and the severity of the experience.

Complex trauma is defined as exposure to multiple traumatic events and includes the wide-ranging, long-term effects of this exposure. Examples of complex trauma include child abuse, abandonment and severe neglect, witnessing repeated domestic violence, substance abuse or the mental illness of a parent.

Children who are exposed to complex trauma may become emotionally detached, distrustful, angry and vigilant. They may also suffer anxiety and depression. They may dissociate themselves from the trauma, may become fearful or aggressive, and in adolescence may engage in extreme risk-taking behaviours. They experience feelings of shame, guilt, low self-esteem and a poor self-image.

For young children, the experience of complex trauma can lead to toxic stress, which has a disruptive effect on the nervous system and stress hormone regulatory systems that can damage developing brain architecture and chemistry. It can lead to lifelong problems in learning, behaviour and both physical and mental health (National Scientific Council on the Developing Child, 2004, pp. 8–10). Without treatment, in adulthood these children may become mentally ill, and engage in violence, substance abuse, illegal activities and prostitution.

Videos: Understanding trauma and adversity

Accommodations

Children and young people who have experienced traumatic events or complex trauma should receive treatment from people who specialise in treating childhood trauma. In school settings, this can be supported by:

- being aware that the student has suffered trauma and is exhibiting signs of traumatic stress (it is not necessary or appropriate to know all of the details related to the student's trauma – this information is confidential)
- making allowances for the student's behaviour (within reason and with clear boundaries)
- allowing the student to take short breaks as needed
- suggesting a buddy or support person who can alert staff if there are any problems in the playground
- working with the student to identify emotional triggers and trying to minimise these or anticipate in order to prepare the student
- focusing on the student's strengths and abilities to develop activities to build self-regulation of emotions and gaining a sense of control
- acting as a trusted mentor and support to the student
- where students have collectively experienced a trauma such as a natural disaster, encouraging students to talk about their experiences, and their emotions and fears, and to work on ways of overcoming these as a group.

Mindfulness

Mindfulness is the ability to pay attention, with judgement given to what we are thinking and feeling in the here and now. As students move into adolescence, factors such as peer pressure, being liked, having friends and being part of a group, and body image influence and shape emotional wellbeing. A student's emotional state will influence how they act, think and learn. Students who are emotionally well adjusted are able to manage negative emotional states with the support of caring adults. Being able to manage emotional states allows individuals to put emotions to one side and focus on the task at hand. This is a developmental skill that must be supported and nurtured by responsive adults. Learning to manage emotions is an essential life skill that can be supported by:

- helping students to recognise and label their emotions
- helping students to choose acceptable and safe behaviours to manage their emotions

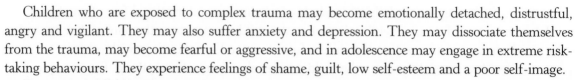

- helping students to recognise how their emotional state influences their thinking, learning and decision-making
- engaging in mindfulness activities
- recognising that experiencing strong emotions can be frightening for children and young people and, regardless of how they react, they need the understanding, guidance and support of caring adults (see **Figure 9.21**).

Figure 9.21 Encourage students to express their emotions via affirmation words

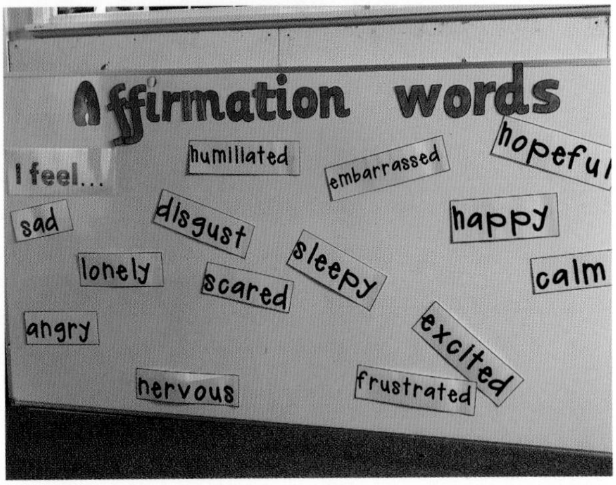

Source: Photo by Tish Okely © Cengage

ESWs can support students by being alert to their emotional wellbeing and alerting the classroom teacher if there are any concerns. They can support mindfulness, which in its simplest form can be described as tuning in to the present moment and focusing on the task at hand.

Be You (2019c) states that mindfulness is a 'clinically proven tool to support your wellbeing and mental health'. The benefits of mindfulness for children include:

- improving resilience (building skills to cope better with stress)
- increasing their ability to self-regulate through breathing and other grounding techniques, especially difficult emotions such as fear and anger
- improving empathy (their ability to understand how another person is feeling, which helps them to build positive relationships).

Mental health education resources for ESWs

Many government and non-government schools have implemented programs specifically designed to promote resilience, mental health and wellbeing.

Social and emotional development red flags

Social and emotional development resources

Keep in mind that red flags in relation to social and emotional development may also indicate issues in other developmental domains. Concerns about development should be based on observations over a period of time and in different situations that show a persistent pattern of behaviours. It's also essential to consider other factors and issues, such as temperament, family and social context, exposure to trauma, adolescence, illicit drugs, alcohol and peer pressure.

Developmental red flags for social and emotional development can be difficult to identify simply because every child or young person will experience anxiety or sadness at some point. For those with healthy social and emotional development these experiences are part of life and the child or young person typically has the resilience to quickly bounce back with the support of caring adults.

Red flags would be indicated by children and young people who display *persistent* signs of anxiety or depression over a period of time. **Figure 9.22** highlights examples of red flags that may be observed in relation to social and emotional development. As you read these red flags try to assign an approximate age range for the development of these skills.

Figure 9.22 Developmental red flags

Anxiety	Depression
> Being very afraid when away from parents (separation anxiety) > Having extreme fear about a specific thing or situation, such as dogs, insects, or going to the doctor (phobias) > Being very afraid of school and other places where there are people (social anxiety) > Being very worried about the future and about bad things happening (general anxiety) > Having repeated episodes of sudden, unexpected, intense fear that come with symptoms like heart pounding, having trouble breathing, or feeling dizzy, shaky or sweaty (panic disorder)	> Feeling sad, hopeless or irritable a lot of the time > Not wanting to do or enjoy doing fun things > Showing changes in eating patterns – eating a lot more or a lot less than usual > Showing changes in sleep patterns – sleeping a lot more or a lot less than normal > Showing changes in energy – being tired and sluggish or tense and restless a lot of the time > Having a hard time paying attention > Feeling worthless, useless or guilty > Showing self-injury and self-destructive behaviour

Source: National Center on Birth Defects and Developmental Disabilities, US Centers for Disease Control and Prevention (2022). Anxiety and depression in children. https://www.cdc.gov/childrensmentalhealth/depression.html#anxiety. Reference to specific commercial products, manufacturers, companies, or trademarks does not constitute its endorsement or recommendation by the U.S. Government, Department of Health and Human Services, or Centers for Disease Control and Prevention.

For younger school age children, signs of anxiety or depression may include:

- lack of interest in playing with others
- unable to share or take turns with other children
- being extremely rigid about routines – becoming extremely upset when routines are changed
- difficulty separating from parent
- very passive or fearful, and does not want to try things other children his age are doing
- extreme fears that interfere with daily activities.

Source: Children's Therapy & Family Resource Centre (n.d.). School aged developmental milestones. http://www.kamloopschildrenstherapy.org/social-emotional-school-aged-milestones

9.6 Social and emotional development and the curriculum

The social and emotional development of children and young people is supported in the Australian Curriculum, particularly within the following three **general capabilities**:

1 personal and social capability
2 ethical understanding
3 intercultural understanding.

A brief summary of the elements of each capability is given here. To read the general capabilities in full, or for more detail on how each of these capabilities is embedded across the curriculum, visit https://www.v9.australiancurriculum.edu.au AC.

Personal and social capability

The personal and social capability is organised into four elements, as shown in **Figure 9.23**.

Each of the four elements is organised into sub-elements, as shown in **Figure 9.24**.

Figure 9.23 Elements for the personal and social capability

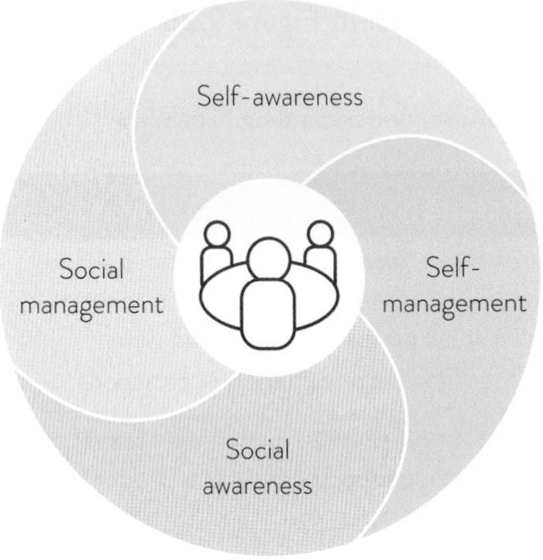

Source: Australian Curriculum, Assessment and Reporting Authority (ACARA) (n.d). Personal and social capability (Version 8.4).

Figure 9.24 Sub-elements of the personal and social capability

Element	Sub-elements
Self-awareness	> Personal awareness > Emotional awareness > Reflective practice
Self-management	> Goal setting > Emotional regulation > Perseverance and adaptability
Social awareness	> Empathy > Relational awareness > Community awareness
Social management	> Communication > Collaboration > Leadership > Decision-making > Conflict resolution

Source: Australian Curriculum, Assessment and Reporting Authority (ACARA) (2022d). Understand this general capability. Personal and social capability.

Ethical understanding

Ethical understanding is organised into three elements (**Figure 9.25**).

Each of the three elements is organised into sub-elements, as shown in **Figure 9.26**.

Figure 9.25 Elements for the ethical understanding capability

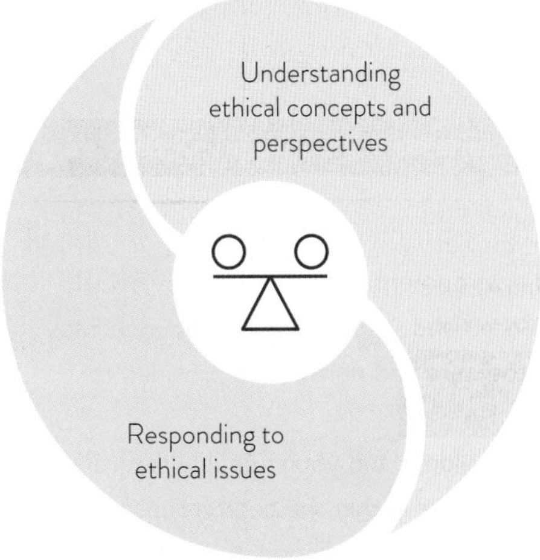

Source: Australian Curriculum, Assessment and Reporting Authority (ACARA) (2022b). Understand this general capability. Ethical understanding.

Figure 9.26 Sub-elements of the ethical understanding capability

Element	Sub-elements
Understanding ethical concepts and perspectives	> Explore ethical concepts > Examine values, rights and responsibilities, and ethical norms > Recognise influences on ethical behaviour and perspectives
Responding to ethical issues	> Explore ethical perspectives and frameworks > Explore ethical issues > Make and reflect on ethical decisions

Source: Australian Curriculum, Assessment and Reporting Authority (ACARA) (2022b). Understand this general capability. Ethical understanding.

Intercultural understanding

Intercultural understanding includes three interrelated elements as shown in **Figure 9.27**. Each of the three elements is organised into sub-elements, as shown in **Figure 9.28**.

Figure 9.27 Intercultural understanding

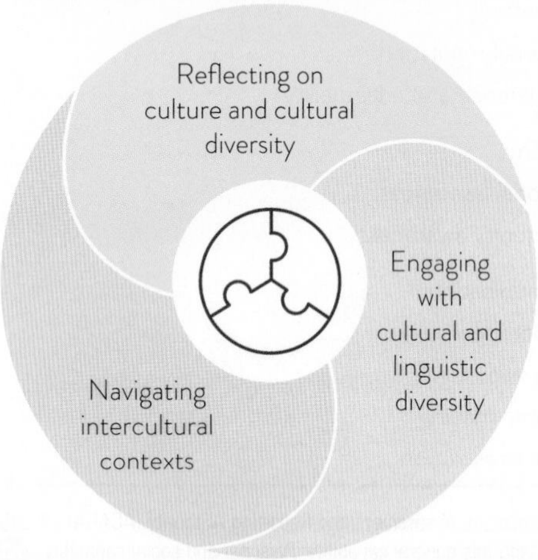

Source: Australian Curriculum, Assessment and Reporting Authority (ACARA) (2022c). Understand this general capability. Intercultural understanding.

Figure 9.28 Sub-elements of the intercultural understanding capability

Element	Sub-elements
Reflecting on culture and cultural diversity	> Reflect on the relationship between cultures and identities > Examine cultural perspectives and world views > Explore the influence of cultures on interactions
Engaging with cultural and linguistic diversity	> Communicate responsively > Develop multiple perspectives > Develop empathy
Navigating intercultural contexts	> Consider responses to intercultural experiences > Respond to biases, stereotypes, prejudices and discrimination > Adapt in intercultural exchanges

Source: Australian Curriculum, Assessment and Reporting Authority (ACARA) (2022c). Understand this general capability. Intercultural understanding.

Together these three capabilities provide a foundation for students to understand themselves and others, and navigate their relationships, lives, work and learning. They are designed to assist students to reflect on the perspective of others and build their ability to regulate their thoughts, emotions and behaviours (ACARA, 2022a).

The general capabilities can be downloaded at: https://v9.australiancurriculum.edu.au/downloads/general-capabilities.

Summary

Social and emotional development involves a complex interplay of psychological and environmental factors. Healthy social and emotional development may be disrupted by childhood trauma. The ability of children and young people to bounce back from trauma and continue along a healthy developmental pathway would depend on the care and nurturance provided to support the child.

Healthy social and emotional development and wellbeing profoundly influence how children and young people regard themselves as learners. Seeing themselves as competent and capable learners, being accepted within the peer group, and developing and sustaining positive relationships with adults will significantly enhance the students' likelihood of reaching their full potential and achieving their life goals.

The Australian Curriculum supports social and emotional development as part of the learning continuum, allowing children and young people to explore a range of concepts related to respect and care of self, others and the broader community.

Self-check questions

1 Define children's and young people's social and emotional development.
2 What are the core skills for social and emotional development (birth to adulthood)?
3 What is the difference between secure and insecure attachment?
4 Define child trauma and list three examples.
5 As an ESW, what is the benefit of being aware of each student's temperament?
6 According to Goleman and Gardner, what are the five core groups of social and emotional competencies that contribute to the development of children's self-regulation?
7 As an ESW, how you can promote children's resilience at school?
8 List two strategies for supporting students with low self-efficacy.
9 What are the four separate steps of learning by observation in Bandura's theory?
10 According to Erikson's theory, what are the five stages of psychosocial development?
11 What are the nine core values of the National Framework for Values Education in Australian Schools?
12 How can practising mindfulness benefit children?

Discussion questions

1 Alison has come to school today with a strong body odour following her. Her Year 8 peers have noticed and started teasing her. As her ESW, you know that deodorant is likely to be a luxury that Alison is not accustomed to.
   a What social and/or emotional factors may be influencing Alison's development?
2 There are two types of attachment. Explain what impact each type has on a student in early primary and a child in early secondary school.
3 Thomas and Ivy are twins in Year 8. Their family life has, at times, been unsteady. Two weeks ago, the police knocked on the door and arrested their mum, Sophie, for theft. Sophie was let out on bail but needs to appear in court in the next month. It is likely that she will serve jail time for her offence.
   a In the scenario, which of the family risk factors applies?
4 During Fatima's late primary years, she experienced bullying from time to time. Later into Year 9, her grandmother and Fatima were reflecting on how little she now retaliates to comments made about her and how proud she is of her heritage and cultural background.
   a Which of the self-concepts most applies to the development of Fatima?

Activities

1 Match the common signs of anxiety or depression children may demonstrate with the appropriate age group of the children.

Age group of children	Common signs of anxiety or depression
Primary school	> Are ambivalent about events > Becoming sexually active > Change in school performance > Development of eating disorders or self-harming behaviours
Upper primary/ lower secondary	> Difficulty concentrating > Difficulty sleeping > Feelings of craziness > Feelings of guilt/shame > Having nightmares > Poor eating and weight loss
Secondary school	> Questioning death > Returning to bedwetting > Screaming/crying a lot > Startled easily > Taking too many risks

2 Match the term to the correct definition

Term	Possible definitions
Positive stress	> Stress responses that have the potential to negatively affect the architecture of the developing brain, but generally occur over limited time periods that allow the brain to recover and thereby reverse potentially harmful effect.
Tolerable stress	> Strong, frequent or prolonged activation of the body's stress-management system
Toxic stress	> Moderate, short-lived stress responses, such as brief increases in heart rate or mild changes in the body's stress hormone levels

Chapter 10

COGNITIVE AND LANGUAGE DEVELOPMENT AND LEARNING

LEARNING OBJECTIVES

When you have completed this chapter, you should be able to demonstrate that, in relation to working in a school environment, you can:

10.1 describe the process of cognitive development and identify the factors that impact on cognitive development

10.2 describe the key theories of cognitive development

10.3 identify aspects of the Australian Curriculum as they relate to cognitive development

10.4 describe how concept development can assist children's learning

10.5 describe the process of language development and identify the factors that influence language development

10.6 describe the process of language

10.7 describe the key stages in the progression of language development

10.8 identify aspects of the Australian Curriculum as they relate to language development.

GO FURTHER

Go Further icons link to extra content for this chapter. Ask your instructor for the **Go Further** resource and deepen your understanding of the topic.

Online resources icons refer to useful weblinks. Ask your instructor for these **Online Resources.**

Introduction

This chapter provides an overview of cognitive and language development. Understanding how thinking and learning develops is critical when supporting student learning in the classroom. Language and cognitive development are interdependent and intricately intertwined. Theories related to these domains of development can be seen in the design of the Australian Curriculum and in the ways teachers engage students as learners.

10.1 Introduction to cognitive development

Cognition is the ability to acquire, understand and apply information through sensory input, thought and life experiences. It is a complex developmental process that occurs on a continuum from birth to death. It involves a range of mental tools, such as knowledge acquisition, language, thinking, memory, retrieval of information, applying existing knowledge to make sense of new knowledge, problem-solving, reasoning and planning.

By the time most children transition to school, they have mastered the fundamentals of language and communication and have developed an astounding range of knowledge and cognitive skills, which lay the foundation for academic learning. Importantly, preschool children have also developed a degree of self-regulation essential for successful transition to school and later academic success.

Like other domains of development, cognitive abilities move from simple to complex, are built over time, and are dependent on and influenced by, all other domains of development. Klein and Knitzer (2006, p. 9) state that 'social-emotional development is the foundation for, and intertwined with, early cognitive development'. Klein and Knitzer found that positive self-esteem and self-confidence are essential for positive school outcomes in areas such as early literacy and maths skills. This is an important finding, which is often overlooked in the rush to prepare children for academic learning. The key message is that later successful academic performance is not dependent on young children being able to identify colours, shapes, numbers or their name, but rather depends on them being emotionally secure, confident learners.

Factors that influence cognitive development

Cognitive development is influenced and shaped by a number of factors, including heredity, the sociocultural environment and the child's growing sense of self. In order to reach their optimum level of cognitive development, children require a warm, caring and stimulating environment in which they can form positive, trusting and loving relationships with their primary carers.

By now, you should be aware that learning takes place in a sociocultural context. Children acquire cognitive abilities only when they actively engage with others – family, peers, older children, teachers and the broader community. With the exception of children who are profoundly cognitively impaired, it is the sociocultural environment that shapes a child's cognitive abilities.

Heredity

Each person has a unique combination of genes that contributes to shaping their cognitive development. Each child matures at their own unique rate and, while environmental factors can influence the rate of maturation, each child will develop according to their own biological clock.

The sociocultural environment

A child's cognitive development is also shaped by their social and cultural environment, including:

- gender roles
- behaviour-management/child-rearing practices
- attitudes to play and exploration as a primary source of learning
- the transmission of cultural beliefs and values

- attitudes towards education
- the degree of appropriate stimulation in the physical environment – children are sensory learners who require 'hands-on' experiences to gather information about, and make sense of, the world
- access to health, welfare and education
- the quality of interactions and early experiences provided by the family.

Relationships: the emotional environment

During the first two years of life, the child's brain is focused on forming and reinforcing connections (neural pathways). These connections are facilitated through positive interactions with others, being active and involved, and learning through exploration and discovery. It is these early experiences and developing relationships that cause the connections in the brain to increase rapidly (Dalli et al., 2011, p. 15).

Social and emotional development

Dalli and colleagues (2011, pp. 52, 60) report that research into brain development has confirmed that the neural mechanisms for cognitive and social development appear to be the same. Optimal brain development is strongly connected to sensitive responsive caregiving. Unresponsive, inconsistent and unstable relationships within the family unit, as well as repeated exposure to highly stressful environments, have a negative impact on brain functioning and overall development.

10.2 Developmental theories

Early developmental theories: a historical perspective

Around the sixteenth century, religious leaders and thinkers began to talk about the 'special qualities' of children. This interest in children was accompanied by a concern about how best to educate children to ensure they became 'good adults'.

- John Locke (1632–1704) believed that newborn babies were like 'blank slates'. What they would become was a result of learning and experience.
- Jean Jacques Rousseau (1712–78) was the first theorist to put forward the idea that development proceeded according to an 'inner biological timetable', and that development followed a series of stages. Part of his 'educational method' relied on the belief that all children are curious: they learn for the sake of learning. If children are allowed to explore and 'deal with physical things', nature will support the child to spontaneously develop skills and understandings without the need for adults to control the process of learning.
- Johann Heinrich Pestalozzi (1746–1827) emphasised the total development of the child: physical, mental, social and emotional.
- Friedrich Fröbel (1782–1852) made a significant contribution by recognising play as a means for children to express themselves, and as a way to imitate and try out various adult roles.

The notion of intelligence

The modern notion of intelligence is probably best recognised through the work of Alfred Binet, who in 1905 developed a test to measure the intelligence of school-age children. With his colleague Theodore Simon, Binet went on to develop tests to identify children who needed additional educational support in school settings. Binet believed that intelligence was the result of environmental as well as hereditary factors, which fuelled the 'nature versus nurture' debate.

Interestingly, Binet predicted that children who had opportunities to interact with materials as part of the learning process would score higher in his tests than children whose experiences were limited.

Binet and Simon developed an intelligence test that they claimed would assess the 'superior faculties' necessary for academic success. They also developed the concept of 'mental age' to compare children's performance in the test to their actual chronological age. For example, a child with a chronological age of eight years who performed well on the IQ test might be said to have a mental age of 12 years. Conversely, a child with a chronological age of 12 years who performed poorly might be said to have a mental age of eight years.

Children's intelligence quotient (IQ) tests commonly include the:

- Wechsler Intelligence Scale for Children (WISC)
- Bayley Scale of Infant Development
- Denver Developmental Screening Test.

Today, these tests and others like them are used primarily to identify serious developmental delays.

Criticism of IQ tests as a measure of intelligence

The usefulness of IQ tests is limited, as they fail to take into account individual differences, or environmental, social, cultural, ethnic or genetic factors. The tests can only measure performance on a given day. IQ tests have been widely criticised as giving false results in relation to culturally or socially disadvantaged groups. Opponents of IQ tests claim they are culturally biased and racist because the language and concepts in the tests are biased towards white, middle-class society.

Performance or achievement tests

A spin-off from IQ tests is performance or achievement tests, which are commonly carried out in schools. For example, in Australia all students are required to undertake National Assessment Program – Literacy and Numeracy (NAPLAN) tests in numeracy and literacy. These tests are designed to measure children's performance in key learning areas (KLAs) of the curriculum, and are age-/grade-related. These tests do not take into account sociocultural factors or individual differences in learning styles.

Jean Piaget (1896–1980)

Jean Piaget made a major contribution to our understanding of cognitive development. Piaget's (1936) constructivist theory of cognitive development focuses on the development of thinking, reasoning, memory and logic. Piaget made a significant advancement in understanding cognitive development by proving that children do not think in the same way as adults.

Piaget's theory of cognitive development includes three key elements:

1. *four stages of cognitive development*: sensorimotor; preoperational; concrete operational; formal operational
2. *schemas*: the building blocks of knowledge (like Lego)
3. *adaptation processes*: allow the learner to transition from one stage to another. He called these: equilibrium, assimilation and accommodation.

When developing these elements of his theory, Piaget focused on a number of underpinning concepts, which are listed in **Figure 10.1**.

Figure 10.1 Piaget's underpinning concepts

Children have different and distinct thinking processes from those of adults – for example, in relation to **object permanence** and conservation
Cognitive or intellectual development is primarily a result of the child's independent interaction with and exploration of the environment Adults do not play a significant role in accelerating cognitive development Free-choice play and discovery learning are relevant ideas here
Development occurs in four sequential, age-related stages Progress through each stage is gradual and predictable and involves long periods of transition. The idea of 'readiness' is relevant here
New knowledge is built on existing knowledge
Mental functioning is seen as the most important factor in determining behaviour – for example, children who are egocentric have great difficulty sharing
Qualitative changes occur because of maturation in thinking

Source: Adapted from Bee & Boyd (2004).

Piaget's stages of cognitive development

According to Piaget (in Hendrick, 1991), Piaget's theory of cognitive development was based on the following beliefs:

- cognitive development occurs in four predictable, sequential stages
- all children pass through the same stages in the same order at roughly the same age
- progress from one stage to another depends on the child's readiness
- movement through each stage is gradual and could involve lengthy transition periods
- there are individual differences in the rate of progress through each stage
- children are hands-on learners engaged in exploring, discovering and problem-solving to learn new knowledge and skills
- self-directed repetition and practice is an important cognitive process.

Videos: Piaget's stages of cognitive development

CONSIDER THIS

READINESS

Piaget believed strongly that adult intervention would not result in acceleration of cognitive development, as development is determined by maturation and therefore could not be accelerated by adult intervention. He argued that if the child is not ready to proceed to the next stage, no amount of intervention would make this learning occur more rapidly.

While this belief has now been challenged by other theorists, it's worth considering what this might mean for children as they are introduced to new knowledge and skills. For example, what might this mean for children who are not yet ready to learn to read, follow 3-4-step directions, speak in a sentence, write, or concentrate for 30 minutes?

How does the modern classroom accommodate readiness?

Piaget developed four age-related stages of development, each characterised by increasingly complex skills. The development of these skills involved the interaction of the child with the environment, as shown in **Figure 10.2**.

Figure 10.2 Piaget's stages of cognitive development

Stage/approximate age	Characteristics
Sensorimotor (birth to 2 years) Understanding the present and the real world	> Involves direct interaction with the environment > Child begins with reflex-dominated responses and continues to the beginning of symbolic thought > Dominated by sensory exploration and motor abilities > Cause-and-effect behaviour develops > Object permanence develops > Reflex actions are gradually replaced by goal-directed activity > Imitation, memory and thought emerge
Preoperational (2 to 7 years) Symbolic representation of the present and real Preparation for understanding concrete operations	> Language develops > Child begins to think independently and hold mental representations > Language and imagination used to extend child's thinking abilities and understand the world around them – characterised by who, what, where, how and when questions > Ability to mentally manipulate symbols develops rapidly – seen through language use > Drawing is used, and reading and writing skills develop > Child can apply logic in one direction only > Foundation laid for the development of concepts of conservation, classification, seriation and reversibility
Concrete operational (7 to 12 years) Organisation of concrete operations – the development of many mathematical concepts	> Child learns to apply logical thought to concrete problems > Development of conservation, reversibility and more complex seriation and classification skills > Child can group objects according to more than one principle and begins to apply logical thinking to solve problems > Perception less dominant in the process of reasoning > Child can think logically in a variety of practical or concrete situations; skills cannot yet be applied to abstract situations > Child understands that mass, weight, length and number remain constant > Child can arrange items in order from greatest amount to least amount > Understanding of terms such as 'smaller than' and 'larger than'
Formal operational (12–15 years) Hypothesis-making; testing the possible	> Abstract thinking develops > Child applies the skills of thinking to more abstract arguments and discussions; thinking is more independent of concrete reality > Child is able to consider alternative possibilities and solutions; development of scientific rational thought > Development of an awareness of social issues; child sees the world not only as it is, but how it could be

Source: Adapted from Hendrick (1991).

COGNITIVE DEVELOPMENT

SCENARIO

SENSORIMOTOR STAGE AND OBJECT PERMANENCE

Milo (2 years) has developed object permanence. He now knows that just because he can't see something, it doesn't mean it no longer exists. When Dad asks *'Where's Zebbie, Milo?'* Milo looks around the room and then runs into his bedroom, returning with Zebbie the Zebra.

PREOPERATIONAL STAGE AND SYMBOLIC REPRESENTATION

Francis (2 years, 6 months) uses off-cuts of timber to represent houses for her little horse. *'One, one, one, one,'* she says as she places a horse on each piece of timber.

CONCRETE OPERATIONAL STAGE AND REVERSIBILITY

Joseph (7 years, 6 months) is able to demonstrate his understanding that a process can be reversed by working backwards through each step.

FORMAL OPERATIONAL STAGE AND ABSTRACT THINKING

Ava (14 years) states that the proverb 'People in glass houses should not throw stones' means that, *'You shouldn't criticise the poor qualities of others when you have the same poor qualities yourself.'*

WHAT DOES THIS TELL US?

Children's and young people's thinking moves from simple to complex as they mature.

Piaget's preoperational, concrete and formal operational stages are most relevant to school-age children and young people. Knowing these stages can assist in understanding how children acquire knowledge through exploration, experimentation and repetition.

Piaget's theory of cognitive development remains a significant contributing factor to our understanding of cognitive development. His theories led to the understanding that children do not think in the same way as adults, and that children play an active role in their own learning through investigation and experimentation. He also emphasised the importance of readiness (the skills, knowledge and disposition needed to acquire a slightly higher level of new skills and knowledge). His central belief that children learn best through hands-on experiences plays an important role in the way in which younger students are introduced to new concepts and knowledge.

GO FURTHER

Find out more about Piaget's theory of knowledge acquisition and the implications for learning in your **Go Further** resource, available through your instructor.

Lev Vygotsky (1896–1934)

Lev Vygotsky's sociocultural theory of cognitive development was based on the belief that each child is born with the skills necessary for learning. Vygotsky (1978) argues that cognitive development is a process of internalising ideas (Bee & Boyd, 2004), which are experienced as a result of interactions with the social/cultural world in which language is a critical factor.

Vygotsky saw the child as a dynamic learner who is facilitated in the learning process by interested adults (parents, extended family, teachers, coach). Vygotsky's theory of cognitive development emphasises the importance of language acquisition and the influence of the child's culture in cognitive development. He argues (Vygotsky, 1978) that learning and development cannot occur outside the social and cultural context, and that social learning plays a critical role in cognitive development.

Vygotsky maintains that more knowledgeable others (such as adults, older children or, in today's context, information accessed electronically) play a crucial role in the development of higher-order knowledge and skills. He stresses social interactions, role modelling, tutoring and instructing as important learning strategies for cognitive development.

Vygotsky believed that cognitive development is the result of genetic factors (lower mental functions), as well as acquired or learned skills (higher mental functions) that could only occur through the socialisation process. He defines lower mental functions as sensation, attention, perception and memory. Through interaction with the environment, these lower-order functions evolve into higher-order functions.

Vygotsky's theory of cognitive development includes three key concepts:

1. zone of proximal development (ZPD)
2. children learn from observing and imitating the behaviours of more knowledgeable others (social learning theory)
3. scaffolding learning.

Figure 10.3 Zone of proximal development

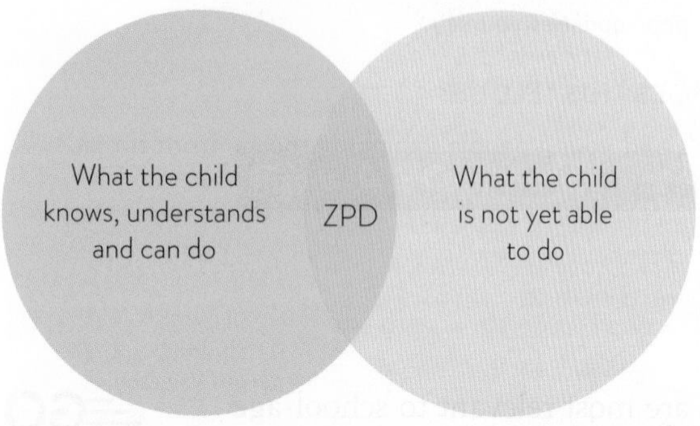

ZPD is the gap between what the student knows, understands and can do independently, and what they can do with the support of more knowledgeable others.

The zone of proximal development (ZPD)

The zone of proximal development (ZPD) is the term used by Vygotsky to describe the period of time when children are almost able to do things and, with the assistance of others, can attain the learning that was previously just out of reach. In other words, the ZPD is the gap between what the student knows, understands and can do independently, and what they can do with the support of more knowledgeable others. Proximal in this context means 'what might come next' in the learning process (see **Figure 10.3**).

The ZPD allows for guided practice as the child becomes a collaborator in the learning process alongside a more knowledgeable person. It allows more knowledgeable others to guide the child to develop skills in order to reach higher mental functioning. The concept is based on Vygotsky's belief that learning and development influence one another.

More knowledgeable others (MKO)

Vygotsky used this term to describe what a child can learn and understand if supported by MKOs (teachers, parents, older children). MKOs support the child to learn new knowledge by building on what the child already knows, understands and can do by modelling, direct instruction and guidance. MKOs engage the child in the ZPD – the child observes, practises and is guided by the MKO.

Scaffolding learning

Videos: Vygotsky sociocultural development and ZPD

Scaffolding includes two processes:

1 breaking a concept into smaller manageable parts so that it can be more easily understood
2 gradually withdrawing support (MKO) from the learner as the learner becomes more competent.

Scaffolding occurs in the ZPD. **Figure 10.4** shows the process of scaffolding.

Figure 10.4 Scaffolding in the ZPD

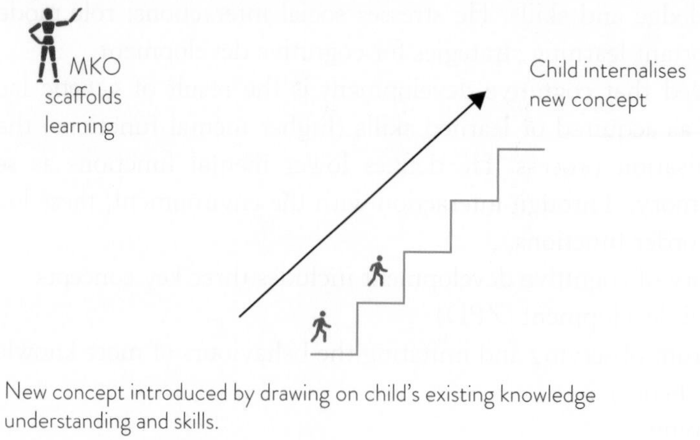

The role of language

Vygotsky's social learning theory emphasised that children learn as a result of interactions in the social world, and that language is critical to this learning process. To explain the relationship between language and learning, Vygotsky used two key terms:

1. **Private speech** (self-talk) used by a child for the purposes of self-direction, self-control and problem-solving. According to Vygotsky, language accelerates thinking and understanding – for example, 'Where is that brown horse? It can go in the truck. Where are you, brown horse? I can just take this white horse. Here you go, horse.'
2. **Public speech** (communicating with others), although still egocentric, is used primarily for communicating with others – for example, 'I'm going to draw a monster with two heads.'

According to Vygotsky's theory, children use language (private speech) to help internalise their knowledge and understanding of the world. Public speech is used to engage in meaningful interactions with MKOs who can assist children to reach a higher level of knowledge and understanding. He emphasised that language development occurs in a social and cultural context and that thought precedes language.

GO FURTHER

Learn how the theories of Vygotsky and Piaget compare in your **Go Further** resource, available through your instructor.

Jerome Bruner (1915–2016)

Bruner's constructivist theory focused on different modes of thinking used to organise knowledge. Bruner (1974) used the representation to describe three developmental modes of thinking:

1. **enactive** – learning through play and discovery (action-based)
2. **iconic** – creating mental images without the need for concrete materials (image-based)
3. **symbolic** – using abstract ideas (language-based).

Bruner believed that, through thinking, children engage in meaning-making. Like Vygotsky, Bruner believed learning is a social and cultural process.

Also similar to Vygotsky, Bruner believed that teacher scaffolding was necessary to assist in the learning process. He argued that children use existing knowledge to build new information by being engaged, active participants in their own learning. As new information is acquired, the child is required to engage in problem-solving and **inductive reasoning** in order to make sense of the new information, which can then be generalised and applied to other aspects of learning. Bruner referred to this process as assisted learning. He advocated that the process of learning allows children to explore, discover, make errors, investigate new possibilities and finally make connections to concepts.

Bruner advocated that learning new information should begin with existing knowledge and, through a process of scaffolding and discovery, lead to the acquisition of new knowledge. He called this model of teaching and learning the spiral curriculum, shown in **Figure 10.5**.

Figure 10.5 Bruner's spiral curriculum model

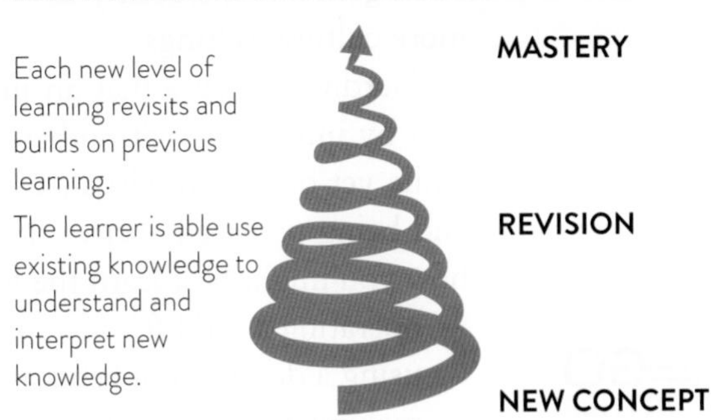

Each new level of learning revisits and builds on previous learning.
The learner is able use existing knowledge to understand and interpret new knowledge.
MASTERY
REVISION
NEW CONCEPT

The role of the educator in Bruner's theory is that of the intentional teacher, actively facilitating, guiding, supporting and challenging children to be active inquirers and learners. Bruner also emphasised the importance of children's self-esteem as a necessary characteristic for effective learning.

Bruner's theory of cognitive development is reflected in pedagogical practices in the classroom such as scaffolding learning and intentional teaching.

Using Bruner's theory in the classroom

Video: Bruner's three steps of learning in a spiral curriculum

Educators use Bruner's theory when they:

- introduce a new concept by building on an existing concept
- provide activities that allow students to explore concepts and make connections with their existing knowledge
- provide repetition which allows students to engage in problem-solving to consolidate their understanding of concepts
- engage students in problem-solving activities that lead to discovery. For example, what would happen if…?

Benjamin Bloom (1913–99)

Applying Bloom's taxonomy in the classroom

Bloom and his colleagues developed a set of three hierarchical, progressively complex processes in three key domains – cognitive domain (knowledge), affective domain (attitudes) and psychomotor domain (skills). Our focus here is on the cognitive domain (Bloom, 1956), which is commonly referred to as Bloom's taxonomy. Bloom's taxonomy classifies thought processes from simple to complex. The original classifications were knowledge, understanding, application, synthesis and evaluation. In 2001, Anderson and Krathwohl updated Bloom's original classifications. Known as Bloom's revised taxonomy, the current classifications are shown in **Figure 10.6**. **Figure 10.7** provides an example of action verbs that can be used at each level of Bloom's taxonomy.

Figure 10.8 shows examples of how Bloom's taxonomy can be applied to a lesson using action verbs.

Anderson and Krathwohl (2001) also added four classifications in relation to the knowledge dimension, and this is described in **Figure 10.9**. Moving from simple concrete to complex abstract, these classifications reflect the stages of development described by Piaget.

Howard Gardner (1950–)

The theory of multiple intelligences (MI) developed by Howard Gardner (1983, p. 34) defines intelligence as the ability to solve problems or to create products that are valued within one or more cultural settings.

Gardner believes that an individual's strengths influence how they learn. Some people learn best by interacting with others, others through reading, asking questions and utilising language, while yet others are visual, using diagrams and drawing and some need to learn through doing and being physically active. For example, if you did not have any prior knowledge, think about how you might best learn the following tasks:

- operating a forklift
- using a desktop publishing program
- making a ceramic pot
- making a stained-glass window.

GO FURTHER

Learn more about Gardner's spheres of intelligence in your **Go Further** resource, available through your instructor.

Some people might choose to observe the process and ask questions, followed by a period of supervised instruction; others may prefer to read about the process, be given verbal or written instructions, or learn by trial and error. For most people, hands-on learning is the most effective method when trying to master new skills, and the same principle applies to children.

Figure 10.6 Bloom's revised taxonomy

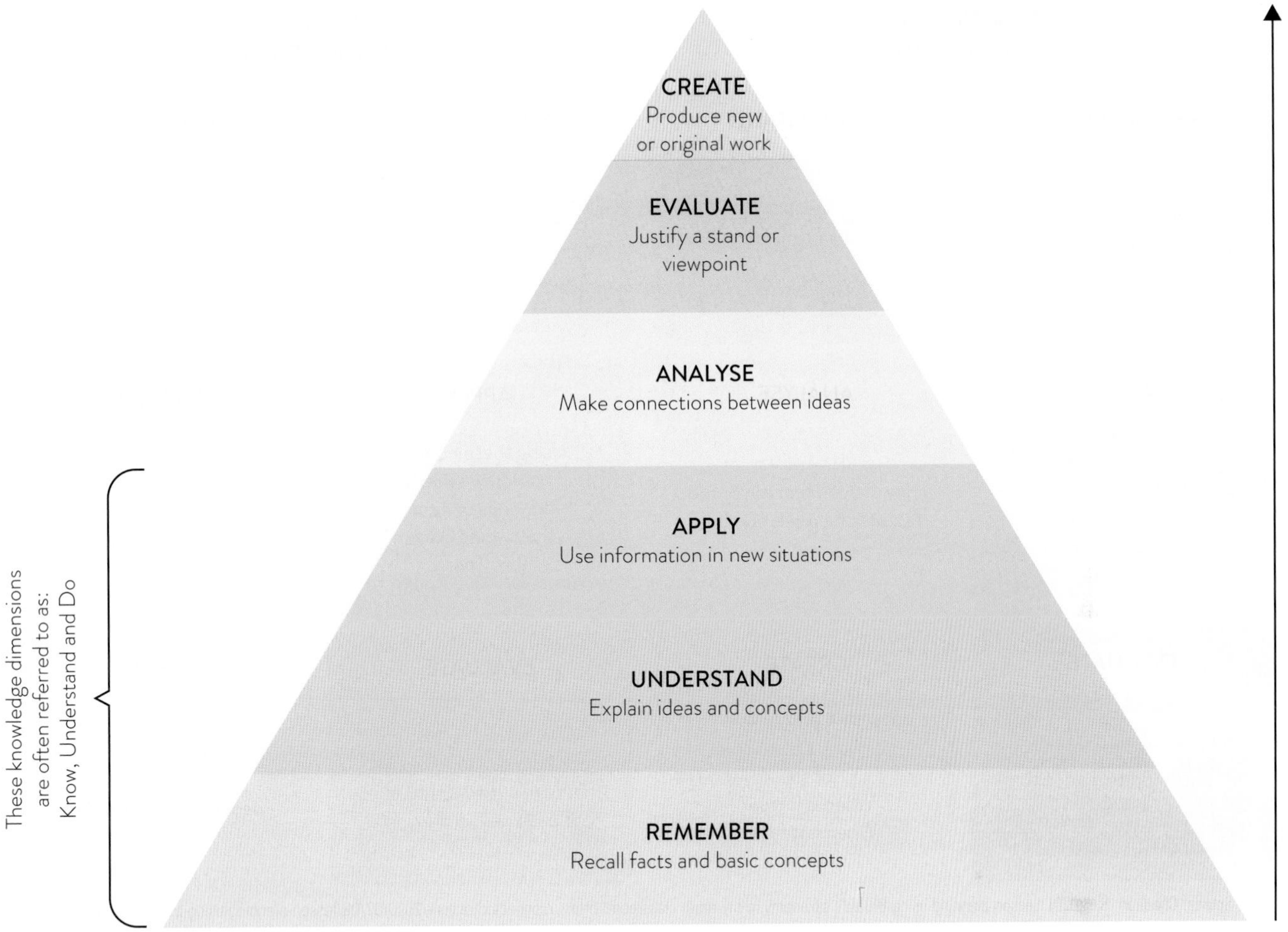

Figure 10.7 Action verbs related to Bloom's taxonomy

Remember	Understand	Apply	Analyse	Evaluate	Create
Retrieve relevant knowledge from long-term memory	Construct meaning from instructional messages, including oral, written and graphic communication	Carry out or use a procedure in a given situation	Break material into foundational parts and determine how parts relate to one another and the overall structure or purpose	Make judgements based on criteria and standards	Put elements together to form a coherent whole; reorganise into a new pattern or structure
Define, Describe, Draw, Identify, Label, List, Match, Memorise, Name, Record, Repeat, State, Write	*Add, Clarify, Compare, Contrast, Explain, Give, Infer, Observe, Predict, Summarise, Translate*	*Adapt, Assign, Calculate, Construct, Employ, Express, Illustrate, Modify, Show, Solve, Use*	*Characterise, Classify, Contrast, Distinguish, Explore, Identify, Investigate, Order, Prioritise*	*Appraise, Assess, Critique, Defend, Determine, Estimate, Explain, Grade, Justify, Rank, Rate*	*Abstract, Assemble, Combine, Compose, Construct, Correspond, Design, Develop, Generate, Integrate, Portray, Produce*

Source: Revised Bloom's taxonomy. https://www.celt.iastate.edu/teaching/effective-teaching-practices/revised-blooms-taxonomy; Cummins, S. (2019). A teacher's guide to Bloom's taxonomy. https://www.innovativeteachingideas.com/blog/a-teachers-guide-to-blooms-taxonomy

Figure 10.8 Lesson plans using Bloom's taxonomy

Prime Numbers using Bloom's Taxonomy

REMEMBERING	UNDERSTAND
What is a Factor? What are Prime numbers?	Why is 11 a Prime number?
APPLY	**ANALYSE**
What are the Prime factors of 135? Can a Prime number be a multiple of 6?	How do you find the prime factors of a given number?
EVALUATE	**CREATE**
Which numbers less than 100 have exactly three factors?	The sum of four even numbers is a multiple of six. When is it true? When is it false?

Area using Bloom's Taxonomy

REMEMBERING	UNDERSTAND
Estimating, measuring, comparing and recording the areas of surfaces in square units of a room.	Finding the area of a number of common household items such as top of tables, front face of door, wall and so on.
APPLY	**ANALYSE**
Using these findings to draw scale drawings of items they would like in their room.	Using their scale drawings to place the items in a given room with the maximum floor space remaining.
EVALUATE	**CREATE**
Calculating the amount of paint needed to repaint the room if they use 10 litres of paint per square unit.	Calculating the length of border tape required if they were to add a decorative panel on the wall.

Source: Chauhan, S. (2020). Lesson planning using Bloom's taxonomy in my math classroom. https://connectedtot.com/2020/07/08/lesson-planning-using-blooms-taxonomy-for-math

Figure 10.9 Progression of knowledge acquisition

Concrete knowledge	——→ Abstract knowledge
Factual	Knowledge of: *terminology* *specific details and elements*
Conceptual	Knowledge of: *classifications and categories* *principles and generalisations* *theories models, and structure*
Procedural	Knowledge of: *subject-specific techniques and algorithms* *subject-specific techniques and methods* *criteria for determining when to use appropriate procedures*
Metacognitive	Strategic knowledge *knowledge about cognitive tasks, including appropriate contextual and conditional knowledge* *self-knowledge*

Source: Iowa State University (2022). Revised Bloom's taxonomy. https://www.celt.iastate.edu/teaching/effective-teaching-practices/revised-blooms-taxonomy

Gardner (1993) emphasises the importance of providing opportunities for children to choose ways of learning to meet their particular intelligences. He describes nine spheres of intelligence and says an individual may have strengths in one or more of these spheres. He does not rate one type of intelligence as higher or lower than another. Gardner's nine spheres of intelligence are shown in **Figure 10.10**.

Figure 10.10 Gardner's nine spheres of intelligence

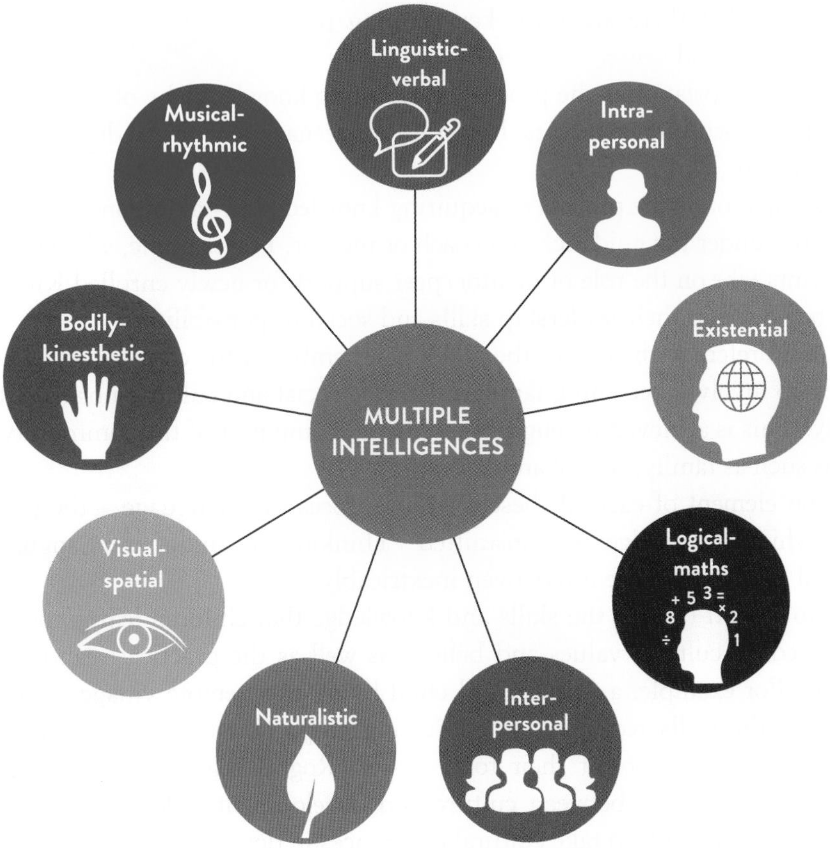

Multiple abilities

Gardner's theory demonstrates that intelligence is not a single trait, but involves multiple abilities that occur on a continuum. Gardner believes that individuals have a unique combination of each intelligence and may have outstanding strengths in one or more areas. An individual's particular blend of intelligences predisposes them to being suitable for a particular vocation or interest.

Video: Nine types of intelligence

Critics of Gardner's theory, including McGreal (2013), argue that no research evidence has been produced to support the theory of multiple intelligences. They argue that if nine spheres of intelligence exist, then there should be nine specific tests that can be used to measure them. Intelligence or spheres of knowledge tend to be integrated rather than segmented as suggested by the multiple intelligences theory. Gardner has not specifically defined what he means by 'intelligence' and has used the terms 'abilities', 'skills' and 'aptitudes' interchangeably when referring to his theory.

Barbara Rogoff (1950–)

Like Vygotsky, Rogoff (2003) regards cognitive development as sociocultural in nature. However, Rogoff (2003, p. 37) regards human development as 'a process in which people transform through their on-going participation in cultural activities'. Rather than culture influencing development, Rogoff argues that people and culture are inseparable, and that each transforms the other: 'Humans develop through their changing participation in the sociocultural activities of their communities, which also change' (p. 11).

Rogoff suggests that there are three key learning processes: **participatory appropriation**, **guided participation** and **apprenticeship**:

1. Participatory appropriation is the process of acquiring knowledge by observing and interacting in sociocultural activities. For example, teenagers copy the dress and language of their cultural icons.
2. Guided participation is the process of acquiring knowledge by taking on new roles and responsibilities under the guidance of a coach or mentor. For example, when senior primary school students take on the role of mentor/peer support for newly enrolled Kindergarten children, they develop their leadership skills and social responsibility.
3. Apprenticeship refers to the role of the child as a member of the community. The process of apprenticeship involves becoming familiar with the social and cultural norms of the community. This is achieved by engaging with and being part of the community through institutions such as family, school and church.

The common element of each of these learning processes is language – the primary cultural tool through which knowledge is transmitted. Thinking, learning and language, and their associated social interactions, are interwoven inextricably.

According to Rogoff (2003), the skills and knowledge that children learn, and when they are learned, are based on cultural values and beliefs, as well as the practical realities of family and community life. For example, a six-year-old child living in a remote village in Africa might be required to learn the skills required for cultivating crops or tending to cattle to support the family's livelihood and to protect their food source. Rogoff argues that much of the current thinking on the relationships between culture and development reflects a white, middle-class, Western perspective that fails to take cultural differences in development into account.

The work of Rogoff and others serves to challenge our traditional view of how children learn and develop. We can no longer assume that traditional developmental stages are universal, because clearly they are not. Rogoff proposes that in order for educators to understand each child's development, we need to look for what is the same and what is different in each child's culture compared with our own.

Rogoff also points to the dangers of generalising about larger groups of people according to the practices observed in a smaller community. Cultural practices are not only acquired as a result of living within a particular community; they can also be acquired because of deliberate choice. That is, each of us has the capacity to adopt new cultural beliefs and practices. Culture is a dynamic process of interactions where children learn through shared practices with members of their family and community.

Cognitive load theory

Cognitive load theory (CLT), developed by John Sweller (1988), addresses the brain's ability to process and store information in the short-term (working) memory. Cognitive overload refers to the amount of information that can be processed at any one time. CLT draws on the model of information processing developed by Atkinson and Shiffrin in 1968. This model is shown in **Figure 10.11**.

Figure 10.11 The 'store model of information processing'

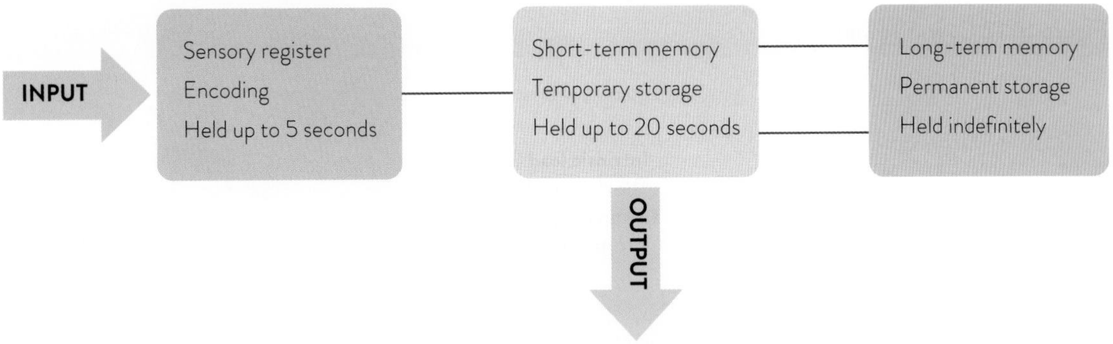

Information processing refers to the way in which information is collected, sorted, stored (in the short and long term) and recalled in a way that is meaningful and allows the individual to make sense of the world. This information processing draws on a number of abilities and skills, which include:

- knowledge of concepts and understanding of relationships
- understanding of the use of symbols such as spoken and written language
- concentration and attention span
- curiosity, intrinsic motivation and persistence
- problem-solving skills
- ability to make choices
- ability to observe, ask questions and evaluate ideas
- ability to work collaboratively with others.

An important part of information processing is the storage and retrieval of information so that it can be recalled easily (memory) when needed. Efficient use of the limited 'space' in the short-term memory relies on converting information into meaningful chunks that take up less 'space', allowing us to work on new information or deal with complex ideas.

Information processing helps us to:

- make connections between past and present experiences
- understand how things work
- make informed predictions or assessments
- label and group things
- generally make sense of the world.

The storage capacity of the working memory is typically limited in young adults to three to five meaningful items at any one time (Cowan, 2010). When the working memory is overloaded students will struggle to process new information.

The CLT has identified three types of cognitive load:

1. *Intrinsic*: this refers to the degree of complexity of the information.
2. *Extraneous*: this refers to the environment in which information is provided and the resources used to provide the information. In a typical classroom, the environment would be the classroom. Students are often distracted in the classroom by other students, movement, external noise, displays in the room and so on. The resources used to provide information may be digital, paper-based or by hands-on investigation. The types of resources used may also distract or overwhelm students. The degree of distraction directly impacts on the extraneous load.

3 *Germane*: this refers to the capacity of the student to draw on existing knowledge (long-term memory) to make sense of new knowledge. The Germane load can be likened to Piaget's schema and the process assimilation, accommodation, adaptation and equilibration.

The three types of cognitive load are shown in **Figure 10.12**.

Figure 10.12 Cognitive load

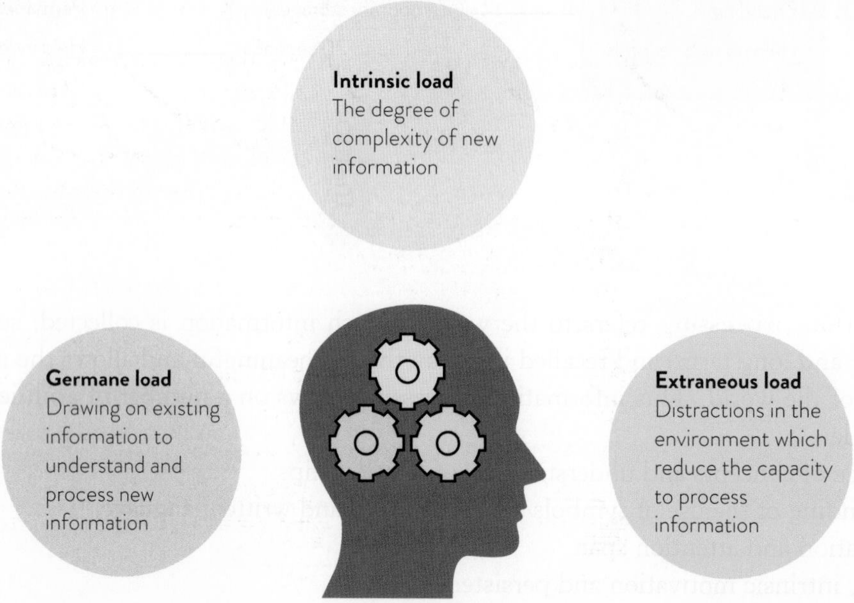

To reduce cognitive loading and maximise learning opportunities, educators can use a range of techniques, examples of which are shown in **Figure 10.13**.

Figure 10.13 Reducing cognitive loading

Unhurried time	Learning goal	Scaffold learning	Chunk information
Ensure there is sufficient time allocated to the lesson	Be clear and concise about the purpose of the lesson	Link new information to what students already know, understand and can do. Provide opportunities for hands-on learning and practice	Break information down into bite-size chunks
Highlight key information	**Declutter**	**Create a series of lessons**	**Use visuals**
Clearly indicate key information so that students aren't sidetracked by less relevant information	Don't include information that is not directly needed	Break down information and deliver it over several lessons; revisit previous lesson	Support new information by presenting it in different ways using visuals such as illustrations, diagrams and graphics

10.3 Cognitive development and the Australian Curriculum

The Australian Curriculum recognises key developmental principles underpinned by a range of development and learning theories. The curriculum is designed to allow students to develop knowledge, understanding and skills in a sequential manner, as highlighted in the following statements from the Australian Curriculum website:

> A considerable body of research shows that optimal learning occurs when learners are presented with challenges just beyond their current level of attainment. This is what Vygotsky (1978) referred to as the 'zone of proximal development' (Masters 2013, p. 15).
>
> Learning is conceptualised not simply as a matter of acquiring more knowledge and skills, but as progressing toward higher levels of competence as new knowledge is linked to existing knowledge, and deeper understandings are developed from, and take the place of, earlier understandings (Pellegrino, Chudowsky & Glaser 2001, p. 115).

Source: Australian Curriculum, Assessment and Reporting Authority (ACARA) (n.d.c). How were the progressions developed?

The curriculum also acknowledges that each student will develop at their own unique pace. This includes recognising that each student begins their school learning journey from a unique perspective; each student brings with them a unique set of social, emotional and cultural experiences; students present with a range of abilities; and students' ways of communicating will vary and may include augmentative and alternative communication.

Examples of how the Australian Curriculum reflects theories of learning and development are shown in **Figure 10.14** and **Figure 10.15**.

Figure 10.14 The Australian Curriculum and theories of learning and development

The curriculum samples reflect the following theories:

- Vygotsky: language is central to learning
- Bruner: new concepts are developed by building on existing concepts
- Piaget: development occurs in predictable stages; learning moves from simple to complex

	Foundation Year	Year 1	Year 1
Mathematics (number and algebra)	Connect number names, numerals and quantities, and position in the sequence of numbers from zero to at least 20	Recognise, represent and order numbers to at least 120, using physical and virtual materials, numerals, number lines and charts	Investigate number sequences, initially those increasing and decreasing by twos, threes, fives and tens from any starting point, then moving to other sequences
	Year 8	**Year 9**	**Year 10**
English (literacy)	Analyse and explain how language has evolved over time and how technology and the media have influenced language use and forms of communication	Analyse how the construction and interpretation of texts, including media texts, can be influenced by cultural perspectives and other texts	Analyse and evaluate how people, cultures, places, events, objects and concepts are represented in texts, including media texts, through language, structural and/or visual choices

Source: Australian Curriculum, Assessment and Reporting Authority (ACARA) (2022a).

Figure 10.15 The Australian Curriculum and theories of learning and development

The curriculum sample reflects	Personal, social and community health: Years 9 and 10
Bloom's revised taxonomy: • Know, understand and do • Action verbs Gardner's spheres of intelligence (learning in different ways) Piaget – children are hands-on learners	*Evaluate factors* that shape identities and *critically analyse* how individuals impact the identities of others *Examine* the impact of changes and transitions on relationships Critically *analyse and apply* health information from a range of sources to health decisions and situations

Understanding how media arts works: Years 7 and 8	Understand how English works: Years 3, 4 and 5
Analyse how technical and symbolic elements are used in media artworks to create representations influenced by story, genre, values and points of view of particular audiences Plan, structure and design media artworks that engage audiences	*Create* literary texts by developing storylines, characters and settings. *Interpret* ideas and information in spoken texts and listen for key points in order to carry out tasks and use information to share and extend ideas and information. *Clarify* understanding of content as it unfolds in formal and informal situations, connecting ideas to students' own experiences and present and justify a point of view.

Source: Australian Curriculum, Assessment and Reporting Authority (ACARA) (2022b). Personal, social and community health; Understanding how English works; Understanding Media Art

10.4 Memory, concept development and critical thinking

The ability to store, recall and retrieve information is central to learning. These processes are developed and refined over time and involve the integration of cognitive, language, social and physical skills. Children and young people must be able to be active participants in classroom tasks and discussion, follow directions, ask and respond to questions, understand and respect that others may have views that are different from their own, listen, pay attention and stay on task.

Memory and recall

Vygotsky believed that the young child's ability to think was bound by their ability to remember. He argued that thinking and remembering were one and the same thing, and that young children's perception of the world was based on their memory of their own concrete experiences. According to Vygotsky, young children's thinking did not involve logic but rather the recall of information.

Some people believe they have a good memory and are easily able to recall things while others consider themselves to have poor memories. However, the person who has a 'good memory' is not necessarily smarter than the person who has a 'poor memory'. Some people can remember faces but not names, or they can remember events but not dates. Others have good verbal recall while others have better visual recall. **Figure 10.16** outlines the main strategies used for remembering.

Figure 10.16 Common strategies involved in remembering

Strategy	Description
Rehearsal	> Involves either mental or verbal repetition, or repetition of movement (such as learning to kick a goal or dance)
Clustering or encoding	> Grouping ideas, objects or words into clusters to help you to remember them – for example, 'all animals'; 'all ingredients used to make a chocolate cake'
Elaboration	> Finding shared meaning or a common reference for two or more things – for example, using a rhyme such as 'Every Good Boy Deserves Fruit' to remember the lines on the treble musical staff, or by associating the name of an object or person > This skill is usually not developed until the late primary or early high school years
Systematic searching	> Involves scanning your memory to search for the required information. For example, you think back and 'relive' a situation or conversation in order to better recall specific facts; you may visualise a scene in your head in order to better describe it to another person > This skill is usually not acquired until late primary school age
Retrieval	> Involves recognition (the clues presented help you to recognise prior experiences) or recall (involves reproducing the information from memory without any clues). For example, if asked, you may not be able to recall the names of the main actors in a recent movie. However, if given a clue – such as multiple-choice answers – you may be able to correctly answer because the clues have prompted your memory > Recognition is easier to achieve than recall, and is used at all levels of development

Existing knowledge, prior experience and interest all play a part in the ability to remember. For example, a five-year-old may be able to recall the correct names of most dinosaurs because this subject is an interest at that particular time, but may have limited recall of this skill by age seven or eight, when dinosaurs are no longer a passion.

Video: The processes of memory

Long-term memory is the largest structure in the cognitive system, and some research suggests we never lose the information stored in the long-term memory; the challenge is to retrieve it at the appropriate time.

Vialle, Lysaght and Verenikina (2005, pp. 85–6) describe three different 'remembering processes' for retrieving information, which seem to occur automatically:

1. *Recognition.* This is an automatic process requiring only a response to a stimulus – for example, the smell of freshly mown grass may instantly take you back to a childhood memory, or a song on the radio may remind you of a significant period in your life.
2. *Recall.* This relies on remembering an absent stimulus (improves with age) – for example, recalling information that has been learned by rote, such as multiplication tables, the order of the planets or the colours of the rainbow.
3. *Reconstruction.* This a process for the storage of information that depends on our existing knowledge base, which in turn influences how we construct information through our memory – for example, learning about child development can be enhanced by drawing on our existing knowledge and life experiences.

Concept development

Concept development requires the ability to recognise relationships between objects and things, apply meaning to objects and things, and apply reasoning skills to sort and assign objects and things. It requires the ability to reason, interpret, deduce and think creatively (see **Figure 10.17**).

Figure 10.17 A student learning the concept of measurement

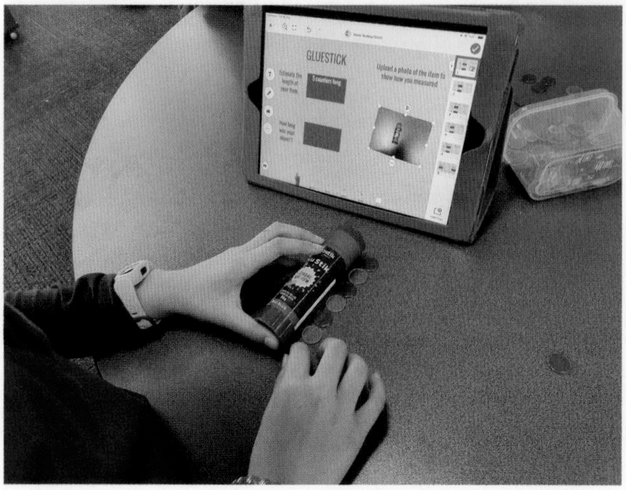

Source: Photo by Tish Okely © Cengage

Concept development is both a cognitive and a language skill. Concepts help us to organise, manage and filter many pieces of information in a meaningful and efficient manner. They allow us to group and sort information based on common attributes.

Concepts develop over time and rely on children drawing on their existing knowledge and reasoning skills to develop new knowledge and understandings. Concept development moves from specific to general – for example, from being able to recognise and label food such as 'apple, orange, banana, pear' to understanding that this collection of food represents fruit. A young child who does not yet have the concept of fruit would be asked, 'Would you like an apple or an orange?' A child who has the concept of fruit would be asked, 'Would you like a piece of fruit?' The skills required for concept development include matching (Can you find the matching sock?), identification (Which object is a square?), naming (What shape is this?), seriating (light to dark/short to tall, wide to narrow) and classifying by one or more attributes (Put all of the large, red, blocks into this container and all of the small red blocks into the other container).

Video: Concept-based learning

Early concept development includes:

- spatial awareness
- symbolic relationships
- quantity, rote and rational counting
- time
- functional relationships (sorting, matching, classifying)
- ordering and seriation
- temporal ordering
- cause and effect.

GO FURTHER

Learn more about each of these eight stages of concept development in your **Go Further** resource, available through your instructor.

Critical and creative thinking

Doyla (2010) suggests that supporting cognitive development in children must focus on higher-order mental functions, and that these can only be developed when adults actively engage with children to support and extend their understandings. Higher-order or critical thinking skills include, for example:

- *mediated perceptions* – for example, distinguishing different shades of green
- *focused attention* – for example, the ability to deliberately focus on one thing to the exclusion of other things present in the environment
- *deliberate memory* – for example, using deliberate strategies to remember something, such as creating a rhyme (i before e except after c)
- *logical thinking* – for example, working through a problem in a planned step-by-step sequence
- *mediation* – for example, recognising the universal meaning of signs and symbols, such as understanding that a skull and cross-bones symbol means 'danger', or an equals (=) sign means 'the same as' (Bodrova & Leong, 2007, pp. 19–20).

Higher-order functions are learned functions that are deliberate, mediated (defining thinking) and internalised behaviours and are reflected in the Australian Curriculum general capability 'Critical and Creative Thinking' (see **Figure 10.18**).

The Critical and Creative Thinking capability includes four elements that are organised into 10 sub-elements, as shown in **Figure 10.19**.

Figure 10.18 The elements of the Critical and Creative Thinking capability

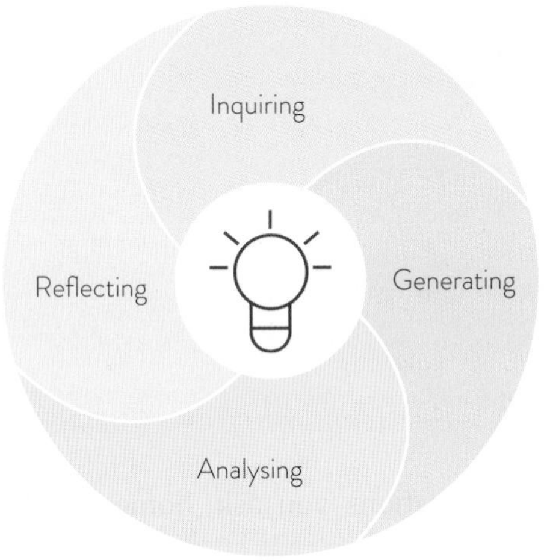

Source: Australian Curriculum, Assessment and Reporting Authority (ACARA) (2023). Critical and creative thinking.

Figure 10.19 Sub-elements of the Critical and Creative Thinking capability

Elements	Sub-elements
Inquiring	> Develop questions > Identify, process and evaluate information
Generating	> Create possibilities > Consider alternatives > Put ideas into action
Analysing	> Interpret concepts and problems > Draw conclusions and provide reasons > Evaluate actions and outcomes
Reflecting	> Think about thinking (metacognition) > Transfer knowledge

Source: Australian Curriculum, Assessment and Reporting Authority (ACARA). (2023). Critical and creative thinking.

Using questions to support creative and critical thinking

Teachers will use a range of questioning strategies to support creative and critical thinking. **Figure 10.20** demonstrates the different scenarios to which they could be applied.

Figure 10.20 Questioning strategies

Type of question	Examples
Reasoning questions Require a student to form relationships of cause and effect, comparison or classification. Reasoning questions challenge students' thinking and encourage investigation and exploration.	'What things go together?/ Why do they go together?' 'What does ... mean?' 'Look at these words; tell me some things about the words that are the same.' 'What is the difference between a soccer ball and a football/a cricket bat and a tennis racquet?'
Creative questions Encourage students to think beyond the ideas and concepts they have developed. Creative questions promote thinking and engage the student in exchanging ideas, problem-solving, hypothesising and imagining.	'How would you ...?' 'What would you do if ...?' 'Suppose ...' 'If ... what would ...?' 'What will happen if ...?' 'How do you think the story is going to end?' 'What do you think the boys could do?' 'What would happen if you were allowed to eat lollies for breakfast, lunch and dinner?' 'Suppose we ran out of water – what would we do?'

Type of question	Examples
Valuing questions Questions that require students to express an opinion, use their imagination, solve problems and to think more deeply in order to express their thoughts and emotions.	'How do you feel when ...?' 'Some people believe Australia should not take refugees. What do you think?' 'If you could invent anything you liked, what would it be?' 'How do you feel when you wake up at night and the house is quiet?' 'If you could only have three foods to eat for 12 months, which foods would you choose? Why?' 'What do you think it will be like going to high school?'
Information questions Encourage students to research facts. Information questions allow teachers to gain insight into the students' existing knowledge and challenge students to investigate and research.	'Where could you find more information about ...?' 'How could you see whether your answer is correct?' 'What can you do to fix this problem?' 'Why do you think the politicians made this decision?' 'Where do butterflies go at night?' 'How does a spider make a web?'
Non-cognitive questions Relate to areas such as management and control, or are rhetorical questions that require a one- or two-word response.	'Does anyone have a question?' 'Have you finished packing away the maths games?' 'How are you today?' 'Has everyone read the question?'

How you answer a question is just as important as the questions you ask. Some tips for answering questions include:

- Make sure the language you use is at the student's level.
- Show genuine interest – look at the student and use the student's name.
- When asked confronting questions, try to reply truthfully and objectively.
- If necessary, after responding, check that the student has understood your response.
- Where appropriate, engage the student in conversation/discussion.

Critical thinking allows children and young people to explore, evaluate and consider alternatives.

SUPPORT HIGHER-ORDER THINKING

SCENARIO

ESW **Evan** is working with a group of Year 7 students to research issues around global warming. Two students, **Liam** and **Jess**, have researched information on the internet, cutting and pasting various texts without using references. The information is jumbled and disjointed.

To support the students, Evan asks Liam and Jess the following questions:

- Which sections of your information do you consider to be most relevant?
- How did you decide which information was most relevant?
- What could you do to check the accuracy of the information?
- Who provided the information? Could the source be in some way biased?
- What gaps do you have in your information?

▶ DISCUSSION

Consider the questions Evan asks the students and explain how they might help the students to organise their information.

Developmental red flags

Specific difficulties in cognitive development can be attributed to a range of factors which are often associated with cognitive disorders – for example, attention-deficit hyperactivity disorder (ADHD), aphasia, dyslexia, dyscalculia and autism spectrum disorder (ASD). Cognitive delays can also be genetic, or the result of an acquired brain injury, serious illness or exposure to toxins.

Concerns about students who have not been diagnosed with cognitive difficulties or delays, may present with behaviours that are atypical for their age/stage of development. Such behaviours may include, for example:

- difficulty paying attention; may appear vague
- easily distracted
- poor memory
- unable to predict and follow daily routines; disorganised
- unable to follow 2-3-step directions
- unable to understand simple cause and effect
- struggling with listening, reading, writing and comprehension
- poor language skills, limited vocabulary for age.

Often the student will present with a number of red flags and may have difficulties in other developmental areas. It is important to observe the child over a period of time to establish if the child persistently presents with behaviour concerns. Cognitive delays and how to support these students will be explored in later chapters.

10.5 Introduction to language development

Language and cognitive development are intricately interwoven, with each domain supporting the development of the other domain. According to Vygotsky (1978), the acquisition of language is the most significant milestone in children's cognitive development. Vygotsky also emphasised that language development occurs in a social context and that children begin to generalise the meaning of words when they are heard repeatedly in a meaningful context.

Language usually is defined as a system of symbols that are combined using a set of rules. For example, the English language uses 26 symbols (letters), 20 vowel sounds and 24 consonant sounds or phonemes. There are over 300 ways of combining letters into sequences to make distinct sounds and around 1000 rules of syntax that dictate how words must be connected to one another to convey meaning. The average adult has a vocabulary in excess of 50 000 words as well as a large repertoire of non-verbal language. By the time children start formal school, they have many of the cognitive skills needed to be logical and independent thinkers; they have mastered the complexities of spoken language and use it to express their thoughts and feelings, and to function successfully in the social world.

Language development is not simply learning about the rules of grammar or developing a vocabulary: it is a social tool used to transmit cultural values, beliefs and practices. It is used to develop relationships with others, to convey meaning, and to share and exchange information, emotions, ideas and thoughts.

The brain is hardwired for language acquisition – the development of language is instinctive and does not require direct instruction. Children learn language by being immersed in it. The environment is critical for shaping and supporting language and cognitive development – the quality and timing of exposure to language will affect the rate and proficiency of language acquisition.

In relation to language development, neuroscience tells us that:

- learning to produce the sounds that will eventually result in language is not completely mastered until around the age of eight years
- babies and young children are better language learners when compared with adults, despite adults' cognitive superiority
- language acquisition is one of the classic examples of a 'critical' or 'sensitive' period of brain development
- the developmental timing of critical periods for learning the mechanics of language varies
- language learning is both a cognitive and social process.

Speech and language: the same or different?

Speech and language are two separate but closely related areas of development. **Speech** is divided into two key areas:

1. **articulation** – the ability to produce speech vowels and consonants
2. **quality of voice** – this refers to how speech sounds when it is spoken. Is the voice loud, soft, husky, fluid, fast, slow or hesitant, or does the voice sound just right? Quality of voice becomes a problem if it is difficult for the child to be understood or if it interferes with the child's ability to interact effectively. Physical problems with the mouth or throat, or a hearing impairment, will affect quality of voice.

Language development refers to how children understand, organise, speak and use words in order to communicate at an effective, age-appropriate level. Language development is divided into two areas: **receptive language** and **expressive language**, as described in **Figure 10.21**.

Figure 10.21 Receptive and expressive language

Receptive language	Expressive language
> Refers to how well the child understands what is said > Develops well before the ability to use spoken language. Babies and toddlers have the ability to understand and respond to spoken language before they are able to use words > Is dependent on the developing brain processing and understanding messages	> Is the ability to communicate thoughts and needs to others so they can be understood > Refers to both verbal and non-verbal communication

Alongside the acquisition of verbal language, children also acquire non-verbal communication skills. Non-verbal communication includes gestures, facial expressions and whole-body movements. Non-verbal communication is used by all cultures and is often a very powerful way of expressing ideas, beliefs and emotions. Bates (1976, cited in Bochner & Jones, 2003) suggests that babies use gestures to express meaning in two ways:

1. to indicate the existence of something (object, person or event), sometimes referred to as deictic gestures
2. to represent things that are known to exist, as in outstretched arms to signify an aeroplane, or for culturally defined meanings such as waving the hand for hello/goodbye.

Factors that influence language development

Theorists and research have identified that language development occurs in a predictable, universal sequence, which moves from simple to complex with earlier development laying the foundation for later development. The rate at which language develops may vary from one child to another. Variations in language acquisition will occur for a variety of reasons, such as sociocultural or physiological factors, life experience and family situation.

Sociocultural context

Language is an integral aspect of culture, and the process of acquiring language is similar across all cultures. Each culture has its own meanings, values and practices in relation to language, which are acquired as part of the socialisation and enculturation process that begins at birth. Language is not simply a form of communication. While children learn the social and cultural functions of language and rules for speaking, language also helps them to learn to understand and make sense of human behaviour.

Rogoff (2003, p. 310) reminds us that while language is universal, the ways in which language is used to communicate vary between cultures: 'everywhere, people use words, silence, gestures, and gaze skilfully to communicate. Yet there also appear to be important differences in how much people talk and in how articulately they communicate non-verbally.'

Young children whose first language is not that of the dominant culture are not necessarily disadvantaged in relation to language development. Bilingualism will be explored in **Chapter 19**.

Physiological influences

To develop oral language, children depend on their ability to hear sounds, differentiate sounds and link meaning to specific words. However, they also require the ability to concentrate, pay attention and interact socially in a meaningful way (National Scientific Council on the Developing Child, 2007b). As a result, any difficulties or disorders related to speech, hearing, vision or cognitive functioning will impact language development.

Shonkoff and Phillips (2000) suggest that there are three types of deviations from the norm that might be expected to have effects on the language-learning process:

1. deviations in the environment that affect the quantity or quality of the linguistic input received by children (e.g. children raised under conditions of relative deprivation of access to linguistic input)
2. deviations in the organism that affect the way children process their linguistic input (e.g. intermittent conductive hearing loss, which affects the way the child processes speech)
3. deviations in the organism that affect the general endowment (capability) of the learner (e.g. children with Down syndrome or children with autism spectrum disorder).

Life experiences

Language development is shaped by the life experiences to which children are exposed. Children who are left alone for long periods of time and are seldom involved in meaningful conversation, and those who have limited exposure to books and stories, are unlikely to acquire language at the same rate as children of a similar age who have been exposed to a language-rich environment and have had a variety of stimulating life experiences:

> From early infancy, [children] naturally reach out for interaction through such behaviours as babbling, making facial expressions, and uttering words, and they develop best when caring adults respond in warm, individualized, and stimulating ways. In contrast when the environment is impoverished, neglectful, or abusive, the result can be a lifetime of increased risk for impairment in learning, behaviour, and health. (National Scientific Council on the Developing Child, 2007a, p.3)

The National Scientific Council on the Developing Child (2007a) confirms that children from socially and educationally disadvantaged backgrounds are less likely to use language for reporting, logical reasoning, anticipating, predicting, recognising problems and reflecting on solutions, and considering the feelings and needs of others. They are also less likely to use language to enrich imaginative play.

The family

The family is the most powerful influence on a child's language development. From birth, the family immerses the child in language. It is within this context that language develops. The quality and timing of exposure to language will affect the rate and proficiency of language acquisition. Families teach children that language can be used in different ways, for example:

- talking is a way of exploring boundaries, finding out information and sharing ideas
- talking is used as a strategy for informing and enriching
- words are used to reassure and comfort
- talking is limited to giving directions
- asking questions leads to conflict, and explanations are not encouraged
- talking may be used as a weapon to upset, humiliate or hurt people.

Physical, social, emotional and cognitive development contribute to, and impact on, language development. Each child will develop language skills at their own pace, and there will be many individual differences in the rate and quality of language acquisition based on culture, ethnicity, health and ability.

GO FURTHER

Find out more about theories of language development in your **Go Further** resource, available through your instructor.

Theories of language development

Traditional theories of language development are generally divided into four perspectives – **nativist**, **cognitivist**, **behaviourist** and **interactionist** – with each contributing to our understanding of how language develops. The theories of language development are briefly described in **Figure 10.22**.

10.6 The process of language

Language is used to communicate a message to the listener. It is useful for educators to be aware of the functions of language to help children to develop the skills they will need to communicate clearly. Halliday (1973, cited in Campbell & Baker, 2006), identified seven functions of language (see **Figure 10.23**). An awareness of these functions of language can be used by ESWs to scaffold children's communication skills by modelling language – demonstrating the function and social aspects of language as a tool for communication.

Figure 10.22 Theories of language development

Nativist

Language is naturally acquired through the presence of a language acquisition device (LAD) that is present from birth.

e.g., Chomsky

Interactionist

Language is acquired as a result of interactions between the environment and (a) information processing and (b) social interactions.

e.g., Bruner, Vygotsky (social constructivist)

Cognitivist

Language is acquired through the process of thinking.

e.g., Piaget

Behaviourist

Language is acquired by operant conditioning – imitation and reinforcement.

e.g., Skinner

Source: (image) iStock.com/Ridofranz

Figure 10.23 The functions of language

Function	Description
Instrumental The 'I want' function	Language is used to get things, to satisfy personal needs.
Regulatory The 'Do as I tell you' function	Language is used to control the behaviour of others.
Interactional The 'Me and you' function	Language is used to begin or maintain interactions.

Function	Description
Personal The 'Here I come' function	Language is used to express awareness of self and personal feelings.
Heuristic The 'Tell me why' function	Language is used to find information and names, to seek knowledge, and to learn the how and why of people, things and events.
Imaginative The 'Let's pretend' function	Language is used to create new worlds, and is used and learned from stories.
Informative The 'I've got something to tell you' function	Language is used to communicate information and express propositions.

Source: Adapted from Campbell & Baker (2006), p. 34.

The components of language

The study of language includes a range of elements, all of which contribute to the literacy skills of reading and writing. We know that language, social and cognitive development are intricately and complexly intertwined. Language is organised hierarchically, from phonemes to morphemes to phrases and sentences that communicate meaning. Obviously, verbal communication requires the production of speech.

To understand language development, it's important to be familiar with the elements shown in **Figure 10.24** and the part they play in both language and literacy development:

Figure 10.24 Elements of language

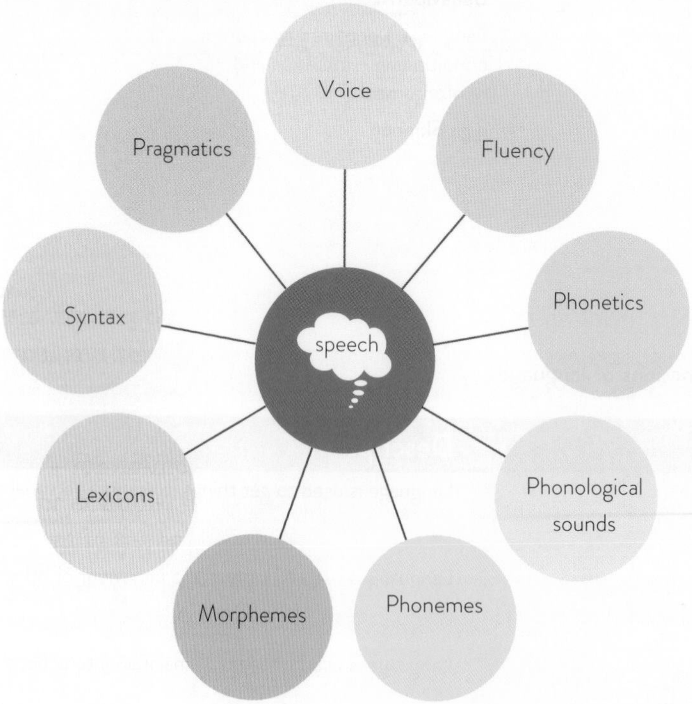

Speech is the production of meaningful sounds to create words that can be understood. Speech consists of three components (voice, fluency and articulation), which must work together in order to produce meaningful sounds.

Voice is the use of the vocal cords to produce sounds. Voice production includes volume (loud to soft), pitch (high to low), quality of sound (clear, rough, hoarse, croaky, strained, breathy) and resonance. **Voice disorders** in children may include talking too loudly, hoarseness, breathiness or weak voice.

Fluency is the rhythm, rate and smoothness of speech. In the typically developing child, each of these components develops naturally over time as the child is immersed in the language of their culture. Common **fluency disorders** include stammering and stuttering, where there is a disruption to the flow of speech due to repetition of sounds, words or phrases.

Articulation is the ability to produce speech sounds. Articulation consists of the following elements:

- *Phonetics* is the physical production of correct sounds, both vowels and consonants to create words; it requires the coordination of the tongue, jaw, lips, teeth and vocal folds. Children with an articulation disorder have difficulty producing the correct sounds; sounds may be substituted or left off, for example, 'ick' instead of 'sick'; 'wabbit' instead of 'rabbit'.
- *Phonology* is the sets of sounds of a particular language. The term phonological awareness is used to describe the ability to be aware of and to manipulate these sounds to produce words.

Phonemes are the smallest distinguishable units in a language that allow us to distinguish a word. Phonemes such as sh, th, oo, ch include combinations of vowels (speech sounds a/e/i/o/u/ sometimes y) and consonants (all other letters of the alphabet). The number of phonemes in any language can vary from around 10 to around 140. There are 44 phonemes in the English language. **Figure 10.25** shows the typical order of phonemic development in English.

Figure 10.25 Order of phonemic development in the English language

Age	Consonants generally acquired	Predictable errors
One to two years	p, m, n, w, h	Omissions of final consonants – 'ca' for 'cat' Substitutions for consonants – 'pall' for 'ball' Reduction of consonant blends – 'sore' for 'store' By two years, intelligibility of 60 per cent
Two to four years	b, d, k, g, f, y	Omission of medial consonants – 'birhouse' for 'birdhouse' Substitutions – 'peder' for 'feather' By four years, intelligibility of 90 per cent
Five to six years	t, ing, r, l	Errors with difficult blends – 'stap' for 'strap' Substitution of 'r' for 'l' – 'yerrow' for 'yellow'
Six to seven years	voiceless th, sh, ch, j	Distortion and substitutions – 'tink' for 'think', 'gar' for 'jar'
Seven to eight years	voiced th, v, z, zh	Substitution of voiceless pair for voiced pair – 'soo' for 'zoo', 'wash' for 'watch' By seven years, 100 per cent intelligibility

Source: Sowers (2000), p. 60.

Morphemes are the smallest meaningful units in a language. Some single morphemes are words, such as 'I' and 'a', while other words have two or more morphemes within them. Morphemes are meaningful parts of words, such as prefixes, suffixes and word stems. For example, the word 'disabled' can be broken up into three morphemes: 'dis', 'able' and 'ed'. Morphemes also indicate ownership (brother's); plurality (shoes); time of occurrence or tense (walks, walking, walked); and comparisons (longer, longest). Other morphemes include prefixes (such as 'anti' or 'dis') and suffixes (such as 'ist' or 'ism'). Morphemes also include irregular past tense verbs such as 'ran', 'gone', 'drank', 'ate' or 'slept'.

Until children learn the correct morphemes, they often make substitutions by applying rules in a universal manner. For example, a three-year-old might say, 'We wented to the shops and Mummy buyed me some new shoes!' A six-year-old might say, 'We went to the shops and Mummy buyed me some new shoes!'. An eight-year-old might say, 'We went to the shops and Mum bought me a new pair of shoes!'

Figure 10.26 shows the typical order of morphological development in the English language.

Figure 10.26 Morphological development in the English language

Morpheme	Grammatical use	Example
-ing	To indicate current actions; used in present progressive verbs	Me play*ing*. No eat*ing*.
-s	To indicate more than one of something; used as a plural noun marker	Big birds. Dogs eating birds.
-'s	To indicate ownership; used as a possessive marker	Taylor's room. Baby's bed.
-ed	To indicate past action; used as a tense marker of verbs	Outside play*ed*. Stay*ed* home.
Entire word	To indicate past action; used as irregular verbs	Baby *ran* away. The girl *ate*.

Source: Sowers (2000), p. 60.

Lexicons are the vocabulary of a particular language. All languages have a lexicon for words such as 'mother' or 'father', but not all languages have lexicons for more complex concepts or specific technical names like 'discrimination', 'democracy' or 'computer'. For example, the Japanese lexicon 'on' is one's responsibility to a kindness that has been done and can never be repaid. There is no single equivalent word in the English language. Lexicons are often borrowed and assimilated from other languages for example, lasagne, kimono and khaki.

The sequence of single words usually appears in the following order: nouns, verbs, adjectives and prepositions. **Figure 10.27** lists the order of development of prepositions and adjectives.

Syntax refers to the system of rules that governs how words can be meaningfully arranged to form phrases and sentences. In the English language, the general rule of syntax is subject (S) first, then the verb (V) and the object (O) last – for example, 'The boy (S) sat (V) on the horse (O)'. As children begin to construct sentences, they may get the word order wrong, for example, 'Daddy car goned' instead of 'Daddy [has] gone [in the] car'. Learning syntax is a developmental task that most children achieve by the age of seven or eight years.

Figure 10.27 Order of lexicon development: prepositions and adjectives in the English language

Phase	Prepositions
1	in, on, under, beside
2	behind, in front of – objects with visible front and back
3	behind, in front of – relationships between people and objects
	Adjectives
1	big, small – to represent any aspect of size
2	tall, short – to describe one dimension of size long, short, high, low
3	thick, thin – to describe a second dimension of size wide, narrow deep, shallow

Source: Sowers (2000), p. 62.

Confusing syntax can change the intended meaning of a message. For example, in the above example, is the child noticing that Daddy's car is missing or that Daddy has gone in the car? **Figure 10.28** describes the order of syntactical development in English.

Figure 10.28 Order of syntactical development in the English language

Length of phrase	Example	Age typically developed
One word	'Drink'	12–18 months
Two words	'Drink gone'	18–24 months
Three words	'More drink me'	24–36 months
Four or more words	'I drink very many milks'	36–42 months

Source: Sowers (2000), p. 64.

Pragmatics, or social language, is the ability to communicate effectively with others for a range of purposes and in a range of situations. Most children require direct training to develop and later refine their pragmatic skills over time. Some children and young people, such as those on the autism spectrum or who have a hearing impairment, may require intensive training. Children and young people who are non-verbal can engage in social language using augmentative and alternative communication.

Verbal language pragmatics are centred around conversational skills. This includes **intent of communication**, which is the ability to generate information such as commenting, asking questions or negotiating in an age-appropriate manner, and **frequency of communication**, which involves engaging in back-and-forth exchange so that one person is not dominating the interaction – for example, active listening and turn-taking, introducing and maintaining a topic and addressing any misunderstanding of what is being communicated.

Pragmatic skills

Politeness and recognition of social roles when communicating are also central in pragmatics. For example, if a student wanted help with a task, they would be expected to ask politely: 'Can you please help me with …?' Recognition of social roles simply refers to how we might automatically vary the way we address others based on their perceived status or relationship to the speaker. For example, we speak differently when addressing partners, children, doctors, police or someone unknown. A central element is the ability to consider and respect the perspective of others, including knowing the level of detail required when communicating with others so that our message is understood – for example, judging when to add detail while at the same time not including irrelevant information.

In addition to verbal communication, children and young people must learn how to recognise, interpret and use non-verbal communication – for example, making eye contact when speaking (this is a culturally based practice), using gestures and facial expressions, recognising and respecting personal space, and understanding social conventions such as not talking on a mobile phone while engaged in a conversation with another person or not interrupting the speaker.

Pragmatics is arguably one of the most challenging skills of communication. Much of what we expect of children and young people in relation to pragmatics is not directly and deliberately taught, but rather acquired through observation, imitation and interactions with family and in a variety of social settings.

Children and young people who have good role models will acquire most pragmatic skills at an age-appropriate level; however, they will still need direction and instruction to refine their skills (adapted from Vicker, 2009).

As you are aware, both Bruner and Vygotsky emphasised the importance of oral language as critical for the development of thinking and learning. Oral language is an essential tool for learning and is crucial for later reading skills development. For example, it is used to share information, give directions, convey emotions, share ideas and problem-solve. While children don't always get the rules of language correct (e.g. wented, goed, feets), the ability to understand that these rules exist demonstrates the brain's ability to notice and make sense of language and speech patterns. Oral language will be explored in **Chapters 13** and **14**.

Understanding the many elements of language and speech is not easy and takes time to acquire. A handy summary of the key elements of language and speech is shown in **Figure 10.29**.

Figure 10.29 Components of language and speech

Component	Description
Speech	The production of meaningful sounds to create words that can be understood
Voice	The use of the vocal cords to produce sounds
Fluency	The rhythm, rate and smoothness of speech
Articulation	The ability to produce speech sounds
Phonetics	The physical act of producing or making sounds, both vowels and consonants
Phonological sounds, or phonemes	The sets of sounds of a particular language
Morphemes	The smallest meaningful units in a language
Lexicon	The vocabulary of a particular language
Syntax	The system of rules that governs how words can be meaningfully arranged to form phrases and sentences
Pragmatics	Social language, is the ability to communicate effectively with others for a range of purposes and in a range of situations

10.7 Progression of language development

Like all other domains of development, language typically develops in a predictable and sequential manner. However, the quality of language development is dependent on the environment. Babies, toddlers and young children need to be exposed to frequent verbal and non-verbal interactions with nurturing adults to support optimum language development. Like other domains of development, language does not develop in isolation. Cognitive and social factors play a critical role in the development of language.

Language and brain development

Neuroscience confirms that early experiences shape brain development, including the development of language. Mustard (2008) highlights that the brain continues to develop over time, and this development is influenced by the interactions between genetics and the environment. Experience in early life affects gene expression and function, and neutral pathways. It shapes:

- temperament and social development
- language and literacy capability
- perceptual and cognitive ability
- how we cope with our daily experiences
- physical and mental health and behaviour, and addiction in adult life
- physical activity and performance.

Neuroscience has allowed researchers to learn more about the acquisition of language. Some key findings are listed in the Consider this box.

CONSIDER THIS

LANGUAGE ACQUISITION RESEARCH FINDINGS

- All babies are born with the innate capacity to acquire language.
- The foetus can hear by the third trimester of pregnancy.
- A newborn baby can recognise their mother's voice.
- Babies babble the same sounds in the same order across all cultures.
- At birth, the brain is wired to acquire any language but by 12 months the ability to distinguish the sounds of a foreign language is greatly diminished.
- The brain codes and remembers the patterns of the baby's native language.
- By six months babies can recognise the individual vowels and consonants of their native language.
- By nine months they can recognise patterns of words.
- There is a critical period for the acquisition of language, which diminishes as the child matures.
- The baby's abilities to distinguish speech sounds and patterns at six months of age correlates with later language abilities, that is, early speech skills predict later language skills.
- There is a strong correlation between oral language skills and later reading development.

Figure 10.30 provides a summary of the typical progression of language acquisition (reflecting a Western sociocultural perspective) that occurs by the time children reach Year 2.

Figure 10.30 Summary of the approximate ages of language acquisition

<table>
<tr><th>Approx. age</th><th>Overview of how language develops</th></tr>
<tr><td>Birth to three months</td><td>Learns the basic skills of communication. Hearing develops, learns to make different sounds, makes eye contact, smiles, responds to sounds.</td></tr>
<tr><td>Three to six months</td><td>Reacts to sound of voice; makes isolated sounds other than cries – 'cooing', e.g. vowels 'ah ah oo oo' and some consonants 'k', 'g'; makes noises at others.</td></tr>
<tr><td>Six to nine months</td><td>'Babbling', a string of connected sounds, uses 'sing-song' sound patterns of adult speech, sings along with favourite music. Recognises common objects by name; recognises some words: 'bottle', 'mummy', 'daddy', 'no'; uses simple gestures such as clapping hands; understands simple requests. Recognises and responds to own name.</td></tr>
<tr><td>Nine to 12 months</td><td>'Jargoning' or long strings of babbled sounds that sound like a foreign language. Begins to copy sounds in environment. May develop first words: 'mama' and 'dada'; by 12 months most children are using five words consistently and understand an increasing number of words.
Language sample at 12 months (while playing with doll's house).
Mostly single words with a few two-word combinations: Matt up, boy, chair, jump, more, that, look, wee, no, sock, shoe, nose, ear, bed.</td></tr>
<tr><td>Twelve to 18 months</td><td>Develops more words and jargoning reduces; often shortens longer words: 'bottle' becomes 'bot'; understands and can follow simple directions; uses short two- to three-word phrases; recognises and identifies common objects. First 50 words usually connected to significant people and objects. Single words used to refer to many objects.
Different word combinations:
> daddy car (subject and object)
> daddy go (subject and action)
> drive car (action and object)
> go car (action and place)
> daddy car (possessor and possessed)
> big car (description and object or person)
> that car (demonstrator and object or person)
> me go car.
Language sample at 18 months (while playing with doll's house)
Uses two-word combinations, nouns, verbs, locatives and adjectives: that doll, boy go, mum there, dolly up, no more, that bed, big bed, me sleep.</td></tr>
<tr><td>Eighteen to 24 months</td><td>Knows about 200 words and uses them to make two- or three-word sentences; asks for help using words or actions; talks in a run-on flow of words while playing; can name some pictures in a book; copies new words and phrases from adult speech, e.g. 'Bye bye Mummy', 'Grandpa's car'; sings simple songs with words and actions; begins to be understood by non-family members; starts to use plurals and past tense (adapted from Healthy Families BC, 2013).</td></tr>
<tr><td>Two to two-and-a-half years</td><td>Uses two- or three-word sentences, understands action words; points to picture to identify actions and family members; knows function of objects; develops listening and turn-taking skills of conversation; responds to directions and questions; can repeat two or more numbers.
Language sample at two years (while playing with variety of toys)
Look duck, oo that duck, sit down, more?, me jump, duck jump, quack quack, pig, look more pig mum, there more, that truck gone, me spoon.</td></tr>
</table>

Approx. age	Overview of how language develops
Two-and-a-half to five years	Develops understanding of variety of rules of vocabulary, word and sentence structure; uses sentences and can tell stories; has extensive vocabulary; can relay information; can report past events; constantly asks questions. **Language sample at three years (looking at book)** Me see dog Mum. That big dog. He's my dog. He's digging a hole. He's going home now. His mum got more bones. His mum cook those bones. Where are more bones? **Language sample at four years (describing game)** I was the mum. A pretend one. Then we were sitting on the blackboard. I hurt my knee. What was the slippery dip for? Why is that slippery dip not working? I get Mark to fix. Mark was the father. He can fix slippery dip. **Language sample at five years (describing what happens at school)** They have lots of books and toys. There's a dolly's house in the corner. I play with dolly house every single day. Then we go outside for lunch. We sit in the shed when it is raining.
Five to seven years	Has developed most language skills; all sounds are produced clearly; some occasional errors with irregular verbs ('broked' instead of 'broken').

Sources: Adapted from Clark & Ireland (1996), p. 25; Mulvaney (1991), pp. 21–37.

Language development in middle childhood

Video: The neuroscience of language

By middle childhood, most children can be easily understood and can usually understand and interpret verbal messages and some non-verbal messages. **Figure 10.31** provides an overview of speech and language skills typically acquired by the time children arrive at school.

Towards the end of middle childhood, children have refined their use of grammar, have a greater knowledge of the rules of language and, according to Duchesne and colleagues (2019, p. 59), have a vocabulary of around 40 000 words. They are better able to adapt their language to meet the needs of their audience and their conversational skills continue to improve. Some specific language skills that are refined during middle childhood include:

- the ability to clarify and expand on what they are saying
- an increasing ability to maintain and contribute to conversations and debates – listen and respond to the comments of others
- an increasing ability to understand and use metaphors (e.g. light as a feather)
- progressive use of slang words
- an increasing ability to notice and interpret body language
- the ability to use silly words to tell jokes as a sense of humour develops
- the ability to create complex storylines
- improved grammar skills
- an increased ability to use language to explain actions and events
- an increased ability to use words specific to concepts such as time, measurement or technology
- an increased ability to use a wide range of verbs to express thoughts, or about cause and effect
- an increased awareness of when and how to use formal language – for example, when talking to the doctor
- a beginning understanding of sarcasm when it is obvious – for example, 'Now that was clever!' (knocks things off table when running inside).

Figure 10.31 Speech and language skills typically acquired by the time children arrive at school

By the time they transition to school, children can:	
Use language to talk about their experiences	☐
Discuss the pictures that they see in storybooks	☐
Recount past experiences in detail; talk about future events or predict what might happen	☐
Follow three-step directions	☐
Mostly use correct grammar and speak so that they can be understood	☐
Initiate communication by smiling and/or eye contact and respond to social greetings	☐
Respond to comments and questions from others and engage in conversation; share their own knowledge and ideas	☐
Use language to help them think, and possibly still use self-talk	☐
Understand and use words to describe opposites – 'full/empty', 'big/small', 'open/closed', 'day/night' and 'high/low'	☐
Use words to describe properties of an object such as shape, colour and size; begin to describe how they are feeling – this is still a challenging task	☐
Use and understand words related to time such as 'today', 'tomorrow', 'yesterday' and 'after lunch'	☐
Provide explanations for events or actions – '*I lost my football because I didn't put it away*'	☐
Ask who, what, how, where and why questions	☐
Explain the use of familiar objects	☐
Use rhyming words, silly words and jokes	☐
Concentrate on stories – answer questions and make predictions	☐
Sometimes mispronounce the letters 's', 'v', 'f' and 'th'	☐
Ask and answer lots of questions	☐
Associate words with actions	☐
Use and interpret non-verbal communication: • Use gestures and facial expressions to communicate • Interpret obvious facial expressions that denote anger, happiness, sadness or fear, but find it more difficult to interpret subtle expressions such as frustration, jealousy and impatience • Use body language to convey their feelings: head bowed, arms crossed, eyebrows furrowed, stamping of feet and hands on hips.	☐

Language development in adolescence

Language development continues to be refined during adolescence and young adulthood. This refinement in the use of language is supported by the growing ability to think abstractly, use logic, persuasion and reasoning, and engage in critical thinking in relation to the acquisition of information and knowledge.

Language development during adolescence and into young adulthood typically includes:

- a growing understanding of sarcasm, irony and plays on words, such as double meanings
- increasing vocabulary and greater complexity in sentence structure
- the ability to adapt language style to suit a particular audience – for example, they may swear and use slang when around their peers but modify their language according to the setting and the audience
- being better able to understand and separate fact from opinion
- being able to better explain more complex ideas, and to use persuasion, better constructed arguments and more sophisticated negotiation skills
- being able to retell events in greater detail, making it more interesting for listeners
- refinement of the rules around communicating in a group context – allowing others to speak, listening without interrupting and respecting others
- being able to understand and follow more complex instructions.

Language develops alongside cognitive, social and emotional development. As students progress through the curriculum, they are introduced to context – specific vocabulary, taught grammar knowledge – and generally exposed to diverse literacy experiences, all of which contribute to language development.

Language development milestones

Red flags and language development

Most students will develop language skills in a predictable, sequential manner. However, it is important to be alert to delays in development that may indicate the need for investigation and intervention. Having a sound knowledge of typical patterns of language and speech development will assist you to identify speech and language problems (see **Figure 10.32**).

Figure 10.32 Language and speech red flags

Red flag	Description
Speech disorders	May include substitutions or distortions such as 'berry' for 'very', lisps, omission of sounds such as 'ellow' for 'yellow', or additional sounds such as 'abble' for 'apple'
Voice disorders	May include a husky, hoarse, breathy or strained voice
Fluency disorders	May include repetitions or interruptions such as stuttering or stammering
Hearing disorders	May be indicated by difficulty in hearing certain sounds, such as beginning, middle or end sounds
Communication disorders	May include problems following two- or three-step directions, an inability to follow or join in conversations with peers and adults, or poor vocabulary
Language processing disorders	May include difficulty in comprehending and/or using spoken words. *Receptive* language disorders may be indicated by a child being unable to follow a sequence of commands, while *expressive* language disorders may present as difficulties with the sequencing of sounds – for example, 'aminal' for 'animal' – or with applying rules such as past tense – 'I wented to the shop'

The impact of language and **speech disorders** on learning and socialising are highlighted in the following Scenario.

SCENARIO

LANGUAGE AND SPEECH DISORDERS

DANE

Dane (6 years) has a severe speech impediment and is becomingly increasingly frustrated by his inability to make himself understood. Most of his peers avoid talking to him in class and complain that they can't understand what he is saying. Some students speak to Dane in a loud voice, assuming he is deaf, while others tell him to talk slowly. Although he is a friendly child, Dane has very few friends. As a developing reader, Dane is struggling. Dane has a schedule of appointments with a speech pathologist; however, his parents have only kept one of the 10 appointments made.

STELLA

Stella (9 years) has verbal dyspraxia – difficulty producing sounds and words. While her condition has improved with speech therapy, she relies on a communication board and sign language as her main form of communication in the classroom. The classroom teacher and many of the students communicate with Stella using verbal language while also signing. Unlike Dane, Stella has a faithful group of friends and is a fluent reader. Her parents ensure that Stella has access to a range of support services.

EMILIA

Emilia (13 years) is in Year 8 and has an auditory processing disorder. This means that in large open-space learning environments where all surrounding class noise, productive or not, impacts what she is able to pick up and understand from her teacher and peers. Added to this are the hard surfaces that reflect noise in the art and home economic rooms as well as the science labs. Often, she misses out on important information because she did not hear all that was said.

WHAT DOES THIS TELL US?

Students who have a speech or language disorder can become isolated from their peers. The inability to engage in two-way communication can be extremely isolating. Not being able to share thoughts and ideas, tell a joke, make a comment or ask for help in a way that can be understood is a significant barrier to socialisation. Using alternative forms of communication can reduce this sense of isolation and increase opportunities for socialisation.

Language disorders are explored in greater detail in Chapter 17.

10.8 Language development and the Australian Curriculum

The Australian Curriculum: English (Foundation to Year 10) AC is designed to support students to: learn to listen to, read, view, speak, write, create and reflect on increasingly complex and sophisticated spoken, written and multimodal texts across a growing range of contexts with accuracy, fluency and purpose. Content is organised under three interrelated strands:

1 Language
2 Literature
3 Literacy.

Source: Australian Curriculum, Assessment and Reporting Authority (ACARA). (n.d.a). Australian Curriculum: English AC

The sub-strands of the Australian Curriculum: English (Foundation to Year 10) AC are shown in **Figure 10.33**:

1 comprehending texts through listening, reading and viewing;
2 composing texts through speaking, writing and creating.

Figure 10.33 The strands and sub-strands of English

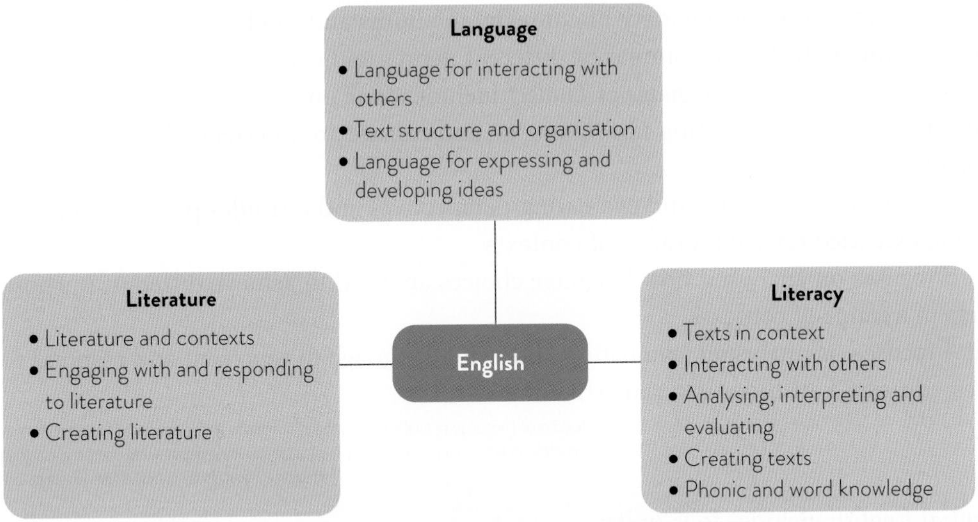

Source: Australian Curriculum, Assessment and Reporting Authority (ACARA). (2022d). Understand this learning area - English.

The English Curriculum is supported by the literacy general capability, which includes three elements (see **Figure 10.34**) and 12 sub-elements (see **Figure 10.35**).

Figure 10.34 Elements of the literacy capability

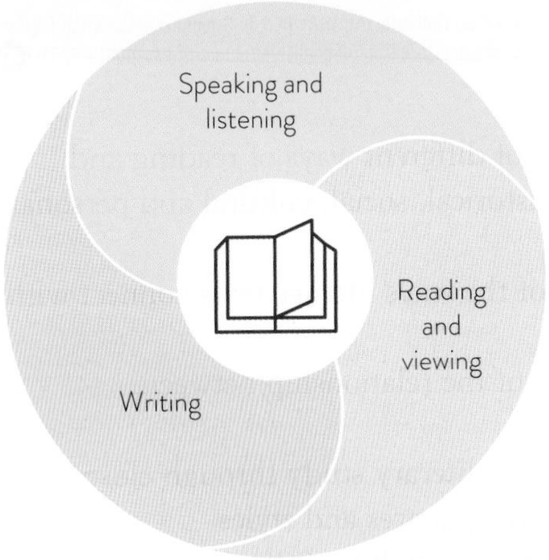

Source: Australian Curriculum, Assessment and Reporting Authority (ACARA). (2022c). Literacy

Figure 10.35 Sub-elements of the literacy capability

Element	Sub-elements
Speaking and listening	> Listening > Interacting > Speaking
Reading and viewing	> Phonological awareness > Phonic knowledge and word recognition > Fluency > Understanding texts
Writing	> Creating texts > Grammar > Punctuation > Spelling > Handwriting and keyboarding

Source: Australian Curriculum, Assessment and Reporting Authority (ACARA). (2022c). Literacy

Senior secondary Australian Curriculum for English

The senior secondary Australian Curriculum for English is presented in four subjects:

- English
- English as an Additional Language or Dialect
- Essential English
- Literature.

English includes three units:

- Unit 1: Investigate the relationships between language, context and meaning
- Unit 2: Compare texts in a variety of contexts, mediums and modes
- Unit 3: Compare texts from similar or different genres and contexts.

English as an Additional Language or Dialect includes four units:

- Unit 1 focuses on investigating how language and culture are interrelated and expressed in a range of contexts.
- Unit 2 focuses on analysing and evaluating perspectives and attitudes presented in texts and creating extended texts for a range of contexts.
- Unit 3 focuses on analysing how language choices are used to achieve different purposes and effects in a range of contexts.
- Unit 4 focuses on analysing, evaluating and using language to represent and respond to issues, ideas and attitudes in a range of context.

Source: Structure of English as an Additional Language or Dialect, Australian Curriculum, Assessment and Reporting Authority (ACARA), https://australiancurriculum.edu.au/senior-secondary-curriculum/english/english-as-an-additional-language-or-dialect/structure-of-english-as-an-additional-language-or-dialect/

Essential English includes four units:

- Unit 1 focuses on students comprehending and responding to the ideas and information presented in texts drawn from a range of contexts.
- Unit 2 focuses on interpreting ideas and arguments in a range of texts and contexts.
- Unit 3 focuses on exploring different points of view presented in a range of texts and contexts.
- Unit 4 focuses on community, local or global issues and ideas presented in texts and on developing students' reasoned responses to them.

Source: Australian Curriculum, Assessment and Reporting Authority (ACARA). (n.d.d). Structure of Essential English. https://australiancurriculum.edu.au/senior-secondary-curriculum/english/essential-english/structure-of-essential-english

Literature includes four units:

- Unit 1 develops students' knowledge and understanding of different ways of reading and creating literary texts drawn from a widening range of historical, social, cultural and personal contexts.
- Unit 2 develops student knowledge and understanding of the ways literary texts connect with each other.
- Unit 3 develops students' knowledge and understanding of the relationship between language, culture and identity in literary texts.
- Unit 4 develops students' appreciation of the significance of literary study through close critical analysis of literary texts drawn from a range of forms, genres and styles.

Source: Australian Curriculum, Assessment and Reporting Authority (ACARA). (n.d.f). Structure of Literature. https://australiancurriculum.edu.au/senior-secondary-curriculum/english/literature/structure-of-literature

The four subject areas include common features:

- the continuing development of students' knowledge
- understanding and skills in listening, speaking, reading, viewing and writing.

Source: Australian Curriculum, Assessment and Reporting Authority (ACARA). (n.d.b.). English (Version 8.4). https://australiancurriculum.edu.au/senior-secondary-curriculum/english

Summary

This chapter provided an overview of theories of cognitive and language development as well as the factors that may influence development. Theories of cognitive development have led to a greater understanding of how thinking and learning progresses in a predictable, sequential and accumulative manner. Theorists have identified how thinking moves from simple to complex, with each stage of development laying the foundation for the next stage. We know that cognitive development does not occur separately but relies on the integration of language, and social and physical development. Brain research has confirmed that the brain develops in a hierarchical manner. While genetics are a major contributing factor for brain development, environmental factors can positively or negatively alter the brain.

The progression of learning and thinking skills relies on the ability to store, sort and recall information. Concept development is critical to being able to organise and make sense of the huge volumes of information with which children are confronted on a daily basis. Higher order mental functions develop best when there is deliberate and intentional teaching that promotes critical thinking, analysis and reflection.

Children develop language in a predictable and sequential manner. By school age, most children are fluent in their home language and can use language to communicate effectively with others. During middle childhood and adolescence, children and young people consolidate their language and are capable of communicating in a variety of ways and for a variety of purposes with a wide audience. Language develops when children and young people are provided with language role models and are given daily opportunities to engage in communication for different purposes.

Self-check questions

1 What factors influence cognitive development?
2 According to Piaget, what are the four developmental principles?
3 What are the three key concepts of Vygotsky's theory of cognitive development?
4 What does Vygotsky's social learning theory refer to?
5 What is the role of the educator in Bruner's theory of cognitive development?
6 According to Sweller's cognitive load theory (CLT), extraneous refers to the environment in which information is provided and the resources used to provide the information. What does this mean in a typical classroom?
7 How does concept development assist children's learning?
8 Define language development and list its two areas.
9 What is the critical factor in Bruner's language development theory?

Discussion questions

1 Discuss how educators use Bruner's theory in classroom.
2 For this task, refer to the scenario 'Language and speech disorders' in this chapter. Discuss the situation of Dane and Stella. What strategies could be used to support students with language and speech disorders?
3 In PE, the class were participating in an introductory task. The teacher asked the students to visit five points on the basketball court, providing instructions like 'Skip over the middle circle', 'Walk back to the key' and 'Get into a circle'. The teacher then ran through each instruction omitting the direction words and asked children to fill in the blanks. Some children could not articulate the correct words.
   a Which of the levels in being able to describe spatial relationships would the children who provided the incorrect responses be sitting at?

Activities

1 Concept development is (select the correct answer):

a A cognitive and physical skill

b A physical and language skill

c A language and cognitive skill

2 Categorise the following three questions into low- or high-order mental functions.

a How do you feel when you see your classmates succeed?

b What colour is the sky?

c What would happen if all the rivers filled up?

Chapter 11

THEORY TO PRACTICE

LEARNING OBJECTIVES

When you have completed this chapter, you should be able to demonstrate that, in relation to working in a school environment, you:

11.1 have a basic knowledge of the Australian Curriculum and how it can be navigated and explored

11.2 have an introductory knowledge of contemporary learning approaches and practices

11.3 have an introductory knowledge of how teachers apply child development and learning theory to a range of pedagogical principles of effective teaching and learning

11.4 are aware of the key elements of a quality learning environment for children and young people

11.5 have a knowledge of how to set up the classroom for small group learning

11.6 have a basic knowledge of how technology is used as a learning tool in the classroom.

Online resources icons refer to useful weblinks. Ask your instructor for these **Online Resources.**

Introduction

This chapter draws together theories of development and learning and explores contemporary approaches to teaching and learning. As an education support worker (ESW), you will not be expected to have an in-depth knowledge of learning theory and how it is applied by teachers in the classroom. You will be required to assist in the facilitation of student learning and contribute to the planning and implementation of education programs.

An introductory knowledge of how theories of development and learning are applied to teaching practices will assist you to understand the wide range of pedagogical practices you will see used by teachers to support and enhance student learning.

You will see a significant number of recommended videos in the Online resources. You are encouraged to view all of these videos as they will enrich your understanding of the many concepts explored in this chapter and help you to understand how learning theories are used in the classroom.

11.1 The Australian Curriculum framework

Melbourne Declaration on Educational Goals for Young Australians

Videos: Australian Curriculum

The framework for the development of the Australian Curriculum is based on the Melbourne Declaration on Educational Goals for Young Australians (MCEETYA, 2008). The Melbourne Declaration reflects the social and economic goals for a democratic and just Australian society with education as central to the achievement of these goals. The Melbourne Declaration includes two key goals that focus on equity, diversity and active participation by children and young people in their education.

Figure 11.1 provides an overview of the key components of the Australian Curriculum. You may also like to review the elements of the Australian Curriculum, which can be found in

Figure 11.1 Components of the Australian Curriculum

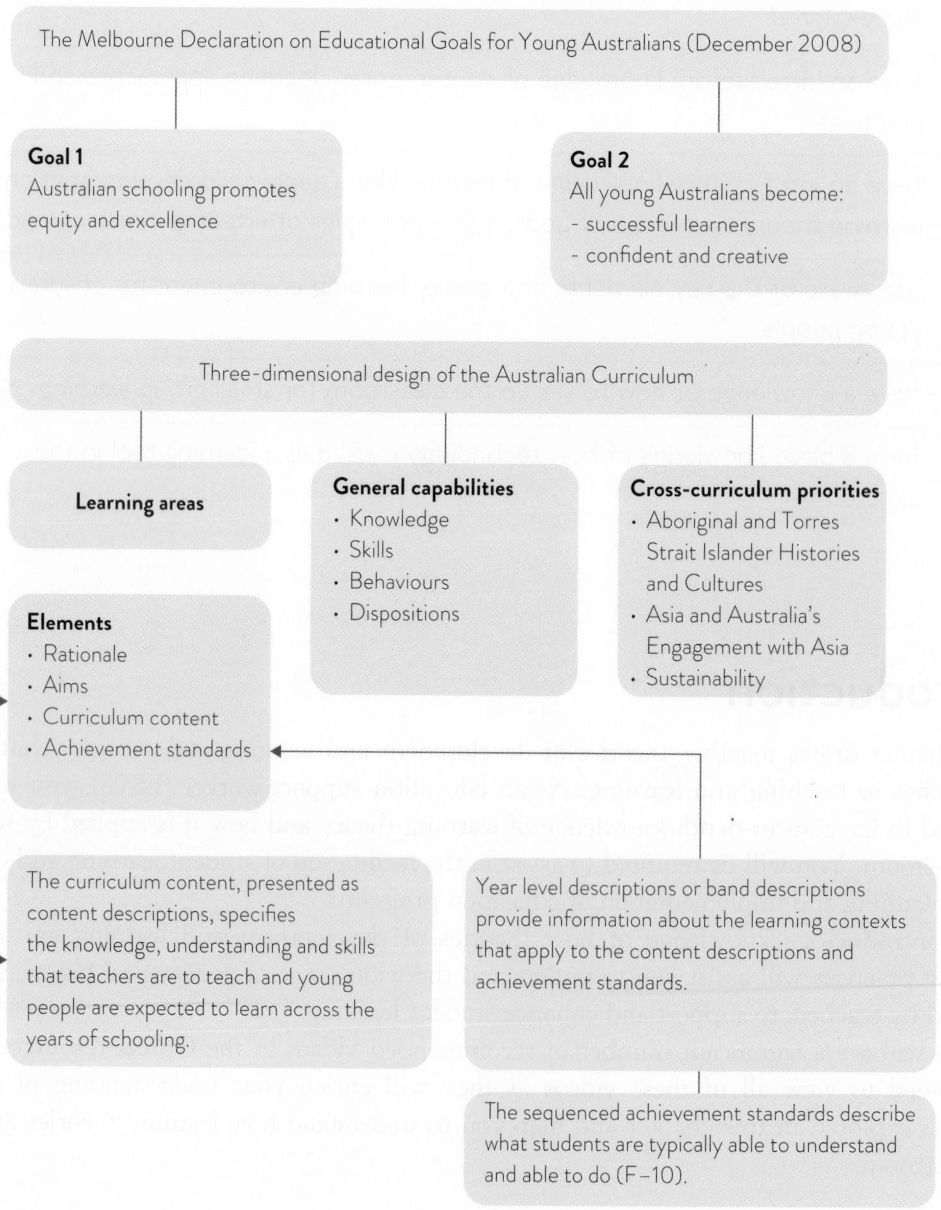
The Melbourne Declaration on Educational Goals for Young Australians (December 2008)
Goal 1
Australian schooling promotes equity and excellence
Goal 2
All young Australians become:
- successful learners
- confident and creative
Three-dimensional design of the Australian Curriculum
Learning areas
General capabilities
· Knowledge
· Skills
· Behaviours
· Dispositions
Cross-curriculum priorities
· Aboriginal and Torres Strait Islander Histories and Cultures
· Asia and Australia's Engagement with Asia
· Sustainability
Elements
· Rationale
· Aims
· Curriculum content
· Achievement standards
The curriculum content, presented as content descriptions, specifies the knowledge, understanding and skills that teachers are to teach and young people are expected to learn across the years of schooling.
Year level descriptions or band descriptions provide information about the learning contexts that apply to the content descriptions and achievement standards.
The sequenced achievement standards describe what students are typically able to understand and able to do (F–10).

Source: Ministerial Council on Education, Employment, Training and Youth Affairs (MCEETYA). (December 2008). Melbourne Declaration on Educational Goals for Young Australians. http://www.curriculum.edu.au/verve/_resources/National_Declaration_on_the_Educational_Goals_for_Young_Australians.pdf (p. 7).

Figure 7.18 in Chapter 7. Also watch the videos in the Online resources, which provide an excellent overview of the various components of the Australian Curriculum.

The Australian Curriculum and CASE

CASE is an acronym in the Australian Curriculum that is used to describe four elements that should be considered when planning learning programs that are adapted to meet the individual needs of students (Australian Curriculum, Assessment and Reporting Authority [ACARA] (n.d) AC).

CASE refers to:

1. Content: Start with learning area content that aligns with students' chronological age to:
   - plan age-appropriate teaching and learning programs
   - develop rigorous programs that challenge and engage all students
   - ensure that all students progress.
2. Abilities: Adjust the teaching and learning programs and classroom instruction to:
   - draw on students' interests and abilities to personalise age-equivalent learning area content
   - use the general capabilities and/or cross-curriculum priorities to adjust the learning focus
   - align age-equivalent learning area content with individual learning goals.
3. Standards: Assess student progress in relation to achievement standards and individual learning goals.
4. Evaluation: Evaluate actions taken to personalise student learning:
   - Teachers review these actions in consultation with the student, their family/carers and other professionals, to evaluate and respond to the impact of personalised learning strategies.
   - Evaluation of these strategies acknowledges successes and determines whether alternative personalised learning strategies are required to ensure the student progresses.

Source: Australian Curriculum, Assessment and Reporting Authority (ACARA) Structure of Literature, https://australiancurriculum.edu.au/senior-secondary-curriculum/english/literature/structure-of-literature

CASE (see **Figure 11.2**) is used as a tool when planning to meet the diverse needs of students.

Figure 11.2 CASE

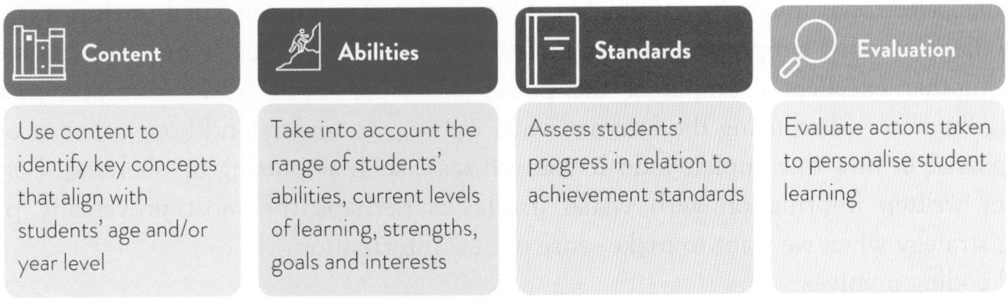

Content
Use content to identify key concepts that align with students' age and/or year level
Abilities
Take into account the range of students' abilities, current levels of learning, strengths, goals and interests
Standards
Assess students' progress in relation to achievement standards
Evaluation
Evaluate actions taken to personalise student learning

Source: Australian Curriculum, Assessment and Reporting Authority (ACARA) (n.d). Steps to personalise learning: CASE. https://www.australiancurriculum.edu.au/resources/student-diversity/planning-for-student-diversity/steps-to-personalise-learning-case AC

CASE reflects an approach to learning that is individualised and best suits the needs of the learner. When teachers adapt learning and teaching strategies that accommodate a diversity of skills and abilities, the needs of each student as a unique learner are recognised and respected. However, it is important to be aware that while CASE promotes individualised planning and

Videos: CASE

learning, teachers are constrained by the age, grade, hierarchical and sequential learning model of the Australian Curriculum. It is also important to acknowledge that where a teacher is working in a classroom without the support of an ESW or without access to additional specialist support teachers, developing and implementing individualised learning plans can be extremely challenging.

11.2 Theories of instruction

Theories of instruction and learning explore the relationship between various pedagogical strategies (teaching practices) and how we learn. When working in a school, you will observe these instructional learning theories in practice. While the teacher is unlikely to say 'I'm going to teach using Sweller's cognitive load theory, Pavio's dual coding theory, Vygotsky's zone of proximal development or Hattie's 'visible teaching and learning' approach', you will see these theories in action. As an ESW, you are not expected to have an in-depth knowledge of theories of instructional learning; however, knowing that these theories underpin best practice in pedagogy will give you a greater appreciation of the range of strategies used by teachers to support learning.

Dual coding theory

Closely related to cognitive load theory (see the discussion of CLT in Chapter 10) is Allen Pavio's dual coding theory. Pavio (1971) was able to demonstrate that our working memory receives and stores visual and verbal input independently. Importantly, he was also able to demonstrate that although they are stored separately, the brain is able to link visual and verbal memories together when retrieving information. When teachers use visual and verbal tools together, Pavio showed that students are able to make associative connections (words and images). Examples of visual formats include posters, drawings, diagrams, timelines and graphic organisers.

Pavio demonstrated that presenting concepts or content in a visual format allows the learner to see key information simultaneously as a single image or graphic. Pavio argued that using visual input helps to reduce the student's cognitive load. Consider, for example, if you wanted to understand how solar panels generate electricity. Would a verbal explanation using words such as photons, electrons, inverters, conductive filaments and atoms make this clear to you? Or would a diagram using simple graphics and a few key words allow you to grasp the process more easily? Another excellent example of the power of visual input is the common practice of accessing 'how to' videos using the internet when wanting to understand how to use or operate a new appliance or how to complete a do-it-yourself task, such as putting up shelving. Combining verbal or written information with visual images is perhaps the most universally preferred learning strategy when we want to make sense of new information.

Dual coding involves:

- breaking new information into smaller chunks
- presenting these chunks in a logical format
- using visuals and key words
- showing the relationship between each chunk.

Video: Dual coding theory

Figure 11.3 summarises the concept of dual coding.

Figure 11.3 Dual coding

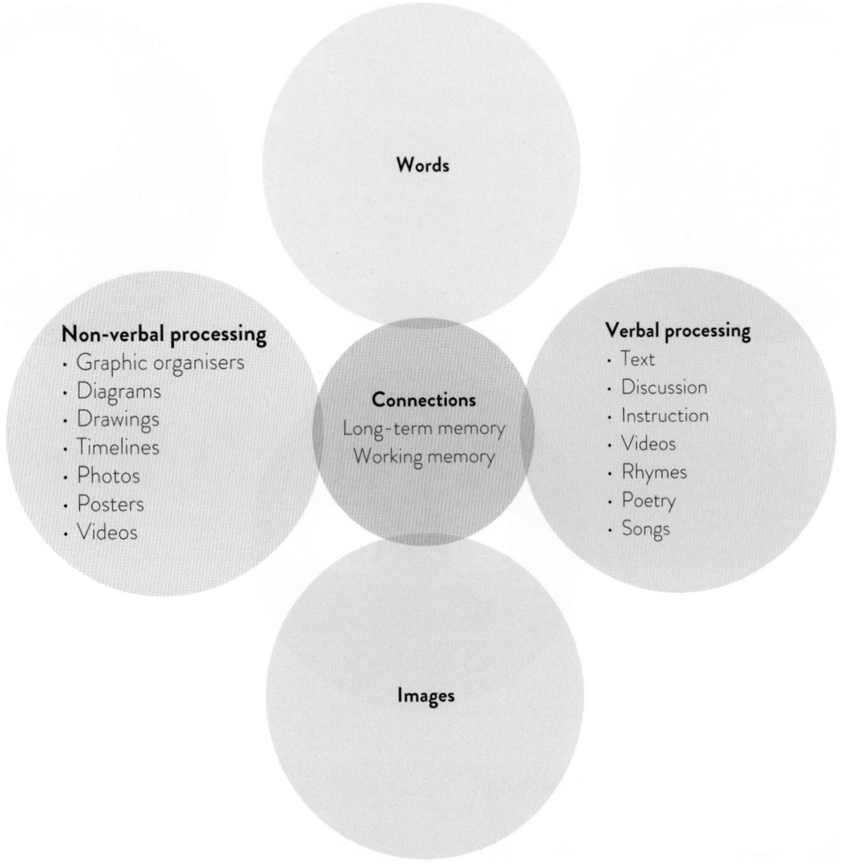

Source: Based on: Education Corner (2023). What is dual coding theory? https://www.educationcorner.com/dual-coding-theory

Visible teaching and learning

Another important pedagogical approach is described by John Hattie (2009) as 'visible teaching and learning' (see **Figure 11.4**). Visible teaching and learning occurs when teachers see learning through the eyes of students and help them to become their own teachers (Visible Learning, 2023).

Hattie (2009) states that what is most important is that teaching is visible to the student and that the learning is visible to the teacher. The teacher must know when learning is correct or incorrect; learn when to experiment and learn from experience; learn to monitor, seek and give feedback; and know to try alternative learning strategies when others do not work. The more the student becomes the teacher and the more the teacher becomes the learner, then the more successful are the outcomes.

Planning for visible learning includes the following steps (see also **Figure 11.5**):

1. reviewing students' prior skills and knowledge and preferred learning styles
2. identifying the learning outcome
3. checking that learning has occurred
4. identifying the progression of learning as it relates to the curriculum
5. teacher reflection.

Figure 11.4 Visible teaching and learning

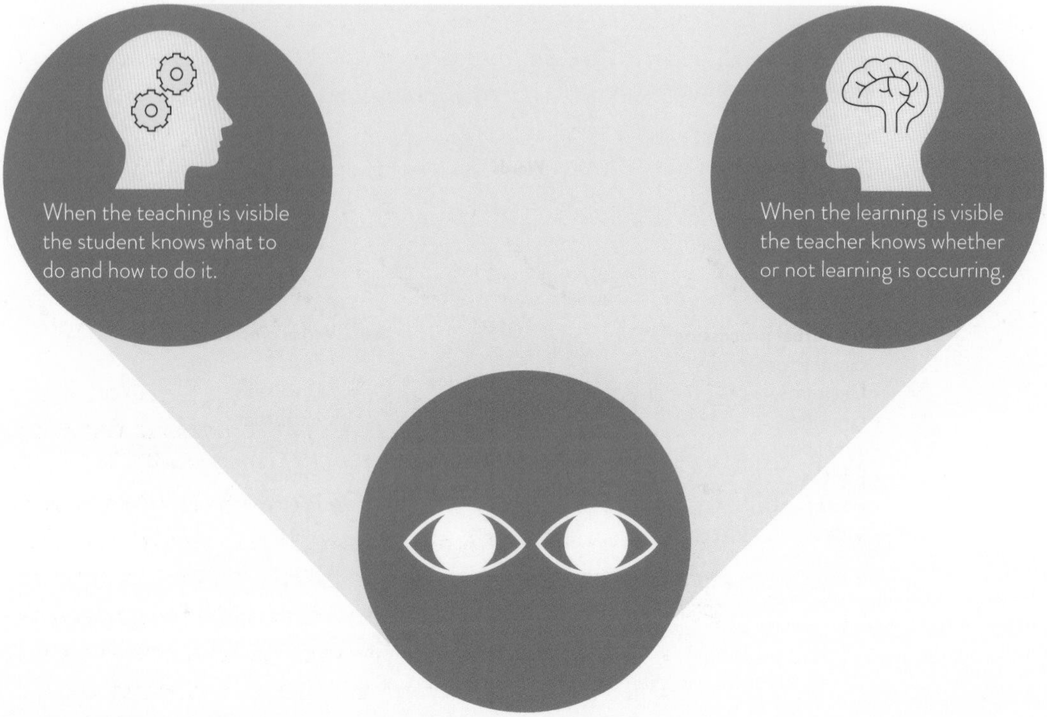

When the teaching is visible the student knows what to do and how to do it.
When the learning is visible the teacher knows whether or not learning is occurring.

Figure 11.5 Steps in visible learning and teaching

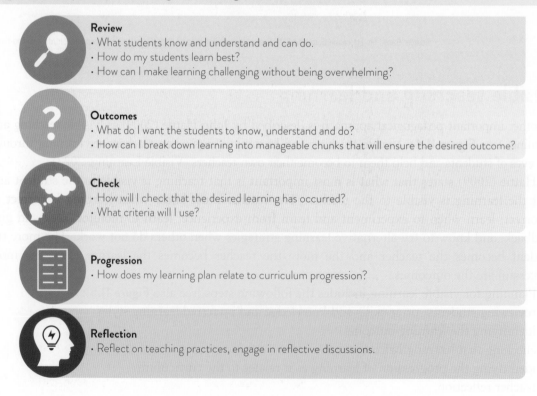

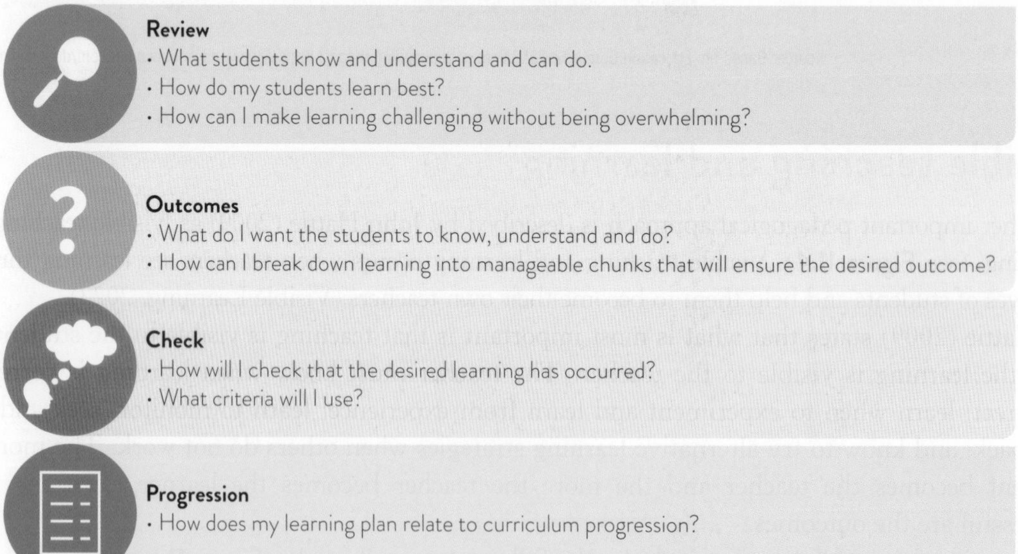

Review
· What students know and understand and can do.
· How do my students learn best?
· How can I make learning challenging without being overwhelming?
Outcomes
· What do I want the students to know, understand and do?
· How can I break down learning into manageable chunks that will ensure the desired outcome?
Check
· How will I check that the desired learning has occurred?
· What criteria will I use?
Progression
· How does my learning plan relate to curriculum progression?
Reflection
· Reflect on teaching practices, engage in reflective discussions.

Visible learning reflects key elements of learning and development theory. For example:

- Piaget's stages of cognitive development focus on the developmental progression of thinking, reasoning, memory and logic. This knowledge allows teachers to identify where each student might be placed along the developmental continuum and understand how students apply thinking, reasoning and logic and the skills they have developed in relation to memory and recall strategies.
- Piaget's schemata (the process of chunking information) and equilibration (assimilation, accommodation, adaptation – the process of acquiring new information by building on existing information), as well as the importance of repetition and practice. This knowledge can guide the teacher when thinking about how to break down information into manageable chunks. It also reminds teachers of the value of repetition and practice to support new learning.
- Vygotsky's zone of proximal development helps teachers to determine how to introduce new information by building on students' existing knowledge, understanding and skills so that learning is challenging but attainable.
- Scaffolding learning (Bruner/Vygotsky) is what the learner can do with and without guidance and support. This knowledge allows teachers to engage in guided learning.
- Bruner's spiral curriculum model (see **Figure 11.6**) encourages teachers to frequently revisit and consolidate existing knowledge and to use this as a framework for developing more complex knowledge.
- Bloom's revised taxonomy classifies thought processes from simple to complex – remember, understand, apply, analyse, evaluate and create – and guides teachers to design lessons that identify the thinking skills needed for students to move from knowledge to the application of knowledge in increasingly complex ways.
- Gardner's theory of multiple intelligences reminds teachers that learning can occur in a wide range of contexts that accommodate many different learning styles.
- Sweller's cognitive load theory reminds teachers that learning occurs best in smaller chunks, allowing the learner to process, store and retrieve information without 'information overload'.

Video: Visible learning

Figure 11.6 Bruner's spiral curriculum model

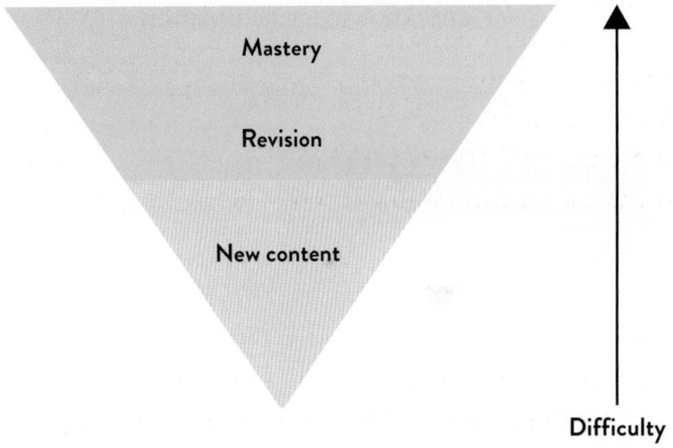

Figure 11.7 Zone of proximal development

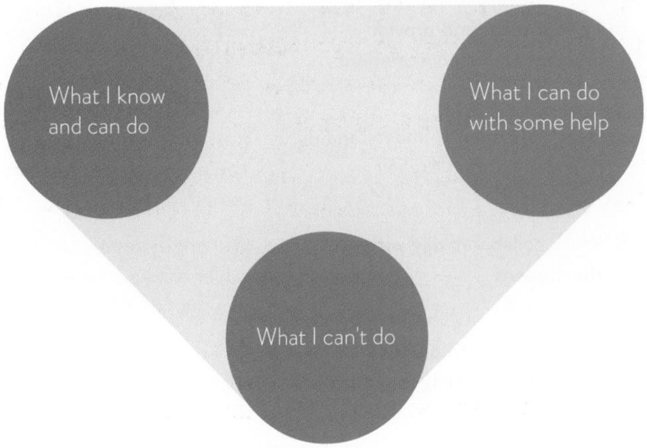

Scaffolding learning

Scaffolding learning is a **pedagogical strategy** based on Vygotsky's (1978) ZPD (see **Figure 11.7**) to describe the process of constructing meaning. As you will recall from Chapter 10, ZPD is the distance between the student's existing skills and knowledge and the level of potential skills and knowledge that can be acquired by a process of problem-solving guided by an adult. ZPD works on a strengths-based model of knowledge acquisition – that is, the starting point is determined by what the student already knows and/or can do.

SCENARIO

SCAFFOLDING LEARNING

Rose (13 years) becomes easily flustered when faced with new information. She tends to panic and immediately use negative self-talk such as *'This is dumb/stupid/too hard/a waste of time.'* Instead of thinking about what she can do, Rose focuses on the negative and predicts failure even before she begins.

The ESW, **Josh**, is familiar with Rose's negative behaviours and always begins any new task by reviewing what Rose knows and can already do in relation to the day's tasks. Josh takes the time to help Rose understand and make the link between existing and new knowledge.

To do this, Josh uses examples of previous work completed by Rose, reinforcing the positive outcomes Rose has achieved: *'Rose, last week we worked on 'sh' words and you did a really good job. This week we are going to add 'ing' to our 'sh' words.'*

WHAT DOES THIS TELL US?

Learning is a cumulative process. While new skills and knowledge are built on existing skills and knowledge, this is not always evident to the learner. In the case of Rose, reminding her to think about what she knows and can do helps her to make connections as she progresses in her learning journey.

Figure 11.8 provides examples of the ways in which teachers use scaffolding to support skills and knowledge acquisition.

Figure 11.8 Scaffolding student learning

1 Model, demonstrate and provide example	Show the student what they will do or learn – 'What does this learning look like?' – for example, 'We are going to work on a word ladder. I have one that I did to show you. Let's look at it together.'
2 Check understanding	Ask open-ended questions that provide students with an opportunity to give feedback and demonstrate their understanding of the task.
3 State the goal or purpose	State the goal or purpose in simple terms – for example, 'We are going to use the clue to subtract a letter and replace it with a different letter to make a new word.'
4 Manageable steps	Chunk or break down the task into manageable steps: 'Let's start with this one. You read the word (bake) and I'll read the clue.'
5 Make connections and provide clues	Talk about what you are thinking and direct the student's thinking – for example, 'Let's see, it says to change the first letter to make this new word. The word clue is something you eat. What's a good way to work on changing the first letter?'
6 Try out ideas and provide practice and encouragement	Trial the student's suggestions (even if you know they won't work). If the student doesn't suggest an idea, suggest yourself – for example, 'Working your way through the alphabet is a great idea. You say the letter and we'll try to make it into a word. The student goes straight to 'C' and says 'cake'.
7 Develop student's understanding to make learning explicit	Restate the aim or goal of the exercise and how the result was achieved – for example, 'Excellent. You changed the first letter "B" into a "C" so it reads "cake" instead of "bake". A cake is certainly something you can eat.'
8 Work collaboratively with the student	Working alongside the student provides the support needed to 'have a go' – for example, 'Let's try the ladder on the next page. It looks a little harder. See, you must change two letters. Are you ready to give it a go? We'll do the first one together.'
9 Allow student to practise new skills/knowledge	When new skills and knowledge are acquired, students need the opportunity to both practise and apply what they have learned.

Scaffolding learning encourages students to focus on their own learning by reflecting on what they already know and can do. Encouraging reflection is often referred to as 'making learning explicit'.

Watkins (2009, p. 3) suggests that educators can help students to focus on their own learning (make learning explicit) by:

- *Noticing learning* – making learning an object of attention. Help students to notice their own learning by pointing out their progress: 'Well done, Dillan! Remember at the beginning of the term you could not spell those words?'
- *Talking about learning* – making learning an object of conversation. Engage students in describing their learning: 'Tell me how you worked out that maths problem. What did you do first? How did you know what to do?'
- *Reviewing experiences of learning* – making learning an object of reflection. This may include talking about learning – for example, 'You worked really hard on those fractions today. What do you think about what you achieved?' With their permission, students' work can also be displayed as a way of reflecting on their achievements.
- *Experimenting with learning* – an important strategy that encourages students to have a go without worrying about whether they get it right or wrong. Use 'What if/what would happen if we tried …?' or 'I wonder what we could do to …?' Use errors as a learning tool: 'Let's see what we need to change.'

Watkins (2009, p. 4) also suggests that older students can be encouraged to think about their own learning by using storyboard themes, such as those shown in **Figure 11.9**.

Videos: Scaffolding examples and working memory.

Figure 11.9 Thinking about learning

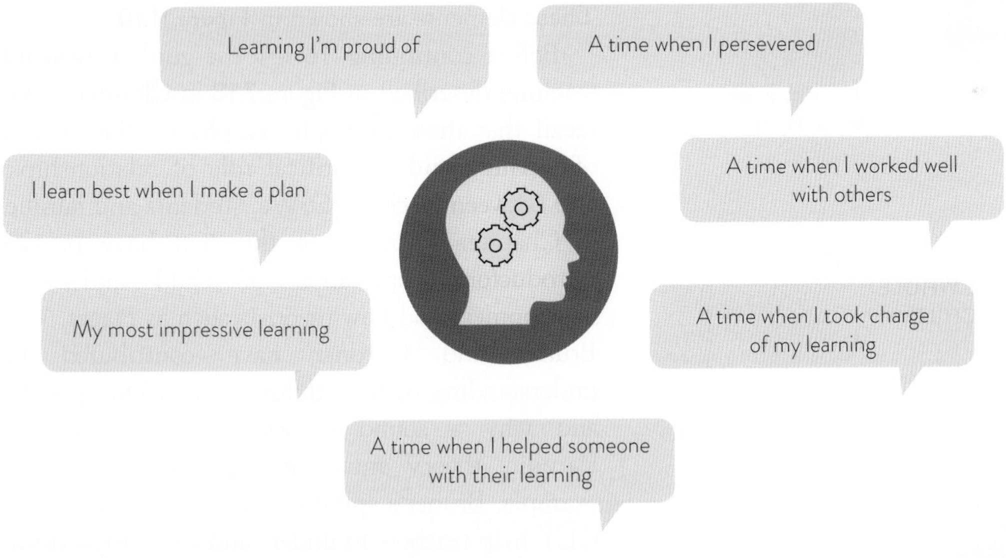

SCENARIO

LEARNING TO LEARN

The classroom teacher and the ESW are sitting together reading the students' responses to the learning-to-learn task, which encourages students to think about their own learning. The students were asked to describe learning they were proud of. Some of the responses from the Year 5 students included:

- *'This week I FINALLY learned not to ask questions for no reason. I took the teacher's advice THINK BEFORE YOU SPEAK!'* **(Kirra)**
- *'Well, I think I did a good job with my maths this week. I even did some revision, which I NEVER do. I know how to work out area. I even measured up our garage at home*

and told Dad the size of the room so we could get the right amount of paint. Dad was really impressed.' **(Zac)**

- *'I am a champion! I got all my spelling words correct! I finally figured out a way to remember hard words. I visualise them and remember their shape.'* **(Corrine)**
- *'Yesterday I read in front of the class. I only made a few mistakes and I didn't even get embarrassed. Mr King, you always say it's okay to make mistakes if we work at fixing them. I get this now.'* **(Bailey)**

WHAT DOES THIS TELL US?

Children can think about and evaluate their own learning. Kirra's response could be used to explore why she thinks her questions are 'stupid'. What does *'Think before you speak'* mean to Kirra? Is she referring to thinking about what she already knows before asking a question or is she referring to her own listening skills?

Asking students to share their thinking about learning can also provide feedback to educators about their learning strategies.

► DISCUSSION

This Scenario highlights the importance of an educator–student partnership in learning. Discuss how encouraging students to talk about and explore their own learning can assist educators to build such a partnership.

11.3 Applying theory to practice

When teachers apply their knowledge of child and adolescent development, the factors that influence and shape development (the concept of 'the whole child'), and their knowledge of learning theory, they put children and young people at the very centre of the pedagogical (teaching) practice. Applying all of this knowledge is essential if children and young people are to engage in education in ways that allow every student to reach their full potential. These elements are shown in **Figure 11.10**.

Figure 11.10 Applying theory to practice

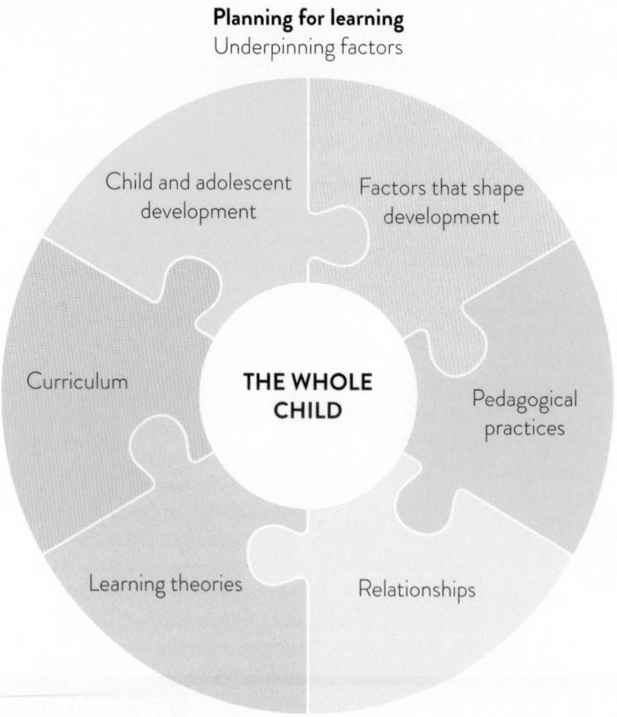

Before continuing, review the guiding principles for teaching described in **Figure 7.18** in Chapter 7. You will recall that these principles emphasise the social nature of learning and the critical role of relationships (with and between teachers, ESWs, students and families).

Chapters 7 to 10 of this text have provided an introductory exploration of child and adolescent development and how theorists such as Piaget, Vygotsky, Bruner and Gardner have contributed to our understanding of how children and young people learn, and why a sound knowledge of development and learning theory must lead planning decisions. For example, Bruner's spiral curriculum model and Sweller's CLT help teachers to understand the complexities of the learning process. Piaget and Vygotsky both demonstrated that children's development occurs in a predictable sequence and, importantly, that new knowledge and skills are developed when children are able to build on existing knowledge and skills through hands-on learning and adult guidance.

Bloom's revised taxonomy is used by teachers to identify learning outcomes that accurately describe:

- *remembering*: what students can recall (knowledge) about a topic/subject matter – for example, 'What are prime numbers?'; 'Name the states and territories of Australia'

- *understanding*: what students can understand (comprehend) about a topic/subject matter – for example, how and why questions
- *applying*: students demonstrate their knowledge and understanding by applying it to a problem or task – for example, measuring volume or surface area, applying word attack strategies
- *analysing*: students ask questions and engage in investigation and problem-solving – for example 'What would happen if…?'; 'Why did the experiment fail?'; 'Why couldn't the little bird find its mother?'
- *evaluating*: students engage in evaluation (assess) when they are asked to predict, anticipate possible outcomes and choose a course of action
- *creating*: students engage in creative thinking to explore their own point of view, question accepted beliefs and generate new ideas – for example, 'What might be the outcome if Australia allowed the use of illegal drugs?; 'Can you think of an alternative to compulsory schooling?'

Differentiated Learning Instruction (DLI)

Differentiated Learning Instruction (DLI) is a strategy used by teachers to tailor learning to meet the individual learning needs of each student. While all students begin with the same learning outcome, the way in which they approach learning is varied. According to Tomlinson and Imbeau (2010), there are four areas where teachers can differentiate instruction (content, process, product and learning environment) as shown in **Figure 11.11**.

Figure 11.11 Elements of DLI

Classroom elements

Readiness
Interests
Learning profile

Content
Content can be differentiated according to readiness and/or interests and/or learning profile
Process
Process can be differentiated according to readiness and/or interests and/or learning profile
Product
Product can be differentiated according to readiness and/or interests and/or learning profile
Learning environment
Learning environment can be differentiated according to learning profile

Learning profile

Learning environment
Learning environment can be differentiated according to learning profile

Student characteristics
There are four types of classroom elements. These include content, process, product and learning environment, which can all be differentiated by teachers according to the readiness, interests and learning profile of students.

Source: Teacher Standards and Accreditation – Differentiating learning, © State of New South Wales (Department of Education), 2023. Adapted under Creative Commons Attribution 4.0 International (CC BY 4.0) https://creativecommons.org/licenses/by/4.0/

Student assessment is an integral part of DLI. Teachers use pre-assessment to determine students' current level of skills and knowledge as a starting point for DLI. Assessment throughout the learning process informs teachers if the DLI is being effective and/or if it needs to be changed or modified. Post-assessment is used to determine if learning outcomes have been met. DLI may include strategies such as think-pair-share strategy (TPS) and retrieval practice.

Videos: Differentiating instruction

Videos: Inquiry-based learning

Inquiry-based learning (IBL)

Inquiry-based learning (IBL) and project-based learning (PBL) are types of **experiential learning** that allow students to be immersed in learning through hands-on investigation and problem-solving. They are the exact opposites of direct teaching and explicit learning. Opponents of IBL argue that students don't develop domain-specific information and instead the working memory becomes overloaded with 'novel' information.

IBL reflects Piaget's theory that children are capable and resourceful and can direct their own learning. It also reflects Vygotsky's belief that learning is a social skill and learning occurs best in social groups. Supporters of IBL argue that it allows students to become immersed in the learning, proves students are able to take ownership and direct their own learning, and that the use of a wide range of learning materials promotes creative thinking.

Figure 11.12 describes the key steps in IBL.

Figure 11.12 Steps in IBL

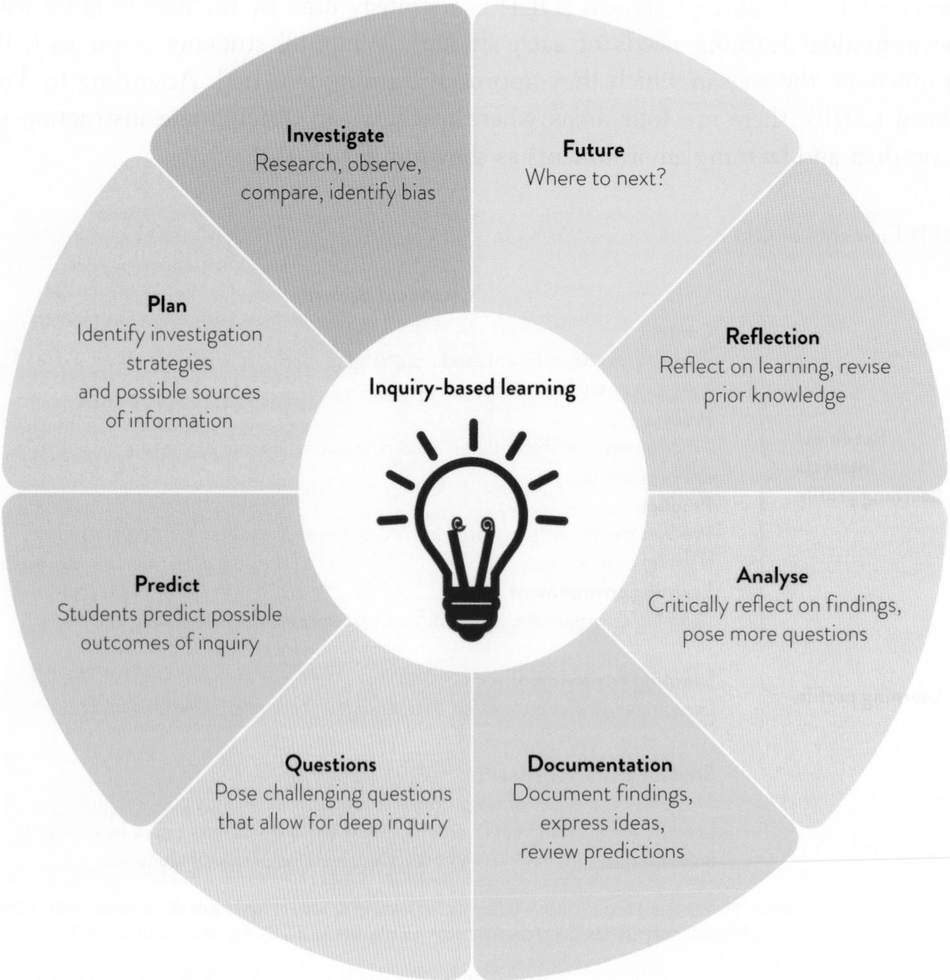

Direct and explicit instruction

You will hear the pedagogical terms **direct instruction** and **explicit instruction** being used by teachers. Often these terms are used interchangeably and while similar, there is a difference in intent. Direct instruction is teacher led. To teach a new concept the teacher follows a set script and students are often asked to repeat information verbatim without any variation. Explicit instruction is also teacher led but differs in that the teacher emphasises or highlights key information that they want students to focus on and remember.

Direct and explicit instruction as a teaching tool includes a clear learning outcome or learning objective and detailed lesson plans that carefully and sequentially introduce information and concepts in small manageable chunks. Explicit teaching practices include:

- telling students what they will be learning, and being clear about the purpose of tasks
- demonstrating or explaining new ideas, and checking that students understand
- giving time for asking and answering questions
- giving specific feedback based on success criteria
- systematically delivering skills, concepts and content knowledge in the right sequence to provide the building blocks towards mastery
- asking students challenging questions, such as 'why, why-not, how, what-if, how does X compare to Y, and what is the evidence for X?'
- assessing and confirming whether students understand what they are learning before progressing
- reviewing learning and explaining how it contributes to related and more complex skills
- providing opportunities for guided, and then independent, practice as students gain proficiency and understanding of concepts and skills.

Source: Centre for Education Statistics and Evaluation (2020). What works best: 2020 update, NSW Department of Education, cese.nsw.gov.au.

Direct and explicit instruction reflect Sweller's cognitive learning theory (CLT) by breaking learning down into smaller parts. This assists information processing and reduces the cognitive load so that students can build deeper understandings of new concepts and information. Direct and explicit instruction also use the process of scaffolding. When students are able to gradually build their knowledge step-by-step, this reduces the risk of misunderstanding and lays a solid foundation for the progression of learning.

Typically, direct and explicit instruction are taught with small groups of students who are at around the same skill level. A key feature of direct and explicit instruction is providing multiple and varied opportunities for practice so that students can apply their learning while they are learning.

In summary, there are five steps in direct and explicit instruction:

1. Develop a clear and explicit learning outcome.
2. Model or provide an example of what you want the student to do/know.
3. Break down complex skills and knowledge into smaller instructional chunks (step-by-step).
4. Provide opportunities for students to practise what they have learned at each step.
5. Provide key information for each step in a single place to make information processing easier. For example, keep written information, and visual information such as graphics and diagrams, to no more than a single side of paper or a single slide. This allows students to 'see' all information at once and makes it easier for students to refer back to information as needed.

Videos: Direct and explicit instruction

Examples of classroom strategies used in direct and explicit instruction include guided learning, modelling and shared learning:

- *Guided learning*: teachers support learning by providing information, preventing errors and answering questions. This allows students to complete a task that they might not normally be able to do without support. The role of the teacher is that of a guide – giving hints and ideas without providing the answer.
- *Modelling*: teachers support learning by completing a task in front of students using a step-by-step process. For example, 'First I'm going to... Next I will ...' When modelling, teachers might ask questions to clarify students' understanding or to predict the next step.

Videos: Guided learning and reading

- *Shared learning*: teachers support learning by working alongside students to complete parts of a task that the students might not normally be able to do without support. In shared learning, both the teacher and the student complete parts of the task.

Strategies such as guided and shared learning and modelling use scaffolding to assist students to move their thinking forward in a way that is just beyond what the students already know, understand or can do.

Videos: Teacher modelling

Think-pair-share strategy (TPS)

Think-pair-share (TPS), also referred to as Turn and Talk, is a pedagogical practice that reflects Vygotsky's belief in social learning. TPS requires students to work in pairs, with the guidance of the teacher to engage in shared problem-solving by thinking independently and then working in pairs to share their knowledge and solve problems.

TPS was first described by Frank Lyman (1981) as an active and collaborative learning process. Teachers follow a series of steps to engage students in TPS, which typically include:

1. Describe what they are going to investigate and why it's being investigated.
2. Acknowledge that the content may be challenging and/or unfamiliar.
3. Pose a question and ask students to think about a document or anything they may know that is relevant to the subject matter being explored.
4. Ask students to share and discuss their information with another student.
5. Ask each pair to summarise their shared knowledge, including points of disagreement.

Retrieval practice

Retrieval practice is a strategy used to assist students to support the development of long-term memory. Based on Sweller's CLT, the process involves asking students to recall information using a range of pedagogical strategies such as:

- self-correcting quizzes
- flashcards with a question on one side and the answer on the other side of the card. Students attempt to answer the question and then check for accuracy by referring to the answer
- writing prompts such as an incomplete sentence. For example, 'Australia's three largest exports are....'; 'The main characters in the story were...'
- concept maps using diagrams and key words to explain a concept
- elaborative interrogation encourages critical thinking by asking students 'how' and 'why' questions to make connections between existing knowledge and new knowledge or concepts. It's a little bit like the concept of '20 Questions' – Why? How do you know?

Videos: Think-Pair-Share

Retrieval practice, particularly with older students, is often undertaken using online tools.

Reflecting on learning (metacognition)

According to the New Zealand Curriculum:

> Reflective learners assimilate new learning, relate it to what they already know, adapt it for their own purposes, and translate thought into action. Over time, they develop their creativity, their ability to think critically about information and ideas, and their metacognitive ability (that is, their ability to think about their own thinking).

Source: The New Zealand Curriculum, Ministry of Education, 2015, https://nzcurriculum.tki.org.nz/The-New-Zealand-Curriculum

Reflection requires students to think about *how* they learn and *why* they are learning (not simply about what they have learned). Reflection encourages students to think about themselves as learners: how they engage in learning; what strategies they use as learners; what they think about their skills and abilities as learners; how they respond when learning is challenging; and what they can do to develop their learning skills.

Tools to support student reflection

Teachers encourage reflection on learning when they ask questions. For example:

- What did you accomplish today?
- What was something you already knew that was reinforced?
- What was the most important thing you learned today?
- What did you appreciate the most today?
- What do you need to learn more about?
- What emotions do you need to be aware of next time?
- What are you most interested in learning about next?

Source: Miller, A. (2019). Treating Reflection as a Habit, Not an Event. Edutopia. https://www.edutopia.org/article/treating-reflection-habit-not-event

Teachers may also encourage students to use an electronic journal to reflect on their learning (see **Figure 11.13**).

Figure 11.13 Examples of journal entries

This week I challenged myself to:	I'm proud of my learning this week because...	My learning goal for next week is....

Videos: Retrieval practice and pre-questions

CONSIDER THIS

REFLECTION

The terms reflection and critical reflection do not have the same meaning. The Critical Reflection Framework (Victorian Education Department, 2007) states:

> Often 'reflection' and 'critical reflection' are used inter-changeably in the literature. However, critical reflection denotes another level of reflection beyond what you might or might not cover in other forms of reflection (e.g. diary, journal). . . . Critical reflection is an extension of 'critical thinking'.

Developing a growth mindset

Carol Dweck developed a growth mindset theory 'using the terms fixed mindset and growth mindset to describe the underlying beliefs people have about learning and intelligence. When students believe they can get smarter, they understand that effort makes them stronger. Therefore they put in extra time and effort, and that leads to higher achievement' (Mindset Works, 2017).

Figure 11.14 provides an overview of Dweck's growth mindset theory.

Students with a growth mindset understand they can get smarter through hard work, the use of effective strategies, and help from others when needed. It is contrasted with a fixed mindset: the belief that intelligence is a fixed trait that is set in stone at birth.

Figure 11.14 Dweck's growth mindset theory

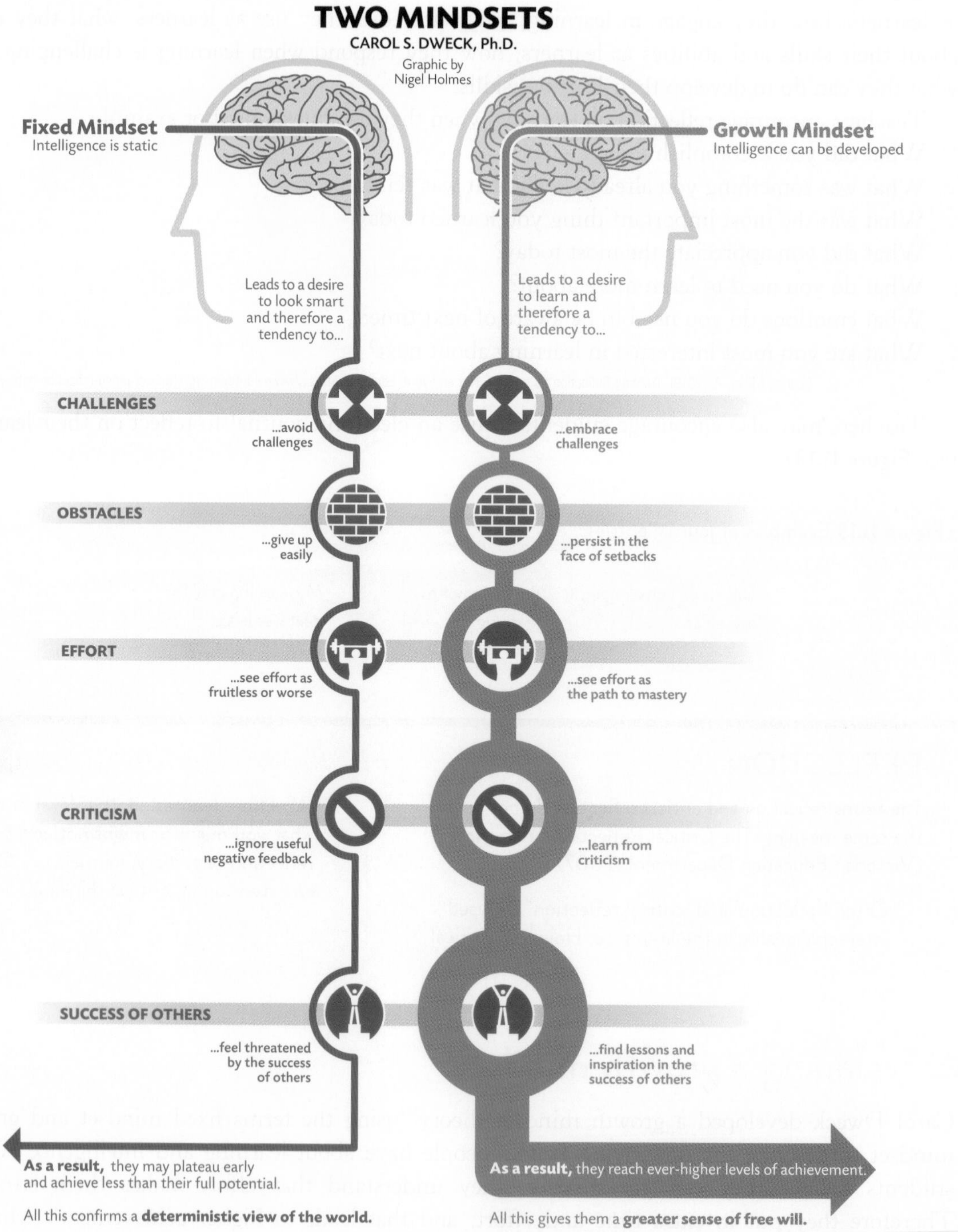
TWO MINDSETS
CAROL S. DWECK, Ph.D.
Graphic by
Nigel Holmes
Fixed Mindset
Intelligence is static
Growth Mindset
Intelligence can be developed
Leads to a desire to look smart and therefore a tendency to...
Leads to a desire to learn and therefore a tendency to...
CHALLENGES
...avoid challenges
...embrace challenges
OBSTACLES
...give up easily
...persist in the face of setbacks
EFFORT
...see effort as fruitless or worse
...see effort as the path to mastery
CRITICISM
...ignore useful negative feedback
...learn from criticism
SUCCESS OF OTHERS
...feel threatened by the success of others
...find lessons and inspiration in the success of others
As a result, they may plateau early and achieve less than their full potential.
As a result, they reach ever-higher levels of achievement.
All this confirms a deterministic view of the world.
All this gives them a greater sense of free will.

Source: Concept by Carol Dweck, graphic by Nigel Holmes, used with permission

Romero (2015) tells us that a student's attitude towards challenges in learning shapes their response to learning. **Figure 11.15** shows the attitude of a student with a fixed mindset versus a student with a growth mindset.

Figure 11.15 Responses to challenging learning

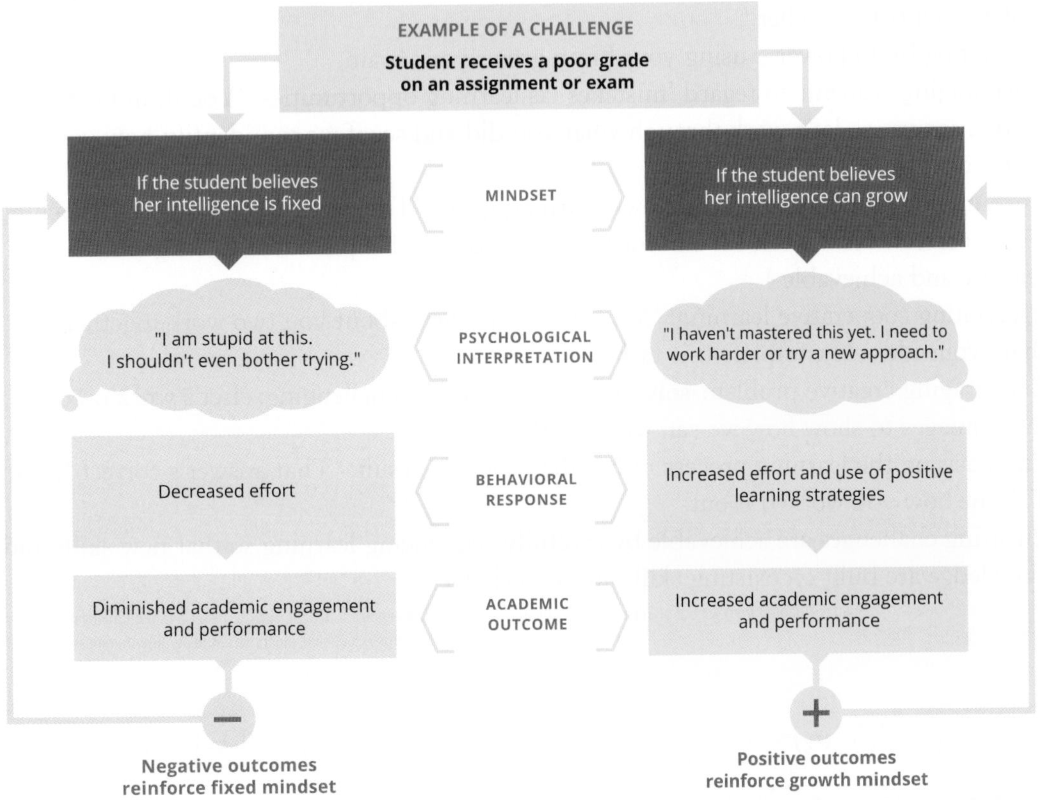

Source: 'What We Know About Growth Mindset from Scientific Research' by Carissa Romero, Student Experience Research Network, July 2015. Licensed under a Creative Commons Attribution-NonCommercial-NoDerivatives 4.0 International (CC BY-NC-ND 4.0), https://creativecommons.org/licenses/by-nc-nd/4.0/

Research on growth mindset reveals that students who are exposed to how their brain develops and what they can do to support their developing brain are more likely to adopt a growth mindset. Romero states:

> Researchers have found that it is possible to promote a growth mindset by teaching students about neuro-science evidence showing that the brain is malleable and gets stronger through effort, trying new strategies, and seeking help when necessary. Researchers have also learned that we can encourage students to adopt more of a growth mindset by changing the way in which we interact with them.

Source: 'What We Know About Growth Mindset from Scientific Research' by Carissa Romero, Student Experience Research Network, July 2015. Licensed under a Creative Commons Attribution-NonCommercial-NoDerivatives 4.0 International (CC BY-NC-ND 4.0), https://creativecommons.org/licenses/by-nc-nd/4.0/

Teachers support a growth mindset when they praise effort rather than outcome. For example, 'I can see that you tried a few different ways to get the answer Josh. That shows me that you're really applying your knowledge'; 'I like the way you went to several sources to get the information. You didn't just rely on one source. That's great critical thinking Ella.'

Using Vygotsky's ZPD allows teachers to offer the right level of challenge for each student. To develop a growth mindset, challenges must require effort but must also be attainable.

Other strategies you may observe being used by teachers to create a growth mindset may include:

- Normalising struggle. Learning can be challenging. Tell students that most of us don't 'get it' immediately when faced with learning new skills and knowledge. Learning requires persistence and effort.
- Encouraging students to see challenges as fun – when there is no challenge learning doesn't stretch our brain!

- Embracing the word 'yet'. When a student says, 'I'm no good at spelling', respond by 'I think you mean you're no good at spelling just yet. I think the effort you're putting in will make you a better speller.'
- Promoting brain power – using your brain grows your brain.
- Encouraging students to regard 'mistakes' as learning opportunities: 'You didn't get the correct answer so let's work through what you did and see if we can identify how you can do better next time.'
- Encouraging students to set their own learning goals: 'This week I got 4 out of 10 spelling words correct. Next week I'll aim for 6 correct words.' (Help student to set goals that are realistic and achievable.)
- Facilitating cooperative learning: 'Max and Sarah, how about you two work together and share your ideas to complete this task.'
- Encouraging creative problem-solving when learning is challenging: 'Let's work on creating a set of images to show how we can work on this problem.'
- Emphasising the learning process rather than the end result: 'That answer's correct Imran. Tell me how you worked it out.'
- Ensuring challenges are achievable by carefully sequencing learning so that new skills and knowledge are built on existing skills and knowledge.

Videos: Student goal setting and self-reflection

Source: Adapted from School of Education. American University, Washington, DC (2020). How to foster a growth mindset in the classroom. https://soeonline.american.edu/blog/growth-mindset-in-the-classroom

11.4 Creating a positive and stimulating learning environment

A positive learning environment is one where every student feels respected, accepted and safe. As discussed in Chapter 5, the Australian Student Wellbeing Framework was designed to support schools as communities that promote student wellbeing, safety and positive relationships so that students can reach their full potential. The Framework includes five elements, as shown in **Figure 11.16**.

Figure 11.16 Elements of the Australian Student Wellbeing Framework

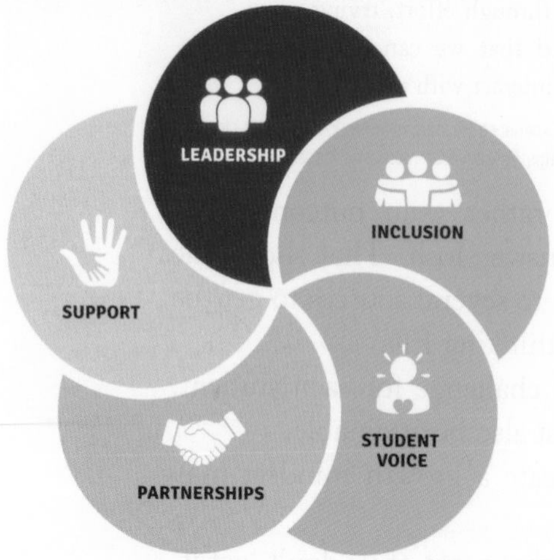

Source: Australian Student Wellbeing Framework, https://studentwellbeinghub.edu.au/educators/framework/. Licensed under Creative Commons Attribution 4.0 International (CC BY 4.0) licence, https://creativecommons.org/licenses/by/4.0/

In relation to a supportive learning environment the Framework states:

- Create and maintain inclusive and interactive learning environments to encourage active student participation to foster a sense of connectedness
- Teach, model and promote values and behaviour in order to create and maintain supportive and safe learning environments
- Foster and maintain positive, caring and respectful student–peer, student–teacher, teacher–parent and teacher–teacher relationships

Source: Australian Student Wellbeing Framework, 2020. Licensed under Creative Commons Attribution 4.0 International (CC BY 4.0) licence. https://creativecommons.org/licenses/by/4.0/

The Framework can be applied in the classroom, and when teachers and ESWs build positive and respectful relationships with each student, students are more likely to feel accepted and happy to engage in learning.

Student wellbeing is embedded in the Australian Curriculum's general capabilities of ethical understanding, personal and social capability, and intercultural understanding.

Elements of a positive and respectful learning environment include:

- *positive teacher–student relationships* – treating each student with kindness, fairness, dignity and respect
- *a nurturing atmosphere* – creating an environment where individual differences are accepted and respected
- *clear and consistent expectations for behaviour* – expected standards of behaviour are communicated clearly, communicated often and communicated consistently
- *routines and rituals* – routines that are predictable provide stability and a sense of control and order for students. For example, routines for greeting students, entering and leaving the room, whole group discussions to resolve issues or problems; rituals may include acknowledge birthdays, sharing something positive about the day before going home, celebrating community events such as a win by the local football team
- *appropriate amounts of structure for specific situations/needs* – for example, creating a balance of teacher-led, small group and self-directed learning, opportunities for free choice activities
- *proactive intervention of problems* – for example, engaging students in setting behaviour standards, problem-solving with students when there are group issues or problems in the classroom.

Source: Adapted from 'Creating a Safe, Fair and Respectful Environment', Asheville City Schools. https://www.ashevillecityschools.net/site/handlers/filedownload.ashx?moduleinstanceid=166&dataid=917&FileName=Creating-a-Safe-Fair-and-Respectful-Environment.pdf

Videos: Problem solving and growth mindset

The Australian Student Wellbeing Framework

11.5 Set up and sustain learning areas

The physical layout of the classroom sends silent messages to students about ways of learning and expected behaviours (see **Figure 11.17**). The classroom should be a welcoming, safe place where students feel a sense of belonging. Spaces that are designed to accommodate the learning, social and emotional needs of students are integral to effective teaching. For example, providing a quiet space allows students to retreat, be alone, calm down, take a break from learning and regather their thoughts, and accommodates the emotional wellbeing of students. Spaces where students can collaborate, problem-solve and engage in hands-on learning accommodate diverse learning styles and diverse abilities. Flexible spaces allow students to take charge of and direct

Figure 11.17 Learning environments can vary in layout and setup. Can you identify the pros and cons of environments like these?

Source: Photos by Tish Okely © Cengage

their own learning. Self-directed learning develops a sense of **agency** and is a key goal in any educational setting.

Flexible spaces allow for the rearrangement of furniture to reflect both learning activities and pedagogical practices for whole, small group and individual learning. For example, differentiated instruction learning centres can be set up to allow for multiple activities at different levels of difficulty. The degree of challenge may be assigned by the teacher, or students may be free to select their own level of challenge.

A key role for ESWs is to work collaboratively to set up and support learning areas. Depending on the teacher's program, the size of the room, and the number and abilities of students, learning areas may be permanent spaces for designated learning in curriculum areas such as reading, maths or investigations; alternatively, learning space may be temporary and changeable.

When working with the teacher to arrange physical learning spaces, other factors that need to be considered include:

- the learning outcomes of each activity
- the nature of the learning activity – for example, working quietly, working with others; will the activity require students to move around? Engage in discussion? Will the activity generate additional noise?
- the pedagogical strategies that will be used
- opportunities to observe student learning
- the materials and equipment needed for the activity (including access to technology)
- adequate and easily accessible storage areas
- the amount and type of furniture and furnishing available – for example, desks, chairs, lounge, bean bags, portable and fixed storage/shelving
- the physical layout of the room – for example, spaces for quiet, independent learning, spaces for small groups, areas for project/investigation work, access to technology
- acoustics, ventilation and natural light
- supervision and safety.

Typically, permanent learning spaces are set up in corners or nooks where students can work alone, in pairs or in small groups. Creating different learning spaces has other benefits, such as:

- helping students to identify how different physical spaces communicate behaviour expectations. For example, in areas where independent learning is taking place, students are expected to work quietly and not interrupt others; in group learning spaces, students learn to work cooperatively and remain on task
- centralising resources and materials for easy and quick access
- creating a learning routine – students become familiar with each learning area and know the type of learning that is expected.

Videos: Safe and positive learning environments

Learning centres provide opportunities for students to practise existing skills and knowledge and to explore new skills and knowledge. Learning centres allow for self-directed learning and also support self-regulation. Learning centres can also be used to support reflective thinking, by encouraging students to develop their own questions for further investigation and deeper learning.

Setting up small group learning areas

Small groups are opportunities for students to engage in direct instruction, collaborative learning with their peers, consolidate or practise existing skills and knowledge, or extend and work on higher-level skills and knowledge. Small groups can be teacher-led, student-led, peer-led or technology-led (e.g. videos, learning programs and computer games; see **Figure 11.18**).

Figure 11.18 Examples of small group learning areas designed effectively in the classroom environment

Source: Photos by Tish Okely © Cengage

Small groups provide an opportunity for students to lead their own learning and build their sense of agency. More skilled and knowledgeable peers can work alongside others using their expertise to scaffold learning. Small groups can also be used by teachers to provide direct instruction when introducing new information, to practise key skills, to address deficits or where intensive instruction is needed (e.g. English language learners, or students with additional learning or behaviour challenges). Where intensive direct instruction is the primary goal, students are usually grouped by ability.

Small groups instruction allows teachers to model thinking and learning strategies, practise skills, build on existing knowledge, learn from a range of sources (including peers) and gain feedback (van Diggele, Burgess & Mellis, 2020).

Bolden (2020) states that when working with small groups, teachers are able to diagnose students' learning deficits and create specific learning plans to meet their needs in content areas. Being in close proximity to students allows the teacher to address misconceptions immediately, in ways that are not possible in whole group instruction. Teachers may engage in a cycle of small group instruction that includes pre-assessment, direct instruction while progress monitoring, post-assessment and reteaching of concepts for mastery. This often includes the pedagogical practice of 'I do, you do, we do' (Bolden, 2020).

CONSIDER THIS

Small group instruction reflects the following theories:

- Vygotsky's ZPD
- Bloom's taxonomy – hierarchical order of thinking skills
- visible learning
- Sweller's CLT.

Teachers typically develop a routine for small group work that helps students to:

- develop time management skills by working to a set time frame (e.g. 30 minutes)
- understand what is acceptable in relation to the completion of tasks, noise level, moving about and asking for help
- access materials/resources
- record their work
- what to do if they finish ahead of other students
- packing away and tidying the workspace
- the standard of work expected
- the behaviour expected – in relation to self and others
- respecting peers as learners.

To reduce the need for teacher instruction when small groups are working independently, teachers commonly use visual prompts such as:

- anchor charts
- digital slides for step-by-step instructions
- posters of things to do if students finish ahead of others
- posters reminding students of required behaviours/rules.

Creating learning environments for secondary schools

In primary school, groups often focus on reading, writing, maths and vocabulary. Examples of small group strategies that can be used with high school students are described in **Figure 11.19**.

Figure 11.19 Examples of group work in high schools

Create a commercial	Students create a 30-second commercial that advertises the subject of the class – emphasising, for example, its value to them (or to the world) and famous people associated with it.
Debate a topic	Four-member groups debate a controversial topic. Two students take one side of the issue and two take the other.
Discuss quotations	Provide a 'hatful of quotes' taken from the text or person being studied. Students in each subgroup take a quote, reflect on it for a few minutes, then read it aloud and comment on it.
Generate questions	Students generate questions for group discussion.
Buzz groups	Students engaging in short, informal discussions, often in response to a particular sentence starter or question.
Think-pair-share	First, students think individually about a particular question or scenario. Then they pair up to discuss and compare their ideas. Finally, they are given the chance to share their ideas in a large class discussion.
Circle of voices	Students form circles of four or five and are given a topic – each student speaks on a topic and engages in group discussion.
Rotating trios	Students form trios, with the groups arranged in a large circle or square formation. Students are given a question and each person takes a turn answering.
Snowball groups/pyramids	Students first work alone, then in pairs, then in fours and so on, progressively doubling in size.

Source: Adapted from: Group Work in the Classroom: Types of Small Groups. Centre for Teaching Excellence, University of Waterloo. https://uwaterloo.ca/centre-for-teaching-excellence/teaching-resources/teaching-tips/developing-assignments/group-work/group-work-classroom-types-small-groups

In addition to the factors considered earlier, when planning small group learning spaces the teacher needs to consider:

- the number, age and abilities of the students
- individual student behaviour – for example, whether students are able to sit, listen and participate; whether some students require a greater level of supervision; whether there are students who are uncooperative, disruptive, impulsive and noisy
- the nature of the task/activity – this will determine the size and nature of the space required. Is the activity active or passive? Will students work independently or collaboratively? Will the activity be messy/noisy/quiet?
- the learning materials/resources that will be used. Will students be required to share learning resources? Will students need access to technology?
- whether the learning activity could be conducted outdoors
- how the students will enter and exit the learning space
- your own role – will you need to stand, sit or move around? Will students come to you? What resources will you require?

Videos: Setting up learning spaces to maximise learning

11.6 Resources for learning

Learning resources include a wide range of materials used to facilitate and support student learning in all curriculum areas, including resources to support students with additional needs – for example, IT equipment, adaptive equipment, play equipment, manipulatives for numeracy, writing materials, texts and other print materials such as charts, posters and graphics, curriculum-specific resources in areas such as music and sport, lab equipment and machines for woodwork and metalwork.

Teachers will select resources for a range of reasons – for example, resources that best suit the required outcomes related to the curriculum, accommodate the diverse needs and abilities of learners, accommodate a range of pedagogical strategies, make planning for differentiated learning easier, add interest and challenge to learning activities, allow for self-directed learning or add an element of novelty and fun to learning.

All schools have a wide range of teaching and learning resources, which increasingly includes the use of technology. Teachers will determine which learning resources best suit the needs of their students and depending on individual needs of students there may be a range of learning resources used throughout the day (see **Figure 11.20**).

Figure 11.20 Students are supported with a diverse range of learning resources

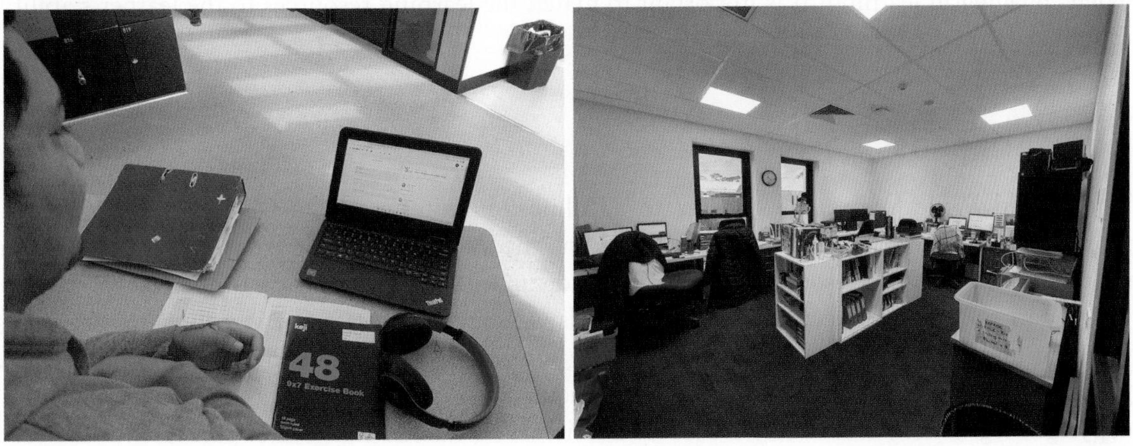

Source: Photos by Tish Okely © Cengage

SCENARIO

USING RESOURCES WELL

PODCAST

ESW **Richard** is working with a group of four Year 7 boys. The English teacher has asked Richard to sit with the group while they listen to a short podcast about poetry. Richard is aware that the boys are likely to be uninterested and disruptive. Richard and the teacher decide that Richard should offer the boys an incentive for staying on task. The lesson goes extremely well as the boys are very motivated by the promise of special time to read the latest skateboard magazines supplied by the teacher.

TABLET

Later that day, Richard works with a small group of Year 7 students using a tablet. The students are required to complete a series of mathematical tasks by working as a team, sharing ideas and using trial and error. The tablet is an effective hands-on resource that keeps the students motivated and on task. Richard takes on the role of facilitator, supporting the students as they work through the tasks.

MESSY FUN

Year 1 students are working on maths tasks. The students work in pairs and are required to cut and paste pictures from magazines to demonstrate their understanding of quantity and classification. ESW **Mira** has been allocated three groups of students – her role is to support and supervise the students, and offer direction and guidance as needed. At the completion of the lesson, the students are having to assist in tidying the room, picking up any paper from the floor and putting all materials back in the correct storage area.

CHOICES

On Wednesday afternoons, the Kindergarten students are free to choose from a range of self-directed art and craft activities. The students are expected to clean up when they are finished. ESW **Jan** is assigned to support **Tia**, who has a mild intellectual impairment. Tia functions best when tasks are highly structured, and she is given step-by-step directions. To encourage Tia to make her own choices, Jan sets Tia up with a range of collage materials and encourages her to create her own design. This is quite challenging for Jan as Tia continually asks her which collage items she should choose. On reflection, Jan thinks that it would have been easier for Tia had she limited the choice of collage materials to three or four items.

WHAT DOES THIS TELL US?

Learning materials and resources can be used in a variety of ways and adapted to suit the desired learning outcome, as well as the diverse needs and abilities of students.

Children and young people benefit from the use of practical hands-on learning resources when engaging in learning. It is important to match the learning resources to the learner's ability as well as to the required learning outcomes.

Digital access to resources

The World Wide Web allows access to an almost infinitesimal range of learning resources. However, not all resources that can be accessed on the Web are fit-for-purpose. As an ESW, you should never download resources to use with students without the approval of the teacher.

As part of governance requirements, schools will have policies and procedures for accessing teaching and learning resources to ensure they are approved for use in the classroom. These governance requirements relate to considerations such as duty of care, ethical behaviour, copyright legislation, sustainable resources and issues of human rights. For example, in the case of multimedia resources, governance requirements will relate to:

- textbooks, novels, plays
- films, videos, radio programs, webinars
- multimedia and digital learning resources including video, audio, podcasts, text, animations and images
- lectures, speeches and performances.

Videos: Small groups in the classroom

Schools will have policies and procedures for vetting the suitability of these resources. These will include factors such as child/young person content suitability, the potential of any content to be offensive to students or parents because of perceived bias in relation to race, ethnicity, religion, sexuality, child-rearing beliefs and human rights. Resources must also be vetted to ensure they don't include offensive or discriminatory language or images (see Victorian Department of Education and Training, 2023).

Multimedia resources such as video games, videos and films, must also meet the Australian Government's Australian Classification for content suitability for children and young people (see **Figure 11.21**).

Figure 11.21 Advisory categories for films and computer games

Icon	Classification
G	General (G) The content is very mild in impact The G classification is suitable for everyone. G products may contain classifiable elements such as language and themes that are very mild in impact.
PG	Parental Guidance (PG) The content is mild in impact The impact of PG (Parental Guidance) classified films and computer games should be no higher than mild, but they may contain content that children find confusing or upsetting and may require the guidance of parents, teachers or guardians.
M	Mature (M) The content is moderate in impact Films and computer games classified M (Mature) contain content of a moderate impact. M-rated films and computer games are not recommended for children under the age of 15. They include portrayals of elements such as violence and themes that require a mature outlook.
MA 15+ RESTRICTED	Mature Accompanied (MA 15+) The content is strong in impact MA 15+ rated material contains strong content and is legally restricted to people over the age of 15. It contains elements such as sex scenes and drug use that could have a strong impact on the viewer.
R 18+ RESTRICTED	Restricted (R 18+) The content is high in impact R 18+ material is restricted to adults as it contains content that is considered high in impact for viewers. This includes content that may be offensive to sections of the adult community. A person may be asked for proof of their age before purchasing, hiring or viewing R 18+ films and computer games at a retail store or cinema.

Source: Australian Classification, https://www.classification.gov.au/for-industry/classification-markings/markings-downloads-and-guides. Licensed under Creative Commons (CC) Attribution 4.0 International licence, creativecommons.org/licenses/by/4.0/

Educational resources must also be sourced ethically. For example, the production of the resource should not involve the exploitation of minority groups or use slave or child labour. The access and use of the resource must also meet the requirements of Australian copyright legislation.

Teaching and learning resources

Each state or territory education department will also have a preferred suppliers list for educational resources, goods and services. School administrators will usually access this list in the first instance when attempting to source the required resources before widening their search. Approved learning resources that meet governance requirements can be accessed digitally and free of charge via education department websites (see **Figure 11.22** and **Figure 11.23**).

Figure 11.22 Free government learning resources

Education department	Weblink
Education ACT	https://www.education.act.gov.au/schooling/resources-for-teachers
Education NSW	https://education.nsw.gov.au/teaching-and-learning/curriculum/pdhpe/life-ready/support-materials#Considerations1
Education NT	https://nt.gov.au/learning/primary-and-secondary-students/nt-school-curriculum

Education department	Weblink
Education QLD	https://education.qld.gov.au/curriculum/learning-at-home/learning-resources
Education Tas	https://www.teaching-learning.utas.edu.au/content-and-resources
Education Vic	https://www.education.vic.gov.au/school/teachers/teachingresources/Pages/default.aspx
Education WA	https://www.education.wa.edu.au/#toc3

Figure 11.23 Free non-government learning resources

Organisation	Weblink
ACER	https://www.acer.org/au/discover/article/selecting-teaching-resources-that-meet-student-needs-a-guide
Australian Human Rights Commission	https://humanrights.gov.au/education/teachers
Cool Australia	https://www.coolaustralia.org/curriculum-materials/?types_k=&types_v=&year_level_k=&year_level_v=&ca_topic_k=&ca_topic_v=&subject_k=&subject_v=&
Inclusion Ed	https://www.inclusioned.edu.au
Life Ed	https://lifeed.org.au
Money Smart	https://moneysmart.gov.au/teaching/teaching-resources
Paying It Forward	https://www.ato.gov.au/General/Education-zone/Paying-It-Forward/
Prime Zone	https://www.primezone.edu.au

When accessing resources from these websites, you should also seek permission from your classroom teacher before use.

Games and activities

Teachers use digital and non-digital games to: deliver curriculum content; assess knowledge and skills; support social and emotional development; promote executive functioning skills, encourage concentration and on-task behaviour; support critical thinking; consolidate skills and knowledge; practise and apply skills and knowledge; challenge and extend high-functioning learners; engage in one-to-one intensive teaching or intervention; enrich curriculum content; differentiate learning; and encourage fun and relaxation. Games can be played alone, in pairs or small groups, and as a whole class activity (see **Figure 11.24**).

Figure 11.24 Digital activities can be used effectively as learning opportunities

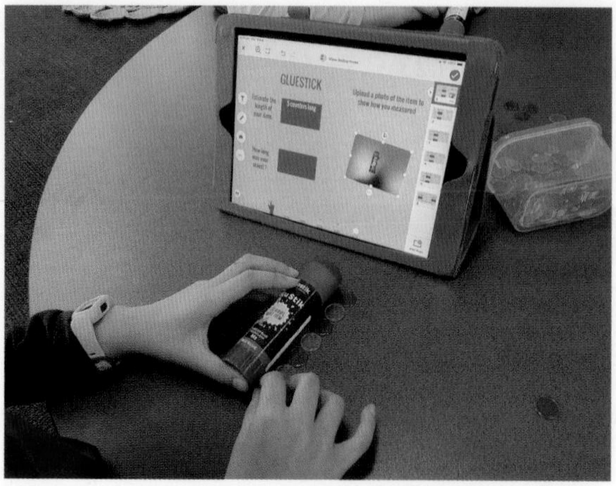

Source: Photo by Tish Okely © Cengage

Board games played in small groups provide opportunities for turn-taking, cooperation, teamwork, negotiation and problem-solving (following rules, solving disagreements) and collaboration. Other social/emotional skills that are facilitated include motivation, perseverance, patience, responsibility, fairness and self-discipline (Upper Elementary Snapshots, n.d.). Games can also be used to ease the anxiety and stress of students who struggle with literacy, have poor language skills, poor concentration skills, are easily distracted or simply find traditional learning strategies too challenging. Digital games promote equity by supporting students with disability to engage in learning alongside their peers. According to Nguyen (2021), research has found that virtual games can improve focus and attention for students with attention deficit hyperactivity disorder (ADHD) and help students with dyslexia improve spatial and temporal attention, which can translate into improved reading.

Games as a learning tool reflect Piaget's theory of cognitive development and our knowledge of the importance of hands-on play as learning for children and young people. The level and challenge of games can be scaffolded to meet the needs of each student. This allows teachers to use Vygotsky's ZPD to accurately, and increasingly challenge, student learning. Games also accommodate Gardner's theory of multiple intelligences.

Copyright resources

When games are used as a learning tool, students are required to use their working memory to recall and apply rules and engage in problem-solving.

Gamification

Gamification is the use of game-design elements and game principles in non-game contexts. Gamification is a tool that classroom teachers can use to complement traditional teaching strategies. Gamification allows the student to explore and learn new information, test their existing knowledge and engage in problem-solving. Gamification can be an effective way for students to apply their knowledge and practice the application of knowledge in a fun, non-threatening learning environment.

Gamification as the name implies, is a games-based approach to online learning. Students typically engage in self-paced games that motivate the player by using rewards such as badges and points tables as the games becomes increasingly challenging. The benefits of gamification include:

- engage students who are not motivated to participate in regular classroom learning strategies
- students can play alone or as part of an online group
- requires minimal supervision
- gamification can be used as a motivator to reward on-target learning behaviour such as completing set tasks in a timely manner, and remaining on-task when tasks are challenging for the student
- for student who suffer anxiety in the classroom, gamification can have a relaxing/calming effect
- the self-paced nature of gamification allows students to set their own learning target or pathway, and is therefore self-motivating (e.g., striving for a personal best)
- students are introduced to new information in a range of different ways and may include real world applications
- new information is built off existing knowledge and skills (scaffolding), allowing student to build knowledge in a non-threatening and fun way
- challenge levels can be monitored and tracked by both the teacher and the student
- allows students to take ownership of their learning
- supports executive functioning skills such as thinking and processing information, planning and decision-making, focusing, remembering and connecting information
- allows for instant and constant feedback
- many games promote creativity by allowing the player to create their own avatars, environments (e.g., playground, town, animals etc.).

Importantly, gamification can add an element of fun to learning.

Source: Adapted from True Education Partnerships (n.d.). Gamification in education: What is it & how can you use It? https://www.trueeducationpartnerships.com/schools/gamification-in-education

Game-based learning

Identifying quality learning resources

Resources must be free of bias, such as racism, sexism, homophobia and religious vilification, and be respectful of human rights. They also must reflect the concepts of inclusion and respect for diversity (social, religious, economic, ethnic, ability). Resources must be fit-for-purpose in relation to learning outcomes, ease of use and be age and ability appropriate. According to Bugler et al. (2017), five key criteria can be used to assess the quality of learning resources (see **Figure 11.25**).

Figure 11.25 Criteria for quality learning materials

Criteria	Description
Accuracy, visual appeal	No errors; correct information Well written Strong visual appeal
Alignment to standards, depth of knowledge	Aligned to standards Efficiently addresses standards Appropriate depth of knowledge, questions and activities
Ease of use, support	Easy for teachers, students and parents to use. For example, if a student is provided with access to an app to assist with spelling, the student must have the necessary skills to use the app Can the resource be adapted to suit the abilities of the student? For example, can a student with a physical disability manipulate the resource? Is the resource easily accessible? Is a website address provided and accurate so the student does not need to engage in an extensive search for the required information? Complete set of instructions, materials, activities, assessments and answers Appropriate support for new teachers
Engagement, ability to meet student needs	Engagement: sparks student interest; relevant Differentiation: appropriate material by skill level, language ability, cognitive capability and learning style. For example, while a 16-year-old may have a reading age of 12 years, it is not appropriate to provide reading material that doesn't reflect the interests of 16-year-olds. The subject matter should reflect the maturity level of the student Cultural and background knowledge: culturally relevant; aligns with prior background knowledge Diverse activities: group and individual, hands-on, requires movement, longer investigations
Trusted sources	Made by and for teachers Include teacher comments, opinions and reviews Ratings based on use by teachers (with information about student characteristics)
Fit for purpose	The resource must be readily useable in the learning context in which it is being provided – for example, an online dictionary for literacy or a calculator for maths; a reference book for research on Australian marsupials contains all the information required by the student in an easy-to-read format. The text size is large enough for the student and language used reflects the student's current reading and comprehension level

Source: Bugler, D., Marple, S., Burr, E., Chen-Gaddini, M. & Finkelstein, N. (2017) How teachers judge the quality of instructional materials. San Francisco, CA: WestEd.

Adapting and modifying learning resources

While schools have access to a wide range of learning resources, there will be occasions when resources will need to be adapted or modified to suit student needs. This includes those students referred to by Rose, Meyer and Hitchcock (2005, cited in Rababate, 2011) as 'students in the margins' whose strengths and barriers are not always obvious. These students tend to be those who need different kinds of supports and scaffolds to learn. They are a heterogeneous group struggling to learn for a wide variety of reasons, such as:

- sensory or physical disabilities
- emotional or behavioural challenges
- learning disabilities or reading difficulties
- autism spectrum disorder
- ADHD
- lack of appropriate background knowledge
- English-language barriers (Rababate, 2011).

A key objective when adapting and modifying learning resources is to remove or reduce barriers to learning so that students can participate in classroom activities alongside their more able peers. When accessing learning resources as fit-for-purpose for each student, the principles of the Universal Design for Learning (UDL) framework provide an approach to designing meaningful learning opportunities that address learner variability. The goal of UDL is to support learners to become 'expert learners' who are, each in their own way, purposeful and motivated, resourceful and knowledgeable, and strategic and goal driven.

> UDL emphasizes three large brain networks that comprise the vast majority of the human brain and play a central role in learning. These networks [see **Figure 11.26**] include: the affective network (how learners monitor the internal and external environment to set priorities, to motivate, and to engage learning and behavior), the recognition network (how learners sense and perceive information in the environment and transform it into usable knowledge), and the strategic network (how learners plan, organize, and initiate purposeful actions in the environment).
>
> Source: UDL guidelines. Frequently asked questions. https://udlguidelines.cast.org/more/frequently-asked-questions#brain

Figure 11.26 The three principles of UDL

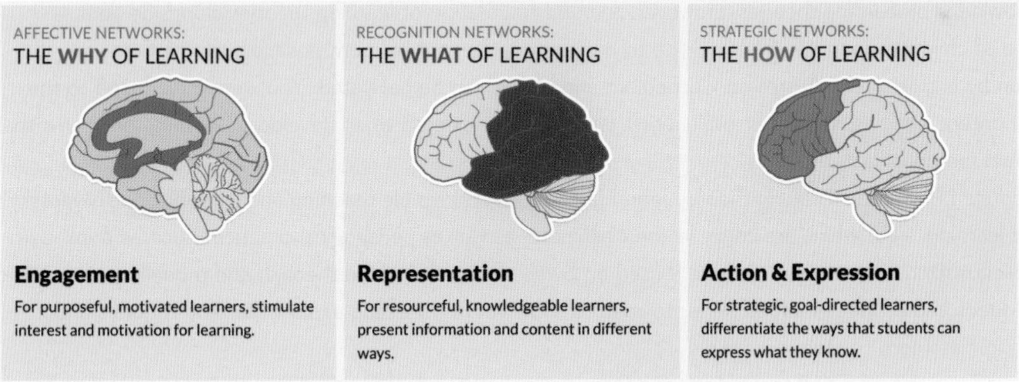

AFFECTIVE NETWORKS:
THE WHY OF LEARNING
Engagement
For purposeful, motivated learners, stimulate interest and motivation for learning.
RECOGNITION NETWORKS:
THE WHAT OF LEARNING
Representation
For resourceful, knowledgeable learners, present information and content in different ways.
STRATEGIC NETWORKS:
THE HOW OF LEARNING
Action & Expression
For strategic, goal-directed learners, differentiate the ways that students can express what they know.

Source: © 2023 CAST, Inc. Used with permission.

Depending on the needs of the student and the available learning resources, strategies that can be used to modify or adapt learning materials may include:

- presenting content visually rather than as text – for example, visual sequences of actions, graphic organisers that highlight only key information, posters, pictures, photos, drawings, real objects (concrete examples), videos
- creating a first–then schedule
- breaking tasks down into steps or a sequence using numbered cards
- reducing the amount of work or the number of tasks that a student needs to complete

Universal Design for Learning guidelines

- providing word banks from which students can select when working on literacy tasks; adding picture symbols to word banks
- highlighting key words in a text using a highlighter pen
- adding pictures to text, enlarging text, reducing the amount of text
- providing a sequential checklist that steps through how to use materials or how to complete a task
- recording instructions, which students can replay as they work
- replacing reading content with visual content – for example, video
- using manipulatives such as magnetic letters as an alternative to writing
- using graph paper to help space letters and numbers in writing and maths
- using technology – including assistive technology, such as communication boards, computers, iPads – to support students to access and record information
- providing low-tech aids such as loop scissors, and grip holders for pencils or paint brushes (Bulloch, 2003).

Adapting teaching strategies

Adapting or modifying learning resources will be an ongoing task and can often be a process of trial and error. Observing students using learning resources and, where possible, talking to them about things they find challenging can assist in determining the best way to modify or adapt materials to facilitate their learning.

Summary

This chapter has drawn together learning theories and their use in the classroom. As an ESW, you will not be expected to have an extensive knowledge of learning theories. However, a sound foundation of learning theories alongside your foundation knowledge of child development will allow you to better understand classroom pedagogical practices.

This chapter began by exploring the Australian Curriculum and how it can be navigated. You were introduced to the elements of CASE (content, abilities, standards, evaluation), which are considered when developing learning programs that can be adapted to meet individual learner needs.

The chapter introduced Pavio's dual coding theory, John Hattie's (2009) 'visible teaching and learning', and Vygotsky's ZPD, and scaffolding learning, all of which are visible in the classroom, as well as pedagogical practices such as think-pair-share, direct and explicit instruction, retrieval practice (based on Sweller's cognitive load theory), and modelling and shared learning. A range of videos and online resources were provided to allow you to 'see' and explore learning theories and pedagogical practices in classroom situations.

The chapter explored the role of digital technology as a learning tool alongside more traditional teaching practices such as games and activities. You were introduced to the importance of promoting a growth mindset with students and encouraging reflective practice as a way students can take ownership of their learning.

The final section of the chapter explored the importance of creating a positive learning environment and your role in creating spaces for small group learning. An essential component of a quality learning environment is the use of quality learning resources. The chapter explored the factors that need to be considered when determining the quality of a learning resource. Finally, the chapter explored how to adapt and modify learning resources to meet the needs of individual learners.

Self-check questions

1 What are two components of the Australian Curriculum that are based on the Melbourne Declaration on Educational Goals for Young Australians?
2 In the Australian Curriculum, what does CASE refer to?
3 What does visible teaching and learning refer to?
4 How can scaffolding learning assist students?
5 Define inquiry-based learning (IBL).
6 Explain how setting up small groups can benefit children's learning.
7 To what extent do schools have policies and procedures for accessing teaching and learning resources?

Discussion questions

1 Just after session one on Tuesdays and Thursdays, the children in Prep and Grade 1 are provided with an opportunity to undertake self-learning. During this time, the classroom has set up a vet clinic, a car wash and a grocery shop.
   a What style of learning are children exposed to in this situation?
2 During a home economics lesson, the Year 7s were asked to look at the demonstration screen and watch and replicate each of the recipe steps as the teacher completed them. The students were able to interject and ask questions as the steps were completed.
   a In relation to direct and explicit instruction, this scenario is an example of what style of teaching?
3 The Year 9s were asked to create a 10-question quiz to review their current topic, using Kahootz. This generated excitement among the class because they love playing games.
   a What are the benefits of using games, activities and gamification in a classroom setting?

Activities

1 Fill in the blanks in the following table by drawing a line from the correct phrase in the first column to the appropriate sentence in the second column, in order to complete the sentences.

positive teacher–student relationships	__________ involves engaging students in setting behaviour standards, and problem-solving with students when there are group issues or problems in the classroom.
proactive intervention of problems	__________ provide stability and a sense of control and order for students.
appropriate amounts of structure for specific situations/needs	__________ creates an environment where individual differences are accepted and respected.
routines and rituals	__________ are to be communicated clearly, communicated often and communicated consistently.
clear and consistent expectations for behaviour	In __________, each student is treated with kindness, fairness, dignity and respect.
a nurturing atmosphere	__________ create a balance of teacher-led, small group and self-directed learning and opportunities for free choice activities.

2 Undertake an online search for three YouTube clips explaining a particular maths concept of your choice. Analyse the suitability of each of the resources using the criteria for quality learning materials. Have this ready to share with peers.

Chapter 12

REPORTING AND ASSESSMENT

LEARNING OBJECTIVES

When you have completed this chapter, you should be able to demonstrate that, in relation to working in a school environment, you can:

12.1	understand the key purposes of assessment, the elements of effective assessment and the importance of record-keeping and reporting
12.2	describe three commonly used types of classroom assessment
12.3	use observation as an assessment tool, professionally record and interpret observations to form a picture of students' skills and knowledge, as directed by the teacher
12.4	understand the purpose of the Individual Education Plan (IEP) and the role of the ESW in supporting, measuring and implementing the strategies and goals of each IEP.

Online resources icons refer to useful weblinks. Ask your instructor for these **Online Resources.**

Introduction

The first part of this chapter focuses on the documentation and reporting requirements of student learning. As an education support worker (ESW), you will not be required to participate in the reporting process. However, it is important to understand school reporting requirements and how they relate to the Australian Curriculum. Understanding reporting requirements concludes the broad overview of the Australian Curriculum that has been presented to you in this textbook. The overview of reporting requirements will also introduce you to some of the key terminology that is used by classroom teachers.

The second part of this chapter explores assessment – the purpose and types of assessment practices and how ESWs can contribute to student assessment. The final section explores Individual Learning Plans – how they are developed and monitored, the stakeholders involved (including ESWs) and their use in directing and guiding planning for learning.

12.1 Documentation and reporting requirements

There are various methods, tools and standards for measuring and reporting student achievement at both state and national levels. These include key performance measures, the Australian Curriculum, Assessment and Reporting Authority (ACARA) achievement standards, student progress reports, the National Assessment Program – Literacy and Numeracy (NAPLAN) and Abilities Based Learning and Educational Support (ABLES).

Key performance measures

The Measurement Framework for Schooling in Australia 2020 sets out the reporting requirements for all schools using a set of key performance measures (KPMs). In relation to learning outcomes, the KPMs include achievement in the National Assessment Program (NAP), with a focus on:

- literacy
- numeracy
- civics and citizenship
- ICT literacy
- science literacy (ACARA, 2020, p. 8).

Achievement standards

The Australian Curriculum achievement standards describe 'the quality of learning (the depth of understanding, extent of knowledge and sophistication of skill) typically expected of students as they progress through schooling. An achievement standard comprises a written description with illustrative student work samples' (ACARA, n.d., p. 1).

Monitoring student progress against curriculum standards is referred to as **standards-referenced assessment**. Linking assessment directly to curriculum standards allows teachers to determine whether a student is progressing at the desired level of knowledge, understanding and skills. The language used in the achievement standards reflects Bloom's taxonomy of measurable verbs – for example, analyses, explains, describes, identifies, plans, uses, selects, constructs, interprets.

Australian Curriculum Achievement Standards

Student Progress Reports

The National Education Agreement (NEA) requires all school to provide parents and carers with a plain English report twice a year using a five-point common grade A–E scale (Council of Australian Governments, 2015). The scale identifies levels of achievement against clearly defined and specific learning standards and must:

- be readily understood by parents/carers
- be confidential
- be timely and given at least once each semester
- address the child's academic and non-academic learning
- be followed by an opportunity for the child and the parents/carers to meet with the child's teachers to discuss all aspects of the report and for the school to give constructive advice about supporting the child's further progress at school (Queensland Studies Authority, 2008).

The NEA reflects the requirements of Schools Assistance (Learning Together – Achievement Through Choice and Opportunity) Regulations 2005. Common grade scale descriptors (F–10) are described in **Figure 12.1**.

Figure 12.1 Grade descriptors (Foundation to Year 10)

A	Demonstrating excellent achievement of what is expected at this year level.
B	Demonstrating good achievement of what is expected at this year level.
C	Demonstrating satisfactory achievement of what is expected at this year level.
D	Demonstrating partial achievement of what is expected at this year level.
E	Demonstrating minimal achievement of what is expected at this year level.

In Years 11 and 12, the specific standards for A–E grades are defined for each course area. Grade descriptors are shown in **Figure 12.2**.

Figure 12.2 Grade descriptors (Years 11 and 12)

A	Awarded to students who have demonstrated a very high level of knowledge and understanding of the full range of concepts and principles of the unit
B	Awarded to students who have demonstrated a high level of knowledge and understanding of the concepts and principles of the unit
C	Awarded to students who have demonstrated a sound level of knowledge and understanding of the basic concepts and principles of the unit
D	Awarded to students who have demonstrated a limited knowledge and understanding of the basic concepts and principles of the unit
E	Awarded to students who have demonstrated a very limited knowledge and understanding of the basic concepts and principles of the unit.

Source: ACT Education and Training (n.d.). Reporting on student achievement and progress to students and parents. http://www.det.act.gov.au/__data/assets/pdf_file/0020/19505/StudentReportingPolicy_updated.pdf

Figure 12.3 provides weblinks to reporting student progress in each state and territory.

Figure 12.3 Reporting student progress

State/territory	Weblink
ACT	ACT student reporting: **https://www.education.act.gov.au/public-school-life/assessment_and_reporting/act-student-reporting**
NSW	New written reports for primary and secondary school students. NSW Education: **https://education.nsw.gov.au/teaching-and-learning/curriculum/reporting-to-parents/report-requirements**
NT	School reports: **https://nt.gov.au/learning/primary-and-secondary-students/school-reports/introduction**
QLD	Queensland Curriculum, Assessment and Reporting (QCAR) Framework December 2008. Queensland Studies Authority: **https://www.qcaa.qld.edu.au/downloads/p_10/guidelines_for_reporting_qcar.pdf**

State/territory	Weblink
TAS	Reporting: **https://www.education.tas.gov.au/parents-carers/parent-fact-sheets/reporting**
VIC	Victorian Curriculum F–10. Revised curriculum planning and reporting guidelines: **https://www.vcaa.vic.edu.au/Documents/viccurric/RevisedF-10CurriculumPlanningReportingGuidelines.pdf**
WA	Reporting on student achievement: **https://k10outline.scsa.wa.edu.au/home/policy/policy-standards/reporting-on-student-achievement**

Students with disability

The common grade scale is used for students with disability who are participating in the standard curriculum. Where students have been provided with an adjusted curriculum to meet their learning needs, a 'P' identifier will be incorporated into the standard grade report. Achievement outcomes for students who have a Personalised Learning Plan (PLP) are reported using a Personalised Reporting Scale (**Figure 12.4**). Descriptors used in a Personalised Reporting Scale may vary across jurisdictions.

Figure 12.4 Personalised Reporting Scale

P4 – Independent	The student can complete a task independently, without assistance. The student maintains the skill or knowledge over time. The student generalises the skill or knowledge to new settings, people or materials.
P3 – Frequent	The student relies on partial prompts to complete a task. The student can regularly perform the skill or demonstrate knowledge. The student uses the skills or knowledge in a variety of familiar settings and situations.
P2 – Occasional	The student understands information, concept and/or can perform skill. The student often relies on physical or verbal assistance when participating in a task. The student has begun to demonstrate the skills in selected, familiar settings.
P1 – Beginning	The student has some existing prior knowledge and/or necessary pre-skills for the task. The student is beginning to participate in a task with maximum teacher assistance. The student uses skills and knowledge in a single setting.

Source: Supporting our students – personalised reporting, St George School, https://stgeorge-s.schools.nsw.gov.au/supporting-our-students/personalised-reporting.html

Diversity in learning

While all schools must comply with the NEA requirements, each state and territory is free to develop a reporting template that best reflects its curriculum framework.

NAPLAN

The National Assessment Program (NAP) is run under the direction of the Education Ministers Meeting. It includes the National Assessment Program – Literacy and Numeracy (NAPLAN) and requires all students in Years 3, 5, 7 and 9 to undertake an online assessment of reading, writing, language conventions (spelling, grammar and punctuation) and numeracy. The NAP also conducts three-yearly sample assessments in science literacy, civics and citizenship, and information and communication technology (ICT) literacy, and participates in international sample assessments.

NAPLAN will be explored in greater detail in the literacy and numeracy chapters in Part 3 of this textbook.

Abilities Based Learning and Educational Support (ABLES)

Abilities Based Learning and Educational Support (ABLES)

ABLES is a curriculum assessment and reporting suite that:

- allows teachers to assess the learning readiness of students with disabilities and additional needs
- generates reports for individualised learning planning
- provides guidance and strategies to help teach students based on their individual learning needs, linked to the Victorian Curriculum and resources
- tracks student progress and achievements over time.

Source: Abilities Based Learning and Educational Support (2022). https://www.education.vic.gov.au/school/teachers/learningneeds/Pages/ables.aspx#link36.

12.2 Assessment

The fundamental purpose of assessment is to establish and understand where learners are in an aspect of their learning at the time of assessment. Assessment clarifies what the learner knows, understands or can do, and highlights what is needed to progress the learner to the required standard of achievement at the end of the year or band of development (ACT Government, 2016).

Assessment is the process of gathering information from a variety of sources that accurately reflects how well a student is achieving the curriculum expectations in a subject (Ministry of Education, 2006, p. 15). Assessment is undertaken for a range of audiences and purposes, as shown in **Figure 12.5**.

Figure 12.5 Purpose of assessment

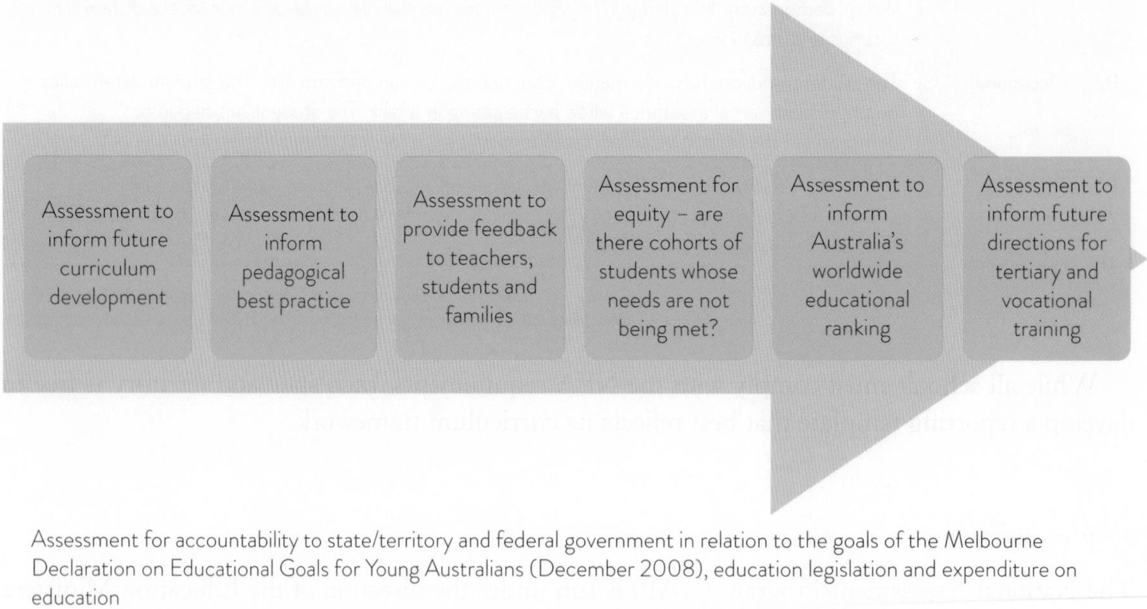

Assessment to inform future curriculum development
Assessment to inform pedagogical best practice
Assessment to provide feedback to teachers, students and families
Assessment for equity – are there cohorts of students whose needs are not being met?
Assessment to inform Australia's worldwide educational ranking
Assessment to inform future directions for tertiary and vocational training
Assessment for accountability to state/territory and federal government in relation to the goals of the Melbourne Declaration on Educational Goals for Young Australians (December 2008), education legislation and expenditure on education

According to the ACT Government (2016), quality assessment:

- allows all students to achieve
- is considered during the design of the teaching and learning task
- is integral to the teaching and learning cycle
- allows opportunities for students to show the extent of their learning
- shows performance and individual progress

- allows measurement of learning gain
- informs, monitors and progresses learning [evidence-based]
- is designed with the learners, the learning goals, curriculum outcomes and the teaching in mind
- has strong validity and reliability
- has inter-rater reliability when evaluated
- shows the benefits of the program and the curriculum through student growth.

Source: ACT Government (2016). *Teachers' Guide to Assessment.* https://ais.act.edu.au/wp-content/uploads/Teachers-Guide-To-Assessment.pdf, p. 6

Assessment in schools is continuous and ongoing. It guides and informs teachers as they plan, implement and evaluate the curriculum. **Figure 12.6** shows the cycle of assessment and evidence-based teaching and learning.

Figure 12.6 Assessment and learning cycle

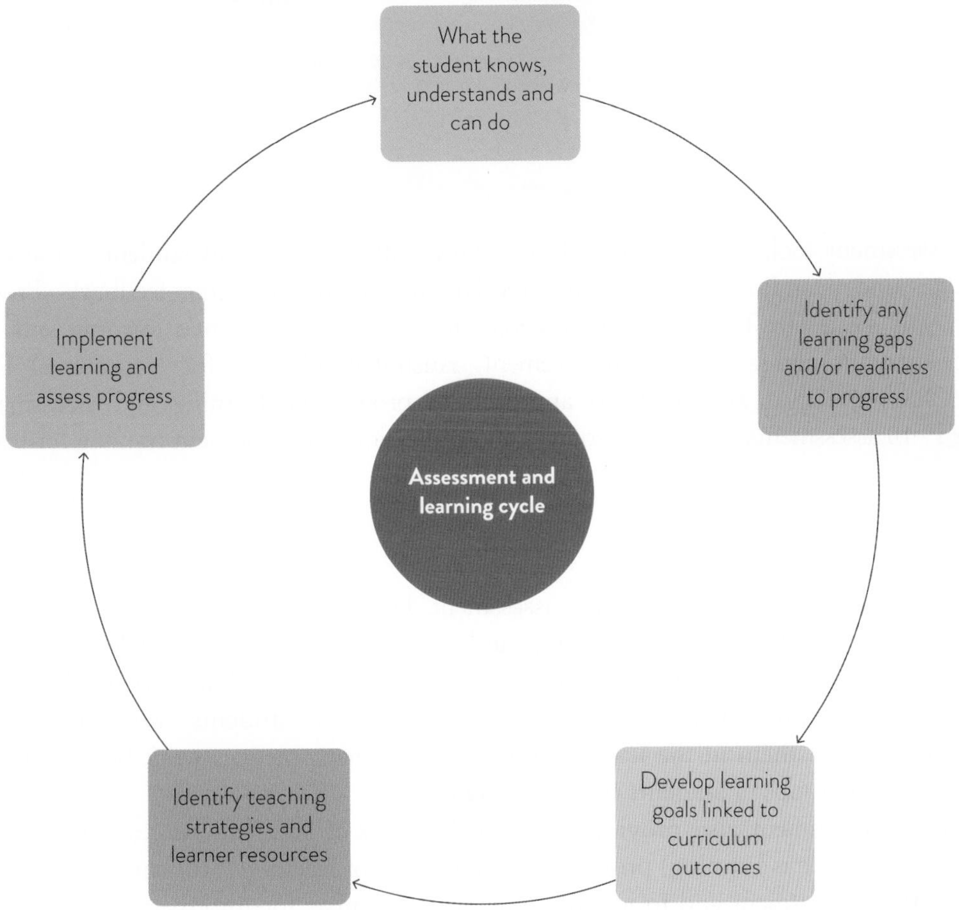

The most commonly used assessments are shown in **Figure 12.7**.

An example of a summative assessment in Australian schools is NAPLAN Online. Examples of formative assessment include impromptu quizzes and student self-assessment. Examples of diagnostics assessment include checklists, surveys and questionnaires. Examples of benching assessment include assessments that compare student outcomes across the globe. Examples of continual assessment include informal quizzes, spelling tests, and teacher-led questions and answers.

Figure 12.7 Types of assessment

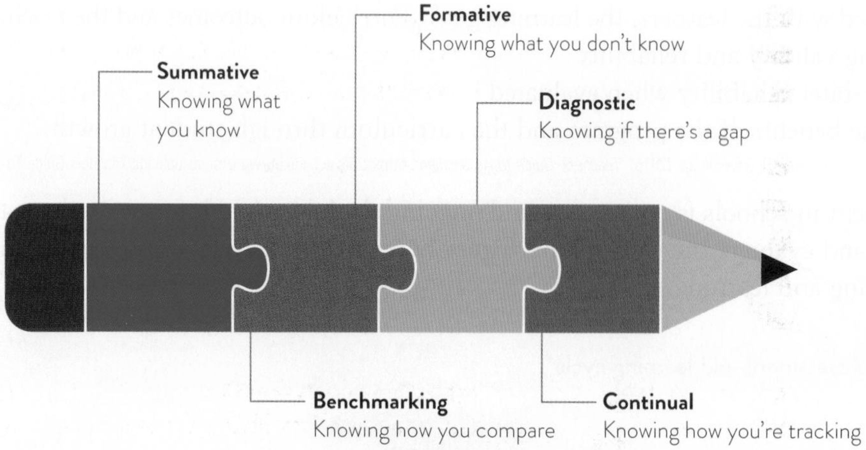

Source: Bently, E. (2021). A guide to 5 school assessment types and their key purposes. https://www.janison.com/resources/post/a-guide-to-5-school-assessment-types-and-their-key-purposes

Technology and assessment

PAT resources

Digital assessment tools using data analytics allow both teachers and students to assess their knowledge, understanding and skills and receive immediate, real-time feedback. Progressive Achievement Tests (PATs) use multiple-choice to assess each student's learning and identify areas of strengths and areas for improvement. Australian Council for Educational Research (ACER) has developed an integrated approach to progressive learning and assessment that includes F–10 assessments, teaching resources and professional development training for teachers.

Classroom assessment

Teachers engage in a process of ongoing assessment, both formal and informal, throughout the school year. As well as understanding and measuring student knowledge, skills and understanding, classroom assessment provides teachers with feedback about their teaching practices – for example, what practices work best for their students, what practices excite students and engage them in the learning process, and what practices work best for individual students or small groups of students (see **Figure 12.8**).

Classroom assessment also provides essential feedback to students as learners. Assessment feedback (assessment as learning) promotes self-reflection of learning. Students can be supported to analyse their assessment and to identify strengths and areas for improvement – for example, 'I know X but I only thought I knew Y. I need to ….'

Three types of assessment commonly used in the classroom are described in **Figure 12.9**.

Assessment *of* learning – summative assessment (knowing what you know)

Making a judgement about student achievement against a set of standards, such as curriculum outcomes, is referred to as assessment of learning. It is also called summative assessment and occurs after teaching has taken place.

Figure 12.8 Assessment practices

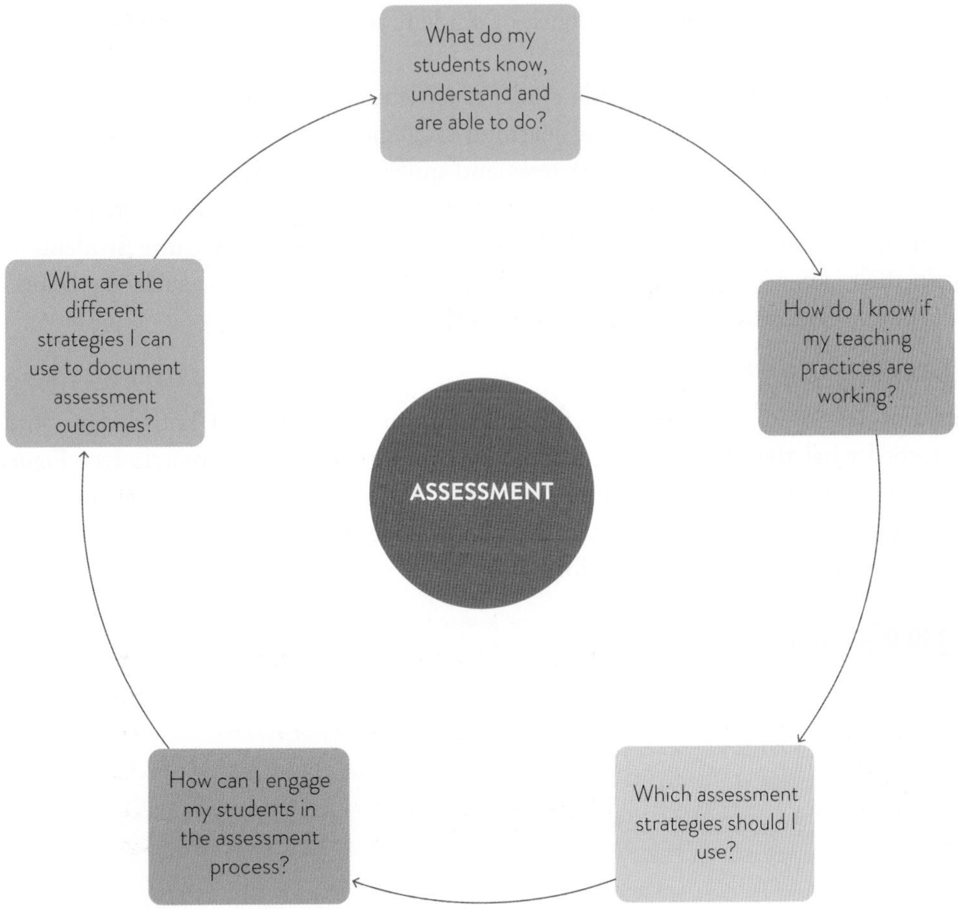

Figure 12.9 Types of assessment

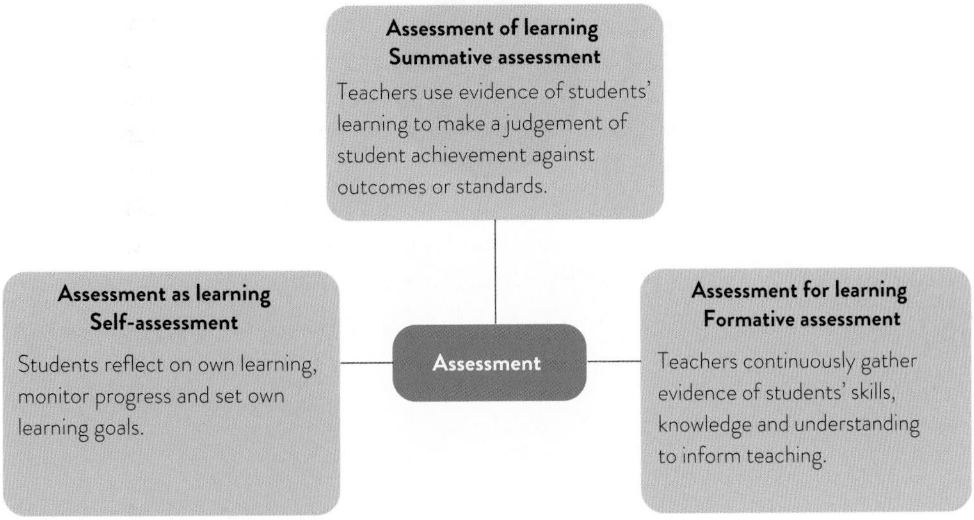

Assessment *of* learning is typically used as a tool to report student progress. It occurs when teachers use evidence of students' learning (what they know, understand and can do) to determine if students have achieved the desired curriculum goals. In order for assessment to be useful and effective, it must have a clearly defined purpose and be based on sound professional principles. Assessment of learning may also be used to plan additional learning goals for individual students and to provide evidence of student achievement to parents, the student and the broader community.

Assessment of learning should enable students to demonstrate what they know and what they can do. Examples of valid assessment of learning strategies in the classroom will vary according to age and grade, but may include short tests and quizzes, projects, essays, report writing, class presentations, work samples, laboratories, design and art projects, and writing summaries. Assessment of learning may also include five-minute strategies that require students to record and check their knowledge and understanding using simple tools such as brain dumps, flashcards, online quizzes and knowledge organisers.

BRAIN DUMP

A brain dump is a quick and easy way for educators to assess student knowledge. Students are asked to record what they know about a topic by completing a simple matrix (see **Figure 12.10**). Typically, students are given a set time frame for this task (e.g. four to five minutes). When completed, students can check for gaps in their knowledge by sharing and discussing their matrix with a peer or by referring to written information.

Figure 12.10 Brain dump

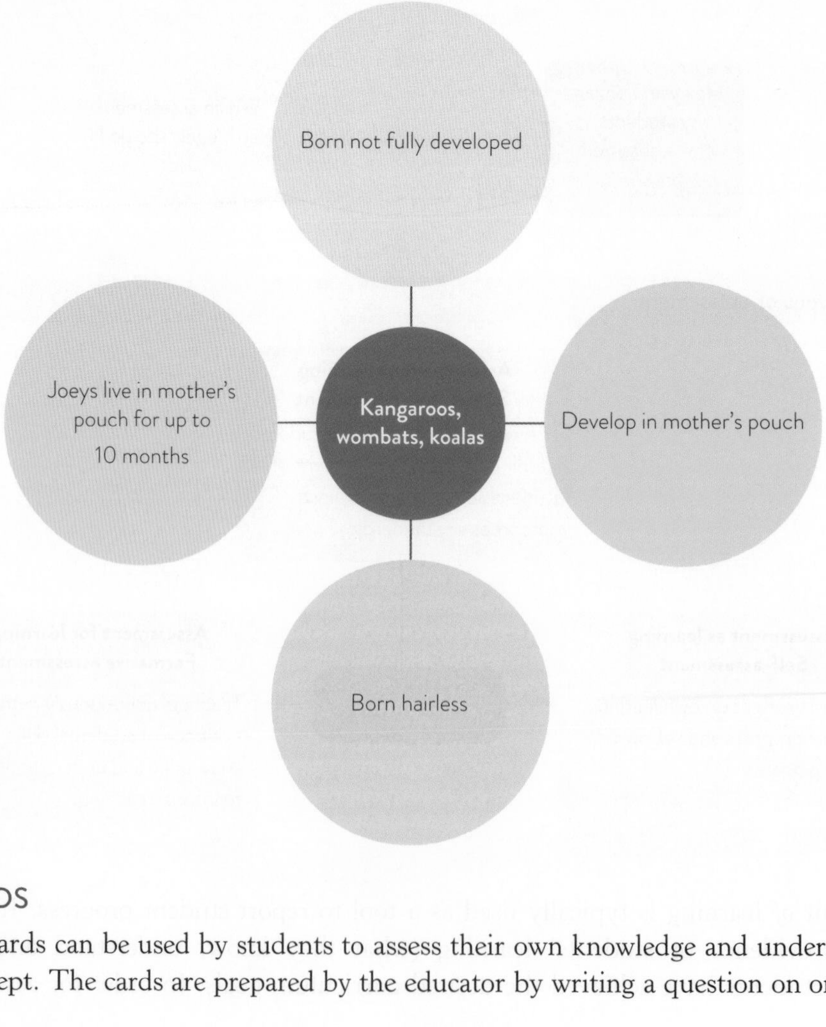

FLASHCARDS

Sets of flashcards can be used by students to assess their own knowledge and understanding of a topic or concept. The cards are prepared by the educator by writing a question on one side of the card and the answer on the reverse side. Students write the answer to the question and then check to see if their answer is correct (see **Figure 12.11**).

QUIZZES

Creating an online multiple-choice quiz using text or images is a fun way for students to quickly assess their knowledge. Quiz scores can be shared with educators to provide instant feedback on student knowledge and understanding. Quizzes can be saved and used at any time to assess and review learning. Examples of quizzes are shown in **Figure 12.12**.

KNOWLEDGE ORGANISER

Similar to a brain dump, a knowledge organiser requires students to record information on a topic or concept within a set time frame (see **Figure 12.13**).

Assessment of student learning is an ongoing process that progressively captures what students know and can do over time.

Assessment *for* learning – formative assessment (knowing what you don't know)

Assessment for learning is quite different from assessment of learning. Also known as **formative assessment**, this form of assessment requires teachers to gather evidence of students' skills, knowledge and understanding as teaching is occurring to determine what students know, understand and can do in order to plan for future learning. Assessment *for* learning requires teachers to make inferences about each student's knowledge, understanding and skills based on careful observation of students as they engage in learning experiences. Assessment for learning includes students actively reflecting on their own learning and providing feedback to the teacher through self-assessment and discussion.

EXIT TICKETS/SLIPS

Exit tickets/slips is a strategy used by teachers to quickly assess learning. They are also a useful tool for challenging students to think about their learning and what they know and can retrieve from their short-term memory. Examples of exit tickets/slips are shown in **Figure 12.14**.

Figure 12.11 Flashcards

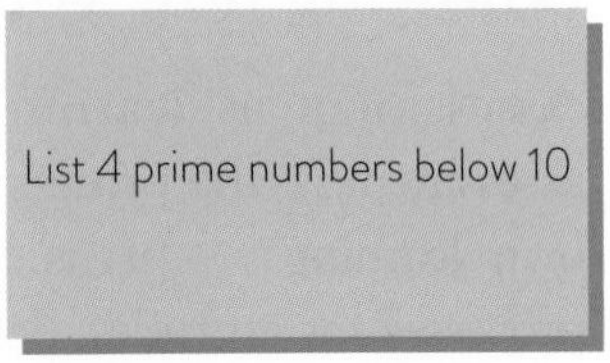

Figure 12.12 Multiple-choice quizzes

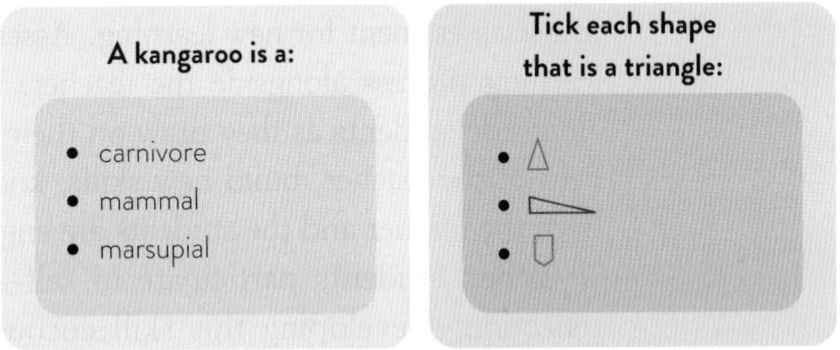

Figure 12.13 Knowledge organiser

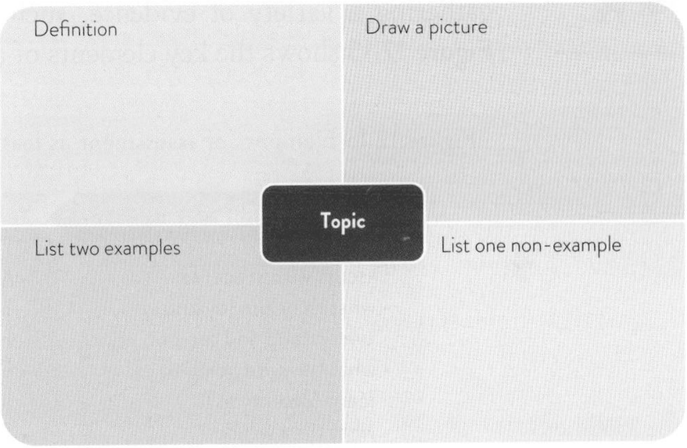

Source: Love to Teach (2020). A collection of retrieval practice research and resources . . . https://lovetoteach87.com/2020/09/09/a-collection-of-retrieval-practice-research-and-resources

Figure 12.14 Exit tickets/slips

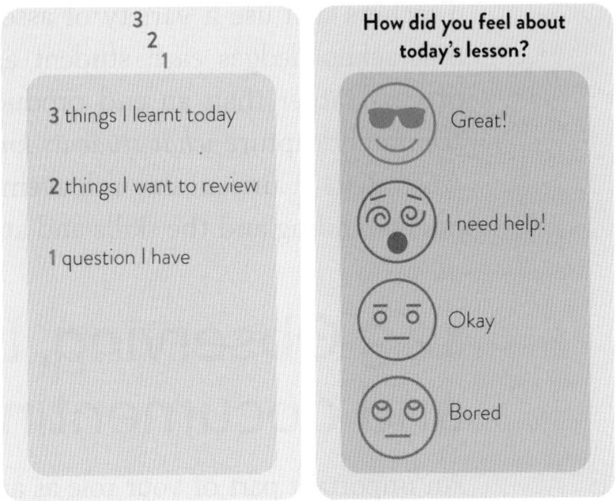

Assessment *as* learning – self-assessment, and peer assessment (knowing how you're on track)

Videos: Types of assessment

Assessment as learning includes both self-assessment and peer assessment. Student self-assessment is 'the process by which the student gathers information about and reflects on his or her own learning ... [it] is the student's own assessment of personal progress in knowledge, skills, processes, or attitudes. Self-assessment leads a student to a greater awareness and understanding of himself or herself as a learner' (Ministry of Education [2006] © Queen's Printer for Ontario).

Formative assessment

Assessment *as* learning occurs when students are their own assessors. Students monitor their own learning, ask questions and use a range of strategies to decide what they know and can do, and how to use assessment for new learning. Assessment *as* learning involves students actively engaging in the learning process alongside the teacher. The role of the teacher is to scaffold learning by working alongside students as they draw on their existing skills, knowledge and understandings, and with the help of the teacher, build new skills, knowledge and understandings. In this method of assessment, both the teacher and the students are engaged in assessing performance.

When students participate in self-assessment, they are developing the skill of critical self-reflection. Developing this skill encourages them to ask themselves questions, such as: 'What skills and knowledge can I demonstrate?'; 'What do I still need to learn?'; 'How am I going to learn these things?'; 'What learning goals can I set?' and 'What support do I need to get there?'

Self-assessment

Students share what they can do and what they understand because of their learning by gathering a variety of evidence, such as work samples or portfolios, journals, logs or videos. **Figure 12.15** shows the key elements of assessment as learning.

Figure 12.15 Elements of assessment as learning

Before	During	After
Discuss with students: • what they already know, understand and can do • what they are going to learn (objectives) • what they will do (outcomes)	• Make a connection between prior knowledge and skills and new knowledge and skills • Provide feedback during the learning process • Scaffold learning	Review: • what they have learned • what was successful • what was challenging • areas for further work • where to next?

Holistic assessment

Teachers will use a variety of assessment strategies to ensure a holistic approach to assessment that acknowledges each student as a unique learner and learning as a dynamic and ongoing process rather than an end product. Using a range of assessment strategies allows teachers to accurately capture *what students know, understand and can do* and meets the requirements of the Australian Curriculum achievement standards to assess essential knowledge, conceptual understanding and the skills and attributes of the general capabilities.

12.3 Observing, listening, questioning and documenting

An important part of your role as an ESW will be to support the teacher to gather evidence of each student's skills, knowledge and understanding. The teacher will systematically undertake formative and summative assessment throughout the year, designed to monitor and report on student progress. In relation to students with an IEP, ESWs can support the teacher to gather information by undertaking observations, noticing and reporting on what students say and do as they work on tasks, identifying tasks that students find particularly challenging, taking notice of how students use equipment and resources, and observing how students work with others.

Figure 12.16 Observing students as they are working can occur formally or informally

Source: Photo by Tish Okely © Cengage

In a classroom setting, observations can be formal or incidental. Incidental observations occur when you observe something about a student's performance while engaged with students as they undertake tasks (see **Figure 12.16**). For example, you may be sitting with a group of students, and supporting them to complete a maths task, when you notice that one student constantly asks you to repeat what you have said. Noting this and informing the teacher would be important, as it may indicate a hearing problem or an auditory processing issue. Incidental observation can also occur when you are having conversations with students. For example, something a student says may raise a concern about their learning and act as a prompt to ask the teacher for further information; it may also indicate that the student is not getting the level of support needed or is not being sufficiently challenged. Incidental observations may also occur when you notice something about a student in the playground on a regular basis – for example, a student who always appears to be sitting alone, a student who runs with an unusual gait, or a student who appears to always speak in a loud voice.

Formal observations

When written objectively, observations can provide valuable evidence of student performance across all curriculum areas and the general capabilities. Observations can provide insight into student thinking, behaviour and relationships with peers. They can provide authentic, context-specific information about each student or group of students because they are a record of what is happening in the here and now. For example, recording what a student says and does as they are interacting with their peers during informal activities is likely to provide greater insight into the student's social skills than the completion of a checklist. Similarly, observing a student engaging in problem-solving with others will provide authentic information about how the student thinks and communicates information and ideas. Observations also reflect the concept of 'the whole child', as the student's behaviour, actions, thinking, communication, use of resources/environment and so on are all taken into account as part of the observation process.

An observation is a snapshot in time and, when gathered over time and in sufficient quantity, can provide valuable evidence about student performance. When added to other forms of evidence, observations can help to complete an authentic picture of a student's development.

If you are required to observe a student, you should understand the purpose of the observation – that is, what information you are attempting to capture. Knowing what you are required to observe will help you to determine when it might be most appropriate to observe.

Observation is a valuable assessment tool. It can be undertaken at any time and provides on-the-spot information about the student's learning. Observations require the observer to gather incidental information about how the student responds to the learning environment, how they go about the task of learning and how they use learning resources. It requires the observer to 'tune in' to the student – that is, to look and listen carefully to what the student does and how they go about a task. Listen to what the student says and also be aware of body language. Look at facial expressions, as they will reveal feelings – for example, whether the task is frustrating or enjoyable.

Observations should be written in an objective manner. They should be free of bias, opinion and assumptions. The key message is to objectively record what you see. Interpretation of the observation is conducted after the observation has been completed. The following statements provide examples of an objective (bias/opinion-free) and a subjective observation (includes personal opinion):

- *Objective observation*: 'When asked to start his maths task, Aaron slumped forward on the desk and put his head on his crossed arms.'
- *Subjective observation*: 'When asked to start his maths task, Aaron slumped forward on the desk and put his head on his crossed arms. Aaron does this because he is quite determined and will try anything to avoid work.'

Statement (a) is factual and does not include an interpretation of Aaron's motives, while statement (b) includes the value judgement of the observer, which may or may not be correct. In this instance, at the time of interpreting the observation, the observer may, for example, comment that Aaron often uses this delaying strategy. This is a statement of fact and avoids any bias. By simply stating that Aaron often uses this strategy, the observer is providing us with additional, factual information.

Observations contribute to the collective knowledge about the student. In essence, they help to form the big picture – who is this student, what are they like, how do they learn, what motivates them as a learner, what are the challenges and barriers to learning for this student?

Observations can be used for several purposes, as described in **Figure 12.17**.

Figure 12.17 Purposes of observation

Purpose	Usefulness
To get to know the student as a unique individual	This will assist in modifying learning experiences to better match the needs of the student – for example, to gain information about the student's temperament, personality, personal routines and rituals, their self-confidence and self-esteem, likes, dislikes, interests, fears and the limits of their comfort zone.
To understand how the student behaves in various situations and how the student uses the environment	This can assist in providing the best possible learning environment and the most effective learning strategies for the student.
To determine the emotional wellbeing of the student	For many students with a disability, the learning environment can be stressful. Monitoring emotional wellbeing will assist in better meeting the emotional needs of each student.
To evaluate the effectiveness of the IEP in meeting the student's interests, preferred learning style and skills	To be successful, the IEP must be implemented in a way that best meets the individual learning style of the student. Everyone will approach new experiences in different ways – some may observe, others may feel confident to use trial and error, still others will rely on adult support and guidance. Does the student persist at tasks, do they give up easily or are they hesitant to take on new challenges?
To understand the student's current level of development and developing skills	Ongoing monitoring and observation of the student's performance will provide direct evidence of their level of functioning, which in turn will assist in matching the learning goals to what is realistically achievable for the student.

While there is no 'best' way of gathering and documenting information about students, it is important that sufficient information is gathered to contribute to informed decision-making. The information gathered should be accurate, unbiased and contribute to future planning. It needs to detail the student's progress towards the stated learning goals in specific curriculum areas.

Observation and professional conduct

Any documentation about a student becomes the property of the school and may eventually be filed with the student's records. Documents may be accessed and read by others – the parents/guardians, teachers and other professionals. It is, therefore, essential that any documentation is recorded in a professional and ethical manner.

Confidentiality

All information gathered about a student should be regarded as confidential and, without the written permission of the parent/s or guardians, should not be discussed or shared with anyone who is not working directly with the student. Parents/guardians also have the right to read any written records, including observations or reports. Students' written records should be kept in a secure place that can be accessed only by authorised staff.

Bias

Observations and reports should be written in an objective manner to avoid bias or stereotyping of students. It would not be appropriate to use words such as 'selfish', 'lazy' or 'spoilt' to describe a student. Such labels are very subjective and may not accurately reflect the student or their situation.

Ensure accurate spelling, grammar and punctuation

Any documentation about a student may be read by parents, colleagues and other professionals. It is, therefore, essential that documentation is free of spelling and grammatical errors. Attention to spelling and grammar reflects a professional approach to the task and also demonstrates respect for those who may read the document. Consider how you might feel if you were a parent and read the following observation: 'Today Anna participated in a group game with three other students. While Anna was reluctant to share he did manage to complete the game and seemed to enjoy the experience. I think it would be good to for Anna to be engaged in more group experiences.'

Avoid jargon and generalisations

Education-specific jargon helps teachers to communicate ideas and concepts in a shorthand way and is acceptable when it is used among colleagues. However, when documenting information about a student, it is important to limit the use of jargon, particularly if the documentation will be read by parents or guardians. It can be useful to develop a bank of words or phrases that are easy to interpret and are not ambiguous. For example, the statement 'Aaron has poor cognitive processing' might be understood more easily if written as 'Aaron has poor memory and recall skills. He often forgets the rules for simple games'.

Generalised terms can be ambiguous and result in misinterpretation. For example, using 'good' or 'poor' to describe a student's work tells the reader very little – for example, 'Aaron did a very poor job on his maths tasks today'. A more informative comment would be, 'Aaron completed two of the 10 maths tasks correctly'.

Careful choice of words can make a remarkable difference when describing student progress. Consider the following examples, which contrast ambiguous statements with clear, easy-to-understand information that provides useful information about student skills and knowledge.

AMBIGUOUS VERSUS CLEARLY EXPRESSED STATEMENTS

SCENARIO

AMBIGUOUS STATEMENTS

- **Anwar** is a complex student whose cognitive skills require further investigation.
- **Nida** has good motor skills.
- **Bella** is a worrier and a real loner.
- **Chidi**'s language skills are poor.

CLEAR AND EASY-TO-UNDERSTAND STATEMENTS

Anwar rarely completes any tasks attempted. He appears to lose concentration and can often be seen sitting and staring at nothing. An assessment to determine Anwar's cognitive skills is recommended.

Nida's gross motor skills are well developed (running, jumping, climbing and ball skills) and are above what might be expected for a student of his age.

Bella tends to spend most of her free time alone. She rarely attempts to interact with her peers.

Chidi's language skills are well below what might be expected for a seven-year-old. He has a very soft voice that is barely audible. He tends to use single words or gestures. When asked to label common objects, he appears to guess the answers. He finds it difficult to follow a two-step direction.

Narratives

Narratives record behaviours and interactions. A narrative observation is a 'story' about a student's learning – it records a learning episode or an incident. It is a record of observable behaviours. Narratives can focus on one student or on a group of students. They may focus on a learning episode, such as counting by 2s, or they may focus on an incident, such as a conversation with a student about their learning.

Narratives may include the following:

- *Jottings* – brief notes made by the observer about significant behaviours or events that are observed. Some observers use 'sticky notes' to quickly jot down a comment made by a student, a verbal exchange between two students or a few words that can be used to later remind the observer what they wish to record. Jottings are done quickly but can be very useful when reflecting on a particular student.
- *Running records* – the most challenging and time-consuming of all observations. They require the observer to dedicate time solely to the task of observing and recording. The observer is required to document exactly what the student does and says within a specific period of time. This is not easy, especially when trying to record language. Consequently, running records are used sparingly and tend to be limited to situations where there are major concerns about a student's learning or where there is a need to look closely at particular dynamics. Generally, running records focus on only one student at a time. They can provide a rich source of information to guide planning decisions.
- *Time sampling* – the observer records specific behaviours of the student at regular, predetermined intervals using a checklist. **Figure 12.18** shows an example of a time sample checklist where the observer records the student's off-task and on-task behaviour every 30 seconds for a period of 15 minutes. This type of observation is often used to verify student behaviour. For example, the teacher may state 'Kyle very rarely engages in on-task behaviour'. A time sample can verify or disprove this statement.
- *Anecdotal observations* – the most common form of observation as they are recorded after the event. Anecdotal observations are simply a story of an event. They provide information about a moment in time as the student or students are engaged in some aspect of learning. The observer is required to recall and document as much detail as possible soon after the observation occurs.

Figure 12.18 Example of a time sample

	Comparison Student (+ or –)	Referred Student (+ or –)	✓ Problem Behaviors (Referred Student): Inattentive	Overactive	Impulsive	Uncooperative	Anxious	Withdrawn	Aggressive	Other Inappropriate			Notes
30 sec													
1 min													
30 sec													
2 min													
30 sec													
3 min													
30 sec													
4 min													
30 sec													
5 min													
30 sec													
6 min													
30 sec													
7 min													
30 sec													
8 min													
30 sec													
9 min													
30 sec													
10 min													
30 sec													
11 min													
30 sec													
12 min													
30 sec													
13 min													
30 sec													
14 min													
30 sec													
15 min													

B. Off-task totals for referred student (number of – marks)

A. Off-task totals for comparison student (number of – marks)

Source: Schrank, F. A., & Woodcock, R. W. (2007). WJ III Normative Update Compuscore and Profiles Program (Version 3.0) [Computer software]. Woodcock-Johnson® III. Rolling Meadows, IL: Riverside Publishing.

In the example in **Figure 12.19**, the ESW was asked to observe Kem's problem-solving skills. To do this, the ESW first chose to observe Kem playing a range of maths games involving problem-solving strategies. While this was an acceptable choice, it did not provide the information required. It did, however, reveal some other relevant information about the student being observed. It is important to be aware that you may not always obtain the desired information – in the case of Kem, he didn't actively participate in the maths games and, therefore, the ESW was unable to contribute to the teacher's knowledge of Kem's problem-solving skills at this time. In the comments section, the ESW suggested the use of a new strategy to observe Kem's problem-solving skills.

A critical element of observations is interpreting or analysing what has been observed and documented. This is a skill that takes time to develop, and it is one that will improve with practice. Notice that the interpretations made by the ESW in this example are factual and objective. The observation provides evidence that Kem is struggling with processing skills, such as memory (he could not recall how to play the games), sequencing skills (he was not able to

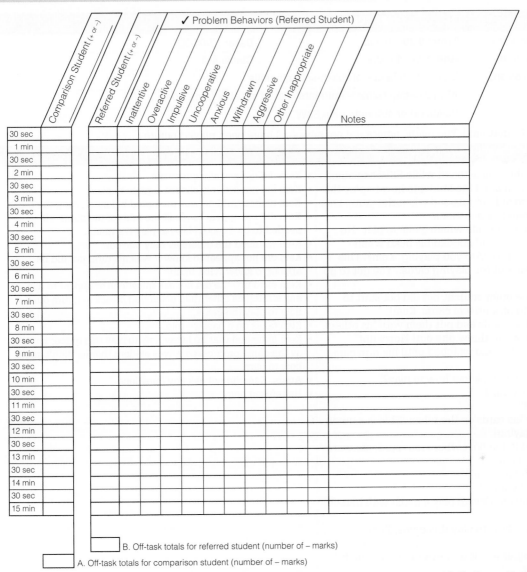

Figure 12.19 Anecdotal observation of student

ANECDOTAL OBSERVATION		
Name of observer: Kate	**Time:** 9.30–10 a.m.	**Date:** 17/04/XX
Name of Student: Kem	**Age:** 8 yrs 4 mths	**Class:** 4M
Purpose of observation:	To observe Kem's problem-solving skills	
Setting:	Maths Group Game – students seated at table or on floor	
Others present:	Seven other students plus ESW	
Other relevant information:	The maths games are not new – all have been played before	

OBSERVATION	INTERPRETATION
▪ Kem sat at the table and listened while ESW explained the activity and reminded the students how to play the three games. Kem did not respond when the group was asked if there were any questions. ▪ Kem did not actively decide which game to play. He remained at the table and nodded his head when another student asked. 'Are you playing, Kem?' This student then dealt out the playing cards. 'You get to go first, Kem.' ▪ Kem looked at the other student but did not start to play. 'You have to pick up two cards, Kem!' ▪ Kem picked up two cards and put them with his others. ▪ 'Kem, now you have to throw one out! Hurry up!' ▪ Kem threw out a card and watched until his turn came around again. ▪ 'Kem, pick up. Don't you know how to play?' ▪ Kem picked up one card. ▪ 'No pick up two!' ▪ Kem then threw his cards on the table: 'This is a dumb game. I'm not playing!' ▪ Kem then moved to the floor where four students were playing another game. ▪ 'Do you want to play, Kem?' ▪ **Kem:** 'No, I'll just watch.' ▪ The ESW then invited Kem to play a game with herself and two others. ▪ 'Do you remember how to play this game, Kem?' ▪ **Kem:** 'Yes.' ▪ As the game progressed, it was evident that Kem did not know to play. ▪ He attempted to copy the other students but his apparent lack of understanding of the rules made it difficult for him to continue. ▪ Each time the ESW asked whether he would like help or whether he had any questions, Kem said, 'No'.	▪ Kem did not ask any questions. ▪ Kem did not actively choose a game to play. ▪ Kem waited until he was prompted before starting the game. ▪ Kem did not appear to recall the rules of the game. He needed to be directed how to play the game. ▪ Kem watched the others as they played. ▪ Kem did not appear to know it was his turn, nor did he appear to know what to do. ▪ Kem gave up – he did not ask questions or appear to use any strategies other than observing others to figure out how to play the game. ▪ Kem takes on a passive role. ▪ Kem indicated that he knew how to play this game; however as the game progressed it was evident that he didn't know how to play. ▪ Again, Kem did not ask any questions. ▪ He refused help.

COMMENT	Kem was not able to demonstrate that he had any recollection of how to play the maths games. He did not seek help or ask questions. He refused help from the ESW. This activity didn't reveal how Kem uses problem-solving skills as he wasn't an active participant in the games. The observation showed that Kem appears reluctant to ask for, or accept, help when needed but did not indicate why this might be the case.
FOLLOW-UP	Prepare some more-structured maths problem-solving tasks for Kem to complete with the ESW. Investigate why Kem is reluctant to seek and accept help as needed.

anticipate when it was his turn) and resilience (Kem was not prepared to seek or accept help; instead, he simply gave up).

Checklists

As an assessment tool, checklists can be used to quickly identify student skills and knowledge. When used before planning learning activities, teachers may use a checklist to confirm a student's existing knowledge and skills. The results are used by the teacher to differentiate the learning needs among students and adapt teaching strategies and materials to meet individual learner needs. For example, a checklist can be used to evaluate the skills a student is using when reading or to assess a student's oral language.

Checklists can also be used to assess knowledge and skills after students have engaged in learning. Students can use a self-assessment checklist to monitor their own performance – for example, a checklist that sets out the sequential steps that must be followed to correctly complete a task.

When used with caution, checklists are a useful tool in the classroom for teachers, ESWs and students. They can provide a quick snapshot of a student's learning skills and knowledge. Where a checklist indicates significant gaps in a student's knowledge and understanding, a more comprehensive assessment process should be used to more accurately identify learner needs. Examples of checklists are shown in **Figure 12.20**. **Figure 12.21** shows a specific language observation checklist template.

Figure 12.20 Checklists

Date	Counting by 10s	Counting by 5s
Asha	✓	✓
Anshu	✓	x
Bella	✓	x

Date	Letter sounds	Decode CVC words
Samir	✓	✓
Zahra	x	x
Zennie	✓	x

U usually S Sometimes R Rarely	Verbal prompt frequently needed			Has difficulty starting a task			Remains on task			Completes task			Participates in discussion		
[Date]	U	S	R	U	S	R	U	S	R	U	S	R	U	S	R
Samir	✓			✓					✓			✓			✓
Esther															
Zennie															
Clarke															
Mia															
Zahra															

Figure 12.21 Language observation checklist template

Language observation checklist template

Student Name:_______________ **Student ID #**_______________
(Last Name, First Name)
School:_______________ **Grade:** _______ **Language:** _______________
(home language other than English)

Compared to *Standard English-speaking* students of the same age, does the student consistently exhibit any of the following characteristics when listening, speaking, reading or writing?

CHARACTERISTICS	Oral		Written	
	Yes	No	Yes	No
a. Uses pronouns, genders correctly.	☐	☐	☐	☐
b. Uses tenses correctly.	☐	☐	☐	☐
c. Uses singular & plural forms correctly.	☐	☐	☐	☐
d. Uses prepositions correctly.	☐	☐	☐	☐
e. Understands teacher directions.	☐	☐	☐	☐
f. Uses appropriate sentence structure.	☐	☐	☐	☐
g. Uses developmentally appropriate vocabulary.	☐	☐	☐	☐

Source: Adapted from Form #05-08-035b, March 2008, Alaska Department of Education & Early Childhood Development

CHECKLISTS

SCENARIO

READING

ESW **Hannah** used a screening checklist to identify the range of skills being used by **Liam** (8 years), a struggling reader. Hannah was not sure whether Liam was applying a range of strategies when attempting to read text. The checklist confirmed that Liam was relying on only one or two key strategies to help him work out challenging words.

BEHAVIOUR

ESW **Amanda** used a behaviour checklist with **Jesse** (10 years) to record the range and frequency of behaviours of concern over a two-week period. The checklist confirmed that Jesse frequently engaged in a wide range of aggressive and anti-social behaviours and that these behaviours tended to occur in the afternoons. Amanda felt that the evidence gathered from the checklist supported her concerns in relation to an escalation in Jesse's aggressive behaviour.

WHAT DOES THIS TELL US?

Checklists can assist in pinpointing concerns in relation to an area of development or a lag in skills and knowledge acquisition. Checklists are useful if used in conjunction with other more authentic forms of assessment, such as observations and work samples.

Analysis and interpretation

When a series of observations have been completed, they can be analysed to form a reasonably accurate picture of the student's current skills, knowledge and understandings. This analysis can then be used as the basis of ongoing planning.

The next step is to 'interpret' or make sense of what has been observed. This is a challenging task that requires the observer to apply their knowledge of child development and how children learn. This knowledge is essential, but it is not enough to accurately interpret and assess a student's learning. The observer must include a holistic perspective that draws on what they already know about the student – the social/cultural context, and their interests, temperament and learning style.

When interpreting, it is important to think about what the observations tell us about the student – their skills and knowledge, learning style, disposition as a learner, visible barriers to learning, confidence, empathy, behaviour, resilience and ability to cope with change, relationships with others, sense of humour, self-esteem, independence, self-care skills, ability to collaborate with others, persistence or flexibility, and communication skills. Noticing these characteristics allows us to capture the essence of the child or young person as a unique individual. In the example of Kem (**Figure 12.19**), his lack of confidence and resilience are significant barriers to learning.

How each ESW sees, understands, interprets and analyses observations will vary according to a range of factors, such as their professional skills and knowledge, cultural and personal values, beliefs and assumptions, and the relationship the ESW has with each student. These factors are referred to as filters or lenses – each of us sees the world through our own unique lens.

Videos: Assessment in the classroom

Reasonable adjustment

All students with disability are entitled to reasonable adjustments to enable them to participate in education on the same basis as other students, as set out in the Disability Standards for Education 2005 (Department of Education and Training [DET], 2005).

In Australia, the Nationally Consistent Collection of Data on School Students with Disability (NCCD) collects data from all schools on students who have received a reasonable adjustment to address the functional impact of a disability. For the purposes of consistency in data collection, the NCCD has identified four levels of reasonable adjustment:

1. *Extensive* – students have very high support needs and are provided with extensive targeted measures and sustained levels of intensive support at all times.
2. *Substantial* – students have substantial support needs, receive essential adjustments and require considerable adult assistance at most times, on most days.
3. *Supplementary* – students receive adjustments in addition to the strategies and resources already available for all students.
4. *Support provided within quality differentiated teaching practice* – students are supported through usual school processes, without drawing on additional resources (NCCD, 2022).

The four levels can be used by schools to determine the resource needs of students with disability to ensure their participation in education. Resources typically include specialist teachers, ESWs and specialist equipment to accommodate each student's learning, wellbeing and healthcare needs. Usually, students classified as requiring reasonable adjustment at levels 1, 2 and 3 will have in place an Individual Education Plan (IEP).

Nationally Consistent Collection of Data (NCCD)

12.4 Working with an Individual Education Plan

The purpose of an IEP is to ensure that each school meets the requirements of the Disability Standards for Education (DET, 2005), which enshrines the right of every student to an education on the same basis as students without disability.

CONSIDER THIS

GUIDING PRINCIPLES OF PERSONALISED LEARNING: QUALITY TEACHING AND LEARNING

Every student has their own aspirations, learning needs, strengths and interests and it is the responsibility of schools to respond to every student and their unique characteristics, with high expectations for achievement. Providing personalised learning and targeted support is one way they achieve this.

The principles underlying personalised learning and support involve:

- All students can learn.
- Every child has a right to a high quality education.
- Effective teachers provide engaging and rigorous learning experiences for all students.
- A safe and stimulating environment is integral to enabling students to explore and build on their talents and achieve relevant learning outcomes.
- For students with disability and additional learning needs, reasonable adjustments should be made where required.

Source: Department of Education and Training (DET) (n.d.). Planning for Personalised Learning and Support: A National Resource. https://www.dese.gov.au/download/2837/planning-personalised-learning-and-support-national-resource/3905/document/pdf, p. 3

An IEP is a personalised plan for learning and inclusion. An IEP identifies and describes reasonable adjustment strategies designed to ensure that students can remain in the classroom, learning alongside others. An IEP may also be referred to as an Individual Learning Plan (ILP) or Personalised Learning Plan (PLP) (One Plan in South Australia).

IEPs are not restricted to students with disability. They can be a valuable tool to use with a range of student needs – for example:

- beginning English language learners
- students who have been displaced, such as refugees, or children who are vulnerable because of child abuse, domestic violence or homelessness
- students who are disengaged from learning
- students who are gifted and not reaching their full potential
- students with long-term chronic illness.

Videos: Individual Education Plan (IEP)

Typically, ESWs do not develop IEPs but are involved in implementation support at the direction of the teacher. For this reason, it is important to have a sound understanding of how IEPs are developed, implemented, monitored, modified and evaluated.

Who has input?

IEPs provide an opportunity for schools to engage in a collaborative approach with a range of stakeholders, including the student and family, specialist services and professionals, and cultural groups. Interested stakeholders can make a contribution to the planning process, and can also act as an ongoing support and resource for teachers, students and families.

The classroom teacher and/or special education teacher is responsible for developing an IEP in collaboration with stakeholders. **Figure 12.22** provides an overview of contributions that can be made by stakeholders.

Gathering information from all stakeholders provides an authentic and comprehensive picture of the 'whole child' – background, family and cultural context, strengths, capabilities, interests, likes and dislikes, personality, temperament, self-regulation skills, behaviours and triggers, language and communication skills, personal and healthcare needs, emotional wellbeing, self-care and independence skills, social skills, rituals and routines. It also indicates the most effective ways to interact for a positive outcome, possible/potential barriers to participation, learning preferences and learning needs.

Figure 12.22 IEP and stakeholder contribution to IEPs

Stakeholder	Role
Parents/guardians	> Provide an overview of the student's personality, temperament, strengths, interests, learning style, developmental history, personal care requirements, health status assessments and treatments, abilities and disabilities > Provide insight into the family's goals and priorities for their child > Describe what a 'good day' or a 'bad day might be like for the student > Provide insight into the student's ability to function socially and in the school environment > Provide information on the student's behaviour and effective strategies to manage behaviours > Provide relevant information about basic care needs (including medications and self-help skills) > Provide information about the student's particular disability and needs, as well as abilities and strengths > Participate as an equal member of the team with regard to planning, decision-making and problem-solving > Identify any modifications to physical facilities that may be required to support the mobility of the student > Identify the specific equipment/aids that may be needed to support the student
Student (where possible)	> Participate in some decision-making and problem-solving, where appropriate > Provide insight into their own ability to function in the school environment > Provide information with regard to own abilities and needs > Participate in setting goals and working towards the achievement of those goals > Cooperate with the teacher, ESW and peers
Teacher (may include principal, deputy principal, school counsellor, specialist teacher)	> Provide leadership in relation to planning, decision-making and problem-solving > Work to support the smooth transition of the student as a member of the class – for example: – creating an atmosphere of acceptance by preparing other students for the arrival of their new class member – talking about how to interact and communicate – providing general information about specific disabilities and answering student questions – explaining modifications or adaptations to the physical environment – explaining how specialist equipment or aids will be used by the student – setting up a buddy system > Document the IEP > Implement and coordinate the program > Plan, adapt and implement learning activities to meet the student's abilities and interests > Demonstrate a willingness to try new ideas and take risks > Act as a role model for students and other staff > Facilitate peer interactions > Direct, guide and support the ESW
Specialist support services, specialist professional, specialist knowledge and expertise medical professional, psychologist, physiotherapist, occupational therapist, speech therapist, cultural adviser	> Participate as an equal member of the team in planning, decision-making and problem-solving > Provide information and support to the classroom teacher > Assist with the dissemination of information to peers and with peer support programs > Assist in the development of the IEP goals > Assist in adapting curriculum, materials and equipment, and provide advice to others as needed > Act as a mentor to the classroom teacher and ESW
ESW	> Contribute written observations > Support the teacher in the implementation phase of the program > Facilitate the student's direct interaction with others > Participate as a valuable member of the team with regard to planning and problem solving > Act as a role model for students and staff > Ensure functional approaches to addressing therapy needs are evident in typical activities and interactions > Support the teacher to implement the IEP goals for the student

Working with families

The person most likely to have comprehensive knowledge of the child or young person is the parent/s, primary carer and/or guardian. Parents are legally entitled to participate in developing an appropriate IEP for their child.

The Family–School Partnerships Framework (Australia) provides a framework for developing effective school–family partnerships based on mutual trust, respect and shared responsibility for the education of the children and young people at the school. The Framework requires teachers to engage in consultative decision-making with parents in the educational decision-making process for their individual child. Teachers must also ensure that parents' values and interests are heard and respected (Department of Education, Employment and Workplace Relations, n.d., pp. 2, 12).

As an ESW, you may or may not have contact with parents – this will depend on the school setting and your designated role. Regardless of contact, it is essential that any interactions, whether written or verbal, are carried out in an ethical manner. For example, when recording information about students it is essential that this is done objectively and professionally – always assume that a parent may read your documentation. Avoid using labels, judgements and assumptions. For example, rather than say 'Imran is lazy and uninterested', a more professional statement might be: 'Imran appeared not to be motivated today. He found it difficult to complete his spelling task.' Objective statements also assist the teacher to understand how the student coped with the planned task/s and to put in place additional strategies for ongoing learning.

Learning barriers

IEPs are used to identify and overcome barriers to learning – for example:

- What is it about the disability or learning need/s that directly affects the learning process and/or makes learning challenging for the student?
- How can the regular program be adjusted to accommodate the learning needs of this student so that the student can continue to learn alongside their peers?

Consider, for example, a student with autism spectrum disorder (ASD) who has limited oral communication skills and may require assistive technology; a student with physical disabilities who may require a walking frame to access the physical environment; or a student with poor impulse control who may require visual cues to support behaviour choices.

Common learning barriers include:

- *motivational* – the student is disengaged from learning
- *personal* – disability, health issues, language barriers, poor social skills, poor or limited communication skills, cultural differences
- *emotional* – poor self-esteem, fear of failure, relationship issues at home, at school, with peers.

Videos: Eliminating barriers to learning

Depending on the nature of the student's disability and learning needs, it is not always possible to overcome all barriers to learning. However, it is possible to minimise some of the barriers so that the student has the opportunity to perform to the best of their ability. Many teachers adopt the principles of the Universal Design for Learning (UDL) framework to adapt or differentiate curriculum delivery to suit diverse needs (refer back to Chapter 11 for more on UDL).

IEP templates and information gathering

Victorian Department of Education IEP template

Each state and territory education department will have a designated IEP template that must be used by schools. While the templates look slightly different across jurisdictions, they typically include the same information. You can go to the website for the education department in your state or territory to access IEP templates and resources.

There are a number of steps that need to be followed when developing an IEP. The first step is to gather information about the student. The goal is not simply to gather a list of the student's needs, but rather to capture the essence of a child or young person – their personality, temperament, likes and aspirations. The information gathered about the student will guide decision-making on educational goals and will inform the development of an IEP. The IEP sets out the measurable goals and objectives for the student and provides a framework for the teacher's program and ongoing evaluation of the student's progress.

Building a profile or picture of the child or young person, and supporting the goals of the IEP, requires a team effort, which may include the child or young person, parents/guardian, teachers, ESWs and specialist support professionals (see **Figure 12.22** earlier). Identifying the needs and capabilities of the student often begins with the teacher talking to those who know most about the child or young person: the parents/guardians. A conversation with the parents/guardians can often reveal details about the student that cannot be identified using formal assessment.

CASE STUDY | Aaron Jones

Part 1: About Aaron

Aaron is 12 years old and has a learning disability. Aaron lives with his parents, his 14-year-old sister and his eight-year-old brother. Aaron and his family recently relocated to the area so that Aaron's mother could take up a professorship at the local university. Aaron's father, a GP, is employed in a local medical centre.

At his previous school, Aaron had been integrated into the regular classroom with the support of an ESW and an itinerant special education teacher, who worked with the teacher and the ESW to plan and monitor Aaron's IEP.

A conversation between the teacher at Aaron's new school and his parents began as follows:

'Tell me about his personality, likes, dislikes, strengths.'
'What would an ideal day look like for Aaron?'
'Tell me how Aaron coped at his previous school.'
'What adjustments do you believe are needed to assist Aaron with his learning?'
'What are your hopes/dreams for Aaron?'
'What are your main concerns/fears for Aaron?'
'What do you believe are Aaron's key learning needs?'
'What do you find works best with Aaron when he is asked to do something he might not like to do?'
'What motivates Aaron?'

Feedback from Aaron's parents

The conversation revealed that Aaron's parents want him to be happy. They would like him to make friends and they hope he can transition to the local high school next year. They also hope he will be able to get a job when he leaves school and learn to live independently.

The parents explained that Aaron is required to do a few jobs around the home to help him develop a sense of responsibility, to practise sequencing a task and support the development of life skills. Each week, Aaron's mother puts ten 50 cent pieces in 'Aaron's jar'. Each time he fails to complete a task, a coin is removed from the jar. He can redeem a coin by doing extra tasks.

Aaron's tasks include setting the table for dinner, feeding the dog, putting out the garbage bins, making his bed, putting his clothes in the laundry basket, hanging up his towel after a shower, helping to prepare the family dinner on Sunday nights and tidying his room.

The information gathered can be used to help determine goals and objectives for the student and will also assist in planning the routine of the school day.

What Aaron said:

'I'm not clever like them [his family].'
'I can draw good but I'm no good at writing.'
'I get confused and forget in class.'
'Sometimes I don't get time to finish [my work].'
'Sometimes I forget things.'
'Mum and Dad say, "Aaron, concentrate!"'
'Other kids don't like me.'

Formal assessments

Aaron has undergone a number of formal assessments. His learning disability has no known medical cause. Aaron was slow to meet early childhood developmental milestones, such as rolling over, sitting up, crawling and walking. His language was also slow to develop. Aaron is able to communicate, and to read and write, although in each area he performs well below the level of his same-age peers. Aaron has a short concentration span (except when drawing); he is easily distracted and disorganised. He finds it difficult to follow directions of more than one step and has difficulty planning and sequencing tasks. Aaron has poor social skills – he finds it difficult to share or take turns. He has difficulty working collaboratively with his peers and often refuses to engage in cooperative tasks or games.

Summary: what was learned about Aaron?

After talking to Aaron's parents, reading the previous teacher's report and various assessment reports, the teacher was able to gain the following picture of Aaron.

Aaron's strengths and capabilities are:

- He is able to communicate needs and wants.
- He can speak in full sentences.
- He is able to ask and answer questions.
- He has a reading age of eight years.
- He is able to write 15 to 20 words legibly if he concentrates and is reminded of correct pen grip.
- He enjoys gardening, swimming and bushwalking.
- He has age-appropriate gross motor skills.
- He is able to cope with most maths tasks.

Aaron's learning needs

- Although he is able to communicate, Aaron has very poor social skills and finds it difficult to make friends.
- His poor concentration means he finds it difficult to stay on task and is easily distracted.
- Aaron finds it difficult to share and wait for a turn in group situations.
- Due to his poor planning skills, Aaron is very disorganised and finds it difficult to sequence tasks.
- He finds it difficult to follow verbal instruction involving more than one step.
- He does not like change – he becomes agitated if his routine is varied. For example, 'It's 6.33 p.m. We have dinner at 6.30 p.m. Dinner is three minutes late!' 'On Tuesdays I have a cheese sandwich for lunch.' 'I sit here every day. This is my chair, and this is my desk.' 'I always have three pencils just in case one breaks.'

The next step

Aaron's new teacher, **Mr Craig**, with the assistance of the Special Education Officer, and in consultation with Dr and Professor Jones, will devise an IEP for Aaron (**Figure 12.23**). The IEP will be discussed with Aaron's parents before implementation to ensure they are happy with the plan. Later, Mr Craig will work with the ESW, **Jodie**, to implement the plan. The Special Education Officer will liaise with Mr Craig and provide support as needed.

Figure 12.23 IEP student profile

INDIVIDUAL EDUCATION PLAN – STUDENT PROFILE

Student: Aaron Jones	**DOB:** 10/11/XX	**Year:** 6	**Teacher:** Mr Craig

Background Information

Aaron recently moved to Blossom Street Primary School from City Primary, where he was referred to Education Support.

Diagnosis

- Specific learning difficulties with no identified medical cause.
- Attention deficit.
- Poor auditory memory – poor planning, organising and sequencing skills.
- Aaron has poor social skills.
- Aaron is able to communicate, read and write, although in each area he performs well below his same-age peers.
- Aaron has a reading and spelling age of 8 years.
- Does not cope with change.

This section provides a summary of disabilities, health issues and learning difficulties (includes any social/behaviour difficulties).

Strengths

- Able to communicate needs and wants.
- Can speak in full sentences.
- Able to ask and answer questions.
- Able to write 15–20 words legibly if he concentrates and is reminded of correct pen grip.
- Enjoys gardening, swimming and bushwalking.
- Has age-appropriate gross motor skills.
- Is able to cope with most maths tasks.

Identifies student's skills and abilities.

Weakness

Reading: Confuses similar words and letters, loses place, repeats words, does not read fluently, persists in using fingers to follow along, does not like to read.
Spelling: Confuses letters and sounds.
Concentration/distractibility: Aaron has a short concentration span (poor working memory); finds it difficult to stay on task and is easily distracted.
Planning and sequencing: Aaron finds it difficult to follow directions of more than one step.
Social skills: Inability to work collaboratively – finds it difficult to share or take turns; also finds it difficult to engage in cooperative games or games with rules.
Resilience: Becomes agitated if routine changes.

Identifies areas where student is struggling and requires specific intervention.

Areas for improvement

Reading

Agencies and personnel involved with Aaron

Kim Bradley (Learning Support Coordinator – City Primary)
Ph: 00023284359
Leon Smith (Area School Psychologist) Ph: 00023484361
Dr Jon (Paediatrician) Ph: 00023284650
Dr Paula (Child Psychologist) Ph: 00023284123

Lists all services/supports currently in place for the student.

PLANNING

Long-term goals

- Development of pro-social friendship skills involving turn-taking, sharing and collaborative interactions.
- Development of resilience to cope with change.

Typically identified in collaboration with parents, educators and other key professionals. Long-term and short-term goals link to the General Capabilities of the Australian Curriculum.

Relationship to curriculum

- Personal and social capability: Self-management, self-awareness, social awareness, social management.
- Development of planning and organisational skills.
- Critical and creative thinking: inquiring – identifying, exploring and organising information and ideas; reflecting on thinking and processes.
- Development of reading and spelling skills: Composing texts through speaking, writing and creating; comprehending texts through listening, reading and viewing.

Typically the starting point for planning. Goals should be specific, measurable, achievable, realistic/relevant and timely (SMART). Goals may also provide specific information for teaching/learning strategies.

This is included to ensure that teacher–parent communication is consistent and ongoing. Acknowledges the key role of parents in supporting student learning.

Identify specific teaching and learning strategies planned to maximise learning outcomes for the student. Can be changed, adapted or modified as needed.

INDIVIDUAL EDUCATION PLAN – STUDENT PROFILE

Short-term goals

- Aaron will work collaboratively (sharing, turn-taking, asking and answering questions, offering ideas) with one other student with the support of the ESW.
- Aaron will follow a two-step instruction using the 'look, listen, plan, act' strategy.
- Aaron will complete daily tasks using a pre-planned sequence developed by Aaron with the support of the ESW.
- Aaron will use a 'to do' list each day to plan and sequence daily tasks.
- Aaron will work with the ESW to identify when he is feeling anxious about change.
- Aaron will work with the ESW to identify strategies he can use to help him remain calm.
- Aaron will use a range of strategies to improve his reading and spelling.

Home–school liaison

- Teacher and parents to communicate weekly via email to share and exchange information.
- Meet with parents, teaching staff and other services (as required) once per term to review progress.
- Parents to implement daily routine tasks for Aaron.

Classroom strategies

- Give clear, specific instructions – pause and ask Aaron to repeat. Implement 'look, listen, plan, act'
- Pair Aaron with more able student to act as a role model for some work tasks.
- Provide positive reinforcement.
- Position Aaron's desk so it is facing away from distractions.
- Source reading material and spelling words that reflect Aaron's interests in gardening, swimming and bushwalking.
- Provide planned breaks between tasks as a reward for on-task behaviour.

Key teaching strategies

- Demonstrate and support the use of explicit strategies to assist Aaron to socialise with peers and participate in small-group learning tasks.
- Use visual cues to sequence tasks.
- Use explicit instruction to teach Aaron 'look, listen, plan, act' strategy.
- Use explicit strategies to improve auditory memory.
- Revisit word attack skills – phonemics (separate sounds within words) and phonics (letter-to-sound relationships).
- Explicitly teach organisational skills.
- Implementation of the major teaching strategies will require the support of an ESW for four hours per day.

Assessment and review

Formative assessment – weekly
Summative – monthly

SMART goals

As shown, an IEP will reflect the collaborative nature of the information-gathering process – for example, between parents, other professionals who are involved with the student, teachers and special education consultants. An IEP should specifically identify:

- the expectations of the family
- the specific learning goals and objectives for the student. Goals should be written using the SMART principle, which ensures that they are clear, unambiguous, easily observable and measurable (**Figure 12.24**).

Figure 12.24 SMART goals

S — **Specific**
- The goal should relate to the acquisition of a specific skill or to specific knowledge and learning strategies that will be used to achieve these goals.
- Aaron will sit at his desk when told it is time to start a new task.

M — **Measurable**
- Goals must be observable or quantifiable, so they can be measured.
- Aaron will complete each task before moving on to a new task.

A — **Achievable**
- Goals must reflect the skills, knowledge and capabilities of the student so that they are realistically achievable.
- 'Aaron is to sit quietly and look at the ESW each time he is given instructions.'

R — **Realistic and relevant**
- Goals must build on the student's current skills, knowledge and capabilities.
- 'Aaron will write three sentences. Each sentence will contain a minimum of eight words.'

T — **Time-limited**
- Goals must be achievable by the student in a reasonable timeframe (reflecting the abilities of the student). This allows goals to be regularly monitored and adjusted if necessary.
- 'Aaron will complete one writing task each day for four weeks.'

PACT

PACT goals are set out in **Figure 12.25**. They are a more contemporary alternative to SMART goals.

Figure 12.25 PACT

Purposeful	The goal should be long-term, relevant and fit-for-purpose to support the student's learning and development
Actionable	The goal must be actionable and achievable by the student with support from educators using scaffolded learning strategies
Continuous	The goal must allow for consistent and continuous improvement over time. There must be opportunity for flexibility and adaptability when determining learning strategies
Trackable	Rather than being measurable, PACT goals are trackable. Student progress is tracked in terms of what the student does, the effort applied and the willingness to work towards the goal. For students with learning challenges, this allows both the teacher and the student to recognise and reward effort as well as outcomes

Source: SMART goals are not so smart: make a PACT instead. https://nesslabs.com/smart-goals-pact

Goals should also be linked to specific curriculum areas and include:

- specific skills and knowledge related to the goals
- conditions under which the goals will be achieved (e.g. working one-on-one with an ESW; working as part of a small group; positioning the student's desk and chair in a way that minimises distractions and assists them to focus on their learning)
- adjustments to the curriculum
- learning resources required
- a time frame for evaluation/review
- criteria for measuring achieved outcomes/student performance (SMART goals): level of competence to be demonstrated; level of accuracy; required output (e.g. amount of work to be completed each day); evaluation strategies, which may include observation, testing, work samples, talking to the student
- requirements of the learning environment – teaching strategies, support resources (including an ESW)
- responsibilities of team members
- overall evaluation of the IEP – implementation, coordination issues, adjustments that could be made.

CASE STUDY | Aaron Jones

Part 2: Individual Education Plan

Figure 12.26 provides a sample of an IEP for Aaron. Please note that this is a sample only and is not a complete IEP. The format and content of an IEP will vary and should be adapted to suit the needs of each school/student.

Figure 12.26 IEP for Aaron

INDIVIDUAL EDUCATION PLAN: PLANNING AND ORGANISING
LEARNING STUDENT AREA
OUTCOMES ▪ Aaron will use a range of identified strategies each day to improve his daily organisational skills. ▪ Aaron will use the 'look, listen, plan, act' strategy each time before commencing a new task.
STRATEGIES ▪ Discuss plans for each learning period (arrival, after recess, after lunch). ▪ With the support of the ESW/teacher, Aaron will create a chronological 'To Do List' using words and/or pictures. ▪ Aaron will use the check box on the 'To Do List' to tick each task as it is completed. ▪ Aaron will refer to the 'To Do List' each time he has completed a task and verbalise to the ESW the next planned task. ▪ Aaron will place his pens, pencils, ruler etc. in the same place on his desk each morning. ▪ Aaron will only place on his desk the worksheet/resources needed for each specific task. ▪ Aaron will look at each new task with the ESW/teacher before commencing. ▪ Aaron will listen to the instructions, ask questions to clarify, and restate what he is required to do. ▪ Aaron will plan the sequence involved in each task. First, next, next... last. ▪ Aaron will use words or pictures to sequence the task and use this as a reminder of the steps he needs to follow. ▪ Aaron will complete each task in the correct sequence.
RESOURCES ▪ 'To Do List' – paper, pens, pictures. ▪ Small cardboard squares, pens, pictures/glue.

INDIVIDUAL EDUCATION PLAN: PLANNING AND ORGANISING

LEARNING STUDENT AREA

STAFF
- ESW
- ESW

EVALUATION
- Daily ESW. Weekly ESW & teacher
- Daily ESW. Weekly ESW & teacher

INDIVIDUAL EDUCATION PLAN: SOCIAL SKILLS

LEARNING STUDENT AREA

OUTCOMES
- Aaron will use specific strategies to help him to remain calm and in control when faced with change.
- Aaron will work collaboratively with his peers when engaged in small group tasks.

STRATEGIES
- With the support of the ESW, Aaron will recognise his own symptoms of stress – feeling anxious, scared, upset, worried – by making a worry poster, 'When I get worried I ...'
- Aaron will work with the ESW to plan things he can do when he experiences feelings on his worry poster to create a list of calming strategies 'To calm myself I can ...'
- With the support of the ESW, Aaron will use one or more of his calming strategies when he is worried by a change in routine.
- With the support of the ESW, Aaron will share limited resources when working in a small group.
- With the support of the ESW, Aaron will contribute to group planning and discussion.

RESOURCES
- Paper/pens
- none

STAFF
- ESW
- ESW

EVALUATION
- Daily ESW. Weekly ESW & teacher
- Daily ESW. Weekly ESW & teacher

Signatures: Student: ______________ Parent/s: ______________
Teacher: ______________ Date: ______________

Implementing the IEP

Once an IEP is in place, the teacher will begin the implementation process. This may involve the support of other professionals as well as the ESW. Where an ESW is employed to assist in the implementation of an IEP, the classroom teacher will:

- discuss the IEP with the ESW, addressing the goals and learning strategies
- identify the lessons and tasks to be undertaken
- identify the learning/teaching strategies that will be used

- discuss how adjustments or modifications to the teaching and learning strategies are to be made and documented
- identify the performance criteria required
- timetable the delivery of learning experiences
- identify the specific resources to be used
- determine the evaluation/record-keeping requirements.

During the initial implementation phase, it is important to keep in mind that a primary goal is inclusion: putting strategies in place that will support the student to participate alongside their peers in the classroom. In collaboration with the classroom teacher, the ESW will need to determine:

- how to get to know the student (establish rapport)
- the most appropriate ways to engage the student in the learning process
- strategies to motivate the student to stay on task (praise/reinforcement/rewards)
- how to provide prompts and feedback during supported learning sessions
- the best strategies to ensure the student is given clear instructions and understands what is required – for example, the use of a communication book for non-verbal students
- how to manage the student's behaviour
- how to assess the student's response to the degree of difficulty and pace of the learning experiences.

Children and young people learn best when they are engaged actively in the learning process. It is important to be aware that the role of the ESW is to support the student as a learner and problem-solver. This requires the ESW to become familiar with the student's current level of functioning, the preferred learning style of the student and the avoidance strategies they may use. You will recall from earlier chapters that Vygotsky (1978) wrote about the importance of scaffolding learning by starting with the known and familiar to support the acquisition of new skills and knowledge.

WRITING

SCENARIO

Hannah (14 years) is developmentally delayed. She has a reading level of 10 years and enjoys stories about animals. Hannah has poor fine motor skills and struggles to write in a legible manner.

ESW **Peta** works with Hannah for two hours each day, with a focus on literacy skills. Currently, the goal for Hannah is to print in a legible manner. Hannah prefers to use cursive style when writing, but does not have the fine motor skills necessary to form and join each letter.

Peta uses Hannah's interest in animals to devise a range of writing experiences. With Peta's support, Hannah is visiting the websites of various zoos and making lists of the foods provided for the different animals. Hannah has noticed that in some zoos the keepers have special food treats for the animals. She asks Peta whether she can help her to write an email to the zoos to ask about the treats. Peta is required to keep samples of Hannah's writing as a tool to evaluate her progress.

WHAT DOES THIS TELL US?

The ESW has used the student's interest in animals to develop a writing program. This helps to motivate the student and can lead to opportunities to extend and challenge the student. In this case, Hannah is supported by the ESW to explore her interest in the food treats used by the zoos.

▶ DISCUSSION

The ESW has used the student's interest in animals to support her handwriting skills. Suggest what Peta could do to expand on this interest and maintain a focus on handwriting.

When planning the implementation of the IEP, consideration must be given to a range of factors – for example, learning strategies, resources, sequencing and timing of tasks, and how to motivate and reward the student.

CASE STUDY | Aaron Jones

Part 3: Planning

ESW **Jodie** has met with Aaron's teacher, **Mr Craig**, to discuss the implementation of Aaron's IEP. During the meeting Jodie, made lots of notes, which she is now using to plan how she will go about working with Aaron. As she reads through her notes, Jodie realises that there is a great deal to consider before starting work with Aaron. Jodie's notes are shown in **Figure 12.27**.

Figure 12.27 Jodie's notes

Jodie's notes	
Identify the learning strategies that will best fit Aaron's learning style and support the achievement of the stated goals. Think about:	
▪ The timing and sequence of tasks.	☐
▪ How to get to know Aaron and understand what motivates him.	☐
▪ Aaron is easily distracted – need to consider the classroom environment and find a place where we can work that minimises distractions.	☐
▪ How will I keep him focused and on-task so that he gets his work finished?	☐
▪ What type of praise and/or rewards will I use?	☐
▪ Aaron has problems listening and understanding – how will I give him instructions and feedback? Use picture cards, signing, maybe?	☐
▪ How can I get Aaron thinking – what prompts might work for him?	☐
▪ What resources will I use? Consider IT resources?	☐
▪ I need to regularly check Aaron's work for accuracy.	☐
▪ Make time to observe Aaron as he's working with the teacher and other students – use these as part of my evaluation.	☐

What does this tell us?

Planning for students with multiple needs requires careful consideration. Teaching and support strategies need to be determined, and the sequencing and presentation of learning activities need to be undertaken. In this case study, Jodie has identified a range of factors that she will need to talk over with the classroom teacher so that she is well prepared to meet Aaron's learning needs. Jodie will also need to be flexible when implementing her planned program. Jodie will need to adapt/adjust her planning based on how well Aaron responds to the planned activities.

The process of evaluation

Regular monitoring and evaluation of the goals and objectives are critical aspects of the IEP. In order to best meet the learning needs of the student and ensure that the student is able to fully engage in the learning experiences, ongoing evaluation is essential. Evaluation will focus on the stated short-term SMART goals, the teaching strategies, the learning resources, the timing and pace of the student's learning program and the response of the student.

Evaluation can be undertaken both formally and informally, and may include written observations, work samples, photographs, feedback from the student and/or their family, and formal assessment.

The Case study (Parts 4 and 5) provides examples of how observations can be analysed and interpreted to build an accurate assessment of Aaron's progress (see **Figures 12.28**, **12.29** and **12.30**). It can also be used to review existing goals and plan new goals.

CASE STUDY | Aaron Jones

Part 4: Examples of types of records

Figure 12.28 Jotting

Date 21/03/21
Aaron completed three of the four tasks set for him today. He stayed on task most of the time and told me he was going to get all his work finished.

Figure 12.29 Running record

RUNNING RECORD

Student Name: Aaron Jones	**Date:** 23/03/XX
Task:	Pattern-making

OBSERVER:

Observation	Time
Aaron is sitting at the table with three other students. The ESW is sitting next to Aaron. The group listens to the instructions for the lesson on pattern-making.	9.20 a.m.
The ESW talks to Aaron about making a pattern using lines and colours. She draws a simple pattern, which Aaron copies.	9.25 a.m.
Aaron looks around, then selects a felt pen and draws three horizontal parallel lines. He pauses and looks at the work of the other students. He draws two vertical lines in the same colour. 	9.39 a.m.
Aaron again looks around at the other students' work. Aaron stands and walks around to stand behind Lilly. 'Show me,' he says to Lilly. Lilly looks up but then returns to her pattern-making without comment. Aaron slowly walks behind each student, pausing to look at their patterns. Aaron returns to his chair, sits down and screws up his paper. 'Stupid!'	9.48 a.m.
The ESW intervenes. 'You've made a good start, Aaron, let's think about what you need to do next to finish your pattern.' **Aaron:** 'I can't do it – it's too hard!' Aaron puts his arms on the desk and his head in his arms.	9.56 a.m.

Figure 12.30 Anecdotal record

Date: 23/03/XX

After recess, Aaron worked on a writing task. He was required to select a topic of interest and write three sentences. Aaron immediately became anxious, saying he had a headache and couldn't write. I referred Aaron to his worry poster and together we identified that he was anxious about the writing task. He used deep breathing and positive statements until he felt calm enough to proceed.

After some discussion, Aaron decided to write about his fishing trip with his father on the weekend. We worked together on sequencing the task and Aaron was able to identify three things he could write about fishing. We also talked about how a sentence is constructed. Aaron was reminded how to hold his pen so that he did not get cramps in his hand. He was assisted to use his personal dictionary.

Aaron wrote, 'I went fishing with Dad. Dad has a big boat and it has a outboard motor. We catched 17 fish and I catched the most.'

CASE STUDY | Aaron Jones

Part 5: Analysis and interpretation

Analysis of the running record for Aaron tells us the following information:

- Aaron was able to sit and listen to the instructions.
- Aaron was able to create a sequence for the task using words and pictures.
- Aaron was able to use his sequence to commence the task, but instead of working through the sequence he looked at the work of other students.
- Even though Aaron had started well by following the correct sequence, he was distracted by the work of the other students. He visually compared his own work with the work of his peers and then screwed up his pattern, declaring it to be stupid. (Other students had completed more steps in their pattern-making.)
- Although Aaron was on track with his pattern-making, he appears to lack confidence in his own abilities.

The ESW, **Jodie**, was able to conclude that Aaron needed to be reminded/encouraged to work through the identified sequence of a task from beginning to end. This will support Aaron to complete a task and gain a sense of accomplishment.

An analysis of the anecdotal record tells us the following information:

- Aaron finds writing tasks stressful. He doubts his abilities, which causes him to become anxious.
- Aaron can use deep breathing and positive 'I' messages to calm himself.
- Aaron was able to complete a task with the support of the ESW.
- Aaron needs assistance to understand what he is required to do, and how to proceed in a systematic manner.
- Aaron demonstrated that he could recall a sequence of events and orally share this information in a logical manner.
- Aaron can use storytelling (oral language) about his fishing trip to assist him to formulate sentences.

The ESW was able to conclude that Aaron needs ongoing support to translate his words into text.

Analysing or interpreting observations should not be over-complicated. The goal is to identify what the students know, what they can do and what they understand. Observations can also be used to identify how the student responds to various teaching strategies and activities. Another important goal of observation and analysis is to gain a deeper understanding of how the student engages in learning and responds to various learning strategies.

Developing learning objectives

Based on the goals of the IEP, the teacher will develop learning objectives for the student. These objectives may be the same as those for other students, or they may be objectives that have been modified to reflect the particular learning needs of the student.

Learning objectives state:

- what the student will learn – for example, the definition of compound words
- the level of achievement – for example, uses compound words in a sentence
- how it will be measured – for example, correctly read aloud and write compound words.

The learning objectives are then used to develop lesson plans, which will detail:

- the relationship to the curriculum
- prior knowledge required of the student
- teaching strategies – how the knowledge/skills will be introduced
- the physical environment/grouping of students
- the lesson plan sequence
- conclusion/transition
- what the student will do – how they will use the knowledge/skills in the classroom
- how the lesson will be evaluated – how the knowledge/skill will be measured
- resources to be used by the teacher/students.

Each teacher will have their own style/template for lesson planning.

Attending a case conference

Where you are working closely with a student with additional needs and participating in observing and documenting the student's learning, you may be asked to participate in a case conference for the student. Case conferences for students with IEPs usually are held once per year (or as necessary).

A case conference brings together all the people who are actively involved in the support of the student and will typically include the class teacher, parents/guardian, specialist support teachers, specialist support professionals/services (e.g. psychologist, physiotherapist, occupational therapist or speech pathologist) and, where appropriate, the student. It may also include the ESW working with the student. Parents may also ask for an independent support person to attend, to act as an advocate for the child and their family.

Case conferences are confidential, and should not be discussed with others who are not in attendance. Case conferences are usually run according to a strict agenda that ensures efficient use of time.

The purpose of a case conference typically is to review the student's progress, raise/address and problem-solve any concerns in the attainment of the goals for the student and discuss new goals. Other matters that may be discussed can include barriers to school attendance and how these are being addressed, funding, specialist equipment and resources, the student's health and wellbeing, behaviour support and curriculum modifications.

Typically, the case conference will be managed and chaired by a senior member of the school executive. This person is also responsible for arranging the case conference, minute-taking and coordination of any follow-up action as a result of the case conference.

Where an ESW is invited to attend a case conference, the role would be one of sharing information about the child's progress and answering questions raised by conference participants. Prior to attending a case conference, it is essential to discuss your role at the case conference with your class teacher. If an ESW has any concerns about the student's IEP, these should be discussed with the teacher/school executive prior to the conference.

Effective case conferences

CASE STUDY | Aaron Jones

Part 6: The case conference

Attending the conference are: **Dr and Professor Jones**; **Ms Brown** (deputy principal and chair); **Mr Craig** (teacher); **Jodie** (ESW); **Kim Bradley** (learning support coordinator – City Primary); **Leon Smith** (area school psychologist); **Dr Paula** (child psychologist).

Jodie is feeling very nervous – this is the first time she has attended a case conference. The purpose of the conference is to discuss strategies to support Aaron's transition to high school. Of specific concern are his poor social skills and inability to cope with change.

Ms Brown steers the conference through a review of Aaron's progress. She asks Leon Smith and Dr Paula for their assessment of Aaron's coping skills and the strategies they recommend to develop these skills.

Jodie is asked to report on Aaron's progress in transitioning to and from recess and lunch, which he finds particularly challenging: *'I give him a 10-minute warning prior to recess and lunch and we talk through what he needs to do. This seems to keep him calm and in control. However, if there's a change due to wet weather or a special event, he can become quite anxious. When this happens, I get him to do his deep breathing and we talk through the change.'*

As they are walking back to the classroom, Jodie asks Mr Craig to give her some feedback on her contribution to the case conference. He replies, *'You did very well, Jodie. Your contribution to the discussion was really valuable and gave everyone a good insight into how Aaron still struggles in the school environment. I know you were very nervous, but you did well – you should be proud of yourself.'*

What does this tell us?

Jodie was able to make a positive contribution to the case conference – she was well prepared and was able to provide concrete examples of Aaron's behaviour.

Summary

This chapter introduced approaches to assessment with a particular emphasis on assessment for learning. IEPs are an example of how assessment for learning can be used to develop learning goals to meet individual student needs. ESWs can support assessment for learning by undertaking observations of students and using their skills and knowledge to analyse and interpret these observations to support the planning process.

IEPs are developed by teachers in consultation with parents/guardians, specialist staff/services and, where appropriate, the student. SMART goals are developed for the students and are used by the teacher to develop learning objectives and lesson plans. ESWs play an important role in supporting the teacher to implement lesson plans, by supporting individual students and/or small groups of students.

Assessment for learning is an effective way of ensuring that planned learning experiences are designed to maximise student participation and student success. This can be achieved only when teachers, with the support of ESWs, observe how students learn, how they function in the classroom environment and how they use equipment and learning tools. It is also important to identify individual barriers to learning – often these barriers are emotional ones, such as poor self-esteem, a lack of resilience or a lack of confidence. ESWs can work with teachers to support students to overcome these barriers to learning.

Self-check questions

1 What is the National Assessment Program – Literacy and Numeracy (NAPLAN)?
2 Define assessment of learning (summative assessment) as one type of assessment commonly used in the classroom.
3 In which method of assessment are both the teacher and the student engaged in assessing performance?
4 Explain the statement 'observations contribute to the collective knowledge about the student'.
5 What is the purpose of an Individual Education Plan (IEP)?
6 As an ESW, outline two contributions you can make to the IEP development process as a stakeholder.
7 What does each letter in the acronym PACT stand for?
8 What methods can be used in undertaking evaluation?
9 Based on the goals of the IEP, the teacher will develop learning objectives for the student. Define learning objectives.
10 What is the role of an ESW when attending a case conference?

Discussion questions

1 For this task, refer to the Scenario 'Ambiguous versus clearly expressed statements' on page 370. Discuss the differences between the two types of statements.
2 For this task, refer to the Scenario 'Writing' on page 386. If you were the ESW working with Hannah, what could you do to develop her writing? Suggest strategies to expand on this interest and maintain a focus on handwriting.

Activities

1 Connect the following concepts to the correct definitions:

Assessment	A quick and easy way for educators to assess student knowledge. Students are asked to record what they know about a topic by completing a simple matrix.
Brain dump	Teachers will use a variety of assessment strategies to ensure a holistic approach to assessment which acknowledges each student as a unique learner and learning as a dynamic and ongoing process rather than an end product.
Exit tickets/slips	A 'story' about a student's learning – it records a learning episode or an incident. It is a record of observable behaviours.
Holistic assessment	The process of gathering information from a variety of sources that accurately reflects how well a student is achieving the curriculum expectations in a subject.
Narrative observation	A strategy used by teachers to quickly assess learning. They are also a useful tool for challenging students to think about their learning and what they know and can retrieve from their short-term memory.

2 For this activity, refer to the 'learning barriers' listed on page 378. Consider, for example, a student with ASD. State what adjustments may be needed for each of the following situations:
- limited oral communication skills
- physical disabilities
- poor impulse control.

PART C

LITERACY AND NUMERACY

Chapter 13

INTRODUCTION TO BECOMING LITERATE

LEARNING OBJECTIVES

When you have completed this chapter, you should be able to demonstrate that, in relation to working in a school environment, you can:

13.1 describe the relationship between reading, oral language and writing

13.2 identify the key structure and concepts of the Australian Curriculum: English (V9.0), including: learning continuum and general capabilities; National Literacy and Numeracy Learning Progressions; achievement standards: English

13.3 describe the purpose of the NAPLAN as it relates to assessment of literacy skills

13.4 describe the elements of the 'big six'

13.5 identify the role of the ESW in supporting literacy development.

GO FURTHER

Go Further icons link to extra content for this chapter. Ask your instructor for the **Go Further** resource and deepen your understanding of the topic.

Online resources icons refer to useful weblinks. Ask your instructor for these **Online Resources.**

Introduction

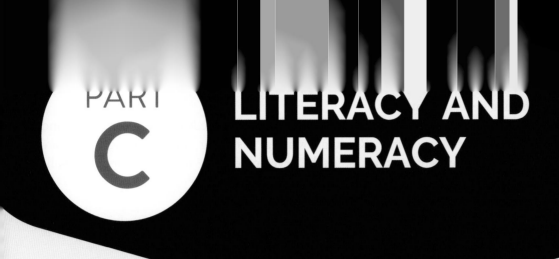

Learning to be literate is not a skill that is acquired naturally; rather, it is something that must be taught. Literacy involves the integration of oral language, listening, reading, writing and critical thinking skills. Regular assessment – both formal and informal – is an important part of

this learning process, as it allows educators and students to track their skills and knowledge and set goals for ongoing development.

Like all other areas of development, the skills and knowledge needed to be a competent and confident reader develop over time. Reading, writing, listening and speaking skills are interrelated and interdependent – that is, skills development in one area supports skills development in all other areas (see **Figure 13.1**).

Figure 13.1 Key literacy skills

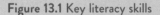

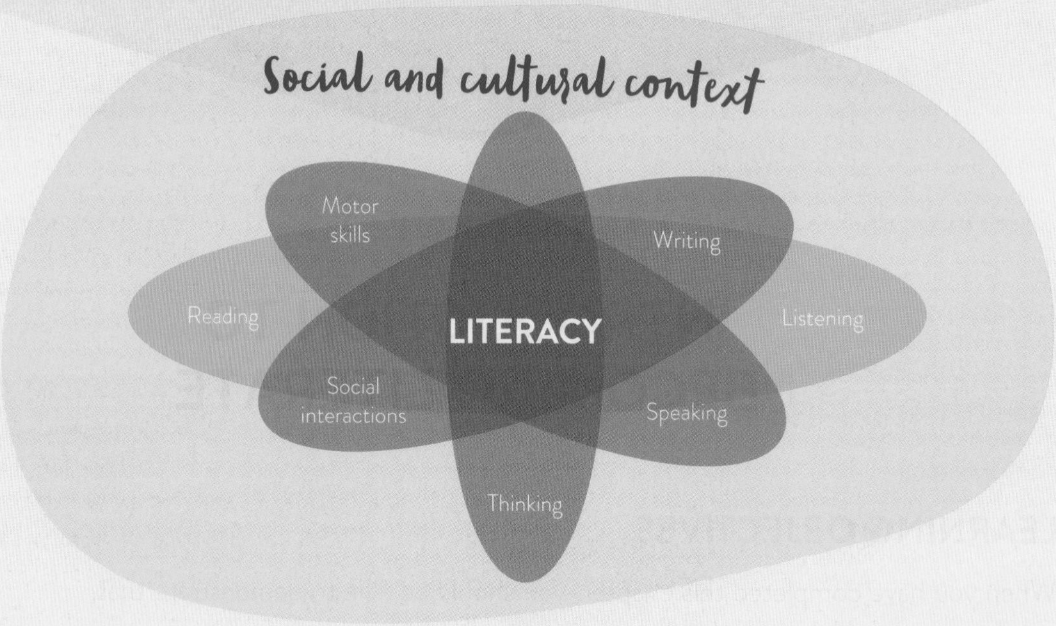

This chapter begins by exploring how reading, oral language and writing are intricately linked. The chapter then looks at the Australian Curriculum: English, assessment for literacy, the 'big six' elements of literacy, and the role of the ESW in supporting literacy development.

13.1 Reading, oral language and writing are intricately linked

Learning to read is a complex task. The brain is biologically primed to acquire language. In contrast to language, there are no brain structures designed by evolution to acquire literacy skills (Centre for Educational Research and Innovation, 2008, pp. 84, 86). To learn new skills and knowledge, the brain also needs frequent opportunities to practise new skills in context. Practising, or rehearsal, in turn supports memory retention. It is important to be aware of these facts when supporting reading development.

Wilson (2014, p. 4) describes the thought process the brain uses to deal with information: reading is 'the process of melding three systems [of the brain] (visual, auditory and understanding/comprehension) that need to work together for children to learn to read'.

CONSIDER THIS

READING AND WRITING ARE COMPLEX DEVELOPMENTAL TASKS

Becoming literate requires the integration of cognitive, language, social and motor skills – for example, to listen without distraction the student must first have acquired skills of self-regulation so they can concentrate, filter out unrelated background noise and pay attention to what is being said.

Understanding and interpreting what is being said is a cognitive process that requires the student to interpret words, sentences and gestures, and apply information-processing skills such as sorting, storing and recalling information.

To read with understanding and recall, and apply what has been read, requires higher-order cognitive skills. Students must draw on their accumulated prior knowledge as readers and apply problem-solving skills when confronted with unknown words.

WHAT DOES THIS TELL US?

All domains of development are interrelated and interdependent. In other words, when supporting the development of new knowledge and skills, educators must take into account the concept of 'the whole child'.

Literacy development

Vygotsky (1978) described language as the primary tool for the development of thinking and reasoning. He believed that language acquisition was the most significant milestone in cognitive development. According to Vygotsky, language (which is developed in a social context) leads learning. It is about communicating and transmitting cultural values, beliefs and practices – it is a social tool. Language is used to develop relationships with others, to convey meaning, and to share and exchange information, emotions, ideas and thoughts in a social and cultural context. Language develops when children are immersed in it from birth. For most children, it is acquired naturally without needing to be taught explicitly.

As well as being fundamental to all aspects of learning, language is the foundation of literacy. Rowe (2006, p. 3) states:

> Because reading involves two basic and complementary processes – learning how to decipher print and understanding what the print means – the purpose of early reading instruction is to help children master the challenges of linking written and spoken language.

Reading supports oral language development which in turn supports reading development. The Department for Education, England (2022) states:

> Children who are good at reading do more of it: they learn more, about all sorts of things, and their expanded vocabulary, gained from their reading, increases their ease of access to more reading. Conversely, those for whom reading is difficult fall behind, not just in their reading but in all subjects and a vicious circle develops.

Source: Department for Education, England (2022). The reading framework. Teaching the foundations of literacy. January, p. 14

In the following Scenario, Alicia discovers an interesting relationship between spoken and written words as she learns about homophones and homographs and, with the help of her father, creates a list (**Figure 13.2**) to show the teacher.

HOMONYMS AND HOMOGRAPHS

SCENARIO

Figure 13.2 Alicia's homonyms

Alicia (6 years, 11 months) has a well-developed vocabulary and at the weekend she discovered **homonyms** (words that sound alike but have different meanings) and **homographs** (words that are spelt the same but have different meanings).

Alicia excitedly tells her kindergarten teacher: *'At the weekend we went to stay at my Nan and Pop's house in the country and we went to a fair. I said to my Dad, "Why is it called a fair?" Is it like being fair? Then we started to think of words that are the same but aren't the same, like a pear that you eat and a pair of shoes. I thought of lots, like bat – cricket bat and animal bat; wave in the surf and wave goodbye; fly like an aeroplane and fly insects. See – Dad helped me make a list. I told him the words and he helped me with the spelling, and I drew the pictures.'*

WHAT DOES THIS CONVERSATION TELL US ABOUT ALICIA'S LITERACY DEVELOPMENT?

Alicia understands homophones – words that sound the same – may have different meanings, depending on the context in which they are used. While at almost seven years of age, most children can accurately use their growing vocabulary in the correct context, Alicia has demonstrated an advanced understanding of word knowledge. Not only can she use words in context as a tool for communication; she is able to think about the sounds of words and make a separate and deliberate mental connection between word sounds and word meanings.

▶ DISCUSSION

Discuss how Alicia's experience with her father supports her literacy development.

Children who have difficulty discerning the sounds of oral language will not only have difficulty in learning to read, but also in learning to write. The interrelationship of reading, writing and oral language is supported by Fountas and Pinnell (2001, p. vi), who state:

> The interconnectedness of reading and writing is profound and inescapable. Fragmenting these complex literacy processes interferes with the greatest goal of literacy education – the construction of meaning from and through text. Using reading and writing together in harmonious concert enables learners to draw on these complementary processes at the same time to construct meaning.

KEEP OUT!

SCENARIO

Joshua (almost 5 years) knows the power of written words. He has two older sisters who tend to alternately boss him around and baby him. It is midway through the summer holidays and Joshua and his sisters have been bickering all morning. After another argument, their father sends the children to their rooms for some quiet

▶

Figure 13.3 Joshua's 'Keep out – no girls' sign

time. Around 25 minutes later, Joshua emerges from his room and asks for some sticky tape. He has made a sign for his bedroom door, directed at his sisters: 'Keep out – no girls' (see **Figure 13.3**).

WHAT DOES THIS POSTER TELL US ABOUT JOSHUA'S LITERACY DEVELOPMENT?

Joshua demonstrates an understanding that he can express his thoughts and feelings using print and images. He also demonstrates awareness of the **alphabetic principle** – understanding that words are composed of letters that represent the sounds (phonemes) in spoken words; uses invented spelling and the relationship between letters and sounds (rules of print – left to right and spacing between words); has an awareness that words are composed of letters that represent the sounds (phonemes) in spoken words; and is able to correctly link letters to sounds (phonological awareness). Furthermore, Joshua is able to draw a picture that symbolises his written message.

Reading, unlike language acquisition, is not typically acquired naturally, and must be taught. Learning to read takes a great deal of time, direct instruction, practice, repetition and support.

13.2 The structure of the Australian Curriculum: English (V9.0)

Through the study of English, individuals learn to analyse, understand, communicate and build relationships with others and the world around them. It helps create confident communicators, imaginative and critical thinkers, and informed citizens.

The English Curriculum (V9.0) aims to ensure that students:

- learn to purposefully and proficiently read, view, listen to, speak, write, create and reflect on increasingly complex texts across a growing range of contexts
- understand how Standard Australian English works in its spoken and written forms, and in combination with non-linguistic forms of communication, to create meaning
- develop interest and skills in examining the aesthetic aspects of texts and develop an informed appreciation of literature
- appreciate, enjoy, analyse, evaluate, adapt and use the richness and power of the English language in all its variations to evoke feelings, form ideas and facilitate interaction with others (Australian Curriculum, Assessment and Reporting Authority [ACARA] AC, 2023c).

The English curriculum is built around the three interrelated strands of *Language*, *Literature* and *Literacy*. Each strand has a number of sub-strands, and these are shown in **Figure 13.4** and **Figure 13.5**.

Figure 13.4 The structure of the English Curriculum

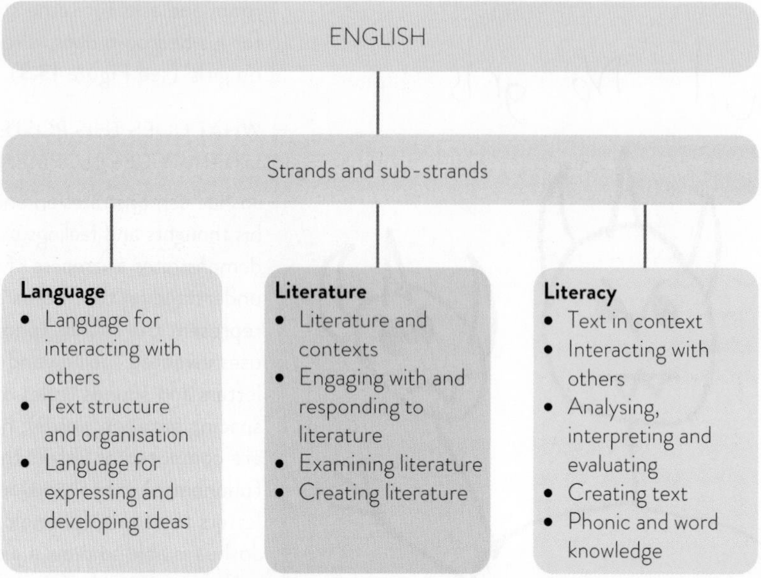

Source: Australian Curriculum, Assessment and Reporting Authority (ACARA) (2023c). Understand this learning area: English. https://v9.australiancurriculum.edu.au/teacher-resources/understand-this-learning-area/english

Figure 13.5 The strands and sub-strands of the English Curriculum

Language strand: students develop their knowledge of the English language and how it works	
Language sub-strands	**Learning**
Language for interacting with others	> Students learn that language varies according to relationships, social setting, purpose and audience, and is a means for expressing personal and social identity.
Text structure and organisation	> Students learn how texts are structured for different audiences and contexts, and to achieve particular purposes. > They learn the techniques that authors use to guide and influence the reader or viewer through effective use of resources at the level of the whole text, paragraph and sentence.
Language for expressing and developing ideas	> Students learn how authors control and use a range of clause structures and word groups as well as combinations of sound, image, movement and layout. > They build vocabulary and learn how to understand and use words according to context.
Literature strand: engages students in the study of literary texts of personal, cultural, social and aesthetic value	
Literature sub-strands	**Learning**
Literature and contexts	> Students learn how characters, events, perspectives and issues in literary texts are shaped by the historical, social and cultural contexts in which they were created.
Engaging with and responding to literature	> Students learn to respond personally to literary texts and make connections to their own lives, other texts and the responses of others.
Examining literature	> Students learn how to explain, analyse and evaluate the ways in which stories, characters, ideas, experiences, opinions and contexts are reflected in texts. > They learn to compare and appraise the ways authors use language and literary devices to influence readers. > They also learn to understand, evaluate, interpret and discuss how certain stylistic choices can create multiple layers of interpretation and effect.

Literature sub-strands	Learning
Creating literature	> Students learn how to use personal knowledge and literary texts as starting points to create texts. > They create texts with imaginative and literary qualities in different genres and forms, and for particular audiences. > Using print, digital and online media, students develop skills that allow them to convey meaning, address significant issues, and heighten engagement and impact.
Literacy strand: students make meaning through application of skills and knowledge from the Language strand	
Literacy sub-strands	**Learning**
Text in context	> Students learn that texts are influenced by historical and cultural contexts, and particular purposes and audiences.
Interacting with others	> Students learn how language is used to express ideas, arguments and opinions in spoken and written presentations by selecting and using linguistic and multimodal elements.
Analysing, interpreting and evaluating	> Students learn to apply text processing skills and strategies to navigate increasingly complex texts. > Students learn to comprehend what they read and view. > They develop more sophisticated processes for interpreting, analysing, evaluating and critiquing ideas, information and issues from different sources. > Students explore how conventions and structures are used in written, digital, multimedia and cinematic texts. > They use their growing knowledge of text structures, language and visual features, and literary devices to explain how texts influence different audiences.
Creating text	> Students apply knowledge and skills they have developed in other strands and sub-strands to create spoken, written and multimodal texts. > They create these texts with clarity, authority and novelty. They do so by selecting key aspects of a topic as well as language and multimodal features. > As part of the process of creating texts, students learn to edit for enhanced meaning and effect. > They develop and consolidate a handwriting style that is legible, fluent and automatic, and that supports sustained writing.
Phonic and word knowledge	> Students develop knowledge about the sounds of English (phonemes) and learn to identify the sounds in spoken words. > They learn the letters of the alphabet and how to write words by using combinations of these letters. > They apply their knowledge of phonemes and graphemes to decode words. > Students learn that patterns and generalisations relate to the spelling of words in English. > They learn to apply phonic knowledge to decode text, especially from Foundation to Year 2. > From Year 7, the strand is called Word knowledge to reflect that students have progressed beyond phonic development.

Source: Australian Curriculum, Assessment and Reporting Authority (ACARA) (2023c). Understand this learning area: English. https://v9.australiancurriculum.edu.au/teacher-resources/understand-this-learning-area/english

Key concepts

Figure 13.6 provides an overview of the key concepts of the Australian Curriculum: English.

The ACARA website https://v9.australiancurriculum.edu.au/downloads/learning-areas#accordion-b71b085f07-item-49001e70bc includes information about the following aspects of the English Curriculum:

Literacy learning and general capabilities

- *Understand the learning area* – provides the aims, rationale, structure, key considerations and key connections for the learning area. Where a learning area has subjects, both the Understand this learning area and Understand this subject materials are available.

Figure 13.6 Key components of the Australian Curriculum: English

Language modes
Listening, speaking, reading, viewing and writing are interrelated.
Each mode supports and builds on all other modes – for example, vocabulary is developed by listening, reading and writing; comprehension and spelling are developed by reading.
Texts include written, spoken, visual, multimodal, and in print or digital/online forms.
They also include all forms of augmentative and alternative communication – for example, gesture, signing, real objects, photographs, pictographs, pictograms and Braille.

Protocols for engaging First Nations Australians
Protocols include the principles, procedures and behaviours for recognising and respecting First Nations Australians and their intellectual property.

Meeting the needs of diverse learners
Diverse learner needs are met when students' learning is inclusive, and relevant to their experiences, abilities and talents.

Students for whom English is an additional language or Dialect (EAL/D)
EAL/D students need to learn English, learn through English and learn about English.
EAL/D students require specific support to learn and build on the English language skills needed to interact at school and to access the curriculum.

Source: Australian Curriculum, Assessment and Reporting Authority (ACARA) (2023c). Understand this learning area: English. https://v9.australiancurriculum.edu.au/teacher-resources/understand-this-learning-area/english ; (images) iStock.com/CurvaBezier; Shutterstock.com/bekulnis; iStock.com/FANDSrabutan; iStock.com/Guzaliia Filimonova.

- *Curriculum content F–6* – provides the level overview, achievement standards, content descriptions and elaborations for each learning area or subject across Foundation to Year 6.
- *Curriculum content 7–10* – provides the level overview, achievement standards, content descriptions and elaborations for each learning area or subject across Years 7 to 10.
- *Scope and sequence* – provides the achievement standards and content descriptions for the learning area or subject across F–10.
- *Glossary* – provides definitions for terms used in the learning area or subject.
- *Comparative information* – shows the differences between Version 8.4 and Version 9.0 achievement standards and content descriptions (ACARA, 2023a).

Learning continuum and general capabilities

The concept of a **learning continuum** reflects what we know and understand from neuroscience about the capacity of the brain to learn continually throughout life. Learning occurs continually and incrementally along a learning continuum. The rate and pace of learning along the continuum is not fixed and constant: there may be plateaus and even setbacks, and different children learn at different rates.

A learning continuum curriculum provides information about the planned sequence of student knowledge and skills in each area of the curriculum – put simply, it tells teachers what comes before and what should come next in relation to curriculum planning. The continuum describes what students will learn (and should know) at each year level, from Foundation to Year 10. By comparing a student's assessment outcome with the continuum, teachers can determine whether student outcomes are at, below or above the required grade level. The continuum will assist teachers to identify where students may require additional support or where they can be extended.

The idea of a continuum reinforces that becoming literate requires the integration of skills, knowledge, disposition and a positive attitude towards learning. Importantly, it also identifies the social context of literacy learning (**Figure 13.7**).

The Literacy continuum incorporates two overarching processes: Comprehending texts through listening, reading and viewing; and Composing texts through speaking, writing and creating. The following areas of knowledge apply to both processes: Text knowledge; Grammar knowledge; Word knowledge and Visual knowledge (ACARA, n.d.b).

In the Australian Curriculum, the general capabilities encompass knowledge, skills, behaviours and dispositions. Students develop capability when they apply knowledge and skills confidently, effectively and appropriately in complex and changing circumstances, in their learning at school and in their lives outside school (ACARA, n.d.a).

Figure 13.7 The learning continuum of the English Curriculum

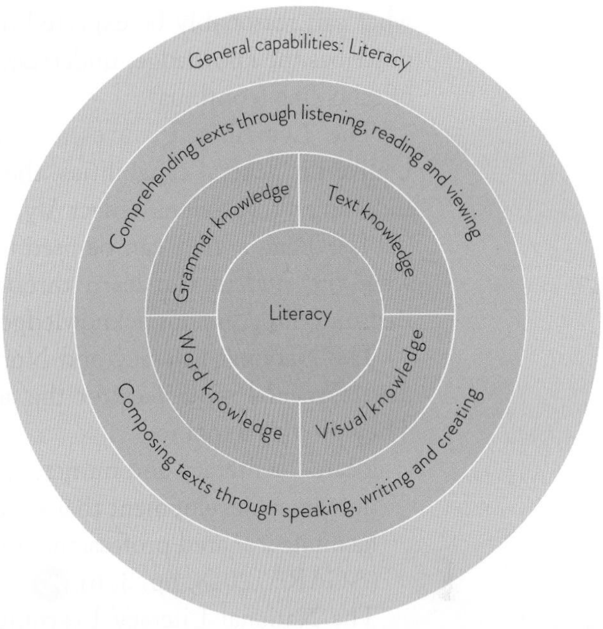

Source: ACARA (2013a).

The Australian Curriculum includes seven general capabilities, shown in **Figure 13.8**.

Becoming literate is not simply about knowledge and skills. Certain behaviours and dispositions assist students to become effective learners who are confident and motivated to use their literacy skills broadly. Many of these behaviours and dispositions are also identified and supported in other general capabilities. They include students:

- managing their own learning in order to be self-sufficient
- working harmoniously with others
- being open to ideas, opinions and texts from and about diverse cultures
- returning to tasks to improve and enhance their work.

To review your knowledge of the Australian Curriculum, go to Chapter 7 of this textbook.

National Literacy Learning Progression

Figure 13.8 The general capabilities

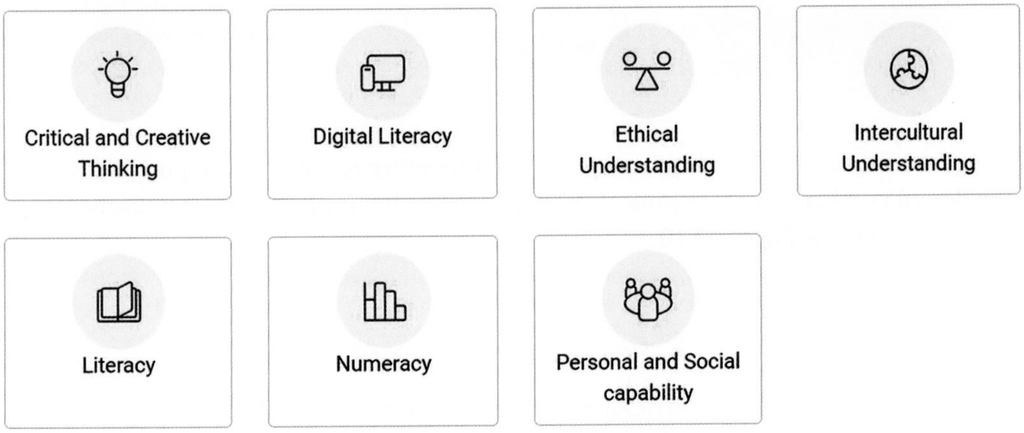

Source: Australian Curriculum, Assessment and Reporting Authority (ACARA) (2023e). The Australian Curriculum Version 9. General capabilities. https://v9.australiancurriculum.edu.au

The National Literacy and Numeracy Learning Progressions

In the Australian Curriculum: English (ACARA, 2023b) the general capabilities describe what can reasonably be expected of students at a particular year/level. The curriculum content describes the knowledge, understanding and skills that are to be taught in each year level or stage of schooling (continua).

The **Learning Progressions** describe the steps of literacy and numeracy development. Unlike the general capabilities, they are not organised by year levels or stages of schooling. The Learning Progressions reflect Vygotsky's (1978) concept of the zone of proximal development (ZPD). That is, they can be used to describe what the student already knows and, with support, what the student can learn through teacher scaffolding, direct instruction and practice. The Learning Progressions acknowledge that each student has their own unique learning pathway.

The National Literacy and Numeracy Learning Progressions describe common pathways or developmental sequences for the acquisition of aspects of literacy and numeracy development. They provide a tool to:

- locate the literacy and numeracy development of students and identify the literacy and numeracy development that should follow
- facilitate a shared professional understanding of literacy and numeracy development (ACARA, 2018, pp. 3, 6).

The National Literacy Learning Progression has three elements, with each element divided into sub-elements, as shown in **Figure 13.9**.

Figure 13.9 The National Literacy Learning Progression elements and sub-elements

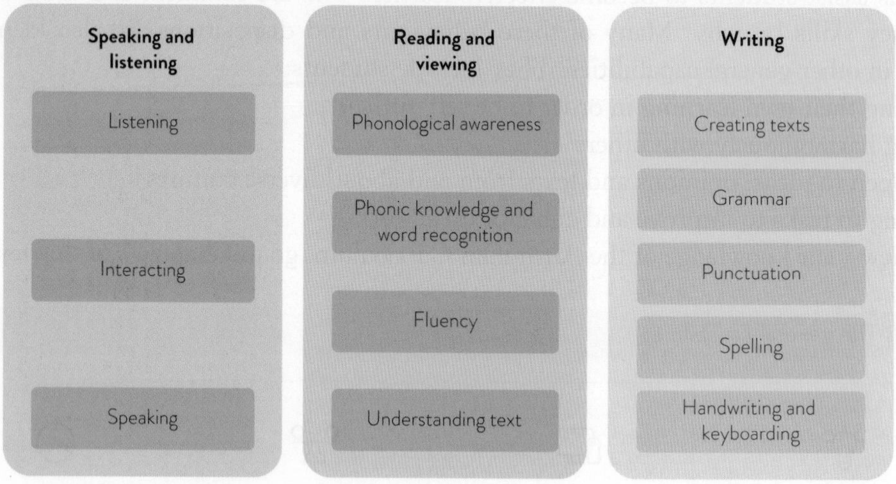

Within each sub-element, indicators are grouped together to form developmental levels. Each indicator describes what a student says, does or produces. Examples of the increasing complexity of learning are shown in **Figure 13.10**.

Achievement standards: English

Sequence of achievement

The final piece of the English Curriculum is the achievement standards. The standards are a series of statements about what students should know and be able to do at the end of the year or band of years. **Figure 13.11** provides examples of these statements.

Figure 13.10 Example of progressions

Listening

Increasing in complexity

LiS1	• Responds to a familiar, simple text structure (e.g. indicates yes/no when asked a commonly recurring question such as 'Are you hungry?') • Uses conventional behaviours to respond, which can include speech, formal gestures and actions (e.g. head nodding and pointing)
LiS8	• Responds to highly complex texts • Identifies and paraphrases key points of a speaker's arguments • Describes their own and others' listening behaviours • Evaluates strategies used by the speaker to elicit emotional responses • Explains any shift in direction, line of argument or purpose made by the speaker • Adopts and re-uses complex abstractions heard in texts • Explains how speaker's language can be inclusive or alienating (e.g. a speaker using language which is only readily understood by certain user groups such as teenagers or people involved in particular pastimes)

Writing

Increasing in complexity

CrT1	Vocabulary searches for and sometimes copies words of personal significance found in written texts or in the environment
CrT7	• Vocabulary uses expressive words to describe action and affect the reader (e.g. tiptoed, instead of walked) • Uses creative wordplay to affect the reader (e.g. repetition, alliteration) • Uses synonyms to replace common and generic words and avoid repetition across a text (e.g. thrilled for excited) • Uses a range of learning area topic words (e.g. environment, equipment)

Source: Australian Curriculum, Assessment and Reporting Authority (ACARA) (2020). This material was downloaded from the (lpofai.edu.au/) website (Website) (accessed May 2023) and was modified. The material is licensed under CC BY-NC 4.0 (https://creativecommons.org/licenses/by-nc/4.0/).

Figure 13.11 Examples of achievement standards

By the end of Foundation	Students listen to texts, interact with others and create short spoken texts, including retelling stories.
By the end of Year 3	Students read, view and comprehend texts, recognising their purpose and audience. They identify literal meaning and explain inferred meaning.
By the end of Year 5	Students read, view and comprehend texts created to inform, influence and/or engage audiences.
By the end of Year 7	Students read, view and comprehend texts created to inform, influence and/or engage audiences.
By the end of Year 10	Students analyse and evaluate representations of people, places, events and concepts, and how interpretations of these may be influenced by readers and viewers.

Source: Australian Curriculum, Assessment and Reporting Authority (ACARA) (2023d). The Australian Curriculum. English. https://v9.australiancurriculum.edu.au/f-10-curriculum/learning-areas/english/foundation-year_year-1_year-2_year-3_year-4_year-5_year-6_year-7_year-8_year-9_year-10?view=quick&detailed-content-descriptions=0&hide-ccp=0&hide-gc=0&side-by-side=1&strands-start-index=0&subjects-start-index=0

13.3 Assessment of literacy

GO FURTHER

Access a sample of the National Literacy Learning Progression in your Go Further resource, available through your instructor.

Literacy is a critical foundation skill that underpins all areas of the curriculum. Literacy is also a fundamental capability essential for lifelong learning and a productive life. To monitor the development and progress of literacy skills the Australian Government has in place the National Assessment Program – Literacy and Numeracy (NAPLAN). Tailored online assessments are conducted each year for all students across Australia in Years 3, 5, 7 and 9. In relation to literacy, all students in the same year level are assessed on the same test items in the assessment domains of reading, writing, language conventions (spelling, grammar and punctuation) and numeracy.

The test results are used by schools to assist in identifying students who require additional literacy and numeracy support. The tests support monitoring and evaluation of the performance of schools and school systems in these fundamental capabilities. They also provide schools, states and territories with information about how education approaches are working, areas to be prioritised for improvement, and those schools requiring support in the teaching and learning of literacy and numeracy. The results can assist teachers by providing additional information to support their professional judgement about students' levels of literacy and numeracy attainment and progress.

NAPLAN tests are one aspect of each school's assessment and reporting process and do not replace the extensive, ongoing assessments made by teachers about each student's performance. The National Literacy Learning Progression is a key tool used by schools when assessing each student's literacy skills (National Assessment Program, 2023a).

Tailored testing

NAPLAN online literacy assessment has been designed to:

> automatically adapt to a student's test performance and ask questions that match the student's achievement level. Tailored testing allows all students to demonstrate their knowledge and encourages students to stay engaged with the test. Tailored testing also provides teachers and schools access to more targeted and detailed information on students' performance in the assessment.

Source: National Assessment Program (2023c). Tailored tests. https://www.nap.edu.au/naplan/understanding-online-assessment/tailored-tests

Figure 13.12 An example of creative writing

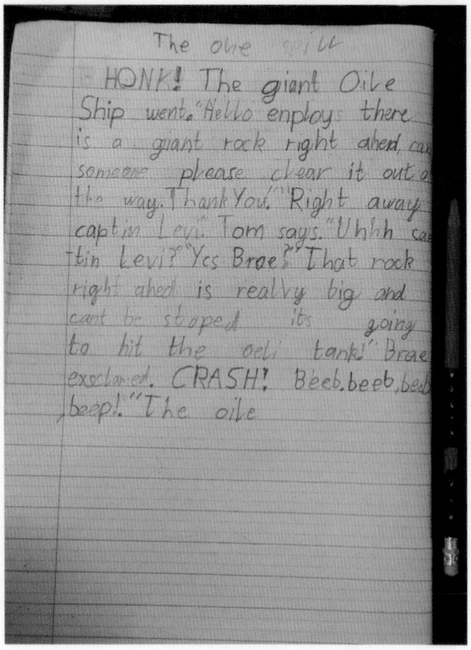

Source: Photo by Tish Okely © Cengage

Key elements of literacy assessment

The NAPLAN literacy assessment is divided into three key elements – reading, writing and the conventions of language (**Figure 13.12**). The NAPLAN literacy assessment is described in **Figure 13.13**.

The NAPLAN results are assessed against national minimum standards for literacy. The assessment scale is divided into 10 bands to record student results in the tests. Band 1 is the lowest band and band 10 is the highest. The national minimum standards encompass one band at each year level and therefore represent a wide range of the typical skills demonstrated by students at this level (National Assessment Program, 2023b).

Figure 13.13 NAPLAN literacy assessment

Reading

Students are provided with a range of texts that illustrate different writing styles. Students read the texts and answer related questions.

Focus

- Reading of written English
- Knowledge and interpretation of language conventions in context

Writing

Students are provided with a 'writing stimulus' (sometimes called a prompt – an idea or topic) and asked to write a response in a particular text type.

Focus

- Imaginative writing (including narrative writing)
- Informative writing
- Persuasive writing

Conventions of language

Students are provided with multiple-choice, text entry and technology-enhanced questions such as drag-and-drop and hot-text.

Focus

- Spelling
- Grammar
- Punctuation
- The understanding of use and knowledge of written standard Australian English

Source: National Assessment Program (2023d). What's in the tests. https://www.nap.edu.au/naplan/whats-in-the-tests

13.4 Literacy and the 'big six'

National minimum standards for literacy

> Reading is an incredibly complex process. It's underpinned by oral language skills and involves very specific skill development (phonemic and decoding strategies) and the application of comprehension strategies.
>
> Source: Brown (n.d.), p. 2.

Over the decades there have been many theories around best practice and reading instruction. According to Konza and colleagues (2015, p. 7), contemporary research on effective reading instruction has concluded that most children benefit from systematic and explicit teaching of each of the **big six** elements (see also **Figure 13.14**).

Figure 13.14 The big six

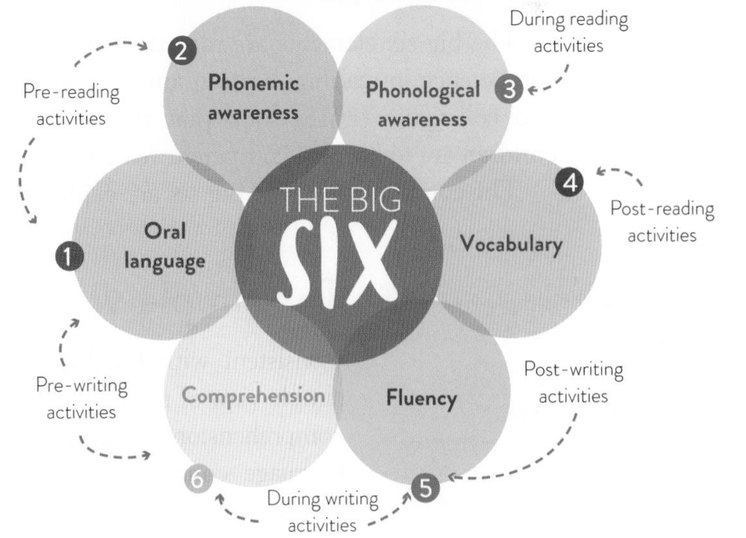

The big six are:

1 **oral language** – the foundation for the development of literacy skills; a strong indicator of later reading, writing and overall academic achievement
2 **phonemic awareness** – the ability to understand that words are made up of individual speech sounds, or **phonemes** (the smallest distinguishable speech sound). Phonemic awareness requires children to focus on the sounds of speech rather than the meaning of words: 'Being able to blend and segment phonemes are the most crucial phonemic skills for reading and spelling' (Brown, n.d., p. 3)

3 **phonological awareness** – understanding the relationship between letters and sounds. Phonics learning focuses on how letters represent sounds, which form patterns for both decoding (reading) and encoding (writing/spelling). Understanding letter–sound and word knowledge is crucial for comprehension. The letter–sound relationship is referred to as the alphabetic principle
4 **vocabulary** – words that are used and understood when heard, read or written. Children who begin school with a rich vocabulary are more likely to be successful readers than children who commence school with a limited vocabulary
5 **fluency** – the ability to read text automatically and accurately. It includes three components: accuracy, rate and prosody (expression). Brown (n.d.) says: 'Fluency involves more than how fast a child can read: it also includes appropriate phrasing and intonation, which reflect comprehension of the material being read' (p. 8). Fluency is the point at which learning to read transforms into reading to learn
6 **comprehension** – the ability to read with understanding; includes skills such as inferring, predicting, summarising key ideas and critical reflection. Comprehension is a complex task that requires children to draw together their skills of oral language, phonemic awareness, phonics, vocabulary and fluency.

According to Konza and colleagues (2015), children need strong vocabularies to understand the broad range of words in texts; they require strong grammatical skills to understand the complex sentences present in many texts; and they require the ability to reason and infer so the necessary links can be made between information in texts.

The National Inquiry into the Teaching of Literacy (2005) stated:

> The Committee recommends that teachers provide systematic, direct and explicit phonics instruction so that children master the essential alphabetic code-breaking skills required for foundational reading proficiency. Equally, that teachers provide an integrated approach to reading that supports the development of oral language, vocabulary, grammar, reading fluency, comprehension and the literacies of new technologies.

The big six elements are regarded as foundational and essential skills for the development of competence in reading, writing and spelling. Based on rigorous evidence-based research, Konza and colleagues (2015) state that these skills must be systematically and explicitly taught if children are to become competent readers.

The components of the big six are explored further in Chapters 14 and 15.

Figure 13.15 The simple view of reading

$RC - D \times LC$
Where *RC* is reading comprehension, *D* is
decoding and *LC* is language comprehension.

Source: Gough & Tunmer (1986)

The simple view of reading

Consistent with the Big Six is a theoretical model of reading known as the simple view of reading (SVR). This model focuses on the progression of reading comprehension: reading accuracy, decoding (accurate word recognition) and language comprehension. Developed by Gough and Tunmer (1986), SVR focuses on what beginning readers need to master to develop a strong foundation as readers (see **Figure 13.15**).

Word recognition first occurs when students use a decoding process, which later becomes automatic word recognition. Language comprehension is the ability to understand spoken language. The SVR is that 'strong word recognition and language comprehension leads to proficient reading comprehension' (Waterford.org, 2022; see also **Figure 13.16** and **Figure 13.17**).

Figure 13.16 Reading comprehension

| Word recognition | × | Language comprehension | = | Reading comprehension |

Phonological awareness · Phonics · Fluency · Comprehension and vocabulary · Language concepts · Communication

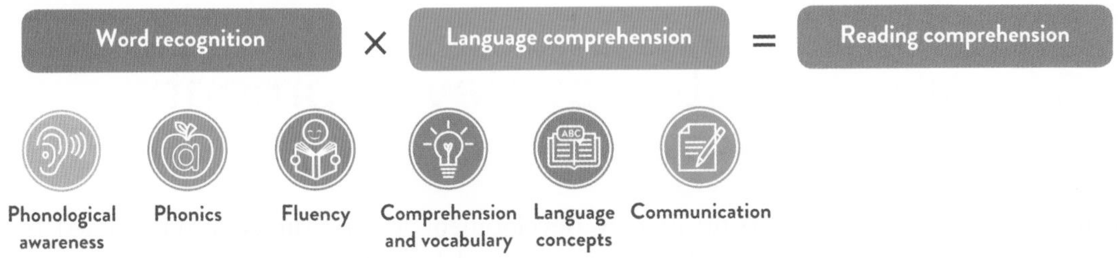

Source: Waterford.org (2022). The simple view of reading: What you need to know. https://www.waterford.org/education/simple-view-of-reading

Figure 13.17 Simple view of reading infographic

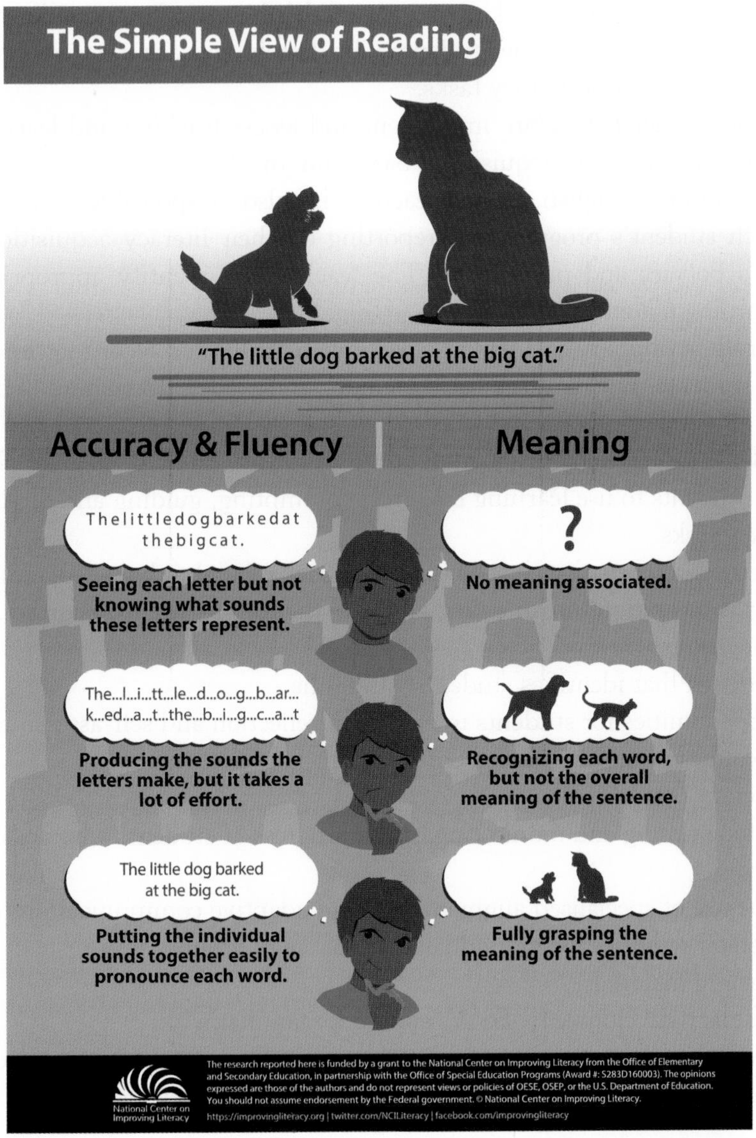

Source: Baker, S. K., Fien, F., Nelson, N. J., Petscher, Y., Sayko, S. & Turtura, J. (2017). Learning to read: 'The simple view of reading'. Washington, DC: US Department of Education, Office of Elementary and Secondary Education, Office of Special Education Programs, National Center on Improving Literacy. Retrieved from https://improvingliteracy.org

Literacy programs in schools typically revolve around the acquisition of skills and knowledge of the big six key areas (refer to **Figure 13.14**).

13.5 Supporting literacy development: the role of the ESW

The Big Six of reading

The role of the ESW in supporting literacy development will be directed and guided by the classroom teacher. ESWs are expected to act as role models to students – for example, to display enthusiasm for and enjoyment of reading; role-model verbal and non-verbal language skills, such as making eye contact when speaking and engaging in back-and-forth conversation; modulating their voice to suit the situation; or using facial expressions to convey meaning. ESWs must be able to read aloud with confidence, taking care to model the use of punctuation when reading. It is important for the ESW to provide students with timely and accurate feedback, support and encouragement as they attempt literacy tasks.

The role of the teacher is to plan, implement and assess teaching and learning programs to support each student's literacy acquisition based on the literacy learning continuum of the Australian Curriculum: English. The teacher is also responsible for monitoring and documenting each student's progress and reporting on their literacy acquisition in accordance with the school's policies and procedures. The teacher will identify appropriate instructional strategies and learning materials.

The ESW's role in supporting literacy development will vary according to the needs of the teacher and the students, but may typically include (under the direction and supervision of the teacher):

- assisting students individually or in small groups – reading to students; listening to students read; helping students to use learning resources; prompting, guiding and directing as students attempt literacy tasks
- providing specific, constructive, just-in-time feedback related to knowledge, understanding and skills that is meaningful to students, allowing them to re-attempt, correct, improve or practise literacy skills
- providing feedback that identifies students' strengths
- facilitating opportunities for students to engage in reflection and self-assessment
- facilitating a calm, unhurried, relaxed environment
- acting as a literacy role model
- contributing to assessing and monitoring of the progress of students who are under-achieving in literacy
- supporting the use of specialised augmentative and adaptive communication technology
- setting up literacy activities for individuals and/or small groups
- preparing learning materials.

To support literacy development, ESWs should be familiar with:

- the elements, sub-elements and level of the Australian Curriculum Literacy continuum
- the National Literacy Learning Progression elements and sub-elements

- the big six elements
- commonly used literacy terminology
- commonly used and evidence-based teaching practices and strategies to support literacy acquisition
- the literacy program used by the school/class
- resources that can be used/made to support literacy acquisition.

While ESWs will work under the direction and guidance of the teacher, having a sound knowledge of the factors that contribute to literacy acquisition is essential.

SCENARIO

SUPPORTING LITERACY ACQUISITION

ESW **Ted** is assisting **Ms Chan**'s Year 2 students as they explore the features of poetry. Ms Chan has been reading 'Feeling sick' by Karen Kearns to the class. The class enjoys the humour. Ted's role is to work with a group of four students with the learning objectives of:

- exploring rhyming words
- listening for a specific purpose.

'FEELING SICK'

By Karen Kearns

I cannot go to school today,
I feel a cold is on the way.
Sneezing, coughing, a sore throat too,
I feel there's nothing I can do!
The best thing is to stay in bed
and cuddle up to my old ted.
What's that you say?
It's out-of-school-uniform day.
A mini-fete and games to play!
Wow! Suddenly I'm feeling great!
Come on mum, we don't want to be late!

Each student is given a printed copy of the poem. Ted asks the students to listen carefully while he reads the poem to the children. He then asks the students to read along with him.

Ted: *'Who can tell me about rhyming words?'*
Izzy: *'I know! It's words that sound the same.'*
Ted: *'That's right, Izzy. Words that sound the same are called rhyming words. Let's see if we can find some rhyming words in our poem.'*

Ted gives the students highlighter pens and they reread the poem aloud, listening for and highlighting rhyming words.

'Good listening! We've found lots of rhyming words. Let's read them together.'

Next, Ted selects a word and challenges the students to help make a list of words that rhyme. Ted then asks the students to select their own word and see how many words they can think of that rhyme.

Ted invites the students to share their rhyming words. The students then work together in the whole group to add to each student's list.

To conclude the lesson, Ted engages the students in a conversation about the poem. He opens the conversation by saying, *'I wonder whether this child was really sick. What do you think?'*

HOW DOES THIS SCENARIO LINK TO THE CURRICULUM?

- Link to Curriculum Content for Year 2 – Learning area content descriptions: English – Literature
- Language devices in literary texts, including figurative language: Identify, reproduce and experiment with rhythmic, sound and word patterns in poems, chants, rhymes and song.

Listening and speaking interactions:

- listens actively to short texts consisting of a few sentences
- recalls one or two ideas
- responds to simple statements, commands or questions
- uses a small range of listening strategies (asking what, when, why questions about a text they have listened to)

Source: Australian Curriculum, Assessment and Reporting Authority (ACARA) (2020). National Literacy Learning Progression, https://www.australiancurriculum.edu.au/resources/national-literacy-and-numeracy-learning-progressions/national-literacy-learning-progression/speaking-and-listening/?subElementId=50559&scaleId=0

Summary

Learning to be literate involves the integration of oral language, listening, reading, writing and critical thinking skills. Literacy must be taught – it is not a skill that is acquired naturally, such as learning to walk or talk. It requires explicit, direct and systematic instruction of the elements of the big six. Literacy skills are built over time through the process of scaffolding – that is, drawing on existing skills and knowledge to acquire new skills and knowledge with teacher instruction and support.

Assessing literacy skills on a regular basis, both formally and informally, allows educators and students to track their skills and knowledge, and to set goals for ongoing development. It also allows educators to plan and implement intervention strategies as needed.

Self-check questions

1 What are the three interrelated strands of the Australian Curriculum: English?

2 Define the three key terms below:
   a language modes
   b EAL/D
   c learning continuum.

3 Explain how diverse learner needs can be met.

4 What are the Australian Curriculum's general capabilities?

5 Explain the National Literacy and Numeracy Learning Progressions.

6 In the English Curriculum, what are the achievement standards?

7 What are the big six elements in literacy?

8 What is the role of the ESW in supporting literacy development?

Discussion questions

1 Elva is supporting Hussain as he works through his phonics worksheet learning to decode the sounds in the words. Hussain's motivation is dropping so Elva suggests a quick stretch and thumb wrestle. She then demonstrated enthusiasm and determination to Hussain.
   a What is the purpose of Elva demonstrating this enthusiasm and determination to Hussain?

2 Discuss the role of ESWs in supporting the literacy development of students. Give an example.

Activities

1 Contemporary research on effective reading instruction shows that most children benefit from systematic and explicit teaching of each of the big six elements. Describe each one.

Chapter 14

ORAL LANGUAGE AND WRITING

LEARNING OBJECTIVES

When you have completed this chapter, you should be able to demonstrate that, in relation to working in a school environment, you can:

14.1 describe oral language and vocabulary skills

14.2 identify teaching strategies for oral language development

14.3 understand the process of writing development and how the Australian Curriculum incorporates writing and literacy

14.4 explain why preparation is important for students before they begin writing, and describe the five stages of writing

14.5 explain some of the elements of writing that are important in your role as an ESW, including grammar and punctuation, spelling and handwriting

14.6 identify strategies that can be used to support the classroom teacher for assessing writing and spelling.

GO FURTHER

Go Further icons link to extra content for this chapter. Ask your instructor for the **Go Further** resource and deepen your understanding of the topic.

Online resources icons refer to useful weblinks. Ask your instructor for these **Online Resources.**

Introduction

The foundation of literacy development is oral language (the first element of the big six, discussed in Chapter 13). Oral language is intricately intertwined with thinking and reasoning and precedes written language. To read you must be able to understand spoken language.

CONSIDER THIS

THE DIFFERENCE BETWEEN SPEECH, LANGUAGE AND COMMUNICATION

Speech refers to:

- speaking with a clear voice, in a way that makes speech interesting and meaningful
- speaking without hesitating too much or without repeating words or sounds Being able to make sounds like 'k' and 't' clearly so people can understand what you say.

Language refers to talking and understanding:

- joining words together into sentences, stories and conversations
- knowing and choosing the right words to explain what you mean
- making sense of what people say.

Communication refers to how we interact with others:

- using language or gestures in different ways, for example to have a conversation or to give someone directions
- being able to consider other people's point of view
- using and understanding body language and facial expressions, such as:
  - > knowing when someone is bored
  - > being able to listen to and look at people when having a conversation
  - > knowing how to take turns and to listen as well as talk
  - > knowing how close to stand next to someone.

Source: The Communication Trust (2012). Misunderstood. Supporting children and young people with speech, language and communication needs. London. https://councilfordisabledchildren.org.uk/sites/default/files/uploads/files/misunderstood-supporting-children-and-young-people-with-speech-language-and-communications-needs.pdf, p. 7.

By the age of four, most children have developed a sound foundation in oral language. They can use sentences, name common objects, and mostly use verbs, adjectives and tense correctly. They can understand and use both verbal and non-verbal language to make their needs known and express their emotions. They can ask and answer questions, describe events, and tell and recall stories. Children have learnt all of these skills without direct instruction; rather they have learnt by being immersed in language. They typically have a vocabulary (number and variety of known words) of around 1500 to 2000 words.

Like all areas of development, each child develops language and vocabulary at their own unique pace. As you are aware, the richness of children's language development is dependent upon their environment. A language-rich environment is one in which children are consistently and frequently exposed to back-and-forth verbal interactions. Age-appropriate conversations, parents who regularly read to and discuss story books with their child, frequent labelling of objects and things, and exposure to new experiences all influence language development. Children who commence school with poor oral language skills are at risk of becoming poor readers.

Factors affecting acquisition of language skills

Chapter 10 of this textbook explored the factors that influence language acquisition. For example, the child's sociocultural context, physiological influences, life experiences and most powerfully, the family unit.

Oral language is the foundation of literacy development. Children who arrive at school with poor oral language and comprehension skills are less likely to reach their full potential as readers and consequently as learners. We also know that early back-and-forth 'conversations' with babies and toddlers are critical for healthy brain development. You will also recall that all domains of development are influenced by all other domains of development. Children with poor oral language skills, limited age-appropriate vocabulary, limited ability to discriminate sounds (phonemic awareness), limited knowledge of print and poor listening skills will struggle on school entry. Typically, these children are over-represented by families experiencing prolonged adversity, such as poverty, domestic violence, poor nutrition, chronic health conditions, unemployment and lack of secure housing.

Children are more likely to reach their full potential as readers and learners when they: experience a language rich environment; engage in conversation; learn the names of objects and things; are provided with speech and communication role models; are engaged by family in playing with words, sounds, rhymes; are read stories, listen to music and learn songs; and have participated in early childhood education services prior to school entry.

Children for whom English is a second (or even third) language may be at risk of later literacy development. However, this would only be true if these children have not been exposed to a language-rich environment (regardless of the language spoken) as previously described.

Children exposed to early childhood programs for at least 12 to 18 hours per week one year prior to school entry are more likely to have developed age-appropriate language skills despite socioeconomic disadvantage. Early childhood play-based programs provide children with planned and incidental learning opportunities based on the individual interests and needs of each child.

This chapter also explores writing development, which occurs in a predictable, sequential manner as children begin to make the association between letters of the alphabet, spoken words and print. The English Curriculum introduces children to a range of writing **genres** that are integrated across all curriculum areas, as well as to handwriting. The English Curriculum also focuses on direct instruction in grammar, punctuation and spelling. Like writing development, learning to spell tends to follow a predictable sequential path as children move from invented spelling to the application of spelling rules. These rules are introduced gradually to students, who must learn their application in order to become 'good' spellers.

Note: The term 'genre' has been replaced with 'text type' in the Australian Curriculum: English; however much of the literature on writing still uses the term 'genre'. Throughout this chapter, 'genre' and 'text type' should be regarded as interchangeable terms.

14.1 Oral language and vocabulary skills

Oral language is our main form of communication and, in the context of the classroom, includes the following broad skills:

- speaking independently using extended talk to describe, recount, retell, present and explain
- listening independently to extended talk and retaining the information to complete tasks
- using social language (pragmatics) to develop conversation and discussion skills
- interpreting academic language to complete learning tasks, which include problem-solving, reasoning, exploring cause and effect, decision-making, expressing ideas, and engaging in self-reflection of own learning.

Videos: Vocabulary

Oral language is made up of several elements, which are shown in **Figure 14.1**.

Styles of oral communication

Teachers use, role model and instruct students on a range of oral language skills. The styles of oral communication explored in the curriculum are described in **Figure 14.2**.

Word knowledge (vocabulary)

Word knowledge develops along a continuum 'ranging from never having seen or heard the word before, to having a deep knowledge of the word and its different meanings, and the ability to use the word confidently and accurately in speaking and writing contexts' (Konza, 2011b, p. 1). Knowing a word, being able to say it, use it in context and identify the sounds in the word makes it easier to read the printed word.

Figure 14.1 The elements of oral language

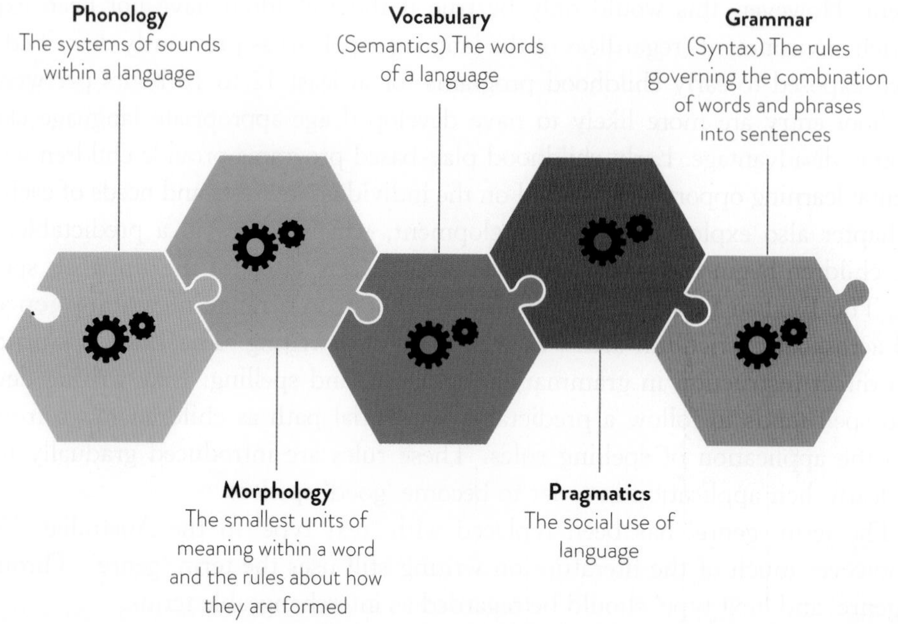

The systems of sounds within a language

(Semantics) The words of a language

(Syntax) The rules governing the combination of words and phrases into sentences
Morphology
The smallest units of meaning within a word and the rules about how they are formed

Figure 14.2 Types of oral communication

Formal language – uses formal words, avoids slang, may include jargon, avoids contraction ('they are', 'who is', rather than 'they're' or 'who's'); avoids figurative language ('the rain is heavy' rather than 'it's pouring cats and dogs'); uses more complex sentences.

Informal language – uses less formal words ('kids' rather than 'children'), slang words ('hi' rather than 'hello'); may include figurative language ('slow as a wet week' rather than 'very slow') and fragmented and shortened sentences ('What's up?', 'I'm off to the shops.').

Formal language is typically used when introducing key concepts, ideas and formulas, such as subtract, analyse, demonstrate and calculate.

'Good morning, please follow me and I'll direct you to the classroom.'
'Hi, I'm Ben, I'll walk you to your classroom.

Transactional language is used to provide information or transfer specific information. It may include clarifying information by asking questions to ensure understanding, confirming and repeating information and explaining.

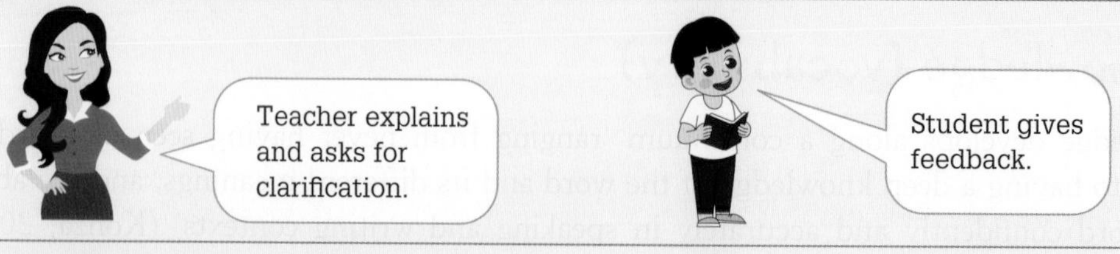

Teacher explains and asks for clarification.
Student gives feedback.

Recounting language is the ability to verbally recall and retell a past event using the correct tense and in the correct chronological order. Students can recount personal events, text (narrative, poem, play, video), a past procedure or a factual account.

'For my holiday we flew to Darwin and then we went on a ship...'

Reciting requires the student to narrate a piece of text (passage, poem, famous quote, rhyme) from memory to an audience using intonation.
Reading aloud requires the student to correctly read text to an audience with fluency and intonation.

'The people upstairs make so much noise you'd think they were bears!'

Questioning skills include:

- clarifying thinking and understanding – 'Can you give me another example?'; 'Do you mean. . .?'
- challenging assumptions – 'What if…'; 'Have you thought about?'; 'I believe that…'
- examining evidence and rationale – 'Why do you say that?'; 'What proof do you have for that …?
- considering alternative perspectives – 'What else could we do?'; 'I wonder what the others think?'
- considering implications and consequences – 'What will happen when you do that?'; 'Who is this going to affect?'
- asking meta questions – 'Why are you asking?'; 'What don't I know?'

Source: Socratic questions revisited. Jamesbowman.me

As they mature, children will continue to acquire new words incidentally through talking and listening within the family unit, and from books and exposure to media, such as television, movies, music, online games and videos. It's also essential for children to be explicitly taught new words so that they can fully engage in the school curriculum. In the classroom context, vocabulary consists of:

- words used when speaking or writing
- words understood when listening
- words that can be decoded and understood when reading
- words automatically recognised and understood when reading (sight vocabulary)

Source: Department of Education WA (2013), p. 87).

Konza (2011b) believes that new words can be taught using a range of classroom strategies:

1 Build vocabulary instruction into everyday routines, for example:
   a reading aloud and engaging students in discussion, modelling words by using them in the context of the lesson
   b explicitly explaining word meaning – 'Jasmina was mortified by her mother's outburst.' mortified means …. outburst means …..
   c engage in small group discussions led by a capable role model (e.g. teacher, ESW, older students, parent volunteers)
   d pre-teach new vocabulary identified in texts or introduced as part of subject-specific content.
2 Select the best context-specific words to teach. The teacher may consider:
   a Which words are most important for understanding the situation or the text?
   b Which words will help build important concept knowledge?

   c. Which words will be encountered frequently outside this particular context? (Time spent teaching these words is well invested.)
   d. Which words have multiple meanings? (Knowing multiple meanings helps students read across contexts.)
   e. Which words can be figured out from the context? (These provide opportunities to demonstrate how to use context to work out word meanings.)
3. Explicitly teach new words by following a sequence of steps:
   a. Read aloud the sentence or mention where the students first met the word.
   b. Show students the word and ask them to say it aloud.
4. Explain the meaning explicitly through a student-friendly definition and use of synonyms:
   a. Provide examples, emphasising the target word.
   b. Ask questions to determine if students understand the word.
   c. Provide sentences that students can judge as being true or false.
   d. Students then write their own sentences to be judged as true or false by other students.
   e. Consciously use the word throughout the following days to reinforce the meaning and different ways in which it can be used.
5. Teach students to use contextual strategies:
   a. Inference – the meaning of the word is not provided. The student must read the whole sentence and try to infer the meaning of the word: 'The band leader is so authoritarian, no one likes him!'
   b. Definition – the meaning of the word is explained in the sentence: 'The band leader is so authoritarian, he loves to boss everyone around!'
   c. Antonym – a word/s with the opposite meaning is used in the sentence or nearby sentence: 'The band leader is so authoritarian. She needs to be more like Joe; she includes everyone in decision-making.'
   d. Synonym – a word/s with a similar meaning is used in the sentence or nearby sentence: 'The band leader is so authoritarian, she thinks she has the right to tell everyone what to do!'
6. Teach the use of graphic organiser. For example:
   a. concept maps, word trees, word maps and Y charts are all different ways of explaining word meanings in detail.

Source: Konza, D. (2011b). Research into Practice Series 1. Paper 1.4 Vocabulary. June 2011. https://www.ecu.edu.au/_data/assets/pdf_file/0004/663700/SA-DECS-Vocabulary-doc.pdf, pp. 3–5.

National Literacy Learning Progression

The continuum of the development and complexity of oral language skills and vocabulary are reflected in both the Australian Curriculum: English and the National Literacy Learning Progression element: Speaking and listening.

14.2 Teaching strategies to support oral language

Teachers engage students in oral language throughout the day for a range of purposes – for example, students are given instructions, directions and explanations, and they are asked to describe, explain, hypothesise and predict. **Figure 14.3** provides a summary of the types of talk that typically occur in classrooms.

Figure 14.3 Classroom talk

Language objective	What is it for?	What does it sound like?
To instruct	Give directions	The first step is . . . The next step is . . . The last part is . . .
To inquire	Asking questions	Who? What? When? Where? How? What do you think?
To test	Deciding if something makes sense	I still have a question about . . . What I learned is . . .
To describe	Telling about something	Using descriptive words and details
To compare and contrast	How two things are alike and different	Here is something they both have in common . . . These things are different from each other because . . .
To explain	Giving examples	This is an example of. . . This is important because. . .
To analyse	Discussing the parts of a bigger idea	The parts of this include. . . We can make a diagram of this.
To hypothesise	Making a prediction based on what is known	I can predict that. . . I believe that ________ will happen because. . . What might happen if . . .?
To deduce	Drawing a conclusion or arriving at an answer	The answer is ________ because. . .
To evaluate	Judging something	I agree with this because. . . I disagree because. . . I recommend that . . . A better solution would be . . . The factors that are most important are. . .

Source: Used with permission of ASCD, from *Content-Area Conversations: How to Plan Discussion-Based Lessons for Diverse Language Learners*, by Douglas Fisher, Nancy Frey and Carol Rothenberg, 2008; permission conveyed through Copyright Clearance Center, Inc.

During classroom talk, students can also be supported to be responsible and accountable for their interactions, as described in **Figure 14.4**. By modifying the language used, these strategies can be applied from foundation to Year 12 students.

Figure 14.4 Accountability

Remember to:	Sounds like
Ask questions when you don't understand a topic.	Can you tell me more? Would you say that again? Can you give me another example so I can understand?
Give a reason why your idea is a good one.	This reminds me of . . . because . . . I believe this is true because . . .
Ask for evidence when something sounds incorrect.	I'm not sure that's right. Can you tell me why you think it's true? Can you show me a place in the book that illustrates that idea?

Remember to:	Sounds like
Give evidence to support your statements.	Read a passage from the book that illustrates your idea. Bring another information source that illustrates your idea.
Use ideas from others to add to your own.	I agree with you because... ...'s idea reminds me of ...

Source: Used with permission of ASCD, from *Content-Area Conversations: How to Plan Discussion-Based Lessons for Diverse Language Learners*, by Douglas Fisher, Nancy Frey and Carol Rothenberg, 2008; permission conveyed through Copyright Clearance Center, Inc.

It cannot be assumed that all students will understand and respond in ways that support and enhance oral language skills. Being mindful of the language used to communicate with students and the ways in which information is communicated are important educator skills. Neuman and Wright (2014) have developed five key principles to guide quality educator communication and support vocabulary development.

Figure 14.5 An example of subject-specific vocabulary

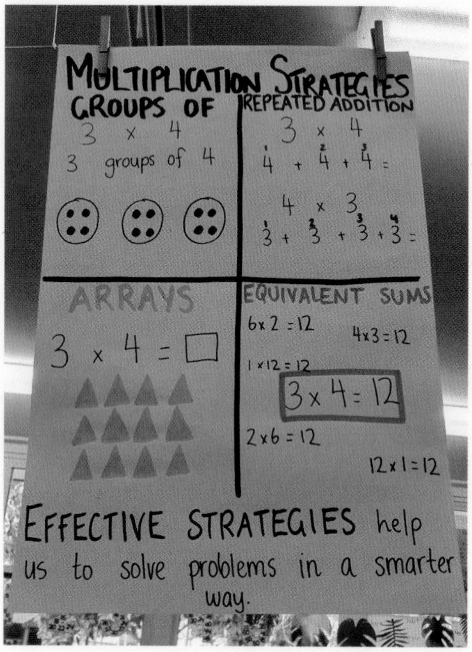

Source: Photo by Tish Okely © Cengage

- *Principle 1: Children need both explicit and implicit instruction*: Students need to practise saying new words and using them in context to make them part of their lexicon (mental dictionary). This can be achieved when new vocabulary is introduced in meaningful ways. For example, when reading a story to kindergarten children, the teacher can highlight new or unfamiliar words and explicitly state their meaning: 'The man with the yellow umbrella *exclaimed*: "Well that's *extraordinary*!" Exclaimed means to shout out loud. Extraordinary means amazing or unusual.'
- *Principle 2: Be intentional in word selection*: Research suggests that using words that are subject/content specific is an effective way to introduce new words (see **Figure 14.5**). For example, a unit exploring sustainability might introduce words in context, such as recycling, climate change, environmental, compost and conservation.
- *Principle 3: Build word meaning through knowledge networks*: Words represent ideas and concepts that are connected to other words and concepts. Helping children to build knowledge networks through words is quite a simple strategy, but one that is extremely effective. For example, if a student tells you she went to the beach on the weekend, you can explore the child's knowledge network by asking what she saw/did. Child: 'We walked on the rocks.' Teacher: 'Did you look in the rock pools? What did you see? How did the rocks feel under your feet?'
- *Principle 4: Children need repeated exposure to gain vocabulary*: Children need repeated and in-context exposure to new words for them to become embedded in their vocabulary. For example, for children to use and understand the word 'extraordinary', they can be asked to use it in a sentence, they may be assigned the task of going home and asking a parent what they think is extraordinary; they can be asked to break down the word and explore the meaning of 'extra' and 'ordinary', and the teacher may read more stories where 'extraordinary' is used.
- *Principle 5: Instructional regime*: Systematic introduction of new vocabulary involves the following steps:
  - Identifying words that need to be taught
  - Defining these words in a child-friendly way

- Contextualizing words in varied and meaningful formats
- Reviewing words to ensure sustainability over time
- Monitoring children's progress and reteaching if necessary.

Source: Neuman, S. & Wright, T. (2014). The magic of words. Teaching vocabulary in the early childhood classroom. *American Educator*. Summer, 4-11, pp. 8–10.

Teaching high-frequency words

CONSIDER THIS

In 2002, Dr Isabel Beck, Dr Margaret McKeown and Dr Linda Kucan developed a three-tier category of words to assist teachers when identifying words for vocabulary instruction.

- *Tier 1:* These are common, everyday words that most children know when they commence formal school
- *Tier 2:* These are words that are used across the curriculum areas and are important for students to know and understand. They include words such as analyse, predict, explain, summarise etc.
- *Tier 3:* These are subject-specific words found in textbooks and are used to build subject knowledge (Beck, McKeown & Kucan, 2013).

ACADEMIC VOCABULARY

By Year 4, most students have shifted from learning to read to reading to learn. Recognising and understanding academic (subject-specific) vocabulary is now essential. This can be challenging for students, especially when such vocabulary is not commonly used in day-to-day communication.

HIGH-FREQUENCY WORDS

High-frequency words are the words used in written English text. They are sometimes called 'irregular words' or 'sight words'. Many common or high-frequency words in English cannot be decoded using sound–letter correspondence because they do not use regular or common letter patterns. These words need to be learnt by sight (for example, 'come', 'was', 'were', 'one', 'they', 'watch', 'many') (Australian Curriculum, Assessment and Reporting Authority [ACARA], n.d.c).

Sight words are words that a student recognises instantly by sight without needing to decode the word (Literacy in Focus, 2019).

Pragmatics

Pragmatics is the social use of language (our daily interactions) and includes both verbal and non-verbal communication. There are three elements of pragmatics:

1. The ability to use language for a range of purposes. For example, to ask for help, provide information, greet others, share information.
2. The ability to adapt or adjust language to meet the needs of the listener or to reflect the situation. For example, talking to a two-year-old versus talking to an adult; talking in a noisy or quiet venue; or sharing knowledge about a topic with a listener who has no knowledge of the topic.
3. Following the social conventions of conversation. For example, taking turns in back-and-forth conversation; pausing to allow time for the listener to respond; respecting personal space; adapting volume of voice to suit the setting; looking at the person with whom you are speaking; and using culturally appropriate non-verbal communication.

Students whose pragmatic skills are poor may have difficulty explaining their thinking or actions, asking questions, engaging in debate, engaging in collaborative problem-solving, seeking additional information, making predictions, stating a problem, and developing and maintaining friendships. If, as Vygotsky (1978) theorised, language is the tool of the mind and social interactions are central to cognitive development, then students with poor pragmatic skills will struggle in the classroom.

Students who struggle with pragmatics may:

- Have difficulty remaining on topic in conversation.
- Not try to gain the attention of adults because they do not know how to or do so inappropriately.

- Tend to stand too close to the speaker and be unaware of personal space.
- Tell stories in a disorganised way.
- Have difficulty looking at the speaker or may look too intensely at the speaker.
- Dominate conversations and not listen.
- Not ask for clarification when they haven't understood.
- Be unable to interpret the tone of voice in others (e.g. do not recognise an angry versus a happy voice).
- Use language in a limited way (e.g. only give directions or make statements but not greet or ask questions).
- Have difficulty understanding another person's point of view.
- Have difficulty making friends.

Source: Kid Sense (2023). Social Communication (Pragmatics). https://childdevelopment.com.au/areas-of-concern/play-and-social-skills/social-communication-pragmatics

Examples of pragmatics used in the classroom with primary school students are shown in **Figure 14.6**.

Figure 14.6 Examples of pragmatics

Pragmatics: 5–12 years	
Introducing communication/responding to others	
> Selecting/introducing topics > Maintaining/changing topics > Sharing and adding information	> Initiating communication > Responding to others > 'Repairing' broken conversations
Social-emotional attunement	
> Tuning-in/responding to others' emotions > Self-regulating emotions, behaviours and thoughts > Considering the perspective of others	> Integrating communicative aspects in context (language used is appropriate to the situation, the setting, the topic, the audience) > Adapting to environmental demands
Non-verbal communication	
> Facial expressions > Gesture	> Body posture > Distance to others (personal space)
Executive functions	
> Attending to content and planning/initiating responses > Interpreting, planning, organising and delivering content	> Creatively interpreting, connecting and expressing ideas > Thinking/articulating complex and abstract ideas
Negotiating	
> Resolving conflict > Cooperating > Engaging/interacting with others > Asserting emotions/opinions	> Expressing feelings > Making suggestions/offering opinions > Disagreeing constructively > Requesting explanations and information

Source: Based on Finocchiaro, C. (n.d.). Pragmatic language for 5-11 year-olds includes (at least) 27 observable behaviours. *Banter.* https://www.banterspeech.com.au/pragmatic-language-for-5-11-year-olds-includes-at-least-27-observable-behaviours. Original source: Cordier, R., Munro, N., Wilkes-Gillan, S., Speyer, R. & Pearce, W. M. Reliability and validity of the Pragmatics Observational Measure (POM): A new observational measure of pragmatic language for children. *Research in Developmental Disabilities*. Vol. 35, Issue 7, July 2014 (pp. 1588–98).

Talking to learn

Talking to, and with, teachers and peers is the primary means by which students actively engage in the learning process. It is also a strategy used by the teacher to promote reasoning and thinking skills.

Encouraging students to think out loud – to make comments, ask questions, **hypothesise** and share information with educators and peers – is an effective way to engage students in the learning process. It promotes deeper understanding and allows students to take a leadership role in their own learning.

A commonly used teaching practice is **exploratory talk**, which requires students to share their thoughts and ideas and justify their thinking. When students engage in exploratory talk, they have the opportunity to extend their thinking. It also provides the teacher with an opportunity to scaffold learning. A successful way to support pragmatic skills is to purposefully include discussion (exploratory talk) when planning learning activities. Exploratory talk can occur with one or two students or with a small group. It may be as simple as saying, 'Tell me what you are thinking'; 'How could we …?' or 'What do you think would be a good way to find out about …?'

CONSIDER THIS

By the teenage years, pragmatics takes on a whole new meaning as teenagers communicate in their own form of social language!

Pragmatics

Encouraging students to engage in exploratory talk by sharing their thoughts and ideas with their peers can be a powerful pedagogical practice. If done effectively, it communicates to students that they are valued as competent, self-directed learners. Students who have poor pragmatic skills will struggle to participate in exploratory talk and will need additional support. They can, for example, be encouraged to use images, diagrams or other visual forms to share their ideas.

When promoting exploratory talk, it is important to take group size into account. Generally speaking, the larger the group, the less opportunity there is for individuals to talk. Group size and group composition are also important considerations for students with poor pragmatic skills. A smaller group of supportive peers is much more conducive to exploratory talk – particularly, where the process is kept low-key. Students with poor pragmatic skills may feel intimidated by their more confident peers, and, in particular, teenagers may feel embarrassed by their lack of skills and may avoid or refuse to contribute in such situations.

Characteristics of exploratory talk include:

- students engage in active listening
- students ask questions and/or challenge ideas
- students share relevant information to build new information
- students listen respectfully to the ideas and opinions of others.

CONSIDER THIS

DO YOU HEAR WHAT I HEAR?

Before continuing, view the following sound videos. How many sounds can you correctly identify?

- Guess the sound game. 20 sounds to guess (5.38 mins): https://www.youtube.com/watch?v=n1m4h79JZso
- Guess the animal sound game. 30 animal sounds. Animal quiz (11.09 mins): https://www.youtube.com/watch?v=nnaqymgi3el

Now that you have played these sound games, think about the sounds you were able to identify. How did you know what these sounds were? Was it because the sounds were familiar, everyday sounds that you instantly recognised? You are unlikely to hear the animal sounds on a regular basis, yet you are likely to have correctly identified many of them. How did you do that? What knowledge did you draw on when identifying the sounds?

Learning to listen

The above exercise allowed you to focus solely on discriminative listening – that is, listening to and interpreting sounds. In a busy classroom, there can be many sounds (and visuals) that distract students from listening. While most students 'hear' teacher explanations, instructions and direction, they may not engage in active listening – that is, hearing and understanding what the speaker is saying.

Video: Types of listening

The video in the 'Go further' margin note describes the five types of listening that move from lower-order to higher-order listening skills. As you watch this video, think about the type of listening that most commonly occurs in a classroom.

In her video *Types of Listening* (2019), Dr Christine Hanlon has used the analogy of a tree to explain the hierarchy of listening skills, as shown in **Figure 14.7**.

Figure 14.7 Hierarchy of listening skills

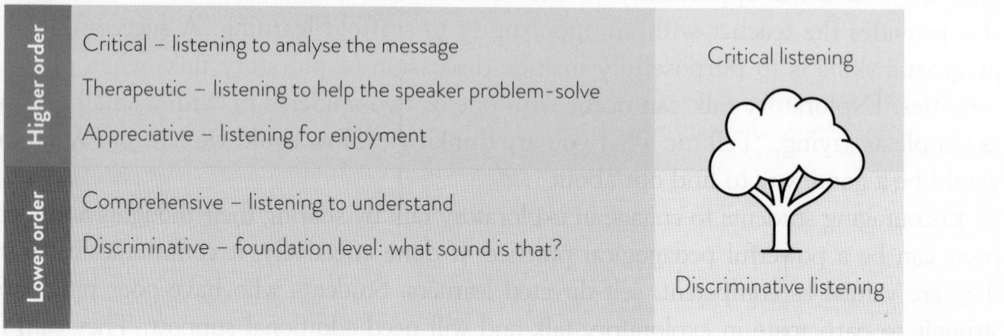

Higher order
Critical – listening to analyse the message
Therapeutic – listening to help the speaker problem-solve
Appreciative – listening for enjoyment
Lower order
Comprehensive – listening to understand
Discriminative – foundation level: what sound is that?
Critical listening
Discriminative listening

Source: Based on: Hanlon, C. (2019). *Types of Listening* (video). https://www.youtube.com/watch?v=G1ULTB5wtjQ

The aim for all students is to engage in comprehensive listening. That is, to attend to the speaker, listen to and interpret what is being said and act on the information as required. At a most basic level, to engage in comprehensive listening students can be taught key listening strategies, as shown in **Figure 14.8**.

Figure 14.8 Key listening strategies

Turn towards the speaker
Look at the speaker
Listen without interruption
If unclear, ask questions to clarify the speaker's message.

Comprehensive listening can be taught when educators:

- role model listening skills (see **Figure 14.8**)
- consistently use the same signal to alert students to stop and listen. When working with small groups, a small bell that tinkles can be enough to signal that you want students to stop and listen. For older students, a talking stick can signal that you want students to stop and listen. A talking stick can also be used in small groups when students are engaged in sharing ideas – only the person holding the talking stick is allowed to speak.
- reinforce listening – 'I can tell you listened carefully Anshul. You completed all the steps in the correct order. Well done.'

- tell students when it's time to listen – 'Let's all listen to Kai, he's going to share his ideas with us.'
- give instructions that are concise, of a limited number, avoid multiple parts and use age-/ability-appropriate language.

Learning listening skills

CONSIDER THIS

BE A GOOD LISTENER

The OWL acronym is a strategy that you can use to develop your own listening skills while at the same time role modelling active listening.

OWL

Observe	Look at the student's facial expression, observe what the student does (e.g. looks to others for an answer, shrugs, looks down, frowns).
Wait	Wait at least five to 10 seconds without further comment. This allows thinking time and takes the pressure off the student to provide an immediate response. Avoid giving extra information or clues.
Listen	Allow the student to respond without interruption. Praise the student's attempt even if incorrect (e.g. 'I can understand your thinking, that was a thoughtful answer/a good guess, on the right track, etc. You said . . . Let's work on this some more so that you can get a better understanding.'

Source: Adapted from Konza (2011a); Pepper & Weitzman (2004).

Supporting oral language: the role of the ESW

To support students' oral language skills, ESWs can use a broad range of strategies described in **Figure 14.9**.

Figure 14.9 Strategies to support oral language skills
Act as a language role model. Speak in sentences; avoid using jargon or slang; make eye contact with listeners/speakers; and model back-and-forth interactions by pausing and **actively listening** to students as they engage in verbal interactions.
Be clear and specific about the purpose of exploratory talk by thinking out loud: 'I'm wondering how the farmer might be feeling about losing his crop.'
Reinforce respect for the thoughts and ideas of others: 'All ideas are welcome as long as you stay on the topic'; 'Axel, let's hear what you're thinking.'
Make it clear that learning is collaborative – sharing thoughts/ideas and problem-solving together helps everyone to learn.
Pair up students who are comfortable talking to each other.
Encourage students to use full sentences when answering questions rather than giving single-word answers.
Avoid putting students 'on the spot' – this can embarrass students and act as a deterrent. Remind students that learning takes time – they aren't expected to 'get it' straight away (that's the purpose of exploratory talk). Remind them there is no wrong answer, just different ways of thinking. Allow time for students to process information and/or respond to questions.
Regularly review the students' ideas: 'Let's look at our ideas/thoughts so far . . .' This reinforces the concept of learning as a cumulative journey.
Engage in scaffolding by asking open-ended questions that challenge and extend thinking: 'What do you already know about multiplying fractions that might help with this question?'
Encourage students to ask questions: 'What questions do you have about this task?'
Help students to refine their exploratory talk by posing questions that challenge their thinking: 'Tell us/show us what you mean when you say . . .'

Demonstrate good communication and conversation skills by speaking clearly, demonstrating respect for the speaker and using responsive body language such as nodding and making eye contact.
Rephrase rather than correct students. For example, a student may tell you: 'I wented to the beach yesterday.' Model correct grammar by responding: 'You went to the beach yesterday. That sounds like fun. What did you do at the beach?'
Encourage children to explain/describe out loud what they are doing: 'Tell me about your poem.'
Reconnect past and present events as a way of extending interactions: 'Remember last year it rained on the day of the school fair. What will happen if it rains again this year?'
Explain new words as they occur. This may relate to stories being read to students, subject-specific words/terminology, words from a song or video.
Elaborate on the student's language by adding additional information: 'I see you've researched Chinese culture. Did you discover any information about the one-child policy?'
Model self-talk by speaking out loud as you demonstrate a task: 'First I'm going to... now I'm going to ...'
Describe events/routines in chronological order. For example, rather than say 'Before you stand at the door to go to the library, please tidy your desk', instead say 'Please tidy your desks and then stand at the door so we can go to the library.'
Provide direct instruction rather than asking a question. For example, 'Can you please put the books back on the shelf?' Instead say, 'Please put the books back on the shelf.'
When asking questions that challenge a student, provide specific information. For example, instead of saying 'Tell me the differences and similarities between the two objects', say 'Tell me about the similarities (or differences) in shape/colour/texture/size.' This allows the student to explore elements of similarity and difference one feature at a time. It allows the student to focus on language to describe each feature. For example, 'This one is dark blue and this one is light blue.'
When asking questions you can also narrow the response by giving the students two clear choices. For example, rather than saying 'What is the boy in the picture doing?', you might say, 'Is the boy running or climbing?'
Encourage students to use their senses – look, listen, touch, etc.

CLASSROOM TALK

SCENARIO

RAP

ESW **Liam** knows that one of the most challenging tasks as an educator is getting students to listen. The group of Year 6 boys with whom he works every day on literacy skills are particularly challenging. It is clear that the boys lack confidence in their own abilities and will often choose to clown around as a way of covering for this lack of confidence. Liam knows the boys are into rap music. With the permission of the classroom teacher, Liam uses rap as a way of motivating the students and grabbing their attention. He says, *'Now listen up dudes, I've got something to say. Are you listening? Are you hearing? ...'* He also challenges the boys to use rap to retell and describe the text they are currently reading. The results have been outstanding. The boys can't wait to share their rap and have been seen working on it during recess and lunch.

THINKING OUT LOUD

ESW **Sarah** is working with a group of Year 8 students to interpret the imagery in a poem. Sarah knows from experience that as soon as she starts to read a poem to the students, they begin tuning out and switching off. Today Sarah has a collection of pictures that reflect the imagery in the poem. Sarah asks the students to select an image and share one or two words that come to mind as they look at the image. Next, Sarah challenges the students to explore how the pictures could be matched to the imagery in the poem. Later, Sarah tells the teacher that the students responded well to the activity and came up with some great words that really captured the imagery in the pictures.

WHAT DOES THIS TELL US?

In both scenarios, the ESW captured the imagination of the students by engaging them in a hands-on way. In the first scenario, the use of rap encouraged students to engage with the text in a fun and creative manner and use their language skills to interpret the text.

In the second scenario, the students were able to make the connection between visual imagery and the imagery created by the use of words. Encouraging students to think aloud and contribute words to describe visual images helped them to make the connection with the imagery used in the poem.

▶ DISCUSSION

How did Liam and Sarah demonstrate their knowledge of child/adolescent development to connect successfully with their students?

Encouraging and supporting oral language and listening skills is a valuable teaching strategy that promotes collaborative learning and allows students to engage actively in the learning process. As an ESW, your most important role is to act as an oral language role model.

Social communication skills and pragmatic language

14.3 Writing development

To understand the purpose of writing, the child must first understand the association between oral and written language – for example, children may see adults writing and using a shopping list, recording telephone numbers or composing an email. Children begin to understand that symbols (the alphabet) can be grouped together to represent words and convey meaning. This awareness is the beginning of the skills needed to crack the alphabetic code.

Children will begin to attempt to make meaning from written words by using simple clues, such as picture association or familiar signs and logos, including those commonly seen in fast-food chains. Next, children learn the alphabet and realise that letters (symbols) have associated sounds. Over time, they develop phonemic awareness, which enables them to experiment with letter sequences and sounds to create words.

Typically, children begin to develop a keen interest in writing during the preschool years. This coincides with a dramatic increase in vocabulary and the ability to use language in quite a sophisticated manner. It is also a time when fine motor skills are refined and the child is able to concentrate and stay on task for longer periods of time. During this time, children become interested in rhyming words and 'silly' words – they begin to understand that words can be fun. They delight in playing with language – for example, by using a familiar word such as 'cat', children are able to produce a string of rhyming words such as 'hat, mat, pat, rat'. Rhyming word games help children to extend and consolidate their phonemic awareness. They begin to understand that by grouping letters together, specific sounds are formed to create words. Students can be encouraged to say words aloud so that they can hear the sounds in the word. This letter–sound relationship is referred to as alphabet coding, and this in turn leads to the development of word recognition.

GO FURTHER

Access examples of student work in each of the stages of writing development in your Go Further resource, available through your instructor.

The link between reading and writing is simply a natural progression of the child's awareness and understanding that print is a meaningful form of communication. This awareness develops on a continuum over an extended period of time and is supported by the child's cognitive, language and motor development. There are three key stages in writing development, described briefly in **Figure 14.10**.

Figure 14.10 The stages of writing development

Emergent stage

- Understands that writing is a form of communication that can convey specific meaning.
- Experiments with print.
- Combines random letters to create 'words'.

Early stage

- Uses print to convey meaning.
- Begins to understand that letters and groups of letters represent sounds.
- Understands directionality when writing.
- Begins to write meaningful words/phrases.

Developing fluency

- Can now write for a variety of purposes and for a specific audience.
- Employs a range of spelling strategies.
- Writes in sentences and paragraphs.

WRITING DEVELOPMENT

SCENARIO

I CAN WRITE!

Asher (2 years, 6 months) is busy with a pen and paper.

'What are you doing?' asks Dad.

'I writing to Mum. See?' Asher holds his page of 'writing' for Dad to see. Asher has created a series of squiggles and lines in random patterns to approximate writing.

'Oh, what does it say?'

'It says, Asher a good boy!'

HOMEWORK

Sari (3 years, 3 months) and **Java** (5 years, 6 months) are sitting at the coffee table. Each has an exercise book and a set of pencils.

Java: *'I'm doing my homework, because I have to write lots of words.'*

Sari: *'Me too!'*

Java: *'No, you can't write words. Only I can.'*

Sari: *'Yes me can! See?'* Sari has written a series of symbols, some of which approximate letters of the alphabet. She has written her symbols from left to right, showing that she has some knowledge of how words are formed. She has in places grouped her symbols and left spaces in between.

By five-and-a-half years, Java has mastered how to write words. He knows that to be meaningful, the symbols must represent the alphabet accurately and be grouped in a specific sequence from left to right.

Java: *'That's not writing that's just scribble.'*

Sari: *'No it not. It says I love my teddy.'*

Java: *'No it doesn't. I'm doing "at" words. Mine says h/a/t, hat, m/a/t, mat, c/a/t, cat, p/a/t, pat, r/a/t, rat.'*(Java sounds and says each word.)

Sari: *'Oh let me see. Oh, that's good writing Java!'*

WHAT DOES THIS TELL US ABOUT HOW WRITING IS DEVELOPED?

Asher, Sari and Java demonstrate the sequential nature of writing acquisition.

At age two, Asher understands that symbols represent words but is not yet able to accurately reproduce letters of the alphabet. He is at the emergent stage of writing development.

Nine months older than Asher, Sari also demonstrates her understanding that there is a relationship between print and oral language, and that print can be created for a specific purpose. Unlike Asher, Sari is now able to more closely approximate the printed alphabet. She is also demonstrating an understanding that to be meaningful, words must be written from left to right, with letters grouped together to form a word. Sari is entering the early stage of writing development.

By age five years and six months, Java has mastered the skill of writing for meaning. Java is entering the fluency stage of writing development. He knows words are formed from left to right. He is able to accurately recreate letters and, most importantly of all, he now understands that letters and combinations of letters represent spoken sounds. This is referred to as the alphabetic principle, or cracking the code.

▶ DISCUSSION

In order for Asher, Sari and Java to develop their writing skills, they must be immersed in print and exposed to print-rich experiences – that is, they must be constantly exposed to the relationship between print and meaning. This occurs when young children are routinely read to, when signs in the community are pointed out and read to them, and when they observe adults reading and writing for a purpose, such as a shopping list.

What might be the consequences for young children who arrive at school without these print-rich experiences?

Creating text (writing)

One of the aims of the Australian Curriculum: English is to ensure that students learn to purposefully and proficiently read, view, listen to, speak, write, create and reflect on increasingly complex texts across a growing range of contexts. The Australian Curriculum (V9) states: as 'part of the process of creating texts, students learn to edit for enhanced meaning and effect. They develop and consolidate a handwriting style that is legible, fluent and automatic, and that supports sustained writing' (ACARA, 2023c).

Speaking and listening, reading and viewing and writing are sub-elements of the Literacy general capability (see **Figure 14.11**). All of these sub-elements have oral language as their foundation.

The Writing element includes five sub-elements, which are described in **Figure 14.12**. Each sub-element moves from simple to complex as the student progresses through each stage of their learning.

The senior secondary English Curriculum (currently V8.4) includes four units. The learning outcomes related to Writing are shown in **Figure 14.13**.

Figure 14.11 Sub-elements of the general capability – Literacy

Source: Australian Curriculum, Assessment and Reporting Authority (ACARA) (2023a). General capabilities. Literacy. https://v9.australiancurriculum.edu.au/f-10-curriculum.html/general-capabilities/literacy?element=0&sub-element=0

Figure 14.12 Sub-elements of the general capability – Literacy learning continuum

Australian Curriculum General Capabilities (Literacy)

Sub-element	Description
Creating text	This sub-element describes how a student becomes increasingly proficient at creating text for a range of purposes and audiences across learning areas. Students' writing moves from representing basic concepts and simple ideas to conveying abstract and complex ideas, in line with the demands of the learning areas.
Grammar	This sub-element describes how a student becomes increasingly proficient at creating coherent and cohesive, grammatically accurate written language. Students develop control over grammar at the whole text, sentence and word group level.
Punctuation	This sub-element describes how a student becomes increasingly proficient at using correct punctuation to ensure clarity and ease of reading in the texts they create. As students write more complex and technical texts, they will use increasingly complex punctuation to support meaning.
Spelling	This sub-element describes how a student becomes increasingly proficient in selecting and arranging letters to form accurately spelt words, to ensure written texts are clear and easily understood. Students develop increasing skill and knowledge in using spelling as a tool to understand and create meaning in text. At higher levels of the progression, students monitor their own spelling and explain how spelling affects meaning.
Handwriting and keyboarding	This sub-element describes how a student uses handwriting and keyboarding skills with increasing speed, accuracy and fluency, to compose and edit texts. It describes how a student develops a fluent, legible handwriting style, beginning with unjoined letters and transitioning to joined handwriting.

Source: Australian Curriculum, Assessment and Reporting Authority (ACARA) (2023b). General capabilities. Literacy. Writing https://v9.australiancurriculum.edu.au/f-10-curriculum.html/general-capabilities/literacy?element=2&sub-element=4

ACARA Senior Secondary Curriculum: English

Video: Low-stakes writing

Figure 14.13 Senior secondary English Writing outcomes

Unit 1	Unit 2	Unit 3	Unit 4
Create oral, written and multimodal texts appropriate for different audiences, purposes and contexts.	Create oral, written and multimodal texts that experiment with text structures and language features for particular audiences, purposes and contexts.	Create, transform and adapt oral, written and multimodal texts in a range of mediums and styles.	Create cohesive oral, written and multimodal texts in a range of forms, mediums and styles.

Source: Australian Curriculum, Assessment and Reporting Authority (ACARA) (n.d.b). English (Version 8.4). https://www.australiancurriculum.edu.au/senior-secondary-curriculum/english/english?unit=Unit+1&unit=Unit+2&unit=Unit+3&unit=Unit+4&page=2 AC

Genres

Genre is defined by ACARA AC as:

> a category used to classify text types and language use; characterised by distinguishing features such as subject matter, form, function and intended audience. Examples of genres typically used in early language learning include greetings, classroom instructions and apologies. More advanced language proficiency includes the ability to use genres such as narrative or persuasive text, creative performance and debates.

Source: Australian Curriculum, Assessment and Reporting Authority (ACARA) (n.d.c). Glossary. https://www.australiancurriculum.edu.au/f-10-curriculum/languages//Glossary/?term=Genre AC

KEY TERMINOLOGY

CONSIDER THIS

To understand the sub-elements of Literacy in the English Curriculum, it is important to be familiar with the key terminology used by teachers.

- *Text*: An identified stretch of language, used as a means for communication or the focus of learning and investigation. Text forms and conventions have developed to support communication with a variety of audiences for a range of purposes. Texts can be written, spoken or multimodal and in print or digital/online forms. Multimodal texts combine language with other systems for communication, such as print text, visual images, soundtrack and spoken word, as in film or computer presentation media.
- *Text processing strategies*: Strategies learners use to decode and understand text. These involve drawing on contextual, semantic, grammatical and phonic knowledge in systematic ways to work out what a text says. They include predicting, recognising words and working out unknown words, monitoring comprehension, identifying and correcting errors, reading on and re-reading.
- *Text structure*: Ways in which information is organised in different types of texts (for example, chapter headings, subheadings, tables of contents, indexes and glossaries, overviews, introductory and concluding paragraphs, sequencing, topic sentences, taxonomies, cause and effect). Choices in text structures and language features together define a text type and shape its meaning. Different languages/cultures structure texts differently in many instances.
- *Textual features and conventions*: Structural components and elements that combine to construct meaning and achieve purpose, and are recognisable as characterising particular text types.

Source: Australian Curriculum, Assessment and Reporting Authority (ACARA) (n.d.c). Glossary. https://www.australiancurriculum.edu.au/f-10-curriculum/languages//Glossary AC

Australian Curriculum: English

The Literature strand of the English Curriculum includes:

- literature and contexts
- engaging with and responding to literature
- examining literature
- creating literature.

Students are required to engage in a variety of texts which 'include literary texts, fiction and non-fiction, media texts, everyday texts, and workplace texts, from increasingly complex and unfamiliar settings, ranging from the everyday language of personal experience to more abstract, specialised and technical language drawn from a range of contexts' (ACARA, n.d.d).

Figure 14.14 An example of an interpretive text

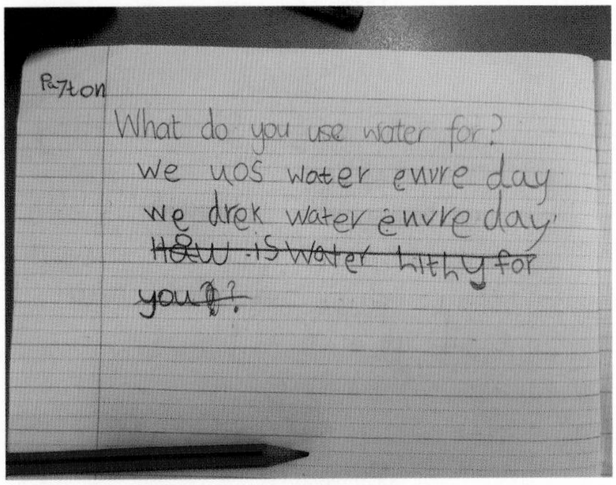

Source: Photo by Tish Okely © Cengage

Types of text

The text types included in the Australian Curriculum: English include imaginative, interpretive (see **Figure 14.14**), analytical or persuasive and multimodal texts (i.e. 'text which involves two or more communication modes; for example, the combining of print, image and spoken text in film or computer presentations' [ACARA, n.d.c]). These text types are detailed in **Figure 14.15**, **Figure 14.17** and **Figure 14.18**.

Figure 14.15 Interpretive texts

The primary purpose of interpretive text is to explain and interpret personalities, events, ideas, representations or concepts. These include autobiography, biography, media feature articles, documentary film and other non-fiction texts. There is a focus on interpretive rather than informative texts in the senior years of schooling (ACARA, n.d.c).

Factual description

Purpose: Describes a place or thing using facts

Features

> Begins with an introductory statement

> Systematically describes different aspects of the subject

> May end with a concluding statement

Example: Landscape description

Factual recount

Purpose: Retells events that have already happened in time order

Features

> Begins with background information – who, when, where

> Describes the series of events in time order

> May end with a personal comment

Example: Historical report

Information report

Purpose: Classifies, describes and gives factual information about people, animals, things or phenomena

Features

> Begins with a general classification or definition
> Lists a sequence of related information about the topic
> Ends with a concluding comment

Example: Facts about whales (see also **Figure 14.16**)

Procedure

Purpose: Gives instructions on how to make or do something

Features

> Begins with a statement of goal (could be the title)
> Lists materials needed in order of use
> Gives a series of steps (instructions) in order
> Each instruction begins with a verb in the present tense

Example: Recipe, instruction manual

Procedural recount

Purpose: Tells how something was made or done in time order and with accuracy

Features

> Begins with a statement of what was made or done
> Tells what was made in order
> Written in the past tense

Example: Documentary, retelling a science experiment and its results

Explanation

Purpose: Explains how or why something happens

Features

> Starts by naming the topic
> Describes items related to the topic in their correct order
> Explains how the items relate to each other and to the topic
> May end with a concluding statement
> May include visual images – for example, flowcharts and diagrams – which support what is written in words
> Written in the present tense

Example: The life cycle of a butterfly, how gears work, labelled diagrams

Source: Department of Education and Communities (2011)

Figure 14.16 An example of an information report

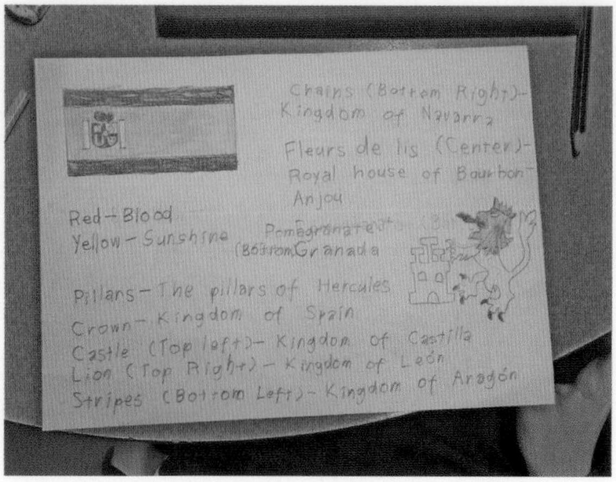

Source: Photo by Tish Okely

Figure 14.17 Persuasive/analytical texts

The primary purpose of analytical text is to identify, examine and draw conclusions about the elements or components that make up other texts. Analytical texts develop an argument or consider or advance an interpretation. Examples of these texts include commentaries, essays in criticism, reflective or discursive responses and reviews (ACARA, n.d.c) AC.

The primary purpose of persuasive text is to put forward a point of view and persuade a reader, viewer or listener. They form a significant part of modern communication in both print and digital environments. They include advertising, debates, arguments, discussions, polemics and essays and articles (ACARA, n.d.c) AC.

Exposition

Purpose: Gives reasons for a point of view to try and convince others

Features

> Begins with a sentence that gives a point of view on a topic
> Lists the arguments giving reasons and evidence for them
> Uses convincing language – for example, 'will damage' instead of 'may damage'

Example: A team's argument for a debate

Discussion

Purpose: Gives different points of view in order to make an informed decision

Features

> Begins with some background information leading to the issue
> Lists arguments for and against, giving evidence for different points of view
> Conclusion might sum up both sides or recommend one point of view

Example: Should cars be banned from the inner city?

Source: Department of Education and Communities (2011)

Figure 14.18 Imaginative texts

The primary purpose of imaginative text is to entertain or provoke thought through their imaginative use of literary elements. They are recognised for their form, style and artistic or aesthetic value. These texts include novels, traditional tales, poetry, stories, plays, fiction for young adults and children including picture books, and multimodal texts such as film (ACARA, n.d.c) AC.

Literary description

Purpose: Describes people, characters, places, events and things in an imaginative way

Features

> Describes characteristic features of the subject – for example, physical appearance, behaviour
> Often forms part of other pieces of writing

Example: Description of a character or setting within a story

Literary recount

Purpose: Retells events from novels, plays, films and personal experiences to entertain others

Features

> Begins with background information – for example, character, time, place
> Describes the events in time order
> May end with a personal comment about the characters or events

Example: A recount of a traditional story – for example, 'The Gingerbread Man'; a humorous and creatively interpreted recount of an ordinary incident that actually took place

Personal response

Purpose: Gives a personal opinion on a novel, play or film, referring to parts within the passage

Features

> Describes how you feel about a novel, film, book or play
> Lists what did and did not appeal to you
> May comment on some of the features of the writing

Example: What did you like about that artwork and why? Describe why you do or do not like this story/poem

Review

Purpose: Summarises, analyses and assesses the appeal of a novel, play or film to a broader audience

Features

> Describes how features – for example, characters, plot, language, humour – may or may not appeal

Example: Commentary on a film, play, book, etc.

Narrative

Purpose: Tells a story using a series of events

Features

> The scene is set in a time and place and characters are introduced

> Usually has a problem that is addressed

> May contain a message for the reader

Example: Picture books, cartoons, mystery, fantasy, adventure, science fiction, historical fiction, fairy tales, myths, legends, fables, plays

SCENARIO

EXAMPLES OF STUDENT TEXT

NARRATIVE

'My dog Rosie is naughty. She digs up mum's plants.'

'Alexa held her laser high above her head. She would not be defeated this time!'

'Harry was dripping wet and smelly. His paws were muddy.'

'The fruit was luscious. Juice dripped off the chin. The taste was an explosion of sweetness.'

RECOUNT

'Yesterday, when I was walking home I saw ...'

'I went to the beach and I found a ...'

PROCEDURAL

'Brushing your teeth for two minutes twice a day will keep them healthy.'

'Cows are milked twice each day. The farmer ...'

PERSUASIVE

'In my opinion we should not have homework because ...'

'I think we should all learn words in our local Aboriginal tribal language because ...'

REPORT

'To make pancakes first you need ...'

'The grass parrot is mainly green, with some purple and orange on the wings.'

EXPLANATION

'The life cycle of a butterfly'

'The Space Shuttle Challenger.'

Everyday text

Everyday text is text that is used on a daily basis to inform, persuade, advise, analyse, argue, describe, instruct, explain and entertain. It includes a wide variety of text materials, often distributed via mass media – for example, emails, Facebook, Twitter, websites, news, opinion pieces and articles, reports, how-to-vote brochures, test results, weather apps, brochures, advertising, junk mail, recipes, manuals, informal notes, invitations, birthday cards, newspapers and magazines.

Students explore contextual information, such as sentence structure and vocabulary used (e.g. formal, informal, jargon, technical), and the style of writing. Students might identify the target audience by, for example, exploring:

- the layout – for example, fun images, colour and selective text may appeal to young people
- the language imperative (words that command attention or instruct the reader) – for example, a numbered step-by-step set of written instruction with images may appeal to a wide cross-section of readers

- formal or informal language designed to appeal to a specific demographic (age, income, social status, ethnicity, etc.)
- tone and emotional appeal – for example, 'Buy one get one free'; 'By popular demand'; 'Scrumptious desserts your family will love'; 'My boyfriend lied!'
- social/cultural values/messages – for example, propaganda (political, religious, commercial) used to incite/promote fear, excitement, spreading of fake news, spending, violence, gender and religious stereotypes, civil rights).

An important aspect of the study of everyday text is to analyse and accurately interpret it for bias and misinformation.

Mass media

Mass media is any form of communication designed to reach a mass audience. Popular platforms for mass media are the internet, Twitter, radio, music, television, billboards, streaming services, media websites, newspapers and magazines. Mass media is used by a wide range of corporations, governments, individuals, political parties, and non-government organisations (NGOs). Mass media is used by both legitimate and unlawful/criminal organisations. The common functions of mass media include:

- shaping world views and bringing people together on a global platform
- bringing world news and events to all corners of the globe
- promoting the distribution of goods and services
- informing, educating and entertaining people on a mass scale
- transmitting social, cultural and political values
- acting as a watchdog of society; for example, by reporting acts of aggression, illegal activity, crimes against humanity and environmental disasters (Team Leverage Edu, 2022).

Multimodal texts

Multimodal texts combine language with other means of communication, such as visual images, soundtrack or spoken words, as in film or computer presentation media. The Australian Curriculum refers to multimedia as the materials and tools that are developed or presented using two or more digital technologies, as described in **Figure 14.19**.

Figure 14.19 Types of media: animation, audio, still and moving images

Curriculum examples:
Create written and/or multimodal texts, including literary texts for different purposes and audiences, expressing and advancing ideas with supporting evidence
Select and experiment with language features including literary devices, and experiment with multimodal features and features of voice
Interact with others, and listen to and create spoken and multimodal texts including literary texts
Comparing images from texts where images of the same subject are represented differently; for example, a cartoon image of an animal, a photograph of an animal and a digital image of an animal in an advertisement
Explore ways that media languages and media technologies are used in in media arts works and practices across cultures, times, places and/or other contexts.

Source: Australian Curriculum, Assessment and Reporting Authority (ACARA), Learning areas

Instructional approaches

As students progress through each stage of schooling, they build on their skills and knowledge to create a range of texts for a variety of purposes. A balanced approach to writing development typically includes five key instructional approaches, each of which is designed to allow students to gradually build their skills and knowledge as writers over an extended period of time. As students progress, they move from a high to a low level of teacher support. **Figure 14.20** shows the five instructional approaches.

Figure 14.20 Instructional approaches to writing

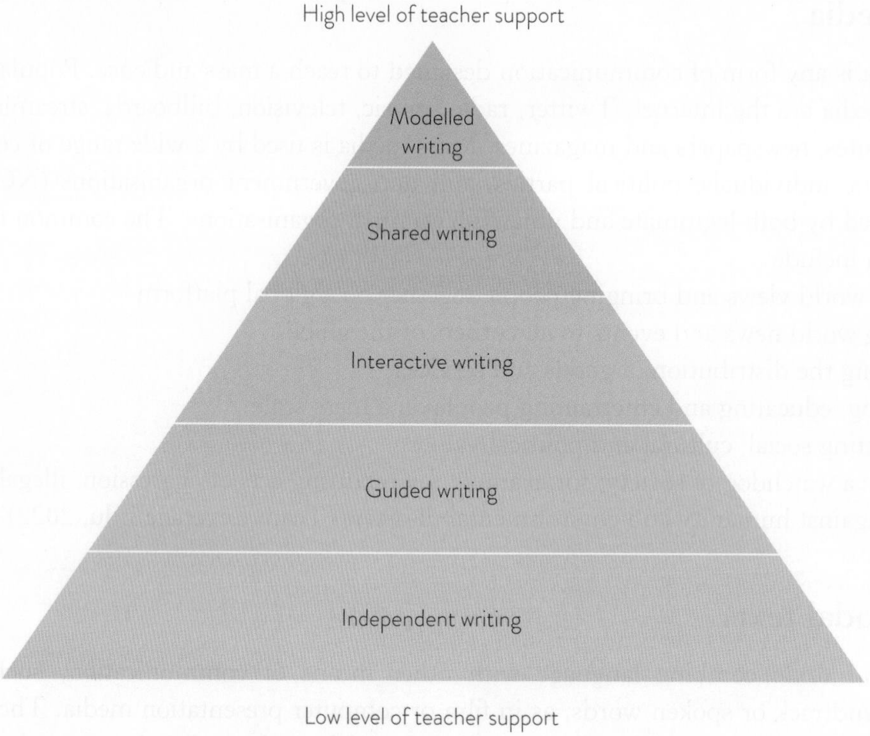

As an ESW, you may be required to use any of these instructional approaches as you support students at different stages with their writing skills.

Modelled writing instruction

Video: Modelled writing

Modelled writing is a process used by the teacher to demonstrate how to create a text. The teacher typically will talk to the students during this process, describe what they are doing and highlight key elements of the text as it is being written. The teacher demonstrates 'think aloud' strategies used by a writer when constructing text: 'I'm going to write about my dog. I'll start with her name …' When assisting beginning writers, the ESW would, for example, talk about where to start on the page – for example, top left – and comment on spacing between words, adding full stops and a capital letter for a new sentence and so on. For more experienced writers, the teacher might model conventions such as the use of speech, word choices or structure of the text. The role of the student during modelled writing is to watch and listen. The ESW may ask questions to reinforce specific writing elements.

Shared writing instruction

Shared writing is a collaborative process where the teacher and students make joint decisions. The teacher and students share the pen so that not all of the scribing is done by the teacher. The role of the teacher is to facilitate collaborative writing through scaffolding – by asking questions, making comments and acting as the scribe.

ESWs can assist in this process by drawing on a shared experience when working with a small group of students – for example, 'Today we are going to write about the colour run that was held yesterday. Let's think of some things we might want to say. You tell me and I'll write them down.' This may be followed, for example, by: 'Good work, some great suggestions. I'll read what we have written and you let me know if you think it makes sense … What should we change?'

Videos: Shared writing

During shared writing, the ESW acts as scribe while students provide the content. For younger students, shared writing may include the use of an easel and a large sheet of paper using a felt pen to write shared text. The ESW might encourage older students to rephrase, add adjectives, reconsider the sequence, challenge word choice and so on: 'I don't think this sentence really captures the emotions of the character. Can anyone suggest how it could be rephrased? What words could we use to better describe how the character is feeling?'

Literacy teaching toolkit

Interactive writing instruction

Interactive writing requires the student to write with support from the teacher and/or ESW, who may also act as a scribe. Interactive writing works best in small groups, where both teacher and students can interact easily. When supporting interactive writing, the ESW may review the process of writing (planning, drafting, revising, editing, publishing) and spelling strategies with the student. The ESW might challenge older students to replace commonly used words or phrases, or discuss print conventions and how to paraphrase and so on. The role of the ESW is to facilitate, scaffold and challenge. The role of the student is to draw on their existing skills and knowledge as a writer, to take risks and to 'have a go'.

Videos: Interactive writing

Guided writing instruction

Guided writing typically is conducted in small groups of students with similar writing abilities. Guided writing is also sometimes referred to as conferencing. When supporting guided writing, the role of the ESW is to scaffold (draw and build on existing skills and knowledge) the skills of each learner, and engage in direct teaching and instruction to address individual learning needs, such as spelling, vocabulary, sentence structure, grammar and organising ideas. With older students, the ESW might focus on the use of pronouns, verbs, adverbs, tense or direct speech. The role of the ESW is one of support and encouragement, while the role of the student is to actively participate in discussion, ask questions and 'have a go'.

Videos: Guided writing and reading

Independent writing

The final stage of writing is independent writing, where the student draws on and applies their accumulated skills, knowledge and experiences as a writer. Students will be required to demonstrate their knowledge of various genres across the curriculum. The role of the ESW is to support, guide and actively encourage critical reflection. The role of the student is to apply the stages of the writing process, research and consult the teacher and seek support as needed.

At this stage, many teachers use a concept known as the author's chair. Students are invited, as authors, to share their writing with a group of peers, whose role is to provide constructive feedback.

Videos: Independent writing

Regardless of the instructional approach, when supporting writing, it is the role of the ESW to facilitate, guide and encourage students. This includes direct instruction and intentional teaching of skills and knowledge. Importantly, ESWs should actively model and demonstrate the link between oral language and writing. ESWs will also play a critical role in observing and documenting students' writing development and provide feedback to the teacher.

14.4 Preparing to be writers

'Learning to write has been likened by one researcher as similar to learning to play a musical instrument, it takes dedication, good teaching and lots and lots of practice to master' (Scull, 2015).

To become *good* writers, students must understand the key purposes of writing: to provide information and facts; to share thoughts, ideas, feelings and experiences; and seek to persuade or influence a variety of audiences. Students must also understand that writing is a dynamic and interactive process. It requires students to draw simultaneously on a range of skills and knowledge, and it requires thinking, planning, reflecting and critical analysis.

To become confident writers, students must be provided with explicit writing instruction. They must learn that writing requires the use of specific techniques. Teachers support writing development by introducing students to three key techniques, which include both skills and knowledge: knowing what good writers like to do; editing; and checking spelling. These processes are outlined in the following Consider this box.

CONSIDER THIS

WRITING TECHNIQUES

WHAT DO GOOD WRITERS LIKE TO DO?

- They like to write.
- They write about things they know about or in which they are interested.
- They draw and 'talk out' their story (rehearsal).
- They decide who they are writing for and what their writing will look like.
- They share their writing with a partner, a conference group or the teacher.
- They read their first draft and ask, 'Does it look right? Does it sound right? Does it make sense?'

WHAT DO GOOD EDITORS DO?

- They use capital letters appropriately.
- They check their punctuation.
- They check their spelling.
- They use complete sentences.
- They write legibly.
- They use interesting words.
- They let somebody else read their story.

WHAT DO GOOD SPELLERS DO?

- They read a lot.
- They write a lot.
- They look for patterns.
- They know many high-frequency words.
- They know if a word looks right.
- They listen for the sounds they hear.
- They know where to look to find a hard word (e.g. word dictionaries).
- They are willing to take risks.

The processes approach

Writing is a process that requires the application of a series of steps. Knowing these steps or procedures, and understanding their purpose, can help students to become effective writers.

Your role as an ESW is to understand the steps in the writing process and provide support to students at each stage of the process as needed.

Figure 14.21 shows the six steps typically used by teachers to develop writing skills. Each step requires students to think, plan and reflect. Students can work on their writing skills individually, in pairs or small groups, or as a whole class. The role of the teacher and the ESW is to provide direct instruction, guidance and support.

Figure 14.21 Components of the writing process

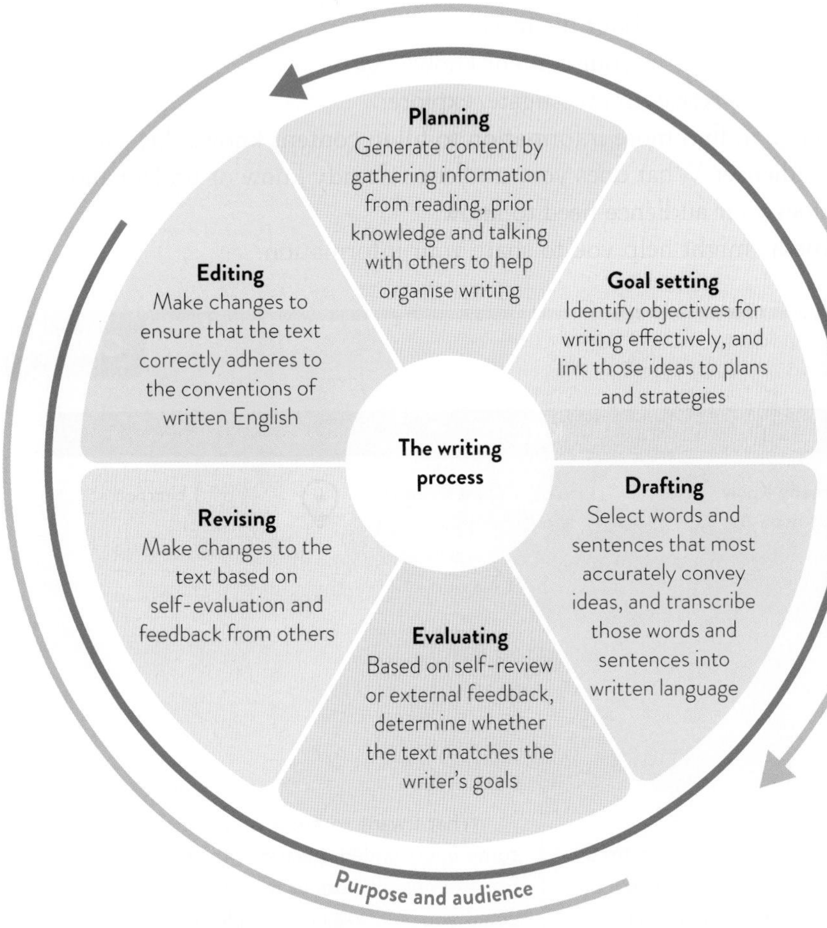

The components may be repeated, implemented simultaneously or implemented in different orders, keeping audience and purpose in mind throughout the writing process.

Source: Institute of Education Sciences (n.d.). Teaching secondary students to write effectively: Practice guide summary. U.S. Department of Education, Institute of Education Sciences, National Center for Education Evaluation and Regional Assistance, What Works Clearinghouse.

Step 1: Planning what to write

This involves thinking and talking about what to write, thus generating ideas. Students must first understand the purpose or reason for writing: 'Why am I writing this text? What is the intended outcome?' – for example, a factual report, a narrative, an adventure story, a list. They must decide on their intended audience: 'Who will read my writing?'

When engaged in creative writing, students will draw on their own experiences and knowledge – for example, texts they have read, or themes and ideas from movies, television, YouTube videos, gaming and theatre. During the planning stage, students will jot down ideas or be assisted to do so by the teacher or ESW.

Students can be assisted with their draft by asking probing questions. These questions will vary depending on the purpose of the writing (e.g. factual description, information report discussion, narrative) – for example:

- What are your goals for this writing task? Are you writing to inform or persuade? Is the purpose to reflect, explain, summarise or analyse?
- What do you already know about the topic?
- Can you identify any gaps in your content knowledge?
- What do you want to research/investigate/explore?
- Where can you go to find more information to fill in content knowledge gaps?
- Who is your audience? What does your audience already know or understand about this topic? What does your audience need to know?
- What visual media might help you to share your information?

KWL

CONSIDER THIS

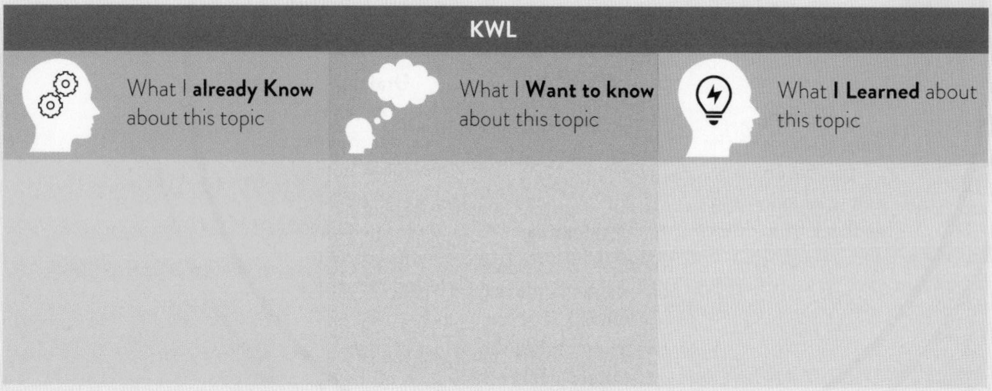
KWL
What I already Know about this topic
What I Want to know about this topic
What I Learned about this topic

KWL is a useful tool for supporting students when attempting persuasive/analytical texts and interpretive text. KWLs are particularly useful for supporting students to organise their thoughts and get started on their writing.

Beginning with K – what I already know – can help students feel more confident and less overwhelmed about completing a writing task. The ESW can act as a scribe and list the student's knowledge in the first column. Record everything the student says, whether it is correct or incorrect. (Incorrect information can be identified by the student as they explore the topic.)

What I want to know may require asking the student some open-ended questions to focus their thinking. For example, 'I wonder if... How does it ...? Where could you ...?' Again, a single response is a good start – as the student explores the topic, they may add to this column.

Finally, what I learned. By reviewing the first column, students can be supported to reflect on what they knew at the beginning of the task and what they now know. This reinforces the student's learning and builds self-esteem.

Step 2: Writing a draft

Videos: KWL

To create a draft, students must be able to transfer their thinking into a logical written sequence. This is challenging for many students. Often the hardest part is getting started: 'Where do I start? How will I sequence my ideas so that there is a logical flow? How much detail do I need? What words and phrases can I use?'

Students who struggle with writing can benefit from seeing an example and/or using a checklist of the required text. **Figure 14.22** provides a sample of some of the information that may be included on a checklist. The content and complexity of the checklist should be adapted to meet the needs of the student. A visual example of how to write a recipe can be found at https://learnenglishteens.britishcouncil.org/skills/writing/a2-writing/recipe. Seeing what the writing task should look like can be extremely helpful for all learners.

Creating a recipe

Figure 14.22 Example of a procedural text checklist

My checklist for procedural writing	*What I need to fix*
▪ Purpose: I stated the purpose of my text	
▪ I used a heading or opening statement	
▪ I listed all of the materials needed for the procedure	I left out two items
▪ I used image and/or diagrams if needed	I could find a picture
▪ Each step in the procedure is written on a new line	
▪ My directions/instructions are clear and easy to follow	I need to add more information to my directions so they are easy to follow
▪ My procedures are in the right order	
▪ I used headings and subheadings	
▪ I used correct terminology	
▪ I checked my spelling	

Students can be reminded that all good writing has a purpose, and a beginning, a middle and an end. Questions that can guide students to write their draft will vary depending on the format being used – for example:

- How will you introduce the topic?
- How will you organise your plan?
- In what sequence will you present the content?
- What subheadings can you use to help you to develop the content?
- What are the key points you want to cover?
- Who will be the intended audience?

Writing a draft allows students to reflect on their writing and make necessary corrections. Sharing a draft with a few other students and seeking feedback using a checklist can be a helpful strategy.

Step 3: Revise the draft

At this stage, students need to engage in critical thinking, which is a higher-order skill that takes time to develop. The aim of revising is to encourage students to read what they have written and ask themselves a series of questions – for example, 'Does it make sense? Does it stay on the intended topic? Is there a logical sequence and flow?' (This is a higher-order skill.) It can be helpful if the student reads their revised draft to another student (or has another student read it) and asks for feedback. Sharing and actively listening to feedback assists students to develop their critical thinking skills: 'Is there a better way to say this? Could I add some adjectives to make my text more interesting? How can I give my writing a style all of my own?'

Step 4: Editing

The revisions are now edited and the necessary changes made. Older students can be encouraged to edit for grammar, spelling, sentence structure and layout. Punctuation can also be checked – capital letters, full stops, commas, question marks, quotation marks and exclamation marks. Depending on the format, the student may also need to include illustrations, graphs or diagrams. When the student is happy with their final draft, they will be ready to publish. Teachers may provide students with editing tools such as a checklist or a list of commonly misspelt words. If using a word program or other computer-based format, remind students that spell-check does not always identify incorrect spelling.

Videos: Instructional strategies and modelled-guided-independent practice

Stage 5: Publishing

Students now prepare their final document in the required format ready for others to read. Students can be encouraged to ask themselves the following questions: 'How should I present my text? Should I add pictures/illustrations/diagrams to highlight or explain key points? Should I use sub-headings?'

GO FURTHER

Access examples of genres that may be used in some curriculum areas for students in all years from Foundation to Year 10 in your Go Further resource, available through your instructor.

Exploring genres

Understanding that there are specific writing styles for specific purposes or functions requires students to explore writing genres. To develop this knowledge, students are exposed to a wide range of genres, which are used across all curriculum areas.

Students explore the unique characteristics of each genre and how they are used for a specific purpose. They also learn, for example, how, where and when to include lists, instructions, graphics, illustrations, photographs and diagrams to support a specific genre – for example, consider the challenge of writing a recipe so that the reader is able to reproduce cooked food with some degree of accuracy and consistency. Following are a series of examples of different genres produced by students.

Procedure

In **Figure 14.23**, Chloe (8 years) writes down her morning procedure. To do this, Chloe draws on high-level thinking skills – she needs to recall and describe the routine and ensure it is written in the correct sequence so it flows in a logical manner.

Compare and contrast

In the next example (**Figure 14.24**), Kai and Asher (both 9 years) are required to compare the attributes of three groups: physical features; likes and dislikes; and favourite things. They are then required to identify whether these attributes are the same or different. This is a complex task that requires the boys to think about, identify, list and describe the sub-elements of physical

Figure 14.23 Example of a procedure written by Chloe (8 years), describing her morning routine

Morning routine procedure	
1 Mum knocks on the door	Morning Routine procedure
	1. Mum knods on the Dar.
2 Get out of bed	2. Get out of Bed
3 Put on slippers and gown	3. Get slippers and gone
4 Eat breakfast	4. Eat Brerfst
5 Brush our teeth	5. Brush ower teeth
6 Get dress(ed)	6. get Dress

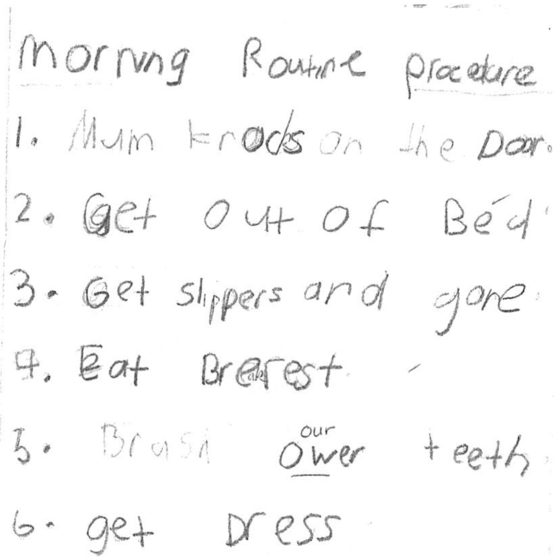

Figure 14.24 Compare and contrast: Kai and Asher

Compare your physical features, likes and dislikes, favourite things with another student				
Comparisons	Kai	Asher	Alike	Different
Hair	Brown and curly	Blonde and straight		☹
Height	140 cm	143 cm		
Weight	33 kg	35 kg		☹
Eye colour	Green	Blue		☹
Favourite sport	Football	Football	☺	
Favourite food	Pizza	Hot chips		☹
Favourite toy	Xbox	Xbox	☺	
Favourite TV program	Cartoons	Cartoons	☺	
Favourite animal	Tiger	Dolphin		☹
Favourite music	Hip hop	Rap	☺	
Dislikes	Homework	Homework	☺	
Likes	Lollies	Lollies	☺	
Add other things				
Favourite footy team	The Swans	The Cats		☹
Favourite book	The day my brain fell out	When dinosaurs walked the Earth	☺	
Things I'm good at	Drawing	Skateboarding		☹
What we learned about our similarities and differences:				

Our main differences were in our physical features like eye colour and hair colour. We like lots of the same things like music and sport. We both don't like homework!

features (hair colour, height, weight and so on). The boys then have to create a table that can easily be read and interpreted and determine a logical process to gather and record the information needed for their table. Finally, they have to interpret and draw conclusions about the information they have recorded: 'We like lots of the same things, like music and sport. We both don't like homework.'

Kai and Asher created a table using the data they collected about their likes and dislikes. It allowed them to easily make comparisons and draw conclusions.

Flow chart

Figure 14.25 shows a flow chart developed by 12-year-old Elliot. Drawing on his own experience of dog-washing, Elliot has identified and recorded each step in the process. Again, this is a complex task requiring a range of cognitive skills, such as recalling, planning and sequencing. Elliot has added his own tips, obviously based on personal experience!

Figure 14.25 Elliot created a flow chart to demonstrate the steps involved in washing his dog

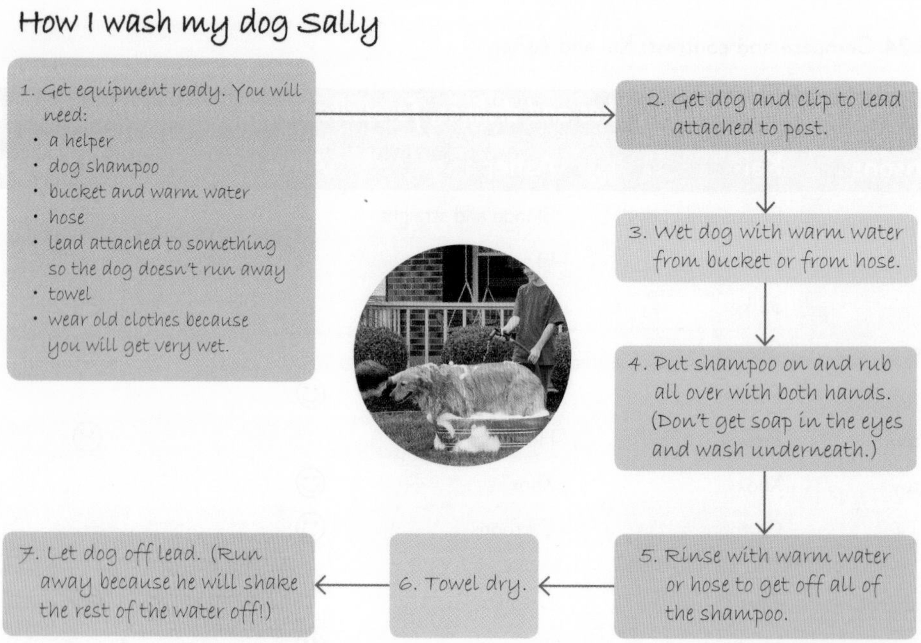

How I wash my dog Sally
1. Get equipment ready. You will need:
• a helper
• dog shampoo
• bucket and warm water
• hose
• lead attached to something so the dog doesn't run away
• towel
• wear old clothes because you will get very wet.
2. Get dog and clip to lead attached to post.
3. Wet dog with warm water from bucket or from hose.
4. Put shampoo on and rub all over with both hands. (Don't get soap in the eyes and wash underneath.)
5. Rinse with warm water or hose to get off all of the shampoo.
6. Towel dry.
7. Let dog off lead. (Run away because he will shake the rest of the water off!)

Source: (image) iStockphoto.com/sonyae

Creating a flow chart also requires students to think about and identify key information or instructions. They need to consider the audience when developing a flow chart – they must assume that the reader will have no knowledge of the task and will be relying on the information in the flow chart. They will also need to consider how much information is required to ensure the flow chart is properly sequenced and easy to follow. It is important to show students an example of a flow chart and to talk about how each step is arranged in a logical manner.

Guided fact file

Figure 14.26 is an example of a guided fact file. In this example, a group of four Year 4 girls are required to research a favourite band and record key facts. The students are also required to

Figure 14.26 A guided fact file

Facts about our favourite girl band
Name of band:______________________________
Names of band members: ______________________________
____
Who is the lead singer?______________________________
Hit songs: __________ __________ __________
Who writes the music? ______________________________
Some interesting facts about band members: ______________________________
How long has the band been together? ______________________________
Where has the band performed? ______________________________
Who writes the lyrics? ______________________________

devise a format to record their facts, identifying what information to record and the order in which it should be recorded so that there is a logical flow. This can be quite challenging. In this example, the students must also collaborate as a team and agree on the information to be presented.

Descriptive narrative

Figure 14.27 and **Figure 14.28** are examples of descriptive narratives. To assist the students, the teachers provided the first sentence and listed ideas and information that might be included in the narrative.

Figure 14.27 A descriptive narrative

Jake and Amy were the first to arrive at the scene of the accident.

Brainstorm ideas

- Type of accident: car accident, plane crash, train derailment, farming accident
- Time: late night, early morning
- Conditions: stormy, icy, raining, thunder, blackout, heat wave, flood, fire storm
- Smells, emotions, reactions etc….

Brainstorm descriptive words or phrases that can be used to convey the scene visually, emotionally, physically.

Brainstorm the sequence of events.

Brainstorm opening sentences, closing sentences, words that can be used.

Work together to **create draft**, edit, and write final narrative.

Figure 14.28 Descriptive narrative planning process

DESCRIPTIVE NARRATIVE PLANNING PROCESS	
I walked into the room not knowing what to expect.	
Brainstorm ideas	Where are you? What can you see? What size is the room? Is it dark or bright? Are there any smells? What can you hear? Are you alone?
Use descriptive words	Below ground, a skyscraper, a space craft, a theatre? Gloomy shapes, blinding light, pulsating blobs The smell of burning oil/dead fish, freshly cut grass Tiny, cavernous, narrow Shadowy figures, a teenager with green hair
Consider the sequence of events	How did you get there? I arrived as if from nowhere. How did you react? I tried to move but it was as if my feet were glued to the floor! The smell made my stomach churn. I stepped with trepidation towards the figure. What happened next? I needed to understand what was happening. I spoke in a trembling voice.
Create sentence starters	Opening sentences: set the scene and introduce the characters. Middle: what the characters said/did. What actions did you take? What did you say/do? Closing sentences: I needed to leave, there was nothing here for me. *Together we …* *Afterwards I felt …*
Support students to develop their first draft, review and edit and finally publish. ▪ Does the narrative make sense? ▪ Is there a beginning, middle and end? ▪ Does it provide descriptive details of the scene/characters/events?	

Figures 14.25 to **14.28** provide examples of a range of genres to which students are introduced as part of the English Curriculum. As an ESW, you may be required to work with students as they practise these genres. Your role will be one of support and guidance. Select one or two of these examples and write a list of open-ended questions that you could ask students to help them identify and organise the content of their writing task. The challenge is to support and guide rather than tell students what to do.

Understanding purpose and context

As part of the planning process, students must consider the context in which they are writing and how context influences what they write. Like all other areas of learning, writing occurs in a social context. Students' values and beliefs are influenced by the social and cultural context in which they live. Writing is a form of written communication and is governed by these social/cultural rules and conventions of communication. As students develop their writing skills, they can be encouraged to engage in self-reflection before they begin writing. **Figure 14.29** includes some of the self-reflection questions students can ask themselves as a way to clearly establish why they are writing a text and what they are going to write.

Figure 14.29 Self-reflection questions

Self-reflection	Key questions
What is the purpose of my writing?	> Why am I writing this text? > What do I know about the topic?
Who is the target audience?	> What do I know about my audience? > What might my audience expect to learn from my text?
How will I organise my text?	> What text form should I use? > How will I set out my text – for example, headings, subheadings? > How will I represent my text?
What content should I include?	> What key information do I need to include? > What can I leave out? > What do I want to highlight or emphasise? > What language should I use? > What do I already know? > What do I need to research before starting? > Will I need to include illustrations?
Describing characters and events	> How will I describe my character/s? > What names will I give my character/s? > How will I describe the emotions/thoughts of my character/s? > Will I use speech in the first person? > How will I describe events? (what, where, when)?

Source: Adapted from: Department of Education WA (2013, pp. 140, 141) © Northern Territory of Australia (Department of Education) 2017. CC-BY-4.0 licence.

Teachers support students to explore purpose and context by providing them with real-life examples to enable them to examine, discuss and identify the features of the text. The teacher facilitates this by asking open-ended questions and encouraging students to discuss and document their findings. Teachers will work with students to develop organisational charts to record the characteristics of a targeted genre. By working together, the teacher encourages students to critically analyse various genres. These charts, like word walls, act as a reminder and guide for students as they attempt writing tasks. **Figure 14.30** shows an example of an organisational chart.

Figure 14.30 Example of a narrative organiser

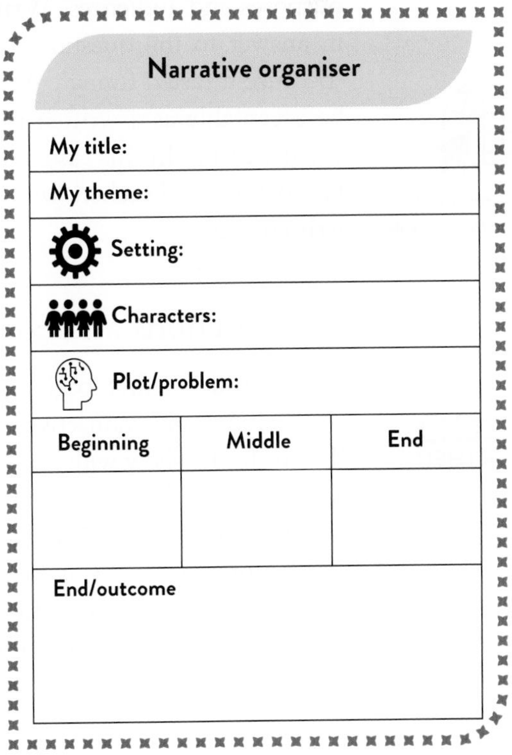

14.5 The elements of writing

There are many structural and stylistic elements of writing that students will learn about during their years of schooling. These include grammar and punctuation, sentence construction, paragraphs and spelling. Students will also learn how to write by hand (handwriting) and by using computers (keyboarding). The following section explains these elements as they are relevant to ESWs.

Figure 14.31 Prepositions worksheet

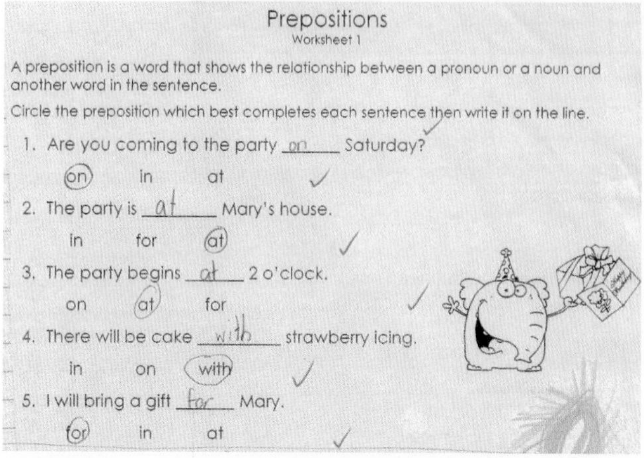
Prepositions
Worksheet 1

A preposition is a word that shows the relationship between a pronoun or a noun and another word in the sentence.

Circle the preposition which best completes each sentence then write it on the line.

1. Are you coming to the party on Saturday?
   on in at
2. The party is at Mary's house.
   in for at
3. The party begins at 2 o'clock.
   on at for
4. There will be cake with strawberry icing.
   in on with
5. I will bring a gift for Mary.
   for in at

Grammar and punctuation

Grammar is the structural rules used when putting words together to create phrases and sentences. A sentence is a group of words that expresses a complete thought. It can be a statement, a question, an exclamation or a command. A sentence tells us what or who, then provides additional detail. Sentences usually contain nouns, verbs, adjectives and pronouns. A sentence begins with a capital letter and ends with a full stop, question mark or exclamation mark.

Like spelling, grammar must be learned in context. Children are exposed to the rules of grammar as they hear others speaking and reading. The rules of grammar – such as sentence structure – as they relate to oral language tend to develop without the need for direct instruction. When speaking, children learn when to pause, to use inflections when asking questions and to convey information in sentences rather than as a single string of spoken words. In contrast, when learning to write (and read) the rules of grammar must be explicitly taught. **Figure 14.31** shows an example of a grammar activity.

GO FURTHER
Access more information on sample lesson plans for writing in your Go Further resource, available through your instructor.

Applying grammar to text

Creating written text is not simply a means of transferring what we say into text. Creating texts requires students to make grammatical choices – that is, 'How will I write this text so that it is fit for purpose and meets the needs of my target audience?' Students who only rely on their knowledge of oral language will find it difficult to create meaningful texts for a variety of purposes and audiences. Written text tends to be more formal than oral language. For example, in answer to the question, 'Why did you throw your apple away?', a student might respond 'Because it tasted funny'. While informal language is acceptable as an oral response, it would not be acceptable as a written response. The expectation is that students will use formal language when writing. In this case, a formal written response would be 'I threw my apple away because it tasted funny'. Teachers will often use sentence starters as a way to help students formalise their written text.

Grammar and punctuation skills

Conjunctions and connections

When students first begin to write, they will often join a series of phrases or thoughts with conjunctions and connectives (joining words) such as 'and', 'because', 'so' and 'but' – for example, 'I went to the show with my brother and Mum and Dad and we had lots of fun /and/ we got two show bags /and/ I ate a hot dog but it made me sick and I threw up and Dad got cranky because it went on his shoes.' (Note: this sentence could be reconstructed into three sentences.)

GO FURTHER
Learn more about writing conventions related to grammar and parts of speech in your Go Further resource, available through your instructor.

Conjunctions such as 'and', 'but', 'when',' how', 'nor', 'or', 'where', 'since', 'why', 'when', 'yet', 'because', 'before', 'after', 'as' and 'if' are placed at the beginning of a clause – for example:

- The boy missed the bus *because* he slept in.
- The game was cancelled *because* it was raining.

Connectives, such as 'after that', 'for example', 'in other words' and 'in the end', can be placed in various parts of the sentence. For example:

- *In the end,* he knew his efforts were futile.
- The earlier ideas, *for example,* using mud bricks, were quickly discounted.

Sentences with two or more independent thoughts or clauses that are joined by a conjunction or connective are called compound sentences. For example:

- I went to school today *and* while there, I fell down the steps.
- I ate a cake today *but* it made me feel sick.

Figure 14.32 shows commonly used connectives and conjunctions.

Figure 14.32 Commonly used connectives and conjunctions

Clarifying

- for example
- for instance
- in other words
- in fact
- in particular
- I mean
- instead

Showing cause and effect

- as a result
- therefore
- because
- however
- unless
- although
- so
- then
- since
- as

Indicating time

- before
- after
- later
- previously
- next
- earlier
- while
- when
- since
- until
- soon
- after a while
- finally

Sequencing ideas

- firstly
- then
- finally
- after that
- afterwards
- in the end
- to conclude
- to summarise
- briefly

Adding information

- also
- as well
- again
- along with
- besides
- too
- in addition

Condition/concession

- still
- however
- yet
- besides
- although
- otherwise
- anyhow
- instead
- if not
- even so
- despite this

Constructing sentences

A sentence must include a subject (noun) and a verb, and express a complete idea, thought or message. It must start with a capital letter and end with a full stop, question mark or explanation mark.

There are three types of sentences:

- *simple* – single clause: 'I went for a swim.'
- *compound* – two independent clauses joined by a conjunction: 'I went for a swim *at* the beach today.'
- *complex* – an independent clause with one or more dependent clauses and a subordinating conjunction: 'I went for a swim at the beach today *because* it was so hot.'

A **sentence** is a word or a group of words that expresses a thorough idea by giving a statement/order, asking a question or exclaiming. A sentence must be written so that it makes sense to the reader. Let's go back to the earlier example: 'I went to the show with my brother and Mum and Dad and we had lots of fun and we got two awesome show bags and I ate a huge hot dog but it made me really sick and I threw up and Dad got cranky because it went on his shoes.' While this sentence certainly gives us quite a lot of information and flows in a logical sequence, there are too many connectives.

Strategies to build sentences

Students can be assisted to progress from simple to compound or complex sentences by using techniques that encourage them to build on their sentence using verbs, adverbs, adjectives and so on. This technique is given a variety of names, such as sentence stretching, power my sentence, make my sentence spark/shine and so on. Consider the examples in **Figure 14.33**.

Figure 14.33 Examples of sentence stretching

Sentence stretchers	
Who?	*My dog* runs fast.
What?	My dog *runs fast* along the wet sand.
Where?	*At the beach* my dog runs fast along the wet sand.
When?	*After school* we go to the beach and my dog runs fast along the wet sand.
Why?	After school we go to the beach because my dog loves to run fast along the wet sand.

THE BEACH

SCENARIO

Brax (10 years) is in Year 4. He finds writing very challenging and uses a number of avoidance strategies: *'My hand hurts, I have a headache, I'm not feeling well, I'm no good at writing.'*

ESW **Helen** has been asked to work with Brax to help him to extend simple sentences to include adjectives and greater detail. Brax has written the following sentence: *'I lke going to the beech'*

Helen: *'Great start, Brax. What do you like about going to the beach?'*

Brax: *'I like going on my boogie board. But sometimes the waves are no good and then me and Dad just swim.'*

Helen: *'What makes a good wave for boogie boarding?'*

Brax: *'Well, sometimes the waves break too far out and then they're too small and sometimes they're too big and rough. They have to be just middle size.'*

Helen: *'Wow, Brax, how do you know so much about waves?'*

Brax: *'Me and my Dad go to Nippers and my Dad does beach patrols. He's a volunteer life saver and he knows lots and he teaches me.'*

Helen: *'Well, Brax, I think I can help you to write about all of these interesting things. How about we have a go together?'*

Brax: *'Okay, but sometimes I don't know how to write things.'*

Helen: *'That's okay, I can help you with the writing if you can tell me what to say. Let's aim for three sentences.'*

WHAT DOES THIS TELL US?

Brax has a great deal of knowledge that he could use for his writing. By asking open-ended questions, the ESW was able to get Brax to share his knowledge. Brax has used complex and descriptive sentences to share this knowledge, and this can be used by the ESW to support the writing process.

The information shared by Brax tells us that he has quite extensive experience in going to the beach. He also shared with Helen that 'he doesn't know how to write things'. This is an important insight into why Brax struggles with his writing. Notice that Helen didn't address spelling or grammar (lke, beech and no full stop).

▶ DISCUSSION

With reference to this Scenario, discuss how taking time to talk to and listen to a student can support literacy development.

Power sentences

Power sentences are also a way of providing students with a framework to build their sentences by using more descriptive words to create a mood or set the scene (**Figure 14.34**).

Figure 14.34 Power my sentence: make it . . . moody/scary/ funny. . . by adding adjectives, adverbs and conjunctions

We walked	through the bush	to the campsite
We walked slowly	through the thick bush	to the now abandoned campsite.
My sprained ankle meant we could only walk slowly	through the thick, dark bush	to the now eerily abandoned campsite.
My sprained and throbbing ankle meant we could only walk slowly	through the thick, spookily dark bush	to the now eerily abandoned and deathly silent campsite!

Figure 14.35 is an example of a simple sentence wheel. Sentence wheels can be developed to reflect the grade/abilities of students. In this example, the sentence wheel provides adjectives that can be used when describing the senses. ESWs encourage students by asking questions that draw on their knowledge and experience: 'Eva, remember yesterday you told me you helped your Nana to make a lemon drizzle cake. What word could you use to describe the taste of the lemons?'

Figure 14.35 Sentence wheel

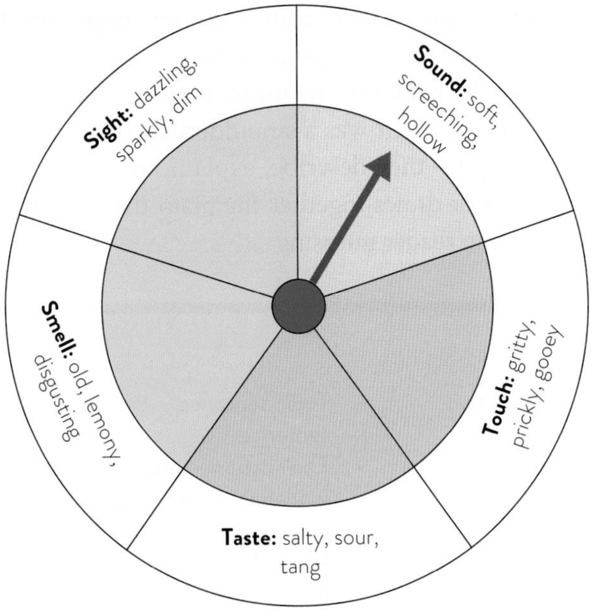

Sentence checklist

Learning the skills to construct a sentence and to progressively build more complex sentences takes time. A checklist can be used to assist students to review and build their sentence-writing skills. **Figure 14.36** provides an example of a simple sentence checklist suitable for Foundation/ Year 1 students.

Figure 14.36 Simple sentence checklist

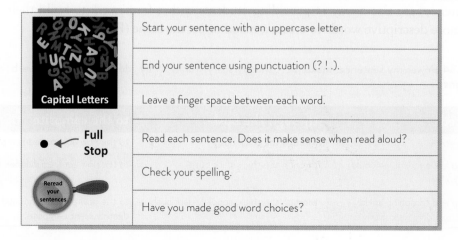

Start your sentence with an uppercase letter.
End your sentence using punctuation (? ! .).
Leave a finger space between each word.
Read each sentence. Does it make sense when read aloud?
Check your spelling.
Have you made good word choices?

Paragraphs and texts

Paragraphs give structure to a piece of writing and organise information to suit the type of text and its purpose. Effective use of paragraphs assists the reader to navigate through the text and tell them when it has moved on to a new point. In formal writing, using the first sentence in a paragraph (the topic sentence) to align your ideas and structure is essential for conveying clear meaning in your writing (NSW Department of Education, 2017).

Each paragraph begins with an idea or topic, which the remaining sentences build on to provide additional information. Students can create a graphic organiser, flow chart or mind map to help them plan a logical sequence for their paragraphs:

- The introduction introduces the reader to the topic. It is the place for an opening attention grabber, for example, 'All that was left was a smouldering, sinking shell!'
- Middle paragraphs are the meat – they describe, explain, investigate, etc.
- The end paragraph concludes or draws together the main theme of the text. Conclusions can also raise questions or leave the reader guessing.

TEEL

CONSIDER THIS

The NSW Smart Teaching Strategies website suggests that students need to be clear about the of purpose of paragraphs – that is, to combine information on a particular idea and demonstrate when there is a change/break.

They must also be clear about the structure of a paragraph. The acronym TEEL is suggested as a useful way of helping students learn about the purpose of a paragraph:

- Topic sentence – the topic, point or focus of the sentence
- Explanation – expand on the point and give more detail
- Evidence – support your idea with quotes, evidence and examples
- Link – link the point back to the overall theme of the text.

Punctuation

Punctuation is a set of marks (e.g. full stop [.], question mark [?], exclamation mark [!], comma [,] and 'quotation mark') that helps the reader to clarify the meaning of the text. Punctuation is a signal to the reader that indicates a pause, places emphasis, alters the function of the language or shows the relationship between elements of the text. Missing, incorrect or wrongly placed punctuation can result in unintentional meaning, as shown in **Figure 14.37**.

Figure 14.38 shows the punctuation sub-element for writing.

Figure 14.37 Is there such a thing as a slow-falling rock?

SLOW FALLING ROCKS AHEAD!	SLOW! FALLING ROCKS AHEAD!

Figure 14.38 Punctuation sub-element for writing

Punctuation	
This sub-element describes how a student becomes increasingly proficient at using correct punctuation to ensure clarity and ease of reading in the texts they create. As students write more complex and technical texts, they will use increasingly complex punctuation to support meaning.	
Level 1	Identifies capital letters in familiar words (e.g. identifies capital letter in own name) Identifies full stops.
Level 2	Writes basic sentence boundary punctuation (e.g. capital letter at beginning, full stop at end) Writes capital letters for familiar names Writes capital letters for some proper nouns.
Level 3	Uses sentence boundary punctuation including question marks or exclamation marks Writes capital letters for proper nouns (e.g. days of the week, addresses).
Level 4	Uses commas in lists of nouns (e.g. 'add the sugar, lemon, water and juice') Uses apostrophes for regular single possessives (e.g. 'girl's') capitalises key events, geographic names, titles (e.g. 'Easter', 'Sydney', 'Ms').
Level 5	Uses quotation marks for simple dialogue (e.g. '"I can't see it," he said.') Uses apostrophes for plural possessives (e.g. 'planes' wings') Follows conventions of use of capitals in headings.
Level 6	Writes commas to separate clauses where appropriate Punctuates more complex dialogue correctly (e.g. '"The team have made some interesting recommendations," she said, nodding. "But I do not want to act upon them before I have read the full report."').
Level 7	Uses complex punctuation conventions (e.g. colons, semicolons, brackets) Uses punctuation conventions for quotations and referencing.
Level 8	Uses punctuation to clarify meaning in complex sentences, drawing on their knowledge of sentence structure (e.g. commas before introductory words, phrases or clauses; semicolons; colons; and dashes) (see Grammar).

Source: Australian Curriculum, Assessment and Reporting Authority (ACARA) F-10 Curriculum | Literacy, https://v9.australiancurriculum.edu.au/f-10-curriculum/general-capabilities/literacy?element=2&sub-element=2. AC

Developing the ability to use punctuation takes time – many students find it difficult to move beyond capitals, full stops and question marks. Students can be supported to develop punctuation knowledge by seeing and talking about punctuation in a passage of text. For example, at Foundation level, students can go on a sentence, capital letter and full stop hunt. Reading aloud and emphasising the use of punctuation are also important. Asking students to listen when a passage is read with and without acknowledging punctuation helps them to better understand its purpose and function. Point out that punctuation helps us to pause and breathe when reading aloud. Older students can be challenged to read a passage where all punctuation has been removed – for example:

> mynameisorlaicametoaustraliafromnorwaywhereitisverycoldinthewinte rilikeaustraliabetterbecauseitiswarmandsunnybutimissmyfriends

Students can then be asked to reinsert punctuation and give a reason for its placement – a new thought/idea/statement; a natural pause; a question or exclamation; first-person speech and so on. Students can also read passages where the punctuation is incorrect and make the necessary changes.

When working with punctuation, it is important to always relate it back to oral language. Listening to or reading a passage with and without punctuation allows students to use sensory information such as sight, sound and breathing to explore punctuation.

Supporting writing: the role of the ESW

The role of the ESW in supporting writing may involve assisting the teacher when they are presenting to the whole class. It may also involve working with individuals or small groups.

When the teacher is working with the whole class, the ESW may be asked to work with students who need support to focus, pay attention and stay on task: 'Liam, we are looking at this paragraph.' This may require the ESW to sit with or near these students. The ESW might simply make eye contact, ask the student to look at the teacher or their work, or reinforce a direction given by the teacher. The ESW might sit with a group of students, give prompts, ask questions and encourage the students to answer questions put by the teacher.

The ESW might also demonstrate the task or tasks, point to information and reinforce the student's actions: 'Good, you've found the right text.' The ESW might clarify the student's understanding of the task or help the student to recall the necessary steps required to complete the task. ESWs can also assist students to access and use the appropriate resources or equipment.

During whole-class lessons, the ESW may be required to observe students' work and provide feedback to the teacher: 'Tess had difficulty following directions/Fahia kept looking at Pia to see what she needed to do/Lennie held his pencil so tight he got cramps in his hand.'

When working with small groups, the ESW will specifically target support to individual students as directed by the classroom teacher. The primary goal is to support students to achieve the required lesson goals/outcomes by working to the best of their ability. The degree of support given to individual students will vary according to ability and teacher requirements.

ESWs can support individual students when they:

- Ensure the student's workspace/environment is work ready:
  - the student has the correct tools for writing (e.g. a student may need to have a special grip attached to their pen, a writing slope or other specialised materials or assistive technologies)
  - the student can see and hear the teacher
  - visual and auditory distractions are minimised
  - the student is seated away from other students who may create a distraction
  - the student is ready to begin work
  - the student is attending to the teacher (by reminding the student to look at and listen to the teacher)
- clarify teacher instructions or directions to ensure the student understands what they are required to do (if necessary modify or adapt the instructions)
- clarify or explain the sequence of a task by breaking it down into logical, achievable steps – 'first, next and then'

- act as a scribe for the student if required (some students may need support to take notes while the teacher is talking or may need the ESW to take notes for the student)
- support the student to access and use available resources such as word walls, sentence openers and/or a dictionary, word processing
- prompt the student when appropriate (by using a range of questions or statements to support writing development). The nature of these prompts will depend on the needs, ability and age/year of the student. Consider, for example, the prompts in **Figure 14.39**, which provide the student with positive feedback or encourage thinking and problem-solving
- encourage the student to develop and use self-correction and self-editing tools.

Figure 14.39 Questions and statements to support writing development

Form of development	Questions/statements
Sentence development	I like this sentence because . . . I can see that in this sentence you have . . . Could you think of an adjective to go here?
Developing content	What other information would you like to add? Let's think about how you have organised the information. What would be a good ending?
Improving writing	What could you add to make your story more interesting? What could you add to make your character more scary/funny? What words could you use to describe your character in more detail? What's another word you could use for . . .? Let's look on the word wall.
Building confidence	I like the way you . . . You have a great idea . . . You've used some very descriptive adjectives. Your story is very interesting/informative/funny. Tell me what you like about your story. What ideas do you have?
Punctuation	Let's check the punctuation together using your checklist.
Spelling	Circle the words you think are not spelt correctly.

It is essential to get to know the strengths of each student, their knowledge and skills, and how they are applied to learning tasks in the classroom. It is also important to understand the objectives, goals and learning outcomes for each lesson. What does the teacher want the students to know, do, practise, learn, explore or research?

GO FURTHER

Learn more about writing programs and resources in your Go Further resource, available through your instructor.

Spelling

Spelling is a sub-element of the English Curriculum and describes how a student becomes increasingly proficient in selecting and arranging letters to form accurately spelt words. Students develop increasing skill and proficiency in using spelling as a tool to understand and create meaning in texts. At higher levels of the progression, students monitor their own spelling and explain how spelling impacts upon meaning. To learn more about the sequential content and elements of spelling in the Australian Curriculum go to the ACARA website at: https://www.australiancurriculum.edu.au. Search for 'National Literacy Learning Progression', follow the link to 'Writing' and select the 'Spelling' sub-element. You will then be able to click on highlighted text to explore definitions of terminology and concepts.

As an ESW, you will not be expected to know each of these elements; however, you should be aware that spelling instruction follows a typical sequence to allow students to gradually build their skills and knowledge as spellers. You should also be aware that progression in spelling is not linear, and students will go back and forth as they develop and build their skills as spellers.

Learning to spell

Encoding or spelling is the ability to hear and identify individual sounds and write a symbol (letters) to represent the sound/s. As they experiment with written words, students begin to realise that for words to be understood, the letters must be placed in the correct sequence – known as **letter knowledge**. This understanding is the beginning of learning to spell. Students acquire this knowledge through direct instruction within a carefully sequenced curriculum that allows them to gain **letter–sound knowledge** of the various combinations and spelling rules in the language. Spelling is integrated across all areas of the curriculum.

Learning to spell occurs alongside learning to read and write and, like reading, requires direct instruction. To become *good* spellers requires students to draw on and apply their accumulated knowledge of language and the way it is used when communicating. Like other areas of development, children's readiness to learn to spell occurs in a typical stage-related sequence as they begin to understand that symbols (letters) represent spoken words. This sequence is shown in **Figure 14.40**.

Figure 14.40 The stages of spelling development

Stage 1
Pre-communicative stage
Children begin to write random letters and shapes that represent letters.

Stage 2
Semiphonetic stage
Children begin to understand that specific letters represent specific sounds – for example, Sophie might write her name as 'Se'.

Stage 3
Phonetic stage
Children use a letter or group of letters to represent every speech sound they hear in a word – for example, beach may be written as 'bech'.

Stage 4
Transitional stage
Children begin to understand and apply common letter patterns. During this stage, we often see invented spelling where a child will draw on their phonetic knowledge to spell a word – for example, 'lik' for 'like' or 'skool' for 'school'.

Stage 5
Correct stage
Children now apply common generalisations and letter–sound combinations; they also begin to remember sight words.

Stages of spelling development

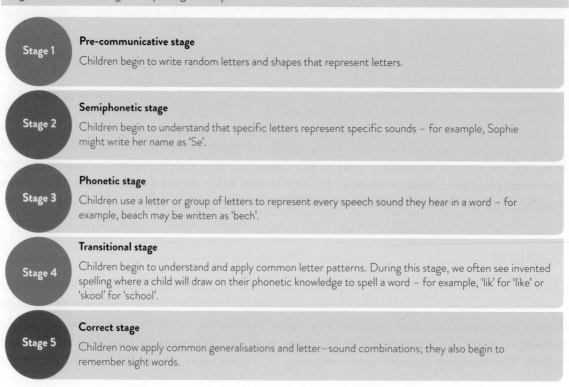

The accompanying figures show the progression of Macky's spelling skills from Kindergarten to Year 1. In **Figure 14.41**, Kindergarten Macky writes, 'I feel happy because learning makes my brain grow big.' This shows that Macky is somewhere around Stage 2/3 in his spelling development. Almost six months later (**Figure 14.42**), Macky has moved to Stage 5. He will still continue to spell some words incorrectly and move between Stages 4 and 5.

Each child will progress through these stages at their own unique pace. Some children will enter school at Stage 2 while others may have reached Stage 3 or 4.

Figure 14.41 The progression of spelling skills – Kindergarten

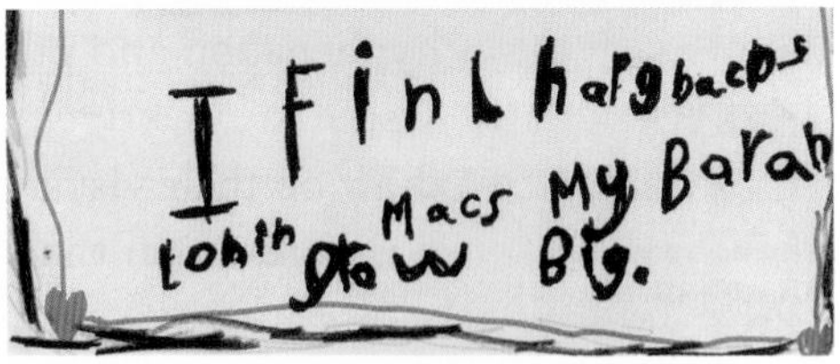

Figure 14.42 The progression of spelling skills – Year 1

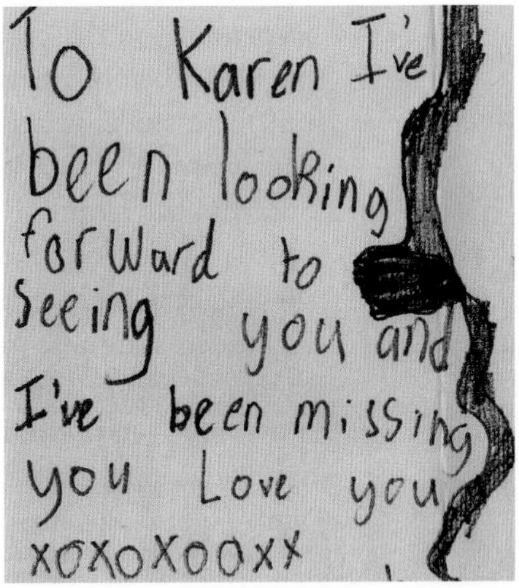

Spelling knowledge

The skills and knowledge acquired when learning to read are also applied when learning to spell. Reading, writing and spelling skills develop concurrently. Learning to spell requires students to continuously build their skills and knowledge as readers, writers and spellers. They must learn spelling rules (and exceptions to spelling rules), as well as sight words, grammar and punctuation. Students must acquire spelling knowledge, as shown in **Figure 14.43**.

Figure 14.43 Spelling knowledge

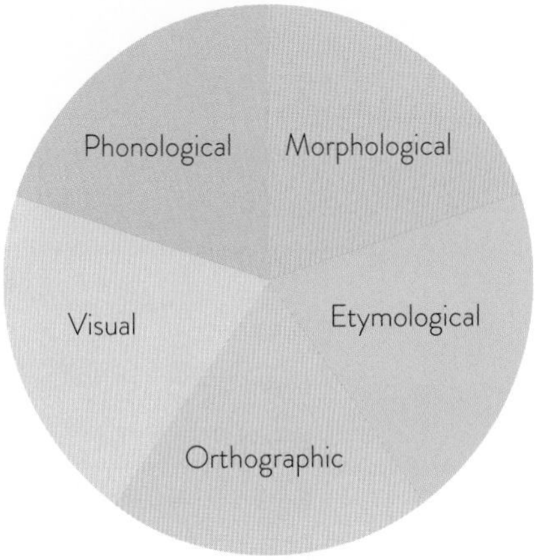

Spelling knowledge includes (Department of Children, Schools and Families, UK, 2009):

- **phonological knowledge** – the relationships between letters (**graphemes**) and sounds (phonemes). Includes:
  - the ability to hear and manipulate individual phonemes (phonemic awareness)
  - knowledge of the different ways that letters go together to make different sounds
  - knowing how to chunk parts of words into sound segments (Hagston, n.d.)
- **morphological knowledge** – the conscious awareness of the sounds of language and the ability to talk about and manipulate those sounds; this includes knowledge of:
  - root words – contain one morpheme and cannot be broken down into smaller grammatical units (e.g. school, chair, boy, dog) and sometimes are referred to as the stem or base form
  - compound words – two root words combined to make a word (e.g. playground, football)
  - suffixes – added after root words, changing the meaning and often the spelling of a word (e.g. beauty – beautiful, happy – happiness); some suffixes, called inflectional suffixes (or inflections), modify words to indicate, for example, plurals (e.g. boy – boys, fox – foxes) or verb tenses (e.g. walk – walks – walking – walked)
  - prefixes – added before a root word, and change the meaning but rarely affect the spelling of a word (e.g. replace, mistake)
- **etymological knowledge** – the origin of words; includes understanding that words with the same base meaning are spelt the same (e.g. bound/boundary) while words that have a different meaning are generally not spelt the same (e.g. seen/scenery)

Videos: Orthographic mapping, morphological awareness and phonological awareness

Decoding resources

- **orthographic knowledge** – knowing how letters go together in written English. It includes knowledge of letter positions, combinations and sequences that make a word; recognition of familiar letter patterns within whole words; it also refers to awareness of capitalisation, hyphenation and punctuation
- **visual knowledge** – understanding the way words and letter combinations look. Students draw on their visual memory when looking to see whether a word 'looks right' – for example, if a word doesn't include a vowel, it is not spelt correctly.

Spelling lists

Teachers are provided with a core list of words for Grades K–6. Teachers and students will add to this list on the basis of interests, current events and curriculum content knowledge. Depending on the grade, students will be introduced to between 10 and 20 new spelling words per week. Before a new list of spelling words is given to students, the teacher will conduct a pre-test. The students are then issued with the spelling list and are able to self-correct their work. Any words that are spelled incorrectly then become the student's spelling goal for the week. Students are required to take their list home and learn their misspelled words using a strategy called 'Look, Say the Word, Cover, Write, Check'. Students are expected to work on their spelling each night in preparation for a post-test scheduled for the following week.

Students are also required to learn around 100 high-frequency and sight words, which are shown in **Figure 14.44**. High-frequency words are those that occur frequently in text, such as 'the', 'my', 'and', 'him' and 'her'. Sight words are words that students learn without the need to apply decoding strategies – that is, they are instantly recognised. Examples include 'came', 'with', 'your' and 'this'. Many, although not all, sight words are also high-frequency words.

Figure 14.44 A sample of high-frequency sight words

a	friend	it	run	two
after	from	like	said	up
again	gave	little	saw	upon
and	get	looked	say	us
at	girl	love	school	use
away	give	made	see	very
because	goes	make	she	was
been	good	me	should	we
before	had	mum	so	went
big	have	my	stayed	were
boy	he	not	that	what
by	her	of	the	when
came	him	off	their	where
come	his	on	them	which

Source: NSW Department of Education (2011)

Spelling strategies

Becoming a good speller requires times and practice. It is important to support students to 'have a go' – that is, use their existing knowledge of words and language to attempt to spell an unknown word. Bear, Invernizzi, Templeton and Johnston (2016) suggest students be taught to analyse words as a way of helping them to understand the many rules associated with English spelling. Referred to as words study, this allows students to:

- examine the logic and consistencies within our written language system
- help students to master recognising, spelling, defining and using specific words
- develop a general knowledge of English spelling patterns and conventions, which assist students to decode unfamiliar words, spell correctly and guess the meaning of unfamiliar words.

Students also require specific word knowledge in order to recall the correct spelling: only specific knowledge of the spelling of 'which' and 'witch' makes it possible to know which witch is which. To be *good* spellers, students need both general and specific knowledge – the two are reciprocal and intertwined.

According to Palmer and Invernizzi (2015), word study is built on the three layers of English spelling:

- the *alphabetic principle* – the relationships between letters and sounds, it includes:
  - the ability to identify letters in different fonts, name the letters, and an awareness of the overall alphabet order and structure. This also includes letter-sound correspondence.
  - the overarching concept that letters and letter patterns represent the sounds of spoken language and that there is a predictable relationship between those letters and letter sounds (The Literacy Nest, 2021)
- **letter patterns** – combining letters to create single sounds such as 'ch', 'sh', 'th'. Single sounds may also be represented by different letters/letter combinations (blends) – for example, 'c', 'k', 'ck'. Letter patterns also relate to meaning – for example, 'which' and 'witch'
- **word meaning** – when students are learning to spell new words, it is also important that they understand the meaning of the word and can use it in the correct context.

Selecting and using the correct word for words that sound the same, are spelt differently and have a different meaning can be challenging for students – for example, 'Queen Elizabeth II *reigned* for over 65 years/'Queen Elizabeth II *rained* for over 65 years.' When spoken, both sentences sound correct; however, when written one of them is obviously wrong!

Perfetti (2007) states that efficient and reliable retrieval of word meanings depends on accurate and complete representations of word features relating to speech sounds (**phonology**), spelling patterns (**orthography**) and word meanings (**semantics**) in memory.

Teaching spelling

Seeing and understanding how words work, how to look for patterns and how to apply generalisations (and exceptions) are important spelling skills for all students. Students also need explicit instruction if they are to be confident spellers. Spelling requires the complex integration of phonological, orthographical, etymological and morphological knowledge. To master this knowledge, students require explicit instruction that acknowledges the interrelationship between oral language, reading, writing and spelling, as shown in **Figure 14.45**.

Explicit spelling instruction includes:

- **Alphabetic principle** – knowledge of which individual letters match up to sounds, in a left to right sequence
- **Pattern information** – which groups of letters function as a pattern to represent sounds, for example, CVC (Consonant/Vowel/Consonant) pattern to form short vowels – 'cat' or CVCe/CVVC patterns to form long vowels as in 'same' or 'meat'

Videos: Teachers engaged in explicit spelling instruction

Figure 14.45 Linguistic knowledge

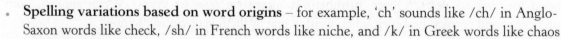

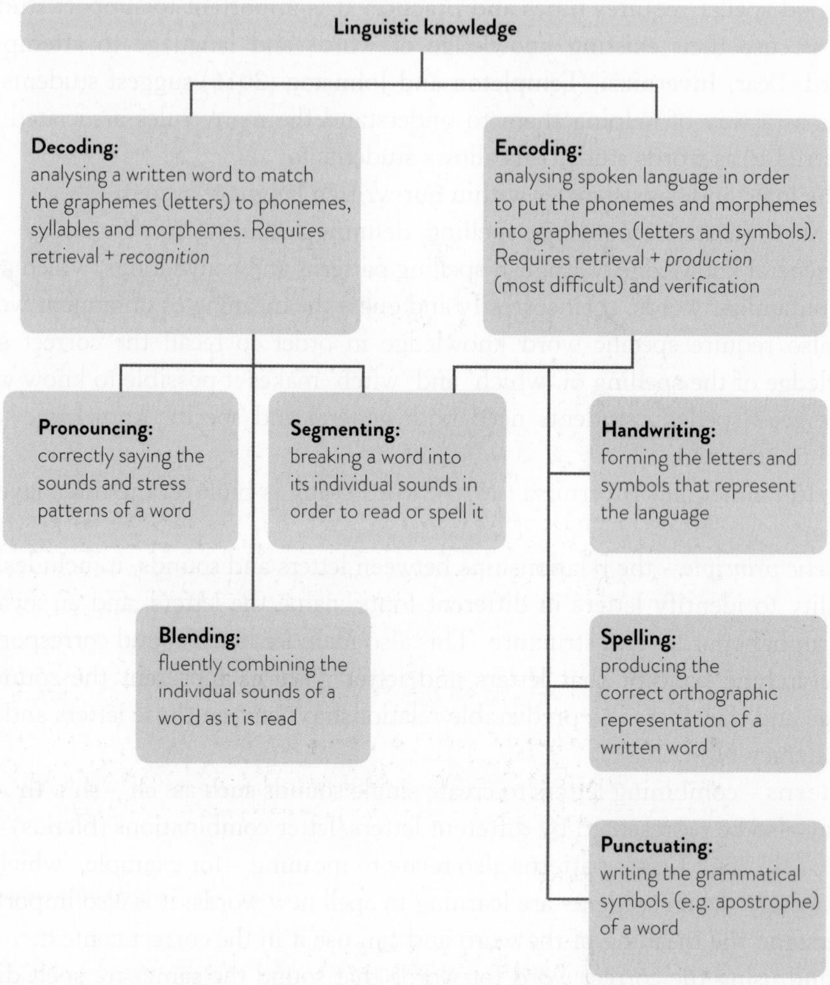
Linguistic knowledge
Decoding:
analysing a written word to match the graphemes (letters) to phonemes, syllables and morphemes. Requires retrieval + recognition
Encoding:
analysing spoken language in order to put the phonemes and morphemes into graphemes (letters and symbols). Requires retrieval + production (most difficult) and verification
Pronouncing:
correctly saying the sounds and stress patterns of a word
Segmenting:
breaking a word into its individual sounds in order to read or spell it
Handwriting:
forming the letters and symbols that represent the language
Blending:
fluently combining the individual sounds of a word as it is read
Spelling:
producing the correct orthographic representation of a written word
Punctuating:
writing the grammatical symbols (e.g. apostrophe) of a word

Source: Reed, D. K. (2012). Why teach spelling? Portsmouth, NH: RMC Research Corporation, Center on Instruction (p. 7).

- **Spelling variations based on word origins** – for example, 'ch' sounds like /ch/ in Anglo-Saxon words like check, /sh/ in French words like niche, and /k/ in Greek words like chaos
- **Meaning information** – which groups of letters represent meaning (the prefix re- as in 'redo' meaning to do again).

Source: Ministry of Education NZ (n.d.). Teach spelling skills explicitly. https://inclusive.tki.org.nz/guides/dyslexia-and-learning/teach-spelling-strategies-explicitly/

GO FURTHER

Access more examples of posters and diagrams to use with decoding strategies for spelling in your **Go Further** resource, available through your instructor.

WORD LADDERS

Rasinski (2012, p. 5) suggests the use of word ladders as a tool to help students explore words in context and decode words: 'when children add, take away, or rearrange letters to make a new word form, one they have just made, they must examine sound symbol relationships closely. Using this kind of analysis helps students to learn how to decode and spell accurately'. Word ladders integrate spelling and word meaning, which builds comprehension and allows words to be explored in context rather than in isolation.

Technology to assist student spelling

Word ladders can be used with the whole class, in small groups or with individual students. Students can work independently or with the support of the teacher and ESW. **Figure 14.46** shows some examples of word ladders. Students start at the bottom of the ladder and work their way up each rung, following the clues, and adding and changing letters as they go.

Figure 14.46 Counting up word ladder

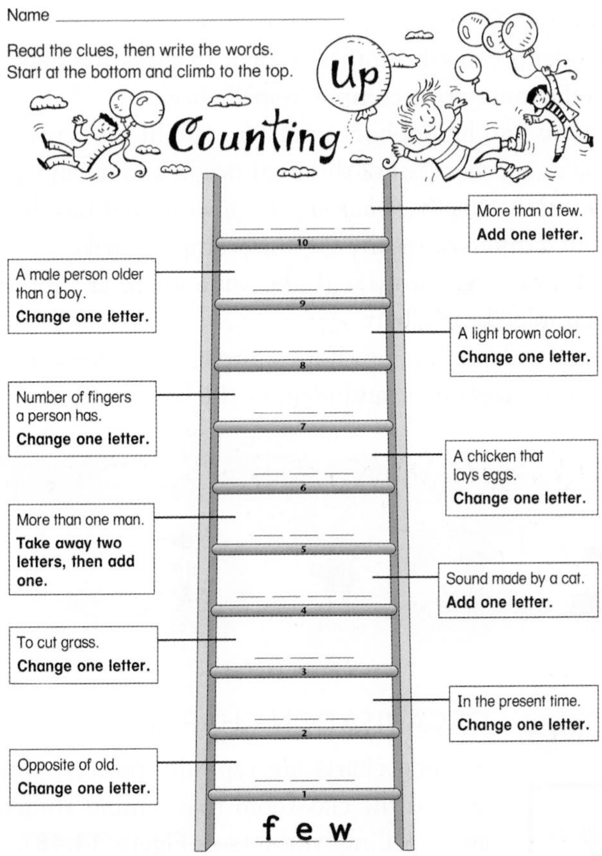

Name
Read the clues, then write the words.
Start at the bottom and climb to the top.
Counting Up
More than a few.
Add one letter.
A male person older than a boy.
Change one letter.
A light brown color.
Change one letter.
Number of fingers a person has.
Change one letter.
A chicken that lays eggs.
Change one letter.
More than one man.
Take away two letters, then add one.
Sound made by a cat.
Add one letter.
To cut grass.
Change one letter.
In the present time.
Change one letter.
Opposite of old.
Change one letter.
few
10
9
8
7
6
5
4
3
2
1
7

Source: From DAILY WORD LADDERS: Grade 2-3 by Tim Raskinski. Copyright © 2005. Reprinted by permission of Scholastic Inc.

The following list provides some examples of spelling strategies used to assist students to develop their spelling knowledge. Using these strategies may not always lead to the correct spelling; however, students typically will get part of the word correct and can then use other strategies, such as word walls, spelling lists and organisational charts, to self-correct their spelling.

- Deconstruct words into syllables and highlight particular sound patterns.
- Word mapping: Use a 'y'-shaped arrow when two letters make one phoneme and no arrows connecting phonemes that make no sound (e.g. silent 'e').
- For a base/root word, first identify the base. When students can identify the base/root word, they can then apply their knowledge of spelling rules to help them spell a word – for example, 'reconstruct', 'unhappy', 'playing', 'bigger'.
- Apply (spelling) analogy of words. When students draw on and apply their existing knowledge of words, it can assist them to spell new words. Students ask themselves: 'Does the word I want to spell sound like a word I already know?' For example, a student may want to write 'black' – it sounds like 'back', which ends in 'ack'. Other strategies might include chunking, word families, and onset and rimes.
- Use/create **mnemonics**, which are short rhymes or phrases that are used to help remember the spelling of irregular words – for example '*Emma* faced a dil*emma*', or 'Please keep *quiet* about my *diet*'. Other examples include:
  - There's a  in separate
  - Sally Ann Is Dancing – SAID.

- Ask, 'Does it look right?' When students write a word and ask themselves, 'Does it look right?' they are drawing on their orthographic memory (mental picture) of the shape of words and letter combination.
- Consult an expert. Students can ask another student to check their spelling, or consult word walls, spelling lists, a dictionary or a computer spell check.
- Homographs, homonyms and homophones must be taught explicitly. A *homograph* is a word with the same spelling as another, but of different origin and meaning, for example wind (the wind blows), wind (wind the clock). A *homonym* is a word that has the same sound and spelling as another, but a different meaning – for example, 'strike' (verb), 'strike' (noun) (see **Figure 14.47**). A **homophone** is a word with the same sound as another but different spelling and meaning – for example, 'bear', 'bare'.
- Morphemic knowledge needs to develop. For example, when decoding words, identify the prefix and suffix with their meanings, and identify the base word.

Figure 14.47 Homonym

Figure 14.48 Example of an organisational chart

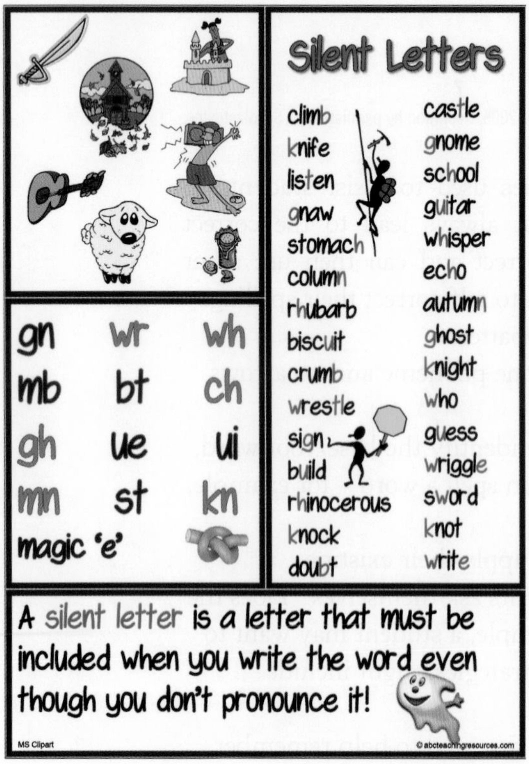

Source: © Copyright ABC Teaching Resources, http://erinschoolfuninfirst.blogspot.com/2013/09/reading-and-writing-organisational-charts.html

ORGANISATION CHARTS

Spelling charts are typically posters, graphics or lists displayed around the classroom that remind students of various grammar and spelling rules (see **Figure 14.48**). Students can refer to them as needed to assist with spelling words they may find challenging.

As an ESW, you will not be expected to have a detailed knowledge of spelling strategies; however, you will be expected to model the strategies used by the teacher to support spelling. Your role is to scaffold spelling skills and knowledge and help students to apply a range of decoding skills.

There is no single best strategy to teach spelling, nor is there a single best strategy to support spellers. Approaches to teaching spelling may vary slightly depending on the program being used by the school. When teaching spelling, teachers will take into account individual differences such as oral language skills, vocabulary and literacy experiences at home. There will be a range of spelling abilities in any classroom, and each student should be supported to work at their own pace and consolidate their spelling knowledge and spelling strategies before moving on to the next stage. Students who struggle with spelling often become anxious, which increases the likelihood of spelling errors. For these students, providing a variety of spelling games that allow for repetition and practice is essential.

CONSIDER THIS

This anonymous poem highlights the complexity of written and spoken English.

Why English is Hard to Learn
We'll begin with *box*; the plural is *boxes*,
But the plural of *ox* is *oxen*, not *oxes*.
One fowl is a *goose*, and two are called *geese*.
Yet the plural of *moose* is never *meese*.
You may find a lone *mouse* in a house full of *mice*,
But the plural of house is *houses* not *hice*.
The plural of *man* is always *men*,
But the plural of *pan* is never *pen*.
If I speak of a *foot*, you show me two *feet*,
And I give you a *book*, would a pair be a *beek*?
If one is a *tooth* and a whole set are *teeth*,
Why shouldn't two *booths* be called *beeth*?
If a singular is this and a plural is *these*,
Should the plural of *kiss* be ever called *kesse*?
We speak of a *brother*, and also a *brethren*,
But though we say *mother*, we never say *methren*.
Then the masculine pronouns are *he*, *his*, and *him*,
But imagine the femine. . . *she*, *shis*, and *shim*!

Anonymous

Source: Orphan Work

Handwriting and keyboarding

Keyboarding is the ability to input information at a keyboard smoothly while typing. Although the curriculum requires students to use Word documents, most states and territories do not have a formal keyboarding program in place. The NSW English Syllabus for Handwriting and Using Digital Technologies includes a range of outcomes related to keyboarding, which consist of demonstrating the use of commonly used software for word processing, keyboard and mouse skills as well as how to access and use images when constructing texts.

Videos: How to teach handwriting

A range of online programs exist that can be used to teach keyboarding skills. Examples can be found at: https://getsmarts.weebly.com/handwritingkeyboarding.html.

Handwriting skills

Research has shown that the act of handwriting is directly related to academic achievement. When children struggle to write letters and words, it takes away from the content of their writing. These children often include less detail, rush through handwritten assignments and show avoidance behaviours.

Handwriting is a complex task that requires the student to coordinate a number of functions – for example, form a meaningful phrase, recall the shape of each letter, recall the order of letters to form words, recall how to form each letter, remember to space each word, coordinate the hand and eye, use the correct grip and remember to move from left to right and from top left to bottom right. All these skills take time to develop and will occur at a unique pace for each student. The ability to produce clear and legible writing requires the coordination of a number of skills, which are outlined in **Figure 14.49**, **Figure 14.50**, **Figure 14.51** and **Figure 14.54**.

Reversals or mirror writing can occur. Some students may write some letters or whole words reversed or upside down. This can be a result of immature internalising of left and right or the lack of a dominant side. The student may not have reached the understanding that letters must be oriented in a particular way and sequenced to make meaning clear.

Figure 14.49 Handwriting skills – sensory-motor

Sensory-motor skills include:

- the ability to separate the functions of the two sides of the hand
- the grip and pinch strength
- fine motor coordination
- hand–eye coordination
- the development of a dominant hand
- spatial awareness/integration – top/bottom, left/right
- posture
- proprioceptive skills – the ability to coordinate movement automatically (sensory integration)
- bilateral control – moving two hands symmetrically to an object or moving two hands asymmetrically (one hand closer or further away) to or from an object – for example, using two hands when writing – one hand to hold the paper, the other hand to write.

Figure 14.50 Handwriting skills – visual-motor

Visual-motor skills include:

- visual tracking – the ability to control the fine eye movements required to follow a line of print
- visual skills – the ability to copy and form letters, numbers and shapes
- visual perception – the ability to use and interpret visual information – for example, the ability to understand that 'a' and 'A' are both the first letter of the alphabet
- the ability to visually discriminate between letters, particularly visually similar letters – for example, db, pq, mw, nm.

Figure 14.51 Handwriting skills – muscle tone and joint stability

Muscle tone and joint stability are necessary for:

- proper writing control, which requires trunk stability and shoulder control (using back and shoulder muscles to steady the body allows greater control of the hand when writing)
- handwriting movement (as handwriting is relatively slow, the shoulder muscles must be strong enough to hold the shoulder in a stable position to allow for smooth writing)
- arm strength
- finger strength and dexterity
- the ability to isolate individual finger movements
- the development of a mature grip, wrist rotation
- the tripod grip (see **Figure 14.52**), which uses the fingers to control the pencil and is the mature grip for handwriting (the pencil is positioned so that there is equal pressure between the thumb, the side of the middle finger and the tip of the index finger, and all fingers are slightly bent. A common error made by children is to grip the pencil too tightly and place too much pressure on the fingers).

Good muscle tone and joint stability allows students to produce consistent:

- *letter alignment*: Letters need to sit on the line rather than drift upwards or drift downwards in order to be legible (see **Figure 14.53**)
- *letter spacing*: Each word must be equally spaced from the next word to make it legible.

  Eachwordmust be equallyspaced fromthenext wordtomakeitlegible
- *letter size*: Keeping letter size consistent makes it easy to read and writing will flow more smoothly.

  KEeping lEttEr sizE consistEnt makeS it Easy to rEad
- *letter slant*: Keeping letter slant consistent makes it easier to read and writing will flow more smoothly.

  Keeping letter slant consistent makes it easier to read.

Figure 14.52 Tripod grip

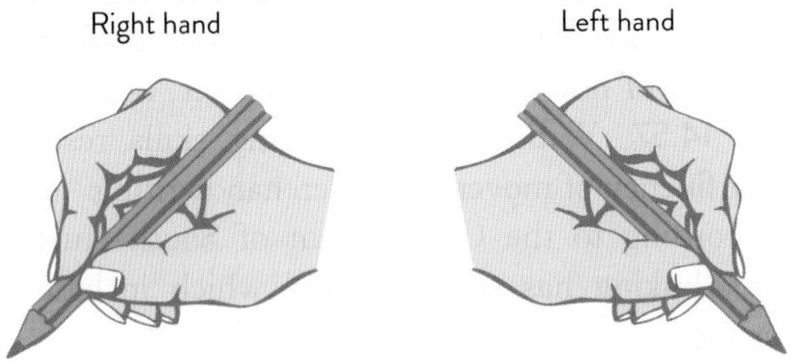

Figure 14.53 Example of incorrect letter alignment

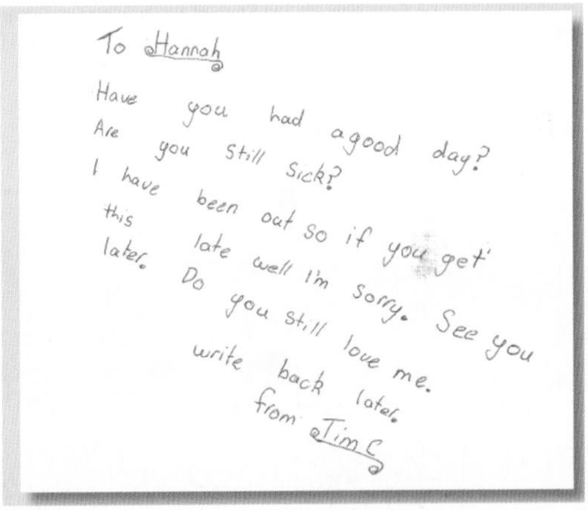

To Hannah
Have you had agood day?
Are you Still Sick?
I have been out so if you get
this late well I'm Sorry. See you
later. Do you Still love me.
write back later.
from Tim C

Figure 14.54 Handwriting skills – cognitive skills

Cognitive skills include:

- recognition and recall of letters, numbers, words and shapes
- form perception – the ability to perceive and recall the shape and form of objects, pictures, letters and numbers
- accurate and consistent letter formation.

LETTER FORMATION

For students with handwriting difficulties, breaking down letters into sub-groups is a useful way to teach handwriting skills. For the purposes of developing handwriting skills, letters are divided into sub-groups based on the similarities of movement – this assists students to develop greater awareness of how letters are formed. These sub-groups are shown in **Figure 14.55**.

Figure 14.55 Sub-groups of letters

anti-clockwise letters	a d g q c e o s u y f
stick letters	l i t j
clockwise letters	m n r h p b
diagonal letters	k v w z

Figure 14.56 Examples of lower case and capital letters in Australian school font

abcdefghi
ABCDEF

Source: Handwriting in South Australian Curriculum, 2nd edition, 2006. © The State of South Australia, Department of Education and Children's Services. CC-BY-4.0 licence

Figure 14.57 An example of cursive writing

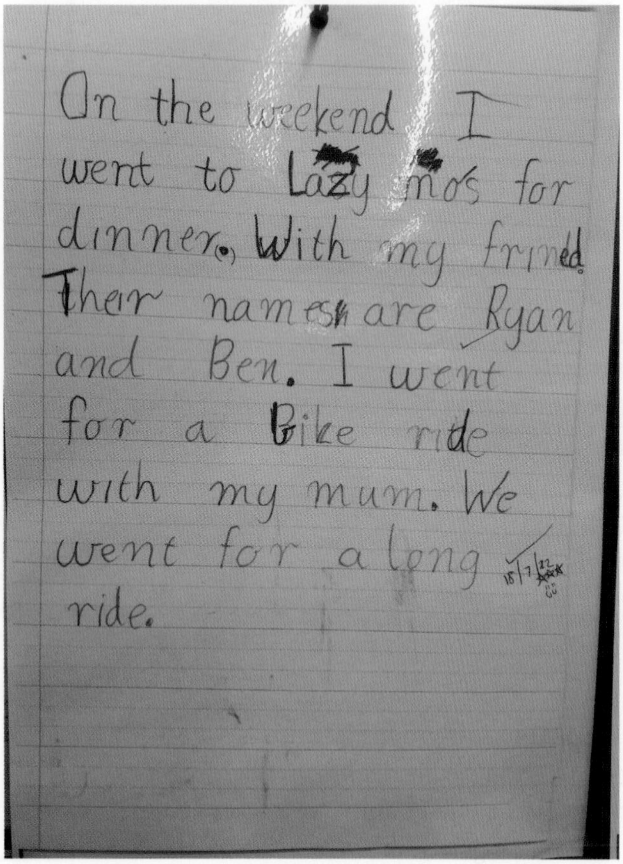
On the weekend I
went to Lazy mo's for
dinner, With my frined
Their names are Ryan
and Ben. I went
for a Bike ride
with my mum. We
went for a long
ride.

Source: Photo by Tish Okely © Cengage

Teaching correct letter formation involves providing learners with opportunities to talk about the names and features of letters and the sounds they represent. In Australia, letter formation is prescribed using the Australian school font, examples of which can be seen in **Figure 14.56**.

Kindergarten students begin to learn Australian school font by tracing over word outlines. In Year 2, students continue to develop these skills with the help of a writing guide.

CURSIVE HANDWRITING

The development of cursive handwriting allows students to write faster. Cursive writing requires the knowledge of how to link letters together, as shown in **Figure 14.57**. With practice, linking skills result in greater fluency of movement when handwriting.

According to the Government of South Australia (2006), linking has specific rules, which include the following:

- There is no link from upper-case letters to lower-case letters.
- The correct starting place and direction of movement for each letter shape are the basis for the development of links.
- The links are the outcome of a flowing handwriting movement rather than drawn deliberately.
- Connections need to exist between letters in a word.
- Any distortion caused to letter shapes through linking should be discouraged.
- Small groups of letters should be practised rather than individual letters, as this is more likely to simulate the movements required for continuous writing.
- Letters that link to the following letter should link directly from the end of the letter to the beginning of the next letter.
- The position at which the letter finishes is important to linking.
- Do not link to g j x y and z.

- The point at which the exit links to the following letter should be no higher than the exit of *o*.
- There is no link from an *s* if you link to it – for example, glasses .
- Do not link to f or z .

The development of cursive handwriting skills requires explicit instruction and practice. As students practise, they should be encouraged to develop a natural rhythm using smooth continuous strokes.

Like any new skill, cursive writing takes time to master. Students should be encouraged to self-monitor their own progress by comparing earlier attempts with later work. Students can also be encouraged to set their own mini-goals for mastering cursive writing.

GO FURTHER

Learn more about the Australian school font and an example of handwriting practice for Kindergarten and Year 2 in your **Go Further** resource, available through your instructor.

Observing handwriting

ESWs may be required to observe, record and evaluate a student's handwriting. This is best achieved by using a checklist (see **Figure 14.58**) which identifies the range of skills that could be observed. Checklists can be used for on-the-spot observation or as a tool to evaluate a sample of

Figure 14.58 Handwritten observation checklist

Handwritten observation checklist	
Student name:	Class:
Classroom teacher:	Date:
Observer's name:	
Look for:	Comments:
Posture ▪ Curve/tilt of head ▪ Distance of head from paper ▪ Placement of feet and legs ▪ Level of shoulders **Hand/arm** ▪ Pencil grip – tripod grip uses the fingers to control the pencil ▪ Bilateral control – position of hand to hold paper while writing ▪ Movement – fluid/jerky ▪ Moves from left to right and top to bottom	☐ ☐ ☐ ☐ ☐ ☐ ☐ ☐
Starts at top left Spacing between words Word formation Word omitted Word spacing Word reversals Writing style – consistent or mixed (combining capitals, lower case, cursive and letter slants)	☐ ☐ ☐ ☐ ☐ ☐ ☐
Hand/arm ▪ Use of lines and margins – consistent or inconsistent, appropriate or inappropriate ▪ Total slope of finished word	☐ ☐
Other comments	☐

Source: Government of South Australia (2006).

a student's handwriting skills. To be considered valid and reliable, the student should be observed on a number of occasions, accompanied by an evaluation of a number of handwriting samples. The combination of observations and writing samples will assist you to identify the strengths and deficits which can be used to formulate appropriate remedial handwriting strategies.

Dysgraphia

Students who consistently struggle to physically form letters and words, or whose writing is consistently messy/illegible, may have a disorder known as **dysgraphia**. This is a handwriting disorder where the individual consistently struggles to write legibly because of poor letter formation (and often poor spelling). An example of dysgraphia is shown in **Figure 14.59**. Unlike students who have mastered the mechanics of writing, those with dysgraphia will often forget what they have written or have difficulty organising their thoughts because they are so busy concentrating on the mechanics of writing.

Video: What is dysgraphia?

There are five recognised forms of dysgraphia, which are described in **Figure 14.60**.

Figure 14.59 An example of dysgraphia

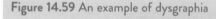

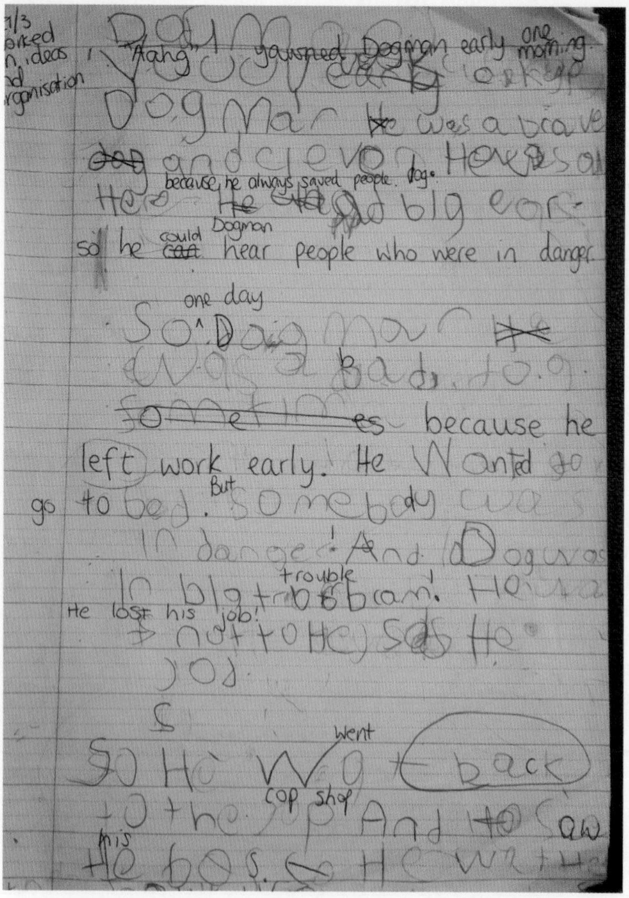

Source: Photo by Tish Okely © Cengage

Figure 14.60 Forms of dysgraphia

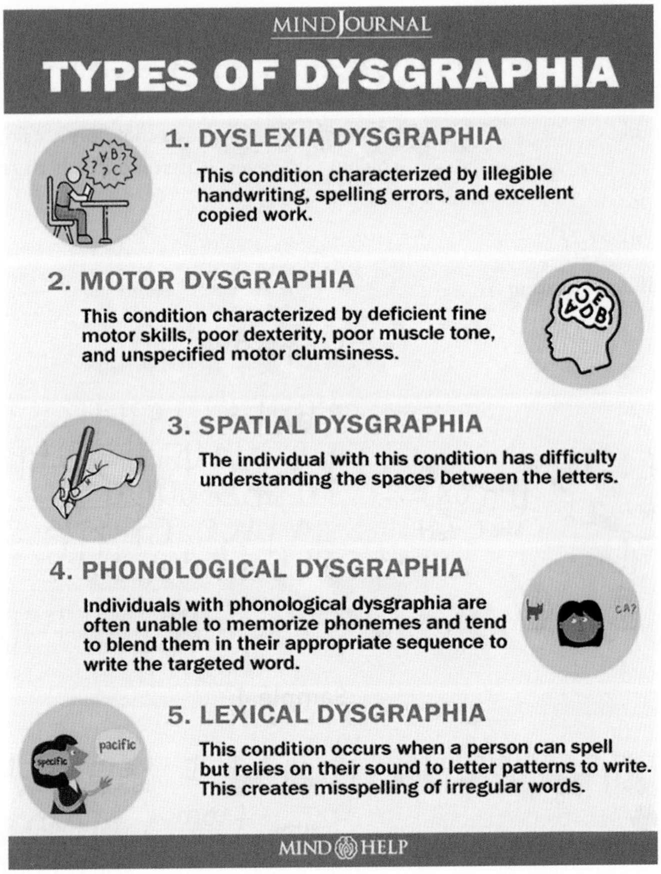

Source: Types of dysgraphia. https://mind.help/topic/dysgraphia/types. Reproduced with permission from Mind Help.

Dysgraphia is assessed by administering a number of tests, including an IQ test, and tests of academic achievement, written responses and visual processing. Students with dysgraphia will often have:

- visual-spatial difficulties such as left-to-right sequencing, writing horizontally, letter spacing (words all run together), writing on a line, discriminating and drawing shapes
- poor fine motor skills, such as holding a pen, tracing, cutting, keyboarding, holding paper steady for writing
- poor language processing skills – remembering their own ideas and directions of others, remembering and following rules of games
- poor spelling skills – difficulty remembering spelling rules; unable to identify words spelt incorrectly; mixing upper and lower case; using a mismatch of print and cursive writing; unable to read their own writing; continually erasing and reattempting writing
- poor grammar – unable to remember and apply grammar rules; mixing up tenses, failing to use punctuation
- poor recall of text – difficulty recalling and retelling stories; sentences are jumbled; leaving out key information or facts (adapted from Patino, 2018).

Students can become extremely anxious and tense, which compounds their writing difficulties. When this occurs, students will become resistant to writing and may engage in a range of avoidance strategies (see **Figure 14.61**).

DYSGRAPHIA

SCENARIO

Jon has dysgraphia. Sample 1 demonstrates his inability to form letters and words.

Sample 2 shows some progress – some words are legible and there is some separation of each word.

Sample 3 demonstrates that Jon can now write in a sentence – he is able to correctly space each word; however, he is unable to spell the words correctly.

In sample 4, we see that Jon is using phonetic spelling; however, it is still difficult to read.

Figure 14.61 Samples of Jon's writing

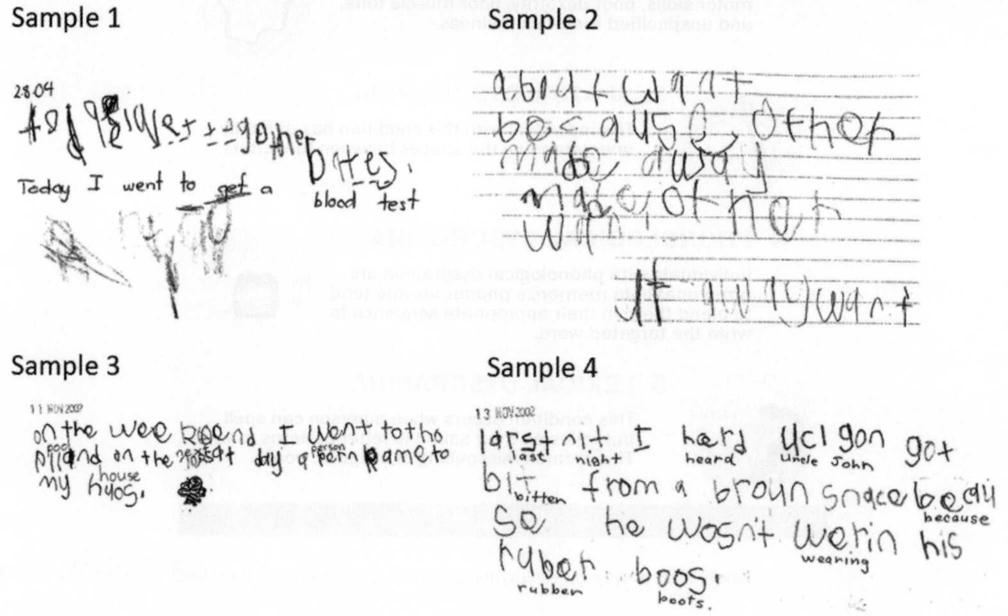

Students with dysgraphia display the following handwriting characteristics:

- inconsistent spacing (or no spacing) between words
- incomplete words or letters and consistently omitting words
- mixed writing style – combining capitals, lower case, cursive and letter slants
- inconsistent use of lines and margins – inappropriate indents
- unusual or extremely tight grip of pen
- slow and laborious letter formation
- poor bilateral coordination (using both hands – one to write, the other to steady the page).

Video: Supporting students with dysgraphia

Figure 14.62 shows the range of strategies that can be used to support students with dysgraphia. Support strategies require a combination of remediation and compensatory strategies to assist cognitive, kinaesthetic and motor development. Children and young people with dysgraphia typically cope better when they can provide information verbally. They may benefit from the use of speech-to-text technology, graphic organisers and paper with raised lines.

Figure 14.62 Supporting students with dysgraphia

- Assist the student to develop fluency – this may include visualising or verbalising the shape and formation of letters – for example a down stroke and circle for 'd' and down stroke for 'b'. It may involve getting the student to practise by air writing or writing in sand or finger paint.
- Provide the student with a printout that shows the direction of each stroke in the formation of a letter.
- Show the student how to physically space words by placing the index finger of the non-dominant hand at the end of the word and placing a dot to indicate where to start the next word.
- Encourage the student to touch the bottom of each letter to the line on the page.
- Draw a line in light pencil above the printed line to indicate the size for lower case letters.
- Draw a second line in another colour to indicate the size of capital letters.
- Have the student pay attention to their posture and pencil grip. A photograph or illustration of correct pencil grip can act as a reminder.
- Have the student try to relax their wrist and use the shoulder for stability.
- Ensure that the chair and desk are at the correct height for the student.
- Use pencil grips, weighted pencils or novelty pencils if this assists the student.
- Show the student how to hold the paper with the non-dominant hand, how to slant the page and how to move the hand across the page and down the page.
- Remind the student to look at what they are writing.
- Encourage the student to verbalise what they find difficult about the mechanics of writing. Does the student:
  - get cramps or soreness in their hand, wrist or back
  - get sweaty palms
  - become anxious
  - find it difficult to see their writing?
- By talking about their symptoms, students can gain a sense of control and take charge of remedial strategies.
- Other strategies may include:
  - encouraging the student to create a draft using key words or phrases to help them retain their thoughts when writing
  - having the student verbalise what they are going to write about (conferencing with another student or ESW).

Proprioceptive dysfunction

Simply put, proprioceptive skills are the ability to coordinate movements automatically. These skills are also referred to as sensory processing skills. An example is the ability to automatically handwrite legibly and fluidly without the need to think about each movement. Students who have difficulty producing legible handwriting may have a **sensory integration dysfunction (SID)**, caused when the brain and central nervous system have difficulty processing, or are unable to process, sensory information required to coordinate movement, and to understand and make sense of the world. The Sound Learning Centre (2023) explains that:

> Sensory Integration Dysfunction can be a difficulty on its own, but often is observed in conjunction with other neurological and physiological conditions, including dyslexia, dyspraxia, Asperger's Syndrome, autistic spectrum disorders, developmental disorders and speech delays.

Students with **proprioceptive dysfunction** tend to be clumsy, awkward and uncoordinated and may inconsistently display a range of behaviours, as listed in **Figure 14.63**.

Figure 14.63 Proprioceptive dysfunction behaviours

Movements appear disjointed, non-fluid or awkward; there is poor balance and coordination
Tactile defensiveness – avoids being touched; doesn't like to get dirty; intensely likes/dislikes certain textures; may like to be dressed or wrapped tightly
Goes about motor tasks in an atypical manner
Unable to pace a task – rushes at turning a page, spills or drips paint because time has not been taken to wipe the brush; holds a pencil too loosely or too tightly; fails to coordinate movement of the arm along the page when writing
Sits or stands in an unusual position when completing a task
Engages in sensory-seeking behaviours such as walking or running too fast or too slowly; bolts at things; bumps into things; drops things; stomps feet when walking; constantly tapping feet or kicking feet against table or chair; loves squishy things such as slime; likes clothing and shoes to be firm rather than loose fitting
Often falls over; has poor balance; may appear floppy or stiff and rigid
Has difficulty with fine motor tasks such as dressing, tying shoelaces, drawing, colouring, completing puzzles, turning pages in a book, undoing cling wrap and unscrewing drink bottles
May be over-stimulated by visual displays in the classroom
Engages in sensory-seeking behaviours such as constantly chewing on things – clothes (collar/sleeve), pens, paper, fingers, nails, lips
Constantly moving – tapping, rocking, swinging or shaking leg, drumming fingers, spinning or twirling
Slouches, puts head in hands, lays upper body across desk
Unable to tune out normal background noise or likes to have loud background noise
May have intense and unusual reactions to certain tastes or smells

Students with proprioceptive dysfunction may be over-sensitive or under-sensitive to sensory information. These are referred to as hypersensitivity (intensive response) or hyposensitivity (low response), respectively. Some students also display both hypersensitivity and hyposensitivity.

Various therapies are available for students with proprioceptive dysfunction – each student will have unique needs and respond to therapies in different ways. Hand-held sensory tools are a useful resource as they provide instant tactile stimulation that can have a calming effect on the student.

14.6 Supporting assessment of writing and spelling: the role of the ESW

As we have explored, learning to write is a developmental task that requires the integration of motor, language and social skills. Like all other areas of development, each student will progress at their own pace with a unique range of skills, strengths and knowledge.

Students who consistently present with difficulties in written communication will usually have difficulty in forming numbers, letters and words. They may find it difficult to write spontaneously, and often their writing consists of jumbled word order or disconnected phrases that are difficult to interpret. Usually their writing will simply not make sense to the reader. Students who have difficulty writing may also have difficulty reading, as well as with information processing and the use of expressive language. They will also have difficulty recalling what letters and numbers look like, so that the end result is illegible.

Students who have an expressive writing disability may:

- have failed to develop hand dominance
- confuse left and right and/or have a poor sense of direction
- frequently reverse letters and numbers
- find it difficult to copy words or numbers
- have poor organisational skills (desktop is disorganised, frequently misplaced belongings, forget where things belong).

Where there is a concern that a student may have an expressive writing disability, the teacher will normally ask for a diagnostic assessment to be conducted by a specialist. The test can confirm the existence of an expressive writing disability but does not provide options for remedial strategies.

Students' writing skills can be assessed by using a rubric, which provides teachers with specific information about a student's ability to:

- understand the sense of audience and the engagement of the reader as they write
- understand and use specific text features of, for example, a persuasive argument or narrative
- organise the text in a meaningful way using a variety of sentence structures, appropriate sequencing and text connectives to control the text
- use typical grammatical features to meet the purpose of the writing
- use a range of language devices and precise vocabulary, spell and punctuate (NSW Department of Education, 2017).

Figure 14.64 shows an example of a checklist that can be used by an ESW to undertake a general assessment of a student's written work. Checklists can be adapted to suit the age, ability level and expected learning outcomes for individuals or groups of students.

Figure 14.64 Assessing writing skills

ASSESSING WRITING SKILLS	
Student name:	Class:
Date:	
Planning skills (pre-writing)	
▪ Able to articulate the purpose/reason for the written task	☐
▪ Able to identify the most appropriate genre	☐
▪ Able to plan a beginning, middle and end	☐
▪ Able to identify key words, phrases or concepts	☐
Written task	
▪ Writing reflects the purpose/reason for the written task	☐
▪ Writing shows an awareness of the audience	☐
▪ Writing reflects pre-planning	☐
Grammar and spelling	
▪ Demonstrates understanding of correct use of grammar and punctuation	☐
▪ Shows evidence of checking spelling of unfamiliar words	☐
▪ Vocabulary reflects topic/purpose of writing	☐
▪ Key words are explained (as appropriate)	☐
▪ Sentence structure is age/stage appropriate	☐

Figure 14.65 is an example of a simple checklist that could be used by students to review their written work. Again, the checklist should be adapted to reflect the skills and abilities of the students.

Figure 14.65 Example of student writing checklist

Reviewing my writing

Things I can check	Things I can do
All words are spelt correctly.	☐
The genre I have used matches the purpose of my writing task.	☐
All sentences start with a capital letter and end with a full stop.	☐
I have used some new words.	☐
I have remained on topic.	☐
Another person has read and can understand my work.	☐
My writing has a beginning, middle and end.	☐
I have used at least one new word.	☐
I have used joining words other than 'and' and 'but'.	☐
I have used the correct tense and plural form for verbs.	☐

Gathering evidence of writing skills

Evidence that may be gathered to assess each student's writing development includes:

- samples of independent writing
- samples of spelling words, including invented spelling
- dated writing samples
- comments from students about their own writing skills (what they feel they do well and what they would like to improve).

A review of writing skills may include an assessment of sentence structure, spelling and grammar. Feedback to the student should focus on how to improve by working with the student to devise strategies that are appropriate to their needs and reflect the goals set by the teacher. When assessing students' writing skills, it is important to be aware that the quality of writing will vary over time and may depend on a range of factors, such as mood, interest, confidence and willingness to have a go.

Students can be encouraged to keep a diary or record of their writing progress. This can be particularly important where the student becomes disheartened when writing tasks become more challenging. By reviewing past work, the student can be reminded of the progress they have made.

Assessment of spelling skills

Most teachers will assess spelling using a weekly spelling list – incorrect words are retested after the student has been given the opportunity to revise. Spelling will also be corrected as students produce text for a range of purposes across the curriculum. Teachers will usually put a line through the word and write the correct spelling above it. Students will then transfer any misspelled words to their personal spelling list and/or dictionary.

Summary

This chapter has explored oral language and its critical role in underpinning literacy development. We have also explored the content and sequence of the Australian Curriculum: English as they relate to oral language and literacy learning.

Learning to write is a skill that develops over time. The foundation of writing skills is oral language and, by extension, vocabulary. Students who struggle with oral language and/or have a limited vocabulary will also struggle with their writing. Talking to students, asking open-ended questions and acting as a scribe can support writing development. Knowledge of genres, grammar, punctuation and spelling also develops over time as students are provided with a wide range of opportunities to read, listen to language and use language in various situations.

Self-check questions

1. What factors influence children's likelihood of reaching their full potential as readers and learners?
2. What are the elements of oral language?
3. Define the terms below:
   a. Transactional language
   b. Recounting language
   c. Pragmatics.
4. Explain the principle 'children need both explicit and implicit instruction' in supporting children's vocabulary development.
5. As an ESW, what is your most important role in supporting the oral language development of children?
6. What are the text types included in the Australian Curriculum: English?
7. What is a KWL? How does it assist students with writing?
8. Define shared writing and explain how ESWs could assist students in this process.
9. Which type of writing is conducted in small groups with students of similar writing abilities? What are the roles of ESWs and students in relation to this?
10. What is the role of the ESW in supporting the writing of the students?
11. How can ESWs best observe, record and evaluate a student's handwriting?
12. Explain the meaning of proprioceptive dysfunction and the characteristics of students with this type of disorder.

Discussion questions

1. The Year 11 students are embarking on a chapter of common law in their legal studies unit. The teacher recognises that words like sovereign, inalienable and arbitrarily are not commonly used words. So as part of the introduction to the lesson, the task set is for pairs of pupils to research two nominated terms and report back to the class.
   a. Which of Neuman and Wright's principles is the teacher applying?
2. Ivan loves to share a good story. He is a confident speaker who tells of his weekend fishing trip. However, he struggles to let other students participate in the conversation, will often talk straight over his peers and is known for changing the location or story in the middle of another one he is telling.
   a. Many people can become distracted during conversations, but when further analysing Ivan's contributions, you note he has a couple of other characteristics of someone struggling with pragmatics. What might these other characteristics be?

Activities

1. Describe a situation where you have listened to what is being said by someone, but not actually heard the message.
2. Describe the tripod grip and a way you may be able to help a child achieve this skill.
3. Collect some student writing samples and note down elements of their handwriting. Discuss with peers.

Chapter 15

READING

LEARNING OBJECTIVES

When you have completed this chapter, you should be able to demonstrate that, in relation to working in a school environment, you can:

15.1 understand the stages of reading development, and access and read and interpret current curriculum documents in relation to reading acquisition

15.2 identify, define and apply the big six elements of reading skills and knowledge: oral language phonemic awareness; phonological awareness; fluency; vocabulary; and comprehension

15.3 identify the strategies to support reading with the guidance of the teacher.

GO FURTHER

Go Further icons link to extra content for this chapter. Ask your instructor for the **Go Further** resource and deepen your understanding of the topic.

Online resources icons refer to useful weblinks. Ask your instructor for these **Online Resources.**

Introduction

This chapter provides an overview of the skills needed to become a competent and confident reader. Learning to read is a significant milestone and is essential for future academic success. An understanding that letters form words and, when put together in a deliberate way, create meaning – like verbal language – is developed during the early years. By school age, most children can recognise and associate groups of letters as words that convey meaning. At this stage, most children can recognise and write their own name and recognise some common words seen in their daily environment. This learning usually occurs because of observation, imitation and immersion in a literacy-rich environment. Reading, however, is a skill that typically requires direct instruction.

By now you are aware that oral language is the foundation for becoming a competent reader, and that oral language, writing and reading are intricately linked. Learning to read is a development task that draws on all domains of development. 'Readiness' in relation to early literacy development not only requires a range of cognitive skills such as self-regulation – the ability to concentrate for periods of time, listen and pay attention without being distracted – it also requires physical skills, such as the hand–eye coordination necessary for writing, visual and auditory discrimination and social-emotional skills, such as positive self-confidence and self-esteem, as well as self-efficacy, which allows children to 'have a go' at learning new things.

SCENARIO

MILLER

Every night, **Miller** (2 years) chooses two bedtime stories from her bookcase. Tonight, Miller has selected one of her favourites, *Dear Zoo*, which she can 'read' herself. Her other selection is a new book she received for her birthday called *Tickle, Tickle*. Miller points to the word 'zoo' and says 'zoo'.

CAN MILLER READ?

Miller is not yet a reader; however, she is demonstrating emergent literacy skills. She knows that printed symbols represent words and that a group of printed words can create a story, which can be read and enjoyed.

15.1 Stages in reading development

Video: Reading difficulties and how parents can assist

Emergent literacy begins at birth, with children attending to the sound of human voices and, by six months, looking intently at pictures in books. Emergent literacy encompasses speaking, listening, looking, thinking, reading and writing.

Children begin to make the connection between the spoken and written word when they are immersed in literacy (**Figure 15.1**). That is, they hear spoken language and see and hear print in many forms, such as fiction and non-fiction books, newspapers, magazines, advertising, food packaging, computers and television, and on clothing and fabric; they see others making and using print, such as writing a shopping list, making a sign or filling in forms; and they use a range of print-making tools like ink and felt pens, pencils, crayons and computers.

Figure 15.1 Exposing children to literature at a young age assists them to make the connection between the spoken and written word

Source: Shutterstock.com/Anton Haurylenka

Each child will arrive at school somewhere along the early literacy continuum. Some children will already be able to read, and most will have sound alphabetic knowledge, be able to write their name, other words and letters, be familiar with books and have favourite stories, have a sound grasp of language, communicate using sentences, identify, label and describe objects and things and have an age-appropriate vocabulary. At the other end of the continuum will be children who have very few of these skills. There will also be children for whom English is a second language who may also fall anywhere along the early literacy continuum. Some children will have disabilities that in various ways have influenced their early literacy skills development. These individual differences present a challenge for foundation level teachers, who must plan a literacy program to meet the unique stage of literacy development of every child.

The stages of early/emergent literacy are described in **Figures 15.2**, **15.3**, **15.4**, **15.5** and **15.6**.

Figure 15.2 Stage 1: Emergent literacy

Reading awareness begins when children become aware that a series of symbols (letters) can represent spoken words and the symbols convey specific meanings. Children usually begin to 'read' familiar sight words before they begin to write. For example, they will recognise their own name and words commonly found in the environment, such as names of fast-food chains, banks, petrol stations and stop signs. At this stage, young children can:

> listen to and discuss storybooks
> understand that print conveys a message
> engage in reading and writing attempts
> identify labels and signs in their environment
> participate in rhyming games
> identify some letters and make some letter–sound matches
> use known letters or approximations of letters to represent written language (especially meaningful words like their name and phrases such as 'I love you').

SCENARIO

THE SHOPPING LIST

Ashlee (3 years) is at the supermarket with her father, who is checking the shopping list as he walks along.

'I think we have everything on the list now, Ashlee.'

'Let me see,' says Ashlee as she takes the shopping list from her father. Looking intently at the list and then at the shopping trolley, she says, *'Ice cream, yoghurt, apples and bread. Mummy writed this for us, didn't she Daddy?'*

What emergent literacy knowledge is Ashlee demonstrating?

Ashlee understands that print has meaning – in this case, Ashlee pretends to read the list written by her mother using clues from the shopping trolley.

Figure 15.3 Stage 2: Experimental reading and writing

Students develop basic concepts of print and begin to engage in and experiment with reading and writing. At this stage, students can:

> retell simple narrative stories or informational texts
> use descriptive language to explain and explore
> recognise letters and letter–sound matches
> show familiarity with rhyming and beginning sounds
> understand left-to-right and top-to-bottom orientation and familiar concepts of print
> match spoken words with written ones
> begin to write letters of the alphabet and some high-frequency words.

SCENARIO

I KNOW!

Harry (4 years) and his father are sharing a familiar picture book. As his father is reading, Harry looks at the illustration and then points to the text, *'That says, "and they pulled and pulled and pulled". I can read, can't I, Dad?' 'Yes, Harry. You're a good reader!'* his father replies.

Harry has memorised the text, which he is able to reproduce accurately. How will this assist Harry to develop reading skills?

Harry has learnt that written words convey meaning. He has also learnt that the illustrations in the book can be used as prompts

Figure 15.4 Stage 3: Early reading and writing

Students begin to read simple stories and can write about a topic that is meaningful to them. At this stage, students can:

> read and retell familiar stories
> use strategies (rereading, predicting, questioning, contextualising) when comprehension breaks down
> use reading and writing for various purposes on their own initiative
> orally read with reasonable fluency
> use letter–sound associations, word parts and context to identify new words
> identify an increasing number of words by sight
> sound out and represent all substantial sounds in spelling a word
> write about topics that are personally meaningful
> attempt to use some punctuation and capitalisation.

WORKING IT OUT!

SCENARIO

Annan (7 years) is reading aloud to his mother from his school reader: *'The car royled down the hill.'*

'I don't think it says "royled", that doesn't make sense,' his mother says. *'Have another look, Annan. What sound do these letters make?'*

'/r/ /o/ /l/l /ed/,' says Annan. *'Ruled – no, rolled. The car rolled down the hill.'*

'Good work, Annan!'

WHAT READING SKILLS IS ANNAN DEMONSTRATING?

Annan demonstrates both phonemic awareness and synthetic phonics skills.

Figure 15.5 Stage 4: Transitional reading and writing

Students begin to read more fluently and write various text forms using simple and more complex sentences. At this stage, students can:

> read with greater fluency
> use strategies more efficiently (rereading, questioning, and so on) when comprehension breaks down
> use word-identification strategies with greater facility to unlock unknown words
> identify an increasing number of words by sight
> write about a range of topics to suit different audiences
> use common letter patterns and critical features to spell words
> punctuate simple sentences correctly and proofread their own work
> spend time reading daily and use reading to research topics.

SHARED READING

SCENARIO

Tyler (10 years): *'Mum, it says in my book that convicts were sent to Australia for stealing a hankie! And it says some convicts were indented. What does that mean, Mum?'*

'How is the word spelled, Tyler?'

'i/n/d/e/n/t/u/r/e/d'.

'You are almost right. The first part of the word is indent. Have another look at the last part of the word and try again.'

'ur/ed, /indent/ur/ed.'

'Indentured. Indentured means they were made to work as unpaid servants.'

'Oh, that's not fair, just for stealing a hankie!'

WHAT READING SKILLS IS TYLER DEMONSTRATING?

Tyler reads with understanding and can isolate unfamiliar words. He can use his phonics skills to try to work out the word. Tyler knows he can get support for his reading by asking questions.

Figure 15.6 Stage 5: Independent and productive reading and writing

Students continue to extend and refine their reading and writing to suit varying purposes and audiences.
Students can:
> read fluently and enjoy reading
> use a range of strategies when drawing meaning from the text
> use word-identification strategies appropriately and automatically when encountering unknown words
> recognise and discuss elements of different text structures
> make critical connections between texts
> write expressively in many different forms (stories, poems, reports)
> use a rich variety of vocabulary and sentences appropriate to text forms
> revise and edit their own writing during and after composing
> spell words correctly in final writing drafts.

GO FURTHER

Access a scenario demonstrating how important it is for children to read for pleasure in your **Go Further** resource, available through your instructor.

Videos: Early literacy

As literacy skills develop, there is a gradual shift from *learning to read* to *reading to learn*. This generally occurs as students move into the primary school years. Typically, most students can engage in silent reading. They usually have developed an extensive sight word vocabulary, can use a range of word-attack skills and are more fluent readers. This coincides with refinement in auditory and visual perception skills, greater self-regulation and self-efficacy skills, and the ability to engage in formal logical thought as the student moves into the concrete operational stage of cognitive development.

Figure 15.7 Students develop independent writing skills when provided with a range of tasks

Source: Photo by Tish Okely © Cengage

Literacy and the Australian Curriculum

One of the key aims of the Australian Curriculum: English is to ensure that students learn to listen to, read, view, speak, write, create and reflect on increasingly complex and sophisticated spoken, written and multimodal texts across a growing range of contexts with accuracy, fluency and purpose (Australian Curriculum, Assessment and Reporting Authority [ACARA], n.d.a) AC.

The literacy component of the English Curriculum includes the communication skills of speaking, writing, creating, listening, reading and viewing, focusing on:

- fluency in letter–sound correspondences of English
- an expanding vocabulary and grasp of grammatical and textual patterns sufficient to understand and learn from texts encountered in and out of school

Literacy glossary

- fluency and innovation in listening to, reading, viewing and creating texts for different purposes and contexts
- the skill and disposition needed to analyse and understand the philosophical, moral, political and aesthetic bases on which many texts are built
- an interest in expanding the range of materials listened to, viewed and read, and in experimenting with ways of expressing increasingly subtle and complex ideas to create effective and innovative texts.

Source: ACARA (n.d.b). Australian Curriculum English: Key ideas.

Figures 15.8, **15.10** and **15.11** outline some of the Australian Curriculum's content descriptions in relation to reading skills development.

Figure 15.8 Content description – Literacy: Foundation – Year 2

Year level	Content description
Foundation	Read **decodable** and **authentic** texts using developing phonic knowledge, and monitor meaning using context and emerging grammatical knowledge (see **Figure 15.9**)
Year 1	Read decodable and authentic texts using developing phonic knowledge, phrasing and fluency, and monitoring meaning using context and grammatical knowledge
Year 2	Read texts with phrasing and fluency, using phonic and word knowledge, and monitoring meaning by re-reading and self-correcting

Source: Australian Curriculum, Assessment and Reporting Authority (ACARA). (2023). Australian Curriculum: English.

Figure 15.9 Foundation year: 'If I gave a pig a cupcake' phonemic awareness example: Foundation

Figure 15.10 Content description – Literacy: Year 3 – Year 6

Year level	Content description
Year 3	Read a range of texts using phonic, semantic and grammatical knowledge to read accurately and fluently, re-reading and self-correcting when required
Year 4	Read different types of texts, integrating phonic, semantic and grammatical knowledge to read accurately and fluently, re-reading and self-correcting when needed
Year 5	Navigate and read texts for specific purposes, monitoring meaning using strategies such as skimming, scanning and confirming
Year 6	Select, navigate and read texts for a range of purposes, monitoring meaning and evaluating the use of structural features; for example, table of contents, glossary, chapters, headings and subheadings

Source: Australian Curriculum, Assessment and Reporting Authority (ACARA). (2023). Australian Curriculum: English. AC

Figure 15.11 Content description – Literacy: Year 7 – Year 10

Year level	Content description
Year 7	Use comprehension strategies such as visualising, predicting, connecting, summarising, monitoring, questioning and inferring to analyse and summarise information and ideas
Year 8	Use interaction skills for identifying purposes and situations, including when supporting or challenging the stated or implied meanings of spoken texts in presentations or discussion
Year 9	Use comprehension strategies such as visualising, predicting, connecting, summarising, monitoring, questioning and inferring to compare and contrast ideas and opinions in and between texts
Year 10	Integrate comprehension strategies such as visualising, predicting, connecting, summarising, monitoring, questioning and inferring to analyse and interpret complex and abstract ideas

Source: Australian Curriculum, Assessment and Reporting Authority (ACARA). (2023). Australian Curriculum: English. AC

CONSIDER THIS

EXAMPLES OF THE LITERACY CONTINUUM IN THE ENGLISH CURRICULUM

1. To see examples of the literacy curriculum for each grade go to: https://v9.australiancurriculum.edu.au/f-10-curriculum/learning-areas/english/foundation-year_year-1_year-2_year-3_year-4_year-5_year-6_year-7_year-8_year-9_year-10
2. To access resources, including work samples, go to: https://v9.australiancurriculum.edu.au/resources

15.2 Reading skills and knowledge

You will recall from Chapter 13 that the big six are regarded as foundational and essential skills for the development of competence in reading, writing and spelling (see **Figure 13.14**). Central to the big six are skills such as the Four Resources Model:

- code-breaking skills (text decoder) – knowledge of letter/sound relationships; concepts about print; spelling; punctuation; grammar; structural conventions and patterns

- **meaning-making skills** (text participant) – knowledge of literal and inferential meanings; use of background information, prior knowledge and previous experiences with similar texts to make meaning
- **text-using skills** (text user) – recognition of the purpose, structure and features of texts; use of texts to increase knowledge and refine understanding; application of knowledge of texts to achieve purposes both inside and outside the school
- **text-analysing skills** (text analyst) – teaching students to identify the techniques used to position readers, viewers and listeners; identification of opinions, bias, points of view; considering reactions to a text from varying perspectives; endorsing a position or presenting an alternative position to that taken by a text.

Source: Victorian Department of Education and Training (2009). Four Resources Literacy Model. https://www.education.vic.gov.au/school/teachers/teachingresources/discipline/english/literacy/readingviewing/Pages/fourres.aspx

Video: Characteristics of a good reader

To support students to become 'good' readers, it is helpful to be aware of the characteristics of a good reader (see **Figure 15.12**).

Figure 15.12 What do good readers do?

Preview

Read the front cover
Read the back cover
Scan the pages to look at any pictures
Look to see how the book is organised

Infer

Use clues to figure out what the author hasn't told you, such as:
- What the setting looks like
- How the characters feel
- Why a character acted in a certain way

Visualise

Make a movie in your mind as you read!
Picture:
- The characters' actions
- The characters' facial expressions
- Where the characters are

Make connections

Consider how the story is similar to, or different from:
- People and events in your life or in the world
- Feelings you've experienced
- Other stories you have read

Ask questions

What is going on in this story?
How does it fit with the rest of the story?
Does what I'm reading make sense?

Summarise

Think about the most important people/events in the book
Retell the events in order

Predict

Think about what you already know
Guess what will happen next

Respond

Write about or discuss:
- Which parts of the book you liked or didn't like and why
- Whether or not you would recommend the book to a friend

Source: Fitzsimons, F. (2017). What 'good readers' do. https://academicliteracy.wordpress.com/2017/12/21/what-good-readers-do

Reading programs

Reading programs focus on the systemic and sequential development of reading skills and knowledge of the elements of the big six. Acquiring these skills requires direct instruction, discussion, reflection and practice. These skills are cumulative and interrelated – that is, students must continually draw on existing skills and knowledge to build new skills and knowledge as readers. They must also develop the ability to apply all of these skills simultaneously as they read. To achieve this, teachers introduce new skills and knowledge and support students to consolidate new skills and knowledge before progressing to the next element. Students are given the opportunity to practise, revisit and apply their developing skills using a variety of reading genres.

Reading is integrated across all curriculum areas. As described in **Chapter 13**, The Big Six elements of reading skills and knowledge include:

1 oral language
2 phonemic awareness
3 phonological awareness
4 fluency
5 vocabulary
6 comprehension.

(Note: Oral language, the foundation of reading development, is explored in Chapter 14 of this text.)

Phonemic awareness

Phonemic awareness is the ability to understand that words are made up of individual speech sounds, or *phonemes*. Phonemes include single letters that represent sound, such as /t/, /k/, /h/ or combinations of *vowels* and *consonants*, such as /sh/, /th/, /oo/, /ch/. The number of phonemes in any language can vary from around 10 to around 140. There are 44 phonemes in the English language. The crucial skills of blending together and segmenting phonemes are essential for reading and spelling.

Videos: Phonemes and phonemic awareness

Phonemic awareness is critical to reading success and allows a student to:

- identify and categorise sounds by recognising which words in a set of words start with the same sound
- combine or blend separate sounds to say the word
- break up or segment a word into its separate sounds
- delete or add sounds to form new words
- substitute sounds to make new words
- isolate the first or last sound in a word.

Figure 15.13 describes the skills demonstrated by students who have mastered phonemic awareness.

Figure 15.13 Phonemic awareness skills

Skill	Example
Identify words that begin with the same sound	For example, 'cat' begins with a /c/ sound and ends with a /t/ sound; 'ball' starts with a /b/ sound and ends with an /all/ sound
Isolate a single sound from within a word	For example, 'tap', 'take', 'time' and 'tin' all have a /t/ at the beginning
Blend individual sounds into a word	For example, /b/ig, /f/ig, /j/ig

Skill	Example
Break a word into individual sounds	For example, 'shout' – /sh/ /out/, 'chip' – /ch/ /ip/, 'fantastic' – /f/ /an/ /tas/ /tic/
Modify, change, or move the individual sounds in a word	For example, 'hat', change the /h/ to /b/.

Figure 15.14 Words could be put to music as an activity to aid phonemic awareness

Figure 15.15 Components of phonemic awareness

1. Recognising which words in a set of words begin with the same sound ('*Bell*, *bike*, and *boy* all have /b/ at the beginning.')
2. Isolating and saying the first or last sound in a word ('The beginning sound of *dog* is /d/.' 'The ending sound of *sit* is /t/.')
3. Combining, or blending the separate sounds in a word to say the word ('/m/, /a/, /p/ – *map*.')
4. Breaking, or segmenting a word into its separate sounds ('up – /u/, /p/.')

Source: Reading Rockets (2023b). Phonological and phonemic awareness. https://www.readingrockets.org/teaching/reading-basics/phonemic

SUPPORTING PHONEMIC AWARENESS

Phonemic awareness can be supported by direct instruction and regular opportunities for practice and application. Playing with language, rhymes, beginning sounds and syllables is an essential first step in the process of learning to read (see **Figure 15.14**).

Figure 15.15 describes the key components of phonemic awareness. Instruction focuses on teaching students to listen to and identify sounds in spoken words so they can be manipulated as a code-breaking skill.

Phoneme blending and segmentation reinforce the connection between spoken and written words. This introduces the concept that single letters and specific letter combinations represent sounds – for example, /all/, as in /b/all, /c/all/, /f/all; or /an/, as in /b/an, /c/an/, /f/an/, /m/an/. Blending and segmentation allow students to play with word sounds – pulling words apart and putting them back together reinforces how phonemes (sounds) work together to create whole words.

Figure 15.16 demonstrates how instruction in phonemic awareness supports other elements of literacy.

Learning to connect phonemes to letter sounds (phonics) requires direct, well-planned instruction. Armbruster, Lehr and Osborn (2001) highlight an accumulation of research that indicates that phonemic awareness instruction improves children's ability to read words, spell, write and comprehend what they are reading. The authors suggest that children who have phonemic awareness understand that sounds and letters are related in a predictable way, which in turn enables children to relate the sounds to letters as they spell words. Learning to blend phonemes with letters helps children to read words, while learning to segment sounds with letters helps them to spell words.

Videos: Elkonin sound boxes

Figure 15.16 The relationships between phonemic awareness instruction and literacy development

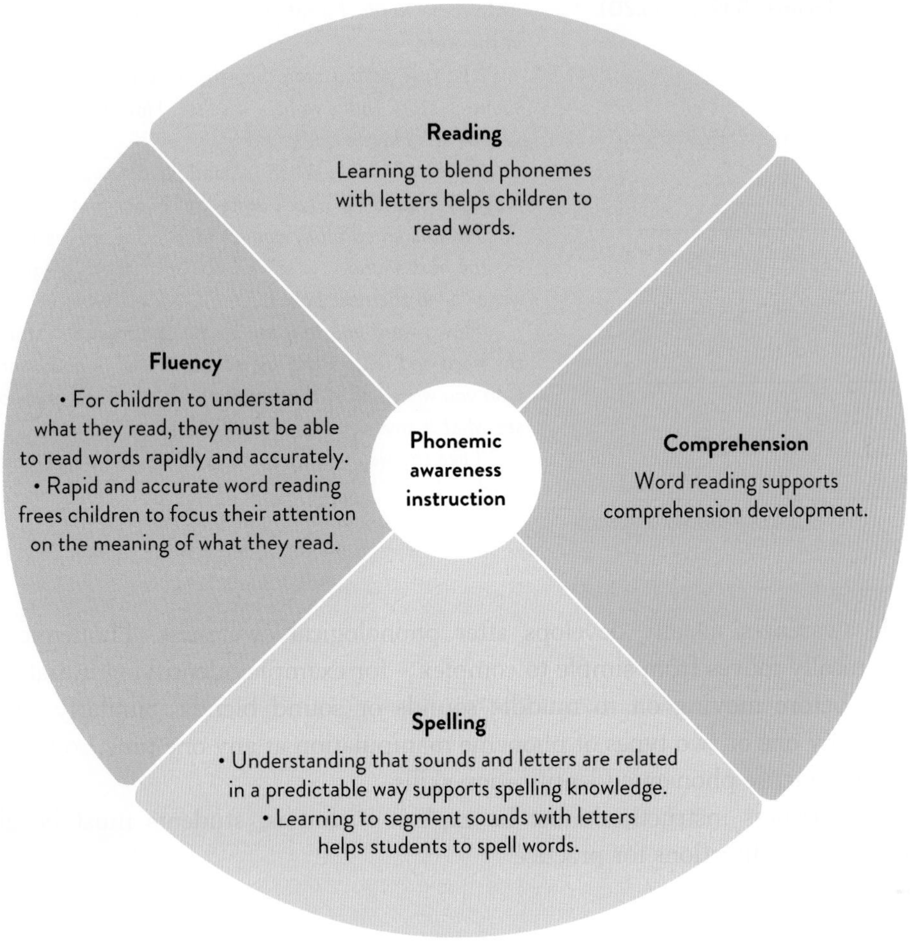

CONSIDER THIS

EXAMPLE OF PHONEMIC AWARENESS ACTIVITY: THE ELKONIN BOX

Elkonin boxes are a common tool used to assist students to develop phonemic awareness (**Figure 15.17**). Elkonin boxes are simply a set of boxes that allow students to physically segment words into phonemes.

Figure 15.17 Elkonin box 1

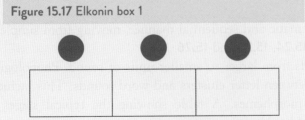

Adapted from Blachman et al. (2000)

Say the word c/a/t – the students move the counters to represent the sounds they hear (**Figure 15.18**).

Figure 15.18 Elkonin box 2

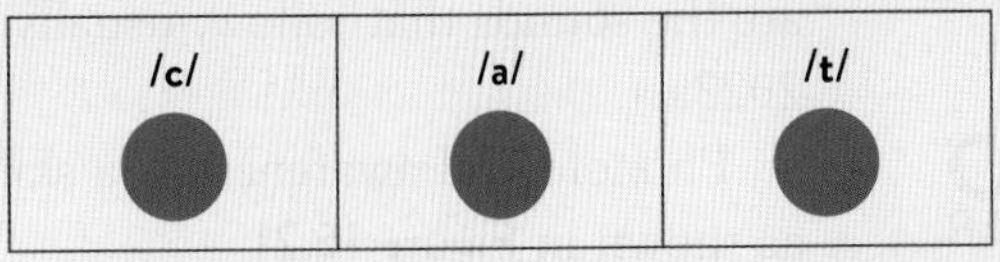

Adapted from Blachman et al. (2000)

Ask the students to listen for beginning, middle and end sounds using the Elkonin box: *'Listen for the /t/ sound in the following words. Place a counter in the first box if you hear the /t/ sound at the beginning of the word; place a counter in the middle box if you hear the sound in the middle of the word; or place it in the last box if you hear the /t/ sound at the end of the word. Listen carefully: mat, top, rat.'*

The Elkonin box can also be used to assist students to listen to, spell and write words (see **Figures 15.19** and **15.20**).

Figure 15.19 Elkonin box 3

●		

Adapted from Blachman et al. (2000)

Figure 15.20 Elkonin box 4

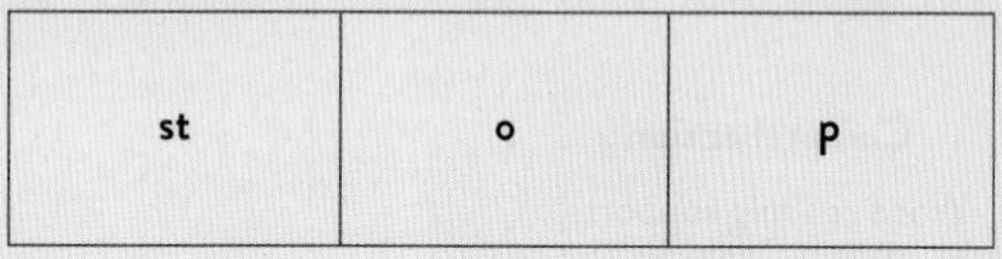

st	o	p

Adapted from Blachman et al. (2000).

For example, '*We are going to use the boxes to help us write some words. I want you to listen carefully to the sounds in the word.*

'*The first word is stop. Say the word and tell me the first sound in stop. That's right – it's "st". How do we write the sound "st". Have a go.*

'*Great, it's "s t". When "s" and "t" are together they make the sound "st". Let's write "st" in our first box.*

'*Now listen carefully again: "stop". Say the word and tell me the next sound . . . "st" . . . o. "O" – that's great! Let's write "o" in the next box.*

'*Now I want you to listen to the end sound – "stop". Say the word and tell me the last sound . . . "p" – good work! Can you write "p" in the last box? Let's look at your box and see what it says . . . "st", "o", "p", stop.*

'*I like the way you listen so carefully. Let's try another word . . .*'

Phonemic awareness usually develops after phonological awareness. Phonemic awareness instruction typically moves from simple to complex – for example, identifying initial sounds and single sounds before moving on to muddle sounds or sound blends. Similarly, students are introduced to only one or two types of phoneme manipulation at any one time, so they can grasp the concept and practise phonemic identification skills.

Phonemic awareness instruction must be explicit – that is, students must be given clear instructions and clear directions for practice.

Phonological awareness

The Reading Rockets website (2023b) describes phonological awareness as 'oral language and is the ability to recognize and manipulate the sounds in spoken words and parts of sentences. Examples include being able to identify words that rhyme, recognizing alliteration, segmenting a sentence into words, identifying the syllables in a word, and blending and segmenting onset-rimes'. (The 'onset' is the initial phonological unit of any word (e.g. c in cat) and the term 'rime' are the sounds that follow, usually a vowel and final consonants (e.g. at in cat) (Reading Rockets, 2023a.)

Phonological awareness is a skill that develops over time and involves listening and speaking, as shown in **Figure 15.21**.

Phonological skills are taught in a systematic and sequential manner, moving from simple to complex as shown in **Figures 15.22**, **15.23**, **15.24**, **15.25** and **15.26**.

Phonological awareness usually proceeds from larger to smaller units of sound. Phonological awareness allows students to make links between letter clusters and word sounds. This includes beginning sounds, onsets, syllables and morphemes. A table showing the typical stages of phonological awareness can be found on the book's website.

GO FURTHER

Learn more about the typical stages of phonological awareness in your Go Further resource, available through your instructor.

Figure 15.21 The development of phonological awareness skills

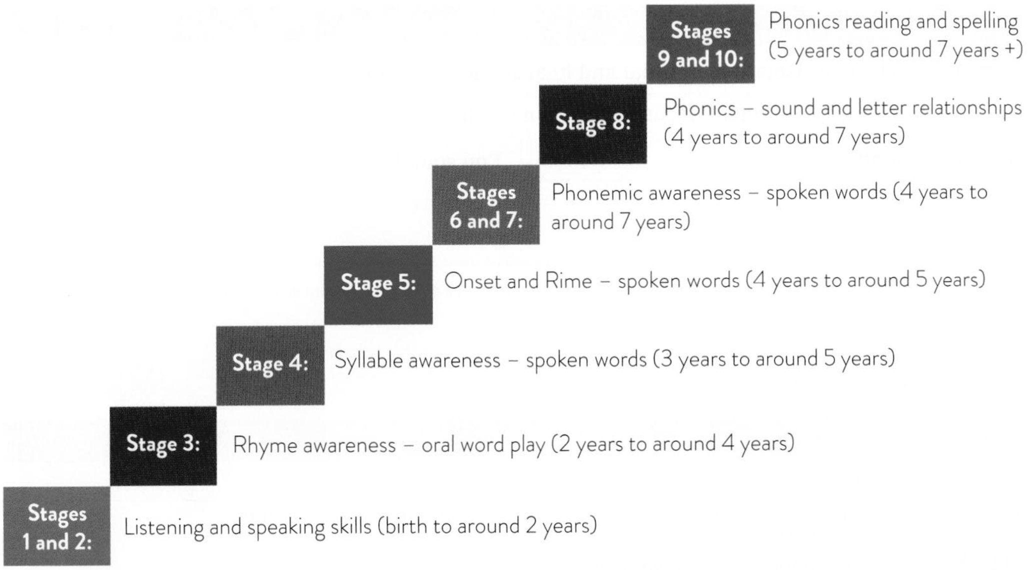

Source: Teach Phonics (2018). What is phonological awareness? https://teachphonics.blog/2018/09/20/what-is-phonological-awareness-2/

Figure 15.22 Syllable awareness

Instructional element: syllable awareness								
Every word can be broken down into syllables where every syllable has at least a vowel (a, e, i, o, u). Most syllables will also have an onset (consonants before vowel) and coda (consonants after the vowel). The vowel and the coda together make up the rime of the syllable (the part that rhymes). Syllable awareness involves activities like counting, tapping, blending or segmenting words into their syllables.								
Single syllable words						**Multi-syllable words**		
yes	no	can	run	cat	sun	yes/ter/day	runn/ing	seg/ment/ing

Source: Department of Education and Training: Victoria (2018a) © State of Victoria (Department of Education and Training). CC-BY-4.0 licence.

Syllable games and phonemic awareness

Figure 15.23 Rhyme awareness and production

Instructional element: rhyme awareness and production
The awareness of words that rhyme and words that do not rhyme. Thinking of and saying words that rhyme.
Words that rhyme
hat/mat/cat/ man/can/fan

Source: Department of Education and Training: Victoria (2018a) © State of Victoria (Department of Education and Training). CC-BY-4.0 licence.

Videos: Words, rhyme and sounds

Figure 15.24 Isolation of initial and final sound in a word

Instructional element: isolation of initial and final sound in a word	
Identifying initial and final sound: focus on the sounds (phonemes) not the letters	
Beginning sound	**End sound**
'f' sound – *phone/fancy* 'b' sound – *b*utterfly/*b*anana	't' sound – ra*t*/womba*t* 'n' sound – pe*n*/he*n*

Sound matching games

Source: Department of Education and Training: Victoria (2018a) © State of Victoria (Department of Education and Training). CC-BY-4.0 licence.

Figure 15.25 Segmentation

Instructional element: segmentation	
Phoneme segmentation is the ability to break words down into individual sounds. To do this, students must: ▪ break the word down into its component sounds ▪ select the letters that represent these sounds.	
Segmenting first sound	
chair – ch/air	sing – s/ing
shirt – sh/irt	sound – s/ound
Segmentation onset-rime	
down: *d/own*	mouse: *m/ouse*
window: *win/dow*	horse: *h/orse*
Segmenting individual sounds	
sh/ar/k	c/u/p
ch/air	f/i/sh

Segmenting and phonological awareness

Source: Department of Education and Training: Victoria (2018a) © State of Victoria (Department of Education and Training). CC-BY-4.0 licence.

Figure 15.26 Deleting and manipulating sounds

Instructional element: deleting and manipulating sounds
Identifying the sounds in words and deleting or swapping sounds to make new words.
star – take away 's' and add 't' – tart
thin – add a 'c' sound – think
mingle – take away 'm' and add 't' – tingle

Source: Department of Education and Training: Victoria (2018a) © State of Victoria (Department of Education and Training). CC-BY-4.0 licence.

SUPPORTING PHONOLOGICAL AWARENESS

CONSIDER THIS

Educators can introduce games that:

- encourage listening and word awareness
- encourage listening to the syllables in words
- encourage onset-rime awareness
- encourage students to use rhyming words.

EXAMPLES IN PRACTICE

'Listen to me say a sentence. How many words did you hear me say?'

'Listen while I say a sentence. Tap the stick to show me how many words I said.'

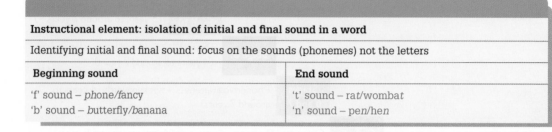

'You say a sentence and I'll tell you how many words you have said. Seven words. Am I right?'

Say compound words and ask the student to tell each part of the word: *'sunflower; moonlight; grandmother; basketball; fireworks'*. Say first word/say second word.

Say a word and ask students to listen carefully, repeat the word slowly, saying and clapping each syllable, and clap each syllable: /veg/e/mite; /choc/o/late; /no/; /pen/cil; /fun/ny; /rabb/it; /name/.

Explore words that have the same middle or end sound but are spelt differently – for example, /eight/ skate/; /four/door/; /two/shoe/.

Say a word and ask students to name a word that rhymes.

Introduce simple rhymes that students can complete: 'The *goat* wore a /coat/; The *dog* jumped a /log/. The *bat* ate the /rat/.' **Figure 15.27** shows an example of a student identifying rhyming words.

Figure 15.27 Rhyming words

Write words that rhyme with... HINT – you can use some words from your spelling list.

love	flip	hop	bin
shove /	hip /	dop /	blin /
above /	_ip	pop /	hin /

LEARNING DISABILITY AND PHONOLOGICAL PROCESSING

CONSIDER THIS

Phonological processing comprises three areas of functioning:

- phonological awareness
- phonological memory – the ability to hold on to speech-based information in short-term memory essential for reading and writing
- rapid automatised naming (RAN) – the ability to quickly identify and name a series of common stimuli (e.g. letters, numbers, colours, objects). Students with poor RAN skills tend to have weaknesses in reading and writing fluency.

Source: Dyslexia – SPELD Foundation Literacy Services (2021). *Understanding Learning Difficulties. A Practical Guide.* Perth (pp. 10 and 11).

Students with learning disabilities generally have difficulties processing information accurately and automatically, and many students have a weakness in working memory. Frequently, older students with dyslexia also demonstrate difficulties in some of these more complex phonological processes (especially in accurate and efficient phoneme identification and manipulation).

AUTISM SPECTRUM DISORDER AND READING

Kaskamanidis (2022) reminds us that:

> children on the autism spectrum have specific core autism features. And one of them is social communication. So, particularly difficulties with pragmatic communication and they also have problems with social interest, or social interaction. [They] also seem to have particular problems with comprehension. So while they might be reading quite well, the actual understanding might not be there. So their particular reading level might mask underlying literacy difficulties.

Source: Kaskamanidis, Z. (August 2022). Effective observation in specialist classroom literacy environments. *Teacher Magazine.* https://www.teachermagazine.com/au_en/articles/effective-observation-in-specialist-classroom-literacy-environments

CHILDREN WITH DYSLEXIA

Dyslexia is a language-based disorder that can affect reading, spelling, writing and maths. Students with dyslexia struggle with decoding – particularly matching letters to sounds and identifying basic morphemic units of sound in written language.

Source: Edutopia (2019). Video: *Debunking the IQ-dyslexia myth* (1.11 mins). https://www.edutopia.org/video/debunking-iq-dyslexia-myth

PHONICS INSTRUCTION

Phonics is the knowledge of letter sounds and the ability to apply that knowledge in decoding unfamiliar printed words. Phonics refers to print. Phonics involves making the connection between the single sounds (phonemes) and their related letter patterns (graphemes) when reading and writing. Phonics skills and phonological awareness are used together for successful reading and writing.

GO FURTHER

Learn more about phonics games and activities teachers might use in your Go Further resource, available through your instructor.

Teaching phonics involves assisting students to understand the relationship between sounds and symbols (letters). When students have grasped blending and segmenting sounds orally, they can be introduced to sound–letter correspondence – that is, the process of translating symbols (alphabetic print) into corresponding sounds. This process is the beginning of learning phonics, also referred to as 'cracking the alphabetic code'. Students should be introduced to single letters/sounds and given the opportunity to play with these, starting with initial letter/sound word activities, an example of which is shown in **Figure 15.28**.

Figure 15.28 Sample of letter/sound activity

	 all	 at	 ug
b	ball	bat	bug
	 ell	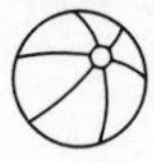 all	 ox
b	bell	ball	box
	 og	 uck	 rum
d	dog	duck	drum
	 ouse	 and	 ammer
h	house	hand	hammer

LETTER–SOUND KNOWLEDGE

Students develop letter–sound knowledge when:

- teachers provide systematic and explicit instruction simultaneously by teaching students how to name, sound and, as soon as possible, blend letters and write them in words
- teachers clearly articulate letter names and sounds
- students have the opportunity to articulate letter names and sounds
- students practise and remember letter names and sounds on a daily basis
- a different letter/phoneme is introduced every day in the students' first term at school
- a multisensory instructional approach is used, such as visual, auditory, kinaesthetic.

Figure 15.29 shows that Macky and his two classmates are beginning to develop phonetic awareness, as evidenced by their writing.

Figure 15.29 Examples of phonetic writing

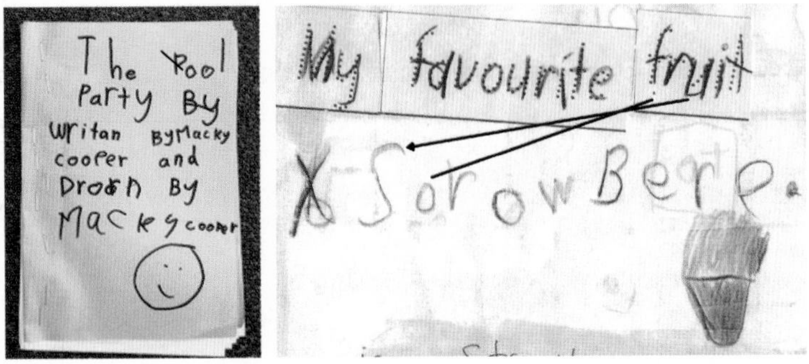

LETTER–SOUND RELATIONSHIPS

CONSIDER THIS

Learning letter–sound relationships is a challenging task for young children because:

- while there are 26 letters in the English alphabet, there are approximately 43–44 sounds
- there is not a one-to-one relationship between letters and sounds, but rather between letter patterns and sounds
- a letter by itself represents no sound; letters represent sounds only when they occur in words
- in written English, one letter may represent more than one sound
- the one sound may be represented by different letters.

Source: Emmit, Hornsby and Wilson (2013).

LETTER–SOUND CORRESPONDENCE

Phonics instruction includes systematic and explicit instruction of all letter–sound correspondence in a well-defined sequence (see **Figure 15.30**). This includes the letter–sound correspondence associated with:

- individual consonants
- individual vowels (short and long vowel sounds)
- vowel and consonant digraphs (e.g. /oi/, /ea/, /ou/, /sh/, /ch/, /th/)
- blends of letter sounds such as those commonly found at the beginning of words (e.g. /st/, /sm/, /bl/, /pr/) or in final stems or rimes (e.g. -ack, -end, -ill, -op)
- vowel digraph spelling patterns (/oi/, /oy/, /ea/) – usually taught in later primary grades.

When planning phonics instruction, teachers begin with letters:

- that appear most frequently in print
- that are most useful to children when they are writing
- that do not look or sound alike – for example, /p/ and /s/
- whose sound can be elongated, either in isolation or within words, for easy identification – for example, *s, m, r, f, n, h, v, w*
- that can be put together easily to create words – for example, word families such as /at/, /cat/, /mat/, hat, /bat/.

Figure 15.30 This student is exploring vowels

Source: Photo by Tish Okely © Cengage

Videos: Tips on teaching letter sounds and the Alphabetic Principle

Over time, students become familiar with letter–sound correspondences such as those shown in **Figure 15.31**, which range from simple to more complex.

Figure 15.31 Letter–sound correspondences, from simple to more complex

t		c	as in *can*	a	as in *father*	oy	
s		b		y	as in *my*	ai	
a	as in *tap*	o–e	as in *rope*	z		ay	
m		c	as in *city*	g	as in *gym*	oa	
i	as in *sit*	k		x		oi	
r		p		th	as in *there*	ar	
d		e	as in *ten*	ch		igh	
a–e*	as in *ate*	u–e	as in *use*	sh		aw	
f		v		wh		ow	as in *cow*
g	as in *good*	w		ph		ew	
o	as in *hop*	j		qu		ir	as in *girl*
l		i–e	as in *five*	th	as in *think*	ng	as in *sing*
n		ee		kn		er	
h		ea		ou		au	as in *author*
u	as in *sun*	y	as in *yes*				

*A vowel followed by a dash and an e indicates the long sound for that vowel in a word where there is a letter between the initial vowel and the final e (e.g. *i–e*, as in *ice, like*; *a–e*, as in *ape, make*).
Source: Ministry of Education. Ontario (2003, pp. 9, 13) © Queen's Printer for Ontario.

CONSIDER THIS

REMINDER!

Phonics and phonemic awareness are *not* the same. as shown in **Figure 15.32**.

Figure 15.32 Key differences between phonemic awareness and phonics

Phonemic awareness	Phonics
• Speech-based • Phonemes (sounds) to graphemes (letters) • Focuses on oral language and auditory discrimination	• Print-based • Graphemes (letters) to phonemes (sounds) • Focus on alphabetic symbols and corresponding letters sounds (visual and auditory discrimination)

Approaches to teaching phonics

As described by the Australian Government (n.d.):

In Australia, phonics is part of the national curriculum and taught in early primary school. There are three elements that are part of a good phonics program:

- the order in which the letters and sounds are taught matters. For example, teaching the letters *s, a, t, p, i, n, m,* and *d* first means that children can already make lots of different words with their first letters, like *sit, sat* and *mat*
- the early introduction of blending (putting different sounds together to make a word) and segmenting (separating a word out into its separate sounds)
- the use of books that can be easily sounded out, giving children the chance to use and practise their phonics.

Source: Australian Government (n.d.). Learning Potential. Learning to read 2: Phonics. https://www.learningpotential.gov.au/articles/learning-to-read-2-phonics

Reading sequence at a glance

ORDER IN WHICH TO TEACH PHONICS SKILLS

There are several approaches to teaching phonics, the most common of which are described below:

- **Synthetic phonics** (whole word). Students are taught the relationship between letters and the speech sounds they represent. This is a part-to-whole approach that teaches children to convert graphemes into phonemes – that is, letters or letter combinations into sounds. For example, students decode a word such as /wombat/ into single sounds – /w/o/m/b/a/t/ – and then blend the sounds into a recognisable word. In this example, students may already recognise /b/a/t/ as /bat/. Synthetic phonics is regarded as the most effective method of instruction for most students. Research of the big six has identified the synthetic approach to phonics – teaching single letters and common letter combinations in an explicit manner, and in an order that helps with blending using easily decodable texts is a beginning point for reading development (Brown, n.d., p. 5).
- **Analytic phonics** (letter–sound). Uses a whole-to-part approach – sounds are not pronounced in isolation; rather, students analyse letter–sound relationships in known words. Students are asked to identify the sound by referring to words they already know – for example, 'What other words do we know that start with /d/? or 'Notice that these words start with the letter /d/.' This is a good process to follow when kids don't know how many sounds there are. Fingers are used to count the sounds (see **Figure 15.33**).
- **Embedded phonics**. Students use letter–sound relationships with context clues to identify and spell unfamiliar words. For example, if reading a story about a wombat, students will learn to decode the word /wombat/ in the context of the story using letter–sound relationships.
- **Analogy phonics**. Students learn to use parts of word families they already know to identify words they don't know that have similar parts. For example, a student may know the word /make/ and use this to decode the unfamiliar word /stake/ by segmenting the shared rime and blending it with a new onset – /m/ake/, /st/ake/.
- **Onset–rime phonics**. Children learn to identify the sound of the letter or letters before the first vowel (the onset) in a one-syllable word and the sound of the remaining part of the word (the rime) (Armbruster, Lehr & Osborn, 2001, pp. 12–13).
- **Phonics through spelling**. Students are taught to segment the word into phonemes (sounds) and write letters for each phoneme.

Figure 15.33 Five-step process for identifying sounds

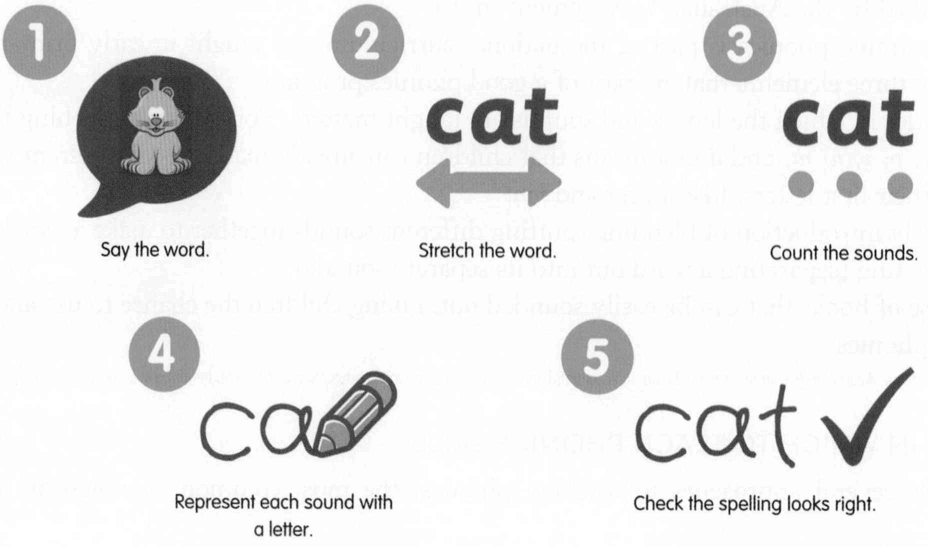

Source: Reproduced with permission from Phonics Hero.

The Victorian Department of Education explains that:

Regardless of which approach is employed, phonics instruction must contain the following:

- explicit teaching of the grapheme and phoneme
- multiple exposures to the grapheme and phoneme through meaningful texts and contexts
- systematic teaching of graphemes and phonemes based on what students need to learn (building on known knowledge)
- explicit links to handwriting and how the upper and lower case grapheme is represented.

Source: Victoria State Government. Education and Training (2023). Literacy Teaching Toolkit: Phonics. https://www.education.vic.gov.au/school/teachers/teachingresources/discipline/english/literacy/readingviewing/Pages/litfocusphonics.aspx#link89

It is important to be aware that while direct phonics instruction will form a significant part of any reading program, it must be complemented by other reading programs.

EXPLICIT INSTRUCTION – PHONICS

SCENARIO

Kindergarten teacher **Christopher** is providing explicit phonics instruction to the whole class.

Today he is introducing the sounds associated with the letter combination /at/.

'I want everyone to look at the words I have written on the smartboard.' Christopher points to and reads each word – '/hat/, /cat/, /mat/, /bat/'.

'Now let's read the words together, '/hat/, /cat/, /mat/, /bat/'. Let's sound out the letters in each word. /h/a/t/, /c/a/t/, /m/a/t/, /b/a/t/. Look at each word and the letters in the word. Tell me which letters are the same in each word.'

Students: *'a/t/.'*

'That's right, /a/t/. Well done! When we put /a/ and /t/ together, what sound does it make?'

Students: *'/at/.'*

'Let's check to see if you are right. We'll all write the word /sat/. Let's say it before we write it. "/sat/".'

Christopher waits while the students write /sat/.

Christopher writes /sat/ on the smartboard: /s/at/

'*Who can think of another word with the sound /at/?*'

The students suggest and write the following words: /fat/, /pat/, /rat/, /sat/.

Christopher uses a Venn diagram to show the relationship between /at/ words (**Figure 15.34**).

What has been the focus of Christopher's lesson?

Christopher has provided explicit phonics instruction, using the rime /at/. He has built on the students' knowledge of single sound phonemes.

To conclude this lesson, Christopher reads a nonsense poem using words that rhyme with /at/.

Figure 15.34 Venn diagram

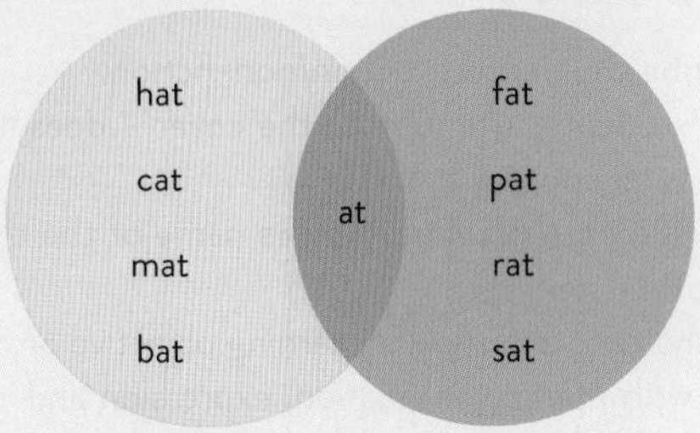

A balanced reading program

Synthetic phonics

In a balanced reading program, teachers read aloud to students, read with students and students read independently. A balanced reading program includes:

- modelled reading
- shared reading
- guided reading
- independent reading
- word study.

MODELLED READING (READ ALOUD)

When reading aloud, the teacher models skills such as rhythm, phrasing, intonation, naturalness and use of voice for different characters/moods. Modelled reading allows students to listen to a fluent reader and hear how the sounds, patterns, intonations and rhythm of spoken language are translated from written language.

Modelled reading also exposes students to different types (genres) and forms of text. It assists students to understand that reading can be a shared experience and is a way of accessing specific information, learning new information and sharing ideas, as well as a source of enjoyment. When teachers read aloud, they can stop and explore new words, investigate meaning and help students to make connections with what they already know, think or understand.

Modelled reading includes three phases – before, during and after:

1. *Before:* Select the text. Identify a clear goal, purpose, objective or learning outcome. Reading aloud to students is not restricted to the English Curriculum – it will occur across the curriculum. For example, the teacher may read a non-fiction book to explore facts in natural science. In this situation, the teacher will have predetermined what information is to be conveyed to students and what students are expected to learn, apply, explore or investigate. The teacher can also identify key words and concepts.
2. *During:* When reading aloud, the teacher may pause and discuss a concept, word or fact. The teacher may ask questions, such as, 'I wonder what might happen next?' or 'What happens if … ?', to generate discussion and allow students to share their ideas and knowledge.
3. *After:* The teacher may not plan any follow-up; they may link the text to other curriculum tasks or ask students to verbally recall the text.

CONSIDER THIS

READING ALOUD TO STUDENTS – SOME THINGS YOU COULD DO

- Describe the genre – fiction/non-fiction.
- Draw students' attention to the cover – does it give any clues as to content?
- Draw students' attention to the name of the text and the author.
- Link the text to a specific learning objective or outcome.
- Read with fluency, intonation, expression and enthusiasm – remember that you are acting as a reading role model.
- Read at a pace that is appropriate to your audience.
- Explore the table of contents, glossary and index, and how they could be used.
- Where relevant, talk about any pictures, illustrations, diagrams, graphs, tables, etc.
- Ask questions to assess students' comprehension: *'What happened when . . .?'; 'How many different species of sharks can you recall?'; 'What did this story make you think about?'; 'How did you feel when . . .?'; 'How could you use the index to help you when you answer these questions?'*

TIPS

Always read the text to yourself before reading it to students. Check that you are familiar with the language and the content. Identify any words that may require explanation.

Notice who asks questions, what students say and how students apply their existing knowledge.

Before you begin, determine how you will measure/evaluate whether you have achieved your key goals/objectives/learning outcomes.

▶ DISCUSSION

Why is it important for ESWs to be good reading role models?

Videos: Reading sessions and shared reading

SHARED READING

Shared reading requires the teacher to read from a selected text, such as a big book or large-text book. Students are required to look at and follow the text as it is being read. Students will be encouraged to read silently, and to mouth or whisper the words as the teacher reads. At a predetermined point, or when students are ready, they read along with the teacher. Shared reading should be a non-threatening and positive experience. Shared reading is an opportunity for students to hear themselves read and to practise reading with fluency and expression. Shared reading should never be hurried – it is an opportunity to explore words in a meaningful context. It also allows the teacher to introduce new vocabulary and more challenging words to students.

Shared reading ideas include:

- *reading bubbles* – use sticky labels to add thought bubbles to images in the text (**Figure 15.35**), and ask students to tell a partner what they think the character is thinking or saying
- *making predictions* – students use the book cover to make a prediction about the content, and after reading the book discuss their prediction with other students.

GUIDED READING

During guided reading, small groups of students who are at around the same level in their reading ability work with the teacher to read a text. The focus is on reading with understanding, using problem-solving to work out unfamiliar words and sentence structures. The role of the teacher is to assist students to apply their existing reading skills by selecting books that are easily read but also offer a degree of challenge. The teacher will use prompts, provide information and ask open-ended questions to help students problem-solve words and meanings.

Figure 15.35 Adding thought bubbles

Carrie's dog had disappeared. Every day Carrie stood at the end of the long road and waited for Dan to come home. Her father said that Dan was a stupid dog and he was never coming back.

Source: iStock.com/bowie15

A guided reading spinner is helpful here – a student spins the arrow and works with a small group to answer a guided reading question (**Figure 15.36**).

Figure 15.36 Spin a question

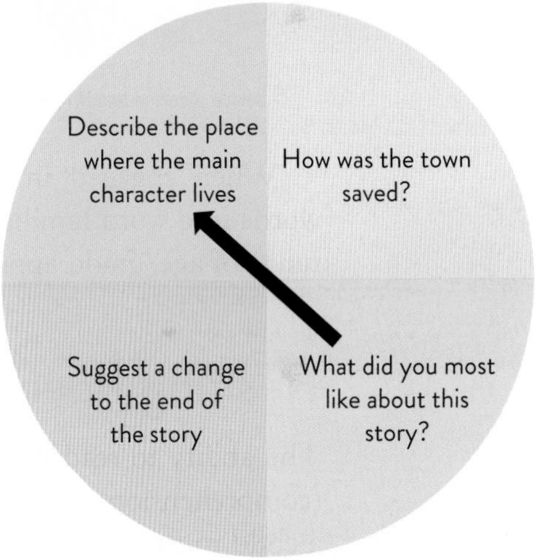

Describe the place where the main character lives
How was the town saved?
Suggest a change to the end of the story
What did you most like about this story?

INDEPENDENT READING

The ultimate goal of any reading program should be to promote the habit of regular, independent reading for both pleasure and learning. When students read for pleasure, they will select their own books and read about topics or subjects in which they are interested and that they enjoy. Where students independently choose books that are above their reading skills level, they can be supported to develop strategies – such as conferencing with other students – to overcome reading challenges. Independent reading can be encouraged by asking students to maintain a reading journal, or create a graphic organiser or a mind map to represent their book, and providing students with the opportunity to share their reading by talking about their book to a group of other students. Teachers can also promote independent reading by implementing the Drop Everything and Read (DEAR) program.

SCENARIO

DEAR OR RRR?

Richard, a Year 2 teacher, is not convinced of the benefits of DEAR. He has several students in his class who are classified as struggling readers. He has observed that these children tend to simply look at the pictures, annoy other students or daydream during DEAR.

Richard decides to introduce Round-Robin-Reading (RRR). This strategy provides an opportunity for all students to read aloud. Richard employs this strategy when students are exploring science and humanities/social science topics. This ensures that students are reading for learning. Richard explains that non-fiction texts offer students the opportunity to attempt new or difficult words as well as to explore new content knowledge. By being on the spot, Richard can guide and support all students. He is also adapting his expectations according to his knowledge of each student's reading level.

WHAT DOES THIS TELL US?

In this Scenario, Richard demonstrates how oral reading can be individualised to reflect each student's ability while still involving a shared reading experience.

Video: Independent reading

WORD STUDY

Word study is an analysis of words that assist the student to identify and understand spelling patterns, and identify and compare words that are phonetically similar. It also supports writing as students gain knowledge of words and meanings (see **Figure 15.37**).

Figure 15.37 Word study

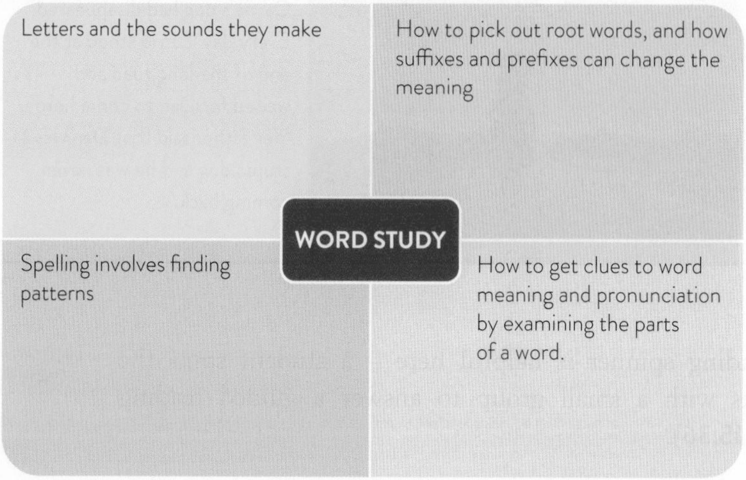

Letters and the sounds they make
How to pick out root words, and how suffixes and prefixes can change the meaning
WORD STUDY
Spelling involves finding patterns
How to get clues to word meaning and pronunciation by examining the parts of a word.

Source: Adapted from K12 Reader (2018). Word study makes language learning fun. https://www.k12reader.com/word-study-makes-language-learning-fun/

When engaged in word study, students explore common patterns, compare and classify words into word families, and explore common prefixes, suffixes and root words. There is a wide range of age/grade-appropriate word study activities that can be used in the classroom.

Reading fluency

The ability to read fluently, accurately and with expression allows students to focus on content (comprehension) rather than on the task of **decoding** each word. When learning to read fluently, a child must know where to pause or where to raise or lower their voice. Instead of reading word by word, the goal is to read words in groups (Konza et al., 2015, p. 2). Fluency develops over time as students become better at word recognition and at seeing connected texts rather than a series of words. The ability to read fluently also contributes to both understanding and enjoyment of reading for its own sake.

Reading fluency includes three components: accuracy, rate and prosody.

- **Reading accuracy** refers to the ability to correctly name words and/or to use key strategies to decode unfamiliar words easily. Reading accuracy is the most important element of reading fluency. Reading accuracy requires students to use 'alphabetic code knowledge and be able to decode words efficiently, whilst also being able to read high frequency words, with automaticity' (Literacy Impact Educational Services, 2023).
- **Reading rate** refers to the speed and fluidity used by the reader while maintaining comprehension of what is being read.
- **Prosody** is the ability to read with expression such as phrasing, stress, pitch, and rhythm.

Fluency will only develop when the student is able to recognise and read words accurately without the need to concentrate primarily on decoding. When this skill is acquired, students can focus on automaticity (automatic word recognition), which allows them to read with fewer pauses. Fluent readers also develop the skill to read several words in a phrase rather than reading each word on its own. Fluency also requires students to use syntactic skills, such as recognising language patterns, using punctuation and phrasing:

- *Syntax* is the sentence structure of a language. It governs how words are meaningfully ordered into phrases, clauses and sentences. For example, in English we say, 'She went to bed' rather than 'Went she to bed'.
- **Syntactic knowledge** is an unconscious understanding of the rules that govern word order. Children typically will acquire syntactic knowledge naturally as they learn to speak – for example, using the correct word order.
- **Syntactic awareness** is a metalinguistics skill that is defined as the conscious ability to manipulate or judge word order within the context of a sentence, based on the application of grammatical rules. For example, if a student were given a series of words such as 'to, went, she, bed', they would demonstrate syntactic awareness by rearranging the words into a meaningful sentence – that is, 'She went to bed'.

Teachers use a range of strategies to support the development of fluency.

In the following Scenario, the teacher demonstrates how reading fluently supports reading comprehension. The teacher assists the students to identify and read short phrases as a strategy to increase fluency.

Videos: Fluency and literacy instruction

GO FURTHER

Read a summary of strategies used to support fluency in your Go Further resource, available through your instructor.

SCENARIO

EXPLICIT FLUENCY INSTRUCTION – READING ACCURATELY AND AT A REASONABLE PACE

Teacher: *'I want you to listen to a poem. I am going to read it in a disjointed manner without pausing at commas or full stops.'*

The teacher reads without fluency to demonstrate difference in sound: *'/Over the hill down/ the road around/ the corner came/ the toad dragonflies/ flitted dragonflies/ droned the toad reached/ the pond but/ was not/ alone/.'*

The teacher asks the class, *'Did the poem make sense? Why not? What could I do to make it easier to understand?'*

The teacher then reads aloud to model fluency: *'Over the hill, down the road, Around the corner, came the toad. Dragonflies flitted, dragonflies droned, The toad reached the pond but was not alone.'*

Teacher: *'What happens when I read fluently and group phrases together? Let's look at the punctuation in the poem. How does it help us to read more fluently?*

A student responds and the teacher says: *'That's right, it shows us where to group words into phrases. "Over the hill,/ down the road,/ around the corner,/ came the toad./" Let's read this together using the commas to pause.'*

In this example, the teacher is explicitly focusing the students' attention on how punctuation can be used to assist in reading a text fluently.

▶ DISCUSSION

Why is it important to combine direct instruction *and* role modelling when focusing on a new reading skill?

Oral Reading Fluency (ORF) Assessment

Reading fluency is measured by the number of words a child can read accurately in one minute. Students can use a timer to challenge themselves to read as many words as they can, with accuracy and speed. Teachers will administer fluency tests throughout the year so that each student's progress can easily be assessed.

Video: Fluency assessment

Vocabulary

Chapter 14 explored vocabulary in the context of oral vocabulary. Vocabulary and reading are also interdependent skills – one builds upon the other. You will recall that skills associated with vocabulary knowledge include:

- word identification (ability to decode words)
- word analysis (understanding letters, sounds and roots, prefixes and suffixes that make up words)
- syntactic awareness (grammatical use of a word)
- pragmatic awareness (how words are used to communicate).

As students move from learning to read to reading to learn, they are exposed to vocabulary that may be new and unfamiliar. To understand and use new vocabulary, students must be able to explore and hear the word meaning in context.

Examples of activities that support vocabulary development are described in **Figure 15.38**.

Figure 15.38 Vocabulary activities

Play barrier games (where students work in pairs using a barrier such as a piece of cardboard). Each student has a similar document, but one student has more information than the other. The students must work together to share information in order to complete the game. For example, students both have a treasure map, but only one student knows the location of the treasure – they must work together, sharing information and asking questions, so the other student can locate the treasure.

WORD OF THE DAY
procrastinate

Challenge students to suggest a 'word of the day' to add to their own vocabulary or that of the class. Compile a key word list and its meaning related to a subject/topic/curriculum area.

Use word cards. Students select a random word card and must talk about the word on the card for 30 to 40 seconds.

Write single words on a piece of paper and the meaning of the word on a separate piece of paper. Crumple the papers and place them all in a bowl. Students must try to beat the clock matching the word and the meaning.

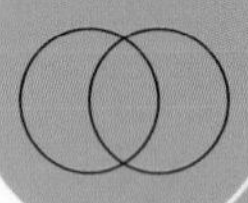

Explore synonyms. Using two overlapping circles (like a Venn diagram), write two words that have a similar meaning, each in a separate circle. In the common area, write words that define or describe similarities, then in each circle write words that identify differences. For example, what might be the similarities and differences between a house and a high-rise unit?

Give each student a picture card. Depending on the age of the student, the pictures may range from simple everyday objects to visual images representing emotions. The students take turns to describe their picture card without revealing the actual image.
Students might also be given a set of cards with each card containing three words that sound similar – for example, 'howl, hole, hot'. The partner student must listen and locate the matching card from the description.

The ____ girl raced _____

- Provide cloze sentences with deleted nouns or adjectives for students to add.
- Explore word families and create word maps.
- Create a story using 'new words' provided by the teacher.
- For older students, discussion starter cards (If I could fly …), visual imagery or sets of cards that can be used to create a story may be useful ways to promote oral language.

Provide unusual and unfamiliar objects for students to describe.

SCENARIO

RESEARCHING WORDS IN THE DICTIONARY

Figure 15.39 shows a list of words that **Chloe** (Year 5) was required to define in a task designed to expand her vocabulary.

Figure 15.39 Chloe expands her vocabulary by researching words in the dictionary

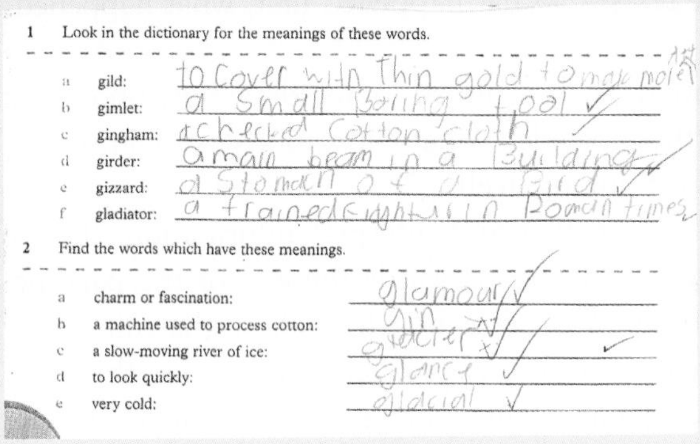

1 Look in the dictionary for the meanings of these words.

a gild: to Cover with Thin gold to make more
b gimlet: a Small Boring tool ✓
c gingham: a checked Cotton cloth ✓
d girder: a main beam in a Building ✓
e gizzard: a Stomach of a Bird ✓
f gladiator: a trained fighter in Roman times

2 Find the words which have these meanings.

a charm or fascination: glamour ✓
b a machine used to process cotton: gin ✓
c a slow-moving river of ice: glacier ✓
d to look quickly: glance ✓
e very cold: glacial ✓

▶ DISCUSSION

Consider the word list – do you consider the words to be relevant to a Year 5 student? Why might these words have been selected? Could you offer a list of words that may be more relevant? How important is it to ensure that new vocabulary is provided in a relevant context that is meaningful to students?

Comprehension

Comprehension is a cognitive reading skill that requires the reader to understand, interpret and respond to what is being read. It is important to be aware that being able to read a word does not necessarily mean the student understands the meaning of the word. Comprehension is developed when students are challenged to explore what has been read – for example, engaging in meaningful discussion and critical reflection and debate.

Comprehension skills in the Australian Curriculum: English

CONSIDER THIS

MISCUE

To **miscue** means to make a reading error. Reading errors can result in:

- *a change in the meaning of the text* – for example, the meaning would change if a student were to read 'The car *cruised* through the gate' instead of correctly reading 'The car *crashed* through the gate'. In this situation, the meaning has been lost and the remaining text will not make sense. In this situation, the teacher would need to encourage self-correction – 'Go back and look at the word – does it make sense in the context of the storyline?'

- *the meaning is lost* – for example, a student might read 'The car *smashed* through the gate'. In this instance, the student may have predicted what was going to happen using visual clues such as an illustration of a car and a smashed gate. In this situation, the teacher may encourage self-correction or may choose not to interrupt the student's flow and can draw attention to the word when the student has finished reading the passage of text.

Various strategies can be used to gain information and meaning from text. Herber (1978) devised a three-level guide continuum to support the development of comprehension skills, which was developed further by Morris and Stewart-Dore (1984). These levels include:

- **literal comprehension** – the reader seeks to understand what is written in the text. For example, locate the title, the author, a heading, locate information in a phrase or sentence: 'Let's see if we can find the section in the text that describes the farmhouse'; 'Who illustrated this text? Can anyone tell what other books this person has illustrated?'
- **interpretive comprehension** – the reader is asked to engage in reflection and draw on existing knowledge to make inferences about the text. This is referred to as 'reading between the lines' and sometimes is referred to as 'hidden comprehension'. Examples of interpretive comprehension skills may include:
  - creating a sequence of events from the texts – 'What happened first, what happened next, then what happened ...?'
  - using visual cues to interpret information, such as illustrations, drawings, photos, graphs and diagrams: 'Look at the photos of these people. What expressions can you see on their faces? What do you think they might be thinking/feeling?'
  - making links between various sentences to gather and interpret information: 'In the first few sentences the author describes the farmhouse. Towards the end of the page he adds information about the animals on the farm. What does he tell us about the animals?'
- using a range of vocabulary to explain key ideas and concepts communicated in the text: 'Let's create a list of words to describe the feeling created when reading this text'; 'Using your own words, write a few sentences to describe your understanding of recycling'.
- **inferential comprehension** (also known as head comprehension) – requires readers to apply and evaluate knowledge from multiple texts, or within different areas of one text, or use their background knowledge about topics. Readers are required to read beyond the lines. Examples of inferential comprehension may include:
  - connect different information across sentences, paragraphs and chapters
  - infer the meaning of information in texts
  - deduce main ideas, themes and concepts in texts
  - use a range of strategies – for example, context cues – to identify the meaning of unknown words
  - identify the purpose and meaning of metaphorical language devices – for example, similes
  - identify similar vocabulary meanings to link and connect ideas: 'What is the main theme of the text?'; 'List the sub-themes of this text'; 'Use your own words to explain the following phrases from the text.'

Critical analysis

Critical analysis is a skill that allows the reader to consider the content of the text beyond what is written – for example, make deductions, theorise or hypothesise. Critical analysis is a higher-order skill. It requires the student not only to draw on their existing knowledge of the text content, concept or ideas, but also to draw on knowledge from other curriculum areas, as well as their own general knowledge and opinions, to inform and make better sense of what is being read. A good example of this might be asking a student to think about what they know happens to their body when undertaking strenuous physical activity, such as football or running, and apply this to help them understand a text related to physiology.

Critical analysis skills are described in **Figure 15.40**.

Figure 15.40 Critical analysis skills

Students demonstrate when they can, for example:

Identify	the intended purpose of a specific part of a text
Identify	the author's point of view or the reader response expected by the author
Identify	their own point of view and either defend or debate it against that of the author
Infer	reasons for the author's use of persuasive language
Demon-strate	an understanding of themes in texts and make critical analysis of them
Connect	and make value judgements between the themes and plots of various texts
Select	alternative titles or manipulate plots for different contexts
Demon-strate	an understanding of characters' motives
Analyse	the use and purpose of layout features and text conventions

Analyse	imagery to assist in deducing meaning
Identify	the authoritative source of information, ideas, points of view and purpose, and how these can affect the validity of the content and/or position of the writer
Identify	the facts that are chosen, left out and changed to form texts – for example, a scientific argument supporting an idea or belief system

Supporting comprehension skills

Direct instruction to support comprehension development includes what is referred to as the 'super six' (shown in **Figure 15.41**).

Figure 15.41 Teaching comprehension: the super six

Element	Approach and examples
Connecting	A process of shared thinking, includes sequencing, problem-solving, relating background knowledge **Teacher** > Provides explicit instruction to teach students to draw on their prior knowledge, or schema, as a strategy to help them comprehend a text **Students** > Make connections: – personal connections from the text with something in their own life (text-to-self) – for example, 'This text reminds me of the time I went on holiday to . . .' – connections with another text (text-to-text) – for example, 'This story is like an article I read about time travel' – connections with something in the known world (text-to-world) – for example, 'This text reminds me of the program I saw on TV about the child soldiers'
Predicting and inferring	Includes comparing and contrasting, drawing conclusions, envisioning, guessing what might happen based on visual/word clues **Teacher** > Draws on students' prior knowledge to make inferences and draw conclusions; asks open-ended questions: 'I wonder what/why/who/how/when/where', etc. **Students** > Use clues such as graphics, text and experiences to anticipate or predict the content of the text and to predict 'what might happen next' as they are reading
Questioning	Includes self-questioning **Teacher** > Models questions of the author, about the text and about own predictions, questions, and understanding of the text **Students** > Pose and answer questions that clarify meaning and promote deeper understanding of the text

Element	Approach and examples
Monitoring	Includes sequencing and checking for understanding **Teacher** > Focuses on the development of metacognition skills (students think about their own thinking): What do I understand? What am I unsure about? What can I do to help me understand? **Students** > Briefly explain or retell the story so far – for example, they can be taught a range of strategies, such as rereading to check for meaning, reading ahead to clarify their predictions, reviewing what they have read, discussing ideas with a peer
Visualising	Creating mental images or pictures **Teacher** > Shares own visual imagery or mental pictures invoked by the text. This may involve drawing on personal experiences **Students** > Visualise and describe a scene or image – for example, 'the cave dripping with purple and green slime'; 'hail hammering, smashing and ripping the roof'; 'the crowd, roaring with excitement as the ball flies towards the goals'
Summarising and synthesising	Identifying key ideas, facts and relevant details **Teacher** > Supports students to identify the key ideas or information contained in the text **Students** > Identify and accumulate the most important ideas and restate them in their own words – for example, 'Write three sentences that summarise this story.' 'In three minutes explain what this story is about to your partner.' 'List three to five facts contained in the story and three to five things you have inferred from the story.' > May use graphic organisers/story maps to illustrate concepts and interrelationships among concepts in a text, using diagrams or other pictorial devices such as maps, webs, graphs, charts, frames and clusters > Add new knowledge generated from the text to their existing knowledge.

Source: NSW Department of Education and Training (2010, pp. 5–6)

Students with effective comprehension skills can:

- understand the purpose of their reading, and so choose a suitable strategy for reading – such as skimming, scanning or reading carefully
- monitor their comprehension, so they can integrate what they are reading with their existing knowledge
- focus on the relevant parts of the text, and are able to distinguish major content from detail
- evaluate content as it is read.

Comprehension skills build over time and can be developed when students are engaged in discussion, questioning, retelling or recalling, summarising and identifying key points and points of interest (see **Figure 15.42**).

Figure 15.42 This student is demonstrating his comprehension skills

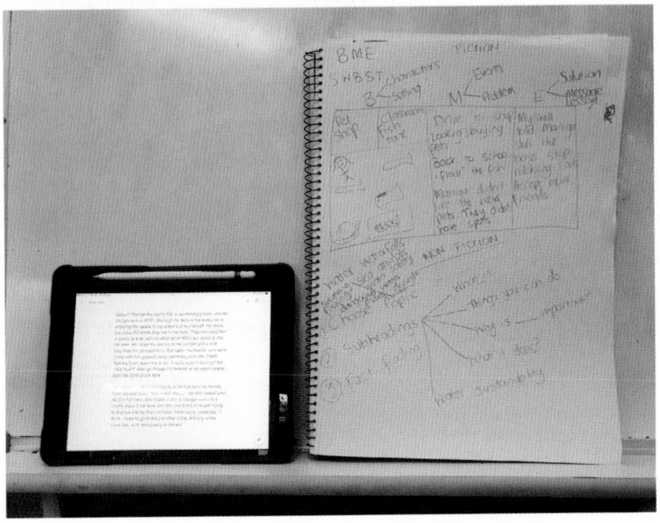

Source: Photo by Tish Okely © Cengage

CONSIDER THIS

LOOKING FOR CLUES: EXPLICIT INSTRUCTION OF COMPREHENSION – THE ABILITY TO READ WITH UNDERSTANDING

Students must be able to identify what they do understand and what they do not understand when reading text. Often a student will say *'I don't understand this/It doesn't make sense to me'*, when what the student means is that they don't understand *some parts of the text*.

Teach students to become detectives and to look for clues that will lead to a better understanding or comprehension of text. Clues may include:

- headings and subheadings
- pictures, diagrams and illustrations
- key words or phrases.

Look at the content that precedes or follows for clues. What are the main ideas? Can you use your background knowledge? Can you identify the key points/main facts?

Comprehension difficulties and high school students

Older students who struggle with comprehension may do so because they have poor word attack skills. As a consequence, student focus on decoding, and lose focus on understanding what they are reading. Students may also have a low level of fluency, which again means they will struggle to focus on the meaning of the text. Students with comprehension difficulties will also struggle to engage in higher-order skills such as interpreting, analysing and synthesising ideas and information, critiquing ideas and issues, and comparing and evaluating. ESWs should be aware that some students are skilled at masking their reading difficulties and as a result may reach high school without being identified as having learning needs.

Videos: Close reading

High school students are required to engage in close reading – that is, analyse and interpret what's in the text to extract and critically analyse the author's meaning.

Strategies that support the comprehension skills of older students include:

- *annotation* – supporting students to highlight or underline key words, phrases, headings and sub-headings, circle words, use question marks, make notes in the margin or on sticky notes, and draw pictures.
- *summarise paragraphs* – read the text aloud together, identify key words and their meaning, use open-ended questions to assist the student to summarise a paragraph or key idea by:
  - categorising information by using coloured pens to identify similar information
  - highlighting new/unfamiliar words – assist the students to explore the context in which the word occurs to help to identify its meaning
  - chunking – breaking complex sentences into shorter chunks (see **Figure 15.43**).
- *talk to the text* – this strategy requires the student to have a conversation with the text as though talking to a person. **Figure 15.44** describes how to 'talk to the text'.

Figure 15.43 An example of chunking

The four super heroes	raced to the cliff top	only to see	that the creature	had disappeared	into the mist

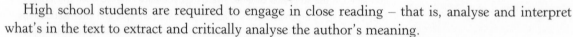

Figure 15.44 Talk to the text

Prediction and preview – use visual clues or what might already be known about the subject matter or author.
- I think you'll be telling me ...
- I already know things about you, so I predict ...

Briefly skim the text
- What are your headings, subheadings, images, diagrams, graphs and so on telling me?

Respond to the text while reading
- You're similar to what I've learned before, because you remind me of ...
- I would have preferred a picture of ... (Students can also sketch, describe, or download a picture, graph, or diagram)
- This is not what I expected, which was ...
- This gives me an idea for ...
- I want to know more about ...
- This information could be useful to me because I'm interested in ...
- I think this will be on the test because ...

According to Willis (2018) talking to the text will not only increase the 'student's pleasure, motivation, curiosity, and engagement, but will also develop stronger confidence in their own abilities as well as resilience, intrinsic motivation, and perseverance'.

It is important to be aware that older students may not know what questions to ask or may feel embarrassed to disclose that they are struggling with comprehension. Let the student know that every reader will, at times, come across unknown words or struggle to understand content (especially if it is unfamiliar or written in formal/academic language). The comprehension strategies are tools that students can use in all subject areas and are also important life skills.

Video: Teaching annotation and context clues

15.3 The role of the ESW: supporting reading in the classroom

Learning to read with understanding is a complex and challenging task that occurs over an extended period of time. Supporting reading development is a collaborative process between the reader and the listener (teacher, ESW, parent). It requires a commitment from the student to make a genuine attempt to read and apply a range of reading strategies. It also requires the listener to support the student by asking questions, prompting and suggesting strategies to the student to help them problem-solve.

While the strategies used to support reading development essentially remain the same regardless of the student's age, the way in which information is conveyed will vary. It is important to be mindful that school-age children are becoming increasingly aware of their own abilities compared with their peers. Students who struggle with reading are very aware that they are not reading at the same level as most of their peers. This can lead to embarrassment, anger and resentment. Students can become reluctant readers because of a fear of failure and a sense of defeat, which can turn into a downward spiral: 'I can't read so I won't try. I don't try so my chances of learning to read are low'. This spiral increases the likelihood of developing poor self-esteem and low self-confidence, which may lead to behaviours such as being the class clown, acting out, distracting others and general uncooperative behaviours. Feeling like a competent learner is critical for every student. As part of your role as an ESW, it is essential to support self-confidence and a 'can do' attitude to learning. This can only occur when you build a relationship with students based on mutual trust and respect.

SCENARIO

Finn (15) has an awesome memory and can recall information shared with him with little error. During his subject selection discussion with his year level coordinator and ESW, he chose subjects that are practical and hands on – Performing Arts, Music and Drama were his three top choices.

When quizzed as to why he was selecting these subjects, Finn said they had far less reading and he was able to demonstrate his understanding, skills and knowledge rather than read and write about them.

WHAT DOES THIS TELL US?

Finn is a student who understands his areas of strength and is prepared to work towards these. The ESW and Careers teacher understand that by this level it is far better to have an engaged learner rather than a student who chooses not to comply with class requirements because reading and writing information are too difficult.

Supporting reluctant readers

It is considered best practice for the ESW to take some time to get to know their students before engaging in a direct support role. While the reality of school funding means that this may not always be possible, it is important to at least establish a rapport with students. You can also ask your teacher to provide you with as much information as possible about the students' strengths, interests and specific learning needs. There may also be an opportunity to meet with the parent/s. Taking time to learn about your students will assist you when planning activities.

SCENARIO

GETTING TO KNOW YOU

It is Term 3, and ESW **Zara Adams** has been appointed to the kindergarten room to work with **Elliott** (5 years), who is struggling with his literacy skills. Zara is introduced to the class, who are told that she is going to be coming in three days a week to help in the classroom: *'Mrs Adams will sometimes work with small groups and sometimes work with one student.'*

Zara is then introduced to Elliott. *'Elliott, please say hello to Mrs Adams. I'd like you to show her where we keep our readers, and then can you show her your writing workbook?'*

Zara sits with Elliott. *'Thanks for showing me around Elliott. It's a really nice classroom. What's your favourite thing to do in class?'*

Elliott: *'I like to play with the Lego and build space jet fighters.'*

Zara: *'Wow! That sounds like lots of fun. What do you like to do at home?'*

Elliott: *'I like to play cricket with my big brother and we play football and ride our bikes.'*

Zara: *'I have a dog at home named Jessie. Do you have any pets?'*

Elliott: *'We have a bird called Charlie, a cat called Rainbow and a dog called Dingo. We used to have a rabbit, but he died.'*

Zara: *'You've got a lot of pets. Maybe I could help you to write about them when we are working together?'*

Zara and Elliott continue to chat, and as they do so Zara is building up a picture of Elliott – his oral language skills, his likes and interests, and some family details. Zara has begun to develop a relationship with Elliott simply by asking questions and responding to his answers with genuine interest.

WHAT CAN ZARA DO WITH THIS INFORMATION ABOUT ELLIOTT?

Zara could plan reading and writing activities that focus on Elliott's interests. For example, she could incorporate the use of Lego in writing games; include topics such as football and cricket; or plan opportunities for mini breaks and/or take lessons outdoors, as Elliott likes outdoor play.

Building rapport with older students can be more challenging. It is important to be open, honest and genuine. Below, ESWs share their tips for working with older students.

> I always offer to shake the student's hand when I first meet them and formally introduce myself.
>
> I like to tell the student that I am really looking forward to working with them.
>
> If appropriate, I try to share some general information about myself – you know, things like my favourite footy team or my role as a surf lifesaver.
>
> I always start the lesson by getting the student to say something positive about their week. They tend to grumble at first but then I find they're looking forward to sharing good news with me.
>
> I try to only give genuine feedback – for example, 'Thanks for paying attention today. I really appreciate it when you work hard' or 'I'm disappointed you didn't put in your best effort today.'
>
> I try to notice and question body language: 'I see you rolled your eyes when I said, "Let's get started". What's that about?
>
> I like to set clear boundaries and expectations. I remind the student of these as needed and I try to be consistent in enforcing them.
>
> I make a point to start each day with a clean slate. I never carry over any negative emotions from a previous lesson. It's best to move forward.
>
> I try to make learning fun.

Students who are struggling readers will usually say they 'hate reading'. In essence, what they hate is being different from other students, feeling nervous, anxious or embarrassed when asked to read, being labelled, not being able to complete their schoolwork, finding ways to disguise their poor reading skills, and struggling to perform academically. As students mature, the anxiety associated with poor reading skills is likely to increase and become self-defeating: 'I can't read, so why bother trying?'

Having a conversation with struggling readers about attitudes and feelings towards reading can provide a great deal of information about the needs of the student and lead to more effective strategies to support reading. Like any other skill, learning to read requires an understanding of the whole child. In the following Scenario, Ellen has developed a reputation as a 'trouble-maker'. Ellen is a struggling reader who wants desperately to fit in with her peers. At this age, being part of the peer group is paramount. Being aware of and sympathetic to this stage of development is an important consideration when determining how best to support Ellen.

SCENARIO

Ellen (13 years) has developed a reputation for being disruptive and a troublemaker. Her English teacher, **Ms Brown**, can see that Ellen struggles with her reading. However, each time Ms Brown attempts to offer additional support, Ellen swears or makes rude comments about Ms Brown's clothing or appearance. Ms Brown is a new graduate and finds this behaviour rather intimidating. For now, Ms Brown decides she will ignore Ellen just to keep the peace.

WHY IS ELLEN REJECTING THE TEACHER'S HELP?

As a young adolescent, Ellen would be very concerned about fitting into her peer group. She would likely find it embarrassing to be singled out from her peers as having reading difficulties. Being disruptive in class and deflecting attention away from her reading may be Ellen's way of coping with her reading difficulties.

▶ DISCUSSION

Older students will often try to hide their lack of skills by acting out in some way. Discuss why it is important for educators to be sensitive to students' feelings of inadequacy, embarrassment or lack of confidence. What might be a way in which Ms Brown could support Ellen without embarrassing her in front of her peers?

CONSIDER THIS

READER SELF-ASSESSMENT FORMS

In reader self-evaluation, students used a standard form to self-assess and record their reading fluency. **Figure 15.45** shows an example.

Figure 15.45 Example of self-assessment form

My fluency self-evaluation

Name:	Date:		
What I read:			
My evaluation	**This needs more work**	**I am improving**	**I did a great job**
Accuracy: ▪ I read words correctly.	☐	☐	☐
Rate: ▪ I read at a good pace – not too fast and not too slow.	☐	☐	☐
Expression: ▪ I use my voice to create different tones.	☐	☐	☐
Punctuation: ▪ I remember to stop at a full stop and pause at commas.	☐	☐	☐
Phrasing: ▪ I read in smooth phrases.	☐	☐	☐
Intonation: ▪ I change the tone of my voice to match the text and make the text sound interesting.	☐	☐	☐
Stress: ▪ I stress key words.	☐	☐	☐

▶ DISCUSSION

Discuss how the use of a self-assessment form not only supports reading skills but also supports social and emotional development. Why might this be important?

A self-assessment checklist for struggling readers can assist students to reflect on their feelings as readers and is an effective way to engage students in examining how their feelings about reading may be impacting their reading progress. A visual questionnaire developed by Kay Dean (1993), from the University of Newcastle in New South Wales, is an example of a simple but very effective and non-threatening way to assess students' attitudes towards reading (see **Figure 15.46**). The short questions can be read to the student, who is able to indicate their response by pointing to or circling a face symbol that indicates a feeling – happy, okay, not sure and worried.

Students who struggle with reading will require ongoing intervention using explicit, direct instruction to acquire the knowledge and skills necessary to be independent readers. Strategies that can be used to support students include:

- introducing new skills and knowledge in a timely manner by building on existing skills and knowledge (scaffolding)
- clearly identifying the level of achievement/mastery required by the student

Figure 15.46 The student's attitude towards reading

How do you feel when your teacher asks you to read aloud?	
How do you feel about your reading skills?	
How do you think your teacher feels about your reading skills?	

- providing regular opportunities for systematic revision and practice
- providing timely and specific corrective feedback to the student
- employing systematic monitoring and documentation of student progress
- sourcing reading material that is age-appropriate and of interest to the student.

For struggling readers to feel they are progressing, goals must be broken down into small steps that allow for rapid mastery. You may recall from Chapter 12 a discussion on SMART goals. SMART goals may need to be reviewed on a weekly or daily basis. For example, when working on phonics it is more effective to start with simple sounds that can quickly be mastered, such as /b/, /m/ and /p/, rather than beginning with more complex sounds such as /sh/, /th/ or /sm/. Small, rapid steps will empower students as learners and promote an 'I can do it' attitude.

Working on SMART goals also provides greater opportunities for adults and students to work collaboratively. As the student achieves mastery of one SMART goal, they can contribute to setting the next mini-goal.

Commencing each lesson with systematic revision and practice of previously achieved goals is an effective learning strategy. Reinforcing existing skills and knowledge helps students to make links with what they already know and are able to do, and move ahead to more advanced skills – for example, 'I can identify /b/, /m/ and /p/; now I'm going to learn to identify harder sounds like /sh/, /sp/ and /th/'. Practice builds confidence and provides opportunities for students to apply their knowledge and skills in different contexts.

SMART GOALS

SCENARIO

In six weeks, **Tom** (13 years) will be able to say the 100 sight words chart automatically with no hesitations or self-corrects.

In three weeks, **Amy** (15 years) will be able to highlight five key words in three subjects: English, Music and Science, with support in these lessons.

In three weeks, **Hayley** (14 years) will increase her concentration on reading tasks from five minutes to 10 minutes with support.

Giving explicit instruction

ESWs will be guided by the classroom teacher to provide reading instruction to individual students and small groups. This chapter has explored a range of strategies to provide explicit reading instruction. To be effective, explicit instruction should be given in small, manageable steps, and reflect the age, development and reading skills of each student. Never make assumptions about a student's understanding – always check: 'Now it's your turn. Show how you …. Tell me what you would do if you don't know a word.'

When introducing new information, try to do so by scaffolding and building on students' existing knowledge to acquire new knowledge – for example, 'I know you can identify the first sound in a word, now we're going to work on listening to and identifying the last sound in a word. Remember when we worked on first sounds I said the word first and then you said the word and then I said it again?' Introduce new concepts one at a time and ensure mastery before moving on to a new concept. This means assisting students to consolidate their knowledge. This can be achieved when students are given multiple opportunities to practise the application of their knowledge in various contexts to ensure it has been generalised.

A wide range of explicit instruction strategies can be used, some of which have already been explored in this chapter. Determining the most effective strategies will depend on the needs of the individual student, the student's age and their abilities. The following list provides a summary of common key strategies. As you gain experience in teaching reading, you will be able to match these and other strategies to individual student needs:

- Read it with your finger – the student points to each word as they read aloud.
- Use coloured highlighters to isolate/highlight each word in a sentence.
- Point to each word as the student reads, pause when an error is made, give the student time to correct the error and/or prompt the student.
- Say the word, tap/clap the syllables.
- Cover the word that has been misread – ask the student to read the sentence and try to work out the missing word.
- Practise working with punctuation: 'I want you to pause every time you see a full stop.'
- If a sentence is misread, ask the student, 'Does that make sense? Let's reread that sentence.'
- Isolate one or two words with two fingers – this allows the student to focus on specific words in isolation from the whole text.
- Construct and deconstruct – the student dictates a sentence which the ESW writes on a piece of paper. Have the student cut the sentence into single words and place these in an envelope; now have the child remove each word, read it aloud and finally reconstruct the sentence.
- Create a personal dictionary/vocabulary – the student builds their own list of new words, which can be revised daily.
- Create personal word banks and flash cards based on the student's interests.
- Have the student use highlighter pen to identify challenging words, which can be added to their personal dictionary.

Listening to students read

An important part of the ESW's role is listening to students reading aloud and providing timely and appropriate support to the reader. *Listening* to a student read requires you to undertake a number of tasks that will allow you to provide feedback, document the student's progress, identify errors and use this information for future planning. These tasks will be carried out *before reading begins,* while the student is reading and when the student has completed the reading task. Students can be supported by the ESW keeping a student reading checklist, as shown in **Figure 15.47**.

Figure 15.47 Reading observation checklist

OBSERVING AND SUPPORTING STUDENT READING: CHECKLIST	
BEFORE READING BEGINS, NOTICE AND DOCUMENT IF THE STUDENT:	
▪ Asks questions or makes any comments about the text: this may demonstrate if the student is able to contextualise the text by identifying features such as title, illustrations, author, headings within the text, key or known words, or similarity to other texts.	☐
▪ Makes predictions: For example, '*I think this book is going to be funny because the dog ends up on the roof.' 'I think this book will have lots of good information about sharks. It's got lots of great photographs and labels.*'	☐
▪ Shows a strong positive or negative response to the reading task: Is the student enthusiastic, confident, ambivalent, anxious or cautious?	☐
The attitude students have towards reading will be a significant influence on their progress as readers.	
WHILE THE STUDENT IS READING, NOTICE AND DOCUMENT IF THE STUDENT:	
▪ Scans each page before reading.	☐
▪ Makes comments about illustrations/photographs/diagrams.	☐
▪ Makes comments to show they're able to draw on prior knowledge.	☐
▪ Uses finger or other aid to track words.	☐
▪ Tracks words with their eyes only.	☐
▪ Notices and uses punctuation correctly by pausing or using voice intonation.	☐
▪ Uses self-correction.	☐
▪ Rereads a sentence or phrase to clarify meaning. For example, '*Alice thought that making a kite would be /sample/. No, Alice thought that making a kite would be /s/im/ple. Alice thought that making a kite would be /simple/.*'	☐
▪ Omits words.	☐
▪ Substitutes unknown words for a word with a similar meaning. For example, '*Jock thought his joke was /funny/ (instead of /hilarious/).*'	☐
▪ Guesses words at random by using visual clues such as the first letter. For example, s/ample, instead of s/imple.	☐
▪ Decodes by sounding out words. For example, correctly identifies beginning and end sounds, recognises common letter patterns such as ough, th, tion, blends sounds to decode whole words.	☐
▪ Reads on when difficult words or phrases are encountered; *or*	☐
▪ Slows down or stops when a difficult word is encountered. For example, looks to adult for help. Does the student respond when asked '*What word do you think it is? What does it start with? What do you think might come next in the story? What makes sense? Look at the picture; does it give you any clues? Can you think of another word that looks like that? What is the word telling us about? What can you do to try to work out the word? You said ______ ; does that sound right?*'	☐
▪ Reads with appropriate fluency and expression; *or*	☐
▪ Reads with poor fluency – pauses, stops, runs sentences together, ignores punctuation.	☐
▪ Demonstrates comprehension of the text by responding appropriately when asked, *What has happened so far? What information have you found out so far about sharks?'*	☐
▪ Makes few errors.	☐
▪ Makes frequent errors.	☐
▪ Reads most high-frequency words.	☐
AFTER READING, NOTICE AND DOCUMENT IF THE STUDENT:	
▪ Recalls and describes the main characters, setting, plot, key events or key information. Offers critical comments. For example, '*The story was interesting, funny, scary.' 'The information was easy/hard to understand.*'	☐
▪ Assesses own performance. For example, 'That was easy for me to read' or '*That was really hard to read. I sounded out the hard words.*'	☐
▪ Makes comparisons with other texts. For example, '*This book is like the one I read about seahorses. I think the other book has more information about rocks than this one.*'	☐

Giving timely corrective feedback

Providing timely and specific corrective feedback to students is critical for struggling readers. Modelling, demonstrating, correcting and explaining are most successful when the student is engaged in the learning process – for example, 'Let's look at this sentence more closely, Callie [10 years]. You said, "The dog barked loudly." Look at this word – what sound does it start with? That's right, it's /s/. What sound does "loudly" start with? Yes, "loudly" starts with /l/. I want you to sound out this word: /s/av/age/ly – "savagely". Good, now read the sentence again. Well done. It says "The dog barked savagely."'

In this example, the feedback is timely because it occurs as the student is reading. It is specific because it addresses the student error. It is corrective because it points out the error and provides a strategy to correct the error. It provides an explanation – the incorrect word does not start with /l/. This strategy also encourages students to attend to detail rather than make assumptions or guesses, and it reinforces Callie's existing skills and knowledge, which she was able to draw upon to correctly read the word 'savagely'. The student and the teacher have worked collaboratively to achieve the desired outcome.

Hattie (2012) suggests that the goal of feedback must be to provide students with insight that helps them to improve their performance. This, says Hattie, requires the educator to:

1 tell the student about their current level of performance – what the student does well and areas for improvement. For example, 'You are very good at recognising the beginning sound of words and now you need to work on recognising the final sound in a word'.
2 tell the student what they can do to improve their performance – this can be used as a goal-setting tool. For older students this can be set as a challenge for them to work towards.

Hattie (2012) suggests there are four key levels of effective feedback:

- level of feedback 1: Task and product
- level of feedback 2: Process level
- level of feedback 3: Self-regulation or conditional level
- level of feedback 4: Self-level.

GO FURTHER

Explore Hattie's four levels of effective feedback in your Go Further resource, available through your instructor.

Video: Hattie's visible learning and feedback

When providing corrective feedback, it should be designed to give the student information that they can use in the 'here and now'. The ESW should think about:

- using the pause-prompt-praise method – give the student time to think and self-correct, prompt self-correction effort, praise self-correction efforts
- speaking in a respectful manner to the student
- ensuring the feedback is easy for the student to understand – keep it simple and to the point
- giving one piece of feedback at a time and checking for understanding and allow time for the student to respond or ask questions
- where possible, following the 'just in time' principle – give feedback as the student is working (if appropriate)
- including demonstration and examples as well as verbal explanations
- offering opportunities for practice
- ensuring student privacy (if needed).

Assisting with targeted reading assessment

Throughout the year, the teacher may direct the ESW to assist in undertaking a range of targeted reading assessment strategies. Strategies used will vary according to teacher preference, age and grade. Targeted assessment strategies include:

- comprehension and accuracy
- cloze assessment
- phonology assessment
- semantic assessment
- syntactic assessment
- miscue analysis
- decoding skills.

GO FURTHER

Explore these targeted reading strategies and access further online reading resources in your Go Further resource, available through your instructor.

Reading strategies and assessment

Ongoing monitoring and documentation

Teachers may ask ESWs to systematically monitor and document individual student progress. The tools used for documentation will be determined by the teacher. ESWs may also engage in informal monitoring strategies, which may include:

- *anecdotal records* – objective documentation of what the student did and said, and how the student performed
- *authentic tasks that provide the student with opportunities to demonstrate specific reading skills* – for example, reading a recipe or reading instructions for a game
- *use of checklists or charts* to record student outcomes
- *discussion with students* to explore their perceived strengths and areas for improvement
- *contracts and contract reviews* – the ESW and student agree on tasks/goals, and review these at set intervals
- *informal reading games* – these allow for observation of reading skills
- *student portfolios* – a collection of the student's work, which shows outcomes of reading skills (adapted from ACT Cross Sectoral Assessment Working Party, 2016).

Systematic documentation is particularly useful in identifying progress, persistent errors or problems, and can be used to direct or modify SMART goals. Typically, teachers will provide ESWs with various checklists and templates to record reading progress. These templates may be developed by the teacher or may be commercially sourced. **Figure 15.48** provides an example of the types of documents that may be used to record student reading.

Where appropriate, documentation of student progress can be shared with the student – this provides opportunities for the student to engage in reflection and goal-setting.

As well as identifying progress, regular monitoring and documentation inform instructional planning. This is important – especially where progress is not adequate to meet desired learning outcomes. The teacher will have a system to monitor and record each student's reading progress. Systems will vary among teachers, schools and grade level. It is important to take the time to familiarise yourself with the system used and work with the teacher to identify the information you are required to document to contribute to the record-keeping system.

As with any student-related documentation, always follow the school's policy and procedures for privacy and confidentiality.

GO FURTHER

Learn more about anecdotal observation by an ESW to assess literacy skills in your Go Further resource, available through your instructor.

GO FURTHER

Access extra reading record examples and a scenario with an example of sharing documentation of student progress with a student in your Go Further resource, available through your instructor.

Figure 15.48 Reading record example

Small group names: Perri Mardi Jordan	**Date:** 21/07/xx
Goal:	To read fluently with 90 per cent accuracy.
What we will work on:	▪ Increasing fluency ▪ Pausing at punctuation ▪ Using inflection in voice
Text used:	Extract from reader – 'The Skate Park'
Perri	▪ Read fluently – no errors ▪ Excellent comprehension ▪ Voice monotone
Follow-up	▪ Work on inflection in voice
Mardi	▪ Tried to read quickly but made 13 errors ▪ Good comprehension despite errors ▪ Needs to work on accuracy
Follow-up	▪ Focus on accuracy
Jordan	▪ Found text very challenging ▪ Needed help with 21 words
Follow-up	▪ Focus on word attack skills

Working with Aboriginal and Torres Strait Islander students

Aboriginal and Torres Strait Islander

According to Creative Spirits (2018):

> the **literacy rate gap** between Aboriginal students and non-Aboriginal students is 'large and persistent' (SBS, 2015), and varies greatly depending on remoteness. Across Australia in 2015, 78.7 per cent of Aboriginal students and 95.6 per cent of non-Aboriginal students achieved the literacy benchmark for Year 3; however, in the Northern Territory, only 42.5 per cent of Aboriginal students achieved the benchmark. The numbers are similar for numeracy in Year 3.

Literacy rates among Aboriginal students are lowest in remote communities. Reasons include low literacy of the parents and poor school attendance. Initiatives like the Accelerated Literacy Program try to bring literacy to a similar level to that of their non-Aboriginal peers (Creative Spirits, 2021).

Low literacy rates, it is thought, can be attributed to failure to provide literacy instruction to previous generations, resulting in whole families with poor literacy skills. They can also be attributed to the way literacy is taught, which does not consider the cultural and learning context of Aboriginal and Torres Strait Islander students. Parents and grandparents from the Stolen Generations remain suspicious of white institutions and may, therefore, refuse to enrol children in school.

Cultural differences mean that Aboriginal and Torres Strait Islander students may not respond to the classroom environment and learning strategies in the same way as other

Australian students. For example, Aboriginal and Torres Strait Islander children are taught not to make direct eye contact with adults, as it is considered disrespectful, which is in contrast to the behaviour expected of non-Aboriginal and Torres Strait Islander students. Aboriginal and Torres Strait Islander students also tend to be shy around unfamiliar adults, so are unlikely to engage in classroom discussion or volunteer an answer to a teacher's question. Learning in Aboriginal and Torres Strait Islander cultures is oral and visual, with storytelling being the main way information is passed from one generation to the next. Aboriginal and Torres Strait Islander children are more likely to remain silent if they are struggling with a concept. This is because they may feel a sense of shame.

It is important not to make assumptions or to generalise when working with Aboriginal and Torres Strait Islander students; however, it is reasonable to assume that they may feel disadvantaged and/or isolated because they form part of a minority group. To support inclusion, there needs to be a genuine attempt to reflect cultural diversity so that students see images of their culture within the school environment. Aboriginal and Torres Strait Islander students typically have a strong sense of community, and older children are expected to care for and teach younger children in the immediate and extended family. Kinship ties are quite complex in Aboriginal and Torres Strait Islander families – for example, Aboriginal and Torres Strait Islander children will refer to many people as 'Auntie' or 'Uncle'.

Sadly, domestic violence, alcohol abuse and child abuse/neglect are common in Aboriginal and Torres Strait Islander families (Australian Institute of Health and Welfare, 2022). Aboriginal and Torres Strait Islander children are more likely to experience out-of-home care than other Australian children. This can lead to high levels of anxiety, mistrust, poor school attendance rates and, ultimately, higher failure and drop-out rates than for other students.

Like all students, Aboriginal and Torres Strait Islander students must be treated with dignity and respect so that they can reach their full potential.

CONSIDER THIS

MIND THE GAP

- The Australian Early Development Census National Report (2018) reports that Aboriginal and Torres Strait Islander children were twice as likely (41%) as non-Indigenous children to be developmentally vulnerable on one or more domains and 26 per cent more developmentally vulnerable in two or more domains. The gap between Aboriginal and Torres Strait Islander children and non-Indigenous children has continued to close; however, many Aboriginal and Torres Strait Islander children remain developmentally vulnerable.
- Being developmentally vulnerable at school entry places children at greater academic risk, particularly in relation to literacy.

Source: Australian Early Development Census National Report 2018. Canberra ACT ©2019 Commonwealth of Australia. https://www.aedc.gov.au/resources/aedc-results

Reading and English language learners

The Australian Early Development Census (2021) reports that 26.8 per cent of children were classified as having a language background other than English. This included Aboriginal and Torres Strait Islander children for whom English is a second language. While around 25 per cent of primary and secondary school students learn English as an additional language or dialect, in some schools this figure can be as high as 90 per cent (ACARA, n.d.c) AC. This information tells us that around 25 per cent of children entering school and 25 per cent of students already attending school speak a language other than English at home.

It has been a long-held belief that students for whom English is an additional language or dialect (EAL/D) will be disadvantaged in terms of reading development. However, the research on whether or not EAL/D students are disadvantaged when it comes to learning to read is mixed.

Ford (2005) says we know that alphabet knowledge and phonological awareness are strong predictors of successful literacy development in children. Ford found that phonological awareness skills developed in the student's home language transfer to and facilitate literacy development in English. This allows children to learn to read in both their home language and in English. Of particular importance to EAL/D students when learning to read is a focus on vocabulary, listening comprehension and syntax.

A 2003 study by Nonie Lesaux (Harvard Graduate School of Education), found that children who speak English as a second language (ESL) are not necessarily at a disadvantage in terms of reading development. The study found that by the end of second grade, the ESL children had attained reading skills that were similar to, and in some cases better than, their native English-speaking peers. Lesaux found that supporting a student's first language will help the student learn to read in English.

What these and many other research findings tell us is that EAL/D students may face additional challenges when learning to read but will not necessarily be disadvantaged. This supports the belief that each student's development and learning needs are unique. Facilitating reading development, like any other milestones, must be supported by planning for and meeting the needs of each learner.

Summary

Learning to read is a complex social and cognitive task that is underpinned by oral language and requires explicit, direct and sequenced instruction, daily practice and timely support. Worldwide research of evidence-based best practice confirms that the big six (oral language, phonemic awareness, phonological awareness, vocabulary, fluency and comprehension) are the essential elements of successful reading programs. Research also confirms that students benefit most from effective reading instruction that is systematic, balanced and explicitly teaches to the elements of the big six. To be effective in supporting reading development, it is important to have a sound knowledge of the big six and be familiar with the strategies used to support each element.

It is also important to be aware that each student will develop reading skills at their own unique pace and along the way may require a range of intervention strategies to consolidate the skills and knowledge necessary to become a confident, independent reader.

Self-check questions

1 What are the stages of writing and reading?
2 What is the Four Resources Model in relation to the big six?
3 What is phonemic awareness, and how can it be supported?
4 What are the benefits of shared reading for students and teachers?
5 Explain guided reading and the role of the teacher in this type of reading.

6 In which type of reading do students read for pleasure, select their own books and read about topics or subjects in which they are interested?

7 Define reading fluency and list its three components.

8 Describe critical analysis skills.

9 As an ESW, how could you support reading in the classroom?

Discussion questions

1 Beth is working through reading her new book. As she reads, she has not been taught blends so is trying to decode the following sounds /k/ /h/ /a/ /i/ /r/.

   a What is the word and what would the blend be in this word?

2 You are working in the Grade 3 room with students who are not able to hear syllables in the words they say.

   a What is a strategy you could use to help the children break up the syllables?

Activities

1 Investigate what reading 'programs' are within the schools where you have worked. Discuss the costs and benefits with your peers.

Chapter 16

SUPPORTING NUMERACY DEVELOPMENT

GO FURTHER

Go Further icons link to extra content for this chapter. Ask your instructor for the **Go Further** resource and deepen your understanding of the topic.

Online resources icons refer to useful weblinks. Ask your instructor for these **Online Resources.**

LEARNING OBJECTIVES

When you have completed this chapter, you should be able to demonstrate that you can understand and apply your knowledge of the numeracy curriculum to:

16.1 support students to develop core numeracy concepts as directed by the classroom teacher

16.2 support students to develop and apply the language of mathematics

16.3 implement numeracy activities as directed by the classroom teacher

16.4 document the numeracy development of students as directed by the classroom teacher

16.5 identify, monitor and support students with difficulties in mathematics.

Introduction

This chapter provides you with an overview of the Australian Curriculum: Mathematics (V9.0) (Australian Curriculum, Assessment and Reporting Authority [ACARA], 2023f AC). It provides examples of curriculum content and the General Capabilities (Numeracy) from Foundation to the Senior curriculum. In your role as an education support worker (ESW), you will not be expected to know or perform many of the higher-order mathematical skills. However, you will be expected to be familiar with the progression of numeracy skills as they are introduced from Foundation to Year 10.

Importantly, this chapter also focuses on an exploration of the basic concepts, underpinning skills, knowledge and concepts needed for numeracy development. While learning about the mathematics curriculum, you should reflect on your knowledge of cognitive development and theories of learning. Remember that knowledge and skills are cumulative, developed over a long period of time, and new knowledge and skills are built on existing knowledge and skills. This last point is particularly important as it is critical to review and establish foundation knowledge of key numeracy concepts (counting, quantity, addition, subtraction, division and multiplication) before introducing new knowledge and skills.

As you explore the numeracy curriculum, you will notice that the terms 'numeracy' and 'mathematics' are often used interchangeably (see **Figure 16.1**).

Figure 16.1 Mathematics versus numeracy

Mathematics	Numeracy
• Mathematics is the study of measurement, properties and relationships of quantities and sets using numbers and symbols. • Mathematics is the formal and broad study of the sciences of numbers, quantities, geometry and form.	• Numeracy is the individual's ability to reason and apply simple numerical concepts. • A person's literacy in mathematics.

Source: Pediaa (2020). Difference between mathematics and numeracy. https://pediaa.com/difference-between-mathematics-and-numeracy

This chapter looks at how ESWs can support numeracy development and explores the importance of using multisensory learning opportunities to support students struggling with numeracy.

Before you begin: exploring your mathematical knowledge

Mathematics tends to be a skill that polarises people – most people either love it or hate it. Those in the latter group might say, 'I was never any good at maths', 'I never saw the point of learning equations', 'I never use them in real life!' Sound familiar? Unfortunately, these people tend not to acknowledge that that they do, in fact, have quite sound numeracy skills, which they use every day – to buy groceries, pay bills, save for a holiday or explore the best deals from utility providers, for example.

Being confident when supporting students with mathematics is essential. If you lack confidence in your own mathematical skills, you may subconsciously transfer this to your students. Maths anxiety is very real, and is defined by Sabnani (2021) in Strong (2021) as 'any sense of anxiety when asked to do a mathematical task'.

When students experience maths anxiety it can become self-perpetuating – that is, 'I'm no good at maths, therefore there's no point in trying, therefore I get poor results'. Research has demonstrated that mathematics anxiety can interrupt working memory, leading to more error-making and reducing the capacity to successfully participate in mathematics. Teachers who experience higher levels of mathematics anxiety are less confident and more likely to avoid teaching mathematics when given the option (Gresham, 2018, in Victorian Government Department of Education and Training, 2021a, p. 3). **Figure 16.2** shows the outcome of maths anxiety.

Figure 16.2 Maths anxiety

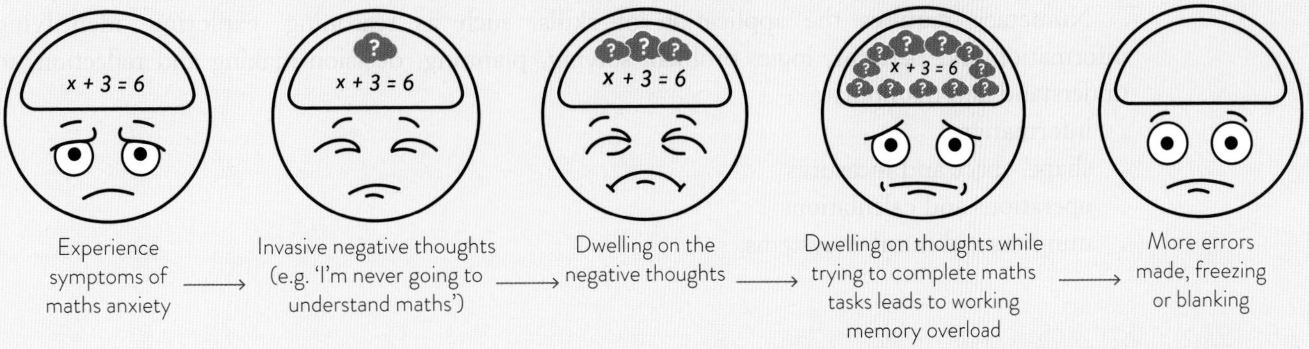
x + 3 = 6
x + 3 = 6
x + 3 = 6
x + 3 = 6
Experience symptoms of maths anxiety
Invasive negative thoughts (e.g. 'I'm never going to understand maths')
Dwelling on the negative thoughts
Dwelling on thoughts while trying to complete maths tasks leads to working memory overload
More errors made, freezing or blanking

Source: Adapted from: Victorian Government Department of Education and Training (2020). Mathematics anxiety. https://www.education.vic.gov.au/school/teachers/teachingresources/discipline/maths/Pages/research_overcomingmathsanxiety.aspx, p. 3

CONSIDER THIS

As an ESW, your role will be to work with the classroom teacher to support students to develop numeracy and mathematical knowledge and skills. To do this effectively, you should have a sound knowledge of each of the numeracy elements and sub-elements of the curriculum, how they are applied in practice and how you can demonstrate these applications to students.

If you fall into the 'I hate maths' category, you will need to reflect on all the ways you competently use maths every day and start telling yourself that maths is okay!

16.1 Numeracy development

Key maths concepts and maths anxiety

Numeracy development begins in early childhood when babies and toddlers begin to explore shapes, patterns, cause and effect, develop object permanence, match and sort like objects, understand words such as 'more', 'up, 'in', 'out' and learn to rote count. During the preschool years, working memory improves. Children begin to engage in symbolic thought, are able to sort and classify objects and things, understand the concept of conservation of length, volume and quantity; they begin to reason from particular to particular and recognise relationships of actions on objects and things, recognise numerals and match these to quantity, develop a basic understanding of time (yesterday, today, tomorrow, after lunch, etc.); they engage in symbolic thought and can substitute one thing to represent another thing; notice and begin to describe differences and similarities; and they apply their growing skills and knowledge in more complex ways (see **Figure 16.3**).

Being aware of the numeracy skills that begin to develop in early childhood allows you to better understand the skills and knowledge that most (but not all) children will have when entering formal schooling.

Numeracy development includes three types of knowledge:

1 **factual knowledge** – number facts that can easily be recalled, such as 2 + 2 = 4
2 **procedural skills** – knowing 'how to', such as pointing at each object when counting or using fingers to help count
3 **conceptual understanding** – knowing 'why', including understanding mathematical relationships – for example, understanding that addition and subtraction are opposite tasks.

The Australian Curriculum includes both mathematical knowledge – for example, knowing the times table, equations and number sense (knowledge) – and numeracy (application of mathematical knowledge). Numeracy is the ability to *apply* mathematical knowledge in a wide range of contexts.

Numeracy requires the application of skills, such as reasoning, exploring, identifying information and patterns, logic, problem-solving, planning, decision-making and reflection, to understand and manipulate:

- information
- shape, space and measures
- operations and calculations
- numbers and number systems.

Figure 16.3 Classroom displays support numeracy skills

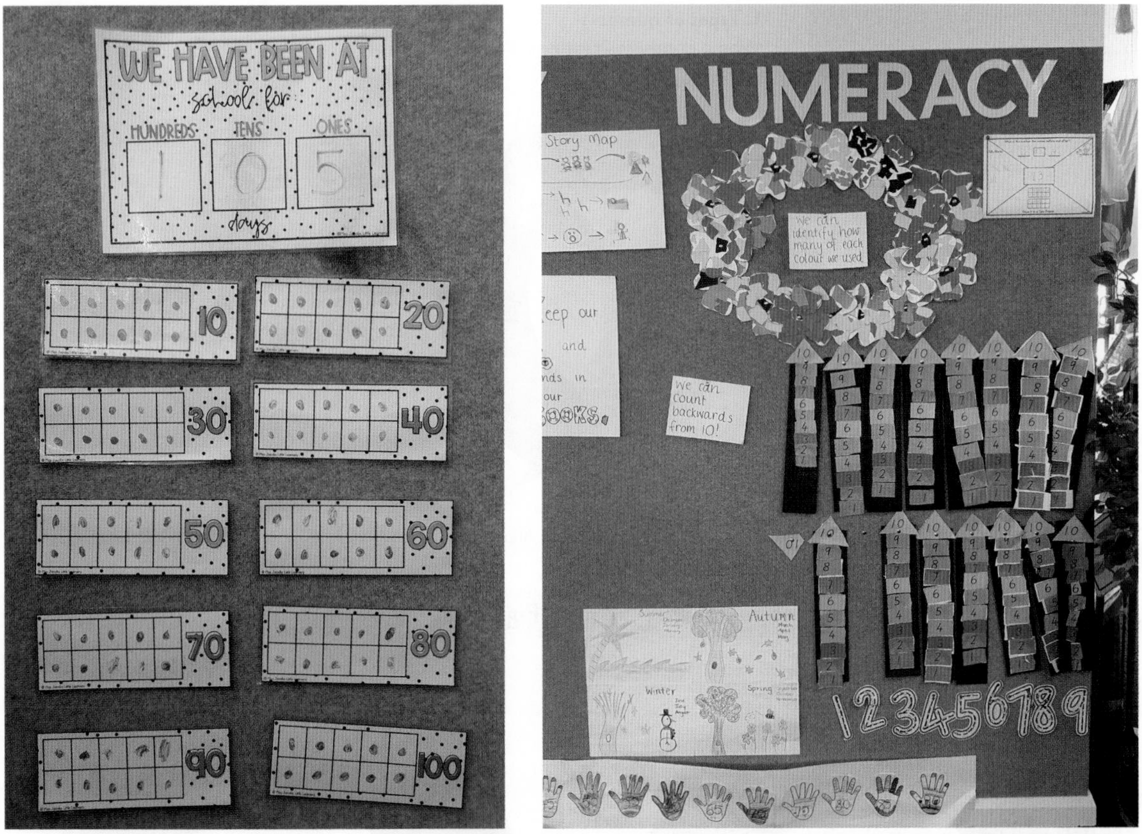

Source: Photos by Tish Okely © Cengage

Numeracy skills are shown in **Figure 16.4**, **Figure 16.5**, **Figure 16.6** and **Figure 16.7**.

Figure 16.4 Operations and calculation

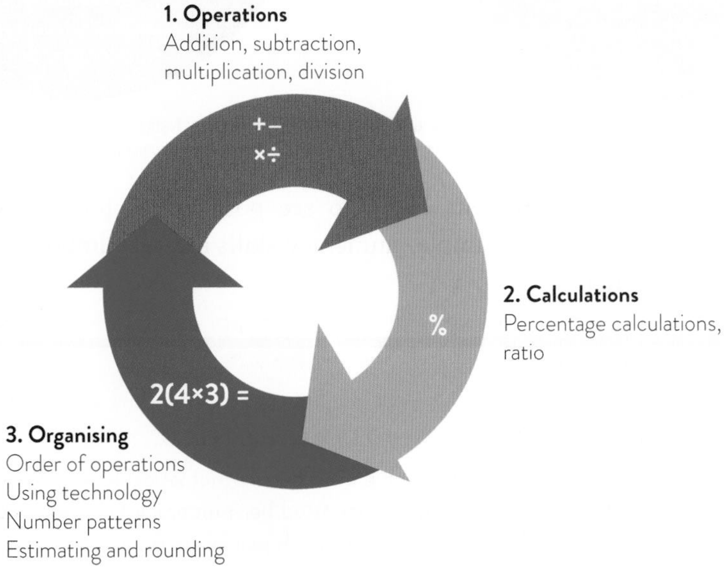

Source: National Numeracy (2023). The essentials of numeracy. https://www.nationalnumeracy.org.uk/what-numeracy/essentials-numeracy

Figure 16.5 Numbers

Source: National Numeracy (2023). The essentials of numeracy. https://www.nationalnumeracy.org.uk/what-numeracy/essentials-numeracy

Figure 16.6 Shape, space and measure

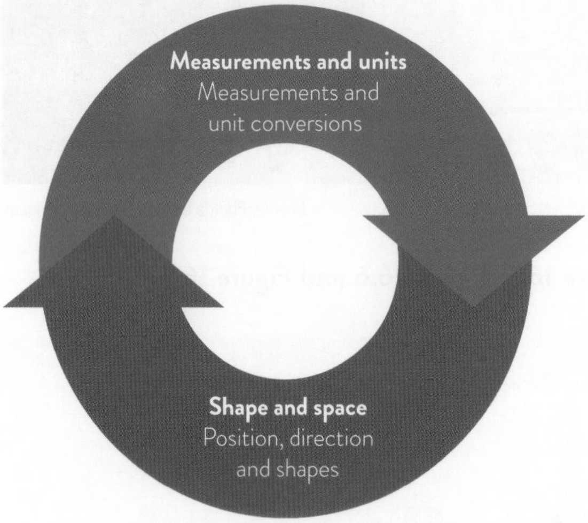

Source: National Numeracy (2023). The essentials of numeracy. https://www.nationalnumeracy.org.uk/what-numeracy/essentials-numeracy

Figure 16.7 Handling data

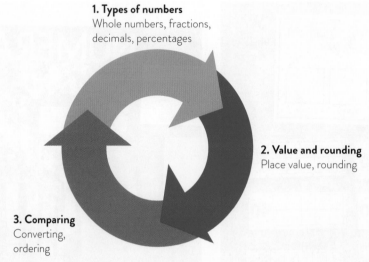

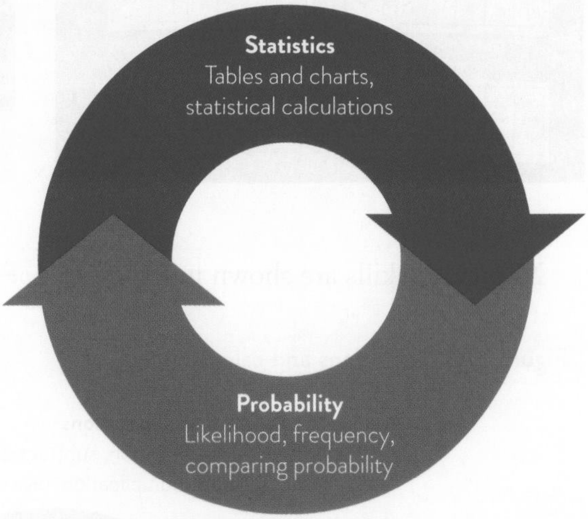

Source: National Numeracy (2023). The essentials of numeracy. https://www.nationalnumeracy.org.uk/what-numeracy/essentials-numeracy

How to improve your maths

Numeracy skills develop as students begin to see possibilities for applying mathematical knowledge in their daily lives – for example, numeracy skills are very important when dividing a bag of lollies between siblings!

SCENARIO

PAIRS

Zephie (5 years) tipped all of her earrings onto her bed, sorted them into pairs and counted how many pairs of earrings she owned. She announced to her mother: *'I have nine pairs of earrings and six other earrings.'*

WHAT DOES THIS TELL US?

Zephie used her mathematical knowledge of quantity and pairs. She used her numeracy knowledge to sort, match and count each pair of earrings. She showed that she understands what constitutes a matching pair and what is *not* a matching pair.

Zephie is likely to have developed this mathematical and numeracy knowledge informally through play, observation and real-life experiences.

SHARING

Dara and **Max** (9 years) are twins. They have each been given a bag of lollies by their grandmother and are busily sharing them so that they each have the same number of lollies. First, they count the lollies. There are 21. Each child takes a turn at selecting and placing a lolly into their own pile.

Dara: *'Now there's one left and I should have it because I'm older than you by three whole minutes!'*
Max: *'No! That's not fair. We have to share.'*
Dara: *'Well we can't because we can't break this one in half – it's too hard.'*
Max: *'I know – let's give that one to Gran. That would be fair to both of us.'*

WHAT DOES THIS TELL US?

Dara and Max demonstrate that they understand the concept of quantity, equal to and half. They also demonstrate that they are able to problem-solve.

The development of mathematical knowledge and numeracy skills and understanding requires the acquisition of:

- *facts* – for example, functions: addition, subtraction, division, multiplication
- *concepts and understanding* – for example, quantity, comparison, measurement, symmetry
- *strategies and procedures* – planning and problem-solving, evaluating, using computations such as addition or subtraction, identifying key information, sequencing, making inferences, applying existing knowledge, asking questions.

Foundational numeracy and algebra concepts include:

- one-to-one correspondence
- sorting, classifying, matching and ordering (patterns)
- basic number sense.

Mathematics and the Australian Curriculum (V9.0)

Mathematics provides students with essential mathematical knowledge, skills, procedures and processes in number, algebra, measurement, space, statistics and probability. It develops the **numeracy** capabilities that all students need in their personal, work and civic lives, and provides the fundamentals on which mathematical specialties and professional applications of mathematics are built.

Mathematics is presented in year levels for each year from Foundation to Year 10. Content is organised under six interrelated strands, as shown in **Figure 16.8** and described in **Figure 16.9**.

Figure 16.8 Mathematics strand

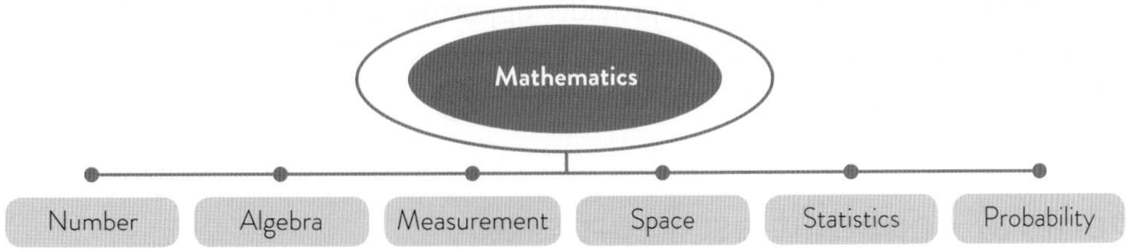

Source: Australian Curriculum, Assessment and Reporting Authority (ACARA) (2023f). Understand this learning area. Mathematics. https://v9.australiancurriculum.edu.au/teacher-resources/understand-this-learning-area/mathematics

Figure 16.9 Mathematics strand descriptors

Strand	Descriptor
 Number	The *Number* strand develops ways of working with mental constructs that deal with correspondence, magnitude and order, for which operations and their properties can be defined.
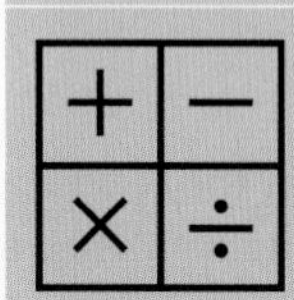 Algebra	The *Algebra* strand develops ways of using symbols and symbolic representations to think and reason about relationships in both mathematical and real-world contexts. It provides a means for manipulating mathematical objects, recognising patterns and structures, making connections, understanding properties of operations and the concept of equivalence, abstracting information, working with variables, solving equations and generalising number and operation facts and relationship.
 Measurement	The *Measurement* strand develops ways of quantifying aspects of the human and physical world. Measures and units are defined and selected to be relevant and appropriate to the context.
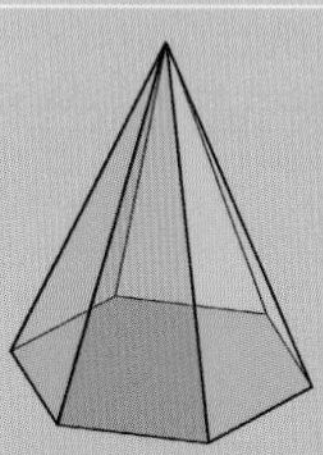 Space	The *Space* strand develops ways of visualising, representing and working with the location, direction, shape, placement, proximity and transformation of objects at macro, local and micro scales in natural and constructed worlds.
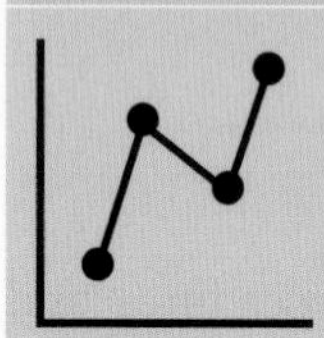 Statistics	The *Statistics* strand develops ways of collecting understanding and describing data and its distribution.
 Probability	The *Probability* strand develops ways of dealing with uncertainty and expectation, making predictions, and characterising the chance of events, or how likely events are to occur from both empirical and theoretical bases.

Source: Australian Curriculum, Assessment and Reporting Authority (ACARA) (2023f). Understand this learning area. Mathematics. https://v9.australiancurriculum.edu.au/teacher-resources/understand-this-learning-area/mathematics

Australian Curriculum: Mathematics

ACARA (2023f) states: 'Mathematics provides opportunities to integrate and connect content to other learning areas, in particular, Science, Technologies, The Arts, Humanities and Social Sciences (HASS) and Health and Physical Education'.

The general capabilities: Numeracy

The general capability Numeracy is organised into three elements:

- Number sense and algebra
- Measurement and geometry
- Statistics and probability.

The key ideas for numeracy are organised into six interrelated elements in the learning continuum, as shown in **Figure 16.10**.

Figure 16.10 General capability: Numeracy

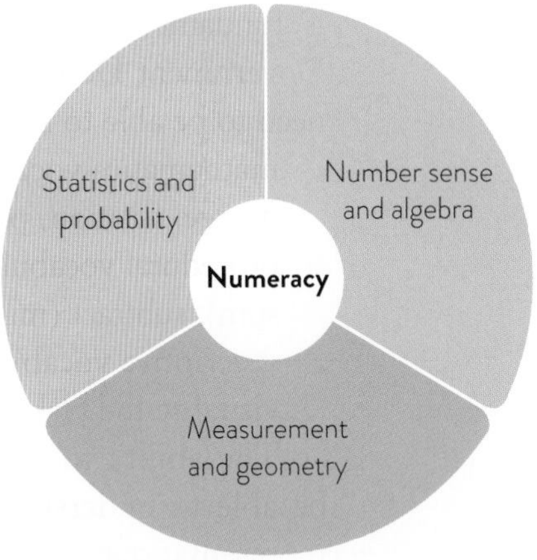

Source: Australian Curriculum, Assessment and Reporting Authority (ACARA) (2023e). Understand this general capability. Numeracy. https://v9.australiancurriculum.edu.au/teacher-resources/understand-this-general-capability/numeracy

The National Literacy and Numeracy Learning Progressions

The National Numeracy Learning Progression 'describes the observable indicators of increasing complexity in the understanding of, and skills in, key numeracy concepts. The numeracy progression includes the elements of Number sense and algebra, Measurement and geometry and Statistics and probability' (ACARA, 2020, p. 3). An example of the numeracy learning progression relating to money and measuring time is described in **Figure 16.11**. These progressions are also described under each element and sub-element in the General Capabilities: Numeracy section of the Australian Curriculum website: https://v9.australiancurriculum.edu.au.

Figure 16.11 National Numeracy Learning Progression (V3.0)

Understanding money	Measuring time
Face value	Units of time
Sorting money	Measuring time
Counting money	Relating units of time
Equivalent money	Converting between units of time
Working with money additively	Measuring time with large and small timescales
Working with money multiplicatively Working with money proportionally	Measuring how things change over time

Source: The National Numeracy Learning Progression © Australian Curriculum, Assessment and Reporting Authority (ACARA) V 3.0 March 2020.

16.2 The language of mathematics

General Capabilities: Numeracy in the Australian Curriculum

The Australian Curriculum: Mathematics introduces students to the language of mathematics. Initially acquired informally through play, exploration and talking to others, the language of mathematics develops over time. Consider the following examples:

- Two-year-old Nora holds out both hands and says, 'More please'. When she has eaten both cubes of cheese, she announces, 'All gone'.
- Five-year-old Java is asked to share his sweets with his sister. He carefully sorts the sweets into two equal groups.
- Three-year-old Ellen is asked to put a cup next to each plate at the lunch table. Ellen demonstrates her understanding of one-to-one correspondence.
- Four-year-old Chelsea is asked to half-fill a small bucket with water.
- The preschool group sings 'Five Little Ducks', counting down from 5 to 1.

These examples demonstrate that by the time most children enter school, they have already acquired some mathematical language, which provides a foundation upon which to build their mathematical vocabulary. The Victorian Government Department of Education (2021a) states: 'Being able to interpret language in a range of mathematical contexts and for different purposes is fundamental to mathematical problem solving'. Di Gisi and Fleming (2005, in Victorian Government Department of Education, 2021a) describe three types of vocabulary that students need to be able to solve word problems:

- mathematics vocabulary, for example counting, **integer**, angle, volume, addition, per cent, degree, fraction, per cent, greater than, volume, etc.
- procedural vocabulary- language used to describe procedures such as counting-on, add (plus, sum), subtract (minus, fewer than, take away), multiply, apply, calculate, compare, analyse, etc.
- descriptive vocabulary – includes words or phrases that describe, explain or help students to visualise the task.

The ability to develop understanding and communicate mathematics requires students to be able to understand and correctly use notation, subject-specific language, conventions and representations.

One of the challenges in the acquisition of this vocabulary is the interchangeable language used to describe a single mathematical application – for example:

- *addition*: add, plus, total, sum of
- *subtraction*: take away, minus, subtract, less, difference between
- *multiplication*: multiple, times, groups of, lots of, multiply, product.

To avoid confusion, it is extremely important that the ESW clarifies with the classroom teacher the mathematical language being used in the classroom and ensures this is reflected in their interactions with students. Always clarify the students' understanding of mathematical language by asking a simple question – for example, 'What's another word we can use for "take away from"?'

SCENARIO

MINUS

Sienna (7 years) is new to the school. Her family has recently moved from interstate. Sienna's school records show that she is a bright student who achieves at above average in all curriculum areas.

This morning, the teacher gave the students a quick verbal maths quiz. The ESW was surprised to see that Sienna correctly answered all questions except those related to subtraction. When the ESW discussed the quiz with Sienna, she discovered that Sienna was not familiar with the term 'minus'. At her last school, she had only ever used the phrase 'take away from' in relation to subtraction.

MATHS SPEAK

ESW **Brian** is working with a group of Year 4 students.

'Today we are going to multiply two-digit numbers. Who remembers what we mean by the word "factor" when we are multiplying?

'Yes, that's right Dane. When we multiply one number by another number these numbers are called factors.

'Who can tell me what the product is?

'Great, Jess, it's the number we get when we multiply one number by another number.

'Here's a simple one: What does the "x" mean?

'Of course, it means times or multiply.'

WHAT DOES THIS TELL US?

Learning mathematical language, and its meaning and application, is an essential skill without which students are not able to participate in meaningful discussion of mathematics concepts.

Mathematical language

Conventions of mathematical language

A mathematical convention is a fact, name, notation, or usage which is generally agreed upon by mathematicians. For instance, the fact that one evaluates multiplication before addition in the expression. A mathematical language uses symbols, instead of words, to communicate mathematical ideas. The syntax and structure can be categorised into five forms:

1 numbers: 0, 1, 2,… (represent quantity; nouns in the alphabet)
2 operation symbols: +, -, *, ÷ (act as connectives in maths sentences)
3 relation symbols: =, ≠, <, ≤, >, ≥ (for comparison, act as verbs)
4 grouping symbols: ( ), [ ], { } (to associate groups of numbers and operators)
5 variables: *x*, *y*, *n*, *A*, *V* (letters to represent quantities; act as pronouns).

Mathematics has its own set of words and symbols that have been allocated a precise meaning that is applied in a universal manner. These words and symbols are used to express quantities, mathematical concepts and ideas and are referred to as mathematical conventions.

GO FURTHER

Explore mathematical conventions in your **Go Further** resource, available through your instructor.

Modelling mathematical language

Modelling mathematical language in the classroom is the most effective way to introduce students to new vocabulary. It is also important to encourage students to use mathematical vocabulary in context as they are working on their numeracy skills. In the Scenario 'Maths speak', the ESW quickly checks the students' prior knowledge of multiplication vocabulary.

Questioning is an effective way of supporting the use and understanding of mathematics vocabulary. Questioning usually occurs informally as students are engaged in tasks. Open-ended questions encourage students to apply their mathematical language in a meaningful context. Consider the following examples:

- How can we work out how many students are here today?
- What could we use to measure the length of the classroom?
- What method will you use to solve this problem?
- What numbers can you make with 1, 7 and 9?
- Are there the same number of even numbers and odd numbers between 11 and 33?
- How can you check to see whether you have the correct answer?
- How are you going to record each step?
- How did you get that answer?
- Can you visualise the ways you could represent the 12?

These types of questions challenge students' thinking and provide them with opportunities to verbalise mathematical ideas, problems and concepts.

CONSIDER THIS

THE LANGUAGE OF MATHEMATICS

Like all subject areas or disciplines, mathematics has its own language, and to be successful in mathematics, students must learn to use this language. They must know the terminology and understand how it is applied. This is not an easy task, however, and many students struggle with this language.

Mathematical language includes many words that sound the same as words with other meanings (or homophones), and many words with the same spelling as everyday words but different meanings as mathematical terms – for example:

- sum and some
- plain and plane
- mode and mowed
- pi and pie
- serial and cereal.

Source: Adams, Thangata and King (2005).

Mathematics also uses words in the English language that may already be familiar to students in their everyday lives but have very different meanings in a mathematical context (Meiers & Trevitt, 2010, pp. 6–7). Consider the examples shown in **Figure 16.12**.

Figure 16.12 Mathematical words and their homophonic everyday meaning

Mathematical term	Everyday meaning
Angle	Point of view
Figure	A female form
Odd	Strange
Order	To make a selection from a menu
Property	Something you own
Rational	Sane
Volume	Sound
Mean	Nasty
Pi	Pie

Word walls

As new mathematical vocabulary is introduced, it is important to explain or demonstrate its meaning, show students how the word/s are written (symbols and print) and add the vocabulary to the relevant word wall. Most primary classrooms will have a maths word wall, to remind students of mathematical vocabulary – an example is shown in **Figure 16.13**. Students may also have their own mathematical vocabulary dictionary to help them to remember words and meanings.

To assist students to make the connection between mathematics vocabulary and their application, word walls can be divided into a range of categories, such as numbers, counting,

Figure 16.13 Mathematics word wall

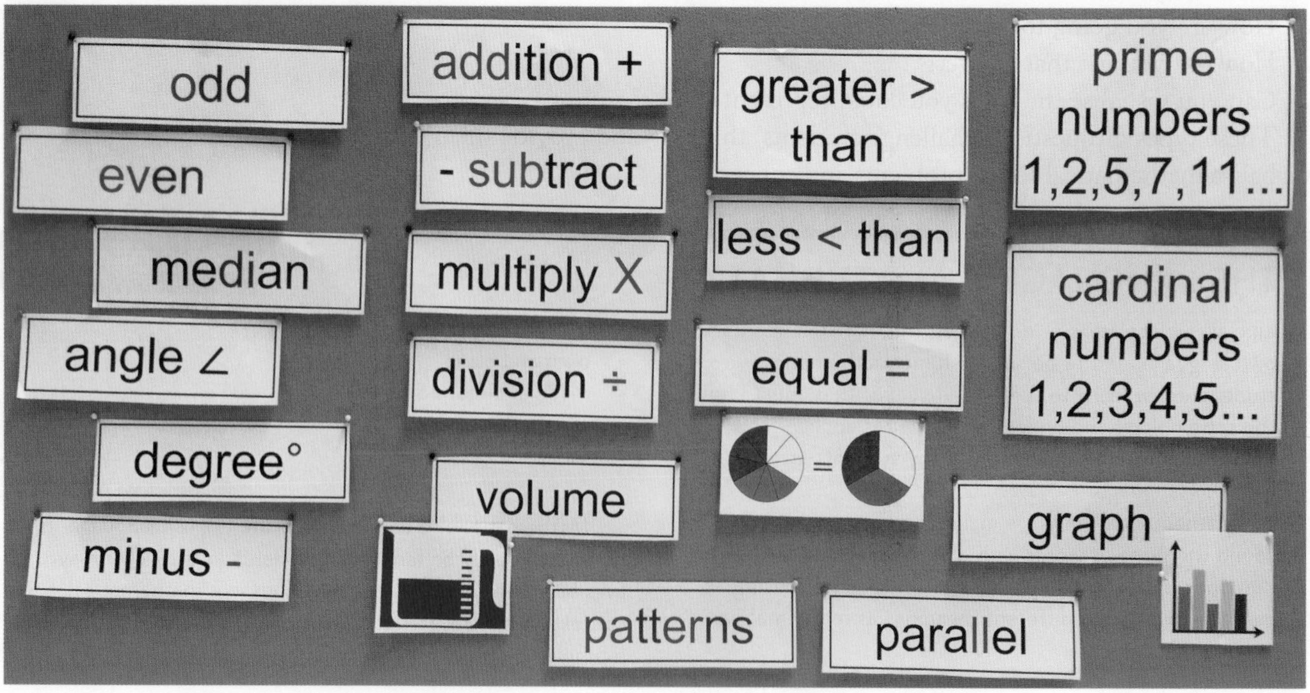

addition, subtraction, multiplication, measurement, patterns, shapes, position, direction, movement, calculations, decimals and fractions.

GO FURTHER

Explore some common terms used in maths word problems in your **Go Further** resource, available through your instructor.

Maths word problems

Maths word problems require students to read, understand and decode information and arrange the problem into a logical sequence of operations to solve the problem. Using concrete materials can assist students to work through the problem. As previously mentioned, as students progress through the curriculum they will be introduced to a range of mathematical terms. Knowing and understanding how these terms apply to maths problems is an essential skill.

Maths word problems

Number sense and algebra

16.3 Numeracy activities

Number sense and algebra

Understanding number sense and algebra begins with recognising and analysing patterns, studying and representing relationships, making generalisations, and analysing how things change (Seeley, 2004). Basic algebraic operations include addition, subtraction, multiplication and division. Later, students learn to manipulate numbers using various symbols and formulas to calculate unknown quantities and solve problems.

The general capability Numeracy element Number sense and algebra includes eight sub-elements, which are described in **Figure 16.14**.

Figure 16.14 General capability: Numeracy – Number sense and algebra sub-elements

Sub-element: Number and place value
This sub-element begins with number sense is the ability to understand numbers and number relationships:
> Students recognise, read, represent, order and interpret numbers within our place value number system, expressed in different ways.

Place value is the value of each digit in a number. For example, 421: 4 stands for four hundred, 2 stands for twenty and one stands for one: 400 + 20 + 1 = 421. In a hundreds chart 421 is represented as:

H	T	O
4	2	1

H: hundred
T: tens
O: ones

Sub-element: Counting processes
> Students are increasingly able to count both verbally, through the stable order of a counting sequence, and perceptually through counting collections.

> Counting sequence: count to 100 by ones and tens; counting forward (or counting on) from a given number; writing the numbers one to ten

1,2, _ 4, 5, _ 7_, 8, 9,10 _

> Understanding that the spoken and written names that are said and read have a fixed order.
> Understand one-to-one correspondence – each item is matched to a number in a counting sequence – the last number counted is the is the final quantity.
> Items counted can be physical or non-physical (e.g. the number of syllables in the word 'hippopotamus' = 5).
> The order in which a collection of objects is counted doesn't change the number of objects.
> The number of objects in a collection remains constant regardless of attributes such as colour, size, shape, etc.

Sub-element: Additive strategies

> Students are increasingly able to think additively, represent a wide range of additive situations, and choose and use computational strategies for different purposes.

Additive strategies are techniques used to solve addition problems from known facts by breaking up and recombining numbers to make addition easier. For example: 9+7 becomes 10+6=16; 47 +93 becomes 50+90=140.

Sub-element: Multiplicative strategies

> Students are increasingly able to think multiplicatively and use multiplicative strategies in computation to solve problems related to a range of multiplicative situations.

The properties of multiplication and division include commutative, distributive, zero, identity, closure and inverse.

Property	Meaning	Example
Commutative	Changing the order does not change the product (outcome)	7 × 2 = 2 × 7 14 = 14
Distributive	When one of the factors is rewritten as the sum of two numbers the product doesn't change.	12 × 3 = 6 × 3 + 6 × 3 36 = 36
Associative	Changing the grouping of factors doesn't change the product	(2 × 8) × 3 = (8 × 3) × 2 16 × 3 = 24 × 2 48 = 48
Inverse	The opposite of multiplication is division	18 × 3 = 54 54 ÷ 3 = 18
Zero	Any number multiplied by 0 equals zero	10 × 0 = 0 1000 × 0 = 0
Identity	Any number multiplied by 1; the product is the number itself	10 × 1 + 10 1000 × 1 + 1000
Closure	When two whole numbers are multiplied the product is always a whole number	5 × 3 = 15 7 × 7 = 49

Sub-element: Interpreting fractions

> Students are increasingly able to recognise the part-whole description of a fraction, but also recognise and use fractions as numbers, measures, operators, ratios and as a division.

Sub-element: Proportional thinking

> The ability to reason proportionally requires students to think multiplicatively and work with percentages, rates and ratios and proportions.

Proportional thinking involves thinking about relationships and making comparisons of quantities and values between two or more things. It involves the ability to consider numbers in different ways. Thinking proportionally requires an understanding of ratio.

Sub-element: Number patterns and algebraic thinking

> Students are increasingly able to identify and describe repeating and growing patterns in the environment and other everyday contexts

Understanding patterns is the foundation skill for algebraic thinking. In mathematics, patterns are a set of numbers arranged in a sequence such that they are related to each other in a specific rule. These rules define a way to calculate or solve problems.

There are two basic divisions to find out the rules in number patterns:

> When the numbers in the given pattern get larger, they are said to be in an ascending order. These patterns usually involve addition or multiplication.

> When the numbers in the given pattern get smaller, they are said to be in a descending order. These patterns usually involve subtraction or division.

Source: Patterns. https://www.cuemath.com/geometry/patterns

Examples of patterns:
> Number patterns: 2, 4, 6, 8, 10 (adding 2)
> Geometric patterns (division and multiplication): 3, 9, 27, 81
> Fibonacci Pattern (each number in the sequence is obtained by adding the two numbers before it, starting with the numbers 0 and 1) 0, 1, 1, 2, 3, 5, 8, 13

Sub-element: Understanding money
Addresses the financial numeracy skills which support students to become financially literate members of society.

Sources: Australian Curriculum, Assessment and Reporting Authority (ACARA) (2023b). General capabilities. Numeracy. Number sense and algebra (V 9.0). https://v9.australiancurriculum.edu.au/f-10-curriculum/general-capabilities/numeracy?element=0&sub-element=0

Place value

Place value is the value represented by a digit in a number on the basis of its position in the number. For example, (2,305) represents two thousands, three one hundreds, no tens and five ones. **Figure 16.15** shows a place value demonstrating the relationship between each place value moving from right to left.

Using a place value chart, students can show the value of each number. **Figure 16.16** shows the place value for 12,361.

Figure 16.15 Place value: example 1

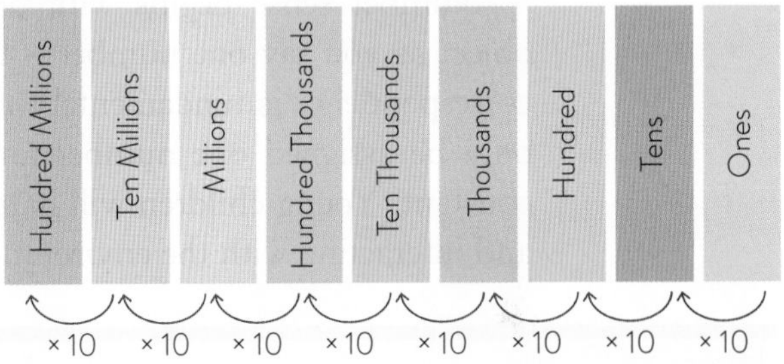

Source: Adapted from: SplashLearn (n.d.a). https://www.splashlearn.com/math-vocabulary/place-value/place-value

Figure 16.16 Place value – example 2

Ten thousands (T Th)	Thousands (H)	Hundreds (H)	Tens (T)	Ones (O)
•	••	•••	••••••	•
1	2	3	6	1

Place value: 12,361

Source: Adapted from: SplashLearn (n.d.a). https://www.splashlearn.com/math-vocabulary/place-value/place-value

Number sense and counting

Number sense is the ability to understand numbers and number relationships. Beginning number sense requires children to understand whole numbers (1–9) and 0. Number sense skills include rote counting, recognising numerals and assigning numerals to a corresponding fixed quantity, identifying and creating number patterns, and understanding **ordinal numbers**.

To count accurately and understand the concept of quantity, students must acquire an understanding of some key numeracy facts, described in **Figure 16.17**.

Figure 16.17 Numeracy facts

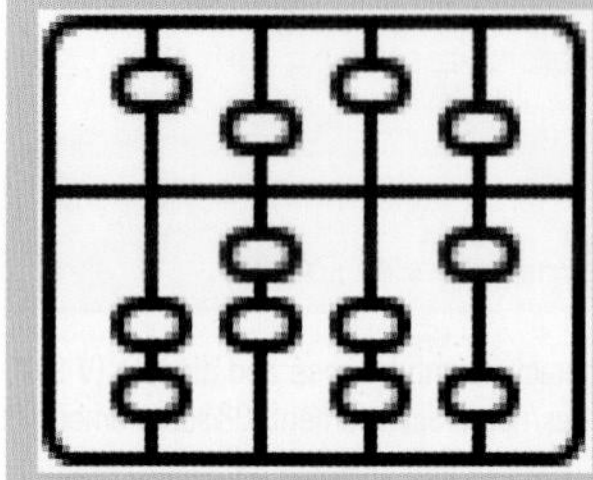

Each object to be counted must be given one and only one number name
The number name list must be used in a fixed order every time a group of objects is counted – that is, you have to say 1, 2, 3, 4 in the same order each time
The order in which the objects are counted doesn't matter
The last number name used gives the number of objects in the set
The arrangement of the objects to be counted remains constant regardless of how they are arranged

Source: Mathematics Developmental Continuum P-10, Learning to Count, http://smartvic.com/teacher/mdc/number/N05001G.html.

Number sense begins with one-to-one correspondence, which is the ability to count one object as you say one number – that is, a number corresponds to a fixed quantity. One-to-one correspondence is fundamental to understanding quantity. Each object that is being counted can only be assigned one number and the quantity of objects being counted in a group remains constant. Young children will naturally engage in one-to-one correspondence as they are playing and interacting with the environment.

SCENARIO

EXAMPLES OF THE PROGRESSION OF ONE-TO-ONE CORRESPONDENCE

Perri (18 months) has two dolls in her pram. She gives each doll a plastic bottle.

Asher (3 years) puts a small plastic animal in each carriage of his train.

Taylor (4 years) helps her mother to set the table. She puts a knife and fork on each placemat.

Sari (5 years) is having a tea party. She places a soft toy animal on each chair.

Connor (7 years) is asked by the teacher to place a set of felt pens on each desk.

Mara (13 years) is on the organising committee for the school play. One of her tasks is to match the number of tickets sold, and those reserved but not yet paid for, with the number of seats required in the auditorium. She must also ensure that there are seats for non-paying guests.

Experimenting with one-to-one correspondence also introduces students to the concept of sets (see **Figure 16.18**). Students can pair each object in one set with one (and only one) object in another set.

Figure 16.18 One-to-one correspondence: which items go together? How many items are in each set?

One-to-one correspondence is an essential first principle in understanding the relationship between quantity and numbers (numerals). For example, if there are five pencils, the child demonstrates one-to-one correspondence by touching each pencil and assigning a corresponding cardinal number. Later, the child is able to demonstrate one-to-one correspondence with numbers by counting a group of objects and matching the quantity to the correct cardinal number (see **Figure 16.19**).

Figure 16.19 Match the number card to the number of objects in each set

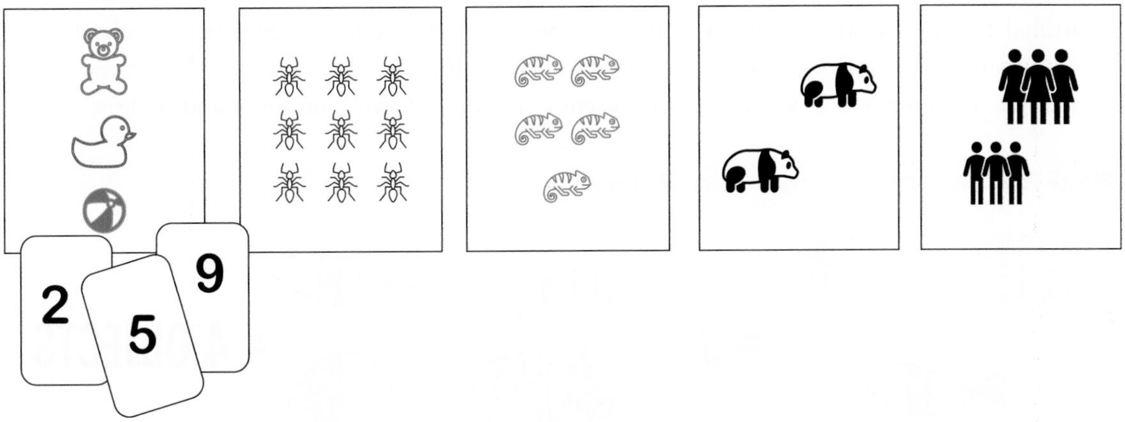

One-to-one correspondence also supports the development of conservation of number (see **Figure 16.20**) – that is, no matter how many ways objects are grouped within the set, the number of objects in the set remains constant.

Figure 16.20 Representation of number conservation – the number of marbles remains constant while looking visually different

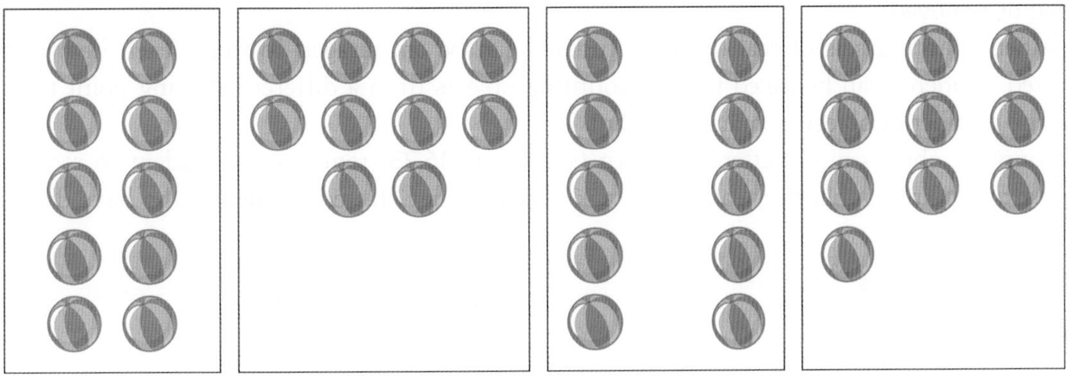

Source: Shutterstock.com/nata_danilenko

Rote counting

Rote counting requires children to understand that counting occurs using a sequence of numbers that remains constant – '1, 2, 3, 4, 5, 6, 7, 8, 9 … 20'. Number sequences can be manipulated when counting, but each number sequence remains constant – '2, 4, 6 …', '5, 10, 15, 20 …' Rote counting and the concept of quantity are not the same. For example, a two-year old may be able to rote count to 10 but may not understand that '3' = three objects.

Figure 16.21 Tell me the number on each card

Recognising numerals

Recognising numerals requires students to identify each numeral by naming numerals when they are shown in a random order (see **Figure 16.21**).

Number symbols (numerals) represent a fixed quantity

A cardinal number denotes quantity – the number in a set. Students develop an understanding that a numeral represents a constant quantity (see **Figure 16.22**), which always remains the same – for example, the numeral '2' will always represent a quantity of two – no more and no less.

Figure 16.22 Numerals as a representation of quantity

Source: Shutterstock.com/LeonART

In the example, the number of fish in each set is also the cardinal number or highest number in the set. The cardinal number is the final number counted in a set.

Students must also understand that the number of objects in the set remains constant regardless of how these objects are arranged (conservation of number). In the above example, the cardinal number for the first group of fish is 3. This number remains constant (unless fish are added or removed).

When counting sets of real objects, students can be encouraged to touch each item as it is counted. Students can be asked to start counting objects from a different starting point to show that the number of objects remains constant.

Counting objects in a scattered pattern (see **Figure 16.23**) requires the student to remember the starting point so that they can keep track of where they started. Students who have difficulty

Figure 16.23 Counting sets

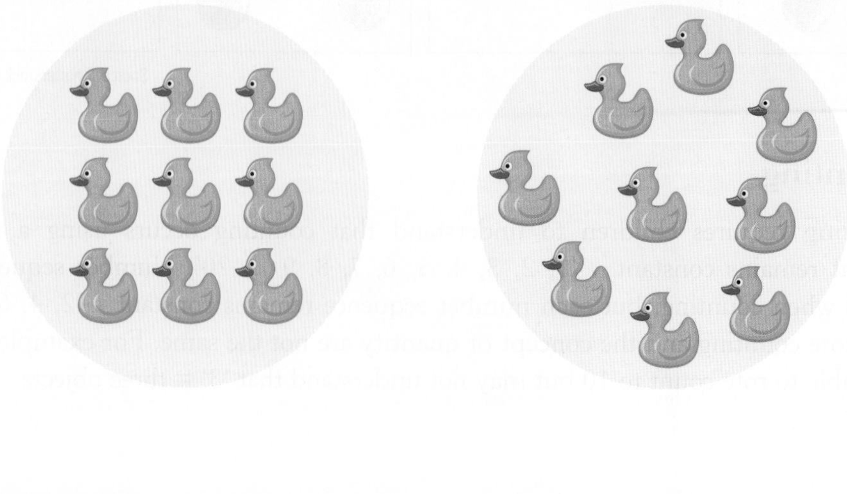

with this task will need to be provided with strategies to help them keep track of each object counted. For example, they may need to move each object out of the circle as it is counted. If counting from a worksheet, the student may need to draw a line through each object counted or place a marker on each object as it is counted.

In a mixed group of items, students can be asked to start counting with a particular item, then move on to another one. For example, in **Figure 16.24**, begin counting with the red circle.

Figure 16.24 Counting activity

Students can be challenged to count objects that are placed randomly around the room – for example, count the number of chairs, doors, windows, paint brushes or red pencils. This requires students to think about how they will go about this task so items aren't missed or counted more than once.

Students can count sets and find a set with the *same number* (an equal number) of objects or students can count objects and match them to the corresponding numeral.

Students can count by posting counters into a container. This requires the student to remember the last number counted; they can only start over by removing all of the counters from the container. This encourages students to concentrate on their counting (see **Figure 16.25**).

Figure 16.25 Using counters can encourage students to concentrate on the task

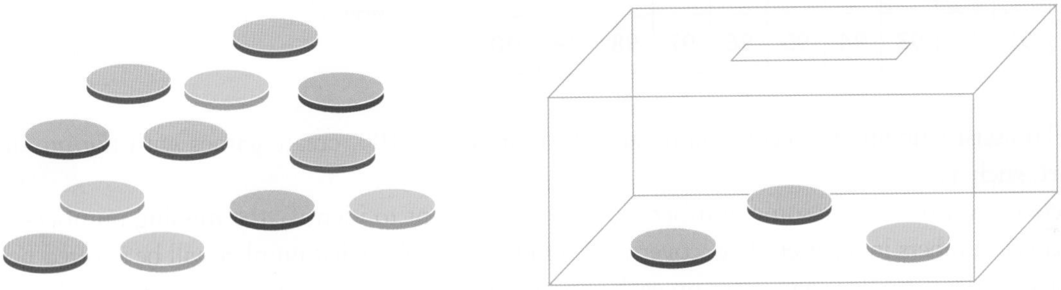

Dominoes can be used to help students recognise and match equal quantities (see **Figure 16.26**).

Figure 16.26 Dominoes require students to count and match

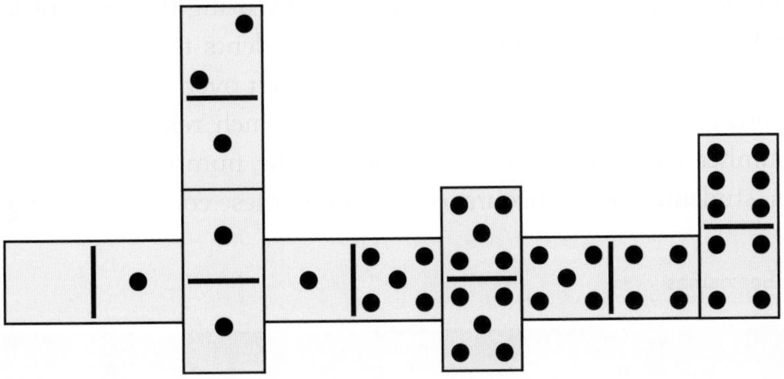

Counting to 100

Students learn the order of numbers and number symbols to 100. This allows them to progress to counting large quantities, counting using two digits and counting by tens.

Again, students must be given lots of opportunities to count large quantities and to use number symbols to 100. Students are usually introduced to a hundreds chart (see **Figure 16.27**) so they can see the sequence of numerals and identify numerals on request.

Figure 16.27 100s chart

1	●	3	●	5	●	7	8	9	10
11	12	13	14	15	16	17	18	19	20
21	22	23	24	25	26	27	28	29	30
31	32	33	34	35	36	37	38	39	40
41	42	43	44	45	46	47	48	49	50
51	52	53	54	55	56	57	58	59	60
61	62	63	64	65	66	67	68	69	70
71	72	73	74	75	76	77	78	79	80
81	82	83	84	85	86	87	88	89	90
91	92	93	94	95	96	97	98	99	100

To assist students to become familiar with numbers to 100, create games with the hundreds chart such as:

- Cover over or remove some numbers and ask the student to identify the missing numbers.
- Cover numbers in a pattern (e.g. cover even numbers 2, 4, 6 – what number will be covered next?).
- Ask students to place a counter on each square containing an identified number (e.g. '4' or '0').
- Familiarise students with mathematical language (e.g. find all of the numbers in the 'twenties').

To assist students to become familiar with numbers to 100, create games with the hundreds chart, such as:

- cover over or remove some numbers and ask the student to identify the missing numbers
- cover numbers in a pattern (e.g. cover even numbers 2, 4, 6 – what number will be covered next?)
- ask students to place a counter on each square containing an identified number (e.g. '4' or '0')
- familiarise students with mathematical language (e.g. find all of the numbers in the 'twenties').

Encourage students to become familiar with number relationships by using the hundreds chart to actively explore number sequences. Students can be challenged to count by tens using the number chart and using tangible materials.

Students can be challenged to count large quantities by using the value of tens. For example, place a large number of blocks in a pile and ask the students to sort them into groups of 10. Count each pile of 10 and then count any others that are left over.

Students can also be introduced to number names, which reinforce the value of tens – for example, 'The number name for 16 is 1 ten and 6. The number name for 23 is …?' Using tangible materials, students can be encouraged to explore these concepts (see **Figure 16.28**).

Figure 16.28 Number names

Tens	Units	
16 1 lot of 10 and 6 units	||||||||||	||||||
23 2 lots of 10 and 3 units	|||||||||| ||||||||||	|||

Understanding complements to 10

Understanding complements to 10 requires students to mentally calculate or count on to 10. For example, show students the numeral card 7 and ask how many more are needed to make 10. Students will initially count on using their fingers; however, as they practise this skill they will be able to state the answer using mental computation. They will also begin to understand commutativity (i.e. 7 + 3 = 3 + 7).

Using 10 frames will assist students to begin to make mental calculations, as shown in **Figure 16.29**. The frames provide a visual clue so that students do not need to resort to counting on their fingers.

Figure 16.29 Using 10 frames

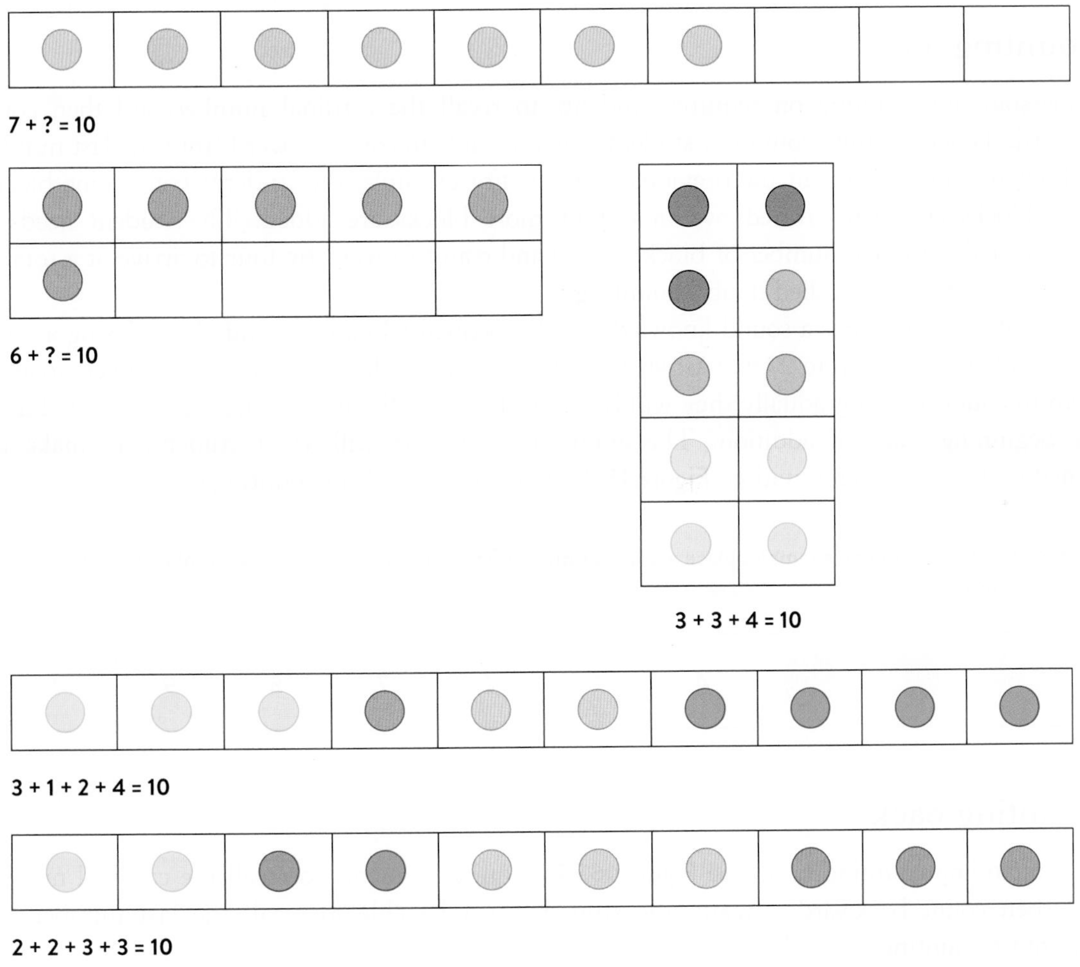

Ten frames can also be used by students to experiment with creating complements to 20 (see **Figure 16.30**), using the same strategies as complements to 10.

Understanding complements to 5 is a natural progression from complements to 10. The most obvious tool for understanding complements of 5 is the use of fingers. Students can easily see that they can make the following complements of 5: 5 + 0 = 5; 4 + 1 = 5; 3 + 2 = 5; 0 + 5 = 5; 1 + 4 = 5; 2 + 3 = 5. Working on complements of 5, 10 and 20 will also develop skills in writing number sentences (2 + 3 = 5).

Figure 16.30 Creating complements to 20

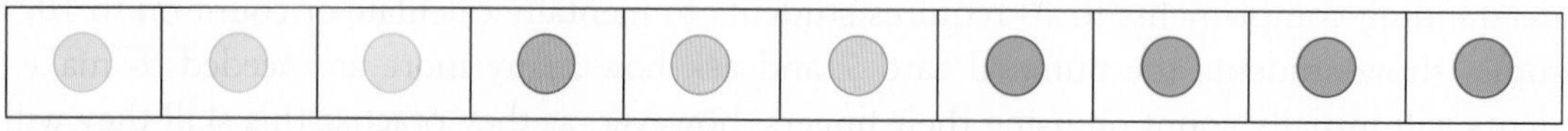

3 + 1 + 2 + 4 = 10

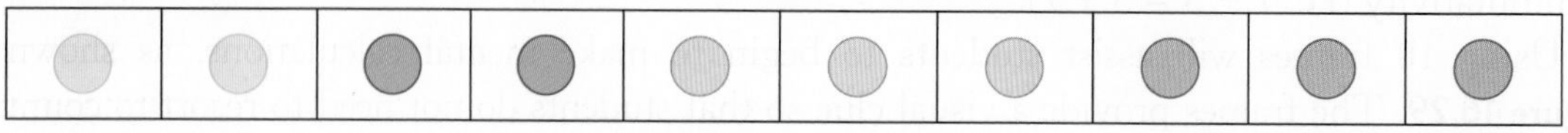

2 + 2 + 3 + 3 = 10

10 + 10 = 20 3 + 1 + 2 + 4 + 2 + 2 + 3 + 3 = 20

Counting on

Understanding counting on requires students to recall the cardinal number and then count forward. To successfully count on, students must be able to count forward from the last number without needing to recount the previous number. For example, the students count nine blocks; these blocks are then covered over and four more blocks are added. The student needs to remember the original number of blocks (nine) and count forward by four to arrive at a total of 13 blocks. This skill is called double counting.

Counting on requires a sound knowledge of the sequential nature of numbers. Using a range of tangible materials up to 20 will assist students. At first, students may use their fingers to assist them to count on but gradually they will begin to do this without any tangible supports. This is the beginning stage of addition. The ability to count on will assist students to make the transition to mental computation. **Figure 16.31** shows an example of counting on.

Figure 16.31 Counting on example: place a counter on the first three numbers of the number line. What number comes next?

| ● | ● | ● | 4 | 5 | 6 | 7 | 8 | 9 | 10 |

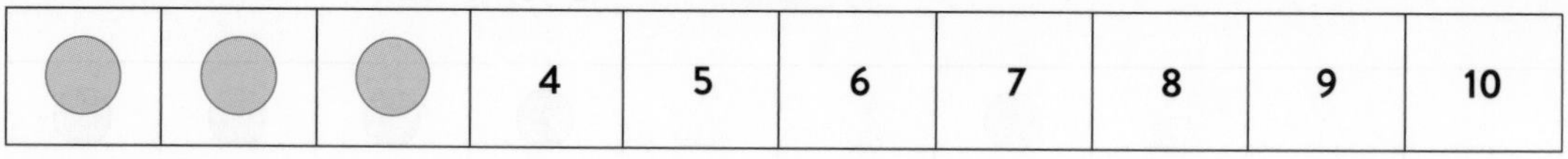

Counting back

Understanding counting back (see **Figure 16.32**) requires students to recall the cardinal number and then count backwards. Again, the student must be able to recall the last number and (without recounting) count backwards.

Figure 16.32 Counting back example: students can be asked to count back from 10, or asked to count back starting from, say, 8

| 1 | 2 | 3 | 4 | 5 | 6 | 7 | ● | ● | ● |

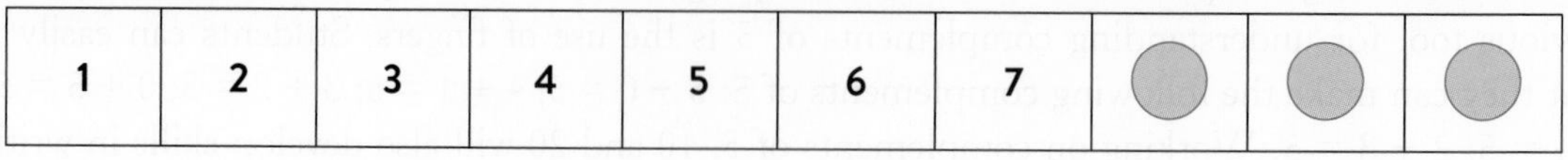

Understanding the concept of rounding whole numbers

To round to the nearest 10 means finding the closest number with all zeros to the right of the tens place. The rule to round up from 5 or more was made so that there would be no ambiguity. When the ones digit is 5, 6, 7, 8 or 9, the number is *rounded up*. When the ones digit is 4, 3, 2 or 1, the number is *rounded down*. For example, 129 rounded to the nearest 10 is 130; 123 rounded to the nearest 10 is 120 (see **Figure 16.33**).

Figure 16.33 Round worksheet

Round each number up or down		
a. 96	rounded up / down	100
b. 22	rounded up / down	
c. 17	rounded up / down	
d. 43	rounded up / down	

Additive strategies

Understanding addition and subtraction begins by using tangible materials that students can manipulate to make addition and subtraction calculations (see **Figure 16.34**).

Figure 16.34 Using concrete materials to demonstrate addition and subtraction

If you have 6 trucks and you take away 2, how many will you have left?

(6 – 2 = 4)

If you have 6 trucks and you add 2 more trucks, how many trucks will you have?

(6 + 2 = 8)

Providing hands-on addition and subtraction tasks will assist students to begin to understand how quantity can be manipulated. It also helps them to understand commutative and associative properties of calculations such as addition, subtraction and later multiplication. For example, 3 + 3 will always equal 6, and 6 – 3 will always equal 3.

Students can also write: 2 + 2 + 2 + 2 = 4 + 4 or 3 + 3 + 2 = 4 + 4 and so on. This strategy also builds number sense. It allows students to play with numbers and begin to realise that number sentences can be written in many different ways and still give the same answer. These number sentences are referred to as *equivalent statements*. Students will be given lots of practice to write their own number sentences and to calculate the correct answer for missing number sentences (see **Figure 16.35**).

Figure 16.35 Number sentences

Missing number sentence	Student's number sentence (multiplication)
17 + □ = 23 – 3 = 20	can also be represented as 2 × 10 = 20
10 – □ = 6 + 2 = 8	can also be represented as 2 × 4 = 8
7 + 3 = 5 + □ = 10	can also be represented as 2 × 5 = 10
12 – 8 = 2 + □ = 4	can also be represented as 2 × 2 = 4

Providing opportunities to practise these calculations will assist students to demonstrate their understanding of maths symbols.

Understanding the law of commutativity

The law of commutativity states that with addition and multiplication of numbers, you can change the order of the numbers in the problem and it will not affect the answer. For example, $(7 + 3)$ is the same as $(3 + 7)$; (7×3) is the same as (3×7).

Understanding this principle allows students to manipulate addition and multiplication tasks to allow the application of skills such as adding on. Students can be encouraged to trial this principle by using tangible materials (see **Figure 16.36**).

Figure 16.36 Practising the law of commutativity with tangible materials

The principle of commutativity can also be illustrated by using a multiplication or addition matrix, as shown in **Figure 16.37**.

Figure 16.37 Using a matrix

	X	=
0	9	0
1	8	8
2	7	14
3	6	18
4	5	20
5	4	20
6	3	18
7	2	14
8	1	8
9	0	0

	+	=
0	9	9
1	8	9
2	7	9
3	6	9
4	5	9
5	4	9
6	3	9
7	2	9
8	1	9
9	0	9

MULTIPLICATION BINGO

SCENARIO

Working with a small group, the ESW gives each student a bingo card with 25 squares in which are written numbers which are multiples of 5.

36	72	24	21	5
18	8	10	15	49
54	81	45	30	28
1	64	48	25	20
35	3	42	32	56

The ESW then uses a set of multiplication fact cards, which are selected and read aloud one at a time.

The students calculate the answer and if the answer is on their card it is covered with a marker. The game continues until a student's card is full.

7×5 5×5

WHAT DOES THIS TELL US?

In this multiplication game, the student is not only required to make a mental calculation; they are also required to listen, which adds a layer of difficulty to the task.

Bingo can be used with any of the four operations (addition, subtraction, multiplication and division) or, to make the task more complex, use a combination of all four operations.

Key maths concepts

Multiplicative strategies

Multiplicative strategies encompass a student's ability to manipulate numbers in multiplicative situations to solve problems (NSW Government. Education, 2023). Citing Siemon et al. (2015), multiplicative thinking is described as:

- a capacity to work flexibly and efficiently with an extended range of numbers (i.e., larger whole numbers, decimals, common fractions, ratio and per cent),
- an ability to recognise and solve a range of problems involving multiplication or division including direct and indirect proportion, and
- the means to communicate this effectively in a variety of ways (e.g., words, diagrams, symbolic expressions, and written **algorithms**).

Source: Adapted from Siemon, D., Beswick, K., Brady, K., Clark, J., Faragher, R., & Warren, E. (2015). *Teaching Mathematics*. South Melbourne: Oxford University Press.

Multiplicative strategies in the Australian Curriculum

Understanding multiplication and division

The basic strategies and language of multiplication and division are shown in **Figure 16.38** and **Figure 16.39**. **Figure 16.40** shows an example of inverse operations.

Figure 16.38 Basic multiplication

4 × 7= 28 or (7 × 4 = 28)
multiplier: 40 multiplicand: 7 product: 28
×: multiple, times

Multiply vertically

320 × 3 | 1102

Hundreds	Tens	Ones	Thousands	Hundreds	Tens	Ones
3	2	0	1	1	0	2
×		3	×			2
9	6	0	2	2	0	4

Multiply vertically (trading, carrying, regrouping)

467 × 2 | 5537 × 2

Hundreds	Tens	Ones	Thousands	Hundreds	Tens	Ones
4	6	7	5	5	3	7
× 2			×			2
8	2	4	10	0	6	4
1	1		1	0	1	
9	3	4	11	0	7	4

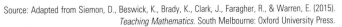

Figure 16.39 Basic division

$12 \div 6 = 2$

divisor: 6 dividend: 12 quotient: 2

÷ divide, divided by

$210 \div 3 = 70$ $5741 \div 4 = $ $\begin{array}{r} 1435\cdot2 \\ 4\overline{)5741\cdot0} \end{array}$

Figure 16.40 Inverse operations

Multiplication and division are inverse operations

$4 \times 7 = 28$	$28 \div 7 = 4$
$7 \times 4 = 28$	$28 \div 4 = 7$

Using arrays

Arrays are simply a grouping of objects or images arranged in rows. Arrays can be used to explore addition, subtraction, multiplication and division. (see **Figure 16.41**).

Figure 16.41 Arrays

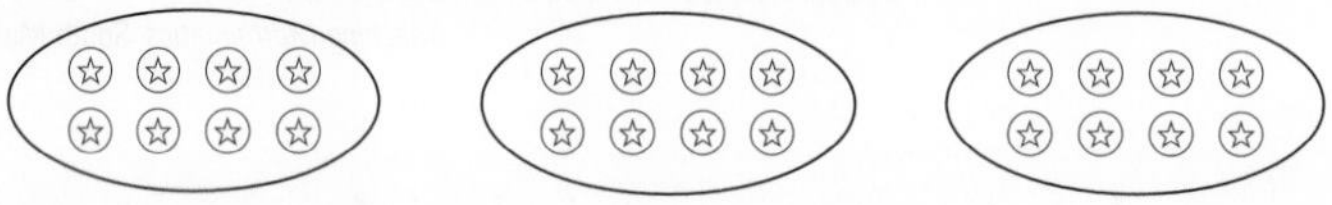

$8 + 8 + 8 = 24$

Factor: number of groups (3)

Product: total number of objects (24)

$(24 \div 3 = 8)$ $24 \div 8 = 3$ $(8 \times 3 = 24)$ $(3 \times 8) = 24$

Using arrays allows students hands-on opportunities to explore and manipulate numbers using word problems. For example:

- If you arrange the objects into two, four or eight groups how many objects will be in each group?
- If you give half of your objects to a friend how many will you have left?
- If there are 24 students in the class how many objects can each student have so that everyone has the same amount?

Visual models for multiplication

Area models also provide students with a visual model for multiplication, as shown in **Figure 16.42**.

Figure 16.42 Area model

$(6 \times 10) + (4 \times 10) =$

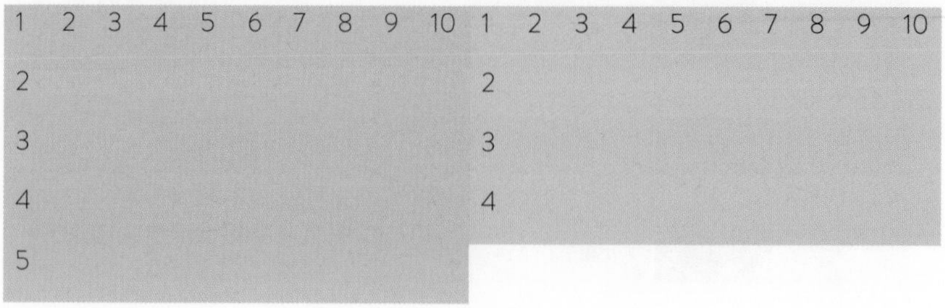

Bar models allow student to demonstrate their understanding of multiplication (see **Figure 16.43**).

Number lines can also be used to visually represent multiplication and division (see **Figure 16.44**).

Multiplication charts allow students to see number patterns as they are multiplied. To see how to explain the use of a multiplication chart to students, view the YouTube videos suggested in the Online Resources.

Figure 16.43 Bar model

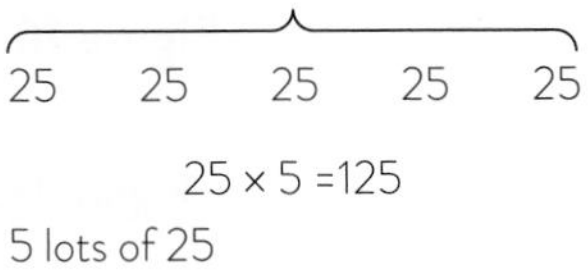

Figure 16.44 Number lines

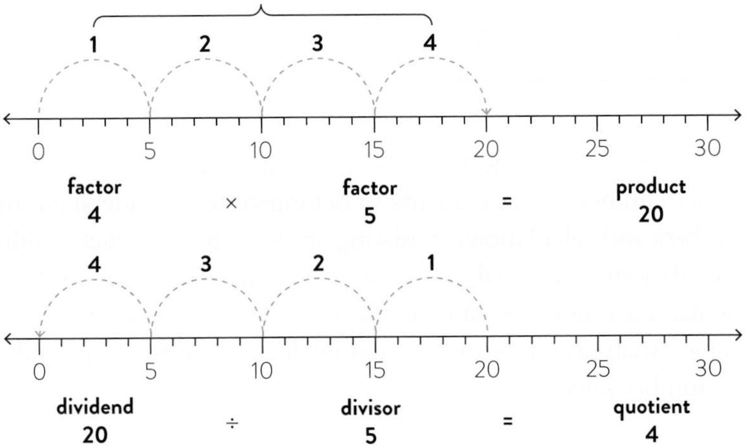

Source: Hogan, J. (2016). Multiplication and division models and strategies. Scholastic Parents. https://www.scholastic.com/parents/school-success/learning-toolkit-blog/multiplication-and-division-models-and-strategies.html

Understanding number fact families

Videos: Multiplication and division

Number facts are basic addition, subtraction, multiplication and division calculations that when committed to memory make maths calculations easier for students to complete.

In maths, a fact family can be defined as a group of maths facts or equations created using the same set of numbers. The fact family shows the relationships between the three numbers involved. In an addition and subtraction fact family, there are four addition and subtraction sentences created using three numbers. Fact families show how a group of numbers is related – for example, for any set of each set of three different numbers, you can create two addition and two subtraction number facts that are related (SplashLearn, n.d.b; see **Figure 16.45**).

Figure 16.45 Examples of addition and subtraction fact families with three numbers

Fact family: 6, 2, 4 **Whole number:** 6 **Parts:** 2 & 4	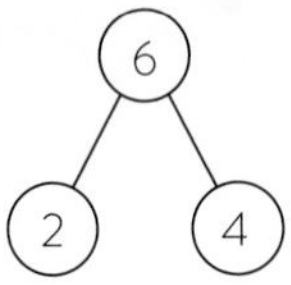	**Fact family: 15, 5, 10** **Whole number:** 15 **Parts:** 5 & 10	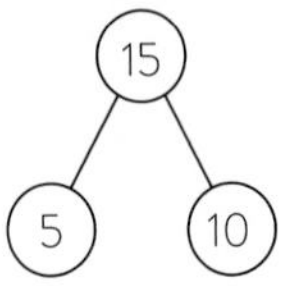
2 + 4 = **6**	6 – 2 = **4**	10 + 5 = **15**	15 –5 = **10**
4 + 2 = **6**	6 – 4 = **2**	5 + 10 = **15**	10 – 5 = **5**

Two numbers can be used in a triangle to show that multiplication and division are inverse operations ($7 \times 3 = 21$ and $21 \div 3 = 7$) and multiplication is commutative ($7 \times 3 = 3 \times 7$) (see **Figure 16.46**).

Figure 16.46 Fact family triangles – example 21, 7, 3

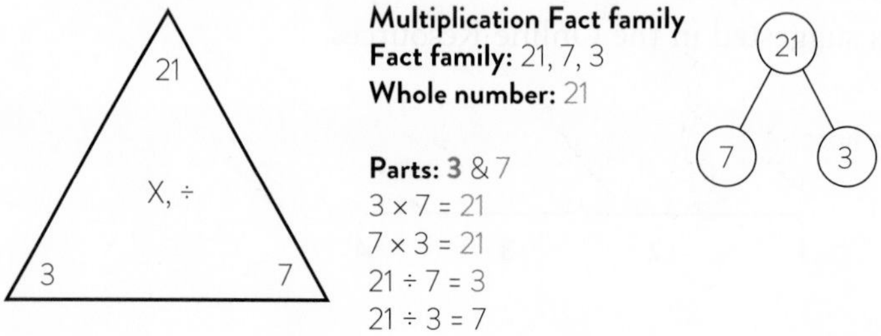

A wide range of fact family worksheets can be accessed online.

Understanding fact families allows students to demonstrate an understanding of relationships between sets of numbers and calculations. Assisting students to write fact families allows them to experiment with calculations using trial and error and at the same time reinforces the concept of number complements. Fact families can be practised at any time and can offer students a worthwhile challenge. Analysing attempts at writing fact families can provide valuable insight into each student's number sense.

Videos: Number rainbows and fact families

Place value and decimals

Operating with decimals in the Australian Curriculum

Place value and decimals

Decimals focus on understanding the use of place value in the base-ten system operating with decimals. While decimals can be written as fractions and fractions can be written as decimals, the two elements are taught separately.

A decimal is a number that includes a whole number and a fraction, like the hundreds chart (**Figure 16.27**) shown on page 538. When writing decimals, the first number is the whole number followed by a dot. The numbers to the right of the dot represent the positional value (tens, hundreds, thousands, etc.). Using a decimal place value chart, students can show the value of each number. **Figure 16.47** shows the place value for 10 453.

Figure 16.47 The place value for 10 453

Whole number	Tenths	Hundredths	Thousandths
	●●●●	●●●●●	●●●
10	4	5	3

Interpreting fractions

Fractions represent part of the whole. This is quite a difficult concept, and it must be introduced using tangible examples. Students who are not yet able to conserve numbers will not be able to understand fractions. Students who are not yet functioning at the concrete level of cognitive development will struggle to conceptualise fractions.

Understanding fractions requires the ability to see the fraction or segment as part of the whole. To understand 7/8, for example, a student must understand that the denominator (the number below the bar) is the quantity that something has been divided into – in this case, eight equal parts – and that the numerator (the number above the bar) in this case 7, represents seven of the eight equal parts (see **Figure 16.48**).

Figure 16.48 Parts of a fraction

numerator 7/8 denominator

vinculum

Types of fractions

Fractions include: proper, improper, mixed and equivalent, as shown in **Figure 16.49**.

Figure 16.49 Types of fractions

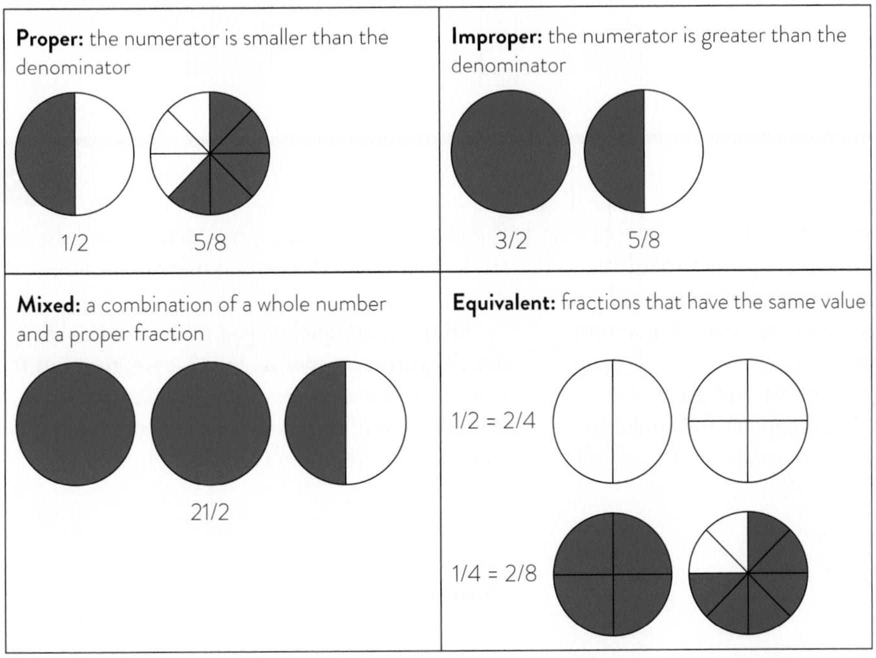

Proper: the numerator is smaller than the denominator
1/2
5/8
Improper: the numerator is greater than the denominator
3/2
5/8
Mixed: a combination of a whole number and a proper fraction
21/2
Equivalent: fractions that have the same value
1/2 = 2/4
1/4 = 2/8

Working with fractions

By beginning with halves and quarters, and using concrete materials, students are able to begin to understand the concepts of portions or segments of the whole. In the example below, students can see that each shape is divided into four equal areas or segments. This is represented by the word quarters. One of the four areas in each shape is coloured. This represents one of four, one quarter, a fourth, ¼ and 0.25 (see **Figure 16.50**). The students can also count the segments that are not coloured – that is, 3 out of 4, which is represented as three-quarters, 3/4 and 0.75.

Figure 16.51 shows examples of fractions.

Figure 16.50 Fractions

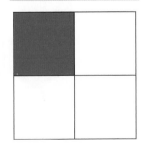

Interpreting fractions in the Australian Curriculum

GO FURTHER

Explore addition, subtraction, multiplication and division rules when working with fractions and how to convert fractions to decimals and percentages in your **Go Further** resource, available from your instructor.

Understanding, multiplying and dividing fractions

Figure 16.51 Examples of fractions

Shade the shapes to help you answer the problems:

a 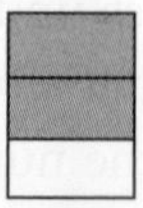 $\frac{1}{2} - \frac{1}{3} = \frac{\boxed{2}}{\boxed{3}}$

b 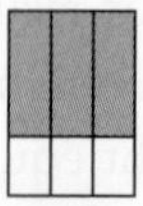 $\frac{3}{9} - \frac{3}{9} = \frac{\boxed{6}}{\boxed{9}}$

c 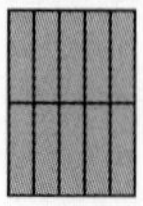 $\frac{4}{10} - \frac{3}{10} = \frac{\boxed{1}}{\boxed{10}}$

d 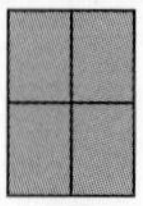 $\frac{5}{8} - \frac{2}{8} = \frac{\boxed{5}}{\boxed{8}}$

Try these. Draw some diagrams if that will help you.

a $\frac{1}{5} + \frac{2}{5} = \frac{\boxed{3}}{\boxed{5}}$

b $\frac{2}{7} + \frac{3}{7} = \frac{\boxed{5}}{\boxed{7}}$

c $\frac{1}{4} + \frac{1}{4} + \frac{1}{4} = \frac{\boxed{3}}{\boxed{4}}$

d $\frac{1}{10} + \frac{5}{10} - \frac{1}{10} = \frac{\boxed{7}}{\boxed{10}}$

FRACTIONS

SCENARIO

The class has been working on fractions for several weeks and the teacher decides to introduce a game to test the students' knowledge. The class is divided into pairs and each pair is given a set of fractions cards (halves, quarters and eighths) and a set of cubes.

Each student draws a fractions card and places it face up. As each card is revealed, it is recorded. The students must then write a number sentence using (>), (<) or (=).

For example, the first student draws ¼ and the second student draws ½. The correct number sentence is: ¼ < ½.

Students are encouraged to use their cubes to work out the correct response. In this case, they put four cubes in a row and then remove three cubes to show ¼. They then would put four cubes in a row and remove two cubes to show ½ (as seen in **Figure 16.52**).

Figure 16.52 Coloured rectangles

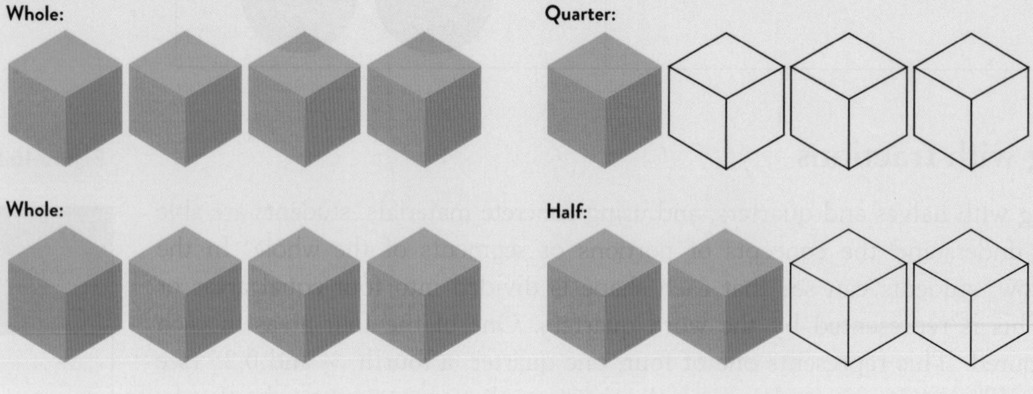

The students can then see that $\frac{1}{4}$ is $< \frac{1}{2}$.

The students play the game for around 20 minutes. They help each other, working together to get the correct answer.

FRACTION LINES

Students are given a worksheet with a number of fraction lines. They are required to write the fraction in the lowest term, as shown in **Figure 16.53**.

Students count the total number of intervals and then count the spaces to the identified interval.

WHAT DOES THIS TELL US?

Maths learning can be presented in many ways. In these examples, the students used hands-on resources and worked collaboratively to solve maths problems.

Figure 16.53 Fraction lines

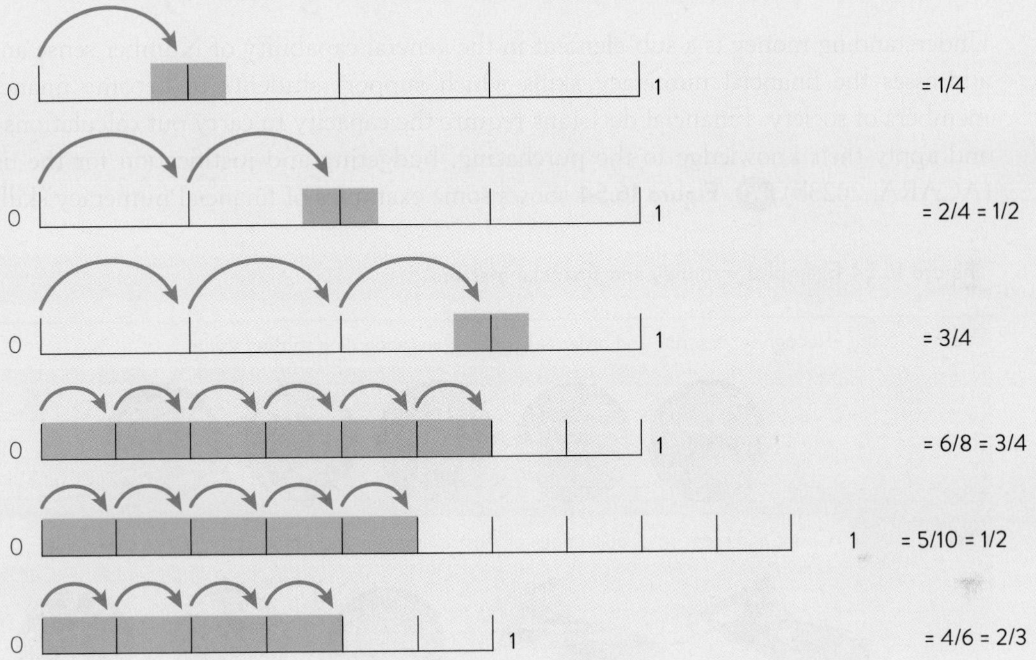

Proportional thinking

Proportional thinking is a sub-element of number sense and algebra in the general capabilities. This sub-element addresses the proportional relationships between quantities. The ability to reason proportionally requires students to think multiplicatively and work with percentages, rates and ratios and proportions (ACARA, 2023b). AC Proportional thinking is a complex cognitive task as it requires students to switch from mainly addition and subtraction to multiplication and division of whole numbers and fractions.

Proportional thinking in the Australian Curriculum

Ratios and rates

Operating with percentages

This sub-element focuses on understanding the use of percentages in representing quantities. It begins with understanding the concept of a percentage, progresses through calculations of a percentage, finding a percentage change first through two steps (calculating the percentage and adding or subtracting) before progressing to one-step methods (10% increase in cost is achieved by multiplying by 1.1) and then to calculating multiple changes (ACARA, 2023b). AC

Operating with percentages in the Australian Curriculum

Operating with percentages includes:

- understanding percentages and relative size
- finding a percentage as a part of a whole
- finding a part of a whole as a percentage
- finding the whole from a percentage and a part
- adding a percentage as multiplying
- repeatedly adding a percentage.

To explore this sub-element, go to the Australian Curriculum website.

Financial literacy and understanding money

Calculating change and budgeting

Understanding money is a sub-element in the general capability of Number sense and algebra. It addresses the financial numeracy skills which support students to become financially literate members of society. Financial decisions require the capacity to carry out calculations with money and apply their knowledge to the purchasing, budgeting and justification for the use of money (ACARA, 2023b) AC. **Figure 16.54** shows some examples of financial numeracy skills.

Figure 16.54 Examples – money and financial matters

Year 1	Recognise, describe and order Australian coins according to their value

Year 2	Count and order small collections of Australian coins and notes according to their value
	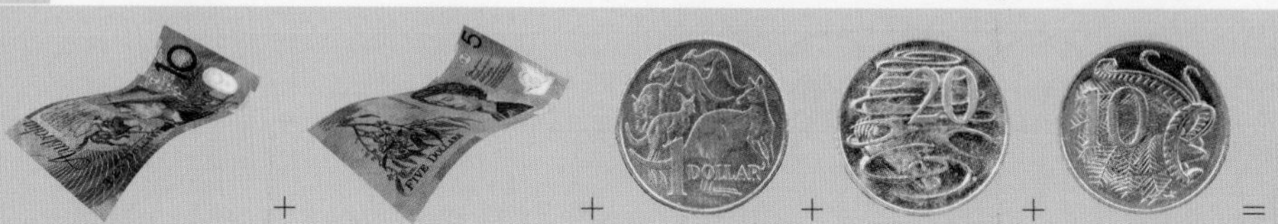 + + + + =
Year 3	Represent money values in multiple ways and count the change required for simple transactions to the nearest ten cents
	\$2.00 = 10 × 20 cents; 20 × 10 cents; 4 × 50 cents
Year 4	Solve problems involving purchases and the calculation of change to the nearest 10 cents with and without digital technologies
At the shops you buy 5 items: > 3 apples – 50 cents each > 2 mangoes – \$2.20 each > How much change will you have from \$20.00?	> (3 × 0.50) + (2 × 2.20) + (4.50) = > 1.50 + 4.40 + 4.50 = 10.40 > 20.00 – 10.40 = ?
Year 5	Model practical problems involving money, such as a budget for a large event, as requiring either addition, subtraction, multiplication or division and justifying the choice of operation in relation to the situation
Year 6	Investigate and calculate percentage discounts of 10%, 25% and 50% on sale items, with and without digital technologies

Source: Australian Curriculum, Assessment and Reporting Authority (ACARA) (2023b). General capabilities. Numeracy. Number sense and algebra (V 9.0). https://v9.australiancurriculum.edu.au/f-10-curriculum/general-capabilities/numeracy?element=0&sub-element=0 AC; (images) Shutterstock.com/hddigital; iStock.com/Marc_Osborne.

Financial literacy

The Australian Securities and Investments Commission (ASIC) (2011) describes financial literacy as 'understanding money and finances and being able to confidently apply that knowledge to make effective financial decisions' (p. 4). ASIC states that 'knowing how to make sound money decisions is a core skill in today's world, regardless of age. It affects quality of life, opportunities we can pursue, our sense of security and the overall economic health of our society' (p. 4).

Education Victoria states:

> A quality financial literacy education provides students with the knowledge, skills and understandings necessary to:
> - make informed decisions about personal consumer and financial choices such as learning why saving is important and how to save, comparing prices of products and services, making good purchase decisions despite strong marketing influences, understanding consumer law and rights, standards, and product safety
> - understand how their consumer and financial decisions affect other individuals, the broader community, and the natural, economic, and business environment
> - learn how to manage financial risks and rewards, avoid identity theft and scams, manage assets, and protect their finances through insurance, savings, and superannuation etc.
> - calculate best buys, solve problems involving profit and loss, and calculate simple and compound interests.
>
> Source: Victorian Government Department of Education and Training (2021b). Financial literacy. https://www2.education.vic.gov.au/pal/financial-literacy/guidance

Financial literacy teaching resources

Figure 16.55 provides an example of a financial literacy task in the senior secondary curriculum.

Figure 16.55 Financial literacy: senior secondary maths example

Senior Secondary: Essential Maths (V9.0)	
Topic 1: Calculations, percentages and rates	**Examples in context** Calculations – for example: > creating a budget for living at home and for living independently > using timesheets, which include overtime, to calculate weekly wages > converting between weekly, fortnightly and yearly incomes.

Source: Australian Curriculum, Assessment and Reporting Authority (ACARA) (n.d.b).Senior secondary: essential maths (V9.0). https://www.australiancurriculum.edu.au/senior-secondary-curriculum/mathematics/essential-mathematics/?unit=Unit+1&unit=Unit+2&unit=Unit+3&unit=Unit+4

SCENARIO

VALUE FOR MONEY?

The Year 6 class has been working on addition and subtraction of decimals. Today the teacher divides the class into pairs and gives each pair a notional $50 and a food catalogue. The students are challenged to spend their $50 wisely to get variety and value for money. They must try to reach as close to or just under the amount allocated. The list of food items includes:

- 1 kg bag of fruit (minimum of three varieties) (price per bag)
- 2 kg bag of vegetables (minimum of four varieties) (price per bag)
- 5 kg of meat (minimum of two types) (price per kg)
- up to 500 g of cheese (price per gram)
- some tinned, frozen or pre-packaged foods (price per item).

The students are required to record their purchases, including the cost of each item, the total amount spent and any change from $50. The task creates a great deal of discussion and the students spend the morning busily completing their shopping list.

While students may be able to count money using tangible strategies, they may become confused when it comes to using a decimal point. As counting using decimals is a higher-order skill, it may be necessary to simply show students how an amount that includes dollars and cents is written.

For example, when counting the money in the above scenario, students may correctly state the total amount as six dollars and 55 cents but may not understand how this is written.

Use a simple explanation, such as whole dollars are written first followed by a dot (or decimal point) and the number of cents. The dot separates the dollars from the cents (e.g. $6.55).

WHAT DOES THIS TELL US?

In this Scenario, the students are presented with the challenge of calculating and recording expenditure, recording their spending in decimal points, and making comparisons and calculations about the best combination of food to buy. The task also involves discussion, problem-solving, negotiation and collaboration.

Number patterns and algebraic thinking

Algebra involves understanding patterns, relations and functions. Recognising and understanding patterns is the beginning of algebraic thinking. Recognising and creating patterns is a complex task that develops over time. Identifying patterns requires students to see similarities and differences within the elements of a pattern. This process requires students to think about the relationships of these elements, make generalisations and predict how the pattern will continue. These skills are said to be the foundation of algebraic thinking. Examples of basic pattern skills include:

- recognising, describing, creating and continuing repeating patterns
- identifying the missing elements in a pattern
- creating, describing and recording number patterns
- recognising and creating increasing and decreasing number patterns
- understanding the relationships between numbers in number patterns
- creating, representing and continuing a variety of number patterns.

Number patterns and algebraic thinking in the Australian Curriculum

Patterns

Understanding simple number patterns can be achieved by engaging students in physical activities, such as copying a pattern of claps, or a sequence of movements, such as 'jump twice', 'hop once', 'clap three times and turn around', and singing songs and rhymes that include number patterns such as 'Five Little Ducks', 'Five Little Speckled Frogs' and 'There Were 10 in the Bed'. Students can also be involved in visually identifying number patterns – for example, '2, 3, 2, 3, 2 …?; 22, 44, 22, 44 …?; 123, 123, 123 …?'

A more complex number pattern can require students to use problem-solving skills to find a solution – for example, '2, 4, 6 …?; 2, 6, 8, 12 …?'

By secondary school, students can work on more complex number patterns – for example, '1, 3, 6 …?' could lead to '? = 6' (by multiplying 1 by 3, then 3 by 2, then 6 by 1); '? = 10' (by adding 2 to 1, then adding 3 to 3, then adding 4 to 6).

Figure 16.56 shows examples of simple patterns that young students may identify and repeat.

Figure 16.56 Recognising patterns requires students to notice relationships of similarity and difference

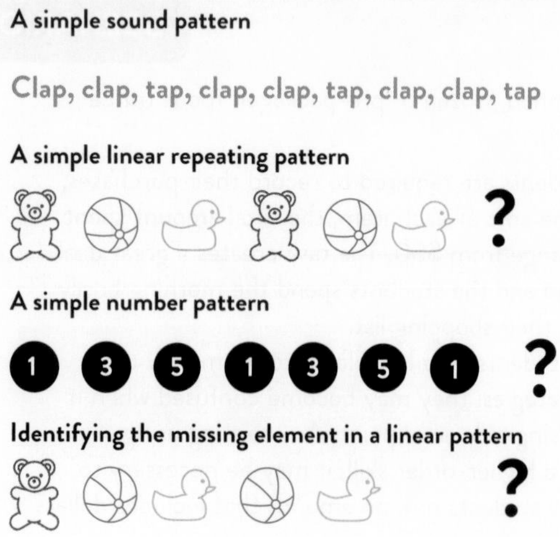

A simple sound pattern
Clap, clap, tap, clap, clap, tap, clap, clap, tap
A simple linear repeating pattern
?
A simple number pattern
1 3 5 1 3 5 1 ?
Identifying the missing element in a linear pattern
?

Ordinal numbers

Ordinal numbers identity the position or order of objects – for example, objects in a line can be assigned a position such as first, second, third … last (see **Figure 16.57**).

Figure 16.57 Example of an ordinal number activity

Source: Shutterstock.com/nata_danilenko

Understanding ordinal numbers requires students to identify the starting point – for example, in the row of monsters in **Figure 16.58**, the first monster will usually be the one on the far left and the last monster will be the one on the far right.

Figure 16.58 Identifying first, last in a row of items

Source: Shutterstock.com/TeddyandMia

Students could be asked to identify the first monster, the third monster and the last monster by writing the abbreviated form of ordinal numbers – for example, 1st, 2nd, 3rd. In this example, the last monster is also the sixth, and if the monsters were arranged in a vertical line rather than a horizontal one, students might identify the first as either the monster at the top or the one at the bottom.

Figure 16.59 provides an example of a Year 4 student demonstrating her understanding of ordinal numbers. This task also requires the student to use her literacy skills to read and follow instructions.

Figure 16.59 Understanding ordinal numbers

For younger students, a simple, fun ordinal activity would be to have students form a line and ask them to call their place in the line – for example, 1st, 2nd, 3rd. Give students tasks: 4th student claps hands; 5th student hops, 3rd student swaps places with 1st student.

Working with sets and subsets

Working with sets and subsets allows students to explore relationships of similarity and provides foundation knowledge for understanding commutative, associative and distributive properties for mental computations. The ability to sort and classify is necessary for understanding sets and subsets.

Students can be assisted to understand that a set can be divided into two or more subsets. In **Figure 16.60**, subsets of Set A might include pink, yellow, red, green and blue circles. It may also include other subsets, such as pink circles in one set and all other circles in another set.

Figure 16.60 Sets and subsets

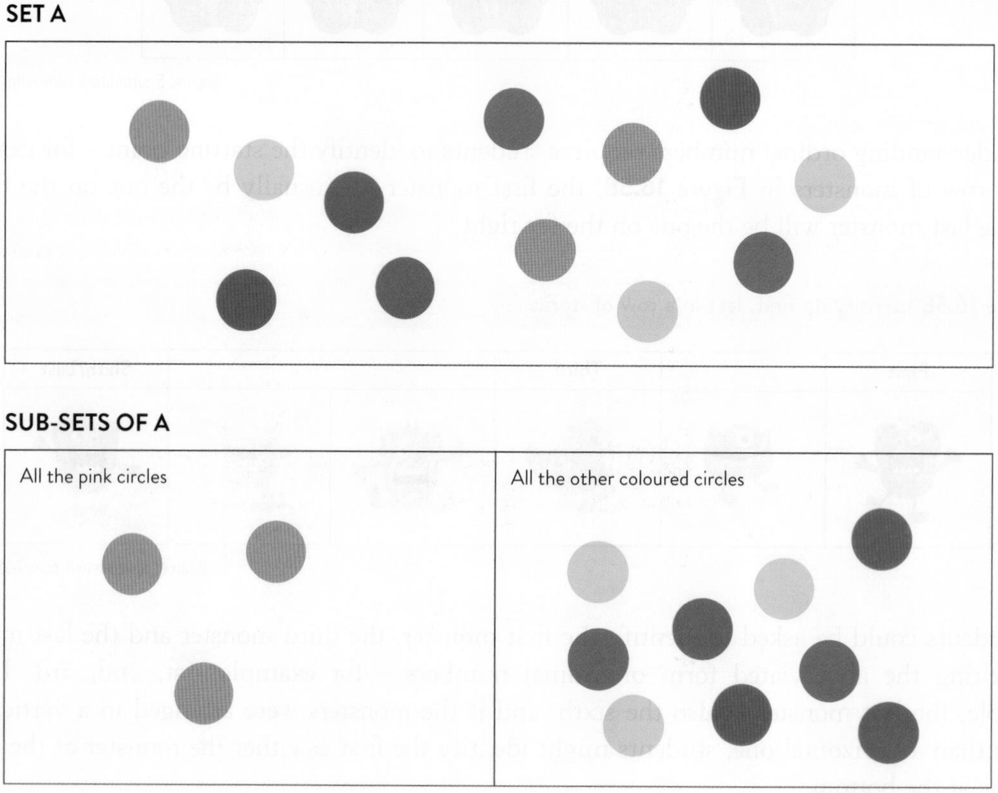

Comparing sets

Students can be encouraged to use numeracy language to compare each set (see **Figure 16.61**) – for example:

- 'There are more buttons in Set B than Set A.'
- 'There are fewer buttons in Set A than in Set B.'

Students can use numeracy language to answer simple questions – for example:

- 'Which set has the most buttons?'
- 'Which set has the fewest buttons?'

Figure 16.61 Comparing sets using numeracy language

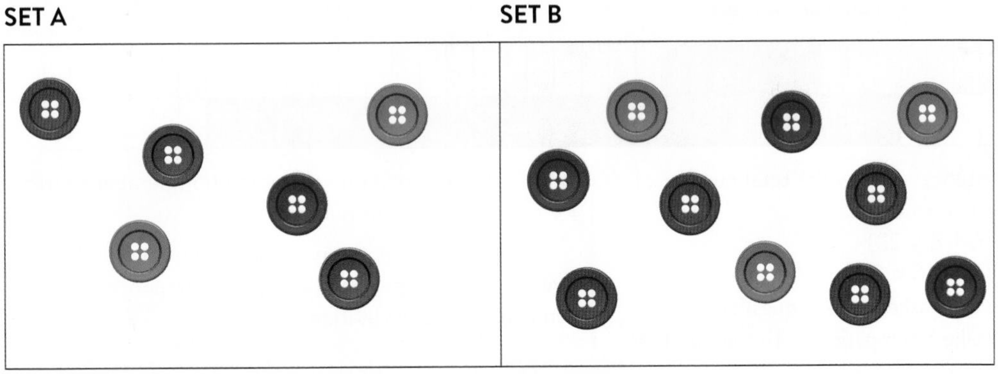

There are more buttons in Set B than in Set A

Source: Shutterstock.com/Igor Shikov

SCENARIO

COMPARING SETS

The ESW works with a group of eight students, dividing them into pairs. Each student is given a set of fish, graph paper and a randomly selected set of five number cards. The students are then asked to make a set of fish to correspond to each number card (see **Figure 16.62**).

Figure 16.62 Comparing sets

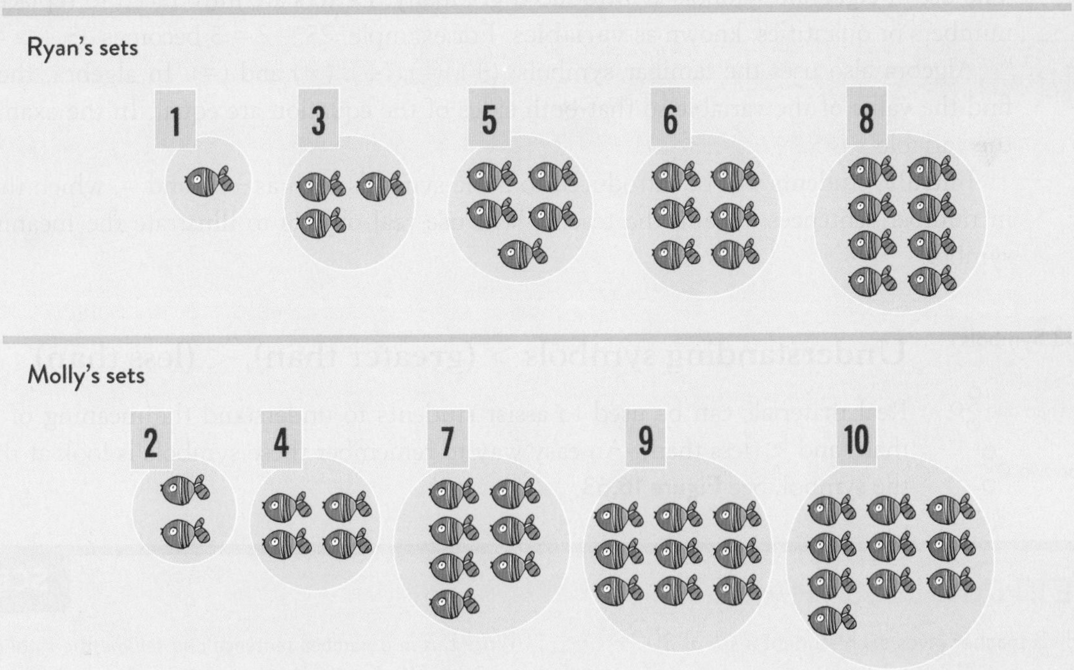

Source: Shutterstock.com/LeonART

The ESW then asks the students to perform the following tasks:

- Create a line graph showing their own fish sets.

Ryan
Molly

- Write a number sentence to show the total number of fish for each of the two students.
  (Ryan: 1 + 3 + 5 + 6 + 8 = 23)
  (Molly: 2 + 4 + 7 + 9 + 10 = 32)

  The students are then asked several questions, requiring them to make a comparison with their partner:
- Who has the most fish?
- How many more fish would be needed so that both students have the same number of fish?
- How many fish are there when both sets are added together?
- Can the fish be divided equally between the two students?
- Write one addition and subtraction number sentence using your set of numbers.

  The students work on a range of number problems with the fish, engaging in counting, comparisons, adding on and basic computation.

WHAT DOES THIS TELL US?

In this activity, the ESW provided the opportunity for the students to explore and represent number sets in different ways. This hands-on approach allows students to explore number, make comparisons and demonstrate their knowledge and understanding of mathematical language.

Algebraic symbols

The use of algebraic symbols is introduced gradually. Letters are introduced to replace unknown numbers or quantities, known as **variables**. For example, 25 ÷ ? = 5 becomes $25 \div x = 5$.

Algebra also uses the familiar symbols: (+), (–), (÷), (×) and (=). In algebra, the goal is to find the value of the variable so that both sides of the equation are equal. In the example above, the variable x *is* 5.

Initially, students will be introduced to basic symbols such as +, – and =, which they will use in number sentences. Again, the teacher will use real objects to illustrate the meaning of each symbol.

Figure 16.63 Symbols

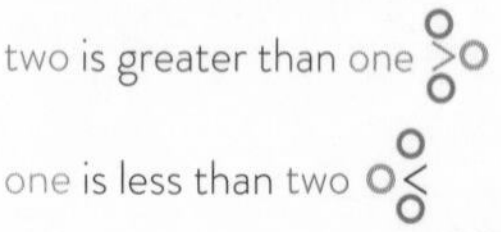
two is greater than one
one is less than two

Understanding symbols > (greater than), < (less than)

Real materials can be used to assist students to understand the meaning of > (greater than) and < (less than). An easy way to remember these symbols is look at the shape of the symbol. See **Figure 16.63**.

SCENARIO

MORE THAN, LESS THAN

The Grade 3 teacher gives each student a set of 30 connecting cubes. The teacher then gives a series of instructions that students must follow, recording the information as they work. The teacher begins: *'I want you to join seven cubes, now I want you to add three cubes. Write this in a number sentence and tell me the total number of cubes (7 + 3 = 10).'*

'Now I want you to remove 4 cubes and write this in a number sentence. Set A: (10 – 4 = 6).'

'Now I want you to join together a new set of cubes that is one more than the set you already have.'

'Write this in a number sentence. Set B: 6 + 1 = 7.

'Now I want you to join together another new set of cubes, which is three less than the last set.'

'Write this in a number sentence. Set C: 7 – 3 = 4.

'Now I want you to join together another new set of cubes, which is 10 more than the last set.'

'Write this in a number sentence. Set D: 4 + 10 = 14.

'Now you should have 4 sets of cubes. Put each set in order from least cubes at the top to most cubes at the bottom.'

Set C: 

Set A: 

Set B: 

Set D: 

A more complex set of questions might include:

- Which set has one less than Set B?
- Which set has two less than Set A?
- Which set has eight more than Set A?
- Which set has three less than Set B?
- Which two sets when added together are one less than Set D?

When the teacher and the ESW were working with the students on this task, they found that several students were confused about the language 'more than, less than'. Some students were not able to follow the teacher's directions and several did not create new sets but rather kept adding to or subtracting from a single set.

WHAT DOES THIS TELL US?

When working on numeracy skills, it is often difficult for students to follow whole-class directions. While the teacher's instructions may be clear, how this information is processed by and acted on by individual students will vary. A more appropriate strategy would be to work with students in small groups, so that on-the-spot support and feedback can be given.

Measurement and geometry

Numbers, algebra and symbols

The measurement and geometry element of the general capability Numeracy includes four sub-elements:

- Using units of measurement
- Shape
- Location and transformation
- Geometric reasoning.

The sub-elements are described in **Figure 16.64**.

Figure 16.64 General capability: Numeracy – Measurement and geometry

Sub-element: Understanding units of measurement	This sub-element describes how students become increasingly able to identify attributes that can be measured and the units by which they are measured.	
	> Describing the size of objects > Comparing and ordering objects > Using informal units of measurement > Estimating measurements > Repeating a single informal unit to measure > Describing turns	> Angles as measures of turn > Using metric units > Converting units > Using metric units and formulas > Circle measurements > Introducing metric units

Sub-element: Understanding geometric properties	This sub-element describes how students become increasingly able to identify the properties of shapes and objects and how they can be combined or transformed.	
	> Familiar shapes and objects > Transformations > Angles	> Properties of shapes and objects > Geometric properties
Sub-element: Positioning and locating	This sub-element describes how students become increasingly able to recognise the attributes of position and location, and to use positional language to describe themselves and objects in the environment using maps, plans and coordinates.	
	> Position to self > Position to other	> Using informal maps and plans > Using proportional thinking for scaling
Sub-element: Measuring time	This sub-element describes how students become increasingly aware of reading and describing the passage of time and how elapsed time or duration can be measured.	
	> Sequencing time > Units of time > Measuring time > Relating units of time	> Converting between units of time > Measuring time with large and small timescales > Measuring how things change over time

Source: Australian Curriculum, Assessment and Reporting Authority (ACARA) (2023a). General capabilities downloads. https://v9.australiancurriculum.edu.au/downloads/general-capabilities#accordion-afa194f119-item-e657062594

Understanding units of measurement

The Measurement strand in the curriculum involves the development of knowledge, procedures and strategies associated with:

- length, mass (weight), area, capacity and volume, which develops understandings of estimation and measurement of these attributes, associated units of measure and the relationships between them
- time, which develops understandings of units and conventions associated with measuring and the recording of the passage (duration) of time, such as calendars, clocks and schedules.

Figure 16.65 shows an example of the progression of understanding units of measurement in the curriculum.

Figure 16.65 Understanding units of measurement

Year 1	Measure the length of shapes and objects using informal units, recognising that units need to be uniform and used end-to-end
Year 3	Measure and compare objects using familiar metric units of length, mass and capacity and instruments with labelled markings
Year 5	Solve practical problems involving the perimeter and area of regular and irregular shapes using appropriate metric units
Year 7	Solve problems involving the volume of right prisms including rectangular and triangular prisms, using established formulas and appropriate units
Year 9	Solve spatial problems, applying angles, properties, scale, similarity, Pythagoras' theorems and trigonometry in right-angled triangles
Year 10	Interpret and use logarithmic scales in applied contexts involving small and large quantities and change

Source: Australian Curriculum, Assessment and Reporting Authority (ACARA) (2023c). Mathematics. https://v9.australiancurriculum.edu.au/f-10-curriculum.html/learning-areas/mathematics/foundation-year_year-1_year-2_year-3_year-4_year-5_year-6_year-7_year-8_year-9_year-10?view=quick&detailed-content-descriptions=0&side-by-side=1&strands-start-index=0&subjects-start-index=0&hide-ccp=0&hide-gc=0

To understand measurement, students must become familiar with standard units of measure and be able to select the correct unit of measure – for example, liquid is measured by volume, distance is measured by linear metres, temperature is measured by degrees and time is measured by seconds, minutes, hours and so on.

Understanding measurement also requires students to develop the language used to describe and compare measurements. For example, students must understand the concepts of height, width, length, volume, weight, capacity and area. They must be able to make comparisons such as longer/shorter, wider/narrower, heavier/lighter and thicker/thinner. They must also understand how these comparisons are applied to length, mass, time, temperature and volume.

Informal measurement

To begin, the exploration of measurement will focus on comparisons that assist students to understand the idea that they are measuring specific attributes of objects. These comparisons should advance from direct to indirect.

Direct comparison involves directly aligning the attributes to be compared, and may include:

- comparing two similar objects (e.g. two boys/girls of different heights – taller/shorter than)
- comparing two dissimilar objects (e.g. the height of a car to the height of a poodle)
- comparing three similar objects – this is more challenging as it requires students to recognise an object as being both bigger and/or smaller than other objects at the same point in time. Comparison such as this leads to transitive reasoning (i.e. if a is bigger than b, and b is bigger than c, then a is bigger than c).

Indirect comparison involves comparing two objects that cannot be aligned directly – for example, the height of a doorway and the length of a desk. An informal, non-standard unit of measure, such as a length of string or ribbon, is required to help with the comparison. Students can be encouraged to use a range of non-standard units to measure length, volume, mass and time. Consider the following examples:

- *Length*: Use hands or a block to measure the height of the bookcase, the teacher's desk, the teacher's chair and the drawers (see **Figure 16.66**). Students can also be asked to make comparisons – for example, the bookcase is 20 hands in height or three and half blocks. The chair is nine hands in height or one and a quarter blocks.

Figure 16.66 Range of non-standard items

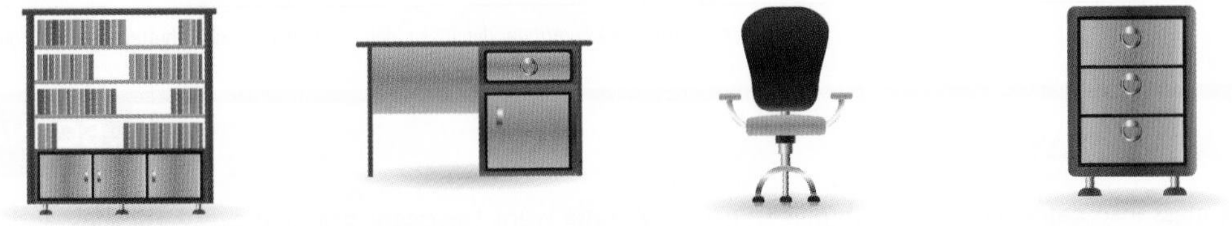

Source: Shutterstock.com/stoyanh

- *Volume*: How many plastic cups of water does it take to fill a small bucket, an ice-cream container, a lunchbox (see **Figure 16.67**).
- *Mass*: Using scales, compare the weight of objects (see **Figure 16.68**).
- *Time*: understanding time (yesterday, today, tomorrow, next week, last week, week days, weekend, etc.); measuring time (count how long it takes to …; faster/slower, etc.).

Figure 16.67 Finding the volume of various containers

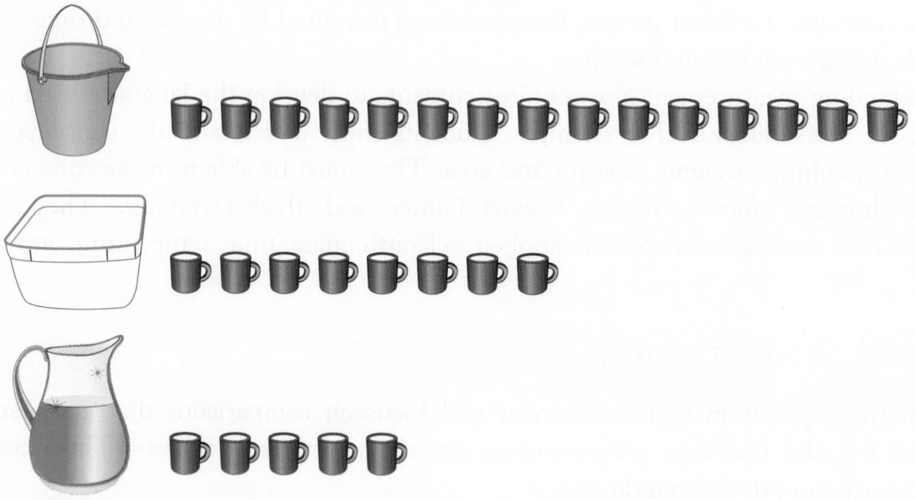

Figure 16.68 Comparing the weight of different objects

Weight of items	Heavier	Lighter	Same weight
Tennis ball Golf ball			
Orange Banana	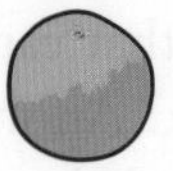		
Teddy bear Doll			
Book DVD			
Robot Duck			

Source: Shutterstock.com/nata_danilenko (doll, teddy bear, duck); Shutterstock.com/fongman (robot)

USING THE CALENDAR

SCENARIO

The teacher divides the class into pairs and gives each pair a calendar for a three-month period. The students are required to answer the following questions:

- **Jack** has to go to the doctor on the third Thursday of each month. List the dates when Jack will attend the doctor.
- **Zennie** went to soccer practice every Tuesday and Thursday for a three-month period. List the dates Zennie went to soccer practice.
- How many Mondays are there in each of the three months?

- **Hassim** went to tutoring every second Monday and every second Thursday for a period of three months. What dates did Hassim attend tutoring?

WHAT DOES THIS TELL US?

This activity requires students to read with understanding so that the question can be translated into a numeracy task. The students are required to count forward, use addition and record information correctly. To do this, they must understand the concept of a calendar and what it represents.

▶ DISCUSSION

The Scenario demonstrates the integrated nature of the Australian Curriculum. As a group, use a calendar to answer the above questions and identify the specific skills and knowledge needed to answer each question.

As students become confident about using various informal units of measure, the teacher will challenge students to estimate measurement outcomes. This encourages them to think about the relationship between the unit of measure and the size of the object being measured. Consider the examples in **Figure 16.69**.

Using informal units of measure

Figure 16.69 Using informal units of measure

Students are given a wide ribbon which is 1 metre in length. They are asked to estimate the length of the ribbon using the following informal units of measure:

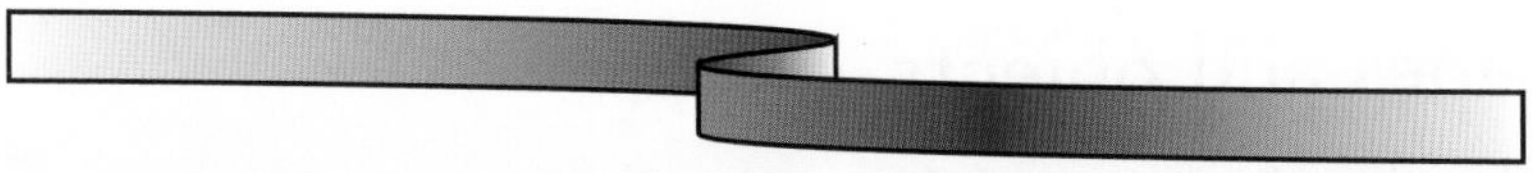

Units of measure	Estimation	Units of measure	Estimation
Wooden block 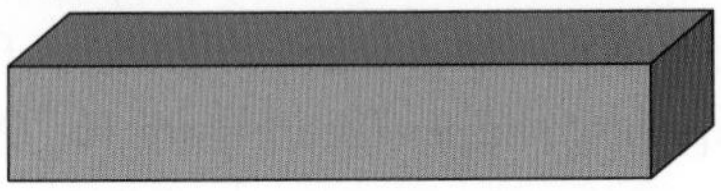		Pencil 	
Pegs 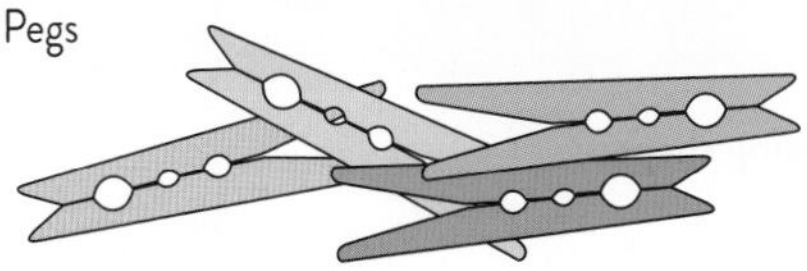		Paper clips 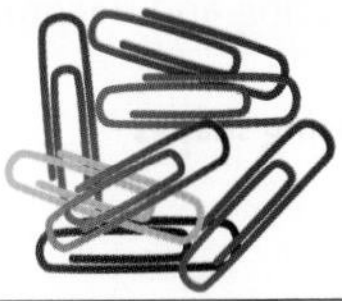	
Feet (heel-to-toe) 		Envelope 	

Source: Shutterstock.com/Genestro (pencil)

Using objects such as those illustrated in **Figure 16.69**, the teacher may also ask the students to *predict* which unit of measure will take the least number and which will take the most number to measure the length of ribbon.

Like informal units of measure, formal units of measure are introduced using tangible, familiar examples, such as a ruler. Students will discover that 10 mm = 1 cm; 100 cm = 1 m; 1000 mm = 1 m and so on. Similarly, the teacher will introduce formal units of measure for volume and mass.

Formal units of measure

As students experiment with measurement, they will become more comfortable with using standard units of measurement. Students who struggle with measurement will need to be provided with hands-on materials to help them understand how a unit of measure relates to a measurement – that is, the unit of measure always remains constant, regardless of what is being measured, which allows comparisons to be made between objects.

Understanding geometric properties

Geometry has two key components – understanding shape and conceptualising space. Understanding shape requires the ability to visually discriminate, compare and contrast the attributes of regular shapes. This is achieved gradually as children play with and use objects with familiar shapes. Learning about shapes includes understanding the properties of shapes, surfaces, points, lines and angles. It involves the ability to recognise and describe the attributes of two-dimensional (2D) and three-dimensional (3D) shapes and describe spatial relationships. Conceptualising spatial relationships (location and transformation) is a more challenging task and requires an understanding of position, direction and distance.

Familiar shapes and objects

Recognising and learning the names of shapes is a fundamental skill that assists students to organise visual information so that it can be easily recalled – for example, recognising that regular 2D shapes remain constant (i.e. the attributes of shape and angles). As students learn the names of shapes, they also become familiar with the language used to describe shapes (circular, curved, right angles, parallel, sides, corner, opposite, etc.). Knowing the attributes of shapes allows children to compare, compose, decompose and manipulate shapes (see **Figure 16.70**).

Figure 16.70 Composing and decomposing shapes

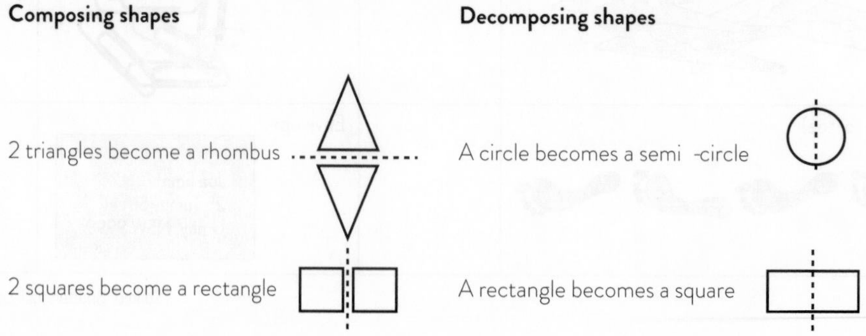
Composing shapes
Decomposing shapes
2 triangles become a rhombus
A circle becomes a semi -circle
2 squares become a rectangle
A rectangle becomes a square

Figure 16.71 shows common 2D shapes.

As children learn about shapes they are acquiring knowledge of their attributes. Some shapes are more easily recognised than others. For example, **Figure 16.72** shows images of two sets of triangles. The triangles in group (a) are exactly the same – they have the same angles and the same lengths. This is a group of congruent triangles. Group (b) are also triangles – they can be

Figure 16.71 Some common 2D shapes

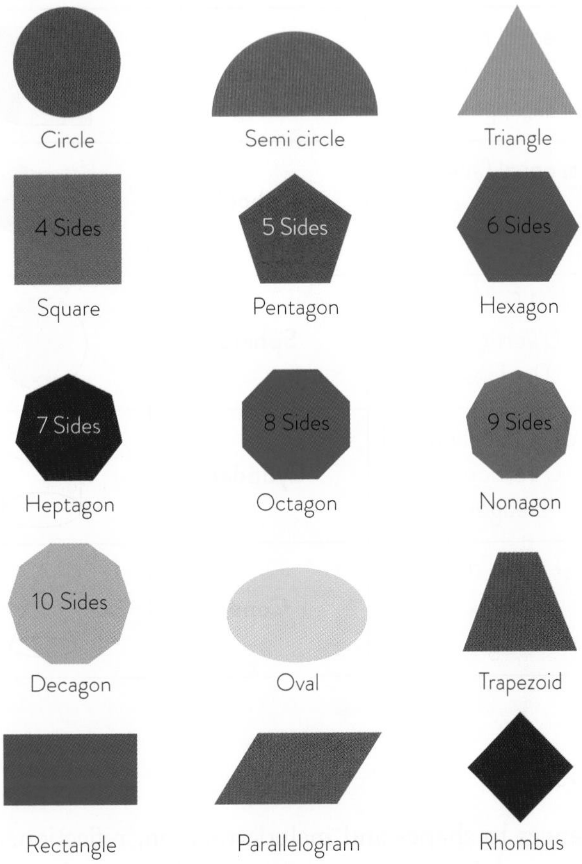

Source: https://monkeypen.com/blogs/news/2d-shapes-posture-for-kids

Figure 16.72 Not all triangles are the same

a This group of triangles are congruent b This group of triangles are incongruent

described as similar but not exactly the same. Both groups are triangles, but for younger students this concept can be confusing.

Playing with and manipulating shapes helps children to understand their attributes.

Shapes and geometry

Properties of shapes and objects

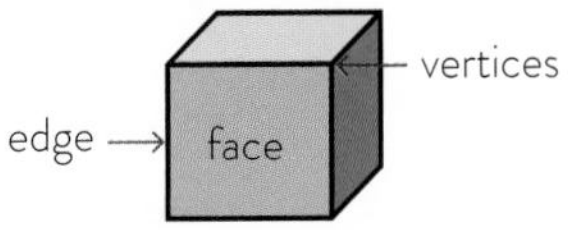

Properties of 2D shapes are described by their shape and angles. Properties of 3D shapes are described by length, width and height. 3D shapes are solid and have:

- faces – any flat surface of the object
- edges – a line where two faces meet
- vertices – the point where two or more lines meet (e.g., a corner)

The amount of space occupied by a 3D shape is called volume (see **Figure 16.73**).

Figure 16.73 Examples of attributes of 3D shapes

6 equal faces 8 vertices 12 edges	**Cube**	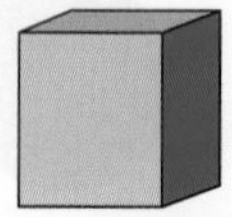
6 equal faces 8 vertices 12 edges	**Cuboid**	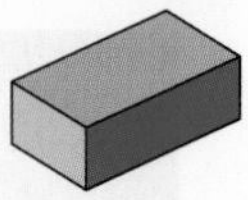
1 face 0 vertices 0 edges	**Sphere**	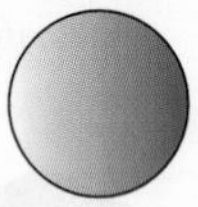
3 faces, 2 flat, 1 curved 0 vertices 2 edges	**Cylinder**	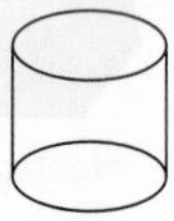
2 faces, 1 flat, 1 curved 1 vertex 1 edge	**Cone**	

Transformations

Transformations are changes to shapes and include rotation, reflection, translation and dilation (see **Figure 16.74**). When studying transformations, students are introduced to transformation formulas.

Figure 16.74 Transformations

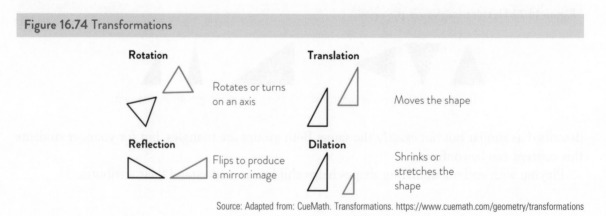

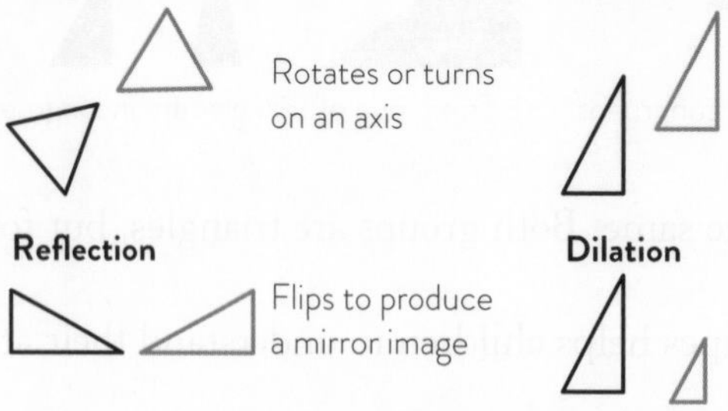

Source: Adapted from: CueMath. Transformations. https://www.cuemath.com/geometry/transformations

Angles

An angle is the space between two rays (lines) extending from a single point. This space is measured in degrees. Angles help to identify common shapes, such as a square, a rhombus or an equilateral triangle. Some of the angles explored in the curriculum are described in **Figure 16.75**.

Figure 16.75 Angles

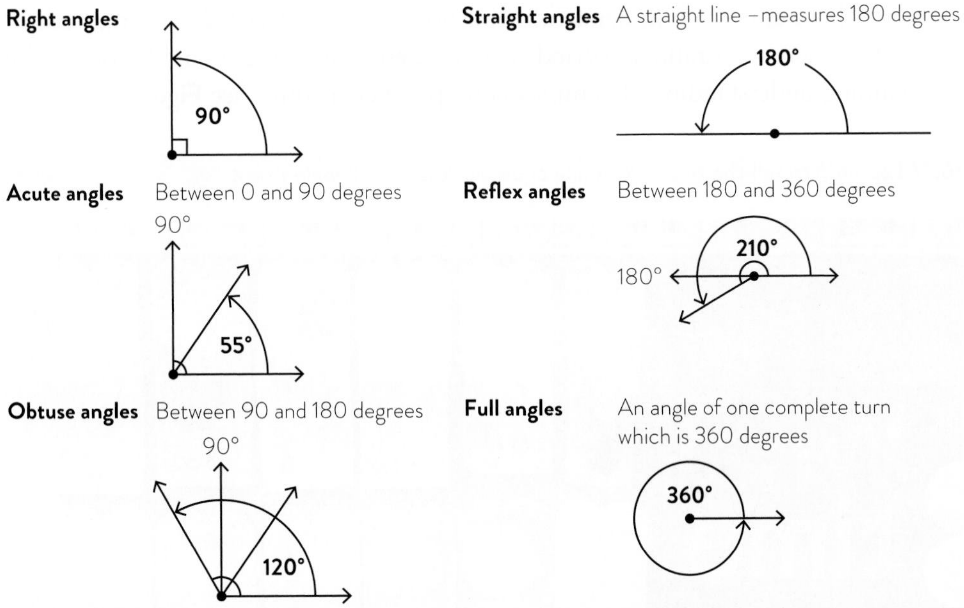

Source: DK Find Out! https://www.dkfindout.com/us/math/geometry/angles

Students learn to identify, compare and measure different types of angles, using a variety of formulas. An example of curriculum content related to angles is shown in **Figure 16.76**.

Figure 16.76 The study of angles

Year 4	Estimate and compare angles using angler names including obtuse, acute, straight angle, reflex and revolution, and recognise their relationship to a right angle
Year 5	Estimate, construct and measure angles in degrees, using appropriate tools including a protractor, and relate these measures to angle names
Year 6	Estimate, angles on a straight line and angles at a point and vertically opposite; se these to determine unknown angles, communicating reasoning

Source: Australian Curriculum, Assessment and Reporting Authority (ACARA). Mathematics. https://v9.australiancurriculum.edu.au/f-10-curriculum.html/learning-areas/mathematics/year-4; https://v9.australiancurriculum.edu.au/f-10-curriculum.html/learning-areas/mathematics/year-5; https://v9.australiancurriculum.edu.au/f-10-curriculum.html/learning-areas/mathematics/year-6

Understanding and measuring time

Children begin to develop a sense of time when they become aware of predictable sequences in their daily routines – for example, eating breakfast, brushing teeth, getting dressed, playing, having morning tea and so on. Very young children are able to distinguish day and night and begin to relate activities and routines to these time frames. Children also begin to understand time when they hear language related to time, such as: in a minute, later, tomorrow, now, first, today, sometimes, before, after and tonight.

The ability to tell the time is a complex task simply because the assigning of seconds, minutes, hours, days, weeks, months and years is an abstract concept. Most children live in the moment and have a very different understanding of time, for example, to an adult who is rushing to get to work on time.

Young children experience time in relation to their day-to-day routines – there is after breakfast, before lunch, after dinner, bedtime and so on. They associate time with various tasks and activities but have almost no understanding of how time is measured. You may recall that it's not until Piaget's concrete operational period that children really begin to apply logical thinking to develop a beginning understanding of complex concepts such as time (see **Figure 16.77**).

Figure 16.77 Learning to tell the time on an analogue clock is a challenging task

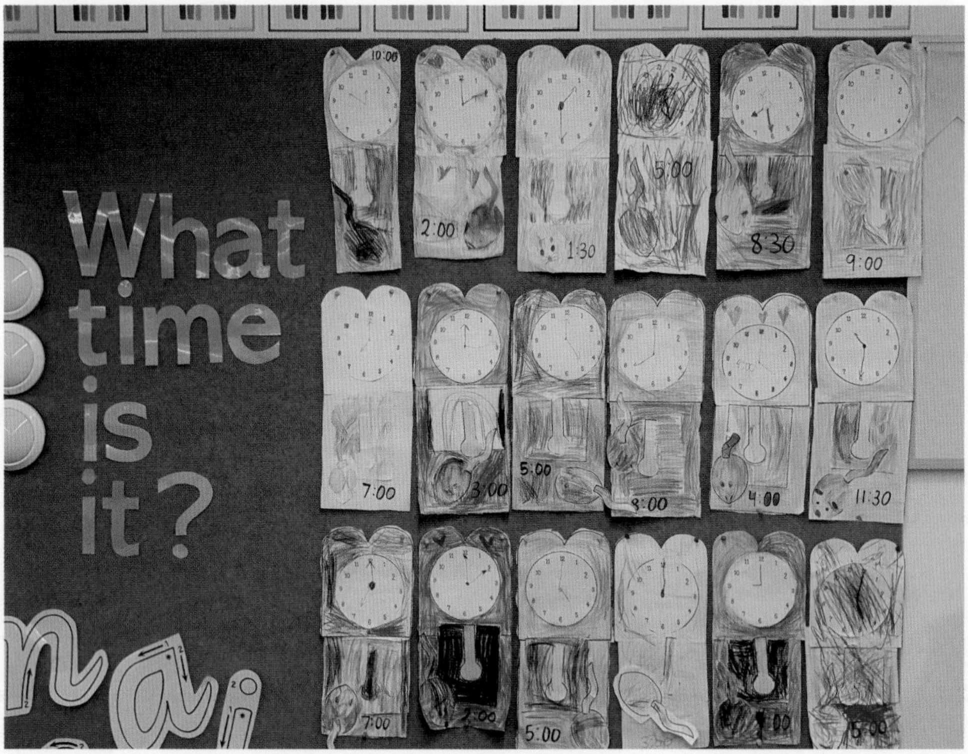

Source: Photo by Tish Okely © Cengage

Foundation skills for understanding and measuring time are concentrated in Foundation to Year 6. Examples of achievement standards for this sub-element are described in **Figure 16.78**.

Figure 16.78 Australian Curriculum. Measurement (time) – sample achievement standards

Foundation	> Sequence days of the week and times of the day including morning, lunchtime, afternoon and night-time, and connect them to familiar events and actions
Year 1	> Describe the duration and sequence of events using years, months, weeks, days and hours
Year 2	> Identify the date and determine the number of days between events using calendars > Recognise and read the time represented on an analogue clock to the hour, half-hour and quarter-hour
Year 3	> Recognise and use the relationship between formal units of time, including days, hours, minutes and seconds to estimate and compare the duration of events > Describe the relationship between the hours and minutes on analogue and digital clocks, and read the time to the nearest minute
Year 4	> Solve problems involving the duration of time including situations involving 'a.m.' and 'p.m.' and conversions between units of time

Year 5	> Compare 12- and 24-hour time systems and solve practical problems involving the conversion between them
Year 6	> Interpret and use timetables and itineraries to plan activities and determine the duration of events and journeys

Source: Australian Curriculum, Assessment and Reporting Authority (ACARA) Mathematics. https://v9.australiancurriculum.edu.au/f-10-curriculum/learning-areas/mathematics/foundation-year_year-1_year-2_year-3_year-4_year-5_year-6?view=quick&detailed-content-descriptions=0&hide-ccp=0&hide-gc=0&side-by-side=1&strands-start-index=0&subjects-start-index=0 AC

Examples of understanding and measuring time activities are shown in **Figure 16.79** and **Figure 16.80**.

Figure 16.79 Measuring and recording time

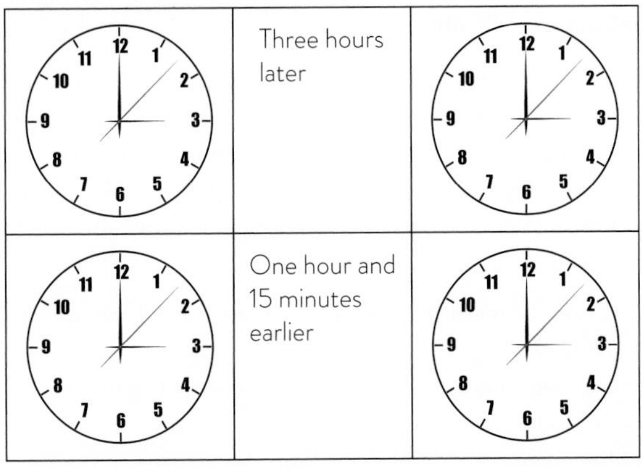

Figure 16.80 Reading and interpreting a timetable

Buses	Blackburn	Greensville	Redhead	Blue Lagoon
School bus	8.00	8.15	8.30	8.45
Tram	8.05	No stop	8.20	8.30
Day tripper	8.15	8.35	8.50	9.10
Z-Express	8.15	No stop	No stop	8.50
Which bus is the quickest from Blackburn to Blue Lagoon?				
How long does it take to get from Greensville to Blue Lagoon in the School bus?				
Where does the Tram not stop?				
Where might the Z-Express be at around 8.45?				
Can you catch the Z-Express from Redhead?				
Which bus is the slowest to reach Blue Lagoon?				
If school starts at 9.00 am which bus would make you late for school?				

Understanding time

Space

The Space strand of the general capability 'develops ways of visualising, representing and working with the location, direction, shape, placement, proximity and transformation of objects at macro, local and micro scales in natural and constructed worlds. It underpins the capacity to make pictures, diagrams, maps, projections, networks, models and graphics that enable the manipulation and analysis of shapes and objects through actions and the senses' (ACARA, 2023f). Examples of the Space strand are shown in **Figure 16.81**.

Figure 16.81 Australian Curriculum. Space strand – sample achievement standards

Year 1	> Make, compare and classify familiar shapes; recognise familiar shapes and objects in the environment, identifying the similarities and differences between them > Give and follow directions to move people and objects to different locations within a space
Year 3	> Make, compare and classify objects, identifying key features and explaining why these features make them suited to their uses > Interpret and create two-dimensional representations of familiar environments, locating key landmarks and objects relative to each other
Year 5	> Connect objects to their nets and build objects from their nets using spatial and geometric reasoning > Construct a grid coordinate system that uses coordinates to locate positions within a space; use coordinates and directional language to describe position and movement > Describe and perform translations, reflections and rotations of shapes, using dynamic geometric software where appropriate; recognise what changes and what remains the same, and identify any symmetries
Year 7	> Represent objects in 2 dimensions; discuss and reason about the advantages and disadvantages of different representations > Classify triangles, quadrilaterals and other polygons according to their side and angle properties; identify and reason about relationships > Describe transformations of a set of points using coordinates in the Cartesian plane, translations and reflections on an axis, and rotations about a given point > Design and create algorithms involving a sequence of steps and decisions that will sort and classify sets of shapes according to their attributes, and describe how the algorithms work
Year 9	> Recognise the constancy of the sine, cosine and tangent ratios for a given angle in right-angled triangles using properties of similarity > Apply the enlargement transformation to shapes and objects using dynamic geometry software as appropriate; identify and explain aspects that remain the same and those that change > Design, test and refine algorithms involving a sequence of steps and decisions based on geometric constructions and theorems; discuss and evaluate refinements

Source: Australian Curriculum, Assessment and Reporting Authority (ACARA) (2023c). Mathematics. https://v9.australiancurriculum.edu.au/f-10-curriculum.html/learning-areas/mathematics/foundation-year_year-1_year-2_year-3_year-4_year-5_year-6_year-7_year-8_year-9_year-10?view=quick&detailed-content-descriptions=0&side-by-side=1&strands-start-index=0&subjects-start-index=0&hide-ccp=0&hide-gc=0

Positioning and locating

Understanding spatial relationships begins when babies begin to crawl under, over and around furniture, when they drop objects from their highchair and when they begin to climb and experiment with their own body in space. By school age, students can typically demonstrate an understanding of spatial relationships by following directions, such as those shown in **Figure 16.82**.

Understanding of direction includes concepts such as back, forward, left, right, top and bottom. This can be demonstrated by asking students to follow the directions shown in **Figure 16.83**.

Figure 16.82 Understanding spatial relationships

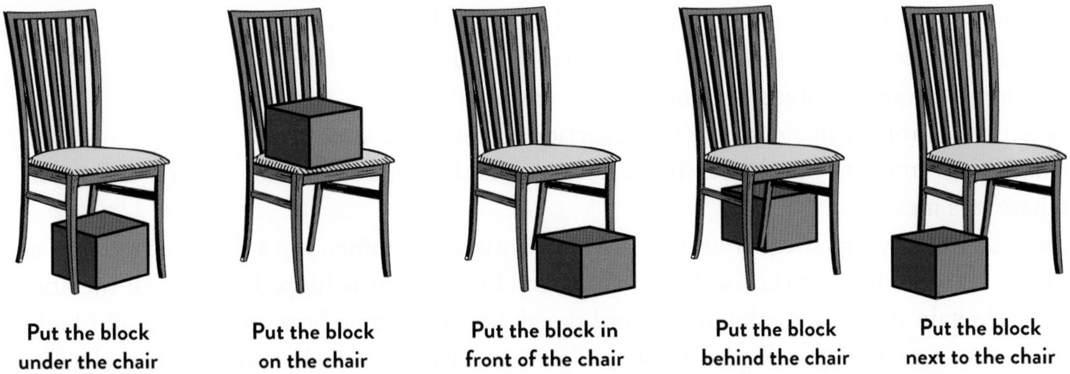

Put the block under the chair
Put the block on the chair
Put the block in front of the chair
Put the block behind the chair
Put the block next to the chair

Figure 16.83 Understanding direction

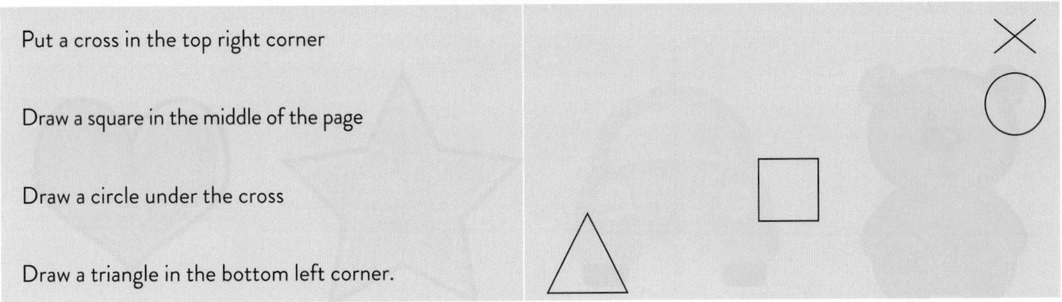

Put a cross in the top right corner
Draw a square in the middle of the page
Draw a circle under the cross
Draw a triangle in the bottom left corner.

Positioning and locating activities

Symmetry

To be symmetrical, one side of an object must be identical to the other if you flip, slide or turn it. There are many examples of symmetry in nature, including flowers, leaves, patterns on rocks, insects and animals. Reflection symmetry occurs when there is a mirror image – a line of symmetry can be drawn through the centre, as seen in **Figure 16.84**.

Figure 16.84 Line of symmetry

Source: iStock.com/Vac1

Some figures also have rotational symmetry, as seen in **Figure 16.85**. For example, a square has rotational symmetry of order 4, which means that if it is rotated through 360° about its centre then it will look exactly like its original shape and position exactly four times through its rotation. In a similar way, an equilateral triangle has rotational symmetry of order 3 and a rectangle has rotational symmetry of order 2.

Figure 16.85 Rotational symmetry

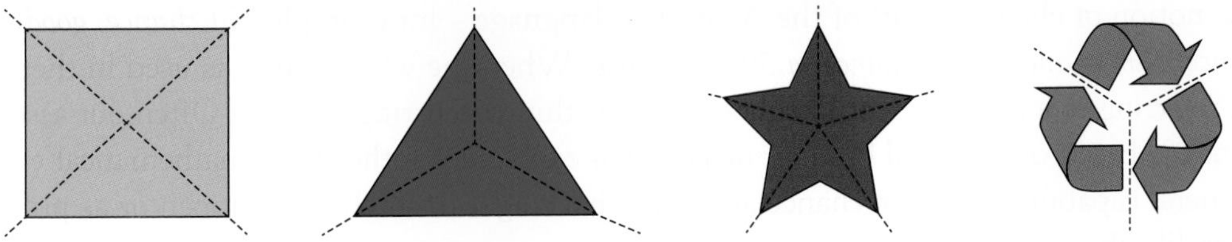

A third type of symmetry is called point symmetry, in which an object has an opposite matching part located the same distance from the central point. An example of point symmetry is the king, queen or jack found in a traditional pack of playing cards.

The study of symmetry includes transformations, which include:

- *rotation* – turning an object around from a central point
- *reflection* – a mirror image where the reflection remains the same size
- *translation* – moving the object: the object remains the same shape and size, regardless of where it is moved to.

Shapes can be symmetrical or asymmetrical. Identifying symmetry is a skill that requires spatial reasoning – the ability to visualise how a shape might look if it is flipped or turned; the ability to create and retain this as a mental image; and the ability to imagine how an object might look from a different perspective (see **Figure 16.86**): 'Can you visualise which letters of the alphabet are symmetrical? Can you visualise a 3D shape such as a pyramid or a cone from above and below?'

Figure 16.86 Symmetrical objects when cut vertically (point symmetry)

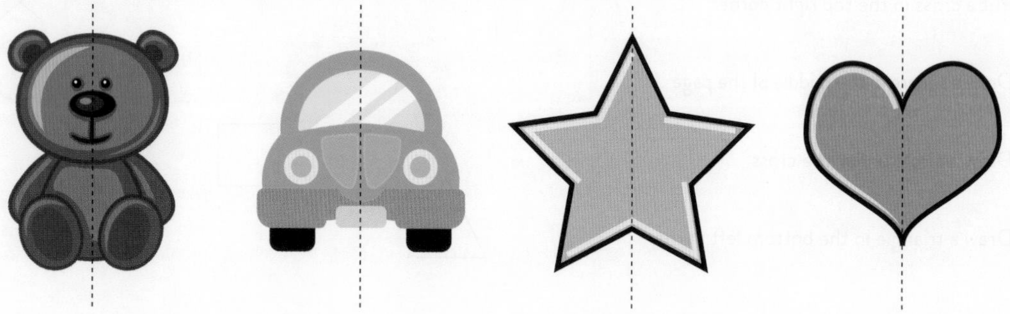

Source: Shutterstock.com/nata_danilenko (bear); Shutterstock.com/sasimoto (car); Shutterstock.com/Elisa Gavi (shapes)

Statistics and probability

The Statistics and probability strand 'develops ways of collecting, understanding and describing data and its distribution'. It includes:

> – *Probability (understanding chance)* – student becomes increasingly able to use the language of chance and the numerical values of probabilities when determining the likelihood of an event and comparing chance events in relation to variation and expectation.
>
> – *Interpreting and representing data* – student becomes increasingly able to recognise, use and interpret visual and numerical displays to describe data associated with statistical investigations, and to critically evaluate investigations by others.
>
> Source: Australian Curriculum, Assessment and Reporting Authority (2023e). Understand this general capability. Numeracy. https://v9.australiancurriculum.edu.au/teacher-resources/understand-this-general-capability/numeracy

Figure 16.87 and **Figure 16.88** show samples of achievement standards for the Statistics and probability strand of the Australian Curriculum.

The notion of chance is part of the Australian language – for example, *fat chance, good chance, no chance, slim chance, not a chance, a 50:50 chance*. When the word chance is used in these ways, we are referring to a possibility or likelihood of something occurring (or not). Often our assessment of chance is based on personal opinion or personal experience rather than mathematical evidence. The general capabilities refer to chance as events that might or might not happen or as predictions based on likelihood.

Figure 16.87 Australian Curriculum – Statistics: sample achievement standards – understanding chance

Year 3	Identify practical activities and everyday events that involve chance; describe possible outcomes and events as 'likely' or 'unlikely' and identify some events as 'certain' or 'impossible' explaining, reasoning
Year 4	Describe possible everyday events and the possible outcomes of chance experiments and order outcomes or events based on their likelihood of occurring; identify independent or dependent events
Year 5	List the possible outcomes of chance experiments involving equally likely outcomes and compare to those which are not equally likely
Year 6	Conduct repeated chance experiments and run simulations with an increasing number of trials using digital tools; compare observations with expected results and discuss the effect on variation of increasing the number of trials
Year 7	Conduct repeated chance experiments and run simulations with a large number of trials using digital tools; compare predictions about outcomes with observed results, explaining the differences
Year 8	Conduct repeated chance experiments and simulations, using digital tools to determine probabilities for compound events, and describe results

Source: Australian Curriculum, Assessment and Reporting Authority (ACARA) (2023c). Mathematics. https://v9.australiancurriculum.edu.au/f-10-curriculum.html/learning-areas/mathematics/foundation-year_year-1_year-2_year-3_year-4_year-5_year-6_year-7_year-8_year-9_year-10?view=quick&detailed-content-descriptions=0&side-by-side=1&strands-start-index=0&subjects-start-index=0&hide-ccp=0&hide-gc=0

Figure 16.88 Examples of how chance is explored by students in Years 3 to 10

Year 3	Predicting what could happen next in practical activities that involve an element of chance, considering possible outcomes and using terms such as 'likely' or 'unlikely' to explain their predictions
Year 4	Experimenting with tossing two coins at the same time, recording and commenting on the chance of outcomes after a number of tosses
Year 5	Discussing supermarket promotions such as collecting stickers or objects and whether there is an equal chance of getting each of them
Year 6	Recognising the language used to describe situations involving uncertainty, such as what it means to be lucky, a 75% chance of rain or a 1-in-100 years flood
Year 7	Conducting simulations using online simulation tools and comparing the combined results of a large number of trials to predicted results
Year 8	Using a random number generator and digital tools to simulate rolling two dice and calculating the difference between them, investigating what difference is likely to occur more often
Year 9	Conducting two-step chance experiments using systematic methods to list outcomes of experiments and to list outcomes favourable to an event
Year 10	Using simulations to gather data on frequencies for situations involving chance that appear to be counter-intuitive, such as the three-door problem or the birthday problem

Source: Australian Curriculum, Assessment and Reporting Authority (ACARA) (2023c). Mathematics. https://v9.australiancurriculum.edu.au/f-10-curriculum.html/learning-areas/mathematics/foundation-year_year-1_year-2_year-3_year-4_year-5_year-6_year-7_year-8_year-9_year-10?view=quick&detailed-content-descriptions=0&side-by-side=1&strands-start-index=0&subjects-start-index=0&hide-ccp=0&hide-gc=0

The general capabilities refer to probability as the number of ways an event can happen out of the total number of possibilities. Probability can be described as fractions of one, for example the probability when rolling a die of an even number is 50% or ½ the time. **Figure 16.89** shows how probability can be shown using a probability line, with 0 being impossible and 1 being a certainty.

Probability explained

Figure 16.89 Probability line

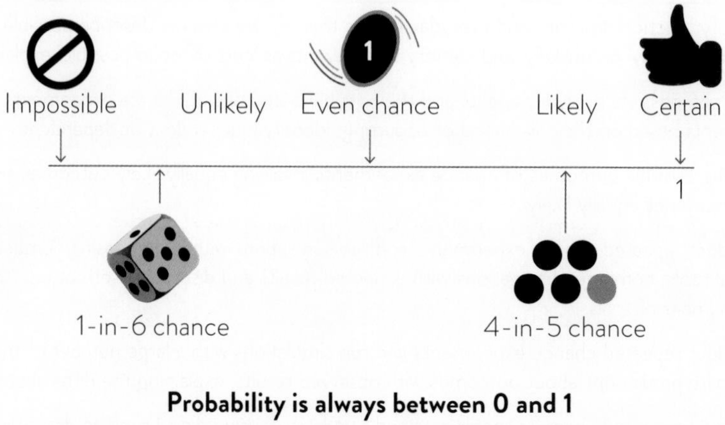

Source: Math Is Fun (2020). https://www.mathsisfun.com/probability_line.html

Interpreting and representing data

The interpreting and representing data sub-element describes how a student becomes increasingly able to recognise and use visual and numerical displays to describe data associated with statistical investigations, and to critically evaluate investigations by others. Making sense of data draws on knowing the concepts and tools that are being used to describe the global features of data. A student understands how these concepts and tools make meaning of data in context, and develops the ability to think critically about any claims, either questioning or confirming them.

The sub-element includes:

- one-to-one data displays
- collecting and displaying data
- interpreting data scales
- shape of data displays
- graphical representations of data
- recognising bias.

Source: Australian Curriculum, Assessment and Reporting Authority (ACARA) (2023b). General capabilities. Numeracy. Number sense and algebra (V 9.0). https://v9.australiancurriculum.edu.au/f-10-curriculum/general-capabilities/numeracy?element=0&sub-element=0

Sample achievement standards for interpreting and representing data are shown in **Figure 16.90**.

Figure 16.90 Australian Curriculum. Statistics: sample achievement standards – interpreting and representing data

Year 1	Acquire and record data for categorical variables in various ways including using digital tools, objects, images, drawings, lists, tally marks and symbols
Year 2	Create different graphical representations of data using software where appropriate; compare the different representations, identify and describe common and distinctive features in response to questions
Year 4	Create and compare different graphical representations of data sets including using software where appropriate; interpret the data in terms of the context
Year 5	Analyse the effectiveness of different displays or visualisations in illustrating and comparing data distributions, then discuss the shape of distributions and the variation in the data

Year 7	Plan and conduct statistical investigations involving data for discrete and continuous numerical variables; analyse and interpret distributions of data and report findings in terms of shape and summary statistics
Year 8	Plan and conduct statistical investigations involving samples of a population; use ethical and fair methods to make inferences about the population and report findings, acknowledging uncertainty

Source: Australian Curriculum, Assessment and Reporting Authority (ACARA) (2023c). Mathematics. https://v9.australiancurriculum.edu.au/f-10-curriculum.html/learning-areas/mathematics/foundation-year_year-1_year-2_year-3_year-4_year-5_year-6_year-7_year-8_year-9_year-10?view=quick&detailed-content-descriptions=0&side-by-side=1&strands-start-index=0&subjects-start-index=0&hide-ccp=0&hide-gc=0

The ability to collect, describe, analyse and interpret data is a complex cognitive task. A progression from sorting, classifying and ordering is the ability to analyse, organise and represent data visually using graphs, charts, tables, symbols and pictures. The ability to collect and analyse data provides a foundation for the development of skills necessary to interpret data to make predictions and explore probability and elementary statistics.

At its simplest, data collection allows students to identify and describe attributes of collections of objects and things – for example, they begin to recognise attributes such as function, colour, shape or volume. Listed below are examples of how children develop and apply data-collecting skills:

- A toddler is asked to find all the socks in the washing basket. The attributes are *socks* or *not socks*.
- A young preschooler is asked to put all the small, coloured blocks into a container. The attributes are *small coloured blocks* and *all other blocks*.
- A Kindergarten student is asked to sort the blocks into separate colours: red, blue and green. The attributes are the individual colours.
- A seven-year-old is asked to sort the blocks in the following manner: colour, shape and thickness. This requires the student to think about the following sets and subsets: sets in red, blue and green blocks; subset – shapes; subset – thickness.
- An eight-year-old is given a set of animal pictures and asked to think about the number of ways in which the animals could be sorted to create subsets.
- A 13-year-old is asked to collect information from each student in the class. She is asked to record the students' favourite foods and the gender of the students.
- A group of 15-year-old students are asked to collect data on preferred options for the school's end-of-term social event. The student may select from five different options. The students collecting the data must record the preferred option, the gender and grade of each student.

Students follow a sequence of data collection and analysis that begins with a question: 'What do we want to know or find out about?' This leads students to determine the information that needs to be collected, how it can be sourced and how it can be collected (survey, samples, measurements, tallies, etc.). **Figure 16.91** shows the cycle of data collection, analysis and conclusion (answering the original question and/or raising further questions for future investigation).

Representing data using simple pictorial charts or graphs is the next stage in working with data. Understanding that a chart or a graph can be used to represent facts is also a complex task.

Figure 16.91 Data collection and analysis cycle

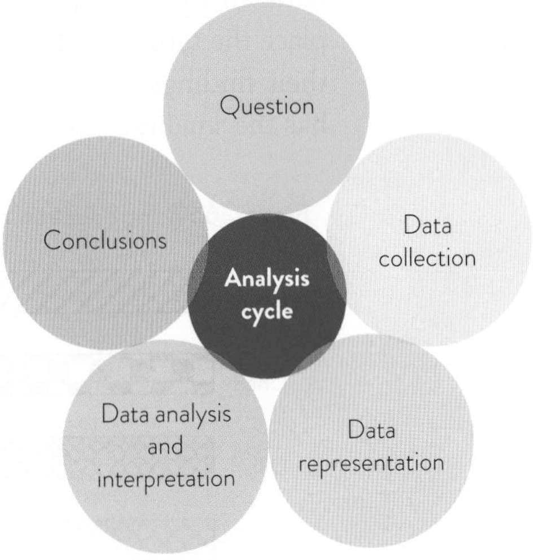

Source: Identifying opportunities to build data literacy in Years 7–10 Health and Physical Education P–10 Australian Curriculum © State of Queensland (QCAA) 2020, https://www.qcaa.qld.edu.au/copyright. Licensed under Creative Commons 4.0, https://creativecommons.org/licenses/by/4.0/

GRAPHS

SCENARIO

EYE COLOUR

The Kindergarten class was given handheld mirrors and asked to identify their eye colour. Each student was then required to colour a picture of an eye, which was used to create a pictorial graph of their data (**Figure 16.92**).

When the graph is completed the teacher works with the students to interpret the graph. The students find:

- There are 11 students with blue eyes.
- There are 5 students with brown eyes.
- There are 3 students with green eyes.
- There are 2 students with hazel eyes.
- The most common eye colour is blue.

Figure 16.92 Pictorial graph

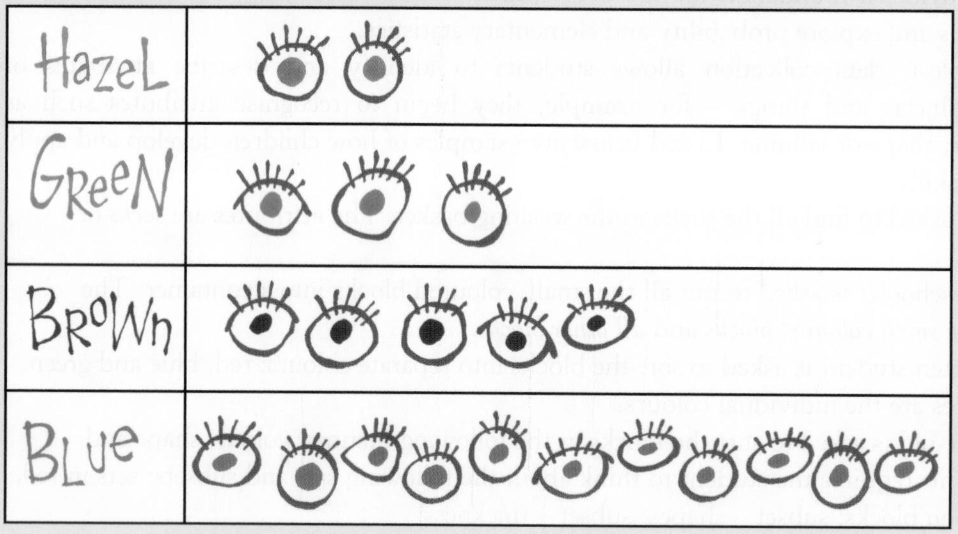

Figure 16.93 is an example of how students begin to collect, represent and interpret simple data. In this example, the students use coloured paper tape to measure around their waist and place the tape in order from longest to shortest. The simple graph allows the student to interpret their findings. Rose has the largest waist, Chen and Dillan have the same-sized waist and Rob has the smallest waist.

Figure 16.93 Introduction to data collection and analysis

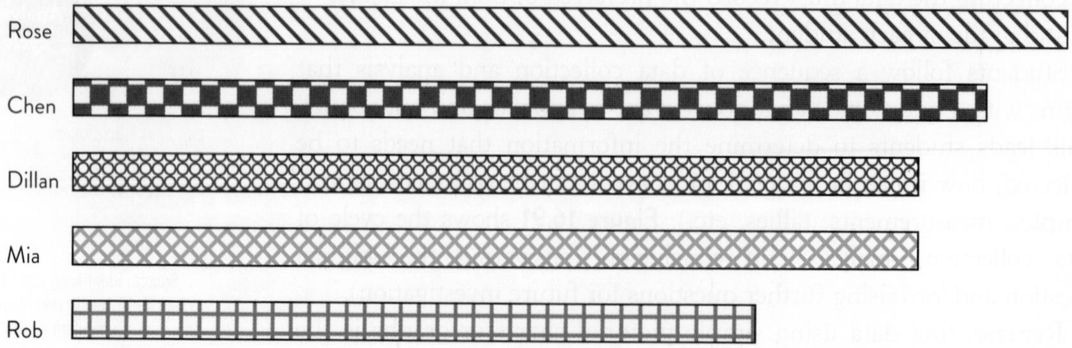

In **Figure 16.94**, students in Year 5 are presented with a bar graph of sales of different ice-cream flavours which student are required to analyse and interpret.

Figure 16.94 Double bar graph work sheet

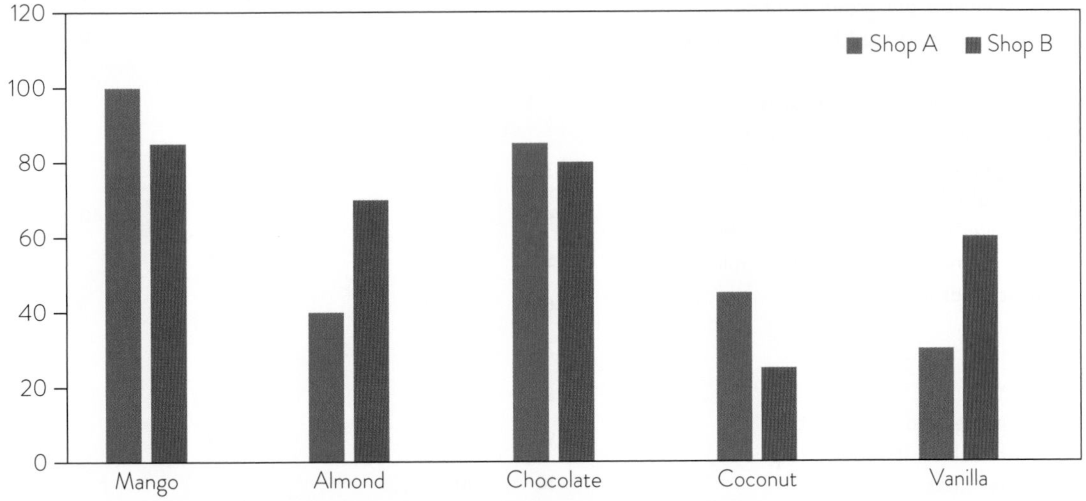

How many mango ice-creams were sold by Shop A?

Which flavour of ice-cream do people like most in Shop A?

Find the total number of chocolate ice-creams sold by Shop A and Shop B.

Which shop sold 25 coconut ice-creams?

Find the total number of coconut ice-creams sold by Shop A and Shop B.

In Shop B which flavour of ice-cream is more popular – vanilla or chocolate?

Find the total number of ice-creams sold by Shop B

How many vanilla ice-creams were sold by Shop A?

Using calculators

Calculators are a useful tool that can be used to support numeracy development. Calculators *should not* replace mental computation or pen and paper, and students should not rely solely on calculators but should be able to use a calculator when it is appropriate to do so. According to Seeley and colleagues (2005, p. 52), research studies have shown that students who use calculators are better at understanding mathematical concepts and solving problems.

Collecting, interpreting and representing data

SCENARIO

USING A CALCULATOR

TASK 1

The teacher divides the class into groups of four. Each student has a calculator, a deck of cards with the picture cards and aces removed (the joker is given the value zero) and a multiplication chart. The students each select two cards from the top of the pile, look at them, then place them face down. Each student is required to use their calculator to multiply the numbers on their cards and record the answer on their multiplication chart. The students are then asked to select one of their cards and complete the multiplication chart for the factor selected.

TASK 2

The students are shown how to play a multiplication game. Each group is given a deck of playing cards with the aces, face cards and jokers removed. The students also have access to one calculator per group and one multiplication chart. The cards are placed face down in six rows of six.

Each player takes turns to turn over two cards at random. The player must multiply the numbers on the cards. If a correct answer is given, the player takes the two cards and fills in the multiplication chart. If the answer is incorrect, the player turns the cards back down on the table. When there are no cards left on the table, the student with the most cards in their own pile wins the game.

WHAT DOES THIS TELL US?

Using calculators to play games allows students to become familiar and comfortable with their use prior to using them for higher-order tasks.

x	0	1	2	3	4	5	6	7	8	9	10
0											0
1					4						
2							12			18	
3											
4											40
5								35	40		
6			12								
7			14		28		42				
8											
9								63			
10		10									

Seeley et al. (2005, p. 52) suggest that calculators are extremely valuable for solving computation problems that students could not otherwise solve. They argue that 'students can develop their decision-making and problem-solving skills far beyond what they would be able to do if they were limited to numbers that they could handle quickly using pencil and paper'.

Calculators can assist students to develop better number sense, support problem-solving and simplify complex tasks. The introduction and use of calculators will vary from classroom to classroom, and will depend on the teacher's assessment of students' basic numeracy concepts.

16.4 Learning and development

As you have explored, the six strands of the Australian Curriculum: Mathematics include key foundation skills and knowledge that students must acquire as a baseline for developing their skills in each strand. The application of mathematical knowledge can only be achieved when students know and understand foundational knowledge of:

- quantity (>, <, =)
- place value
- addition
- subtraction
- multiplication
- division
- fractions.

However, the development of mathematical skills and knowledge is a complex cognitive task that requires skills such as problem-solving, inductive reasoning, the ability to process and store information in the short-term (working) memory, and the ability to recall and retrieve information, and understand and use language to explore concepts. When considering the skills needed for the application of mathematical concepts, it is also useful to think about Bloom's revised taxonomy of classifying thought processes from simple to complex:

- Remember: recall facts and basic concepts
- Understand: explain ideas and concepts

- Apply: use information in new situations
- Analyse: make connections between ideas

Clements and Sarama (2021), citing Kilpatrick, Swafford and Findell (2001), state that mathematical proficiency requires:

> – conceptual understanding – comprehension of mathematical concepts, operations, and relations
> – procedural fluency – skill in carrying out procedures flexibly, accurately, efficiently, and appropriately
> – strategic competence – ability to formulate, represent, and solve mathematical problems
> – adaptive reasoning – capacity for logical thought, reflection, explanation, and justification
> – productive disposition – habitual inclination to see mathematics as sensible, useful, and worthwhile, coupled with a belief in diligence and one's own efficacy.
>
> Source: Clements, D. & Sarama, J. (2021). *Learning and Teaching Early Math: The Learning Trajectories Approach.* 3rd edn. New York: Routledge (p. 10).

You may also recall that it is not until children have reached Piaget's concrete operational stage of cognitive development that they can master many of the foundational mathematical concepts. The ability to hypothesise and think abstractly (needed for higher-order algebra or problem-solving requiring the use of logic) doesn't develop until children have reached the formal operational stage.

We also know that:

- new knowledge must be built on existing knowledge (scaffolding)
- repetition and practice are essential for consolidating understanding of concepts (conceptual knowledge includes facts, operations/methods, relationships [e.g. 2 × 6 is the same as 6 × 2]) and understanding of how these can be applied to solve a variety of mathematical problems
- when the working memory is overloaded, students will struggle to process new information
- language is central to learning (the language of mathematics – words, numbers, symbols, pictures and graphs).

Maths glossary

Teaching strategies

Each school will have a range of instructional models for teaching mathematics based on the needs of the student cohort as well as individual student needs. Many schools will use a combination of online programs as well as direct, teacher-led instruction. To ensure consistency in instruction across all grades, schools may also have an established instructional protocol that identifies the instructional models to be used, as well as expectations in relation to assessment, testing and data collection.

An example of a numeracy protocol and instructional procedures are shown in **Figure 16.95**. In this example, instruction begins by tuning in to mathematics using a warm-up game. The teacher then uses direct instruction followed by planned small group and individual tasks that allow students to apply new knowledge and practise existing skills and knowledge. Open-ended investigations that include multiple entry and exit points provide differentiated instruction to meet each student's learning needs. The lesson concludes with a reflection that allows students to talk about their learning and engage in self-assessment of their learning needs. The protocol also allows opportunities for students to engage in hands-on investigation and learning that reflects best practice in relation to learning theory and child development knowledge.

Examples of maths programs used in schools

The protocol used in **Figure 16.95** includes a combination of modelled, shared, guided and natural mathematics.

Figure 16.95 Example of numeracy protocols and instructional procedures

NUMERACY PROTOCOLS

- Students will have a minimum of five hours on Numeracy each week
- Consistent Mathematics language will be used across the school
- The Numeracy Instructional Model will be used for Numeracy sessions
- Explicit learning intentions and success criteria will be displayed and referred to, throughout the lesson Activities will focus on the development of the relevant skills and concepts
- Daily fluency time will be embedded into the Numeracy block
- The Numeracy Assessment Schedule and timelines for data collection will be adhered to
- Testing and data will be used to inform planning and determine student growth
- Manipulatives are to be used regularly in all classes from Prep to Year 6
- Open-ended tasks and planning documents will reflect pre-planned questions.

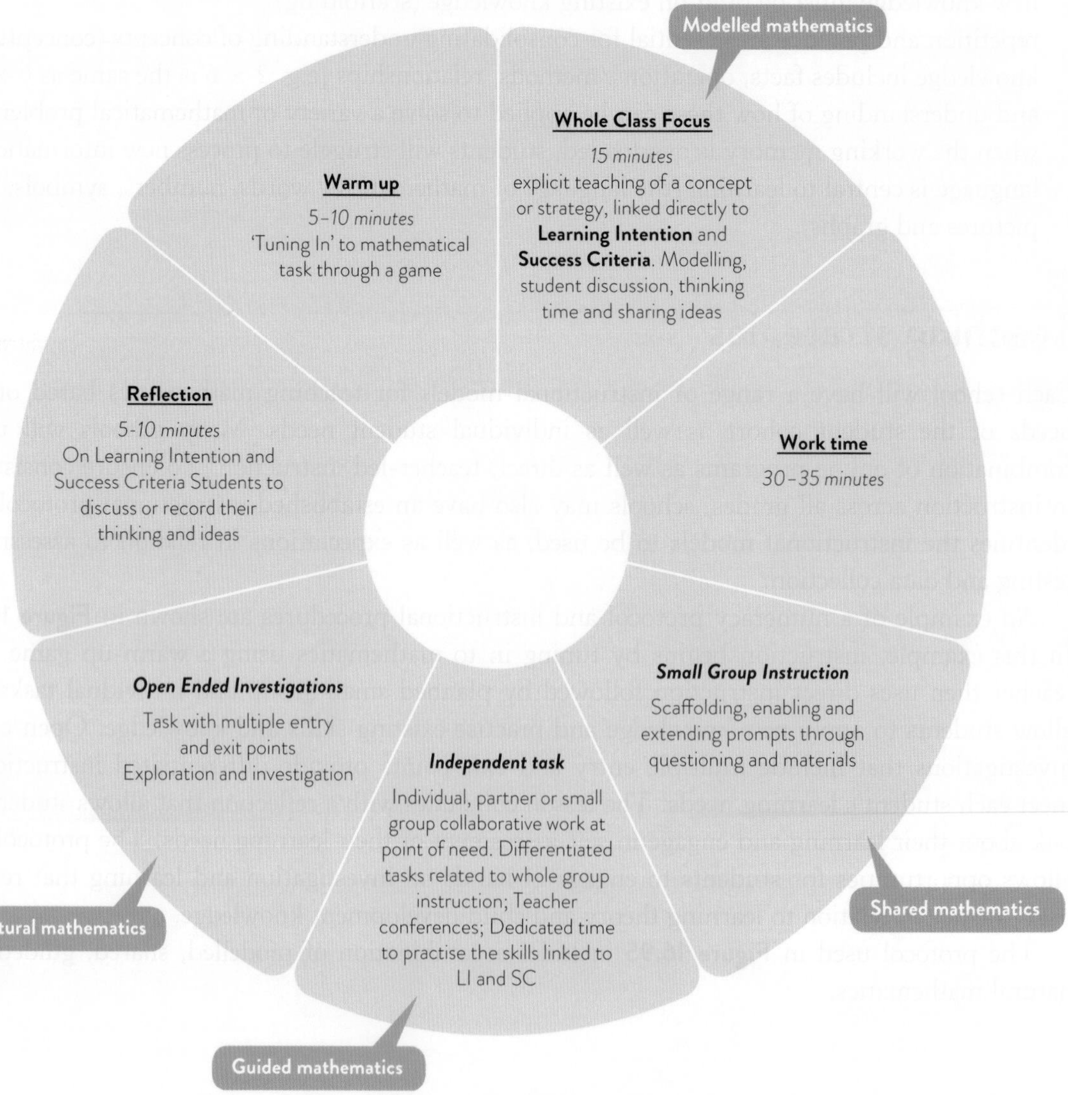
Modelled mathematics
Whole Class Focus
15 minutes
explicit teaching of a concept or strategy, linked directly to Learning Intention and Success Criteria. Modelling, student discussion, thinking time and sharing ideas
Warm up
5–10 minutes
'Tuning In' to mathematical task through a game
Work time
30–35 minutes
Reflection
5-10 minutes
On Learning Intention and Success Criteria Students to discuss or record their thinking and ideas
Small Group Instruction
Scaffolding, enabling and extending prompts through questioning and materials
Open Ended Investigations
Task with multiple entry and exit points
Exploration and investigation
Independent task
Individual, partner or small group collaborative work at point of need. Differentiated tasks related to whole group instruction; Teacher conferences; Dedicated time to practise the skills linked to LI and SC
Shared mathematics
Natural mathematics
Guided mathematics

Source: Horsham West & Haven Primary School, Victoria. https://www.horshamwps.vic.edu.au/teaching-and-learning/numeracy

Modelled mathematics involves *adult-directed small group instruction*. The teacher:

- introduces the learning experience by explaining its real-life significance, its relationship to other areas of maths and the steps involved in learning the skill
- uses the students' prior knowledge as a starting point to actively model and describe the knowledge/skills/procedures using tangible, hands-on materials. This strategy uses Vygotsky's zone of proximal development where new knowledge is introduced by drawing on existing knowledge and skills
- makes explicit the links between what students see, how the task is described and how the task is represented symbolically
- provides support for students to explore, using trial and error, and practice
- uses language prompts to promote thinking and problem solving, such as:
  - 'Look at me while I …'
  - 'Do you recall how we …?'
  - 'Listen while I explain …'
  - 'Let's see if we can now …'
  - 'Now, you try …'
  - 'What is different? How is it the same?'
  - 'In your own words tell me …'

In modelled mathematics, students are encouraged to draw on prior knowledge, ask questions, and engage in discussion and hands-on practice/exploration and problem-solving. Students are encouraged to verbalise the task, make connections with prior knowledge and, if appropriate, use written symbols to represent the task.

In **shared mathematics**, learning is made explicit by highlighting key ideas and encouraging students to explore connections with other mathematical ideas. The teacher introduces the learning experience and asks students to engage in brainstorming to identify and link prior knowledge and skills to the new task: 'Tell me what you know about …'; 'Do you remember when we …?' Students are also encouraged to use tangible materials to explore the task and use written symbols to represent it. Shared mathematics usually occurs with the whole class or with small groups.

Video: Modelling numeracy lessons

Guided mathematics requires minimal input from adults. The teacher introduces the learning experience and reviews relevant skills and understandings related to the experience. Students are encouraged to discuss their ideas and understanding, and problem-solve using a range of support materials. The teacher or ESW scaffolds learning by asking questions and encouraging students to verbalise their thinking. The teacher or ESW uses language prompts to promote thinking and problem solving, such as:

- 'Today we will …'
- 'Outline the differences for me …'
- 'What are the similarities?'
- 'How have you used this concept before?'
- 'Tell me about …'
- 'If this happened, would it affect the outcome?'

Video: Why do objects sink or float?

Natural mathematics consists of three discrete parts:

1 The teacher directs the students to engage in mental routines (tuning-in). For example:
  - Ask the students to count backwards by 10s starting from 100.
  - Ask specific questions requiring a mental calculation: 'What is 29 minus 7?'
  - Ask open-ended questions, which may have more than one correct response: 'I multiplied two single-digit numbers and the answer was less than 10. What number or numbers could they be?'

– Ask questions that give students the chance to practise the language of mathematics: 'I am thinking of a number between 10 and 40. You may ask questions to find out what my number is. I can only answer yes/no and higher/lower.'

2 The teacher presents students with an open-ended real-life problem (investigations). For example, students are required to work in small groups to find a solution: 'You have $12 and your two friends each have $8. You decide to pool your money to buy pizza and hire a DVD. You can hire three DVDs for $10 or hire a latest release for $8. Small individual pizzas (four slices) cost $8 or you can buy a family combo for $22, which includes garlic bread, one large pizza (10 slices) and soft drink. How will you work out what might be the best value for money for you and your friends?'

3 The teacher invites the students to reflect on and discuss their solutions and how they arrived at the outcome. For example, open-ended questions are used to promote thinking and discussion: 'How did you decide which option would be most cost effective?'; 'What did you need to think about when making your decision?'

These models may be used interchangeably and will depend on the skills and knowledge being introduced and the learning abilities/needs of the students.

CONSIDER THIS

INTRINSIC AND EXTRINSIC MOTIVATION

Posamentier (2013) suggests using both intrinsic and extrinsic motivation to encourage an interest in mathematics. *Extrinsic motivation* involves the attainment of a reward that is outside the student's control – for example, earning free time for a computer game. *Intrinsic motivation* is based on self-fulfilment – doing it because it is rewarding and provides a sense of satisfaction and achievement.

Students can feel motivated when educators:

- develop a positive relationship with students built on mutual trust and respect – always greet every student by their first name
- show empathy – for example, 'I know this is a hard concept to grasp so let's just take it slowly, there is no need to rush'
- are active listeners – listen without interrupting and show genuine interest in what the student is saying
- recognise students' efforts by providing genuine and constructive feedback – for example, 'I like the way you're thinking'; 'I can see you've really thought about your answer'; 'Good response, Tom! Let's just see if you can take it a step further'
- match the task to the student's skill level – providing a challenge that is achievable
- promote collaborative learning – remember that students learn from each other as well as the teacher
- adapt material so that it is relevant to the students – for example, create maths problems around student interests, such as saving up to buy a car, skateboarding, music and dance
- use technology and/or provide hands-on learning opportunities
- offer choices – for example, 'Decide who you will work with today'; 'You need to complete three tasks; you can do them in any order'; 'You can hand your work in any time during the next three weeks; the final due date is . . .'; 'How about you choose which question you want to start with?'
- make themselves available to students – for example, 'If you need extra help or just want to check that you're on the right track, I'm usually free during the second half of lunch.'
- thank students for their participation – let them know their efforts are appreciated
- take a break and add some fun to maths – for example challenge students with brain teasers such as Cool Maths 4 Kids: https://www.coolmath4kids.com/brain-teasers or brain-twisting paradoxes: http://listverse.com/2010/05/28/11-brain-twisting-paradoxes.

When students are struggling, it can be useful to identify and share common problems – for example, 'I have noticed that just about everyone is finding this a challenge. How about we talk about what you understand and don't understand, and we can work it out together as a group?'

▶ DISCUSSION

Discuss the use of extrinsic rewards as a motivator for learning. Do you agree or disagree with the use of rewards? What might be the advantages and disadvantages of using extrinsic rewards in a classroom setting?

Documenting numeracy development

Each teacher will record student outcomes as they relate to the National Numeracy Learning Progression using a preferred online tool. Typically, evidence of numeracy development will be drawn from a variety of contexts, which allow students to demonstrate their application of mathematical knowledge and skills – for example, written observations, work samples, formative and summative assessment tasks, anecdotal records, checklists, quizzes and examinations. Teachers will usually gather this evidence over time and in a number of different learning situations.

Evidence will include formative assessment (students' progress at regular intervals) and summative assessment. For students who present with learning difficulties, teachers may also request a diagnostic assessment, which can be used to identify specific learning difficulties.

Numeracy progress and assessment

Students can participate in their own assessment of skills and knowledge using tools such as 'I Can' Statements as used in NSW schools: https://calculate.org.au/2017/11/03/i-can-statements/ .

16.5 Supporting students who struggle with mathematics

The executive function skills required to be competent at mathematics include holding and manipulating information in mind (working memory), flexible thinking (shifting), focusing on relevant information and ignoring distractions (inhibition). Students who struggle with numeracy may present with executive functioning and sensorimotor difficulties, such as poor visual processing skills (see **Figure 16.96**), poor fine motor skills, poor working memory needed to store, recall and use information, poor organisational skills, limited skills in thinking flexibly, or an inability to identify and focus key information and ignore irrelevant information. Students may demonstrate:

- difficulty using number symbols
- difficulty working towards a solution in a logical and sequential manner
- poor memory and processing skills
- difficulty understanding and using mathematical language
- difficulty remembering and/or applying number facts
- poor problem-solving skills (lack of attack strategies)
- difficulty understanding number operations, particularly multi-step operations.

Figure 16.96 Visual motor processing issues

Visual processing issue	Explanation
Visual discrimination	Difficulty seeing the difference between two similar letters, symbols, shapes or objects – for example, confusing 5 and 3, or 6 and 8
Visual figure–ground discrimination	Inability to identify a shape or symbol from its background, making it difficult to find a specific piece of information on a page
Visual sequencing	Difficulty telling the order of symbols, words or images, making it difficult to read a calculation. They may reverse or misread letters, numbers and words
Visual–motor processing	Difficulty using feedback from the eyes to coordinate the movement of other parts of the body – for example, difficulty writing within the lines or copying information

Visual processing issue	Explanation
Long- or short-term visual memory	Difficulty recalling what they have seen. This can make it hard for students to visualise a problem, and to recall and apply existing knowledge
Visual–spatial	Difficulty telling where objects are in space as well as judging distance
Visual closure	Difficulty identifying an object when only parts are visible – for example, they may not be able to recognise when a calculation is incomplete
Letter and symbol reversal	Switching letters or numbers when writing

Source: Arky, B. (2014). Understanding visual processing issues. Understood. https://www.understood.org/en/learning-attention-issues/child-learning-disabilities/visual-processing-issues/understanding-visual-processing-issues

SCENARIO

STUDENTS WHO STRUGGLE WITH MATHS

JACKSON

Jackson (10 years) struggles with numeracy. He has difficulty writing numerals, often confusing 3 and 5. He uses his fingers for addition and subtraction, but often forgets to count his thumbs. Jackson has difficulty understanding sets and does not understand the concept of filling in a missing number in simple number calculation. Even when using tangible materials, Jackson will become confused as he is working through a problem because he seems to forget what he is doing and has to start over. As his anxiety level increases, he resorts to making wild guesses.

EMMA

Emma (14 years) says she hates maths. She struggles with basic mathematical concepts and tries to cover her lack of skills and knowledge by acting out. She disrupts the class by talking loudly, making jokes and generally making a nuisance of herself. Emma doesn't complete any homework or assignments. Her teacher has all but given up trying to help Emma.

WHAT DOES THIS TELL US?

Students who struggle with maths often find themselves in a downward spiral. They become anxious and fearful about their lack of progress and typically engage in negative self-talk such as, 'I hate maths'; 'I'm no good at maths'. They often resort to guessing, acting out or avoidance, which in turn compounds the problem.

▶ DISCUSSION

Discuss your experience with mathematics in high school. Were you 'good' at maths or did you struggle or simply get by? How did this make you feel about your own abilities?

Strengths and deficits

Very often, students with mathematical difficulties will have both strengths and weaknesses. Gaps or weaknesses in any one area will impact overall performance – for example, a student may be able to apply a formula to obtain the correct answer but may have no understanding of what the answer represents. A student can apply a formula to obtain the circumference of a circle but cannot explain the meaning of the term circumference.

Often mathematical difficulties can be attributed to the problems with conceptualising or understanding the big picture. Consider, for example, the problem $(21 - 5) + 2 = ?$ To answer this correctly, the student must first understand that it is both a subtraction and addition task. The student must be able to correctly sequence the task – that is, deduct 5 from 21 (16) and then add 2 to arrive at the correct answer (18). Students who are not able to do this calculation correctly can be assisted by providing them with concrete materials such as counters, so they can make the calculation manually.

It is easy to make assumptions that students understand what the teacher is saying or demonstrating. This often occurs when instructions are given to students without checking that the students understand what is required. For example, consider the instructions given to Year 3 students in **Figure 16.97**.

Figure 16.97 Instructions

Working in pairs, use your ruler to measure and record the width of each of the objects listed on your worksheet. When you have measured each object, rank them in order of width. (1 = widest)		
Object	**Measurement**	**Ranking**
Door		
Lost and found box		
Windowsill		
Whiteboard		
Library lounge		
Paper cupboard		
Science table		
Your desk		
Blue bookcase		
LEGO crate		
Teacher's desk		
Magazine rack		

In this example, it should not be assumed that every student will understand the term 'width' as it relates to three-dimensional objects. It would also be necessary to check that students know how to use their ruler to measure objects longer in length than their ruler. Student may not understand the word 'rank' and may not know what to do if two objects are the same width.

Establishing a baseline

Before assisting a student, the teacher will have determined a range of factors to establish a baseline for the development of differentiated learning strategy for the student. **Figure 16.98** lists examples of some baseline factors the teacher may consider. These factors may be quite broad and will reflect the concept of 'the whole child'.

The teacher may obtain this information from observing and working with the student, assessment and feedback from the student. Identifying the student's learning needs allows the teacher to set measurable learning goals that will allow progress to be monitored and assessed. It also ensures that differentiated instruction is targeted and time effective. As part of this process, the teacher will identify the most effective teaching strategies. These strategies are explained in **Figure 16.99**.

Figure 16.98 Baseline facts

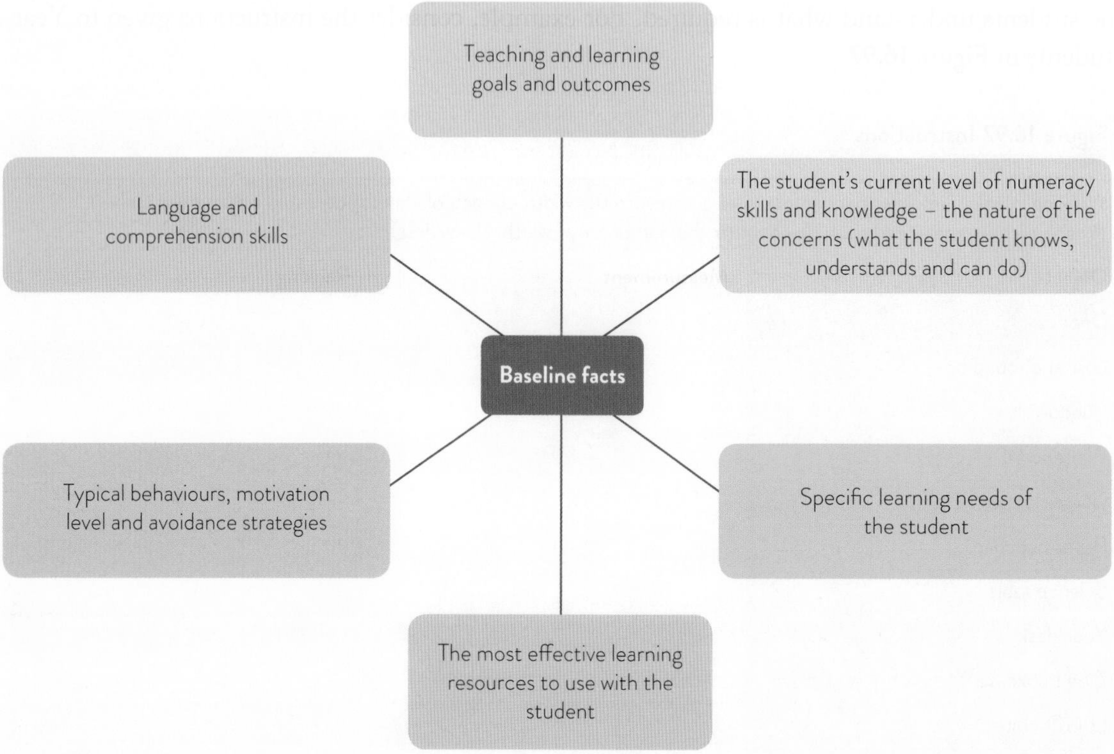

Figure 16.99 Teacher support strategies

Engage in maths conversations

Ask/remind students what they already know and can do: 'Yesterday you showed me that you have a good understanding of fractions. Today we're going to use that knowledge to add fractions. I think you're ready for this challenge.'

Give clear step-by-step instructions

This may include listening to verbal instructions which should focus on the step-by-step procedures rather than a final answer. Students who are struggling need time to process each step and practise each step. For example:

> 'Let's take a look at this problem. I'll read it to you and then we'll work through it together: (10 × 9) ÷ (5 × 2) = (90) ÷ ( ) = ?
> 'We start at the left, just like when you are reading. The brackets tell us that we need to do whatever is inside them first. So, the first brackets say 10 × 9. Can you tell me another word we use instead of "times"? Great – multiply and times are the same thing.
> 'Can you do the first part? What is 10 × 9? Good – let's write 90 underneath on the next line.
> 'Let's use your times table chart:
> (10 × 9) ÷ (5 × 2) = (90) ÷ ( ) =
> 'Now let's move across. What is the next part of this calculation? Yes, that's right – it is (5 × 2). Good – write your answer in the next bracket.
> (10 × 9) ÷ (5 × 2) = (90) ÷ (10) =
> 'Okay, can you tell me what our last calculation is? Excellent – it's 90 divided by 10. Remember "divided by" means how many lots of 10 are in 90.
> 'Let's use the counters to work this out. We need 90 counters. Now let's put the counters in groups of 10. Great, now I want you to count how many sets of 10 we have made. Nine – that's right: 90 divided by 10 is 9. Where do we need to write 9?
> (10 × 9) ÷ (5 × 2) = (90) ÷ (10) = 9
> 'Well done! Let's go over what we did. Tell me how we started?'

Help students to plan and follow a logical sequence of steps to complete a task

This requires knowing the end goal. For example, 'I need to read each problem and work out the correct answer.' Reading the problem aloud to the students and then asking them to read it aloud will help them to focus on the task. Tell or ask the students the first step: 'First we need to... and then.... Good, next we need to.... Great! Now we need to...' (Remind them that knowing the steps is the key to getting the correct outcome. There is no need to rush, allow the students to work at their own pace). As you are working through the task ask the students what they already know and demonstrate how this knowledge can be applied to the task. For example, 'You already know how to count by 5s ....'

Ask probing questions that encourage reflection and problem-solving

For example: 'Look at the maths wall – which fact can we use to help us?'; 'What happens to a number when we add 0?'; 'Let's count the segments in the circle. Yes, there are 4. How many segments do we need to make half?' Ask students to recall facts – for example, 'What's 9 × 10?' Ask students to explain a process – for example, 'What formula will you use?' Ask students to predict or estimate an answer – for example, 'Do think the answer will be more than or less than 100?' Ask for an explanation to check for understanding – for example, 'You've done a good job on the graph. Tell me what these two bars represent.' Ask students to think of alternative strategies – for example, 'How could you have solved this problem a different way?'

Maher (2021) provides an example of how questioning can be used to explore a maths problem.

> Teacher: Can you show me what you are working on today?
> Student: I am trying to solve the word problem.
> Teacher: Tell me about it.
> Student: I think I need to multiply.
> Teacher: How do you know?
> Student: It says that the bakery has five kinds of cupcakes and that they have four of each cupcake in the window.
> Teacher: OK, why do you think you should multiply?
> Student: We need to find out how many cupcakes in all are in the window, and there are equal numbers of each cupcake.
> Teacher: OK... so how might you solve this problem?

Use hands-on learning resources and multisensory learning strategies to encourage students to use some or all of their senses as part of the learning process

It's hands-on in nature, and allows students to practise, experiment and problem-solve. Multisensory learning is particularly relevant for students with learning disabilities such as dyslexia and dysgraphia.

Talk about what the student is doing and ask the student to explain their thinking to obtain insight into the student's understanding of the task or concept

This allows you to assist the student to develop more effective problem-solving strategies.

Figure 16.100 provides examples of multisensory mathematics learning.

Hott, Isbel and Montani (2014) identify the following effective intervention strategies:

- *Talk about the resources and point out their attributes.* A multisensory approach using tangible materials can assist students to build their skills. It allows them to manipulate materials to create visual representations, which can then be translated into written symbols. For example, 'Have you noticed that if I join these two-semi circles I can make a circle?'; 'I can use these 12 counters to make different but equal sets (4 × 4 × 4). How else can we make some equal sets?' Also make use of online resources, such as maths games that include both verbal and visual information and maximise student interactions.
- *Model and explain mathematical language and symbols to reinforce conceptual knowledge.* (Conceptual knowledge is a deep understanding of a concept that allows students to use and transfer that knowledge in different situations.) For example, consider the concept of addition and subtraction. The answer to a specific calculation remains constant: (5 – 3 = 2) and (3 + 2 = 5) – the answer will always remain the same. The concept also remains the same – that is, if I take away from a number, I will have a lower number; if I add to a number, I will have a higher number. This knowledge is transferable – for example, if I have five oranges and I give three away, I will have two oranges left. 'Another word for "times" is multiply'; '10 is more than 5, so we can say 10 is greater than 5. We can also write this '10 > 5'.

Figure 16.100 Multisensory learning

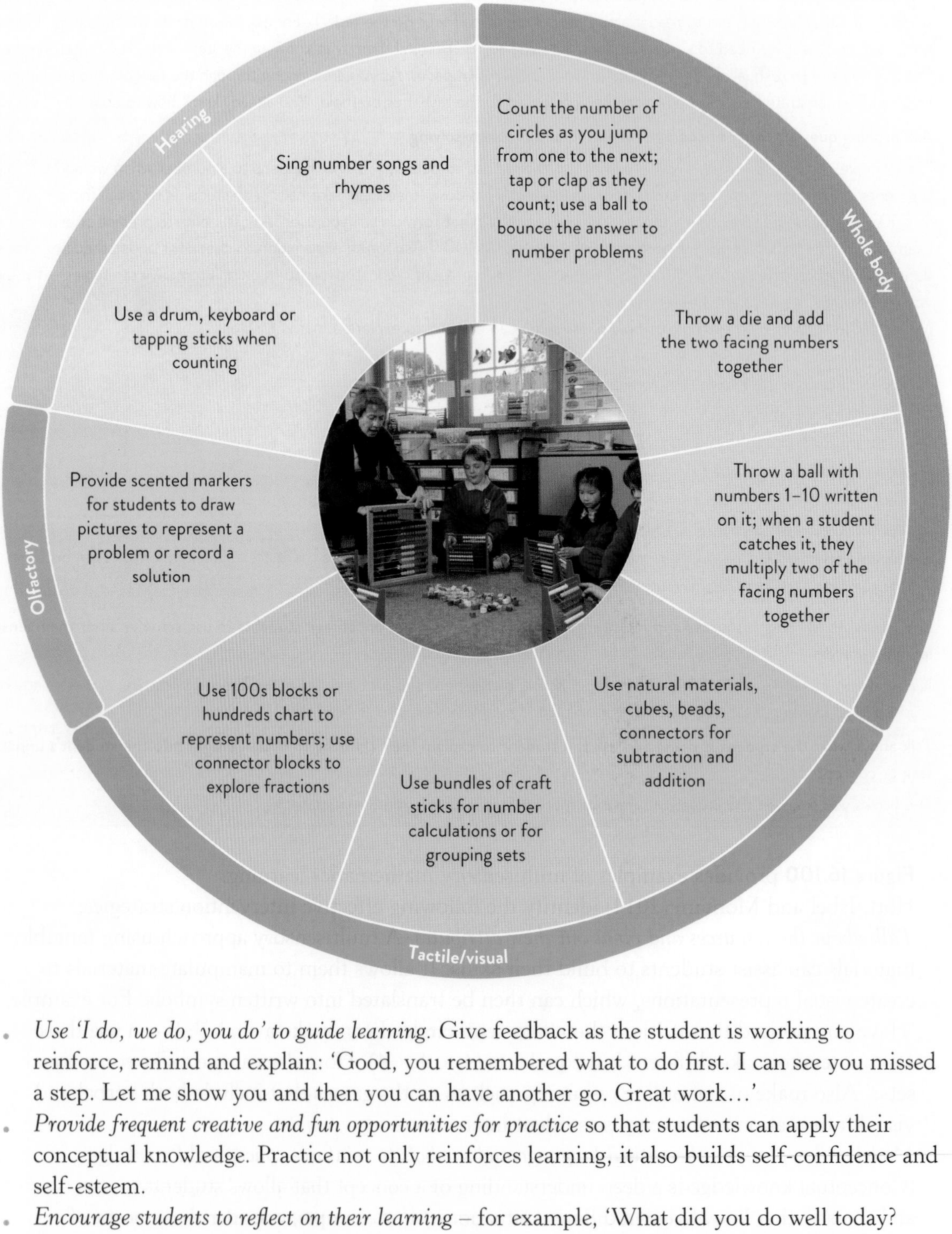

- *Use 'I do, we do, you do' to guide learning.* Give feedback as the student is working to reinforce, remind and explain: 'Good, you remembered what to do first. I can see you missed a step. Let me show you and then you can have another go. Great work…'
- *Provide frequent creative and fun opportunities for practice* so that students can apply their conceptual knowledge. Practice not only reinforces learning, it also builds self-confidence and self-esteem.
- *Encourage students to reflect on their learning* – for example, 'What did you do well today? What do you need to work on? Why do you think you've been able to complete this task without my help today?'
- *Regularly monitor student progress and share this with student.* Students who are struggling can be motivated by seeing their progress.

Teaching practices and supports

Source: Adapted from Hott, B., Isbel, L. & Montani, T. (2014). Strategies and interventions to support students with mathematics disabilities. https://www.council-for-learning-disabilities.org/wp-content/uploads/2014/12/Math_Disabilities_Support.pdf

SCENARIO

PROBLEM-SOLVING

After a brainstorming session, students in Grade 3 created a number of posters that were displayed in the room to remind them of various ways to problem-solve mathematics tasks. Their ideas included:

- Talk it over with a friend, share ideas or role-play.
- Draw the problem with pictures, charts, graphs, symbols or diagrams.
- Use concrete materials to represent the problem.
- Guess and check.
- Use a calculator and apps.
- Look for clues – patterns and relationships.
- Write down what you know – the facts.
- Write down what you don't know.
- Make a list.
- Work backwards.
- Hypothesise, predict, experiment, use trial and error.

WHAT DOES THIS TELL US?

Becoming a problem-solver is an important mathematical skill. Encouraging the use of a variety of problem-solving strategies allows students to explore a wide range of mathematical processes in a fun, hands-on way.

▶ DISCUSSION

Discuss/share the strategies that you use when faced with a problem. For example, consider how you would manage your time and undertake preparation if you were employed part-time at two schools. What strategies would you use to manage your time and ensure you were well prepared?

As you are now aware, each developmental domain impacts on and is influenced by development in all other domains. Students who present with lags in development in one or more domains, such as language, memory, processing or visual motor skills, may struggle with some aspects of mathematics development. Older students with poor planning and organisational skills are also likely to become anxious and stressed when attempting mathematical tasks, and this serves to reinforce their negativity and lack of self-confidence as mathematicians.

Identifying learning needs

Using best-practice principles, the first step in supporting numeracy development with an individual student is to identify their skills, knowledge, weaknesses and gaps in knowledge. This typically will be carried out by the class teacher, who can identify the knowledge and skills that need to be developed. Importantly, this process should also identify the student's existing skills and prior knowledge, which form the foundation for ongoing learning – that is, work from the known and use this as a framework for scaffolding new knowledge and skills. This process is referred to as the KISS principle. The KISS principle is simply a planning strategy that focuses on adjusting learning goals to individual needs. It involves planning based on the information in **Figure 16.101**.

Developing competency in numeracy requires the student to acquire, understand and apply basic mathematical facts and computations. Without this knowledge, students will not be able to progress through the mathematics curriculum. It is essential to engage the student in explicit learning so that a solid foundation for the recall and application of basic mathematical knowledge is developed.

According to the Qualifications and Curriculum Authority UK (2011, p. 6), mathematics offers students with learning difficulties opportunities to:

- build on their awareness of events and actions to recognise changes in pattern, quantity and space in their immediate environment and in the wider world
- use their developing awareness to anticipate and predict changes
- use their awareness and develop an understanding of pattern, space, shape and number, and to develop problem-solving skills that contribute to making choices, taking decisions and gaining control over their immediate environment

Figure 16.101 The KISS principle

KISS

K

What students need to KNOW and do with regard to numeracy

- The teacher will determine what support is needed to assist each student in the learning process to achieve the learning outcomes as they relate to the core content of the syllabus. The teacher will also determine any adjustments needed for individual students, identify what is important for the student to learn, determine how the knowledge will be presented and decide on the most effective teaching and learning strategies.

I

INTERACTIONS to support and scaffold learning

- Interactions will include teacher–student, student–student, student–teacher. The teacher will consider what, if any, adjustments need to be made in relation to interactions, how to best communicate expectations of learning and how feedback will be provided.

S

SITUATIONS in which the learning will occur

- The teacher will determine how best to support the learning process by planning a wide range of learning opportunities that cater for individual differences. This will include consideration of when, where and how learning will take place as well as the required level of participation by each student as an active learner.

S

Ways to demonstrate SUCCESS in learning

- The teacher will determine how evidence of learning will be gathered and documented, including strategies to help students demonstrate their knowledge and skills.
- In order to facilitate learning, the teacher will also determine the range of resources that will be used to support the learning process. Numeracy programs generally use a wide range of resources to promote hands-on learning, as well as written tasks and computer-based programs. Learning materials will vary across the grades and will reflect the interests of the students.

- extend mathematical skills, experiences and understanding, which allows students to visualise, compare and estimate; for some pupils, this will be achieved in abstract as well as tangible contexts
- begin to think about the strategies they use and explain them to others
- develop a powerful set of thinking tools to help students increase their knowledge and understanding of the world and, during the school years, to learn effectively in different subjects across the curriculum.

Summary

Mathematical literacy encompasses the ability to:

- estimate in numerical or geometric situations
- know and understand mathematical concepts and procedures
- question, reason and solve problems
- make connections within mathematics and between mathematics and life
- generate, interpret and compare data
- communicate mathematical reasoning (Expert Panel on Student Success in Ontario, 2004, p. 24).

The skills and knowledge of mathematical literacy occurs on a continuum over a long period of time. To develop mathematical literacy, students must have the opportunity to engage in a wide range of learning experiences that allows for the practice of existing skills as well as investigation of new knowledge and skills. Students must also have opportunities to apply mathematical skills in a wide range of contexts, which can be applied to real-life problems and situations.

To support mathematics skills and knowledge, ESWs must have a sound general knowledge of the National Numeracy Learning Progression and be familiar with the strategies used by teachers to implement the mathematics curriculum. It is also essential for ESWs to be aware of their own attitude towards mathematics and be mindful not to express any anxieties related to mathematics learning.

Self-check questions

1. What are the three types of knowledge in numeracy development?
2. Explain mathematics based on the Australian Curriculum.
3. What are the six mathematics strands?
4. Explain the concept of the National Numeracy Learning Progression.
5. Define procedural vocabulary in mathematics.
6. What are the benefits of modelling mathematical language in the classroom?
7. Define number facts in mathematics.
8. What is understanding money and how does it apply to financial literacy?
9. What are the required factors of mathematical proficiency?
10. Explain the four models of instruction according to numeracy protocol at schools.
11. List three support strategies teachers may use in identifying a student's learning needs.
12. What does the KISS principle refer to in supporting a student's numeracy development?

Discussion questions

1 One of the challenges in the acquisition of the language of mathematics is the range of words used to describe a single mathematical application. Why might this be confusing for students with cognitive disability or students for whom English is an additional language?

2 For this task, refer to the Scenario 'Value for money?' on page 551. Analyse what students learn from this activity and what skills are exercised.

Activities

1 Connect the following concepts to the correct definition:

Multiplicative strategies	knowing 'why', including understanding mathematical relationships
Number sense	number facts that can easily be recalled
Conceptual understanding	student's ability to manipulate numbers in multiplicative situations to solve problems
Factual knowledge	ability to understand numbers and number relationships

2 Investigate what mathematics 'programs' are at the schools where you have worked. Discuss the costs and benefits with your peers.

3 Explain the strategies that could be used to help students understand spatial relationships and directions. Give an example for each.

4 Describe the mathematical proficiency required criteria as stated by Clements and Sarama (2021).

5 For this activity, refer to the video 'Modelling numeracy lessons' (published by AITSL) at: **https://www.youtube.com/watch?v=psRSjbXd02I&t=21s**. Discuss the strategies and models utilised by the teacher to enhance the learning experience of the students.

6 For this activity, refer to **Figure 16.98** 'Baseline facts' on page 584. Explain the most effective teaching strategies to support students' learning needs. Give examples for each strategy.

PART D SUPPORTING STUDENTS WITH ADDITIONAL NEEDS

Chapter 17

SUPPORT FOR STUDENTS WITH DISABILITY

LEARNING OBJECTIVES

When you have completed this chapter, you should be able to demonstrate that, in relation to working in a school environment, you can:

17.1 describe the concept of inclusion and inclusive practices including personal attitudes, values and beliefs towards disability and inclusion

17.2 describe the features of best practice in inclusive education

17.3 describe the barriers to inclusion for students with disability

17.4 identify different types of disability and describe the key learning strategies that can be put in place to support learning for students with disability

GO FURTHER

Go Further icons link to extra content for this chapter. Ask your instructor for the **Go Further** resource and deepen your understanding of the topic.

Online resources icons refer to useful weblinks. Ask your instructor for these **Online Resources.**

Introduction

It is not possible in the context of this textbook to provide comprehensive information about all disability; instead, this chapter provides an overview of the common characteristics of disabilities that you may encounter in your role as an education support worker (ESW). The chapter includes links to videos and websites to support your knowledge and understanding of disability. Online resources to support learning are also included.

By now you are familiar with the concept of the 'whole child' and the importance of acknowledging each student as a unique individual with a unique set of interests, strengths and needs. It should never be assumed that simply because a student has been diagnosed with or identified as having a disability or additional needs that the child or young person will present with a certain set of strengths and limitations. Remember, development occurs along a continuum and this continuum is unique to each child, regardless of ability. When exploring disability, it is important to bear in mind that every student should be supported to reach their full potential by making best use of their strengths and abilities.

The following information provides a snapshot of the most common characteristics of disabilities and additional needs. When working with students, you should research additional information as needed.

17.1 Inclusion

In 2017, as part of its Agenda for Sustainable Development, the United Nations Educational, Scientific and Cultural Organization (UNESCO) developed a guide to inclusion and equity to support countries to embed inclusive education policies. *Inclusion* is defined as a process that helps overcome barriers limiting the presence, participation and achievement of learners. **Equity** is defined as ensuring that there is a concern with fairness, such that the education of all learners is seen as having equal importance (UNESCO, 2017, pp. 12, 13, 32).

UNESCO identifies four overlapping dimensions that need to be embedded in education systems to ensure inclusion and equity: Concepts; Policy Statements; Structures; and Practices. The Practices dimension focuses on the role of educators (teacher and support staff) and is described in **Figure 17.1**.

Figure 17.1 Practices dimension of inclusion

1. Schools and other learning centres have strategies for encouraging the presence, participation and achievement of all learners from their local community.
2. Schools and other learning centres provide support for learners who are at risk of underachievement, marginalisation and exclusion.
3. Teachers and support staff are prepared to respond to learner diversity during their initial training.
4. Teachers and support staff have opportunities to take part in continuing professional development regarding inclusive and equitable practices.

Source: United Nations Educational, Scientific and Cultural Organization (UNESCO) (2017). *A Guide for Ensuring Inclusion and Equity in Education.* http://unesdoc.unesco.org/images/0024/002482/248254e.pdf

The central message of UNESCO is that every learner matters and matters equally. The Practices dimension highlights the importance of both a commitment to inclusion and equity, and initial and continued professional development of teachers and ESWs to equip them to meet the needs of children with additional needs.

Inclusion of students with disability is enshrined in legislation. The *Disability Discrimination Act 1992* and the *Disability Standards for Education 2005* describe disability as being a wide range of physical, mental health or learning conditions, including:

- total or partial loss of the person's bodily or mental functions
- total or partial loss of a part of the body
- the presence in the body of organisms causing disease or illness
- the presence in the body of organisms capable of causing disease or illness
- the malfunction, malformation or disfigurement of a part of the person's body
- a disorder or malfunction that results in the person learning differently from a person without the disorder or malfunction
- a disorder, illness or disease that affects a person's thought processes, perception of reality, emotions or judgment or that results in disturbed behaviour.

and includes a disability that:

- presently exists; or
- previously existed but no longer exists; or
- may exist in the future (including because of a genetic predisposition to that disability); or
- is imputed to a person.

To avoid doubt, a disability that is otherwise covered by this definition includes behaviour that is a symptom or manifestation of the disability.

Source: *Disability Discrimination Act* 1992, https://www.legislation.gov.au/Details/C2018C00125. Based on content from the Federal Register of Legislation at 13 June 2023. For the latest information on Australian Government law please go to https://www.legislation.gov.au.

The Disability Standards for Education (Department of Education and Training [DET], 2015a) aim to protect the rights of children with a disability to an education *on the same basis* as students without a disability. 'On the same basis' means:

1. A student with a disability should have access to the same opportunities and choices in their education that are available to a student without disability. Students with disability are entitled to rigorous, relevant and engaging learning opportunities drawn from the Australian Curriculum and set in age-equivalent learning contexts.
2. While all students will access age-equivalent content, how they access it and the focus of their learning may vary according to their individual learning needs, strengths, goals and interests.

Source: Student diversity – students with a disability, Tasmanian Catholic Education Office. https://curriculum.catholic.tas.edu.au/studentdiversity/students-with-disability

'On the same basis' does not mean that every student has the same experience; rather, they are entitled to equitable opportunities and choices to access age-equivalent content from all learning areas of the Australian Curriculum. The NCCD states:

Participating in education *on the same basis* as other students means that students with disability:

- have the same, or very similar, opportunities to take part in education as other students
- do not face unnecessary barriers that limit these opportunities
- have the opportunity to succeed and show their learning
- are provided with adjustments that make education accessible to them.

On the same basis does not mean all students have to be educated in exactly the same way. Teachers may have to do things differently for students with disability to ensure they have access to the curriculum.

Source: Nationally Consistent Collection of Data on School Students with Disability (NCCD) (2022c). On the same basis. https://www.nccd.edu.au/wider-support-materials/same-basis

Video: 'On the same basis' (NCCD)

The Standards cover enrolment, participation, curriculum development, accreditation and delivery, student support services and elimination of harassment and victimisation. Each part of the Standards sets out the:

- rights of students with disability in relation to education and training to help people understand what is fair and reasonable under the Standards
- legal obligations or responsibilities of education providers
- measures that may be implemented to comply with the requirements of the Standards (DET, 2015a).

The Standards set out three key obligations for education providers, which are described in **Figure 17.2**.

Figure 17.2 Key obligations of education providers

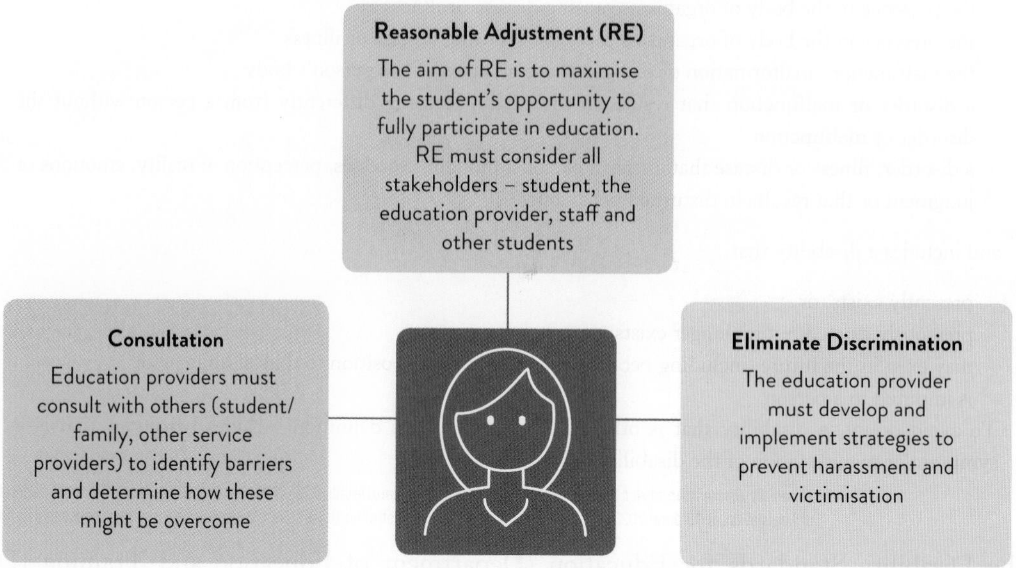

Reasonable Adjustment (RE)
The aim of RE is to maximise the student's opportunity to fully participate in education. RE must consider all stakeholders – student, the education provider, staff and other students
Consultation
Education providers must consult with others (student/family, other service providers) to identify barriers and determine how these might be overcome
Eliminate Discrimination
The education provider must develop and implement strategies to prevent harassment and victimisation

Source: Department of Education and Training (2015a, pp. 1, 2).

The Standards require all schools – public and private – to make every effort to accommodate students with a disability and continue to monitor, support and make adjustments as needed. Reasonable adjustment requires schools to balance the student's learning needs with the interests of all parties affected, including those of the student with disability, the education provider, staff and other students. Education providers are not required to make adjustments where those adjustments would result in unjustifiable hardship for the education provider, such as financial hardship.

The Australian Human Rights Commission provides examples of reasonable adjustment, including:

- modifying educational premises – for example, making ramps, modifying toilets and ensuring that classes are in rooms accessible to the person with a disability
- modifying or providing equipment – for example, lowering lab benches, enlarging computer screens, providing specific computer software or an audio loop system
- changing assessment procedures – for example, allowing for alternative examination methods such as oral exams, or allowing additional time for someone else to write an exam for a person with a disability
- changing course delivery – for example, providing study notes or research materials in different formats or providing a sign language interpreter for a deaf person.

The NCCD

The Nationally Consistent Collection of Data on School Students with Disability (NCCD):

> gives Australian schools, parents, guardians and carers, education authorities and the community information about the number of students with disability in schools and the adjustments they receive. The Australian Education Regulation 2013 requires all schools to report the data collected for the NCCD to the Australian Government on an annual basis.

Source: Nationally Consistent Collection of Data on School Students with Disability (NCCD) (2022c). What is the NCCD?. https://www.nccd.edu.au/wider-support-materials/what-nccd?parent=/understanding-nccd&activity=/wider-support-materials/what-nccd&step=-1

Students who are included in the NCCD are defined in **Figure 17.3**.

Figure 17.3 Students included in the NCCD

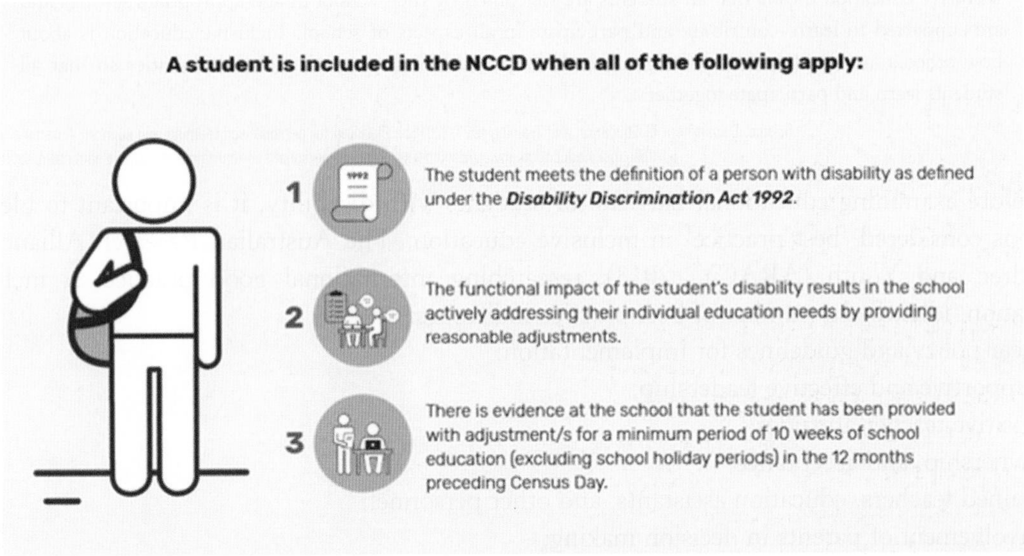

Source: Supported by the Australian Government Department of Education. © 2020 Education Services Australia Ltd, unless otherwise indicated. Creative Commons BY 4.0, https://creativecommons.org/licenses/by/4.0/

To support schools in meeting their obligations under the Standards, the NCCD website provides case studies to showcase how schools can apply reasonable adjustment for students with disability.

NCCD case studies and resources

17.2 School inclusion policies

To meet legislative requirements, all schools must have policies and practices in relation to inclusion. Inclusion policies address legislative requirements, and also seek to guide attitudes about inclusion. Examples of school inclusion policies are included in **Figure 17.4**.

Figure 17.4 Examples of school inclusion policies

Students with Disability	https://www2.education.vic.gov.au/pal/students-disability/policy
Equity and Inclusion Charter	https://www.education.wa.edu.au/dl/x1p863d
Inclusive education policy statement	https://education.qld.gov.au/student/inclusive-education/Documents/policy-statement-booklet.pdf
Inclusive Education Statement for students with disability	https://education.nsw.gov.au/content/dam/main-education/teaching-and-learning/disability-learning-and-support/our-disability-strategy/inclusive-education/Inclusive-Education-Statement.pdf

Best practice in inclusive education

The Department of Education and Training describes inclusive education:

> Inclusive education means that all students are welcomed by their school in age-appropriate settings and are supported to learn, contribute and participate in all aspects of school. Inclusive education is about how schools are developed and designed, including classrooms, programmes and activities so that all students learn and participate together.

Source: Department of Education and Training (DET) (2015b). Planning for personalised learning and support: A national resource. https://docs.education.gov.au/documents/planning-personalised-learning-and-support-national-resource-0, p. 2

Before examining educational barriers for students with disability, it is important to identify what is considered 'best practice' in inclusive education. The Australian Research Alliance for Children and Youth (ARACY, 2013), researching international good practice in inclusive education, identified a number of best practice indicators:

- clear policy and guidelines for implementation;
- supportive and effective leadership;
- positive teacher attitudes;
- ownership, and acceptance;
- trained teachers, education assistants, and other personnel;
- involvement of parents in decision making;
- engagement of learners;
- flexible curriculum responding to individual need;
- a plan for ongoing teacher development; and
- the nurturing of communities of lead practice.

Source: Australian Research Alliance for Children and Youth (ARACY) (2013). Inclusive education for students with disability. A review of the best evidence in relation to theory and practice, p. 17.

ARACY identified several features of the learning environment that positively contribute to positive outcomes for students with disability. These features include:

1. quality teaching:
   - collaboration between student, teachers and family
   - alignment of goals and resources (including ICT)
   - the use of scaffolding and feedback
   - a focus of supporting self-regulation and support for the student to develop metacognitive strategies to reflect on their own learning
2. inclusive pedagogy – the what, why and how of teaching to support students with disability
3. differentiating the curriculum to cater for individual needs and differing behaviours
4. use of alternative curriculum or resources to assist students with significant disability to achieve outcomes appropriate to their future environments
5. use of assistive and adaptive technologies that allow students with disability to access physical environments, be mobile, communicate effectively, access computers, and enhance functional skills that may be difficult without the technology
6. Universal Design for Learning (UDL) – the conscious and deliberate creation of lessons and outcomes that allow all students access to and participation in the same curriculum
7. individual planning – development of Individual Education Plans (IEPs) in collaboration with all stakeholders that identify outcomes matched to the needs and strengths of each student.

Source: Australian Research Alliance for Children and Youth (ARACY) (2013). Inclusive education for students with disability. A review of the best evidence in relation to theory and practice, pp. 32–5

Inclusion in practice

According to Strnadová, Arthur-Kelly and Foreman (2022), five underlying 'principles have formed the basis of policy and practice for the inclusion of students with a disability and other forms of diversity. School systems have used these principles to develop system-wide policies; school leaders have used them as a basis for school policy and practice, and classroom teachers have used them in the preparation and implementation of programs' (p. 3). The principles are shown in **Figure 17.5**.

Figure 17.5 Underlying principles of inclusion

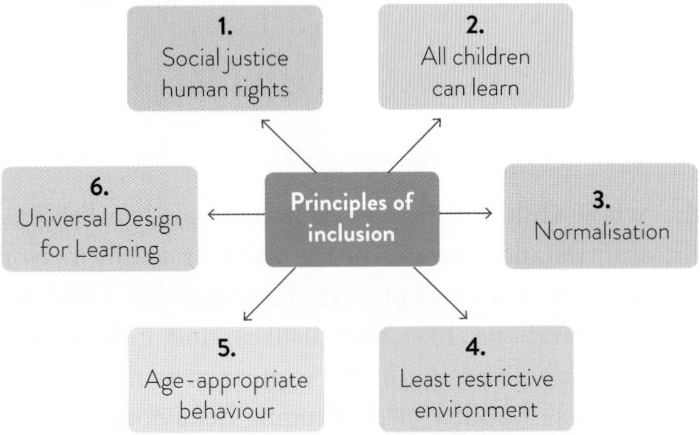

Source: Strnadová, I., Arthur-Kelly, M. & Foreman, P. (2022). *Inclusion in Action*. South Melbourne: Cengage Learning Australia (pp.1–13).

In the context of these principles, normalisation refers to 'the concept that all people, regardless of disability, should be able to live a life that is as normal as possible for their culture. In education, the principle of normalisation suggests that all children should have the opportunity to attend the local school' (Strnadová, Arthur-Kelly & Foreman, 2022, p. 3). Least restrictive environment refers to 'the opportunity for people with a disability to live in environments that give them the greatest range of choices; that is, the fewest restrictions'. The concept of age-appropriate argues that students 'should be provided with opportunities to perform tasks that are seen by their peers and themselves to be positive and valuable' (p. 3). For example, providing age and content appropriate reading material for older students who struggle with reading.

UDL includes three key education principles: (1) engagement and interaction; (2) representation; and (3) action and expression. Its aim is to provide a barrier-free educational environment, accessible to all student (Strnadová, Arthur-Kelly & Foreman, pp. 1–13). (UDL is explored in Chapter 18.)

The Australian Alliance for Inclusive Education (2018) describes inclusion as:

- all students included in the general education classroom all day, every day
- all students working in naturally supportive, flexible structures and groupings with other students, regardless of individual ability
- all students presumed competent
- students supported (where needed), such as through curriculum adaptations and differentiated teaching, to access the core curriculum
- all students known and valued as full members of the school community, developing meaningful social relationships with peers and able to participate in all aspects of the life of the school.

Importantly, the Alliance also defines what inclusion is *not*:

- students only being allowed to participate in the class if they are 'keeping up' academically – this includes:
  - frequent 'pull-outs'
  - working separately in a corner of the classroom with the education assistant while the teacher instructs the rest of the class, or
  - students being given a separate 'special curriculum' or 'program' (as opposed to being supported where needed, including through curricular adjustments, to access the same core curriculum), or
  - being required to demonstrate independence or self-sufficiency as a condition of entry.

Video: What is inclusion?

Inclusion not only includes students with disability but also students with other forms of diversity.

Person-centred principles

Like the concept of the 'whole child', principles of **holistic and individual-centred care** focus on the strengths, skills, abilities and interests of the child or young person and take social and cultural factors into account. It is a concept that recognises the child or young person as an individual with rights and aspirations, likes and dislikes, and individual ways of thinking and being. The goal is to 'see' the whole person in the context of their lived experiences and culture rather than simply focusing on a disability or challenging behaviours.

According to Life Without Barriers (2018), person-centred principles encompass 10 concepts, which are described in **Figure 17.6**.

Figure 17.6 Person-centred principles

Principle	Definition
Person at the centre	The person with disability is central to all planning and decision-making.
Inclusive and accessible	Support is provided for inclusion in all areas of life and accessibility to all areas of the community.
Focus on outcomes	The focus is on achieving positive outcomes for people with a disability.
Inclusion of others	As identified by the individual, recognition of family members, friends, significant others and other service providers in supporting the individual and fostering connections with the community.
Personal priorities and strengths	There is a strong focus on the person's abilities, interests, dreams and aspirations, and the supports required to realise them. There is also strong recognition of the person as a unique individual who is influenced by age, gender, culture, ethnicity, belief system, social and income status, education, family and any other factors that make them unique.
Shared commitment	There is a strong commitment to supporting the individual to realise their goals and aspirations.
Respect for culture	There is respect for the individual's social customs and traditions, language, culture, and religious beliefs and practices.
Continuous process	There is recognition that support and care require a continuous process of listening, learning and further action, and are not a one-off event. There is also recognition that people with disability have futures, and that their aspirations will change and grow with their experiences.

Principle	Definition
Regular review and continuous improvement	The individual's program is reviewed regularly with the person and their support network to assess ongoing changes and learnings, and to ensure that planned activities are being achieved and are still relevant to the person's goals.
One person, one plan	Planning is coordinated across all domains of a person's life, including all specialist services being accessed as well as informal supports and networks, insofar as the person wants this to happen (NSW Department of Family and Community Services, Ageing, Disability and Home Care, Lifestyle Planning Policy, March 2011, amended 2012).

Source: Life Without Barriers (2018).

Person-centred principles require a commitment to collaboration and respect for the individual as well as a commitment to acting in the best interests of the individual so that they can reach their full potential. They also centre on ethical practices and a willingness to work in partnership with the child or young person's family or carers.

These principles recognise the rights of the individual to contribute to the development of their individual goals and outcomes, and to have some say in how these are implemented. According to Life Without Barriers (2018, pp. 6–7), person-centred outcomes include:

- individuality – everyone's differences are recognised and respected
- choice – the right of individuals to make informed choices, and to take responsibility for those choices and related risks, is supported
- privacy – information and activities are kept confidential
- independence – individuals are empowered to do activities for themselves and their dignity should be treated in a respectful way
- inclusion – people are supported to fully participate in all aspects of the community that they choose, and to be viewed as valued and equal citizens.

Consultation and consent

A person-centred approach also extends to including the voice of the student (where possible) when determining reasonable adjustments that allow the student to participate *on the same basis* as other students. **Figure 17.7** demonstrates the voice of the student.

Figure 17.7 The voice of the student

I am a ... student with disability
I expect that:

- The school will ask about my needs
- The education staff will listen respectfully when I explain how the school can meet my needs
- I will know how the education staff will teach me and keep me informed.

I can contribute by:

- Talking to the school about my needs
- Telling the school how the adjustment is working for me.

Source: Nationally Consistent Collection of Data on School Students with Disability (NCCD) (2022a). https://www.nccd.edu.au/wider-support-materials/consultation?parent=%2Fdisability-standards-education&activity=%2Fwider-support-materials%2Fworking-together&step=0

The right of a student (or their associate relative/carer) to be consulted is enshrined in:

- Convention on the Rights of Persons with Disabilities (United Nations, 2016)
- *Disability Discrimination Act 1992*
- Disability Standards for Education 2005.

Barriers to consultation and consent may be a factor for students with communication, behavioural, emotional and cognitive impairments. According to Tancredi (2020), these barriers present in several ways – for example:

> – The way questions are worded. Questions need to use vocabulary that is familiar to and understood by the student. The linguistic structure of the questions posed also needs to be simple, direct and able to be comprehended by the student.
> – The requirement to engage with reflective questioning. Students may require support to recall experiences and express their opinions.
> – Excessive demands on cognitive load. Students must hold the interviewer's questions in their verbal working memory, in order to use this information to formulate a response.
> – Requisite access to vocabulary to express opinions and ideas. For students to share their insights, they must be able to access the vocabulary they wish to use to express their insights and to convey their message with specificity.

Source: Tancredi, H.A. (2020). Consulting students with disability: A practice guide for educators and other professionals. The Centre for Inclusive Education QUT. https://research.qut.edu.au/c4ie/practice-guide-student-consultation

Strategies for effective consultation with students

Classroom inclusion

Accommodating the needs of students with disability and providing equitable access to the classroom begins with a positive attitude towards inclusion. Policy statements alone cannot ensure successful inclusion. A powerful contributor to the success of inclusion is teacher attitudes. Our attitudes are reflected consciously and subconsciously in how we act, respond and behave around and towards others. Attitudes reflect our values and beliefs, which are often developed in childhood and influenced by family, culture and personal experience. Attitudes can be positive, negative or neutral. Attitudes towards those who are perceived to be different from us can manifest in different ways – for example, acceptance, embracing, tolerance, pity, intolerance, bias and **prejudice**. Malaquias (2018) suggests that:

> … prejudice and bias operate at an explicit, conscious and controllable level and at a residual, implicit, subconscious and spontaneous or uncontrollable level … implicit or unconscious bias and prejudice is by definition not consciously controllable – and manifests itself in body language and spontaneous behaviours – particularly when an individual is fatigued or under stress.

Studies have revealed that teacher attitudes and expectations are significant barriers to the successful implementation of inclusive classrooms and equitable participation of all students. The more severe the child's disability, the less positive teachers' attitudes towards inclusion tend to be.

In general, teachers were found to be more supportive of including children with physical and sensory disabilities than those with intellectual, learning and behavioural disabilities. Factors that contribute to teacher attitudes vary, but commonly include the availability of support and how the teacher regards their own teacher competence when working with students with disabilities.

Teachers' attitudes towards inclusion are also based on practical concerns, such as: accommodating the individualised time demands of students with disability without disadvantaging other students in the classroom; being apprehensive of the quality and quantity of work output of children with disabilities; lacking adequate support services; and limited training and competence in supporting inclusive educational practice (Vaz et al., 2015, pp. 2–3).

Shaddock, Giorcelli and Smith (2007, pp. 5–6) suggest that educators who are competent at including children with disability:

- work predominantly from the basis of student strengths and not their disabilities
- focus on the student's strengths
- adapt a flexible approach to learning by offering interesting learning challenges for all students
- modify the pace of work, building activities gradually and in clear stages
- adopt a team approach, such as co-teaching or team-teaching
- use a variety of teaching techniques – for example, problem-solving, investigative learning, direct instruction, hands-on learning and teaching, multimedia and technology. These approaches may allow students with a disability to demonstrate their strengths and further promote their acceptance
- insist that students (and their efforts) not be devalued or marginalised by allowing them to be pigeonholed – for example, by a medical diagnosis
- focus on the social and the typical (e.g. 'He is 14 years old and most 14 year olds enjoy *x*').
- support students to develop a sense of belonging and form friendships with peers
- use a wide range of teaching strategies that reflect best practice for all students
- work collaboratively with colleagues, parents and support services
- engage in ongoing planning, evaluation and review
- adapt plans to meet changing needs of the student
- use a range of resources.

Richards and Armstrong (2008, p. 42) suggest that to support inclusion, adults can:

- act as positive role models and support the right of all students to a positive future
- actively value each student and support the right of each student to be a valued member of the school community
- actively support the right to privacy of students who need assistance with personal and intimate care, and for these students to feel safe and protected
- actively support the right of students to have their physical needs met and to have input into how this can best be achieved
- model and support the use of augmentative communication and technology to ensure students with communication and language problems are listened to and have a voice
- actively work to support student learning in the regular classroom by ensuring that learning materials, resources and physical facilities are appropriate to individual student needs
- actively support students to build friendships
- support students to have a voice in the school and ensure the views of students are listened to and respected.

PRACTICAL ADVOCACY

CONSIDER THIS

Advocacy may include making every student feel welcome and respected; having the same high expectations for all students; encouraging students to support and value each other and work collaboratively; supporting students to explore and understand differences; and actively addressing behaviours such as bullying, racism, sexism and homophobia. Further examples of practical advocacy include:

- Speak to the student directly; never speak 'over' the student in their presence.
- Treat every student with the dignity and respect they deserve.
- Ensure, as much as possible, the same expectations and routines for all students.
- Draw attention to the student's achievements and strengths.
- Try not to isolate students who are receiving individualised instruction.
- Encourage peers, rather than adults, to assist the student.
- Doing things *with*, rather than *for*, the student when they need assistance to foster independence.

▶ DISCUSSION

Alongside the teacher, ESWs will typically play a key role in supporting students with disabilities and additional needs; however, this requires genuine commitment and teamwork from all stakeholders. Discuss how each of the above examples demonstrates a commitment to advocacy for the rights of students with additional needs.

People in an inclusive environment will also:

- use correct terminology and inclusive language
- use the child-first principle
- use flexible grouping
- use appropriate resources
- use appropriate communication methods
- work collaboratively with family and other professionals.

Correct terminology and inclusive language

The words we use to refer to people matter. When used as labels, words often come with a preconceived set of beliefs or assumptions that may or may not be accurate. When labels are used to describe individuals, they may limit how that person is perceived. For example, labels such as 'disabled', 'refugee', 'old' or 'mentally ill' all carry particular stereotypes with them.

When labels are used to describe people with disability, they can result in negative stereotypes. Often, labels are used to describe individuals, the individual becomes secondary to the label, so that the focus is on the disability rather than the individual. This practice dehumanises people with disability. Every student with disability has a unique personality, temperament, strengths, likes, dislikes and needs. Using a label to define a student limits how others *see* the student, which, in turn, may limit the student from reaching their full potential.

Children who have been diagnosed with disability (or multiple disabilities) are usually assigned a label that is universally used to indicate a group of attributes that are characteristic of the disability – for example, Down syndrome, autism spectrum disorder (ASD) or cerebral palsy. However, like any child or young person, individual skills and abilities occur along a continuum. Remember, every child is on their own unique trajectory in terms of learning and development, regardless of ability (or disability). When labels are assigned to children and young people they may lead to assumptions and a preconceived set of beliefs that may or may not be accurate and may limit how that child or young person is perceived.

Labels also tend to reinforce negative stereotypes – the disability becomes the focus rather than the individual. This practice dehumanises people with disability and may, in turn, create barriers that limit the child or young person from reaching her full potential. Strategies that can be adopted to minimise stereotyping include:

- acting as a positive role model and supporting the rights of all students
- actively valuing each student and supporting the right of each child to be a valued member of the group
- actively supporting the right to privacy of students who require assistance with personal and intimate care, and for these students to feel safe and protected, and to have input into how this can best be achieved
- modelling and supporting the use of augmentative and alternative communication (AAC) technology to ensure students with communication and language barriers are listened to and have a voice
- actively working to support student learning by ensuring that learning materials, resources and physical facilities are appropriate to individual needs
- actively supporting students to build and sustain friendships
- supporting students to have a voice in their education and ensuring the views of children and young people are listened to and respected.

The 'child-first' principle

How you refer to and interact with students with disability will greatly influence how those students are perceived by their peers. Students will take their cues from the adults they trust and respect. You can minimise stereotyping by modelling and supporting inclusive language and behaviours. Keep in mind the importance of 'the child-first' principle – that is, refer to the child first and the disability second; 'the student with disability' rather than 'the disabled student'.

Video: The language of disability and accessibility

Flexible grouping

Students with disability benefit from working with their peers. Including mixed ability groupings as a regular practice encourages peer support and peer mentoring. As you will recall, Vygotsky (1978) emphasised that learning occurs in a social context. Being part of a group of learners allows students with disability to participate in education on the same basis as other students: that is, as a member of a class, with same-age peers in an environment that fosters friendship and respectful relationships.

Appropriate communication practices

All students benefit when conversation, instructions, information and feedback are communicated in a variety of ways. While verbal and written communication is used most of the time, non-verbal communication including gestures, facial expressions, sign language, visuals (images, photos, graphics, video and interactive games) are also used. Alternative and augmented communication (AAC; see Chapter 18) can also be incorporated into these communication strategies. Varying instruction methods accommodates the needs of differing abilities and allows students to engage in a range of communication strategies.

Appropriate resources

All students benefit from concrete, hands-on learning that allows them to explore, manipulate, investigate and experiment. Hands-on resources also allow students to take charge of their own learning as they work with various materials. Teachers also make use of a broad range of technologies to present information, introduce concepts and review learning. Providing students with access to engaging technology that accommodates both visual and auditory needs gives them opportunities to work independently at a pace that best suits their needs. Technology can also create a more equitable learning environment, particularly for students with disability who may not otherwise be able to engage in learning activities alongside their peers.

Collaboration with families and other professionals

The people who have the most expertise in relation to the child's strengths and needs are typically the parents/guardians. Parents of children with disability are likely to have faced and overcome many challenges when advocating for their child's needs and access to services. Students with disability will typically be involved with a number of professionals and/or medical specialists. Each individual or agency contributes to the care and wellbeing of the child and often acts as a valuable support to the family. These services may, for example, be provided by speech pathologists, paediatric occupational therapists, physiotherapists, specialist doctors, assistive technology specialists and audiologists. Each professional involved with the child will have knowledge about the child's functioning as it relates to their specialist area. Being aware of who is working with the student and what services/support they are providing is part of the collaborative process that enables teachers and support staff to develop a holistic understanding of how these services contribute to the student's care and wellbeing.

Videos: Family and parent involvement

The benefits of inclusion

Inclusion is based on the concept of equity and social justice. All children and young people are entitled to access on an equal basis to all educational opportunities, irrespective of disability or any form of disadvantage (Vaz et al., 2015, p. 2).

Konza (2008) and Foreman and Arthur-Kelly (2014) suggest some of the benefits of inclusion:

- It supports the normalisation of society: 'the practice of inclusion promotes attitudes of inclusion. It provides opportunities for other children to engage with children with a disability, which promotes understanding, empathy and acceptance of differences and, importantly, an awareness of similarities, strengths and interests'.
- Children are educated within their own community and can form friendships with peers in the neighbourhood; they are thus more likely to engage in after-school, weekend and holiday activities with peers.
- Children without disabilities are able to act as role models in areas such as social interactions, classroom behaviour, problem-solving and conflict resolution.
- It provides access for older children with a disability to broader educational choices and a wider range of specialist teachers.
- It provides children with greater access to a more diverse range of extra-curricular activities, such as music, drama, dance and sport.

- It provides older children with greater access to specialist educational facilities such as art, technology, science and food technology.
- It provides teachers with opportunities for professional growth as they develop the skills necessary to support children with additional needs.

Benefits for the child or young person

Like any other child or young person, a student with disability will find school both rewarding and challenging. The most obvious benefit is that the child or young person begins to develop an identity outside the family unit by interacting with others, developing friendships and learning to negotiate social interactions.

Another important benefit is peer modelling. Children with disability may have had limited experience with other, more able children. Participation in a mainstream school allows the child to interact with their peers, build a sense of belonging, develop resilience and build positive self-esteem.

Benefits for the family

Inclusion allows the family to access a local school just like any other family, lessening the sense of isolation and helping to bring about a sense of normality that can be missing when a child with disability is involved in an endless round of intervention services.

SCENARIO

BUILDING RELATIONSHIPS: THE INVITATION

Yasmin's mother was overwhelmed when Yasmin received an invitation from a Year 1 classmate to her birthday party. The note from Milly's mother read:

> Dear Mrs Brown,
> Milly talks incessantly about Yasmin and she really wants her to come to her party. Milly tells me that Yasmin is 'special and can't talk much but is lots of fun'. I explained to Milly that we needed to ask Yasmin's mum first before we invite her to the party. I hope you will say yes. Yasmin will be in good hands and will be well looked after. You are quite welcome to come along.
> Regards, Beth Smith

Yasmin's mother cried when she read the invitation and couldn't wait to ring her partner and share the news. She had never thought that Yasmin would be invited to a party! She felt like a 'normal' mum for the first time ever.

WHAT DOES THIS TELL US?

Inclusion is not simply about access. More importantly, it is about acceptance, kindness and empathy for others. In this Scenario, Yasmin's mother was overwhelmed by an invitation that most families would take for granted. It demonstrates the power of looking beyond the disability to seeing the child's strengths and character.

Benefits for educators

Educating and caring for a child with disability provides an opportunity to build professional knowledge while also learning new skills and knowledge through hands-on experience. When educators have the opportunity to work collaboratively with parents and specialist support staff, there can be a rich exchange of information.

Video: A parents' perspective

EDUCATOR BENEFITS: LEARNING CURVE

SCENARIO

Alice, **Yasmin**'s Year 1 teacher, was initially very uncertain and apprehensive about her ability to meet Yasmin's needs as she had very limited experience with children with disability. Alice worked with a special education teacher to identify gaps in her skills and knowledge and devised a professional development plan. She also spent several sessions observing how the specialist teacher and Yasmin communicated using a digital augmented communication program. This gave Alice much-needed confidence and many practical strategies to support Yasmin's learning. Alice describes her time with Yasmin as a journey of discovery about herself, about Yasmin and about the many demands made on Yasmin's family. Alice keeps a journal to document her fears, disappointments and many small triumphs. More and more she begins to see what Yasmin can do rather than what she cannot do.

WHAT DOES THIS TELL US?

Working with students with disability supports both professional and personal growth and development. It requires a collaborative effort that includes the child, the family, the educator team and other support services.

Benefits for other students

Learning to get along with others and to respond appropriately to individual differences is a social skill that benefits all children and young people. Compassion, cooperation, kindness and empathy are vital skills for successful social development. Importantly, other students learn that their peers with disability also have individual strengths, likes, dislikes and unique personalities.

Where there are obvious differences, young children are likely to be curious and may ask questions related to the physical appearance or abilities of the child with disability. These questions should be answered honestly and in an age-appropriate manner. Helping children to focus on similarities as well as differences will support acceptance and respect: for example, 'Yasmin can't speak as well as you but she's really good at using her iPad to communicate'.

BENEFITS FOR CHILDREN

SCENARIO

YASMIN IS OUR FRIEND

Yasmin has become a favourite among the students in Year 1. She has a beautiful smile and her engaging personality has endeared her to her peers. Generally, the other students are very patient and caring towards Yasmin. Several children have asked why Yasmin 'can't talk properly' and are keen to learn how Yasmin uses her iPad to communicate. With the support of Yasmin and her parents, the teacher has explained Yasmin's disability in a way that is easily understood by her peers.

WHAT DOES THIS TELL US?

Young children do notice differences, are curious and will ask questions about those differences. When questions are answered honestly, in ways that children can understand, they are usually satisfied and accepting of differences.

Benefits for the broader community

Inclusion benefits the broader community by making diversity visible. Inclusive practices allow others to experience diversity, help to challenge stereotypes and break down social and cultural barriers. Inclusion promotes tolerance and acceptance of differences as well as recognition of similarities and strengths. Where individuals feel awkward or unsure about how to behave towards a person with disability, inclusive practices can provide a model for effective interactions. Inclusion also allows children with additional needs and their families the right to be an integral part of the community and supports a sense of belonging.

SCENARIO

COMMUNITY BENEFITS: CELEBRATIONS

Yasmin and her family are attending Carols by Candlelight, held at the local park. Yasmin is very excited as the family is having a picnic dinner. A group of children, accompanied by several adults, are walking around the crowd giving out songbooks. Yasmin's friend **Milly** is with the group. She spots Yasmin and asks if Yasmin can join the group.

Yasmin's mother tells Milly that Yasmin can't go with the group because she might get lost.

Milly responds, *'No, she won't get lost because we will look after her. She can hold my hand and my big sister's hand.'*

Milly's sister, **Kate** (16 years) sees Yasmin: *'Hello, Yasmin, I remember you. You came to Milly's party and I let you try on my necklaces.'* Kate turns to Yasmin's mother, saying, *'I'll take good care of her, but if you're worried I'll walk back later with Milly and the girls can play for a while. I know Milly loves Yasmin. She's always talking about her.'*

WHAT DOES THIS TELL US?

Inclusive practices modelled in a school setting can have the flow-on effect of breaking down barriers within the broader community.

17.3 Students with disability

The Australian Bureau of Statistics (ABS) 2022 *Survey of Disability, Ageing and Carers* (SDAC) states that 'a person has a disability if they have at least one of a list of limitations, restrictions or impairments, which has lasted, or is likely to last, for at least 6 months and restricts everyday activities' (Australian Institute of Health and Welfare [AIHW], 2023). Limitations include 'self-care, mobility, communication, cognitive or emotional tasks, health care, reading or writing tasks, transport, household chores, property maintenance, meal preparation, schooling and employment'. The severity of disability is defined by SDAC as 'whether a person needs help, has difficulty, or uses aids or equipment with 3 core activities – self-care, mobility, and communication – and is grouped for mild, moderate, severe, and profound limitation'.

While data collected by ABS tells us that 10 per cent of children and young people in Australia have a disability and that the majority attend a mainstream school, it is important to be aware that attendance does not necessarily equate to inclusion. The 2021 Royal Commission into Violence, Abuse, Neglect and Exploitation of People with Disability makes it clear that students with disability who attend mainstream schools continue to face barriers.

GO FURTHER

Explore some statistics about children and young people with disability in your **Go Further** resource, available through your instructor.

Barriers and challenges for students with disability

Barriers for students with disability typically begin with lack of awareness, stereotyping and discrimination. Awareness of how to accommodate the needs of students with disability is essential if students are to access educational opportunities on the same basis as students without disability. Stereotyping occurs when educators and other students are not exposed to accurate information about disability and make decisions or take action based on incorrect and often biased beliefs. Discrimination occurs when students with disability are excluded from participation in education because of misinformation, failure to make reasonable adjustments or simply not recognising and acting to eliminate discrimination as and when it occurs.

Barriers can typically be attributed to a number of key factors, described in **Figure 17.8**.

Figure 17.8 Types of barriers

Barrier	Description
Institutional	Legislation, policies and practices that create barriers to participation
Physical	Accessibility to buildings, classrooms, bathroom/toilet facilities, outdoor play spaces, transport
Informational and communication	Access to information using different types of communication (verbal, written, visual, technical, Auslan, Braille, different languages)
Attitudinal	Lack of knowledge, bias, stereotyping
Cultural	Lack of knowledge of customs/beliefs related to disability and child rearing practices; language barriers
Internalised barriers	The student/family believe that barriers encountered can't be overcome/are overwhelming and there is a sense of hopelessness

Source: Adapted from: WeCapable (2023). Accessibility: Definition, meaning, examples and types of barriers. https://wecapable.com/accessibility-definition-meaning-examples-barriers

In 2021, the Royal Commission into Violence, Abuse, Neglect and Exploitation of People with Disability identified a number of concerns in relation to inclusive education:

- schools failing to follow policies and laws when denying or discouraging enrolment of students with disability;
- schools failing to identify and implement appropriate reasonable adjustments for students with disability;
- students with disability being inappropriately and repeatedly suspended by schools;
- defective appeal decisions and inadequate complaints and appeal procedures for students with disability who are suspended;
- inadequate collection and analysis of data to understand and address the scope of the barriers and problems faced by students with disability.

Source: Royal Commission into Violence, Abuse, Neglect and Exploitation of People with Disability (Nov. 2021). Students with disability face serious barriers to accessing safe, quality and inclusive education: https://disability.royalcommission.gov.au/news-and-media/media-releases/students-disability-face-serious-barriers-accessing-safe-quality-and-inclusive-education

Children and Young People with Disability Australia (CYDA, 2019) also reported barriers including:

- exclusion from events or activities at school such as excursions, sports, and special events such as incursions, carnivals, surveys and NAPLAN testing
- financial burden – to enable access to, and participation in, education families of students with disability feel obliged to pay personally for specific supports or equipment required (e.g. specialist allied health: occupational therapist, speech therapist, psychology, individual support worker, transport)
- bullying of students with disability both verbal and physical.

Source: Children and Young People with Disability Australia (CYDA) (2019). Time for change: The state of play for inclusion of students with disability. Results from the 2019 CYDA National Education Survey Children and Young People with Disability Australia October 2019. https://www.cyda.org.au/images/pdf/time_for_change_2019_education_survey_results.pdf, pp. 10, 15

Additional barriers to inclusion in the Australian context may include living in remote areas, which makes access to school and specialist support difficult.

Cultural barriers are also an important consideration. Attitudes towards people with disability vary across cultures. The Royal Commission identified that people with disability from culturally and linguistically diverse backgrounds were viewed and treated in negative ways or stigmatised. For example, a child with a disability may be regarded by the family as shameful and this results in the child being hidden in the house or restrained in a bedroom (Royal Commission into Violence, Abuse, Neglect and Exploitation of People with Disability, 2021).

For culturally and linguistically diverse families, language barriers are a key issue. For example, access to information about educational options may not be available in the family's home language. There may also be a lack of interpreters and a general distrust of government agencies.

Video: Barriers to accessing a safe, quality and inclusive education

17.4 Types of disability

This section provides you with a *general overview* of a range of disabilities. The information provided will give you a beginning understanding of various disabilities and provide you with an overview of some of the common characteristics and potential learning challenges that present in classrooms. Students may present with a single or multiple disabilities and/or learning difficulties.

Students with disability may also present with a range of health issues and challenges that impact on:

- their quality of life, including mental health and wellbeing
- care practices
- opportunities to interact, play and socialise with their peers
- opportunities to participate in learning alongside their peers.

As you explore these disabilities, you must keep in mind the importance of the concept of the whole child. You must also draw on your child development knowledge, which emphasises that development occurs along a continuum unique to each child. Like any other child or young person, a student with disability will have their own unique strengths, abilities and learning needs. The goal when working with any student is to support them to reach their full potential by focusing on their strengths and abilities.

Imputed disability

The NCCD (2021) describes **imputed disability** as 'an undiagnosed disability the school team considers a student to have that is having a functional impact on their learning'. Red flags that may indicate an imputed disability will vary greatly. Examples of indicators of imputed disability are shown in **Figure 17.9**. It is important to note that these examples must be considered in the context of 'the whole child/young person', should be consistently observable over an extended period of time, and take into account any external factors that may impact student performance or behaviours.

Figure 17.9 Examples of red flags for imputed disability

The student is not achieving outcomes consistent with the range of achievement for their age group, despite receiving, at a minimum, quality differentiated teaching practice
The student's growth in literacy and/or numeracy is significantly or substantially below expectations for a student of that age or stage of development
The student's level of literacy and/or numeracy has a functional impact on their ability to participate in learning on the same basis as their peers
The student has significant difficulty understanding or using language in different conditions that might suggest oral language or hearing concerns
The student presents with vision difficulties – for example, find near (or far) work difficult to see, or obscure a part of their vision in order to focus and concentrate better
The student's hearing or vision is inconsistent throughout the day
The student's parents, guardians or carers have disclosed that they suspect the student may have a disability

The student may be presenting with signs of an underlying social/emotional disability that is having a functional impact on their learning
The student's schooling history provides evidence of adjustment(s) to address the functional impact of imputed disability
The student has been unwell for an extended period of time with a condition that has a functional impact on their learning
The student participated in an evidence-based intervention for at least 10 weeks and did not make the progress that would be expected of a child of that age/stage of development
The student required ongoing support from the school wellbeing team/counsellor/psychologist/community-based mental health service for at least 10 weeks in the last 12 months of schooling
The student received support from an external provider, resulting in the collaborative identification of adjustment(s) to be implemented by the school team, but with no diagnosis made

Source: Nationally Consistent Collection of Data on School Students with Disability (NCCD) (2021). Imputing disability for the NCCD. Advice document. August. https://www.nccd.edu.au/sites/default/files/Imputing%20Disability%20for%20the%20NCCD.pdf, pp. 8–9. Licensed under Creative Commons 4.0, https://creativecommons.org/licenses/by/4.0/

Being aware of the general nature of a student's disability and learning needs is an important beginning point when teachers, parents, the student, and other professionals work together to develop a learning plan for the student. This core group of people, including the child or young person, can be a great source of knowledge that allows for the development of a deep and authentic understanding of the whole child or young person.

It is also important to be aware that 'the most successful form of intervention that improves student outcomes is feedback, not only to the students but also to the teacher via the student' (Ashman, 2015, pp. 16–17). Hattie (2009) reminds us that 'teachers must observe and listen to their students – about what they know and understand, where they make errors, and when they're not engaged in the teaching–learning process'. Observation also helps educators to understand how students learn best, how they communicate and what motivates them as learners.

Neurodevelopmental disorders

The Murdoch Children's Research Unit (n.d.) describes **neurodevelopmental disorders** as 'disorders of early brain development where the integrity and function of the nervous system is damaged during critical periods of brain development: while growing in the womb, or during the first two years of life'. Some neurodevelopmental disorders are shown in **Figure 17.10**.

Figure 17.10 Neurodevelopmental disorders

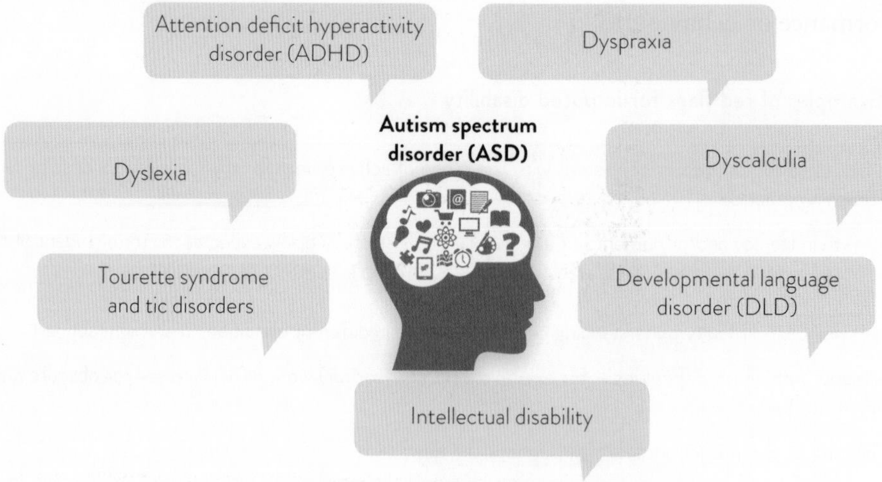

Source: Autism Toolbox (2019a). What does neurodiversity mean? http://www.autismtoolbox.co.uk/what-does-neurodiversity-mean

Children and young people with these disorders can present with a variety of indicators from mild to severe, such as poor emotional regulation, low muscle control, problems with social integration, and learning difficulties.

Autism spectrum disorder (ASD)

Autism is a lifelong neuro-developmental difference that affects the development of the brain. Autism affects the way a person communicates and interacts with others, how information is processed and how the person makes sense of the world (Organization for Autism Research, 2023). **Figure 17.11** describes children with ASD.

Figure 17.11 Children with ASD

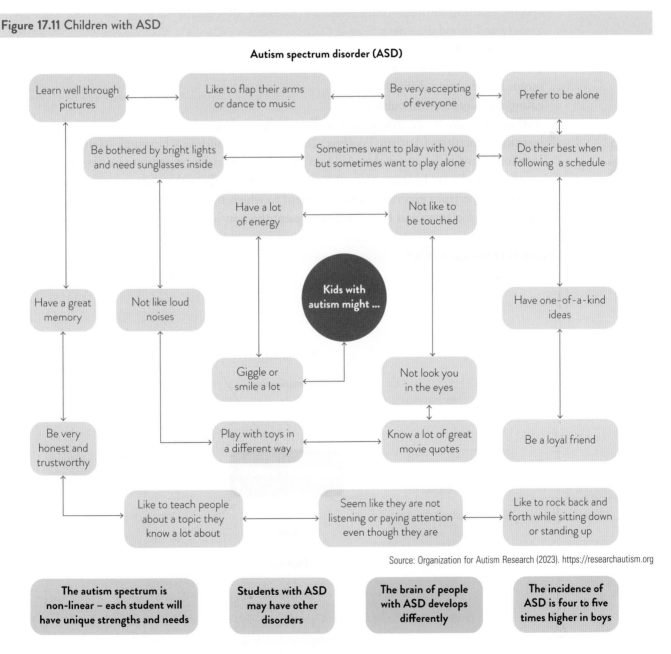

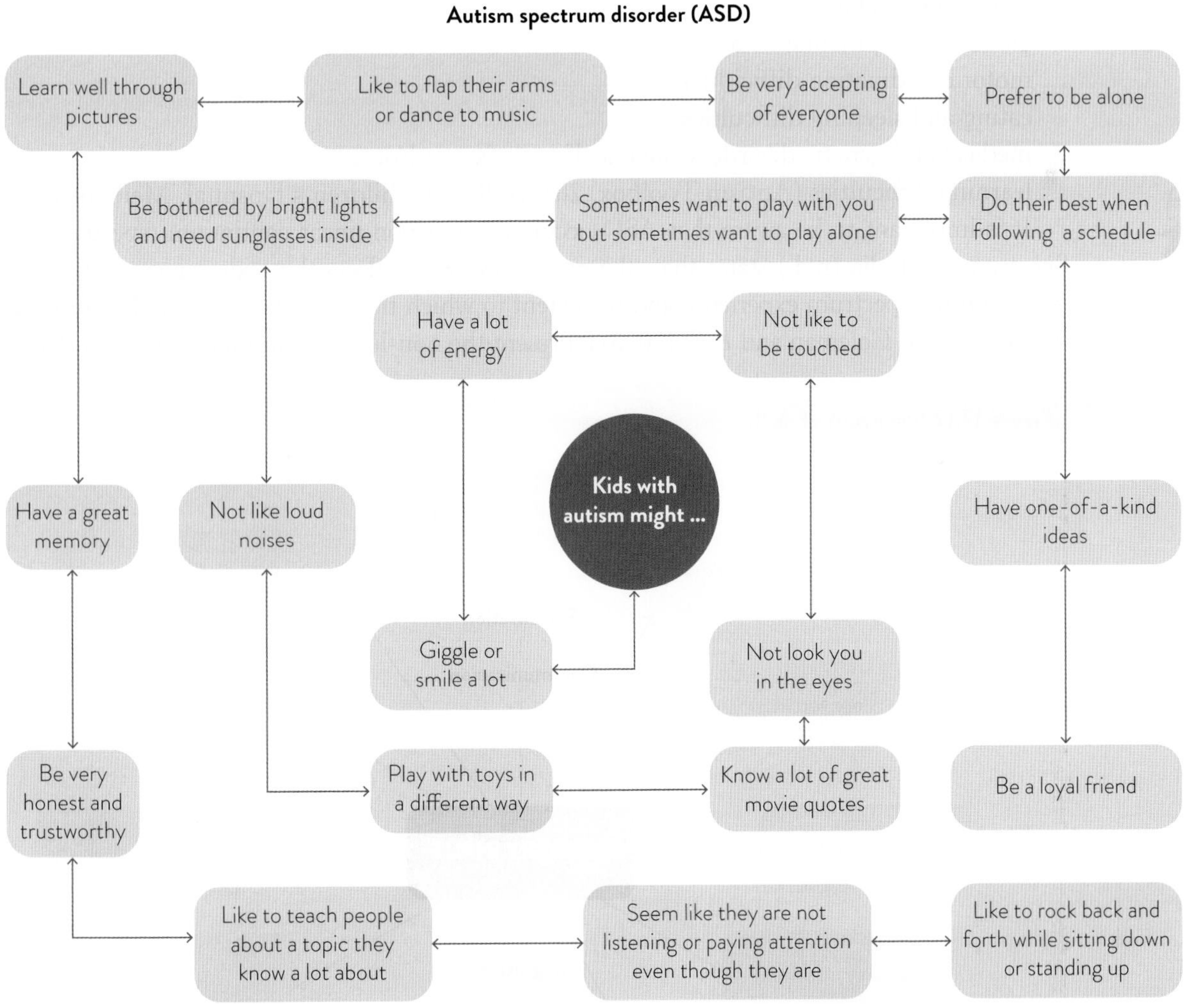

Source: Organization for Autism Research (2023). https://researchautism.org

The autism spectrum is non-linear – each student will have unique strengths and needs

Students with ASD may have other disorders

The brain of people with ASD develops differently

The incidence of ASD is four to five times higher in boys

To date researchers have not been able to identify why the brain of people with ASD develops differently. Families with one child with autism have an increased risk of having another child with autism when compared with the general population. According to research undertaken by Maenner et al. (2020), cited in Gallagher, Coleman and Kirk (2023), approximately 33 per cent of children and young people with ASD also have intellectual disabilities. Other conditions that may occur alongside ASD include:

- attention deficit hyperactivity disorder (ADHD)
- developmental coordination disorder (DCD), also referred to as dyspraxia
- developmental language disorder (DLD)
- epilepsy
- foetal alcohol spectrum disorder
- intellectual disability
- Tourette syndrome and tic disorders
- specific learning disorder/differences (e.g. dyslexia, dyscalculia)
- anxiety and mood disorders
- challenging behaviour
- global developmental delay
- motor coordination difficulties
- eating and sleeping difficulties
- medical and genetic disorders, such as Fragile X syndrome
- learning difficulties (Autism Toolbox, 2019b; Royal Children's Hospital, Melbourne, 2021).

Videos: Understanding autism

It is important to be aware that ASD occurs along a non-linear continuum (spectrum). Autism Spectrum Australia (n.d.) states that 'the word spectrum reflects the wide range of challenges that people on the spectrum experience and the extent to which they may be affected'. **Figure 17.12** shows how Gallagher, Coleman and Kirk (2023) represent the non-linear continuum across six domains.

Figure 17.12 Spectrum of skills

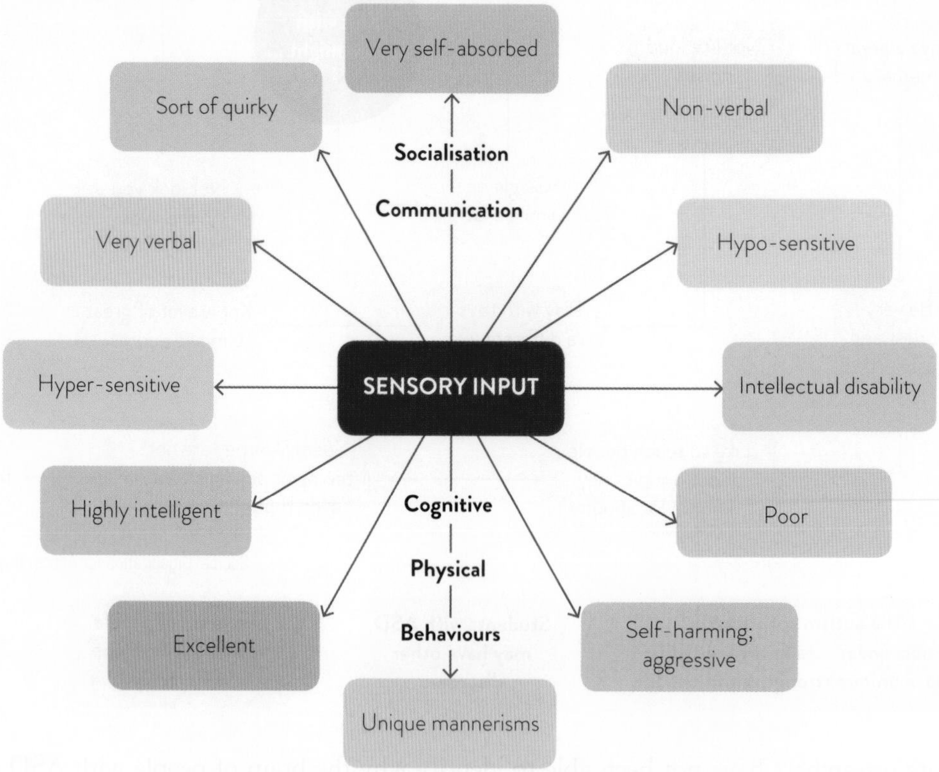

Source: Adapted from Gallagher, J., Coleman, M. & Kirk, S. (2023). *Educating Exceptional Children.* Cengage Learning, p. 149.

Scheuermann, Webber and Lang (2019) describe a range of behaviours that may be present in people with ASD. These behaviours are listed in **Figure 17.13**.

Figure 17.13 Range of ASD behaviours

Strengths and interests

> Logical or visual thinking > Persistence > Eye for detail > Good skills with technology > Memory for facts and figures	> Very strong focus on interest areas > Deep interest in typical topic such as Pokémon, sport, Disney, trains or more unusual topics (e.g. air conditioners, bins) > Around 20 per cent of people with ASD have exceptional or above average skills in areas such as reading, maths, art, mechanics, music, memory

Behavioural excesses and deficits

Social interaction > Indifference to people, places, events and objects around them > Limited use and understanding of non-verbal communication, such as eye gaze, facial expression and gestures > Difficulties forming and sustaining friendships > A lack of seeking to share enjoyment, interest and activities with other people > Difficulties with social and emotional responsiveness, including showing empathy	**Communication** > A lack of functional communication > Delayed language development > Use of nonsense speech > Echolalia – repeating what others say > Use of stereotypic phrases – repeating the same phrase over and over and out of context so it makes no sense > Difficulties initiating and sustaining conversations > Stereotyped and repetitive use of language such as repeating phrases from television > Limited imaginative or make-believe play
Repetitive behaviours > Stereotyped and repetitive body movements such as hand flapping and spinning, walking on tiptoes > Repetitive use of objects such as repeatedly flicking a doll's eyes or lining up toys > Extreme inability to cope with change > Adherence to non-functional routines or rituals, such as insisting on travelling the same route home each day, or avoiding walking on lines in tiles, carpet, footpath; only eating certain foods	**Sensory** > Hyper-reactivity or **hyporeactivity** to sensory input or unusual interests in sensory aspects of the environment > Extreme sensitivity to noise, light, touch – the sound of a ticking clock, the clackity-clack of a fan, the sound of an idling engine or the soft hum of a machine may cause an extreme reaction > Unusual sensory interests such as sniffing objects or staring intently at moving objects > Sensory sensitivities including avoidance of everyday sounds and textures; and intellectual impairment or learning difficulties
Learning difficulties > Students are likely to have learning difficulties (although this is not always the case) > Students may have problems with processing and generalising information, problem-solving > May need direct instruction to develop self-help skills such as toileting, using utensils to feed self, dressing/undressing, putting on and removing shoes and socks, dressing according to the weather conditions, following simple routines such as meals, bathing, brushing teeth, or washing and drying hands	**Excessive behaviours** > Tantrums, screaming, **stimming**, self-abuse, aggression, **echolalia**, **perseveration**, refusing to follow directions > Self-harm such as head-banging, squeezing or pinching parts of their own body until a bruise is formed; biting, scratching or hitting self > Physical aggression – biting, scratching or biting others > Poor sleep

Sources: Scheuermann, B., Webber, J. & Lang, R. (2019). *Autism. Teaching Makes a Difference.* 2nd edn. Cengage Learning; Autism Spectrum Australia (n.d.). How do we describe autism? https://www.autismspectrum.org.au

Diagnosing ASD

Videos: About ASD

The National Guidelines for the Assessment and Diagnosis of Autism Spectrum Disorders provide a nationally consistent and unified approach to assessment of ASD in Australia and include:

- comprehensive needs assessment to identify individual strengths, challenges and needs. It includes:
  - an assessment of functioning (cognitive abilities, speech and language function, daily living skills, friendships and school)
  - a medical evaluation (physical examination to determine any medical causes for behaviours)
- diagnostic evaluation to determine whether behaviours are consistent with a diagnosis of ASD (Autism CRC, 2018).

ASD and behaviour

Video: National Guidelines for the Assessment and Diagnosis of ASD

Students with ASD often present with several challenging behaviours, and do not respond to commonly used behaviour-management strategies. Often, the only way students with ASD can let you know how they are feeling is by engaging in extreme maladaptive behaviours such as flapping, screaming, physical aggression and self-harming.

It is best practice to address one behaviour of concern at a time. An Individual Behaviour Plan (IBP) can be put in place. The IBP should focus on one particularly challenging/maladaptive behaviour – usually determined by the class teacher in collaboration with parents and therapists.

According to Willis (2006), when considering how best to respond to unwanted behaviours, it is essential to consider the way the student behaves (form) and why the behaviour is occurring (function). Eliminating the function or cause of the behaviour is often the most effective way to reduce the unwanted behaviour. Eliminating the cause assists the student to calm down and avoids any direct intervention with the student, which can often result in an increase in unwanted behaviour. Consider the examples of Jude and Eric in the following Scenario.

RESPONDING TO BEHAVIOUR

SCENARIO

JUDE

Jude (12 years) is screaming and flapping his hands. This is something he does regularly. His piercing screams are unsettling the other students. ESW **Luke** noticed that Jude had been watching the ceiling fan as it went around and around; however, the fan has since been switched off.

- The *form* of Jude's behaviour is screaming and hand flapping.
- The *function* (reason) for his behaviour is because the fan has been switched off.

To manage Jude's behaviour, Luke turns the fan back on – Jude immediately begins to calm down.

ERIC

Eric (11 years) was making patterns with coloured tiles when another student approached and stood at the table facing him. Eric began to pinch himself and make a wailing sound. Without commenting on Eric's behaviour, ESW **Luke** immediately moved the student to another activity. As soon as the other student was away from Eric, the behaviour stopped.

- The *form* of Eric's behaviour is pinching himself and wailing.
- The *function* of Eric's behaviour is the invasion of his personal space by another student.

▶ DISCUSSION

Discuss how applying an analysis of the function and form of a student's behaviour can assist in planning an appropriate response and/or modifications to the physical environment or daily routines.

Modifying the behaviour of any student can be a challenge. Modifying the behaviour of a student with ASD is even more challenging. There is a wide range of evidence-based practices that can be used to modify behaviours when working with students with ASD. There is no single best strategy – educators need to work with the student, the family and therapists to determine the most effective strategy for each individual. **Figure 17.14** provides examples of some evidence-based practices that may be used. To be effective, any strategy used must be implemented exactly the way it has been designed, which may require specialised training.

Figure 17.14 Examples of evidence-based practices

Functional behaviour assessment (FBA)	Information gathered from an FBA can be used to devise a response to the behaviour with the aim of reducing the severity of the behaviour or eliminating it. Steps include determining: > the exact nature of the behaviour (what the student does) > what triggers the behaviour > the immediate consequences of the behaviour for the student (and others) > the function of the behaviour – what is the student trying to communicate? Factors to consider may include: > changing some aspects of the environment (triggers) > anticipating and intervening before the behaviour occurs > identifying an alternative behaviour (what could the student be taught to do as an alternative to extreme behaviour?) > identifying alternative responses to the behaviour (changing your own behaviour).
Least-to-most prompting (prompting)	A system that uses a hierarchy of prompts (from least amount of help to most amount of help) to correct, modify or change a behaviour (see **Figure 17.15**).
Social skills training (SST)	Group or individual instruction designed to teach learners with ASD ways to interact appropriately with peers, adults and other individuals. Most social skill meetings include instruction on basic concepts, role-playing or practice, and feedback to help learners with ASD acquire and practise communication, play or social skills to promote positive interactions with peers.
Task analysis (TA)	A process in which an activity or behaviour is divided into small, manageable steps to assess and teach the skill – for example, toileting or handwashing.
Visual support (VS)	Any visual display that supports the learner engaging in a desired behaviour or skills independently of prompts. Examples of visual supports include pictures, written words, objects within the environment, arrangement of the environment or visual boundaries, schedules, maps, labels, organisation systems, and timelines.

Source: Wong et al. (2012, pp. 20, 21).

Supporting students with ASD

Guided Functional Behaviour Assessment Tool

According to Willis (2006, p. 22), five key strategies are used to work with students with ASD. These strategies include:

- **early intervention** – structured support programs (home and/or centre based) for children prior to entering school
- **structured behaviour intervention** – development of a plan to assist the student to manage their behaviour
- **sensory integration therapy** – a program developed by an occupational therapist designed to assist the student to manage sensory input

Figure 17.15 Hierarchy of prompting

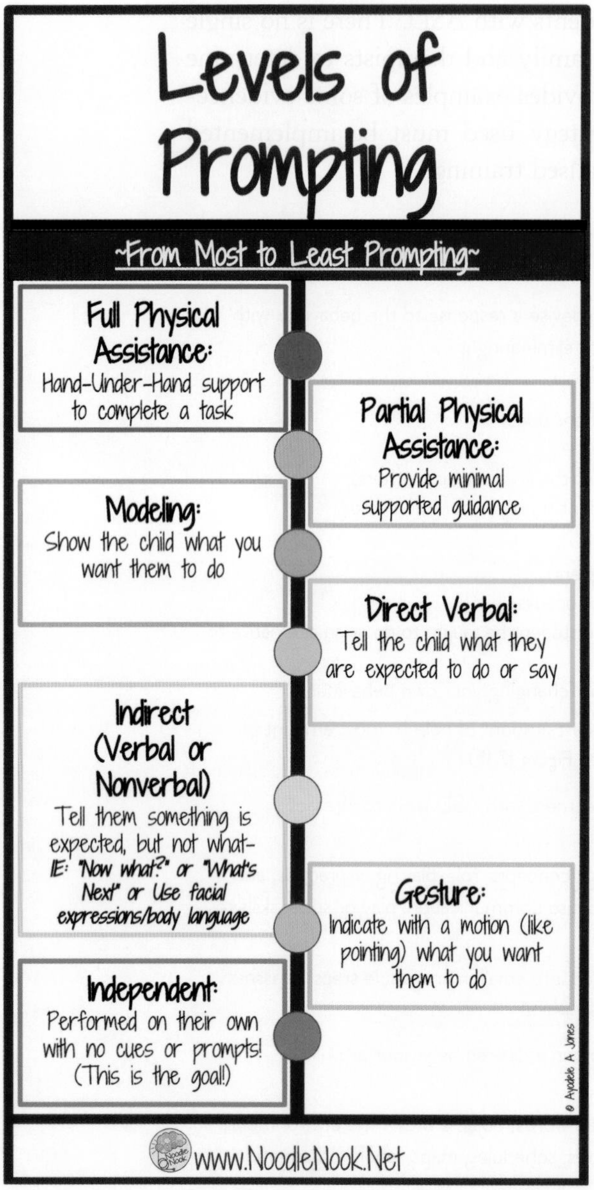

Source: NoodleNook (2018). Copyright @ NoodleNook.

- **speech/language therapy** – a speech pathologist works with the student to develop a program to facilitate language and communication
- **special education** – the student is placed in a regular school setting or a special unit. An IEP is developed to assist the student to reach their full learning potential.

A program to support a student with ASD may include any combination of the above strategies, which may vary over time.

Educational goals for students with ASD will typically address behavioural excesses and behavioural deficits, focusing on communication, social competence, behaviour management and functional life skills. Scheuermann, Webber and Lang (2019) suggest that applied behaviour analysis (ABA) is a strategy that can be used to support skills development in students with ASD. The authors state (p. 2):

> Behaviour does not occur in isolation and does not originate solely from within an individual student. Instead, most behaviors exhibited by students with autism – both appropriate and challenging behaviours – are related to events in the environment that occur either before the behavior is exhibited (called antecedents) or immediately after a given behavior occurs (consequences–positive/negative).

An example of how ABA might be applied in the classroom is shown in **Figure 17.16**.

The key to a successful ABA approach is to observe the student and identify both positive and negative antecedents with a view to maximising the positives and reducing or eliminating the negatives. Being aware of triggers or antecedents that have negative outcomes for the student is not an easy task; however, by getting to know the student, it is possible to reduce some of these triggers – for

Figure 17.16 Applying ABA in the classroom

Antecedent: event/s that occur/s to trigger the behaviour	Behaviour	Consequence
The teacher gives Harvey his favourite magnetic letters for a spelling task (positive).	Harvey immediately begins to use the magnetic letters to create a series of words (positive).	The teacher gives Harvey a sticker to reinforce desired behaviour. Harvey stays on task for several minutes.
A student walks by and accidentally bumps Harvey's desk, causing some of the letters to fall to the floor.	Harvey jumps up hits the student and begins to scream.	The teacher responds by sternly saying, 'Harvey no hitting'. Harvey drops to the floor and continues to scream.

example, providing an ordered, quiet space that allows the student to be part of the class but at the same time allows the student their own space.

The use of consequences can be an effective strategy when working with students with ASD. Positive consequences might be something tangible, like a sticker, a special fidget toy, or a favourite activity or task. It may also be something intangible like praise or a thumbs up.

Negative consequences are not the same as punishment. Using negative consequences for a student with ASD often includes allowing the student to avoid a task they don't like doing – for example, 'If you finish your worksheet, I won't give you any homework today/you can take a ten-minute break'. In these examples, the consequences are negative because the student gets to avoid something they dislike.

An important part of ABA is targeting and teaching desired behaviours. This may take the form of offering alternatives for undesirable behaviours and direct instruction. Scheuermann, Webber and Lang (2019) state that 'stereotypic behaviours include spinning objects, body rocking, repetitive vocalizations, flapping hands' (p. 3) and these can be reduced by offering the student alternatives, which are described in **Figure 17.17**.

Figure 17.17 Alternatives to stereotypic behaviours

Sensory system	Alternative behaviours
Visual	Prism, pinwheel, kaleidoscope, toys that make flashing lights, View-Master, Lite-Brite, Slinky, lava lamp, windup toys, perpetual motion balls, string puppets, or yo-yos
Auditory	Talking toys, music boxes, music through headphones, noisemakers, clickers, seashells, talking through a microphone (amplification), using headphones to listen to recordings of the child's own voice, animal noises (whales, dolphins) or white noise
Tactile	Pieces of cloth with a variety of textures (velvet, burlap, chenille, suede, satin, fur), Silly Putty, Slime, squishy balls, bean bags, Beanie Babies, plastic bubble wrap, hand exercise balls, 'worry' beads or rocks
Vestibular	Rocking horse, rocking chair, hammock, swing, tyre swing, trampoline, rolling on large therapy balls or in barrels, somersaults
Proprioceptive	Wrist or ankle weights, isometric exercises, hand weights, gymnastic exercises (headstands, handstands, cartwheels, somersaults, etc.), or grip-strengthening exercise tool, foot chair band, wiggle seat, scoop rockers, weighted vests
Olfactory	Cologne or aftershave either worn on the student's body or offered in small vials; or other fragrances offered in vials (e.g. scents used in making potpourri or dropped on light bulbs)
Gustatory	Small bite-size foods that can be chewed. Chewy toys – for examples go to: https://sensoryreadystore.com.au/collections/sensory

Source: Scheuermann, B., Webber, J. & Lang, R. (2019). *Autism: Teaching Makes a Difference*. 2nd edn. Cengage Learning Inc., pp. 29, 75

Teaching strategies, accommodations and modifications

Videos: Secondary students and ASD

When working with students with ASD, teachers will use a range of instructional strategies customised to meet the needs of learners. There is no single 'best practice' model for teaching students with ASD, simply because each student will have their own strengths and learning needs that reflect the continuum of ASD.

The learner environment should be set up to avoid sensory overload from noise, smells, movement, bright lights, multi-colours and windows. Seating should be comfortable and allow plenty of personal space. Students with ASD often struggle with handwriting – using a keyboard or a voice-to-text device for students who are verbal can be useful.

Children and young people with ASD may be verbal or non-verbal. They may use unusual forms of communication, such as words or phrases from music or television. They may respond to a question by making a statement that does not relate to the question. They may be echolalic – repeating the speaker's sentence or repeating a phrase or a single word. In the following Scenario, Liliya is echolalic and Joe responds to an invitation to play in a manner that his peers may find hard to interpret.

TUNING IN TO COMMUNICATION

SCENARIO

LILIYA

Liliya (13 years) is sitting at the table ready for her morning tea.

ESW: *'Liliya, would you like some apple or banana?'*
Liliya: *'Liliya, would you like some apple or banana?'*
ESW: *'I'll give you some of both.'*
Liliya: *'10-4, 10-4.'* (The ESW knows this is Liliya's term for 'okay'.)

JOE

Joe (14 years) is outdoors watching two students, **Kirra** and **Jesse**, kicking a ball to each other.

Jesse: *'Want to play, Joe?'*
Joe: *'I count cars. I count cars. I count cars.'* Joe also signs 'no'.

This is Joe's way of responding to Jesse and telling him he doesn't want to play.

WHAT DOES THIS TELL US?

Liliya and Joe have their own unique ways of communicating. Their aversion to socialisation and poor communication skills often result in students with ASD being socially isolated.

ACC technologies

Non-verbal students will require access to ACC technology such as Picture Exchange Communication System (PECS), Key Word Sign or speech generating devices.

Explicit or direct instruction

A common characteristic of students with ASD is the need for consistent and predictable routines. Extending this to the way instruction is provided can support students with ASD to engage in learning and stay on-task. Predictability and consistency also contribute to reducing stress and anxiety in students with ASD.

An example of a consistent teaching strategy is direct instruction, which was explored in Chapter 11. Direct instruction can be a useful instructional model because it uses structured, systematic, predictable and sequential teaching strategies. It is designed to break down information into small steps or increments. Ninety per cent of direct instruction lessons focus on what the student already knows, understands and can do. The remaining 10 per cent of a direct instruction lesson introduces new knowledge and skills. The pace of lessons is based on the individual learning needs of each student. Direct instruction involves clear instructions, modelling, demonstrating and practice.

When working with ASD students, it is important to be explicit – that is, clearly state the purpose of the lesson and the learning outcome. Students should be given explicit instruction, the degree of which will depend on the student. For example, you may begin by saying, 'Dylan, I want you to listen closely to me. Are you ready? We are going to work on multiplication.' Using clear, unambiguous language will support the student to understand and attend to the task. Students with ASD typically interpret information in a very literal way. Depending on the needs of each student, instruction may need to be repeated or broken down into micro steps.

Instruction may be verbal, written, graphic (use photos rather than line drawings as these can be difficult for students with ASD to interpret), tactile/concrete materials or technology using a roller ball or toggle. It is important to be aware that students with ASD may only be able to attend to one information source at a time. For example, they may not be able to listen to you read and follow along by looking at printed text at the same time.

Students with ASD may have difficulty generalising their skills and knowledge, making it difficult for them to extend on and build new skills and knowledge. Providing opportunities for students to apply their skills and knowledge in a wide range of situations can help them to generalise and engage in problem-solving. Students with ASD often have difficulty sequencing tasks, and visual sequence cards can be used to support independent learning (see **Figure 17.18**).

Task initiation

Figure 17.18 Visual cues

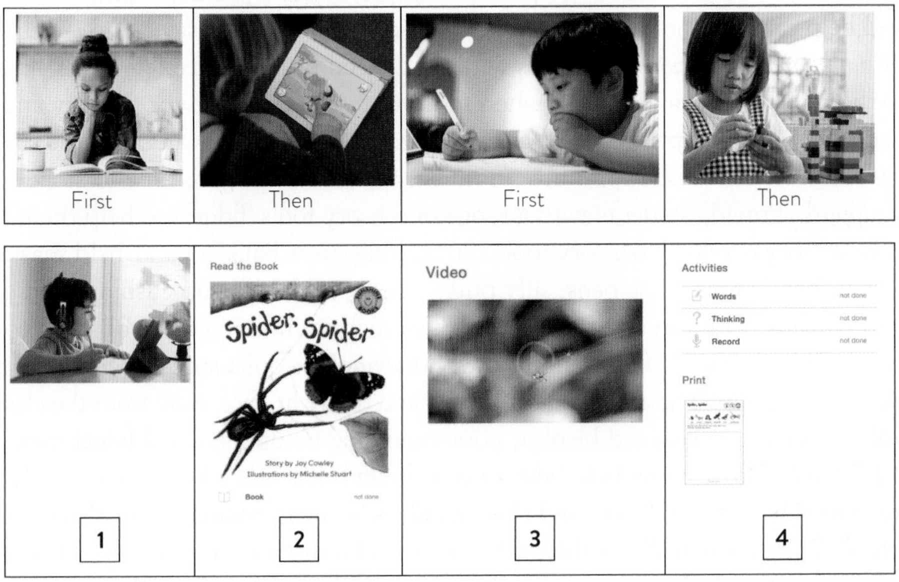

Source: Adapted from: Autism Classroom. News and resources. https://autismclassroomresources.com/visual-schedule-series-first-then/; (images) iStock.com/Poike (child reading); Alamy Stock Photo/Agencja Fotograficzna Caro (child iPad); iStock.com/Thai Liang Lim (writing); Shutterstock.com/Meaw_stocker (puzzle); Shutterstock.com/Ann in the uk (child tablet); (book cover; website screenshot) Wendy Pye Publishing Ltd (Sunshine Books).

Examples of accommodations and modifications

A wide range of accommodations and modifications can be developed to support the learning needs of students with ASD. Some of these are described below:

- *Create a predictable daily routine:* Providing students with a daily and weekly schedule will reduce anxiety in relation to transitions and give students a sense of control. Visual schedules can reduce anxiety by supporting the student to anticipate and understand the daily sequence of lessons and breaks.
- *Provide a consistent physical environment:* This is an environment where everything remains in the same place. While other students may cope with moving around the room students with ASD are more secure if their working space remains fixed.
- *Communication aids:* Use assistive technology, visual aids or tactile aids alongside verbal communication and gestures to communicate information and support learning.
- *Information processing:* Students with ASD will need more time to process information and instructions. Use visual aids, such as a sequence of photos to show steps in a task or to give step-by-step instructions paced to reflect the student's needs. Slowing down can help the student

to understand, process and remember information. Use explicit instruction, demonstrate, model, show and repeatedly check for understanding. Use 'first, then, next' instruction. Before giving instructions always get the student's attention – for example, 'Layla, look at me. I am going to read each word on this page (pause). When I say the word you will point to it (pause); look at the page (pause) "horse". Layla point to the word horse'. Provide positive reinforcement when the student follows the instructions. This technique will vary based on the student's needs.

- *Support to stay on-task:* According to Larkey and Tulleman (2021), each task should be clear, concise and as concrete as possible. Remember that students with ASD find it difficult to generalise and think abstractly. They often approach tasks from particular to particular. They may not understand 'the bigger picture' and may often interpret statements in a very literal way.
- *Support asking for help:* Students with ASD may not recognise when they need help and may not consider asking for help. Larkey and Tulleman (2021) suggest providing a visual prompt and instructions on how to ask for help. For example, 'When you don't know what to do, get your need help card and hold it up so the teacher can see. You can say "I need help please".'
- *Allow for unhurried transitions:* Students with ASD need time to complete tasks, arrange and organise their workspace, and choose when to move to the next activity. Larkey and Tulleman (2021) suggest providing a series of visual cues that you can show the students, for example, 5 minutes to finish, 3 minutes to finish, 1 minute to finish, time to stop.
- *Sensory support:* Provide students with a range of sensory tools/fidgets to help them manage and relieve sensory overload. Sensory tools can include stress balls, a hand-held massager, balloon balls, bendy toys, blow pens, silly putty, chewy toys, blow-up cushions and foot pads, and weighted pads. This can also include activities such as climbing or an obstacle course.
- *Quiet area:* Students with ASD benefit from withdrawing to a quiet space where they can be alone, calm down and regroup. The area should be quiet and dimly lit, face away from the classroom and include objects such as a weighted blanket, noise-cancelling headphones and fidget toys.
- *Regular time-out:* Allow students to take a five-minute break every hour, or as needed. This helps students refresh and refocus, and thus avoid meltdowns. Students can also be provided with a choice board, which allows them to choose a calming/timeout activity. This gives students a sense of control and encourages them to monitor and manage their own stress levels.
- *Reduce noise and bright light:* Provide seating that allows for indirect light and reduced noise (such as away from door or busy areas).
- *Emotional/stress monitor:* Provide students with a visual prop so that they can easily signal if they are becoming distressed.
- *Unhurried time:* Provide students with unhurried time to complete tasks without the pressure of time constraints.
- *Organisation:* Students with ASD may have poor organisational and planning skills. Provide a plastic bin under the student's desk where they can store personal items and school work.
- *Break down tasks:* Students with ASD may need to have a task broken down into small, manageable steps. This can be done using visual prompts, or by providing templates or verbal cues.
- *Social skills instruction:* Students with ASD often lack the ability to form friendships and understand social rules, such as turn-taking, saying please and thank you, asking rather than taking, sharing and so on. Providing daily reminders by demonstrating, modelling and using role-play assists students to apply these skills.
- *Create visuals:* Visuals may include, for example, daily schedules, 'first/then' instructions, reminders of class rules, how to ask for help, a task broken down into a series of steps, etc.

Practical ideas and tips for ESWs

Accommodations and modifications must be individualised for each student. Often parents will be able to assist in identifying strategies that will best support their child in the classroom.

Asperger's syndrome

In 2013, Asperger's syndrome became part of one umbrella diagnosis of ASD in the *Diagnostic and Statistical Manual of Mental Disorders 5 (DSM-5)* (American Psychiatric Association, 2013). Asperger's syndrome occurs on a continuum and is typically characterised by individuals who have normal to above normal intelligence and have persistent impairments in socialisation, communication, cognition and sensation.

Australian expert on Asperger's syndrome Professor Tony Attwood takes a neurodiversity approach to Asperger's syndrome. Attwood states:

> children and adults with Asperger's syndrome have a different, not necessarily defective, way of perceiving, thinking, learning and relating. The person usually has a strong desire to seek knowledge, truth and perfection, with a different set of priorities than would be expected with other people. The overriding priority may be to solve a problem rather than satisfy the social or emotional needs of others. The person values being creative rather than co-operative, and may perceive patterns, errors and solutions that are not apparent to others. The person is usually renowned for speaking their mind and being honest and determined, with a strong sense of social justice and a distinct sense of humour.
>
> Source: Attwood, T. (2023). What is Asperger's syndrome/ASD – Level 1? https://tonyattwood.com.au/about-aspergers-asd-level-1/what-is-aspergers-asd-level-1

Video: Is Asperger's syndrome the next stage of human evolution?

Figure 17.19 lists the range of presenting behaviours that may be present in children and young people with Asperger's syndrome.

Figure 17.19 Common challenges and characteristics of people with Asperger's syndrome

Challenge	Characteristic
Social	> Lack of understanding of social cues and subtleties > *Literal interpretation of others' words* > Difficulty engaging in reciprocal conversation > Tendency to speak bluntly without regard for impact of words on others > Universal application of social rules to all situations > Focus on single topic of interest that may not be of interest to others
Communication	> Difficulty understanding social nuances such as sarcasm or metaphor > Echolalia – may repeat last words heard without regard for meaning > Poor judge of personal space – may stand too close to other students > Abnormal inflection and eye contact > Inappropriate facial expressions or gestures > Difficulty interpreting others' nonverbal communication cues
Cognition	> Poor problem-solving and organisational skills > Concrete, literal thinking > Difficulty differentiating relevant and irrelevant information > Obsessive and narrowly defined interests > Difficulty generalising and applying learned knowledge and skills across different situations, settings and people
Sensory and motor challenges	> Over- or under-sensitivity to different sensory stimuli, including pain > Difficulty with fine-motor skills, such as handwriting

Source: Organization for Autism (2016). Life Journey Through Autism: An Educator's Guide to Asperger Syndrome. Arlington, VA (p. 6).

Accommodations for high school students with Asperger's syndrome are shown in **Figure 17.20**.

Figure 17.20 Accommodations for high school students

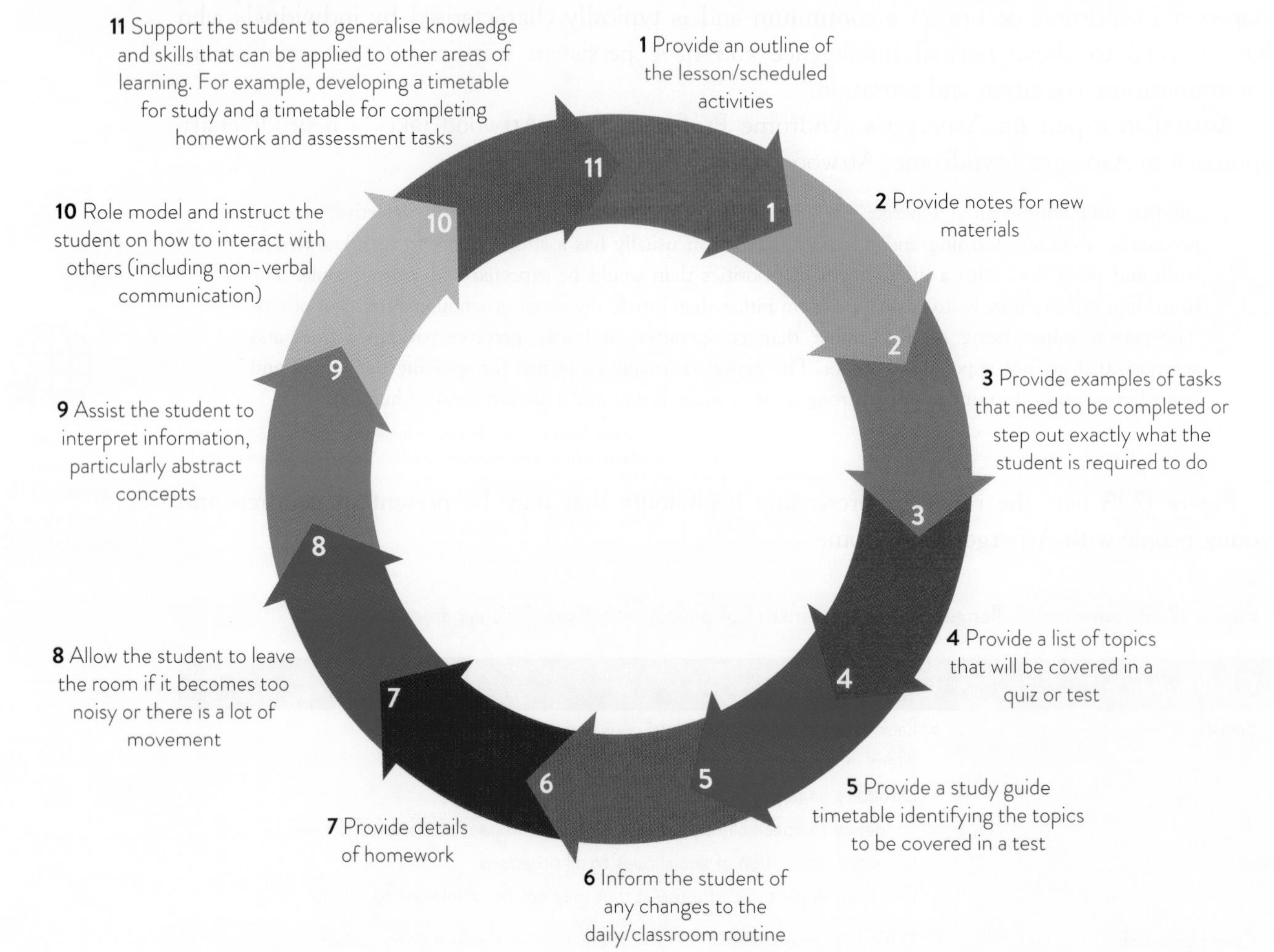

1 Provide an outline of the lesson/scheduled activities
2 Provide notes for new materials
3 Provide examples of tasks that need to be completed or step out exactly what the student is required to do
4 Provide a list of topics that will be covered in a quiz or test
5 Provide a study guide timetable identifying the topics to be covered in a test
6 Inform the student of any changes to the daily/classroom routine
7 Provide details of homework
8 Allow the student to leave the room if it becomes too noisy or there is a lot of movement
9 Assist the student to interpret information, particularly abstract concepts
10 Role model and instruct the student on how to interact with others (including non-verbal communication)
11 Support the student to generalise knowledge and skills that can be applied to other areas of learning. For example, developing a timetable for study and a timetable for completing homework and assessment tasks

Working with students with ASD

Schools and support for students with ASD

The individual websites for state and territory schools, listed in the Online Resources, have information about ASD and how students are supported in schools. An exploration of these sites reveals there are quite significant differences in information and resources to support educators. By far the most outstanding site is the Autism Hub (Queensland), which is worth exploring regardless of your location.

State/territory school resources for students with ASD

Attention deficit hyperactivity disorder

Attention deficit hyperactivity disorder (ADHD) is a neurobiological developmental disorder that results in poor concentration, impulsivity and hyperactivity. The cause of ADHD remains unknown. It may be linked to genetic and environmental factors. **Figure 17.21** shows common characteristics and interventions for children with ADHD.

Figure 17.21 Characteristics of and interventions for ADHD

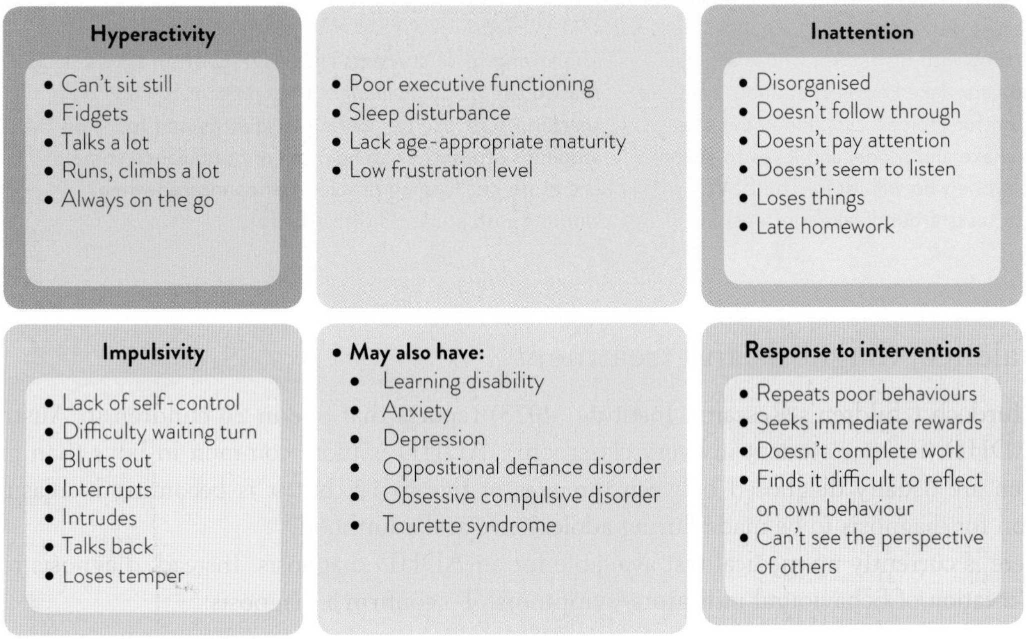

Hyperactivity
• Can't sit still
• Fidgets
• Talks a lot
• Runs, climbs a lot
• Always on the go
• Poor executive functioning
• Sleep disturbance
• Lack age-appropriate maturity
• Low frustration level
Inattention
• Disorganised
• Doesn't follow through
• Doesn't pay attention
• Doesn't seem to listen
• Loses things
• Late homework
Impulsivity
• Lack of self-control
• Difficulty waiting turn
• Blurts out
• Interrupts
• Intrudes
• Talks back
• Loses temper
• May also have:
• Learning disability
• Anxiety
• Depression
• Oppositional defiance disorder
• Obsessive compulsive disorder
• Tourette syndrome
Response to interventions
• Repeats poor behaviours
• Seeks immediate rewards
• Doesn't complete work
• Finds it difficult to reflect on own behaviour
• Can't see the perspective of others

Source: Adapted from: Neurodivergent Insights. https://neurodivergentinsights.com

ADHD is characterised by:

- **inattention** – inability to concentrate, inability to complete tasks, flitting from one thing to another, disorganised, unable to estimate the time needed to complete a task, often unsure of where to start
- **impulsivity** – risk-taking/reckless behaviour, inability to listen to and follow instructions, extremes of emotions, accident prone, unable to wait for a turn, fails to consider consequences of actions for self or others, difficulty playing with others
- **hyperactivity** – restless, fidgeting, making inappropriate noises or talking incessantly, can't sit or stand still, climbs on everything.

According to the DSM-5 (APA, 2013), there are three main subtypes of ADHD:

- *Inattentive presentation* – characterised by challenges predominantly relating to concentration, memory and organisation.
- *Hyperactive/impulsive presentation* – characterised by challenges predominantly in self-control, restlessness and sitting still.
- *Combined presentation* – characterised by challenges in a combination of inattentive and hyperactive/impulsive symptoms.

It is not uncommon for children with ADHD to also have one or more comorbidities such as learning disabilities, anxiety, depression, sensory processing disorder, and oppositional defiant disorder. Students with ADHD may also show strengths in areas such as creative/out-of-the-box thinking, curiosity and resourcefulness in exploring a topic of interest.

Video: What is ADHD?

SCENARIO

STRENGTHS-BASED APPROACH TO ADHD

Jake (12 years) has ADHD and has been taking medication for many years to manage his symptoms. Jake is a bright boy but struggles in class. He finds it difficult to stay on task and is easily distracted.

Jake likes to spend time with his father, who is a mechanic, restoring old cars. Jake knows a lot about car engines and has a passion for Holden cars. He knows the details of almost every make and model and loves to share this information with anyone who will listen. The ESW plans maths and literacy tasks around Jake's interest in cars. He will often bring in car magazines for in-class reading and comprehension tasks.

WHAT DOES THIS TELL US?

The strengths of students with ADHD often take a back seat to the many challenges they present to classroom teaching staff. Remembering to identify and focus on the student's strengths can help to counterbalance some of the more challenging problems encountered when working with students with ADHD.

Prevalence, diagnosis and treatment

The Murdoch Children's Research Institute (2023) reports that one in 20 children in Australia have ADHD (i.e. one student in every classroom). ADHD is more common in boys than girls. Children are usually diagnosed between the ages of five to 12, but it is becoming increasingly common for diagnosis to be made during adolescence and adulthood.

There is currently no medical test available for an ADHD diagnosis. Instead, diagnosis relies on observation of behavioural indicators/symptoms. To confirm a diagnosis:

- children should have six or more symptoms of the disorder that have been consistently displayed over a period of six months
- symptoms must be present before the age of 12
- symptoms need to be excessive for the developmental age of the individual
- symptoms are present in more than one setting
- symptoms must be causing significant impairment in at least two settings (e.g. home and school).

Source: The Murdoch Children's Research Institute (Melbourne) (2023). ADHD. https://www.mcri.edu.au/impact/a-z-child-adolescent-health/a/adhd

According to ADHD Support Australia (2022), assessment of ADHD may also include:

- developmental, learning, educational or IQ checks
- language, speech and movement checks
- general health checks
- vision and hearing tests.

Video: ADHD medication

Understanding ADHD

In Australia, the most common approved medications used to treat ADHD are psychostimulants. These drugs may include dexamfetamine, methylphenidate and lisdexamfetamine. According to NSW Health (2018), 'psychostimulant medication is thought to work by altering the availability of particular brain chemicals or neurotransmitters (dopamine and noradrenaline) in regions of the brain involved with behaviour inhibition, impulse control, attention and working memory'. Non-stimulant medications include atomoxetine and guanfacine and typically the effects can last up to 24 hours.

Treatment for ADHD may include drug therapy, behaviour therapy, special diets and nutritional supplements. Behaviour therapy often will involve the whole family.

Accommodations and modifications

Each student with ADHD will present with a unique set of strengths, needs, behaviours and challenges. Teachers often work with parent/s, therapists and other support professionals as a starting point to understand the student's strengths, challenges, current medication/treatment, typical behaviours and behaviour triggers as well as behaviour management strategies that work. A wide range of strategies can be used to support ADHD students – not all will be successful, and often it is a matter of trial and error. Closely observing the student and getting to know their strengths, likes, dislikes and triggers is an important beginning point and will help to build a positive working relationship.

Figure 17.22 lists some examples of things that might be observed to gain a better understanding of how ADHD affects student behaviour and learning.

Figure 17.22 Observing students with ADHD

Students with ADHD

- ☐ Antecedents of challenging behaviours (environment, peers, transitions, curriculum areas)
- ☐ Which calming strategies does the student respond to best?
- ☐ What acting out, distracting, avoidance behaviours does the student employ?
- ☐ What are the student's interests/favourite activities?
- ☐ Which behaviour management strategies appear to be most effective/least effective?
- ☐ Is there a pattern to the student's behaviour?
- ☐ Does the student seem to tire at particular times during the day?
- ☐ How does the student make use of sensory/fidget toys?
- ☐ What behaviours does the student display when procrastinating starting/staying on task/completing activities?
- ☐ Is the student able to take themself to a quiet area for some time out when needed?
- ☐ What signs of anxiety does the student display?
- ☐ Is the student able to ask for help when needed?

Through observation, you can gain a great deal of information about how the student functions, what motivates the student, what triggers undesirable behaviours and what works best to calm the student. Observation must be a key priority in planning for the needs of ADHD students.

Practical considerations when working with students with ADHD may include the following:

- *Use positioning:* sit the student near the teacher or ESW and face them away from visual distractions.
- *Use communication:* work with the student on an agreed communication signal as a reminder to stay on task.
- *Manage behaviour:* use a range of techniques such as setting clear limits, offering rewards; use hands-on learning resources or behaviour contracts.
- *Don't use multiple instructions:* break down instructions (and tasks) into single steps.
- *Don't offer choices unless you are prepared to accept the outcome:* for example, 'Can you open your book to chapter 3?' If the student says, 'No', you are left with a challenge. It's better to say, 'Open your book to Chapter 3'.
- *Use tangible rewards for on-task behaviour:* such as 10 minutes on a computer game.
- *Have realistic expectations:* Dukette and Cornish (2009, in Thoonsen & Lamp, 2022, p. 100), state that 'the average time someone can concentrate without getting distracted varies from 3 to 5 minutes for young children and up to 20 minutes for adults'.

SCENARIO

ACCOMMODATIONS FOR ADHD

Charan (14 years) has ADHD. He takes regular medication to manage his condition and attends cognitive therapy. ESW **Kate** has been assigned to support Charan in class.

Before commencing work with Charan, Kate spent time observing him in different classrooms. Kate's observations revealed that Charan:

- takes around 10–15 minutes to settle in each new class
- always heads for a desk at the back of the room
- always attempts to engage other students in silly behaviour as he moves from one room to another for class (such as taunting, shoving, speaking loudly about other students)
- is slow to follow teacher directions in class and looks around to see what others are doing
- appears to be not 'with it' on many occasions
- mutters to himself when students are asked to work independently
- 'drops' books, pens, ruler, etc. to gain attention or as a strategy to move about
- fails to take notes from the teacher or from the whiteboard
- often does not have the right textbooks and materials for the particular class
- rarely completes any homework.

To better accommodate Charan, Kate decides to:

- use a reward system to encourage responsible behaviour when moving from room to room
- teach Charan to check his timetable before each class so that he knows what he needs to take with him
- work with teachers to allocate a desk that Charan uses for each class that minimises distraction and is towards the front of the room
- review teacher instructions with Charan to ensure he knows what he is required to do – write step-by-step instructions and break down each task into manageable chunks
- work with teachers to provide notes in point form for Charan
- recommend that Charan be allowed to take short breaks during class time
- recommend that homework for Charan be reduced or eliminated – as an alternative, Kate can provide one-on-one tutorial support for each subject.

WHAT DOES THIS TELL US?

Taking the time to observe students allows the ESW to better plan specific accommodations to meet individual needs.

▶ DISCUSSION

Think about the observations and accommodations for Charan. Discuss how the accommodations will support Charan's learning.

High school students

The challenges for students with ADHD are often compounded as they reach adolescence because they are coping with the emotional roller coaster of puberty as they strive towards independence. It is also during the teenage years that the brain begins to reconstruct itself to refine executive functioning skills. This period of brain development is characterised by impulsive behaviours, defiance, sullenness and, sometimes, reckless behaviours. During this period, students must also cope with significant changes to the school learning environment, such as:

- being assigned a different teacher for each subject and coping with the different teaching style and personality of teachers
- moving to different rooms according to a timetable and remembering which textbooks and learning resources are needed for each subject
- being assigned multiple homework and assessment tasks with different due dates
- engaging in independent learning to complete projects alone or with a partner/small group
- working with small groups requires students to draw on their executive functioning skills, such as organising, prioritising, problem-solving, time management, etc.

- demands on self-regulation – students must now balance the demands of study, sport, social activities, family and part-time job. Peer pressure is also a significant factor as teenagers are faced with pressures of drugs, antisocial behaviour, alcohol, social media and sexual activity
- being an effective communicator with teachers, family, friends, workplace supervisor etc. – this is challenging for teens at a time when the brain is under reconstruction.

The above points remind us that the teenage years are challenging! For young people with ADHD (and other forms of neurodiversity), providing strategies to help them navigate this period of development is critical. These strategies may include the following:

- *Time management*: creating a weekly schedule with blocks of time allocated for study, sport, friends, downtime, social media, etc. Being able to see what their week or day might look like can help students to stay focused and on track. For homework assignments and in-class project work chunking small amounts of time that suit the individual needs of the student interspersed with regular breaks can be a helpful strategy.
- *Helping students to get organised and get started*: what is the task? What do you need to do (broken into small steps)? What resources will you need? Where will you set up? Create a step-by-step checklist that students can refer to as needed.
- *Teach research and note-taking skills*: ADHD students are typically disorganised and need support and direction when attempting more complex tasks (e.g. first, then, now, next).
- *Asking for help*: remind students that it is OK to ask for help at any time. Provide students with a few written sentence starters to help them ask for support (see **Figure 17.23**).

Figure 17.23 Asking for help

I need help with:

- ☐ Understanding the question/assignment/project
- ☐ Working with my small group
- ☐ The steps I need to follow
- ☐ Finding resources
- ☐ Knowing which information to use
- ☐ Setting out, layout and headings
- ☐ Recording my references

Students with ADHD require consistent, calm and sensitive support. Their behaviour can be challenging, trying and sometimes simply annoying, making it easy to forget that there is a genuine underlying reason for the lack of self-control. It is also important to be aware that students with ADHD may have poor sleep patterns and often will not get the amount of rest their growing body needs. Being tired can exaggerate or compound the behaviours of students with ADHD. The families of students with ADHD are also often tired and stressed, simply because raising a child with ADHD is extremely challenging. A supportive school environment is essential for both the student and the family.

Accommodations and teaching strategies for students with ADHD

Dyscalculia

Dyscalculia is a maths learning disability. It impairs an individual's ability to learn number-related concepts, perform accurate calculations, reason and problem-solve, and perform other basic maths skills (Additude, 2023). Students with dyscalculia struggle to recall and retain maths facts and calculations (see **Figure 17.24**).

Videos: What is dyscalculia?

The Australian Dyslexia Association has identified indicators of dyscalculia that may occur as the child progresses through school. These indicators are shown in **Figure 17.25**.

Figure 17.24 Characteristics of dyscalculia

Dyscalculia	Dyscalculia is a neurodevelopmental disorder resulting in an inability to see, handle and understand numbers. There is thought to be a genetic and neurological link to dyscalculia.
Individuals with dyscalculia have trouble with the mechanics of doing mathematics, such as being able to recall basic mathematics facts.	Students with dyscalculia may not understand quantities or concepts like biggest versus smallest. They may not understand that the numeral 5 is the same as the word 'five'.
Dyscalculia is a lifelong condition. Dyscalculia tends to run in families.	Symptoms of dyscalculia may vary from individual to individual.

Source: Australian Dyslexia Association (2023). Dyslexia, dysgraphia and dyscalculia? https://dyslexiaassociation.org.au/support/dyslexiadysgraphia-and-dyscalculia

Figure 17.25 Indicators of dyscalculia

School level	Indicators
Early school	> Has difficulty learning and recalling basic maths facts, such as 2 + 4 = 6 > Struggles to identify +, and other signs, and to use them correctly > May still use fingers to count instead of using more advanced strategies, like mental maths > Struggles to understand words related to maths, such as greater than and less than > Has trouble with visual-spatial representations of numbers, such as number lines
Primary school	> Has difficulty understanding place value > Has trouble writing numerals clearly or putting them in the correct column > Has trouble with fractions and with measuring things, like ingredients in a simple recipe > Struggles to keep score in sports games
High school	> Struggles to apply maths concepts to money, including estimating the total cost, making exact change and figuring out a tip > Has a hard time grasping information shown on graphs or charts > Has difficulty measuring things like ingredients in a simple recipe or liquids in a bottle > Has trouble finding different approaches to the same mathematical problem

Source: Australian Dyslexia Association (2023). Dyslexia, dysgraphia and dyscalculia? https://dyslexiaassociation.org.au/support/dyslexiadysgraphia-and-dyscalculia

Assessment and diagnosis

Typically, dyscalculia is assessed by a psychologist focusing on four key areas of maths:

1 *computation skills* – assesses the ability to do maths operations efficiently and accurately
2 *maths fluency* – assesses the ability to recall maths facts quickly and accurately
3 *mental computation* – assesses the ability to complete a maths operation in your head
4 *quantitative reasoning* – assesses the ability to understand quantitative relationships and solve maths word problems (Understood, n.d.).

Assessors may also consider the results of an assessment to a child's IQ test.

Accommodations and modifications

Students with dyscalculia find it difficult to recall maths facts, computations and maths word problems. They struggle to recall maths information and will require many opportunities for practice.

Accommodations and modifications will vary according to the ability and needs of each student. It's important to remember that accommodations and modifications not only support the development of maths skills – they can also contribute to reducing maths anxiety, which many students with dyscalculia experience. Examples of accommodations and modifications are shown in **Figure 17.26**.

Dyscalculia resources for ESWs

Figure 17.26 Examples of accommodations and modifications

Accommodations and modifications
Provide concrete objects for counting, subtraction, comparing and seriating.
Provide foam numerals and number signs that students can manipulate to help them to see and manipulate numbers.
Provide cards showing different number patterns, numerals and words. ☺☺ five ☺☺☺ 5 2 + 3 = 5
Play games with dice and dominoes.
Allow the use of a calculator (teach the student how it can be used).
Use assistive technology such as online self-paced maths games.
Provide graphic organisers – number facts, 100s chart, maths vocabulary, common synonyms (e.g. subtract, minus, takeaway, reduce, less than, fewer than), formulas, multiplication charts.
Break down maths tasks into small manageable sequence of steps.
Provide graph paper so the student can keep columns of numbers in line.
Present maths tasks using concrete objects or graphics.
Provide a written example of the task.
Highlight/emphasise key words to remind the student of what they are required to do.
Use technology, such as talking measuring tapes and scales.
Allow additional time for the student to complete tasks and/or reduce the quantity of tasks.

Developmental language disorder

Gallagher, Coleman and Kirk (2023) remind us that communication 'involves input (hearing or seeing), central processing and executive functioning skills (thinking about and understanding, decision-making), and output (speaking, signing, writing, etc.)' (p. 301).

Developmental language disorder (DLD) is characterised by difficulty thinking about, understanding and using and developing age-appropriate language skills without any known underlying cause. Children and young people with DLD present with persistent grammar errors, difficulty with speech sounds, poor vocabulary for their age, difficulty expressing thoughts and feelings, not being able to remember words that describe objects or things, difficulty speaking in sentences, difficulty understanding the meaning of words, and difficulty understanding instructions, reading and spelling. Without intervention and support, children and young people with DLD are at greater risk of school failure because language is central to learning.

Figure 17.27 describes some characteristics that children and young people with DLD may display.

Figure 17.27 Common characteristics of children and young people with DLD

Speech difficulties	Language difficulties	Communication difficulties
> Speech is difficult to understand > Difficulties discriminating similar speech sounds, such as 'bat and batch' or 'found and fought' > May stammer or **stutter** > May have a consistently harsh or high-pitched voice > May have difficulty using intonation – for example, used when asking a question or expressing an emotion > Hearing impairment > Articulation disorders	> Immature sentence structures > Difficulty linking sentences using joining words such as 'and', 'but', 'then' > Difficulty in sequencing sentences so that they are meaningful to the listener > Difficulty acquiring new vocabulary and using new words in the correct context > Difficulty finding the right words to use > Limited vocabulary to describe emotions > Difficulty understanding complex sentences > Difficulty understanding idioms such as 'it cost an arm and a leg' or getting 'cold feet' > Aphasia (difficulty in articulating and understanding words)	> Limited eye contact with listener > Problems refocusing on a topic of conversation if the conversation goes off track > Difficulty 'reading' the speaker/listener – for example, doesn't pick up on non-verbal cues > Difficulty keeping to the topic of discussion > Difficulty using language for problem-solving, negotiation and conflict resolution > Problems with language comprehension

Source: Adapted from The Communication Trust (2011).

Assessment and diagnosis

Thomas and Thorne (2011) identify a number of 'red flags' that may indicate a student is experiencing language difficulties. These include:

- The student says the teacher is always talking too quickly.
- The student gets mixed up when listening to multi-step instructions or states frequently that the instructions are too complicated.
- The student can do maths quite well until it comes to problems expressed in words.
- The student has problems with sounding out new words or remembering what words mean.
- It is hard for the student to put ideas in writing.
- The student knows what they want to say; they just can't get the words out.
- The student avoids answering questions in class.

It is important to be aware that no two students will have identical DLD – even those with a diagnosed disability. DLD is typically assessed and diagnosed by a speech pathologist using a standardised test as well as observing the child interacting with a parent.

DLD resources for ESWs

Acquired brain injury

National Disability Services (n.d.) describes acquired brain injury (ABI) as 'multiple disabilities arising from damage to the brain acquired after birth results in deterioration in cognitive, physical, emotional or independent functioning. May be as a result of accidents, stroke, brain tumours, infection, poisoning, lack of oxygen or degenerative neurological disease'.

The Royal Children's Hospital, Melbourne reports that in Australia, the most common causes of ABI in children are:

- traumatic brain injury (from falls, motor vehicle accidents, sports)
- infections around the brain, such as meningitis and encephalitis
- stroke in childhood
- a lack of oxygen to the brain (also called hypoxic-ischaemic events), which can result from near-drowning accidents, prolonged seizures or cardiac (heart) complications.

Source: Royal Children's Hospital, Melbourne (2018). Acquired brain injury (ABI). https://www.rch.org.au/kidsinfo/fact_sheets/Acquired_Brain_Injury_ABI

Research undertaken by The Children's Trust (UK) has found children with ABI may present with one or more of the following (depending on the severity of the injury):

- Weakness of limbs, difficulties getting around
- Tiredness – often talked about as 'fatigue' by professionals
- Changes in behaviour – irritability (a 'short fuse'), behaving impulsively or inappropriately
- Difficulties learning new things (and learning difficulties)
- Problems with memory
- Difficulty processing information
- Difficulty with concentration
- Emotional difficulties such as anxiety or depression
- Difficulties understanding and using language, difficulties keeping up with conversations
- Difficulties organising and planning – difficulties carrying out everyday tasks
- Difficulty with empathy – putting themselves 'in someone else's shoes'.

Source: The Children's Trust. For children with brain injury (2023). Acquired brain injury explained. https://www.thechildrenstrust.org.uk/brain-injury-information/info-and-advice/what-is-acquired-brain-injury/acquired-brain-injury-explained

Diagnosis and treatment

ABI is a medical emergency: 'Doctors use many methods to determine the severity of a brain injury, including the rate of recovery, the area of the brain affected, the response to treatment or rehabilitation, and the time following the injury when they are confused, disorientated and have a poor day-to-day memory (post-traumatic amnesia)' (Royal Children's Hospital, Melbourne, 2018).

Treatment and ongoing support for children and young people with ABI may include a team of professional supports and services, including:

- *social workers* who may work with the family to coordinate support services
- *physiotherapists* who may assist with areas such as balance, motor skills, and mobility fatigue and fitness
- *occupational therapists* who may focus on supporting the student to regain or relearn everyday skills like dressing and handwriting, as well as prescribe splints, equipment or assistive technology as needed
- *neuropsychologists* who will identify how the ABI might have affected the student's thinking, cognitive and learning skills and the support that may be needed in the classroom
- *clinical psychologists* who can support both the student and the family in areas such as grief, self-esteem, social skills and getting back to everyday life
- *speech pathologists* who will work with the student needing support with language, speaking, expression, and literacy (Novita, n.d.).

Medical needs

Students with ABI may have complex medical needs. The Queensland Government (Children's Health Queensland Hospital and Health Service, 2023) states that children and young people with ABI may need treatment for:

- epilepsy/seizures – may experience post-traumatic epilepsy
- hydrocephalus – a condition that results in build-up of the fluid around the brain due to a blockage or poor natural absorption of the fluid. Hydrocephalus is usually treated through the insertion of a shunt. Difficulties with the shunt such as a blockage or disconnections can cause symptoms including:
  - headache, vomiting, fever, dizziness
  - irritability and personality/behavioural changes

– deterioration in performance (e.g. school work, balance, concentration)
– lethargy and drowsiness
– in more severe cases, visual disturbances and seizures
– changes in muscle tone or movement patterns
– hormone and growth changes (sexuality). The hormones that regulate growth and sexual development may develop more slowly or more rapidly as a result of an ABI. In some instances students may be prescribed medication to regulate hormonal changes.

Source: Children's Health Queensland Hospital and Health Service (2023). Medical considerations for students with an acquired brain injury. https://www.childrens.health.qld.gov.au/chq/health-professionals/paediatric-health-resources/abi-resources/

ABI resources

To support the medical and health needs of students with ABI, schools will typically require a medical advice form completed by the student's medical practitioner. This form may also include instructions for the first aid required if a student experiences a medical episode. To view an example of a medical advice form, go to: https://www.education.vic.gov.au/Documents/school/principals/spag/health/braininjury.doc.

Accommodations and modifications

In a review of the impact of ABI, Martin, Campbell and Shields (2018) found that a number of symptoms 'profoundly and negatively impact on a child's ability to learn at school and interact with peers' (**Figure 17.28**). The authors suggest that the emotional, cognitive and social symptoms common after an ABI can be addressed by putting in place a range of accommodations and modifications specific to the needs of each student. These are shown in **Figure 17.28**.

Figure 17.28 Strategies and external aids to support a student with cognitive deficits

Cognitive impairment	Symptoms	Teaching/learning strategies	External aids
Attention	> Difficulty concentrating > Easily distracted > Hard to multitask > Easily bored > Unable to complete things > Can't remember > Changes subject often	> Control noise and activity > Preferential seating > Simple instructions > Slow pace > Allow breaks and rest > Small sections of work > Use cues (verbal gestural, visual) to remind > Repeat instructions	> Earplugs to reduce noise > Timer to focus attention > Place symbols and signs to remind students
Memory	> Forgets people, places, things > Forgets specific routines and rules > Forgets instructions > Frequently loses things	> Repeat new information > Teach visual imagery > Simplify information > Task analysis > Use fact cards and cue sheets > Teach study skills > Teach note-taking > Teach self-questioning	> Checklists, Post-it notes > Keep items in specific locations > Use labels, maps, journals, calendars, planners > Memory notebook > Timers and alarms

Cognitive impairment	Symptoms	Teaching/learning strategies	External aids
Organisation	> Forgets specific routines and rules > Frequently loses things > Difficulty starting or finishing a task > Difficulty sequencing tasks	> Review daily routines > Specific locations and labels > Assign an in-class peer buddy > Involve an older student mentor/learning coach	> Use a visual schedule > Highlighting and colour-coding > Checklists for tasks > Binder with subject sections and homework pockets > Daily planner to record homework > Graphic organisers for sequencing > Timelines for assignment completion
Writing and information processing	> Difficulty starting writing > Losing place and confusion	> Reduce written work > Allow extra time > Allow verbal response > Enlarge print on worksheets > A catch-up period at end of the day	> Use digital recorders > Assign peer note-taker > Use word processor > Use peer scribe

Source: Martin, T.J., Campbell, S. & Shields, M. (2018). Traumatic brain injury: Informed accommodation in the classroom. *TEACH Journal of Christian Education*, vol. 12, iss. 1, article 2. https://research.avondale.edu.au/teach/vol12/iss1/2 (p. 7).

Dyslexia

Dyslexia can have a profound effect on educational outcomes for students because it involves difficulties with language, reading, spelling and writing. **Figure 17.29** describes dyslexia.

Figure 17.29 Strategies and external aids to support a student with cognitive deficits

Dyslexia	The International Dyslexia Association (2013, p. 3) defines dyslexia as a language-based learning disability.
1 in 10 Australians have dyslexia	Dyslexia is a specific learning disorder that is neurological in origin, meaning that it is brain-based. It is characterised by difficulties with accurate and fluent word reading and by poor spelling and decoding abilities that do not progress as expected with the provision of well-intentioned and targeted intervention (Dyslexia – SPELD Foundation Australia, 2022).
Dyslexia may be diagnosed at around the age of 7 years, but can also be diagnosed as late as 11 or 12 years.	Dyslexia occurs on a continuum from mild to severe. Each student with dyslexia will have a unique set of strengths and difficulties.

Source: Cotterill, T. (2017). *Principles and Practices of Working with Pupils with Special Educational Needs and Disability*. UK: Routledge Taylor & Francis Group (p. 171).

Gallagher, Coleman and Kirk (2023, p. 6) define dyslexia as a 'specific learning disability that is neurobiological in origin'. The authors state that children and young people with dyslexia 'have difficulties with language-based tasks (i.e., reading, spelling, writing, and phonological awareness), many have well-developed abilities in visual, spatial, motor, and nonverbal problem solving'.

Videos: What is dyslexia?

Early signs of dyslexia are shown in **Figure 17.30**.

Figure 17.30 Early signs of dyslexia

Preschool age	First years of school
> Late talking and/or learning new words slowly > Problems with pronunciation, such as reversing sounds in words or confusing words that sound alike > Being unable to recognise letters in their own name > Mispronouncing familiar words or using 'baby talk' > A family history of reading and/or spelling difficulties (dyslexia has a genetic component and often runs in families) > Switching compound word sounds around – e.g. got for instead of forgot	> Difficulty sounding out basic words like 'cat', 'map', 'nap' > Not having a strategy for reading new words > Not associating letters with sounds, such as the letter 'b' with the 'b' sound > Difficulty seeing (and occasionally hearing) similarities and differences in letters and words > Difficulty spelling > Spending an unusually long time completing tasks that involve reading or writing > Avoiding reading out loud or any activities that involve reading > Complaining that reading is hard
Primary and high school years	
As students progress through the grades, they may develop a range of avoidance behaviours to mask their learning difficulties. For example: > spending a long time preparing to start a task > asking for further instructions > complaining or being argumentative > engaging in disruptive behaviours with other students > focusing on another task > attempting to access their phone > complaining they are tired and putting head on desk > complaining of headache, stomach ache, etc. All of these behaviours are designed to avoid attempting the learning task. They also serve another, and more important goal – to save face and avoid the embarrassment of being seen by their peers as not keeping up with the rest of the class. Students who continuously engage in avoidance behaviours are usually masking stress and anxiety. Unfortunately, educators may focus on the behaviour rather than the underlying causes. It is important to remember the concept of 'the whole child' – it is important to look beyond the behaviour to determine underlying issues.	

Source: Learning Links (2023). Empowering children to learn. https://www.learninglinks.org.au/resources/signs-of-dyslexia/

Dyslexia may impact all areas of learning for some students, and students with dyslexia may feel anxious, have poor self-esteem and see themselves as failures. The International Dyslexia Association (2013, pp. 4–5) states that in the classroom, students with dyslexia may present with some, or all, of the following difficulties:

- learning letters and their sounds
- organising written and spoken language
- memorising number facts
- reading quickly enough to comprehend
- keeping up with and comprehending longer reading assignments
- spelling
- learning a foreign language
- correctly doing maths operations.

Assessment and diagnosis

Dyslexia is assessed using a combination of screening tools that evaluate IQ and literacy skills. Standardised reading tests are used to evaluate skills such as phonetic decoding skills, word reading ability and reading comprehension.

Accommodations and modifications

When devising accommodations and modifications for students with dyslexia, it is important to incorporate the student's strengths, such as problem-solving, art, design and creativity, computing, spatial awareness and lateral thinking. The International Dyslexia Association (2013) suggests a range of accommodations that can be used to support students with dyslexia, which are described in **Figure 17.31**.

Figure 17.31 Accommodations for students with dyslexia

Accommodations
Keep written directions short and specific and back them up with oral directions
Break tasks down into small chunks so the student is only required to focus on one element at a time
Decrease distractions – where there is a lot of information, emphasise key points and/or provide the student with a reading guide and a glossary
Assist the student to keep their place when working through a workbook by using a place marker, such as a small diagonal cut at the bottom of the page
Allow the student additional time to complete tasks and offer opportunities for practice
Use assistive technology if this suits the needs of the student
Actively support learning by stepping out the tasks to be completed, demonstrating, providing samples, guiding and coaching
Use a graphic organiser when giving instructions
Encourage students to create mind maps, drawings, diagrams or flowcharts to summarise key information
Provide subject-specific key words in classroom handouts
Encourage the use of personalised dictionaries

Source: International Dyslexia Association (2023). Accommodations for students with dyslexia. https://dyslexiaida.org/accommodations-for-students-with-dyslexia/

Dyslexia resources for ESWs

A multisensory approach, known as Multisensory Structured Language or the Orton-Gillingham instructional approach, encourages teachers to use a combination of auditory, visual and kinaesthetic-tactile learning strategies that maximise outcomes for students.

Multisensory Structured Language (MLS) and Structured Literacy (SL)

MSL and SL involve the simultaneous use of visual, auditory and kinaesthetic-tactile pathways to enhance memory and learning of written language. They include the six essential components of reading/literacy for students with dyslexia. The multisensory approach allows students to make links between the visual (language we see), auditory (language we hear), and kinaesthetic-tactile (language symbols we feel) pathways in learning to read and spell, all of which are essential components when learning to read (see **Figure 17.32**).

Figure 17.32 Learning to read

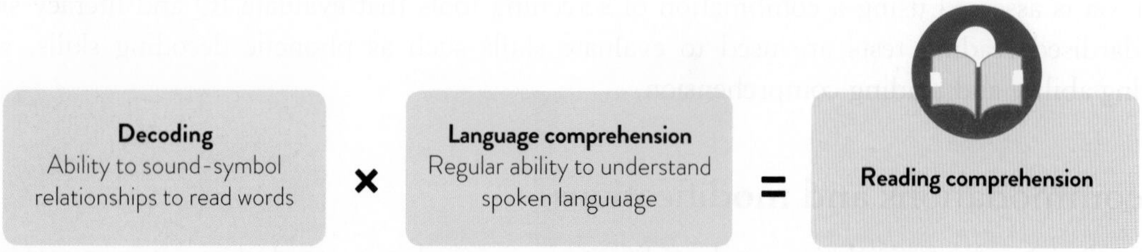

MSL acknowledges that students with dyslexia have difficulty recognising phonemes, and this makes it difficult for them to blend sounds to make words or segment words into sounds. MSL techniques include using a mirror so students can see speech sounds (phonemes) as they are saying words with similar sounds. Students look at the printed words to identify letters that represent the phoneme. Students then trace or write the words while saying the words aloud. The teacher reinforces the phonemes by saying the sounds aloud. Students then use the words to write a sentence.

MSL includes six key features:

- **simultaneous** multisensory approach: visual, auditory and kinetic
- systematic and **cumulative**: follow a logical and sequential order
- direct teaching of concepts through continuous student-teacher interactions
- **diagnostic** teaching: ongoing assessment of each student as they participate in the MSL approach
- synthetic and analytic instruction: synthetic instruction identifies the parts of the language (e.g. phonemes) and then teaches how the parts work together to form a whole (e.g. blending sounds to form a word). Analytic instruction presents the whole and teaches how this can be broken down into its component parts (e.g. segmenting words into sounds).
- comprehensive and inclusive: all levels of language are addressed together (e.g. including sounds (phonemes), symbols (graphemes), meaningful word parts (morphemes), word and phrase meanings (semantics), sentences (syntax), longer passages (discourse), and the social uses of language (pragmatics).

Video: Multisensory structured language

Source: The International Dyslexia Association (2009). Multisensory Structured Language Teaching. Baltimore. https://www.multisensoryeducation.net.au/images/cms/What%20is%20MSL%20Teaching%20Fact%20Sheets.PDF

Developmental language disorder (DLD)

DLD is characterised by:

- severe language problems that interfere with communication in everyday life and/or affects educational progress
- severe language problems that do not resolve spontaneously and are likely to persist over time.

Source: Developmental Language Disorder (DLD) (2017). The consensus explained RALD. https://www.youtube.com/watch?v=OZ1dHS1X8jg

Figure 17.33 provides some key facts related to DLD.

Students with DLD may be assisted by a range of specialist support services, such as physiotherapists, speech pathologists and occupational therapists. Students may also be supported by itinerant teachers who are trained to provide specialised support to the classroom teacher and the student.

Figure 17.33 DLD facts

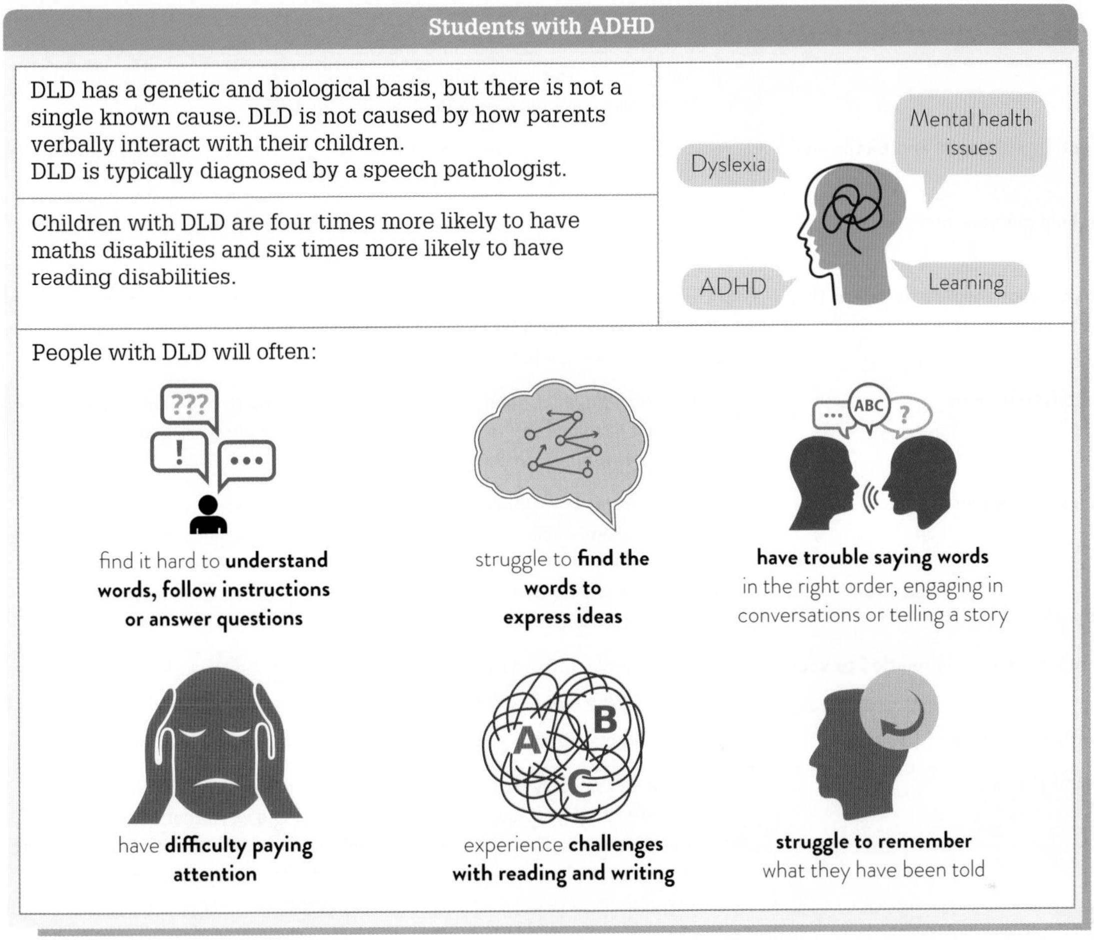

Students with ADHD
DLD has a genetic and biological basis, but there is not a single known cause. DLD is not caused by how parents verbally interact with their children.
DLD is typically diagnosed by a speech pathologist.
Children with DLD are four times more likely to have maths disabilities and six times more likely to have reading disabilities.
Dyslexia
Mental health issues
ADHD
Learning
People with DLD will often:
???
!
find it hard to understand words, follow instructions or answer questions
struggle to find the words to express ideas
ABC
?
have trouble saying words in the right order, engaging in conversations or telling a story
have difficulty paying attention
A
B
C
experience challenges with reading and writing
struggle to remember what they have been told

Source: Adapted from DLD Project (n.d.). Developmental Language Disorder. https://thedldproject.com/wp-content/uploads/2022/05/DLD-Awareness-Flyer-The-DLD-Project.pdf

The specific support needs of each student will vary. Some students will require AAC programs (see Chapter 16), others may be supported with an ESW in a regular classroom, while yet others may require a high level of support in a special school or unit. When working directly with students with DLD, strategies that can be used by ESWs are described in **Figure 17.34**.

Figure 17.34 Examples of specific strategies for supporting language and communication

Gain the student's attention before talking and get down to the student's eye level when talking	Sit next to the student when talking (see **Figure 17.35**). Position yourself so that the student can watch your face as well as listen. You may need to tell the student to keep looking at you while you are talking and remind the student to look at you when they are talking.
Speak clearly, using a normal speech pattern and voice tone	For example, 'Look at me because I'm going to give you some information'. Pause and wait for the student to look at you. 'We are going to work on addition.' Pause and ensure the student is still looking at you. 'You need to get out your counters.' Pause and wait for the student to get the counters. 'Now we are going to work together on this worksheet.' Pause. 'Let's look at the first question together.' Point to the question and check that the student is looking at the worksheet.
Use words and phrasing appropriate to the student's level	Where a student has difficulty with comprehension, use short sentences – for example, 'We are going to do some maths. Here are your counters.'

Give one instruction at a time and give instructions or information in a sequential order	Give the student time to listen, process and respond to instructions. Limit the amount of information – keep it simple by chunking information and then pausing to allow the student time to process instructions. If necessary, check with the student to make sure the message has been received accurately – for example, 'Put your pencil down. Good, now put your book on the shelf. Well done, Zac! Now go and sit on your chair.'
Combine verbal instruction with visual and tactile aids	This may include written instructions, AAC, symbols, drawings, prompt cards, videos, photos, graphic organisers and objects.
Use body language to help get your message across	Facial expressions and gestures such as pointing can help with communication.
Tell the student what you want them to do rather than telling them what not to do	For example, 'Keep your feet on the floor when sitting on your chair' tells the student what you want them to do, while 'Don't swing on your chair' does not tell the student what to do.
Repeat information in different ways	For example, a first statement might be, 'It's time to pack away.' The second statement might be, 'Hari, put your pencils back into their container. Great work! Now put your book on the shelf.'
Give clear, unambiguous information	Some students may not be able to interpret a message unless it is very concrete and explicit – for example, if you said, 'I expect students in my class to put their belongings away' a student with DLD may not understand that you were talking directly to them. A more explicit statement would be, 'Owen, please put your jumper in your bag.'
Give direct and specific information in relation to your expectations	For example, instead of saying, 'I hope you're going to work hard today', say, 'Alexi, I want you to write two sentences.'
Provide the student with an example of the task	For example, 'We are going to do a crossword together. I have one to show you.'
Emphasise key aspects of the task	Students may only hear the first part of the instruction and may miss key information. If you say, 'Write a sentence using a word that begins with "w",' the student may only hear 'Write a sentence'. Provide the student with a list of key vocabulary (and meaning) as appropriate. Restate information/instructions as needed and highlight key points.
Provide visual cues	These may be written in numbered points, a flowchart or a series of pictures – for example, 'What do you need to do first?' The student can point to or name a picture/symbol. Then say, 'What do you need to do next?'
Break down words into manageable speech sounds (syllables)	'Listen while I say the word "com-mun-i-cat-ion". Let's say the first part of the word.'
Act as a language role model	Avoid correcting the student's language – simply paraphrase it. For example, the student might say, 'Don't wanna do it. Too hard!' Rephrase by saying, 'Oh, you don't want to do it because you think it's too hard. Let's look at each step and see just what you can do.'
Provide 'here-and-now' feedback	Comment on what the student is doing: 'I can see you're using your picture dictionary to help with your writing, Perri. That's very good thinking.'
Use AAC, where appropriate, to assist the student	If, for example, you are working with a student on a maths task, have a set of numbers in words and numerals. If the student is required to undertake a task with multiple steps, use symbols or characters to show the sequence of tasks. Provide students with a simple system for communicating their understanding (see **Figure 17.36**).
Ask for clarification	Where a student makes a statement or asks a question and it is difficult to interpret, ask the student for clarification by saying, 'Can you tell me what you mean? Could you tell me again? Can you repeat what you just said so that I can listen carefully? Can you show me? Can you tell me what you need to do?'
Teach self-talk to students	Students can be encouraged to engage in self-talk, which can help them to remember an oral instruction: 'First I have to read the first question and ask for help if I need it.'

Model patience	Students who struggle with words, can't find the right words or have difficulty forming a sentence require the listener to be patient: 'Take your time, don't rush. Think about what you want to say before you speak.' Try not to jump in and finish sentences for the student – this doesn't help their confidence or their oral language development.
Define/explain or demonstrate the meaning of new or unfamiliar words	Put the word in several different sentences so that it can be understood in context. Ask the student to put the word in a sentence. Write the word on a card and place it on the word wall or in the student's personal dictionary. If the new word is a preposition or action verb, the meaning of the word can be shown in a concrete manner.
If possible, face the student away from distractions	Where possible, arrange the seating so that the student is facing away from the main classroom. Also try to work in an area that is relatively quiet.
Manage behaviour	Be aware that non-compliance, acting out or off-task behaviour may simply be a result of the student not understanding what is required and not having the language and/or confidence to ask for help. Praise appropriate behaviours.
Avoid putting students on the spot	Students who struggle with language and communication should not be placed in a situation where they may feel embarrassed in front of their peers.
Model and coach oral communication	For example, James tends to talk over the top of others or interject. The ESW reminds James to remain quiet and not interrupt when others are speaking. In some group discussions, the ESW uses a talking stick. The only person who can speak is the holder of the talking stick.
Allow extra time for the student to get organised and begin tasks	Students with DLD usually take longer to process information and will perform many tasks at a slower pace than their peers.
Revise with the student	Often a DLD student will miss words but not be able to see this. Pointing at each word and reading aloud (one to one) allows the student to hear their words and provides a better chance of identifying whether they have missed some words – for example, 'The boxer fell hit head hard on, does that sound right? Let's read that again.'
Acknowledge that some tasks are challenging	Encourage the student to have a go: 'I know you find it really hard to retell the story, but I know you can do it. Let's start at the beginning. Tell me what happened first?'

Figure 17.35 The ESW should get down to the student's eye level to communicate effectively

Figure 17.36 Communication visuals

	Got it!
	I need to ask some questions.
	I don't get it. Please help!

Communication underpins learning and social interactions. Students will DLD face many challenges.

Voice disorders

The major types of voice disorders are caused by:

- vocal misuse or abuse
- change of vocal cord mass; polyps, nodules, contact ulcers, haemorrhagic cords
- vocal cord paralysis
- neurological disorders – for example, Parkinson's disease
- removal of or damage to the larynx due to cancer or trauma.

Early signs and symptoms of voice disorders are:

- any intermittent or progressive change in voice quality – for example, the voice may sound hoarse, husky, breathy, nasal or monotonous
- a complete or transient loss of voice
- persistently inappropriate voice quality, pitch or loudness.

Articulation disorder

Articulation disorders are characterised by errors or omission of sounds, substitution of one sound for another and distortion of sounds. These occur during the production of isolated speech sounds (phonemes) and are misarticulated at both the syllable and word level. Early signs and symptoms are:

- the child not babbling but using a wide variety of sounds by 18 months
- speech that is unintelligible to familiar people at three years
- difficulty with later developing sounds (/s/, /sh/, /l/, /r/, /z/, /v/, /th/) by five years
- the child being frustrated by their inability to make themselves understood
- the parents being concerned about and unable to understand the child's speech
- disturbance of sucking, chewing or swallowing at any age.

Articulation errors are typical of preschoolers, and are usually not cause for concern; however, some therapists believe early remediation prevents the errors becoming habits that can be difficult to change.

Central Auditory Processing Disorder

Central Auditory Processing Disorder (CAPD) is a receptive language disorder involving difficulties in the decoding and storing of auditory information (typically incoming verbal messages). This type of receptive language disorder is a result of genetic factors and/or early otitis media, though it may not be possible to find causal factors. There are many signs and symptoms of CAPD; however, a skilled audiologist would best be able to provide technological testing at age seven and beyond.

Early signs and symptoms are:

- difficulty following verbal directions
- difficulty following a conversation
- echolalia (repeating back words and phrases without comprehension)
- re-auditorisation (repeating back what was heard, and then showing comprehension)

- a student who says 'Huh?' or 'What?' and requires more repetitions of verbal input messages
- speech–sound discrimination difficulties, especially in noisy situations
- being highly distractable and active
- unintelligible speech, but with adequate vocal inflection and gestures
- difficulty memorising names and places
- difficulty repeating words or numbers in sequence
- an appearance of being tuned out or not paying attention
- difficulty with reading, spelling and writing
- appearing disorganised and forgetful
- possible difficulty remembering auditory information
- possible speech or language 'delays' (adapted from Porter, 2002).

SCENARIO

ACCOMMODATIONS TO THE PHYSICAL ENVIRONMENT

Ronan (11 years) has CAPD. To assist him in the classroom, the teacher and ESW have created a quiet zone with enough room for four students, located in a carpeted area with screens to absorb sound. Ronan uses a communication board to assist him to remember and sequence tasks. He also wears headphones to reduce background noise when working independently.

WHAT DOES THIS TELL US?

Simple accommodations can be made to the physical environment to maximise participation of students with specific learning needs.

Childhood apraxia of speech (CAS)

CAS is a rare and usually lifelong condition. Children with CAS have problems saying sounds, syllables and words. Although a child with CAS knows what they want to say, their brain struggles to correctly move their lips, jaw and tongue in order to speak clearly and be understood (Centre of Research Excellence in Child Language, 2018).

Children with CAS may also present with poor fine and gross motor skills, and have literacy difficulties, including reading, writing and spelling. Treatment for CAS is ongoing speech therapy.

Intellectual disability

Gallagher, Coleman and Kirk (2023) refer to the DSM-5 (APA, 2013) to define intellectual disability as 'neurodevelopmental disorders that begin in childhood and are characterised by intellectual difficulties as well as difficulties in conceptual, social, and practical areas of living' (p. 33).

Assessment and diagnosis

Assessment for intellectual disability includes clinical evaluation and individualised standard IQ testing by a psychologist. The diagnosis of intellectual disability requires satisfying the following criteria:

- deficits in intellectual functioning: reasoning, problem-solving, planning, abstract thinking, judgement, academic learning and learning from experience

- deficits in adaptive behaviours:
  - conceptual skills: language and literacy; money, time and number concepts; and self-direction
  - social skills: interpersonal skills, social responsibility, self-esteem, gullibility, naïveté (i.e. wariness), social problem-solving, and the ability to follow rules/obey laws and to avoid being victimised
  - practical skills: activities of daily living (personal care), occupational skills, healthcare, travel/transportation, schedules/routines, safety, use of money, use of the telephone (Gallagher et al., 2023, p. 116).

The classifications of ID include:

- Mild limitations in adaptive behaviours or intellectual functioning
- Moderate limitations in adaptive behaviours or intellectual functioning
- Severe limitations in adaptive behaviours or intellectual functioning
- Profound limitations in adaptive behaviours or intellectual functioning

Source: Gallagher et al. (2023), p. 117.

Causes of intellectual disability

Both genetic and environmental factors can contribute to intellectual disability. Examples include:

- Down syndrome: a chromosomal abnormality in which the individual has an extra copy of chromosome 21, resulting in mild to moderate intellectual as well as a range of hearing, skeletal and heart problems
- Fragile X syndrome: a chromosomal abnormality that leads to moderate to severe intellectual and developmental disabilities
- Prader-Willi syndrome: a chromosomal abnormality is caused by deletion or lack of several genes on chromosome 15
- Rett syndrome: a genetic disorder almost exclusive to females where the brain fails to mature by halting early development
- Foetal alcohol spectrum disorder (FASD): a spectrum disorder that presents as a continuum of permanent birth defects caused by maternal consumption of alcohol during pregnancy
- extremely premature birth: some babies born before 28 weeks are at greater risk of developmental problems, including intellectual, sensory sensitivity, physical, social, language and development
- brain infections: such as the rubella and encephalitis virus, both of which can destroy healthy brain cells (Gallagher et al., 2023).

Environmental factors include the impact of chronic poverty, malnutrition and exposure to trauma and chronic stress.

Chromosomal abnormalities and intellectual development

Children and young people with intellectual disability often require a range of health services to support their development, such as early intervention for babies, toddlers and preschool children, physiotherapy, occupational therapy and speech therapy, as well as respite care (for families), and transitional to adulthood and vocational programs. Students with intellectual disability will have their own unique pattern of strengths and challenges.

Specific learning disorders, learning difficulties and learning disability – the same or different?

The terms specific learning disorders, learning difficulties and learning disability appear to be used interchangeably, which can be quite confusing!

Learning difficulties are defined by Dyslexia – SPELD Foundation (n.d.) as: 'a generic term which refers to the 20 to 25% of students who exhibit problems acquiring academic skills as a consequence of a range of causes. These include: intellectual disability, physical or sensory deficits (e.g. hearing impairment), emotional or behavioural difficulties, and inadequate environmental experiences'.

Specific learning disorder (SLD) refers to significant difficulty in one or more academic areas while coping well, or even excelling, in other areas of academic, sporting or artistic achievement. SLDs are not intellectual impairments. Examples of SLDs include:

- *dyslexia*: difficulties with reading and writing
- *dysgraphia*: difficulties with spelling and handwriting
- *dyscalculia*: difficulties with numbers and calculations
- *dysphasia*: difficulties with speaking and understanding others' speech
- *auditory processing disorder*: difficulty hearing differences between sounds
- *visual processing disorder*: difficulty interpreting visual information.

The *Disability Standards for Education 2005* define disability related to learning as a 'disorder or malfunction that results in a person learning differently from a person without a disorder or malfunction' (DET, 2005).

Learning disabilities refer to a disorder or malfunction that results in a person learning differently from a person without a disorder or malfunction. Students with learning disabilities are of average or above average intelligence and there is often a gap between a student's potential and their achievement at school (NCCD, 2022b). Learning disability typically includes difficulties in understanding, processing, remembering, focusing and staying on-task, and recalling information – either slow to recall or no recall at all). Learning disability may include:

- *language processing*: difficulty listening and understanding language; and speaking
- *phonological processing*: difficulty using, manipulating or breaking down phonemes (sounds of language) – see also the Go further
- *visual and spatial processing*: difficulty understanding and interpreting what you see; locating objects in space relative to self. It includes visual discrimination, visual memory, figure-ground and visual closure – for example, difficulty in identifying patterns and geometric shapes, not understanding that (2 + 4) is the same as (4 + 2); difficulty estimating length; difficulty formulating letters
- *perceptual motor integration*: difficulty integrating sensory information within the brain to perform movements such as handwriting, changing direction, moving arms or legs across the body, hand–eye and hand–foot coordination, understanding left/right, up/down, top/bottom, etc. Tracking words on a page, completing a number sentence, locating the starting point for a task, moving around the room, listening to and following verbal instructions, and using visual cues all require perceptual motor integration
- *executive functioning*: difficulty planning, prioritising and organising skills, self-monitoring, on-task behaviour, task initiation (getting started), focusing, ignoring distractions, emotional control, working memory, recalling and applying information.

To overcome these barriers to learning, the learning skills and needs of children and young people with learning disability will require support along a continuum from simple reminders to intensive intervention. Many of the accommodations and modifications already discussed in this chapter can be used to assist learning.

Videos: Phonological, visual and spatial processing

Developmental delay

Developmental delay is a lag in reaching developmental milestones at the expected rate based on the child's age/stage of development. Developmental delay can occur in one or more domains of development – language, physical, social, cognitive and emotional. The term global developmental delays refers to a delay in all domains of development.

Examples of factors that contribute to developmental delay may include:

- extremely premature birth
- exposure to toxins such as drugs, alcohol in the womb
- lead poisoning
- severe neglect and malnutrition
- chronic/toxic stress such as child abuse.

Developmental delays are usually evident as a baby matures into a toddler as this is the period when key developmental milestones occur – sitting, crawling, pulling to standing positions, walking, engaging in play with objects, responding to sounds and speech, feeding self, vocalising and beginning language.

Children with developmental delay are typically supported by interventions such as speech therapy, physiotherapy, occupational therapy and early intervention. With intervention, children with developmental delay may 'catch up' to their same-age peers; however, this will depend on the contributing factors and access to intervention services. In the classroom, children with developmental delay will require a range of supports to participate in learning alongside their peers.

Sensory processing disorders

Sensory processing is the way that a person perceives, processes and organises the information they receive through their senses – hearing, sight, touch, smell, taste and movement. The brain uses sensory information to make sense of the world and respond in an appropriate manner. This process is called **sensory integration**, which allows the body to:

- receive sensory information
- interpret and process sensory information to determine an appropriate response.

Figure 17.37 shows the process of sensory integration.

Figure 17.37 Sensory integration

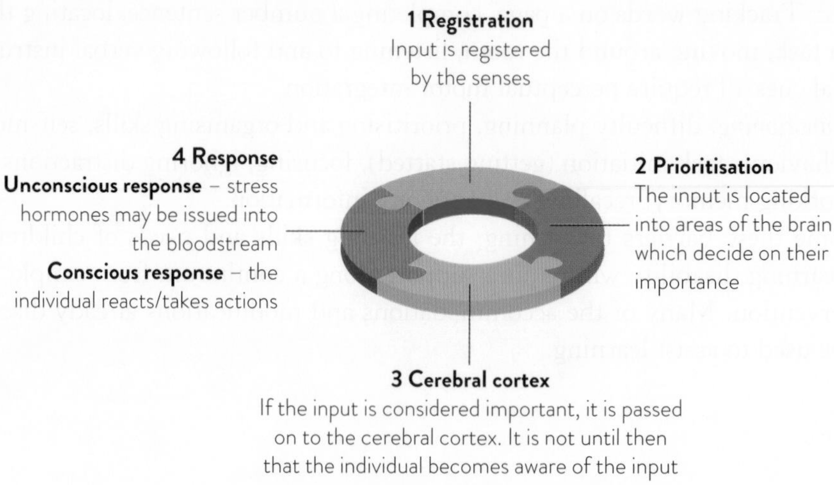

1 Registration
Input is registered by the senses
2 Prioritisation
The input is located into areas of the brain which decide on their importance
3 Cerebral cortex
If the input is considered important, it is passed on to the cerebral cortex. It is not until then that the individual becomes aware of the input
4 Response
Unconscious response – stress hormones may be issued into the bloodstream
Conscious response – the individual reacts/takes actions

Source: Thoonsen, M. & Lamp, C. (2022). *Sensory Solutions in the Classroom.* Jessica Kingsley Publisher.

Sensory modulation is the term used to describe the way the body responds to sensory stimulation and information. Children and young people with atypical sensory modulation (SPD) have difficulty functioning in the regular environment because of their response to sensory stimuli. The term *sensory processing disorder* is commonly substituted for SPD. Children and young people with autism will typically have sensory processing issues.

Atypical sensory modulation, or SPD, includes the following elements:

- **Sensory over-responsivity** (hypersensitivity): occurs when an individual has an exaggerated negative response to sensory input, often leading to avoidance and hypervigilance of the stimulus – for example, unable to tolerate wearing clothing where seams or tags touch the skin; unable to tolerate loud noise, bright light, certain flavours and smells, and certain physical environments; has a fear of crowds and movement.
- **Sensory under-responsivity** (hyposensitivity): occurs when an individual may seem to be unaware of, or slow to respond to, a stimulus that would typically be expected to elicit a response – for example, under-responsive to pain, which can lead to injury when the person continues to engage in a behaviour that would normally elicit a strong pain response, such as touching a hot stove.
- **Sensory-seeking behaviour**: occurs when an individual has an unusual craving for, or preoccupation with, certain sensory experiences – for example, a person may repeatedly sniff their fingers or put non-food items in their mouth (Autism Spectrum Australia, 2017).

Some children and young people may have symptoms of both hypersensitivity and hyposensitivity.

The consequences for children and young people with a sensory processing disorder may include anxiety, fear and avoidance, ritualistic behaviours and a tendency for sameness, and functional difficulties in areas such as self-care, behaviour and school participation. They may have extreme meltdowns, such as screaming, holding their hands over their ears or running away from sources of stimulation. Again, those with ASD often present with some of these issues.

Assessment and diagnosis

SPD is typically assessed by an occupational therapist, who will usually develop a sensory diet or at-home treatment activities to address the child's sensory needs.

Sensory resources and strategies

Children and young people with SPD will each present with their own unique set of symptoms and behaviours, as described in **Figure 17.38**.

Figure 17.38 SPD behaviour examples

Resistance and extreme reactions to change – an unplanned change in routine often causes stress and may lead to a meltdown
Avoidance or reacting negatively to noises in the environment, such as a hairdryer, vacuum cleaner, drill, crying or screaming of other children or loud music
Avoidance of certain foods or only eating certain foods – a fixation on texture, taste, smell or temperature of foods, may obsessively smell and eat non-food items
Speaking loudly but often tuning out to what is being said
Difficulty paying attention, and commencing and finishing a task – starting and stopping requires change, which causes a great deal of stress
Tactile defensiveness – distress at having hair combed/cut or nails clipped. Students avoid touch, including manipulating objects – this can result in reduced fine motor skills and poor coordination

Impulsive behaviours – hypersensitive students may react without warning due to anxiety and stress associated with over-stimulation, putting themselves or others at risk
Focusing on detail but not being aware of the bigger picture
Constantly moving/fidgeting/rocking/swaying/spinning, sliding/climbing, running rather than walking, chews on everything, enjoys being upside down, engaging in risk-taking behaviours, easily excitable
Noticing and watching fast-moving objects such as fans
Vestibular (sense of balance and movement) dysfunction

Accommodations and modifications

Accommodations should be individualised to match the sensory issues – examples are shown in **Figure 17.39**.

Figure 17.39 Examples of accommodations

Sensory issue	Accommodations
Auditory	> Provide noise-reducing headphones > Use a sound machine or a fan to provide white noise > Provide quiet spaces for independent work > Simplify verbal directions to 1–2 words or steps at a time
Visual	> Provide coloured overlays for reading > Cut out a 'window' (rectangle in an index card) for the child to use to keep words and sentences in focus while blocking other material that can be distracting on the page > Use wide-ruled paper or adaptive paper to help students form letters in the right space > Write directions in different colours
Flexible seating	> Exercise balls, adjustable tables or desks that allow students to stand or sit while working, textured mats or wedge cushions for the seats > Wrapping therapy bands around the legs of chairs or desks to give sensory feedback when students swing their legs
Writing	> Slant boards (you can use the side of a three-ring binder also) > Finger spacers (you can use small wood craft sticks or just have the student use their finger between words for spacing in sentences) > Weighted pencil or pens > Text-to-speech software
Sensory breaks	> Every 15 or 20 minutes for younger students and every 30 to 45 minutes for older students > Send the student to take a note to the office or retrieve a book from the library > Movement breaks during a lesson such as: standing up and reaching high and then touching the floor; wall push-ups; star jumps; yoga or stretches
Sensory stations	> Sensory bin or sensory table > Body socks or body tubes > Mini trampoline > Bubble wrap for popping

Sensory issue	Accommodations
Tactile wall	> Old CDs, sandpaper, bubble wrap, cotton balls, textured foam, velcro, fabric, sponges, pompoms, pipe cleaners, sequined fabric, wallpaper samples, paint swatches, contact paper, (sticky) artificial turf, corrugated cardboard
Regulation station	> Bean bag, rocking chair, oil and water calming bottle, crash pads, fidgets, slime, silly putty, headphones with soft, calming music

Source: Greutman, H. & Kostelyk, S. (2018). Sensory Processing Explained. A Handbook for Parents and Educators. Growing Hands-On Kids. https://sensoryprocessingexplained.com/wp-content/uploads/woocommerce_uploads/2019/08/Sensory-Processing-Explained-FINAL.pdf, pp. 111–19.

Developmental coordination disorder

Developmental coordination disorder (DCD) (previously referred to as dyspraxia) is a disorder that affects physical coordination. Children and young people with DCD may present as uncoordinated, clumsy and slow to perform simple motor tasks. **Figure 17.40** provides some key facts about DCD.

Figure 17.40 Developmental coordination disorder

Developmental coordination disorder	DCD (also referred to as dyspraxia) is a neurodevelopmental coordination disorder that is characterised by difficulty with coordination, including fine motor skills, hand–eye coordination, balance and manual dexterity	
DCD is thought to affect approximately 5% of the population and is more common in males (3:1)	DCD does not affect an individual's level of intelligence	DCD is a lifelong disorder
Children with DCD may have poor motor planning resulting in difficulties with: > handwriting > sport, physical play > self-care – dressing, tying laces, washing hair > using equipment such as scissors, pencil sharpener, keyboard and mouse, manipulatives such as counters > organisational skills		Children and young people with DCD may avoid any form of physical activity

Source: Adapted from: Developmental Coordination Disorder Australia Inc. (2022). Understanding DCD. https://dcdaustralia.org.au/what-is-dcd-2

Children and young people with DCD have poor motor planning (or praxis) skills – that is, the ability to plan, organise and carry out movements. Motor planning requires the integration of the brain and the senses. You may like to review your knowledge of motor skills development by referring to Chapter 8 of this textbook.

Motor planning usually occurs at a subconscious level – for example, using a knife and fork to eat, picking up a pencil dropped on the floor or walking up stairs. As we carry out these movements, our brain is busy planning and directing our movements almost instantaneously. It calculates how to move, how to balance while moving, the sequence of movements and the speed of the movements. Difficulties with motor planning mean that children and young people with DCD struggle with many basic day-to-day tasks, such as getting dressed, brushing their teeth, washing their hands or making a sandwich.

Motor planning requires complex interactions between the brain, the senses and the muscles, as well as balance, coordination and memory. Motor planning is also necessary for the production of speech.

Assessment and diagnosis

According to Developmental Coordination Disorder Australia Inc. (2022), there are four criteria for a diagnosis of DCD, as defined by the DSM-5 (APA, 2013). These criteria are shown in **Figure 17.41**.

Figure 17.41 Criteria for DCD diagnosis

Criterion A	Criterion B	Criterion C	Criterion D
Movement skills are substantially below that expected for age and opportunity for learning and use.	Movement difficulties identified significantly and persistently interfere with daily living and impact school productivity, prevocational and vocational activities, leisure and play.	Movement difficulties are present from early childhood.	Movement difficulties are not better explained by intellectual delay, visual impairment or other neurological conditions that affect movement (e.g., cerebral palsy, muscular dystrophy).

Source: Developmental Coordination Disorder Australia Inc. (2023). How is DCD diagnosed? https://dcdaustralia.org.au/diagnosis-therapy

DCD resources and strategies

Accommodations and modifications

Supporting students with DCD will require teachers and ESWs to collaborate with the student, the parent/s and the student's therapist to identify the needs of the student in the classroom. Older students may be able to identify what modifications or accommodations work best to support their learning needs. Each student's support needs will be unique and should be regularly reviewed with key stakeholders. **Figure 17.42** provides examples of how students can be supported in the classroom.

Figure 17.42 DCD accommodations and modifications

DCD issue	Suggested accommodations/modifications
I have poor fine motor skills. I find it hard to: > write neatly > use a keyboard and handheld devices > manage buttons and zips > use utensils and scissors	**Accommodation or modification that may assist me:** > Writing paper with wide and/or raised lines > Graph paper to use when writing numbers to keep them in line > Slant board for writing > A variety of pencil grips > Voice-to-text software > A spacing tool for writing such as a craft stick > Notes/summaries to reduce the need for writing – use a highlighter for important information or to draw a left and right margin to indicate area for writing > Templates for written work
I have poor gross motor skills. I find it hard to: > throw and catch a ball, play ball sports > ride a bike, scooter or skateboard > hop and skip > maintain dynamic balance and change direction > perform tasks involving awareness of position in space	**Accommodation or modification that may assist me:** > Actively teach physical skills and provide time for practice > Allow student to move around > Position seating to minimise distractions

DCD issue	Suggested accommodations/modifications
I have poor organisational skills. I find it hard to: > follow directions > start and complete a task > plan and sequence tasks > follow rules for games > recall information > keep my work neat	**Accommodation or modification that may assist me:** > Review and practise rules for games before starting > Give only one- or two-step directions and check comprehension before proceeding > Have the student repeat instructions to clarify understanding > Create a checklist so the student can tick steps when completed > Provide a written or visual daily timetable so the student can anticipate the daily routine > Ensure consistency of routines as much as possible > Keep tasks short so the student feels a sense of accomplishment > Work one-on-one to create simple mind maps > Provide unhurried time to complete tasks > Use visual cues to remind student of task sequence
I have difficulty with communication. I find it hard to: > follow and contribute to conversations > adapt my volume and pitch to suit the situation > read non-verbal communication > work collaboratively in a small group	**Accommodation or modification that may assist me:** > Use software to record instructions so that student can listen multiple times as needed > Create graphic organisers and/or communication devices to support communication > Provide a pictorial or text-based checklist of tasks to undertake when working in a small group

Source: Adapted from: Kid Sense (2023). Planning and sequencing (praxis). https://childdevelopment.com.au/areas-of-concern/organisation/planning-and-sequencing-praxis/

Note: Dysgraphia (handwriting disorder) is explored in Chapter 14.

GO FURTHER

Learn more about physical disabilities in your **Go Further** resource, available through your instructor.

Summary

When working with students with disability, always begin by considering the strengths, interests and abilities of the student – that is, what the student already knows, understands and can do. This reflects the principles of holistic and individual-centred care. Remember: all learning begins with what we already know – that is, we draw on our existing knowledge and skills to learn new knowledge and skills. This principle is particularly important when working with students with disability.

It is important to seek as much information as possible about the student and the particular disability so that you are well informed and prepared when supporting the student in the classroom. You will find working with students with a disability both challenging and rewarding. The many challenges will require you to be patient, thoughtful and supportive of even the smallest steps. The rewards will occur as you celebrate with the students the many small but important steps in their learning journey.

Chapter 18 explores the principles for Universal Design for Learning, development of IEPs and the use of augmented communication to support learning.

Self-check questions

1 Define the following terms:
  a inclusion
  b equity
  c inclusive education
  d Universal Design for Learning (UDL)
  e imputed disability.
2 What are the benefits for educators of educating and caring for a child with disability?
3 List all types of barriers for students with disability.
4 List five key strategies that are used to work with students with ASD.
5 What is a common characteristic of students with ASD? How can direct instruction benefit students with ASD?
6 List three accommodations and modifications that can be developed to support the learning needs of a student with ASD.
7 Define the following disorders related to students with disability:
  a ASD
  b Asperger's syndrome
  c attention deficit hyperactivity disorder (ADHD)
  d dyscalculia
  e dyslexia.
8 Define the following language-related disorders:
  a developmental language disorder (DLD)
  b articulation disorder
  c childhood apraxia of speech (CAS).
9 What is intellectual disability and how is it characterised?
10 Explain developmental coordination disorder (DCD) in children and young people.
11 Describe some of the characteristics that may be present in children with cerebral palsy (CP).
12 What is visual Impairment? List three common eye conditions in childhood.
13 Define otitis media (OM). What group of children are at higher risk of OM?

Discussion questions

1 Watch the following video that demonstrates a reading strategy called text chunking, which can be used with some students who are dyslexic to improve their reading fluency. **Video**: Text Chunking (3.33 mins) **https://www.youtube.com/watch?v=85lWhXaVqlA**
  a What outcome is the teacher hoping to achieve with the student?
  b How does the teacher introduce chunking?
  c What rule must the student apply?
  d Discuss how this process might not only improve fluency, but also improve confidence and self-esteem.
2 For this task, refer to the Scenario 'Tuning in to communication' on page 618. Discuss the best strategy to respond to students with unusual forms of communication skills?

Activities

1 Connect each term to the correct definition

Imputed disability	Disorders of early brain development where the integrity and function of the nervous system is damaged during critical periods of brain development: while growing in the womb, or during the first two years of life.
Neurodevelopmental disorders	The student is placed in a regular school setting or a special unit. An IEP is developed to assist the student to reach their full learning potential.
Early intervention	An undiagnosed disability the school team considers a student to have that is having a functional impact on their learning.
Special education	Structured support programs (home and/or centre based) for children prior to entering school

2 For this task, refer to 'Barriers and challenges for students with disability' on page 607. Explore how each type of barrier might impact students with disability in your classroom setting.

3 For this task, refer to the characteristics of an inclusive environment on page 602. Discuss each characteristic and give examples.

4 For this task, refer to **Figure 17.7** 'The voice of the student'. Discuss how a person-centred approach helps students to reach their full potential, focusing on outcomes.

Chapter 18

SUPPORTING BEHAVIOUR

LEARNING OBJECTIVES

When you have completed this chapter, you should be able to demonstrate that, in relation to working in a school environment, you can:

18.1 identify the legislative and policy guidelines for managing and supporting student behaviour

18.2 identify your own responsibilities as an ESW when supporting behaviour and use self-reflection as a tool to develop your own behaviour management skills

18.3 identify the factors that influence behaviour

18.4 describe learning environments that support positive behaviour

18.5 identify key behaviour management frameworks

18.6 describe the elements of trauma-informed care

18.7 describe the process of observing, documenting and analysing student behaviours

18.8 describe the elements of a Behaviour Intervention Plan

18.9 identify some common challenging behaviours that may be encountered in a school environment

18.10 describe the strategies used to engage in problem-solving, negotiation and conflict resolution.

Online resources icons refer to useful weblinks. Ask your instructor for these **Online Resources.**

Introduction

Learning to behave in a socially acceptable manner is a developmental skill that begins in early childhood and continues into adulthood. It requires the child to develop social and emotional competence and self-regulation through consistent, loving and respectful relationships – first within the family unit, through the transmission of cultural values, beliefs and child-rearing practices, and later with peers, teachers, coaches and important others. Relationships in the school environment will contribute significantly to the child's social and emotional development, and are critical for shaping independent and emotionally healthy young adults.

Kaweski (2014, p. 42) defines **behaviour** as 'the actions or reactions of a person, in relation to his or her environment, experiences or needs. Behaviour can be conscious or unconscious, overt or covert, voluntary or involuntary'. This definition places behaviour in a context that helps us to understand that children and young people may not always be in control of their behaviour, and reminds us that behaviour occurs not in isolation but in a social context where external influences shape behaviour. Kaweski argues that behaviour is not a problem that must be fixed; instead, it is a reaction to an unmet need. In turn, the ways children and young people experience reactions to and consequences of their behaviour will influence future behaviours.

18.1 Legislation and policy

Legislation, policy and procedures relating to discipline and support for behaviour in Australian schools include state/territory legislation, departmental policy and whole-of-school behaviour management plans. They also include national frameworks to support the mental health and wellbeing of students. Documents that directly and/or indirectly guide behaviour management decision-making will include:

1. state and territory Education Acts
2. codes of conduct/ethics
3. school discipline and anti-bullying policies (including Commonwealth legislation relevant to bullying, harassment, discrimination and violence)
4. duty-of-care requirements
5. The National Safe Schools Framework and the Australian Student Wellbeing Framework (discussed later in this chapter)
6. *Australian Education Act 2013*
7. child protection legislation
8. UN Convention on the Rights of the Child.

Bullying

Government and non-government schools in each state and territory have policies to address bullying. To explore these policies, go to https://bullyingnoway.gov.au/responding-to-bullying/legislation-and-policy and click on your state or territory. The policies reflect Commonwealth legislation relevant to bullying, harassment, discrimination and violence, including:

- *Disability Discrimination Act 1992*
- *Human Rights and Equal Opportunity Commission (HREOC) Act 1986*
- *Racial Discrimination Act 1975*
- *Racial Hatred Act 1995*
- *Sex Discrimination Act 1984*
- Bullying. No Way! legislation and policy.

Bullying is an ongoing and deliberate misuse of power in relationships through repeated verbal, physical and/or social behaviour that intends to cause physical, social and/or psychological harm. It can involve an individual or a group misusing their power over one or more persons. Bullying can happen in person or online, and it can be obvious (overt) or hidden (covert) (Bullying. No Way!, n.d.a).

Unfortunately, bullying continues to be a problem in schools. Bullying. No Way! states research has found that students often do not report bullying because they fear not being believed or not having their concerns appropriately and thoughtfully addressed by relevant adults. Australia's Safe and Supportive School Communities Working Group reports that one

Bullying in schools

student in four reports bullying occurring in person, and one student in five reports online bullying. However, these figures do not include the unknown number of students who do not report bullying (Bullying. No Way!, n.d.b).

The Australian Institute of Health and Welfare (AIHW, 2020) reports that 'bullying is more common among children with disability from culturally and linguistically diverse backgrounds or who identify as lesbian, gay, bisexual, trans and gender diverse, or children who have intersex variations' (p. 369).

State and territory Education Acts

Each state and territory government requires government and non-government schools to have policies and procedures for discipline and wellbeing. These policies usually define serious violent conduct as reasonable grounds for suspension or expulsion of a student. The NSW *Education Act 1990* is provided as an example:

> NSW *Education Act 1990* No. 8 (December 2020)
>
> **Division 3 Directions about enrolment and attendance**
>
> (2) The Minister may give a non-attendance direction to a student only if—
>
> (a) the Minister believes on reasonable grounds that—
>
> (i) there is a significant risk that the student will engage in serious violent conduct, or
>
> (ii) the student supports terrorism or violent extremism, and
>
> (b) the Minister believes on reasonable grounds that issuing the non-attendance direction is necessary to protect the health or safety of the students or staff of any school.
>
> (3) While a non-attendance direction in relation to a student is in force, the Minister—
>
> (a) must assess whether the attendance of the student at school constitutes a risk to the health or safety of any person (including the student), and
>
> (b) must, if appropriate, develop strategies to eliminate or minimise that risk and to enable the student to attend school, and
>
> (c) must, in accordance with the guidelines, develop and implement a plan to support the student while the student is not attending school under the direction.
>
> (4) In subsection (2) (a) (i), ***serious violent conduct*** means conduct constituting any of the following offences (regardless of whether the student cannot, or might not, be held to be criminally responsible for the conduct)—
>
> (a) an offence involving—
>
> (i) loss of a person's life or serious risk of loss of a person's life, or
>
> (ii) serious physical or psychological injury to a person or serious risk of such injury to a person, or
>
> (iii) serious damage to property in circumstances endangering the safety of any person,
>
> (b) a serious offence of a sexual nature,
>
> (c) an offence involving serious animal cruelty.

Source: NSW Government. NSW *Education Act 1990* No. 8 (December 2020). https://legislation.nsw.gov.au/view/whole/html/inforce/current/act-1990-008#pt.5A

In addition to state and territory Acts, the Commonwealth Government can provide behaviour management support to schools. The *Australian Education Act 2013*, Division 3, allows for additional funding in schools where there are students:

- with disability loading
- who identify as Aboriginal and Torres Strait Islander
- from low socioeconomic communities
- for whom English is a second language.

School discipline/ behaviour policies

Additional funding to support students who may be disadvantaged is an example of indirect support. The Act acknowledges that students who are disadvantaged will have a range of needs that may require additional support in the school setting, which may include additional behaviour intervention/support strategies.

CONSIDER THIS

DISADVANTAGED

Research over the past three decades has consistently shown suspensions and expulsions disproportionately target students from diverse or minority backgrounds (Graham et al., 2020). This is particularly the case for those with a disability or those from specific racial, ethnic and class backgrounds. For example, in NSW in 2021, while 3.3% of all students were suspended, 10% of Aboriginal students and 8.4% of all students with disability were suspended.

Source: Miller, P. (2022). If Australian schools want to improve student discipline, they need to address these 5 issues. *The Conversation.* 4 August 2022. https://theconversation.com/if-australian-schools-want-to-improve-student-discipline-they-need-to-address-these-5-issues-187993

Child protection legislation

Schools must also comply with state and territory child protection legislation. This legislation outlines the role and responsibilities of schools to act in the best interest of the child or young person and meet the requirements of the National Framework for Protecting Australia's Children 2021–2031.

The AIHW (2020) states that child abuse and neglect can have a wide range of significant adverse impacts on a child's development and later outcomes, including, but not limited to:

- reduced social skills
- poor school performance
- impaired language ability
- higher likelihood of criminal offending
- negative physical health outcomes
- mental health issues such as eating disorders, substance abuse, depression and suicide (ABS 2019; AIFS 2014).

Source: Australian Institute of Health and Welfare (2020). Australia's children. Cat. no. CWS 69. Canberra: AIHW (p. 328)

The AIHW (2020, p. 338) also reported that:

> being exposed to family violence can have a wide range of detrimental impacts on a child's development, mental and physical health, housing situation and general wellbeing. More specifically, research has found exposure to family violence is associated with a range of outcomes, including:
> - diminished educational attainment
> - reduced social participation in early adulthood
> - physical and psychological disorders
> - suicidal ideation
> - behavioural difficulties
> - homelessness
> - future victimisation and/or violent offending.

CONSIDER THIS

KEY FINDINGS FROM THE AIHW (2020)

- In 2017–18, approximately 26 400 children aged 0–12 had one or more child protection notifications substantiated (excluding New South Wales as data was not available).
- Emotional abuse was the most commonly reported primary abuse type for substantiations (59%).
- More than one-third (35%) of children aged 0–12 who had at least one substantiation were in the lowest socioeconomic group.
- Indigenous children were more likely than non-Indigenous children to have had a substantiation in 2017–18 (48 per 1000 children compared with 7.2 per 1000).

Source: Australian Institute of Health and Welfare (AIHW) (2020). Australia's children. Cat. no. CWS 69. Canberra: AIHW (pp. 327, 332)

UN Convention on the Rights of the Child

Australia is a signatory to the UN Convention on the Rights of the Child. The government is responsible for ensuring that these rights are upheld in all areas of society, including schools. Of particular relevance to behaviour support are Conventions 3 and 19:

> Convention 3. Best interests of the child: When adults make decisions, they should think about how their decisions will affect children. All adults should do what is best for children.
>
> Convention 19. Protection from violence: Governments must protect children from violence, abuse and being neglected by anyone who looks after them.

Source: UN Convention on the Rights of the Child. https://www.unicef.org/media/60981/file/convention-rights-child-text-child-friendly-version.pdf

Legislation and policy play a central role in decision-making in relation to guiding, supporting and managing student behaviour. It's important to remember that challenging behaviour always has an underlying cause and there are many factors that contribute to the ways students behave. These factors range from health (including mental health), disability, poverty, domestic and family violence, parental drug and alcohol abuse, parental chronic illness and poor mental health to child-rearing practices, cultural values and beliefs, victimisation, racism and bullying. Understanding these contributing factors will help ESWs to better understand what motivates behaviour. Feeling unsafe, isolated, frightened, angry, jealous, anxious, out-of-control, sad, embarrassed or hopeless – these are all feelings that students may experience as they navigate their way in the world. Many vulnerable children and young people are in situations where there is a huge disconnect between their home life and the school environment.

Duty of care

All educators have a duty of care to students. The Legal Services Commission of South Australia states:

> A teacher's relationship with a student is based on the **common law doctrine** that, while the child is at school, the teacher is *in loco parentis* (that is, the teacher takes over the role of the parents) and is entitled to use the parents' authority to carry out his or her duties in relation to the child. Education and care providers must also adhere to legislated child safe environment requirements. Schools have a duty of care and supervision to children and young people attending the school, which includes taking reasonable steps to protect students from harm or injury (including harm caused by other students). Schools are required to respond to all behaviours of concern, including behaviour that takes place outside school hours or off school grounds, where there is a reasonable connection between the behaviour and the school, or school relationships. This can include online behaviour towards another student that occurs out of school hours (for example, cyber-bullying).

Source: Legal Services Commission of South Australia (2021). School discipline. https://lawhandbook.sa.gov.au/ch06s06s03.php

Codes of conduct

To ensure duty of care and professional conduct, all schools have a code of conduct/ethical standards for educators. In the example in **Figure 18.1**, the Department of Education WA (2021), describes core values and a clear set of standards to guide the behaviour and decision-making of educators. The document states: 'The actions of staff are to be guided by our values which

Figure 18.1 Values: Education WA

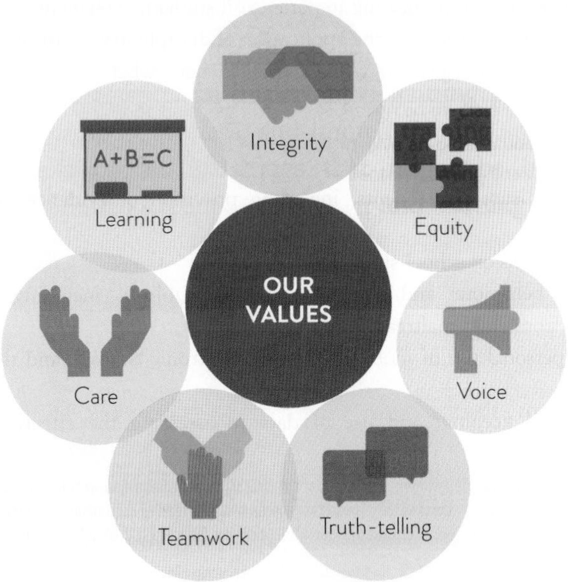

Source: Adapted from Department of Education WA (2021). Code of Conduct. Shaping the Future. East Perth. Licensed under Attribution 2.5 Australia (CC BY 2.5 AU. https://creativecommons.org/licenses/by/2.5/au/

reflect the social responsibilities owed to students, parents and carers, communities, stakeholders and each other' (p. 3).

The WA Code of Conduct includes 12 core standards, four of which are:

- **Behave professionally and with integrity:** We are honest and trustworthy in our relationships, and demonstrate dignity and integrity at all times, both at work and in the community.
- **Create cultural safety:** We create and sustain culturally safe and responsive work and learning environments.
- **Embrace equity, diversity and inclusion:** We celebrate and embrace people from all backgrounds and value every person as an individual.
- **Maintain safety and wellbeing:** We maintain the safety and wellbeing of ourselves, our students, our colleagues and our stakeholders.

Source: Department of Education WA (2021). Code of Conduct. Shaping the Future. East Perth. Licensed under a Creative Commons Attribution 4.0 International (CC BY 4.0) licence, https://creativecommons.org/licenses/by/4.0/

To support the code of conduct, Education WA also has a handbook for staff titled 'How to Comply with Our Code of Conduct'. This document supports compliance with the code of conduct and, in part, sets out behaviours that are unacceptable in relation to professional staff–student interactions. The document states: 'As an employee of the Department you are responsible for maintaining a professional role with the students you come into contact with. This means establishing clear professional boundaries with students that help to protect everyone from misunderstandings or a violation of the professional relationship' (Department of Education WA, 2011, p. 5).

Education WA also has a document titled 'Student Behaviour in Public Schools Procedures', which requires principals to develop a whole school plan to support positive student behaviour that includes:

- a school code of conduct stating the behaviours that students are required to learn and maintain at the school;
- the roles and responsibilities of staff in implementing whole school behaviour support;

- teaching and classroom management strategies that support positive student behaviour including:
  – the management of the school environment to promote positive student behaviour;
  – the school's strategy for communicating to parents on students' behaviour;
  – the school's strategy for deciding on the application of disciplinary measures;
  – the school's approach to coordinating with external agencies where required;
- measures to address:
  – all forms of bullying;
  – aggression;
  – drug and alcohol misuse by students, including provision of evidence-based drug and alcohol education;
  – the presence of weapons on school sites;
  – risks of suicidal behaviour and/or non-suicidal self-injury, including risks associated with cumulative harm from child maltreatment;
- the rules regarding personal use of mobile and other electronic devices, and responses to breaches of these rules; and
- the strategy for record keeping, and use of data in assessing the effectiveness of whole school behaviour support.

Source: Department of Education WA (2023). Student Behaviour in Public Schools Procedures. Effective date: 17 July 2023. Version: 2.7. These procedures must be read in conjunction with the Student Behaviour in Public Schools Policy.

18.2 Role and responsibilities

All educators in school settings have a duty of care to children and young people. This extends to ESWs, who must always act in the best interest of the student. In relation to behaviour management, this means following the policies and procedures of the school when guiding and managing behaviour and reporting any concerns about student behaviour to the teacher.

ESWs should maintain a friendly, respectful and professional relationship with students. Interactions with students should be fair and consistent. Students should be given clear boundaries and expectations in relation to expected behaviour. When challenging behaviour occurs, students, where possible, should be given the opportunity to step away, calm down and start over.

Maintaining respectful, consistent and positive relationships with students is the foundation for effective behaviour management. Building relationships of trust provides a pathway for engaging in interactions with students that communicate your intention to act in ways that support student wellbeing while also supporting them to develop the skills needed to manage their own behaviour in a socially acceptable manner.

Self-reflection

As you begin your journey as an ESW, you can build your behaviour management skills by observing experienced educators who manage behaviour with respect and empathy. Observe the techniques used by these educators – the way they greet students, how they engage students as learners, how they ask questions, how they reinforce positive behaviours, how they create positive relationships with each student and how they manage challenging behaviours. When you observe best practice, ask questions and engage in discussions around behaviour management, you are continually building and refining your own skills.

Another important way to develop your behaviour management skills is to engage in regular self-reflection. Each time you make a decision about how you will respond to manage student behaviour provides an opportunity for self-reflection and learning. Taking some time each day to think about your interactions, and perhaps keeping a reflective journal, allows you to tap into your own **emotional intelligence** and become more aware of how you respond and relate to others. **Figure 18.2** provides examples of self-reflection questions that can be used to guide your thinking and examine your interactions with students in relation to:

- your own emotional response
- your level of consistency when responding to behaviours
- how you encourage students to take responsibility for their own behaviour
- how you use positive reinforcement.

The figure also includes examples of how different responses to student behaviours result in different behaviour outcomes.

Figure 18.2 Self-reflection and behaviour management

Reflective questions	Examples of strategies you can try
Emotional responses	
> What changes can I make in my own behaviour that might change the student's behaviour? > Did I overreact? Was my reaction driven by my assumptions/judgement of this student? (e.g. I don't particularly like this student, I find this student annoying.) Am I simply asserting my power? > Do I use **proximity control** by simply standing/sitting near the student and making eye contact? > Would it have been better to have simply ignored the behaviour? > Do I know each student well enough to anticipate their behaviours by picking up on their cues?	> Samir (12 years) is tapping his ruler on the table. Rather than tell him to stop, redirect Samir's attention: 'Samir, your writing topic last week was really interesting. Could you write some more about your trip to India? I would love to know more about your experiences.' > If a student behaviour invokes an emotional response such as anger or frustration, turn away and take some deep breaths before addressing the student. > Sometimes the best strategy is to do nothing, ignore the behaviour and be ready to reinforce positive behaviour when it occurs.
Consistency	
> Do I verbalise inappropriate behaviour as a learning tool? > Do I use effective non-verbal messages or cues such as raised eyebrows or shaking my head, frowning, placing a finger on my lips, placing hands on my hips or signalling 'no' or 'stop' with my hand to indicate that the behaviour must stop? > Do I use assertive statements when required? > Do I use redirection where appropriate? > Do I always set clear limits and discourage students from arguing about tasks or directions I have given? > Am I consistent in reminding students of classroom rules? > How do I use questioning to remind students of the required behaviour? > Do I always ensure consistent and predictable routines when working with students? > Do I always let the students know when there is a change in routine or alteration to the planned schedule?	> 'Tarren, you are speaking too loudly. You need to use a quiet voice, so you don't disturb others.' > 'Kai, please listen to me. I want you to sit down now.' > 'Omar, remember the classroom rule is to ask to borrow things from other students rather than simply taking them.' > 'Sara, tell me the rule about returning books to the shelf.' > 'We won't be going to the library after our session today because the teacher is away. You can choose a game to play until it's time for lunch.'

Reflective questions	Examples of strategies you can try
Encouraging responsibility	
> Are there ways I could have helped this student to start over rather than focusing on the behaviour? > Should I be actively teaching this student coping strategies? > How do I encourage students to tune into their bodies and recognise the signs of anger or tension, such as tightening jaw, clenching fists and change in heartbeat? > How do I help students to constructively manage their feelings? > What choices can I offer which will allow the students to have more control over their environment? > How do I promote trust and respect for all individuals? > How can I encourage students to understand how their actions or words affect others? > Am I encouraging positive self-talk by helping students to use self-talk to work their way through a problem? > Do I really encourage students to ask for help and to help each other? > Do I encourage students to take responsibility for their behaviour? > Am I a good model?	> Teach the students to say, 'Stop. I don't like it when you take my things without asking.' > Talk about ways to handle anger by deep breathing, writing in a journal, creating a poster with ideas to manage anger or talking to someone who can help. > 'I can see you're getting tense because you're clenching your jaw. How about we take a break? Close your eyes and try to breathe deeply.' > It is important that, within the limitations of their skills and abilities, students are assisted to acknowledge and take 'ownership' of their behaviour. This strategy supports students to reflect on their behaviour and, with support, to identify ways they might better manage their behaviour. > Encourage students to listen when others are speaking; remind students that name calling or making a joke about a student who walks, talks, dresses or learns differently is not acceptable. > 'Talk to me about what you're doing.' > 'Don't forget to let me know if you need help, Marnie.' > Talk in a quiet voice; use materials and equipment with care; speak to others in a respectful manner.
Positive reinforcement	
> Do I notice and praise positive behaviours when they occur? > What sort of concrete rewards could I use to motivate students to behave in a positive manner? > How can I make learning fun? > Do I try to incorporate student interests when planning my work with the students? > Do I consistently use positive language when communicating with students? > What positive motivation strategies do I use? Do I tell the students that I believe in their skills and praise their efforts? > How can I encourage older students to accept their limitations but also recognise their strengths? > Do I make sure I break tasks down into small achievable chunks so the task is manageable and achievable? > Do I have a well-stocked supply of resources such as fidget toys and quick calm down strategies?	> 'I noticed that you helped Sarim put all the books away this morning. That was very kind of you.' > Rather than saying, 'If you don't listen you won't know what to do', you might say, 'I need you to listen so that you'll know what to do.' > 'I know you find maths hard. You should be very proud of your effort today. Well done!'

SCENARIO

SETTING CLEAR BOUNDARIES

Pat has been working as an ESW for 20 years. He says managing student behaviour has been his biggest challenge and steepest learning curve. Pat likes to pass his knowledge and experience on to newly appointed ESWs:

- I can tell you that no two situations will ever be exactly the same and no two students will respond in the same way to management strategies.
- I try to give students choices. Like choosing the order in which assigned tasks are completed.
- I use role-plays – they can work well with some students and it adds an element of fun. I might say, *'Today I'll be you and you can be me. I'll start.'* They sometimes reply, *'Mr Pat this is too hard for me – can't we do something else?'*
- Where appropriate, I use humour. I believe a light, funny comment or statement can often defuse tension or frustration and allow everyone to feel a bit more comfortable. Be careful, because what you think is funny may not be funny to the student involved. You don't want them to think that you are laughing at their expense. Never use sarcasm and don't embarrass students.

- I use rewards targeted at the interests of the student: *'When you complete the set tasks you can spend five minutes playing a game on the iPad.'*
- I have learned over the years that students are very focused on the concept of 'fairness' and it is essential that you act in a way that is seen to be fair to everyone. I always try to apply behaviour-management strategies consistently. Students are very quick to point out any inconsistencies in behaviour management strategies!'
- I talk to students with a 'can do' attitude. I get them talking about what they can do rather than what they can't do. I will say to a student who is worried about a task, *'Okay, you might find this hard but let's give it a go and see what happens. I'm here to help.'*
- I let students know I mean business by changing the tone of my voice. It usually works for me. When I use my formal voice, they know I mean business!
- I try to use only genuine, timely and specific praise and try to catch the student doing the right thing. For example, I might say, *'I noticed you helped Anton to clean up his paints this morning. That was really kind of you Thomas.'*
- I encourage the student to work with me to problem-solve. Working collaboratively with a student sends a very clear message that you respect and value the student as a problem-solver.
- I try to appeal to students' values. I try to build relationships with the students based on mutual trust and respect and then use this to appeal to their sense of responsibility. I might say, *'I know when you swear at me that you are angry and upset but I still don't like it, it makes me feel uncomfortable.'* Or, *'I know you're feeling frustrated, but if you tear up your work you will have to do it again.'* Or, *'I know you want your friends to like you. When you get loud and bossy they don't want to be with you.'*
- Every time I work with a group of students, I establish clear rules for behaviour. I make it clear what is and isn't acceptable so that students know what is expected of them without any surprises.
- My best advice is to reflect on how you interact with students and how you react to their behaviours. Talking to colleagues and taking advantage of professional development has really helped me to develop my behaviour-management skills.

WHAT DOES THIS TELL US?

Managing behaviour is a daily challenge – the skills required are built over time and can be improved through self-reflection, discussion with colleagues and professional development.

▶ DISCUSSION

Discuss the examples of behaviour management strategies described in this Scenario and in **Figure 18.2**. Explore which you would feel most comfortable using and which you find challenging. Share ways that you can build on your behaviour-management strategies.

18.3 Behaviour and the curriculum

Chapter 9 of this textbook explored the Personal and Social general capability in the Australian Curriculum. You will recall that this capability included self-awareness, self-management, social awareness and social management (see **Figure 18.3**).

A sub-element of the Personal and social capability is Emotional awareness (see **Figure 18.4**), which is designed to support students to think about how their emotional responses influence their behaviour and the impact this behaviour has on others. Placed in the context of brain development, particularly during the teenage years, engaging in self-reflection and analysing emotions is quite a challenge. You may also recall Bloom's revised taxonomy, from Chapter 10, which places the ability to analyse as a higher-order skill. You may also recall from Chapter 7 that during adolescence the prefrontal cortex of the brain undergoes significant development. It is thought that

Figure 18.3 General capability: Personal and social

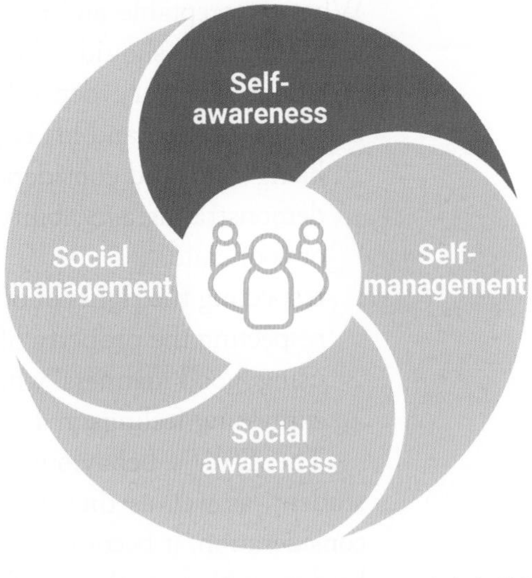

Source: Australian Curriculum, Assessment and Reporting Authority (ACARA) (2023). Australian Curriculum V9. Personal and Social Capability. https://v9.australiancurriculum.edu.au/f-10-curriculum.html/general-capabilities/personal-and-social-capability?element=0&sub-element=0

Figure 18.4 Sub-element: Emotional awareness

This sub-element supports students to explore the factors that influence emotions in themselves and in others, and how emotional responses affect behaviour in a range of contexts.	
Level 1a	Identify a range of emotions across different situations
Level 1 (Foundation)	Identify their own emotional responses
Level 2 (Years 1–2)	Describe the emotional responses of themselves and others
Level 3 (Years 3–4)	Explain the influence that their own behaviour has on the emotional responses of others
Level 4 (Years 5–6)	Analyse the influence of different factors and situations on their emotional responses
Level 5 (Years 7–8)	Evaluate how emotional responses influence behaviour and consider the consequences of these responses
Level 6 (Years 9–10)	Reflect on their emotional responses to different situations

Source: Australian Curriculum, Assessment and Reporting Authority (ACARA) (2023). Australian Curriculum V9. Personal and Social Capability. https://v9.australiancurriculum.edu.au/f-10-curriculum.html/general-capabilities/personal-and-social-capability?element=0&sub-element=0

many of the less desirable attributes of adolescent development, such as recklessness, challenging rules, poor organisational skills and emotional outbursts, are related to this final stage of brain development.

You may recall that the brain is also responsible for the development of executive functioning skills (thinking and processing information, decision-making, impulse control, emotional control, focusing, filtering distractions and self-monitoring). It is important to be aware that the development of executive functioning skills occurs over time, with each child developing at their own unique pace. Students who have not yet developed executive functioning in one or more areas at an age-appropriate level are likely to experience difficulty in managing their own behaviour and meeting the behaviour expectations of adults.

Australian Curriculum: Personal and Social Capability

Factors that influence behaviour

What is acceptable and responsible behaviour for students aged five to 18 years? What does it look like? How should children and young people behave in a school setting? Responses to these questions will vary depending on your personal values, family practices, cultural values and beliefs, education and life experience. For example, you might include behaviours such as:

- being kind, and considerate of others
- demonstrating age/ability-appropriate prosocial skills, such as the ability to share, take turns or cooperate
- respecting the rights of other people
- respecting the property of others
- using 'good manners' when speaking to adults
- expressing feelings in a socially acceptable manner.

The ESW's behaviour expectations must vary based on the development and age of the student, as well as their social, environmental and cultural background. Taking all of this into consideration, it becomes clear that managing student behaviour is quite a complex task if it is to be done with empathy and fairness.

Ultimately, the goal of behaviour-management practice should be to support the development of self-regulation, which is a critical factor in the development of socially acceptable behaviours. As you will recall from Chapter 9, self-regulation is the ability to persist at new and/or challenging tasks; the ability to cope emotionally with life's challenges, frustrations and disappointments; the ability to calm down after feeling angry or upset; and the ability to monitor and control one's own behaviours.

Students will not always make the right behaviour choices – this is a normal part of development. When students make 'wrong' choices, it can be used as a learning opportunity: 'Why did you make that choice? What might be a better choice the next time you're in a similar situation? What can you do to redeem yourself? How can you make it better for the other person?' Encouraging this type of reflection must be done in an age-appropriate way. It can be helpful for some, although not all, children and young people, simply because the ability to reflect on and talk about one's own behaviour can be a very difficult and often confronting task.

Rudolf Dreikurs (1968) studied human behaviour, particularly misbehaviour in children. His theoretical approach, which is referred to as interactionalist, focuses on both internal and environmental influences. The most important contribution made by Dreikurs was his rationale for misbehaviour, which he referred to as '**mistaken behaviour**'. He argued that mistaken behaviour occurred because of the child's basic needs not being met and a need to fit in to the social group. He believed that mistaken behaviour had one of four goals:

1. *attention* – the desire to be noticed; this behaviour may be passive or aggressive
2. *power* – the desire to have power over others if the need for attention is not met: the child or young person may engage in a power struggle with a target adult, such as a parent or teacher
3. *revenge* – the need to seek revenge when needs are not met: verbal or physical abuse, destruction of property
4. *avoidance of failure* – acting out to avoid tasks that may result in a sense of failure or inadequacy; this may also include displays of self-imposed helplessness ('It's too hard', 'I can't do it') or self-imposed avoidance.

Dreikurs believed that if adults regarded inappropriate behaviour as *mistaken* behaviour, they would have a realistic framework with which to work with the student – for example, ensuring that the child or young person received a reasonable amount of positive attention, therefore avoiding the need for acting-out behaviour. Power struggles can be avoided by providing children and young people with opportunities to be involved in decision-making and to be given age-appropriate choices. He also suggested encouraging students to support each other and work as a team. Valuing students' contributions, skills and efforts would help to avoid students' need to act out.

Based on the work of Dreikurs, Gartrell (2004) argues that regarding the unacceptable behaviours as 'mistaken behaviours' places behaviour in the context of incomplete development of a skill. To support this idea, Gartrell argues that if a student makes a cognitive or language error, teachers will use their professional knowledge and appropriate learning strategies to guide the student towards developing an understanding or skill. For example, you would never consider 'punishing' a younger student who said, 'I wented to the beach yesterday'. Gartrell suggests that a child who 'behaves mistakenly' to solve a problem or conflict should not be punished, but rather guided towards learning appropriate behaviour.

Gartrell's argument is a compelling one, as it reminds us that children and young people are learners when it comes to self-regulation. The expectation that a child will behave in a socially appropriate manner increases as the child matures. However, this expectation should be accompanied by an understanding of social and emotional development and how the developing brain impacts on the ability to make the 'right' behaviour choices. We know, for example, that repeated exposure to stresses that are overwhelming may result in significant maladaptation or disorder. We also know that the frontal lobe, which in part controls behaviour and impulse control, is not fully mature until the early 20s. As students approach adolescence and move into young adulthood, they must also cope with peer pressure, which has a powerful influence on behaviour.

It is important for all students to acquire developmentally appropriate skills to manage their own behaviour. Consideration of each student's level of development, personality, temperament, self-esteem, self-concept and self-efficacy will provide an insight into the factors that may contribute to the student's behaviour. Children and young people with low self-esteem are more likely to engage in antisocial behaviours, while those with low self-efficacy are likely to be extremely negative about their own achievements and reluctant to try new things for fear of failure. These students are more likely to be loners, lack resilience and find it difficult to make and maintain friendships. Resilience allows children and young people to cope with setbacks and attempt new challenges (see Chapter 9).

Understanding why a student behaves in certain ways should not in itself become an excuse for poor behaviour. Rather, it should serve to guide decision-making in relation to the most appropriate strategies to respond to and manage the behaviour. Your job as an ESW is to support the teacher as directed when strategies are put in place to address underlying issues. Many of these underlying issues are, like icebergs, largely below the surface (see **Figure 18.5**).

Figure 18.5 Unseen underlying issues

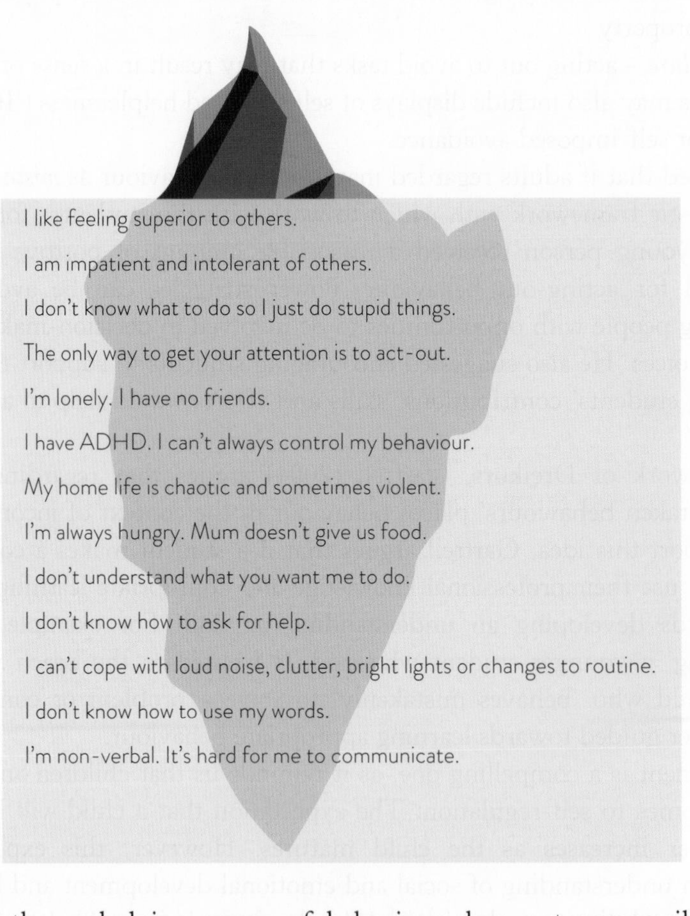

I like feeling superior to others.
I am impatient and intolerant of others.
I don't know what to do so I just do stupid things.
The only way to get your attention is to act-out.
I'm lonely. I have no friends.
I have ADHD. I can't always control my behaviour.
My home life is chaotic and sometimes violent.
I'm always hungry. Mum doesn't give us food.
I don't understand what you want me to do.
I don't know how to ask for help.
I can't cope with loud noise, clutter, bright lights or changes to routine.
I don't know how to use my words.
I'm non-verbal. It's hard for me to communicate.

Being aware of the underlying causes of behaviour does not necessarily make managing behaviour any less challenging; however, understanding what motivates and triggers behaviours helps educators to develop realistic expectations of what can be achieved in the school environment to modify and/or change some behaviours. Where there are serious underlying emotional issues, behaviours are unlikely to change until these issues have been addressed. Unfortunately, this is often outside the role and expertise of teachers and school counsellors.

The family

A child's relationship within their family is the single most important influence on social and emotional competence. The AIHW (2020) states that socially and emotionally competent children:

- are confident
- have good relationships
- communicate well
- do better at school
- take on and persist with challenging tasks
- develop the necessary relationships to succeed in life.

Source: Australian Institute of Health and Welfare (AIHW) (2020). Australia's children. Cat. no. CWS 69. Canberra: AIHW (p. 122)

Social and emotional competence also supports children and young people to be more resilient when faced with stressors that occur within the family and/or as a result of external factors, such as natural disasters or pandemics. Social competence is also influenced by factors such as cultural identity, community wellbeing, socio-economic status and access to health and welfare support.

Child-rearing practices

Child-rearing practices guide how families socialise children and put in place expectations, standards and boundaries for behaviour. Child-rearing practices are influenced by many factors, such as values, beliefs and cultural norms. Variations in child-rearing practices means that there will be occasions when the behaviour-management strategies used by the school conflict with those of the family. This will usually occur where there are extreme differences – for example, overly permissive parents or harsh disciplinarians who, in extreme cases, may physically and/or emotionally abuse the child or young person.

Culture

Expectations in relation to children's behaviour and discipline practices vary between and within cultures. In Australia, teachers typically manage behaviour based on white, middle-class expectations of how children should behave. Understanding how a student's culture influences their behaviour can assist teachers to better understand student behaviour and take this into account when managing behaviour. There are a number of cultural variations in behavioural expectations, including the following.

- *Eye contact.* In some cultures – for example, Aboriginal and Torres Strait Islander, Chinese, Japanese and Iranian – children are taught that it is not polite to make direct eye contact with persons of authority as this is a sign of disrespect to those in authority. In contrast, most Western countries believe that eye contact is a sign of politeness and interest in the speaker.
- *Directing questions to the teachers.* In some Asian cultures, asking the teacher questions is considered to be impolite or disrespectful.

- *Language barriers.* In homes where English is a second or third language, students may misunderstand or simply not understand behavioural expectations. When asked whether they understand what they are required to do, students will answer 'Yes' to be polite or to 'save face', when in fact they have not understood the teacher.
- *Smiling.* In some cultures, such as those of Aboriginal and Torres Strait Islander peoples, children may smile when being reprimanded as a sign of respect for authority or to avoid offence.
- *Sense of time.* In some cultures, such as in India or countries in Africa, time, deadlines and schedules are of limited importance. Students may appear lazy or uninterested because they arrive late or don't hand in tasks in the timeframe set by the teacher.
- *Saving face and shaming the family.* Many Asian countries, particularly China, place great emphasis on 'face' and humility. A common behaviour-management practice in junior classrooms is the use of a sticker system to reinforce each student's positive behaviours on a classroom notice board. For some Asian-Australian families, this may be a source of public humiliation and loss of face, especially if the child has none or very few stickers.

Emotional literacy

By school age, most children have a beginning understanding of the cultural and social 'rules' and expectations related to behaviour. The development of **emotional literacy** – the ability to express and manage emotions and know how to respond appropriately to the emotions of others – is a long-term developmental task.

Examples of child-rearing attitudes and behaviours that positively shape children's emotional literacy include:

- love, respect, trust and support versus criticism and violence
- guidance versus punishment
- positive versus negative feedback
- discipline versus natural and logical consequences
- role modelling/demonstrating versus telling/directing/taking over
- respectful two-way communication versus dominant one-way communication
- empathy and respect versus bias
- using mistakes/failures as opportunities for learning versus judgement.

Temperament

The Australian Temperament Project (ATP) defines temperament as 'the differences between individuals, visible from birth, in how they typically behave and react to their social surroundings' (Vassallo & Sanson, 2013, p. 4).

Temperament is a lifelong trait which is thought to be a product of both biology and life experience. It relates to *how* children and young people behave – their style of behaviour – rather than *what* they do, and plays an important role in how children develop and how they adjust to various contexts (family, school and so on) throughout their lives (Prior et al., 2000, pp. 3–4). The Australian Temperament Project research identified several key dimensions of temperament, including:

> sociability – the tendency of a child to be shy or outgoing in new situations and when meeting new people; reactivity – how strongly a child reacts to experiences and to frustration; and persistence – the extent to which a child can stay on task and control their attention, despite distractions and difficulties …

> These dimensions also reflect the capacity of an individual to manage, or self-regulate, their own feelings, attention and behaviour. (Sanson & Oberklaid, 2013, p. 4)

The ATP research (Prior et al., 2000) found that no single adverse temperamental characteristic predicted later behavioural difficulties; instead, a number of adverse temperamental characteristics combined with environmental factors contribute to difficult behaviours. On average, boys were found to be more aggressive than girls. Behaviours at age three to four years that were found to be indicators of later behavioural issues included both internalising behaviours (anxiety, depression and social withdrawal) and externalising behaviours (aggression, oppositional behaviour, hyperactivity and attention problems).

Prior and colleagues (2000, p. 27) point out that children who show 'serious levels of aggressive and antisocial behaviour such as destructiveness, fighting, lying, and defiance when they are young' are at risk of significant problems later in life. Intervening during the early years of these children's lives is crucial.

SCENARIO

RESPONDING TO BEHAVIOURS OF CONCERN

FAMILY VIOLENCE

Frank (12 years) lives with his mother and her partner. He has two siblings, a younger sister and a half-brother. The relationship between his mother and her partner is characterised by domestic violence and alcohol abuse. Frank used to have regular contact with his natural father until his father moved interstate. Frank's mother and partner use rough discipline – they yell and swear at Frank and tell him he is worthless and useless. He has been locked out and left to sleep on the verandah on several occasions. Frank has little regard for authority. He is rude and disrespectful to his teachers and is often involved in playground fights.

CULTURAL DIFFERENCES

Raveen (14 years) and her family have lived in Australia for 10 years. Raveen's father is extremely strict with his children and believes that girls must be quiet and submissive. Raveen has reacted to this by becoming more and more rebellious. Recently she was caught smoking in the girls' toilets. She begs the teacher not to tell her parents, saying that she will be beaten by her father.

LEARNING DISABILITY

Harry (15 years) has learning difficulties. It takes Harry a long time to learn new information and he struggles with reading and spelling. Harry covers up his learning difficulties by being the class clown. He will do almost anything to win the favour of his peers. He constantly shows off and commits various offences such as 'tagging' the classroom wall or deliberately breaking school equipment. When questioned about his behaviour, Harry is rude to his teachers, often swearing at them.

OUT-OF-HOME CARE

Sara (14 years) lives with her aunt and uncle and their four children. Sara was in and out of foster care for the first 10 years of her life, due to neglect by her parents, until finally settling with her aunt and uncle. Sara sees her mother intermittently but has no contact with her father. Although her family are loving and caring, Sara is very distrustful of others. She is often angry and tends to flare up over seemingly minor things. Sara's temper has caused her a great deal of bother with the teachers, who regard her as a troublemaker. Sara is often on lunchtime detention and lately she has been refusing to go to school. Her aunt and uncle are finding it difficult to manage her behaviour.

WHAT DOES THIS TELL US?

Understanding the personal circumstances of each student provides valuable information about the factors that contribute to inappropriate and/or unacceptable behaviours.

Pitonyak (2005) notes, 'Trying to understand someone's behaviour outside of the context of the person's life is fundamentally disrespectful to the person'.

While Frank, Raveen, Harry and Sara must demonstrate appropriate behaviour standards, it is important to consider contributing factors when determining how best to respond.

18.4 Learning environments

To function at their best, students must feel emotionally safe and secure. A safe, emotionally supportive educational environment will include consideration of physical and emotional/social dimensions which contribute to students' health, safety and sense of wellbeing.

To create an emotionally safe learning environment, adults working with children and young people must convey a genuine sense of respect, trust and commitment to student wellbeing. Each student must feel valued as a unique individual with unique abilities, strengths and interests. There must be respect for the student's family, including cultural and religious beliefs and home language/s. To support children's mental health and wellbeing, the school should be an environment where students are able to seek and receive support that empowers them to work through personal issues and concerns.

Adults must act as positive role models, assist students to problem-solve, apply appropriate conflict-resolution strategies and work towards age/ability-appropriate self-regulation. Adults must be empathic and consider each situation from the perspective of the student. **Figure 18.6** describes key features of a safe, emotionally supportive school environment.

Cassel (2018) states that strong relationships increase student motivation and reduce behavioural issues, and they improve student achievement and classroom climate. According to Be You (2019), relationships of trust are fostered when teachers work with students to support them to explore and build a range of skills, including:

- **self-awareness** – recognising their own feelings and building self-confidence
- *social awareness* – understanding and respecting similarities and differences
- *self-management* – developing self-regulation
- **responsible decision-making** – thinking and choosing wisely
- *relationship skills* – learning how to get along with others, including learning effective communication skills, developing conflict-resolution skills, learning to cooperate with others, understanding how to build friendships.

RESPECTFUL LEARNING ENVIRONMENT

SCENARIO

The school sports carnival included a Special Olympics for students attending the Special Education Unit at the school. Students from the unit were honoured alongside their peers at an awards assembly. Each student who participated in the Special Olympics was awarded a certificate of appreciation by the school principal and the school captains. Parents were invited to attend and one of the students from the Special Education Unit spoke on behalf of her peers. The presentation was followed by a special morning tea.

WHAT DOES THIS TELL US?

In this example, the school is modelling and demonstrating respect for diversity. The presentation sends a clear message to the school community that every student, regardless of ability, is valued and respected.

▶ DISCUSSION

Discuss how an event such as the Special Olympics promotes positive whole school student behaviour.

The difference between guidance, discipline and punishment

Guidance can be defined as supporting a student to develop an understanding of what is expected in terms of socially acceptable behaviour, considering the individual student's ability,

Figure 18.6 Features of a safe environment

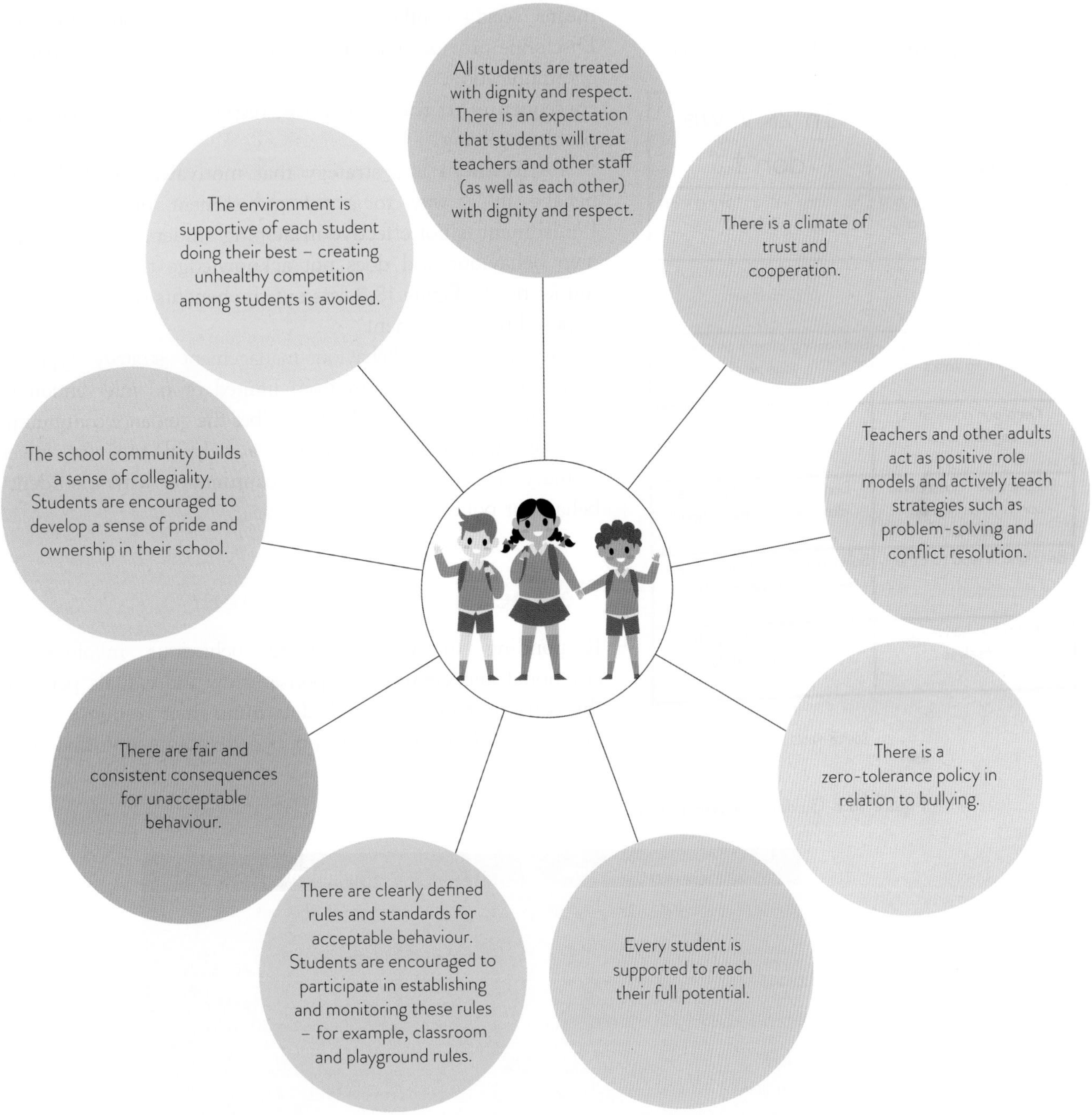

age, circumstances and the context in which the behaviour occurs. Guidance is a positive behaviour-management strategy that helps the student develop the skills to monitor and regulate their own behaviour without the need for adult intervention (see **Figure 18.7**). It acknowledges that unacceptable behaviour is a function of unmet needs.

Figure 18.7 Posters can be used to remind students of expected and agreed behaviours

2KV Classroom Agreement
In 2KV we do...
In 2KV we don't...
Listen to the teacher and others when they are talking
No calling out or talking over others
Ask the teacher before leaving the room
Leave the room without permission
Stay focused on your learning tasks
Distracting others or avoiding your work
Keep our noise at a sensible level
No yelling or swearing
Respect our classroom, our friends and our teacher
Damage property in the classroom or the school
Be a kind friend to others
Bullying, name calling or nasty behaviour towards others
Keep our hands to ourselves
Hurt others or touch them inappropriately

Source: Photo by Tish Okely © Cengage

Desautels (2018) reminds us that, unlike punishment, discipline is proactive and begins before there are problems. It means seeing conflict as an opportunity to problem-solve. Discipline provides guidance, focuses on prevention, enhances communication, models respect and embraces natural consequences. It teaches fairness, responsibility, life skills and problem-solving.

Punishment is a strategy that motivates the student to behave in a way to avoid punishment or disapproval. Punishment is not effective in helping students regulate their own behaviour and does not acknowledge the existence of unmet needs. **Figure 18.8** sets out the benefits of 'guidance' as opposed to 'punishment'.

Guidance as a behaviour-management strategy typically occurs along a continuum from limited or no intervention to direct intervention. **Figure 18.9** describes the guidance continuum.

The guidance continuum is a helpful tool for lower primary students when used in conjunction with a student-behaviour policy.

Perspectives on behaviour

Responding to and managing behaviour involves an emotional and cognitive response. How individuals perceive the behaviour of others will determine their response to the behaviour. Kaweski (2014, pp. 47–8) points out that 'two

Figure 18.8 Guidance versus punishment

Guidance/discipline	Punishment
Emphasises what to do and sets an example to follow	Often emphasises what not to do by adults who frequently insist on blind obedience
An ongoing process of interaction between adults and students	May be a spontaneous on-the-spot reaction of adults who decide and act
Seen as a positive response, which helps students develop responsibility and self-control	Often negative and punitive in ways that may undermine trust, autonomy and initiative
Fosters a student's ability to think and problem-solve, which bolsters self-esteem	Has the potential to diminish self-esteem when adults depend on extreme controls
Based on a caring, nurturing approach, which acknowledges and respects student's feelings and needs	Frequently spontaneous and impulsive, often causing feelings of shame and humiliation
Viewed as collaboration	Often results in power assertion by adults

Source: Gordon & Browne (1996) *Guiding Young Children in a Diverse Society*. p. 18.

Figure 18.9 The guidance continuum

1 = least intervention 10 = most intervention

1 Ignore	Let the students sort it out for themselves. This option can be used when the educator assesses that the students are safe and will benefit from trying to resolve the problem themselves. For example, if you see two students arguing over shared resources, don't rush in: wait and see whether they can sort it out themselves.
2 Listen and watch	Make sure you hear what the students are saying. Become aware of the issues. Make sure students see you are watching and available to offer support if needed.
3 Act as reporter	Say what you notice and hear: *'It looks like there's a problem'*, *'I can hear that you are arguing about who should go first'*.
4 Acknowledge desirable behaviour	Catch students when they are behaving well and acknowledge/encourage this behaviour so they develop an understanding of what you want them to do: *'I see that you worked out your argument, well done!'* This is probably the most important strategy when guiding behaviour. Appropriate behaviour will persist if students are given timely, specific feedback about what they did well.
5 Step in/set limits	Educators can help students to understand what behaviours are acceptable and what behaviours are not acceptable by giving clear and appropriate explanations that take into account the child/young person's age and abilities. Protect physical or emotional security: *'Please keep your hands by your side'*, *'Swearing is unacceptable'*
6 Ask questions	This is helpful where students are able to discuss their behaviour and can assist in identifying ways to try to change the behaviour. *'Is there a problem?'*, *'How do you feel about that?'*, *'What can I do to help?'*
7 Brainstorm	Encourage students to state what to do: *'How could we solve this problem?'*, *'Who has a good idea?'*, *'What could you do so that you will both be happy?'*, *'What could you do instead of pushing?'* Offer ideas: *'Maybe you need to ask another student for help'*
8 Offer choices	*'You have two choices. You can .... Or ....you can ....* 'This strategy is particularly effective for children who are disorganised and disruptive.
9 Take action alongside	The educator takes the lead, is firm and directs students by taking action and enforcing consistent boundaries: *'Here's what we'll do together'*, *'I want you to ...'*
10 Do it yourself	Take command and tell students what to do: *'It seems too difficult for you to work at this table. You need to go and sit at the other table so you can concentrate.'*

Source: Adapted from Gordon & Browne (1996).

different people can view the same behaviour and come away with entirely different interpretations of what happened and why. We tend to jump to conclusions without thoroughly understanding the numerous factors that would help us to arrive at a more valid conclusion'.

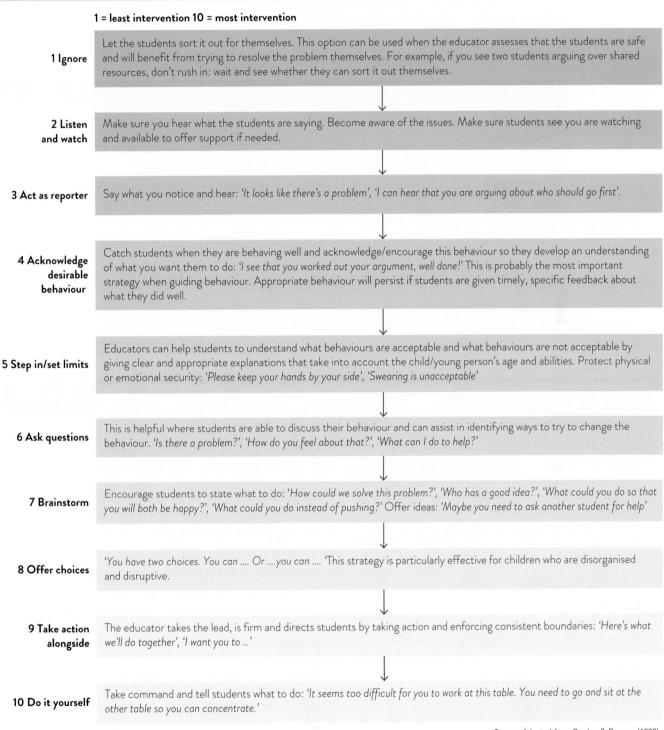

Just as individual personality and temperament will influence children's and young people's behaviour, individual personality and temperament will also influence how adults respond to behaviours – this is simply the human factor. To balance the human factor, Kaweski suggests that before deciding how to respond to unacceptable behaviour, educators should consider 'nine respectful notions' (described in **Figure 18.10**).

Figure 18.10 Nine respectful notions

Notion	Description
Understanding	Does the student understand the required behaviours?
Communication	What is the student attempting to communicate by their behaviour?
Unmet needs	What are the unmet needs of the student?
Self-determination	What actions have been put in place to include the student in decision-making?
Hidden benefit	What are the benefits to the student of the consequences or actions taken as a result of the behaviour?
Survival strategies	Did the student's behaviour stem from a sense of survival or self-preservation?
Family and cultural practices	In what ways is the student's behaviour a reflection of their family and cultural background?
Roles	Does the student behave in a positive manner around some people? Ask who and why.
Medication	Is the student on medication which may have side-effects? Is the behaviour a result of not taking medication?

Source: Kaweski, W. (2014, p. 49).

SCENARIO

RESPECTFUL NOTIONS

UNDERSTANDING

Adam (14 years) has been diagnosed with Asperger's syndrome. He does not understand how to generalise rules. When stopped by a teacher for running along the verandah and reminded of the 'no running inside' rule, he responds, *'I know that rule. No running inside. This is not inside, this is the verandah. It's not strictly inside. The rule should say no running inside or on the verandah – that would be correct.'*

SURVIVAL STRATEGIES

Sara (10 years) has been caught stealing food and money from the backpacks of other students. Sara lives with her mother and two younger siblings. Her mother often gambles what little money she has on poker machines. There is often no food in the house.

CULTURAL PRACTICES

Ishmal (8 years) has three older sisters. As the only male child in the family, he is very much indulged. There are very few limits placed on his behaviour. As a result, Ishmal becomes angry and abusive when his needs and wants are not immediately met at school.

ROLES

Connie (13 years) is considered to have many challenging behaviours. She is often sullen and uncooperative in class. However, when in Ms Brown's science class, she is a model student. Connie says, *'Ms Brown treats me like a real person. She says she wishes she had my beautiful red hair. She makes everyone feel special. I like Ms Brown. I wish she could be my teacher all the time.'*

WHAT DOES THIS TELL US?

The behaviour of Adam, Sara, Ishmal and Connie is shaped by powerful factors that are outside their control. Applying Kaweski's 'nine respectful notions' is a sound example of how these behaviours can be explored, interpreted and understood from varying perspectives. Being aware of what contributes to a student's behaviour is an important consideration when determining an appropriate response strategy.

▶ DISCUSSION

Each of these students behaves in a way that reflects their unique abilities and social context. Explain why it is important to be aware of what drives or motivates student behaviours.

The notion of respect is also championed by Bailey (2021), who uses the term 'conscious discipline' to describe a values-based approach to supporting positive behaviours. Conscious discipline is a brain-based approach that teaches self-regulation, problem-solving and healthy teacher–student relationships, and fosters social-emotional learning (emotional intelligence) in educators and students to develop a whole-of-school culture around discipline. Conscious discipline is built on the following beliefs:

1. Controlling and changing ourselves is possible and has a profound impact on others.
2. Connectedness governs behaviour.
3. Conflict is an opportunity to teach.

Bailey states that conscious discipline is based on seven skills, as described in **Figure 18.11**.

Figure 18.11 The seven skills of conscious discipline

SEVEN SKILLS

1. **Composure**
Being the person you want others to become: no one can make you angry without your permission
2. **Assertiveness**
Saying 'No' and being heard: setting limits respectfully
3. **Encouragement**
Building the school family: we are all in this together
4. **Choices**
Building self-esteem and willpower: the only person you can make change is you
5. **Empathy**
Teaching children to manage their emotions (self-regulation)
6. **Positive intent**
Creating teaching moments with oppositional, shut-down and aggressive children
7. **Consequences**
Helping children to learn from their mistakes

Source: Based on Bailey, B. (2021). *Conscious Discipline. Building Resilient Classrooms.* USA. Loving Guidance, LLC (pp. 15, 16, 28).

Figure 18.12 outlines the conscious discipline core values and beliefs.

Figure 18.12 Conscious discipline

Belief	Value it teaches
Changing ourselves is possible.	It is our choice whether or not to change.
We are in charge of ourselves.	We can become the person we want to be.
We are empowered by choosing to control ourselves instead of others.	Power comes from within.
When things don't go our way, we will seek solutions.	We are responsible for our feelings and actions. Our choices impact others.
We must teach children in order for them to learn to behave.	We teach others how to treat us. We cannot expect them to magically know how.
Conflict is an essential part of life.	Conflicts and mistakes present us with the opportunity to learn a missing skill or let go of a limiting belief.
Love is the best motivator for learning and growth.	Love is more powerful than fear, cooperation is more effective than coercion and compassion is more powerful than competition.

Belief	Value it teaches	
	Traditional discipline compliance model	**Conscious discipline community model**
Motivation	Rewards and punishment	Connection and contribution
Goal	Obedience	Problem solvers
Foundation	Rules	Community
Power	External control	Internal self-regulation
Skills	Consequences	Seven skills of conscious discipline
Philosophy	Rejection	Acceptance

Source: Bailey, B. (2021). *Conscious Discipline. Building Resilient Classrooms.* USA. Loving Guidance, LLC (pp. 15, 16 and 28).

The conscious discipline model is holistic because it focuses on ourselves as educators – our values and beliefs about children and young people and our expectations of behaviour. It challenges educators to reflect on their own emotional intelligence as the point for supporting and guiding behaviour.

18.5 Behaviour management frameworks

There is a variety of behaviour management frameworks that may be adopted by schools. The values and principles embedded in various models should be central to determining how best they meet the needs of the school and support children and young people to develop age-appropriate behaviours and self-regulation. Ideally, a primary goal of any effective framework is to guide and support students to make positive choices, learn from mistaken behaviours and build positive self-esteem. Examples of behaviour management frameworks that may be found in schools in Australia include:

- Positive Behavioural Interventions and Supports (PBIS)
- school-wide positive behaviour support framework (SWPBS)
- National Safe Schools Framework
- Australian Student Wellbeing Framework.

Positive Behavioural Interventions and Supports (PBIS)

Positive Behavioural Interventions and Supports (PBIS) is an evidence-based, tiered framework for supporting students' behavioural, academic, social, emotional, and mental health. The three-tier framework is based on a continuum of 'all', 'some' and 'few', in which around 80 per cent of students experience positive academic, behavioural, social and emotional support.

Tier 1: Universal, Primary Prevention (All)
Tier 1 practices include:
- Collaborating with students, families, and educators to define positive school/program-wide expectations and prioritize appropriate social, emotional, and behavioral skills
- Aligning classroom expectations with school/program-wide expectations
- Explicitly teaching expectations and skills to set all students up for success
- Encouraging and acknowledging expected behavior
- Preventing and responding to unwanted behavior in a respectful, instructional manner
- Fostering school/program-family partnerships

Tier 2: Targeted, Secondary Prevention (Some)

Tier 2 practices include:

– Providing additional instruction and practice for behavioral, social, emotional, and academic skills
– Increasing adult support and supervision
– Providing additional opportunities for positive reinforcement
– Increasing prompts or reminders
– Increasing access to academic supports
– Increasing school-family communication

Tier 3: Intensive and Individualized, Tertiary Prevention (Few)

Tier 3 practices include:

– Engaging students, educators, and families in functional behavioral assessments and intervention planning
– Coordinating support through wraparound and person-centered planning
– Implementing individualized, comprehensive, and function-based support

Source: Center on PBIS (2023). What is PBIS? https://www.pbis.org/pbis/what-is-pbis

Elements of PBIS

PBIS has five interrelated elements, shown in **Figure 18.13** and described in **Figure 18.14**.

Figure 18.13 The elements of PBIS

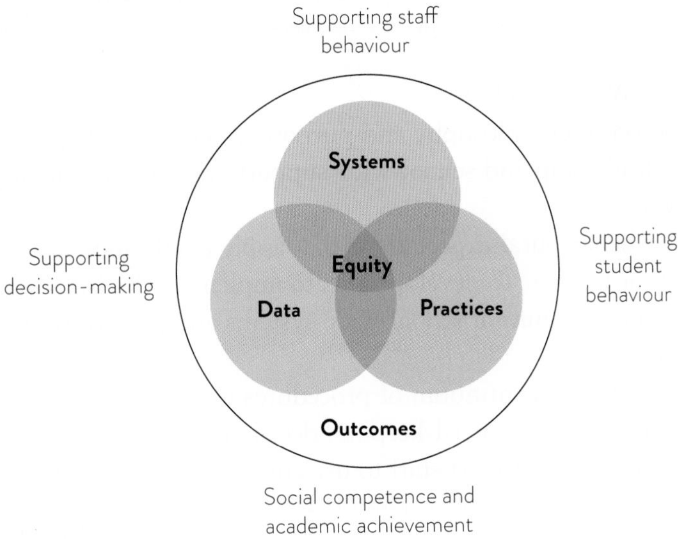

Source: Center on PBIS (2023). What is PBIS. https://www.pbis.org/pbis/what-is-pbis

Figure 18.14 PBIS interrelated elements

Element	Description
Equity	> Working collaboratively with all stakeholders (students, families, educators and community) > Implementing and adapting strategies that meet the individual needs of students > The reduction of risk for exclusionary discipline, such as office discipline referrals and suspensions based on individual characteristics like race/ethnicity or special education status (Centre on PBIS, 2023)
Systems	> School-wide, consistent approach to discipline > Training, coaching and mentoring for educators

Element	Description
Data	Data is collected and used to: > analyse and diagnose problems or gaps (Centre on PBIS, 2023) > identify strategies that are most effective in supporting students' behavioural, social, emotional and academic growth.
Practices	Behaviour management practices and behaviour interventions should be designed to create a positive school climate where all stakeholders feel safe and supported.
Outcomes	Stakeholders work together to achieve effective outcomes based on clearly defined goals.

Source: Center on PBIS (2023). What is PBIS. https://www.pbis.org/pbis/what-is-pbis

School-wide positive behaviour support framework (SWPBS)

Video: Evidence-based practices for behavioural support

The SWPBS draws on the PBIS framework. It is similar to the concept of Education WA's whole school plan to support positive student behaviour. SWPBS uses a three-tier intervention framework:

- Tier 1: Primary prevention – supports for all students, staff and settings
- Tier 2: Secondary prevention – additional specialised group systems for students with at-risk behaviour
- Tier 3: Tertiary prevention – specialised, individualised systems for students with high-risk behaviour, provided in addition to primary and secondary prevention.

Source: Education Victoria (2022). Behaviour – Students. https://www2.education.vic.gov.au/pal/behaviour-students/guidance/5-school-wide-positive-behaviour-support-swpbs-framework

The key features of SWPBS include:

- establishment of a common philosophy and purpose in relation to behaviour support
- establishment of a leadership and school-wide support system to implement, monitor and review the framework
- a set of three to five behavioural expectations that apply at all times
- providing support for teachers to develop skills to implement the framework
- implementation of a continuum of school-wide systems and procedures to encourage expected behaviours
- development of school-wide continuum of procedures to discourage inappropriate behaviour
- development of procedures for record-keeping, decision-making and ongoing monitoring
- development of strategies to support staff to use effective classroom practices.

Source: Education Victoria (2022). Behaviour – Students. https://www2.education.vic.gov.au/pal/behaviour-students/guidance/5-school-wide-positive-behaviour-support-swpbs-framework

The National Safe Schools Framework

The National Safe Schools Framework (Ministerial Council on Education, Early Childhood Development and Youth Affairs, 2010) is:

> The Framework provides a vision and a set of guiding principles for safe and supportive school communities that also promote student wellbeing and develop respectful relationships. It identifies nine elements to assist Australian schools to continue to create teaching and learning communities where all members of the school community both feel and are safe from harassment, aggression, violence and bullying. It also responds to new and emerging challenges for school communities such as cybersafety, cyberbullying and community concerns about young people and weapons.

Source: National Safe Schools Framework (revised 2011). Supported by the Australian Government Department of Education, Employment and Workplace Relations. © 2010 Education Services Australia as the legal entity for the Ministerial Council on Education, Early Childhood Development and Youth Affairs (MCEECDYA). http://www.curriculum.edu.au/verve/_resources/NSSFramework.pdf, p. 2

The guiding principles of the National Safe Schools Framework are based on the provision of a safe and supportive school environment. The principles are described in **Figure 18.15**.

Figure 18.15 National Safe Schools Framework principles

Australian schools:

> affirm the rights of all members of the school community to feel safe and be safe at school
> acknowledge that being safe and supported at school is essential for student wellbeing and effective learning
> accept responsibility for developing and sustaining safe and supportive learning and teaching communities that also fulfil the school's child protection responsibilities
> encourage the active participation of all school community members in developing and maintaining a safe school community where diversity is valued
> actively support young people to develop understanding and skills to keep themselves and others safe
> commit to developing a safe school community through a whole-school and evidence-based approach.

Source: Supported by the Australian Government Department of Education, Employment and Workplace Relations. © 2010 Education Services Australia as the legal entity for the Ministerial Council on Education, Early Childhood Development and Youth Affairs (MCEECDYA). http://www.curriculum.edu.au/verve/_resources/NSSFramework.pdf p.3

The Framework includes nine elements:

1 Leadership commitment to a safe school
2 A supportive and connected school culture
3 Policies and procedures
4 Professional learning
5 Positive behaviour management
6 Engagement, skill development and safe school curriculum
7 A focus on student wellbeing and student ownership
8 Early intervention and targeted support
9 Partnerships with families and community

Source: Ministerial Council on Education, Early Childhood Development and Youth Affairs (MCEECDYA). National Safe Schools Framework (revised 2011) 2010 Education Services Australia as the legal entity for the Ministerial Council on Education, Early Childhood Development and Youth Affairs (MCEECDYA). http://www.curriculum.edu.au/verve/_resources/NSSFramework.pdf, p. 4.

Element 5 – Positive Behaviour Management is characterised by:

5.1 Careful selection of evidence-informed positive behaviour management approaches that align with the school community's needs.
5.2 The promotion and recognition of positive student behaviour.
5.3 A clear understanding and consistent implementation by all staff of the school's selected positive behaviour management approaches within both the school and classroom context.
5.4 Effective risk prevention plans for the use of technology in the classroom and for playground organisation and supervision.
5.5 Effective risk prevention plans for student behaviour management during off-campus and school-related out-of-hours activities.

Source: Ministerial Council on Education, Early Childhood Development and Youth Affairs (MCEECDYA). National Safe Schools Framework (revised 2011) 2010 Education Services Australia as the legal entity for the Ministerial Council on Education, Early Childhood Development and Youth Affairs (MCEECDYA). http://www.curriculum.edu.au/verve/_resources/NSSFramework.pdf, p. 6

National Safe Schools Framework

Australian Student Wellbeing Framework

The Australian Student Wellbeing Framework (Student Wellbeing Hub, 2020; see **Figure 18.16**) supports Australian schools to provide every student with the strongest foundation possible for them to reach their aspirations in learning and in life.

It includes five key principles, as described in **Figure 18.17**.

Figure 18.16 Australian Student Wellbeing Framework

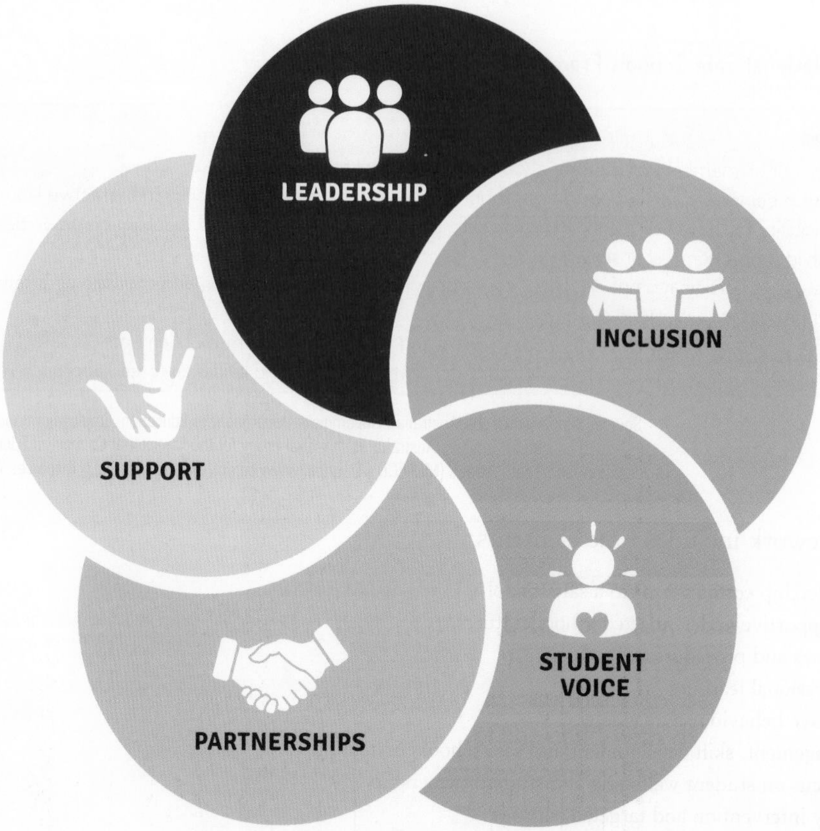

Source: Australian Student Wellbeing Framework. https://studentwellbeinghub.edu.au/educators/framework/. Licensed under Creative Commons Attribution 4.0 International (CC BY 4.0), https://creativecommons.org/licenses/by/4.0/

Figure 18.17 Student Wellbeing Principles

Leadership: Visible leadership to inspire positive school communities. Principals and school leaders play an active role in building a positive learning environment where the whole school community feels included, connected, safe and respected.

Student Voice: Authentic student participation. Students are active participants in their own learning and wellbeing, feel connected and use their social and emotional skills to be respectful, resilient and safe.

Support: Wellbeing and support for positive behaviour. School staff, students and families share and cultivate an understanding of wellbeing and positive behaviour and how this supports effective teaching and learning.

Inclusion: Inclusive and connected school culture. All members of the school community are active participants in building a welcoming school culture that values diversity, and fosters positive, respectful relationships.

Partnerships: Effective family and community partnerships. Families and communities collaborate as partners with the school to support student learning, safety and wellbeing.

Source: Australian Student Wellbeing Framework. https://studentwellbeinghub.edu.au/educators/framework/. Licensed under Creative Commons Attribution 4.0 International (CC BY 4.0), https://creativecommons.org/licenses/by/4.0/

Australian Student Wellbeing Framework

Mental health and behaviour

Mental health is defined by the World Health Organization (WHO) as 'a state of wellbeing in which an individual realises their own abilities, can cope with the normal stresses of life, can work productively and make a contribution to their community. Poor mental health can impact on the potential of young people to live fulfilling and productive lives' (WHO, 2022; see **Figure 18.18**).

Mental health is measured on a continuum, along which most people move up and down. Be You (2023) describes this continue as: Flourishing, Going OK, Struggling and Severe impact on everyday activities. To read about the mental health continuum go to: https://beyou.edu.au/resources/mental-health-continuum.

Figure 18.18 Students' mental health is supported by focusing on feelings

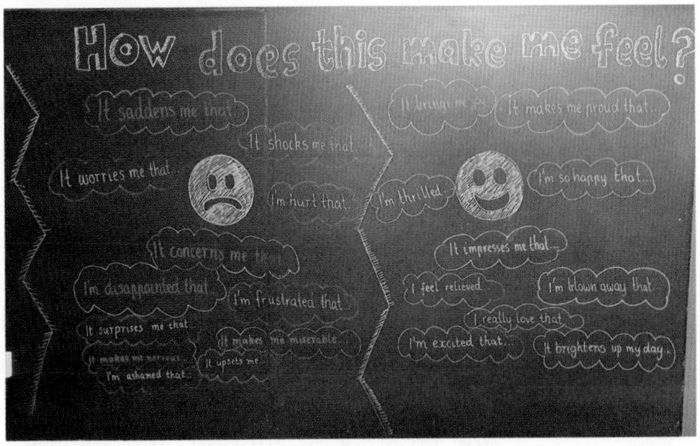

Source: Photo by Tish Okely © Cengage

CONSIDER THIS

CHILDREN AND YOUNG PEOPLE'S MENTAL HEALTH

The Australian Institute of Health and Welfare 2020 reports:

- Mental health and many common mental illnesses are influenced by social, economic and physical environment factors.
- Children's social and emotional wellbeing (SEWB) is a key component of mental health and wellbeing.
- There is strong evidence that mental disorders in childhood and adolescence predict mental illness in adulthood (WHO 2014b; Lahey 2015; NMHC 2019a).
- In 2015, for children aged 5–14, three of the five leading causes of the total burden of disease were mental disorders:
  - anxiety disorders ranked second
  - depressive disorders third
  - conduct disorders fourth (AIHW Burden of Disease database)
  - ADHD was the most common disorder for children.
- Mental disorders were also more common among children living in families with poor family functioning.
- Children living in families with two parents or carers were less likely to have mental health disorders than children living in families with one parent or carer.
- Average NAPLAN test scores were lower for students with mental disorders.
- Mental illness was more common among children born in Australia (14%) compared with children born overseas.
- Children in households where parents had lower levels of education, lower household income, or were living in public housing also had higher proportions of mental disorders.

Source: Australian Institute of Health and Welfare (2020). Australia's children. Cat. no. CWS 69. Canberra: AIHW (pp. 86, 88, 90, 122).

The AIHW (2020) reported also that the Australian Early Development Census (AEDC) identifies mental health competence in children and young people as reflected in:

- overall social competence
- responsibility and respect
- approaches to learning
- readiness to explore new things
- prosocial behaviour.

Source: Australian Institute of Health and Welfare (AIHW) (2020). Australia's children. Cat. no. CWS 69. Canberra: AIHW (p. 126)

Resilience, mental health and supporting cultural diversity

Being aware of the relationship between mental health and behaviour is essential. While ESWs are not required to address student mental health issues, it is important to be aware that stress, anxiety and depression can trigger a cycle of emotional responses that may result in challenging behaviours and despair. ESWs can support students by showing empathy, compassion and respect, while helping students to name their emotions – angry, embarrassed, sad, worried and so on.

To learn more about mental health, you should access the resources in Go further.

18.6 Trauma-informed care

You will recall that the impact of trauma on children and young people (explored in Chapter 9) can be examined in the context of 'the three Es':

- Event – the actual event or threat that has taken place
- Experience – the emotional response to the event
- Effect – the short- and long-term adverse effects of the traumatic event/s.

Trauma can be categorised as either 'simple' or 'complex'. Simple trauma is described as a one-time event, such as a natural disaster or serious injury. In Australia, natural disasters such as floods, bushfires, severe storms and drought are becoming recurring events that require the need for emergency support and government assistance to help displaced communities to recover, often over a number of years.

Complex trauma, referred to by the Center on the Developing Child, Harvard University as adverse childhood experiences (ACEs), results in toxic stress that has a long-term detrimental impact on brain development. These complex traumatic childhood experiences include physical and emotional abuse and neglect, carer mental illness, household violence, persistent bullying, homelessness, chronic poverty and food insecurity, and displacement from country of origin/refugees because of war, or persecution or violence. Studies have shown that the more ACEs experienced, the greater the chance of poor outcomes later in life, including dramatically increased risk of heart disease, diabetes, obesity, depression, substance abuse, smoking, poor academic achievement, time out of work and early death. ACEs can trigger excessive and long-lasting activation of stress response systems, which impact on the child's developing brain, as well as the immune system, metabolic regulatory systems and cardiovascular system (Center on the Developing Child, Harvard University, 2023).

The National Association of School Psychologists (2015) in the US states that 'childhood traumatic experiences have the power to undermine child and adolescent development in myriad areas that threaten academic success: communication skills, coherent sense of self, coping skills, peer and adult relationships, the ability to attend to classroom tasks and instructions, organizing and remembering information, and grasping cause-and-effect relationships' (p. 2).

According to the NSW Department of Education (2020, p. 6), possible indicators of complex trauma may include:

- increased tension and irritability
- anxiety

- low self-esteem
- aggressive or violent behaviour
- inability to feel or control emotions
- tired in class due to sleep disturbances
- over- or under-reaction to noises, lights and sudden movements
- difficulty forming positive relationships with peers.

For young people, additional indicators may include personality changes, substance abuse, acute psychological distress and self-harm (Victoria State Government, 2012; National Child Traumatic Stress Network Schools Committee, 2008).

The listed indicators are not conclusive, as many students will, from time to time, display some of the above behaviours. Indicators must also be considered alongside the context of the child's or young person's life situation.

Understanding the short-term and long-term implications of ACEs in children and young people is essential for all educators. As an ESW, you will not be required to engage in counselling these students. However, you may be required to support these students in the classroom. Trauma-informed classroom practices will include:

- providing a safe and predictable environment with clearly defined rules and boundaries
- building trusting, respectful and supportive relationships with students
- supporting students to build resilience and develop age-appropriate coping strategies
- supporting students to develop safe ways to express their emotions
- treating students with empathy and kindness.

What does a 'safe' environment look like for children and young people experiencing ACEs? According to the Australian Childhood Foundation (2018, p. 32), a safe school environment is one where children and young people can build positive relationships with caring adults, in which there is:

> – a consistent approach to communication
> – acknowledgement and validation of children and young people's feelings
> – experiences where adults act in protective ways even when behaviour is challenging and complex.

Source: Australian Childhood Foundation (2018). Making spaces for learning. Trauma informed practices in schools. Richmond, Victoria. https://www.theactgroup.com.au/documents/makingspaceforlearning-traumainschools.pdf, p. 32

The resource 'Making spaces for learning. Trauma informed practices in schools' (Australian Childhood Foundation, 2018) offers a range of suggestions by practising teachers to support students who have experienced trauma. Examples are shown in **Figure 18.19**.

Figure 18.19 Examples of teacher trauma-informed classroom practices

> Create spaces for the student to move into and still be part of the class group. Tactile corners in the classroom that have bean bags or a rocking chair, stress balls or a plush rug can support students to participate in class activity and calm down at the same time. > Utilise buddy programs to enable students to manage change with some support. > Provide a range of methods to reinforce behavioural expectations, including visual, auditory, sensory, words and pictures.	> Provide 'cool down' time and space for the student that is not described as discipline > Build in regular resources that enable the teacher to spend one-on-one time listening, talking and/or drawing with the student. > Use a digital camera in class to 'catch' students doing the right thing and help them to reflect on their own strengths and commitments. > Find an activity the child is good at and facilitate them being able to invite others into it.

Source: Australian Childhood Foundation (2018). Making spaces for learning. Trauma informed practices in schools. Richmond, Victoria. https://www.theactgroup.com.au/documents/makingspaceforlearning-traumainschools.pdf, pp. 65, 66, 69, 73

Trauma-informed practices

Building positive, caring and supportive relationships is the most important way you can support students who have, or are, experiencing ACEs.

18.7 Observing, documenting and analysing behaviour

The most effective way to understand student behaviour is to closely observe the student over time, at different periods of the day, in different physical spaces and in different learning/social situations. It is important to look closely at the factors that influence student behaviour, such as the physical setting, routines/timetable and the influences of other adults and students.

An accurate, holistic picture of each student is developed when the following 'principles' of observation are followed:

- Allow sufficient time to get to know the student and establish a relationship before beginning 'formal' observations.
- Take into account how the presence of the observer impacts the student's behaviour and what is recorded. Often, the ESW will be a partner in the experience; at other times, observations will need to be made from a distance.
- Decide on the best time to observe development and learning – this is usually during normal classroom activities.
- Collect information over time and in different settings to ensure an accurate representation of the student's behaviour. 'One-off' observations can be misleading. Frequent observation is essential for monitoring and assessing student progress, changing abilities and interests.

Observations must be accurate and should include the following details:

- the student's name, age and/or date of birth
- date and time of observation
- situation or setting in which the observation is occurring
- names and ages of other students present
- what the student does as well as language and interactions that occurred.

Observers must look for, 'notice', listen carefully and record all the relevant details necessary to understand the student's needs and interests. Curtis and Carter (2000) provide guidelines for recording information about students in this way, as outlined in **Figure 18.20**.

Figure 18.20 Guidelines for recording observations

Focus	Requirements
Objectivity	When observing students, you should strive to be objective and non-judgemental; however, observing without judging is a very difficult task. It is almost impossible to be totally objective. What we 'see' is coloured by our cultural values, beliefs and life experiences. Consider the following observation of Kane: 'Kane is gripping his pencil tightly as he writes. He is frowning and leaning over his work. Suddenly he slams his fist on the table, screws up his page and throws it on the floor, saying "This is just stupid!"'
Specificity	Include specific details, such as the context of the observation – for example, 'It is just after recess and all the students in the class are working on their story writing. Kane is sitting at a table with three other students who are all working quietly.'
Directness	Record direct quotes. These can provide a lot of information about the student's learning – for example, 'After the angry outburst Kane lays his head on the table and covers his eyes. "I hate writing – it's dumb and stupid and I don't have to do it!"'

Focus	Requirements
Mood	Identifying the student's mood can be helpful. It tells us a lot about how a student is feeling – for example, 'Kane was frowning as he wrote. He appeared to be gripping the pencil tightly.'
Completeness	Behaviour usually has a beginning, a middle and an end. Observations should describe the setting, who was involved, the actions in the order they occurred, the responses, interactions and the ending; for example, 'After a few minutes the ESW asked Kane if he would like to go with her to get a drink of water. Kane stood up and walked to the door. He waited for the ESW and they left the room together.'

Source: Curtis, D. & Carter, M. (2000). *The Art of Awareness: How Observation Can Transform Your Teaching.* St Paul, MN: Redleaf Press.

When gathering information to describe and document behaviour, it is important to put aside any assumptions you may have about the student so that a clear 'picture' of the behavioural concerns can be documented. The bigger picture – that is, the social and cultural context – can then be considered when determining how to move forward to support and guide the student to develop appropriate behaviours that will be sustained in the long term and lead to positive outcomes for the student.

Documentation of student behaviour must be reliable, valid and free from bias:

- *Reliable.* To be considered reliable, documentation must be accurate and consistent. This can only be achieved by drawing on a range of information collected over time and in different situations.
- *Valid.* Documentation is valid only when it is based on observations that contain sufficient information to form a fair 'picture' of student behaviour.
- *Free from bias.* Observations and interpretations must be accurate, objective and free of bias and prejudice.

Documenting behaviours of concern is a first step in the process of planning behaviour intervention strategies.

NOTE: The next section of this chapter includes observations of 12-year-old Kane, which will be used to develop an example of a behaviour intervention plan.

CASE STUDY | Kane

Part 1: About Kane

Kane (12 years) lives with his mother and two older sisters (14 years and 16 years) in a rented apartment. The family is on income support and his mother has chronic asthma. Kane's mother left her husband four years ago, because of alcohol-fuelled domestic violence, taking the children with her. Kane has witnessed a great deal of domestic violence – on many occasions, neighbours called police to intervene. Kane's mother has needed medical treatment on numerous occasions after being assaulted by her former husband.

Kane sees his father intermittently – they sometimes go to a football game or to the movies. Kane's 16-year-old sister has run away from home twice, constantly argues with her mother and regularly truants from school.

Kane's development is uneven. He has a reading and spelling age of eight years. Kane is a loner – he finds it difficult to relate to other students and is easily frustrated. Kane has a short temper and lashes out when he finds himself in a difficult situation. He will swear at other students and punch them if he is angry. When he becomes frustrated with written work, he will tear out pages from his workbook and rip them into tiny pieces or screw them into a tight ball and throw them across the room. The teacher often responds to Kane's angry outbursts by sending him to sit alone in the book area.

Kane has a vivid imagination and is a talented storyteller. He can produce very detailed drawings of dragons and other mythical creatures.

Event sampling

Another simple way to record specific behaviours is the use of event sampling to record the time, place and frequency of specific, pre-selected behaviour. Identifying the conditions under which a particular behaviour/s occurs and the frequency of the behaviour provides valuable information that can be used when determining why certain behaviours occur, as well as what strategies can be put in place to eliminate undesirable behaviours.

Figure 18.21 shows an event sample that records Kane's behaviours of concern:

- out of seat
- disrupting others
- physical taunting.

Figure 18.21 Event sample

Target Student: Kane			**Age:** 12 yrs			**Date:** 02.03.XX	
Time: 9–10:45 a.m.			**Place:** Classroom				
Observer: Educational Support Worker							
Behaviour	9–9.15	9.15–9.30	9.30–9.45	9.45–10.00	10–10.15	10.15–10.30	10.30–10.45
Out of seat		III	I	II	III	II	I
Disrupting others		II	I	I	II	II	
Physical taunting	I					I	
Verbal taunting	II		I	I	I	I	
Kane was very unsettled. He displayed frequent out-of-seat behaviour and disrupted the work of other students as he wandered around the room. On three occasions he tapped students on the head to gain their attention. He made negative comments about the work of others. He also used name calling such as 'dumbhead', 'idiot' and 'ugly face' when taunting others.							

If repeated over a period of time, event sampling can reveal persistent patterns in behaviour. In the example of Kane, it shows that his behaviours of concern occur from around 9.15 a.m. and begin to diminish around 10.30 a.m. By identifying what is happening in the classroom during this time period (and what changes at 10.30 a.m.), educators can pinpoint what is triggering this behaviour and take action to change the environment or routine for Kane.

Time sampling

Figure 18.22 is an example of a time sample. Observations are taken at set times and for a particular length of time – for example, the ESW observes and records Kane's behaviour for two minutes every half hour between 9 a.m. and 10.45 a.m.

The eight-minute time sample reveals quite a lot about Kane and the way he responds to activities and instructions – he appears not to follow the directions of the teacher, doesn't engage in activities in the expected way and engages in behaviour to gain negative attention from his teacher.

Figure 18.22 Time sample

Target Student: Kane	**Age:** 12 yrs	**Date:** 01.03.XX
Place: Classroom		
Observer: Educational Support Worker		

9.15 a.m.	The students have been asked to select a book, read it and then write about it. Kane is at the reading table looking through a book about wild animals. He is alone. He takes the book back to his table, flips the pages quickly then closes the book. He begins to draw a picture (of a tiger?).
9.45 a.m.	Kane is working with some sorting materials. He has sorted the counters into colours and is lining each set of counters into rows. He is talking softly to himself (cannot hear what he is saying). Mrs Brown approaches: '*Kane you're supposed to be using those counters to do your maths. Now please get started.*' Kane looks directly at Mrs Brown and using his arm in a sweeping motion scatters the counters across the table and onto the floor. He maintains direct eye contact with Mrs Brown. Mrs Brown: '*Kane pick the counters up and then go and sit by my table.*' Kane flops to the floor and starts to pick up the counters. He throws them onto his desk. Mrs Brown: '*Kane, that's not the way to pick up the counters. Go and sit next to my table now.*' Kane smiles and walks to the table and lies underneath it. Mrs Brown ignores this behaviour.
10.15 a.m.	Kane is at his desk. He has lined all of the items on his desk in a row and is touching each one in a repetitious action. The other students are working on patterns. Kane picks up his ruler and starts to tap it on the table. He looks at the teacher. Mrs Brown ignores this behaviour. The tapping gets louder. Mrs Brown walks over to Kane and takes the ruler. Kane then begins to drum on the table with his fingers.
10.45 a.m.	The students are told they may go outside for recess. Kane runs to the door, pushing others out of the way, saying '*Move dumbheads*'.

Analysing behaviour

While ESWs are not responsible for analysing behaviour or developing behaviour plans, it is important to have skills that can assist you to identify the underlying causes and triggers for behaviours of concern. This is particularly important for students with disability such as ADHD, ASD, sensory processing disorders and developmental coordination disorder that contributes to behaviours of concern. Two effective models that can be used to analyse behaviour are the:

- Applied Behaviour Analysis (ABC) Model
- Functional Behaviour Assessment.

Applied Behaviour Analysis (ABC) Model

The Applied Behaviour Analysis Model, also referred to as the Antecedent-Behaviour-Consequence (ABC) Model, is a systematic and objective way of observing and recording student behaviour. The model is shown in **Figure 18.23**.

The ABC Model allows educators to analyse and better understand student behaviour in an objective manner. It lets the educator take a step back and not allow their own emotional response to influence behaviour analysis.

Figure 18.23 ABC Model

A

A is the antecedent that leads to the behaviour – that is, what occurs immediately before the behaviour.

The antecedent is the trigger – the before part of the behaviour. Triggers might include people (other students, teachers, ESWs), the environment (loud noise, inadequate or poorly functioning resources, an unexpected change in the daily routine), learning tasks (student does not like/feels inadequate or anxious about particular task/learning area, working in groups)

B

B is the behaviour – that is, what the student did.

The behaviour is the student's response to the trigger. Behaviours may be positive or negative.

C

C is the consequence or outcomes of the behaviour – that is, what happened immediately after the behaviour occurred.

The consequence/s of the behaviour may also be positive or negative.

SCENARIO

USING THE ABC MODEL IN THE CLASSROOM

IZZY

Izzy (11 years) has an intellectual disability and has poor oral language skills. She finds it difficult to express her thoughts and needs. She is easily frustrated and tends to act out when faced with challenging tasks or tasks that she doesn't want to do. At home Izzy's parents report that when Izzy acts out they simply give in – there are no consequences. Izzy has learned that to get what she wants she simply has to act out.

Today Izzy is in a group with three other children and is supported by ESW **Helen**. The class is investigating insects and Izzy's group is exploring spiders. The students have black cardboard and are drawing a web using white markers. Izzy's attempt to draw her web is not going well. Helen offers to help but Izzy refuses. Izzy looks around at the work of her peers and sudden screws her cardboard up and throws it on the floor. She then sweeps the container of markers onto the floor. She folds her arms across her chest and declares in a loud voice, *'Spiders are ugly!'* Helen asks Izzy to pick up the things from the floor but Izzy refuses. Helen then tells Izzy to go back to her desk.

Antecedents	Behaviours	Consequences	Outcomes
> Small group task drawing spider web. > Drawing task too challenging for Izzy	> Attempts to draw web > Refuses assistance from Helen > Screws up her work and throws it on floor > Sweeps markers onto floor > Declares spiders are ugly > Refuses to pick up items from floor	> Returns to her own desk	> Doesn't complete task

In this scenario Izzy is faced with a challenging task. She refuses Helen's assistance and instead becomes frustrated and destroys her work. As a consequence she is asked to return to her desk.

Helen could have avoided this situation by offering alternative tasks to Izzy and the group. This would have allowed Izzy to participate alongside her peers without feeling frustrated.

THE MATHS CLASS

Eddie (14 years) is failing at maths. He finds the work hard to understand and says he's 'no good at maths'. Today **Ms Jenkins** is introducing a new concept to the class. As Ms Jenkins is talking, Eddie purposely knocks his books onto the floor. As he bends down to pick them up, he hits Ellen on the leg. Ellen shouts: *'Eddie get lost! That hurt you idiot!'* The entire class erupts into laughter. Ms Jenkins, speaking firmly says: *'Eddie! Come and sit at the front of the room.'* Eddie smiles to himself and as he walks to the front of the room he taps several boys on the head. Ms Jenkins responds: *'Eddie, take a behaviour slip and go to Mr Brown's office!'*

Antecedents	Behaviours	Consequences	Outcomes
> Maths class > New maths concept being introduced by teacher	> Drops books > Hits Ellen > Taps others on the head	> Disrupts the class > Upsets Ellen > Gets the attention of the teacher > Eddie is sent from room	**Ms Jenkins** > Eddie is no longer a disruption > Asserts her authority **Eddie** > Gets a reaction from his peers and teacher > Doesn't have to participate in maths class

The ABC Model is effective in describing what happens before, during and immediately after a behaviour incident. This can be useful when attempting to eliminate some manageable triggers, such as environmental factors. However, it doesn't identify underlying factors that contribute to negative behaviours. In this case, Eddie regards himself as a failure at maths – his solution is to behave in a way that will ensure he is removed from the class. Eddie doesn't get the extra help he needs; he isn't supported to ask for help; and his attitude towards his skills in maths is not addressed. In the case of Izzy, she has learned that she can control her environment by acting out with zero consequences for poor behaviour.

Functional Behaviour Assessment (FBA)

FBA is similar to the ABC Model and is typically used in the development of a Behaviour Intervention Plan. An FBA:

1 specifically describes behaviours of concern – for example, refusing to follow directions, yelling and hitting. A precise description of the behaviour/s is necessary when implementing an intervention plan to reduce or eliminate undesirable behaviours or to increase desirable behaviours

2 includes analysis of triggers and consequences as a way of determining underlying causes. For example, Eddie acts out during maths – the underlying cause is his lack of confidence in his maths skills, as well as his lack of knowledge and understanding of maths concepts

3 identifies strategies that that can be put in place to support changes in behaviour that are measurable and time limited.

An FBA begins by collecting a number of observations that are sufficient in number to identify an ongoing pattern of behaviour. **Figure 18.24** provides an example of a form that can be used to collect observations. As you can see, the process is relatively simple – you are only required to record what you see happening.

Figure 18.24 FBA observation form

Date/time	Activity	Antecedent	Behaviour	Consequence
When	**What**	**What happened right before that may have triggered the behaviour**	**What the behaviour looked like**	**What happened after the behaviour, or as a result of the behaviour**
9.15	Reading and book report	Directions from teacher	Briefly flipped through book and started to draw a picture	Task not completed
9.45	Working with sorting materials and pattern making	Transition from reading to maths	Sorted counters and placed them in lines Talking quietly to self	
		Directed by teacher to start maths activity	Looks at teacher and sweeps counters onto the floor	Non-compliance
		Asked to pick up the counters	Flops to floor and throws counters onto his desk	Teacher directs Kane to sit next to teacher's desk
		Directed to sit next to teacher's desk	Smiles and goes and lies under the teacher's desk	Ignored by teacher
10.15	Returned from under teacher's desk. Lines items in rows on his desk. Touches each one using a repetitious action	Begins tapping on desk with ruler	Teacher takes away the ruler	Kane drums on desk with fingers
10.45	Seated at desk	Directed by teacher to go outside for recess	Runs to door and pushes others, name calling	

Source: Understanding the Antecedent Behaviour Consequence (ABC) Data Model. https://www.educationandbehavior.com/wp-content/uploads/2017/12/ABC-Chart.pdf

The data collected through observation can be analysed to identify patterns of behaviour and indicate possible underlying causes. Typically, analysis will be carried out by a team such as the teacher, specialist support staff, parent/s, ESW and, if appropriate, the student.

The data is used to develop a Behaviour Intervention Plan. In the case of Kane, his behaviours may indicate a number of concerns. For example, he is unable to follow directions, he may not understand what he is required to do, he may not hear what the teacher is saying, he may find the task too difficult, he may not be able to process verbal messages and he uses inappropriate behaviours to gain the attention of the teacher.

The teacher will use the data, along with the student's existing knowledge and skills, as a beginning point for intervention. This may involve further assessment to determine a starting point. To support a Behaviour Intervention Plan, accommodations (changes in the way a student learns the same materials as the rest of the class) and modifications (changes to the content of what the student is expected to learn or do) will be made. For example, accommodations for Kane may be to provide him with visual cue cards, a graphic organiser or direct demonstration by the teacher. Modifications may include asking him to draw a character from a book or copy patterns using pattern cards.

Video: Managing challenging behaviours

18.8 Behaviour Intervention Plans

A Behaviour Intervention Plan, like an IEP, is a plan of inclusion. It defines the behavioural barriers to participating in an educational setting. It includes behaviour management strategies, accommodations and modifications that can be put in place to support the student to modify and change their behaviour.

The Behaviour Intervention Plan is typically developed by the teacher, and will include consultation with other stakeholders, including parent/s, the ESW and other support staff, and therapists involved with the student. Where appropriate it may also include input from the student. The plan will require similar information to an IEP – for example, the student's background, health issues, diagnosed disabilities, assessment results, strengths, interests and weaknesses; as well as agencies involved, long-term and short-term goals and home–school liaison. In addition, a Behaviour Intervention Plan will include:

- a description of the behaviours of concern – what the student does/says; where the behaviour typically occurs; the frequency and duration of the behaviour; the intensity of the behaviour; whether there are any identifiable patterns to the behaviour
- identification of the student's needs – what are the needs that are not being met and how can these be identified and acted upon?
- the behaviour-management strategies that have been used in the past and their effectiveness
- a list of known behaviour triggers – what are the typical circumstances?
- a description of any early warning signs, such as talking quickly, becoming agitated, pacing, mumbling to self
- how the student currently communicates needs, concerns and distress
- how the student responds to adult intervention and consequences
- whether the student is able to make the connection between their behaviour and the consequences
- identification of short-term goals, including the behaviours required, and the skills the student needs – for example, how to calm oneself when angry or upset, how to communicate when upset, anxious, worried, angry and so on
- adaptations and modifications, such as reducing or removing potential triggers
- the positive consequences that can be applied for desired behaviours
- the strategies that will be used to modify or reduce the behaviour
- the consequences that will be applied for behaviours.

Behaviour support planning

CASE STUDY | Kane

Kane Part 2: Observing and recording Kane's behaviour

An anecdotal record is a descriptive recollection of an observed behaviour or event. It does not record every detail, but rather highlights the most relevant points. An anecdotal record is recorded after the event. **Figure 18.25** is an example of an anecdotal record.

A running record gives a written account of everything a student does or says in a fixed period (**Figure 18.26**). Running records are very time-consuming and often difficult to compile, especially if there is a lot of action taking place. They also require the observer to be fully occupied with the recording.

Figure 18.25 Anecdotal record

Name: Kane	**Age:** 12 yrs	**Date:** 27.02.XX
Time: 10 a.m.	**Place:** Classroom	
Observer: Educational Support Worker		

Kane was assigned to work on some maths tasks with a group of six students. The students were working with counters to solve addition and subtraction tasks. For around 10 minutes Kane simply observed the other students. He did not make any comments, nor did he attempt any tasks. The following incident then occurred.

Max: *'Kane, you'd better hurry up and help or else you'll be in big trouble.'*

Kane did not respond to Max.

Max: *'I'm telling on you Kane. We're all supposed to be helping and you're just watching!'*

As Max stood up to go to the teacher, Kane grabbed his legs and Max fell to the floor. Max retaliated by punching Kane. The two boys wrestled on the floor until the class teacher intervened. Kane was sent to sit alone at his desk. Kane put his head in his arms and repeatedly said to himself (in a quiet voice), *'I hate Max. I hate Mrs Brown.'*

Figure 18.26 Running record

Target Student: Kane	**Age:** 12 yrs	**Date:** 01.03.XX
Time: 11.30 a.m.	**Place:** Library	
Observer: Educational Support Worker		

Kane is sitting at a table with three other students, Nardia, Jessie and Dillan. Kane is slightly turned away from the students with his body twisted at an awkward angle. Nardia and Jessie are listening to Dillan who is talking animatedly about his book on dinosaurs.

Kane appears to be listening to Dillan but does not make eye contact with him or make any comments.

Mr Green, the library teacher, approaches the group. *'Dillan, this is quiet reading time.'*

As soon as Mr Green walks away Kane turns to Dillan: *'That's a baby book you're reading. Dinosaurs are for babies!'*

Dillan: *'No they're not! You just got a stupid book about dogs!'*

Kane quickly grabs Dillan's book and knocks it to the floor. Nardia and Jessie tell Kane he's naughty. Nardia goes off to find Mr Green.

Kane stands up and walks behind a bookcase and sits on the floor.

What we know so far about Kane:

- Kane has difficulty relating to same-age peers – appears to lack age-appropriate social skills, making it difficult for him to relate well to others.
- Kane finds it difficult to follow directions.
- Kane seems unable to ask for help when needed.
- Kane engages in inappropriate behaviour to gain the attention of his teacher.
- Kane often responds to interaction with peers in an aggressive manner.
- Kane finds it difficult to start new tasks.

Setting goals and objectives

CASE STUDY | Kane

Part 3: Goals for Kane

Behaviours of concern include:

- poor social skills
- anger and aggression towards others (poor self-regulation)
- low self-esteem
- task avoidance – Kane tends to give up easily when faced with challenging tasks.

Goals for Kane might focus on:

- supporting his social and emotional development in order to build his self-esteem
- successfully completing set tasks
- using words instead of hitting others
- identifying his emotions and expressing them in a socially acceptable manner.

Based on the goals, a number of specific strategies can be put in place to help Kane to achieve the stated goals. For example:

- Kane will sit at his allocated table and complete two set tasks each morning between 9.15 a.m. and 10.15 a.m., without touching others.
- When feeling angry, Kane will remove himself to the calm-down area and rejoin the class when ready.

A primary task for the teacher is to support Kane's social and emotional development. For example, developing self-confidence is essential if Kane is to fully engage in learning and attempt more challenging tasks, as well as develop friendships, improve his ability to interact positively with peers and use his language to express his emotions rather than lash out at others.

It is also important at this point to look closely at Kane's strengths and interests, and to incorporate these into planned activities. For example, knowing Kane enjoys drawing and storytelling – a goal might be to work with the ESW to create a graphic novel. The ESW could act as a scribe and record text dictated by Kane, which he could later illustrate.

The teacher reports that Kane has poor spelling skills and becomes easily frustrated when he makes mistakes. The ESW could work with Kane to use spell-check and create a personal dictionary of frequently misspelled words. Creating opportunities for Kane to complete tasks and feel positive about his achievements will in turn contribute to modifying negative behaviours.

To be effective, goals for a Behaviour Intervention Plan should consider what is realistically achievable by the student within a specific timeframe. The outcome of the plan should be to change the student's behaviour in ways that promote self-regulation and self-esteem. Goals should be easily measurable as part of a cycle of evaluation and ongoing goal setting.

Videos: Calm-down centres

An easy-to-use acronym for goal writing is PACT, shown in **Figure 18.27**.

Figure 18.27 PACT goals

PACT goals

P Purposeful

Purposeful: The goal directly addresses your identified concern/s in relation to student behaviour.

Identified concern

- Kane lashes out verbally and physically when angry/upset.
- Kane has poor social skills and poor self-regulation.

A Actionable

Actionable: The goal you set is based on a concrete action that is realistic for the student.
State what you want Kane to do.

C Consistent

Consistent: The actions must be able to be maintained by the student over time.

T Trackable

Trackable: The actions must be observable.

PACT goal for Kane

Each time Kane becomes angry he will take himself to the calm-down area and rejoin the class when he feels calm.

This goal is **purposeful** as it relates directly to the behaviour of concern.

This goal is **actionable** as Kane is able to remove himself from the situation.

This goal is **consistent** as Kane is required to take action every time he feels angry.

This goal is **trackable** as it can be easily observed.

Implementing the goal

- Kane has poor self-regulation skills and will need prompting and support to begin the process of identifying when he is angry and removing himself from the situation.
- To be effective Kane needs to believe that this goal will help him to manage his behaviour. The motivator for Kane may be that the calm-down area includes some fidget toys that he likes.
- He may need support from the teacher or ESW such as a hand signal to indicate that he needs to move to the calm-down area.
- He may need support to identify when he feels calmer.

Consistency

Kane may not always be agreeable to this strategy. Initially it may only work sometimes because he must unlearn his usual response to anger. However, like any attempt to change behaviours, persistence and consistency are crucial.
It is important to assist Kane to review and reflect on how well he is able to implement the goal. For example: 'Kane, this week you took yourself away to calm down three times without needing any reminders. Great work! You must be very proud of how well you are managing angry feelings.'

CASE STUDY | Kane

Part 4: Documenting Kane's Behaviour Intervention Plan

Figure 18.28 provides an example of information that may be included in a Behaviour Intervention Plan. In this example, the behaviours of concern are clearly identified (purposeful), and the strategies that will be used to support changes in behaviour are actionable and trackable. Kane will be required to work with the ESW to document how his behaviour is improving, as well as identify setbacks and what he can do to change his behaviour – promoting consistency.

Figure 18.28 Behaviour Intervention Plan

Name of Student: Kane Smith **Class Teacher:** Mrs Brown **Date:** 22/03/XX

GOAL

Description of behaviours
- Physically and verbally abusing others
- Non-completion of written tasks
- Destroying written tasks
- Out-of-seat behaviour

Behaviour goals
- Kane will complete all tasks in the time allocated.
- Kane will accept errors or mistakes by not destroying his work.
- Kane will follow teacher directions, routines, class rules.
- Kane will follow the classroom conflict resolution strategies.
- Kane will use positive interactions with his peers.
- Kane will share ideas, information, and complete tasks when working in a small group.

Strategies
- Arrange seating so that Kane is facing the teacher.
- Teacher/ESW to give verbal praise for appropriate behaviour.
- Teacher/ESW to ignore minor inappropriate behaviours where possible.
- Teacher/ESW to give verbal reminders and/or use cue cards.
- Teacher/ESW to provide Kane with ongoing strategies to manage temper and aggressive outbursts.
- Teacher/ESW to implement a reward system.
- Kane to set daily goal for improvement.
- Provide a quiet retreat area where Kane will withdraw from the class for five minutes, calm himself and prepare to rejoin the class.
- Kane will develop a portfolio about himself, his family and his achievements.

Evaluation strategies
- Daily tally sheet to record compliance and non-compliance (this is to be completed by teacher and Kane). Written observations.
- Kane will be required to use a behaviour journal to record his progress, identify any setbacks and suggest things he can do to change his behaviour (on a weekly basis). To assist Kane with this task the ESW will act as a scribe.
- It is expected that all students will behave responsibly in accordance with the school's Code of Conduct.
- Consequences for unacceptable behaviour will be withdrawal of afternoon free-choice activity time; writing an apology; email sent to parents; in extreme situations sent to Principal to explain poor behaviour.
- Principal on positive progress, work on project of interest for 15 minutes with another student, listen to music or recorded stories for 15 minutes.
- Consequence of not meeting set goal: Withdrawal of a special privilege.

Teacher: ______________________ **Student:** ______________________

Parent: ______________________ **Review date:** ______________________

Figure 18.29 Cycle of planning: Behaviour Intervention Plan

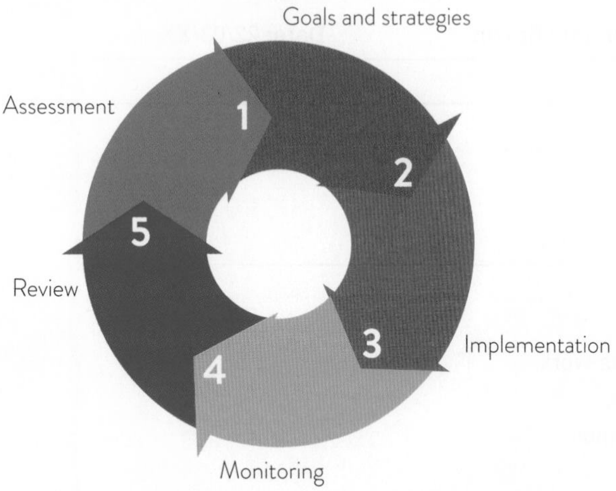

Strategies to monitor and evaluate progress

An essential element of any behaviour management plan is the cycle of assessment, goals and strategies, monitoring and review, as shown in **Figure 18.29**.

The process of monitoring and reviewing a student's progress (tracking) will require ongoing observation and other tracking measures such as event sampling, checklists and observations. Monitoring must also include an assessment of the quality of the intervention from the perspective of the student and educators; for example, positive relationships with peers and teachers, increased sense of wellbeing, and increased personal control through positive decision-making.

The review process measures the effectiveness of the strategies used to achieved the stated goals. The review will identify what's working well and what needs to be changed or modified. It may also include assessing the external factors, identified during data collection, that trigger student behaviours, such as the classroom physical environment, timetable, routines and transitions.

The review is an opportunity to examine changes that have taken place – what the behaviours/s looked like before intervention and what they look like after intervention. For example:

- changes/decreases in challenging behaviours (quality and quantity)
- evidence of new positive behaviours and/or skills
- evidence of achievement or working towards primary goals (in Kane's case social and emotional development)
- consistency in the effectiveness of the behaviour management strategies as well as changes/modifications to the environment
- the student's perspective (if appropriate) – in the case of Kane, he can be encouraged to reflect on how his behaviours have changed and the positive benefits of these changes, such as developing friendships.

CASE STUDY | Kane

Part 5: Kane's progress

Feedback from ESW **Pete**, who has been working with **Kane**, has focused on helping Kane to build his social skills. Pete states: *'For creative writing, I paired Kane with Jarrod, who is very easygoing and keen on drawing dragons. Working alongside Jarrod was great for Kane. When Jarrod made a mistake or wasn't happy with his drawing, he said so, laughed or expressed frustration but then just got on with fixing it. He was also very supportive of Kane and didn't let him get away with giving up if something went wrong. Jarrod was great for Kane. He'd say, "Come on Kane, give it a rest, no one's perfect man, not even me!" Jarrod made Kane laugh. It was wonderful to see Kane gaining some real confidence.'*

'I've also been working with Kane to identify the skills needed to make and sustain friendships. I had to spell it out for Kane as he didn't really have a clue how to make friends. We actually made a list of things that people do to be friendly and then Kane tried to put some of these into practice. We're not there yet but I see Kane making a real effort to use the skills we've been working on. The skills I've observed him using include:

- *complimenting others*
- *sharing ideas and listening to the ideas of others*
- *when someone talks to you, saying something back to keep the conversation going (this has been tough for Kane – he often can't think of what to say so we are working on open-ended questions)*
- *being aware that not everyone will want to be your friend and that's okay.'*

Feedback from Kane: *'Mr Pete has been helping me to make friends and not be so angry all the time. It's been good because I never thought anyone would want to be my friend but now I think Jarrod is my friend and so are some of the other kids. Jarrod is a funny guy. He says to me, "Hey man, don't get all heated up, just stay cool".'*

Discussion

Revisit and discuss each case study entry/observation to build an understanding of the factors that contribute to Kane's behaviour. Discuss the strategies used by the teacher and ESW to modify Kane's behaviour and develop his self-esteem.

18.9 Challenging behaviours in the school environment

Most students behave in a socially acceptable manner in the school environment. While rules of behaviour may be bent or challenged and sometimes broken, most students respond positively to guidance and direction. You may recall Bronfenbrenner's ecological systems theory of development in which development is influenced by the child's interaction with the social and cultural environment. Bronfenbrenner argues that the family is the primary socialising agent, and even though external factors become increasingly important as the child matures, the family remains the cornerstone for social and emotional development. In the Australian context, schools reflect the **prevailing social norms** of society. It can be argued that most families expect their children to behave within these social norms, requiring children and young people to follow school rules and show respect for their educators.

Children and young people will demonstrate behaviours that range from delightful to self-destructive. The range of behaviours that may be encountered in the classroom will be as broad and varied as the characterisitics of the students themselves. At one end of the continuum are students whose behaviour is well-regulated. These students are generally happy, cooperative and respectful. In between are a range of behaviours that may be regarded as annoying or frustrating. At the other extreme end, students can display behaviours that are violent, abusive, bullying and threatening. There will also be students who engage in self-destructive behaviours due to depression or other forms of mental illness.

School communities also reflect the social context of the broader community in which some members of society engage in challenging behaviours. Education Victoria (2020) describes challenging behaviours in the school context as behaviour that 'either interferes with the safety or learning of the student or other students, or interferes with the safety of school staff'. Examples of challenging behaviour include:

- Withdrawn behaviours such as shyness, rocking, staring, anxiety, school phobia, truancy, social isolation or hand flapping.
- Disruptive behaviours such as being out-of-seat, calling out in class, tantrums, swearing, screaming or refusing to follow instructions.

- Violent and/or unsafe behaviours such as head banging, kicking, biting, punching, fighting, running away, smashing equipment or furniture/fixtures.
- Inappropriate social behaviours such as inappropriate conversations, stealing, being over-affectionate, inappropriate touching or masturbation.

Source: Education Victoria (2020). Behaviour – Students. https://www2.education.vic.gov.au/pal/behaviour-students/guidance/3-challenging-behaviour-influences-and-triggers

Education Victoria identifies factors that may contribute to challenging behaviours. These include:

- biophysical factors – medical conditions and disability
- psychological factors – emotional trauma, lack of social skills
- behavioural/social factors – including where a student's problem behaviour has been learned through reinforcement, consequences or adaptation to social practices
- historical community factors – family members have experienced past difficulties/trauma in school system
- cultural factors – cultural differences in values and beliefs
- student group dynamics – bullying, cliques that exclude others
- environmental factors – quality of physical facilities
- classroom organisation issues – inconsistent routines, non-inclusive
- teacher behaviour – poor classroom management skills, disorganised.

Source: Education Victoria (2020). Behaviour – Students. https://www2.education.vic.gov.au/pal/behaviour-students/guidance/3-challenging-behaviour-influences-and-triggers

Our perception of what is or is not a behaviour that challenges occurs on a continuum and will depend on the situation in which the behaviour occurs. For example, it may be appropriate for students to talk, walk around and share ideas if they are working on a collaborative project. However, the same behaviour may be considered unacceptable if the expectation is that students should sit quietly and work independently.

Our perception of behaviours that challenge will also depend on the skills, knowledge and experience of those working with the student – ESWs who are highly skilled in managing behaviour may have a different perspective on what is a challenging behaviour compared with less-skilled or novice ESWs. Our definition of behaviours that challenge will also be influenced by cultural values and beliefs about what might be considered acceptable/unacceptable.

The abilities, age and skills of each student will also influence our perceptions – for example, a student with ADHD is likely to have many more challenging behaviours than a student without ADHD. The next section explores some challenging behaviours you may encounter in the school environment, and provides suggestions for responding to or supporting these behaviours.

Withdrawn, over-cautious or timid behaviour

Some students are reluctant to attempt new tasks because of fear of failure or lack of confidence. They may avoid participating in group work and worry about making mistakes. These students may need support to form friendships, develop confidence and promote self-esteem. Provide positive reinforcement by breaking tasks down into small steps to promote confidence; pair the student with a more confident buddy; work with students to identify strengths; and acknowledge that making 'mistakes' is simply part of the learning process.

SCENARIO

ANXIOUS

Udo (12 years) is an average student but lacks confidence in her abilities. She becomes extremely anxious when faced with a new task to a point where she becomes unable to perform. As soon as the teacher asks the class to work on a new task, Udo panics: *'I don't know what to do. Can you help me? I forgot what we have to do.'*

Udo gets herself so worked up that at times she becomes physically ill. The teacher provides Udo with notes for each new task and the ESW works with Udo to create step-by-step instructions. The ESW also reminds Udo of her existing skills and knowledge and how these can be applied to the new task. This strategy has helped Udo to be less anxious.

WHAT DOES THIS TELL US?

Anxiety can reduce student participation and limit the student's ability to reach their full potential. Working with the student to develop strategies to cope with anxiety is an effective way to build the student's self-confidence.

Attention-seeking and disruptive behaviour

The term **attention-seeking behaviour** is often used to describe a wide range of behaviours, such as repeatedly calling out, talking over others and out-of-seat behaviour. The term 'attention-seeking' is not a helpful one, as it usually implies *nuisance* behaviours when, in fact, this type of behaviour indicates the student has an unmet need. The first goal should be to identify that unmet need rather than simply focusing on eliminating the behaviour. Putting in place consequences for attention seeking may only serve to reinforce the attention-seeking behaviour. Identifying and responding to the student's need for attention is more likely to change the behaviour than applying negative consequences for the behaviour. For example, praising and acknowledging on-task behaviour is more likely to result in a reduction in attention-seeking behaviour than applying negative consequences. Other strategies include ensuring that the tasks the student is being asked to complete match the skills and ability level of the student and engaging the student in collaborative goal-setting for the completion of tasks, which signals that the student is valued and trusted.

Lack of confidence – complains work is too hard

Students may lack confidence, or have planning and/or processing difficulties – difficulty understanding the directions given by the teacher, difficulty sequencing or knowing where to start or simply finding the task too difficult. In these circumstances, it will be necessary to assess the abilities and strengths of each student to more closely match the tasks to their abilities and learning style – for example, breaking tasks down step by step and using a graphic organiser to support sequencing of tasks into manageable chunks.

SCENARIO

ASSESSING LEARNING NEEDS

Linh (5 years, 6 months) is not coping with Kindergarten. The teacher has noticed that Linh is often disorganised and never seems to be quite 'with it'. Linh looks to other students to see what she is supposed to be doing and even then she struggles to complete (or even commence) a task.

Linh's teacher arranges a formal assessment where it is revealed that she has extensive auditory processing difficulties. Linh is now supported in class by an ESW following an IEP developed by the class teacher and the special education resource teacher.

WHAT DOES THIS TELL US?

While it was clear that Linh was not coping, the underlying cause was not clear. Referring Linh for an assessment identified her learning needs and allowed the teacher to put in place an individual plan to support Linh's learning needs.

Persistent teasing, tormenting or annoying others

Often students who display this kind of behaviour lack confidence, have poor self-esteem and have not developed the skills needed to develop and sustain friendships. This behaviour can be addressed by working with the student to name and describe these inappropriate behaviours and devise alternative behaviours for the student to attempt. For example, instead of saying something negative, thinking of something positive to say.

CHANGING BEHAVIOURS

SCENARIO

Reggie (10 years) is regarded as annoying by teachers and students. He always seems to be tormenting others, making negative comments and generally being unpleasant. His teacher, **Mr Humphries**, has observed that Reggie does not have the social skills necessary to interact effectively with others.

Reggie is not a team player, and he blames others if he doesn't succeed. He tells tales, laughs when others make mistakes and rarely praises others. As a result, Reggie has no close friends and most of the time he is excluded or simply tolerated by his peers.

Mr Humphries has started to work with Reggie on the development of prosocial skills. The goal is to help Reggie develop the skills needed to form positive relationships with others. Each week, Mr Humphries and Reggie set a behaviour goal. This week Reggie is required to make one positive comment to another student each day.

Together, Reggie and Mr Humphries review his progress. Next week, Reggie will be required to notice and make a list of the positive behaviours of others. Reggie is making slow but consistent progress.

WHAT DOES THIS TELL US?

It should not be assumed that all students know how to develop and sustain friendships. Children and young people who lack the skills to relate positively to others often become isolated and engage in various acting-out behaviours. To change these behaviours, it is necessary to use direct instruction that provides students with the opportunity to practise and reflect on their behaviour with a supportive mentor.

Regular outbursts of anger

This behaviour may include yelling out, swearing, verbal abuse, name-calling, whining, nagging and sulking. It indicates low self-esteem and a lack of confidence. The student may be feeling frustrated at not being able to keep up with classmates and they may be unable to express their feelings in a socially acceptable manner. Stop for a moment and think about what it might be like to go to school each day knowing that the work is too hard, you can't understand the instructions and you don't have the skills needed to ask for help – this would be enough to make anyone angry and unhappy!

There is no point attempting to reason with a student who is angry. It is important to pick your battles and let some behaviour go unchallenged, however annoying or frustrating that may be. Where possible, create a space where the student can withdraw, calm down, regroup and later rejoin the class. Later, when the situation has calmed down, talk to the student to try to identify the cause of the anger, what you can do to reduce or eliminate this cause and how you can help the student to express their emotions in a more acceptable manner. (This strategy will depend on the ability of the student as well as the student's age.)

SCENARIO

CHILLOUT ZONE

Shah (15 years) has Asperger's syndrome. He attends the local high school, which also has a special education unit attached. Shah copes quite well at school as long as he is able to maintain his daily routines and rituals.

He has committed his weekly timetable to memory and knows the exact time when each bell should ring throughout the day. If any bell is late, he will announce this to anyone who might be listening: *'It's 12.02 Australian Eastern Daylight Saving Time, the bell should ring at 12. Two minutes late, two minutes late. That's not good.'*

Shah does not like any form of physical contact and if he is accidentally touched or pushed he can go into meltdown. To manage this, Shah is allowed to leave the room five minutes before the bell so he can move to the next room before the corridors become crowded.

Today, however, he encounters a Year 7 class returning to their room after doing some maths problems outdoors. Shah becomes extremely distressed when the students bump him as they are going upstairs. He sits on the stairs and curls himself into a ball with his hands over his head, screaming and rocking. The bell has now gone, and other students start moving onto the stairs, making the situation worse for Shah.

Shah eventually calms down enough to accompany a teacher to the 'chillout zone' – a private area in the library that has been set up to allow Shah and other students to sit quietly. The area has been set up with a beanbag, armchair, cushions and a variety of sensory objects, such as squeezy balls, oil and water wheels, fidget pads, sensory putty, spinning tops and wooden massagers. Shah immediately takes a squeezy ball in each hand and sits on the beanbag.

WHAT DOES THIS TELL US?

Students who are easily angered or rapidly become distressed lack the self-regulation necessary to manage their own behaviour, and therefore need guidance and support from caring adults. Having a chillout zone where students can be alone, calm down and regroup gives them a sense of control. It also allows students to take ownership of their own behaviour and conveys respect for the student's need for quiet time away from others.

Students with complex behaviour support needs

Videos: Challenging behaviours

Students with disability may present with a range of issues that directly influence behaviour. For example, students with sensory issues, limited expressive and receptive language, poor social skills, poor self-regulation, cognitive processing issues, childhood trauma or exposure to domestic violence may engage in a range of behaviours that are challenging. These behaviours may be triggered by sensory overload, changes in routine, unfamiliar people, hunger, fear, excitement or frustration. These behaviours are often referred to as dysregulated behaviour – that is, the inability to self-regulate emotional responses. Behaviours of concern may include stimming, making loud noises, intense angry outbursts, screaming, tantrums, verbal or physical abuse, self-harm or running away as an emotional response to external triggers.

As previously explored, positive behaviour support (PBS) is a strategy that focuses on increasing positive behaviours and adjusting the environment to reduce negative behaviour triggers. For students with complex behaviour support needs, proactively identifying potential triggers is an important intervention strategy. Environmental triggers can include noise, clutter, flickering lights, the hum of fluorescent lighting, bright light, sudden loud noises, smells, crowding or close proximity of others, changes in routine, changes in seating arrangement, wall displays and certain textures.

Video: How ADHD causes emotional dysregulation

Figure 18.30 describes the behaviours associated with extreme sensory sensitivities, most commonly seen in some students with ASD.

Figure 18.30 Behaviours commonly seen in some students with ASD

Hyper-sensitivity (unable to filter sensory stimuli) – extreme over-reaction. This may include students who are: > **Sensory avoidant:** over-responsive to sensory input and responds by avoiding it or escaping from it > **Sensory defensive:** over-responsive to sensory input and responds in a negative way in an attempt to reduce the sensory input and to protect himself from the sensory input > **Tactile defensive:** cannot tolerate specific touch input e.g. people standing too close, the feeling of some materials in messy play and art or the texture of some food > **Auditory defensive:** cannot tolerate specific noises – e.g. school bell, musical instruments or hand dryer	
Behaviour examples	
> Defensiveness – e.g. pushing someone who is standing too close > Avoidance – e.g. running out of the classroom, hiding in a corner of the playground > Easily upset, anxious, distractable > Attempts to 'shut down' and block out all input > Sensory avoidant behaviour – leaving the room	> Avoids close physical proximity to others > Flapping hands or flicking fingers in front of eyes > Pacing up and down room > Rocking in chair > Tapping pencil on desk > May engage in disruptive behaviours in order to get removed from the situation which is causing sensory overload and distress
Hypo-sensitivity – extreme under-reaction. This may include students who are: **sensory under-responsive** – i.e. not registering and responding to the sensory input around them	
Behaviour examples	
> Disengaged and uninterested in activities, especially more passive activities such as sitting at a desk to listen/read/write > Appears lethargic > Slow processing of information, difficulty completing work	> Delayed or no response to questions and instructions > Becomes more alert and engaged in more active tasks and multisensory activities – e.g. PE, playground, art, music
Sensory seeking – unusual interest in aspects of the sensory environment. This includes students who crave increased sensory stimulation – e.g. movement input, noise, tactile input	
Behaviour examples	
> Frequently stands or moves around the classroom instead of sitting > Swings in chair > Enjoys fast movement > Frequently fidgets > Likes to hold a fidget object > Sniffs objects and people	> Makes noise in quiet environments – e.g. assembly, independent work time, exam hall > Enjoys 'rough and tumble' play > Repeating a favourite noise, song or script from a film > Focusing intently on a preferred object – e.g. spinning coin, light switch > Frequently touching objects and people

Source: Middletown Centre for Autism (2023). Examples of atypical responses to sensory stimuli. https://sensory-processing.middletownautism.com/background/examples-of-atypical-responses-to-sensory-stimuli/

Responding to confrontation and violence

Classroom adaptations and sensory strategies

Anger, confrontation and violence are an extreme reaction to underlying emotional stress. Gallagher, Coleman and Kirk (2023, pp. 259, 273) state that a 'dynamic system' that includes 'a combination of academic problems, attention difficulties, coercive family relations, and poor parental monitoring can contribute to aggressive student behaviour'. Anger can be a response to frustration, hurt feelings, feeling disrespected, afraid, disappointed, isolated, humiliated or helpless. Children and young people with poor impulse control, poor social skills and/or a lack of appropriate emotional role models role may express anger in the form of violence and extreme confrontational behaviour.

CONSIDER THIS

REPORTS OF VIOLENCE

A publication by the Australian Institute for Teaching and School Leadership (AITSL, 2020), 'National strategy to address the abuse of teachers, school leaders and other school staff', stated that:

- 80% of surveyed teachers had experienced bullying and harassment in the preceding 9–12-month period;
- over half (55.6%) of those surveyed reported unacceptable behaviour coming from both students and parents;
- 84% of school leaders surveyed reported being subjected to some form of offensive behaviours by parents or students in the last year; of the school leaders who reported abuse, 36.8% reported experiencing threats of violence exclusively from students, and 24.5% from parents;
- 12% of Australian principals report at least weekly intimidation of their staff.

Source: Australian Institute for Teaching and School Leadership (AITSL) (2020). National strategy to address the abuse of teachers, school leaders and other school staff. December. https://www.aitsl.edu.au/docs/default-source/abuse-strategy/national-strategy-to-address-the-abuse-of-teachers-school-leaders-and-other-school-staff.pdf?sfvrsn=6bb0d93c_2, pp. 7, 10 11.

WHAT DOES THIS TELL US?

Violence and intimidation of teachers, school leaders and other school staff is perpetrated not only by students but also by parents. This reinforces the view of Gallagher, Coleman and Kirk (2023) that student violence is partly a product of the broader social system. Students whose experience of personal and social problems within the family unit being solved via violence are likely to resort to violence as a means to address problems in the school setting. In this context, violence in schools is much more difficult to address and manage.

Dahlberg and Krug (2002, cited in Queensland Schools Alliance Against Violence [QSAAV], 2010, p. 5) define 'interpersonal violence' as:

> The intentional use of physical force or power, threatened or actual, against another person or against a group or community that results in or has a high likelihood of resulting in injury, death, psychological harm, maldevelopment or deprivation.

According to QSAAV, this definition links 'intention' to committing the act, regardless of the outcome. The definition also includes all acts of violence, whether public or private, reactive or proactive, criminal or non-criminal. QSAAV also states that there may be a considerable disparity between intended behaviour and intended consequences. For example, if a six-year-old with poor self-regulation physically lashed out at another student, would this be considered intentional? If a 15-year-old student punched a hole in the wall out of sheer frustration, would that be seen as intentional? If a 10-year-old with ADHD upended his desk and accidentally injured another student, would that be considered intentional?

Videos: Conduct disorder and ODD

When students become extremely angry, they can be confrontational and may resort to acts of physical or verbal aggression. As an ESW, try to remain calm but assertive, and try not to escalate the student's behaviour. Maintain eye contact with the student, use the student's name and talk in a calm manner. Don't argue with the student – simply listen. If the student becomes aggressive, tell them in a firm voice to lower their arms or step back.

If there are other students in the immediate area, direct them to move away quickly and quietly. Seek help as quickly as possible. To protect yourself, you may need to back away (do not turn your back on the student). If possible, place a barrier between yourself and the student – for example, stand behind a desk.

If a fight occurs between students, you should not attempt to physically intervene. Again, move other students away from the immediate area and call for help.

Gantz (2009, pp. 128–34) has developed a model to describe stages of misbehaviour and related stages of discipline (as seen in **Figure 18.31**). The Gantz model suggests that behaviours such as aggression, immorality and defiance would fall into what could be considered *challenging behaviours*. Gantz describes the use of preventative, supportive and corrective discipline to address behaviours but also acknowledges the need to consider both the external factors that may contribute to *misbehaviour* as well as assessing the *needs* of each student.

Figure 18.31 Five levels of misbehaviour and three stages of discipline

FIVE LEVELS OF MISBEHAVIOUR	**Aggression**	The most severe form of misbehaviour, including physical or verbal attacks by students
	Immorality	Acts such as cheating, lying and stealing
	Defiance of authority	Refusal to follow directions and rules
	Class disruption	Calling out, getting out of seat, general fooling around
	Goofing off	For example, daydreaming, failure to attend/participate and non-completion of tasks
THREE STAGES OF DISCIPLINE	**1 Preventative discipline** This refers to the steps that can be taken to preclude misbehaviour occurring in the first place	• Ensuring that the tasks developed match the ability and interests of the student • Arranging the physical environment to take into account student needs, minimise distractions and create a pleasant working environment • Developing age/ability-appropriate rules that are stated in positive rather than negative terms • Using positive reinforcement – both verbal ('You have done an excellent job on the maths tasks, Liam') and non-verbal (smile, thumbs up or handshake) • Use of graphic reinforcements, such as star charts and smiley faces • Use of tangible reinforcers – for example, a token system that can be traded for a special reward such as extra time on the computer
	2 Supportive discipline This refers to the steps that can be taken at the first sign of misbehaviour	• Responding immediately with a warning or reminder: 'Lucy, remember you need to ask permission to be out of your seat. Please sit down.' • Using non-verbal communication, such as a frown, stare or gesture • Using physical proximity – walk nonchalantly to the student and stand close
	3 Corrective discipline This refers to steps taken to restore order once misbehaviour occurs	• Invoking consequence of misbehaviour: 'Lucy I have already reminded you not to leave your seat without permission. This afternoon you will miss out on free activity time.' • Contracting by meeting with the student after the incident has occurred and developing a mutually agreed contract – the contract should include the target behaviour, consequences of non-compliance, reward for compliance and a timeframe • Using time out – the student is removed from the situation and relocated to a designated area. The goal of time out should be to allow the student to calm down, think about their behaviour and prepare to start over. Remember that the goal is to work towards self-regulation rather than punitive action that embarrasses or humiliates a child.

Source: Based on Gantz (2009, pp. 128–34).

Prevention of violence

A key preventative measure is recognising warning signs and triggers that may lead to violent outbursts. According to the Association of Teachers and Lecturers (ATL, 2011, p. 9), factors that may indicate signs of violent or dangerous student behaviour include:

- a previous history of violence, possibly under the influence of alcohol, drugs or solvents
- tense or agitated appearance; dilated pupils; exhibiting an over-sensitive reaction to correction or instruction; giving abrupt replies to questions, often with gesticulations; exhibiting increased voice pitch and volume; showing signs of muscular tension in the face and limbs
- unnaturally quiet and withdrawn or alternatively excitable and boisterous restless behaviour involving pushing, noisiness or jostling
- being threatening or verbally abusive – deliberately provocative behaviour such as name-calling and attention-seeking.

Student violence can be frightening for everyone involved – including the student who is violent. Responding to student violence is the responsibility of the principal, teacher, school counsellors and parents/guardians. However, as an ESW, you may experience or witness student violence.

18.10 Classroom behaviour-management strategies

Teachers in schools will develop a range of strategies to guide and manage the behaviours of students in their class. These strategies will reflect the whole-of-school behaviour plan.

Managing behaviour is a skill that develops over time. Everyone who works with children and young people will be challenged at some point by inappropriate and challenging student behaviours. There is no single best solution and no single best response. A good way to develop your behaviour-management skills is to observe the classroom teacher and continually reflect on your own practices.

Problem-solving, negotiation and conflict resolution

In school settings, problem-solving and negotiation occur throughout the day as educators and students engage in interactions, and accommodate changes or adjustments to the planned activities and the daily routine. Students will engage in negotiation and problem-solving as they work together, and share resources and learning spaces.

Learning to negotiate when there are differing opinions about how to resolve a problem provides an opportunity to learn from others as they share different ways of thinking. Teachers and ESWs support students to develop negotiation and problem-solving skills when they demonstrate active listening, encourage exploration of the perspective of others, and work towards a solution that has the consensus of all those involved. Consistently implementing a series of steps when negotiating and problem-solving is a way of ensuring fairness and inclusion. These steps are shown in **Figure 18.32**.

Figure 18.32 Negotiation and problem-solving with students

IDENTIFY OR CLARIFY THE PROBLEM OR ISSUE	**Identify or clarify the problem or issue** **1** Encourage the student to be specific by asking open-ended questions. For example, 'You say you hate maths because it's too hard. Give me an example of something you find hard to do. What part of this is hard for you?' Probing questions can assist students to reflect on the problem, break it down and identify the problem more clearly.
	2 Identify why it's a problem. Again, ask open-ended questions. For example, 'Is it a problem because … you don't understand the question/don't know where to start/don't know how to apply the formula/feel rushed?'
	3 Identify how the problem impacts on the student/others. For example, 'How do you feel when …? 'What happens if you don't finish the task?'
	4 Identify and understand the desired outcomes. This last part is determined by answers to 1, 2 and 3.
	When asking open-ended questions always seek to clarify what the student means: 'Are you saying …?', 'Do you mean …?', 'I hear you saying you are worried about …' It's also important to take notice of the student's non-verbal communication: 'You say you're happy to … but I can see by your expression that you're still concerned.'
CONSIDER ALL OPTIONS	• Brain-storm ideas/solutions: 'What can we do together to work on/resolve this problem?', 'What can you do?', 'What can I do to help/support you?' • Work cooperatively to reach a mutually agreed outcome. This may not immediately resolve the problem; however, by putting strategies in place the student can work towards a resolution. • Implement the agreed solution and decide how and when the solution will be reviewed.

Supporting conflict resolution

Conflict between students or between students and the educator may occur for a variety of reasons, including misunderstanding, tension, poor communication, lack of respect, adaptability to change, differences in values and beliefs, resistance to change, inability to be flexible, and differences in levels of motivation, enthusiasm, and personal and professional goals. Conflict may occur between work colleagues, between educators and parents, between educators and students, and among students.

The goal of **conflict resolution** should not be about power (being right, having a better idea, exerting seniority or authority); rather, it should be about finding a solution that best fits the goals of the school, the needs of the individuals involved and the best interests of the school community. This can be challenging as the very nature of conflict means that stakeholders have different responsibilities, interests, motivations and needs.

It is important to recognise that in school settings there is an embedded imbalance of power between educators, students and, to an extent, parents. Where conflict resolution involves students and educators, there should be mutual respect and a willingness to be open-minded, objective and empathic. Conflict resolution requires participants to actively listen to and consider the perspectives of others. However, it is also important to recognise that students may not yet have these skills and may find it difficult to listen to and consider the perspectives of others. This is particularly the case during adolescence, when the brain is undergoing major refinement of areas such as impulse control and emotional self-regulation.

Conflict resolution is an opportunity for learning – the goal is not winning, but rather it is about reaching a consensus that all parties agree to accept. Typically, this requires the ability to compromise (a give-and-take attitude).

When conflict occurs, having in place consistently applied, clear strategies to resolve conflict allows educators to role-model skills such as listening, respect, negotiating, fairness and empathy. These skills support self-regulation and create an opportunity for students to develop the life skills needed as they grow and mature.

Conflict resolution skills and games

Engaging in conflict resolution with students is also an opportunity to build positive relationships. It communicates a message of concern and respect for the rights and wellbeing of every student. It is also important to keep in mind that, for some students, learning how to respectfully negotiate conflict is a skill they may not have been exposed to – particularly in situations where students experience, for example, family violence or adult mental illness.

Figure 18.33 shows the elements of conflict resolution.

Figure 18.33 Elements of conflict resolution

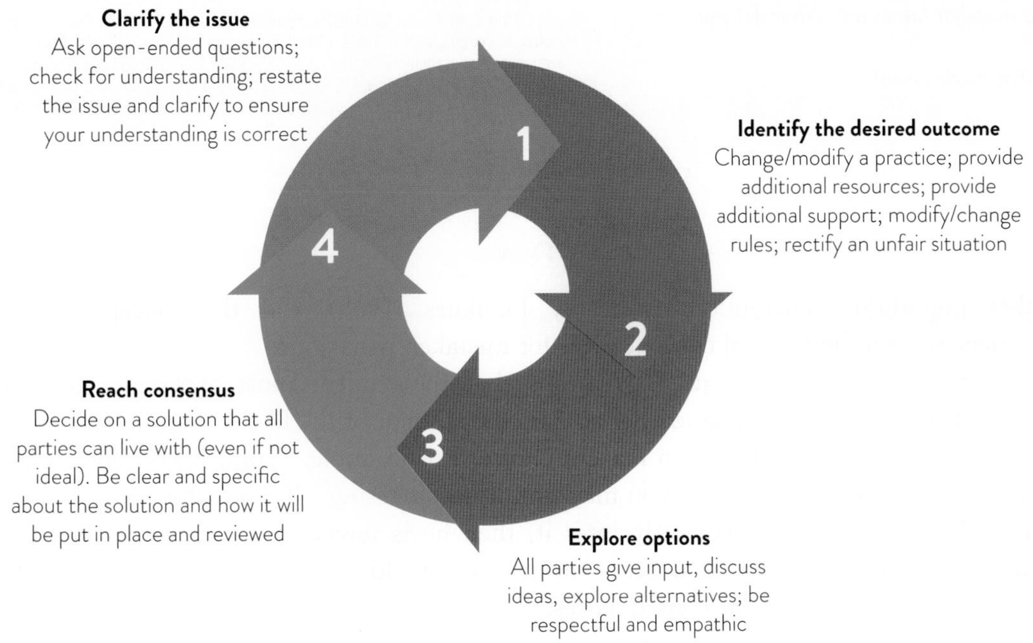

Clarify the issue
Ask open-ended questions; check for understanding; restate the issue and clarify to ensure your understanding is correct
1
Identify the desired outcome
Change/modify a practice; provide additional resources; provide additional support; modify/change rules; rectify an unfair situation
2
Explore options
All parties give input, discuss ideas, explore alternatives; be respectful and empathic
3
Reach consensus
Decide on a solution that all parties can live with (even if not ideal). Be clear and specific about the solution and how it will be put in place and reviewed
4

The 4 WHATS

In his work with children and young people with ADHD, Michael Manos (2019, in Keath, 2021) has developed a technique that he calls 'The 4 WHATS'. The focus of this technique is self-reflection. Asking the student to describe their behaviour makes it more difficult for them to blame others and helps them to take ownership of their actions as a strategy to develop self-awareness. The technique involves asking the student four questions:

1 What did you do? Identifies the behaviour of concern.
2 What happened when you did that? Identifies the immediate consequences of the behaviour in relation to the environment and/or others.
3 What could you have done instead? Focuses on alternative actions.
4 What would have happened if you'd done that? Asks the student to think of an alternative.

Manos argues that this technique can be helpful for students who find it difficult to recognise cause and effect. Manos refers to this 'helping children join the dots' between their behaviour and the consequences of their behaviour. Manos points out that this technique may take time to work as many children will immediately blame others rather than talk about their own actions.

SCENARIO

THE 4 WHATS

Mitch (14 years) has ADHD. As the class was walking to the library, Mitch punched **Imran** in the back of the neck, bringing them both to the attention of the teacher, who tells Mitch to walk with him. When they arrive at the library, the teacher takes Mitch aside.

Teacher: *'Mitch what did you do to Imran?'*

Mitch: *'He kept stopping so I'd run into him. He was doing it on purpose.'*

Teacher: *'OK, but what did you do?'*

Mitch: *'He's always tormenting me. He's a jerk!'*

Teacher: *'You've told me what Imran did. What did you do Mitch?'*

Mitch: *'I gave him what he deserved!'*

Teacher: *'What did you do Mitch?'*

Mitch: *'I punched his neck.'*

WHAT DOES THIS TELL US?

In this Scenario, the teacher needed to ask Mitch four times what he did before getting the desired response. Using the '4 WHATS' can be a slow process. It takes patience and persistence. It's important to remain calm and remember the end goal – getting the student to verbalise and take ownership of their actions.

Sources: Manos, M. Center for Pediatric Behavioral Health at Cleveland Clinic Children's Hospital, in Keath, L. (2021). The 4 'whats' of negative behavior. Teaching children self-awareness and accountability. The Carolina Institute for Developmental Disabilities at the University of North Carolina. https://www.verywellmind.com/teaching-children-with-the-4-whats-20733

Using behavioural consequences

Another important contribution, made by Dreikurs (1968), was the concept of natural consequences, including logical consequences for mistaken behaviour.

The use of **natural consequences** means that the student must experience the natural outcome of their behaviour. The teacher advises the student of the likely natural consequence of the action but allows the student to make a choice. For example, 'Tom, if you don't put your phone in your locker during sport, you may find it goes missing.' If Tom chooses not to put his phone in his locker and subsequently loses it, then he is forced to take responsibility for his actions. Tom will be angry and upset – the teacher would remind Tom that he had made a choice and now must accept the consequences.

Natural consequences help students take responsibility for their own actions and can be used to help them think through their actions and anticipate possible outcomes. The application of natural consequences can be challenging for adults who must resist 'rescuing' the child or young person from their own actions and allow them to experience natural consequences.

Logical consequences are similar to natural consequences but include adult intervention in applying the consequence. Logical consequences focus on the student's behaviour and should be applied consistently each time the behaviour occurs. Logical consequences work well during middle childhood because students are able to understand cause and effect: *if you do A, then B will happen.* For example, 'If you don't hand in your homework you will be given extra work to complete over the weekend.' Logical consequences help students to develop self-discipline and to think about the effects of their behaviour on themselves and others.

Dreikurs also emphasised the role of encouragement rather than praise. Duchesne and colleagues (2019, p. 658) state that, 'Encouragement focuses on effort rather than achievement and removes a value-based judgment about a student. In contrast praise often arises after the child has completed a task and makes a direct link to the value of the person because they acted in a praiseworthy way.' For example, when praising, an adult might say, 'Good girl, Yannie', while when using encouragement the adult might say, 'I liked the way you kept trying, Yannie, you've made great progress with your handwriting.' In this example, the adult encourages Yannie's persistence at the writing task rather than simply praising the end-product.

Dreikurs believed that punishment was not an appropriate response to mistaken behaviour. He advocated that the adult be proactive in providing an environment that encouraged children and young people to be cooperative and successful. The role of the adult should be to anticipate behaviour and provide opportunities for students to correct their behaviour. Examples of natural and logical consequences are provided in the following Scenario.

SCENARIO

NATURAL AND LOGICAL CONSEQUENCES

EXAMPLES OF NATURAL CONSEQUENCES

Mirra (10 years) tends to become loud and bossy when working in a small group. As a natural consequence, the students in her group respond by excluding her from their discussion. Mirra feels upset and angry that she has been excluded.

Harley (6 years) has brought along his special animal figures to show the class. The teacher suggests that Harley put the figures in his bag before going to lunch because they might get lost when he is playing. Harley ignores this advice and is now crying because three figures are missing. Harley feels upset that his animal figures are missing.

EXAMPLES OF LOGICAL CONSEQUENCES

Julia (15 years) repeatedly fails to complete her English projects. As a logical consequence, she fails her mid-year assessment. Julia is worried about how her parents will respond to her mid-year report.

Ussef (10 years) always acts out during assembly. He talks loudly, pokes and pushes other students and generally makes a nuisance of himself. As a logical consequence, Ussef must sit next to his teacher, away from the other students in his class. Ussef feels embarrassed that he is not able to sit with his class.

▶ DISCUSSION

Discuss the use of natural and logical consequences – do they both have a place in school behaviour-management strategies?

Things to consider when using natural and logical consequences:

- There should be a clear cause-and-effect relationship.
- Logical consequences should be applied in a timely manner: *'You ignored the timer and continued playing on the computer. The consequences are that you won't be able to play computer games for one week.'*
- Consequences should be firm but not punitive or threatening: *'I asked you to put your monster figure in your bag until recess. Now I will look after it and give it back to you at lunchtime.'*
- Consequences should directly reflect the behaviour: *'You took Ella's calculator without first asking permission and now it is broken. You need to work out how you are going to replace it.'*
- Where appropriate, students can be given a choice: *'You can either put your monster figure in your bag until recess or give it to me to mind.'*
- Consequences should be reasonable – that is, the consequence should be proportionate to the behaviour. Remember that the goal is to assist the student to change or modify their behaviour.

Bailey (2021) states consequences should be a tool for teaching children to 'examine their behaviour, reflect on the impact of their choices and make changes until they reach their highest goals'.

Using behavioural consequences as a teaching tool can help students to build their self-regulation skills and begin to take responsibility for their own behaviour. Consequences help students to make a link between their own actions and the outcomes of those actions. It also assists students to reflect on past experiences in order to modify their own behaviour. For students with additional needs, such as ASD or ADHD, making the relationship between action and consequences (cause and effect) explicit is essential. Bailey reminds us that consequences act as positive or negative motivators.

Using appropriate behaviour consequences will, over time, assist the students to modify their behaviour and develop the skills required to make positive behaviour choices. It is important to be aware that the specific behaviour consequences should be individualised to reflect the needs and abilities of each student. An essential consideration is the student's ability to manage their own behaviour – for example, a student with ADHD will have less control over their own behaviour than a student who does not have ADHD.

Managing big emotions

There will be occasions when students aren't able to control their emotions and may become angry, despondent and/or upset. Remember, children and young people are still developing self-regulation skills. Remain calm, allow time for the student to settle, ask how they are feeling: 'I can see you're angry/upset/anxious. How about we do some deep breathing together/do you want to take a break and get a drink of water; what would you like to happen now?'

Avoid getting into a power struggle with the student: 'I'm sorry you feel that way. I am here to support you. I want to work with you.' Avoid also blaming or telling the student what to do. For example, 'You should apologise. You need to take responsibility for your behaviour. You always seem to be in trouble.' These statements can inflame an already angry or upset student. Ask the student what they could do or what others could do to help reach a positive outcome: 'When Liam torments you what could you do instead of retaliating?'

Behaviour-management strategies to avoid

The role of educators is to support students to develop socially acceptable behaviour and age/ability-appropriate self-regulation. This will naturally develop for most students, as they mature and are guided by social interactions with family, friends, school and the broader community. Some students, however, will struggle to self-regulate without direct instruction.

Adults who are responsible for the care and wellbeing of students should always treat every student with dignity and respect. This can sometimes be difficult when a student behaves in ways that challenge our fundamental beliefs and confront our personal values. However, the role of adults is not to judge but to manage students and guide them to develop behaviours that will allow them to be accepted members of the school community and to reach their full potential.

Often students will act out because they feel powerless. It may not seem this way when a student is being physically or verbally abusive, but the reality is that these students are usually extremely vulnerable and have unmet emotional needs. Being out of control is not a pleasant state, and rarely leads to a person feeling better about themselves. In fact, students and young people can become frightened by their own anger and lack of self-control.

The goal of behaviour management is to provide students with a consistently safe environment where the focus is learning the skills of self-regulation. With this in mind, there are some behaviour-management practices that are at best unhelpful and at worst quite damaging. For example:

- Never use any form of physical punishment. When managing behaviour, avoid any form of physical contact with students. Even putting your hand on a student's shoulder as a gesture of comfort can be misconstrued.
- Never use sarcasm or humiliate a student, especially in front of their peers. This type of behaviour is unethical and disrespectful – it's simply an assertion of power and has no place in a school environment.
- Avoid threatening body language such as pointing, rolling your eyes, gesturing, standing over the student and folding your arms, or invading the student's personal space. Covert eye contact can, however, be a very useful strategy. For example, making eye contact with the student and giving a subtle shake of the head or a reinforcing nod can be a very valuable management strategy.
- Never turn your back on a student who is talking to you. This is simply common courtesy, which should be afforded to every student. If you have to quickly attend to a situation, always excuse yourself (as you would if speaking to another adult): 'Excuse me please, Harry. I will just be a few moments.' When returning: 'Sorry Harry, please continue. I'm really interested in what you have to say.'
- Never deliberately put a student in a situation where you know they will fail. Again, this is simply asserting power over the student and may result in a student feeling embarrassed, ashamed or angry. For example, never ask a student who is a struggling reader to read aloud to others.
- Never label a student as a liar, cheat, thief, stupid, slow or incompetent. Labels tend to stick. It is not your role to judge students. It is your role to support students.
- Never immediately demand that the student explain their behaviour. First, try to make the situation safe for the student, other students and yourself. Leave the discussion until after the student has calmed down and you can talk to the student in private.
- Never openly compare a student with others. Comparisons serve no purpose. Students are very astute at knowing where they rank in the class. Comparisons should only be made privately about the student's own progress: 'Elise, you got 18 out of 20 for your spelling. That's such a big improvement. You should be very proud!'
- Never engage in an argument with a student – adults rarely win! It is better to walk away when a student begins to argue. Talk about the issue at a later time.
- Never make negative comments about the student's family/culture. Again, this is simply showing the student courtesy and respect.
- Avoid dwelling on past behaviours. Address inappropriate behaviours as they occur and then move on. A good rule of thumb is to start each day with a clean slate. You may have had a bad day with a student the day before, but dwelling on it or carrying over those feelings will not help. It is better to greet the student with a smile and expectations of a good day. This also helps the student to move on, save face and start over – an opportunity we all deserve.

Being aware of what to avoid is just as important as knowing what to do when managing behaviour. Remember, all behaviour is learned – students learn behaviour by observing and copying from others, and this includes inappropriate or undesirable behaviour.

Summary

Managing behaviour is a skill that develops over time. There is no single best solution and no single best response. Everyone who works with children and young people will be confronted with behaviours that challenge their skills, their values and their ability to remain calm and respectful. The most important thing to remember is that every adult working with children and young people has the opportunity to build positive and respectful relationships that lay the foundation for supporting them to develop skills for self-regulation and resilience appropriate to the age, abilities and family circumstances of each student.

Teachers in schools use a range of strategies to guide and manage the behaviours of students. These strategies adhere to legislative obligations, policies and practice. They are also guided by whole-of-school behaviour plans that reflect various wellbeing and behaviour frameworks and initiatives.

Understanding the many factors that influence behaviour allows educators to respond in ways that support children and young people to develop the social and emotional skills necessary to make positive behaviour choices. Individual Behaviour Support Plans recognise that many students face unique challenges in managing their own behaviour and require additional support to develop age and ability appropriate behaviour skills. Like all other areas of learning and development, behaviour is best managed when the unique needs, circumstances and abilities of each student are identified and used to develop appropriate strategies to guide and manage behaviour.

Responding appropriately and respectfully to the emotional needs of children and young people as they navigate their way to becoming socially competent is an ongoing challenge (and learning journey) for all educators.

Self-check questions

1. Explain the school's duty of care to students.
2. What factors could contribute to the student managing their own behaviour?
3. Define the development of emotional literacy.
4. What is the difference between guidance/discipline and punishment?
5. What are the nine respectful notions educators should consider before deciding how to respond to unacceptable behaviour?
6. Explain Positive Behavioural Interventions and Supports (PBIS) and its three-tier framework.
7. What is the National Safe Schools Framework?
8. List the five Student Wellbeing Principles according to the Australian Student Wellbeing Framework.
9. As an ESW, how can you support students' mental health?
10. What does a 'safe' environment look like for children experiencing ACEs?
11. Explain the Applied Behaviour Analysis Model. What does ABC refer to?
12. What is an essential element of any behaviour management plan?
13. What are the benefits of conflict resolution for students. How could ESWs engage in conflict resolution?
14. What is the goal of behaviour management?
15. What is the difference between sensory avoidant and sensory defensive in students with ASD?

Discussion questions

1. Discuss eye contact as a behavioural expectation in different cultures.
2. Discuss how schools can provide a safe learning environment for students to function at their best and feel emotionally safe and secure.
3. Discuss the seven skills of conscious discipline model in **Figure 18.11**. As an ESW, give an example of a time you have used this model for supporting and guiding behaviour.
4. Discuss the five interrelated elements of PBIS in **Figure 18.13**. As an ESW, how can these elements assist you in supporting student behaviour?

Activities

1 For this task, refer to the Scenario 'Responding to behaviours of concern' on page 667. Discuss the factors that are contributing to inappropriate and/or unacceptable behaviours of each student that need to be considered in responding to these behaviours.

2 For this task, refer to the Scenario 'Respectful notions' on page 672. Explore these behaviours based on Kaweski's nine respectful notions and reflect on each student's behaviour.

3 For this task, refer to the **Figure 18.20** 'Guidelines for recording observations' on page 682. Discuss the guidelines and give examples for each aspect of focus in recording observations.

4 For this task, refer to the Gantz model in 'Responding to confrontation and violence' on page 702. Discuss the three stages of discipline to address challenging behaviours.

Chapter 19

SUPPORT STUDENTS WITH ENGLISH AS AN ADDITIONAL LANGUAGE

GO FURTHER

Go Further icons link to extra content for this chapter. Ask your instructor for the **Go Further** resource and deepen your understanding of the topic.

Online resources icons refer to useful weblinks. Ask your instructor for these **Online Resources.**

LEARNING OBJECTIVES

When you have completed this chapter, you should be able to demonstrate that, in relation to working with EAL/D learners, you can:

19.1 identify some of the issues and challenges that may affect immigrants and refugees, and describe the impact of culture shock, trauma and cultural disorientation experienced by new arrivals

19.2 identify the features of EAL/D learning progressions and EAL/D programs

19.3 identify strategies to support EAL/D students, particularly in relation to the oral language, reading and writing

19.4 identify and access a range of resources to use when working with EAL/D students

19.5 identify ways in which educators can build and support partnerships with families.

Introduction

Teaching students for whom English is an additional language/dialect (EAL/D) requires highly specialised skills and knowledge gained through targeted training. This chapter provides a brief overview of some of the features of EAL/D programs and strategies that can be used to support English language learners in school settings. Throughout this chapter, we provide video links as tools to explore concepts and examples of practice. There are also links to online resources which you may find useful. If you take up an EAL/D support role, you will find it helpful to become a member of an EAL/D support network and undertake specialist training offered either online or in your local area.

The most important role you will have when working with EAL/D is being a language role model. Engaging students in **authentic** conversations allows them to hear and practise their English in a relaxed, informal manner.

Australia is one of the most culturally diverse countries in the world. Our population is made up of people from many cultures, who together speak over 300 different languages. The Australian Government uses the phrase 'cultural and linguistic diversity' (CALD), which considers 'the person's country of birth, their ancestry, where their parents were born, what language/s they speak, and their religious affiliation' (Australian Institute of Health and Welfare [AIHW], 2022).

CONSIDER THIS

ENGLISH AS AN ADDITIONAL LANGUAGE OR DIALECT IN AUSTRALIAN SCHOOLS

The Australian Curriculum, Assessment and Reporting Authority (ACARA; n.d.) states that 'around 25 per cent of primary and secondary school students in Australia learn English as an additional language or dialect'. These may include Aboriginal and Torres Strait Islander students, permanent and temporary immigrants from non-English-speaking countries, refugees and children of adults who do not use English as their first language at home (including children of deaf adults who use Auslan as their primary language).

As of 30 June 2018, an estimated 4.7 million children aged 0–14 and 1.4 million young people 15–19 years lived in Australia.

39% of Australian children (0–14) had one or both parents born overseas (ABS, 2016).

Aboriginal and Torres Strait Islander children made up 5.9% (an estimated 278,000) of the total child population in Australia.

Source: Based on AIHW (2022), p. 1

19.1 Immigration issues and challenges

Cultural diversity in Australia

Currently, new arrivals wishing to resettle in Australia from overseas are divided into two streams: the Migration Program (which includes skilled and family migrants) and the Humanitarian Program (for refugees and humanitarian entrants).

Refugees

The meaning of a 'refugee' in the *Migration Act 1958* (the Act) is a person in Australia who is:

- outside their country of nationality or former habitual residence (their home country) and
- owing to a 'well-founded fear of persecution', is unable or unwilling to return to their home country or to seek the protection of that country

To have a well-founded fear of persecution, a person must fear serious harm because of their:

- race
- religion
- nationality
- membership of a particular social group, or
- political opinion

Serious harm includes, but is not limited to:

- a threat to the person's life or liberty
- significant physical harassment of the person
- significant physical ill treatment of the person
- significant economic hardship that threatens the person's capacity to subsist (ability to survive)
- denial of access to basic services, where the denial threatens the person's capacity to subsist (ability to survive)
- denial of capacity to earn a livelihood of any kind, where the denial threatens the person's capacity to subsist (ability to survive).

Source: Department of Home Affairs (n.d.). Refugee and Humanitarian Program. https://immi.homeaffairs.gov.au/what-we-do/refugee-and-humanitarian-program/about-the-program/seek-protection-in-australia/australia-protection-obligations

In Australia, refugees and humanitarian entrants are supported by the Humanitarian Settlement Program, which includes the following services:

- Adult Migrant English Program (AMEP)
- complex case support (CCS)
- Humanitarian Settlement Program (HSP)

- Settlement Engagement and Transition Support (SETS) Program
- translating and interpreting service (TIS).

Programs for refugees and humanitarian entrants are also supported by a range of non-government organisations and multicultural services.

CONSIDER THIS

REFUGEES

The United Nations High Commissioner for Refugees (UNHCR) reported in 2021:

- 82.4 million people forcibly displaced worldwide
- 26.6 million refugees
- 48 million displaced within their own countries
- 4.4 million asylum seekers
- 135 countries supported by emergency funding.

Close to half of all refugee children – 48 per cent – remain out of school (p. 5).

Immigration detention

The Roads to Refuge website (2020) explains that:

> Immigration detention forms a part of the Australian immigration policy under the *Migration Act 1958 (Cth)*. People who arrive in Australia intending to seek asylum, without already having been granted a refugee protection visa or on another valid visa, are placed in mandatory detention while their application for refugee status is considered.

Australia's immigration detention facilities include:

- Immigration Detention Centres (IDCs) including Regional Processing Centres, currently located in Nauru and Manus Island (in Papua New Guinea)
- Immigration Transit Accommodation (ITAs)
- Alternative Places of Detention (APODs)
- community detention.

Children in onshore immigration detention

As of 30 June 2022 there were:

- 170 children living in community detention
- 1426 children in the community living on bridging visas
- no children (aged less than 18 years) in Immigration Residential Housing, Immigration Transit Accommodation and Alternative Places of Detention (Department of Home Affairs, 2022).

Roads to Refuge (2020) further explains that:

Videos: Refugees and asylum seekers

> Following the Australian Human Rights Commission's National Inquiry into Children in Immigration Detention in 2014, changes were made to Australian immigration policy regarding the detaining of children in immigration detention. Families with children are usually detained in the community to allow children to attend school.

Bryant et al. (2018) say that 'child and adolescent refugees, who account for more than half of the world's refugees, have a higher prevalence of mental disorders than children and adolescents who are not refugees' (p. 249).

Post-traumatic stress

Many refugees and humanitarian entrants have experienced traumatic events prior to coming to Australia. Post-traumatic stress disorder (PTSD) is defined by the Black Dog Institute (2023) as 'a group of stress reactions that can develop after we witness a traumatic event, such as death, serious injury or sexual violence to ourselves or to others'. Potentially traumatic events involve actual or threatened death, serious injury or sexual violence to oneself or others – for example, war, terrorism, assaults, car accidents, natural disasters: 'PTSD can occur as a result of direct (experienced a personal trauma or witnessed a traumatic event) or indirect (hear/learn about a traumatic event) exposure to a traumatic event' (Black Dog Institute, 2023). **Figure 19.1** describes the signs and symptoms of PTSD.

Figure 19.1 The signs and symptoms of PTSD

Signs	Symptoms
Reliving the traumatic event	The person relives the event through unwanted and recurring memories, often in the form of vivid images and nightmares. There may be intense emotional or physical reactions, such as sweating, heart palpitations or panic when reminded of the event.
Being overly alert or wound up	The person experiences sleeping difficulties, irritability and lack of concentration, becoming easily startled and constantly on the lookout for signs of danger.
Avoiding reminders of the event	The person deliberately avoids activities, places, people, thoughts or feelings associated with the event because they bring back painful memories.
Feeling emotionally numb	The person loses interest in day-to-day activities, feels cut off and detached from friends and family, or feels emotionally flat and numb.

Source: Beyond Blue (2022). Post-traumatic stress disorder (PTSD). https://www.beyondblue.org.au/the-facts/anxiety/types-of-anxiety/ptsd

Anxiety and insecurity

Feeling anxious, insecure and unsafe are characteristics of children and young people who have been refugees. Restoring a sense of safety and control is a core goal for professionals working with victims of trauma. In a school setting, supporting children and young people to feel secure and safe is a first step in helping newly enrolled refugee students. This can be achieved when educators:

- provide a predictable environment – for example, a daily timetable with predictable routines, a physical space that is welcoming and clear guidelines for behaviour (including strategies for students who are feeling particularly stressed on any given day)
- provide a quiet play space as a safe alternative to the playground
- explain the purpose of activities and set realistic expectations for performance – for example, telling students what they will be doing, why it is important, and what they will learn
- accommodate individual learning needs and develop realistic goals in collaboration with the student
- provide opportunities for students to safely share their concerns and problems and work collaboratively on solutions.

Source: Victorian Foundation for Survivors of Torture Inc (2000). *Guide to Working with Young People Who Are Refugees* (p. 37).

Research has shown that PTSD in refugee children and young people is closely associated with the severity of PTSD in their caregivers. PTSD in refugees is also associated with harsh parenting styles, leading to adverse effects on their children's mental health. Bryant et al. (2018) explain: 'the anger and frustration difficulties associated with PTSD symptoms of refugees might directly contribute to the harsh parental behaviour that affects their children's internalising and externalising problems' (p. 249).

This cycle of stress, attributed to the life-threatening experiences of being forced from home, community and family, the threat and terror of violence, forced migration and detention in a foreign land, creates an environment that is toxic to children's mental health and wellbeing. After resettlement, children and their families may also experience culture shock, which compounds the already poor mental health of children.

The National Inquiry into Children in Immigration Detention (2014) found that children in detention facilities were commonly exposed to adults suffering from mental health problems including depression, stress and anxiety, where incidents of violence, self-harm and psychotic behaviour, resulting in negative emotional trauma (Australian Human Rights Commission [AHRC], 2014, p. 134). The report also stated that clinicians from the Children's Hospital at Westmead Refugee Clinic also reported evidence of trauma and PTSD in children exiting detention: 'More than half of all the asylum seeker children we are currently seeing are suffering from post-traumatic stress, nightmares and self-harming' (p. 205).

Research by clinicians working to support the mental health of refugee children and young people at the Royal Children's Hospital, Melbourne has also identified the negative impact of childhood refugee trauma, described in **Figure 19.2**.

Figure 19.2 Examples of the impact of childhood and adolescent refugee trauma

Children	Adolescents
> Behavioural issues including irritability or aggression > Difficulties making friends, engaging in play or joining group activities > Attention or concentration, hyperactive behaviour, learning difficulties > Avoidance behaviour, including school refusal > Anxiety, depression, intrusive thoughts/images, a 'frozen' appearance, mutism or perceptual abnormalities (e.g. hearing voices) > Sexualised behaviour, which may indicate that a child or young person has witnessed or been exposed to sexual abuse > Developmental delay, lack of expected developmental progress, worsening of pre-existing developmental concerns or regression	> Irritability or anger, sadness, hopelessness > Sense of guilt/worthlessness, low self-esteem, anxiety symptoms, panic symptoms/attacks > Self-harm/suicide, risk-taking behaviour

Source: Royal Children's Hospital, Melbourne (n.d.). Mental health. https://www.rch.org.au/immigranthealth/clinical/Mental_health_resources

The Royal Children's Hospital, Melbourne has developed a set of general principles to guide health, welfare and education needs for professionals working with refugee children/adolescents experiencing trauma. Some of the principles relevant to the school setting include:

- Ensuring predictability – through maintaining routine, including school attendance, and preparing for changes; reassuring children about the future.
- Encouraging play in younger children, enjoyable activities or sports in older children/adolescents, and peer connections and experiences of success at all ages.
- Encouraging expression of emotions and asking what children/young people are thinking/feeling.

- Setting realistic goals for behaviour and avoiding overreacting to difficult behaviour during transition periods.
- Promoting engagement with school and community, and maintenance of first language alongside English language learning.

Source: Royal Children's Hospital, Melbourne (n.d.). Mental health. https://www.rch.org.au/immigranthealth/clinical/Mental_health_resources

Figure 19.3 provides a summary of the causes of stress for refugees and new arrivals.

Figure 19.3 Causes of stress for refugees and new arrivals

Stressor	Definition	Possible cause
Trauma	Child experiences an intense event that threatens or causes harm to their emotional and physical wellbeing	> War and persecution > Displacement from home > Flight and migration > Poverty > Family and community violence
Acculturation	Children and families experience acculturation as they try to navigate between their new cultural values and their culture of origin	> Conflicts between children and parents over new and old cultural values > Conflicts with peers related to cultural misunderstandings > The necessity to translate for family members who are not fluent in English > Problems trying to fit in at school > Struggle to form an integrated identity including elements of their new culture and their culture of origin
Resettlement	Children and families who have relocated try to make a new life for themselves	> Financial stressors > Difficulties finding adequate housing > Difficulties finding employment > Loss of community support > Lack of access to resources > Transportation difficulties
Isolation	Children and families experience isolation as new immigrants in a new country	> Discrimination > Experiences of harassment from peers, adults or law enforcement > Experience of mistrust with host population > Feelings of not 'fitting in' with others > Loss of social status

Sources: US Department of Education (2017). Newcomer toolkit. https://www2.ed.gov/about/offices/list/oela/newcomers-toolkit/ncomertoolkit.pdf, p. 108. Retrieved from: National Child Traumatic Stress Network (n.d.). Refugee services toolkit. http://learn.nctsn.org/mod/book/view.php?id=4518&chapterid=36

Culture shock and cultural disorientation

Refugee stories and resources

The transition to a new country is not merely a physical one – it is also very stressful emotionally. This is true for people participating in planned migration as well as for refugees and humanitarian entrants. Before continuing, you may like to refer to **Chapter 3**, which explores the concept of culture, cultural competence and cultural safety. It's also useful to reflect on the dimensions of diversity as described by Samson, Donnet and Daft (2018).

Culture shock is a term used to describe the stress, anxiety and disorientation of relocation to a new country and a new culture. It includes experiences related to everyday life – for example:

- language barriers
- adjustment to climate, pace of life, lifestyle, work–life balance
- housing, transport, shopping, money, banking
- accessing and using services – medical, school, childcare
- isolation and sense of loss of family and friends
- changes in diet – lack of familiar foods, new foods (taste, texture, smell)
- adjustment to eating habits – packing lunch for school or work, different types of utensils, different ways of buying, storing and cooking food
- sounds – traffic, language, music, birds, etc.
- differences in values and beliefs related to gender roles, particularly in relation to the expected behaviours (and freedoms) of males and females, within and outside the family unit.

In essence, disorientation reflects the strangeness of being confronted with a new way of life where everything that is familiar and makes us feel safe has changed.

There are five distinct stages of culture shock, as shown in **Figure 19.4**.

Figure 19.4 Five stages of culture shock

Honeymoon phase	This reflects the initial excitement of the new country.
Rejection phase	Reality sets in and immigrants must now deal with day-to-day difficulties such as not understanding colloquial expressions (e.g. 'bring a plate'), not being able to buy the types of foods they could in their country of origin, feeling different and isolated, and second-guessing the decision to migrate.
Regression phase	Immigrants retreat to the known – only mixing with people from the same culture, resisting new experiences, complaining about the new country and its strange ways.
Recovery phase	Immigrants become more comfortable with the new country – learning the language, getting used to the customs, trying new experiences.
Reverse cultural shock phase	Immigrants return to their homeland and revisit their native culture.

Every immigrant will experience some level of culture shock. It is natural to miss one's home and lifestyle, loved ones and friends. Refugees and humanitarian entrants, who have likely experienced a great deal of trauma and may have lived a very stressful existence in their country of origin (and/or in refugee camps), will also suffer culture shock and homesickness.

Not being around the familiar and the known, the experience of unfamiliar sights, sounds and smells, the loss of extended family and friends all contribute to disorientation for children and young people. This is compounded by the experience of adjusting to the school environment and to a new language. For some families, school and formal learning will be an entirely new experience. Families may find it difficult to understand school routines – for example, school uniforms, packing snacks and lunches, or understanding school rules. Teachers and ESWs should be aware that these families and children may experience racism and various forms of discrimination.

Culture shock may also extend to the classroom. Consider, for example, the following changes that students may experience when adjusting to schooling in Australia:

- students may not have prior experience of attending school or of attending school for full days
- school rules, routines and timetables may appear to be extremely relaxed compared with other cultures
- problem-solving, collaboration and group learning may be regarded as unusual ways of 'teaching', particularly in contrast to other cultures where teacher-led/directed rote learning is common
- students may feel put-on-the-spot if asked a direct question by the teacher
- students may not be used to receiving individual praise in front of other students and may feel embarrassed
- students may not have experienced mixed gender classes
- students may not have experienced sitting at tables in small learning groups
- students may not have experienced a male/female teacher
- students may not have experienced interactive learning where they are expected to take responsibility for their own learning.

It is important to be aware that EAL/D students who are also adjusting to a new culture and learning a new language will need a great deal of support.

Adolescent children, who typically are striving for self-identity and independence, are a particularly vulnerable group among new immigrants. Children in this group may struggle with their traditional cultural identity as well as their 'new' identity within their peer group. Adolescents have a great need to 'fit in' and be a part of the norm (as evidenced in the following Scenario). This may lead to a rejection of their own culture and subsequent conflict within the family unit. It often leads to identity confusion. Rejection of both the old and the new culture can lead to behaviour problems until the adolescent is able to reach a stage of being comfortable with elements of both cultures.

Biculturalism enables adolescents to operate with ease in two cultural contexts, while maintaining a sense of pride in their own ethnic background and identity.

SCENARIO

CULTURE SHOCK

Twins **Deka** and **Ekon** (14 years), their sister **Jamille** (11 years) and their parents have lived in four refugee camps during the last five years. The children have not been to school for around six years and are finding it difficult to adjust to school in Australia. Although still learning English, the children are able to communicate sufficiently to be understood; however, they are finding the Australian accent difficult to understand.

The children were very excited to come to Australia but the school environment is extremely challenging for them. They are fearful of authority and have learned not to make eye contact or ask questions. They tell their father that Australian children are very naughty in school because they ask many questions of their teachers and they don't always pay attention. The children are also amazed that so many students have mobile phones and lots of money to spend every day. They tell their father that the students must come from very rich families.

WHAT DOES THIS TELL US?

Adjusting to a new country and culture can cause culture shock. Deka, Ekon and Jamille are not only adapting to a new country and a new language; they are also adjusting to school life and to the Australian teenage subculture.

▶ DISCUSSION

Discuss the concept of cultural shock. Think about the typical lifestyle of Australians. What might people coming from dissimilar cultures find confusing, confronting or challenging? How might you react if you were transported to a totally different culture? How might you go about adjusting to that culture?

Migrant integration issues

The IOM United Nations *World Migration Report 2022* estimates that there 'were around 281 million international migrants in the world in 2020, which equates to 3.6 per cent of the global population'. The report identified a number of dimensions that assist immigrants to integrate into their new community. These dimensions are measured internationally using the Migrant Integration Policy Index (MIPEX), which assesses policies to integrate migrants in countries across six continents, including Australia. The MIPEX includes eight dimensions:

- Access to nationality – how easily can immigrants become citizens?
- Anti-discrimination – is everyone effectively protected from racial/ethnic, religious, and nationality discrimination in all areas of life?
- Education – are education systems responsive to the needs of immigrant children?
- Family reunification – how easily can immigrants reunite with family?
- Health – is the health system responsive to immigrants' needs?
- Labour market mobility – do immigrants have equal rights and opportunities to access jobs and improve their skills?
- Permanent residence – how easily can immigrants become permanent residents?
- Political participation – are immigrants granted the right and opportunity to participate in political life?

In 2019, it was reported that Australia had scored MIPEX rating of 65 out of a possible 100 points, making it one of the 'Top Ten' countries with a well-developed comprehensive approach to integration:

- In relation to education, Australia was ranked in the top 5: 'all children in Australia have the implicit right to access education. Children from culturally and linguistically diverse backgrounds (CALD) benefit from specific support to access early childhood education and care.'
- In relation to health, Australia ranked in the top 10: 'immigrants in Australia are entitled and able to access healthcare benefits from a system well-adapted to their specific needs. However, immigrants still face some obstacles in accessing healthcare in Australia, depending on their legal status.'

Figure 19.5 shows Australia's MIPEX for the 2019 reporting period.

Figure 19.5 Migrant Integration Policy Index outcomes – Australia (2019)

Source: Australia – Key findings, Migrant Integration Policy Index 2020, https://www.mipex.eu/australia

IMMIGRANT CHILDREN

CONSIDER THIS

In 2015, the Organisation for Economic Co-operation and Development (OECD) undertook research on the school experiences of immigrant children in 43 countries, and reported that:

- Around 80 per cent of first- and second-generation immigrant students in Australia reported that they feel like they belonged at school.
- In most OECD countries, immigrant students who arrived at the age of 12 or older – and have spent at most four years in their new country – lag farther behind students in the same grade in reading proficiency than immigrants who arrived at younger ages.
- In Australia, immigrant children are slightly less likely than non-immigrant children to have attended pre-primary education.
- Immigrant students who have not attended pre-primary education have a gap that is equivalent to about one and a half years of learning.
- Immigrant students are 3.4 times more likely than non-immigrant students to repeat a grade either in primary or secondary school.

Source: OECD (2015). Helping Immigrant Students to Succeed at School – and Beyond. https://www.oecd.org/education/Helping-immigrant-students-to-succeed-at-school-and-beyond.pdf, pp. 3, 6, 7, 10

The report states that schools play a crucial role in integrating immigrant children and building communities and how well children feel they belong in school is a good indicator of how they are integrating into their wider community (OECD, 2015, p. 4).

SCENARIO

EDUCATION – DIFFERENT PERSPECTIVES

Hua (16 years) has arrived in Australia to complete the final two years of her education. Hua is living with an aunt and uncle, Mr and Mrs Zhōu, who settled in Australia from Hong Kong 15 years ago and have two adult children who no longer live at home. Although Hua could speak English, it took some time to adjust to the Australian accent.

The primary cause of Hua's culture shock was the teaching style of some of her teachers. Her schooling experience in her country had been lecture-style teaching, where students were not invited to engage in discussion or self-directed learning. Students were expected to rote learn knowledge that was tested weekly. She regularly completed three hours of homework each night. Hua told her aunt and uncle that her Australian teachers expected her to ask questions in class, work with other students in small groups and engage in learning projects. Hua judged the teachers harshly for not teaching properly! 'I get only one hour of homework!' She told her aunt and uncle they should go to the school and complain that the teachers were not teaching properly.

WHAT DOES THIS TELL US?

Culture shock can be experienced in many different ways. For Hua, her experience of teaching and learning was very different to that of Australian schools where the focus is learning rather than knowledge acquisition.

The Australian Government's Access and Equity policy supports the integration of migrants by providing access to a range of services designed to meet the needs of people from culturally and linguistically diverse backgrounds so that they can participate fully in economic, social and cultural life in Australia. Support for immigrants includes translation and interpreter services, orientation services, such as intensive English-language classes for adults and school-age children, registration with Medicare and Centrelink, medical support, enrolment of children in school and accommodation assistance. Families are also assisted with applying for a tax file number, opening a bank account, applying for a driver's licence and accessing support services in their local area.

19.2 EAL/D programs

The Australian Curriculum defines EAL/D students as 'those whose first language is a language or dialect other than English and who require additional support to develop proficiency in Standard Australian English (SAE)'.

> These students may include:
> - Aboriginal and Torres Strait Islander students
> - immigrants to Australia and temporary visa holders from non-English speaking countries
> - students with a refugee background
> - children born in Australia of migrant heritage where English is not spoken at home
> - English-speaking students returning to Australia after extended periods in non-English speaking settings
> - children of deaf adults who use Auslan as their first language
> - international students from non-English speaking countries.

The curriculum requires a number of points to be considered when developing personalised learning plans for EAL/D students:

- EAL/D students need to:
  - learn English
  - learn through English
  - learn about English.

- EAL/D students' experiences, understandings and expectations may be different from those that are assumed to be 'common knowledge' in Australian classrooms and must therefore be taken into account.
- EAL/D students may have additional or alternative understandings that need to be considered when teaching aspects of the Australian Curriculum.
- EAL/D students require specific support to learn and build on the English language skills needed to access the general curriculum, in addition to learning area-specific language structures and vocabulary.
- EAL/D students may not require additional support to engage with age-appropriate content.
- EAL/D students can achieve educational standards commensurate with their peers.
- EAL/D students may have different levels of language proficiency across the modes of listening, speaking, reading and writing.
- EAL/D students are already language learners in at least one other language.

Source: Australian Curriculum, Assessment and Reporting Authority (ACARA) (n.d.). Meeting the needs of students for whom English is an additional language or dialect. https://www.australiancurriculum.edu.au/resources/student-diversity/meeting-the-needs-of-students-for-whom-english-is-an-additional-language-or-dialect

Competence in ESL

The acquisition of English as a second language requires students to develop competence in listening, speaking, reading and writing in three key areas, as shown in **Figure 19.6**.

Figure 19.6 ESL competencies

Pragmatic competence	Organisational competence	Strategic competence
The ability to use language appropriately and acceptably according to particular purposes, audiences and situations.	The ability to control correctly and coherently the formal structures of language. It focuses on the relationship between language and its expressed meanings.	The ability to assess, respond to and negotiate meanings as part of a dynamic process of language use.

Source: Curriculum Corporation (1994). ESL Scales. Carlton South: NSW Department of Education and Training (pp. 5, 6)

EAL/D learning progression Foundation to Year 10

The EAL/D learning progression describes characteristics of students as they progress through five stages as English language learners in reading/viewing and writing behaviours (ACARA, 2015). The stages are described in **Figure 19.7**.

ESL scales

The ESL scales provide a detailed description of English language progression for learning with EAL/D to assist teachers to track EAL/D student progress against key learning areas from Foundation to Year 10. However, these scales may not be used in all states and territories.

Figure 19.7 EAL/D learning progression

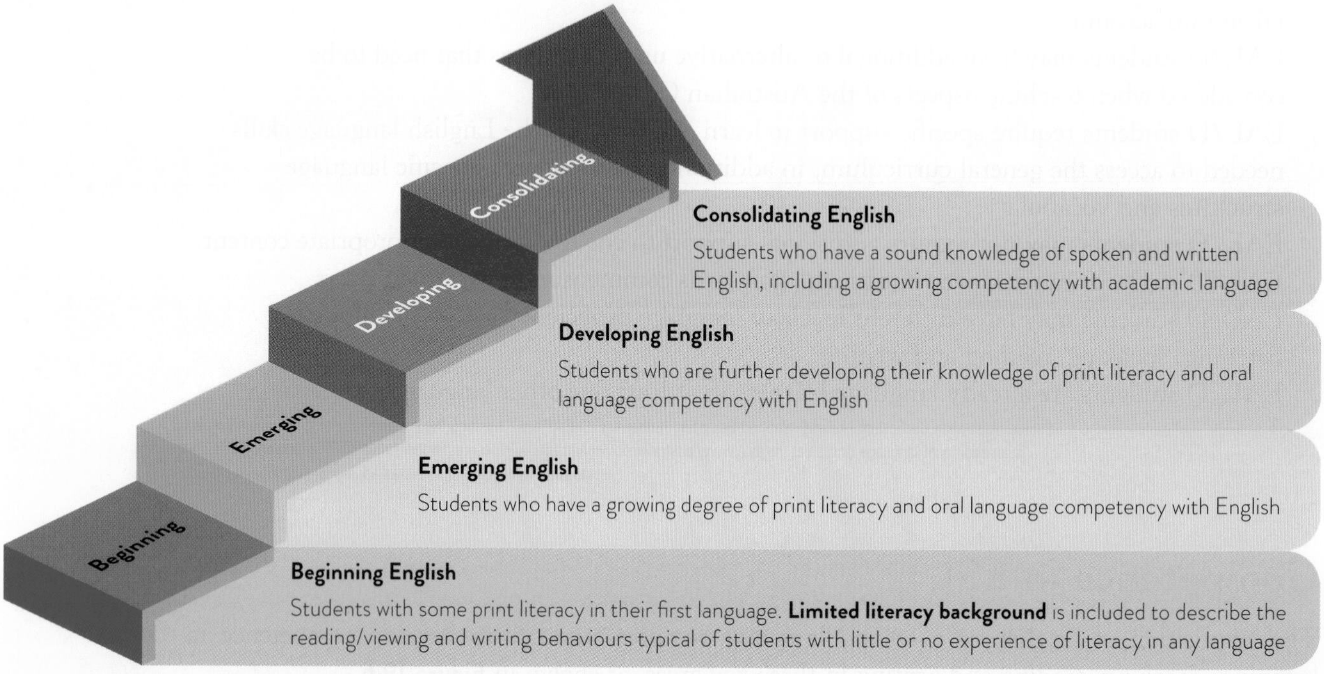

Consolidating
Developing
Emerging
Beginning
Consolidating English
Students who have a sound knowledge of spoken and written English, including a growing competency with academic language
Developing English
Students who are further developing their knowledge of print literacy and oral language competency with English
Emerging English
Students who have a growing degree of print literacy and oral language competency with English
Beginning English
Students with some print literacy in their first language. **Limited literacy background** is included to describe the reading/viewing and writing behaviours typical of students with little or no experience of literacy in any language

Source: Australian Curriculum, Assessment and Reporting Authority (ACARA) (2015). *English as an Additional Language or Dialect Teacher Resource: EAL/D Learning Progression Foundation to Year 10.* https://docs.acara.edu.au/resources/EALD_Learning_Progression.pdf. Image source: EAL/D Learning Progression.

The purpose of the ESL scales is to:

- provide a set of benchmarks against which the full range of ESL learners' achievements in English may be set
- develop a shared language among teachers of ESL learners in specialist and generalist contexts
- assist teachers throughout Australia in making consistent formative and summative judgements about ESL learners' achievements
- enhance students' access to the eight key learning areas
- help in identifying ESL learners' achievements and needs to assist program and curriculum development.

Source: Curriculum Corporation (1994). ESL Scales. Carlton South: NSW Department of Education and Training

ESL scales

Figure 19.8 shows the structure of the ESL scales.

Figure 19.8 Structure of ESL scales

ESL scales	
> 1 Three strands > 2 Oral interaction (listening and speaking): levels 1–8 > 3 Reading and responding: levels 1–7 > 4 Writing: levels 1–7	**Strand organisers** **Communication** How the student interacts with the English-speaking environment and communicates in the new code of English. > English communication for social and cultural participation > English communication for learning

ESL scales	
Level statements > A holistic description of student performance at each level within the scales > Summary of outcomes > Provide teachers with a broad description of a student's performance and a way into using the scales	**Language and cultural understanding** What the student understands about the situational and sociocultural contexts that affect the way English is used and interpreted. > Understanding how spoken and written English is used for particular purposes and audiences > Understanding how values, attitudes and world views are communicated through spoken and written language
Outcome statements > Outcome statements are given for each organiser at every level > They are the building blocks of the scale, reflecting the distinctive and essential elements of knowledge and skills in ESL > Outcome statements are based on observable student behaviour	**Language structures and features** The linguistic structures and features the student uses to create and comprehend texts. > Elements of language relating to texts > Features such as grammar, vocabulary, morphemes and aspects of the sound and writing systems
Pointers > Pointers indicate or signal the achievement of an outcome > Show the teacher what to look for in deciding whether an outcome has been achieved > Illustrate an outcome's meaning by giving examples of typical behaviours that demonstrate its achievement	**Strategies** How the student goes about operating in English and acquiring English. > Participating in, sustaining, planning, managing and refining communication > Techniques used to enhance their learning of English

Source: NSW Department of Education and Training. ESL Scales. Carlton South: Curriculum Corporation 1994. https://education.nsw.gov.au/content/dam/main-education/teaching-and-learning/curriculum/multicultural-education/eald/ESL-scales.pdf, pp. 3, 9, 10, 11

Reviewing student progress

EAL/D learning progressions and assessment

The EAL/D learning progression can be used as a guide to identify where an EAL/D student is located on the progression and the nature of their speaking, listening, reading/viewing and writing skills. Each state/territory will have formal assessment strategies for measuring EAL/D proficiency. However, the most effective strategy to measure and monitor student progress is through informal observation, discussion and documentation of students as they engage in a range of learning activities. This type of assessment is perhaps a more authentic or natural way to assess students' talking, listening, writing and reading skills.

Examples of classroom review strategies are outlined below:

- Observing the student in a variety of contexts – for example, whole-class activities, group or project work and working collaboratively with another student, and across all curriculum areas. This allows the observer to gain information about the student's receptive and expressive language skills. Observations can provide evidence of:
  - receptive language proficiency – for example, the student's ability to listen to, interpret and follow teacher directions and instructions
  - how the student engages with resources and equipment
  - how the student interacts with peers
  - expressive language proficiency – for example, asking and answering questions, labelling.
- Informal questioning while students are engaged in various tasks can be used to assess understanding of language, comprehension, concepts, relationships and application of knowledge and ability to sort, order, classify and problem-solve.

- To assess reading and comprehension skills, students can be provided with cloze texts including sentences where a word is left blank and the student fills in the missing word.
- Written work samples can be used to assess word skills, understanding, vocabulary, grammar, spelling and sentence structure.
- Oral reading assessment may include single words, phrases, sentences or short passages, depending on the English proficiency of the student.
- Dictation can be used to assess comprehension, spelling and auditory processing skills.
- Strip stories are a strategy that assesses comprehension. The student is required to read a number of sentences, each of which is written on a single cardboard strip and place the sentences in a logical sequence.
- Using KWL charts, the teacher can work collaboratively with the student to identify existing skills, knowledge and understanding at the beginning of a unit of study and again at the completion of a unit of study. (KWL stands for I know/what I want to know/what I've learned.)

19.3 Preparing for EAL/D students

Working with EAL/D students requires a whole-school approach to supporting bilingualism by modelling attitudes of respect and acceptance of all languages. Before a student arrives at the school, it can be very helpful to access information on the student's culture, including the culture's child-rearing practices and a list of its key words.

Elgas and colleagues (2002, p. 18) believe that children and young people who are learning English as an additional language should be provided with:

- open-ended concrete learning experiences that allow students to easily engage in play without needing to speak English (e.g. play dough, art, craft, matching and sorting games)
- long periods of uninterrupted play time with frequent opportunities to interact with other students and adults
- a curriculum that provides opportunities for students to reuse and practise learned words and phrases in a range of different contexts (e.g. following up a story with a related dramatic play scenario)
- an organised room where materials are visible, inviting and accessible
- a predictable routine that offers opportunities to label actions and objects and to hear and use key phrases associated with routines (songs or non-verbal gestures will give students visual and auditory clues so they can follow routines with the class)
- an atmosphere of 'welcome' where all students and adults are treated with respect
- experiences that match the student's cognitive skills – experiences must remain challenging and satisfying for the student
- experiences in which the teacher can observe, listen to and respond to the student's verbal and non-verbal communication by labelling, gesturing, paraphrasing and explaining using single words, short phrases and full sentences, and opportunities to engage in singing and rhyme that involve repetition of words and phrases
- opportunities to engage in teacher-led small-group experiences to promote communication.

Imagine what it feels like to enter a room where everything is unfamiliar and the people do not speak your language. The room contains furniture and furnishings that reflect a culture very different from your own. As you gaze around, you cannot see anything that is familiar to you. Even the smells are different. For most of us, that would be a very daunting experience. For children, it can also be a very frightening one. To overcome this, schools can create an environment that reflects a multicultural perspective by including images and objects from a variety of different cultures. This can help students to feel more comfortable and welcomed. Feeling accepted, valued and part of the school is essential for all students. A whole-school approach promotes acceptance, exploration, celebration and respect for differences.

CASE STUDY | Lavindra

Part 1

Lavindra (7 years) is from Sri Lanka and speaks Tamil. Her family fled their home eight years ago to avoid internal conflict between warring factions. Lavindra was born in a refugee camp and has never attended school. She has lived with her mother, father, maternal grandmother, aunt and four siblings in a variety of camps, all characterised by extreme poverty, violence and corruption. Until her arrival in Australia, Lavindra had never lived in a house, had never had more than one set of clothes or shoes and had no toys or books. The family practises the Hindu religion. Lavindra's father was an experienced, well-respected tailor before leaving his country.

Lavindra is watching the other students at the collage table. The ESW approaches and says, *'Lavindra, would you like to do a collage?'* As she talks, she points and gestures at the collage table.

Lavindra smiles and nods as the ESW motions for her to sit down at the table.

The ESW stays nearby, saying to the other students, *'Lavindra is going to join you and do a collage'.*

Lavindra continues to watch the other students.

Lilly says, *'Lavindra, here's a brush for you. You have to put the paste on first and then you stick things on. Okay?'*

Lavindra smiles and begins to create her collage. Lilly periodically smiles and encourages her.

'Good work, Lavindra!'

When she is finished, Lilly shows Lavindra where to put her collage to dry.

Later the ESW says to Lilly, *'Lilly, I saw you helping Lavindra at the collage table. Thank you for helping her. It was very kind of you to be her friend.'*

Lilly smiles broadly and skips away saying, *'Lavindra is my friend.'*

What does this tell us?

- The ESW assumes Lavindra can participate with the group without direct support and encourages her to do so.
- By scaffolding (using gestures and phrases), the ESW adjusts her communication to facilitate Lavindra's understanding and to help her participate.
- Lavindra learns that this is a place where she can participate alongside her peers. The environment is safe and supportive.
- The ESW positively reinforces Lilly for supporting Lavindra and encourages this developing friendship.

Lavindra is a beginning English language learner. She is now living in a culture that is totally foreign. The language is unfamiliar and there are different sounds, sights and smells. Lavindra has lived her life in a tent or in makeshift accommodation with no running water or electricity. She has never been away from her family – has never been to a school, a park, a supermarket; she has never lived in a house, had toys or books or even slept in her own bed. Culture shock will be an inevitable part of Lavindra's experience. She will require high levels of emotional and social support.

Getting to know the EAL/D student

The starting point for assessing EAL/D students is getting to know the student, the family and the culture. This includes the student's background information, such as the student's journey; how the student came to be in Australia – immigration, refugee, illegal immigrant, temporary visa; the experiences of the student and the family – many refugees and illegal immigrants have experienced great hardship, deprivation, religious persecution, terrorism and extreme ill-treatment.

Knowing the student's story can assist teachers and ESWs to better understand and meet the needs of each student.

Background information on the student will usually include:

- date of birth, country of birth, country/countries of residence prior to arrival in Australia; this may include refugee camps and detention centres
- date of arrival in Australia and visa status
- family situation – parents/guardians/siblings; whether the family is together or separated
- language/s spoken at home (mother and father). Where families have lived in more than one country before arriving in Australia, children may have acquired a second or third language
- whether anyone speaks/reads/writes English in the home
- key cultural and religious practices/beliefs. This information will assist in understanding and meeting the cultural/religious needs of the student
- education history – what, if any, formal education the student has experienced
- initial language assessment (listening, speaking, reading, writing).

Gathering information about the student allows teachers and ESWs to gain a greater understanding of the student and their family. It will also assist in building respectful and trusting relationships with the student and their family.

Acquisition of English language

When children and young people are learning English as an additional language or dialect, they are not only acquiring knowledge of the spoken language, but also acquiring knowledge of the dominant culture. They must learn the often quite subtle social rules of language and how to apply these rules when interacting with peers.

In a report on EAL/D children, the Department for Education and Skills, UK (2006, p. 15) states:

> Generally speaking, children learning an additional language can become conversationally fluent in the new language in two to three years but may take five years or longer to catch up with monolingual peers in the development of cognitive and academic language.

The acquisition of a second language generally occurs in one of two ways (Papadaki-D'Onofrio, 2003, p. 46). *Simultaneous acquisition* occurs when children are exposed to a second or third language from birth. *Sequential* or *successive acquisition* occurs when children begin to learn a second language after a first language is partially or fully established.

Research indicates that students' levels of language and literacy competence in their first language influence their rate of second language learning, possibly their ultimate levels of attainment in the language and the success with which they perform cognitively demanding literacy tasks in the second language.

Maintenance of first language

Family, language and culture provide the foundation of a child's identity and sense of belonging. Language is not simply a form of communication – it is the primary way in which an individual's culture is transmitted. As children learn the rules of language, they are also learning the social and cultural functions of language. Rogoff (2003, p. 310) reminds us that while language is universal, how it is used to communicate varies between cultures: 'Everywhere, people use words, silence, gestures, and gaze skillfully to communicate. Yet there also appear to be important differences in how much people talk and in how articulately they communicate non-verbally.'

It is essential to encourage students to be proud of their cultural heritage and demonstrate genuine respect for the student's first language. Students whose first language is not that of the dominant culture are not necessarily disadvantaged in relation to language development. They are, however, at risk of losing their cultural identity if their first language is not respected and maintained.

While it is extremely important for children to be fluent in their first language, it is equally important that they be fluent in the language of the dominant culture – that is, Standard Australian English (SAE). The ability to use the language of the dominant culture, while still maintaining one's home language, is a goal that should be supported by all educators. Children who are fluent in their native language are more successful at learning a second language. As long as children have a sound foundation in their first language, they usually have little difficulty in acquiring a second language. Similarly, children who are **bilingual** are able to acquire new words in both languages and use new words in the correct context.

Bilingual students who are learning English are simultaneously learning the cultural values and social behaviours associated with each language. They will often mix words from both languages in the same sentence when answering a question or explaining a concept. This practice is called *code switching*. Drawing on their first language helps students to better understand and process knowledge.

Some families have concerns about the effect of maintaining their children's first language. Often parents will stop using their first language around their children, thinking this will help their children to learn English. Misinformation about the benefits of maintaining the child's home language, and its importance in relation to learning a second language, are common.

Research confirms that 'bilingual children are *not* more likely than monolingual children to have difficulties with language, to show delays in learning, or to be diagnosed with a language disorder. Just like some monolingual children have a language delay or disorder, a similar proportion of bilinguals will have a language delay or disorder' (Byers-Heinlein & Lew-Williams, 2013). Parents should be encouraged to speak their children's native language in the home to ensure the children develop proficiency in their first language (see the Scenario box).

It is very reassuring for children and families to be able to converse in their home language when they first commence in a school. Although it is not always possible, some schools have bilingual staff or can access support staff or interpreter services. Other schools may find that they have to rely on the goodwill of other parents or members of the community to assist as interpreters. If such support is not available, it would be necessary to access a commercial interpreter service.

SCENARIO

SPEAKING ENGLISH

After settling in Australia, Ethiopian parents *Ashebir* and *Niyyat* were determined that their children would learn to speak both Amharic and English. However, after only one year in Australia, they tend to speak mostly English to their children.

Ashebir: *'My boss told me I should only speak English to my children. He says, "You are in Australia now mate, you must speak English!"'*

Niyyat: *'I worry about my children suffering at school. I don't want the other children to make fun of them. Children can be so cruel at times. We are confused about what to do. We have been told different things. My oldest child's teacher said we should speak English at home so that the children can learn English. But at the child-care centre they tell me it is important to speak our own language at home so that the children can speak both languages. I don't know what to do. I worry for my children. I want them to be happy and to fit in. It is hard enough that they have different-coloured skin. They must be able to speak like the other children.'*

WHAT DOES THIS TELL US?

Families are often under a great deal of pressure to learn and speak English. There is a general misperception that bilingualism is a disadvantage for children whose first language is not that of the dominant culture.

Aboriginal and Torres Strait Islander EAL/D students

Aboriginal and Torres Strait Islander students may have, as their first language, a language other than English. However, their needs as First Australians are considered to be different from those of EAL/D students born overseas.

Indigenous people contribute to Australia's cultural diversity and provide a rich history of beliefs, values and cultural practices that are yet to be fully recognised and embraced by other Australians. Many Aboriginal and Torres Strait Islander people still face substantial barriers that are, in part, a result of other Australians' failure to recognise and value the unique nature of Aboriginal and Torres Strait Islander culture and differences in learning style.

Consider the following statement (cited in Fleer and Williams-Kennedy, 2001, p. 69) by an Aboriginal parent when talking about formal education: 'When the children go to school, they take their families with them.' This is quite a powerful statement that reflects beliefs about learning as a shared responsibility that goes well beyond that which is taught in schools. Even though the child is physically in a different place, the spirit of the family – the values, beliefs and ways of learning – go with the child.

While it is important not to generalise, and to consider the strengths and abilities of each student (Aboriginal and Torres Strait Islander or students of other backgrounds) as a unique individual, there remain significant gaps in educational opportunities and outcomes for Aboriginal and Torres Strait Islander students.

According to the Queensland Department of Education, Training and Employment (DETE QLD), Aboriginal and Torres Strait Islander EAL/D learners are likely to have first languages that are:

> – traditional languages – Aboriginal and Torres Strait Islander languages that originated prior to European colonisation, some of which continue to be spoken today
> – Creole languages – new languages that have formed since colonisation. There are creole languages spoken by Aboriginal and Torres Strait Islander people across Australia
> – Aboriginal English – dialects of English spoken by many Aboriginal people across Australia.

Source: State of Queensland, Department of Education, Training and Employment (2013). Capability Framework: Teaching Aboriginal and Torres Strait Islander EAL/D learners. https://education.qld.gov.au/student/Documents/capability-framework-teaching-aboriginal-torres-strait-islander-eald-learners.pdf, p. 4

Creoles are languages that develop from pidgin languages. Pidgin languages emerge as a way for people who do not have a common language to communicate. If a pidgin develops into a more complex, stable language and is acquired by children as a first language, it is then defined as a creole. Creoles adopt elements of the languages spoken in the surrounding environment. They are equal to any of the world's languages – they are complex, rule-governed systems of communication and can express an infinite range of ideas.

Features of Aboriginal English

While Aboriginal English is used throughout Australia, there are variations in dialect that are localised to specific geographic areas. Some common features of Aboriginal English described by Eades (2000, pp. 4–5) include:

- There is no /h/ sound – for example 'ow are you?' rather than 'How are you?'; 'e' for 'he' or 'she'.
- Replace the /f/ sound with a /p/ or /b/ sound.
- Replace the /v/ sound with /b/ or /p/.
- Replace the /th/ sound with /t/ or /d/.
- There is no use of verb for present/past – 'e ome' rather than 'He's gone home.'
- The word 'deadly' is used to mean 'very good/excellent'.
- Avoid asking direct questions; instead, wait politely until others are ready to share information. This is very different from SAE, in which direct questioning is seen as an important learning strategy.
- The use of pauses or silence in a conversation is considered to be a sign of comfortable interaction in Aboriginal English. This contrasts with SAE, where silences in conversation are often considered to be awkward and something that should be avoided.

Read more about Aboriginal and Torres Strait Islander languages in Chapter 6.

Code-switching

Code-switching occurs when an English language learner reverts to their home language when speaking. This occurs when the speaker doesn't know the correct English word or phrase. It can also occur unintentionally as the person speaking is usually thinking in their home language and converting their thoughts into English. There will also be occasions when there is no word or phrase in English that is deemed to be equivalent to the home language word or phrase.

In the Aboriginal context, code-switching occurs when a speaker uses SAE in formal settings such as school or work and then switches to Aboriginal English or their own language when at home or within the Aboriginal community. Doing this successfully requires the speaker to understand and apply subtle differences in the cultural meanings of words and expressions.

Code-switching can also occur within a single sentence. This type of code-switching may occur because the student is unable to think of the appropriate word in English or in response to the cultural context in which the spoken language is being used. For example, an Aboriginal student may switch from SAE to Aboriginal English when another Aboriginal student joins in a discussion.

Ways of communicating are culturally bound. For example, when asked a direct question, the student may feel a sense of shame because they have been 'singled out' from the group. Other cultural practices related to communication, such as long periods of silence when communicating, being silent before responding to a question and avoiding eye contact with Elders, should be acknowledged and respected. Aboriginal and Torres Strait Islander students may not ask for help if they are unsure of what to do or how to respond to a question, and may respond only briefly when asked to share information – not because they are unable to elaborate, but because brevity is valued. Knowing and respecting these cultural ways of communicating are essential when working with Aboriginal and Torres Strait Islander students.

Eades (2000, p. 6) states:

> Although the differences between Aboriginal English and Standard English may not seem great in many areas, there are subtle differences, especially in the way that language is used, which are important to

the identity of Aboriginal children. Respecting, valuing and understanding Aboriginal ways of using English is a significant step in respecting, valuing and understanding the identity and self-esteem of these children.

Capability Framework Teaching Aboriginal and Torres Strait Islander EAL/D learners

Aboriginal and Torres Strait Islander children and young people for whom English is a second language are likely to have been exposed to variations of Australian and American English through television, videos, music, movies and the internet and, like most children and young people, will have a repertoire of vocabulary related to popular culture.

English-language programs for Aboriginal and Torres Strait Islander students recognise that the student's home language/dialect differs from SAE. Programs may focus on specific grammar and vocabulary knowledge as well as academic language (see **Figure 19.9**).

Figure 19.9 Students are read stories in Standard Australian English

Source: [L] Alamy Stock Photo/Janine Wiedel Photolibrary; [R] Alamy Stock Photo/Bill Bachman

ABORIGINAL ENGLISH

SCENARIO

Freddy (11 years) lives with his mother, older brothers, younger sister and maternal grandmother in a small country town. Freddy's mother works part-time at the Aboriginal preschool. His older brothers are both working on rural properties. His older sister is in Year 12 and wants to be a primary school teacher.

Freddy loves fishing. He has four fishing rods and has asked his sister to buy him a new one for his birthday. Freddy tries to go fishing every day. He has several favourite spots on the river and tells his mother that he has some secret spots.

Despite his mother's efforts, Freddy communicates using Aboriginal English. He says he hates school because it's too hard and he can't understand the teacher. He is not looking forward to transitioning to high school in a nearby town and tells his mother that high school is *'only for the white fellas'*. Freddy's mother tells him that he has to get a good education so he can get a good job.

'Na, gunna go fishin' when I get big man. Fishin's deadly!'

'Well, you're not a big man yet and I want you to go to that school.'

Freddy smiles and looks across to his grandmother.

'Whadda you think, Nanna? Fishin's deadly, ain't it?'

Nanna responds to Freddy in her Aboriginal language and her comment makes Freddy laugh.

WHAT DOES THIS TELL US?

Although Freddy has good role models, he does not see formal education as a useful pathway. He speaks in mainly Aboriginal English and is also able to understand and speak the Aboriginal language of his mother and grandmother.

▶ DISCUSSION

Freddy's lack of skills in using and understanding SAE will become an increasing barrier as he moves into high school. Discuss what could be done to support students like Freddy to acquire the language skills he will need to succeed academically.

Stages of English language acquisition

To become fluent in a second language takes many years. When learning a first language, children are immersed in language; they hear and observe how people communicate, and acquire language in a very natural and predictable manner. Children and young people learning English later don't have this same immersion language. As beginning language learners, they are likely to speak their first language at home and English only when at school or during intensive English classes.

The stages in the development of a second language tend to follow a predictable sequence. Gonzalez (2021) states that this sequence may vary depending on factors such as:

- the student's first language proficiency (listening, speaking, reading, and writing),
- the student's current English language proficiency,
- the student's background knowledge and opportunities,
- the student's access to language at home, and
- similarities and differences between the student's first language and English (cognates and written features).

Source: Gonzalez, V. (2021). An asset-based approach to supporting English learners' reading skills. Edutopia. https://www.edutopia.org/article/asset-based-approach-supporting-english-learners-reading-skills

There are commonly six stages in the development of a second language for EAL/D students. These stages are described in **Figure 19.10** and **Figure 19.11**.

Figure 19.10 Stages 1–3 of English language acquisition

6 months ⟷ 3 years		
Stages		
Pre-production	**Early-production**	**Speech emergent**
Also referred to as 'The Silent Stage' where the student may not speak in either their first language or English Student may understand some spoken English Students are looking, listening and absorbing language ready for the time when they will speak Non-verbal: nods 'yes' and 'no', draws and points more weeks	May mix words and sounds from both languages even if the person they are talking to is using only one language Student does not yet have a sufficient vocabulary in one or both languages to express themselves entirely in one language May use single words and short phrases Borrowing of words from each language is temporary Limited comprehension One- or two-word responses Uses key words Present-tense verb usage	English becomes more frequent, words and sentences are longer Student still relies heavily on context clues and familiar topics Vocabulary continues to increase and errors begin to decrease, especially in common or repeated interactions Good comprehension Simple sentence, grammatical and pronunciation errors Misunderstands jokes/idioms

Support strategies		
Demonstrate/point/ gesture/use visual cues to emphasise meaning Speak slowly Show me… Circle the… Where is…? Who has …?	Yes/no questions Either/or questions Lists and labels One- or two-word answers Ask students to point to pictures and say the new word Model a phrase and have the student repeat it and add modifications. Teacher says, 'This book is very interesting.' The student repeats it and says, 'This book is very boring.' Continue with as many modifications as possible Avoid excessive error correction. Reinforce learning by modelling correct usage	Why …? How …? Explain … Begin to introduce academic vocabulary Ask questions that require a short answer and are fairly literal Introduce charts and graphs by using easily understood information such as a class survey of food preferences Have students retell stories or experiences and have another student write them down In writing activities, provide the student with a fill-in-the-blank version of the assignment with the necessary vocabulary listed on the page Focus only on correction that directly interferes with meaning

General support strategies

- *The quality of interactions with adults is very important*
- *Pressuring the student to speak will interfere with their language development and extend the period of silence*
- *Talk to the student even if there is no response*
- *Small groups with two or three students*
- *Ask a variety of questions*
- *Include other students as the focus of conversation*
- *Use popular songs*
- *Learn a few simple phrases and counting in the student's first language*
- *Encourage the student to respond non-verbally*
- *Give lots of praise for effort*
- *Offer opportunities for the student to repeat what has been said (if willing)*
- *Provide many opportunities for interaction with other students*
- *Provide lots of opportunity to role-play – a good way to practise language*

Source: Robertson, K. & Ford, K. (n.d.). Language acquisition: An overview. https://www.colorincolorado.org/article/language-acquisition-overview

Figure 19.11 Stages 4–6 of English language acquisition

3 years ⟷ 7 years		
Stages		
Beginning fluency	**Intermediate fluency**	**Advanced fluency**
Speech is fairly fluent in social situations with minimal errors New contexts and academic language are challenging and students may struggle to express themselves due to gaps in vocabulary and appropriate phrases	Excellent comprehension Fewer grammatical errors Able to speak almost fluently in new situations or in academic areas, but there will be gaps in vocabulary knowledge and some unknown expressions There are very few errors, and the individual is able to demonstrate higher-order thinking skills in the second language such as offering an opinion or analysing a problem	When student is fluent in both languages, they are easily able to shift confidently from one language to the other Communicates fluently in all contexts The student may still have an accent and use idiomatic expressions incorrectly at times, but the individual is essentially fluent and comfortable communicating in the second language
Support strategies	***Support strategies***	***Support strategies***
Work in pairs and groups to encourage discussion 'Think, pair, share' Ask questions and repeat student response to check for understanding Ask questions that require inference and justification of the answer Ask students if they agree or disagree with a statement and why Model more advanced academic language structures such as, 'I think', 'In my opinion' and 'When you compare' Have students repeat the phrases in context Rephrase incorrect statements in correct English, or ask the student if they know another way to say it Provide opportunities for students to give short presentations on a topic of interest Focus on pronunciation and discuss the sound of words	What would happen if …? Why do you think? Introduce key academic vocabulary and skills such as brainstorming, prioritising, categorising, summarising and compare and contrast Use graphic organisers and thinking maps Explore word families such as 'important, importance, importantly' Have a 'guessing time' during silent reading where they circle words they don't know and write down their guess of the meaning	Decide whether… Retell … Offer challenge activities to expand the student's vocabulary knowledge such as identifying antonyms, synonyms and the use of a thesaurus
General support strategies		
Some students will insist on speaking only in English as they do not want to appear different. They may also be reluctant to use their first language at home. Encourage maintenance of first language *Continue to develop language skills as gaps arise*		

Source: Robertson, K. & Ford, K. (n.d.). Language acquisition: An overview. https://www.colorincolorado.org/article/language-acquisition-overview

SCENARIO

A MATTER OF INTERPRETATION

Dhakir (5 years) has lived in Australia for three years. He speaks fluent Arabic and conversational English. Dhakir came home from his first day of Kindergarten and told his mother that his teacher thinks he is red. Dhakir explained that when the Kindergarten students were lining up to go back into class after lunch, his teacher pointed to him and said, '"*Dhakir, you are Kinder Red – you need to be in this line with the red children." I am not red! I am brown!*'

WHAT DOES THIS TELL US?

Although Dhakir speaks conversational English, his interpretation of his teacher's comments shows us that he is not yet understanding the idioms of the language.

Awareness of English language

Awareness of English language begins with listening to the sounds of the language. Listening is also the process for beginning to produce words and sentences for communication. Horwitz (2020) describes the three stages of listening development of EAL/D students and the strategies that can be used to support listening skills at each stage (see **Figure 19.12**).

Figure 19.12 Stages of listening development and support strategies

Stage	Description	Support strategies
1: Recognition of the target language	At this stage learners can distinguish English from other languages	> Listening to songs, rhymes, commercials, movies, podcasts or extended conversations to get used to the sounds of the language > Having students pretend they are speaking English
2: Recognition of isolated words	Learners begin to notice isolated words	> Listening to short passages that contain familiar phrases > Listening for familiar phrases or words while listening to commercials, familiar nursery rhymes or descriptions of famous people, places or events > Using digital materials that allow students to click on objects or phrases and hear pronunciations, transcriptions and/or translations
3: Recognition of phrase boundaries	Learners begin to recognise and distinguish individual words, phrases and sentence boundaries (but do not yet understand much of what is being said)	> Having students select pictures that correspond to oral descriptions > Having students summarise conversations they have heard > Asking students their opinions of what they have heard

Source: Horwitz, E. (2020). *Becoming a Language Teacher. A Practical Guide to Second Language Learning and Teaching.* 2nd edn. Melbourne, Castledown (pp. 92, 94, 95).

As students progress they begin to understand the overall topic and have some understanding of what is being said. In the final stage 'learners are able to follow the meaning of a passage and are better able to process the listening material in chunks rather than word by word' (Horwitz, 2020, p. 95).

As well as listening development, EAL/D students must be supported to develop their comprehension skills. Comprehension skills develop alongside the six stages in the development of a second language. However, it is important to keep in mind the concept of the 'whole child', the continuum of learning and development, and the uneven nature of development. Each student will develop at their own unique pace and will likely have strengths in some areas while needing support in other aspects of English language acquisition.

It is important to have realistic expectations as students progress their comprehension skills. It is also important to reassure students that learning to understand and speak English takes a very long time. Reminding students of what they have already achieved can be helpful if they express disappointment or impatience as English language learners.

Reading, speaking and listening with EAL/D learners

Materials used to support comprehension skills should reflect the age, culture and interests of the students. This is particularly important for older students, who should not be given materials that are clearly targeted at a younger age group. When working with students, it is also important to be aware that listening for comprehension is both demanding and exhausting. Always ensure students have regular relaxation breaks and fun activities throughout the day. Some useful listening comprehension strategies are outlined in **Figure 19.13**.

Figure 19.13 Listening comprehension strategies

Strategy	Implementation
Background knowledge	Exploring a student's pre-existing knowledge of a topic: > What words do they know in English and/or first language related to the topic? > What knowledge can they draw on about the topic? (share information in first language with another student)
Previewing	Helping students anticipate the content they are about to listen to or read: > Talk about the title – what do you think it means? > Explore any illustrations or graphics that may give clues about the content
Advance organiser	This process is an example of scaffolding where the teacher links new information to what students already know and understand: > Link the text to a learning area > Refer to previous activities > Refer to a word wall
Meaning support	Using a range of resources to aid understanding. For example, photos, real objects, sound effects, etc.
Recall	Students are asked to recall what they remember of the text. This can be done in the students' first language or in English. Students who speak the same first language could also verbally share what they recall (recalling information may not necessarily indicate understanding)
Recall question	Teacher asks a question about the text – students verbally respond in English
Inference questions	An **inference** question requires the students to demonstrate understanding of the text (rather than simply recalling)
Intonation	Teacher reads using rise and fall of voice to stress words or concepts

Source: Horwitz, E. (2020). *Becoming a Language Teacher. A Practical Guide to Second Language Learning and Teaching* 2nd edn. Melbourne, Castledown (pp. 92, 94, 95).

19.4 Resources for working with EAL/D students

The process of learning English occurs in a planned sequence that moves from mainly spoken English to written/text-based language. According to Harper and Feez (2021):

> this allows students to ground their learning experiences in familiar language, either everyday English or their home language or dialect, at the same time as they are given opportunities to listen to and practise unfamiliar technical or subject-specific language. Teachers can then introduce written language in ways that support both understanding of the topic and students learning to use language to talk and write about the topic.

Source: Harper, H. & Feez, S. (2021). *An EAL/D Handbook*. Newtown, NSW. Primary English Teaching Association Australia (PETAA), p. 214.

Beginning EAL/D learners should be encouraged to use their first language to build their skills as English language learners. This allows students to draw on and apply their knowledge and skills to new learning. Known as **translanguaging**, this process allows students to draw on their first language as well as English to communicate. Translanguaging:

- recognises the importance of the student's first language
- allows students to explore complex tasks and new information in their language which supports deeper understandings
- allows students to draw on their existing academic language as they learn new academic language
- recognises the importance of 'the whole child' – that is, a competent communicator in their first language and a learner of English
- recognises and respects the student's linguistic heritage.

Videos: Multilingualism and translanguaging

When students engage in translanguaging, they are able to draw from all of their language resources as part of the learning process. A range of communication strategies that can be used with EAL/D students are described in **Figure 19.14**.

Figure 19.14 Communication strategies

Strategy	Implementation and results
Allow for wait time	EAL/D students will typically translate spoken English into their own language before responding. Allow time for this to occur by pausing at the end of each sentence.
Use short sentences	Repeat the sentence if the student appears not to understand what is being said. Repeating a short sentence rather than immediately rephrasing a sentence gives the student the opportunity to hear the sentence more than once. Constant rephrasing introduces new words, which may be very confusing for the student.
Avoid the use of jargon and Australian slang	EAL/D students will have difficulty finding an equivalent meaning for jargon and slang words or colloquial sayings. For example, new English learners may find words such as 'fridge', 'footy' and 'hassle' hard to understand.
Explain key words in context	This is particularly important in subject areas where words have a specific meaning.
Encourage practice	Provide opportunities for EAL/D students to use new vocabulary through ongoing practice.
Check for comprehension	Before continuing, stop and check the student's understanding. For example, observe what the student is doing and observe their language and facial expression. (A blank or puzzled look would indicate a lack of understanding.)
Use written and spoken language simultaneously	Write or highlight key words.
Use visual aids	Help the student make associations between spoken and written words.
Communicate with the student in their first language (where possible)	Do this to check progress and understanding.
Give specific and timely feedback	Address errors in grammar and pronunciation by rephrasing rather than correcting. For example, the student may say, 'To shop I went.' Rephrase by saying, 'I went to the shop.'
Engage EAL/D students in small-group learning experiences	This allows them to practise their skills and promotes peer interaction.

Scaffolding

Scaffolding is a technique that draws on what the student already knows, understands and can do to build new knowledge and skills. In the context of EAL/D students, scaffolding can be used to develop specific academic English language skills at grade and subject content level by sequencing activities and allowing students to use words and phrases in their first language to make sense of new learning in English. Using an EAL/D student's 'native language in a strong, supportive learning environment can build student confidence as learners, build English skills, and help them acquire academic content to become successful in school' (US Department of Education, 2017, p. 11).

When scaffolding for EAL/D students, the goal is to gradually move from intensive support (controlled by teacher) in the early stages and gradually move to guided support before eventually becoming an independent learning. The pace of gradual reduction in support should be guided by the needs of each individual student.

Scaffolding strategies may include the following:

- Briefly explain the learning outcome or purpose of the activity. For example, 'We are going to learn about Australian money'; 'We are going to look at pictures of animals and learn names in English.'
- Identify prior knowledge and skills – students use their first language to make connections with new information. For example, using photographs, drawings or interactive graphic organisers to build new understanding.
- Direct a question to the most advanced student – remind everyone to listen. Ask the small group to recall what the student said. This builds both listening and oral language skills.
- Scaffold within an activity – move the students through a logical sequence – first, then, next.
- Encourage interaction and collaboration – this allows students to learn from each other and provides opportunities for practice.
- Provide opportunities for independent learning so that each student can work at their own pace.
- Scaffold the degree of challenge or difficulty within activities. More advanced students can be given additional challenges.

Scaffolding is a strategy that allows teachers to work within the student's zone of proximal development (ZPD) by drawing on existing knowledge to develop new knowledge. Scaffolding for both oral language and reading development is a way of ensuring the EAL/D students are learning at a pace that best meets their needs. Huynh (2017) describes three ways of scaffolding for EAL/D students that immerses them in English and reflects the concept of 'the whole' by providing a variety of ways for learning to take place:

1. Sensory scaffolding allows students to engage in active, hands-on experiences with oral and written language.
2. Interactive scaffolding provides opportunities for student-led discussion, collaboration and sharing of ideas, opinions and interpretations of text and word meanings.
3. Scaffolding using graphics allows students to represent and interpret oral and written English in different ways to explore meaning and build relationships between words, phrases and concepts.

Figure 19.15 and **Figure 19.16** describe these approaches to scaffolding. The following link provides examples of a range of scaffolding options that can be used with students to support their learning. For example, graphs, timelines, infographics, tables and number lines: https://tankhuynh.com/scaffolding-instruction.

Videos: Graphic organisers and differentiation

Figure 19.15 Sensory scaffolding

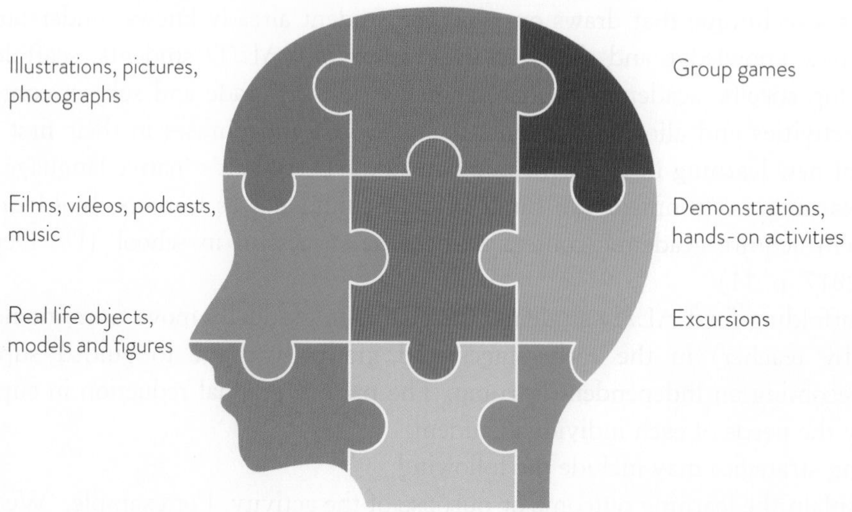

Source: Huynh, T. (2017). Three types of scaffolding: There's a scaffold for that. https://tankhuynh.com/scaffolding-instruction

Figure 19.16 Interactive scaffolding

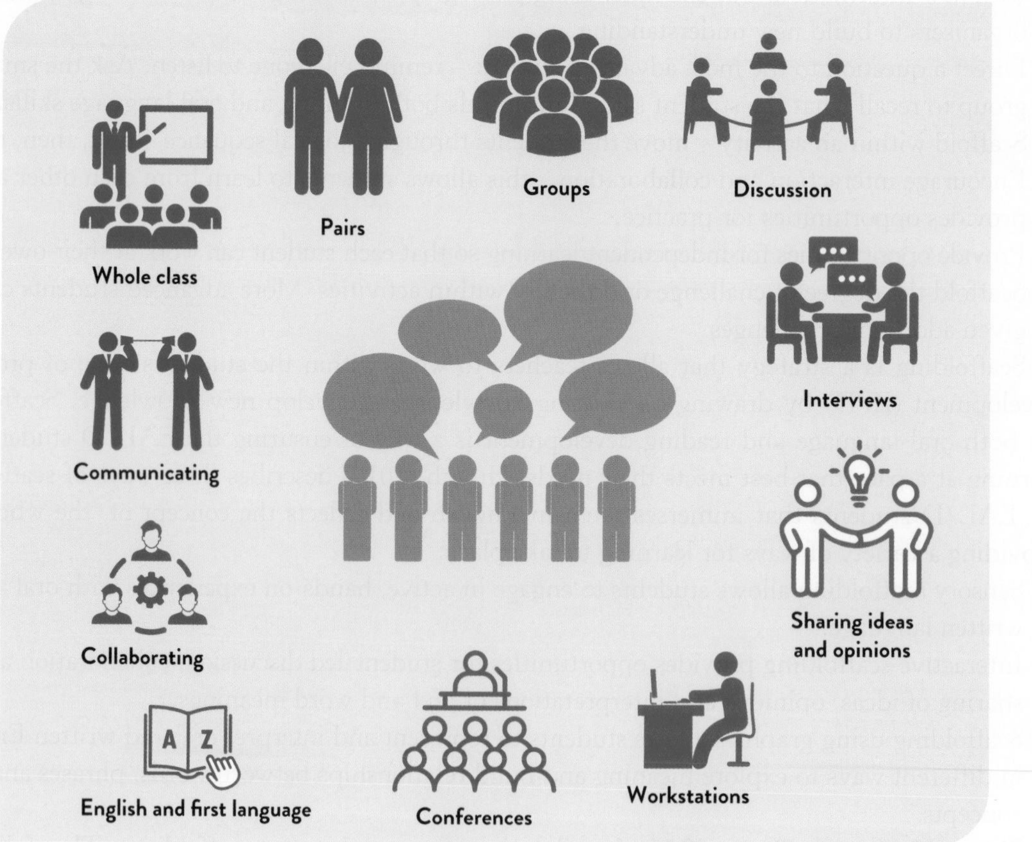

Source: Huynh, T. (2017). Three types of scaffolding: There's a scaffold for that. https://tankhuynh.com/scaffolding-instruction

Dialogic teaching

Using a strategy called dialogic teaching, teachers engage in teacher talk, providing opportunities for students to listen to and practise English. Harper and Feez (2021, p. 15) say that dialogic teacher talk may include:

- asking students to share their thinking and engage in problem-solving and recounting
- asking open-ended questions that promote an extended answer
- drilling and repetition
- talk for instructing and explaining
- using dialogue to build shared understandings
- expressing feelings and opinions
- narrating, speculating and imagining
- exploring and evaluating ideas
- discussing, reasoning, justifying, and negotiating.

Dialogic teaching principles are:

- collective – the teacher and students work on tasks together
- reciprocal – the teacher and students listen to each other, and consider different points of view
- supportive – students share their ideas and help each other, without worrying about being right or wrong.

Educational content is represented in ways that are:

- cumulative – the teacher and students build on and share ideas
- purposeful – the teacher plans the talk and guides the dialogue towards a specific educational goal.

Harper and Feez (2021) state that as EAL/D students learn the language needed to participate in interactive classroom talk, they are 'able to shift between making meanings about their everyday shared experience and the more specialised meanings used to achieve educational goals' (p. 16).

Dialogic teaching

Development of vocabulary

Learning new words and using them in context takes time. EAL/D students need to hear, say, see and write new words in a range of contexts before they will become part of the student's vocabulary. Beck, McKeown and Kucan (2013) devised three tiers, or categories, of words to assist teachers to identify words that require direct, explicit instruction. Typically, words in Tier 1 are common everyday words used in social interactions and for the most part don't require explicit instruction (even for EAL/D who usually develop these words through peers and other social encounters). Tier 2 and 3 words are more complex in meaning and are less frequently used in a social context. In the context of the classroom, these words are theme, topic or learning area specific, and will require explicit teaching and exploration (see **Figure 19.17**).

Flanigan and Greenwood (2007, in NSW Department of Education and Communities, n.d., p. 1) developed a system to help teachers organise, categorise and prioritise the many types of content words they must teach at Tier 2 and Tier 3. These are typically words that:

- students *must know* in order to understand what they read.
- students *are likely to use and encounter frequently*.
- are not adequately defined in context.
- are not in students' background knowledge.
- students may not know based on structure. (Emphasis in original)

Source: NSW Department of Education and Communities. Vocabulary: Selecting words to teach. https://cer.schools.nsw.gov.au/content/dam/doe/sws/schools/c/cer/localcontent/selecting_words_final.pdf, p.2.

Figure 19.17 Three tiers of vocabulary

Type	Definition	Examples	Instruction
Tier 1: Common , everyday words	Basic words used often in everyday conversation	> Dog > Go > Happy > Drink > Phone > Play > Afraid	These words do not need to be explicitly taught, especially in upper grades with native English speakers.
Tier 2: Words that are needed in an academic context, and provide access to more complex topics and discussions outside of the everyday. Words that are useful across multiple topic and subject areas.	More complex, frequently occurring words in academic settings.	> Compare > Neutral > Contrast > Admire > Plead > Represent > Environment > Collaborate	Teach these words. Students will see and use these words often as sophisticated language users.
Tier 3: Content-specific words	Highly specialised words that are related to a specific discipline.	> Pogrom > Quagmire > Locution > Polyglot > Sonata > Isosceles	Teach these words when a specific lesson requires knowledge of the word and underlying concept.

Source: Beck, McKeown and Kucan (2013).

Videos: Vocabulary and using sentence frames

Figure 19.18 provides an example of how new vocabulary can be introduced using explicit instruction.

Academic language

Academic language is formal language related to concepts and specific content areas of the curriculum. Academic language includes many high-frequency Tier 2 and 3 words and phrases in general instructions, such as: define, describe, identify, label, list, predict, explain, match, compare, contrast, summarise, construct, rank and rate. It also includes words specific to learning areas – for example, multiply, divide, square root, parallel lines, equation, debate, argue, predict, reflect, voltage and velocity. It cannot be assumed that EAL/D students know or understand these words in their first language, nor can it be assumed that students will have any contextual or background knowledge related to the learning area or the related academic language.

Not only do EAL/D students need to learn the meaning of these words, they also need to learn how to pronounce the words and apply them to their learning task. Students who are not able to acquire formal academic language used in schools are more likely to have poor educational outcomes.

Figure 19.18 Explicit instruction

Teacher says the word – e.g. excited.

Students repeat the word.

Teacher writes and says the word.

Teacher explains the meaning of the word and part of speech – e.g. verb, adjective, noun: 'Excited is an adjective. Excited describes a feeling (a describing word).'

The teacher uses synonyms familiar to the student to assist them to understand the meaning of the word – e.g. very happy, pleased.

Teacher uses the word in a sentence. The children were excited to be at the beach.

Where possible the teacher provides a visual representation of the word.

The teacher asks the students if they can think of a similar word in their first language and use it in a sentence.

The teacher asks the students to say the word again.

The teacher says the word in a different sentence and asks the students to repeat the word.

The students write the word, its meaning and a sentence.

Word	Meaning	Sentence
excited	**very happy**	**The children were excited to be at the beach.**

'Excited' is added to the word wall.

Source: Horwitz, E. (2020).

Academic language requires direct and explicit instruction. Beck, McKeown and Kucan (2013) say that 'Explicit instruction of spoken vocabulary is a high impact strategy that increases comprehension and enhances learning outcomes for all students'. The authors suggest that a student's knowledge about a word can be described as occurring along a continuum, described in **Figure 19.19**.

Vocabulary instruction

Beck, McKeown and Kucan (2013) have identified key elements of vocabulary instruction necessary to ensure that newly introduced words are understood and can be used by students. These elements are listed in **Figure 19.20**.

Figure 19.19 Word knowledge continuum

No knowledge → Rich knowledge

STAGE 1: Never saw it before
- No knowledge

STAGE 2: Heard of it but don't know what it means
- General sense, e.g. *background* checking something out

STAGE 3: Recognises it in context as having something to do with...
- Narrow, context-bound knowledge

STAGE 4: Knows it well
- Rich knowledge of a word's meaning; its relationship to other words

Source: Beck, I., McKeown, M. & Kucan, L. (2013).

Figure 19.20 Elements of effective vocabulary instruction

Multiple encounters are required before a word is really known.Provide a range of **robust** instructional activities that allow students to explore, see and use the word in a variety of contexts.
Ask students to attempt to define the word – what do they already know about the word?
Talk about and describe various situations where the word could be used (e.g. She was *delighted* with the gift; I was *delighted* with myself! We were *delighted* with the performance).
Require students to provide examples and non-examples: delighted non-example. 'The boys say they were not happy with the way they played the match.'
Establish relationships among words. For example, is there a relationship between *delighted* and *pleased*?
Provide more than one definition of a word to ensure understanding. For example, delighted: feeling great pleasure; delighted: feeling extremely pleased and excited; delighted: a high degree of pleasure or enjoyment.
Students add word to their personal dictionary.
Students write the word in a sentence.
Create a classroom dictionary or word wall (including visuals).
Revisit words and challenge students to use them in context in various activities.
Have each student suggest a new word for the class to explore.
Explore word families – feeling words, action words, etc.

Source: Beck, L., McKeown, M. & Kucan, L. (2013). pp. 83, 84, 85, 109.

Vocabulary, reading and writing

Videos: Introducing and using new words

As you are by now aware, oral language, vocabulary, reading and writing are all related. For EAL/D students, hearing and speaking English (oral language) is the first challenge. Spoken words must be comprehensible – that is, what the speaker is saying must be reasonably able to be understood by the listener even if not all of the words used are understood. In other words, what the student is hearing is slightly ahead of their stage of English language comprehension.

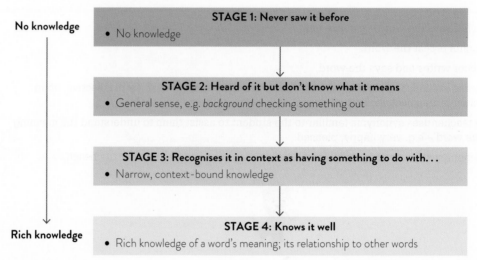

When working with EAL/D students, helping them to understand and comprehend meaning requires a multisensory approach. You will recall that in Chapter 17 the concept of Multisensory Structured Language (MSL) was explored. MSL uses direct and explicit instruction that engages the senses to understand and explore language. In a similar way, a multisensory approach can be an effective strategy when teaching EAL/D students. **Figure 19.21** describes this multisensory approach.

Figure 19.21 Multisensory approach for English language learners

Supporting English language comprehension		
Connect with each student – look at the student to gauge their level of comprehension	Ask multiple questions to check and confirm comprehension	Slow down! Ensure at least 10–15 seconds of wait time before expecting the student to respond to a question.
Rephrase (ask the question or provide an explanation in a different way	Simplify sentences: > Use fewer words > Break the information down into a few shorter sentences rather than one long sentence	Shelter vocabulary – try to use words that you know students already understand (this shelters them from the stress of not understanding any part of what is being said).
Use visuals, sounds, props, real objects, videos, songs, etc. to support comprehension	Link meaning of words to words students already know and understand	Use facial expressions and gestures to help convey meaning.
Circling - the instructional practice of asking a series of prescribed questions in the target language about a statement in the target language (see **Figure 19.22**)	Signal understanding – students quickly signal if they understand what the teacher is saying: > Thumbs up – yes > Arm out hand with palm down – I understand some of what you said > Thumbs down – I don't understand	Write, draw, tell it: > Students describe their understanding by writing (if able) in English or first language > Draw a picture to illustrate meaning > Share understanding with a peer who speaks same first language

Figure 19.22 Example of circling

Circling is used to help students understand and process spoken English – the teacher makes a statement and then uses a number of questions to clarify student understanding	
There were three pigs. The three pigs lived in a forest. A wolf also lived in the forest. The pigs were afraid of the wolf.	There were three pigs. The three pigs lived in a forest. A wolf also lived in the forest. The pigs were afraid of the wolf.
> Teacher: There were three pigs. Class, were there three pigs? > Class: Yes. > Teacher: Yes, there were three pigs. > Teacher: Were there four pigs? > Class: No. > Teacher: No, there were not four pigs. There were three pigs! > Teacher: Were there three pigs or were there three elephants? > Class: Three pigs. > Teacher: There were not three elephants, there were three pigs! Were there three pigs or were there six pigs? > Class: Three pigs. > Teacher: Correct! There were three pigs! There were not six pigs, there were three pigs! Were there three wolves? > Class: No. > Teacher: No, there were not three wolves, there were three pigs. How many pigs were there? > Class: Three.	> Teacher: There were three pigs. Class, how many pigs were there? > Class: Three. > Teacher: Yes, there were three pigs. The three pigs lived in a forest. Class, did the three pigs live in a forest? > Class: Yes. > Teacher: Yes, the three pigs lived in a forest. Dinah, do you live in a forest? > Dinah: No. > Teacher: No, you don't live in a forest. What do you live in? > Dinah: A house. > Teacher: Class, Dinah lives in a house! She does not live in a forest, she lives in a house. Where did the three pigs live? > Class: In a forest. > Teacher: Yes, the three pigs lived in a forest. A wolf also lived in the forest. Class, what animals lived in the forest? > Class: Three pigs and a wolf.

Source: The Comprehensible Classroom LLC (2014). What is circling? A tutorial for language teachers. https://www.comprehensibleclassroom.com, p. 4

Figure 19.23 Picture and letter displays can be used to support EAL/D students

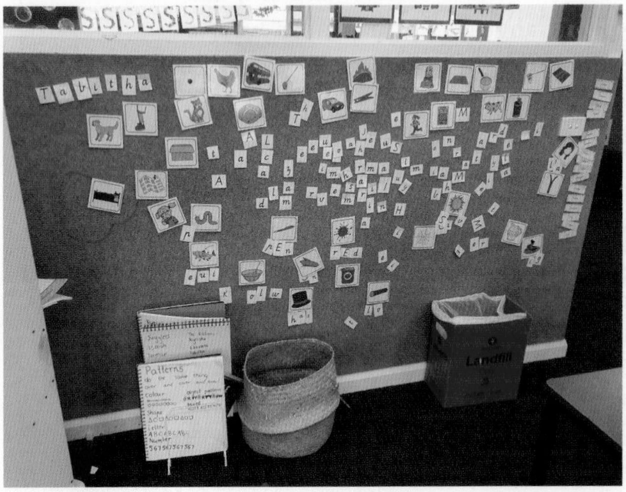

Source: Photo by Tish Okely © Cengage

Examples of vocabulary activities

- Typically, vocabulary is built by beginning with survival words needed by EAL/D students to navigate the school day (**Figure 19.23**).
- Using real objects, photographs, drawings, picture dictionaries, and video or online graphics allows students to make the connection between the English word and their first language. (It's important to be aware that some English words may not have an equivalent word in the student's first language.)
- Picture sequences – students are given a set of pictures to put into a logical sequence using the 'first, next, then' concept.
- Using written speaking frames to retell a story. Working in a small group read a short story a few times and then ask students to recall the story using speaking frames. 'The dog…', 'Anna was…' Students can work collaboratively to share their ideas.
- Playing games, such as bingo, scrabble and memory word game.
- Creating individual word dictionaries using English words and first language words.
- Working in small groups where each student must contribute two English words related to a theme or topic.

Reading strategies and checking for understanding

Figure 19.24 Using photos

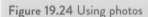

Source: iStock.com/Brostock

- Matching word cards to picture cards and using the words in a sentence. Images and words should be easily relatable and group in ways that make them easy to access and use. Students can be encouraged to create their own lists.
- Using photos (see **Figure 19.24**):
  - Students can label things they see in the photo.
  - Students can create 'thought bubbles' for characters in photos. For example, 'What might the people in this picture be thinking?'
  - Teachers can generate questions using question frames. For example, 'The girl is feeling …'
  - Students can respond to written questions:
  - Knowledge: what items or people can you name with the vocabulary you know?
  - Comprehension: What is happening in the photo?
  - Application: What one sentence caption would you write?
  - Analysis: Where do you think they are?
  - Synthesis: What might they be thinking?
  - Evaluation: Are they too young to play soccer? Why or why not?
  - Students can identify the similarities and differences between two different images using sentence frames as: Both pictures have ______. One difference is __________. In the first picture there is __________, but in the second picture there is __________.

- Creating vocabulary folders containing A4 pages of images and single words nouns, verbs, adjectives, adverbs, themes, etc. that students can use as they begin to increase their vocabulary knowledge (see **Figure 19.25**).

Figure 19.25 Examples of lists for vocabulary folder

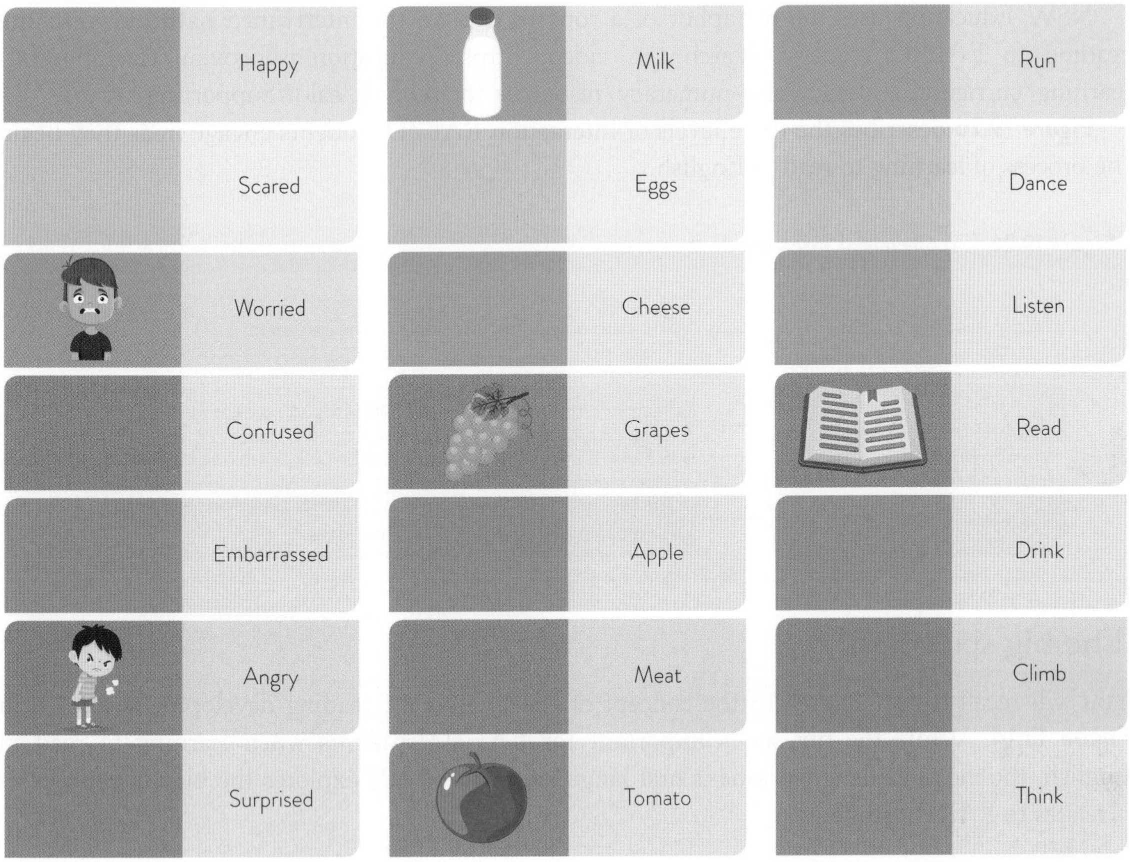

Sources: Shutterstock.com/Viktorija Reuta (milk); Shutterstock.com/Nicoleta Ionescu (worried); Shutterstock.com/Wat cartoon (angry); Shutterstock.com/HardtIllustrations (grapes); Shutterstock.com/Kilroy79 (tomato); Shutterstock.com/FOTOSPLASH (book).

Learning to read in a second language

Learning to read in a second language, while also learning to speak in a second language, is an extraordinarily difficult task. Approaches to reading instruction for EAL/D students include both top-down and bottom-up strategies. Horwitz (2020, p. 135) explains: Bottom up reflects a phonics-based approach to reading where 'students learn to read by sounding out individual words and attempting to understand a text by individually processing every sound and word'. A top-down approach involves learners 'applying their background knowledge and focus on understanding a written text as a whole. They use their understanding of the text and the predictability of the grammatical patterns in their target language to guess the meaning of unfamiliar words or phrases'.

Education Victoria states that EAL/D students:

> need to learn reading skills at the levels of sub-word, word, phrase, sentence, paragraph and text. These include:
> – recognising letters and understanding the direction of writing
> – learning the connections between letters and sounds in order to sound out words
> – knowing the meaning of words (and parts of words)

- making meaning from sentences and larger sections of text
- connecting literal meanings to cultural and content knowledge
- reading and viewing text to find information, predict and infer
- applying these skills to increasingly technical or formal texts.

Source: Department of Education and Training Victoria (2021). Reading and viewing and EAL/D learners. https://www.education.vic.gov.au/school/teachers/teachingresources/discipline/english/literacy/readingviewing/Pages/reading-and-viewing-and-eald-learners.aspx

NSW Education uses the metaphor of a rope to explain the intertwined nature of teaching reading to EAL/D readers. Watch the video: https://education.nsw.gov.au/teaching-and-learning/curriculum/literacy-and-numeracy/resources-for-schools/eald#Supporting2.

Figure 19.26 describes the three levels of interaction EAL/D students engage in as they begin the process of learning to read in English.

Figure 19.26 Three levels of interaction

Word level interactions	⟶	Translate only unfamiliar single nouns and verbs
Sentence level	⟶	Search for detail – find nouns and verbs and search for how, when, where and why.
Page level interactions	⟶	The teacher reads the text aloud, students read aloud and search for meaning. Students discuss their ideas.

The big six

You will recall from Chapter 13 the concept of the 'big six' of reading development, shown in **Figure 13.14**. While the big six is important for EAL/D students when learning to read in English, the most challenging issue is oral language. **Figure 19.27** explores the big six concept as it relates to EAL/D students.

Figure 19.27 EAL/D readers and the big six

Oral language is the foundation for the development of literacy skills and is a strong indicator of later reading, writing and overall academic achievement. We also know that children who begin school with a rich vocabulary are more likely to be successful readers than children who commence school with a limited vocabulary. We also know that EAL/D students who can read in their first language are more likely to be successful readers as they acquire English.

Phonemic awareness is the foundation for spelling and word recognition skills. It is the ability to hear and manipulate the sounds in language.

Challenge for EAL/D students: may not be able to hear the sounds in a word and/or may not be able to reproduce these sounds and are therefore not able to link sounds to letter patterns.

Phonics is understanding that letters and letter patterns represent the sounds of spoken language.

Challenge for EAL/D students: Students who have not learned to read in their native language may struggle to put together the sound/symbol correspondence concept, new words, and new sounds all at once. For example:

- letter recognition
- beginning and ending sounds
- blends
- rhyming words
- silent letters
- homonyms.

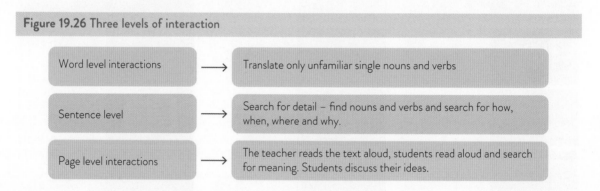

Vocabulary is recognising and understanding words in context.

Challenge for EAL/D students: before students can read words they must be part of the students' existing vocabulary. If students can't say the word, they will struggle to read and understand the word. Learning to read begins with known words. EAL/D students may not know any words in English.

To 'know' a word means:

> the ability to define a word
> the ability to recognise when to use that word
> knowledge of its multiple meanings
> the ability to decode and spell that word
> the ability to use different definitions of that word accurately in different contexts.

Fluency is the ability to read a text accurately and quickly.

Challenge for EAL/D students: Reading for comprehension rather than fluency is a priority for EAL/D students. Reading with understanding while trying to decode words is a challenging task for EAL/D students. To develop fluency EAL/D students should be encouraged to engage in independent reading; read aloud the same passage numerous times to practise intonation and inflection.

Comprehension is the understanding and interpretation of what is read. It requires students to:

> decode what they read
> make connections between what they read and what they already know
> think deeply about what they have read.
> *Challenge for EAL/D students*: They may not have the vocabulary needed for reading, may struggle to decode words, may be unfamiliar with content, and may struggle to read at a pace that allows the student to make sense of the text.

Source: Robertson, K. & Breiseth, L. (n.d.). Reading 101 for English language learners. https://www.colorincolorado.org/article/reading-101-english-language-learners

Guided reading

As you will recall, in guided reading, small groups of students who are at around the same level in their reading ability work with the teacher to read a text. The focus of guided reading is reading with understanding, and using problem-solving to work out unfamiliar words and sentence structures.

Guided reading for EAL/D students is most effective if it is carried out on a one-to-one basis with the student and teacher or ESW. The role of the adult is to scaffold the individual student's existing reading skills, such as decoding, pronunciation, fluency and intonation. The adult can also support the student to look at the text before reading, perhaps using the images and pictures or the title to predict what the text might be about or scan for any known words.

Texts for guided reading for EAL/D students should be culturally relevant and reflect a degree of familiarity or prior knowledge. Texts should not be too complex or contain too many new words. The goal of guided reading is to build content knowledge (usually related to a learning area) and demonstrate understanding by completing a guided writing activity. Guided reading can also include inferencing and predicting.

Videos: Guided reading and choral reading

Reading aloud and choral reading

Reading aloud has a number of benefits for EAL/D students. It:

- models correct pronunciation
- allows students to hear fluent reading
- allows students to follow along
- demonstrates the use of intonation and inflection to add meaning to text
- allows for both prediction and inferencing

- allows students to hear words and phrases in context rather than in isolation
- provides opportunities for discussion, which builds comprehension.

Reading aloud also builds enjoyment of literature, particularly if texts are chosen that will appeal to the students' interests and cultural background (Adapted from Huynh, 2018).

Choral reading is reading aloud in unison with a whole class or group of students. Choral reading builds reading fluency and supports correct pronunciation. Reading in a group means students feel less self-conscious and are supported by more able students. Texts can include popular songs, short poems and short stories of a few paragraphs. Each student should have their own printed copy. Students should be given several opportunities to read the same text.

To begin, the teacher reads the text to the students using intonation. Next, the teacher might ask the meaning of some words or phrases to gauge comprehension. The teacher reads aloud again, and finally asks the group to read aloud with the teacher. The teacher should set a pace that supports fluency but also accommodates the needs and skills of the students.

Inferencing

An important skill that is typically taught alongside learning to read is inferencing, which Huynh (2016a) describes as 'creating a thought or opinion that can be supported by the text'. Inferencing supports the development of critical thinking, a skill that is used in all learning areas. Inferencing allows EAL/D students to draw on their existing knowledge, to express their opinions and demonstrate their background knowledge and thinking (in the first language and/or English). Often, it requires combining one's background knowledge and life experience with the text-based evidence.

Huynh draws on the work of Beers (2003), who suggests a strategy she termed 'It Says – I Say – So' to break down the process of inferencing into manageable steps. These steps are described in **Figure 19.28**.

Figure 19.28 Beers 'It Says – I Say – So'

1	2	3	4
• Write and say the question • Create an inferral question about the subject matter	• 'It says' • Find information from the text to answer the question	• 'I Say' • Students think about what they already know	• 'So' • Students state their own opinion based on the text and what they already know or think

Sources: 'It Says – I Say – So'. Reading Rockets. https://www.readingrockets.org/pdfs/inference-graphic-organizer.pdf; Beers, K. (2003). *When Kids Can't Read: What Teachers Can Do.* Portsmouth, NH: Heinemann.

Student-led discussion

Video: How to facilitate a Harkness discussion

The most important element in reading programs for EAL/D students is student-led discussion (known as The Harkness Discussion), which allows students to pose questions, provide answers and evaluate shared ideas. Huynh (2016b) suggests that student-led discussion facilitates:

- student-centred instruction
- students listening to each other
- students answering each other's questions

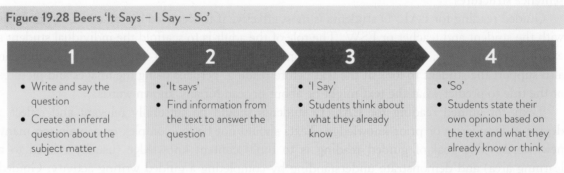

- students strengthening interpersonal skills
- students developing critical thinking skills.

Source: Huynh, T. (2016b). The Harkness Discussion: Where everyone has a voice at the table. https://tankhuynh.com/a7-teaching-harkness

In other words student-led discussion is collaborative and student-centred.

Practical strategies to support EAL/D learners

The role of the ESW in relation to EAL/D students will typically be one of support and the preparation of learning resources. **Figure 19.29** describes the main role and responsibilities of the classroom teacher and the role of the ESW when working with EAL/D students.

Figure 19.29 Supporting EAL/D students

The role and responsibilities of the teacher	The role of the ESW
• Adapts learning experiences/resources to meet EAL/D needs • Supports EAL/D students as English-language learners • Adapts assessment strategies to meet EAL/D needs • Keeps assessment records of learning that occurs in home language as well as in English • Works collaboratively with parents • Provides opportunities for students to explore their own culture • Provides activities that reflect a multicultural perspective • Promotes anti-bias in the classroom	• Assists in adapting learning resources to meet EAL/D needs • Engages in team-teaching by translating tasks to EAL/D students by working alongside teacher • Supports EAL/D students in their learning by explaining concepts or directions in the learners' first languages (if possible) • Supports the participation of EAL/D students in the classroom • Assists teachers to communicate with parents and other family members if possible • Acts as a language role model – uses accurate pronunciation and grammar

As well as specific teacher-directed tasks, EAL/D students will benefit from role models. They will look to the ESW, teacher or classmate models for an example of what to do, how to do it (including the sequence of a task) and what materials or resources to use.

GO FURTHER

Access examples of the wide range of teaching support resources that can be used to support EAL/D students to develop English language skills in your **Go Further** resource, available through your instructor.

ESWs can support EAL/D students in a variety of ways – for example, by:

- speaking slower, not louder – students need to process the words separately and form an understanding; for EAL/D students, this requires some extra time
- checking for understanding by asking questions
- keeping instructions short, preferably starting with action verbs: 'Draw …'; 'Pick up …' Long instructions overwhelm EAL/D students
- making sure to pause frequently when giving instructions. This provides time for students to think about the instructions and ask questions
- introducing new concepts and vocabulary in a meaningful context – for example, using pictures of common objects to name and classify
- writing key vocabulary on a word wall
- setting up learning centres that focus on a theme or concept
- engaging in one-to-one conversation and questioning
- engaging in small-group role-plays
- developing a range of visual prompts to guide student learning – for example, creating a flow chart to show steps in making a craft item or steps in the daily routine/timetable

- using concrete materials to support concept development – for example, plastic numbers, counters, number cards (numerals and words) to aid in learning names of numerals, items of clothing to label, plastic fruit and vegetables, tools, household items, different types of balls/bats
- using music and movement to introduce new words (e.g. 'Heads and shoulders, knees and toes')
- reading to the student; listening to the student read and asking questions – for example, 'What happens when …?'; 'What was the dog's name?'
- acting as a scribe to model writing – for example, Gharam (8 years) dictates, 'Me have brother. He baby.' The ESW writes and reads aloud, 'I have a baby brother.'

CASE STUDY | Lavindra

Part 2

The classroom teacher, specialist EAL/D teacher and ESW have identified a range of teaching strategies that can be used with **Lavindra**.

Teaching strategies for Lavindra

- Role-playing part of a story using repetitious dialogue from the text – for example, a picture book.
- Naming and displaying real objects and asking Lavindra to choose a similar thing from a set of picture cards: *'This is a plate. Show me another plate.'*
- Using a repetitive chorus with visual cues or prompts to model target language: *'My name is Miss Jenkins, hello, hello, hello. My name is Lavindra, hello, hello, hello.'*
- Naming colour cards and matching objects to colour cards – crayons, counters, teddies.
- Sitting opposite Lavindra and using the whole hand to point to your own eyes, nose, mouth, etc. Indicate that Lavindra should mirror and say words.
- Using common objects for 'feely box' activities. Lavindra pulls an object from the box, the ESW labels the object, then Lavindra repeats, *'This is a dog.' 'This is a spoon.' 'This is a pen.'*
- Listening to rhymes and imitating gestures – for example. *'Everybody do this, do this, do this. Everybody do this just like me.'*
- Using sequencing pictures and placing in the correct order.
- Focusing on language, identifying who, what, where and when during shared reading of a picture book – for example, *Who Sank the Boat?* by Pamela Allen.

19.5 Supporting partnerships with families

Mutually respectful relationships between home and school are a key contributing factor in positive outcomes for EAL/D students.

Facilitating student, school and home interactions

Research demonstrates that there is no 'one-size-fits-all' approach to engagement with families. Just as every student is unique, the pathway to developing respectful relationships with each family will be unique. Student outcomes are improved when schools and families work together towards a set of common goals. Partnerships with families help to build a concept of 'the whole child' and allow educators to better meet individual needs.

Education and Training, ACT Government (2015) suggests adopting a philosophy of 'doing with' rather than 'doing to' to build partnerships with EAL/D families. This philosophy includes the following beliefs and practices:

- Positive communication empowers EAL/D families. Give messages which stress the important role EAL/D families have to play in enriching the school's life, as well as their own child's unique learning.
- Involve EAL/D families in the design and implementation of a culturally responsive and respectful environment with a focus on equal access and participation in school life.
- Create a warm and welcoming environment with parent-friendly spaces that encourage interaction between the school and parents, and between all parents.
- Actively create a range of opportunities for EAL/D families to share their stories, cultural perspectives, food and customs.
- Ensure there is a person working in the school who is known in the community to have a broad understanding of the issues faced by EAL/D families, who takes the time to connect with families, is a familiar person for families to seek support from, and an advocate.
- Regularly use the Translating and Interpreting Service (www.tisnational.gov.au) to share important information and clarify misunderstandings, without concern about cost.

Source: Education and Training. ACT Government (2015). Progressing Parental Engagement School Fact Sheet. https://www.education.act.gov.au/?a=807433, p. 2.

The Victorian Foundation for Survivors of Torture Inc., in conjunction with the Department of Education and Training Victoria, has developed a guide for working in partnership with refugee families. The guide provides a definition of parent engagement with schools as: 'A two-way collaboration between families and schools based on good communication, trusting relationships and respectful partnerships, with the goal of enhancing children's education.'

The foundation recommends that to support effective and respectful two-way communication with families, it is important to provide regular access to trained interpreters to facilitate one-to-one communication with families and translations of school documents. It's also important to be aware that some parents may have limited literacy skills in their first language.

Translators can also be used to support the orientation process by developing videos about the school community, the curriculum and the learning environment in a variety of languages. An orientation program that allows families to visit the school is an important step in building respectful relationships. **Figure 19.30** describes the information that might be shared (via a translator) for families during an orientation visit.

Figure 19.30 Sharing information with families

Orientation information sharing may include:

> A tour of the school and its facilities – library, hall, outdoor spaces, canteen, sporting facilities etc.
> Observation of classrooms in action – the focus on hands-on learning, student activities, play as learning etc.
> Textbooks and learning resources
> Brief overview of the curriculum and special school programs such as music, dance, drama
> How parents can support home–school partnership
> Language learning support for students
> Healthy eating habits, including culturally appropriate food for lunch boxes
> Meet and greet of principal, school executive, school counsellor, classroom teachers and ESWs
> Relevant school policies – absences, illness, behaviour expectations etc.
> School-community social events

Source: Victorian Foundation for Survivors of Torture Inc. (2015). Schools and Families in Partnership: A Desktop Guide to Engaging Families from Refugee Backgrounds in their Children's Learning. (pp. 2, 4) https://sifr.foundationhouse.org.au/app/uploads/2020/07/SCHOOLS_FAMILIES_PARTNERSHIP_DESKTOP-GUIDE_WEB_cr.pdf

NAMING CONVENTIONS

CONSIDER THIS

Something as simple as taking the time to learn the correct pronunciation of names and understanding cultural naming conventions demonstrates respect for EAL/D families.

ARABIC

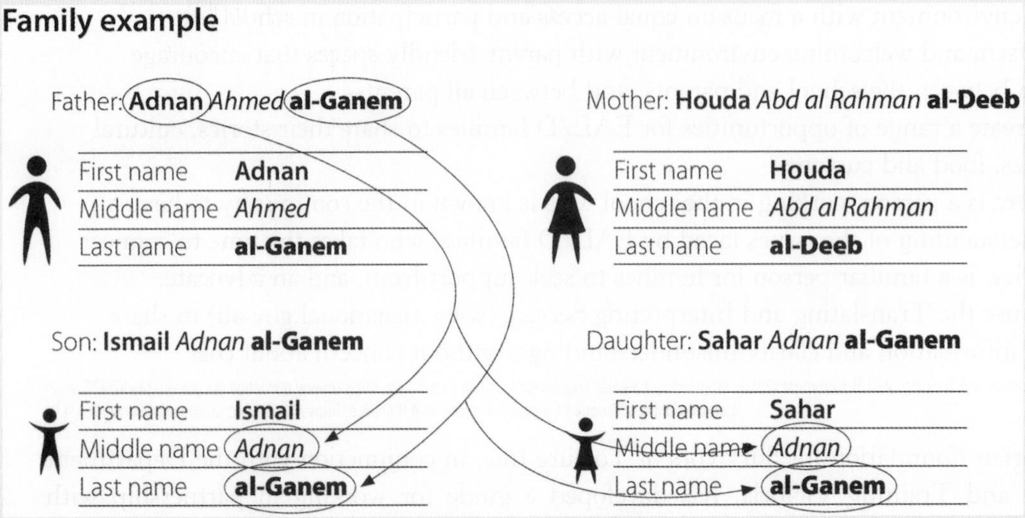

CHINESE

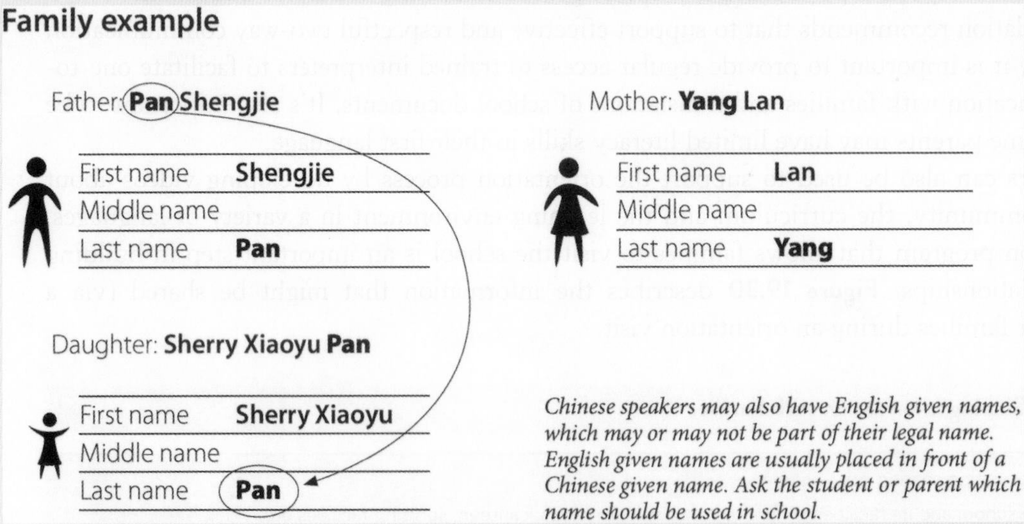

Family example
Father: Pan Shengjie
First name Shengjie
Middle name
Last name Pan
Mother: Yang Lan
First name Lan
Middle name
Last name Yang
Daughter: Sherry Xiaoyu Pan
First name Sherry Xiaoyu
Middle name
Last name Pan
Chinese speakers may also have English given names, which may or may not be part of their legal name. English given names are usually placed in front of a Chinese given name. Ask the student or parent which name should be used in school.

Source: Greenberg Motamedi, J., Jaffery, Z., Hagen, A. & Yoon, S. Y. (2017). Getting it right: Reference guides for registering students with non-English names, 2nd edition. (REL 2016-158 v2). Washington, DC: US Department of Education, Institute of Education Sciences, National Center for Education Evaluation and Regional Assistance, Regional Educational Laboratory Northwest. Retrieved from http://ies.ed.gov/ncee/edlab (pp. 6, 8).

The role of the ESW

Some schools will employ specialist multicultural education aides (MEAs), whose role with families may include:

- Keeping parents informed of school events and activities and encouraging them to participate
- Helping parents to make school appointments and reminding them shortly before
- Translating school notices, letters and newsletters (written or verbal) as appropriate, and not as a replacement for the use of professional translating services [see **Figure 19.31**]
- Helping parents to complete forms such as those used during enrolment
- Liaising between teachers and parents: advise parents if a child is having a problem at school and encourage parents to speak with the teacher
- Attending home visits with student wellbeing coordinators
- Providing liaison between families and community organisations.

Source: State of Queensland. Department of Education (2023). Advice for parents. https://education.qld.gov.au/students/inclusive-education/english-language-support/advice-for-parents; Victorian Foundation for Survivors of Torture Inc. (2015). *Schools and Families in Partnership: A Desktop Guide to Engaging Families from Refugee Backgrounds in their Children's Learning* (p. 8). https://sifr.foundationhouse.org.au/app/uploads/2020/07/SCHOOLS_FAMILIES_PARTNERSHIP_DESKTOP-GUIDE_WEB_cr.pdf

MEA guidelines

Figure 19.31 Translated document for parents

致家长的建议书

家长在为孩子学习提供支持方面扮演着重要角色。研究不断表明，如果家长参与孩子的教育，孩子的学业表现会更好。您无需精通英语即可为孩子求学提供帮助和支持。

帮助孩子学习英语

我们强烈建议家长通过以下方式帮助孩子学习英语：

- 经常使用母语和 / 或英语为孩子朗读
- 鼓励孩子积极学习并坚持使用你们的母语
- 熟悉澳大利亚课程和孩子在校学习目标
- 与孩子谈论其在校体验
- 若对学习计划或孩子的学习进展有任何疑问或担心，随时与孩子的老师或有关教职人员进行沟通
- 参加家长老师座谈会

拜访孩子所在学校时，您可以通过学校前台预约与老师交谈。如果您的第一语言不是英语，而且您更习惯使用自己的母语，您可以让某位家人或朋友陪您一起去学校，帮助您与学校工作人员沟通。或者，您也可以通过翻译与口译服务请求学校提供口译员。此服务免费提供。

使用你们的母语

作为家长，您在家里必须持续使用你们的母语，这很重要。

孩子的第一语言或方言与其认同感密切相关。鼓励孩子不断学习其第一语言，有助于他们进入新的学习环境后顺利完成社交和情感转型。

持续使用孩子的第一语言让孩子能够学习与其年龄相符的世界知识和词汇，而无需等到其英语语言能力达到了解这些话题所需的水平。

一家颇有实力的研究机构指出，第一语言基础坚实的学员往往能够更快地掌握英语，并在学业上取得更好的成绩。孩子学习另一语言时，如果第一语言的基础不扎实或未得到巩固，则很难学好另一语言。建立并巩固孩子的母语基础对于成功培养其英语语言知识和技能至关重要。

帮助孩子学习学校开设的课程

如果您的孩子仍在学习英语口语、阅读和写作，则他们被视为英语作为另一语言或方言课程（EAL/D）学员，并将获得额外支持以帮助其学习课程内容。

澳大利亚学校的所有学生均学习澳大利亚课程内容。

由于您的孩子一边学习英语，一边学习新内容，所以学校会根据其英语水平调整学习任务。随着他们的英语水平不断提高，他们获得的支持类型将发生变化。

家庭作业

每所学校都有各自的家庭作业制度。家庭作业让学生有机会巩固其课堂学习内容，养成良好的学习习惯，并让家人参与其学习过程。如果您的孩子看不懂其家庭作业，您应该向任课教师反映这一情况。

在家里进行趣味阅读是一项非常有益的家庭作业活动。阅读的形式可以是您为孩子朗读，您和孩子一起阅读，也可以是他们自己阅读。阅读的书籍可以是英文书籍或者你们的母语书籍，也可以是从学校图书馆或当地公共图书馆免费借阅的书籍。

Source: Advice for parents Arabic and Chinese Simplified 2018 © The State of Queensland (Department of Education) CC BY 4.0.

Getting to know families

To build a partnership with families of EAL/D students it is essential to be well informed about the students and families who will be part of your school community. If you are employed in a specialist MEA role, it will be also important to be aware of the range of support services available to EAL/D students and families. Building a network around families can lead to better outcomes for families, especially where families are isolated and have little or no knowledge of the systems that can support their transition and settlement in Australia. **Figure 19.32** provides information about the types of networks that you can connect with to support families. These networks can also assist you in your role by providing information and resources to support your role with both students and the families.

Naming conventions and translation

Figure 19.32 Knowing and supporting families

Knowing	Supporting
Ask for correct pronunciation of name/s	Multicultural resource centres
Learn naming conventions	Multicultural family support /play groups
Check names are spelt correctly	Child health clinics
What countries do families come from?	English language classes for adults
Are families refugees or immigrants?	Interpreter services
If refugees what was their journey? What trauma may they have experienced? How long have they been refugees?	Ethnic welfare/housing services
What languages are spoken by the families?	Ethnic women's groups
Who are the members of the family?	
What are the common cultural practices and beliefs? What special events are typically celebrated by the family?	
Are there any specific cultural practices that must be observed? Are there gender-specific roles/expectations for behaviour/ responsibilities?	
Have the children had prior education?	
What are the family's dreams and aspirations for their children?	

Summary

This chapter has provided a brief overview of the background knowledge and practices required to effectively support EAL/D learners. Before working with EAL/D students, it is essential to have some background knowledge about the challenges faced by refugee and immigrant families. Issues such as culture shock, post-traumatic stress, separation from family and friends, and adjustment to a new culture are all major life stressors for children, young people and families. Background information is essential when considering the concept of 'the whole child', rather than simply seeing the student as an English language learner.

You were introduced to the EAL/D Learning Progressions Foundation to Year 10 and the ESL Scales, which guide teachers when working with EAL/D students. The acquisition of English for second language learners is a challenging and complex task that takes many years to achieve. Students typically move through predictable stages of English language learning; however, the rate of progression will be unique to each student.

Teaching EAL/D learners requires specialist skills and knowledge that can't be adequately covered in a single chapter. Instead, you were provided with a brief overview of the strategies that can be used to support the development of oral language, reading and writing.

Finally this chapter looked at the importance of working in partnership with families and the role of the ESW. Throughout this chapter you have been provided with a variety of links to resources that provide additional knowledge and practical resources. Should you decide to work in this specialist area, it is recommended that you undertake additional training, and access an experienced mentor to guide your practices.

Self-check questions

1. Define post-traumatic stress disorder (PTSD) and list four signs and symptoms of PTSD.
2. How can educators help newly enrolled refugee students to feel secure in a school setting?
3. List three general principles to guide health, welfare and education professionals working with refugee children/adolescents experiencing trauma according to the Royal Children's Hospital, Melbourne.
4. Define acculturation and explain the possible causes.
5. Define the term culture shock and describe its five distinct stages.
6. Define English as an additional language or dialect (EAL/D) based on the Australian Curriculum and list the students included in this category.
7. What are the purposes of the English as a Second Language (ESL) scales?
8. Identify whether each of the following statements is true (T) or false (F):
   a. Bilingual children are not more likely than monolingual children to have difficulties with language, to show delays in learning or to be diagnosed with a language disorder. Just as some monolingual children have a language delay or disorder, a similar proportion of bilinguals will have a language delay or disorder.
   b. Translanguaging is the process where EAL/D students draw only on English language to communicate.
   c. Students who are not able to acquire formal academic language used in schools are more likely to have poor educational outcomes.
9. What are the three stages of listening development of EAL/D students?
10. What is dialogic teaching and its principles?
    In dialectic teaching, how is educational content represented?
11. Academic language requires direct and explicit instruction. Define explicit instruction.
12. What are the challenges for EAL/D students in oral language when they are learning to read?

Discussion questions

1 The Australian Curriculum requires a number of points to be considered when developing personalised learning plans for EAL/D students (refer back to section 19.2 EAL/D programs). Discuss each point.

2 Discuss the most effective strategies ESWs can use to measure and monitor EAL/D students' progress. Give an example for each.

3 Discuss your main role and responsibilities as an ESW in relation to EAL/D students. Give examples.

Activities

- For this task, refer to the Scenario 'Culture shock' on page 719. Discuss how as an ESW you could help Deka, Ekon and Jamille with their adjustment to their new country and culture.
- For this task, go to **Figure 19.14** 'Communication strategies' on page 738 and discuss each strategy. Give examples based on your knowledge and experience working with EAL/D students.

Chapter 20

SEARCH AND ACCESS ONLINE INFORMATION AND RESOURCES

LEARNING OBJECTIVES

When you have completed this chapter, you should be able to demonstrate that you can:

- 20.1 identify and use organisational policies and procedures for internet access and use, including cybersecurity strategies to protect information from accidental or illegal corruption, theft or damage
- 20.2 define the concept of 'information for educational use' as designed by copyright legislation
- 20.3 accurately reference materials that have been sourced from books, journals, videos, online, photocopies, etc. to ensure basic aspects of copyright, moral and intellectual property rights in relation to educational use
- 20.4 research and evaluate credible sources of information
- 20.5 access information on your school's intranet according to the school's policies and procedures
- 20.6 use search engines and key words to source information
- 20.7 define research requirements and objectives and determine methods for documentation and presentation of information.

Online resources icons refer to useful weblinks. Ask your instructor for these **Online Resources.**

Introduction

This chapter will explore how to search for and access online information as directed by the teacher. Information may be used for a wide range of purposes – for example, to support the development of learning resources and materials; to identify appropriate sites for students and/or provide information to students for assignments, projects, homework and classroom-based learning; to research current knowledge and or best practice; to identify learning resources and materials for students with special learning needs (e.g. English as a second language/dialect [EAL/D] learners) and students with disability, or to access information that reflects diversity.

Protocols for correctly referencing and attributing ownership as well as ensuring compliance with copyright requirements will also be examined.

20.1 Organisational policies and procedures

Organisational policies and procedures will include:

- internet access and use
- copyright, including moral and intellectual property rights
- referencing and crediting information.

Procedures for accessing and using the internet

All schools will have policies and procedures for employees when accessing and using information on the internet for teaching and learning purposes. Education Victoria's 'Teaching and learning resources – Selecting appropriate materials' policy states:

> – Schools must ensure that teaching and learning resources provide challenging and engaging learning programs for students but do not offend students or the wider school community due to their obscene, offensive or controversial nature.
> – Schools must not use teaching and learning resources created by inappropriate organisations for classroom use.
> – The department provides guidelines to inform teachers' and principals' decisions regarding the selection of teaching and learning resources, available on the Guidance tab.
> – These guidelines also outline how schools should respond to objections raised about the use of specific teaching and learning resources.

Source: Education Victoria (2023). Teaching and learning resources – Selecting appropriate materials. https://www2.education.vic.gov.au/pal/selecting-suitable-teaching-resources/print-all © State of Victoria (Department of Education and Training). Licensed under Creative Commons Attribution 4.0 international licence, https://creativecommons.org/licenses/by/4.0/

The policy states that students should 'not be exposed to highly offensive or obscene materials or themes and information must not be accessed from "inappropriate" organisations' (Education Victoria, 2023). The policy defines offensive or obscene material as 'material about which there is a consensus that it is unacceptable'. To determine acceptability, schools are encouraged to pose questions such as:

> – Are the proposed materials/themes within the resource likely to be regarded as highly offensive or overly obscene by the school community?
> – Have the proposed materials been created by an inappropriate organisation(s) for classroom use
> – Are the proposed materials/themes within the resource controversial or likely to be regarded as inappropriate by some students or their parents?

Source: Education Victoria (2023). Teaching and learning resources – Selecting appropriate materials. https://www2.education.vic.gov.au/pal/selecting-suitable-teaching-resources/print-all © State of Victoria (Department of Education and Training). Licensed under Creative Commons Attribution 4.0 international licence, https://creativecommons.org/licenses/by/4.0/

In relation to controversial themes, the policy states that 'topics will often be appropriate and important subjects of study in schools and, at times, cannot be avoided in the context of teaching and learning'. Possible topics that may meet with objections may include:

> – themes related to magic or fantasy
> – racial and religious themes
> – sexual activity, nudity and related themes
> – drug misuse or addiction
> – crime, violence or cruelty
> – suicide and excessively bleak scenarios
> – the depiction of revolting or abhorrent phenomena
> – satirical or comparative perspectives on race, religion or gender.

Source: Education Victoria (2023). Teaching and learning resources – Selecting appropriate materials. https://www2.education.vic.gov.au/pal/selecting-suitable-teaching-resources/print-all © State of Victoria (Department of Education and Training). Licensed under Creative Commons Attribution 4.0 international licence, https://creativecommons.org/licenses/by/4.0/

Inappropriate organisations are those listed in the Sponsorship policy and Financial Literacy policy and include:

- political parties
- tobacco companies
- gaming venues
- companies involved in the sale or promotion of alcohol
- companies involved in the sale or promotion of weapons, including firearms
- companies that encourage unhealthy food choices by young people
- religious organisations, excepting for the delivery of Special Religious Instruction
- authorised deposit-taking institutions such as banks.

Source: Education Victoria (2023). Teaching and learning resources – Selecting appropriate materials. https://www2.education.vic.gov.au/pal/selecting-suitable-teaching-resources/print-all © State of Victoria (Department of Education and Training). Licensed under Creative Commons Attribution 4.0 international licence, https://creativecommons.org/licenses/by/4.0/

Education WA's 'Telecommunications use' policy states, in part:

> Staff and contractors must restrict their usage of Departmental online services for personal reasons, and use discretion in the content involved. Such usage must not:
> - interfere with the employee's job functions;
> - place undue demands on the network;
> - involve deliberately accessing, sending or downloading of materials that are unacceptable in terms of legislation, Public Sector and Department policy. This includes material that carries content that may be considered to be of a pornographic, racist, sexist, inflammatory, hateful, obscene or abusive nature.

Source: Telecommunications Use Policy, v. 1.0, effective 1 August 2003, https://www.education.wa.edu.au/web/policies/-/telecommunications-use-policy. Licensed under Attribution 2.5 Australia (CC BY 2.5 AU)

Cybersecurity

Schools will also have policies and procedures related to cybersecurity to protect information from accidental or illegal corruption, theft or damage. Types of cybersecurity threats are shown in **Figure 20.1**.

According to Business.gov, common online threats to watch out for include:

- Phishing – external site: fake messages to trick you into giving out your private personal, commercial or financial details. They can even pretend to be from an organisation you trust, such as a large business or government agency.
- Malware – external site: malicious software most commonly used by criminals to steal your confidential information, hold your system or device to ransom or install damaging programs onto your device without your knowledge.
- Ransomware – external site: a type of malicious software that makes your computer or files unusable unless you pay a fee to unlock them.

Source: Australian Government. Business (2023). Cyber security and your business. https://business.gov.au/online/cyber-security/cyber-security-and-your-business

Figure 20.2 provides information on cybersecurity that can be downloaded at Cyber Security NSW: https://www.digital.nsw.gov.au/sites/default/files/2022-09/top-10-cyber-security-tips.pdf.

20.2 Information for educational use

According to Copyright Agency, an education statutory licence allows people working in education institutions to copy, adapt, share and store materials for students, including for online learning.

Figure 20.1 Cybersecurity threats

Figure 20.2 Tips for cybersecurity

Online security is becoming more important than ever. While there's no bulletproof way to prevent a cyber attack, here are some easy tips from Cyber Security NSW to help you keep your personal information safe and secure.

Choose unique passwords
Use it for just one account. If an attacker gets hold of one of your passwords, they can't get access to all your other accounts.

Don't follow links or open attachments from untrusted sources
Phishing emails are designed to look legitimate so always think before you click on links or open attachments. Always check if you know who the email is from and never give out personal information such as credit card details, bank account details or passwords.

Never leave your devices unattended
Never leave your devices unattended. If you are stepping away from your desk, lock your screen with a unique password.

Keep your operating systems up to date
Updates often fix vulnerabilities that attackers can find and use to access your system. It's an effective way to help keep them out.

Set up multifactor authentication on your devices
Choose to get a code sent to another device like your phone when logging in online. This is an added layer of security helping stop attackers getting into your accounts.

Avoid using your work email on public facing internet websites
Limit the use of your work email address on public facing internet websites.

Avoid the use of public wi-fi especially to conduct business
Try not to use free wi-fi or internet hot spots unless necessary. When doing so, avoid sending or receiving valuable or sensitive information and identify that it is a 'public' network type if prompted.

Stay smart with social media
What you post on social media can give cyber criminals information that they can use against you. Set your privacy so only friends and family can see your details.

Check bank statements/quotes regularly
Keep an eye on work and personal bank statements and bank account numbers to check you know the source of the transaction.

Make sure to familiarise yourself with your agency's acceptable use policy or speak to your local IT Security contact
If you see something of concern, report it immediately to your Chief Information Security Officer (CISO) or your IT Security contact. Your IT security contact is: _____

Subject matter that is automatically protected by copyright in Australia includes:

- 'works', being literary works (textual material), dramatic works, musical works and artistic works;
- and 'subject matter other than works', being sound recordings, films, television and sound broadcasts and published editions.

Copyright does not protect ideas, but instead it protects the particular expression of the ideas in a material form. Importantly, copyright exists separately from the physical work, and as such the sale of the physical work does not automatically include the copyright.

Source: Arts Law Centre of Australia (2023). Copyright. https://www.artslaw.com.au/information-sheet/copyright/

Figure 20.3 sets out the copyright requirements.

Figure 20.3 Copyright requirements for an educational licence

Requirement	What this means
1 The institution is covered by an agreement with Copyright Agency	There are payment arrangements in place for: > nearly all Australian schools > TAFEs > members of Universities Australia > other education institutions, such as registered training organisations If you don't have a licence, education institutions can apply for a licence online on our RightsPortal.
2 The material is copied and/or shared for educational purposes	Education purposes includes: > made or retained for use, or is used, in connection with a particular course of instruction provided by the institution > made or retained for inclusion, or is included, in the collection of a library of the institution.
3 The material is not used for any other purpose	Education institutions need to take steps to make sure that materials are not used for any other purposes, for example by: > using secure servers to ensure that materials are only available to the relevant students and parents assisting them > telling students and parents how they can and can't use the materials (e.g. no sharing with others) > not retaining material any longer than needed for educational purposes.
4 The education institution does not copy or share more than a reasonable portion of a publication that is available for purchase	An education institution copying from a publication that is available for purchase can copy and share 10% of the pages, or a chapter, per student per course. An institution may be allowed to copy and/or share more if that is reasonable, and not detrimental to the content creators if done at scale. For example, if lots of people copy 80% of a book available for sale, instead of buying it, then that is likely to be detrimental to the content creators.
Provided these requirements are met, people working in an education institution can copy, adapt, share and store any text and images that they have access to, including digital and print material. They can: > photocopy, print and scan > duplicate digital copies, and upload to a server > share material on a server to students, and email to students, provided the material is only available to the relevant students, and for the necessary time > adapt, and include in teacher-made resources.	
Moral rights There are legal obligations to attribute creators and treat their work with respect. These creators' rights are known as 'moral rights'. They mean you must: > attribute (give credit to) the creator > not say a person is a creator of a work when they're not > not do something with a work (such as change or add to it) that would have a negative impact on the creator's reputation.	

Sources: Copyright Agency (2022). Copying under an education licence. https://www.copyright.com.au/licences-permission/educational-licences/copying-under-education-licence; Copyright Agency (2023). Moral rights. https://www.copyright.com.au/about-copyright/moral-rights

20.3 Referencing and crediting information

When using any materials belonging to another person or entity you must reference the source. This protects and respects the rights of the author/s and avoids plagiarism. The University of NSW (2022c) defines plagiarism as 'using the words or ideas of others and passing them off as your own. Plagiarism is a type of intellectual theft'. The university explains that 'plagiarism can take many forms, from deliberate cheating to accidentally copying from a source without acknowledgement. Consequently, whenever you use the words or ideas of another person in your work, you must acknowledge where they came from'.

Paraphrasing, summarising and quoting

Common ways that the work of others is used include:

Paraphrasing:
- does not match the source word for word
- involves putting a passage from a source into your own words
- changes the words or phrasing of a passage, but retains and fully communicates the original meaning
- **must** be attributed to the original source.

Summarising:
- does not match the source word for word
- involves putting the main idea(s) into your own words, but including only the main point(s)
- presents a broad overview, so is usually much shorter than the original text
- **must** be attributed to the original source.

Quotations
- match the source word for word
- are usually a brief segment of the text
- appear between quotation marks
- **must** be attributed to the original source.

Source: University of NSW (2022b). Paraphrasing, summarising and quoting. https://www.student.unsw.edu.au/paraphrasing-summarising-and-quoting

Figure 20.4 describes the Harvard referencing system.

Figure 20.4 The Harvard referencing system

Books

Include information in the following order:
> author's surname, and initial(s)
> year of publication
> title of publication (in italics and with minimal capitalisation)
> edition (if applicable. Abbreviated as 'edn')
> publisher
> place of publication.

Karskens, G 1997, *The Rocks: life in early Sydney*, Melbourne University Press, Carlton.
Ward, R 1966, *The Australian legend*, 2nd edn, Oxford University Press, Melbourne.

Websites

Include information in the following order:
> author (the person or organisation responsible for the site)
> year (date created or revised)
> site name (in italics)
> name of sponsor of site (if available)

- accessed day month year (The accessed date is the date you viewed or downloaded the source. As online materials can change or disappear at any time, you must cite the date on which you accessed the information)
- URL or internet address (between pointed brackets). If possible, ensure that the URL is included without a line-break.

Department of Social Services 2020, *Department of social services website*, Australian government, accessed 20 February 2020, <**https://www.dss.gov.au/**>.

Online articles

Include information in the following order:

- author
- year of publication
- article title (between single quotation marks)
- publication title (in italics with maximum capitalisation)
- date of article (day, month)
- page number.

Williamson, S 1998, 'UNSW gains top ranking from quality team', *Sydney Morning Herald*, 30 February, p. 21.

Journals

Include information in the following order:

- author's surname and initial
- year of publication
- title of the article (between single quotation marks and with minimal capitalisation)
- title of the journal or periodical (in italic font using maximum capitalisation)
- volume number (vol.)
- issue number (no.)
- page range of the article
- DOI (Digital Object Identifier), if available.

Kozulin, A 1993, 'Literature as a psychological tool', *Educational Psychologist*, vol. 28, no. 3, pp. 253–265, DOI:10.1207/s15326985ep2803_5.

Government websites

If there is no obvious author or editor, cite the sponsoring agency as the author:

(Department of Education, Science & Training 2000)

List of references

Give the name of the ministry or agency that has issued the document:

Department of Education, Science & Training 2000, *Annual Report 1999–2000*, AGPS, Canberra.

Videos and films

Include the full title and date of production:

- (My Brilliant Career, 1979)
- (Four Corners, 9 July 2001)

References

Include information in the following order:

- title (if part of an ongoing series, list the episode title first, then the series name)
- year of recording
- format
- publisher/distributor
- place of recording
- date of recording (if applicable).
- *My Brilliant Career*, 1979, motion picture, New South Wales Film Corporation, distributed by Australian Video, Australia.

Blog posts

Include information in the following order:

- the name (or alias) of the author
- year of post

> the title of the posting (if applicable) between single quotation marks
> the title of the site (in italics)
> format
> the date of posting (day month)
> accessed day month year (the date you viewed the site)
> the URL of the blog post (between pointed brackets).

Bartlett, A 2007, *The Bartlett diaries*, weblog, accessed 22 May 2007, <**http://andrewbartlett.com/blog/**>.

A blog post

If you are citing a group blog, cite the author of the post:

Bahnisch, M 2007, 'The commentariat vs. the people?', *Larvatus Prodeo*, weblog post, 11 May, accessed 22 May 2007, <**http://larvatusprodeo.net/2007/05/11/the-commentariat-vs-the-people**>.

Podcasts

> When referring to the speaker:
> Jill Kitson (Lingua Franca 2007) reported that . . .

References

List a podcast as you would a radio program. Include information in the following order:

> name of the podcast (in italics)
> year
> format (podcast)
> publisher
> date of podcast (day, month)
> accessed day month year
> the URL (between pointed brackets).

Lingua Franca 2007, podcast radio program, ABC Radio National, 28 April, accessed 25 May 2007, <**http://abc.net.au/rn/podcast/feeds/lin.xml**>.

Creative Commons (CC) is an internationally active non-profit organisation that provides free licences for creators to use when making their work available to the public. These licences help the creator to give permission for others to use the work in advance under certain conditions. Every time a work is created, such as when a journal article is written or a photograph taken, that work is automatically protected by copyright. Copyright protection prevents others from using the work in certain ways, such as copying the work or putting the work online (Smart Copying, 2023).

Source: University of NSW (2022a). Citing different sources with Harvard referencing. https://www.student.unsw.edu.au/citing-different-sources

Copyright, referencing and Creative Commons

Photocopying existing printed materials/resources

It is not uncommon to see forms, activities and so on that are not referenced being used in the classroom. Often this material has been 'around' for some time and the original author is unknown. Best practice in this situation is to state: 'Source unknown'. This avoids the material being wrongly attributed to the current user.

20.4 Researching and evaluating credible sources of information

A source is credible when it is trustworthy. Sometimes it is hard to determine whether a source is credible or not; voicing an opinion or presenting false information as fact without any credentials or proof is easy for anyone to do, especially online. Sources can often appear as credible even when they are not. Following are a few points to consider when evaluating sources for credibility.

Be sceptical

Just because something is presented as a fact, it doesn't mean that it is true. Examine the source and author's credentials and affiliations. Beware of sources that use vague terms like 'recent studies show' or 'many people believe', without backing up these claims with citations.

Beware of bias

Always consider the source. For example, information about a product or resource that is authored by the creator may be biased. Check whether the author is able to cite research to support any claims being made.

Analysing web resources

The World Wide Web is now the 'go to' destination for information. Determining whether the information being sourced is authentic, unbiased, current and accurate is an important consideration. **Figure 20.5** explores the factors that should be considered when sourcing information from the internet and considering its authenticity. After carefully reviewing the site, you can decide whether or not you believe the source to be credible.

Examples of credible websites are shown in **Figure 20.6**.

Figure 20.5 Authenticity and the World Wide Web

Authority

- Is the publisher reputable? Reliable publisher = reliable content and authors
- Is the sponsorship clear?
- Is contact address available?
- Is there a link to the sponsoring organisation?
- Is the author qualified to write on this topic?

Who wrote it?

- Is the author/source qualified to write about the topic?
- Look for a link or About Me/About Us/Background page that will tell you more about them
- Who is accountable for the information?
- Find the author/organisation responsible for the content
- Look for info on their education and experience
- Evaluate what you know about them and decide if you believe they are

Currency

- Is the publication current?
- Is there a date for the last update?
- Is the topic one that does not change frequently?
- Look at how sources are cited and what type of source is used

Objectivity

- Does the sponsor have commercial interests?
- Is advertising included on the page?
- Are there obvious biases?

Accuracy

- Are sources listed for the facts?
- Can information be verified through another source?
- Has the site been edited for grammar, spelling, etc.?

Coverage

- Are the topics covered in depth?
- Does the content appear to be complete?

Links to the site

- Are there links to other credible sites? – Links to other sites help to validate the credibility of the information.

Wikipedia

Wikipedia has a wide range of information that can be useful to read when you are first trying to understand a topic. Wiki pages sometimes also have references or links to further information that could be useful for your assignments. However, as Wikipedia content can be altered or updated by anyone, it's not considered to be a credible source of information.

Internet 'domain names'

The domains .gov, .edu and .ac can only be registered by government and educational institutions.

- Government.gov
- Education.edu
- Organisation.org
- Commercial.com
- Academic.ac
- Network.net

For this reason, they reflect a higher order of authority than .com, .org or .net sites.

Sources: Adapted from: Paperpile (2023). https://paperpile.com/g/find-credible-sources; University of Adelaide (2014). Credibility. Writing Centre Learning Guide. https://www.adelaide.edu.au/writingcentre/sites/default/files/docs/learningguide-sourcecredibility.pdf

Figure 20.6 Examples of credible websites

Source: Australian Curriculum, Assessment and Reporting Authority (ACARA) (2023). The Australian Curriculum V9. https://v9.australiancurriculum.edu.au

Source: Australian Teacher Aide (2023). https://www.australianteacheraide.com.au

20.5 Accessing information on your school's intranet

Unlike the internet, a school intranet is not publicly accessible. Information on the internet sits on the World Wide Web. Information on an intranet is situated on the organisation's server and is password protected. Typically, the intranet will include a range of information and communication tools that can be accessed by all employees. There may also be some areas of the intranet that are locked and only available to authorised staff – for example, personnel files, finance or student records.

The intranet will include a wide range of information, for example:

- documents and shared files – policies, procedures, forms, templates
- a student management system – records, reports, assessment results, etc.
- third-party school apps
- licensed programs
- learning tools
- a teacher–student portal where students can log-on to access learning programs and access/post assignments, homework, projects, etc.
- school calendar highlighting key dates, events, holidays, exams, etc.
- staff and student wellbeing – access to programs to support wellbeing, mindfulness, relaxation, etc.
- professional learning – access to subscribed learning sites, journals, teacher blogs, conference and professional development opportunities, etc.
- parent/guardian portal.

All schools will have policies for safe and ethical access of the internet and the intranet. An example is provided in the Online resource.

Examples of acceptable use of ICT policies

20.6 Using search engines and key words

There are a number of search engines that can be accessed via the internet. The most commonly used and well-known are Google Chrome, Internet Explorer, Bing, Safari, Yahoo! and Firefox.

Search engines allow you to search broadly or to narrow your search – for example, you can click 'search all', 'search images' or 'search videos'.

Using key words

Key words are the words you use to find information on the internet. Using key words helps to focus your search and reduce the likelihood of unwanted information. **Figures 20.7** and **20.8** show different results simply by changing a few words. For example, if you wanted to search for phonics activities for Year 1 students you might include: 'free phonics activities' – see **Figure 20.8** for results.

This search includes results from the USA, which include American spelling. Alternatively, you could search for 'free phonics activities Year 1 au'. By adding

Figure 20.7 Search X: free phonics activities (27 700 results)

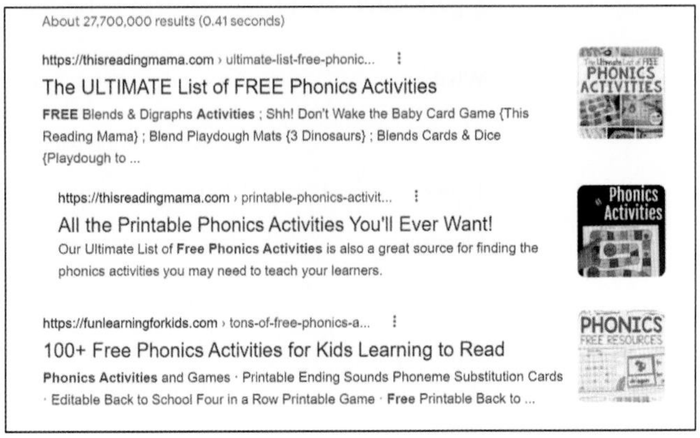
About 27,700,000 results (0.41 seconds)

https://thisreadingmama.com › ultimate-list-free-phonic...
The ULTIMATE List of FREE Phonics Activities
FREE Blends & Digraphs **Activities** ; Shh! Don't Wake the Baby Card Game {This Reading Mama} ; Blend Playdough Mats {3 Dinosaurs} ; Blends Cards & Dice {Playdough to ...

https://thisreadingmama.com › printable-phonics-activit...
All the Printable Phonics Activities You'll Ever Want!
Our Ultimate List of **Free Phonics Activities** is also a great source for finding the phonics activities you may need to teach your learners.

https://funlearningforkids.com › tons-of-free-phonics-a...
100+ Free Phonics Activities for Kids Learning to Read
Phonics Activities and Games · Printable Ending Sounds Phoneme Substitution Cards · Editable Back to School Four in a Row Printable Game · **Free** Printable Back to ...

Source: GOOGLE search engine

Figure 20.8 Search 'free phonics activities Year 1 au' (20 000 results)

About 16,200,000 results (0.42 seconds)

Ad · https://www.3plearning.com/phonics/resources ▾

Printable Phonics Resources - Phonics Worksheets & Games

Download hundreds of **free** maths, literacy and classroom management **resources**! Reading, writing and comprehension **teaching resources** from Reading Eggs. **Phonics Activities**. **Phonics** Printables. Brands: 3P Learning, Mathletics, Mathseeds, Reading Eggs.

Ad · https://www.coolaustralia.org/teacher/resource ▾

Aligned with Aus Curriculum - Free Resources & Lesson Plans

Teachers love our real-world learning topics that are easily integrated into classes. Since 2008, we have been supporting teachers with learning **activities** and **resources**.
Teaching Resources · Teaching Inspiration · Digital Library · Professional Development

Ad · https://www.speldnsw.org.au/ ▾

SPELD NSW - Phonics Teaching Resources

Instruction With Evidence-Based Methods. Join SPELD NSW. Dyslexia, ADHD, Reading. Learning Difficulty Help. Types: Phonemic Kits, Maths **Activities** Kits, Maths x10 Kits.
Teachers Certificate 2023 · Professional Development · Parents · Assessments

'au' (Australia), only Australian sites are found, and by adding 'free' you are less likely to return commercial sites which may require payment for resources.

Remove unnecessary stop words, such as prepositions (in, of, on), conjunctions (and, but) and articles (a, the). Quotation marks should be used when searching for a single word or a phrase. Quotation marks narrow the search – for example, if researching the history of the relationship between dogs and humans, different results will be returned if 'human' is not included.

Adding a plus sign (+) will ensure that 'and' is included – for example, 'large dogs+and small dogs' will ensure that all returns relate to both large and small dogs.

You can also conduct wildcard searches: use the * symbol as a placeholder for another word. For example, searching for * man in the world returns results for the richest man in the world, the tallest, the oldest, and so on. Wildcard searches are also useful when, for example, you don't know the full text of a quote (Mindtools, 2023).

You can also search a known site for key words. For example, you could search how to report incidents at Safe Work Australia by typing: https://www.safeworkaustralia.gov.au/reporting incident. This can save time if you know exactly what you're looking for on a particular site.

The best way to develop your search techniques is to try different ways of searching and see what works best for you. You can add sites that you use regularly to 'bookmarks', which creates shortcut links to these sites. To find out how to set up your favourites, type 'Create, view & edit bookmarks' into your preferred search engine and follow the directions.

20.7 Research requirements and objectives

When you are asked to research information, it's essential to identify the exact requirements, as this will avoid wasting time gathering irrelevant information. Best practice is to ask for written instructions and to review and clarify these instructions with the person concerned. **Figure 20.9** provides an example of the criteria that should be confirmed before commencing the research.

Figure 20.9 Identifying research criteria

What	Knowledge/information – this needs to be specific and clearly defined. What is the purpose of the research? How will the information be used/applied? You should identify what must be included and what can be excluded.
Type of information	Written information only; examples; links to websites; podcasts, videos, etc.
Quantity	How much detail is required? Does the person want information from a broad range of sources? Is the required information simple or complex? Is the person expecting brief notes or a comprehensive report?
Currency	Is there a specific source where information must be accessed? For example, a current school/departmental policy, a government website, a trusted commercial source.

Demographics	Will the information be sourced from Australia, a state/territory or worldwide?
Delivery method	Hard copy (written); electronic; PowerPoint.
Recommendations	Does the person require you to summarise the information and make recommendations based on the information gathered?

Documenting and presenting the information

Before commencing any research, it is essential to be clear about the required reporting format. This may depend on the purpose and use of the research. For example:

- Does the person want a written report?
- Does the person want a summary of key points using headings/subheadings?
- How does the person want sources to be recorded – electronic files, printed, scanned?
- Does the person want links to other relevant information?
- Does the person want verbal feedback or a presentation?

If you are working on a time-consuming research task, it can be helpful to regularly check in with the person to ensure you are 'on track' and the style of presentation is suitable. When undertaking research all sources should be documented for future reference/review. This can be done by creating a simple spreadsheet (see **Figure 20.10**).

When accessing information from the internet, it is good practice to copy and paste the web address so that you have an accurate record of the source. It can also be useful to take a screen shot as a reminder of the content on the site.

Figure 20.10 Documented references

Date accessed	Name	Source	Notes

Referencing apps

There are a number of free apps that can be used to document, organise and safeguard your references if you are working on a project where you are sourcing a large volume of reference materials. Examples of these apps include Zotero and Mendeley. Both are compatible with Word.

Presenting the information in a logical manner

The format for presenting information should reflect the original instructions. Information should be presented in a logical order. Using key headings and subheadings can be helpful as it allows you to group similar content from various sources. Information can also be presented visually, if applicable, by using graphics, charts, diagrams and images.

All information should be free of spelling and grammar errors. Where there are gaps in information, this should be noted. For example, 'Unable to source information from Australian content'; 'Unable to source any information less than 5 years old'.

When researching and gathering information, you may also find inconsistencies or **discrepancies**. For example, you may find that statistics vary widely (e.g. 10% of boys are likely to…./50% of boys are likely to….). A source may also identify significant differences in relation to how information is interpreted or applied. Where discrepancies occur, it's important to highlight these in your notes.

Summary

This chapter provided an overview of reliable sources of information and resources. As you gain experience as an ESW, you will build your skills in working with teachers and students. Adopting an attitude of continuous professional development will help you to build your skills and expand your knowledge.

Throughout this textbook you have been provided with a broad range of online links to information, resources and professional learning. Hopefully, you have taken the time to visit these sites and explore what each site has to offer. Keeping track of online resources and professional reading will allow you to revisit information as needed. You will find that over time you will have a customised database of 'go-to' resources that you can access at any time to support your role in the workplace.

This section of the textbook provides examples of websites where you can access resources to support your role as an ESW. Many of the links and online resources provided in the textbook will support your studies and be useful sources of information as you develop in your role. Adding websites to your 'favourites' and keeping a record of what each site has to offer is a great way to build your own portfolio of resources.

Pinterest

Pinterest is a free site where you can create virtual boards to pin and save images, articles, websites etc. You may like to check out my Pinterest page, which has around 30 boards dedicated to Education Support. Go to Pinterest and search for 'Kearns Resources' (see **Figure 20.11**). Scroll down until you come to 'School TA' – there you'll see all the boards created for your use. You can save any pins to your own board.

Creating presentations

- Best classroom tools for presentations and slideshows: **https://www.commonsense.org/education/top-picks/best-classroom-tools-for-presentations-and-slideshows**
- Teachers' essential guide to showing movies and videos in the classroom: **https://www.commonsense.org/education/articles/teachers-essential-guide-to-showing-movies-and-videos-in-the-classroom**

Accessing and using social media/video games

- Keeping your students (and yourself) safe on social media: A checklist: **https://www.commonsense.org/education/articles/keeping-your-students-and-yourself-safe-on-social-media-a-checklist**
- How to find learning opportunities in video games kids and teens love: **https://www.commonsense.org/education/articles/how-to-find-learning-opportunities-in-video-games-kids-and-teens-love**

IT information and advice

- EdTech Focus on K–12: **https://edtechmagazine.com/k12**

English language learners

- Common Sense Education: ELA tools aligned to common core standards: **https://www.commonsense.org/education/top-picks/ela-tools-aligned-to-common-core-standards**

Figure 20.11 Kearns resources on Pinterest

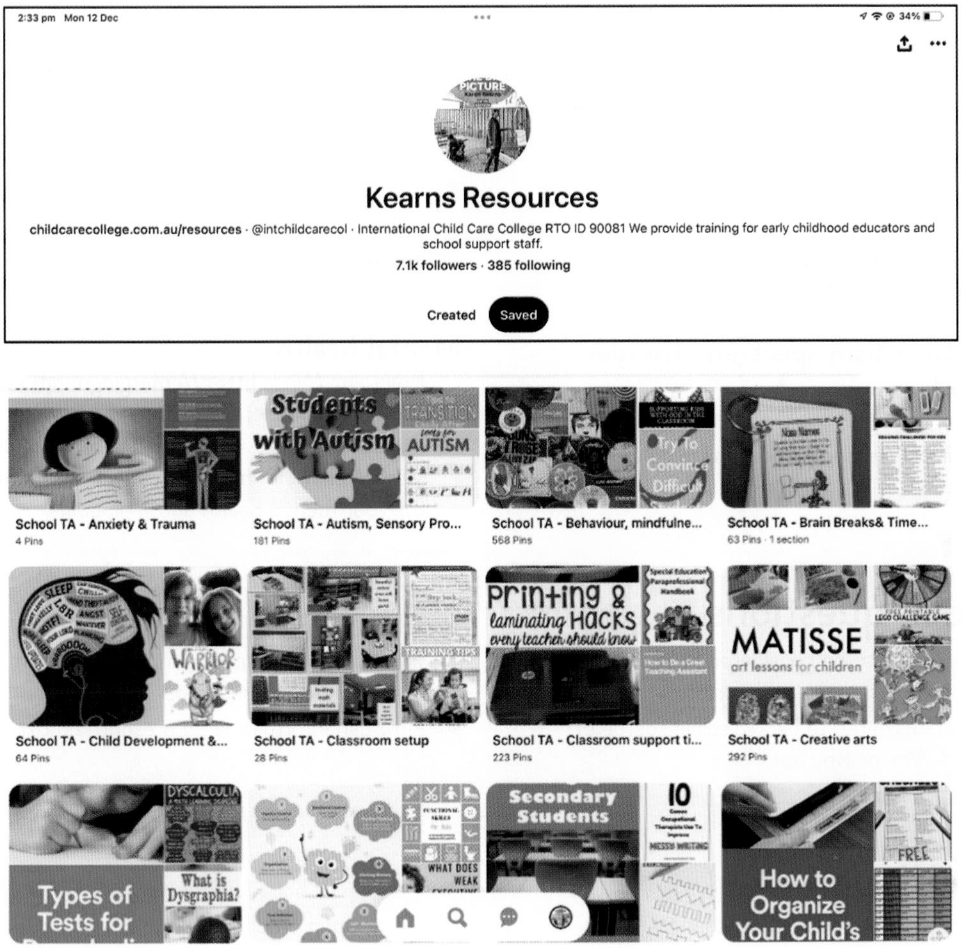

Source: Pinterest

Helpful tools to ease learners back into maths, reading, and writing

- Common Sense Education: **https://www.commonsense.org/education/articles/helpful-tools-to-ease-learners-back-into-math-reading-and-writing**
- Cool Australia: **https://www.coolaustralia.org**: a wide range of resources for all learning areas
- Developing core literacy proficiencies Grades 6–12: Odell Education: **https://www.odelleducation.com/curriculum/oer/?utm_source=pocket_saves**
- Edutopia: **https://www.edutopia.org**: articles, videos, links to resources
- Language & Learning: **https://www.languageandlearning.com.au/library**
- National Numeracy (UK): **https://www.nationalnumeracy.org.uk**: a wide range of free numeracy resources
- Sparkle Box: **https://www.sparklebox.co.uk**: a wide range of free printable resources
- Teachers Pay Teachers: **https://www.teacherspayteachers.com/Browse/Search:special+education+paraprofessionals/Price-Range/Free**: free resources for paraprofessionals; also includes resources for purchase
- Teachit: **https://www.teachit.co.uk**: a range of free resources to explore
- TeAchnolgy: **https://www.teach-nology.com**: provides free and easy-to-use resources for teachers dedicated to improving the education of today's generation of students: Foundation – Year 12

Students with additional needs

- Video: How to develop accommodations and modifications for learners. Accommodations and modifications (6.36 mins): **https://www.youtube.com/watch?v=O0xdaCEqrU0**
- Dyslexia – SPELD Foundation: **https://dsf.net.au**: provides information and resources to support children with learning difficulties:
  - NSW: **https://www.speldnsw.org.au/about**
  - South Australia: **https://www.speldsa.org.au**
  - Victoria: **https://www.speldvic.org.au**
  - WA: **https://auspeld.org.au**

Learners with autism spectrum disorder and sensory learner needs

- Centre for Autism Middletown: Sensory Processing Resource: **https://sensory-processing.middletownautism.com/resources**
  - 'How to' videos to manage sensory needs
  - PDFs: Printables such as 'I need a break', calm down ideas, volume control
- The National Center on Accessible Educational Materials for Learning: **https://aem.cast.org**: this centre at CAST provides technical assistance, coaching, and resources to increase the availability and use of accessible educational materials and technologies for learners with disabilities across the lifespan.
- IRIS Resource Locator: **https://iris.peabody.vanderbilt.edu/resources/iris-resource-locator**: provides a wide range of easy-to-read information, resources and videos

Mental health

- Emerging Minds **https://emergingminds.com.au**: advancing the mental health and emotional wellbeing of Australian infants, children, adolescents and their families
- Very Well Mind: **https://www.verywellmind.com**: caring for your mental health and wellbeing

Self-check questions

1 What factors need to be considered to ensure the authenticity of internet-based information sources?
2 Is Wikipedia considered to be a credible source of information? Why or why not?
3 What is the benefit of using key words in Search and what are unnecessary stop words?
4 How can information be presented most effectively?

Discussion question

1 Discuss the importance of being sceptical and aware of bias when evaluating credible sources of information.

Activities

1 Connect each term to the correct definition.

using the words or ideas of others and passing them off as your own	Summarising
involves putting a passage from a source into your own words	Quotations
involves putting the main idea(s) into your own words, but including only the main point(s)	Paraphrasing
are usually a brief segment of the text	Plagiarism

GLOSSARY

Academic language Formal language related to specific content areas of the curriculum.

Academic self How do I perform at school? What subjects do I like? What am I good at? What are my goals for the future?

Accommodation The individual adjusts their existing scheme when the scheme does not fit a new object.

Accommodations Adaptations, adjustments or changes to curriculum or the learning environment to overcome barriers to learning.

Acronym Abbreviation.

Actively listening Using skills that demonstrate to a speaker that the listener is really trying to understand their message.

Adaptation The individual uses prior knowledge and skills to acquire new knowledge and skills.

Agency Ability to reflect on own learning, set goals and make choices about own learning.

Albinism An inherited condition that results from the body's inability to produce normal amounts of a pigment called melanin. It affects the eyes and skin of some individuals, and only the eyes of others.

Algebra Involves understanding patterns, relations and functions.

Algorithm A process that can be carried out mechanically, using a well-defined set of instructions, to perform a particular task or solve a type of problem.

Allegation A statement without proof that someone has perpetrated abuse against a child or young person.

Alphabetic principle Understanding that words are composed of letters that represent the sounds [phonemes] in spoken words.

Amblyopia Often referred to as 'lazy eye'; one eye is weaker than the other, and the other eye takes over. Usually treated by placing a patch on the stronger eye to strengthen the weaker eye.

Analogy phonics Students learn to use parts of word families they already know to identify words they don't know that have similar parts.

Analytic phonics Uses a whole-to-part approach – sounds are not pronounced in isolation; rather, students analyse letter–sound relationships in known words.

Anxiety A feeling of being overwhelmed by the expectations of oneself and others; having irrational fears and generally lacking self-confidence.

Apprenticeship A term used by Rogoff to refer to the role of the child as a member of the community. The process of apprenticeship involves becoming familiar with and participating in the social and cultural norms of the community.

Area model A rectangular diagram used in mathematics to solve multiplication problems, in which the factors being multiplied define the length and width of a rectangle.

Articulation The ability to produce speech sounds.

Assessment The process of evaluating skills and knowledge.

Assessment as learning Includes self-assessment and peer-assessment of the student's progress; intended to generate new learning.

Assessment for learning *see* Formative assessment

Assessment of learning *see* Summative assessment

Assimilation The process of incorporating a new object or event into an existing schema or way of dealing with the world.

Ataxic cerebral palsy Associated with a lack of balance and coordination, such as unsteady or shaky movements (tremors).

Athetosis A form of cerebral palsy characterised by uncontrolled extra movements that occur particularly in the arms, hands and feet, and around the mouth. Children may appear floppy when carried.

Attachment issues An inability to trust others and difficulty forming healthy relationships throughout life.

Attention deficit hyperactivity disorder (ADHD) Typically includes excessive, impulsive, restless and sometimes aggressive behaviour.

Attention-seeking behaviour May include behaviours such as repeatedly calling out, talking over others and out-of-seat behaviour.

Attitudes Learned predispositions of thinking or reacting towards a situation, group or concept.

Auditory perception The process of making sense out of what one hears.

Australian Education Act 2013 The principal legislation for the provision of Australian Government funding to Government and non-government schools; sets out broad expectations for compliance, to ensure funding accountability to the Commonwealth and to school communities.

Australian Education Regulation 2013 Outlines the financial accountability and other conditions that are required by approved authorities in order to receive funding under the *Australian Education Act 2013.*

Authentic Genuine, realistic.

Authentic text Real, living or natural language texts that may entertain, inform and/or persuade.

Balance The ability to maintain an upright position without falling over.

Behaviour The actions or reactions of a person in relation to their environment, experiences or needs; can be conscious or unconscious, overt or covert, voluntary or involuntary.

Behaviour Intervention Plan (BIP) Similar to an IEP. A plan of inclusion that defines the barriers to participating in an educational setting and allows teachers (and families) to identify what makes the school environment challenging for the student; also defines the adaptations or adjustments that can be made to support the student to modify and change their behaviour.

Behaviourist (language development) Language is acquired by operant conditioning – imitation and reinforcement.

Bias Attaching preconceived or prejudiced beliefs, values and attitudes to a person or particular group.

Big six Elements of reading instruction: oral language, phonemic awareness, phonological awareness, vocabulary, fluency and comprehension.

Bilingual The ability to use two languages in everyday life.

Binge eating disorder A mental illness characterised by regular episodes of binge eating. This involves eating an excessive amount of food, which may take place in a rapid space of time, or may be more of an extended grazing. These episodes can feel chaotic, uncontrollable and highly distressing.

Care and protection order A legal order or arrangement that gives child protection departments some responsibility for a child's welfare.

Central Auditory Processing Disorder (CAPD) A receptive language disorder involving difficulties in the decoding and storing of auditory information (typically incoming verbal messages).

Cephalocaudal development The direction of the body's physical growth, reflected in the order in which parts of the body become larger and the order in which functions and structures become more complex. Cephalocaudal development progresses from head to foot.

Cerebral palsy (CP) A non-progressive, permanent disorder of movement and posture caused by damage to the developing brain.

Childhood trauma An event that results in immediate and long-term emotional stress.

Chronosystem The outermost circle of Bronfenbrenner's ecological systems theory; the social and historical timeframe in which the child's life is set.

Code-breaking skills Use knowledge of letter/sound relationships, concepts about print, spelling, punctuation, grammar, structural conventions and patterns.

Code-switching In the Aboriginal context, occurs when a speaker uses Standard Australian English (SAE) in formal settings such as school or work and then switches to Aboriginal English when at home or within the Aboriginal community.

Cognition The ability to acquire, understand and apply information through sensory input, thought and life experiences.

Cognitivist In language development, language is acquired through the process of thinking.

Common law doctrine Law that is based on court-established legal precedents and commonly held beliefs.

Communication Ability to use and respond to spoken and written English in a social context and an academic context.

Communication disorders Speech and language problems that may include difficulties following two- or three-step directions, an inability to follow or join in conversations with peers and adults, or poor vocabulary.

Complex trauma A series of or repeated ongoing traumatic events.

Comprehension The ability to read with understanding; includes skills such as inferring, predicting, summarising key ideas and critical reflection.

Conceptual understanding Knowing 'why', including understanding mathematical relationships – for example, understanding that addition and subtraction are opposite tasks.

Conflict of interest An individual's personal interests and/or values clash with professional responsibilities.

Conflict resolution The process of handling conflict and resolving a disagreement between people.

Conservation The understanding that something stays the same in quantity even though its appearance changes.

Continuous process There is recognition that support and care require a continuous process of listening, learning and further action, and are not a one-off event, as well as recognition that people with disability have futures, and that their aspirations will change and grow with their experiences.

Core strength The development of the muscles in the abdomen, pelvis, shoulders and back necessary for posture control.

Critical analysis Allows the reader to consider the content of the text beyond that which is written.

Critical periods Periods in which learning is optimal or at its best; these are the periods in which experience will provide maximum benefits.

Cultural awareness The ability to reflect on how our own cultural practices and views influence our beliefs and values.

Cultural competence The ability to understand, communicate and interact with people across cultures.

Cultural diversity The variation between people in terms of ancestry, ethnicity, ethno-religiosity, language, national origin, race and/or religion.

Cultural protocol Ethical principles that guide behaviour in a particular situation; designed to protect Aboriginal and Torres Strait Islander cultural and intellectual property rights.

Cultural safety An environment that is safe for people: where there is no assault, challenge or denial of their identity, of who they are and what they need.

Cultural sensitivity Awareness of the sensitivities around cultural differences, requiring critical self-reflection on one's own cultural values, attitudes and beliefs, as well as the beliefs and biases of other cultures.

Culture A common set of norms and values shared by a group.

Culture shock A term used to describe the emotional stress of migration or even temporary relocation to a new country and a new culture.

Cumulative Building or adding on.

Curriculum Typically specifies *content and skills* – that is, what children should know (knowledge content) and what they should be able to do (skills content). It often describes the type of learning that will take place and the expected outcomes that will be achieved by the learners.

Custody order Generally refers to orders that place children in the custody of the state or territory department responsible for child protection, or a non-government agency.

Dangerous incident ('near-miss') Any incident in relation to a workplace that exposes a worker or any other person to a serious risk to that person's health or safety or that is likely to create a serious risk to health or safety in the future – for example, exposure to a toxic chemical.

Decodable text Text that is written for the beginning reader that contains the specific grapheme (letter)–phoneme (sound) correspondence.

Decoding The skill required to make sense of written words.

Demographics Related to a population or specific group or location.

Descriptive narrative A written narrative that describes an event, thing or action.

Developmental red flags A term used to describe behaviours of concern in relation to a child's development, particularly in relation to developmental milestones.

Diagnostic Detect, identify.

Differentiated Learning Instruction A strategy used by teachers to tailor learning to meet the individual learning needs of each student.

Direct comparison Involves directly aligning the attributes to be compared.

Direct instruction Teacher-led instruction where to teach a new concept, the teacher follows a set script and students are often asked to repeat information verbatim without any variation.

Disclosure Revealing that some form of child abuse has occurred.

Discrepancy Inconsistent, illogical or dissimilar.

Discrimination Unfair treatment in the workplace involving a person's identity – for example, sex, age, culture, religion, sexual preference, disability, politics or medical condition.

Diversity Understanding that each individual is unique and recognising our individual differences.

Domains of development Also referred to as 'areas of development'; includes the social, cognitive, language, emotional and physical domains.

Due diligence Taking all reasonably practical precautions to minimise the risk of accidents and injury in the workplace.

Duty of care The requirement to act with due care and consideration for the welfare and wellbeing of others.

Dyscalculia Difficulty with doing maths problems, understanding time and using money.

Dysgraphia A handwriting disorder where the individual consistently struggles to write legibly because of poor letter formation (and often poor spelling).

Dyskinetic cerebral palsy Includes *dystonia* and *athetosis*.

Dyslexia A language-based learning disability; refers to a cluster of symptoms that result in people having difficulties with specific language skills, particularly reading.

Dystonia A type of cerebral palsy characterised by sustained muscle contractions that frequently cause twisting or repetitive movements, or abnormal postures.

Early intervention Structured support programs (home and/or centre based) for children prior to entering school.

Echolalia Repetition of another's spoken words as a symptom of a disability.

Embedded phonics Students use letter–sound relationships with context clues to identify and spell unfamiliar words.

Emergent literacy The developing skills required to understand the meaning of words in print. These include speaking, listening, looking, thinking, reading and writing.

Emotional development Learning to express feelings; development of a sense of self, self-esteem and self-concept.

Emotional intelligence Identifying one's own emotions and those of others for the purpose of managing and guiding one's own behaviour.

Emotional literacy The ability to express and manage emotions and knowing how to respond appropriately to the emotions of others.

Emotional wellness The child/young person's ability to develop positive relationships, overcome adversity and regulate their own emotions in an age-appropriate manner.

Employment contract A contract between an employer and an employee to establish the rights and responsibilities between the two parties, including wages and conditions.

Enactive stage Bruner's stage of cognitive development – learning through play and discovery (action-based).

Encoding (or spelling) The ability to hear and identify individual sounds and write a symbol (letters) to represent the sound/s.

Equilibration The most general developmental principle in Piaget's theory, which states that an organism always tends towards biological and psychological balance. Development progresses towards an ideal state of equilibrium, which is never fully achieved.

Equity Ensuring fairness, so the education of all learners is seen as having equal importance.

Ethical dilemma A choice between two moral imperatives – neither of which is clearly acceptable or preferable.

Etymological knowledge The origin of words; includes understanding that words with the same base meaning are spelt the same while words that have a different meaning are generally not spelt the same.

Exosystem The third circle in Bronfenbrenner's ecological systems theory; the social system one step removed from the child – for example, family friends, parents' workplaces.

Experiential learning A continuous process in which students bring their own knowledge, ideas, beliefs and practices – at different levels – to their understanding and interpretation of new information (Bartle, 2015).

Explicit instruction Teacher-led instruction where the teacher emphasises or highlights key information that they want students to focus on and remember.

Exploratory talk A teaching practice that requires students to share their thoughts and ideas and justify their thinking.

Expressive language The ability to use spoken language to communicate needs, feelings and ideas.

Factual knowledge Number facts that can easily be recalled, such as 2 + 2 = 4.

Finalised guardianship or custody order An order involving the transfer of legal guardianship to the relevant state or territory department or non-government agency.

Fine motor development The development of small muscle groups – for example, in the hands, fingers, toes and around the lips and tongue.

Flexible thinking The ability to think outside of the box and adapt to change or the unexpected.

Fluency Comprises three components: accuracy, rate and prosody (expression).

Fluency disorders Speech and language problems that may include repetitions or interruptions such as stuttering or stammering.

Focus on outcomes The focus is on achieving positive outcomes for people with disability.

Formal language Uses formal words, avoids slang, may include jargon, avoids contraction, avoids figurative language and uses more complex sentences.

Formative assessment Gathering evidence of students' skills, knowledge and understanding as teaching is occurring to determine what students know, understand and can do in order to plan for future learning.

Foster care A form of out-of-home care where the caregiver is authorised and reimbursed by the state/territory for the care of the child.

Frequency of communication Involves engaging in back-and-forth exchange so that one person is not dominating the interaction.

Gamification The use of game-design elements and game principles in non-game contexts.

General capabilities In the Australian Curriculum, encompass knowledge, skills, behaviours and dispositions that, together with curriculum content in each learning area and the cross-curriculum priorities, will enable students to live and work successfully in the 21st century. AC

Generalised anxiety disorder Worrying and feeling anxious about almost everything.

Genre A category of literary writing.

Governance Systems, legislation, policies and procedures by which schools operate.

Grammar The structural rules used when putting words together to create phrases and sentences.

Grapheme The smallest element of writing. A unit of sound of one or more letters – for example, 'l', 'a', 'in'.

Gross motor development The development of the large muscle groups – for example, in the legs, arms, back and chest.

Guardianship order Conveys responsibility for the welfare of the child to the guardian.

Guidance Supporting a student to develop an understanding of what is expected in terms of socially acceptable behaviour, taking into account the individual student's development, circumstances and the context in which the behaviour occurs.

Guided mathematics Requires minimal input from adults. The teacher/ESW introduces the learning experience and reviews relevant skills and understandings related to the experience. Students are encouraged to discuss their ideas and understanding and problem-solve using a range of support materials.

Guided participation Knowledge that is acquired by taking on new roles and responsibilities under the guidance of a coach or mentor.

Harm Where abuse is an action against a child, refers to the detrimental effect or impact of that action on the child.

Hazard Any object, action, process or system that could lead to someone developing an illness or becoming injured.

Hearing disorders Problems with hearing that may be indicated by difficulty in hearing certain sounds, such as beginning, middle or end sounds.

Heredity The genetic blueprint passed down from one generation to the next.

High-frequency words The words used in written English text. They are sometimes called 'irregular words' or 'sight words'.

Higher-order functions Learned functions that are deliberate, mediated (defining thinking) and internalised behaviours.

Holistic and individual-centred care Focuses on the strengths, skills, abilities and interests of the child or young person, and takes social and cultural influences into account.

Homograph A word with the same spelling as another but a different meaning.

Homonym A word that has the same sound and spelling as another, but a different meaning.

Homophone A word with the same sound as another but different spelling and meaning.

Human agency The individual's ability to think and act in ways that shape their experiences and life chances.

Hyperactivity Restless, fidgeting, making inappropriate noises or talking incessantly, can't sit or stand still, climbs on everything.

Hyporeactivity Underresponsive to sensory input.

Hypothesise Predict meaning or outcome based on known facts.

Iconic stage Bruner's stage of cognitive development – creating mental images without the need for concrete materials (image-based).

Ideal self A set of beliefs each individual has about the qualities they would like to have as a person.

Impulsivity Risk-taking/reckless behaviour, inability to listen to and follow instructions, extremes of emotion, accident prone, unable to wait for a turn, fails to consider consequences of actions on self or others, difficulty playing with others.

Imputed disability An undiagnosed disability the school team considers a student to have that is having a functional impact on their learning.

Inattention Inability to concentrate, inability to complete tasks, flitting from one thing to another, disorganised, unable to estimate the time needed to complete a task, often unsure of where to start.

Inclusion Attitude or act of acceptance of diversity and differences. The term is used to embrace all aspects of diversity within the school community and the broader community.

Inclusion of others As identified by the individual, recognition of family members, friends, significant others and other service providers in supporting the individual and fostering connections with the community.

Inclusive and accessible Support is provided for inclusion in all areas of life and accessibility to all areas of the community.

Inclusive workplace A workplace that embraces the diversity of its employees.

Indirect comparison Involves comparing two objects that cannot be aligned directly – for example, the height of a doorway to the length of a desk.

Individual Behaviour Management Plan (IBMP) A plan tailored to an individual student with the goal of systematically modifying their environment with the goal of changing their behaviour over time.

Individual differences While development generally occurs in a predictable sequence, each child will develop at their own unique pace.

Individual Education Plan (IEP) A document that identifies a student's unique learning needs, details the educational goals for the student and outlines the specific strategies that will be used to work towards achievement of the goals.

Inductive reasoning Thinking from specific to general; for example, every Christmas we go to our grandparents' house. My friend's family does the same.

Inference Interpreting, suggesting or explaining the meaning of the text.

Inferential comprehension (also known as head comprehension) Requires readers to apply and evaluate knowledge from multiple texts, or within different areas of one text, or to use their background knowledge about topics.

Informal language Uses less formal words, slang words, may include figurative language, and fragmented and shortened sentences.

Information processing The way in which information is collected, sorted, stored (in the short and long term) and recalled in a way that is meaningful and allows the individual to make sense of the world.

Inhibitory/impulse control The skill we use to master and filter our thoughts and impulses so we can resist temptations, distractions and habits, and learn to pause and think before we act.

Integer A whole number (not a fractional number) that can be positive, negative or zero.

Intent of communication The ability to generate information, such as commenting, asking questions or negotiating in an age-appropriate manner.

Interactionist In relation to language development, language is acquired as a result of interactions between the environment and (a) information processing or (b) social interactions.

Interpretive comprehension The reader is asked to engage in reflection and draw on existing knowledge to make inferences about the text.

Investigation The process whereby the relevant department obtains more detailed information about a child who is the subject of a notification.

Keyboarding The ability to input information at a keyboard smoothly while typing.

Language A system of symbols that are combined using a set of rules.

Language processing disorders Problems with processing language that may include difficulty in comprehending and/or using spoken words. Receptive language disorders may be indicated by a child being unable to follow a sequence of commands, while expressive language disorders may present as difficulties with the sequencing of sounds.

Law of commutativity States that with addition and multiplication of numbers, you can change the order of the numbers in the problem and it will not affect the answer.

Learning continuum Learning occurs continually and incrementally throughout life, although the rate and pace are neither fixed nor constant.

Learning difficulties Students who exhibit problems acquiring academic skills due to causes including intellectual disability, physical or sensory deficits, emotional or behavioural difficulties or inadequate environmental experiences.

Learning disabilities A condition that has a dominating influence on a person's capacity to learn and who is generally assessed as having reduced cognitive capacity.

Learning Progressions Describe the steps of literacy and numeracy development in the Australian Curriculum: English. Unlike the general capabilities, they are not organised by year level or stage of schooling.

Learning Support Plan (LSP) A document that sets out specific areas of academic support for a particular student.

Legally blind Indicates that a person has less than 20/200 vision in the better eye or a very limited field of vision (20 degrees at its widest point).

Letter knowledge Understanding of upper and lower case.

Letter patterns Combining letters to create single sounds.

Letter–sound knowledge Phonics instruction is an essential component of a comprehensive literacy program because it is a high-yield strategy to draw upon when attempting to name words that are not immediately known.

Literacy rate gap The large and persistent difference in literacy levels between Aboriginal and non-Aboriginal students in Australia; increases with remoteness.

Literal comprehension The reader seeks to understand what is written in the text.

Logical consequences Similar to *natural consequences* but include adult intervention in applying the consequences.

Low vision Generally refers to a severe visual impairment, not necessarily limited to distance vision.

Macrosystem The second outer circle of Bronfenbrenner's ecological systems theory; includes cultural values, laws and customs of the community in which the child and family live.

Maltreatment Non-accidental behaviour towards another person that is outside the norms of conduct and entails a substantial risk of causing physical or emotional harm.

Mathematics Specific mathematical knowledge and skills – for example, knowing the times table, equations and number sense.

Maturation A person's biologically determined developmental pathway.

Mental health A positive capacity relating to the social and emotional wellbeing of individuals and communities.

Mesosystem The second inner circle of Bronfenbrenner's ecological systems theory; serves as links among microsystems, such as the relationship between home and school, parents and friends.

Microsystem The innermost circle of Bronfenbrenner's ecological systems theory; includes roles and interpersonal relationships – especially family.

Mindfulness The ability to pay attention, with judgement given to what we are thinking and feeling in the here and now.

Miscue In reading, saying something that is not actually in the text.

Mistaken behaviour Dreikurs argued that 'mistaken behaviour' occurred because of the child's basic needs not being met and a need to fit in to the social group.

Mixed-type cerebral palsy May involve a combination of types of cerebral palsy.

Mnemonics Short rhymes or phrases that are used to help remember the spelling of irregular words.

Modelled mathematics Using adult-directed small-group instruction, students are encouraged to draw on prior knowledge, ask questions, engage in discussion and hands-on practice/exploration and problem-solving.

Moral development The understanding of right and wrong related to societal expectations; the development of a conscience and self-imposed standards of behaviour.

Morality Concerned with fundamental questions of right and wrong, justice, fairness and basic human rights.

Morphological knowledge The conscious awareness of the sounds of language and the ability to talk about and manipulate those sounds.

Motor planning The ability to plan, organise and carry out movements.

Motor response or motor output Using sensory information to produce movement.

Multimodal texts Combine language with other means of communication such as visual images, soundtrack or spoken words, as in film or computer presentation media.

Nativist Language is acquired naturally through the presence of a Language Acquisition Device (LAD) that is present from birth.

Natural consequences The student experiences the natural outcomes of their behaviour.

Natural mathematics Consists of three discrete parts: the teacher directs students to engage in mental routines; students are presented with a real-life problem; and students are invited to discuss their solutions and how they arrived at the outcome.

Near-sightedness A lack of ability to see distant objects (the child usually will hold objects up close to their eyes).

Neglectful behaviour Failure (usually by a parent) to provide for a child's basic needs.

Neurodevelopmental disorder A disorder of early brain development where the integrity and function of the nervous system is damaged during critical periods of brain development.

Non-verbal communication Using body language and behaviour to communicate – for example, through gestures or facial expressions.

Not substantiated Where an investigation concludes that there was no reasonable cause to suspect prior, current or future abuse, neglect or harm to the child.

Notifiable incident The death of a person, a 'serious injury or illness' or a 'dangerous incident' arising out of work carried out by a business or undertaking or at a workplace.

Notification Contacts made to an authorised department by persons or other bodies making allegations of child abuse or neglect, child maltreatment or harm to a child.

Numeracy The knowledge and application of number concepts.

Object permanence The understanding that objects continue to exist even when they cannot be perceived directly.

Obsessive compulsive disorder (OCD) An anxiety disorder in which people have unwanted and repeated thoughts, feelings, images and sensations (obsessions) and engage in behaviours or mental acts in response to these thoughts (compulsions), often in an attempt to get rid of the obsessions.

One person, one plan Planning is coordinated across all domains of a person's life, including all specialist services being accessed as well as informal supports and networks, insofar as the person wants this to happen.

Onset–rime phonics Children learn to identify the sound of the letter or letters before the first vowel (the onset) in a one-syllable word and the sound of the remaining part of the word (the rime).

Opportunistic occasional predators More likely to commit abuse when a lack of appropriate controls, such as a code of conduct or reporting procedures, obscures personal responsibility for the abuse.

Optic nerve atrophy Deterioration of the optic nerve.

Oral language The foundation for the development of literacy skills; considered to be a strong indicator of later reading, writing and overall academic achievement.

Ordinal number A number that indicates the place or order in a sequence.

Orthographic knowledge Knowing how letters go together in written English.

Orthography Spelling patterns.

Otitis media (OM) A term used for middle ear infections; also referred to as 'glue ear'.

Paragraphs Give structure to a piece of writing and organise information to suit the type of text and its purpose.

Partially sighted Indicates some type of visual problem that has resulted in a need for additional support.

Participatory appropriation Knowledge that is acquired through observation and interaction in sociocultural activities.

Pedagogical strategy A teaching practice.

Peer-assessment A form of assessment as learning undertaken by fellow students.

Perceptual motor development The ability to receive, interpret and respond successfully to sensory information.

Perceptual motor learning The ability to make sense of what we see, hear, feel, taste and smell.

Perpetrator A person who has been determined to have caused (intentionally or unintentionally) by acts of omission or knowingly the maltreatment of a child.

Perseveration Saying the same thing or behaving in the same way over and over to the point where it makes no sense.

Person at the centre The person with disability is central to all planning and decision-making.

Person conducting a business or undertaking (PCBU) A person conducting a business or undertaking alone or with others, whether or not for profit or gain – for example, a self-employed person, each partner within a partnership, a company. In children's services, the PCBU will be the approved provider.

Personal priorities and strengths There is a strong focus on the person's abilities, interests, dreams and aspirations, and the supports required to realise them. There is also strong recognition of the person as a unique individual who is influenced by age, gender, culture, ethnicity, belief system, social and income status, education, family and any other factors that make them unique.

Personality The traits that make each person unique.

Phobia An intense and irrational fear of an object, thing or event.

Phoneme The smallest distinguishable speech sound.

Phonemic awareness The ability to understand that words are made up of a sequence of sounds.

Phonics Involves making the connection between the single sounds (phonemes) and their related letter patterns (graphemes) when reading and writing.

Phonics through spelling Students are taught to segment the word into phonemes (sounds) and writing letters for each phoneme.

Phonological awareness Recognition that a word may contain a number of different sounds; understanding the relationship between letters and sounds.

Phonology Speech sounds.

Physical development (motor development) A complex process involving muscle tissue, tendons, bones, joints and nerves.

Physical self What do I look like compared with others? What physical skills do I have? Am I attractive?

Physically abusive behaviour Any non-accidental physically aggressive act towards a child.

Place value The value represented by a digit in a number on the basis of its position in the number.

Plasticity The brain's ability to reorganise and adapt to influences, interactions and challenges in the environment.

Positive outlook A focus on positives rather than negatives; having a 'can do' attitude.

Post-traumatic stress disorder (PTSD) Can develop as a consequence of a traumatic experience or event such as a serious accident, a natural disaster, witnessing extreme violence, being attacked or bullied; often accompanied by flashbacks and extreme mood swings.

Pragmatics Also known as social language. The ability to communicate effectively with others for a range of purposes and in a range of situations.

Predictable text Early readers that contain repetitive words and sentences.

Prejudice Pre-judgement; making up your own mind about something or someone without adequate knowledge or information; a belief that is often founded on incorrect information, biased values and family beliefs based on fear, ignorance and misinformation.

Prevailing social norms Standards of behaviour generally accepted by the community.

Private speech A child uses private speech for the purposes of self-direction, self-control and problem-solving.

Procedural skills Knowing 'how to', such as pointing at each object when counting or using fingers to help count.

Professional knowledge Specialised knowledge and its application to practice.

Proprioception An innate sensory motor skill that allows infants to become aware of their body by receiving sensory feedback from involuntary movement of the joints and muscles.

Proprioceptive dysfunction Students tend to be clumsy, awkward and uncoordinated, and will display a number of sensory and tactile behaviours; they may be over-sensitive or under-sensitive to sensory information.

Prosody The ability to read with expression.

Proximity control A behaviour management strategy where the educator positions themself close to the student as a way of encouraging on-task behaviour.

Proximodistal development The progression of physical and motor development from the centre of the body towards the extremities.

Psychological/emotional self Am I likeable? How do I manage my emotions? How do I deal with disappointment or conflict? Am I happy, kind, friendly, helpful, empathic?

Public speech A child's public speech, although still egocentric, is used primarily for communicating with others.

Punctuation Symbols, such as full stops, commas and question marks, used to divide written text into sentences and clauses.

Punishment A strategy that motivates the student to behave in a way to avoid punishment or disapproval.

Quality of voice How speech sounds when it is spoken.

Reading accuracy Assesses the number of errors made by the student when reading a selected text.

Reading fluency Develops over time as students become better at word recognition and at seeing connected texts rather than a series of words; includes three components – accuracy, rate and prosody.

Reading rate The speed and fluidity used by the reader while maintaining comprehension of what is being read.

Reasonably practical In relation to WHS, that which is, or was at a particular time, reasonably able to be done to ensure health and safety, taking into account all relevant issues.

Receptive language Understanding or comprehending the meaning of spoken language.

Reciprocal determinism A person's behaviour both influences and is influenced by personal factors and the social environment.

Recounting language The ability to verbally recall and retell a past event using the correct tense and in the correct chronological order.

Regular review and continuous improvement The individual's program is reviewed regularly with them and their support network to assess ongoing changes and learnings, and to ensure that planned activities are being achieved and are still relevant to their goals.

Relationship skills Include learning effective communication skills, developing conflict-resolution skills, learning to cooperate with others, understanding how to build friendships.

Residual current devices (RCDs) Safety switches, such as a circuit breaker, reduce the risk of electrical shock because they are designed to immediately switch off the supply of electricity when electricity 'leaking' to earth is detected at harmful levels.

Resilience An individual's ability to overcome setbacks and persevere in the presence of difficulty or hardship.

Respect for culture Respect for the individual's social customs and traditions, language, culture, and religious beliefs and practices.

Responsible decision-making Thinking and choosing wisely.

Risk An action with the potential to result in harm to persons or property.

Risk assessment A systematic evaluation of the potential risks that may be involved in a projected activity or undertaking.

Robust Instruction where students are required to think about and use the word to demonstrate understanding.

Rote counting The number words are repeated in the correct sequence without reference to the actual quantity of objects.

Safety Data Sheet (SDS) A document that provides detailed information about a hazardous chemical.

Scaffolding Providing structure and support; a method of teaching, designed to teach a child something new by utilising what they already know or can do.

Schema Mental concept developed by the child to understand and make sense of objects, things, actions and events.

School refusal Children who develop school refusal are usually so anxious about going to school that they will develop psychosomatic illnesses, such as a headache or upset tummy.

Self-assessment A process where the student gathers information about and reflects on their own learning.

Self-awareness The realisation that one is a separate being; recognising one's own feelings and building self-confidence.

Self-concept The process of evaluating oneself – 'Who am I, what am I like, what do others think of me, what will I become?' Self-concept is multidimensional – it is a process of thinking critically in order to evaluate oneself in a range of areas.

Self-confidence Trust in one's own abilities, judgement and actions.

Self-control Control over oneself or one's actions and feelings.

Self-efficacy An understanding of one's own personal competence to deal with challenging situations.

Self-esteem The measure of how much an individual likes or values the characteristics that make up the image they have of themselves and their ability.

Self-management Regulating one's emotions to handle stress, control impulses and persevere in overcoming obstacles; setting and monitoring progress towards personal and academic goals; expressing emotions appropriately.

Self-regulation Includes the ability to persist at tasks; the ability to cope with challenges, frustration and disappointment; being able to calm down after being hurt, angry or upset; and the ability to control one's behaviour and manage conflict.

Semantics Word meanings.

Sense of agency An individual's sense of control or self-confidence.

Sense of responsibility/participation A feeling of purpose and self-motivation to attempt challenges.

Sensitive periods Periods of development during which an organism is most likely to be susceptible to a particular influence.

Sensorimotor development The ability to receive, interpret and respond successfully to sensory information.

Sensory input The use of sensory information by the brain.

Sensory integration The process by which the brain uses sensory information to make sense of the world and respond in an appropriate manner.

Sensory integration dysfunction (SID) Caused when the brain and central nervous system have difficulty processing, or are unable to process, sensory information required to coordinate movement, and to understand and make sense of the world.

Sensory integration therapy A program developed by an occupational therapist to assist the student to manage sensory input.

Sensory modulation The term used to describe the way the body responds to sensory stimulation and information.

Sensory over-responsivity Occurs when an individual has an exaggerated negative response to sensory input, often leading to avoidance and hypervigilance of the stimulus.

Sensory Processing Disorder A neurological condition where the brain has difficulty processing and responding to sensory information such as sound or touch, resulting in the individual feeling overwhelmed.

Sensory under-responsivity Occurs when an individual may seem to be unaware of, or slow to respond to, a stimulus that would typically be expected to elicit a response.

Sentence A word or a group of words that expresses a thorough idea by giving a statement/order, asking a question or exclaiming.

Separation anxiety Difficulty separating from the family without becoming anxious.

Serial perpetrator predators High-frequency chronic offenders who choose victims based on situational factors and are likely to actively manipulate environments to create opportunities to abuse.

Sexually abusive behaviour Any sexual activity between an adult and a child below the age of consent; non-consensual sexual activity between minors; sexual activity between a child under 18 years and a person in a position of power or authority; or any sexual activity that a child does not fully comprehend, is unable to give informed consent to or for which the child is not developmentally prepared.

Shared commitment A strong commitment to supporting the individual to realise their goals and aspirations.

Shared mathematics Learning is made explicit by highlighting key ideas and encouraging students to explore connections with other mathematical ideas.

Sight words Words that a student recognises instantly by sight without needing to decode the word.

Simultaneous At the same time.

Situational perpetrators Commit abuse in reaction to environmental factors and often behave impulsively when overcome by temptation or a temporary failure of self-control.

Social awareness Understanding and respecting similarities and differences.

Social environment Family, education, religion, culture and economic status.

Social interaction An exchange between two people; an important part of social functioning.

Social justice The concept that all people have the right to opportunities that will increase their 'life' chances and allow them to be happy, productive members of society.

Social self Do I have a range of social networks and friendships? Do I participate in a range of activities and experiences with others? Can I communicate effectively with people of different ages? What are my core values and beliefs?

Social skills Students become aware of the human interaction skills involved in effective group cooperation when working in a small group.

Social values Those values that society as a whole supports or rejects – for example, gun laws, capital punishment, homosexual marriages or euthanasia. Social values are often the basis for developing laws or codes of conduct for particular professions. In this way, social values influence the legal and ethical framework in which we live and work. ESWs need to be aware of their own 'social values' – for example, the view that same-sex couples should not be allowed to adopt children.

Socialisation The process of psychologically growing into a society, in which an individual acquires the behaviours, attitudes, values and roles expected of them.

Sociocultural context All the factors that influence a person's development and behaviour.

Spastic cerebral palsy The most common type of cerebral palsy, associated with stiffness or tightness of muscles.

Special education The student is placed in a regular school setting or a special unit. An IEP is developed to assist the student to reach their full learning potential.

Specific Learning Disorder (SLD) Significant difficulty in one or more academic areas while coping well, or even excelling, in other areas of academic, sporting or artistic achievement.

Speech The spoken form of language; the production of sounds (articulation) and voice quality.

Speech disorders Speech and language problems that may include substitutions or distortions.

Speech/language therapy A speech pathologist works with the student to develop a program to facilitate language and communication.

Spina bifida A congenital orthopaedic impairment that means 'cleft spine' – an incomplete closure in the spinal column.

Standards-referenced assessment Monitoring student progress against curriculum standards.

Stereotype A standardised idea or concept, or preconceived image or view, of a person based on certain characteristics. Stereotypes do not take individual differences into consideration, which can result in discrimination.

Stimming Self stimulation.

Strabismus A misalignment of the eyes because of an imbalance in the eye muscles; often one or both eyes appear to be crossed.

Structured behaviour intervention Development of a plan to assist the student to manage their behaviour.

Stutter A speech disorder of fluency that often involves sound repetition, delayed sound production or the elongation of some speech sounds (Gallagher et al., 2023).

Substantiated After investigation, it is concluded that there is reasonable cause to believe that the child has been, was being or is likely to be abused, neglected or otherwise harmed.

Summative assessment Making a judgement about student achievement against a set of standards such as curriculum outcomes (also known as assessment of learning).

Symbolic stage Bruner's stage of cognitive development – using abstract ideas (language-based).

Syntactic awareness A metalinguistics skill that is defined as the conscious ability to manipulate or judge word order within the context of a sentence, based on the application of grammatical rules.

Syntactic knowledge An unconscious understanding of the rules that govern word order.

Syntax The sentence structure of a language. It governs how words are ordered meaningfully into phrases, clauses and sentences.

Synthetic phonics Students are taught the relationship between letters and the speech sounds they represent. This is a part-to-whole approach that teaches children to convert graphemes into phonemes.

Temperament The traits that determine how an individual reacts, interacts and behaves.

Thinking and problem-solving The ability to engage in problem-solving and finding new ways to approach challenges.

Think-pair-share (TPS) A pedagogical practice that requires students to work in pairs, with the guidance of the teacher, to engage in shared problem-solving by thinking independently and then working in pairs to share their knowledge and solve problems.

Totally blind Students who have no light perception and learn via Braille or other non-visual media.

Transactional language Used to provide information or transfer specific information.

Transductive reasoning Reasoning that moves from particular to particular, and results in thinking that lacks adult logic.

Translanguaging Using both first language and English when communicating and thinking.

Unacceptable risk of significant harm Siginificant harm that has not yet occurred but is likely in the future, given risk factors identified in the present.

Value(s) The worth placed on an object, behaviour or custom; the judgements we make about what is important; our personal 'standards' – for example, that all children should be taught manners.

Variables The use of algebraic symbols in mathematics: letters replace unknown numbers or quantities.

Visual acuity Clearness or clarity of vision.

Visual discrimination Includes the ability to perceive depth, colour and movement.

Visual impairment Diminished ability to see clearly.

Visual knowledge Understanding the way words and letter combinations look.

Visual perception The ability to make sense and meaning out of what you see.

Vocabulary The words that are understood when language is heard or read.

Voice disorders Speech and language problems that may include a husky, hoarse, breathy or strained voice.

Whole child Each domain of development is influenced by, and dependent on, all other domains of development.

WHS management system A system of managing, recording, analysing and ensuring the health and safety of individuals in the workplace.

Witnessing family violence A form of psychologically abusive behaviour.

Word meaning When students are learning to spell new words, it is also important that they understand the meaning of the word and can use it in the correct context.

Work health and safety (WHS) legislation Occupational health and safety law aimed at protecting the health, safety and welfare of people in the workplace.

Working memory The capacity to hold and manipulate information in our minds over short periods.

Zone of proximal development (ZPD) Referred to by Vygotsky as the lower limit that the child can achieve in terms of learning without adult support, compared with the upper limit that the child can achieve in terms of learning with support from an adult or more knowledgeable older child.

REFERENCES

CHAPTER 1

Australian Human Rights Commission (AHRC) (2016). Topic 8: Legal and ethical considerations of service delivery. https://humanrights.gov.au/sites/default/files/VET%20Disability%20Unit%20Trainers%20Manual%20-%20Topic%208.pdf

Australian Teacher Aide (2023). Australian Standards for Paraprofessional Educators in Schools. https://www.australianteacheraide.com.au/australian-standards-paraprofessional-educators-schools

Berkeley Compliance Services (2023). Conflict of interest. https://compliance.berkeley.edu/conflict-of-interest

Conflict Resolution Network (n.d.). Conflict resolution skills: 12 skill summary. https://www.crnhq.org/12-skill-summary

Department of Education and Training (DET) (2005). *Disability Standards for Education 2005*. https://www.education.gov.au/disability-standards-education-2005

Eurich, T. (2018). The right way to respond to negative feedback. *Harvard Business Review*. https://hbr.org/2018/05/the-right-way-to-respond-to-negative-feedback

Fair Work Ombudsman (2018). *National Employment Standards*. https://www.fairwork.gov.au/employee-entitlements/national-employment-standards

How to handle negative feedback: 6 ways to accept criticism. https://www.masterclass.com/articles/how-to-handle-negative-feedback#why-is-it-important-to-accept-negative-feedback

Markkula Center for Applied Ethics (2010). What is ethics? https://www.scu.edu/ethics/ethics-resources/ethical-decision-making/what-is-ethics

Office of the Australian Information Commission (n.d.). Australian Privacy Principles. https://www.oaic.gov.au/privacy/australian-privacy-principles

Office of the Commonwealth Ombudsman (2017). Conflict of interest guideline. September. https://www.ombudsman.gov.au/__data/assets/pdf_file/0030/29919/Conflict-of-Interest-Guidelines-September-2017.pdf

Victoria State Government Education and Training (2017). Conflict of interest toolkit. General information (July). https://www.education.vic.gov.au/hrweb/Documents/COI-Toolkit-General.pdf

CHAPTER 2

Australian Government Department of Education (2022). What is the Quality Schools package and what does it mean for my school? Fact sheet. https://www.dese.gov.au/quality-schools-package/fact-sheets/what-quality-schools-package-and-what-does-it-mean-my-school

Australian Human Rights Commission (AHRC) (2012). About us. Know your rights. https://humanrights.gov.au/sites/default/files/content/about/publications/brochure/about-us.pdf

Australian Human Rights Commission (2019). Good practice, good business – A quick guide to Australian discrimination laws © Australian Human Rights Commission 2019.

Department of Education and Children's Services, SA (2007). Duty of care owed by teachers. Section 1 of *Administrative Instructions & Guidelines*. SA Government, Adelaide. http://www.decd.sa.gov.au/docs/documents/1/DutyofCare.pdf

Department of Education and Early Childhood Development, Victoria (2011). *ICT Acceptable Use Policy*. Victorian Government, Melbourne. http://www.education.vic.gov.au/Documents/school/principals/infrastructure/ictacceptableusepolicy.pdf

Department of Education, Qld (2022). Information security policy. https://ppr.qed.qld.gov.au/attachment/information-security-policy.pdf

Department of Education, WA (2018). *Duty of Care for Students*. http://det.wa.edu.au/policies/detcms/navigation/safety-and-welfare/duty-of-care-for-students

Department of Education and Training (DET) (2005). *Disability Standards for Education 2005*. https://www.education.gov.au/disability-standards-education-2005

Department of Families, Housing, Community Services and Indigenous Affairs (2013). © Commonwealth of Australia. Released under CC BY 3.0 AU, link to licence: https://creativecommons.org/licenses/by/3.0/au

United Nations (1990). *Convention on the Rights of the Child*. United Nations, Geneva; Australian Human Rights Commission. https://www.ohchr.org/en/professionalinterest/pages/crc.aspx

Williams, A. & McWilliams, C. (2014). *MGMT2*, 2nd Asia-Pacific edn. Cengage Learning, Melbourne.

CHAPTER 3

Ashman, A. & Elkins, J. (2012). *Education for Inclusion and Diversity*, 4th edn. Pearson, Sydney.

Australian Bureau of Statistics (ABS) (2018). Estimates of Aboriginal and Torres Strait Islander Australians. https://www.abs.gov.au/statistics/people/aboriginal-and-torres-strait-islander-peoples/estimates-aboriginal-and-torres-strait-islander-australians/jun-2016

Australian Bureau of Statistics (ABS) (2019). Disability, ageing and carers, Australia: Summary of findings. https://www.abs.gov.au/statistics/health/disability/disability-ageing-and-carers-australia-summary-findings/latest-release

Australian Bureau of Statistics (ABS) (2022). Statistics. https://www.abs.gov.au/statistics/people/population

Australian Catholic University (2015). 15 idioms commonly used in Australia. https://internationalblog.acu.edu.au/15-idioms-commonly-used-in-australia

Australian Human Rights Commission (AHRC) (n.d.). Religion. https://humanrights.gov.au/quick-guide/12091

Australian Human Rights Commission (AHRC) (2003). Social justice and human rights for Aboriginal and Torres Strait Islander Peoples, information sheet. AHRC, Sydney. http://www.humanrights.gov.au/sites/default/files/content/social_justice/infosheet/infosheet_sj.pdf

Australian Human Rights Commission (AHRC) (2010). *Bringing Them Home*. AHRC, Canberra. https://www.humanrights.gov.au/sites/default/files/content/education/bringing_them_home/Individual%20resources%20and%20activities/10_RS_Australia_overview.pdf

Australian Human Rights Commission (AHRC) (2012). Face the facts: Some questions and answers about Indigenous peoples, migrants and refugees and asylum seekers. AHRC, Sydney. http://www.humanrights.gov.au

Australian Human Rights Commission (AHRC) (2014). Face the facts: Cultural diversity. AHRC, Sydney. https://www.humanrights.gov.au/sites/default/files/FTFCulturalDiversity.pdf

Australian Human Rights Commission (AHRC) (2015). Face the facts: Lesbian, gay, bisexual, trans and intersex people. https://humanrights.gov.au/our-work/education/face-facts-lesbian-gay-bisexual-trans-and-intersex-people

Australian Human Rights Commission (AHRC) (2016). Workplace cultural diversity tool. https://humanrights.gov.au/our-work/race-discrimination/projects/workplace-cultural-diversity-tool

Australian Human Rights Commission (AHRC) (2016). Willing to Work: Report of the National Inquiry into Employment Discrimination Against Older Australians and Australians with Disability © Australian Human Rights Commission 2016.

Australian Institute of Health and Welfare (AIHW) (2012). *A Picture of Australia's Children 2012*. AIHW, Canberra. http://www.aihw.gov.au/WorkArea/DownloadAsset.aspx?id=10737423340

Australian Network on Disability (2016). Employing people with disability. http://www.and.org.au/pages/tapping-into-talentemploying-people-with-disability.html

Ball, J. (2015). *Cultural Safety in Practice with Children, Families and Communities*. School of Child and Youth Care, University of Victoria, Victoria, Canada. http://www.ecdip.org/docs/pdf/Cultural%20Safety%20Poster.pdf

Black Dog Institute (2019). Signs and symptoms of anxiety. https://www.blackdoginstitute.org.au/docs/default-source/factsheets/signs-and-symptoms-of-anxiety.pdf?sfvrsn=0

Black Dog Institute (2020). Facts & figures about mental health. https://www.blackdoginstitute.org.au/wp-content/uploads/2020/04/1-facts_figures.pdf

Charles Sturt University (n.d.). Guide to working with Indigenous Australian staff. https://cdn.csu.edu.au/__data/assets/pdf_file/0006/851415/Working-with-Indigenous-Australian-Staff.pdf

Cooper, J., He, Y. & Levin, B.B. (2011). *Developing Critical Cultural Competence: A Guide for 21st-Century Educators*. Corwin Press, Thousand Oaks, CA.

Department of Education, Queensland (2018). Proud at work: Including and supporting LGBTIQ+ staff. https://qed.qld.gov.au/workfordet/induction/det/humanresources/Documents/workforceinclusion-strategy.pdf

Diversity Council of Australia (2023). Inclusion. https://www.dca.org.au/topics/inclusion

Dodson, M. (1993). *Annual Report of the Aboriginal and Torres Strait Islander Social Justice Commission*. Human Rights and Equal Opportunity Commission (HREOC). Sydney. http://www.austlii.edu.au/au/other/IndigLRes/1993/3/index.html

Eckermann, A.-K., Dowd, T. & Jeffs, L. (2009). Culture and nursing practice. In J. Crisp & C. Taylor (eds), *Potter and Perry's Fundamentals of Nursing*, 3rd edn. Mosby Elsevier, Sydney, pp. 118–24.

Equal Opportunity Commission of South Australia (2011). *Equal Opportunity at Work: A Handbook for Employers in South Australia*. Government of South Australia, Adelaide. https://eoc.sa.gov.au/sites/default/files/inline-files/EO%20at%20Work_1.pdf

Fair Work Ombudsman (2016). Protection from discrimination at work. https://www.fairwork.gov.au/employee-entitlements/protections-at-work/protection-from-discrimination-at-work

Jalongo, M.R. & Isenberg, J.P. (2012). *Exploring Your Role in Early Childhood Education*, 4th edn. Pearson Education, London.

Koori Human Services Unit (2008). *Improving Care for Aboriginal and Torres Strait Islander Patients: Resource Kit*. Secretariat of National Aboriginal and Islander Child Care (SNAICC). Sydney. http://www.supportingcarers.snaicc.org.au/connecting-to-culture/cultural-safety

LeBaron, M. (2003). Cross-cultural communication. In G. Burgess & H. Burgess (eds), *Beyond Intractability*. Conflict Research Consortium, University of Colorado, Boulder, CO. http://www.beyondintractability.org/essay/cross-cultural_communication

Lindh, S. (2012). Embedding Aboriginal & Torres Strait Islander perspectives. *Reflections*, 49, pp. 6–7.

Martin, K. (1999). When 'why?' becomes 'why not?': Cultural safety and Aboriginal early childhood services. *Every Child*, vol. 5, no. 4, pp. 6–7.

National Mental Health Consumer & Carer Forum (2018). Aboriginal and Torres Strait Islander Social and Emotional Wellbeing, Advocacy Brief. https://nmhccf.org.au/sites/default/files/docs/aboriginal_and_torres_strait_islander_social_and_emotional_wellbeing_ab_1.pdf

NSW Health (2004). *Communicating Positively: A Guide to Appropriate Aboriginal Terminology*. NSW Health, Sydney. http://www.health.nsw.gov.au/aboriginal/Publications/pubterminology.pdf

Oxfam Australia (2015). Aboriginal and Torres Strait Islander cultural protocols. https://www.oxfam.org.au/wp-content/uploads/2015/11/2015-74-atsi-cultural-protocols-update_web.pdf

Pride in Diversity (2013). *A Manager's Guide to LGBTI Workplace Inclusion*. https://www.westernsydney.edu.au/__data/assets/pdf_file/0009/1114857/Managers-Guide-to-LGBTI-Workplace-Inclusion-WEB_2.pdf

Racism. It stops with me. https://itstopswithme.humanrights.gov.au

Roth, K. & McCracken Jarrar, A. (2021). In the world. Amnesty International Australia (May). https://www.amnesty.org.au/justice-for-george-floyd-a-year-of-global-activism-for-black-lives-and-against-police-violence/?cn=trd&mc=click&pli=23501504&PluID=0&ord={timestamp}&gclid=EAIaIQobChMIuu-sqqCy9AIV2hwrCh0f6AprEAAYAyAAEgJ1ifD_BwE

Safe Work Australia (2018). Mental health. https://www.safeworkaustralia.gov.au/topic/mental-health

Samson, D., Donnet, T. & Daft, R. (2018). *Management*, 6th edn. Cengage Learning, Melbourne.

Scott, E. (2022). What is spirituality? The Very Well Mind. https://www.verywellmind.com/how-spirituality-can-benefit-mental-and-physical-health-3144807

Secretariat of National Aboriginal and Islander Child Care (SNAICC) (2012). *What is Cultural Safety?* http://www.supportingcarers.snaicc.org.au/connecting-to-culture/cultural-safety

Stibich, M. (2022). What is religion? The psychology of why people believe. https://www.verywellmind.com/religion-improves-health-2224007

The Conversation (June 2021). Australia's news media play an important role reminding the country that Black lives still matter. https://theconversation.com/australias-news-media-play-an-important-role-reminding-the-country-that-black-lives-still-matter-161412

United Nations, Universal Declaration of Human Rights, Article 2. https://www.un.org/en/about-us/universal-declaration-of-human-rights

Victorian Equal Opportunity and Human Rights Commission (VEOHRC) (2013). *Reporting Racism: What You Say Matters.* http://www.humanrightscommission.vic.gov.au/media/k2/attachments/Reporting_Racism_Web_low_res.pdf

Wentling, R.M. & Palma-Rivas, N. (1998). Current status and future trends of diversity initiatives in the workplace: Diversity experts' perspective. *Human Resource Development Quarterly*, vol. 9, no. 3, pp. 235–53.

Williams, R. (1998). *Cultural Safety: What Does It Mean for Our Work Practice?* Faculty of Aboriginal & Torres Strait Islander Studies, Northern Territory University, Darwin.

Zion, S., Kozleski, E. & Fulton, M. (2005). *Understanding Culture.* National Institute for Urban School Improvement, Olympia, WA. http://www.urbanschools.org/pdf/understanding.culture.LETTER.pdf

CHAPTER 4

Black Dog Institute (2014). Workplace wellbeing fact sheet. http://www.blackdoginstitute.org.au/docs/WorkplaceWellbeing.pdf

Comcare (2008). *Officewise: A Guide to Health and Safety in the Office.* Commonwealth of Australia, Canberra. https://www.comcare.gov.au/__data/assets/pdf_file/0006/39570/Officewise_OHS1_Apr_10.pdf

Comcare (2021). Workplace sexual harassment. https://www.comcare.gov.au/office-safety-tool/workplace-safety/workplace-sexual-harassment

Guetzloe, E. (2006). Practical strategies for working with students who display aggression and violence. CYC Online. Issue 86, March. http://www.cyc-net.org/cyc-online/cycol-0306-guetzloe.html

National Health and Medical Research Council (NHMRC) (2012). *Staying Healthy: Preventing Infectious Diseases in Early Childhood Education and Care Services*, 5th edn. NHMRC, Canberra.

NSW Department of Education and Communities (2012). Legal liability and rights of staff in relation to serious incidents which involve potential risk of injury to persons on departmental premises. *Legal Issues Bulletin*, no. 19, p. 2.

NSW Department of Education and Training (2018). *Guidelines Issued Under Part 5a of the* Education Act 1990 *for the Management of Health and Safety Risks Posed to Schools by a Student's Violent Behaviour*. NSW Government, Sydney. https://www.det.nsw.edu.au/media/downloads/legislation/mhsguidelines.pdf

Product Safety Australia (2015). *Chemicals in Consumer Products.* https://www.productsafety.gov.au/content/index.phtml/itemId/975127/fromItemId/973881

Safe Work Australia (2011a). *Model Code of Practice: Hazardous Manual Tasks, Code of Practice: Hazardous Manual Tasks*. Safe Work Australia, Canberra. http://www.safeworkaustralia.gov.au/doc/model-code-practice-hazardous-manual-tasks

Safe Work Australia (2011b). *How to Manage Work Health and Safety Risks Code of Practice*. Safe Work Australia, Canberra. https://www.safeworkaustralia.gov.au/system/files/documents/1702/how_to_manage_whs_risks.pdf

Safe Work Australia (2012). *Guide to the Model Work Health and Safety Act*. Safe Work Australia, Canberra. http://www.safeworkaustralia.gov.au/sites/SWA/about/Publications/Documents/621/Guide_Model_WHS_ Regulations.pdf

Safe Work Australia (2016). *Guide for Preventing and Responding to Workplace Bullying*. Safe Work Australia, Canberra. https://www.safeworkaustralia.gov.au/doc/guide-preventing-and-responding-workplace-bullying

Safe Work Australia (2018). *Hazardous Manual Tasks: Code of Practice.* Safe Work Australia, Canberra. https://www.safeworkaustralia.gov.au/system/files/documents/1905/model-cop-hazardous-manual-tasks.pdf

Safe Work Australia (2019). Guide to the Model Work Health and Safety Act. https://www.safeworkaustralia.gov.au/doc/guide-model-work-health-and-safety-act

Standing Council on School Education and Early Childhood (SCSEEC) (2013). *National Safe Schools Framework*. Education Services Australia, Melbourne. http://www.safeschoolshub.edu.au/documents/nationalsafeschoolsframework.pdf

Workfast (2017). *Safe Lifting in the Workplace*. https://workfast.com.au/blog/toolbox-talk-safe-lifting-information

WorkSafe ACT (2010). *Safe Work Procedures*. http://www.health.gov.au/internet/main/publishing.nsf/Content/9D831D9E6713F92ACA257BF0001F5218/$File/0-5yrACTIVE_Brochure_FA%20SCREEN.pdf

WorkSafe ACT (2012). *Making Your Small Business Safer & Healthier*. WorkSafe ACT, Canberra. http://www.worksafety.act.gov.au/publication/view/1099

WorkSafe Victoria (2014). *A Guide for Employers Preventing and Responding to Work-related Violence*. http://www.worksafe.vic.gov.au/safety-and-prevention/health-andsafety-topics/occupational-violence

WorkSafeAct (2023) *Health and Safety Advice – Safe work procedures, Australian Capital Territory (ACT)*. https://www.worksafe.act.gov.au/health-and-safety-portal/safety-by-industry/hospitality-and-tourism/safe-work-procedures

CHAPTER 5

ACT Government (n.d.). Responding to student accidents/incidents: Support, reporting and insurance arrangements procedure. https://www.education.act.gov.au/__data/assets/pdf_file/0019/810136/RespondingStudentsAccidentsIncidentsProcedure.pdf

Association of Independent Schools South Australia (2016). *Student Health, Safety & Wellbeing: Policy Guidelines*. https://www.ais.sa.edu.au/wp-content/uploads/Pages/Policy_Resources/Student-Health-Safety-Wellbeing-Policy-Guidelines.pdf

Australasian Society of Clinical Immunology and Allergy (ASCIA) (2013). Action plan for anaphylaxis. ASCIA, Sydney. http://www.allergy.org.au/images/stories/anaphylaxis/2013/ASCIA_Action_Plan_Anaphylaxis_EpiPen_Personal_2013.pdf

Australian Bureau of Statistics (ABS) (2017). ABS 2071.0 – Census of Population and Housing: Reflecting Australia – Stories from the Census, 2016 (June 2017).

Australian Government (2022). Information about cleaning and disinfection for schools. https://www.health.gov.au/sites/default/files/documents/2022/02/information-about-cleaning-and-disinfection-for-schools.pdf

Australian Human Rights Commission (AHRC) (2019). *Children's Rights Report 2019. In Their Own Right: Children's Rights in Australia*. https://www.humanrights.gov.au/our-work/childrens-rights/publications

Australian Institute of Family Studies (AIFS) (2018). *Growing Up in Australia: The Longitudinal Study of Australian: Children Annual Statistical Report 2017 (2018)*.

Australian Institute of Health and Welfare (AIHW) (2022). Chronic conditions and burden of disease. Australia's children. 25 February. https://www.aihw.gov.au/reports/children-youth/australias-children/contents/health/chronic-conditions-and-burden-of-disease

Cancer Council Victoria (2014). *Sample SunSmart Policy for Schools*. http://www.sunsmart.com.au

Cherry, C. (2022). Types of nonverbal communication. Verywell Mind. https://www.verywellmind.com/types-of-nonverbal-communication-2795397

Department of Education, New South Wales (2023). 'Letter to parents confirming arrangements' from 'Health and physical care'. https://education.nsw.gov.au/student-wellbeing/health-and-physical-care/health-care-procedures/administering-medication/frequently-asked-questions#Can3

Department of Education, Queensland (n.d.). Administration of medications in schools procedure. https://ppr.qed.qld.gov.au/pp/administration-of-medications-in-schools-procedure

Department of Education, Queensland (2016). Guidelines for the administration of medications in schools. January. https://ppr.qed.qld.gov.au/attachment/guidelines-for-the-administration-of-medications-in-schools.docx

Department of Education, Queensland (2022). Curriculum Activity Risk Assessment (CARA) process. CARA planner. https://education.qld.gov.au/curriculum/stages-of-schooling/CARA

Department of Education, SA (2022). Health care plans for individual care – information for health professionals. https://www.education.sa.gov.au/working-us/service-providers/health-care-plans-individual-care-information-health-professionals

Department of Education and Training (DET) (n.d.). Effective consultation: Improving outcomes for students with disability. Fact sheet. https://www.dese.gov.au/download/2338/fact-sheet-4-effective-consultation/19614/document/pdf

Department of Education and Training (DET) (2014). Disability Standards for Education 2005. Fact sheet. Modified 2022. https://www.dese.gov.au/download/2336/fact-sheet-2-disability-standards-education-2005/19610/document/pdf

Department of Employment and Workplace Relations (2006). Getting students to work . . . safely. https://www.safeworkaustralia.gov.au/system/files/documents/1702/gettingstudentstoworksafely_2006_pdf.pdf

Department of Health (WA) (2013). Food poisoning. WA Government, Perth. http://www.public.health.wa.gov.au/3/1613/2/food_poisoning.pm

Diocese of Broken Bay (2016). Administration of medication in schools procedures. https://www.skmvdbb.catholic.edu.au/wp-content/uploads/2017/12/Medication-Procedures-2016.pdf

Education NSW (n.d.a). Accident to school student visitor. https://education.nsw.gov.au/content/dam/main-education/policy-library/associated-documents/sup_doc.pdf

Education NSW (n.d.b). Request for student to carry his/her own EpiPen®, Anapen® or asthma reliever medication. https://education.nsw.gov.au/content/dam/main-education/student-wellbeing/health-and-physical-care/media/documents/parent_request_form.pdf

Education NSW (2020). Health and physical care. Frequently asked questions. Education NSW. https://education.nsw.gov.au/student-wellbeing/health-and-physical-care/health-care-procedures/administering-medication/frequently-asked-questions

Education Victoria (2022). Managing and reporting school incidents (including emergencies). 20 June. https://www2.education.vic.gov.au/pal/reporting-and-managing-school-incidents-including-emergencies/policy

Hand Hygiene Australia (n.d.). What is hand hygiene? https://www.hha.org.au/hand-hygiene/what-is-hand-hygiene

healthdirect (2022). School exclusion periods. https://www.healthdirect.gov.au/school-exclusion-periods

International Union for Health Promotion and Education (n.d.). *Promoting Health in Schools: From Evidence to Action*. https://doh.health.tas.gov.au/__data/assets/pdf_file/0007/117385/PHiSFromEvidenceToAction_WEB1.pdf

Kidsafe Queensland (2016). Playground safety. http://www.kidsafeqld.com.au/playground-safety

National Asthma Council Australia (2013a). Symptoms and triggers. http://www.nationalasthma.org.au/understanding-asthma/symptoms-triggers

National Asthma Council Australia (2013b). What is asthma? http://www.nationalasthma.org.au/understanding-asthma/what-is-asthma

National Health and Medical Research Council (NHMRC) (2013). *Staying Healthy: Preventing Infectious Diseases in Early Childhood Education and Care Services*, 5th edn. NHMRC, Canberra. Updated and reprinted June 2013.

NSW Department of Education and Communities (2015). The Wellbeing Framework for Schools. https://education.nsw.gov.au/content/dam/main-education/student-wellbeing/whole-school-approach/Wellbeing_Framework_for_Schools.pdf

NSW Government (2020). Primary school enrolment. https://education.nsw.gov.au/public-schools/going-to-a-public-school/enrolment/primary-school-enrolment

NSW Ministry of Health (2018). Immunisation enrolment toolkit. For primary and secondary schools from 1 April 2018. https://www.health.nsw.gov.au/immunisation/Publications/school-immunisation-enrolment-toolkit.pdf

Queensland Government (2021). Managing risks in school curriculum activities procedure. CARA information sheet. https://education.qld.gov.au/curriculum/stages-of-schooling/CARA

Robertson, C. (1998). *Safety, Nutrition, and Health in Early Education*. Delmar, Albany, NY.

Student Wellbeing Hub (2020). Australian Student Wellbeing Framework. https://studentwellbeinghub.edu.au/educators/framework

World Health Organization (2022). Health promoting schools. https://www.who.int/health-topics/health-promoting-schools#tab=tab_1

CHAPTER 6

Australian Human Rights Commission (AHRC) (2018). National Principles for Child Safe Organisations. https://childsafe.humanrights.gov.au/sites/default/files/2019-02/National_Principles_for_Child_Safe_Organisations2019.pdf

Australian Institute of Family Studies (AIFS) (2014a). Australian legal definitions: When is a child in need of protection? CFCA Fact Sheet. AIFS, Canberra. https://aifs.gov.au/cfca/publications/australian-legal-definitions-when-child-need-protection

Australian Institute of Family Studies (AIFS) (2014b). Who abuses children? https://aifs.gov.au/cfca/publications/who-abuses-children

Australian Institute of Health and Welfare (AIHW) (2013). National Framework for Protecting Australia's Children 2009–2020, August 2013. AIHW, Canberra.

Australian Institute of Health and Welfare (AIHW) (2014). Child Protection Australia: 2012–13, Child Welfare Series No. 58. Cat. No. CWS 49. Canberra. http://www.aihw.gov.au/WorkArea/DownloadAsset.aspx?id=60129548164

Australian Institute of Health and Welfare (AIHW) (2018a). Child protection Australia 2016–17. Child welfare series no. 68. Cat. no. CWS 63. AIHW, Canberra.

Australian Institute of Health and Welfare (AIHW) (2018b). Family, domestic and sexual violence in Australia 2018. Cat. no. FDV 2. AIHW, Canberra. https://www.aihw.gov.au/reports/domestic-violence/family-domestic-sexual-violence-in-australia-2018/summary

Australian Institute of Health and Welfare (AIHW) (2021a). Child protection Australia 2019–20. Child welfare series no. 74. Cat. no. CWS 78. AIHW, Canberra.

Australian Institute of Health and Welfare (AIHW) (2021b). Child protection Australia 2019–20 (18 May). https://www.aihw.gov.au/reports/child-protection/child-protection-australia-2019-20/summary

CFCA (2014). Effects of child abuse and neglect for children and adolescents. CFCA fact sheet. January. https://www3.aifs.gov.au/cfca/publications/effects-child-adolescents-and-neglect-children-and-adolescents

Children's Hospital Westmead (2014). Shaken baby syndrome, kids' health fact sheet. http://www.schn.health.nsw.gov.au/parents-andcarers/fact-sheets/shaken-baby-syndrome

Department of Communities, Child Safety and Disabilities Services Qld (2015). *Practice Guide: The Assessment of Harm and Risk of Harm*. https://www.communities.qld.gov.au/resources/childsafety/practice-manual/pg-assess-risk-of-harm.pdf

Dolgin, K. (2014). *The Adolescent. Development, Relationships and Culture*, 13th edn. Pearson Education, Essex, England.

Dwyer, J., O'Keefe, J., Scott., P. & Wilson, L. (2012). *Literature Review: A Trauma-Sensitive Approach for Children Aged 0–8 Years*. Women's Health Goulburn North East, Goulburn, NSW. https://www.whealth.com.au/documents/work/trauma/LiteratureReview.pdf

Family and Community Services (NSW) (2011). *Child Wellbeing and Child Protection: NSW Interagency Guidelines. Making a Child Protection Report: How Do I Know if a Child or Young Person is Being Abused or Neglected?* http://www.community.nsw.gov.au/kts/guidelines/documents/signs_abuse.pdf

Government of South Australia (2017). *Protective Practices for Staff in Their Interactions with Children and Young People*. Department for Education, Adelaide.

Lamont, A. (2010). *Effects of Child Abuse and Neglect for Children and Adolescents*. Australian Institute of Family Studies, Melbourne. http://www.aifs.gov.au/nch/pubs/sheets/rs17/rs17.html

Lamont, A. (2011). Who abuses children? Australian Institute of Family Studies, Melbourne. http://www.aifs.gov.au/nch/pubs/sheets/rs7/rs7.pdf

Miller, D. & Brown, J. (2014). *'We Have the Right to Be Safe': Protecting Disabled Children from Abuse*. National Society for the Prevention of Cruelty to Children, London. http://www.nspcc.org.uk/preventing-abuse/research-and-resources/right-to-be-safe

NSW Government, Office of the Children's Guardian (2020). The Child Safe Standards. https://ocg.nsw.gov.au/sites/default/files/2021-12/g_CSS_GuidetotheStandards.pdf?Embed=Y

Price-Robertson, R. (2015). *What is Child Abuse and Neglect?* AIFS, Canberra. http://www.aifs.gov.au/cfca/pubs/factsheets/a142091/index.html

Royal Commission into Institutional Responses to Child Sexual Abuse (2016). *Final Report*. https://www.childabuseroyalcommission.gov.au

Scott, D. (2012). Pre-employment screening: Working with children checks and police checks. Australian Institute of Family Studies, Canberra. http://www.aifs.gov.au/cfca/pubs/factsheets/a141887

Scott, D. & Nair, L. (2013). Child protection and Aboriginal and Torres Strait Islander children. Australian Institute of Family Studies, Canberra. http://www.aifs.gov.au/cfca/pubs/factsheets/a142117

United Nations (1990). Convention on the Rights of the Child. http://www.ohchr.org/en/professionalinterest/pages/crc.aspx

United Nations International Children's Emergency Fund (UNICEF) (2018). A Summary of the Rights Under the Convention on the Rights of the Child, Fact Sheet. https://www.unicef.org/crc/files/Rights_overview.pdf

CHAPTER 7

Australian Curriculum, Assessment and Reporting Authority (ACARA) (2022). Australian Curriculum Version 9. https://v9.australiancurriculum.edu.au

Briceño, E. (2015). Growth mindset: Clearing up some common confusions. KQED. https://www.kqed.org/mindshift/42769/growth-mindset-clearing-up-some-common-confusions

Bronfenbrenner, U. (1979). *The Ecology of Human Development: Experiments by Nature and Design*. Harvard University Press, Cambridge, MA.

Dolgin, K. (2014). *The Adolescent: Development, Relationships, and Culture*, 13th edn. Pearson Education, Harmondsworth.

Ertmer, P.A. & Newby, T.J. (2013). Behaviorism, cognitivism, constructivism: Comparing critical features from an instructional design perspective. *Performance Improvement Quarterly*, vol. 26, no. 2, pp. 43–71. https://lidtfoundations.pressbooks.com/chapter/behaviorism-cognitivism-constructivism

Feinstein, S. (2009). *Secrets of the Teenage Brain*. Skyhorse, New York.

Gable, S. & Hunting, M. (2001). Nature, nurture and early brain development: Information sheet GH6115. MU Extension, University of Missouri-Columbia, New York. http://extension.missouri.edu/p/GH6115

Gerdes, J., Durden, T. & Poppe, L. (June 2013). *Brain Development and Learning in the Primary Years*. University of Nebraska–Lincoln Extension, Institute of Agriculture and Natural Resources. https://extensionpublications.unl.edu/assets/pdf/g2198.pdf

Guerra, N.G., Williamson, A.A. & Lucas-Molina, B. (2012). Normal development: Infancy, childhood, and adolescence. In J.M. Rey (ed.), *IACAPAP e-Textbook of Child and Adolescent Mental Health*. International Association for Child and Adolescent Psychiatry and Allied Professions, Geneva.

Immordino-Yang, M.H., Darling-Hammond, L. & Krone, C. (2018). *The Brain Basis for Integrated Social, Emotional, and Academic Development: How emotions and social relationships drive learning*. The Aspen Institute National Commission on Social, Emotional, and Academic Development. https://www.aspeninstitute.org/wp-content/uploads/2018/09/Aspen_research_FINAL_web.pdf

McCandliss, B. & Toomarian, E. (2020). Putting neuroscience in the classroom: How the brain changes as we learn. Pew. April. https://www.pewtrusts.org/en/trend/archive/spring-2020/putting-neuroscience-in-the-classroom-how-the-brain-changes-as-we-learn

Mustard, J. (2008). *Investing in the Early Years: Closing the Gap Between What We Know and What We Do*. Adelaide Thinker in Residence. Department of the Premier and Cabinet, Adelaide. http://www.thinkers.sa.gov.au/lib/pdf/Mustard_Final_Report.pdf

National Scientific Council on the Developing Child (2004). Center on the Developing Child at Harvard University (2007). A Science-Based Framework for Early Childhood Policy: Using Evidence to Improve Outcomes in Learning, Behavior, and Health for Vulnerable Children. http://www.developingchild.harvard.edu

Rogoff, B. (2003). *The Cultural Nature of Human Development*. Oxford University Press, New York.

Schiller, P. (2010). Early brain development research review and update. Exchange. November/December (pp. 26–30). https://www.childcareexchange.com/library/5019626.pdf

Shonkoff, J. & Phillips, D. (2000). *From Neurons to Neighborhoods: The Science of Early Childhood Development*. National Academy Press, Washington, DC.

Sprenger, M. (2008). *The Developing Brain: Birth to Age Eight*. Corwin Press, Thousand Oaks, CA.

Understood (2013). Executive Function 101. The National Center for Learning Disabilities Inc. https://www.understood.org/en/learning-attention-issues/child-learning-disabilities/executive-functioning-issues/ebook-executive-function-101

University of Pittsburgh (2022). Curriculum: Guiding principles. University Child Development Centre. http://www.childdevelopment.pitt.edu/node/225

CHAPTER 8

Australian Curriculum, Assessment and Reporting Authority (ACARA) (2022a). Health and Physical Education (Version 9). Understand this learning area: Health and Physical Education. Structure: Focus areas. https://v9.australiancurriculum.edu.au/teacher-resources/understand-this-learning-area/health-and-physical-education

Australian Curriculum, Assessment and Reporting Authority (ACARA) (2022b). Understand this learning area: Health and Physical Education. Key considerations: Health and Physical Education propositions. https://v9.australiancurriculum.edu.au/teacher-resources/understand-this-learning-area/health-and-physical-education

Australian Institute of Health and Welfare (AIHW) (2020). Australia's children. Cat. no. CWS 69. AIHW, Canberra: AIHW, pp.131–5.

Beyond Blue (2022). Body image. https://beyou.edu.au/fact-sheets/mental-health-issues-and-conditions/body-image

Butterfly Foundation, The (2022). Body Image Explained. https://butterfly.org.au/body-image/body-image-explained/

Capon, J. (1984). Perceptual-motor lesson plans, level 1. Front Row Experience. Byron, CA.

Charlesworth, L., Wood, J. & Viggian, P. (2011). Middle childhood. In Elizabeth D. Hutchinson, *Dimension of Human Behavior. The Changing Life Course*. Sage Publications, Thousand Oaks, CA.

Dolgin, K. (2014). *The Adolescent: Development, Relationships, and Culture*, 13th edn. Pearson Education, Harmondsworth.

Eating Disorders Victoria (2022a). What is anorexia nervosa? https://www.eatingdisorders.org.au/eating-disorders-a-z/anorexia-nervosa

Eating Disorders Victoria (2022b). What is binge eating? https://www.eatingdisorders.org.au/eating-disorders-a-z/binge-eating-disorder

Eating Disorders Victoria (2022c). What is bulimia nervosa? https://www.eatingdisorders.org.au/eating-disorders-a-z/bulimia-nervosa

Eating Disorders Victoria (2023). Key research and statistics. https://www.eatingdisorders.org.au/eating-disorders-a-z/eating-disorder-statistics-and-key-research/?gclid=EAIaIQobChMIoIWxmrqu9wIVLplmAh3oyQOQEAAYAiAAEgK67_D_BwE

Jackson, S. & Goossens, L. (2006). *Handbook of Adolescent Development*. Psychology Press, Bristol.

Jensen, E. (2005). *Teaching with the Brain in Mind*, 2nd edn. Association for Supervision and Curriculum Development, Alexandria, VA.

Jensen Arnett, J. & Arnett Jensen, L. (2019). *Human Development: A Cultural Approach*, 3rd edn. Pearson, New York.

Kids Sense (2022). Developmental delay. https://childdevelopment.com.au/areas-of-concern/diagnoses/developmental-delay

Murdoch Children's Research Institute (2019). Aussie pre-teens spend most of their day sitting still, study shows. https://www.mcri.edu.au/news/aussie-pre-teens-spend-most-their-day-sitting-still-study-shows

Queensland Human Rights Commission (2020). Trans@School. https://www.qhrc.qld.gov.au/__data/assets/pdf_file/0019/24535/QHRC_TransAtSchool_forschools.pdf

Royal Children's Hospital, Melbourne (2020). Gender dysphoria. https://www.rch.org.au/kidsinfo/fact_sheets/Gender_dysphoria

Sigelman, C.K. (1999). *Lifespan Human Development*. Brooks Cole, Pacific Grove, CA.

CHAPTER 9

Alberg, J. (2018). Social development. In J. Lenihan (ed.). *Preparing to Teach, Committing to Learn: An Introduction to Educating Children Who are Deaf/Hard of Hearing*. https://www.infanthearing.org/ebook-educating-children-dhh/chapters/Chapter%204%202018.pdf

Australian Curriculum, Assessment and Reporting Authority (ACARA) (n.d). Personal and social capability (Version 8.4). https://www.australiancurriculum.edu.au/f-10-curriculum/general-capabilities/personal-and-social-capability

Australian Curriculum, Assessment and Reporting Authority (ACARA) (2022a). Australian Curriculum: General capabilities – Personal and social capability Version 9.0. About the general capability. https://v9.australiancurriculum.edu.au/downloads/general-capabilities#accordion-afa194f119-item-a9a4b7ac87

Australian Curriculum, Assessment and Reporting Authority (ACARA) (2022b). Understand this general capability. Ethical understanding. https://v9.australiancurriculum.edu.au/teacher-resources/understand-this-general-capability/ethical-understanding

Australian Curriculum, Assessment and Reporting Authority (ACARA) (2022c). Understand this general capability. Intercultural understanding. https://v9.australiancurriculum.edu.au/teacher-resources/understand-this-general-capability/intercultural-understanding

Australian Curriculum, Assessment and Reporting Authority (ACARA) (2022d). Understand this general capability. Personal and social capability. https://v9.australiancurriculum.edu.au/teacher-resources/understand-this-general-capability/personal-and-social-capability

Bandura, A. (1986). *Social Foundations of Thought and Action*. Prentice Hall, Englewood Cliffs, NJ.

Be You (2019a). Resilience fact sheet. https://beyou.edu.au/factsheets/wellbeing/resilience

Be You (2019b). Anxiety fact sheet. https://beyou.edu.au/fact-sheets/mental-health-issues-and-conditions/anxiety

Be You (2019c). Mindfulness fact sheet. https://beyou.edu.au/factsheets/wellbeing/mindfulness

Bee, H. & Boyd, D. (2004). *The Developing Child*, 10th edn. Pearson Education, Sydney.

Bowlby, J. (1969). *Attachment and Loss, Volume 1: Attachment*. Basic Books, New York.

Center for Child Trauma Assessment Services and Interventions (CCTASI) (2023). What is child trauma? Chicago. https://cctasi.northwestern.edu/child-trauma

Center on the Developing Child, Harvard University (n.d.). What is executive function? And how does it relate to child development? https://developingchild.harvard.edu/resources/what-is-executive-function-and-how-does-it-relate-to-child-development

Cherry, K. (2022). What is attachment theory? The importance of early emotional bonds. Very Well Minds. https://www.verywellmind.com/what-is-attachment-theory-2795337

Children's Therapy & Family Resource Centre (n.d.). School-aged developmental milestones. http://www.kamloopschildrenstherapy.org/social-emotional-school-aged-milestones

Collaborative for Academic, Social, and Emotional Learning (CASEL) (2007). Background on social and emotional learning (SEL). December. CASEL Briefs. University of Illinois, Chicago. http://casel.org/wp-content/uploads/2011/04/EDC_CASELSELResearchBrief.pdf

Collaborative for Academic, Social, and Emotional Learning (CASEL (2020). What are the core competence areas and where are they promoted? 1 October 2020. https://casel.org/casel-sel-framework-11-2020/

Dolgin, K. (2014). *The Adolescent: Development, Relationships, and Culture*, 13th edn. Pearson Education, Harmondsworth.

Duchesne, S., McMaugh, A., Bochner, S. & Krause, K. (2019). *Educational Psychology for Learning and Teaching*, 6th edn. Cengage Learning, Melbourne.

Erikson, E. (1963). *Childhood and Society*. W.W. Norton, New York.

Gardner, H. (1993). *Multiple Intelligences: The Theory in Practice*. Basic Books, New York.

Georgetown University Center for Child and Human Development (n.d.). What is social and emotional health? Center for Early Childhood Mental Health Consultation. https://www.ecmhc.org/tutorials/social-emotional/mod1_0.html

Goleman, D. (2006). *Emotional Intelligence*. Bantam Books, New York.

Health Direct (2021). Kids and mental health. https://www.healthdirect.gov.au/kids-mental-health

Hunter Institute of Mental Health (2010). *Response Ability Vocational Education & Training Resources: Children's Services*. Hunter Institute of Mental Health, Newcastle.

Immordino-Yang, M.H., Darling-Hammond, L. & Krone, C. (n.d.). The brain basis for social-emotional learning also supports academic learning. UNESCO MGIEP. https://mgiep.unesco.org/article/the-brain-basis-for-social-emotional-learning-also-supports-academic-learning

Jackson, S. & Goossens, L. (2006). *Handbook of Adolescent Development*. Psychology Press, Bristol.

Keogh, B. (2009). Temperament in the classroom: Helping each child find a good fit. Great Schools. https://www.greatschools.org/gk/articles/temperament-in-the-classroom-helping-each-child-find-a-good-fit

Mcleod, S. (2023). Mary Ainsworth: Strange situation experiment & attachment theory. https://simplypsychology.org/mary-ainsworth.html

National Center on Birth Defects and Developmental Disabilities, US Centers for Disease Control and Prevention (2022). Anxiety and depression in children. https://www.cdc.gov/childrensmentalhealth/depression.html#anxiety

National Child Traumatic Stress Network (n.d.). About child trauma: Trauma types. https://www.nctsn.org/what-is-child-trauma/trauma-types

National Child Traumatic Stress Network (2018). About child trauma: The National Child Traumatic Stress Network. https://www.nctsn.org/what-is-child-trauma/about-child-trauma

National Scientific Council on the Developing Child (2004). *A Science-Based Framework for Early Childhood Policy: Using Evidence to Improve Outcomes in Learning, Behavior, and Health for Vulnerable Children*. http://www.developingchild.harvard.edu

National Scientific Council on the Developing Child (2005). Excessive stress disrupts the architecture of the developing brain, Working paper no. 3. Center on the Developing Child, Harvard University, Cambridge, MA. http://www.developingchild.net

NSW Centre for Parenting and Research (2004). Aggression in children and young people, factsheet. http://www.imagineeducation.com.au/files/CHC30113/DOCS._20Agggression_20in_20Children_20and_20Young_20People.pdf

Pennsylvania State University, The (2016). Emotional wellness: Understanding its importance. http://bkc-od-media.vmhost.psu.edu/documents/tips1303.pdf

Prior, M., Sanson, A., Smart, D. & Oberklaid, F. (2000). *Pathways from Infancy to Adolescence: Australian Temperament Project 1983–2000*. Australian Institute of Family Studies, Melbourne.

Thomas, A., Chess, S. & Birch, H.G. (1970). The origin of personality. *Scientific American*, vol. 223, no. 2, pp. 102–9.

Values Education Good Practice Schools Project (2008). *At the Heart of What We Do: Values Education at the Centre of Schooling. The Final Report of the Values Education Good Practice Schools Project – Stage 2*. http://www.curriculum.edu.au/verve/_resources/VEGPSP-2_final_3.pdf

Yeo, M. & Sawyer, S. (2005). Chronic illness and disability. *BMJ*. 26 March, vol. 330, no. 7493, pp. 721–3. https://www.ncbi.nlm.nih.gov/pmc/articles/PMC555640

CHAPTER 10

Anderson, L.W. & Krathwohl, D.R., et al. (eds) (2001). *A Taxonomy for Learning, Teaching, and Assessing: A Revision of Bloom's Taxonomy of Educational Objectives*. Allyn & Bacon. Boston, MA.

Atkinson, R.C. & Shiffrin, R.M. (1968). Human memory: A proposed system and its control processes. In K.W. Spence & J.T. Spence, *The Psychology of Learning and Motivation: II*. Academic Press. https://doi.org/10.1016/S0079-7421(08)60422-3

Australian Curriculum, Assessment and Reporting Authority (ACARA) (n.d.a). Australian Curriculum: English. https://australiancurriculum.edu.au/f-10-curriculum/english/?strand=Language&strand=Literature&strand=Literacy&capability=ignore&priority=ignore&elaborations=true

Australian Curriculum, Assessment and Reporting Authority (ACARA) (n.d.b). English (Version 8.4). https://australiancurriculum.edu.au/senior-secondary-curriculum/english

Australian Curriculum, Assessment and Reporting Authority (ACARA) (n.d.c). How were the progressions developed? https://www.australiancurriculum.edu.au/resources/national-literacy-and-numeracy-learning-progressions/how-were-the-progressions-developed

Australian Curriculum, Assessment and Reporting Authority (ACARA) (n.d.d). Structure of Essential English. https://australiancurriculum.edu.au/senior-secondary-curriculum/english/essential-english/structure-of-essential-english

Australian Curriculum, Assessment and Reporting Authority (ACARA) (n.d.e). Structure of English as an Additional Language or Dialect. https://australiancurriculum.edu.au/senior-secondary-curriculum/english/english-as-an-additional-language-or-dialect/structure-of-english-as-an-additional-language-or-dialect

Australian Curriculum, Assessment and Reporting Authority (ACARA) (n.d.f). Structure of Literature. https://australiancurriculum.edu.au/senior-secondary-curriculum/english/literature/structure-of-literature

Australian Curriculum, Assessment and Reporting Authority (ACARA) (2022a). Australian Curriculum. https://v9.australiancurriculum.edu.au

Australian Curriculum, Assessment and Reporting Authority (ACARA) (2022b). Australian Curriculum: Overview. https://v9.australiancurriculum.edu.au/f-10-curriculum/f-10-curriculum-overview

Australian Curriculum, Assessment and Reporting Authority (ACARA) (2022c). Literacy. https://v9.australiancurriculum.edu.au/f-10-curriculum.html/general-capabilities/literacy?element=2&sub-element=0

Australian Curriculum, Assessment and Reporting Authority (ACARA) (2022d). Understand this learning area. English. https://v9.australiancurriculum.edu.au/teacher-resources/understand-this-learning-area/english

Australian Curriculum, Assessment and Reporting Authority (ACARA) (2023). Critical and creative thinking. https://v9.australiancurriculum.edu.au/f-10-curriculum.html/general-capabilities/critical-and-creative-thinking?element=3&sub-element=0

Bates, E. (1976). *Language and Context: The Acquisition of Pragmatics*. Academic Press, New York.

Bee, H. & Boyd, D. (2004). *The Developing Child*, 10th edn. Pearson Education, Sydney.

Bloom, B.S. (1956). *Taxonomy of Educational Objectives, Handbook I. The Cognitive Domain*. David McKay Co Inc, New York.

Bochner, S. & Jones, J. (2003). *Child Language Development: Learning to Talk*, 2nd edn. Whurr, London.

Bruner J.S. (1974). *Toward a Theory of Instruction*. Harvard University Press, Cambridge, MA.

Campbell, R. & Baker, C. (2006). Children learning language. In R. Campbell & D. Green (eds), *Literacies and Learners: Current Perspectives*, 3rd edn. Pearson Australia, Sydney.

Chauhan, S. (2020). Lesson planning using Bloom's taxonomy in my math classroom. https://connectedtot.com/2020/07/08/lesson-planning-using-blooms-taxonomy-for-math

Clark, L. & Ireland, C. (1996). *Learning to Talk, Talking to Learn*. Angus & Robertson, Sydney.

Cowan, N. (2010). The magical mystery four: How is working memory capacity limited, and why? National Library of Medicine. https://www.ncbi.nlm.nih.gov/pmc/articles/PMC2864034

Cummins, S. (2019). A teacher's guide to Bloom's taxonomy. https://www.innovativeteachingideas.com/blog/a-teachers-guide-to-blooms-taxonomy

Dalli, C., White, E.J., Rockel, J., Duhn, I., Buchanan, E., Davidson, S., Ganly, S., Kus, L. & Wang, B. (2011). *Quality Early Childhood Education for Under-Two-Year-Olds: What Should It Look Like? A Literature Review*. Report to the Ministry of Education, Wellington, NZ. http://www.educationcounts.govt.nz/publications

Dolya, G. (2010). *Vygotsky in Action in the Early Years*. Routledge, Abingdon.

Duchesne, S., McMaugh, A., Bochner, S. & Krause, K. (2019). *Educational Psychology for Learning and Teaching*, 6th edn. Cengage Learning, Melbourne.

Gardner, H.E. (1983). *Frames of Mind: The Theory of Multiple Intelligences*. Basic Books, New York.

Gardner, H.E. (1993). *Multiple Intelligences: The Theory in Practice*. Basic Books, New York.

Healthy Families BC (2013). Toddlers' language development from 18–24 months. http://www.healthyfamiliesbc.ca/home/articles/toddlers-language-development-18-24-months

Hendrick, J. (1991). *Total Learning: Developmental Curriculum for the Young Child*, 3rd edn. Allyn & Bacon/Merrill Education, Boston, MA.

Iowa State University (2022). Revised Bloom's taxonomy. https://www.celt.iastate.edu/teaching/effective-teaching-practices/revised-blooms-taxonomy

Klein, L. & Knitzer, J. (2006). *Effective Preschool Curriculum and Teaching Strategies*. Pathways to Early School Success: Issue Brief No. 2, National Center for Children in Poverty, New York.

McGreal, S. (2013). The illusory theory of multiple intelligences. *Psychology Today*, November. https://www.psychologytoday.com/intl/blog/unique-everybody-else/201311/the-illusory-theory-multiple-intelligences

Mulvaney, A. (1991). *Look Who's Talking! How to Help Children with Their Communication Skills*. Simon & Schuster, Sydney.

Mustard, J. (2008). *Investing in the Early Years: Closing the Gap Between What We Know and What We Do*. Adelaide Thinker in Residence. Department of the Premier and Cabinet, SA Government, Adelaide. http://www.thinkers.sa.gov.au/lib/pdf/Mustard_Final_Report.pdf

National Scientific Council on the Developing Child (2007a). A science-based framework for early childhood policy: Using evidence to improve outcomes in learning, behavior, and health for vulnerable children. Center on the Developing Child, Harvard University, Cambridge, MA. http://www.developingchild.net

National Scientific Council on the Developing Child (2007b). The science of early childhood development: Closing the gap between what we know and what we do. Center on the Developing Child, Harvard University, Cambridge, MA. http://www.developingchild.net

Piaget, J. (1936). *Origins of Intelligence in the Child*. Routledge & Kegan Paul, London.

Podium School (n.d.). 9 multiple intelligences types by Howard Gardner. https://learn.podium.school/personality-development/9-multiple-intelligences-types-by-howard-gardner/#htoc-9-existential-intelligence

Rogoff, B. (2003). *The Cultural Nature of Human Development*. Oxford University Press, New York.

Shonkoff, J. & Phillips, D. (2000). *From Neurons to Neighborhoods: The Science of Early Childhood Development*. National Academy Press, Washington, DC.

Sowers, J. (2000). *Language Arts in Early Education*. Delmar/Thomson Learning, Melbourne.

Sweller, J. (1988). Cognitive load during problem solving: Effects on learning. *Cognitive Science. A Multidisciplinary Journal*, vol. 12, no. 2, April, pp. 257–85.

Vialle, W., Lysaght, P. & Verenikina, I. (2008). *Handbook on Child Development*, 2nd edn. Social Science Press, Katoomba.

Vicker, B. (2009). *Meeting the Challenge of Social Pragmatics with Students on the Autism Spectrum*. Indiana University Press, Bloomington, IN. https://www.iidc.indiana.edu/pages/Meeting-the-Challenge-of-Social-Pragmatics-with-Students-on-the-Autism-Spectrum

Vygotsky, L. (1978). *Mind in Society: The Development of Higher Mental Processes*. Harvard University Press, Cambridge, MA.

CHAPTER 11

Australian Curriculum, Assessment and Reporting Authority (ACARA) (n.d). Steps to personalise learning: CASE. https://www.australiancurriculum.edu.au/resources/student-diversity/planning-for-student-diversity/steps-to-personalise-learning-case

Australian Government. Department of Infrastructure, Transport, Regional Development, Communications and the Arts (n.d.). The advisory categories for films and computer games. https://www.classification.gov.au/classification-ratings/what-do-ratings-mean

Australian Student Wellbeing Framework (2020). https://studentwellbeinghub.edu.au/educators/framework/.

Bartle, E. (2015). *Experiential Learning: An Overview*. Institute for Teaching and Learning Innovation, Queensland.

Bolden, F. (2020). How to implement effective small group instruction. https://www.teachhub.com/classroom-management/2020/03/how-to-implement-effective-small-group-instruction

Bugler, D., Marple, S., Burr, E., Chen-Gaddini, M. & Finkelstein, N. (2017). How teachers judge the quality of instructional materials. Selecting instructional materials: Brief 1 – Quality. WestEd. March.

Bulloch, K. (2003). *Adapting Materials and Strategies for Special Needs Students*. http://www.educationoasis.com/visitor-resources/articles/adapting-special-needs

Centre for Education Statistics and Evaluation (2020). NSW Department of Education. What works best: 2020 update. https://education.nsw.gov.au/about-us/educational-data/cese/publications/research-reports/what-works-best-2020-update

Education Corner (2023). What is dual coding theory? https://www.educationcorner.com/dual-coding-theory

Hattie, J. (2009). *Visible Learning. A Synthesis of over 800 Meta-Analyses Relating to Achievement*. Routledge, New York.

Kelly, S. (2020). Introduction to Universal Design for Learning (UDL). Michigan State University. http://edtech.cal.msu.edu/introduction-to-universal-design-for-learning-udl

Lyman, F. (1981). The responsive classroom discussions: The inclusion of all students. In A. Anderson (ed.), *Mainstreaming Digest*. University of Maryland Press, College Park.

Miller, A. (2019). Treating reflection as a habit, not an event. Edutopia. https://www.edutopia.org/article/treating-reflection-habit-not-event

Mindset Works (2017). Dr Dweck's research into growth mindset changed education forever. https://www.mindsetworks.com/science

Ministerial Council on Education, Training, Employment and Youth Affairs (MCEETYA) (December 2008). *Melbourne Declaration on Educational Goals for Young Australians*. http://www.curriculum.edu.au/verve/_resources/National_Declaration_on_the_Educational_Goals_for_Young_Australians.pdf

Nguyen, H.P. (2021). How to use gameplay to enhance classroom learning. Edutopia. https://www.edutopia.org/article/how-use-gameplay-enhance-classroom-learning

NSW Government (2022). Education. Differentiating learning. https://education.nsw.gov.au/teaching-and-learning/professional-learning/teacher-quality-and-accreditation/strong-start-great-teachers/refining-practice/differentiating-learning

Rababate, P. (2011). Universal Design for Learning: Meeting the needs of all students. https://www.readingrockets.org/article/universal-design-learning-meeting-needs-all-students

Romero, C. (2015). What we know about growth mindset from scientific research. http://studentexperiencenetwork.org/wp-content/uploads/2015/09/What-We-Know-About-Growth-Mindset.pdf

Rose, D.H., Meyer, A. & Hitchcock, C. (eds). *The Universally Designed Classroom: Accessible Curriculum and Digital Technologies* (pp. 13–35). Harvard Education Press, Cambridge, MA.

School of Education. American University Washington, DC (2020). How to foster a growth mindset in the classroom. https://soeonline.american.edu/blog/growth-mindset-in-the-classroom

Student Wellbeing Hub (2020). Australian Student Wellbeing Framework. https://studentwellbeinghub.edu.au/educators/framework

Tomlinson, C. & Imbeau, M. (2010). *Leading and Managing a Differentiated Classroom*. ASCD, Alexandria, VA.

True Education Partnerships (n.d.). Gamification in education: What is it & how can you use It? https://www.trueeducationpartnerships.com/schools/gamification-in-education

University of Waterloo (n.d.). Centre for Teaching Excellence. Group work in the classroom: Types of small groups. https://uwaterloo.ca/centre-for-teaching-excellence/teaching-resources/teaching-tips/developing-assignments/group-work/group-work-classroom-types-small-groups

Upper Elementary Snapshots (n.d.). Why you should be using games in the classroom. https://www.upperelementarysnapshots.com/2018/01/why-you-should-be-using-games-in.html

van Diggele, C., Burgess, A. & Mellis, C. (2020). Planning, preparing and structuring a small group teaching session. *BMC Medical Education*, pp. 1– 8. https://bmcmededuc.biomedcentral.com/track/pdf/10.1186/s12909-020-02281-4.pdf

Victorian Department of Education and Training (2023). School operations. Teaching and learning resources – Selecting appropriate materials. https://www2.education.vic.gov.au/pal/selecting-suitable-teaching-resources/policy

Victorian Education Department (2007). A 'critical' reflection framework. https://www.education.vic.gov.au/Documents/childhood/professionals/support/reffram.pdf

Visible Learning (2023). Hattie ranking: 252 influences and effect sizes related to student achievement. https://visible-learning.org/hattie-ranking-influences-effect-sizes-learning-achievement

Vygotsky, L. (1978). *Mind in Society: The Development of Higher Mental Processes*. Harvard University Press, Cambridge, MA.

Watkins, C. (2009). School leadership today: Leading learning: pedagogy. *Learning About Learning*, vol. 1, no. 3. http://www.teachingtimes.com

CHAPTER 12

Abilities Based Learning and Educational Support (2022). https://www.education.vic.gov.au/school/teachers/learningneeds/Pages/ables.aspx#link36

ACT Education and Training (n.d.). Reporting on student achievement and progress to students and parents. http://www.det.act.gov.au/__data/assets/pdf_file/0020/19505/StudentReportingPolicy_updated.pdf

ACT Government (2016). *Teachers' Guide to Assessment*. https://ais.act.edu.au/wp-content/uploads/Teachers-Guide-To-Assessment.pdf

Australian Curriculum, Assessment and Reporting Authority (ACARA) (n.d.). Structure of the Australian Curriculum. Information sheet. https://docs.acara.edu.au/resources/Information_Sheet_Structure_of_the_Foundation_to_Year_10_Australian_Curriculum.pdf

Australian Curriculum, Assessment and Reporting Authority (ACARA) (2020). Measurement Framework for Schooling in Australia. https://www.acara.edu.au/docs/default-source/default-document-library/measurement-framework-2020-for-pubafa92e404c94637ead88ff00003e0139.pdf?sfvrsn=1c3d4d07_0

Bently, E. (2021). A guide to 5 school assessment types and their key purposes. https://www.janison.com/resources/post/a-guide-to-5-school-assessment-types-and-their-key-purposes

Council of Australian Governments (COAG) (2015). *National Education Agreement*. Commonwealth Government, Canberra.

Department of Education, Employment and Workplace Relations (n.d.). The Family – School Partnerships Framework. A guide for schools and families. http://www.familyschool.org.au/files/3013/8451/8364/Family-school_partnerships_framework.pdf

Department of Education and Training (DET) (n.d.). Planning for personalised learning and support: A national resource. https://www.dese.gov.au/download/2837/planning-personalised-learning-and-support-national-resource/3905/document/pdf

Department of Education and Training (DET) (2005). *Disability Standards for Education 2005*. https://www.education.gov.au/disability-standards-education-2005

Love to Teach (2020). A collection of retrieval practice research and resources... https://lovetoteach87.com/2020/09/09/a-collection-of-retrieval-practice-research-and-resources

Ministry of Education [Canada] (2006). *The Ontario Curriculum, Grades 1–8: Language*. Queen's Printer for Ontario, Toronto, ON.

Nationally Consistent Collection of Data on School Students with Disability (NCCD) (2022). What's reasonable? https://www.nccd.edu.au/wider-support-materials/whats-reasonable

Queensland Studies Authority (2008). Queensland Curriculum, Assessment and Reporting (QCAR) Framework December 2008. https://www.qcaa.qld.edu.au/downloads/p_10/guidelines_for_reporting_qcar.pdf

St George School (n.d.). Personalised reporting. Decisions about reporting for students with disability are made in consultation with parents/carers and report on personalised goals and outcomes identified through the collaborative curriculum planning. https://stgeorge-s.schools.nsw.gov.au/supporting-our-students/personalised-reporting.html

Vygotsky, L. (1978). *Mind in Society: The Development of Higher Mental Processes*. Harvard University Press, Cambridge, MA.

CHAPTER 13

Australian Curriculum, Assessment and Reporting Authority (ACARA) (n.d.a). General capabilities (Version 8.4). https://www.australiancurriculum.edu.au/f-10-curriculum/general-capabilities

Australian Curriculum, Assessment and Reporting Authority (ACARA) (n.d.b). Literacy (Version 8.4). https://www.australiancurriculum.edu.au/f-10-curriculum/general-capabilities/literacy

Australian Curriculum, Assessment and Reporting Authority (ACARA) (2020). National Literacy Learning Progression Version 3.0. March. https://www.ofai.edu.au/media/01nixkio/national-literacy-progressions-v3-for-publication.pdf

Australian Curriculum, Assessment and Reporting Authority (ACARA) (2023a). Learning area downloads. https://v9.australiancurriculum.edu.au/downloads/learning-areas#accordion-b71b085f07-item-49001e70bc

Australian Curriculum, Assessment and Reporting Authority (ACARA) (2023b). Understand this general capability. Literacy. https://v9.australiancurriculum.edu.au/teacher-resources/understand-this-general-capability/literacy

Australian Curriculum, Assessment and Reporting Authority (ACARA) (2023c). Understand this learning area: English. https://v9.australiancurriculum.edu.au/teacher-resources/understand-this-learning-area/english

Australian Curriculum, Assessment and Reporting Authority (ACARA) (2023d). The Australian Curriculum. English. https://v9.australiancurriculum.edu.au/f-10-curriculum/learning-areas/english/foundation-year_year-1_year-2_year-3_year-4_year-5_year-6_year-7_year-8_year-9_year-10?view=quick&detailed-content-descriptions=0&hide-ccp=0&hide-gc=0&side-by-side=1&strands-start-index=0&subjects-start-index=0

Australian Curriculum, Assessment and Reporting Authority (ACARA) (2023e). The Australian Curriculum Version 9. General capabilities. https://v9.australiancurriculum.edu.au

Baker, S.K., Fien, F., Nelson, N.J., Petscher, Y., Sayko, S. & Turtura, J. (2017). Learning to read: 'The simple view of reading'. US Department of Education, Office of Elementary and Secondary Education, Office of Special Education Programs, National Center on Improving Literacy, Washington, DC. https://improvingliteracy.org/files/briefs/Learning-to-Read-The-Simple-View-of-Reading-Infographic.png

Brown, C. (n.d.). The reading process and the big six. Compiled by Chris Brown, Assistant Principal, Bacchus Marsh Primary School, Victoria. Pearson.

Centre for Educational Research and Innovation (2008). *Understanding the Brain: The Birth of a Learning Science*. OECD, Geneva. https://www.oecd.org/site/educeri21st/40554190.pdf

Department for Education, England (2022). *The Reading Framework. Teaching the Foundations of Literacy*. January. https://assets.publishing.service.gov.uk/government/uploads/system/uploads/attachment_data/file/1102800/Reading_framework_teaching_the_foundations_of_literacy_-_Sept_22.pdf

Fountas, I.C. & Pinnell, G.S. (2001). *Guiding Readers and Writers, Grades 3–6*. Heinemann, Portsmouth, NH.

Gough, P.B. & Tunmer, W.E. (1986). Decoding, reading, and reading disability. *Remedial and Special Education*, vol. 7, pp. 6–10.

Government of South Australia Department of Education (n.d.). Integrating the big 6 of reading. The simple view of reading. https://www.richmondps.sa.edu.au/app/uploads/2020/11/integrating-the-big-6-of-reading.pdf

Konza, D., Pond, L., Michael, M. & Fried, L. (2015). *Implementing the Big Six: Practical Applications for the Classroom*. Fogarty Learning Centre, Edith Cowan University, Perth. https://www.pall.asn.au/wp-content/uploads/2015/09/5-Implementing-the-Big-Six.pdf

National Assessment Program (NAP) (2023a). NAPLAN. https://www.nap.edu.au/naplan

National Assessment Program (NAP) (2023b). National minimum standards. https://www.nap.edu.au/naplan/whats-in-the-tests/national-minimum-standards

National Assessment Program (NAP) (2023c). Tailored tests. https://www.nap.edu.au/naplan/understanding-online-assessment/tailored-tests

National Assessment Program (NAP) (2023d). What's in the tests. https://www.nap.edu.au/naplan/whats-in-the-tests

National Inquiry into the Teaching of Literacy (2005). *Final Report*. Attorney-General's Department, Canberra.

Rowe, K. (2006). Teaching reading: Findings from the National Inquiry. *Research Developments*, no. 15, art. 2. https://research.acer.edu.au/cgi/viewcontent.cgi?article=1030&context=resdev

Vygotsky, L. (1978). *Mind in Society: The Development of Higher Mental Processes*. Harvard University Press, Cambridge, MA.

Waterford.org (2022). The simple view of reading: What you need to know. https://www.waterford.org/education/simple-view-of-reading

Wilson, L. (2014). *The Second Principle: A Dozen Important Brain-based Concepts*. http://thesecondprinciple.com/teaching-essentials/a-dozen-important-brain-based-concepts

CHAPTER 14

Australian Curriculum, Assessment and Reporting Authority (ACARA) (n.d.a). Australian Curriculum. Curriculum connections. Multimedia. https://www.australiancurriculum.edu.au/resources/curriculum-connections/portfolios/multimedia

Australian Curriculum, Assessment and Reporting Authority (ACARA) (n.d.b). English (Version 8.4). https://www.australiancurriculum.edu.au/senior-secondary-curriculum/english/english?unit=Unit+1&unit=Unit+2&unit=Unit+3&unit=Unit+4&page=2

Australian Curriculum, Assessment and Reporting Authority (ACARA) (n.d.c). Glossary. Version 8.4. https://www.australiancurriculum.edu.au/f-10-curriculum/english/glossary

Australian Curriculum, Assessment and Reporting Authority (ACARA) (n.d.d). Texts. https://www.australiancurriculum.edu.au/senior-secondary-curriculum/english/english?unit=Unit+1&unit=Unit+2&unit=Unit+3&unit=Unit+4&page=2

Australian Curriculum, Assessment and Reporting Authority (ACARA) (2023a). General capabilities. Literacy. https://v9.australiancurriculum.edu.au/f-10-curriculum.html/general-capabilities/literacy?element=0&sub-element=0

Australian Curriculum, Assessment and Reporting Authority (ACARA) (2023b). General capabilities. Literacy. The writing element. https://v9.australiancurriculum.edu.au/f-10-curriculum.html/general-capabilities/literacy?element=2&sub-element=4

Australian Curriculum, Assessment and Reporting Authority (ACARA) (2023c). Understand this learning area: English. https://v9.australiancurriculum.edu.au/teacher-resources/understand-this-learning-area/english

Bear, D., Invernizzi, M., Templeton, S. & Johnston, F. (2016). *Words Their Way: Word Study for Phonics, Vocabulary, and Spelling Instruction*, 6th edn. Pearson Education, Harmondsworth.

Beck, I., McKeown, M. & Kucan, L. (2013). *Bringing Words to Life*, 2nd edn. Robust Vocabulary Instruction, 2nd edn. Guildford Press, New York. https://www.speld.org.au/files/blog/robust_vocab_instruction_beck_mckeown_kucan_2.pdf

Bilingual Kidspot. Why English is hard to learn. https://www.facebook.com/bilingualkidspot/posts/and-this-is-why-english-is-so-hard-to-learn/1611834605520295

British Council (n.d.). A recipe. https://learnenglishteens.britishcouncil.org/skills/writing/a2-writing/recipe

Communication Trust, The (2012). Misunderstood. Supporting children and young people with speech, language and communication needs. London. https://councilfordisabledchildren.org.uk/sites/default/files/uploads/files/misunderstood-supporting-children-and-young-people-with-speech-language-and-communications-needs.pdf

Department for Children, Schools and Families, UK (2009). *Support for the National Strategies – Primary: Spelling*, 2nd edn. UK Government, London.

Department of Education and Children's Services (2006). *Handwriting in the South Australian Curriculum*, 2nd edn. Hyde Park Press, Adelaide. https://www.australianschoolfonts.com.au/assets/resources/handwriting-2nd-ed-2007-sa.pdf

Department of Education, WA (2013). *First Steps: Writing Resource Book*. Department of Education WA, Perth.

Finocchiaro, C. (n.d.). Pragmatic language for 5–11 year-olds includes (at least) 27 observable behaviours. Banter. https://www.banterspeech.com.au/pragmatic-language-for-5-11-year-olds-includes-at-least-27-observable-behaviours

Fisher, D., Frey, N. & Rothenberg, C. (2008). *Content-area conversations: How to plan discussion-based lessons for diverse language learners. association for supervision and curriculum development*. Alexandria, VA. Extract: Chapter 5. Procedures for classroom talk. https://www.washoeschools.net/cms/lib/NV01912265/Centricity/Domain/253/Math%20K-6/Fisher%20Article.pdf, pp. 2–3.

Government of South Australia (2006). *Handwriting in the South Australian Curriculum*, 2nd edn. https://www.australianschoolfonts.com.au/assets/resources/handwriting-2nd-ed-2007-sa.pdf

Hagston, J. (n.d.). Spelling knowledges: Taking a strategic approach. https://www.qcal.org.au/wp-content/uploads/2019/03/QCAL-Spelling-workshop-March-2019-slides.pdf

Kid Sense (2023). Social communication (pragmatics). https://childdevelopment.com.au/areas-of-concern/play-and-social-skills/social-communication-pragmatics

Konza, D. (2011a). Research into Practice Series 1. Paper 1.1 Oral language. June 2011. https://www.ecu.edu.au/__data/assets/pdf_file/0004/663700/SA-DECS-Vocabulary-doc.pdf

Konza, D. (2011b). Research into Practice Series 1. Paper 1.4 Vocabulary. June 2011. https://www.ecu.edu.au/__data/assets/pdf_file/0004/663700/SA-DECS-Vocabulary-doc.pdf

Literacy in Focus (2019). Tiered vocabulary. What it is and why does it matter? https://www.litinfocus.com/tiered-vocabulary-what-is-it-and-why-does-it-matter

Literacy Nest, The (2021). What is the alphabetic principle? https://www.theliteracynest.com/2021/04/whats-so-important-about-the-alphabetic-principle.html

Mind Help (2023). Types of dysgraphia. https://mind.help/topic/dysgraphia/types

Ministry of Education NZ (n.d.). Teach spelling skills explicitly. https://inclusive.tki.org.nz/guides/dyslexia-and-learning/teach-spelling-strategies-explicitly

National Literacy Learning Progression. Punctuation description. https://www.australiancurriculum.edu.au/resources/national-literacy-and-numeracy-learning-progressions/national-literacy-learning-progression/writing/?subElementId=50959&searchNodeId=50961&searchTerm=punctuation#dimension-content

Neuman, S. & Wright, T. (2014). The magic words. Teaching vocabulary in the early childhood classroom. *American Educator.* Summer, 4–11.

NSW Department of Education (2017). Smart teaching strategies: Paragraphs. https://education.nsw.gov.au/teaching-and-learning/student-assessment/smart-teaching-strategies/literacy/writing/stage-4/paragraphing/internal-structure-paragraphs

Palmer, J. & Invernizzi, M. (2015). *No More Phonics and Spelling Worksheets*. Heinemann, New York.

Patino, E. (2018). Understanding dysgraphia. Understood. https://www.understood.org/en/learning-attention-issues/child-learning-disabilities/dysgraphia/understanding-dysgraphia

Pepper, J. & Weitzman, E. (2004). *It Takes Two to Talk®: A Practical Guide for Parents of Children with Language Delays*, 2nd edn. The Hanen Centre, Toronto.

Perfetti, C.A. (2007). Reading ability: Lexical quality to comprehension. *Scientific Studies of Reading*, no. 11, pp. 357–83.

Rasinski, T. (2012). *Daily Word Ladders: 80+ Word Study Activities That Target Key Phonics Skills to Boost Young Learners' Reading, Writing & Spelling Confidence*. Scholastic, New York.

Reed, D.K. (2012). Why teach spelling? RMC Research Corporation, Center on Instruction, Portsmouth, NH.

Scull, J. (2015). Learning to write in Year 1 is vital. Edu Research Matters. https://www.aare.edu.au/blog/?tag=teaching-writing

Sound Learning Centre (2023). Sensory integration dysfunction (SID). https://www.thesoundlearningcentre.co.uk/diagnosis/sensory-integration-dysfunction-sid

Team Leverage Edu (2022). Types of mass media. Blog. https://leverageedu.com/blog/types-of-mass-media

Vygotsky, L. (1978). *Mind in Society: The Development of Higher Mental Processes*. Harvard University Press, Cambridge, MA.

CHAPTER 15

ACT Cross Sectoral Assessment Working Party (2016). *Teachers' Guide to Assessment*. https://www.education.act.gov.au/_data/assets/pdf_file/0011/297182/Teachers-Guide-To-Assessment.pdf

Armbruster, B.B., Lehr, F. & Osborn, J. (2001). *Put Reading First: The Research Building Blocks for Teaching Children to Read*. University of Illinois Press, Champaign, IL.

Australian Curriculum, Assessment and Reporting Authority (ACARA) (n.d.a). Australian Curriculum: English. Aims. https://australiancurriculum.edu.au/f-10-curriculum/english/aims

Australian Curriculum, Assessment and Reporting Authority (ACARA) (n.d.b). Australian Curriculum. English. Key ideas. https://www.australiancurriculum.edu.au/f-10-curriculum/english/key-ideas

Australian Curriculum, Assessment and Reporting Authority (ACARA) (n.d.c). Meeting the needs of students for whom English is an additional language or dialect. https://www.australiancurriculum.edu.au/resources/student-diversity/meeting-the-needs-of-students-for-whom-english-is-an-additional-language-or-dialect

Australian Curriculum, Assessment and Reporting Authority (ACARA) (2023). Australian Curriculum: English. https://v9.australiancurriculum.edu.au/f-10-curriculum/learning-areas/english/foundation-year_year-1_year-2_year-3_year-4_year-5_year-6_year-7_year-8_year-9_year-10?view=quick&detailed-content-descriptions=0&hide-ccp=0&hide-gc=0&side-by-side=1&strands-start-index=0&subjects-start-index=0

Australian Early Development Census National Report (2018). AEDC results. Canberra, ACT. https://www.aedc.gov.au/resources/aedc-results

Australian Early Development Census National Report (2021). Early childhood development in Australia. https://www.aedc.gov.au/resources/detail/2021-aedc-national-report

Australian Government (n.d.). Learning potential. Learning to read 2: Phonics. https://www.learningpotential.gov.au/articles/learning-to-read-2-phonics

Australian Institute of Health and Welfare (2022). Child protection Australia 2020–21. 15 June. https://www.aihw.gov.au/reports/child-protection/child-protection-australia-2020-21/contents/about

Blachman, B.A., Ball, E.W., Black, R. & Tangel, D.M. (2000). *Road to the Code: A Phonological Awareness Program for Young Children*. Brookes, Baltimore, MD.

Brown, C. (n.d.). The reading process and the big six. Compiled by Chris Brown, Assistant Principal, Bacchus Marsh Primary School, Victoria. Pearson.

Creative Spirits (2018). Aboriginal literacy rates. https://www.creativespirits.info/aboriginalculture/education/aboriginal-literacy-rates#ixzz50Ax17PHF

Creative Spirits (2021). Aboriginal literacy rates. https://www.creativespirits.info/aboriginalculture/education/aboriginal-literacy-rates

Department of Education and Training Victoria (2018a). *Literacy Teaching Toolkit: Phonological Awareness*. https://www.education.vic.gov.au/school/teachers/teachingresources/discipline/english/literacy/readingviewing/Pages/litfocusphonological.aspx#link27

Dyslexia – SPELD Foundation Literacy Services (2021). *Understanding Learning Difficulties. A Practical Guide*. Perth.

Edutopia (2019). Video: Debunking the IQ-dyslexia myth (1.11 mins). https://www.edutopia.org/video/debunking-iq-dyslexia-myth

Emmitt, M., Hornsby, D. & Wilson, L. (2013). *The Place of Phonics in Learning to Read and Write*. ALEA, Sydney. https://www.alea.edu.au/documents/item/773

Ford, K. (2005). Fostering literacy development in English language learners. https://www.colorincolorado.org/article/fostering-literacy-development-english-language-learners

Hanlon, C. (2019). *Types of Listening* (video). https://www.youtube.com/watch?v=G1ULTB5wtjQ

Harvard Graduate School of Education (2003). Study finds ESL students attain fundamental reading skills similar to or better than native English speaking peers. https://www.gse.harvard.edu/news/03/11/proper-intervention-esl-students-not-learning-disadvantage

Hattie, J. (2012). *Visible Learning for Teachers: Maximising Impact on Learning*. Routledge, Abingdon.

Herber, H. (1978). *Teaching Reading in the Content Areas*. Prentice-Hall, Englewood Cliffs, NJ.

K12 Reader (2018). Word study makes language learning fun. https://www.k12reader.com/word-study-makes-language-learning-fun

Kaskamanidis, Z. (August 2022). Effective observation in specialist classroom literacy environments. *Teacher Magazine*. https://www.teachermagazine.com/au_en/articles/effective-observation-in-specialist-classroom-literacy-environments

Konza, D., Pond, L., Michael, M. & Fried, L. (2015). *Implementing the Big Six: Practical Applications for the Classroom*. Edith Cowan University. https://www.pall.asn.au/wp-content/uploads/2015/09/5-Implementing-the-Big-Six.pdf

Literacy Impact Educational Services (2023). Repeated reading: A high impact strategy for improving reading fluency. https://www.literacyimpact.com.au/repeated-reading-a-high-impact-strategy-for-improving-reading-fluency

Ministry of Education, Ontario (2003). *A Guide to Effective Reading Instruction: Kindergarten to Grade 3*. http://www.eworkshop.on.ca/edu/resources/guides/reading_k_3_english.pdf

Morris, A. & Stewart-Dore, N. (1984). *Learning to Learn from Text: Effective Reading in the Content Areas*. Addison-Wesley, Sydney.

NSW Department of Education and Training (2010). *Teaching Comprehension Strategies*. NSW Government, Sydney.

Reading Rockets (2023a). Onset/rime games. https://www.readingrockets.org/strategies/onset_rime

Reading Rockets (2023b). Phonological awareness and phonemic. https://www.readingrockets.org/teaching/reading-basics/phonemic

Teach Phonics (2018). What is phonological awareness? https://teachphonics.blog/2018/09/20/what-is-phonological-awareness-2

Victoria State Government. Department of Education and Training (2023). Literacy teaching toolkit: Phonics. https://www.education.vic.gov.au/school/teachers/teachingresources/discipline/english/literacy/readingviewing/Pages/litfocusphonics.aspx#link89

Victorian Department of Education and Training (2009). Four Resources Literacy Model. https://www.education.vic.gov.au/school/teachers/teachingresources/discipline/english/literacy/readingviewing/Pages/fourres.aspx

Victorian Department of Education and Training (2018). *Four Resources Model for Reading and Viewing*. https://www.education.vic.gov.au/school/teachers/teachingresources/discipline/english/literacy/readingviewing/Pages/fourres.aspx

Willis, J. (2018). Aiding reading comprehension with Post-its. Edutopia. https://www.edutopia.org/article/aiding-reading-comprehension-post-its

CHAPTER 16

Adams, T., Thangata, F. & King, C. (205). 'Weigh' to go! Exploring mathematical language. *Mathematics Teaching in Middle School*, vol. 10, no. 9, pp. 444–8.

Arky, B. (2014). Understanding visual processing Issues. Understood. https://www.understood.org/en/learning-attention-issues/child-learning-disabilities/visual-processing-issues/understanding-visual-processing-issues

Australian Curriculum, Assessment and Reporting Authority (ACARA) (n.d.a). National Numeracy Learning Progression. Measuring time description. https://www.australiancurriculum.edu.au/resources/national-literacy-and-numeracy-learning-progressions/national-numeracy-learning-progression/measurement-and-geometry/?subElementId=50827&scaleId=0

Australian Curriculum, Assessment and Reporting Authority (ACARA) (n.d.b). Senior secondary: Essential maths (V9.0). https://www.australiancurriculum.edu.au/senior-secondary-curriculum/mathematics/essential-mathematics/?unit=Unit+1&unit=Unit+2&unit=Unit+3&unit=Unit+4

Australian Curriculum, Assessment and Reporting Authority (ACARA) (2020). National Numeracy Learning Progression. https://www.ofai.edu.au/media/iiwbecoj/national-numeracy-progression-v3.pdf

Australian Curriculum, Assessment and Reporting Authority (ACARA) (2023a). General capabilities downloads. https://v9.australiancurriculum.edu.au/downloads/general-capabilities#accordion-afa194f119-item-e657062594

Australian Curriculum, Assessment and Reporting Authority (ACARA) (2023b). General capabilities. Numeracy. Number sense and algebra (V 9.0). https://v9.australiancurriculum.edu.au/f-10-curriculum/general-capabilities/numeracy?element=0&sub-element=0

Australian Curriculum, Assessment and Reporting Authority (ACARA) (2023c). Mathematics. https://v9.australiancurriculum.edu.au/f-10-curriculum.html/learning-areas/mathematics/foundation-year_year-1_year-2_year-3_year-4_year-5_year-6_year-7_year-8_year-9_year-10?view=quick&detailed-content-descriptions=0&side-by-side=1&strands-start-index=0&subjects-start-index=0&hide-ccp=0&hide-gc=0

Australian Curriculum, Assessment and Reporting Authority (ACARA) (2023d). The Australian Curriculum. https://v9.australiancurriculum.edu.au

Australian Curriculum, Assessment and Reporting Authority (ACARA) (2023e). Understand this general capability. Numeracy. https://v9.australiancurriculum.edu.au/teacher-resources/understand-this-general-capability/numeracy

Australian Curriculum, Assessment and Reporting Authority (ACARA) (2023f). Understand this learning area. Mathematics. https://v9.australiancurriculum.edu.au/teacher-resources/understand-this-learning-area/mathematics

Australian Securities and Investments Commission (2011). Report 229: National financial literacy strategy. March. https://asic.gov.au/media/1343576/rep229-national-financial-literacy-strategy.pdf

Clements, D. & Sarama, J. (2021). *Learning and Teaching Early Math: The Learning Trajectories Approach*, 3rd edn. Routledge, New York.

Department of Education and Training, Victoria (2018). Learning to count. https://www.education.vic.gov.au/school/teachers/teachingresources/discipline/maths/continuum/Pages/learntocount.aspx

Expert Panel on Student Success in Ontario (2004). *Leading Math Success*. http://www.edu.gov.on.ca/eng/document/reports/numeracy/numeracyreport.pdf

Hogan, J. (2016). Multiplication and division models and strategies. Scholastic Parents. https://www.scholastic.com/parents/school-success/learning-toolkit-blog/multiplication-and-division-models-and-strategies.html

Hott, B., Isbel, L. & Montani, T. (2014). *Strategies and Interventions to Support Students with Mathematics Disabilities*. https://www.council-for-learning-disabilities.org/wp-content/uploads/2014/12/Math_Disabilities_Support.pdf

Maher, Z. (2021). How to differentiate math instruction with one-on-one conferences. Edutopia. https://www.edutopia.org/article/how-differentiate-math-instruction-one-one-conferences

Math Is Fun (2020). https://www.mathsisfun.com/probability_line.html

Meiers, M. & Trevitt, J. (2010). Language in the mathematics classroom. *The Digest*, no. 2, pp. 6–7. https://research.acer.edu.au/cgi/viewcontent.cgi?article=1006&context=digest

National Numeracy (2023). The essentials of numeracy. https://www.nationalnumeracy.org.uk/what-numeracy/essentials-numeracy

NSW Government. Education (2023). Multiplicative strategies. https://education.nsw.gov.au/teaching-and-learning/curriculum/literacy-and-numeracy/teaching-and-learning-resources/numeracy/multiplicative-strategies

Patterns. https://www.cuemath.com/geometry/patterns

Pediaa (2020). Difference between mathematics and numeracy. https://pediaa.com/difference-between-mathematics-and-numeracy

Posamentier, A. (2013). 9 strategies for motivating students in mathematics. https://www.edutopia.org/blog/9-strategies-motivating-students-mathematics-alfred-posamentier

Qualifications and Curriculum Authority (QCA) (2011). *Planning, Teaching and Assessing the Curriculum for Pupils with Learning Difficulties: Mathematics*. QCA, London.

Seeley, C. (2004–2006). A journey in algebraic thinking. National Council of Teachers of Mathematics. https://www.nctm.org/News-and-Calendar/Messages-from-the-President/Archive/Cathy-Seeley/A-Journey-in-Algebraic-Thinking

Seeley, C., Hagelberger, B., Schielack, J. & Krehbiel, K. (2005). *Using Calculators in Elementary School: Teaching Children Mathematics*. National Council of Teachers of Mathematics. Reston, VA.

Siemon, D., Beswick., K, Brady, K., Clark, J., Faragher, R. & Warren, E. (2015). *Teaching Mathematics: Foundations to Middle Years*, 2nd edn. Oxford University Press, Melbourne.

SplashLearn (n.d.a). Place value. https://www.splashlearn.com/math-vocabulary/place-value/place-value

SplashLearn (n.d.b). What is a fact family? https://www.splashlearn.com/math-vocabulary/number-sense/fact-family

Strong, S. (2021). When teachers overcome math anxiety, students benefit. Edutopia. https://www.edutopia.org/article/when-teachers-overcome-math-anxiety-students-benefit

Victorian Government Department of Education (2020). Mathematics anxiety. https://www.education.vic.gov.au/school/teachers/teachingresources/discipline/maths/Pages/research_overcomingmathsanxiety.aspx

Victorian Government Department of Education (2021). Developing understanding in mathematics. https://www.education.vic.gov.au/school/teachers/teachingresources/discipline/english/literacy/Pages/developing_mathematical_understanding.aspx

Victorian Government Department of Education and Training (2021). Financial literacy. https://www2.education.vic.gov.au/pal/financial-literacy/guidance

CHAPTER 17

Additude (2023). What is dyscalculia? https://www.additudemag.com/what-is-dyscalculia-overview-and-symptom-breakdown

ADHD Support Australia (2022). Getting an ADHD diagnosis. https://www.adhdsupportaustralia.com.au/what-is-adhd/adhd-diagnosis

American Psychiatric Association (2013). *Diagnostic and Statistical Manual of Mental Disorders 5 (DSM-5)*, 5th edn. APA.

Ashman, A. (Ed.) (2015). *Education for Inclusion and Diversity*. Pearson Australia, Melbourne.

Attwood, T. (2023). What is Asperger's syndrome/ASD – Level 1? https://tonyattwood.com.au/about-aspergers-asd-level-1/what-is-aspergers-asd-level-1

Australian Alliance for Inclusive Education (2018). What is inclusive education? http://allmeansall.org.au/for-educators

Australian Dyslexia Association (2023). Dyslexia, dysgraphia and dyscalculia? https://dyslexiaassociation.org.au/support/dyslexiadysgraphia-and-dyscalculia

Australian Institute of Health and Welfare (AIHW) (2023). People with disability in Australia. https://www.aihw.gov.au/reports/disability/people-with-disability-in-australia/contents/people-with-disability/prevalence-of-disability

Australian Research Alliance for Children and Youth (ARACY) (2013). Inclusive education for students with disability. A review of the best evidence in relation to theory and practice. https://www.aracy.org.au/publications-resources/command/download_file/id/246/filename/Inclusive_education_for_students_with_disability_-_A_review_of_the_best_evidence_in_relation_to_theory_and_practice.pdf

Autism CRC (2018). *National Guideline for the Assessment and Diagnosis of Autism Spectrum Disorders*. https://www.autismcrc.com.au/access/national-guideline

Autism Spectrum Australia (n.d.). How do we describe autism? https://www.autismspectrum.org.au

Autism Spectrum Australia (2017). Sensory processing. https://www.autismspectrum.org.au/sites/default/files/Factsheet_Sensory%20processing_20170306.pdf

Autism Toolbox (2019a). What does neurodiversity mean? http://www.autismtoolbox.co.uk/what-does-neurodiversity-mean

Autism Toolbox (2019b). What is autism? http://www.autismtoolbox.co.uk/what-autism

Centre of Research Excellence in Child Language (2018). Childhood apraxia of speech. http://dyspraxiakidsaustralia.org.au/wp-content/uploads/2016/07/fact_sheet_childhood_apraxia_of_speech-copy.pdf

Cerebral Palsy Alliance (2018a). Manual Ability Classification System. https://www.cerebralpalsy.org.au/what-is-cerebral-palsy/severity-of-cerebral-palsy/manual-ability-classification-system

Cerebral Palsy Alliance (2018b). What is cerebral palsy? How cerebral palsy affects people. https://www.cerebralpalsy.org.au/what-is-cerebral-palsy/how-cerebral-palsy-affects-people

Cerebral Palsy Australia (2023). Website. https://cpaustralia.com.au

Cerebral Palsy League (2018). Types of cerebral palsy. http://www.cpl.org.au/news/learning-centre/cp/types-of-cerebral-palsy

Children and Young People with Disability Australia (CYDA) (2019). Time for change: The state of play for inclusion of students with disability. Results from the 2019 CYDA National Education Survey Children and Young People with Disability Australia October 2019. https://www.cyda.org.au/images/pdf/time_for_change_2019_education_survey_results.pdf

Children's Health Queensland Hospital and Health Service (2023). Medical considerations for students with an acquired brain injury. https://www.childrens.health.qld.gov.au/chq/health-professionals/paediatric

Children's Trust, The. For children with brain injury (2023). Acquired brain injury explained. https://www.thechildrenstrust.org.uk/brain-injury-information/info-and-advice/what-is-acquired-brain-injury/acquired-brain-injury-explained

Communication Trust, The (2011). *Don't Get Me Wrong*. https://www.thecommunicationtrust.org.uk/media/174/dontgetmewrong.pdf

Cotterill, T. (2017). *Principles and Practices of Working with Pupils with Special Educational Needs and Disability*. Routledge Taylor & Francis Group, UK.

Department of Education, SA (2023). Spina bifida and hydrocephalus health support for children and young people. https://www.education.sa.gov.au/schools-and-educators/health-safety-and-wellbeing/specific-conditions-and-needs/spina-bifida-and-hydrocephalus-health-support-children-and-young-people

Department of Education and Training (DET) (2005). *Disability Standards for Education 2005*. https://www.education.gov.au/disability-standards-education-2005

Department of Education and Training (DET) (2015a). Fact sheet 2: Disability Standards for Education 2005. https://docs.education.gov.au/documents/fact-sheet-2-disability-standards-education-2005

Department of Education and Training (DET) (2015b). Planning for personalised learning and support: A national resource. https://docs.education.gov.au/documents/planning-personalised-learning-and-support-national-resource-0

Developmental Coordination Disorder Australia Inc. (2022). Understanding DCD. https://dcdaustralia.org.au/what-is-dcd-2

Developmental Coordination Disorder Australia Inc. (2023). How is DCD diagnosed? https://dcdaustralia.org.au/diagnosis-therapy

Developmental Language Disorder (DLD) (2017). The consensus explained RALD. https://www.youtube.com/watch?v=OZ1dHS1X8jg

DLD Project (n.d.). Developmental language disorder. https://thedldproject.com/wp-content/uploads/2022/05/DLD-Awareness-Flyer-The-DLD-Project.pdf

Disability Discrimination Act 1992. https://www.legislation.gov.au/Details/C2018C00125. Based on content from the Federal Register of Legislation at 13 June 2023. For the latest information on Australian Government law please go to https://www.legislation.gov.au.

Dyslexia – SPELD Foundation Australia (n.d.). Learning difficulties. https://dsf.net.au/learning-difficulties/?gclid=EAIaIQobChMI8ZTx9q31-gIVwRErCh1JvADIEAAYASAAEgJ1EPD_BwE&utm_source=pocket_mylist

Dyslexia – SPELD Foundation Australia (2022). What is dyslexia? https://dsf.net.au/what-is-dyslexia/?gclid=EAIaIQobChMIqKvlr6yA_wIVT66WCh1Rig94EAAYAiAAEgKOXvD_BwE

Foreman, P. & Arthur-Kelly, M. (2014). *Inclusion in Action*, 4th edn. Cengage Learning, Melbourne.

Gallagher, J., Coleman, M. & Kirk, S. (2023). *Educating Exceptional Children*. Cengage Learning, Melbourne.

Greutman, H. & Kostelyk, S. (2018). *Sensory Processing Explained. A Handbook for Parents and Educators. Growing Hands-On Kids.* https://sensoryprocessingexplained.com/wp-content/uploads/woocommerce_uploads/2019/08/Sensory-Processing-Explained-FINAL.pdf

Hattie, J.A. (2009). *Visible Learning: A Synthesis Of Over 800 Meta-Analyses Relating To Achievement*. Routledge, Abingdon, UK.

International Dyslexia Association (2009). Multisensory Structured Language teaching. Baltimore. https://www.multisensoryeducation.net.au/images/cms/What%20is%20MSL%20Teaching%20Fact%20Sheets.PDF

International Dyslexia Association (2013). *Dyslexia in the Classroom: What Every Teacher Needs to Know*. IDA, Baltimore, MD.

International Dyslexia Association (2023). Accommodations for students with dyslexia. https://dyslexiaida.org/accommodations-for-students-with-dyslexia

Kid Sense (2023). Planning and sequencing (praxis). https://childdevelopment.com.au/areas-of-concern/organisation/planning-and-sequencing-praxis

Konza, D. (2008). Inclusion of students with disabilities in new times: Responding to the challenge. University of Wollongong. http://ro.uow.edu.au/cgi/viewcontent.cgi?article=1036&context=edupapers

Larkey, S. & Tulleman, A. (2021). *Teacher Assistants BIG Red Book of Ideas for Supporting Students with ASD/Autism/Asperger)*. Sue Larkey Learning Media.

Learning Links (2023). Empowering children to learn. https://www.learninglinks.org.au

Life Without Barriers (2018). Person-centred practice approach. https://www.lwb.org.au/about-us/publications-and-resources/person-centred-practice-approach

Malaquias, C. (2018). Recognition of unconscious prejudice as a barrier to inclusion of students with disability. Australian Alliance for Inclusive Education. http://allmeansall.org.au/recognition-involuntary-implicit-prejudice-barrier-high-expectations-inclusion-students-disability

Martin, T.J., Campbell, S. & Shields, M. (2018). Traumatic brain injury: Informed accommodation in the classroom. *TEACH Journal of Christian Education*, vol. 12, iss. 1, art. 2. https://research.avondale.edu.au/teach/vol12/iss1/2

Murdoch Children's Research Institute (n.d.). Neurodevelopment. https://www.mcri.edu.au/research/strategic-collaborations/flagships/neurodevelopment

Murdoch Children's Research Institute (2023). ADHD. https://www.mcri.edu.au/impact/a-z-child-adolescent-health/a/adhd

National Disability Services (n.d.) Disability types and description. https://www.nds.org.au/disability-types-and-description

National Dissemination Center for Children with Disabilities (2004). Blindness/visual impairment fact sheet 13 (FS-13). http://www.parentcenterhub.org/repository/visualimpairment/#types

Nationally Consistent Collection of Data on School Students with Disability (NCCD) (2021). Imputing disability for the NCCD. Advice document. August. https://www.nccd.edu.au/sites/default/files/Imputing%20Disability%20for%20the%20NCCD.pdf

Nationally Consistent Collection of Data on School Students with Disability (NCCD) (2022a). Definitions of disability and the NCCD categories. https://www.nccd.edu.au/wider-support-materials/definitions-disability-and-nccd-categories

Nationally Consistent Collection of Data on School Students with Disability (NCCD) (2022b). Learning differences, learning difficulties, learning disabilities and the NCCD. https://www.nccd.edu.au/wider-support-materials/learning-differences-learning-difficulties-learning-disabilities-and-nccd

Nationally Consistent Collection of Data on School Students with Disability (NCCD) (2022c). On the same basis. https://www.nccd.edu.au/wider-support-materials/same-basis

Noodlenook (2018). Prompting hierarchy – How I got duped! http://www.noodlenook.net/prompting-hierarchy

Novita (n.d.). Acquired brain injury. https://www.novita.org.au/disability/acquired-brain-injury

NSW Health (2018). ADHD – frequently asked questions. https://www.health.nsw.gov.au/pharmaceutical/patients/Pages/faq-adhd-consumers.aspx#bookmark2

Organization for Autism (2016). *Research Life Journey Through Autism: An Educator's Guide to Asperger Syndrome*. Arlington, VA.

Organization for Autism Research (2023). https://researchautism.org

Porter, L. (2002). *Educating Young Children with Additional Needs*. Allen & Unwin, Sydney.

Richards, G. & Armstrong, F. (2008). *Key Issues for Teaching Assistants. Working in Diverse and Inclusive Classrooms*. Routledge, New York.

Royal Children's Hospital, Melbourne (2008). *Cerebral Palsy: An Information Guide for Parents*, 5th edn. Department of Developmental Medicine, Royal Children's Hospital, Melbourne. https://www.mcri.edu.au/sites/default/files/media/documents/cres/cpbooklet_0.pdf

Royal Children's Hospital, Melbourne (2018). Acquired brain injury (ABI). https://www.rch.org.au/kidsinfo/fact_sheets/Acquired_Brain_Injury_ABI

Royal Children's Hospital, Melbourne (2021). Autism spectrum disorder. https://www.rch.org.au/kidsinfo/fact_sheets/Autism_spectrum_disorder

Royal Commission into Violence, Abuse, Neglect and Exploitation of People with Disability (Nov. 2021). Students with disability face serious barriers to accessing safe, quality and inclusive education. https://disability.royalcommission.gov.au/news-and-media/media-releases/students-disability-face-serious-barriers-accessing-safe-quality-and-inclusive-education

Royal Institute for Deaf and Blind Children (RIDBC) (2018). Vision. https://www.ridbc.org.au/blindness

Scheuermann, B., Webber, J. & Lang, R. (2019). *Autism. Teaching Makes a Difference*, 2nd edn. Cengage Learning.

See/Hear (1998). *Orientation and Mobility Training: The Way to Go*. http://www.tsbvi.edu/seehear/fall98/waytogo.htm

Shaddock, A., Giorcelli, L. & Smith, S. (2007). Students with disabilities in mainstream classrooms. A resource for teachers. Australian Government Department of Education, Employment and Workplace Relations.

Spina Bifida Hydrocephalus Queensland (2016). *Educating a Child with Spina Bifida and/or Hydrocephalus P–12*. https://static1.squarespace.com/static/5926168ef7e0ab55ef3dc982/t/593e519dd482e99f138140f2/1497256351020/Booklet+Educating+a+Child+with+SBH.pdf

Statewide Vision Resource Centre (2018). *Educational Support for Vision Impaired Students with Additional Impairments*. http://svrc.vic.edu.au/wp-content/resources/PLvi_additional-booklet.pdf

Strnadová, I., Arthur-Kelly, M. & Foreman, P. (2022). *Inclusion in Action*. Cengage Learning, Melbourne.

Tancredi, H.A. (2020). Consulting students with disability: A practice guide for educators and other professionals. The Centre for Inclusive Education, QUT. https://research.qut.edu.au/c4ie/practice-guide-student-consultation

Thomas, A. & Thorne, G. (2011). What are some common problems with language? Centre for Development and Learning. http://www.cdl.org/resource-library/articles/problems_language.php?type=subject&id=7

Thoonsen, M. & Lamp, C. (2022). *Sensory Solutions in the Classroom*. Jessica Kingsley Publisher.

Understood (n.d.). Types of tests for dyscalculia. https://www.understood.org/en/articles/test-for-dyscalculia

United Nations Educational, Scientific and Cultural Organization (UNESCO) (2017). *A Guide for Ensuring Inclusion and Equity in Education*. http://unesdoc.unesco.org/images/0024/002482/248254e.pdf

Vaz, S., Wilson, N., Falkmer, M., Sim, A., Scott, M., Cordier, R. & Falkmer, T. (2015). Factors associated with primary school teachers' attitudes towards the inclusion of students with disabilities. *PLoS ONE*, vol. 10, no. 8, pp. 1–12.

Vision Australia (2018). Vision tests. https://www.visionaustralia.org/information/eye-health/vision-tests

Vygotsky, L. (1978). *Mind in Society: The Development of Higher Mental Processes*. Harvard University Press, Cambridge, MA.

WeCapable (2023). Accessibility: Definition, meaning, examples and types of barriers. https://wecapable.com/accessibility-definition-meaning-examples-barriers

Willis, C. (2006). *Teaching Young Children with Autism Spectrum Disorder*. Gryphon House, Beltsville, MA.

Wong, C., Odom, S.L., Hume, K., Cox, A.W., Brock, M.E., Plavnick, J.B., Schultz, T.R., Fettig, A. & Kucharczyk, S. (2012). *Evidence-based Practices Update: Reviewer Training*. University of North Carolina, Frank Porter Graham Child Development Institute, Chapel Hill, NC. https://autismpdc.fpg.unc.edu/sites/autismpdc.fpg.unc.edu/files/imce/documents/table7_working_definition_ebp.pdf

CHAPTER 18

Association of Teachers and Lecturers (ATL) (2011). *Violence, Threatening Behaviour and Abuse: Advice and Information for Members in England and Wales*. The Education Union, London. http://www.new2teaching.org.uk/tzone/images/ATL_Violence_threatening_behaviour_and_abuse_tcm7-26211.pdf

Australian Childhood Foundation (2018). Making spaces for learning. Trauma-informed practices in schools. Richmond, Victoria. https://www.theactgroup.com.au/documents/makingspaceforlearning-traumainschools.pdf

Australian Curriculum, Assessment and Reporting Authority (ACARA) (2023). Australian Curriculum V9. Personal and social capability. https://v9.australiancurriculum.edu.au/f-10-curriculum.html/general-capabilities/personal-and-social-capability?element=0&sub-element=0

Australian Curriculum, Assessment and Reporting Authority (ACARA, n.d.). Meeting the needs of students for whom English is an additional language or dialect. https://www.australiancurriculum.edu.au/resources/student-diversity/meeting-the-needs-of-students-for-whom-english-is-an-additional-language-or-dialect

Australian Institute of Health and Welfare (AIHW) (2020). Australia's children. Cat. no. CWS 69. AIHW, Canberra.

Australian Institute for Teaching and School Leadership (AITSL) (2020). National strategy to address the abuse of teachers, school leaders and other school staff. December. https://www.aitsl.edu.au/docs/default-source/abuse-strategy/national-strategy-to-address-the-abuse-of-teachers-school-leaders-and-other-school-staff.pdf?sfvrsn=6bb0d93c_2

Bailey, B. (2021). *Conscious Discipline. Building Resilient Classrooms.* Loving Guidance, LLC, USA.

Be You (2019). KidsMatter valuation: final report. http://resources.beyondblue.org.au/prism/file?token=BL/0717

Be You (2023). Mental health continuum. https://beyou.edu.au/resources/mental-health-continuum

Bullying. No Way! (n.d.a). Research snapshot from a literature review by Australia's Safe and Supportive School Communities Working Group. What is bullying, including online bullying? https://bullyingnoway.gov.au/understanding/Documents/research-snapshot-what-is-bullying.pdf

Bullying. No Way! (n.d.b). What is the prevalence of bullying in schools? Research snapshot from a literature review by Australia's Safe and Supportive School Communities Working Group. https://bullyingnoway.gov.au/understanding/Documents/research-snapshot-prevalence-of-bullying-in-schools.pdf

Cassel, S. (2018). Simple relationship-building strategies. Edutopia. https://www.edutopia.org/article/simple-relationship-building-strategies

Center on the Developing Child, Harvard University (2023). ACEs and toxic stress: Frequently asked questions. https://developingchild.harvard.edu/resources/aces-and-toxic-stress-frequently-asked-questions

Center on PBIS (2023). What is PBIS? https://www.pbis.org/pbis/what-is-pbis

Curtis, D. & Carter, M. (2000). The art of awareness: How observation can transform your teaching. Redleaf Press, St Paul, MN.

Department of Education WA (2011). How to comply with our code of conduct. Standards and Integrity Directorate. East Perth, WA. https://highgateps.wa.edu.au/sites/highgateps.wa.edu.au/files/users/user2/Handbook%20-%20Code%20of%20Conduct.pdf

Department of Education WA (2016). Student behaviour in public schools procedures. Effective date: 26 April 2016. Version: 2.7. https://www.education.wa.edu.au/o/article/pdf/web/policies/-/student-behaviour-in-public-schools-procedures

Department of Education WA (2021). *Code of Conduct. Shaping the Future*. East Perth, WA. https://www.education.wa.edu.au/dl/4noov3q

Desautels, L. (2018). Aiming for discipline instead of punishment. Edutopia. https://www.edutopia.org/article/aiming-discipline-instead-punishment

Dreikurs, R. (1968). *Psychology in the Classroom*, 2nd edn. Harper & Row, New York.

Duchesne, S., McMaugh, A., Bochner, S. & Krause, K. (2019). *Educational Psychology for Learning and Teaching*, 6th edn. Cengage Learning, Melbourne.

Education Victoria (2020). Behaviour – Students. https://www2.education.vic.gov.au/pal/behaviour-students/guidance/3-challenging-behaviour-influences-and-triggers

Education Victoria (2022). Behaviour – Students. https://www2.education.vic.gov.au/pal/behaviour-students/guidance/5-school-wide-positive-behaviour-support-swpbs-framework

Gallagher, J., Coleman, M. & Kirk, S. (2023). *Educating Exceptional Children*. Cengage Learning, Melbourne.

Gantz, J. (2009). *Teaching 101*, 2nd edn. Corwin Press, Thousand Oaks, CA.

Gartrell, D. (2004). *The Power of Guidance: Teaching Social-emotional Skills in Early Childhood Classrooms*. Delmar, Clifton Park, NY.

Gordon, A. & Browne, K. (1996). *Guiding Young Children in a Diverse Society*. Allyn and Bacon, Boston, MA.

Graham, L.J., McCarthy, T., Killingly, C., Tancredi, H. & Poed, S. (2020). *Inquiry into Suspension, Exclusion and Expulsion Processes in South Australian Government Schools: Final Report*. The Centre for Inclusive Education, QUT, Brisbane, Qld. https://www.education.sa.gov.au/sites/default/files/report-of-an-independent-inquiry-into-suspensions-exclusions-and-expulsions-in-south-australian-government-schools.pdf

Kaweski, W. (2014). *Teaching Adolescents with Autism: Practical Strategies for the Inclusive Classroom*. Skyhorse Publishing, New York.

Keath, L. (2021). The 4 'whats' of negative behavior. Teaching children self-awareness and accountability. The Carolina Institute for Developmental Disabilities at the University of North Carolina. https://www.verywellmind.com/teaching-children-with-the-4-whats-20733

Lahey, B. (2015). Editorial: Why are children who exhibit psychopathology at high risk for psychopathology and dysfunction in adulthood? *JAMA Psychiatry*, vol. 72, no. 9, pp. 865–6.

Legal Services Commission of South Australia (2021). School discipline. https://lawhandbook.sa.gov.au/ch06s06s03.php

Manos, M. (2021). Center for Pediatric Behavioral Health at Cleveland Clinic Children's Hospital, in Keath, L. (2021), The 4 'whats' of negative behavior. Teaching children self-awareness and accountability. The Carolina Institute for Developmental Disabilities at the University of North Carolina. https://www.verywellmind.com/teaching-children-with-the-4-whats-20733

Middletown Centre for Autism (2023). Examples of atypical responses to sensory stimuli. https://sensory-processing.middletownautism.com/background/examples-of-atypical-responses-to-sensory-stimuli

Miller, P. (2022). If Australian schools want to improve student discipline, they need to address these 5 issues. *The Conversation*, 4 August. https://theconversation.com/if-australian-schools-want-to-improve-student-discipline-they-need-to-address-these-5-issues-187993

Ministerial Council on Education, Early Childhood Development and Youth Affairs (MCEECDYA) (2011). National Safe Schools Framework (revised 2011). 2010 Education Services Australia as the legal entity for the Ministerial Council on Education, Early Childhood Development and Youth Affairs (MCEECDYA). http://www.curriculum.edu.au/verve/_resources/NSSFramework.pdf

National Association of School Psychologists (2015). Creating trauma-sensitive schools: Supportive policies and practices for learning [Research summary]. Bethesda, MD.

National Child Traumatic Stress Network Schools Committee (2008). Child Trauma Toolkit for Educators, National Center for Child Traumatic Stress.

National Mental Health Commission (2019). *Monitoring Mental Health And Suicide Prevention Reform: National Report 2019*. NMHC, Sydney.

NSW Department of Education (2020). Trauma-informed practice in schools: An explainer. https://education.nsw.gov.au/about-us/educational-data/cese/publications/research-reports/trauma-informed-practice-in-schools

NSW Government (2020). *NSW Education Act 1990 No. 8* (December). https://legislation.nsw.gov.au/view/whole/html/inforce/current/act-1990-008#pt.5A. Based on content from the New South Wales Legislation website at 14 June 2023. For the latest information on New South Wales Government legislation please go to https://www.legislation.nsw.gov.au

Pitonyak, D. (2005) in Kaweski, W. (2014). *Teaching Adolescents with Autism. Practical Strategies for the Inclusive Classroom*. Skyhorse Publishing, New York.

Prior, M., Sanson, A., Smart, D. & Oberklaid, F. (2000). *Pathways from Infancy to Adolescence: Australian Temperament Project 1983–2000*. Australian Institute of Family Studies, Melbourne. http://www.aifs.gov.au/institute/pubs/resreport4/main.html

Queensland Schools Alliance Against Violence (QSAAV) (2010). *Working Together: Understanding Student Violence in Schools*. Queensland Government, Brisbane. http://apo.org.au/files/Resource/5310t3410.pdf

Sanson, A. & Oberklaid, F. (2013). Infancy and early childhood. In S. Vassallo & A. Sanson (eds), *The Australian Temperament Project: The First 30 Years*. AIFS, Melbourne, p. 4.

Slee P.T., Lawson M.J., Russell A., Askell-Williams H., Dix K.L., Owens L., Skrzypiec G., Spears B. (2009). KidsMatter Primary Evaluation Final Report. Centre for Analysis of Educational Futures, Flinders University of South Australia. © Copyright Beyond Blue Limited December 2009.

Student Wellbeing Hub (2020). Australian Student Wellbeing Framework. https://studentwellbeinghub.edu.au/educators/framework

UN Convention on the Rights of the Child. https://www.unicef.org/media/60981/file/convention-rights-child-text-child-friendly-version.pdf

Vassallo, S. & Sanson, A. (eds) (2013). *The Australian Temperament Project. The First 30 Years*. AIFS, Melbourne.

Victoria State Government (2012). Child development and trauma: Best interests case practice model and specialist practice resource. Department of Human Services.

WHO (2014). Social determinants of mental health. WHO, Geneva. https://apps.who.int/iris/bitstream/handle/10665/112828/9789241506809_eng.pdf;jsessionid=24E1328393F9FF4556281B616E4F1D29?sequence=1

WHO (2022). Mental health. Key facts. June. https://www.who.int/news-room/fact-sheets/detail/mental-health-strengthening-our-response

CHAPTER 19

Australian Bureau of Statistics (2016). *Cultural Diversity: Who We are Now*. http://www.abs.gov.au/ausstats/abs@.nsf/Latestproducts/2024.0Main%20Features22016

Australian Curriculum, Assessment and Reporting Authority (ACARA) (n.d.). Meeting the needs of students for whom English is an additional language or dialect. https://www.australiancurriculum.edu.au/resources/student-diversity/meeting-the-needs-of-students-for-whom-english-is-an-additional-language-or-dialect

Australian Curriculum, Assessment and Reporting Authority (ACARA) (2015). *English as an Additional Language or Dialect Teacher Resource: EAL/D Learning Progression Foundation to Year 10*. https://docs.acara.edu.au/resources/EALD_Learning_Progression.pdf

Australian Human Rights Commission (AHRC) (2014). *The Forgotten Children: National Inquiry into Children in Immigration Detention 2014*. Author, Sydney.

Australian Institute of Health and Welfare (AIHW) (2022). Reporting on the health of culturally and linguistically diverse populations in Australia: An exploratory paper. Cat. no. PHE 308, AIHW, Australian Government.

Beck, I., McKeown, M. & Kucan, L. (2013). *Bringing Words to Life*, 2nd edn. Robust Vocabulary Instruction, 2nd edn. Guildford Press, New York. https://www.speld.org.au/files/blog/robust_vocab_instruction_beck_mckeown_kucan_2.pdf

Beers, K. (2003). *When Kids Can't Read: What Teachers Can Do*. Heinemann, Portsmouth, NH.

Beyond Blue (2022). Post-traumatic stress disorder (PTSD). https://www.beyondblue.org.au/the-facts/anxiety/types-of-anxiety/ptsd

Black Dog Institute (2023). Understanding post-traumatic stress disorder. https://www.blackdoginstitute.org.au/resources-support/post-traumatic-stress-disorder

Bryant, R., Edwards, B., Creamer, M., O'Donnell, M., Forbes, D., Felmingham, K., Silove, D., Steel, Z., Nickerson, A., McFarlane, A., Van Hooff, M. & Hadzi-Pavlovic, D. (2018). The effect of post-traumatic stress disorder on refugees' parenting and their children's mental health: A cohort study. *The Lancet Public Health*, May, vol. 3, pp. 249–58.

Byers-Heinlein, K. & Lew-Williams, C. (2013). Bilingualism in the early years: What the science says. *Learning Landscape*, Autumn, vol. 7, no. 1, pp. 95–112. National Library of Medicine, https://www.ncbi.nlm.nih.gov/pmc/articles/PMC6168212

Comprehensible Classroom, The, LLC (2014). What is circling? A tutorial for language teachers. https://www.comprehensibleclassroom.com

Curriculum Corporation (1994). ESL scales. NSW Department of Education and Training. https://education.nsw.gov.au/content/dam/main-education/teaching-and-learning/curriculum/multicultural-education/eald/ESL-scales.pdf

Curriculum Corporation (2006). ESL scales. http://www.itcouldnthappentome.com.au/microsites/DECDC/resources/otherResources/ESL%20Scales.pdf

Department for Education and Skills, UK (2006). *Excellence and Enjoyment: Learning and Teaching for Bilingual Children in the Primary Years: Introductory Guide*. Belmont Press, Norwich.

Department of Home Affairs (n.d.). Refugee and Humanitarian Program. https://immi.homeaffairs.gov.au/what-we-do/refugee-and-humanitarian-program

Department of Home Affairs (2022). Immigration Detention and Community Statistics Summary 30 June 2022. https://www.homeaffairs.gov.au/research-and-stats/files/immigration-detention-statistics-30-june-2022.pdf

Eades, D. (2000). *Aboriginal English*. Primary English Teaching Association, Sydney.

Education and Training. ACT Government (2015). Progressing parental engagement school fact sheet. Government. https://www.education.act.gov.au/?a=807433

Education and Training Victoria (2021). Reading and viewing and EAL/D learners. https://www.education.vic.gov.au/school/teachers/teachingresources/discipline/english/literacy/readingviewing/Pages/reading-and-viewing-and-eald-learners.aspx

Elgas, M., Prendeville, J., Moomaw, S. & Kretchmer, R. (2002). Building a sense of belonging. *Child Care Information Exchange*, no. 143.

Fleer, M. & Williams-Kennedy, D. (2001). *Building Bridges: Literacy Development in Young Indigenous Children*. Australian Early Childhood Association, Canberra.

Gonzalez, V. (2021). An asset-based approach to supporting English learners' reading skills. Edutopia. https://www.edutopia.org/article/asset-based-approach-supporting-english-learners-reading-skills

Greenberg Motamedi, J., Jaffery, Z., Hagen, A. & Yoon, S.Y. (2017). *Getting It Right: Reference Guides for Registering Students with Non-English Names*, 2nd edn. US Department of Education, Institute of Education Sciences, National Center for Education Evaluation and Regional Assistance, Regional Educational Laboratory Northwest, Washington, DC. http://ies.ed.gov/ncee/edlab

Harper, H. & Feez, S. (2021). *An EAL/D Handbook*. Primary English Teaching Association Australia (PETAA), Newtown, NSW.

Horwitz, E. (2020). *Becoming a Language Teacher. A Practical Guide to Second Language Learning and Teaching*, 2nd edn. Castledown, Melbourne.

Huynh, T. (2016a). Four steps of teaching inferencing to MLs (multilinguals). https://www.empoweringells.com/a6-teaching-inferencing

Huynh, T. (2016b). The Harkness Discussion: Where everyone has a voice at the table. https://tankhuynh.com/a7-teaching-harkness

Huynh, T. (2017). Three types of scaffolding: There's a scaffold for that. https://tankhuynh.com/scaffolding-instruction

Huynh, T. (2018). Reading aloud to EALs, not just for little ones. https://tankhuynh.com/readalouds

IOM United Nations (2022). *World Migration Report 2022*. https://worldmigrationreport.iom.int/wmr-2022-interactive

National Child Traumatic Stress Network (n.d.). Refugee services toolkit. http://learn.nctsn.org/mod/book/view.php?id=4518&chapterid=36

NSW Department of Education and Communities (n.d.). Vocabulary: Selecting words to teach. https://cer.schools.nsw.gov.au/content/dam/doe/sws/schools/c/cer/localcontent/selecting_words_final.pdf

OECD (2015). Helping immigrant students to succeed at school – and beyond. https://www.oecd.org/education/Helping-immigrant-students-to-succeed-at-school-and-beyond.pdf

Papadaki-D'Onofrio, E. (2003). Bilingualism/multiculturalism and language acquisition. *Theories in Child Care Information Exchange*, no. 153.

Queensland, Department of Education (2023). Advice for parents. https://education.qld.gov.au/students/inclusive-education/english-language-support/advice-for-parents

Queensland, Department of Education, Training and Employment (2013). Capability Framework: Teaching Aboriginal and Torres Strait Islander EAL/D learners. https://education.qld.gov.au/student/Documents/capability-framework-teaching-aboriginal-torres-strait-islander-eald-learners.pdf

Roads to Refuge (2020). Immigration detention. https://www.roads-to-refuge.com.au/journeys/journeys-detention.html

Robertson, K. & Breiseth, L. (n.d.). Reading 101 for English language learners. https://www.colorincolorado.org/article/reading-101-english-language-learners

Robertson, K. & Ford, K. (n.d.). Language acquisition: An overview. https://www.colorincolorado.org/article/language-acquisition-overview

Rogoff, B. (2003). *The Cultural Nature of Human Development*. Oxford University Press, New York.

Royal Children's Hospital, Melbourne (n.d.). Mental health. https://www.rch.org.au/immigranthealth/clinical/Mental_health_resources

Samson, D., Donnet, T. & Daft, R. (2018). *Management*, 6th edn. Cengage Learning, Melbourne.

United Nations High Commissioner for Refugees (UNHCR) (2021). *Annual Report 2021*. https://www.unrefugees.org.au/media/1meg1nar/2021-annual-report-web-final_compressed.pdf

US Department of Education (2017). Newcomer toolkit. https://www2.ed.gov/about/offices/list/oela/newcomers-toolkit/ncomertoolkit.pdf

Victorian Foundation for Survivors of Torture Inc. (2000). *Guide to Working with Young People Who Are Refugees*. Author.

Victorian Foundation for Survivors of Torture Inc. (2015). *Schools and Families in Partnership: A Desktop Guide to Engaging Families from Refugee Backgrounds in their Children's Learning*. https://sifr.foundationhouse.org.au/app/uploads/2020/07/SCHOOLS_FAMILIES_PARTNERSHIP_DESKTOP-GUIDE_WEB_cr.pdf

CHAPTER 20

Arts Law Centre of Australia (2023). Copyright. https://www.artslaw.com.au/information-sheet/copyright

Australian Curriculum, Assessment and Reporting Authority (ACARA) (2023). The Australian Curriculum V9. https://v9.australiancurriculum.edu.au

Australian Government. Business (2023). Cyber security and your business. https://business.gov.au/online/cyber-security/cyber-security-and-your-business

Australian Teachers Aide (2023). https://www.australianteacheraide.com.au

Copyright Agency (2022). Copying under an education licence. https://www.copyright.com.au/licences-permission/educational-licences/copying-under-education-licence

Copyright Agency (2023). Moral rights. https://www.copyright.com.au/about-copyright/moral-rights

Cyber Security NSW (n.d.). https://media-storage.easygenerator.com/document/89ffe44d-0164-4bd1-ab87-7467c1cce6c8.pdf

Department of Education, WA (2013). Telecommunications use. https://www.education.wa.edu.au/dl/l6km3go

Education Victoria (2023). Teaching and learning resources – Selecting appropriate materials. https://www2.education.vic.gov.au/pal/selecting-suitable-teaching-resources/print-all

Foundation House (2023). School's in for refugees. https://sifr.foundationhouse.org.au

Mindtools (2023). Seven ways to find what you want on the internet. https://www.mindtools.com/abtmh5z/seven-ways-to-find-what-you-want-on-the-internet

Paperpile (2023). https://paperpile.com/g/find-credible-sources

Safe Work Australia (n.d.). Model WHS laws. https://www.safeworkaustralia.gov.au

Smart Copying (2023). What is Creative Commons? https://smartcopying.edu.au/what-is-creative-commons

University of Adelaide (2014). Credibility. Writing Centre Learning Guide. https://www.adelaide.edu.au/writingcentre/sites/default/files/docs/learningguide-sourcecredibility.pdf

University of NSW (2022a). Citing different sources with Harvard referencing. https://www.student.unsw.edu.au/citing-different-sources

University of NSW (2022b). Paraphrasing, summarising and quoting. https://www.student.unsw.edu.au/paraphrasing-summarising-and-quoting

University of NSW (2022c). What is plagiarism? https://www.student.unsw.edu.au/what-plagiarism

INDEX